W9-BSO-714

M

Macy's
Maddock Douglas
Marsh Groceries
Massey Energy Company
Memorial Hospital
Merck
MGM Grand Hotel and Casino
Microsoft
Mid American Credit Union
Midvale Steel Company
Miller Brewing Company
MIM Software
Montclair Hospital
MTI

N

National EMS
Netflix
Next Media Animation
Nick's Pizza & Pub
Nike
Nokia-Siemens Networks
Nortel
Novo Nordisk
Nucor Corporation

O

Ocean Spray Cranberries
Ooma
Oriental Trading Company

P

Partners + Napier
Patience and Nicholson
Pixar Studios
Priceline.com
Prime View International
Priority Designs
Progressive Insurance
Pullman Company

R

Red Door Interactive
Red Stream Technology
REI
Research In Motion
Ryla Teleservices

S

7-Eleven
S.C. Johnson
Savilis
Scharffen Berger Chocolate Maker
Single Source Systems
Sky Factory
SoBe
Sodexo
Southwest Airlines
Staff Management
Summit Entertainment
Supervalu
Sysco

T

24 Hour Fitness USA
37signals.com
3M
Tasty Catering
Trader Joe's
Troy Lee Designs
Tupperware
Turner Broadcasting

U

UBS AG
Unilever
UPS
USA Today

W

Walt Disney Company
Waste Management, Inc.
We Energies
West Paw Design
Winn Dixie

Y

Yum! Brands

MANAGEMENT 7e

CHUCK WILLIAMS

Butler University

SOUTH-WESTERN
CENGAGE Learning·

Australia · Brazil · Japan · Korea · Mexico · Singapore · Spain · United Kingdom · United States

SOUTH-WESTERN
CENGAGE Learning·

Management, 7e
Chuck Williams

Vice President of Editorial, Business: Jack W. Calhoun

Executive Editor: Scott Person

Developmental Editor: John Choi, B-Books

Sr. Editorial Assistant: Ruth Belanger

Marketing Manager: Jonathan Monahan

Sr. Content Project Manager: Holly Henjum

Media Editor: John Rich

Manufacturing Planner: Ron Montgomery

Marketing Coordinator: Julia Tucker

Production Service: MPS Limited, a Macmillan Company

Sr. Art Director: Tippy McIntosh

Cover and Text Design: Stratton Design

Cover Image: © Yamada Taro, Getty Images

Rights Acquisitions Specialist: John Hill

Photo Research: Terri Miller/E-Visual Communications, Inc.

For product information and technology assistance, contact us at
Cengage Learning Customer & Sales Support, 1-800-354-9706

For permission to use material from this text or product, submit all requests online at **www.cengage.com/permissions**
Further permissions questions can be emailed to
permissionrequest@cengage.com

Library of Congress Control Number: 2011941255

ISBN-13: 978-1-111-96981-3

ISBN-10: 1-111-96981-7

South-Western
5191 Natorp Boulevard
Mason, OH 45040
USA

Cengage Learning products are represented in Canada by Nelson Education, Ltd.

For your course and learning solutions, visit **www.cengage.com**

Purchase any of our products at your local college store or at our preferred online store **www.cengagebrain.com**

Printed in the United States of America
1 2 3 4 5 6 7 15 14 13 12 11

Brief Contents

Contents

Planning   164

Organizing 336

⑤ Controlling   662

About This Edition

Welcome to *Management*, 7e! Please take a few minutes to read the preface and familiarize yourself with the approach (combining theory with specific stories and examples), features, pedagogy, and end-of-chapter assignments in *Management*. This is time well spent. After all, besides your instructor, this book will be your primary learning tool.

The Approach

Combining Theory with Specific, Up-to-Date Stories and Examples Say "theory" to college students and they assume that you're talking about complex, arcane ideas and terms that have nothing to do with the "real world," but which need to be memorized for a test and then forgotten (at least until the final exam). However, students needn't be wary of theoretical ideas and concepts. Theories are simply good ideas. And good theories are simply good ideas that have been tested through rigorous scientific study and analysis.

Where textbooks go wrong is that they stop at theory and read like dictionaries. Or they focus on theoretical issues related to research rather than practice. However, good management theories (i.e., good ideas) needn't be complex, difficult to understand, or irrelevant. In fact, the late Rensis Likert, of the University of Michigan, once said that there is nothing as practical as a good theory.

So, to make sure you're exposed to good ideas (i.e., good theories) that you can refer to for practical, theory-driven advice, and which encourage you to put theory-driven knowledge into practice for yourselves, each chapter in this book contains 50 to 60 specific stories and examples that illustrate how managers are using management ideas in their organizations.

The stories and examples you'll read in each chapter are relevant and up to date. You'll read how FedEx, a global leader in shipping, is using new airplanes to deliver more packages faster than it ever did before. By switching to a cargo version of Boeing's 777 jet, FedEx can load 14,000 more pounds of cargo and travel 2,100 more miles per planeload, allowing it to make global connections faster than ever. You'll learn how companies like Nordstrom are using developments in information technology to give shoppers a convenient experience and increase sales. At Nordstrom.com, users can access real-time, nationwide inventory information. Customers can see how many of a particular item are in stock at each of Nordstrom's 115 stores nationwide. Because customers see that the items they want are available in a store, the percentage of people who bought an item after searching for it on the website has doubled. You'll also learn how companies are fulfilling their social responsibility by committing to environmental responsibility. A number of leaders in the banking industry have committed to limit the financing they give to companies that undertake environmentally hazardous projects. Bank of America, Wells Fargo, Morgan Stanley, and Citibank recently announced that they will no longer finance companies that mine for coal by blasting off the tops of mountains. London-based HSBC announced that it will no longer finance the production of palm oil, which is blamed for massive deforestation and pollution in developing

countries. As these stories show, each chapter has been updated with dozens of new real-world business examples, straight from the latest pages of *Businessweek, Fortune, Forbes, Fast Company,* and *Inc.,* as well as *The Wall Street Journal, The New York Times,* and other leading newspapers, to help you understand how management concepts are being used.

In short, research and theory *and* stories and examples are important for effective learning. Therefore, this book contains over a thousand specific examples and stories to make management theories and ideas more interesting. So, to get more out of this book, read and understand the theories and theoretical ideas. Then read the stories or examples to learn how those ideas should or should not be used in practice. You'll find that both are current and up to date.

Learning System

Because of their busy schedules, very few students have the opportunity to read a chapter from beginning to end in one sitting. Typically, it takes students anywhere from two to five study sessions to completely read a chapter. Accordingly, at the beginning of each chapter, you'll find a detailed chapter outline in which each major part in the chapter is broken out into numbered sections and subsections. For example, the outline for the first part of Chapter 4, on ethics and social responsibility, looks like this:

Chapter 4 : Ethics and Social Responsibility

What Is Ethical and Unethical Workplace Behavior?
 1. Ethics and the Nature of Management Jobs
 2. Workplace Deviance
 3. U.S. Sentencing Commission Guidelines for Organizations
  3.1 Who, What, and Why?
  3.2 Determining the Punishment

The numbered information contained in the chapter outline is then repeated in the chapter as learning objectives (at the beginning of major parts of the chapter) and as numbered headings and subheadings (throughout the chapter) to help students remember precisely where they are in terms of the chapter outline.

Finally, instead of a big summary at the end of the chapter, students will find detailed reviews at the end of each section.

Together, the chapter outline, numbering system, learning objectives, section headings (which mark the beginning of a section), and section reviews (which mark the end of a section) allow students to break the chapter into smaller, self-contained sections that can be read in their entirety and digested during a single study session if needed. Furthermore, the numbered headings and outline should make it easier for instructors and students to know what is being assigned or discussed in class ("In Section 3.1 of Chapter 3 . . .").

So What's New?

If you are already familiar with the previous editions' approach of reinforcing research and theory with stories and examples, you may be asking yourself, "So what's new?" The answer is quite a bit.

What's New Companies   So many new examples are in the Seventh Edition that we've created a list of What's New Companies at the beginning of each chapter. Throughout the chapter, we've highlighted new examples with the design located in the margin.

What Would You Do?   Each chapter opens with an engaging case outlining actual management problems facing a well-known company. After students read the case, they are presented several questions to help guide their thinking about the issues, and are ultimately asked, "If you were the manager at this company, what would you do?" Putting students in the place of the manager personalizes the dilemma and forces students to solve common managerial problems. The solution to the case, or What Really Happened? is in the Instructor Manual. Allowing students to compare what they would have done to what the managers really did provides a great learning opportunity.

This edition presents 17 new "What Would You Do?" chapter-opening sections featuring companies like NetFlix, Cessna, Apple, 3M, and DuPont, among others.

Study Tips   Knowing how to study effectively is not an innate talent. So, to prepare students for studying the material, a detailed study tip appears in the chapter opener. Eighteen different tips give students many options for reviewing key concepts and mastering chapter content. Students are challenged to write their own tests and exchange them in a study group, explain the chapter concepts to a friend who is not in class, cut up the text glossary to make a quiz-bowl game, and much more.

Doing the Right Thing   Numerous studies and well-known corporate scandals make clear the distressing state of managerial ethics in today's business world. And because managers set the standard for others in the workplace, unethical behavior and practices quickly spread when they don't do the right thing. Therefore, in each chapter you'll find practical, useful advice to help you become a more ethical manager or businessperson in Doing the Right Thing sections. Topics include ethical competitive analysis, avoiding the slippery slope of cheating, dealing with gifts from suppliers, avoiding conflicts of interest, not cheating on travel expenses, and many more.

What Really Works   Understanding how to interpret data is important for every manager, but unfortunately, sometimes research findings on the same topic present exactly opposite results. That's why we introduce students to *meta-analysis*. Additionally, one primary advantage of meta-analysis over traditional significance tests is that you can convert meta-analysis statistics into intuitive numbers that anyone can easily understand. Indeed, each meta-analysis reported in the What Really Works sections of this textbook is accompanied by an easy-to-understand statistic called the *probability of success*. Of course, no idea or technique works every time and in every circumstance. However, in today's competitive, fast-changing global marketplace, few managers can afford to overlook proven management strategies like those discussed in the What Really Works feature of this book.

Management Facts and Trends   Short boxes keep students up to date on current trends facing managers, as well as interesting facts about managers and management. Chapters contain one or more of these interesting, focused, and concise examples.

Key Terms   Key terms appear in boldface in the text, with definitions in the margins to make it easy for students to check their understanding. A complete alphabetical list of key terms appears at the end of each chapter as a study checklist, with page citations for easy reference.

End-of-Chapter Assignments

In most textbooks, there are only two or three end-of-chapter assignments. By contrast, at the end of each chapter in *Management 7e*, there are five assignments from which to choose. (But if you count the opening case, What Would You Do?, and its answer, What Really Happened?, there are really six assignments.) This gives instructors more choice in selecting just the right assignment for their classes. It also gives students a greater variety of activities, making it less likely that they'll repeat the same kind of assignment chapter after chapter.

Self-Assessments   The chapter-ending cases and assignments begin with a related assessment questionnaire to help students consider how their own perspectives influence their management skills. Basic scoring information follows each questionnaire, and the Instructor Manual contains directions for using the assessment tools in class.

Management Decision   Management Decision assignments are focused on a particular decision. Students must decide what to do in the given situation and then answer several questions to explain their choices. For example, students must decide how to manage cutting perks in difficult economic times, whether to mine employees' personal data to find out how to motivate them, and more. Some Management Decision features have optional extensions that turn the exercises into mini-projects. Information on how to do these is in the Instructor Manual.

Management Team Decision   Management Team Decision assignments are similar to Management Decision assignments in that students face a problem, must decide what to do, and then answer several questions to explain their choices. The difference, however, is that Management Team Decision assignments are designed to be completed by student teams or groups. Teams have the opportunity to practice the group decision-making techniques outlined in Chapter 5 (Planning and Decision Making). Student management teams will decide, for example, how to find a balance between productivity and customer service, encouraging employees to deal with work-life issues in a healthy manner, and how to determine an executive's salary.

Practice Being a Manager   Working through management issues before you even get to the workplace can be a beneficial way to practice being a manager. Each exercise gives students the opportunity to role-play management scenarios, discuss management dilemmas, and resolve management problems. Some of the exercises have components that require individual, take-home preparation, but most are designed to be started and completed during the class session. Students can explore management issues and problems in context and with other students. The guided exercises are supported by detailed teaching notes and role-playing instructions in the Instructor Manual.

Develop Your Career Potential   Develop Your Career Potential assignments have one purpose: To help students develop their present and future capabilities as managers. What students learn through these assignments is not traditional "book-learning" based on memorization and regurgitation, but practical knowledge and skills that help managers perform their jobs better. Assignments include interviewing managers, dealing with the press, conducting a personal SWOT analysis, learning from failure, developing leadership skills, 360-degree feedback, and more.

Reel to Real Videos   Each chapter of *Management*, 7e, contains two video options. The first is a film clip from a popular Hollywood movie that relates to the chapter content. For example, students will see a Biz Flix clip from *Charlie Wilson's*

War for Chapter 3 on organizational culture, from *Inside Man* for Chapter 5 on planning, and from *Friday Night Lights* for Chapter 15 on managing service and manufacturing operations, to name a few. The second video option is comprised of longer segments, called Management Workplace, that run approximately 10 minutes and provide a deeper look at a single company, its operations, and how it addresses various management issues every day. In the Seventh Edition, we go inside Barcelona Restaurant Group (fine dining), Plant Fantasies (landscape design), Holden Outerwear (winter-sports equipment retailer), Modern Shed (construction), and Mitchell Gold + Bob Williams (custom furniture). Both the Biz Flix and the Management Workplace features guide students on what to look for and think about as they watch the video.

Instructor Supplements

Comprehensive Instructor Manual The Instructor Manual to accompany the Seventh Edition has been completely redone to help instructors with a variety of class types. In addition to the chapter outlines, additional activities, and solutions you expect, each chapter of the manual includes a grid detailing all of the pedagogy choices for the chapter and the companies and teaching points presented. A selection of lesson plans is also included, as are detailed chapter outlines (lecture notes). The lecture notes include teaching notes for key concepts and for feature boxes, prompts where relevant PowerPoint slides correspond to chapter content, and prompts for where to show the video. Solutions for chapter features are included.

In addition to all of these teaching tools, an appendix titled *Teaching Your First Management Course* can be found at the end of the instructor manual. This appendix is designed specifically to meet the needs and concerns of the first-time instructor.

Test Bank The Test Bank for the Seventh Edition of *Management* builds on the solid foundation of previous editions. Each test bank chapter contains at least 150 questions in a variety of types: true/false, multiple-choice, short-answer, and critical-thinking questions, and a scenario section that asks students to answer questions based on detailed management situations. Difficulty ratings are provided, as are tags correlating to AASCB outcomes and page references for where solutions appear in the text.

ExamView A computerized version of the Test Bank (called ExamView) is available on your Instructor Resource CD-ROM and by special request. ExamView allows you to add or edit questions, instructions, and answers. You can create, edit, store, print, and otherwise customize all your quizzes, tests, and exams. The system is menu driven, making it quick and easy to use.

Course Pre- and Post-Assessments To help you better determine your students' baseline understanding of management principles, we have created an assessment test for your use at the beginning of the term. The 200-question pre-test covers the basic management concepts that students need to understand. As a conclusion to your course, you can administer the 200-question post-test. These tests are designed to help you track your students' proficiency levels semester to semester. Pre- and post-assessments are also broken down by chapter, so if you prefer, you can administer throughout the semester for each chapter of the text. Assessment tests are available in both Word and ExamView formats.

Reel to Real Video Nothing helps students master management concepts like seeing them put into practice in the real world. Both the Biz Flix and Management

Workplace videos are available on DVD. The Instructor Manual includes detailed teaching notes so that you can incorporate video into your class in a meaningful way.

PowerPoint® Slides

A rich set of PowerPoint slides, with teaching notes, will make class preparations easy and interesting. The approximately 40 to 50 slides per chapter cover all key concepts, terms, features, cases, and even some exhibits from the text. Ample teaching notes offer additional insights and examples plus important points to cover in lectures. For instructors wishing to integrate various media, we have also created a set of video PowerPoint slides in which the Biz Flix movie clips are embedded in appropriate slides.

Self-Assessment PowerPoint Slides

To support the Self-Assessment Appendix, we have created a separate set of PowerPoint files that enable professors to use the assessment inventories in the classroom setting. In each Self-Assessment PowerPoint chapter, individual assessment items are placed on separate slides. Excel spreadsheets embedded on each slide allow instructors to use the data from a simple show of hands to create distributions for each assessment item. Students can see where they fit in the distribution, making the assessment tool more interesting and relevant.

Who Wants to Be a Manager?

Games are an increasingly popular classroom review tool, so the Seventh Edition of *Management* includes a quiz game that uses JoinIn™ clicker technology. Each chapter has two rounds of 25 questions each, organized into five categories. Category names are fun, but the questions in each category are serious review of chapter concepts. A mixture of true/false and multiple-choice questions keep students working through this enjoyable classroom review.

Instructor Resource CD-ROM (IRCD)

For your convenience, the Instructor Manual, Test Bank, Course Pre- and Post-Assessments, ExamView Software, PowerPoint presentations, and Who Wants to Be a Manager? are available on a single CD-ROM, the IRCD.

The Business and Company Resource Center

Put a complete business library at your fingertips with the Business & Company Resource Center (BCRC). The BCRC is a premier online business research tool that allows you to seamlessly search thousands of periodicals, journals, references, financial information, industry reports, company histories, and much more. The BCRC is a powerful and time-saving research tool for students—whether they are completing a case analysis, preparing for a presentation, creating a business plan, or writing a reaction paper. Instructors can use the BCRC like an online coursepack, quickly and easily assigning readings and research projects without the inconvenience of library reserves, permissions, and printed materials. BCRC filters out the "junk" information students often find when searching the Internet, providing only the high-quality, safe, and reliable news and information sources. Contact your local representative for pricing and optional bundling information for the Business & Company Resource Center with your text.

Web Tutor™ (for both WebCT® and Blackboard®)

Online learning is growing at a rapid pace. Whether you are looking to offer courses at distance or to offer a Web-enhanced classroom, South-Western/Cengage Learning offers you a solution with WebTutor. WebTutor provides instructors with text-specific content that interacts with the two leading systems of higher education course management—WebCT and Blackboard.

WebTutor is a turnkey solution for instructors who want to begin using technology like Blackboard or WebCT but who do not have Web-ready content available, or those who do not want to be burdened with developing their own content.

WebTutor uses the Internet to turn everyone in your class into a front-row student. WebTutor offers interactive study guide features such as quizzes, concept reviews, flashcards, discussion forums, additional video clips, and more. Instructor tools are also provided to facilitate communication between students and faculty.

Williams Web site (www.cengage.com/management/williams) The Williams Web site contains a wealth of resources for both instructors and students. Here is what's available only for professors at the Instructor Resource page of the Williams Web site:

> » The full PowerPoint presentations with teaching notes.
> » Files for the full Test Bank in Word.
> » Files for the full Instructor Manual are also available online. If you don't have your materials on hand, you can download the chapters you need and customize them to suit your lesson plan.

Student Resources The *Management* package has many resources to help reinforce the concepts in each chapter.

CengageNOW for Williams *Management*, 7e, has a dedicated CengageNOW study tool that tightly integrates the material in the text with a myriad of review opportunities. Students can test their understanding, concentrate their review on their weakest areas, and then verify their progress using the latest technology.

Premium Student Website New to this edition of *Management* is student access to the Premium Student Website. Students can access interactive quizzes, flashcards, PowerPoint slides, learning games, and more to reinforce chapter concepts. Access to the Williams *Management*, *7e*, Premium Student Website is pincode protected. Learn more by adding *Management*, *7e*, to your bookshelf at www.cengagebrain.com. Ask your local Cengage Learning sales representative about this optional package item.

Acknowledgments

Let's face it: Writing a textbook is a long and lonely process. It's surely the most difficult (and rewarding) project I've ever tackled. And as I sat in front of my computer with a rough outline on the left side of my desk, a two-foot stack of journal articles on the floor, and a blank screen in front of me, it was easy at times to feel isolated. But, as I found out, a book like this doesn't get done without the help of many other talented people.

First, I'd like to thank the outstanding team of supplement authors: Amit Shah (Frostburg State University), for the outstanding test bank; Colin Grover (B-books, Ltd.), for the superb PowerPoint slide designs and the great content.

I'd like to thank the world-class team at Cengage for the outstanding support (and patience) they provided while I wrote this book: Scott Person, who heads the Management group at Cengage, was calm, collected, and continuously positive through the major ups and downs of this project; Jonathan Monahan, who was in charge of marketing the book, did an outstanding job of developing marketing themes and approaches; and Holly Henjum, who managed the production process. Authors are prone to complain about their publishers. But that hasn't been my experience at all. Pure and simple, everyone at Cengage has been great to work with throughout the entire project. However, special thanks on this team goes to

Jamie Gleich Bryant, of B-books, Ltd., who was my developmental editor and with whom I had the most contact while writing the book. Jamie and her team worked with reviewers, edited the manuscript, managed the development of supplements, provided superb feedback and guidance at every stage of the book, and nudged and prodded me to write faster, make improvements, and maintain the high quality standards that were set when I began writing. Jamie's enthusiasm, professionalism, commitment, and attention to detail made me a better writer, made this a better book, and made me appreciate my good fortune to work with such an outstanding talent. Thanks, Jamie, and here's to many more editions.

I'd like to thank an excellent set of reviewers whose diligent and thoughtful comments helped shape the earlier editions and whose rigorous feedback improved the Seventh Edition.

Ali Abu-Rahma
United States International University

William Acar
Kent State University

David C. Adams
Manhattanville College

Bruce R. Barringer
University of Central Florida

Gayle Baugh
University of West Florida

James Bell
University of Texas–Austin

Greg Blundel
Kent State University–Stark

Katharine A. Bohley
University of Indianapolis

Santanu Borah
University of North Alabama

Angela Boston
University of Texas–Arlington

Michael Boyd
Owensboro Community College

Jon L. Bryan
Bridgewater State College

Wayne Buchanan
Defiance College

Bruce Byars
University of North Dakota–Grand Forks

Diane P. Caggiano
Fitchburg State College

David Cassidy
College of Eastern Utah

Dan Cochran
Mississippi State University

C. Brad Cox
Midlands Technical College

Kathy Daruty
Pierce College

Nicolette DeVille
Christensen *Guilford College*

Michael DiVecchio
Central Pennsylvania College

Jennifer Dose
University of Minnesota–Morris

Jason Duan
Cameron University

Joyce A. Ezrow
Anne Arundel Community College

Kimborough Ferrell
Spring Hill College

Charles R. Franz
University of Missouri–Columbia

Paul R. Gagnon
Central Connecticut State University

Franco Gandolfi
Cedarville University

Janice Gates
Western Illinois University

Anu A. Gokhale
Illinois State University

Barry Allen Gold
Pace University

Martin Grossman
Bridgewater State College

Susan C. Hanlon
University of Akron

Russell F. Hardy
New Mexico State University

David Hennessey
Mount Mercy College

Dorothy Hetmer-Hinds
Trinity Valley Community College

Roger W. Hutt
Arizona State University at the Polytechnic Campus

Joseph Izzo
Alderson Broaddus College

Jim Jawahar
Illinois State University

Kathleen Jones
University of North Dakota

Paul N. Keaton
University of Wisconsin–La Crosse

Ellen Ernst Kossek
Michigan State University

Nancy E. Kucinski
Hardin-Simmons University

Lowell H. Lamberton
Central Oregon Community College
Linfield College

Donald R. Leavitt
Western Baptist College

Lee W. Lee
Central Connecticut State University

Jerrold Leong
Oklahoma State University

Randy Lewis
Texas Christian University

Bob Livingston
Cerritos College

Linda Livingstone
Baylor University

Thomas P. Loughman
Columbus State University

Larry Maes
Davenport University

George Marron
Arizona State University

Lynda Martin
Oklahoma State University

David McCalman
University of Central Arkansas

Robert McGowan
University of Denver

Don Mosley
University of South Alabama

Sherry Moss
Florida International University

Jaideep Motwani
Grand Valley State University

Victoria T. Mullennex
Davis & Elkins College

John J. Nader
Grand Valley State University

Charlie Nagelschmidt
Champlain College

Patrick J. Nedry
Monroe County Community College

Stephanie Newport
Austin Peay State University

Don A. Okhomina
Fayetteville State University

James S. O'Rourke IV
University of Notre Dame

Rhonda S. Palladi
Georgia State University

Lynne Patten
Clark Atlanta University

Jane Pettinger
Minnesota State University–Moorhead

Clifton D. Petty
Drury University

John Poirier
Bryant University

David M. Porter Jr.
UCLA

Michael Provitera
Barry University

Abe Qastin
Lakeland College

Robert Raspberry
Southern Methodist University

Levi Richard
Citrus Community College

Kim Rocha
Barton College

Linda Ross
Cleveland Community College

Penni F. Sikkila
Baker College

Amit Shah
Frostburg State University

Thomas Shaughnessy
Illinois Central College

Michelle Slagle
University of South Alabama

James Smas
Kent State University

Finally, my family deserves the greatest thanks of all for their love, patience, and support. Writing a textbook is an enormous project with incredible stresses and pressures on authors as well as their loved ones. However, throughout this project, my wife, Jenny, was unwavering in her support of my writing. She listened patiently, encouraged me when I was discouraged, read and commented on most of what I wrote, gave me the time to write, and took wonderful care of me and our family during this long process. My children, two in college and one in a business career, also deserve special thanks for their patience and for understanding why Dad was locked away at the computer for all of this time.

Meet the Author:

Chuck Williams *Butler University*   Chuck Williams is Dean of the College of Business at Butler University. Previously he was Dean of the Eberhard School of Business at the University of the Pacific and an Associate Professor of Management at the M.J. Neeley School of Business at Texas Christian University, where he has also served as an Associate Dean and the Chair of the Management Department. He received his B.A. in Psychology from Valparaiso University and specialized in the areas of Organizational Behavior, Human Resources, and Strategic Management while earning his M.B.A. and Ph.D. in Business Administration from Michigan State University. Previously, he taught at Michigan State University and was on the faculty of Oklahoma State University.

His research interests include employee recruitment and turnover, performance appraisal, and employee training and goal setting. Chuck has published research in the *Journal of Applied Psychology*, the *Academy of Management Journal*, *Human Resource Management Review*, *Personnel Psychology*, and the *Organizational Research Methods Journal*. He was a member of the *Journal of Management*'s Editorial Board, and serves as a reviewer for numerous other academic journals. He was also the webmaster for the Research Methods Division of the Academy of Management (http://division.aomonline.org/rm.joomla). Chuck is also a corecipient of the Society for Human Resource Management's Yoder-Heneman Research Award.

Chuck has consulted for a number of organizations: General Motors, IBM, JCPenney, Tandy Corporation, Trism Trucking, Central Bank and Trust, StuartBacon, the City of Fort Worth, the American Cancer Society, and others. He has taught in

executive development programs at Oklahoma State University, the University of Oklahoma, and Texas Christian University.

Chuck teaches a number of different courses but has been privileged to teach his favorite course, Introduction to Management, for nearly 20 years. His teaching philosophy is based on four principles: (1) courses should be engaging and interesting; (2) there's nothing as practical as a good theory; (3) students learn by doing; and (4) students learn when they are challenged. The undergraduate students at TCU's Neeley School of Business named him instructor of the year. He has also been a recipient of TCU's Dean's Teaching Award.

MANAGEMENT 7e

Introduction
to Management

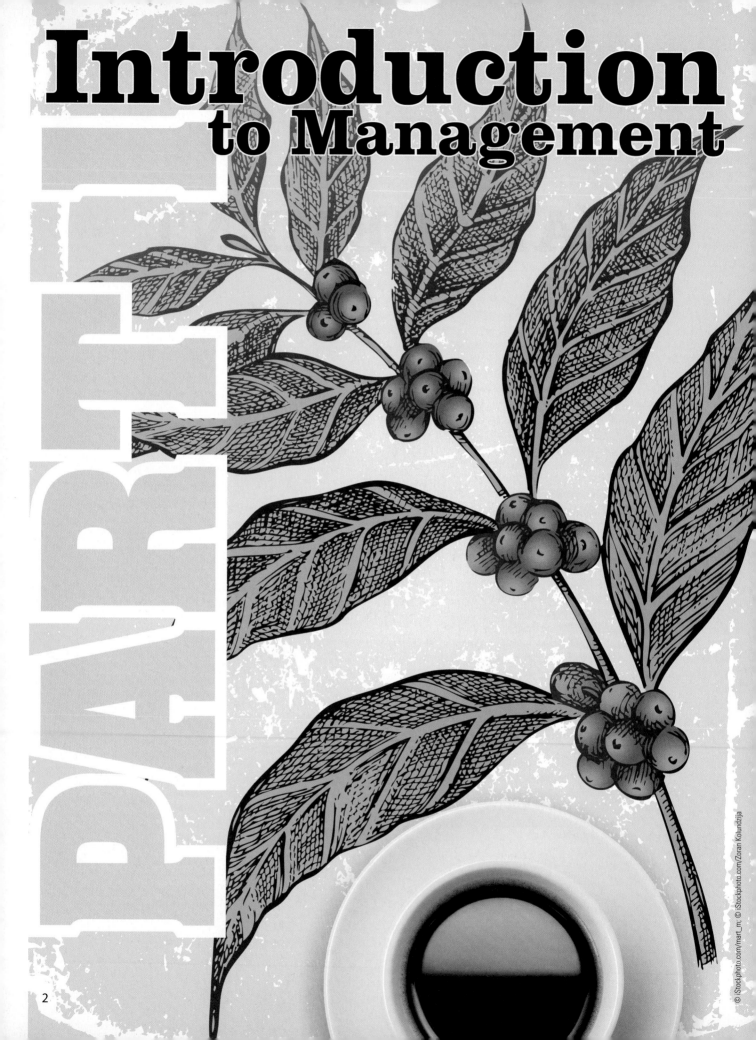

Chapter 1
Management

This chapter begins by defining management and discussing the functions of management. We look at what managers do, what it takes to be a manager, what companies look for in their managers, the most serious mistakes managers make, and what it is like to make the tough transition from being a worker to being a manager.

Netflix

Chapter 2
The History of Management

This chapter reviews the historical origins of management ideas and practice and the historical changes that produced the need for managers. You'll learn about various schools of management thought and the key contributions made by important management theorists.

ISG Steelton

Chapter 3
Organizational Environments and Cultures

Chapter 3 examines the internal and external forces that affect business, including how those forces affect the decisions and performance of a company. We cover the general environment that affects all organizations and the specific environment unique to each company.

Waste Management

Chapter 4
Ethics and Social Responsibility

This chapter examines ethical behavior in the workplace and explains how unethical behavior can expose a business to legal penalties. You'll read about the influences on ethical decision making and learn the practical steps that managers can take to improve ethical decision making.

American Express

CHAPTER 1

Management

Learning Outcomes

1. Describe what management is.
2. Explain the four functions of management.
3. Describe different kinds of managers.
4. Explain the major roles and subroles that managers perform in their jobs.
5. Explain what companies look for in managers.
6. Discuss the top mistakes that managers make in their jobs.
7. Describe the transition that employees go through when they are promoted to management.
8. Explain how and why companies can create competitive advantage through people.

what would you do?

"what's new" companies

Netflix

HCL Technologies

FedEx

Campbell Soup

Johnson & Johnson

Intuit

UPS

Corkd.com

EMI Group

Netflix Headquarters, Los Gatos, California.[1]

CEO Reed Hastings started Netflix in 1997 after becoming angry about paying Blockbuster Video $40 for a late return of *Apollo 13*. Hastings and Netflix struck back with flat monthly fees for unlimited DVDs rentals, easy home delivery and returns via prepaid postage envelopes, and no late fees, which let customers keep DVDs as long as they wanted. Blockbuster, which earned up to $800 million annually from late returns, was slow to respond and lost customers in droves.

When Blockbuster, Amazon, and Walmart started their own mail-delivery video rentals, Hastings recognized that Netflix was in competition with "the biggest rental company, the biggest e-commerce company, and the biggest company, period." With investors expecting it to fail, Netflix's stock price dropped precipitously to $2.50 a share. But with an average subscriber cost of just $4 a month compared to an average subscriber fee of $15, Netflix, unlike its competitors, made money from each customer. Three years later, Walmart abandoned the business, asking Netflix to handle DVD rentals on Walmart.com. Amazon, by contrast, entered the DVD rental business in Great Britain, expecting that experience to prepare it to beat Netflix in the United States. But, like Walmart, Amazon quit after four years of losses. Finally, 13 years after Netflix's founding, Blockbuster declared bankruptcy. With DVDs mailed to 17 million monthly subscribers from 50 distribution centers nationwide, Netflix is now the industry leader in DVD rentals.

© Jin Lee/Bloomberg via Getty Images

However, its expertise in shipping and distributing DVDs won't provide a competitive advantage when streaming files over the Internet. Indeed, Netflix's Watch Instantly download service is in competition with Amazon's Video on Demand, Apple's iTunes, HuluPlus at Hulu.com, Time-Warner Cable's TV Everywhere, and DirectTV Cinema, all of which offer movie and TV downloads. Moreover, unlike DVDs, which can be rented without studio approval, U.S. copyright laws require streaming rights to be purchased from TV and movie studios before downloading content into people's homes. And that creates two new issues. First, does Netflix have deep enough pockets to outbid its rivals for broad access to the studios' TV and movie content? Second, can it convince the studios that it is not a direct competitor? HBO, for instance, won't license any of its original shows, like *The Sopranos*, for Netflix streaming. It also has exclusive rights for up to eight years for content from Twentieth Century Fox and Universal Pictures. HBO co-president Eric Kessler says, "There is value in exclusivity. Consumers are willing to

study tips

ⓧ

Learning a new subject can be challenging. To help you master the principles in this textbook, each chapter opener contains a student resource list that alerts you to the materials outside your book that can help you better understand assignments, work on group projects, and study for exams and tests.

© iStockphoto.com/Ivan Burmistrov

© iStockphoto.com/Alex Slobodkin

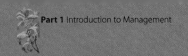

pay a premium for high-quality, exclusive content." If other studio executives think this, Netflix will not acquire the video content it needs to satisfy its customers. Planning involves determining organizational goals and a means for achieving them. So, how can Netflix generate the cash it needs to pay the studios? How can it convince them it's not a competitor so they will agree to license their content?

Netflix must also address the significant organizational challenges accompanying accelerated growth. Hastings experienced the same problem in his first company, Pure Software, where he admitted, "Management was my biggest challenge; every year there were twice as many people and it was trial by fire. I was underprepared for the complexities and personalities." With blazing growth on one hand and the strategic challenge of obtaining studio content on the other, how much time should he and his executive team devote directly to hiring? Deciding where decisions will be made is a key part of the management function of organizing. So, should he and his executive team be directly involved, or is this something that he should delegate? Finally, what can Netflix, which is located near Silicon Valley, home to some of the most attractive employers in the world, Google, eBay, Apple, Hewlett-Packard, and Facebook, provide in the way of pay, perks, and company culture that will attract, inspire, and motivate top talent to achieve organizational goals?

If you were in charge of Netflix, what would you do?

The management issues facing Netflix are fundamental to any organization: What's our plan? What are top management's key responsibilities? How can we best position the company against key competitors? How can we attract, motivate, and lead talented employees? Good management is basic to starting, growing, and maintaining a business once it has achieved some measure of success.

We begin this chapter by defining management and discussing the functions of management. Next, we look at what managers do by examining the four kinds of managers and reviewing the various roles that managers play. Then we investigate what it takes to be a manager by reviewing management skills, what companies look for in their managers, the most serious mistakes managers make, and what it is like to make the tough transition from being a worker to being a manager. We finish this chapter by examining the competitive advantage that companies gain from good management. In other words, we learn how to establish a competitive advantage through people.

What Is Management?

To understand how important *good* management is, think about mistakes like these: Mistake # 1: A new Chinese plant manager at a factory in South Carolina publicly

After reading the next two sections, you should be able to

1. *Describe what management is.*
2. *Explain the four functions of management.*

berates his workers when they make mistakes, creating resentment and alienation among his American workers.[2] Mistake # 2: Managers at McNeil Laboratories, a division of Johnson & Johnson, discovered that a large batch of the Motrin pain reliever had failed a number of quality-control tests. But instead of warning consumers and issuing a public recall, Mc-Neil hired people to go to stores and purchase every bottle of Motrin they could find. The people hired to "buy" the faulty drugs were instructed by managers to "simply 'act' like a regular customer while making these purchases," and, furthermore, *"There must be no mention of this being a recall of the product."*[3]

Ah, bad managers and bad management. Is it any wonder that companies pay management consultants nearly $250 billion a year for advice on basic management issues such as how to lead people effectively, organize the company efficiently, and manage large-scale projects and processes?[4] This textbook will help you understand some of the basic issues that management consultants help companies resolve. (And it won't cost you billions of dollars.)

1 Management is . . .

Many of today's managers got their start welding on the factory floor, clearing dishes off tables, helping customers fit a suit, or wiping up a spill in aisle 3. Similarly, lots of you will start at the bottom and work your way up. There's no better way to get to know your competition, your customers, and your business. But whether you begin your career at the entry level or as a supervisor, your job as a manager is not to do the work, but to help others do theirs. **Management** is getting work done through others. Vineet Nayar, CEO of IT services company **HCL Technologies**, doesn't see himself as the guy who has to do everything or have all the answers. Instead, he sees himself as "the guy who is obsessed with enabling employees to create value." Rather than coming up with solutions himself, Nayar creates opportunities for collaboration, peer review, and employee feedback on ideas and work processes. Says Nayar, "My job is to make sure everybody is enabled to do what they do well."[5]

Nayar's description of managerial responsibilities suggests that managers also have to be concerned with efficiency and effectiveness in the work process. **Efficiency** is getting work done with a minimum of effort, expense, or waste. At **FedEx**, efficiency means delivering more packages in less time—but always on time—for less cost. To increase its efficiency, FedEx ordered 12 cargo versions of Boeing's 777 jets to replace the MD-11s, which had been its primary long-distance cargo plane. Why? Because the 777 carries 178,000 pounds of cargo and has a maximum range of 1,675 miles—14,000 pounds and 2,100 miles more than the MD-11. And because the 777 can fly from the United States to Asia, without stopping for fuel, it can make the trip three hours faster than the MD-11. This gives FedEx's Asian customers two extra hours to manufacture products and still get them shipped out for next-day delivery. The company calls the planes a "game changer" in the international package delivery market.[6]

© Peter Foley/Bloomberg via Getty Images

< **"what's new" companies**

management getting work done through others.

efficiency getting work done with a minimum of effort, expense, or waste.

< **"what's new" companies**

Efficiency alone, however, is not enough to ensure success. Managers must also strive for **effectiveness**, which is accomplishing tasks that help fulfill organizational objectives such as customer service and satisfaction. John F. Kennedy International Airport in New York City was notorious for crowded runways, resulting in delays which trapped passengers on idling airplanes with no access to food, water, or bathrooms (by law, passengers are required to stay in their seats until the plane is safely in the air). That changed, however, when the airport instituted a runway reservation system where each flight is assigned a takeoff time and no plane is allowed to leave the gate until its assigned time. How effective is the new system? Instead of 40 planes queuing on the runway, now only 6 to 8 planes wait in line for takeoff. And although flight delays are still common, passengers now experience them at the terminal, where they have access to food, bathrooms, and lounges. The airlines have also benefitted because they burn less fuel and save wear and tear on engines.[7]

Review **1**	**Management Is . . .** Good management is working through others to accomplish tasks that help fulfill organizational objectives as efficiently as possible.

② **Management Functions**

"Could you imagine, say, running a book publisher if you didn't read? Or running a movie studio if you don't watch TV or go to the movies?"

JON RICCITIELLO, CEO OF
ELECTRONIC ARTS

Henri Fayol, who was a managing director (CEO) of a large steel company in the early 1900s, was one of the founders of the field of management. You'll learn more about Fayol and management's other key contributors when you read about the history of management in Chapter 2. Based on his 20 years of experience as a CEO, Fayol argued that "the success of an enterprise generally depends much more on the administrative ability of its leaders than on their technical ability."[8] For example, John Riccitiello, CEO of Electronic Arts, the world's leading computer game maker, is a serious "gamer." Says Riccitiello, "Could you imagine, say, running a book publisher if you didn't read? Or running a movie studio if you don't watch TV or go to the movies?"[9] Although it certainly helps that Riccitiello understands EA's products and its hardcore "gamer" customers, EA succeeds not for those reasons, but because of his capabilities as a manager.

Managers need to perform five managerial functions in order to be successful, according to Fayol: planning, organizing, coordinating, commanding, and controlling.[10] Most management textbooks today have updated this list by dropping the coordinating function and referring to Fayol's commanding function as "leading." Fayol's management functions are thus known today in this updated form as planning, organizing, leading, and controlling. Studies indicate that managers who perform these management functions well are more successful, gaining promotions for themselves and profits for their companies. For example, the more time CEOs spend planning, the more profitable their companies are.[11] A 25-year study at AT&T found that employees with better planning and decision-making skills were more likely to be promoted into management jobs, to be successful as managers, and to be promoted into upper levels of management.[12]

The evidence is clear. Managers serve their companies well when they plan, organize, lead, and control. So we've organized this textbook based on these functions of management, as shown in Exhibit 1.1. The major sections within each chapter of this textbook are numbered using a single digit: 1, 2, 3, and so on. The subsections are consecutively numbered, beginning with the major section number. For example, "2.1" indicates the first subsection under the second major section. This numbering system

effectiveness accomplishing tasks that help fulfill organizational objectives.

should help you easily see the relationships among topics and follow the topic sequence. It will also help your instructor refer to specific topics during class discussion.

Now let's take a closer look at each of the management functions: **2.1 planning, 2.2 organizing, 2.3 leading,** and **2.4 controlling**.

2.1 Planning

Planning involves determining organizational goals and a means for achieving them. As you'll learn in Chapter 5, planning is one of the best ways to improve performance. It encourages people to work harder, work hard for extended periods, engage in behaviors directly related to goal accomplishment, and think of better ways to do their jobs. But most importantly, companies that plan have larger profits and faster growth than companies that don't plan.

For example, the question "What business are we in?" is at the heart of strategic planning. You'll learn about this in Chapter 6. If you can answer the question "What business are you in?" in two sentences or less, chances are you have a very clear plan for your business. But getting a clear plan is not so easy. Sometimes even very successful companies stray from their core business. This happened when eBay paid $2.6 million to acquire Skype, which makes software for free phone and video calls over the Internet. However, eBay eventually sold Skype to a group of investors for $1.9 billion. Why? Because eBay's new CEO realized it was a poor fit with its core e-commerce business, meaning eBay's Internet auction site and its PayPal online payment service business.[13]

You'll learn more about planning in Chapter 5 on planning and decision making, Chapter 6 on organizational strategy, Chapter 7 on innovation and change, and Chapter 8 on global management.

2.2 Organizing

Organizing is deciding where decisions will be made, who will do what jobs and tasks, and who will work for whom in the company. On average, it costs more than $10 billion to bring a new pharmaceutical drug to market. So when Pfizer, the second-largest pharmaceutical firm in the world, acquired Wyeth, the 11th largest, CEO Jeffrey Kindler decided to restructure Pfizer's research and development unit into two parts, one for small molecules or traditional pills and one for large molecules or drugs made from living cells. Kindler said, "Creating two distinct, but complementary, research organizations, led by the top scientist from each company, will provide sharper focus, less bureaucracy and clearer accountability in drug discovery."[14] In

Exhibit 1.1   Management Functions and Organization of the Textbook

Part 1: Introduction to Management

Chapter 1: Management
Chapter 2: The History of Management
Chapter 3: Organizational Environments and Cultures
Chapter 4: Ethics and Social Responsibility

Part 2: Planning

Chapter 5: Planning and Decision Making
Chapter 6: Organizational Strategy
Chapter 7: Innovation and Change
Chapter 8: Global Management

Part 3: Organizing

Chapter 9: Designing Adaptive Organizations
Chapter 10: Managing Teams
Chapter 11: Managing Human Resource Systems
Chapter 12: Managing Individuals and a Diverse Work Force

Part 4: Leading

Chapter 13: Motivation
Chapter 14: Leadership
Chapter 15: Managing Communication

Part 5: Controlling

Chapter 16: Control
Chapter 17: Managing Information
Chapter 18: Managing Service and Manufacturing Operations

© Cengage Learning 2013

planning determining organizational goals and a means for achieving them.

organizing deciding where decisions will be made, who will do what jobs and tasks, and who will work for whom.

© iStockphoto.com/Hans Martens

what really works
Meta-Analysis

Some studies show that having two drinks a day increases life expectancy by decreasing the chances of having a heart attack. Yet other studies show that having two drinks a day shortens life expectancy. For years, we've "buttered" our morning toast with margarine instead of butter because margarine was supposed to be better for our health. Now, however, new studies show that the trans-fatty acids in margarine may be just as bad for our arteries as butter. Confusing scientific results like these frustrate ordinary people who want to eat right and live right. They also make many people question just how useful most scientific research really is.

Managers also find themselves questioning the conflicting scientific research published in journals like the *Academy of Management Journal*, the *Academy of Management Review*, the *Strategic Management Journal*, the *Journal of Applied Psychology*, and *Administrative Science Quarterly*. *The Wall Street Journal* may quote a management research article from one of these journals that says that total quality management is the best thing since sliced bread (without butter or margarine). Then, just six months later, *The Wall Street Journal* will quote a different article from the same journal that says that total quality management doesn't work. If management professors and researchers have trouble deciding what works and what doesn't, how can practicing managers know?

Thankfully, a research tool called **meta-analysis** is helping management scholars understand how well their research supports management theories. It is also useful for practicing managers because it shows what works and the conditions under which management techniques may work better or worse in the real world. Meta-analysis involves studying the scientific studies themselves. It is based on this simple idea: If one study shows that a management technique doesn't work and another study shows that it does, an average of those results is probably the best estimate of how well that management practice works (or doesn't work). For example, medical researchers Richard Peto and Rory Collins averaged all of the different results from several hundred studies investigating the relationship between aspirin and heart attacks. Their analysis, based on more than 120,000 patients from numerous studies, showed that aspirin lowered the incidence of heart attacks by an average of 4 percent. Prior to this study, doctors prescribed aspirin as a preventive measure for only 38 percent of heart-attack victims. Today, because of the meta-analysis results, doctors prescribe aspirin for 72 percent of heart-attack victims.

Fortunately, you don't need a Ph.D. to understand the statistics reported in a meta-analysis. In fact, one primary advantage of meta-analysis over traditional significance tests is that you can convert meta-analysis statistics into intuitive numbers that anyone can easily understand. Each meta-analysis reported in the "What Really Works" sections of this textbook is accompanied by an easy-to-understand statistic called the *probability of success*. As its name suggests, the probability of success shows how often a management technique will work.

For example, meta-analyses suggest that the best predictor of a job applicant's on-the-job performance is a test of general mental ability. In other words, smarter people tend to be better workers. The average correlation (one of those often misunderstood statistics) between scores on general mental ability tests and job performance is 0.60. However, very few people understand what a correlation of 0.60 means. What most managers want to know is how often they will hire the right person if they choose job applicants based on general mental ability test scores. Likewise, they want to know how much difference a cognitive ability test makes when hiring new workers. The probability of success may be high, but if the difference isn't really that large, is it worth a manager's time to have job applicants take a general mental ability test?

Well, our user-friendly statistics indicate that it's wise to have job applicants take a general mental ability test. In fact, the probability of success, shown in graphical form here, is 76 percent. This means that an employee hired on the basis of a good score on a general mental ability test stands a 76 percent chance of being a better performer than someone picked at random from the pool of all job applicants. So chances are you're going to be right much more often than wrong if you use a general mental ability test to make hiring decisions.[15] In summary, each What Really Works section in this textbook is based on meta-analysis research, which provides the best scientific evidence that management professors and researchers have about what works and what doesn't work in management. We will use the easy-to-understand index known

as the *probability of success* to indicate how well a management idea or strategy is likely to work in the workplace. Of course, no idea or technique works every time and in every circumstance. Nevertheless, the management ideas and strategies discussed in the What Really Works sections can usually make a meaningful difference where you work. In today's competitive, fast-changing, global marketplace, few managers can afford to overlook proven management strategies like the ones discussed in What Really Works.

General Mental Ability

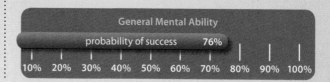

all, the new company will consist of nine businesses, including primary care, vaccines, oncology, consumer and nutritional products, and pharmaceuticals.

You'll learn more about organizing in Chapter 9 on designing organizations, Chapter 10 on managing teams, Chapter 11 on managing human resources, and Chapter 12 on managing individuals and a diverse workforce.

2.3 Leading

Our third management function, **leading**, involves inspiring and motivating workers to work hard to achieve organizational goals. For Alan Mulally, CEO of Ford Motor Company, a critical part of keeping his employees motivated is to "Communicate, communicate, communicate. Everyone has to know the plan, its status, and areas that need special attention." Accordingly, Mulally distributed a set of cards with Ford's mission on one side and the company's four most important goals on the other. He also hosts a Business Plan Review each week with his top executives to check on performance company wide, which is tracked via 280 charts, each with the name and picture of the manager responsible. Mulally's leadership brought Ford back from the brink of bankruptcy. In a series of timely maneuvers and shrewd business deals, Mulally secured a $23.6 billion loan and then sold off several noncore brands to raise $23.6 billion prior to the recession, which kept Ford sufficiently capitalized as the world economy slowed. And although General Motors and Chrysler were forced to seek government loans and eventually file for bankruptcy, Ford stayed afloat on its own, posting healthy profits in 2009 and 2010, well ahead of Mulally's promise to make Ford profitable by 2011.[16]

You'll learn more about leading in Chapter 13 on motivation, Chapter 14 on leadership, and Chapter 15 on managing communication.

2.4 Controlling

The last function of management, **controlling**, is monitoring progress toward goal achievement and taking corrective action when progress isn't being made. The basic control process involves setting standards to achieve goals, comparing actual

meta-analysis a study of studies, a statistical approach that provides one of the best scientific estimates of how well management theories and practices work.

leading inspiring and motivating workers to work hard to achieve organizational goals.

controlling monitoring progress toward goal achievement and taking corrective action when needed.

performance to those standards, and then making changes to return performance to those standards. At $410 billion a year in annual sales, Mike Duke, Walmart's CEO, runs the largest company in the world (which will be even larger when you read this). Duke, an engineer by education, is well-known for being organized and meticulous in his attention to detail. He maintains a red folder, eight in all, for each of the executives who reports to him. On the outside of each folder, his assistant will write the executive's name and the time of Duke's next meeting with him. The inside of each folder contains a set of goals, problems, and follow-up items related to that manager's responsibilities. For example, the folder for Brian Cornell, who runs Sam's Club, Walmart's discount warehouse chain, contains recent sales figures, a question that Duke has regarding the strategy Sam's is using to purchase real estate for new locations, and an email from a Sam's Club member who wrote to Duke complaining that the Member's Mark facial tissue (a private brand sold by Sam's) gets stuck in the box and doesn't pull out easily. Regarding the tissue, Duke said, "Brian's team identified that as a real problem. And I said, 'Great, now that we've identified the problem, when are we going to solve it?' And I keep this in here until Brian tells me it's solved. It's a follow-up mechanism."[17]

You'll learn more about the control function in Chapter 16 on control, Chapter 17 on managing information, and Chapter 18 on managing service and manufacturing operations.

Review 2

Management Functions Henri Fayol's classic management functions are known today as planning, organizing, leading, and controlling. Planning is determining organizational goals and a means for achieving them. Organizing is deciding where decisions will be made, who will do what jobs and tasks, and who will work for whom. Leading is inspiring and motivating workers to work hard to achieve organizational goals. Controlling is monitoring progress toward goal achievement and taking corrective action when needed. Studies show that performing these management functions well leads to better managerial performance.

doing the right thing

Making a Great Workplace

Good managers focus not only on the bottom line, but on the people they manage. One of the most important tasks that a manager has is to make sure that the people that they are supposed to manage are taken care of. Yvon Chouinard, the founder of the outdoor clothing company Patagonia, says that the key to her company's success is making sure that employees feel physically and emotionally secure at work, and that they are given the freedom to be creative and solve problems. Patagonia also has an extensive benefits policy that includes child care and flexible scheduling, so that employees don't have to worry about how personal issues might conflict with work. Although some might worry that these expenses hurt the company's bottom line, Chouinard views them as necessary expenses for building a family atmosphere. So, as a manager, do the right thing and make sure to take care of the people that you manage.[18]

Exhibit 1.2   Jobs and Responsibilities of Four Kinds of Managers

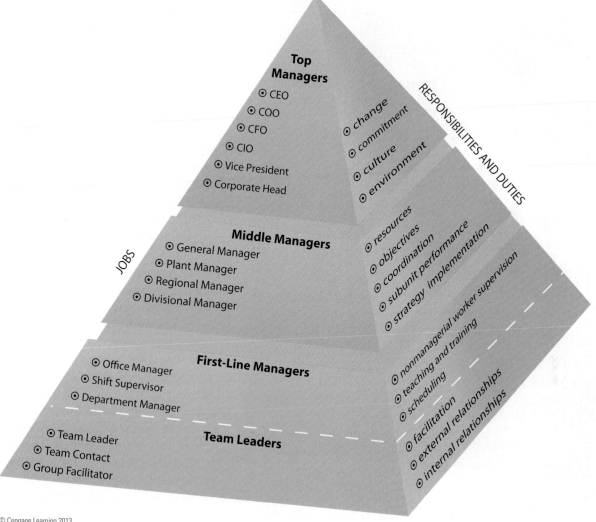

Top Managers
- ⊙ CEO
- ⊙ COO
- ⊙ CFO
- ⊙ CIO
- ⊙ Vice President
- ⊙ Corporate Head

Middle Managers
- ⊙ General Manager
- ⊙ Plant Manager
- ⊙ Regional Manager
- ⊙ Divisional Manager

First-Line Managers
- ⊙ Office Manager
- ⊙ Shift Supervisor
- ⊙ Department Manager

Team Leaders
- ⊙ Team Leader
- ⊙ Team Contact
- ⊙ Group Facilitator

JOBS

RESPONSIBILITIES AND DUTIES
- ⊙ change
- ⊙ commitment
- ⊙ culture
- ⊙ environment
- ⊙ resources
- ⊙ objectives
- ⊙ coordination
- ⊙ subunit performance
- ⊙ strategy implementation
- ⊙ nonmanagerial worker supervision
- ⊙ teaching and training
- ⊙ scheduling
- ⊙ facilitation
- ⊙ external relationships
- ⊙ internal relationships

© Cengage Learning 2013

What Do Managers Do?

Not all managerial jobs are the same. The demands and requirements placed on the CEO of Sony are significantly different from those placed on the manager of your local Wendy's restaurant.

3 Kinds of Managers

As shown in Exhibit 1.2, there are four kinds of managers, each with different jobs and responsibilities: **3.1 top managers, 3.2 middle managers, 3.3 first-line managers,** and **3.4 team leaders.**

top managers executives responsible for the overall direction of the organization.

3.1 Top Managers

Top managers hold positions like chief executive officer (CEO), chief operating officer (COO), chief financial officer (CFO), and chief

After reading the next two sections, you should be able to

3. *Describe different kinds of managers.*

4. *Explain the major roles and subroles that managers perform in their jobs.*

© Michael Asselin/Corbis

"what's new" companies >

> "The CEO has a very specific job that only he or she can do: Link external world with the internal organization."
>
> A. G. LAFLEY, FORMER CEO, PROCTER & GAMBLE

information officer (CIO) and are responsible for the overall direction of the organization. Top managers have the following responsibilities:[19] First, they are responsible for creating a context for change. In fact, the CEOs of AIG, British Petroleum, General Motors, and Massey Energy were all fired precisely because they had not moved fast enough to bring about significant changes in their companies.[20]

Indeed, in both Europe and the United States, 35 percent of all CEOs are eventually fired because of their inability to successfully change their companies.[21] Creating a context for change includes forming a long-range vision or mission for the company. As one CEO said, "The CEO has to think about the future more than anyone."[22] Once that vision or mission is set, the second responsibility of top managers is to develop employees' commitment to and ownership of the company's performance. That is, top managers are responsible for creating employee buy-in. Campbell Soup's CEO, Douglas Conant, says, "To win in the marketplace, we believe you must first win in the workplace. I'm obsessed with keeping employee engagement front and center and keeping up energy around it." Indeed, Conant put that into action in a highly symbolic way when he joined **Campbell Soup** as its new CEO. "When I first got to Camden, N.J., our facility there was surrounded by barbed wire. It looked and felt more like a minimum-security prison than a corporate headquarters. I didn't waste any time taking down the fences and replacing them." Said Conant, "Campbell as an organization needed to demonstrate its commitment to its people before they could be expected to demonstrate their own extraordinary commitment to it and its success. This understanding became the basis of what we call the Campbell Promise, which is summed up by the phrase, 'Campbell valuing people, people valuing Campbell.'"[23]

Third, top managers must create a positive organizational culture through language and action. Top managers impart company values, strategies, and lessons through what they do and say to others both inside and outside the company. Indeed, no matter what they communicate, it's critical for CEOs to send and reinforce clear, consistent messages.[24] A former *Fortune* 500 CEO said, "I tried to [use] exactly the same words every time so that I didn't produce a lot of, 'Last time you said this, this time you said that.' You've got to say the same thing over and over and over."[25] Likewise, it's important to actively manage internal organizational communication. Kimberly Till, CEO of Harris Interactive, a New York–based market research company, emphasizes the importance of frequent communication, saying, "I keep all the employees in the loop through weekly emails, town hall meetings and forums, video clips of big decisions and visits to the offices."[26]

Finally, top managers are responsible for monitoring their business environments. A. G. Lafley, former CEO of Procter & Gamble, believes that most people do not understand the CEO's responsibilities. Says Lafley, "Conventional wisdom suggests that the CEO was primarily a coach and a utility infielder, dropping in to solve [internal] problems where they crop up. In fact, however, the CEO has a very specific job that only he or she can do: Link the external world with the internal organization."[27] This means that top managers must closely monitor customer needs; competitors' moves; and long-term business, economic, and social trends.

3.2 Middle Managers

Middle managers hold positions like plant manager, regional manager, or divisional manager. They are responsible for setting objectives consistent with top management's goals and for planning and implementing subunit strategies for achieving those objectives.[28] One specific middle-management responsibility is to plan and allocate resources to meet objectives.

A second major responsibility is to coordinate and link groups, departments, and divisions within a company. In February 2008, a tornado destroyed a Caterpillar plant in Oxford, Mississippi, the only plant in the company that produced a particular coupling required for many of Caterpillar's machines. The disaster threatened a worldwide production shutdown. Greg Folley, a middle manager in charge of the parts division that included the plant, gave workers two weeks to restore production to pre-tornado levels. He said, "I was betting on people to get it done." He contacted new vendors, sent engineers from other Caterpillar locations to Mississippi to check for quality, and set up distribution operations in another facility. Meanwhile, Kevin Kempa, the plant manager in Oxford, moved some employees to another plant, delivered new training to employees during the production hiatus, and oversaw reconstruction of the plant. The day before the two-week deadline, the Oxford plant was up and running and produced 8,000 parts.[29]

A third responsibility of middle management is to monitor and manage the performance of the subunits and individual managers who report to them. After **Johnson & Johnson's** (J&J) McNeil Consumer Healthcare division experienced repeated manufacturing problems that led to a recall of children's Tylenol, Motrin, and Benadryl, J&J's Ajit Shetty, who runs the company's oversight group, was given the responsibility for maintaining quality standards in the company's consumer, medical device, and pharmaceutical segments. The chief quality officers from each business group and the 120 managers of J&J's manufacturing facilities around the world will continue to maintain responsibility for producing safe, high-quality products, but having all of these middle managers work together and report directly to Ajit Shetty should help J&J maintain its high standards in a uniform way.[30]

< **"what's new" companies**

Finally, middle managers are also responsible for implementing the changes or strategies generated by top managers. Why? Because they're closer to the managers and employees who work on a daily basis with suppliers to effectively and efficiently deliver the company's product or service. In short, they're closer to the people who can best solve problems and implement solutions. Brad Heath, founder and CEO of VirTex Assembly Services, an Austin, Texas–based firm that provides engineering and manufacturing services to electronics firms, says of middle managers, "They're very important because I can't focus on all the different areas that they [i.e., middle managers] do and give those [areas] adequate attention. If I try to do that, I can't focus on my mission, which is charting the direction of the company."[31]

3.3 First-Line Managers

First-line managers hold positions like office manager, shift supervisor, or department manager. The primary responsibility of first-line managers is to manage the performance of entry-level employees who are directly responsible for producing a

middle managers managers responsible for setting objectives consistent with top management's goals and for planning and implementing subunit strategies for achieving these objectives.

first-line managers managers who train and supervise the performance of nonmanagerial employees who are directly responsible for producing the company's products or services.

company's goods and services. Thus, first-line managers are the only managers who don't supervise other managers. The responsibilities of first-line managers include monitoring, teaching, and short-term planning.

**"what's new"
companies** >

First-line managers encourage, monitor, and reward the performance of their workers. Jennifer Lepird is the human resources staffer on a team at **Intuit** that manages the acquisitions of companies that Intuit buys. When Intuit bought Paycycle, one of its competitors, Jennifer stayed up all night, putting together a spreadsheet that showed how the salary structure for Paycycle's managers and employees should be integrated with Intuit's. Her acquisition team manager, a first-line manager, sent her a thank-you email and a gift certificate for several hundred dollars. Jennifer was thrilled by her boss's reward, saying, "The fact that somebody took the time to recognize the effort made the long hours just melt away."[32] First-line managers also teach entry-level employees how to do their jobs. Damian Mogavero's company, Avero LLC, helps restaurants analyze sales data for each member of a restaurant's wait staff. Restaurant managers who use these data, says Mogavero, will often take their top-selling server to lunch each week as a reward. The best managers, however, will also take their poorest-selling servers out to lunch to talk about what they can do to improve their performance.[33] Likewise, Coca-Cola manager Tom Mattia says, "I try to make every interaction I have with someone on my team a teaching experience. There are always specific work issues that need to get addressed, but then I try to explain my thinking behind an approach so people can get more experience."[34]

First-line managers also make detailed schedules and operating plans based on middle management's intermediate-range plans. By contrast to the long-term plans of top managers (three to five years out) and the intermediate plans of middle managers (6 to 18 months out), first-line managers engage in plans and actions that typically produce results within two weeks.[35] Consider the typical convenience-store manager (e.g., 7-Eleven) who starts the day by driving past competitors' stores to inspect their gasoline prices and then checks the outside of his or her store for anything that might need maintenance, such as burned-out lights or signs, or restocking, like windshield washer fluid and paper towels. Then comes an inside check, where the manager determines what needs to be done for that day. (Are there enough coffee and donuts for breakfast or enough sandwiches for lunch?) Once the day is planned, the manager turns to weekend orders. After accounting for the weather (hot or cold) and the sales trends at the same time last year, the manager makes sure the store will have enough beer, soft drinks, and Sunday papers on hand. Finally, the manager looks seven to ten days ahead for hiring needs. Because of strict hiring procedures (basic math tests, drug tests, and background checks), it can take that long to hire new employees. Said one convenience-store manager, "I have to continually interview, even if I am fully staffed."[36]

3.4 Team Leaders

The fourth kind of manager is a team leader. This relatively new kind of management job developed as companies shifted to self-managing teams, which, by definition, have no formal supervisor. In traditional management hierarchies, first-line managers are responsible for the performance of nonmanagerial employees and have the authority to hire and fire workers, make job assignments, and control resources. In this new structure, the teams themselves perform nearly all of the functions performed by first-line managers under traditional hierarchies.[37]

Team leaders have a different set of responsibilities than traditional first-line managers.[38] **Team leaders** are primarily responsible for facilitating team activities toward accomplishing a goal. This doesn't mean team leaders are responsible for team performance. They aren't; the team is. Team leaders help their team members plan and schedule work, learn to solve problems, and work effectively with each

team leaders managers responsible for facilitating team activities toward goal accomplishment.

other. Management consultant Franklin Jonath says, "The idea is for the team leader to be at the service of the group." It should be clear that the team members own the outcome. The leader is there to bring intellectual, emotional, and spiritual resources to the team. Through his or her actions, the leader should be able to show the others how to think about the work that they're doing in the context of their lives. It's a tall order, but the best teams have such leaders.[39]

Relationships among team members and between different teams are crucial to good team performance and must be well managed by team leaders, who are responsible for fostering good relationships and addressing problematic ones within their teams. Getting along with others is much more important in team structures because team members can't get work done without the help of other teammates. For example, studies show that it's not the surgeon but the interactions between the surgeon and all operating room team members that determine surgical outcomes. However, at 20 hospitals, 60 percent of the operating room team members—nurses, technicians, and other doctors—agreed with the statement "In the ORs here, it is difficult to speak up if I perceive a problem with patient care."[40] And when operating room team members don't speak up, serious mistakes can occur, no matter how talented the surgeon. Consequently, surgeons are using "safety pauses" to better involve members of their surgical teams. The surgeon will pause, ask whether anyone has concerns or comments, and address them if need be. Studies show that safety pauses reduce mistakes, such as operating on the wrong leg or beginning surgery with key surgical instruments missing.[41]

Team leaders are also responsible for managing external relationships. Team leaders act as the bridge or liaison between their teams and other teams, departments, and divisions in a company. For example, if a member of Team A complains about the quality of Team B's work, Team A's leader is responsible for solving the problem by initiating a meeting with Team B's leader. Together, these team leaders are responsible for getting members of both teams to work together to solve the problem. If it's done right, the problem is solved without involving company management or blaming members of the other team.[42]

So the team leader's job involves a different set of skills than traditional management jobs typically do. For example, a Hewlett-Packard ad for a team leader position says, "Job seeker must enjoy coaching, working with people, and bringing about improvement through hands-off guidance and leadership."[43] Team leaders who fail to understand how their roles are different from those of traditional managers often struggle in their jobs. A team leader at Texas Instruments said, "I didn't buy into teams, partly because there was no clear plan on what I was supposed to do. . . . I never let the operators [team members] do any scheduling or any ordering of parts because that was mine. I figured as long as I had that, I had a job."[44]

You will learn more about teams in Chapter 10.

Kinds of Managers There are four different kinds of managers. Top managers are responsible for creating a context for change, developing attitudes of commitment and ownership, creating a positive organizational culture through words and actions, and monitoring their company's business environments. Middle managers are responsible for planning and allocating resources, coordinating and linking groups and departments, monitoring and managing the performance of subunits and managers, and implementing the changes or strategies generated by top managers. First-line managers are responsible for managing the performance of nonmanagerial employees, teaching direct reports how to do their jobs, and making detailed schedules and operating plans based on middle management's intermediate-range plans. Team leaders are responsible for facilitating team performance, managing external relationships, and facilitating internal team relationships.

Review 3

4 Managerial Roles

Although all four types of managers engage in planning, organizing, leading, and controlling, if you were to follow them around during a typical day on the job, you would probably not use these terms to describe what they actually do. Rather, what you'd see are the various roles managers play. Professor Henry Mintzberg followed five American CEOs, shadowing each for a week and analyzing their mail, their conversations, and their actions. He concluded that managers fulfill three major roles while performing their jobs—interpersonal roles, informational roles, and decisional roles.[45]

In other words, managers talk to people, gather and give information, and make decisions. Furthermore, as shown in Exhibit 1.3, these three major roles can be subdivided into ten subroles. Let's examine each major role—**4.1 interpersonal, 4.2 informational**, and **4.3 decisional roles**—and their ten subroles.

4.1 Interpersonal Roles

More than anything else, management jobs are people-intensive. Estimates vary with the level of management, but most managers spend between two-thirds and four-fifths of their time in face-to-face communication with others.[46] If you're a loner, or if you consider dealing with people a pain, then you may not be cut out for management work. In fulfilling the interpersonal role of management, managers perform three subroles: figurehead, leader, and liaison.

In the **figurehead role**, managers perform ceremonial duties like greeting company visitors, speaking at the opening of a new facility, or representing the company at a community luncheon to support local charities. Wichita, Kansas–based Cessna is the largest manufacturer of general aviation planes in the world. When Cessna opened a new 101,000-square-foot jet service facility employing 77 workers in Mesa, Arizona, CEO Jack Pelton flew in to join Mesa's mayor, Cessna managers, and local workers and their families to celebrate the grand opening.[47]

In the **leader role**, managers motivate and encourage workers to accomplish organizational objectives. At RedPeg Marketing, cofounder Brad Nierenberg motivates his employees with company perks, such as a three-bedroom beach house that is available to all 48 employees for vacations, cold beer in the refrigerator, free breakfast at staff meetings, and trophies and awards for great performance. Once, after the company had met a critical goal, Nierenberg walked into the office with $38,000 in cash, or $1,000 each for his then 38 employees. Said Nierenberg, "I thought, 'I've got to make a big deal out of this; I can't just put it in their checking account because that's not as fun.' I thought it would be cool for them to see $38,000 in cash."[48]

In the **liaison role**, managers deal with people outside their units. Studies consistently indicate that managers spend as much time with outsiders as they do with their own subordinates and their own bosses. When Mike Tannenbaum, general manager of the New York Jets, headed across town to the headquarters of J.P. Morgan Chase, he wasn't paying J.P. Morgan CEO Jamie Dimon a social call. Tannenbaum had scheduled the meeting to discuss J.P. Morgan's risk assessment and acquisition processes. The appointment with Dimon was part of a much broader initiative in which members from all levels of the Jets organization were encouraged to interact with professionals outside of their fields, such as firefighters, storm chasers, and bankers like Dimon, for the purpose of learning better management and decision-making

---

figurehead role the interpersonal role managers play when they perform ceremonial duties.

leader role the interpersonal role managers play when they motivate and encourage workers to accomplish organizational objectives.

liaison role the interpersonal role managers play when they deal with people outside their units.

Exhibit 1.3
Mintzberg's Managerial Roles and Subroles

Interpersonal Roles
- Figurehead
- Leader
- Liaison

Informational Roles
- Monitor
- Disseminator
- Spokesperson

Decisional Roles
- Entrepreneur
- Disturbance Handler
- Resource Allocator
- Negotiator

Source: Reprinted by permission of Harvard Business Review (an exhibit) from "The Manager's Job: Folklore and Fact," by Mintzberg, H. *Harvard Business Review*, July–August 1975. Copyright © by the President and Fellows of Harvard College. All rights reserved.

processes. The Jets are also planning opportunities in the future for J.P. Morgan employees to visit their facilities. In this case, the liaison role operates in both directions, as managers are initiating interactions with outsiders and outsiders are coming to them.[49]

The same holds true for the convenience-store managers discussed earlier. Even first-line managers spend much of their time dealing with outsiders as they deal with vendors who make store deliveries and set up product displays, work with computer technicians who help with computer glitches and satellite connections to headquarters, order from sales representatives who supply the mops and deli aprons used in the store, and even call the sheriff about stolen credit cards.[50]

4.2 Informational Roles

Not only do managers spend most of their time in face-to-face contact with others but they spend much of it obtaining and sharing information. Indeed, Mintzberg found that the managers in his study spent 40 percent of their time giving and getting information from others. In this regard, management can be viewed as processing information, gathering information by scanning the business environment and listening to others in face-to-face conversations, processing that information, and then sharing it with people both inside and outside the company. Mintzberg described three informational subroles: monitor, disseminator, and spokesperson.

In the **monitor role**, managers scan their environment for information, actively contact others for information, and because of their personal contacts, receive a great deal of unsolicited information. Besides receiving firsthand information, managers monitor their environment by reading local newspapers and *The Wall Street Journal* to keep track of customers, competitors, and technological changes that may affect their businesses. Now, managers can also take advantage of electronic monitoring and distribution services that track the news wires (Associated Press, Reuters, and so on) for stories related to their businesses. These services deliver customized electronic newspapers that include only stories on topics the managers specify. Business Wire (www.businesswire.com) monitors and distributes daily news headlines

monitor role the informational role managers play when they scan their environment for information.

mgmt:trends

As McDonald's looks to grow in China's booming markets, it knows that a key to its success will be the quality of its managers. That's why it recently opened up a training center, Hamburger University, in Shanghai, with the goal of recruiting and retaining top workers. With an investment of about $23 million, McDonald's created a center where it could train about 1,000 people per year for junior and senior management positions. The center also helps franchise owners learn how to operate their restaurants effectively and efficiently. And all of this investment is intended to serve as a foundation for the company's plans to expand aggressively by opening 1,000 new stores in China. Hamburger University is great for employees too, because it gives them an opportunity to move up in the McDonald's hierarchy. An entry-level employee can rise to store manager, and with training from Hamburger University, rise to middle and senior management in the organization, making McDonald's an ideal place for people looking for steady career paths.[51]

from major industries (e.g., automotive, banking and financial, health, high tech).[52] CyberAlert (www.cyberalert.com) keeps round-the-clock track of new stories in categories chosen by each subscriber.[53] FNS NewsClips Online (www.news-clips.com) provides subscribers daily electronic news clips from more than 5,000 online news sites.[54]

Because of their numerous personal contacts and their access to subordinates, managers are often hubs for the distribution of critical information. In the **disseminator role**, managers share the information they have collected with their subordinates and others in the company. At Telephonica 02, a British-based telecommunications firm ranked as one of the best places to work in London, managers sit down twice a year with their employees to review a pocket-sized pamphlet outlining the company's goals and objectives. The discussions center around how the employees' personal development and growth plans can be linked to the company's goals.[55] Although there will never be a complete substitution for face-to-face dissemination of information, Serena Software, based in Redwood City, California, uses Facebook to communicate worldwide with its 850 employees. On "Facebook Fridays," employees are given an hour, should they choose, to spend time using Facebook to communicate about themselves or learn about others in the company. Serena Software relies on Facebook so much for recruiting new employees and marketing its products that it has become the company's de facto intranet.[56] (You'll read more about intranets in Chapter 15 on communication.)

In contrast to the disseminator role, in which managers distribute information to employees inside the company, managers in the **spokesperson role** share information with people outside their departments and companies. One of the most common ways CEOs serve as spokespeople for their companies is at annual meetings with company shareholders or the board of directors. CEOs also serve as spokespeople to the media when their companies are involved in major news stories. When Steve Jobs, chairman and former CEO of Apple, gave a keynote address or made a product presentation, he was acting as a spokesperson for the company. Jobs' speeches were rigorously well rehearsed and were famous for capturing the attention of industry experts, Apple fans, potential customers, and analysts alike. When the iPhone was launched in 2007, Jobs described the device as a "revolutionary and magical product that is literally five years ahead of any other mobile phone." At the unveiling of the iPhone 4 in 2010, Jobs described it as "the biggest leap since the original iPhone."[57] As Apple's spokesperson, Steve Jobs used his platform to communicate Apple's technology vision to customers and competitors.

4.3 Decisional Roles

Mintzberg found that obtaining and sharing information is not an end in itself. Obtaining and sharing information with people inside and outside the company is useful to managers because it helps them make good decisions. According to Mintzberg, managers engage in four decisional subroles: entrepreneur, disturbance handler, resource allocator, and negotiator.

In the **entrepreneur role**, managers adapt themselves, their subordinates, and their units to change. When **UPS** found nearly 30 percent of its driver candidates were flunking its driver training program, it abandoned traditional classroom training, based on lectures and books, for high-tech, interactive training methods. UPS training now includes video-game simulators, and "kinetic learning" modules designed to allow recruits to practice specific scenarios such as walking on ice. It even has an 11,500-square-foot facility with a real driving course that teaches and tests UPS's driving techniques. Thanks to its new, interactive training methods, only 10 percent

disseminator role the informational role managers play when they share information with others in their departments or companies.

spokesperson role the informational role managers play when they share information with people outside their departments or companies.

entrepreneur role the decisional role managers play when they adapt themselves, their subordinates, and their units to change.

"what's new" companies >

of driver trainees fail, leading Allen Hill, UPS's senior vice president of human resources, to conclude that the new training methods have "enhanced the probability of success of these new drivers."[58]

< **"what's new" companies**

In the **disturbance handler role**, managers respond to pressures and problems so severe that they demand immediate attention and action. When computer hackers replaced wine critic Gary Vaynerchuk's website, **Corkd.com**, with pornographic images, Vaynerchuk immediately recorded an apology video, posted it on another website, and then tweeted about the apology video to his 900,000 followers. He also communicated directly with the 65 people who mentioned the incident on their own Twitter accounts. Said Vaynerchuk, "Every person that mentioned Corkd on Twitter got a message from me and a link to the video." Although it took eight hours to restore the Corkd.com website, there was no drop-off in terms of sales or website visits. Furthermore, he received 75 emails from customers who appreciated his quick explanation about what had happened.[59]

In the **resource allocator role**, managers decide who will get what resources and how many resources they will get. For instance, as the recession that began in the fall of 2008 deepened, companies slashed production by closing facilities, laying off workers, and cutting pay for surviving workers and managers. But when it came to research and development (R&D) spending, the largest firms spent as much on R&D as they did before, despite revenues falling by nearly 8 percent. Why did they allocate an even larger part of their budgets to R&D spending in the middle of a recession? Because in prior economic downturns, continued investments in R&D led to the development of successful products such as the iPod and fuel-efficient jet engines. Says Jim Andrew, of the Boston Consulting Group, "Companies by and large realized that large reductions in R&D are suicidal." Therefore, companies such as Intel, which saw a 90 percent drop in its net income, still spent $5.4 billion on R&D. Likewise, 3M, which cut capital spending by 30 percent and laid off 4,700 workers, slightly increased its R&D spending so as not to sacrifice future profits from new, innovative products.[60]

In the **negotiator role**, managers negotiate schedules, projects, goals, outcomes, resources, and employee raises. For example, after years of lawsuits, it only took two days for Roger Faxon, the new CEO of **EMI Group Ltd.**, which owns the rights

disturbance handler role the decisional role managers play when they respond to severe problems that demand immediate action.

resource allocator role the decisional role managers play when they decide who gets what resources.

negotiator role the decisional role managers play when they negotiate schedules, projects, goals, outcomes, resources, and employee raises.

< **"what's new" companies**

After years of lawsuits, it took Roger Faxon, CEO of EMI Group Ltd., just two days to negotiate the rights to sell Beatles' music on Apple's iTunes stores.

to sell the Beatles' music, to negotiate a deal to make the legendary band's music available for sale at Apple's iTunes store. It had been long thought that the surviving band members, Paul McCartney and Ringo Starr, and the widows of deceased band members John Lennon and George Harrison, who have veto rights over how the music is distributed, would never permit digital downloads of the band's music. But, in the end, they agreed. Just two months after the agreement was negotiated, 5 million Beatles' songs and two million Beatles' albums had been sold and downloaded via iTunes.[61]

Review 4

Managerial Roles Managers perform interpersonal, informational, and decisional roles in their jobs. In fulfilling the interpersonal role, managers act as figureheads by performing ceremonial duties, as leaders by motivating and encouraging workers, and as liaisons by dealing with people outside their units. When managers perform their informational role, they act as monitors by scanning their environment for information, as disseminators by sharing information with others in the company, and as spokespeople by sharing information with people outside their departments or companies. In decisional roles, managers act as entrepreneurs by adapting their units to incremental change, as disturbance handlers by responding to larger problems that demand immediate action, as resource allocators by deciding resource recipients and amounts, and as negotiators by bargaining with others about schedules, projects, goals, outcomes, and resources.

What Does It Take to Be a Manager?

I didn't have the slightest idea what my job was. I walked in giggling and laughing because I had been promoted and had no idea what principles or style to be guided by. After the first day, I felt like I had run into a brick wall. (Sales Representative No. 1)

Suddenly, I found myself saying, "Boy, I can't be responsible for getting all that revenue. I don't have the time." Suddenly you've got to go from [taking care of] yourself and say, "Now I'm the manager, and what does a manager do?" It takes awhile thinking about it for it to really hit you . . . a manager gets things done through other people. That's a very, very hard transition to make. (Sales Representative No. 2)[62]

The preceding statements were made by two star sales representatives who, on the basis of their superior performance, were promoted to the position of sales manager. As their comments indicate, at first they did not feel confident about their ability to do their jobs as managers. Like most new managers, these sales managers suddenly realized that the knowledge, skills, and abilities that led to success early in their careers (and were probably responsible for their promotion into the ranks of management) would not necessarily help them succeed as managers. As sales

After reading the next three sections, you should be able to

5. *Explain what companies look for in managers.*

6. *Discuss the top mistakes that managers make in their jobs.*

7. *Describe the transition that employees go through when they are promoted to management.*

representatives, they were responsible only for managing their own performance. But as sales managers, they were now directly responsible for supervising all of the sales representatives in their sales territories. Furthermore, they were now directly accountable for whether those sales representatives achieved their sales goals.

If performance in nonmanagerial jobs doesn't necessarily prepare you for a managerial job, then what does?

5 What Companies Look for in Managers

When companies look for employees who would be good managers, they look for individuals who have technical skills, human skills, conceptual skills, and the motivation to manage.[63] Exhibit 1.4 shows the relative importance of these four skills to the jobs of team leaders, first-line managers, middle managers, and top managers.

Technical skills are the specialized procedures, techniques, and knowledge required to get the job done. For the sales managers described above, technical skills involve the ability to find new sales prospects, develop accurate sales pitches based on customer needs, and close the sale. For a nurse supervisor, technical skills include being able to insert an IV or operate a crash cart if a patient goes into cardiac arrest.

Technical skills are most important for team leaders and lower-level managers because these people supervise the workers who produce products or serve customers. Team leaders and first-line managers need technical knowledge and skills to train new employees and help employees solve problems. Technical knowledge and skills are also needed to troubleshoot problems that employees can't handle. Technical skills become less important as managers rise through the managerial ranks, but they are still important.

Human skills can be summarized as the ability to work well with others. Managers with human skills work effectively within groups, encourage others to express their thoughts and feelings, are sensitive to others' needs and viewpoints, and are good listeners and communicators. Human skills are equally important at all levels of management, from first-line supervisors to CEOs. However, because lower-level managers spend much of their time solving technical problems, upper-level managers may actually spend more time dealing directly with people. On average, first-line managers spend 57 percent of their time with people, but that percentage increases to 63 percent for middle managers and 78 percent for top managers.[64]

Conceptual skills are the ability to see the organization as a whole, to understand how the different parts of the company affect each other, and to recognize how the company fits into or is affected by its external environment such as the local community, social and economic forces, customers, and the competition. Good

technical skills the ability to apply the specialized procedures, techniques, and knowledge required to get the job done.

human skills the ability to work well with others.

conceptual skills the ability to see the organization as a whole, understand how the different parts affect each other, and recognize how the company fits into or is affected by its external environment.

Exhibit 1.4 Relative Importance of Managerial Skills to Different Managerial Jobs

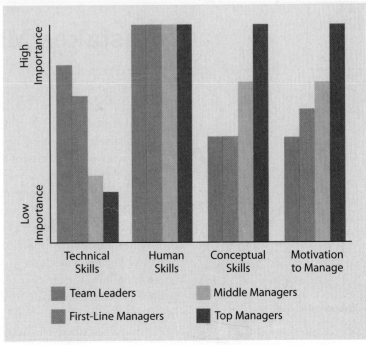

© Cengage Learning 2013

managers have to be able to recognize, understand, and reconcile multiple complex problems and perspectives. In other words, managers have to be smart! In fact, intelligence makes so much difference for managerial performance that managers with above-average intelligence typically outperform managers of average intelligence by approximately 48 percent.[65] Clearly, companies need to be careful to promote smart workers into management. Conceptual skills increase in importance as managers rise through the management hierarchy.

Good management involves much more than intelligence, however. For example, making the department genius a manager can be disastrous if that genius lacks technical skills, human skills, or one other factor known as the motivation to manage. **Motivation to manage** is an assessment of how motivated employees are to interact with superiors, participate in competitive situations, behave assertively toward others, tell others what to do, reward good behavior and punish poor behavior, perform actions that are highly visible to others, and handle and organize administrative tasks. Managers typically have a stronger motivation to manage than their subordinates, and managers at higher levels usually have a stronger motivation to manage than managers at lower levels. Furthermore, managers with a stronger motivation to manage are promoted faster, are rated as better managers by their employees, and earn more money than managers with a weak motivation to manage.[66]

Review 5

What Companies Look for in Managers Companies do not want one-dimensional managers. They want managers with a balance of skills. They want managers who know their stuff (technical skills), are equally comfortable working with blue-collar and white-collar employees (human skills), are able to assess the complexities of today's competitive marketplace and position their companies for success (conceptual skills), and want to assume positions of leadership and power (motivation to manage). Technical skills are most important for lower-level managers; human skills are equally important at all levels of management; and conceptual skills and motivation to manage increase in importance as managers rise through the managerial ranks.

6 Mistakes Managers Make

Another way to understand what it takes to be a manager is to look at the mistakes managers make. In other words, we can learn just as much from what managers shouldn't do as from what they should do. Exhibit 1.5 lists the top ten mistakes managers make.

Several studies of U.S. and British managers have compared "arrivers," or managers who made it all the way to the top of their companies, with "derailers," or managers who were successful early in their careers but were knocked off the fast track by the time they reached the middle to upper levels of management.[67] The researchers found that there were only a few differences between arrivers and derailers. For the most part, both groups were talented and both groups had weaknesses. But what distinguished derailers from arrivers was that derailers possessed two or more fatal flaws with respect to the way they managed people. Although arrivers were by no means perfect, they usually had no more than one fatal flaw or had found ways to minimize the effects of their flaws on the people with whom they worked.

The No. 1 mistake made by derailers was that they were insensitive to others by virtue of their abrasive, intimidating, and bullying management style. The authors of one study described a manager who walked into his subordinate's office and interrupted a meeting by saying, "I need to see you." When the subordinate tried to

motivation to manage an assessment of how enthusiastic employees are about managing the work of others.

24

explain that he was not available because he was in the middle of a meeting, the manager barked, "I don't give a damn! I said I wanted to see you now."[68] Not surprisingly, only 25 percent of derailers were rated by others as being good with people, compared to 75 percent of arrivers.

The second mistake was that derailers were often cold, aloof, or arrogant. Although this sounds like insensitivity to others, it has more to do with derailed managers being so smart, so expert in their areas of knowledge, that they treated others with contempt because they weren't experts too. For example, AT&T called in an industrial psychologist to counsel its vice president of human resources because she had been blamed for "ruffling too many feathers" at the company.[69] Interviews with the vice president's co-workers and subordinates revealed that they thought she was brilliant, was "smarter and faster than other people," and that she "generates a lot of ideas" and "loves to deal with complex issues." Unfortunately, these smarts were accompanied by a cold, aloof, and arrogant management style. The people she worked with complained that she does "too much too fast," treats coworkers with "disdain," "impairs teamwork," "doesn't always show her warm side," and has "burned too many bridges."[70]

The third mistake made by derailers involved betraying a trust. Betraying a trust doesn't mean being dishonest. Instead, it means making others look bad by not doing what you said you would do when you said you would do it. That mistake, in itself, is not fatal, because managers and their workers aren't machines. Tasks go undone in every company every single business day. There's always too much to do and not enough time, people, money, or resources to do it. The fatal betrayal of trust is failing to inform others when things will not be done on time. This failure to admit mistakes, quickly inform others of the mistakes, take responsibility for the mistakes, and then fix them without blaming others clearly distinguished the behavior of derailers from arrivers.

The fourth mistake was being overly political and ambitious. Managers who always have their eye on their next job rarely establish more than superficial relationships with peers and coworkers. In their haste to gain credit for successes that would be noticed by upper management, they make the fatal mistake of treating people as though they don't matter. An employee with an overly ambitious boss described him this way: "He treats employees coldly, even cruelly. He assigns blame without regard to responsibility, and takes all the credit for himself. I once had such a boss, and he gave me a new definition of shared risk: If something I did was successful, he took the credit. If it wasn't, I got the blame."[71]

The fatal mistakes of being unable to delegate, build a team, and staff effectively indicate that many derailed managers were unable to make the most basic transition to managerial work: to quit being hands-on doers and get work done through others. Two things go wrong when managers make these mistakes. First, when managers meddle in decisions that their

Exhibit 1.5 Top Ten Mistakes That Managers Make

1.	Insensitive to others: abrasive, intimidating, bullying style.
2.	Cold, aloof, arrogant.
3.	Betrayal of trust.
4.	Overly ambitious: thinking of next job, playing politics.
5.	Specific performance problems with the business.
6.	Overmanaging: unable to delegate or build a team.
7.	Unable to staff effectively.
8.	Unable to think strategically.
9.	Unable to adapt to boss with different style.
10.	Overdependent on advocate or mentor.

Source: M. W. McCall, Jr., and M. M. Lombardo, "What Makes a Top Executive?" *Psychology Today* (February 1983): 26–31.

© Hill Street Studios/Blend Images/Jupiterimages

Managers who fail to delegate will not have enough time do to anything well.

subordinates should be making—when they can't stop being doers—they alienate the people who work for them. Rich Dowd, founder of Dowd Associates, an executive search firm, admits to constantly monitoring and interrupting employees because they weren't doing the job "in the way I saw fit, even when their work was outstanding." According to Richard Kilburg of Johns Hopkins University, when managers interfere with workers decisions, "You . . . have a tendency to lose your most creative people. They're able to say, 'Screw this. I'm not staying here.'"[72] Indeed, one employee told Dowd that if he were going to do her job for her, she would quit. Second, because they are trying to do their subordinates' jobs in addition to their own, managers who fail to delegate will not have enough time to do much of anything well.

Review 6	**Mistakes Managers Make** Another way to understand what it takes to be a manager is to look at the top mistakes managers make. Five of the most important mistakes made by managers are being abrasive and intimidating; being cold, aloof, or arrogant; betraying trust; being overly ambitious; and failing to build a team and then delegate to that team.

7 The Transition to Management: The First Year

In her book *Becoming a Manager: Mastery of a New Identity*, Harvard Business School professor Linda Hill followed the development of 19 people in their first year as managers. Her study found that becoming a manager produced a profound psychological transition that changed the way these managers viewed themselves and others. As shown in Exhibit 1.6, the evolution of the managers' thoughts, expectations, and realities over the course of their first year in management reveals the magnitude of the changes they experienced.

Initially, the managers in Hill's study believed that their job was to exercise formal authority and to manage tasks—basically being the boss, telling others what to do, making decisions, and getting things done. One of the managers Hill interviewed said, "Being the manager means running my own office, using my ideas and thoughts." Another said, "[The office is] my baby. It's my job to make sure it works."[73] In fact, most of the new managers were attracted to management positions because they wanted to be in charge. Surprisingly, the new managers did not believe that their job was to manage people. The only aspects of people management mentioned by the new managers were hiring and firing.

Exhibit 1.6 The Transition to Management: Initial Expectations, after Six Months, and after a Year

MANAGERS' INITIAL EXPECTATIONS			AFTER SIX MONTHS AS A MANAGER			AFTER A YEAR AS A MANAGER					
JAN	FEB	MAR	APR	MAY	JUN	JUL	AUG	SEP	OCT	NOV	DEC

MANAGERS' INITIAL EXPECTATIONS	AFTER SIX MONTHS AS A MANAGER	AFTER A YEAR AS A MANAGER
⊙ Be the boss	⊙ Initial expectations were wrong	⊙ No longer "doer"
⊙ Have formal authority	⊙ Fast pace	⊙ Communicating, listening, and giving positive reinforcement
⊙ Manage tasks	⊙ Heavy workload	⊙ Learning to adapt to and control stress
⊙ Job is not managing people	⊙ Job is to be problem-solver and troubleshooter for subordinates	⊙ Job is people development

After six months, most of the new managers had concluded that their initial expectations about managerial work were wrong. Management wasn't just about being the boss, making decisions, and telling others what to do. The first surprise was the fast pace and heavy workload involved. Said one of Hill's managers, "This job is much harder than you think. It is 40 to 50 percent more work than being a producer! Who would have ever guessed?" The pace of managerial work was startling too. Another manager said, "You have eight or nine people looking for your time . . .coming into and out of your office all day long." A somewhat frustrated manager declared that management was "a job that never ended . . . a job you couldn't get your hands around."[74]

Informal descriptions like this are consistent with studies indicating that the average first-line manager spends no more than two minutes on a task before being interrupted by a request from a subordinate, a phone call, or an email. The pace is somewhat less hurried for top managers, who spend an average of approximately nine minutes on a task before having to switch to another. In practice, this means that supervisors may perform 30 different tasks per hour, whereas top managers perform 7 different tasks per hour, with each task typically different from the one that preceded it. A manager described this frenetic level of activity by saying, "The only time you are in control is when you shut your door, and then I feel I am not doing the job I'm supposed to be doing, which is being with the people."[75]

The other major surprise after six months on the job was that the managers' expectations about what they should do as managers were very different from their subordinates' expectations. Initially, the managers defined their jobs as helping their subordinates perform their jobs well. For the managers, who still defined themselves as doers rather than managers, assisting their subordinates meant going out on sales calls or handling customer complaints. One manager said, "I like going out with the rep, who may need me to lend him my credibility as manager. I like the challenge, the joy in closing. I go out with the reps and we make the call and talk about the customer; it's fun."[76] But when the managers "assisted" in this way, their subordinates were resentful and viewed their help as interference. The subordinates wanted their managers to help them by solving problems that they couldn't solve. Once the managers realized this distinction, they embraced their role as problem solver and troubleshooter. Thus, they could help without interfering with their subordinates' jobs.

After a year on the job, most of the managers thought of themselves as managers and no longer as doers. In making the transition, they finally realized that people management was the most important part of their job. One of Hill's interviewees summarized the lesson that had taken him a year to learn by saying, "As many demands as managers have on their time, I think their primary responsibility is people development. Not production, but people development."[77] Another indication of how much their views had changed was that most of the managers now regretted the rather heavy-handed approach they had used in their early attempts to manage their subordinates. "I wasn't good at managing . . ., so I was bossy like a first-grade teacher." "Now I see that I started out as a drill sergeant. I was inflexible, just a lot of how-to's." By the end of the year, most of the managers had abandoned their authoritarian approach for one based on communication, listening, and positive reinforcement. One manager explained, "Last night at five I handed out an award in the boardroom just to the individual. It was the first time in his career that he had [earned] $100,000, and I gave him a piece of glass [a small award] and said I'd heard a rumor that somebody here just crossed over $100,000 and I said congratulations, shook his hand, and walked away. It was not public in the sense that I gathered everybody around. But I knew and he did too."[78]

Finally, after beginning their year as managers in frustration, the managers came to feel comfortable with their subordinates, with the demands of their jobs, and with their emerging managerial styles. Although being managers had made them acutely

aware of their limitations and their need to develop as people, it also provided them with an unexpected reward of coaching and developing the people who worked for them. One manager said, "It gives me the best feeling to see somebody do something well after I have helped them. I get excited." Another stated, "I realize now that when I accepted the position of branch manager that it is truly an exciting vocation. It is truly awesome, even at this level; it can be terribly challenging and terribly exciting."[79]

Review 7

The Transition to Management: The First Year Managers often begin their jobs by using more formal authority and fewer people management skills. However, most find that being a manager has little to do with bossing their subordinates. After six months on the job, the managers were surprised at the fast pace and heavy workload and that "helping" their subordinates was viewed as interference. After a year on the job, most of the managers had come to think of themselves not as doers, but as managers who get things done through others. And because they finally realized that people management was the most important part of their job, most of them had abandoned their authoritarian approach for one based on communication, listening, and positive reinforcement.

Why Management Matters

If you walk down the aisle of the business section in your local bookstore, you'll find hundreds of books that explain precisely what companies need to do to be successful. Unfortunately, the best-selling business books tend to be faddish, changing dramatically every few years. One thing that hasn't changed, though, is the importance of good people and good management: Companies can't succeed for long without them.

After reading the next section, you should be able to

8. *Explain how and why companies can create competitive advantage through people.*

8 Competitive Advantage Through People

In his books *Competitive Advantage through People* and *The Human Equation: Building Profits by Putting People First*, Stanford University business professor Jeffrey Pfeffer contends that what separates top-performing companies from their competitors is the way they treat their workforce—in other words, their management style.[80]

Pfeffer found that managers in top-performing companies used ideas like employment security, selective hiring, self-managed teams and decentralization, high pay contingent on company performance, extensive training, reduced status distinctions (between managers and employees), and extensive sharing of financial information to achieve financial performance that, on average, was 40 percent higher than that of other companies. These ideas, which are explained in detail in Exhibit 1.7, help organizations develop workforces that are smarter, better trained, more motivated, and more committed than their competitors' workforces. And—as indicated by the phenomenal growth and return on investment earned by these companies—smarter, better trained, and more committed workforces provide superior products and service

Exhibit 1.7   Competitive Advantage through People: Management Practices

1.	Employment Security—Employment security is the ultimate form of commitment that companies can make to their workers. Employees can innovate and increase company productivity without fearing the loss of their jobs.
2.	Selective Hiring—If employees are the basis for a company's competitive advantage, and those employees have employment security, then the company needs to aggressively recruit and selectively screen applicants in order to hire the most talented employees available.
3.	Self-Managed Teams and Decentralization—Self-managed teams are responsible for their own hiring, purchasing, job assignments, and production. Self-managed teams can often produce enormous increases in productivity through increased employee commitment and creativity. Decentralization allows employees who are closest to (and most knowledgeable about) problems, production, and customers to make timely decisions. Decentralization increases employee satisfaction and commitment.
4.	High Wages Contingent on Organizational Performance—High wages are needed to attract and retain talented workers and to indicate that the organization values its workers. Employees, like company founders, shareholders, and managers, need to share in the financial rewards when the company is successful. Why? Because employees who have a financial stake in their companies are more likely to take a long-run view of the business and think like business owners.
5.	Training and Skill Development—Like a high-tech company that spends millions of dollars to upgrade computers or research and development labs, a company whose competitive advantage is based on its people must invest in the training and skill development of its people.
6.	Reduction of Status Differences—These are fancy words that indicate that the company treats everyone, no matter what the job, as equal. There are no reserved parking spaces. Everyone eats in the same cafeteria and has similar benefits. The result: much improved communication as employees focus on problems and solutions rather than on how they are less valued than managers.
7.	Sharing Information—If employees are to make decisions that are good for the long-run health and success of the company, they need to be given information about costs, finances, productivity, development times, and strategies that was previously known only by company managers.

Source: J. Pfeffer, *The Human Equation: Building Profits by Putting People First* (Boston: Harvard Business School Press, 1996).

to customers. Such customers keep buying and, by telling others about their positive experiences, bring in new customers.

According to Pfeffer, companies that invest in their people will create long-lasting competitive advantages that are difficult for other companies to duplicate. Indeed, other studies clearly demonstrate that sound management practices can produce substantial advantages in four critical areas of organizational performance: sales revenues, profits, stock market returns, and customer satisfaction.

In terms of sales revenues and profits, a study of nearly 1,000 U.S. firms found that companies that use *just some* of the ideas shown in Exhibit 1.7 had $27,044 more sales per employee and $3,814 more profit per employee than companies that didn't. For a 100-person company, these differences amount to $2.7 million more in sales and nearly $400,000 more in annual profit! For a 1,000-person company, the difference grows to $27 million more in sales and $4 million more in annual profit![81]

Another study that considers the effect of investing in people on company sales found that poorly performing companies were able to improve their average return on investment from 5.1 percent to 19.7 percent and increase sales by $94,000 per employee. They did this by adopting management techniques as simple as setting performance expectations (establishing goals, results, and schedules), coaching (informal, ongoing discussions between managers and subordinates about what is being done well and what could be done better), reviewing (annual, formal discussion about results), and rewarding employee performance (adjusting salaries and bonuses based on employee performance and results).[82] So, in addition to significantly improving the profitability of healthy companies, sound management practices can turn around failing companies.

By taking care of employees, with great perks, companies can create long-lasting competitive advantage.

To determine how investing in people affects stock market performance, researchers matched companies on *Fortune* magazine's list of "100 Best Companies to Work for in America" with companies that were similar in industry, size, and—this is key—operating performance. Both sets of companies were equally good performers; the key difference was how well they treated their employees. For both sets of companies, the researchers found that employee attitudes such as job satisfaction changed little from year to year. The people who worked for the "100 Best" companies were consistently much more satisfied with their jobs and employers year after year than were employees in the matched companies. More importantly, those stable differences in employee attitudes were strongly related to differences in stock market performance. Over a one-year period, an investment in the "100 Best Companies to Work for" would have resulted in an 82 percent cumulative stock return compared with just 37 percent for the matched companies.[83] This difference is remarkable given that both sets of companies were equally good performers at the beginning of the period. Even more impressive, however, is that from 1998 to 2009, a $100,000 investment in the "100 Best Companies to Work for" would have grown to $266,536 compared to just $134,392 invested in the Standard & Poor's 500, which is a stock index of the 500 largest public companies in the United States.[84] In other words, over those ten years an investment in the "100 Best" companies doubled investors' money. Finally, research also indicates that managers have an important effect on customer satisfaction. Many people find this surprising. They don't understand how managers, who are largely responsible for what goes on inside the company, can affect what goes on outside the company. They wonder how managers, who often interact with customers under negative conditions (when customers are angry or dissatisfied), can actually improve customer satisfaction. It turns out that managers influence customer satisfaction through employee satisfaction. When employees are satisfied with their jobs, their bosses, and the companies they work for, they provide much better service to customers.[85] In turn, customers are more satisfied too. Indeed, customers of companies on *Fortune*'s list of "100 Best Companies to Work for," where employees are much more satisfied with their jobs and their companies, have much higher customer satisfaction scores than do customers of comparable companies who are not on *Fortune*'s list. Over an eight-year period, that difference in customer satisfaction also resulted in a 14 percent annual stock market return for the "100 Best" companies compared to a 6 percent return for the overall stock market.[86]

You will learn more about the service–profit chain in Chapter 18 on managing service and manufacturing operations.

Review 8

Competitive Advantage Through People Why does management matter? Well-managed companies are competitive because their workforces are smarter, better trained, more motivated, and more committed. Furthermore, companies that practice good management consistently have greater sales revenues, profits, and stock market performance than companies that don't. Finally, good management matters because it leads to satisfied employees who, in turn, provide better service to customers. Because employees tend to treat customers the same way that their managers treat them, good management can improve customer satisfaction.

SELF-ASSESSMENT

Is Management for You?

Each chapter has a related self-assessment to help you consider how your own perspectives influence your management skills. Each assessment tool starts with a short description and ends with basic scoring information. (Your instructor will have interpretations of your scores.) As you advance through the book, take time to review your assessment scores together. Doing so will help you see patterns in your own perceptions and behaviors and give you insights into how those perceptions may affect your performance as a manager.

As you learned in Section 7 of this chapter, many managers begin their careers in management with specific ideas about what it means to be the boss. Although you may want to be a manager because of excitement, status, power, or rewards, knowing how to manage is not automatic; it requires specific skills and competencies, as well as a desire to manage. This assessment is meant to establish your baseline ability in the skills covered in the chapter. It will not tell you whether you should or should not be a manager, or whether you have "what it takes" to be a manager. It will, however, give you feedback on general skills that influence your overall managerial style.[87]

Be candid as you complete the assessment by circling the appropriate responses.

ML = Most like me

SL = Somewhat like me

NS = Not sure

SU = Somewhat unlike me

MU = Most unlike me

1. I can get others to do what I want them to do.
   ML   SL   NS   SU   MU

2. I frequently evaluate my job performance.
   ML   SL   NS   SU   MU

3. I prefer not to get involved in office politics.
   ML   SL   NS   SU   MU

4. I like the freedom that open-ended goals provide me.
   ML   SL   NS   SU   MU

5. I work best when things are orderly and calm.
   ML   SL   NS   SU   MU

6. I enjoy making oral presentations to groups of people.
   ML   SL   NS   SU   MU

7. I am confident in my abilities to accomplish difficult tasks.
   ML   SL   NS   SU   MU

8. I do not like to write.
   ML   SL   NS   SU   MU

9. I like solving difficult puzzles.
   ML   SL   NS   SU   MU

10. I am an organized person.
    ML   SL   NS   SU   MU

11. I have difficulty telling others they made a mistake.
    ML   SL   NS   SU   MU

12. I like to work set hours each day.
    ML   SL   NS   SU   MU

13. I view paperwork as a trivial task.
    ML   SL   NS   SU   MU

14. I like to help others learn new things.
    ML   SL   NS   SU   MU

15. I prefer to work alone.
    ML   SL   NS   SU   MU

16. I believe it is who you know, not what you know, that counts.
    ML   SL   NS   SU   MU

17. I enjoy doing several things at once.
    ML   SL   NS   SU   MU

18. I am good at managing money.
    ML   SL   NS   SU   MU

KEY TERMS

conceptual skills 23	liaison role 18
controlling 11	management 7
disseminator role 20	meta-analysis 10
disturbance handler role 21	middle managers 15
effectiveness 8	monitor role 19
efficiency 7	motivation to manage 24
entrepreneur role 20	negotiator role 21
figurehead role 18	organizing 9
first-line managers 15	planning 9
human skills 23	resource allocator role 21
leader role 18	spokesperson role 20
leading 11	team leaders 16
	technical skills 23
	top managers 13

19. I would rather back down from an argument than let it get out of hand.
    ML   SL   NS   SU   MU

20. I am computer literate.
    ML   SL   NS   SU   MU

Scoring

Start by reversing your scores for items 5, 8, 11, 15, and 16. For example, if you used ML, change it to MU, and vice versa; if you used SL, change it to SU, and vice versa. Now assign each answer a point value.

Number of ML answers ___8___ times 5 points each = __40__

Number of SL answers ___6___ times 4 points each = __24__

Number of NS answers ___3___ times 3 points each = __9__

Number of SU answers ___3___ times 2 points each = __6__

Number of MU answers ___5___ times 1 point each = __5__

TOTAL = __84__

You can find the interpretation for your score at www.cengagebrain.com.

Source: From P. Hunsaker, *Management; A Skills Approach*, 2nd ed., p 24–25. Copyright © 2005. Used by permission Pearson Education, Inc., Upper Saddle River, NJ.

MANAGEMENT DECISION

Making decisions is part of every manager's job. To give you practice at managerial decision making, each chapter contains a Management Decision assignment focused on a particular decision. You'll need to decide what to do in the given situation and then answer several questions to explain your choices.

Should We Try to Make More Money?[88]

To say that the airline industry has experienced some struggles would be a huge understatement. Faced with fears over terrorist attacks and sharp rises in the price of oil, airlines have been losing money at historic rates. In 2009, only four domestic airlines were able to turn a profit, while the five largest carriers lost more than $3 billion combined.

In the midst of these struggles, the industry found an unexpected, but highly lucrative, source of revenue—baggage. For many years, passengers were allowed to travel with up to three pieces of luggage—one item to carry on the plane, and two larger items that could be checked into the storage area. In 2008, American Airlines became the first major airline to charge passengers who wanted to check their baggage. Though this additional fee was much reviled, other airlines quickly followed suit, charging $15–$35 per bag for each portion of a roundtrip flight.

The net effects of baggage fees have been incredible. In 2009, the airlines combined to collect nearly $2 billion in baggage fees alone; Delta Airlines led the entire industry with $550 million. The baggage fees have also led passengers to check fewer bags. This has allowed airlines to dedicate more space to cargo, which commands a premium price. What is more, there has been a reduction in the number of mishandled bags, which led to an additional $94 million in savings. Best of all, all of this is essentially "free money"—the airlines did not lower their fares after charging for checked baggage, and they have not had to increase other expenses (such as labor) to collect the fees.

All told, the checked bag fees have been such a success that Spirit Airlines now charges $45 for carry-on baggage that is stored in overhead bins. You are a manager of the lone holdout, Southwest Airlines, which allows passengers to check two bags with no charge. Although Southwest has remained profitable during the industry's struggles, it is difficult to see competitors rake in millions of dollars in additional revenue with virtually no labor. You begin to wonder whether your company shouldn't also charge for bags so that it can maintain a competitive edge. After all, as you well know, the airline industry is unpredictable, and your company could find itself in deep struggles very quickly.

Questions

1. How is this decision emblematic of your job as a manager?

2. What are the advantages and disadvantages of following competitors by charging for checked baggage?

MANAGEMENT TEAM DECISION

From sports to school to work to civic involvement, working in teams is increasingly part of our experience. But although working in teams is more and more common, making decisions as teams is not necessarily any easier. You will learn more about managing teams in Chapter 10, but to give you more experience with teamwork, a Management Team Decision exercise designed for a group of three to five students is included in each chapter. As a group, you must come to a mutually agreeable decision on the scenario presented. Each Management Team Decision will focus on a management topic presented in the chapter. For Chapter 1, you'll work with the management function of planning and organizing as you decide how to interact with a large investor.

Saying No to an Investor[89]

You never though much about soft drinks before, but since your kids started going to junior high school and ordering their own lunches, you've become more and more concerned about how much sugary, calorie-loaded drinks they consume every day. And not just with your own kids, you wanted to do something to help kids and parents find delicious alternatives to unhealthy carbonated drinks. So it seemed quite fortunate when you got a management position at Honest Tea, a beverage company that is dedicated to providing wholesome, healthy teas and juices that use all natural, organic, unprocessed ingredients. The company proudly displays its commitment to natural, wholesome ingredients by including a label on all of its products that says "No High Fructose Corn Syrup," a sweetener that has been heavily criticized for increasing obesity, diabetes symptoms, liver disease, and even containing trace amounts of mercury.

Although the label is a small, but very public, part of the company's overall strategy of highlighting the company's commitment to quality ingredients, it's caused a serious conflict with a huge investor. When Seth Goldman and Barry Nalebuff started Honest Tea, they had a great time inventing new flavor combinations. What was hard for them was finding stores that would sell their products. They went from store to store with their teas in insulated containers, or sample bottles made from empty Snapple bottles.

A few years ago, however, Coca-Cola bought a 40 percent stake in Honest Tea for $43 million. And while the cash infusion was great for the company, what was even better was that Coca-Cola was able to give a huge boost in distribution. Honest Tea was able to take advantage of Coca-Cola's nationwide network of distributors, so that it could find a place for its products in stores, restaurants, and cafes all over the country.

But the investment from Coca-Cola had its downside, as well. Coca-Cola executives were quite disturbed by the "No High Fructose Corn Syrup" label. Although it was meant to tout the healthiness of Honest Tea's products, Coca-Cola people saw it as an implicit criticism of its own products, most of which use high fructose corn syrup. So senior managers from Coca-Cola approached Honest Tea with a request—change the label so that it says "sweetened with organic cane sugar" or "no fake stuff," or better yet, just get rid of the label altogether.

Although you and the other managers at Honest Tea want to maintain a good relationship with Coca-Cola, you're worried that any changes to the label will violate the company's philosophical commitments. Some worry that removing the label altogether will go against the company commitment of letting people know that the products contain no hidden ingredients. Others argue that changing the label at all will be misleading, because it wouldn't be crystal clear to consumers that the ingredients are not artificial or highly processed. But at the same time, you and the other managers don't want to anger Coca-Cola, which not only owns 40 percent of your company but also has an option to purchase all of it in the future.

You and other senior managers have been assigned to a team that will engage in negotiations with Coca-Cola. How will you respond to your biggest investor? Will you give in to Coca-Cola's wishes, and if so, how? Or, will you decide just to stick to your guns and do nothing? For this exercise, assemble a team of five students to act as the management team.

Questions

1. How is this decision emblematic of a manager's role as a liaison?

2. How would your team choose to respond to Coca-Cola's request?

3. If you respond positively to Coca-Cola's request for changes to the label, how would you explain the change to consumers? If you respond negatively to the request, how would you explain your decision to Coca-Cola? What would you do to make sure your relationship does not turn hostile?

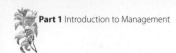

PRACTICE BEING A MANAGER

Finding a Management Job

Management is a wide-ranging and exciting area of work. One way to gain a sense of the possibilities is to study the advertisements for management job openings. Companies advertise their management openings in a variety of ways, including print advertisements in such newspapers as *The Wall Street Journal* (especially its Friday career section) and online ads at job sites like Monster.com and CareerBuilder.com.

Step 1: Find a job you'd like to have. Search through the newspaper and online ads and locate several detailed job descriptions for management positions. Select the one that you find most appealing—a job that you could picture yourself interviewing for either in the near future or later in your career. Do not be too concerned about your current qualifications in making your selection, but you should see realistic prospects of meeting the qualifications over time (if a job requires an MBA, for example, you should see yourself completing this degree sometime in the future). Print your selected detailed job description and bring it to your next class session.

Step 2: Share your job description. In class, your professor will assign you to a pair or group of three. Write your name on your selected management job description, and exchange your job description with your partner(s). Each member of the pair or triad should now have a job description other than their own.

Step 3: Think like a hiring manager. Read the job description you received from your partner. Imagine that you are the manager responsible for hiring someone to fill this position. A human resources specialist in your company has already screened the applicants' résumé and background. Thus, you may assume that your partner has met all the basic qualifications for the job. Your job as a senior manager is to ask questions that might get beyond the résumé to the person—what might you ask to learn whether someone is well suited to thrive in this management job and in your company?

Step 4: Take turns interviewing. Each member of the group should be briefly interviewed (5–10 minutes) for the job he or she selected.

Step 5: Debrief. Discuss your experiences with your partner(s). What was it like to be interviewed for your selected position? What was it like to role-play interviewing someone for a management position? Now imagine the real thing. Brainstorm about how you might prepare yourself over time to be the top candidate for an attractive management position and to be a senior manager responsible for hiring the best-qualified managers for your company.

Step 6: Discuss with the class. Share your interview experiences and brainstorming ideas with the class. Do you hear any similarities across the pairs/triads? What ideas or questions are most significant to you as you consider management job interviews?

DEVELOP YOUR CAREER POTENTIAL

Interview Two Managers

Welcome to the first Develop Your Career Potential activity! These assignments have one purpose: to help you develop your present and future capabilities as a manager. What you will learn through these assignments is not traditional "book learning" based on memorization and regurgitation, but practical knowledge and skills that help managers perform their jobs better. Lessons from some of the assignments—for example, goal setting—can be used for immediate benefit. Other lessons will obviously take time to accomplish, but you can still benefit now by making specific plans for future improvement.

Step 1: Interview two practicing managers. In her book *Becoming a Manager: Mastery of a New*

Identity, Harvard Business School professor Linda Hill conducted extensive interviews with 19 people in their first year as managers.[90] To learn firsthand what it's like to be a manager, interview two managers whom you know, asking them some of the same questions, listed here, that Hill asked her managers. Be sure to interview managers with different levels of experience. Interview one person with at least five years' experience as a manager, and then interview another person with no more than two years' experience as a manager. Ask the managers these questions:

1. Briefly describe your current position and responsibilities.
2. What do your subordinates expect from you on the job?
3. What are the major stresses and challenges you face on the job?

4. What, if anything, do you dislike about the job?
5. What do you like best about your job?
6. What are the critical differences between average managers and top-performing managers?
7. Think about the skills and knowledge that you need to be effective in your job. What are they, and how did you acquire them?
8. What have been your biggest mistakes thus far? Could you have avoided them? If so, how?

Step 2: Prepare to discuss your findings. Prepare to discuss your findings in class or write a report (if assigned by your instructor). What conclusions can you draw from your interview data?

END NOTES

[1]M. Anderson & M. Liedtke (Associated Press), "Hubris—and late fees—doomed Blockbuster," *MSNBC*, September 23, 2010, accessed January 29, 2011, from www.msnbc.msn.com/id/39332696/ns/business-retail/; M. Copeland, "Reed Hastings: Leader of the Pack," *Fortune*, December 6, 2010, 120–130; J. Heilemann, "Showtime for Netflix," *Business 2.0* (March 2005): 36; R. Grover, "Netflix: Premium Cable's Worst Nightmare," *Bloomberg Businessweek*, September 20, 2010, 21–22; and J. Surowiecki, "The Financial Page: The Next Level," *The New Yorker*, October 18, 2010, 28.

[2]S. Prasso, "American made . . . Chinese owned," *Fortune*, May 24, 2010, 92.

[3]Mina Kimes "Why J&J's Headache Won't Go Away," *Fortune*, September 6, 2010, 100–108.

[4]"Business Services: Global Industry Guide," *Data Monitor*, January 21, 2010, accessed April 18, 2009, from www.marketresearch.com.

[5]V. Nayar, "Corner Office: He's Not Bill Gates, or Fred Astaire," interview by A. Bryant, *The New York Times*, February 13, 2010, accessed June 22, 2010, from www.nytimes.com/2010/02/14/business/14cornerweb.html.

[6]Jennifer Levitz "FedEx Looks to 777s to Deliver an Edge," *The Wall Street Journal*, July 14, 2010, B1, B2.

[7]S. McCartney, "At JFK, More Flying, Less Waiting on the Tarmac," *The Wall Street Journal*, July 29, 2010, D3.

[8]D. A. Wren, A. G. Bedeian, and J. D. Breeze, "The Foundations of Henri Fayol's Administrative Theory," *Management Decision* 40 (2002): 906–918.

[9]S. Totilo, "The Unexpected Gamer Who Runs EA," *Kotaku*, accessed January 26, 2011, from http://kotaku.com/5568591/the-unexpected-gamer-who-runs-ea.

[10]H. Fayol, *General and Industrial Management* (London: Pittman & Sons, 1949).

[11]R. Stagner, "Corporate Decision Making," *Journal of Applied Psychology* 53 (1969): 1–13.

[12]D. W. Bray, R. J. Campbell, and D. L. Grant, *Formative Years in Business: A Long-Term AT&T Study of Managerial Lives* (New York: Wiley, 1993).

[13]G. Fowler, "eBay to Unload Skype in IPO, Citing Poor Fit," *The Wall Street Journal*, April 15, 2009, B1; G. Fowler and E. Ramstad, "EBay Looks Abroad for Growth—Online Auctioneer to Buy Korean Site as It Refocuses on E-Commerce, PayPal," *The Wall Street Journal*, April 16, 2009, B2; and G. Fowler, "EBay's Earnings Soar with Sale of Skype," *The Wall Street Journal*, January 21, 2010, B3.

[14]A. Johnson, "Pfizer Outlines Post-Wyeth R&D Structure—Company Splits Research on Traditional Drugs from Biologics and Strives to Retain Scientists," *The Wall Street Journal*, April 8, 2009, B4.

[15]R. J. Grisson, "Probability of the Superior Outcome of One Treatment over Another," *Journal of Applied Psychology* 79 (1994): 314–316; and J. E. Hunter and F. L. Schmidt, *Methods of Meta-Analysis: Correcting Error and Bias in Research Findings* (Beverly Hills, CA: Sage, 1990).

[16]A. Taylor III, "Fixing Up Ford," *Fortune*, May 25, 2009, 44–51 (para 1); N. Bunkley, "Ford Profit Comes as Toyota Hits a Bump," *The New York Times*, January 28, 2010, accessed June 23, 2010, from www.nytimes.com/2010/01/29/business/29ford.html; and A. Taylor III, "Fixing Up Ford" (para 2).

[17]B. O'Keefe and D. Burke, "Meet the CEO of the Biggest Company on Earth," *Fortune*, September 27, 2010, 80–94.

18"A Little Enlightened Self-Interest," Inc.com, June 8, 2010, accessed July 5, 2010, from www.inc.com/top-workplaces/2010/a-little-enlightened-self-interest.html.

19H. S. Jonas III, R. E. Fry, and S. Srivastva, "The Office of the CEO: Understanding the Executive Experience," *Academy of Management Executive* 4 (1990): 36–47.

20D. Mattioli, "The Year In Review: CEO Changes: Crises Trigger Dramatic Departures—From H-P's Hurd to Pfizer's Kindler, 'Surprise Exits' Stunned Many in 2010, Though Turnover at Top Was Low Overall," *The Wall Street Journal*, December 26, 2010, B6.

21Jonas et al., "The Office of the CEO."

22Ibid.

23T. Waghorn, "How Employee Engagement Turned Around Campbell's: An interview with Douglas Conant, CEO of Campbell Soup Co.," *Forbes*, June 23, 2009, January 17, 2011, from www.forbes.com/2009/06/23/employee-engagement-conant-leadership-managing-turnaround.html.

24M. Porter, J. Lorsch, and N. Nohria, "Seven Surprises for New CEOs," *Harvard Business Review* (October 2004): 62.

25M. Murray, "As Huge Firms Keep Growing, CEOs Struggle to Keep Pace," *The Wall Street Journal*, February 8, 2001, A1.

26T. Gutner, "Career Journal—90 Days: Plotting a Smooth Course When You Take the Helm," *The Wall Street Journal*, March 24, 2009, D5.

27E. Byron, "P & G's Lafley Sees CEOs As Link to World," *The Wall Street Journal*, March 23, 2009, B6.

28Q. Huy, "In Praise of Middle Managers," *Harvard Business Review* (September 2001): 72–79.

29I. Barat, "Rebuilding After a Catastrophe: How Caterpillar Is Responding to Tornado's Lesson," *The Wall Street Journal*, May 19, 2008, B1–B2.

30J. Rockoff, "J&J, Bruised by Recalls, Aims Higher—CEO Weldon Offers Prescription to Regain Consumers' Trust by Revamping Drug Manufacturing, Adding Quality Overseer," *The Wall Street Journal*, August 19, 2010, B10.

31M. Henricks, "Go-Betweens," *Entrepreneur*, March 2007, 91–92.

32T. Demos, "Motivate Without Spending Millions," *Fortune*, April 12, 2010, 37–38.

33J. Adamy, "A Menu of Options: Restaurants Have a Host of Ways to Motivate Employees to Provide Good Service," *The Wall Street Journal*, October 30, 2006, R1, R6.

34C. Hymowitz, "Today's Bosses Find Mentoring Isn't Worth the Time and Risks," *The Wall Street Journal*, March 13, 2006, B1.

35S. Tully, "What Team Leaders Need to Know," *Fortune*, February 20, 1995, 93.

36B. Francella, "In a Day's Work," *Convenience Store News*, September 25, 2001, 7.

37L. Liu and A. McMurray, "Frontline Leaders: The Entry Point for Leadership Development in the Manufacturing Industry," *Journal of European Industrial Training* 28, no. 2–4 (2004): 339–352.

38"What Makes Teams Work?" *Fast Company*, November 1, 2000, 109.

39K. Hultman, "The 10 Commandments of Team Leadership," *Training & Development*, February 1, 1998, 12–13.

40L. Landro, "The Informed Patient: Bringing Surgeons Down to Earth—New Programs Aim to Curb Fear That Prevents Nurses from Flagging Problems," *The Wall Street Journal*, November 16, 2005, D1.

41Ibid.

42N. Steckler and N. Fondas, "Building Team Leader Effectiveness: A Diagnostic Tool," *Organizational Dynamics* (Winter 1995): 20–34.

43Tully, "What Team Leaders Need to Know."

44Ibid.

45H. Mintzberg, *The Nature of Managerial Work* (New York: Harper & Row, 1973).

46C. P. Hales, "What Do Managers Do? A Critical Review of the Evidence," *Journal of Management Studies* 23, no. 1 (1986): 88–115.

47"Cessna CEO Joins Mesa Mayor to Open New Jet Center," *Business Wire*, for February 2009, available online at www.Reuters.com.

48C. Penttila, "Employee Benefits in Today's Economy," *Entrepreneur* 37, no. 1 (January 2009): 51–55.

49K. Clark and R. Sidel, "Gang Green Meets Wall Street," *The Wall Street Journal*, May 5, 2010, accessed June 22, 2010, from http://online.wsj.com/article/SB100014240527487030866670457522 4480779342098.html?mod=WSJ_hpp_MIDDLENexttoWhatsNewsForth.

50Francella, "In a Day's Work."

51"Getting into Harvard Easier Than McDonald's University in China," *Bloomberg Businessweek*, January 26, 2011, accessed February 2, 2011, from www.bloomberg.com/news/2011-01-26/getting-into-harvard-easier-than-mcdonald-s-hamburger-university-in-china.html.

52"News by Industry," *Business Wire*, accessed March 11, 2009, from www.businesswire.com/portal/site/home/news/industries/.

53"Media Monitoring," *CyberAlert*, accessed March 11, 2009, from www.cyberalert.com.

54"What Is FNS News Clips Online?" *FNS NewsClips*, accessed March 11, 2009, from www.news-clips.com.

55"100 Best Companies to Work for 2009," *The Sunday Times* (London), March 8, 2009, 20.

56S. Humphries, "Grapevine Goes High-Tech," *The Courier Mail*, January 10, 2009.

57A. Lashinsky, "The Decade of Steve," *Fortune*, November 23, 2009, 114; and Y. Iwatani Kane and I. Sherr, "Apple Unveils iPhone 4," *The Wall Street Journal*, June 8, 2010, accessed June 8, 2010, from http://online.wsj.com/article/SB1 0001424052748703303904575292703491815956.html?mod=WSJ_hps_MIDDLETopStories.

58J. Levitz, "UPS Thinks Out of the Box on Driver Training," *The Wall Street Journal*, April 6, 2010, accessed June 22, 2010, from http://online.wsj.com/article/SB1000142405270 23039121045751645738234188844.html?mod=WSJ_hp_editorsPicks.

59S. Needleman, "Entrepreneurs 'Tweet' Their Way Through Crises—Twitter

Helps Companies Cope With Site Crashes, Weather Delays: 'You Can't Do That With a 1-800 Number,'" *Wall Street Journal*, September 15, 2009, B5.

60 J. Scheck, "R&D Spending Holds Steady in Slump—Big Companies Invest to Grab Sales in Recovery: The iPod Lesson," *The Wall Street Journal*, April 6, 2009, A1.

61 L. Greenblatt, "Beatles Sales on iTunes Hit New Milestone," *MusicMix*, January 14, 2011, accessed January 17, 2011, from http://music-mix.ew.com/2011/01/14/beatles-sales-itunes/; and E. Smith, "Day in the Life of Deal—How EMI's New CEO Helped Beatles Clear iTunes Hurdles," *The Wall Street Journal*, November 17, 2010, B12.

62 L. A. Hill, *Becoming a Manager: Mastery of a New Identity* (Boston: Harvard Business School Press, 1992).

63 R. L. Katz, "Skills of an Effective Administrator," *Harvard Business Review* (September–October 1974): 90–102.

64 C. A. Bartlett and S. Ghoshal, "Changing the Role of Top Management: Beyond Systems to People," *Harvard Business Review* (May–June 1995): 132–142.

65 F. L. Schmidt and J. E. Hunter, "Development of a Causal Model of Process Determining Job Performance," *Current Directions in Psychological Science* 1 (1992): 89–92.

66 J. B. Miner, "Sentence Completion Measures in Personnel Research: The Development and Validation of the Miner Sentence Completion Scales," in H. J. Bernardin and D. A. Bownas (eds.), *Personality Assessment in Organizations* (New York: Praeger, 1986), 147–146.

67 M. W. McCall, Jr., and M. M. Lombardo, "What Makes a Top Executive?" *Psychology Today*, February 1983, 26–31; and E. van Velsor and J. Brittain, "Why Executives Derail: Perspectives across Time and Cultures," *Academy of Management Executive* (November 1995): 62–72.

68 McCall and Lombardo, "What Makes a Top Executive?"

69 A. K. Naj, "Corporate Therapy: The Latest Addition to Executive Suite Is Psychologist's Couch," *The Wall Street Journal*, August 29, 1994, A1.

70 Ibid.

71 P. Wallington, "Management2 Toxic!" *Financial Mail*, July 28, 2006, 48.

72 J. Sandberg, "Overcontrolling Bosses Aren't Just Annoying: They're Also Inefficient," *The Wall Street Journal*, March 30, 2005, B1.

73 Hill, *Becoming a Manager*, p. 17.

74 Ibid., p. 55.

75 Ibid., p. 57.

76 Ibid., p. 64.

77 Ibid., p. 67.

78 Ibid., p. 103.

79 Ibid., p. 161.

80 J. Pfeffer, *The Human Equation: Building Profits by Putting People First* (Boston: Harvard Business School Press, 1996); and *Competitive Advantage through People: Unleashing the Power of the Work Force* (Boston: Harvard Business School Press, 1994).

81 M. A. Huselid, "The Impact of Human Resource Management Practices on Turnover, Productivity, and Corporate Financial Performance," *Academy of Management Journal* 38 (1995): 635–672.

82 D. McDonald and A. Smith, "A Proven Connection: Performance Management and Business Results," *Compensation & Benefits Review* 27, no. 6 (January 1, 1995): 59.

83 I. Fulmer, B. Gerhart, and K. Scott, "Are the 100 Best Better? An Empirical Investigation of the Relationship between Being a 'Great Place to Work' and Firm Performance," *Personnel Psychology* (Winter 2003): 965–993.

84 "Financial Results," *Great Place to Work*, January 22, 2011, accessed January 22, 2011, from www.greatplacetowork.com/what_we_believe/graphs.php.

85 B. Schneider and D. E. Bowen, "Employee and Customer Perceptions of Service in Banks: Replication and Extension," *Journal of Applied Psychology* 70 (1985): 423–433; and B. Schneider, J. J. Parkington, and V. M. Buxton, "Employee and Customer Perceptions of Service in Banks," *Administrative Science Quarterly* 25 (1980): 252–267.

86 "How Investing in Intangibles—Like Employee Satisfaction—Translates into Financial Returns," Knowledge@Wharton, January 9, 2008, accessed January 24, 2010, from http://knowledge.wharton.upenn.edu/article.cfm?articleid=1873.

87 P. L. Hunsaker, *Management: A Skills Approach* (Upper Saddle River, NJ: Pearson Prentice Hall, 2005), 24–25.

88 "Airlines Make a Bundle Through Separate Charges," *The Seattle Times*, April 7, 2010, accessed June 30, 2010, from http://seattletimes.nwsource.com/html/travel/2011539200_webtroubleshooter06.html/; Hugo Martin "Spirit Airlines Launches $45 Carry-on Fee," *The Los Angeles Times*, April 7, 2010, accessed July 1, 2010, from http://articles.latimes.com/2010/apr/07/business/la-fi-spirit7-2010apr07; and Christine Negroni "Less Baggage, Big Savings to Airlines" *The New York Times*, April 6, 2010, from www.nytimes.com/2010/04/07/business/07bags.html?src=me.

89 Elizabeth Olson "Can Honest Tea Say No To Coke, Its Biggest Investor?" *The New York Times*, July 7, 2010, accessed August 15, 2010, from www.nytimes.com/2010/07/08/business/smallbusiness/08sbiz.html?dbk.

90 Hill, *Becoming a Manager*.

reel to real

© GreenLight

© Cengage Learning

© iStockphoto.com/Oner Döngel

BIZ FLIX

In Good Company

When a sports magazine gets taken over by a media conglomerate, a seasoned and successful ad sales executive named Dan Foreman (Dennis Quaid) is stunned by his demotion. Carter Duryea (Topher Grace)—a business school prodigy who is half Dan's age and talks a lot about "corporate synergy"—is brought in as his new boss. Dan has spent years developing good relationships with his clients, but Carter thinks it's more expedient to cross-promote the magazine with the corporation's cell phone division. In this clip from the film, Carter has come to appreciate Dan's work ethic and relationship skills, but his superior, Mark Steckle (Clark Gregg), wants to fire him. Carter stands up for Dan, even though it may mean he has to follow him out the door. Carter and Dan will have to work together if they're going to find a way to save their jobs.

What to Watch for and Ask Yourself

1. Which management skills discussed in this chapter does the character Mark Steckle seem to lack?

2. The sequence shows three people who represent different hierarchical levels in the company. Based on this scene, which of the four kinds of managers do you think each of them might be?

3. Which of the characters in this clip exhibited the strongest human skills?

MANAGEMENT WORKPLACE

Camp Bow Wow: Innovative Management for a Changing World

Sue Ryan, a Camp Bow Wow franchisee from Colorado, knows the ins and outs of managing a care center for pets. To help launch her business a few years ago, Ryan recruited experienced pet-care worker Candace Stathis, who came on as a camp counselor. Ryan soon recognized that Stathis was a star performer with a natural ability to work with clients and pets alike, and today Stathis serves as the camp's general manager. At Camp Bow Wow, store managers have distinct roles from camp counselors. Whereas counselors typically take care of dogs, answer phones, and book reservations, managers must know how to run all operations and mange people as well. To keep camp running as efficiently as possible, Stathis maintains a strict daily schedule for doggie baths, nail trimmings, feedings, and play time.

Discussion Questions

1. Identify three skills that companies look for in managers and explain which might be most needed for the Camp Bow Wow leaders highlighted in the video.

2. Which activities at Camp Bow Wow require high efficiency? Which activities require high effectiveness?

3. List two activities that leaders at Camp Bow Wow perform daily, and identify which of the managerial roles discussed in the chapter figure prominently for each.

CHAPTER 2

History of Management

Learning Outcomes

1. Explain the origins of management.
2. Explain the history of scientific management.
3. Discuss the history of bureaucratic and administrative management.
4. Explain the history of human relations management.
5. Discuss the history of operations, information, systems, and contingency management.

what would **you do?**

ISG Steelton–International Steel Group, Steelton, Pennsylvania[1]

As the day-shift supervisor at the **ISG Steelton** steel plant, you summon the six college students who are working for you this summer, doing whatever you need done (sweeping up, sandblasting the inside of boilers that are down for maintenance, running errands, and so forth). You walk them across the plant to a field where the company stores scrap metal. The area is stacked with organized piles of metal. You explain that everything they see has just been sold. Metal prices have finally risen enough that the company can earn a small profit by selling its scrap.

You point out that railroad tracks divide the field into parallel sectors, like the lines on a football field, so that each stack of metal is no more than 15 feet from a track. Each stack contains 390 pieces of metal. Each piece weighs 92 pounds and is about a yard long and just over 4 inches high and 4 inches wide. You tell the students that, working as a team, they are to pick up each piece, walk up a ramp to a railroad car that will be positioned next to each stack, and then neatly position and stack the metal for shipment. That's right, you repeat, *92* pounds, *walk* up the ramp, and *carry* the metal onto the rail car. You explain that a forklift could be used only if the metal were stored on wooden pallets (it isn't); if the pallets could withstand the weight of the metal (they would be crushed); and if you, as their supervisor, had forklifts and people trained to run them (you don't). In other words, the only way to get the metal into the rail cars is for the students to carry it.

© Greg Pease/Taxi/Getty Images

Based on an old report from the last time the company sold some of the metal, you know that workers typically loaded about 30 pieces of metal parts per hour over an 8-hour shift. At that pace, though, it will take your six students *6 weeks* to load all of the metal. But the purchasing manager who sold it says it must be shipped in *2* weeks. Without more workers (there's a hiring freeze) and without forklifts, all of the metal has to be loaded by hand by these six workers in 2 weeks. But how do you do that? What would motivate the students to work much, much harder than they have all summer? They've gotten used to a leisurely pace and easy job assignments. Motivation might help, but motivation will only get so much done. After all, short of illegal steroids, nothing is going to work once muscle fatigue kicks in from carrying those 92-pound pieces of metal up a ramp all day long. What can you change about the way the work is done to deal with the unavoidable physical fatigue?

If you were the supervisor in charge, what would you do?

study tips ⊗

Build a management time line that shows the evolution of management theory. Divide a piece of paper with a line down the middle. Place management theories on one side and overall historical theories on the other so that you can see what was happening in management as a part of general history. Examining theories in context can help you identify trends that might emerge in the future.

© iStockphoto.com/Ivan Burmistrov

© iStockphoto.com/Alex Slobodkin

The problems that the ISG steel plant supervisor is facing in the What Would You Do? case are certainly difficult, but they aren't unique. Each day, managers are asked to solve challenging problems and are given only a limited amount of time, people, or resources. Yet it's still their responsibility to get things done on time and within budget. Most of the management ideas and practices that today's managers use to solve their daily problems have their roots in the people and ideas you'll read about in this chapter on the history of management. Indeed, reading the theories in this chapter will enable you to figure out a solution to the ISG supervisor's problems.

We begin this chapter by reviewing the origins of management ideas and practice throughout history and the historical changes that produced the need for managers. Next, you'll learn about various schools of management thought. Beginning with scientific management, you'll learn about the key contributions made by Frederick Taylor, Frank and Lillian Gilbreth, and Henry Gantt. Next, you'll read about Max Weber and bureaucratic management and then about Henri Fayol and administrative management. Following that, you'll learn about human relations management and the ideas of Mary Parker Follett (constructive conflict and coordination), Elton Mayo (Hawthorne Studies), and Chester Barnard (cooperation and acceptance of authority). Finally, you'll learn about the history of operations management, information management, systems management, and contingency management.

In the Beginning

In this textbook, you've already learned that *management* is getting work done through others; *strategic* plans are overall plans that clarify how a company will serve customers and position itself against competitors over the next two to five years; and *just-in-time inventory* is a system in which the parts needed to make something arrive from suppliers just as they are needed at each stage of production. Today's managers would undoubtedly view those ideas and many of the others presented in the book as self-evident. For example, tell today's managers to "reward workers for improved production or performance," "set specific goals to increase motivation," or "innovate to create and sustain a competitive advantage," and they'll respond, "Duh! Who doesn't know that?" A mere 125 years ago, however, business ideas and practices were so different that today's widely accepted management ideas would have been as self-evident as space travel, cell phones, and the Internet. In fact, management jobs and careers didn't exist 125 years ago, so management was not yet a field of study. Now, of course, managers and management are such an important part of the business world that it's hard to imagine organizations without them. So if there were no managers 125 years ago, but you can't walk down the hall today without bumping into one, where did management come from?

After reading the next section, you should be able to

1. Explain the origins of management.

1 The Origins of Management

Management as a field of study may be just 125 years old, but management ideas and practices have actually been used from the earliest times of recorded history. For example, 2,500 years before management researchers called it *job enrichment*, the

Greeks learned that they could improve the productivity of boring, repetitious tasks by performing them to music. The basic idea was to use a flute, drum, or song lyrics to pace people to work in unison using the same efficient motions, stimulate them to work faster and longer, and make the boring work more fun.[2] Although we can find the seeds of many of today's management ideas throughout history, not until the last two centuries did systematic changes in the nature of work and organizations create a compelling need for managers.

1.1 Management Ideas and Practices Throughout History

Examples of management thought and practice can be found throughout history.[3] For example, the earliest recorded instance of information management dates to ancient Sumer (modern Iraq), ca. 8000–3000 B.C.E. Sumerian businessmen used small clay tokens to calculate quantities of grain and livestock—and later value-added goods like perfume or pottery—they owned and traded in temples and at city gates. Different shapes and sizes represented different types and quantities of goods. The tokens were also used to store data. They were kept in small clay envelopes, and the token shapes were impressed on the outside of the envelope to indicate what was inside. Eventually, someone figured out that it was easier to just write these symbols with a stylus on a tablet instead of using the tokens. In the end, the new technology of *writing* led to more efficient management of the business of Sumerian temples.[4]

A task as enormous as building the great pyramids in Egypt was bound to present practical problems that would lead to the development of management ideas. Egyptians recognized the need for planning, organizing, and controlling; submitting written requests; and consulting staff for advice before making decisions. The enormity of the task they faced is evident in the pyramid of King Khufu, which contains 2.3 million blocks of stone. Each block had to be quarried, cut to precise size and shape, cured (hardened in the sun), transported by boat for two to three days, moved onto the construction site, numbered to identify where it would be placed, and then shaped and smoothed so that it would fit perfectly into place. It took 20,000 workers 23 years to complete this pyramid; more than 8,000 were needed just to quarry the stones and transport them. A typical quarry expedition might include 100 army officers, 50 government and religious officials, and 200 members of the king's court to lead the expedition; 130 stonemasons to cut the stones; and 5,000 soldiers, 800 barbarians, and 2,000 bond servants to transport the stones on and off the ships.[5]

Exhibit 2.1 shows how other management ideas and practices throughout history relate to the management functions in the

© sculpies/Shutterstock.com

Exhibit 2.1   Management Ideas and Practices throughout History

Time	Individual or Group	Planning	Organizing	Leading	Controlling	Contributions to Management Thought and Practice
5000 B.C.E.	Sumerians				√	Record keeping.
4000 B.C.E. to 2000 B.C.E.	Egyptians	√	√		√	Recognized the need for planning, organizing, and controlling when building the pyramids. Submitted requests in writing. Made decisions after consulting staff for advice.
1800 B.C.E.	Hammurabi				√	Established controls by using witnesses (to vouch for what was said or done) and writing to document transactions.
600 B.C.E.	Nebuchadnezzar		√	√		Wage incentives and production control.
500 B.C.E.	Sun Tzu	√		√		Strategy; identifying and attacking opponent's weaknesses.
400 B.C.E.	Xenophon	√	√	√	√	Recognized management as a separate art.
400 B.C.E.	Cyrus		√	√	√	Human relations and motion study.
175 B.C.E.	Cato the Elder		√			Job descriptions.
284	Diocletian		√			Delegation of authority.
900	Alfarabi			√		Listed leadership traits.
1100	Ghazali			√		Listed managerial traits.
1418	Barbarigo		√			Different organizational forms/structures.
1436	Venetians				√	Numbering, standardization, and interchangeability of parts.
1500	Sir Thomas More			√		Critical of poor management and leadership.
1525	Machiavelli		√	√		Cohesiveness, power, and leadership in organizations.

Source: C. S. George, Jr., *The History of Management Thought* (Englewood Cliffs, NJ: Prentice-Hall, 1972).

textbook. Besides the achievements of the Sumerians and Egyptians, we might note the Babylonian King Hammurabi, who established controls by using witnesses and written documents; King Nebuchadnezzar, who over a millennium later pioneered techniques for producing goods and using wages to motivate workers; Sun Tzu, author of *The Art of War*, who emphasized the importance of strategy and identifying and attacking an opponent's weaknesses; the Greek author Xenophon, who recognized management as a distinct and separate art; King Cyrus of Persia, who recognized the importance of human relations and used motion study to eliminate wasteful steps and improve productivity; Cato the Elder, who emphasized the importance of job descriptions; the Roman emperor Diocletian, who mastered the art of delegation by dividing the widespread Roman Empire into 101 provinces grouped into 13 dioceses, which were in turn grouped into four geographic divisions; the

medieval Arab scholars al-Farabi and al-Ghazali, who began defining what it takes to be a good leader or manager; Barbarigo, who discussed the different ways in which organizations could be structured; the Venetians, who used numbering and standardization to make parts interchangeable; Sir Thomas More, who emphasized the negative societal consequences associated with poor leadership in his book *Utopia*; and the Italian philosopher and politician Machiavelli, who wrote about the importance of cohesion, power, and leadership in organizations.

1.2 Why We Need Managers Today

Working from 8 A.M. to 5 P.M., coffee breaks, lunch hours, crushing rush hour traffic, and punching a time clock are things we associate with today's working world. Work hasn't always been this way, however. In fact, the design of jobs and organizations has changed dramatically over the last 500 years. For most of humankind's history, for example, people didn't commute to work.[6] Work usually occurred in homes or on farms. In 1720, almost 80 percent of the 5.5 million people in England lived and worked in the country. And as recently as 1870, two-thirds of Americans earned their living from agriculture. Even most of those who didn't earn their living from agriculture didn't commute to work. Blacksmiths, furniture makers, leather goods makers, and other skilled tradespeople or craftspeople who formed trade guilds (the historical predecessors of labor unions) in England as early as 1093, typically worked out of shops in or next to their homes.[7] Likewise, cottage workers worked with each other out of small homes that were often built in a semicircle. A family in each cottage would complete a different production step, and work passed from one cottage to the next until production was complete. For example, textile work was a common cottage industry: Families in different cottages would shear the sheep; clean the wool; comb, bleach, and dye it; spin it into yarn; and weave the yarn into cloth. With no commute, no bosses (workers determined the amount and pace of their work), and no common building (from the time of the ancient Egyptians, Greeks, and Romans through the middle of the nineteenth century, it was rare for more than 12 people to work together under one roof), cottage work was very different from today's jobs and companies.[8] And because these work groups were small and typically self-organized, there wasn't a strong need for management.

During the Industrial Revolution (1750–1900), however, jobs and organizations changed dramatically.[9] First, unskilled laborers running machines began to replace high-paid, skilled artisans. What made this possible? The availability of power (steam engines and later electricity) as well as numerous related inventions, including Darby's coke-smelting process and Cort's puddling and rolling process (both for making iron), as well as Hargreave's spinning jenny and Arkwright's water frame (both for spinning cotton). Whereas artisans made entire goods by themselves by hand, this new production system was based on a division of labor: Each worker, interacting with machines, performed separate, highly specialized tasks that were but a small part of all the steps required to make manufactured goods. Mass production was born as rope- and chain-driven assembly lines moved work to stationary workers who concentrated on performing one small task over and over again. While workers focused on their singular tasks, managers were needed to coordinate the different parts of the production system and optimize its overall performance. Productivity skyrocketed at companies that understood this. At **Ford Motor Company**, where the assembly line was developed, the time required to assemble a car dropped from 12.5 man-hours to just 93 minutes after switching to mass production.[10]

< *"what's new" companies*

Second, instead of being performed in fields, homes, or small shops, jobs occurred in large, formal organizations where hundreds, if not thousands, of people worked under one roof.[11] In 1849, for example **Chicago Harvester** (the predecessor of International Harvester) ran the largest factory in the United States, with just 123 workers. In 1870, the **Pullman Company**, a manufacturer of railroad sleeping cars, was the largest factory, with only 200 employees. Yet by 1913, Henry Ford employed 12,000 employees in his Highland Park, Michigan, factory alone. Because "the number of people working in manufacturing quintupled from 1860 to 1890," and individual factories employed so many workers under one roof, companies now had a strong need for disciplinary rules to impose order and structure. For the first time, they needed managers who knew how to organize large groups, work with employees, and make good decisions.

"what's new"
companies >

"The number of people working in manufacturing quintupled from 1860 to 1890."

Review 1

The Origins of Management Management as a field of study may be just 125 years old, but management ideas and practices have actually been used since the beginning of recorded history. From the Sumerians, as early as 8000 B.C.E., to sixteenth-century Europe, there are historical antecedents for each of the functions of management discussed in this textbook: planning, organizing, leading, and controlling. Despite these early examples of management ideas, there was no compelling need for managers until systematic changes in the nature of work and organizations occurred in the nineteenth and twentieth centuries. During this time, work shifted from families to factories; from skilled laborers to specialized, unskilled laborers; from small, self-organized groups to large factories employing thousands under one roof; and from unique, small batches of production to large standardized mass production. Consequently, managers were needed to impose order and structure, motivate and direct large groups of workers, and plan and make decisions that optimized overall company performance by effectively coordinating the different parts of organizational systems.

The Evolution of Management

Before 1880, business educators taught only basic bookkeeping and secretarial skills, and no one published books or articles about management.[12] Over the next 25 years, however, things changed dramatically. In 1881, Joseph Wharton gave the University of Pennsylvania $100,000 to establish a department to educate students for careers in management. By 1911, 30 business schools—including those at Harvard, the University of Chicago, and the University of California—had been established to teach managers how to run businesses.[13] In 1886, Henry Towne, president of the Yale and Towne Manufacturing Company, presented his ideas about management to the American Society of Engineers. In his talk, entitled

After reading the next four sections, which review the different schools of management thought, you should be able to

2. *Explain the history of scientific management.*

3. *Discuss the history of bureaucratic and administrative management.*

4. *Explain the history of human relations management.*

5. *Discuss the history of operations, information, systems, and contingency management.*

"The Engineer as Economist," he emphasized that managing people and work processes was just as important as engineering work that focused on machines.[14] Towne also argued that management should be recognized as a separate field of study, with its own professional associations, journals, and literature, where management ideas could be exchanged and developed.

Today, because of the forethought and efforts of Joseph Wharton and Henry Towne, you can turn to dozens of academic journals (such as the Academy of Management's *Journal* or *Review*, *Administrative Science Quarterly*, the *Strategic Management Journal*, and the *Journal of Applied Psychology*), hundreds of business school and practitioner journals (such as *Harvard Business Review*, *Sloan Management Review*, and the *Academy of Management Perspectives*), and thousands of books and articles if you have a question about management. In the next four sections, you will learn about other important contributors to the field of management and how their ideas shaped our current understanding of management theory and practice.

2 Scientific Management

Bosses, who were hired by the company owner or founder, used to make decisions by the seat of their pants—haphazardly, without any systematic study, thought, or collection of information. If the bosses decided that workers should work twice as fast, little or no thought was given to worker motivation. If workers resisted, the bosses often resorted to physical beatings to get workers to work faster, harder, or longer. With no incentives for bosses and workers to cooperate with one another, both groups played the system by trying to take advantage of each other. Moreover, each worker did the same job in his or her own way with different methods and different tools. In short, there were no procedures to standardize operations, no standards by which to judge whether performance was good or bad, and no follow-up to determine whether productivity or quality actually improved when changes were made.[15]

This all changed, however, with the advent of **scientific management**, which involved thorough study and testing of different work methods to identify the best, most efficient ways to complete a job. Let's find out more about scientific management by learning about **2.1 Frederick W. Taylor, the father of scientific management; 2.2 Frank and Lillian Gilbreth and motion studies;** and **2.3 Henry Gantt and his Gantt charts.**

2.1 Father of Scientific Management: Frederick W. Taylor

Frederick W. Taylor (1856–1915), the father of scientific management, began his career as a worker at **Midvale Steel Company**. He was later promoted to pattern maker, supervisor, and then chief engineer. At Midvale, Taylor was deeply affected by his three-year struggle to get the men who worked for him to do, as he called it, "a fair day's work." Taylor, who had worked alongside the men as a coworker before becoming their boss, said, "We who were the workmen of that shop had the quantity output carefully agreed upon for everything that was turned out in the shop. We limited the output to about, I should think, one-third of what we could very well have done." Taylor explained that, as soon as he became the boss, "the men who were working under me . . . knew that I was onto the whole game of **soldiering**, or deliberately restricting output."[16] When Taylor told his workers, "I have accepted a

< "what's new" companies

scientific management thoroughly studying and testing different work methods to identify the best, most efficient way to complete a job.

soldiering workers deliberately slowing their pace or restricting their work output.

1856-1915

Frederick W. Taylor

© Bettman/Corbis; © iStockphoto.com/I.P. images

"Almost every act of the workman should be preceded by one or more preparatory acts of the management."

FREDERICK W. TAYLOR, MIDVALE STEEL COMPANY

rate buster a group member whose work pace is significantly faster than the normal pace in his or her group.

job under the management of this company and I am on the other side of the fence … I am going to try to get a bigger output," the workers responded, "We warn you, Fred, if you try to bust any of these rates [a **rate buster** was someone who worked faster than the group], we will have you over the fence in six weeks."[17]

Over the next three years, Taylor tried everything he could think of to improve output. By doing the job himself, he showed workers that it was possible to produce more output. He hired new workers and trained them himself, hoping they would produce more. But "very heavy social pressure" from the other workers kept them from doing so. Pushed by Taylor, the workers began breaking their machines so that they couldn't produce. Taylor responded by fining them every time they broke a machine and for any violation of the rules, no matter how small, such as being late to work. Tensions became so severe that some of the workers threatened to shoot him. Looking back at the situation, Taylor reflected, "It is a horrid life for any man to live, not to be able to look any workman in the face all day long without seeing hostility there and feeling that every man around one is his virtual enemy." He said, "I made up my mind either to get out of the business entirely and go into some other line of work, or to find some remedy for this unbearable condition."[18]

The remedy that Taylor eventually developed was scientific management. Taylor, who once described scientific management as "seventy-five percent science and twenty-five percent common sense," emphasized that the goal of scientific management was to use systematic study to find the "one best way" of doing each task. To do that, managers had to follow the four principles shown in Exhibit 2.2.[19] The first principle was to "develop a science" for each element of work. Study it. Analyze it. Determine the "one best way" to do the work. For example, one of Taylor's controversial proposals at the time was to give rest breaks to factory workers doing physical labor. We take morning, lunch, and afternoon breaks for granted, but in Taylor's day, factory workers were expected to work without stopping.[20] When Taylor said that breaks would increase worker productivity, no one believed him. Nonetheless, through systematic experiments, he showed that workers receiving frequent rest breaks were able to greatly increase their daily output.

Second, managers had to scientifically select, train, teach, and develop workers to help them reach their full potential. Before Taylor, supervisors often hired on the basis of favoritism and nepotism. Who you knew was often more important than what you could do. By contrast, Taylor instructed supervisors to hire "first-class" workers on the basis of their aptitude to do a job well. In one of the first applications of this principle, physical reaction times were used to select bicycle ball-bearing

Exhibit 2.2 Taylor's Four Principles of Scientific Management

First	Develop a science for each element of a man's work, which replaces the old rule-of-thumb method.
Second	Scientifically select and then train, teach, and develop the workman, whereas in the past he chose his own work and trained himself as best he could.
Third	Heartily cooperate with the men so as to ensure all of the work being done is in accordance with the principles of the science which has been developed.
Fourth	There is an almost equal division of the work and the responsibility between the management and the workmen. The management take over all the work for which they are better fitted than the workmen, while in the past almost all of the work and the greater part of the responsibility were thrown upon the men.

Source: F. W. Taylor, *The Principles of Scientific Management* (New York: Harper, 1911).

inspectors who had to be able to examine and reject poor-quality ball bearings as fast as they were produced on a production line. For similar reasons, Taylor also recommended that companies train and develop their workers—a rare practice at the time.

The third principle instructed managers to cooperate with employees to ensure that the scientific principles were actually implemented. Labor unrest was widespread at the time; the number of labor strikes against companies doubled between 1893 and 1904. As Taylor knew from personal experience, workers and management more often than not viewed each other as enemies. Taylor's advice ran contrary to the common wisdom of the day. He said, "The majority of these men believe that the fundamental interests of employees and employers are necessarily antagonistic. Scientific management, on the contrary, has for its very foundation the firm conviction that the true interests of the two are one and the same; that prosperity for the employer cannot exist through a long term of years unless it is accompanied by prosperity for the employee and vice versa; and that it is possible to give the workman what he most wants—high wages—and the employer what he wants—a low labor cost—for his manufactures."[21]

The fourth principle of scientific management was to divide the work and the responsibility equally between management and workers. Prior to Taylor, workers alone were held responsible for productivity and performance. But, said Taylor, "Almost every act of the workman should be preceded by one or more preparatory acts of the management which enable him to do his work better and quicker than he otherwise could. And each man should daily be taught by and receive the most friendly help from those who are over him, instead of being, at the one extreme, driven or coerced by his, bosses, and at the other left to his own unaided devices."[22]

Above all, Taylor felt these principles could be used to determine a "fair day's work," that is, what an average worker could produce at a reasonable pace, day in and day out. Once that was determined, it was management's responsibility to pay workers fairly for that fair day's work. In essence, Taylor was trying to align management and employees so that what was good for employees was also good for management. In this way, he felt, workers and managers could avoid the conflicts he had experienced at Midvale Steel. And one of the best ways, according to Taylor, to align management and employees was to use incentives to motivate workers. As Taylor wrote:

> In order to have any hope of obtaining the initiative of his workmen the manager must give some special incentive to his men beyond that which is given to the average of the trade. This incentive can be given in several different ways, as, for example, the hope of rapid promotion or advancement; higher wages, either in the form of generous piecework prices or of a premium or bonus of some kind for good and rapid work; shorter hours of labor; better surroundings and working conditions than are ordinarily given, etc., and, above all, this special incentive should be accompanied by that personal consideration for, and friendly contact with, his workmen which comes only from a genuine and kindly interest in the welfare of those under him. It is only by giving a special inducement or "incentive" of this kind that the employer can hope even approximately to get the "initiative" of his workmen.[23]

In other words, Taylor believed in piece-rate incentives in which work pay was directly tied to how much workers produced.

Although Taylor remains a controversial figure among some academics who believe that his ideas were bad for workers, his key ideas have stood the test of time.[24] These include using systematic analysis to identify the best methods; scientifically selecting, training, and developing workers; promoting cooperation between management and labor; developing standardized approaches and tools; setting specific tasks or goals and then rewarding workers with financial incentives; and giving workers shorter work hours and frequent breaks. In fact, his ideas are so well accepted and widely used that we take most of them for granted. As eminent management scholar Edwin Locke says, "The point is not, as is often claimed, that he was 'right in the context of his time,' but is now outdated, but that *most of his insights are still valid today.*"[25]

2.2 Motion Studies: Frank and Lillian Gilbreth

The husband and wife team Frank and Lillian Gilbreth are best known for their use of motion studies to simplify work, but they also made significant contributions to the employment of disabled workers and industrial psychology. Like Frederick Taylor, their early experiences significantly shaped their interests and contributions to management.

Though admitted to MIT, Frank Gilbreth (1868–1924) began his career as an apprentice bricklayer. While learning the trade, he noticed the bricklayers using three different sets of motions—one to teach others how to lay bricks, a second to work at a slow pace, and a third to work at a fast pace.[26] Wondering which was best, he studied the various approaches and began eliminating unnecessary motions. For example, by designing a stand that could be raised to waist height, he eliminated the need to bend over to pick up each brick. Turning to grab a brick was faster and easier than bending down. By having lower-paid workers place all the bricks with their most attractive side up, bricklayers didn't waste time turning a brick over to find it. By mixing a more consistent mortar, bricklayers no longer had to tap each brick numerous times to put it in the right position. Together, Gilbreth's improvements raised productivity from 120 to 350 bricks per hour and from 1,000 bricks to 2,700 bricks per day.

As a result of his experience with bricklaying, Gilbreth and his wife Lillian developed a long-term interest in using motion study to simplify work, improve productivity, and reduce the level of effort required to safely perform a job. Indeed, Frank Gilbreth said, "The greatest waste in the world comes from needless, ill-directed, and ineffective motions."[27] **Motion study** broke each task or job into separate motions and then eliminated those that were unnecessary or repetitive. Because many motions were completed very quickly, the Gilbreths used motion-picture films, then a relatively new technology, to analyze jobs. Most film cameras at that time were hand cranked and thus variable in their film speed, so Frank Gilbreth invented the microchronometer, a large clock that could record time to 1/2,000th of a second. By placing the micro chronometer next to the worker in the camera's field of vision and attaching a flashing strobe light to the worker's hands to better identify the direction and sequence of key movements, the Gilbreths could use film to detect and precisely time even the slightest, fastest movements. Motion study typically yielded production increases of 25 to 300 percent.[28] It was even used in hospitals to clearly identify the large amount of time that surgeons wasted looking for the next surgical instrument they needed. Frank Gilbreth improved this process by making a nurse responsible for organizing, retrieving, and handing surgical instruments to surgeons, a process still in use today.[29]

Frederick W. Taylor also strove to simplify work, but he did so by managing time rather than motion as the Gilbreths did.[30] Taylor developed time study to put an end to soldiering and to determine what could be considered a fair day's work. **Time study** worked by timing how long it took a "first-class man" to complete each part of his job. A standard time was established after allowing for rest periods, and a

motion study breaking each task or job into its separate motions and then eliminating those that are unnecessary or repetitive.

time study timing how long it takes good workers to complete each part of their job.

worker's pay would increase or decrease depending on whether the worker exceeded or fell below that standard.

One of the Gilbreths' most overlooked accomplishments was the critical role they played in rehabilitating and employing disabled workers.[31] After World War I, there were 13 million wounded and disabled soldiers in the United States and Europe. Frank Gilbreth worried, "What is to be done with the millions of cripples, when their injuries have been remedied as far as possible, and when they are obliged to become again a part of the working community?"[32] The Gilbreths were particularly sensitive to this issue because Frank himself had recovered from a rheumatism attack that had left him temporarily paralyzed from the neck down. So they applied motion study to identify the kinds of tasks that disabled workers could effectively perform. Nearly 75 years before the Americans with Disabilities Act became law (see Chapter 12 for more information), the Gilbreths argued that the government, employers, and engineers had an important role to play in employing disabled workers. The government's job, they said, was to provide vocational training. Indeed, in 1918 the U.S. Congress passed the Vocational Rehabilitation Act, adopting most of the Gilbreths' key recommendations. Employers, they said, should identify jobs that disabled people could perform. To help employers do this, the Gilbreths created a large slide show of pictures documenting the hundreds of ways in which disabled people could effectively perform jobs. Also, according to the Gilbreths, engineers had a responsibility to adapt and design machines so that disabled workers could use them.

Lillian Gilbreth (1878–1972) was an important contributor to management in her own right. She was the first woman to receive a Ph.D. in industrial psychology as well as the first woman to become a member of the Society of Industrial Engineers and the American Society of Mechanical Engineers. When Frank died in 1924, she continued the work of their management consulting company (which they had shared for over a dozen years) on her own. Lillian, who was concerned with the human side of work, was one of the first contributors to industrial psychology, originating ways to improve office communication, incentive programs, job satisfaction, and management training. Her work also convinced the government to enact laws regarding workplace safety, ergonomics, and child labor.

2.3 Charts: Henry Gantt

Henry Gantt (1861–1919) was first a protégé and then an associate of Frederick Taylor. Gantt is best known for the Gantt chart, but he also made significant contributions to management with respect to pay-for-performance plans and the training and development of workers. As shown in Exhibit 2.3, a **Gantt chart** visually indicates what tasks must be completed at which times in order to complete a project. It accomplishes this by showing time in various units on the x-axis and tasks on the y-axis. For example, Exhibit 2.3 shows that the following tasks must be completed by the following dates: In order to start construction on a new company headquarters by the week of November 18, the architectural firm must be selected by October 7, architectural planning done by November 4, permits obtained from the city by November 11, site preparation finished by November 18, and loans and financing finalized by November 18.

Though simple and straightforward, Gantt charts were revolutionary in the era of seat-of-the-pants management because of the detailed planning information they provided to managers. As Gantt wrote, "By using the graphical forms its [the Gantt chart's] value is very much increased, for the general appearance of the sheet is sufficient to tell how closely the schedule is being lived up to; in other words, whether the plant is being run efficiently or not. . . . Such sheets show at a glance where the

Gantt chart a graphical chart that shows which tasks must be completed at which times in order to complete a project or task.

Exhibit 2.3   Gantt Chart for Starting Construction on a New Headquarters

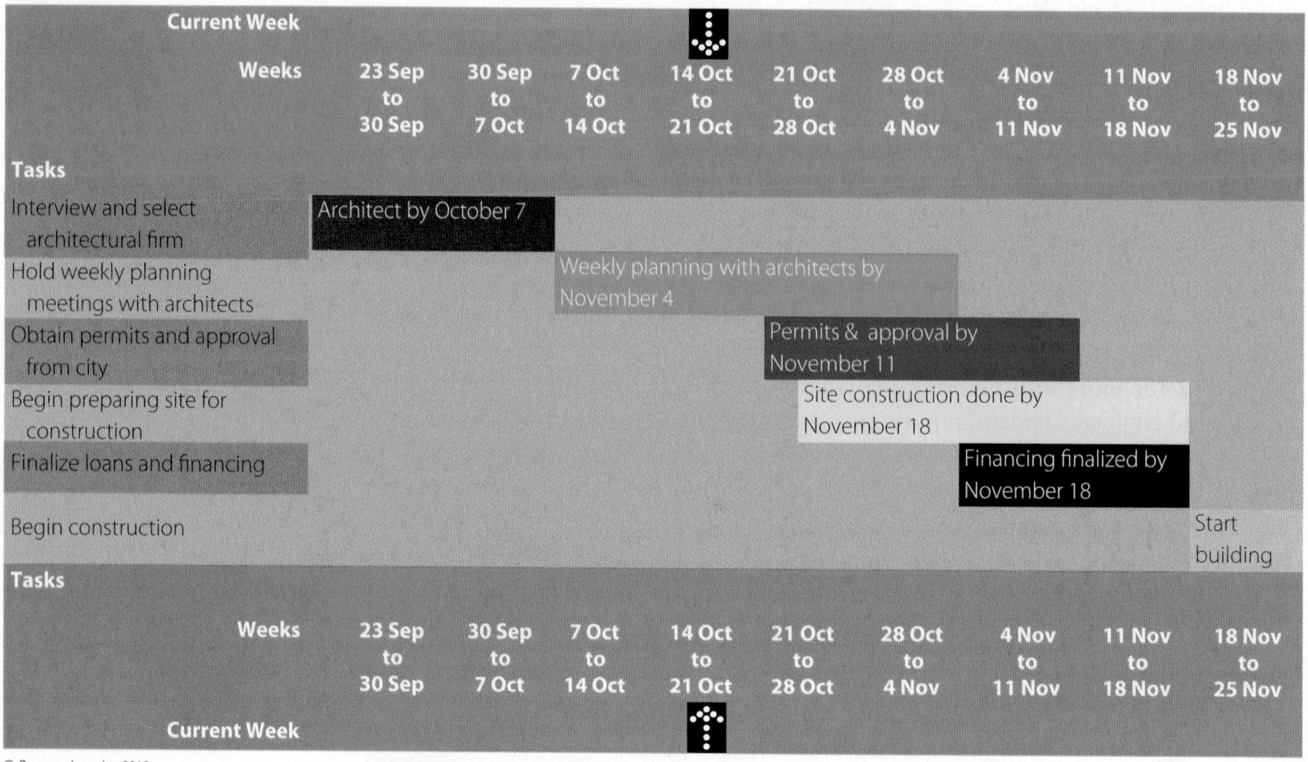

Current Week				⋮					
Weeks	23 Sep to 30 Sep	30 Sep to 7 Oct	7 Oct to 14 Oct	14 Oct to 21 Oct	21 Oct to 28 Oct	28 Oct to 4 Nov	4 Nov to 11 Nov	11 Nov to 18 Nov	18 Nov to 25 Nov
Tasks									
Interview and select architectural firm		Architect by October 7							
Hold weekly planning meetings with architects				Weekly planning with architects by November 4					
Obtain permits and approval from city					Permits & approval by November 11				
Begin preparing site for construction						Site construction done by November 18			
Finalize loans and financing							Financing finalized by November 18		
Begin construction									Start building
Tasks									
Weeks	23 Sep to 30 Sep	30 Sep to 7 Oct	7 Oct to 14 Oct	14 Oct to 21 Oct	21 Oct to 28 Oct	28 Oct to 4 Nov	4 Nov to 11 Nov	11 Nov to 18 Nov	18 Nov to 25 Nov
				Current Week					

delays occur, and indicate what must have our attention in order to keep up the proper output."[33] The use of Gantt charts is so widespread today that nearly all project management software and computer spreadsheets have the capability to create charts that track and visually display the progress being made on a project.

Gantt was much more sympathetic toward workers than Frederick Taylor was, and he introduced a significant change to Taylor's well-known piece-rate reward system. Unlike Taylor's system, in which payment was completely dependent on production—if you produced at substandard levels, you got substandard pay—Gantt's task and bonus system did not punish workers for not achieving higher levels of production. Workers who produced more received a daily bonus, but those who didn't simply received their standard daily pay. The key, according to Gantt, was that his task-and-bonus system didn't punish workers for lower production as they took time to learn how to increase their production efficiency. Production usually doubled under Gantt's system.[34]

Finally, Gantt, along with Taylor, was one of the first to strongly recommend that companies train and develop their workers.[35] In his work with companies, he found that workers achieved their best performance levels if they were trained first. At the time, however, supervisors were reluctant to teach workers what they knew for fear that they could lose their jobs to more knowledgeable workers. Gantt overcame the supervisors' resistance by rewarding them with bonuses for properly training all of their workers. Said Gantt, "This is the first recorded attempt to make it in the financial interest of the foreman to teach the individual worker, and the importance of it cannot be overestimated, for it changes the foreman from a driver of men to their friend and helper."[36] Gantt's approach to training was straightforward: "(1) a scientific investigation in detail of each piece of work, and the determination of the best method and the shortest time in which the work can be done. (2) A teacher capable of teaching the best method and the shortest time. (3) Reward for both teacher and pupil when the latter is successful."[37]

Scientific Management   In contrast to an unsystematic, seat-of-the-pants approach to management, scientific management recommended studying and testing different work methods to identify the best, most efficient ways to complete a job. According to Frederick W. Taylor, the father of scientific management, managers should follow four scientific management principles: (1) study each element of work to determine the "one best way" to do it; (2) scientifically select, train, teach, and develop workers to reach their full potential; (3) cooperate with employees to ensure implementation of the scientific principles; (4) divide the work and the responsibility equally between management and workers. Above all, Taylor felt these principles could be used to align managers and employees by determining a fair day's work, or what an average worker could produce at a reasonable pace, and a fair day's pay, or what management should pay workers for that effort. Taylor felt that incentives were one of the best ways to align management and employees.

The husband and wife team of Frank and Lillian Gilbreth are best known for their use of motion studies to simplify work. Whereas Taylor used time study to determine a fair day's work, based on how long it took a "first-class man" to complete each part of his job, Frank Gilbreth used film cameras and microchronometers to conduct motion study to improve efficiency by categorizing and eliminating unnecessary or repetitive motions. The Gilbreths also made significant contributions to the employment of disabled workers, encouraging the government to rehabilitate them, employers to identify jobs that they could perform, and engineers to adapt and design machines they could use. Lillian Gilbreth, one of the first contributors to industrial psychology, originated ways to improve office communication, incentive programs, job satisfaction, and management training. She also convinced the government to enact laws regarding workplace safety, ergonomics, and child labor. Henry Gantt is best known for the Gantt chart, which graphically indicates when a series of tasks must be completed to perform a job or project, but he also developed ideas regarding pay-for-performance plans (where workers were rewarded for producing more but were not punished if they didn't) and worker training (all workers should be trained and their managers should be rewarded for training them).

Review 2

3 Bureaucratic and Administrative Management

The field of scientific management developed quickly in the United States between 1895 and 1920 and focused on improving the efficiency of manufacturing facilities and their workers. At about the same time, equally important ideas about bureaucratic and administrative management were developing in Europe. German sociologist Max Weber presented a new way to run entire organizations (bureaucratic management) in *The Theory of Economic and Social Organization*, published in 1922. Henri Fayol, an experienced French CEO, published his ideas about how and what managers should do in their jobs (administrative management) in *General and Industrial Management* in 1916. Although they were developed at the same time as scientific management, the ideas of Weber and Fayol would not begin to influence American ideas about management until after World War II, when their books were translated into English and published in the United States in 1947 and 1949, respectively.

Let's find out more about the contributions Weber and Fayol made to management by learning about **3.1 bureaucratic management** and **3.2 administrative management**.

3.1 Bureaucratic Management: Max Weber

Today, when we hear the term *bureaucracy*, we think of inefficiency and red tape, incompetence and ineffectiveness, and rigid administrators blindly enforcing nonsensical rules. When German sociologist Max Weber (1864–1920) first proposed the idea of bureaucratic organizations, however, these problems were associated with monarchies and patriarchies rather than bureaucracies. In monarchies, where kings, queens, sultans, and emperors ruled, and patriarchies, where a council of elders, wise men, or male heads of extended families ruled, the top leaders typically achieved their positions by virtue of birthright. For example, when the queen died, her oldest son became king regardless of his intelligence, experience, education, or desire. Likewise, promotion to prominent positions of authority in monarchies and patriarchies was based on whom you knew (politics), who you were (heredity), or ancient rules and traditions.

It was against this historical background of monarchical and patriarchic rule that Weber proposed the then new idea of bureaucracy. *Bureaucracy* comes from the French word *bureaucratie*. Because *bureau* means desk or office and *cratie* or *cracy* means to rule, *bureaucracy* literally means to rule from a desk or office. According to Weber, **bureaucracy** is "the exercise of control on the basis of knowledge."[38] Rather than ruling by virtue of favoritism or personal or family connections, people in a bureaucracy would lead by virtue of their rational-legal authority—in other words, their knowledge, expertise, or experience. Furthermore, the aim of bureaucracy is not to protect authority, but to achieve an organization's goals in the most efficient way possible.

Exhibit 2.4 shows the seven elements that, according to Weber, characterize bureaucracies. First, instead of hiring people because of their family or political connections or personal loyalty, they should be hired because their technical training or education qualifies them to do the job well. Second, along the same lines, promotion within the company should no longer be based on whom you know (politics) or who you are (heredity), but on your experience and achievements. And to further limit the influence of personal connections in the promotion process, *managers*, rather than organizational owners, should decide who gets promoted. Third, each position or job is part of a chain of command that clarifies who reports to whom throughout the organization. Those higher in the chain of command have the right, if they so choose,

bureaucracy the exercise of control on the basis of knowledge, expertise, or experience.

Exhibit 2.4 Elements of Bureaucratic Organizations

Qualification-based hiring	Employees are hired on the basis of their technical training or educational background.
Merit-based promotion	Promotion is based on experience or achievement. Managers, not organizational owners, decide who is promoted.
Chain of commands	Each job occurs within a hierarchy, the chain of command, in which each position reports and is accountable to a higher position. A grievance procedure and a right to appeal protect people in lower positions.
Division of labor	Tasks, responsibilities, and authority are clearly divided and defined.
Impartial application of rules and procedures	Rules and procedures apply to all members of the organization and will be applied in an impartial manner, regardless of one's position or status.
Recorded in writing	All administrative decisions, acts, rules, or procedure will be recorded in writing.
Managers separate from owners	The owners of an organization should not manage or supervise the organization.

Source: M. Weber, *The Theory of Economic and Social Organization*, trans. A. Henderson & T. Parsons (New York Free Press, 1947), 329–334.

to give commands, take action, and make decisions concerning activities occurring anywhere below them in the chain. Unlike many monarchies or patriarchies, however, those lower in the chain of command are protected by a grievance procedure that gives them the right to appeal the decisions of those in higher positions. Fourth, to increase efficiency and effectiveness, tasks and responsibilities should be separated and assigned to those best qualified to complete them. Authority is vested in these task-defined positions rather than in people, and the authority of each position is clearly defined in order to reduce confusion and conflict. If you move to a different job in a bureaucracy, your authority increases or decreases commensurate with the responsibilities of that job. Fifth, because of his strong distaste for favoritism, Weber felt that an organization's rules and procedures should apply to all members regardless of their position or status. Sixth, to ensure consistency and fairness over time and across different leaders and supervisors, all rules, procedures, and decisions should be recorded in writing. Finally, to reduce favoritism, "professional" managers rather than company owners should manage or supervise the organization.

When viewed in historical context, Weber's ideas about bureaucracy represent a tremendous improvement in how organizations should be run. Fairness supplanted favoritism; the goal of efficiency replaced the goal of personal gain; and logical rules and procedures took the place of traditions or arbitrary decision making. Today, however, after more than a century of experience, we recognize that bureaucracy has limitations as well. Weber called bureaucracy the "iron cage" and said, "Once fully established, bureaucracy is among those social structures which are the hardest to destroy."[39] In bureaucracies, managers are supposed to influence employee behavior by fairly rewarding or punishing employees for compliance or noncompliance with organizational policies, rules, and procedures. In reality, however, most employees would argue that bureaucratic managers emphasize punishment for noncompliance much more than rewards for compliance. Ironically, bureaucratic management was created to prevent just this type of managerial behavior. By encouraging managers to apply well-thought-out rules, policies, and procedures impartially and consistently to everyone in the organization, bureaucratic control is supposed to make companies more efficient, effective, and fair. But, as you'll read in Chapter 16 on control, it can sometimes have just the opposite effect. Managers who use bureaucratic control often put following the rules above all else. Too much emphasis on rule- and policy-driven decision making can make companies highly resistant to change and slow to respond to customers and competitors.

3.2 Administrative Management: Henri Fayol

Though his work was not translated and widely recognized in the United States until 1949, Frenchman Henri Fayol (1841–1925) was as important a contributor to the field of management as Frederick Taylor. Like Taylor and the Gilbreths, Fayol's work experience significantly shaped his thoughts and ideas about management. But, whereas Taylor's ideas changed companies from the shop floor up, Fayol's ideas were shaped by his experience as a managing director (CEO) and generally changed companies from the board of directors down.[40] Fayol is best known for developing five functions of managers and 14 principles of management, as well as for his belief that management can and should be taught to others.

Like his father, Henri Fayol enrolled in France's National School of Mines, graduating with an engineering degree at the age of 19.[41] His first job as a mining engineer was spent learning how to contain and put out underground fires. In this job, he began the valuable habit of recording notes about actions or happenings that either improved or decreased the productivity of the mine and its workers.[42] For instance, he wrote this note to himself about the cause of a work stoppage that occurred when his boss, the managing director, was gone: "May 1861. The horse on the sixth level of the St. Edmund pits broke its leg this morning. I made out an order for its replacement. The stableman refused to accept the order because it did not bear the Director's signature. The Director was absent. No one was designated to replace him. Despite my entreaties, the stableman persisted in his refusal. He had express orders, he said [not to provide a replacement horse unless the managing director ordered]. The injured horse was not replaced and production at the sixth level was lost."[43] It's very possible that this experience helped him form the now widely accepted management principle that a manager's authority should equal his or her responsibility.[44] In other words, because he was responsible for the productivity and production of coal at the St. Edmund's pit, his boss, the managing director, should have given him the authority to take actions commensurate with that responsibility, such as signing for a replacement horse. (See Chapter 9 for more on delegation, authority, and responsibility.)

"what's new" companies >

The most formative events in Fayol's business career came during his 20-plus years as the managing director (CEO) of Compagnie de Commentry-Fourchambault-Decazeville, commonly known as **Comambault**, a vertically integrated steel company that owned several coal and iron ore mines and employed 10,000 to 13,000 workers. Fayol was initially hired by the board of directors to shut down the "hopeless" steel company. The company was facing increased competition from English and German steel companies, which had lower costs, and from new steel mills in northern and eastern France, which were closer to major markets and thus could avoid the large shipping costs incurred by Fayol's company, located in central France.[45] In the five years before Fayol became CEO, production had dropped more than 60 percent, from 38,000 to 15,000 annual metric tons. Comambault had exhausted a key supply of coal needed for steel production, had already shut one steel mill down, and was losing money at another.[46] The company had quit paying dividends to shareholders and had no cash to invest in new technology, such as blast furnaces, that could lower its costs and increase productivity.

So the board hired Fayol as CEO to quickly dissolve and liquidate the business. But, after "four months of reflection and study," he presented the board with a plan, backed by detailed facts and figures, to save the company.[47] With little to lose, the board agreed. Fayol then began the process of turning the company around by obtaining supplies of key resources such as coal and iron ore; using research to develop new steel alloy products; carefully selecting key subordinates in research, purchasing, manufacturing, and sales and then delegating responsibility to them; and cutting costs by moving the company to a better location closer to key markets.[48] Looking back ten years later, Fayol attributed his and the company's success to changes in management practices. He wrote, "When I assumed the responsibility for the restoration of Decazeville, I did not rely on my technical superiority. . . . I relied on my ability as an organizer [and my] skill in handling men."[49] Fayol concluded, "With the same [coal] mines, the same [steel] mills, the same financial resources, the same markets, the same Board of Directors and the same personnel, solely *with the application of a new way of running the company* [italics added], the firm experienced a rise [in its performance] comparable to its earlier decline."[50]

"[T]he success of an enterprise generally depends much more on the administrative ability of its leaders than on their technical ability." —Henri Fayol

Based on his experience as a CEO, Fayol argued that "the success of an enterprise generally depends much more on the administrative ability of its leaders than on their technical ability."[51] And, as you learned in Chapter 1, Fayol argued that managers need to perform five managerial functions if they are to

Exhibit 2.5 Fayol's 14 Principles of Management

1.	**Division of work**	Increase production by dividing work so that each worker completes smaller tasks or job elements.
2.	**Authority and responsibility**	A manager's authority, which is the "right to give orders," should be commensurate with the manager's responsibility. However, organizations should enact controls to prevent managers from abusing their authority.
3.	**Discipline**	Clearly defined rules and procedures are needed at all organizational levels to ensure order and proper behavior.
4.	**Unity of command**	To avoid confusion and conflict, each employee should report to and receive orders from just one boss.
5.	**Unity of direction**	One person and one plan should be used in deciding the activities to be used to accomplish each organizational objective.
6.	**Subordination of individual interests to the general interest**	Employees must put the organization's interests and goals before their own.
7.	**Remuneration**	Compensation should be fair and satisfactory to both the employees and the organization; that is, don't overpay or underpay employees.
8.	**Centralization**	Avoid too much centralization or decentralization. Strike a balance depending on the circumstances and employees involved.
9.	**Scalar chain**	From the top to the bottom of an organization, each position is part of a vertical chain of authority in which each worker reports to just one boss. For the sake of simplicity, communication outside normal work groups or departments should follow the vertical chain of authority.
10.	**Order**	To avoid conflicts and confusion, order can be obtained by having a place for everyone and having everyone in their place; in other words, there should be no overlapping responsibilities.
11.	**Equity**	Kind, fair, and just treatment for all will develop devotion and loyalty. This does not exclude discipline, if warranted, and consideration of the broader general interest of the organization.
12.	**Stability of tenure of personnel**	Low turnover, meaning a stable work force with high tenure, benefits an organization by improving performance, lowering costs, and giving employees, especially managers, time to learn their jobs.
13.	**Initiative**	Because it is a "great source of strength for business," managers should encourage the development of initiative, the ability to develop and implement a plan, in others.
14.	**Esprit de corps**	Develop a strong sense of morale and unity among workers that encourages coordination of efforts.

Source: H. Fayol, *General and Industrial Management* (London: Pittman & Sons, 1949); M. Fells, "Fayol Stands the Test of Time," *Journal of Management History* 6 (2000); and C. Rodrigues, "Fayol's 14 Principles of Management Then and Now: A Framework for Managing Today's Organizations Effectively," *Management Decision* 39 (2001), 880–889.

be successful: planning, organizing, coordinating, commanding, and controlling.[52] Because most management textbooks have dropped the coordinating function and now refer to Fayol's commanding function as "leading," these functions are widely known as planning (determining organizational goals and a means for achieving them), organizing (deciding where decisions will be made, who will do what jobs and tasks, and who will work for whom), leading (inspiring and motivating workers to work hard to achieve organizational goals), and controlling (monitoring progress toward goal achievement and taking corrective action when needed). In addition, according to Fayol, effective management is based on the 14 principles in Exhibit 2.5.

Finally, Fayol, along with Joseph Wharton, was one of the first to argue that management could and should be taught to others. In short, Fayol believed that the principles of management could be taught in colleges and universities and that managers are not born, but can be made through a combination of education and experience.

Review 3

Bureaucratic and Administrative Management Today, when we hear the word *bureaucracy*, we think of inefficiency and red tape. Yet according to German sociologist Max Weber, bureaucracy—or running organizations on the basis of knowledge, fairness, and logical rules and procedures—would accomplish organizational goals much more efficiently than monarchies and patriarchies, where decisions were made on the basis of personal or family connections, personal gain, and arbitrary decision making. Bureaucracies are characterized by seven elements: qualification-based hiring; merit-based promotion; chain of command; division of labor; impartial application of rules and procedures; recording rules, procedures, and decisions in writing; and separating managers from owners. Nonetheless, bureaucracies are often inefficient and can be highly resistant to change.

The Frenchman Henri Fayol, whose ideas were shaped by his 20-plus years of experience as a CEO, is best known for developing five management functions (planning, organizing, coordinating, commanding, and controlling) and 14 principles of management (division of work, authority and responsibility, discipline, unity of command, unity of direction, subordination of individual interests to the general interest, remuneration, centralization, scalar chain, order, equity, stability of tenure of personnel, initiative, and esprit de corps). He is also known for his belief that management can and should be taught to others.

4 Human Relations Management

As we have seen, scientific management focuses on improving efficiency; bureaucratic management focuses on using knowledge, fairness, and logical rules and procedures; and administrative management focuses on how and what managers should do in their jobs. The human relations approach to management focuses on *people*, particularly the psychological and social aspects of work. This approach to management sees people not as just extensions of machines but as valuable organizational resources in their own right. Human relations management holds that people's needs are important and understands that their efforts, motivation, and performance are affected by the work they do and their relationships with their bosses, coworkers, and work groups. In other words, efficiency alone is not enough. Organizational success also depends on treating workers well.

Let's find out more about human relations management by learning about **4.1 Mary Parker Follett's theories of constructive conflict and coordination; 4.2 Elton Mayo's Hawthorne Studies;** and **4.3 Chester Barnard's theories of cooperation and acceptance of authority.**

4.1 Constructive Conflict and Coordination: Mary Parker Follett

Mary Parker Follett (1868–1933) was a social worker with a degree in political science who, in her fifties, after 25 years of working with schools and nonprofit organizations, began lecturing and writing about management and working extensively as a consultant for business and government leaders in the United States and Europe. Although her contributions were overlooked for decades, perhaps because she was a woman or perhaps because they were so different, many of today's "new" management ideas can clearly be traced to her work.

Follett is known for developing ideas regarding constructive conflict and coordination. Constructive conflict, also called cognitive conflict, is one of Follett's most important contributions and is discussed further in Chapter 5 on decision making and Chapter 10 on teams. Unlike most people, then and now, who view conflict as bad, Follett believed that conflict could be beneficial. She said that conflict is "the appearance of difference, difference of opinions, of interests. For that is what conflict means—difference." She went on to say, "As conflict—difference—is here in this world, as we cannot avoid it, we should, I think, use it to work for us. Instead of condemning it, we should set it to work for us. Thus we shall not be afraid of conflict, but shall recognize that there is a destructive way of dealing with such moments and a constructive way."[53]

Follett believed that managers could deal with conflict in three ways: domination, compromise, and integration. She said, "Domination, obviously, is a victory of one side over the other. This is the easiest way of dealing with conflict, the easiest for the moment but not usually successful in the long run. . . . As for the second way of dealing with conflict, that of compromise, we understand [it] well, for it is the way we settle most of our controversies; each side gives up a little in order to have peace, or, to speak more accurately, in order that the activity which has been interrupted by the conflict may go on."[54] Follett continued, "Yet no one really wants to compromise, because that means a giving up of something. Is there then any other method of ending conflict? There is a way beginning now to be recognized at least, and even occasionally followed: when two desires are *integrated*, that means that a solution has been found in which both desires have found a place that neither side has had to sacrifice anything."[55]

So, rather than one side dominating the other or both sides compromising, the point of integrative conflict resolution is to have both parties indicate their preferences and then work together to find an alternative that meets the needs of both. According to Follett, "Integration involves invention, and the clever thing is to recognize this, and not to let one's thinking stay within the boundaries of two alternatives which are mutually exclusive." Indeed, Follett's ideas about the positive use of conflict and an integrative approach to conflict resolution predate accepted thinking in the negotiation and conflict resolution literature by six decades.[56]

Follett's writing on the role of coordination in organizations is another of her important contributions. She lists four fundamental principles of organizations:

1. Coordination as reciprocal relating all the factors in a situation
2. Coordination by direct contact of the responsible people concerned
3. Coordination in the early stages
4. Coordination as a continuing process

Follett's <u>first</u> principle recognizes that most activities and events in an organization are interrelated. Make just one change, and other changes, some expected but some not, will occur. Cut costs, and quality may be affected. Change the raw ingredients used to make a product, and manufacturing procedures may no longer work. Marketing offers customers special incentives to buy more products, and operations has to work overtime to keep up with the increased demand. Because of

domination an approach to dealing with conflict in which one party satisfies its desires and objectives at the expense of the other party's desires and objectives.

compromise an approach to dealing with conflict in which both parties give up some of what they want in order to reach agreement on a plan to reduce or settle the conflict.

integrative conflict resolution an approach to dealing with conflict in which both parties indicate their preferences and then work together to find an alternative the meets the needs of both.

these interrelations, leaders at different levels and in different parts of the organization must coordinate their efforts to solve problems and produce the best overall outcomes in an integrative way. In short, managers cannot manage their part of the organization while ignoring its other parts. What each manager does affects other parts of the organization and vice versa.

Follett explains her second principle, coordination by direct contact of the people concerned, and her third principle, coordination in the early stages, this way: "Direct contact must begin in the earliest stages of the process. ... If the heads of departments confront each other with finished policies, agreement will be found difficult. . . . But if these heads meet while they are forming their policies, meet and discuss the questions involved, a successful co-relation is far more likely to be reached. Their thinking has not become crystallized. They can still modify one another."[57] In other words, better outcomes will be achieved if the people affected by organizational issues and problems meet early and directly to address them. Working with those involved or affected will produce more effective solutions than will isolating or ignoring them.

With respect to her fourth principle, coordination as a continuing process, Follett said: "It is a fallacy to think that we can solve problems—in any final sense. The belief that we can do so is a drag upon our thinking. What we need is a process for meeting problems. When we think we have solved one, well, by the very process of solving, new elements or forces come into the situation and you have a new problem on your hands to be solved."[58] Consequently, there is always a need for early, integrative coordination of the people affected by organizational situations, problems, or issues. The need for coordination never goes away.

Exhibit 2.6 summarizes Follett's contributions to management in her own words. She casts power as "with" rather than "over" others. Giving orders involves discussing instructions and resentment. Authority flows from job knowledge and experience rather than position. Leadership involves setting the tone for the team rather than being aggressive and dominating, which may be harmful. Coordination and control should be based on facts and information. In the end, Follett's contributions added significantly to our understanding of the human, social, and psychological sides of management. Peter Parker, the former chair of the London School of Economics, said about Follett: "People often puzzle about who is the father of management. I don't know who the father was, but I have no doubt about who was the mother."[59]

4.2 Hawthorne Studies: Elton Mayo

Australian-born Elton Mayo (1880–1948) is best known for his role in the famous Hawthorne Studies at the Western Electric Company. His ideas became popular during the early twentieth century when labor unrest, dissatisfaction, and protests (some of them violent) were widespread in the United States, Europe, and Asia. In 1919 alone, for example, more than 4 million American workers went on strike.[60]

Working conditions contributed to the unrest. Millions of workers in large factories toiled at boring, repetitive, unsafe jobs for low pay. Employee turnover was high and absenteeism was rampant. With employee turnover approaching 380 percent in his automobile factories, Henry Ford had to double the daily wage of his manufacturing workers from $2.50, the going wage at the time, to $5.00 to keep enough workers at their jobs. Workers joined labor unions to force companies to improve their pay and working conditions.

In 1913, the federal government created the U.S. Department of Labor "to foster, promote and develop the welfare of working people, to improve their working conditions and to enhance their opportunities for profitable employment."[61] In 1935,

Exhibit 2.6 Some of Mary Parker Follett's Key Contributions to Management

Constructive conflict	• "As conflict—difference—is here in this world, as we cannot avoid it, we should, I think, use it to work for us. Instead of condemning it, we should set it to work for us."
Power	• "Power might be defined as simply the ability to make things happen, to be a causal agent, to initiate change."
	• "It seems to me that whereas power usually means power-over, the power of some person or group over some other person or group, it is possible to develop the conception of power-with, a jointly developed power, a co-active, not a coercive power."
The giving of orders	• "Probably more industrial trouble has been caused by the manner in which orders have been given than in any other way."
	• "But even if instructions are properly framed, are not given in an overbearing manner, there are many people who react violently against anything that they feel is a command. It is often the command that is resented, not the thing commanded."
	• "An advantage of not exacting blind obedience, of discussing your instructions with your subordinates, is that if there is any resentment, any come-back, you get it out into the open, and when it is in the open you can deal with it."
Authority	• "Indeed there are many indications in the present reorganization of industry that we are beginning to rid ourselves of the over and under idea, that we are coming to a different conception of authority, many indications that there is an increasing tendency to let the job itself, rather than the position occupied in a hierarchy, dictate the kind and amount of authority."
	• "Authority should go with knowledge and experience, that is where obedience is due, no matter whether it is up the line or down."
Leadership	• "Of the greatest importance is the ability to grasp a total situation.... Out of a welter of facts, experience, desires, aims, the leader must find the unifying thread. He must see a whole, not a mere kaleidoscope of pieces. . . . The higher up you go, the more ability you have to have of this kind."
	• "The leader makes the team. This is pre-eminently the leadership quality—the ability to organize all the forces there are in an enterprise and make them serve a common purpose."
	• "[It is wrong to assume] that you cannot be a good leader unless you are aggressive, masterful, dominating. But I think not only that these characteristics are not the qualities essential to leadership but, on the contrary, that they often militate directly against leadership."
Coordination	• "One which I consider a very important trend in business management is a system of cross-functioning between the different departments. . . . Each department is expected to get in touch with certain others."
	• "Many businesses are now organized in such a way that you do not have an ascending and descending ladder of authority. You have a degree of cross-functioning, of inter-relation of departments, which means a horizontal rather than a vertical authority."
	• "The most important thing to remember about unity is—that there is no such thing. There is only unifying. You cannot get unity and expect it to last a day—or five minutes. Every man in a business should be taking part in a certain process and that process is unifying."
Control	• "Control is coming more and more to mean fact-control rather than man-control."
	• "Central control is coming more and more to mean the co-relation of many controls rather than a super-imposed control."

Source: M. P. Follett, *Mary Parker Follett—Prophet of Management: A Celebration of Writings from the 1920s*, ed. P. Graham (Boston: Harvard Business School Press, 1995).

Congress passed the National Labor Relations Act (also known as the Wagner Act), which gave workers the legal right to form unions and collectively bargain with their employers, but prevented companies from engaging in unfair labor practices to "bust" unions. In this historical context, Mayo's work on the Hawthorne Studies proved highly relevant as managers looked for ways to increase productivity as well as improve worker satisfaction and working conditions.[62]

The Hawthorne Studies were conducted in several stages between 1924 and 1932 at a Western Electric plant in Chicago. Although Mayo didn't join the studies until

Although Mayo's studies used several variables like lighting and incentives to increase productivity, it turned out that productivity increased no matter what changes were made. Mayo concluded that paying more attention to the workers and the development of the workers into a cohesive group produced higher levels of productivity and job satisfaction.

1928, he played a significant role thereafter, writing about the results in his book *The Human Problems of an Industrial Civilization*.[63] The first stage of the Hawthorne Studies investigated the effects of lighting levels and incentives on employee productivity in the Relay Test Assembly Room, where workers took approximately a minute to put "together a coil, armature, contact springs, and insulators in a fixture and secure the parts by means of four machine screws."[64]

Two groups of six experienced female workers, five to do the work and one to supply needed parts, were separated from the main part of the factory by a 10-foot partition and placed at a standard work bench with the necessary parts and tools. Over the next five years, the experimenters introduced various levels and combinations of lighting, financial incentives, and rest pauses (work breaks) to study the effect on productivity. Curiously, however, production levels increased whether the experimenters increased or decreased the lighting, paid workers based on individual production or group production, or increased or decreased the number and length of rest pauses. In fact, Mayo and his fellow researchers were surprised that production steadily increased from 2,400 relays per day at the beginning of the study to 3,000 relays per day five years later. The question was: Why?

Mayo and his colleagues eventually concluded that two things accounted for the results. First, substantially more attention was paid to these workers than to workers in the rest of the plant. Mayo wrote, "Before every change of program [in the study], the group is consulted. Their comments are listened to and discussed; sometimes their objections are allowed to negate a suggestion. The group unquestionably develops a sense of participation in the critical determinations and becomes something of a social unit."[65]

For years, the "Hawthorne Effect" has been *incorrectly* defined as increasing productivity by paying more attention to workers.[66] But it is not simply about attention from management. The Hawthorne Effect cannot be understood without giving equal importance to the social units, which became intensely cohesive groups. Mayo said, "What actually happened was that six individuals became a team and the team gave itself wholeheartedly and spontaneously to cooperation in the experiment. The consequence was that they felt themselves to be participating freely and without afterthought, and were happy in the knowledge that they were working without coercion from above or limits from below."[67] Together, the increased attention from management and the development of a cohesive work group led to significantly higher levels of job satisfaction *and* productivity.

Mayo and his research colleagues concluded:

> » "There has been an important increase in contentment among the girls working in the test-room conditions.
> » "There has been a decrease in absences of about 80 percent among the girls since entering the test-room group.

> » "The changed working conditions have resulted in creating an eagerness on the part of the operators to come to work in the morning.
> » "The operators have no clear idea as to why they are able to produce more in the test-room; but as shown in the replies to the questionnaires … there is the feeling that better output is in some way related to the distinctly pleasanter, freer, and happier work conditions.[68]

For the first time, human factors related to work were found to be more important than the physical conditions or design of the work. In short, the Hawthorne Studies found that workers' feelings and attitudes affected their work.

The next stage of the Hawthorne Studies was conducted in the Bank Wiring Room, where "the group consisted of nine wiremen, three solderers, and two inspectors. Each of these groups performed a specific task and collaborated with the other two in completion of each unit of equipment. The task consisted of setting up the banks of terminals side-by-side on frames, wiring the corresponding terminals from bank to bank, soldering the connections, and inspecting with a test set for short circuits or breaks in the wire. One solderman serviced the work of the three wireman."[69] Although productivity increased in the Relay Test Assembly Room no matter what the researchers did, productivity dropped in the Bank Wiring Room. Again, the question was, Why?

Mayo and his colleagues found that group effects were just as responsible for the decline in performance in the Bank Wiring Room as they were for the increased performance in the Relay Test Assembly Room. The difference was that the workers in the Bank Wiring Room had been an existing work group for some time and had already developed strong negative norms that governed their behavior. For instance, despite a group financial incentive for production, the group members decided that they would wire only 6,000 to 6,600 connections a day (depending on the kind of equipment they were wiring), well below the production goal of 7,300 connections that management had set for them. Individual workers who worked at a faster pace were socially ostracized from the group or "binged" (hit on the arm) until they slowed their work pace. Thus, the group's behavior was reminiscent of the soldiering that Frederick Taylor had observed. Mayo concluded, "Work [was] done in accord with the group's conception of a day's work; this was exceeded by only one individual who was cordially disliked."[70]

In the end, the Hawthorne Studies demonstrated that the workplace was more complex than previously thought, that workers were not just extensions of machines, and that financial incentives weren't necessarily the most important motivator for workers. By highlighting the crucial role, positive or negative, that groups, group norms, and group behavior play at work, Mayo strengthened Mary Parker Follett's point about coordination—make just one change in an organization and others, some expected and some unexpected, will occur. Thanks to Mayo and his colleagues and their work on the Hawthorne Studies, managers better understood the effect that group social interactions, employee satisfaction, and attitudes had on individual and group performance.

4.3 Cooperation and Acceptance of Authority: Chester Barnard

Like Henri Fayol, Chester Barnard (1886–1961) had experiences as a top executive that shaped his views of management. Barnard began his career in 1909 as an engineer and translator for AT&T, becoming a general manager at Pennsylvania Bell Telephone in 1922 and then president of New Jersey Bell Telephone in 1927.[71] Barnard's ideas, published in his classic book *The Functions of the Executive*, influenced companies from the board of directors down. He is best known for his ideas about cooperation and the acceptance of authority.

Barnard proposed a comprehensive theory of cooperation in formal organizations. In fact, he defines an **organization** as a "system of consciously coordinated activities or forces of two or more persons."[72] In other words, organization occurs whenever two people work together for some purpose, whether it is classmates working together to complete a class project; Habitat for Humanity volunteers donating their time to build a house; or managers working with subordinates to reduce costs, improve quality, or increase sales. Why did Barnard place so much emphasis on cooperation? Because cooperation is *not* the normal state of affairs: "Failure to cooperate, failure of cooperation, failure of organization, disorganization, disintegration, destruction of organization—and reorganization—are characteristic facts of human history."[73]

Barnard argued that managers can gain others' cooperation by completing three executive functions: securing essential services from individuals, formulating an organization's purpose and objectives, and providing a system of communication. By "securing essential services from individuals," Barnard meant that managers must find ways to encourage workers to *willingly* cooperate with each other and management to achieve organizational goals. According to Barnard, managers can gain workers' willing cooperation by offering them *material incentives* such as money or tangible rewards; *nonmaterial incentives* such as recognition, prestige, personal power, improved working conditions, or satisfaction of personal ideals or needs; and *associational incentives* such as the chance to work with people they like or to be more directly involved or associated with key events or processes in the organization.[74]

Top executives unify people in the company by "formulating an organization's purpose and objectives," or making clear what needs to be accomplished. If the organization's purpose is clear, then each person in each job at each level of the company should understand how his or her daily activities, behaviors, and choices contribute to the accomplishment of that purpose. This is the ultimate form of cooperation in an organization. If, however, the organization's purpose is not clear, then departmental or personal objectives may become more important than organizational objectives. The result is a less cohesive organization in which workers are less likely to cooperate to accomplish the organization's goals.

By "providing a system of communication," Barnard meant that managers must create an organizational structure with a clear hierarchy (one that delineates responsibilities, tasks, and jobs) and hire and promote the right people into management—that is, talented people with the right skills and education who will put the organization's needs before their own. Those managers, in turn, are responsible for promoting cooperation by effectively communicating the organization's purpose and objectives and by minimizing organizational politics.

Finally, the extent to which people willingly cooperate in an organization depends on how workers perceive executive authority and whether they're willing to accept it. According to Barnard, there is a *zone of indifference* for many managerial requests or directives in which acceptance of managerial authority is automatic. For example, if your boss asks you for a copy of the monthly inventory report, and compiling and writing that report is part of your job, you think nothing of the request and automatically send it. In general, people will be indifferent to managerial directives or orders if they (1) are understood, (2) are consistent with the purpose of the organization, (3) are compatible with the people's personal interests, and (4) can actually be carried out by those people.

organization a system of consciously coordinated activities or forces created by two or more people.

doing the right thing

More Than a Pair of Hands

When problems come up in the workplace, it's often tempting, as a manager, just to tell your employees what to do. After all, you're the manager, you're the boss, you're supposed to have all the answers to problems, and the employees should recognize your brilliance and obey at all times. But Joe Scanlon, a labor leader in the 1930s, argued that managers and companies benefit when they view the employee as more than a "pair of hands." Scanlon argued that, more often than not, the people who are closest to the problem, the employees, often have the best and simplest solution to a problem. What is more, if the employee is more involved in the solution, then he or she is more likely to implement solving the problem successfully. So, the next time a problem comes up, do the right thing—make sure you involve your employees when you're looking for a solution. They just might have the perfect solution.[75]

Acceptance of managerial authority (i.e., cooperation) is not automatic, however. Ask people to do things contrary to the organization's purpose or to their own benefit and they'll put up a fight. So, although many people assume that managers have the authority to do whatever they want, Barnard, referring to the "fiction of superior authority," believed that workers ultimately grant managers their authority. Consequently, Barnard maintained that it is more effective to induce workers' willing cooperation through incentives, clearly formulated organizational objectives, and effective communication throughout the organization than it is to threaten them into cooperation.

Human Relations Management Unlike most people who view conflict as bad, Mary Parker Follett, the mother of modern management, believed that conflict could be a good thing and that it should be embraced rather than avoided. She noted three ways of dealing with conflict—domination, compromise, and integration—and argued that the latter was best because it focuses on developing creative methods for meeting conflicting parties' needs. Follett also used four principles to emphasize the importance of coordination in organizations. She believed that the best overall outcomes are achieved when leaders and workers at different levels and in different parts of the organization directly coordinate their efforts to solve problems in an integrative way.

Elton Mayo is best known for his role in the Hawthorne Studies at the Western Electric Company. In the first stage of the Hawthorne Studies, production went up because the increased attention paid to the workers in the study and their development into a cohesive work group led to significantly higher levels of job satisfaction and productivity. In the second stage, productivity dropped because the workers had already developed strong negative norms in which individual "rate busters" who worked faster than the rest of the team or cooperated with management were ostracized or "binged." The Hawthorne Studies demonstrated that workers' feelings and attitudes affected their work; that financial incentives weren't necessarily the most important motivator for workers; and that group norms and behavior play a critical role in behavior at work.

Review 4

Chester Barnard, president of New Jersey Bell Telephone, emphasized the critical importance of willing cooperation in organizations and said that managers could gain workers' willing cooperation through three executive functions: securing essential services from individuals (through material, nonmaterial, and associational incentives), unifying the people in the organization by clearly formulating the organization's purpose and objectives, and providing a system of communication. Finally, although most managerial requests or directives will be accepted because they fall within the zone of indifference, Barnard maintains that it is more effective to induce cooperation through incentives, clearly formulating organizational objectives, and effective communication throughout the organization. Ultimately, he says, workers grant managers their authority, not the other way around.

5 Operations, Information, Systems, and Contingency Management

In this last section, we review four other significant historical approaches to management that have influenced how today's managers produce goods and services on a daily basis, gather and manage the information they need to understand their businesses and make good decisions, understand how the different parts of the company work together as a whole, and recognize when and where particular management practices are likely to work.

To better understand these ideas, let's learn about **5.1 operations management, 5.2 information management, 5.3 systems management,** and **5.4 contingency management.**

5.1 Operations Management

In Chapter 18, you will learn about *operations management*, which involves managing the daily production of goods and services. In general, operations management uses a quantitative, or mathematical, approach to find ways to increase productivity, improve quality, and manage or reduce costly inventories. The most commonly used operations management tools and methods are quality control, forecasting techniques, capacity planning, productivity measurement and improvement, linear programming, scheduling systems, inventory systems, work measurement techniques (similar to the Gilbreths' motion studies), project management (similar to Gantt's charts), and cost-benefit analysis.[76]

Today, with those tools and techniques, we take it for granted that manufactured goods will be made with standardized, interchangeable parts; that the design of those parts will be based on specific, detailed plans; and that manufacturing companies will aggressively manage inventories to keep costs low and increase productivity. These key elements of operations management have some rather strange origins: guns, geometry, and fire.

Since 1526, in Gardone, Italy, the descendants of Bartolomeo Beretta have been making world-renowned **Beretta** firearms and gun barrels. Throughout most of the company's history, skilled craftspeople made the lock, stock, and barrel of a Beretta gun by hand. After each part was made, a skilled gun finisher assembled the parts

"what's new" companies >

66

into a complete gun. But the gun finisher did not simply screw the different parts of a gun together, as is done today. Instead, each handmade part required extensive finishing and adjusting so that it would fit together with the other handmade gun parts. Hand fitting was necessary because, even when made by the same skilled craftspeople, no two parts were alike. In fact, gun finishers played a role similar to that of fine watchmakers who meticulously assembled expensive watches—without them, the product simply wouldn't work. Today, we would say that these parts were low quality because they varied so much from one part to another. You'll learn more about variation and quality in Chapter 18 on managing service and manufacturing operations.

All this changed in 1791, when the U.S. government, worried about a possible war with France, ordered 40,000 muskets from private gun contractors. Like Beretta, all but one contractor built handmade muskets assembled by skilled gun finishers who made sure that all the parts fit together. Thus, each musket was unique. If a part broke, a replacement part had to be handcrafted. But one contractor, Eli Whitney of New Haven, Connecticut (who is better known for his invention of the cotton gin) determined that if gun parts were made accurately enough, guns could be made with standardized, interchangeable parts. So he designed machine tools that allowed unskilled workers to make each gun part the same as the next. Said Whitney, "The tools which I contemplate to make are similar to an engraving on copper plate from which may be taken a great number of impressions perceptibly alike."[77] Years passed before Whitney delivered his 10,000 muskets to the U.S. government. But he demonstrated the superiority of interchangeable parts to President-elect Thomas Jefferson in 1801 by quickly and easily assembling complete muskets from randomly picked piles of musket parts. Today, because of Whitney's ideas, most products, from cars to toasters to space shuttles, are manufactured using standardized, interchangeable parts.

But even with this advance, manufacturers still could not produce a part unless they had seen or examined it firsthand. Thanks to Gaspard Monge, a Frenchman of modest beginnings, this soon changed. In Monge's time, maps were crude, often inaccurate, and almost never up-to-date. In 1762, however, the 16-year-old Monge drew a large-scale map of the town of Beaune, France. He developed new surveying tools and systematic methods of observation so that every feature on the map was in proportion and correctly placed. Monge's advanced skills as a draftsperson led to his appointment to the prestigious École Militaire de Mézières, a military institute, where one of his first assignments was to determine the proper placement of cannons for a military fortress. This task normally involved long, complicated mathematical computations. But Monge used the geometrical principles he had developed as a draftsperson to calculate his estimates so quickly that, at first, commanders refused to believe they were accurate. Soon, however, they realized the importance of his breakthrough and protected it as a military secret for more than a decade.[78]

Monge's greatest achievement was his book *Descriptive Geometry*. In it, he explained techniques for drawing three-dimensional objects on paper. For the first time, precise drawings permitted manufacturers to make standardized, interchangeable parts without first examining a prototype. Today, thanks to Monge, manufacturers rely on CAD (computer-aided design) and CAM (computer-aided manufacturing) to take three-dimensional designs straight from the computer to the factory floor.

Once standardized, interchangeable parts became the norm, and once parts could be made from design drawings alone, manufacturers ran into a costly problem that they had never faced before: too much inventory. *Inventory* is the amount and number of raw materials, parts, and finished products that a company has in its possession. In fact, large factories were accumulating parts inventories sufficient for two to three months, much more than they needed on a daily basis to run their manufacturing operations.

A solution to this problem was found in 1905, when the Oldsmobile Motor Works in Detroit burned down. At a time when cars were far too expensive for most Americans, Oldsmobile had become the leading automobile manufacturer in the United States by being the first to produce an affordable car. When the Oldsmobile factory burned down, management rented a new production facility to get production up and running as quickly as possible. But because the new facility was much smaller, there was no room to store large stockpiles of inventory (which the company couldn't afford anyway as it was short on funds). Therefore, the company made do with what it called "hand-to-mouth inventories," in which each production station had only enough parts on hand to do a short production run. Fortunately, because all of its parts suppliers were close by, Oldsmobile could place orders in the morning and receive them in the afternoon (even without telephones), just like today's computerized, just-in-time inventory systems.

> Once standardized, interchangeable parts became the norm, and once parts could be made from design drawings alone, manufacturers ran into a costly problem that they had never faced before: too much inventory.

So, contrary to common belief, just-in-time inventory systems were not invented by Japanese manufacturers. Instead, they were invented out of necessity a century ago because of a fire. You can learn more about just-in-time inventory management in Chapter 18.

5.2 Information Management

The earliest known use of written information occurred nearly 60,000 years ago when Cro-Magnons, from whom modern humans descended, created and recorded a lunar calendar. The calendar consisted of 28 symbols carved into a reindeer antler and indicated when the waters would be high. The calendar was used to track and kill deer, bison, and elk that would gather at river crossings.[79] For most of recorded history, information has been costly, difficult to obtain, and slow to spread. Because of the immense labor and time it took to hand-copy information, books, manuscripts, and written documents of any kind were rare and extremely expensive. Word of Joan of Arc's death in 1431 took 18 months to travel from France across Europe to Constantinople (now Istanbul, Turkey). Most people literally heard news and information from the town crier ("Hear ye! Hear ye!") or from minstrel and acting groups who relayed information as they traveled from town to town.

Yet, as you will learn in Chapter 17, accurate, timely, relevant, and complete information has been important to businesses throughout history. Indeed, as we discussed at the beginning of this chapter, most of the clay tablets unearthed in our earliest cities are business and economic texts. Consequently, throughout history, organizations have pushed for and quickly adopted new information technologies that reduce the cost or increase the speed with which they can acquire, store, retrieve, or communicate information.

The first technologies to truly revolutionize the business use of information were paper and the printing press. In the fourteenth century, water-powered machines were created to pulverize rags into pulp to make paper. Paper prices, which were already lower than those of animal-skin parchments, dropped dramatically. Less than a half-century later, Johannes Gutenberg invented the printing press, which greatly reduced the cost and time needed to copy written information. In fifteenth-century Florence, Italy, a scribe would charge 1 florin (an Italian unit of money) to hand-copy one document page. By contrast, a printer would set up and print 1,025 copies

of the same document for just 3 florins. Within 50 years of its invention, Gutenberg's printing press cut the cost of information by 99.8 percent!

What Gutenberg's printing press did for publishing, the manual typewriter did for daily communication. Before 1850, most business correspondence was written by hand and copied using the letterpress. With the ink still wet, the letter would be placed into a tissue-paper book. A hand press would then be used to squeeze the book and copy the still-wet ink onto the tissue paper. By the 1870s, manual typewriters made it cheaper, easier, and faster to produce and copy business correspondence. Of course, in the 1980s, slightly more than a century later, typewriters were replaced by personal computers and word processing software for identical reasons.

© Paul Orr/Shutterstock.com

As the volume of printed information increased, businesses needed new ways to organize and make sense of it. Vertical file cabinets and the Woodruff file, invented in 1868, represented major advances in information storage and retrieval. Once sales orders or business correspondence were put in the proper file drawer, they could be found easily and quickly by anyone familiar with the system. The cash register, invented in 1879, kept salesclerks honest by recording all sales transactions on a roll of paper securely locked inside the machine. But managers soon realized that the cash register's most important contribution was better management and control of their business. For example, department stores could track performance and sales by installing separate cash registers in the food, clothing, and hardware departments. Time clocks, introduced in the 1890s, helped businesses keep track of worker hours and costs.

Finally, businesses have always looked for information technologies that would speed access to timely information. The Medici family, which opened banks throughout Europe in the early 1400s, used posting messengers to keep in contact with their more than 40 branch managers. The post messengers, who predated the U.S. Postal Service Pony Express by 400 years, could travel 90 miles per day, twice what average riders could cover, because the Medicis were willing to pay for the expense of providing them with fresh horses. This need for timely information also led companies to quickly adopt the telegraph in the 1860s; the telephone in the 1880s; and, of course, Internet technologies in the last two decades. See Chapter 17 for more on how companies are using today's technologies to lower the cost and increase the speed with which accurate, timely, relevant, and complete information is acquired.

5.3 Systems Management

Today's companies are much more complex than they used to be. They are larger and employ more people. They most likely manufacture, service, *and* finance what they sell, not only in their home markets but in foreign markets throughout the world too. They also operate in complex, fast-changing, competitive, global environments that can quickly turn competitive advantages into competitive disadvantages. How, then, can managers make sense of this complexity, both within and outside their organizations?

One way to deal with organizational and environmental complexity is to take a systems view of organizations. The systems approach is derived from theoretical models in biology and social psychology in the 1950s and 1960s.[80] A **system** is a set of interrelated elements or parts that function as a whole. Rather than viewing one part of an organization as separate from the other parts, a systems approach

system a set of interrelated elements or parts that function as a whole.

encourages managers to complicate their thinking by looking for connections between the different parts of the organization. Indeed, one of the more important ideas in the systems approach to management is that organizational systems are composed of parts, or **subsystems**, which are simply smaller systems within larger systems. Subsystems and their connections matter in systems theory because of the possibility for managers to create synergy. **Synergy** occurs when two or more subsystems working together can produce more than they can working apart. In other words, synergy occurs when 1 + 1 = 3.

Systems can be open or closed. **Closed systems** can function without interacting with their environments. But nearly all organizations should be viewed as **open systems** that interact with their environments and depend on them for survival. Therefore, rather than viewing what goes on within the organization as separate from what goes on outside it, the systems approach also encourages managers to look for connections between the different parts of the organization and the different parts of its environment. Successful interaction with organizational environments is critical because open systems tend toward **entropy**, which is the inevitable and steady deterioration of a system.

As shown in Exhibit 2.7, organizations operate in two kinds of complex environments. The *general environment* consists of the economy and the technological, sociocultural, and political and legal trends that indirectly affect all organizations. Changes in any sector of the general environment eventually affect most organizations. In addition, each organization has a specific environment that is unique to that firm's industry and directly affects the way it conducts day-to-day business. The *specific environment* includes customers, competitors, suppliers, industry regulation, and advocacy groups. Both the general and specific environments are discussed in detail in Chapter 3. As Exhibit 2.7 shows, organizational systems obtain inputs from both the general and specific environments. Managers and workers then use their management knowledge and manufacturing techniques to transform those inputs into outputs, such as products and services. These outputs are then consumed by persons or organizations in the environment, which in turn provide feedback to the organization, allowing managers and workers to modify and improve their products or services.

subsystems smaller systems that operate within the context of a larger system.

synergy two or more subsystems working together to produce more than they can working apart.

closed systems systems that can sustain themselves without interacting with their environments.

open systems systems that can sustain themselves only by interacting with their environments, on which they depend for their survival.

entropy the inevitable and steady deterioration of a system.

Exhibit 2.7 Systems View of Organizations

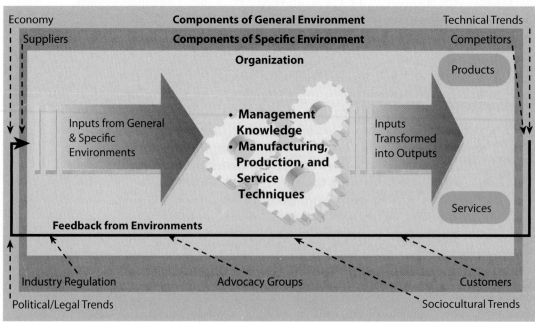

© Cengage Learning 2013

A systems view of organizations offers several advantages. First, it forces managers to view their organizations as part of and subject to the competitive, economic, social, technological, and legal and regulatory forces in their environments.[81] Second, it also forces managers to be aware of how the environment affects specific parts of the organization. Third, because of the complexity and difficulty of trying to achieve synergies among different parts of the organization, the systems view encourages managers to focus on better communication and cooperation within the organization. Finally, it makes managers acutely aware that good internal management of the organization may not be enough to ensure survival. Survival also depends on making sure that the organization continues to satisfy critical environmental stakeholders such as shareholders, employees, customers, suppliers, governments, and local communities. For more on ideas related to the systems view of management, see Chapter 3 on environments and cultures, Chapter 4 on ethics and social responsibility, Chapter 6 on organizational strategy, and Chapter 8 on global management.

5.4 Contingency Management

Earlier, you learned that the goal of scientific management was to use systematic study to find the one best way of doing each task and then use that one best way everywhere. The problem, as you may have gathered from reading about the various approaches to management, is that no one in management seems to agree on what that one best way is. Furthermore, more than 100 years of management research has shown that there are clear boundaries or limitations to most management theories and practices. No management ideas or practices are universal. Although any theory or practice may work much of the time, none works all the time. How, then, is a manager to decide what theory to use? Well, it depends on the situation. The **contingency approach** to management clearly states that there are no universal management theories and that the most effective management theory or idea depends on the kinds of problems or situations that managers or organizations are facing at a particular time.[82] In short, the best way depends on the situation.

One of the practical implications of the contingency approach to management is that management is much harder than it looks. In fact, because of the clarity and obviousness of management theories (okay, most of them), students and workers often wrongly assume that a company's problems would be quickly and easily solved if management would take just a few simple steps. If this were true, few companies would have problems.

A second implication of the contingency approach is that managers need to look for key contingencies that differentiate today's situation or problems from yesterday's situation or problems. Moreover, it means that managers need to spend more time analyzing problems, situations, and employees before taking action to fix them. Finally, it means that as you read this text and learn about management ideas and practices, you need to pay particular attention to qualifying phrases such as "usually," "in these situations," "for this to work," and "under these circumstances." Doing so will help you identify the key contingencies that will help you become a better manager.

A system is a set of interrelated elements or parts that function as a whole. Organizational systems obtain inputs from the general and specific environments. Managers and workers then use their management knowledge and manufacturing techniques to transform those inputs into outputs, such as products and services, which are then consumed by persons or organizations in the environment, which in turn provide feedback to the organization, allowing managers and workers to modify and improve their products or services. Organizational systems must also address the issues of synergy, open versus closed systems, and entropy.

contingency approach holds that there are no universal management theories and that the most effective management theory or idea depends on the kinds of problems or situations that managers are facing at a particular time and place.

Finally, the contingency approach to management precisely states that there are no universal management theories. The most effective management theory or idea depends on the kinds of problems or situations that managers or organizations are facing at a particular time. This means that management is much harder than it looks and that managers need to look for key contingencies by spending more time analyzing problems and situations before they take action to fix them.

Review 5

Operations, Information, Systems, and Contingency Management Operations management uses a quantitative, or mathematical, approach to find ways to increase productivity, improve quality, and manage or reduce costly inventories. The manufacture of standardized, interchangeable parts; the graphical and computerized design of parts; and the accidental discovery of just-in-time management were some of the most important historical events in operations management.

For most of recorded history, information has been costly, difficult to obtain, and slow to spread. Consequently, throughout history, organizations have pushed for and quickly adopted new information technologies that reduce the cost or increase the speed with which they can acquire, store, retrieve, or communicate information. Historically, some of the most important technologies that have revolutionized information management were the use of horses in Italy in the 1400s, the creation of paper and the printing press in the fourteenth and fifteenth centuries, the manual typewriter in 1850, the telegraph and vertical file cabinets for storage of information in the 1860s, cash registers in 1879, the telephone in the 1880s, time clocks in the 1890s, the personal computer in the 1980s, and the Internet in the 1990s.

SELF-ASSESSMENT

KEY TERMS

bureaucracy 54
closed systems 70
compromise 59
contingency approach 71
domination 59
entropy 70
Gantt chart 51
integrative conflict
resolution 59
motion study 50
open systems 70
organization 64
rate buster 48
scientific management 47
soldiering 47
subsystems 70
synergy 70
system 69
time study 50

Dealing with Conflict

Conflict is an inevitable part of work life (and life in general), and the success of individual employees, teams, and entire organizations depends on how they manage interpersonal conflict. How do you deal with conflict? Do you look for it, avoid it, or something in between? This 20-question assessment is designed to provide insight into how you manage conflict.[83] This information will provide you with a baseline for future development of conflict-management skills.

You can also use this self-assessment as a precursor to the Management Team Decision exercise that follows. At a minimum, it will raise your awareness of how you handle differences of opinion before you begin working in a team. It may even inspire you to make conscious changes in your conflict-management style, helping you—and your team—be more effective.

Rate each statement, using the following scale:

1 Strongly disagree

2 Disagree

3 Not sure

4 Agree

5 Strongly agree

When I have a conflict at work, I do the following:

1. I give in to the wishes of the other party.
   1   2   3   4   5

2. I try to realize a middle-of-the-road solution.
   1   2   3   4   5

3. I push my own point of view.
   1   2   3   4   5

4. I examine issues until I find a solution that really satisfies me and the other party.

    1   2   ③   4   5

5. I avoid a confrontation about our differences.

    1   ②   3   4   5

6. I concur with the other party.

    1   2   3   ④   5

7. I emphasize that we have to find a compromise solution.

    1   2   3   ④   5

8. I search for gains.

    1   2   3   ④   5

9. I stand for my own and others' goals and interests.

    1   2   3   ④   5

10. I avoid differences of opinion as much as possible.

    1   ②   3   4   5

11. I try to accommodate the other party.

    1   2   ③   4   5

12. I insist we both give in a little.

    1   2   3   ④   5

13. I fight for a good outcome for myself.

    1   2   3   ④   5

14. I examine ideas from both sides to find a mutually optimal solution.

    1   2   3   ④   5

15. I try to make differences loom less severe.

    1   2   ③   4   5

16. I adapt to the other parties' goals and interests.

    1   2   ③   4   5

17. I strive whenever possible toward a 50–50 compromise.

    1   2   3   4   ⑤

18. I do everything to win.

    1   ②   3   4   5

19. I work out a solution that serves my own as well as others' interests as much as possible.

    1   2   3   ④   5

20. I try to avoid a confrontation with the other person.

    1   ②   3   4   5

Scoring

This inventory can be broken down into five sections:

1. Add together your scores for items 1, 6, 11, and 16: _12_

2. Add together your scores for items 2, 7, 12, and 17: _19_

3. Add together your scores for items 3, 8, 13, and 18: _13_

4. Add together your scores for items 4, 9, 14, and 19: _15_

5. Add together your scores for items 5, 10, 15, and 20: _9_

You can find the interpretation for your score at www.cengagebrain.com.

MANAGEMENT DECISION

Tough Love?

The first job you had, on an auto-parts assembly line, was an absolute nightmare, mostly because of your boss. If you were one minute late for your shift, he docked you a half-hour of pay. If you weren't ten minutes early for every staff meeting, he would yell at you, in front of everyone else, for being late. If you took a sick day, he would call you three or four times a day to make sure you were bedridden at home. He once even called your doctor!

So when you became a manager at a software firm, you decided that you would never be that kind of boss. Even though there was much pressure to meet deadlines and quality standards, you always tried to make your place a relaxed atmosphere. You didn't set a dress code, you let your staff set their own hours, and you never even thought of yelling at them or calling them out in public.

Lately, though, you wonder whether maybe you've been a little too lax. Several employees have been showing up really late for work, or taking days and even weeks off with no advance notice. What's worse, they are giving really odd excuses for not showing up for work. One of your quality control engineers, who repeatedly showed up for work late, blamed his cat for hiding his car keys. One of his software engineers said that she couldn't show up for work for three days because she dyed her hair blond, and it looked "tragic." Even your Human Resources (HR) director got in on the act, saying that she had to have two weeks off because she broke up with her boyfriend and had to take a trip to Hawaii with another guy to deal with the pain.

Needless to say, you're getting frustrated, not only because your employees' absences are killing your productivity but also because you feel like they are treating you like a moron with their excuses. You want to find a way to bring some discipline back into your company, but you don't want to end up being authoritarian like your first boss.

Questions

1. How would you resolve the situation described in this scenario?
2. What is an effective way for a manager to balance the need for supporting employee morale with the need for establishing discipline and authority?

MANAGEMENT TEAM DECISION

Resolving Conflicts[84]

As a manager with lots of experience in negotiations, you've experienced a lot of different conflicts. There was one case where a worker argued that he should be allowed to smoke his (legally prescribed) marijuana at his desk. Another time, someone asked you to mediate between two executives who were having a strategic disagreement—one thought that the company should invest in tulip futures, while the other thought that pork bellies were the future. But even with all of this experience, you haven't seen a case like the one going on at a Mott's apple juice factory that you've been called in to consult on.

Mott's, a division of Dr. Pepper Snapple Group, employs 305 people at its juice factory in Williamson, N.Y., near Rochester. All 305 employees, however, have been on strike for more than 3 months. They are protesting the fact that the company wants to make severe cuts in pay and benefits—a reduction of wages by $1.50 (about $3,000 per year), a pension freeze, a reduction in 401K contributions, and a decrease in the health insurance subsidy.

On the surface, these cuts seem to make some business sense, because companies all over the world are struggling. But what is so unusual in this case is that Dr. Pepper Snapple Group is more profitable than it ever has been. In the last year, its net income was $550 million, a dramatic improvement from the previous year, when it lost $312 million. Because of this success, employees are accusing the company of being greedy. Stuart Applebaum, the president of the factory workers' union, says "[Dr. Pepper Snapple doesn't] even show the respect to lie to us. They just came in and said, 'We have no financial need for this, but we just want it anyway because we figure we can get away with it.'"

The company, meanwhile, defends the pay and benefits cut by arguing that its current labor costs are considerably higher than other local companies. The average pay at the Mott's plant is $21, whereas other factories and transportation companies in the area pay closer to $14. In a public statement, the company defends the move, saying in part, "As a public company, Dr. Pepper Snapple Group has a fiduciary responsibility to operate in the best interests of all its constituents, recognizing that a profitable business attracts investment, generates jobs and builds communities."

You have been assigned to a task force with representatives from management and labor that has been charged with resolving the crisis. As all of you review the files, you realize this is a critical case; if the employees lose, other companies might be motivated to take similar actions and cut labor costs (and increase profits) even when they are not struggling financially.

For this Management Team Decision, form a group of three or four with other students, to act as the task force, and answer the following questions.

Questions

1. How could you help steer negotiations between labor and management so that the conflict between them is healthy and productive? Is that even possible?
2. Is the company justified in trying to cut costs even when it has made a huge profit? Are the employees justified in not working to protest what they perceive as unfair cuts?

PRACTICE BEING A MANAGER

Observing History Today

The topic of management history may sound like old news, but many of the issues and problems addressed by Max Weber, Chester Barnard, and other management theorists still challenge managers today. *How can we structure an organization for maximum efficiency and just treatment of individuals? What is the basis for, and limits to, authority in organizations?* It is rather amazing that these thinkers of the late nineteenth and early twentieth centuries generated such a wealth of theory that still influences our discussion of management and leadership challenges in the twenty-first century. This exercise will give you the opportunity to draw upon some ideas that trace their roots back to the pioneers of management thinking.

Preparing in Advance for Class Discussion

Step 1: Find an observation point. Identify a place where you can unobtrusively observe a group of people as they go about their work. You might select a coffee shop, bookstore, or restaurant.

Step 2: Settle in and observe. Go to your selected workplace and observe the people working there for at least 20 minutes. You should take along something like a notebook or PDA so that you can jot down a few notes. It is a good idea to go during a busy time, so long as it is not so crowded that you will be unable to easily observe the workers.

Step 3: Observe employees at work. Observe the process of work and the interaction among the employees. Consider some of the following issues:

- Identify the steps that employees follow in completing a work cycle (e.g., from taking an order to delivering a product). Can you see improvements that might be made, particularly steps that might be eliminated or streamlined?

- Observe the interaction and mood of the workers. Are they stressed? Or are they more relaxed? Does it seem to you that these workers like working with each other?

- Listen for signs of conflict. If you see signs of conflict, is the conflict resolved? If so, how did the workers resolve their conflict? If not, do you think that these workers suppress (bottle up) conflict?

- Can you tell who is in charge here? If so, how do the other workers respond to this person's directions? If not, how does the work group sort out who should be doing each task, and in what order?

Step 4: Consider what you saw. Immediately after your observation session, look through this chapter on management history for connections to your observations. For example, do you see any signs of the "Hawthorne Effect"? Would Frederick Taylor approve of the work process you observed, or might he have suggested improvements? What might Chester Barnard's theory have to say about how the workers you observed responded to instructions from their "boss"? Write a one-page paper of bullet-point notes describing possible connections between your observations and the thinking of management pioneers such as Mary Parker Follett.

Class Discussion

Step 5: Share your findings as a class. Discuss the various points of connection that you found between pioneering management thinkers and your own observations of people at work. Are some of the issues of management "timeless"? If so, what do you see as timeless issues of management? What are some ways in which work and management *have changed* since the days of the management pioneers?

DEVELOP YOUR CAREER POTENTIAL

Know Where Management Is Going

As you read in the chapter, management theories are dynamic. In other words, they change over time, sometimes very rapidly. In addition, management theories have often been cumulative, meaning that later theorists tend to build on theories previously advanced by other scholars. Thus, a new theory becomes the starting point for yet another theory that can either refine or refute the management thinking of the day.

One way to prepare for your career as a manager is by becoming aware of management trends today. The best (and easiest) way to do that is by regularly combing through business newspapers and periodicals. You will always find at least one article that relates to management concepts, and as you scan the business press over time, you will see which theories are influencing current management thinking the most. By understanding management history and management today, you will be better able to anticipate changes to management ideas in the future. This exercise is designed to introduce you to the business press and to help you make the connection between the concepts you learn in the classroom and real-world management activities. Done regularly, it will provide you with invaluable insights into business activities at all types of organizations around the world.

Activities

1. Find a current article of substance in the business press (for example, *The Wall Street Journal*, the *Financial Times, Fortune, Businessweek, Inc.*) that discusses topics covered in this course. Although this is only Chapter 2, you will be surprised by the amount of terminology you have already learned. If you are having trouble finding an article, read through the Table of Contents on pages iv–x to familiarize yourself with the names of concepts that will be presented later in the term. Read your article carefully, making notes about relevant content.

2. Write a one-paragraph summary of the key points in your article. List the terms or concepts critical to understanding the article, and provide definitions of those terms. If you are unfamiliar with a term or concept that is central to the article, do some research in your textbook or see your professor during office hours. Relate these key points to the concepts in your text by citing page numbers.

3. How does your article relate to the management theories covered in this chapter? Explain the situation detailed in your article in terms of the history of management.

END NOTES

[1] J. Hough and M. White, "Using Stories to Create Change: The Object Lesson of Frederick Taylor's 'Pig-Tale,'" *Journal of Management* 27 (2001): 585–601; E. Locke, "The Ideas of Frederick W. Taylor: An Evaluation," *Academy of Management Review* 7 (1982): 14–24; F. W. Taylor, *The Principles of Scientific Management* (New York: Harper, 1911); C. Wrege and R. Hodgetts, "Frederick W. Taylor's 1899 Pig Iron Observations: Examining Fact, Fiction, and Lessons for the New Millennium," *Academy of Management Journal* 43 (2000): 1283–1291; and D. Wren, *The History of Management Thought*, 5th ed. (New York: Wiley, 2005).

[2] G. Glotz, *Ancient Greece at Work* (New York: Alfred A. Knopf, 1926).

[3] C. S. George, Jr., *The History of Management Thought* (Englewood Cliffs, NJ: Prentice-Hall, 1972).

[4] D. Schmandt-Besserat, *How Writing Came About* (Austin: University of Texas Press, 1997).

[5] A. Erman, *Life in Ancient Egypt* (London: Macmillan & Co., 1984).

[6] J. Burke, *The Day the Universe Changed* (Boston: Little, Brown, 1985).

[7] S. A. Epstein, *Wage Labor and Guilds in Medieval Europe*, (Chapel Hill: University of North Carolina Press, 1991).

[8] "History of the Organization of Work: Organization of Work in Preindustrial Times: The Ancient World," *Britannica Online*, accessed January 15, 1999, from www.eb.com.

[9] R. Braun, *Industrialization and Everyday Life*, trans. S. Hanbury-Tenison (Cambridge: Cambridge University Press, 1990).

[10] J. B. White, "The Line Starts Here: Mass-Production Techniques Changed the Way People Work and Live throughout the World," *The Wall Street Journal*, January 11, 1999, R25.

[11] R. B. Reich, *The Next American Frontier* (New York: Times Books, 1983).

[12] J. Mickelwait and A. Wooldridge, *The Company: A Short History of a Revolutionary Idea* (New York: Modern Library, 2003).

[13] "How Business Schools Began," *Businessweek*, October 12, 1963, 114–116.

[14] "Industrial Management," *The Engineering Magazine* 61 (1921): 232.

[15] H. Kendall, "Unsystematized, Systematized, and Scientific Management," in *Scientific Management: A Collection of the More Significant Articles Describing the Taylor System of Management*, C. Thompson, ed. (Easton, PA: Hive Publishing, 1972), 103–131.

[16] United States Congress, House, Special Committee, *Hearings to Investigate the Taylor and Other Systems of Shop Management*, vol. 3. (Washington, DC: Government Printing Office, 1912).

[17]Ibid.

[18]Ibid.

[19]Taylor, *The Principles of Scientific Management*.

[20]A. Derickson, "Physiological Science and Scientific Management in the Progressive Era: Frederic S. Lee and the Committee on Industrial Fatigue," *Business History Review* 68 (1994): 483–514.

[21]United States Congress, House, Special Committee, 1912.

[22]Taylor, *The Principles of Scientific Management*.

[23]Ibid.

[24]Wrege and Hodgetts, "Frederick W. Taylor's 1899 Pig Iron Observations"; Hough and White, "Using Stories to Create Change."

[25]Locke, "The Ideas of Frederick W. Taylor."

[26]George, *The History of Management Thought*.

[27]F. Gilbreth and L. Gilbreth, "Applied Motion Study," in *The Writings of the Gilbreths*, W. R. Spriegel and C. E. Myers, eds., (1917; reprint, Homewood, IL: Irwin, 1953), 207–274.

[28]Ibid.

[29]"Frank and Lillian Gilbreth: Motion Study Pioneers," *Thinkers*, December 2000.

[30]D. Ferguson, "Don't Call It 'Time and Motion Study,'" *IIE Solutions* 29, no. 5 (1997): 22–23.

[31]F. Gilbreth and L. Gilbreth, "Motion Study for the Crippled Soldier," *American Society of Mechanical Engineers Journal* 37 (1915): 669–673.

[32]Ibid.

[33]H. Gantt, "A Graphical Daily Balance in Manufacture," *Transactions of the American Society of Mechanical Engineers* 24 (1903): 1325.

[34]H. Gantt, "A Bonus System for Rewarding Labor," *Transactions of the American Society of Mechanical Engineers* 23 (1901): 373.

[35]P. Peterson, "Training and Development: The View of Henry L. Gantt (1861–1919)," *SAM Advanced Management Journal* (Winter 1987): 20–23.

[36]H. Gantt, "Industrial Efficiency," *National Civic Federation Report of the 11th Annual Meeting*, New York, January 12, 1991, 103.

[37]Ibid.

[38]M. Weber, *The Theory of Economic and Social Organization*, trans. A. Henderson and T. Parsons (New York: Free Press, 1947).

[39]M. Weber, *The Protestant Ethic and the Spirit of Capitalism* (New York: Scribner, 1958).

[40]George, *The History of Management Thought*.

[41]D. Wren, "Henri Fayol As Strategist: A Nineteenth Century Corporate Turnaround," *Management Decision* 39 (2001): 475–487.

[42]D. Reid, "Fayol: From Experience to Theory," *Journal of Management History* 3 (1995): 21–36.

[43]H. Fayol, "Observations et expériences personnelles," *Archives Fayol*, no date, 4–11.

[44]Wren, "Henri Fayol As Strategist"; Reid, "Fayol: From Experience to Theory."

[45]Wren, "Henri Fayol As Strategist."

[46]Ibid.

[47]Ibid.

[48]Ibid.

[49]F. Blancpain, "Les Cahiers Inédits d'Henri Fayol," trans. D. Wren, *Extrait du Bulletin de l'Institut International d'Administration Publique* 28–29 (1974): 1–48.

[50]H. Verney, "Un Grand Ingénieur: Henri Fayol," *La Fondateur de la Doctrine Administrative: Henri Fayol* (Paris: Dunod, 1925), as cited in Wren, "Henri Fayol As Strategist."

[51]D. A. Wren, A. G. Bedeian, and J. D. Breeze, "The Foundations of Henri Fayol's Administrative Theory," *Management Decision* 40 (2002): 906–918.

[52]H. Fayol, *General and Industrial Management* (London: Pittman & Sons, 1949); Wren, Bedeian, and Breeze, "Foundations."

[53]M. P. Follett, *Mary Parker Follett— Prophet of Management: A Celebration of Writings from the 1920s*, ed.

P. Graham (Boston: Harvard Business School Press, 1995).

[54]Ibid., p. 68.

[55]Ibid., p. 69.

[56]See the best-selling book by Roger Fisher, William Ury, and Bruce Patton, *Getting to Yes: Negotiating Agreement without Giving In*, 2nd ed. (New York: Penguin, 1991).

[57]Follett, p. 69.

[58]Ibid, p. 222.

[59]D. Linden, "The Mother of Them All," *Forbes*, January 16, 1995, 75.

[60]E. O'Connor, "The Politics of Management Thought: A Case Study of the Harvard Business School and the Human Relations School," *Academy of Management Review* 24 (1999): 117–131.

[61]J. MacLaury, "A Brief History: The U.S. Department of Labor," United States Department of Labor, accessed June 27, 2011, from www.dol.gov/oasam/programs/history/dolhistoxford.htm.

[62]M. Losey, "HR Comes of Age," *HRMagazine* 43, no. 3 (1998): 40–53.

[63]J. H. Smith, "The Enduring Legacy of Elton Mayo," *Human Relations* 51, no. 3 (1998): 221–249.

[64]E. Mayo, *The Human Problems of an Industrial Civilization* (New York: Macmillan, 1933).

[65]Ibid.

[66]"Hawthorne Revisited: The Legend and the Legacy," *Organizational Dynamics* (Winter 1975): 66–80.

[67]E. Mayo, *The Social Problems of an Industrial Civilization* (Boston: Harvard Graduate School of Business Administration, 1945).

[68]Mayo, *The Social Problems of an Industrial Civilization*, 65–67.

[69]"Hawthorne Revisited: The Legend and the Legacy."

[70]Mayo, *The Social Problems of an Industrial Civilization*, 45.

[71]George, *The History of Management Thought*.

[72]C. I. Barnard, *The Functions of the Executive* (Cambridge, MA: Harvard University Press, 1938), 4.

[73]C. I. Barnard, *The Functions of the Executive: 30th Anniversary Edition* (Cambridge, MA: Harvard University Press, 1968), 5.

[74]S. Parayitam, M. White, and J. Hough, "Juxtaposition of Chester I. Barnard and Frederick W. Taylor: Forerunners of Management," *Management Decision* 40 (2002): 1003–1012.

[75]J. Dunkelberg and D. Jessup, "So Then Why Did You Do It?" *Journal of Business Ethics* 29 (2001): 422–426.

[76]J. Fuller and A. Mansour, "Operations Management and Operations Research: A Historical and Relational Perspective," *Management Decision* 41 (2003): 422–426.

[77]D. Wren and R. Greenwood, "Business Leaders: A Historical Sketch of Eli Whitney," *Journal of Leadership & Organizational Studies* 6 (1999): 131.

[78]"Monge, Gaspard, Comte de Péluse," *Britannica Online*, accessed January 9, 2005, from www.britannica.com/bps/search?query=Gaspard+Monge,+count+de+Péluse&blacklist=389244.

[79]D. Whitehouse, "Oldest Lunar Calendar Identified," BBC News, October 16, 2000, accessed April 25, 2009, from http://news.bbc.co.uk/2/hi/science/nature/975360.stm.

[80]D. Ashmos and G. Huber, "The Systems Paradigm in Organization Theory: Correcting the Record and Suggesting the Future," *Academy of Management Review* 12 (1987): 607–621; F. Kast and J. Rosenzweig, "General Systems Theory: Applications for Organizations and Management," *Academy of Management Journal* 15 (1972): 447–465; and D. Katz and R. Kahn, *The Social Psychology of Organizations* (New York: Wiley, 1966).

[81]R. Mockler, "The Systems Approach to Business Organization and Decision Making," *California Management Review* 11, no. 2 (1968): 53–58.

[82]F. Luthans and T. Stewart, "A General Contingency Theory of Management," *Academy of Management Review* 2, no. 2 (1977): 181–195.

[83]C. K. W. de Dreu, A. Evers, B. Beersma, E. S. Kluwer, and A. Nauta, "A Theory-Based Measure of Conflict Management Strategies in the Workplace," *Journal of Organizational Behavior* 22 (2001) 645–668.

[84]Steven Greenhouse, "In Mott's Strike, More than Pay at Stake" *The New York Times*, August 17, 2010, accessed October 10, 2010, from www.nytimes.com/2010/08/18/business/18motts.html?_r=1&adxnnl=1&adxnnlx=1297947774-W3u9XoLkFQ6q+a7OmuVx1A.

BIZ FLIX

Casino

Martin Scorcese's film *Casino* is a complex and beautifully photographed study of Las Vegas gambling casinos and their organized crime connections during the 1970s. It completes his trilogy that began with *Mean Streets* (1973) and continued with *Goodfellas* (1990). In *Casino*, ambition, greed, drugs, and sex ultimately destroy the mob's gambling empire. The film includes a memorable performance by Robert De Niro as Sam Rothstein. This scene, which comes from the beginning of "The Truth about Las Vegas" sequence, opens the film and establishes important background about casino operations. Listen carefully to Rothstein's voice-over as he describes the casino's operation and explains how it tries to reach its goals.

© GreenLight

What to Watch for and Ask Yourself

1. Do you think the casino owners make discipline (clearly defined rules and procedures) a high priority in the way they run their business? Why?

2. Mary Parker Follett believed that managers could deal with conflict in three ways: domination, compromise, and integration. Which of these is most likely employed by the casino management in this film?

3. How important is employee order (having a place for everyone and having everyone in their place) in this clip?

MANAGEMENT WORKPLACE

Barcelona Restaurant Group: The Evolution of Management Thinking

Andy Pforzheimer is himself a renowned chef and the co-owner of Barcelona Restaurant Group, a collection of seven wine and tapas bars in Connecticut and Atlanta, Georgia. When customers dine at any of Pforzheimer's restaurants, they experience the local color and personal touch of a neighborhood eatery. The waitstaff is personable and strives to get to know customers' tastes. Delivering this unique dining experience requires a unique approach to management. The company gives employees the freedom and control they need to impress customers. It recruits self-confident individuals who can take ownership over the establishment and its success. Further, Pforzheimer is adamant that his staff be mature and willing to take responsibility for their work and success.

© Cengage Learning

Discussion Questions

1. What aspects of restaurant work are especially challenging to waitstaff, and how does Barcelona's approach to management help employees overcome the downsides of the job?

2. What steps do the leaders of Barcelona Restaurant Group take to insure cooperation and acceptance of authority from their employees?

3. Would the management style of Barcelona Restaurant Group best be described as scientific management or contingency management?

CHAPTER 3

Organizational Environments and Culture

Learning Outcomes

1. Discuss how changing environments affect organizations.
2. Describe the four components of the general environment.
3. Explain the five components of the specific environment.
4. Describe the process that companies use to make sense of their changing environments.
5. Explain how organizational cultures are created and how they can help companies be successful.

what would **you do?**

Waste Management Headquarters, Houston, Texas[1]

Americans generate a quarter billion tons of trash a year, or 4.5 pounds of trash per person per day. Thanks to nearly 9,000 curbside recycling programs, a third of that is recycled. But, that still leaves 3 pounds of trash per person per day to be disposed. In the past, trash was incinerated, often in local neighborhoods. John Waffenschmidt, vice president for Covanta Energy Corp., remembers that when he delivered newspapers in the 1960s, "I'd go out in the morning and there would be little flakes coming down because there were 4,000 or 5,000 apartment-building incinerators." The rest was incinerated in large power plants, like the one on the east side of the Hudson River that burns 1,900 tons of New York City garbage each day.

With 20 million customers; 273 municipal landfills; 91 recycling facilities; and yes, 17 waste-to-energy facilities—that's what large power-generating incinerator plants are called today—Waste Management, Inc., is the largest waste-handling company in the world. It generates 75 percent of its profits from 273 landfills, which can hold 4.8 billion tons of trash. And because it only collects 110 million tons a year, it has plenty of landfill capacity for years to come.

You joined the company a decade ago, and, after three and a half short years as deputy general counsel and then chief financial officer, became CEO. That quick promotion prompted you to joke, "I needed to go to a bookstore to see whether I could find a book called *CEO-ing for Dummies*." Instead, Waste Management sent you to Harvard for an executive program for CEOs, where the most important lesson you learned was to listen, because, as you tell your executive team, "This company and this industry aren't very good at that." And with all of the changes taking place in your industry, Waste Management won't succeed unless it listens. However, corporations, cities, and households are greatly reducing the amount of waste they generate, and thus the amount of trash that they pay Waste Management to haul away to its landfills. Subaru of America, for instance, has a zero-landfill plant in West Lafayette, Indiana, that hasn't sent any waste to a landfill since 2004. None! And Subaru isn't exceptional in seeking to be a zero-landfill company. Walmart, the largest retailer in the world, has also embraced this goal, stating, "Our vision is to reach a day where there are no dumpsters behind our stores and clubs, and no landfills containing our throwaways." Like

"what's new" companies

Waste Management, Inc.
Dow Chemical
Prime View International
Activision-Blizzard
Harrah's
Ooma
Gatorade
Knights Apparel
AxleTech International
Novo Nordisk
Partners+Napier

< **"what's new" companies**

study tips

ⓧ

Create your own diagram of the business environment, and compare it with the example in the chapter.

Read several articles in the business press, and list the environmental factors at play in each of the articles.

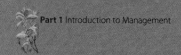

those at Subaru and Walmart, corporate leaders worldwide are committed to reducing the waste produced by their companies. Because that represents a direct threat to Waste Management's landfill business, what steps could it take to take advantage of the trend toward zero waste that might allow it to continue growing company revenues?

Another significant change for Waste Management is that not only are its customers reducing the waste they send to its landfills, they're also wanting what is sent to landfills to be sorted for recycling and reuse. For instance, food waste, yard clippings, and wood—all organic materials—account for roughly one-third of the material sent to landfills. Likewise, there's growing demand for waste companies to manage and recycle discarded TVs, computer monitors, and other electronic waste that leaks lead, mercury, and hazardous materials when improperly disposed. However, the high cost of collecting and sorting recyclable materials means that Waste Management loses money when it recycles them. What can the company do to meet increased customer expectations, on one hand, while still finding a way to earn a profit on high-cost recycled materials?

Finally, advocacy groups, such as the Sierra Club, regularly protest Waste Management's landfill practices, deeming them irresponsible and harmful to the environment. Should Waste Management take on its critics and fight back, or should it focus on its business and let the results speak for themselves? Should it view environmental advocates as a threat or an opportunity for the company?

If you were in charge of Waste Management, what would you do?

From changing social attitudes about waste and recycling, to anti–Waste Management websites, everywhere that Waste Management's top managers look, they see changes and forces outside the company that directly affect how they do business.

This chapter examines the internal and external forces that affect business. We begin by explaining how the changes in external organizational environments affect the decisions and performance of a company. Next, we examine the two types of external organizational environments: the general environment that affects all organizations and the specific environment unique to each company. Then, we learn how managers make sense of their changing general and specific environments. The chapter finishes with a discussion of internal organizational environments by focusing on organizational culture.

External Environments

external environments all events outside a company that have the potential to influence or affect it.

After reading the next four sections, you should be able to

1. *Discuss how changing environments affect organizations.*
2. *Describe the four components of the general environment.*
3. *Explain the five components of the specific environment.*
4. *Describe the process that companies use to make sense of their changing environments.*

External environments are the forces and events outside a company that have the potential to influence or affect it. From Sony Walkmans to PlayStation video games and consoles, to its top-of-the-line televisions, Sony's ability to innovate made it one of the world's top electronics companies. However, because of intense competition in its external environment from Apple (iPods, iPhones, and iPads), Microsoft (Xbox 360), Samsung, and

Vizio (high-definition TVs), Sony has been forced to cut costs, lay off workers, and try to change its internal culture in order to restore profits (more on that later in the chapter).[2]

1 Changing Environments

Let's examine the four basic characteristics of changing external environments: **1.1 environmental change; 1.2 environmental complexity; 1.3 resource scarcity;** and **1.4 the uncertainty that environmental change, complexity, and resource scarcity can create for organizational managers.**

1.1 Environmental Change

Environmental change is the rate at which a company's general and specific environments change. In **stable environments,** the rate of environmental change is slow. Apart from occasional shortages due to drought or frost, the wholesale food distribution business—where dairy items, fresh produce, baked goods, poultry, fish, and meat, are processed and delivered by trucks from warehouses to restaurants, grocers, and other retailers—changes little from year to year. Distributors take shipments from farmers, food manufacturers, and food importers, consolidate them at warehouses, and then distribute them to retailers. Although recent adoption of global positioning satellite (GPS) systems and radio frequency identification (RFID) devices might be seen as "change," wholesale food distributors began using them because, like the trucks they bought to replace horse-drawn carriages in the early 1900s, GPS and RFID improved the core part of their business, getting the freshest food ingredients to customers as quickly and inexpensively as possible, which has not changed in over a century.[3]

Whereas wholesale food distribution companies have stable environments, EA Sports, whose best-selling products are sports games like *Madden NFL* (football), *NBA Live* (basketball), *NHL* (hockey), *Tiger Woods PGA Tour* (golf), and *FIFA* (soccer), competes in an extremely dynamic external environment: video games. In **dynamic environments,** the rate of environmental change is fast. The external environment of Microsoft's Xbox 360 gaming platform is highly dynamic because of intense competition that brings rapid changes in gaming technology. When Nintendo's Wii console, which uses motion from its wireless controller to play games, sold 74 million units worldwide the year it was introduced, Microsoft and Sony saw their Xbox 360 and PS3 game system sales fall far behind.[4] At the 2010 E3 Expo videogame tradeshow, Microsoft introduced its Kinect motion technology for the Xbox. In contrast to Nintendo's Wii, the Kinect, captures motion without a controller. Players move in response to games, and the Kinect scans those motions and uses them as input. Although Microsoft sold 8 million Kinects in its first two months, Nintendo and Sony are working on the next advance in gaming, 3-D technology.[5] Furthermore, Microsoft's Xbox faces competition from new gaming devices, such as Apple's iPhone and iPad, where low-cost best sellers like *Angry Birds* have sold 50 million copies. Together, these trends portend intense competition and dynamic changes in the gaming industry.[6]

Although you might think that a company's external environment would be either stable or dynamic, research suggests that companies often experience both. According to **punctuated equilibrium theory,** companies go through long periods of stability (equilibrium) during which incremental changes occur, followed by short, complex periods of dynamic, fundamental change (revolutionary periods), finishing with a return to stability (new equilibrium).[7]

environmental change the rate at which a company's general and specific environments change.

stable environment an environment in which the rate of change is slow.

dynamic environment an environment in which the rate of change is fast.

punctuated equilibrium theory the theory that companies go through long periods of stability (equilibrium).

Exhibit 3.1   Punctuated Equilibrium: U.S. Airline Profits since 1979

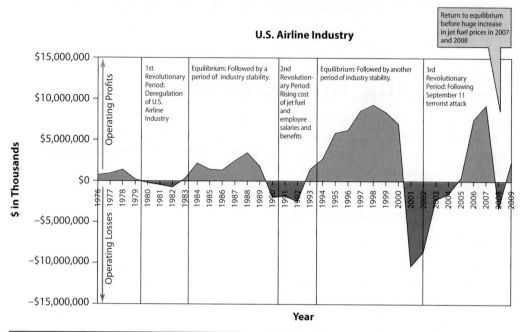

Source: "Table 1072: U.S. Scheduled Airline Industry—Summary," *The 2011 Statistical Abstract: The National Data Book*, U.S. Census Bureau, December 15, 2010, accessed February 2, 2011, from www.census.gov/compendia/statab/cats/transportation/airline_operations_and_traffic.html.

> Although you might think that a company's external environment would be *either* stable *or* dynamic, research suggests that companies often experience both.

Exhibit 3.1 shows one example of punctuated equilibrium—the U.S. airline industry.

Three times in the last 30 years, the U.S. airline industry has experienced revolutionary periods. The first, from mid-1979 to mid-1982, occurred immediately after airline deregulation in 1978. Prior to deregulation, the federal government controlled where airlines could fly, how much they could charge, when they could fly, and the number of flights they could have on a particular route. After deregulation, these choices were left to the airlines. The large financial losses during this period clearly indicate that the airlines had trouble adjusting to the intense competition that occurred after deregulation. By mid-1982, however, profits returned to the industry and held steady until mid-1989.

Then, after experiencing record growth and profits, U.S. airlines lost billions of dollars between 1989 and 1993 as the industry went through dramatic changes. Key expenses, including jet fuel and employee salaries, which had held steady for years, suddenly increased. Furthermore, revenues, which had grown steadily year after year, suddenly dropped because of dramatic changes in the airlines' customer base. Business travelers, who had typically paid full-price fares, comprised more than half of all passengers during the 1980s. However, by the late 1980s, the largest customer base had changed to leisure travelers, who wanted the cheapest flights they could get.[8] With expenses suddenly up and revenues suddenly down, the airlines responded to these changes in their business environment by laying off 5 to 10 percent of their workers, canceling orders for new planes, and eliminating unprofitable routes. Starting in 1993 and lasting till 1998, these changes helped the airline industry achieve profits far in excess of their historical levels. The industry began to stabilize, if not flourish, just as punctuated equilibrium theory predicts.[9]

The third revolutionary period for the U.S. airline industry began with the terrorist attacks of September 11, 2001, in which planes were used as missiles to bring down the World Trade Center towers and damage the Pentagon. The immediate effect was a 20 percent drop in scheduled flights, a 40 percent drop in passengers, and losses so large that the U.S. government approved a $15 billion bailout to keep the airlines in business. Heightened airport security also affected airports, the airlines themselves, and airline customers. Five years after the 9/11 attacks, United Airlines, U.S. Airways, Delta, and American Airlines had reduced staffing by 169,000 full-time jobs to cut costs after losing a combined $42 billion.[10] Due to their financially weaker position, the airlines restructured operations to take advantage of the combined effect of increased passenger travel, a sharply reduced cost structure, and a 23 percent reduction in the fleet to return their businesses to profitability.[11] But just as the airlines were heading toward a more stable period of equilibrium in 2006 and 2007, the price of oil jumped dramatically, doubling, if not tripling, the price of jet fuel, which prompted the airlines to charge for luggage (to increase revenues and discourage heavy baggage) and cut flights using older, fuel-inefficient jets.

1.2 Environmental Complexity

Environmental complexity refers to the number and the intensity of external factors in the environment that affect organizations. **Simple environments** have few environmental factors, whereas **complex environments** have many environmental factors. The dairy industry is an excellent example of a relatively simple external environment. Even accounting for decades-old advances in processing and automatic milking machines, milk is produced the same way today as it was 100 years ago. And although food manufacturers introduce dozens of new dairy-based products each year, U.S. milk production has grown a meager 1.25 percent per year over the last decade. In short, producing milk is a highly competitive but simple business that has experienced few changes.[12]

At the other end of the spectrum, few industries find themselves in more complex environments today than the newspaper business. For a century, making money selling newspapers was relatively simple: sell subscriptions for daily home delivery, and then sell classified ads and retail ads to reach those subscribers. In today's digital age, however, that business model doesn't work. First, revenue from classified ads, which were extremely profitable for local newspapers, dropped 29 percent last year, because of popular sites like craigslist.com that allow free posting of classified ads.[13] Second, digital ads bring in only about 10 percent of the revenue of one-time, print, newspaper ads, and don't generate enough revenue to cover the cost of "free" online versions newspapers. Finally, because digital content is very inexpensive to distribute relative to print, most consumers expect Internet-based news to be free. Although a few online newspapers, such as *The Wall*

environmental complexity the number and the intensity of external factors in the environment that affect organizations.

simple environment an environment with few environmental factors.

complex environment an environment with many environmental factors.

© David Adamson/Alamy

Street Journal and *The Times of London* have had success charging for online access, it may be difficult for other newspapers to do so. *Mediaweek* senior editor Mike Shields said, "The *Journal* is not free. They never wavered or changed that. That is as key to the success as the content they deliver. That precedent is enviable and hard for someone [else] to copy, particularly if you've been giving away your content for 10 years." [14]

1.3 Resource Scarcity

The third characteristic of external environments is resource scarcity. **Resource scarcity** is the abundance or shortage of critical organizational resources in an organization's external environment. For example, the primary reason flat-screen, LCD TVs with lifelike pictures were initially six times more expensive per inch than regular TVs, two times more expensive than rear projection TVs, and 25 percent more expensive than plasma TVs was that there weren't enough LCD screen factories to meet demand. As long as this condition persisted, LCD TV prices had to remain high. With building costs at $2 billion to $4 billion each year, LCD factories were at first a scarce resource in this industry. [15] But as sales of LCD TVs soared, more LCD factories were built to meet demand, and so prices came down as the critical resource, manufacturing capacity for flat screens, became less scarce. Likewise, in many locations throughout the world, water is a scarce resource. This is why a **Dow Chemical** plant in Texas, faced with water shortages each summer, hired Nalco, a firm that helps companies reduce energy, water, and other natural resource consumption. Nalco's water management systems reduced water consumption at Dow's Texas plant by 1 billion gallons per year. [16] Likewise, working with the Marriott in Mumbai, India, Nalco was able to install a water recycling system which saves 300 million glasses of drinkable water per year from that single hotel.

"what's new" companies >

resource scarcity the abundance or shortage of critical organizational resources in an organization's external environment.

uncertainty the extent to which managers can understand or predict which environmental changes and trends will affect their businesses.

1.4 Uncertainty

As Exhibit 3.2 shows, environmental change, environmental complexity, and resource scarcity affect environmental **uncertainty**, which is how well managers can understand

Exhibit 3.2 Environmental Change, Environmental Complexity, and Resource Scarcity

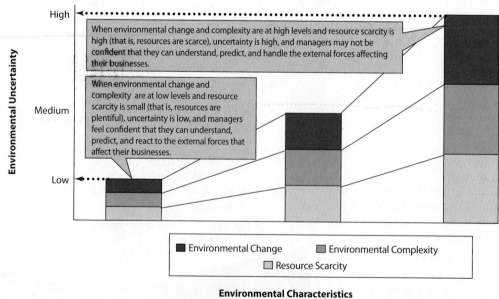

Environmental Uncertainty

When environmental change and complexity are at high levels and resource scarcity is high (that is, resources are scarce), uncertainty is high, and managers may not be confident that they can understand, predict, and handle the external forces affecting their businesses.

When environmental change and complexity are at low levels and resource scarcity is small (that is, resources are plentiful), uncertainty is low, and managers feel confident that they can understand, predict, and react to the external forces that affect their businesses.

■ Environmental Change ■ Environmental Complexity ■ Resource Scarcity

Environmental Characteristics

or predict the external changes and trends affecting their businesses. Starting at the left side of the figure, environmental uncertainty is lowest when environmental change and environmental complexity are at low levels and resource scarcity is small (i.e., resources are plentiful). In these environments, managers feel confident that they can understand, predict, and react to the external forces that affect their businesses. By contrast, the right side of the figure shows that environmental uncertainty is highest when environmental change and complexity are extensive and resource scarcity is a problem. In these environments, managers may not be confident that they can understand, predict, and handle the external forces affecting their businesses.

Changing Environments Environmental change, complexity, and resource scarcity are the basic components of external environments. Environmental change is the rate at which conditions or events affecting a business change. Environmental complexity is the number and intensity of external factors in an external environment. Resource scarcity is the scarcity or abundance of resources available in the external environment. The greater the degree of environmental change, environmental complexity, and resource scarcity, the less confident managers are that they can understand, predict, and effectively react to the trends affecting their businesses. According to punctuated equilibrium theory, companies experience periods of stability followed by short periods of dynamic, fundamental change, followed by a return to periods of stability.

Review 1

2 General Environment

As Exhibit 3.3 shows, two kinds of external environments influence organizations: the general environment and the specific environment. The **general environment** consists of the economy and the technological, sociocultural, and political/legal trends that indirectly affect *all* organizations. Changes in any sector of the general environment eventually affect most organizations. For example, when the Federal Reserve lowers its prime lending rate, most businesses benefit because banks and credit card companies often lower the interest rates they charge for loans. Consumers, who can then borrow money more cheaply, might borrow more to buy homes, cars, refrigerators, and plasma or LCD flat-screen TVs.

By contrast, each organization also has a **specific environment** that is unique to that firm's industry and directly affects the way it conducts day-to-day business. After more than 20 million unsafe toys, many of them produced in Chinese factories, were recalled, the toy industry spent $200 million to increase the safety of its products.[17] But because that change came from the specific environment (which only influences this industry) and not the general environment (which influences all businesses), only toy manufacturers and retailers, such as Toys "R" Us, were affected. The specific environment, which will be discussed in detail in Section 3 of this chapter, includes customers, competitors, suppliers, industry regulation, and advocacy groups. But first let's take a closer look at the four components of the general environment: **2.1 the economy** and **2.2 the technological, 2.3 sociocultural,** and **2.4 political/legal trends** that indirectly affect all organizations.

general environment the economic, technological, sociocultural, and political trends that indirectly affect all organizations.

specific environment the customers, competitors, suppliers, industry regulations, and advocacy groups that are unique to an industry and directly affect how a company does business.

2.1 Economy

The current state of a country's economy affects virtually every organization doing business there. In general, in a growing economy, more people are working and

Exhibit 3.3   General and Specific Environments

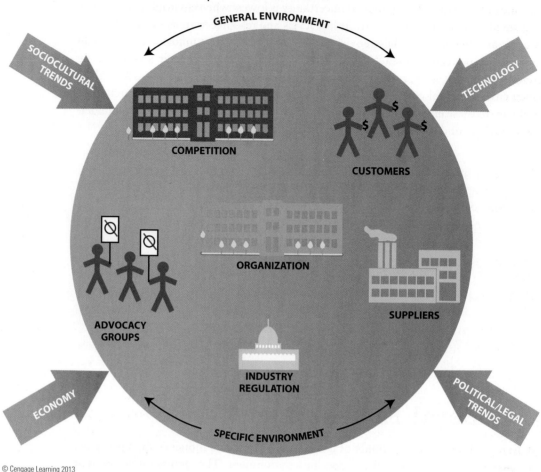

© Cengage Learning 2013

wages are growing, and therefore consumers have relatively more money to spend. More products are bought and sold in a growing economy than in a static or shrinking economy. Though an individual firm's sales will not necessarily increase, a growing economy does provide an environment favorable to business growth. In contrast, in a shrinking economy, consumers have less money to spend and relatively fewer products are bought and sold. Thus, a shrinking economy makes growth for individual businesses more difficult.

Because the economy influences basic business decisions, such as whether to hire more employees, expand production, or take out loans to purchase equipment, managers scan their economic environments for signs of significant change. Unfortunately, the economic statistics that managers rely on when making these decisions are notoriously poor predictors of *future* economic activity. A manager who decides to hire ten more employees because economic data suggest future growth could very well have to lay off those newly hired workers when the economic growth does not occur. In fact, a famous economic study found that at the beginning of a business quarter (a period of only three months), even the best economic forecasters could not accurately predict whether economic activity would grow or shrink *in that same quarter*![18]

Because economic statistics can be poor predictors, some managers try to predict future economic activity by keeping track of business confidence. **Business confidence indices** show how confident actual managers are about future business growth. For example, the Conference Board's CEO Confidence Index is a quarterly survey of 100 CEOS in large companies across a variety of different industries that examines attitudes regarding future growth in the economy or particular

> The current state of a country's economy affects virtually every organization doing business there.

business confidence indices indices that show managers' level of confidence about future business growth

industries.[19] Another widely cited measure is the Small Business Research Board's Business Confidence Index, which asks 500 small business owners and managers to express their optimism (or pessimism) about future business sales and prospects.[20] Managers often prefer business confidence indices to economic statistics because they know that other managers make business decisions that are in line with their expectations concerning the economy's future. So if the Conference Board or Small Business Research Board business confidence indices are dropping, a manager might decide against hiring new employees, increasing production, or taking out additional loans to expand the business.

2.2 Technological Component

Technology is the knowledge, tools, and techniques used to transform inputs (raw materials, information, and so on) into outputs (products and services). For example, the inputs of authors, editors, and artists (knowledge) and the use of equipment like computers and printing presses (technology) transformed paper, ink, and glue (raw materials) into this book (the finished product). In the case of a service company such as an airline, the technology consists of equipment, including airplanes, repair tools, and computers, as well as the knowledge of mechanics, ticketers, and flight crews. The output is the service of transporting people from one place to another.

Changes in technology can help companies provide better products or produce their products more efficiently. For example, advances in surgical techniques and imaging equipment have made open-heart surgery much faster and safer in recent years. Although technological changes can benefit a business, they can also threaten it. For example, **Prime View International**, based in Taipei, Taiwan, makes the E Ink screens used in the leading e-reader devices, Amazon.com's Kindle, Barnes & Noble's Nook, and Sony's Reader. Their popularity stems from their uncanny likeness to newsprint (i.e., black and white), which makes the screens much easier to read for longer periods; no backlighting, which means devices using E Ink screens can be read in direct sunlight without reflection or washing out; and incredibly low power consumption that allows e-readers to go four weeks between charges. The E Ink screens have become so popular that within 33 months of its introduction, Amazon.com was selling 143 Kindle books for every 100 hardcover books, and 115 Kindle books for every 100 paperback books. Although print-based books will be with us for some time, in the long run the Kindle, other e-readers, and tablet computers, like the iPad, clearly started a trend away from print-based books.[21]

< **"what's new" companies**

Companies must embrace new technology and find effective ways to use it to improve their products and services or decrease costs. If they don't, they will lose out to those companies that do. Indeed, although Prime View's E Ink screens are leading to a decline in print-based books, its stronghold on the screen market for e-readers is being challenged by Qualcomm's mirasol display technology that, like E Ink, uses low power and can be read in direct sunlight, but unlike E Ink's black-and-white screens, displays in color.[22] In response, Prime View has developed a color version of its E Ink technology that delivers high-contrast screens that are readable in sunlight and use little power.

Chapter 7, on organizational change and innovation, provides a more in-depth discussion of how technology affects a company's competitive advantage.

2.3 Sociocultural Component

The sociocultural component of the general environment refers to the demographic characteristics, general behavior, attitudes, and beliefs of people in a

technology the knowledge, tools, and techniques used to transform input into output.

Exhibit 3.4 Demographics: Percentage of Married Women (with Children) Who Work

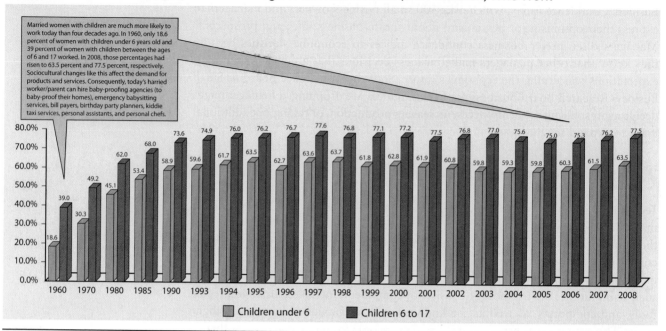

Married women with children are much more likely to work today than four decades ago. In 1960, only 18.6 percent of women with children under 6 years old and 39 percent of women with children between the ages of 6 and 17 worked. In 2008, those percentages had risen to 63.5 percent and 77.5 percent, respectively. Sociocultural changes like this affect the demand for products and services. Consequently, today's harried worker/parent can hire baby-proofing agencies (to baby-proof their homes), emergency babysitting services, bill payers, birthday party planners, kiddie taxi services, personal assistants, and personal chefs.

Children under 6   Children 6 to 17

Source: U.S. Census Bureau, *Statistical Abstract of the United States,* 1999 and 2001 (Washington, DC: U.S. Government Printing Office, 1999 and 2001); "Employment Status of Women by Marital Status and Presence and Age of Children: 1960 to 1998," Table No. 631: U.S. Census Bureau, *Statistical Abstract: The National Data Book,* 2009, "Employment Status of Women by Marital Status and Presence and Age of Children: 1970 to 2007," Table No. 598, accessed April 27, 2009, from www.census.gov/compendia/statab/2011/tables/11s0598.pdf.

particular society. Sociocultural changes and trends influence organizations in two important ways.

First, changes in demographic characteristics, such as the number of people with particular skills or the growth or decline in particular population segments (marital status, age, gender, ethnicity), affect how companies staff their businesses. Married women with children are much more likely to work today than four decades ago, as illustrated in Exhibit 3.4. In 1960, only 18.6 percent of women with children under the age of 6 and 39 percent of women with children between the ages of 6 and 17 worked. By 2009, those percentages had risen to 63.6 percent and 77.5 percent, respectively.

Second, sociocultural changes in behavior, attitudes, and beliefs also affect the demand for a business's products and services. Today, with more married women with children in the workforce, traffic congestion creating longer commutes, and both parents working longer hours, employees are much more likely to value products and services that allow them to recapture free time with their families, and families are deliberately selective about how they spend their free time. Thus people—especially working mothers—use numerous services to help reduce the amount of time they spend doing chores and household management tasks.

Priscilla La Barbera, a marketing professor at New York University, says, "People are beginning to realize that their time has real value."[23] Brian Wheeler, who runs a concierge service in Washington, D.C., that performs personal tasks for company employees, said, "Many households have two adults working full time, people are working longer hours, and traffic in our region gets worse each year. When you combine these things, there isn't much time for anything outside of work and life maintenance stuff. We give them a hand and magically get things done for them during the day so that when they get home they can actually unwind or spend quality time with their family."[24] For example, at McGraw Wentworth, a provider of group healthcare benefits, employees can get their laundry picked up and returned on site. IT staffing firm Akraya provides employees with professional home cleaning services.[25]

2.4 Political/Legal Component

The political/legal component of the general environment includes the legislation, regulations, and court decisions that govern and regulate business behavior. New laws and regulations continue to impose additional responsibilities on companies. Unfortunately, many managers are unaware of these new responsibilities. For example, under the 1991 Civil Rights Act (www.eeoc.gov/policy/cra91.html), if an employee is sexually harassed by anyone at work (a supervisor, a coworker, or even a customer), the company—not just the harasser—is potentially liable for damages, attorneys' fees, and back pay.[26] Under the Family and Medical Leave Act (www .dol.gov/whd/fmla), employees who have been on the job one year are guaranteed 12 weeks of unpaid leave per year to tend to their own illnesses or to their elderly parents, a newborn baby, or a newly adopted child. Employees are guaranteed the same job, pay, and benefits when they return to work.[27]

Many managers are also unaware of the potential legal risks associated with traditional managerial decisions like recruiting, hiring, and firing employees. Increasingly, businesses and managers are being sued for negligent hiring and supervision, defamation, invasion of privacy, emotional distress, fraud, and misrepresentation during employee recruitment.[28] More than 14,000 suits for wrongful termination (unfairly firing employees) are filed each year.[29] In fact, wrongful termination lawsuits increased by 77 percent during the 1990s.[30] One in four employers will at some point be sued for wrongful termination. It can cost $300,000 to settle such a case once it goes to court, but employers lose 70 percent of court cases, and the former employee is awarded, on average, $1 million or more.[31] On the other hand, employers who settle before going to court typically pay just $10,000 to $100,000 per case.[32]

Companies also face a variety of potential legal risks from customer-initiated lawsuits. Toyota, for instance, reached an undisclosed settlement with the relatives of four people who were killed when their Lexus, on loan from a dealership, sped up to 100 miles per hour, hit an SUV, crashed through a fence, and burst into flames after flipping over. It's alleged that an oversized floor mat designed for another car became stuck against the accelerator when pressure was applied to the brake pedal, thus accidentally accelerating the car. Several months later, the U.S. Department of Transportation reported ten similar reports from consumers. Although none of those reports were verified, Toyota addressed widespread consumer concerns about sudden acceleration in its vehicles by issuing a recall to replace the car mats and electronic throttle controls in 8 million cars.[33]

Although most of these Toyotas were just a few years old, under product-liability law, manufacturers are liable for products made decades ago. Furthermore, product-liability law, as written, does not consider whether manufactured products have been properly maintained and used by the customer. Plaintiffs only have to demonstrate that they were injured by the manufacturer's product. Under the concept of "strict liability," the burden of proof is shifted to the company, which must prove that the product was safe and not defective.[34] Thus, once injuries have been shown, the company is assumed guilty until it proves its innocence. Today, jury verdicts in product-liability cases cost companies an average of $6.8 million per case.[35]

Not everyone agrees that companies' legal risks are too severe. Indeed, many believe that the government should do more to regulate and restrict business behavior and that it should be easier for average citizens to sue dishonest or negligent corporations. From a managerial perspective, the best medicine against legal risk is

prevention. As a manager, it is your responsibility to educate yourself about the laws, regulations, and potential lawsuits that could affect your business. Failure to do so may put you and your company at risk of sizable penalties, fines, or legal charges.

Review 2

General Environment The general environment consists of economic, technological, sociocultural, and political and legal events and trends that affect all organizations. Because the economy influences basic business decisions, managers often use economic statistics and business confidence indices to predict future economic activity. Changes in technology, which transforms inputs into outputs, can be a benefit or a threat to a business. Sociocultural trends, like changing demographic characteristics, affect how companies run their businesses. Similarly, sociocultural changes in behavior, attitudes, and beliefs affect the demand for a business's products and services. Court decisions and new federal and state laws have imposed much greater political and legal responsibilities on companies. The best way to manage legal responsibilities is to educate managers and employees about laws and regulations and potential lawsuits that could affect a business.

3 Specific Environment

As you just learned, changes in any sector of the general environment (economic, technological, sociocultural, and political and legal) eventually affect most organizations. Each organization also has a specific environment that is unique to that firm's industry and directly affects the way it conducts day-to-day business. For instance, if your customers decide to use another product; your main competitor cuts prices 10 percent; your best supplier can't deliver raw materials; federal regulators mandate reductions in pollutants in your industry; or environmental groups accuse your company of selling unsafe products, the impact from the specific environment on your business is immediate.

Let's examine how the **3.1 customer, 3.2 competitor, 3.3 supplier, 3.4 industry regulation**, and **3.5 advocacy group components of the specific environment affect businesses.**

3.1 Customer Component

Customers purchase products and services. Companies cannot exist without customer support. Monitoring customers' changing wants and needs is critical to business success. There are two basic strategies for monitoring customers: reactive and proactive.

Reactive customer monitoring involves identifying and addressing customer trends and problems after they occur. One reactive strategy is to listen closely to customer complaints and respond to customer concerns. The online forums for **Activision-Blizzard's** World of Warcraft (WoW), the most popular web-based role-playing game, are infamous for trolls—users who take advantage of the anonymous nature of the forums to post insulting and hateful messages for no obvious reason. To discourage this behavior, Activision-Blizzard announced forum posters would have to start using their real names. Forum users protested that what they posted on the WoW forum could be searched with Google for anyone, including their employers, to see. Others worried that hackers might track down their personal information to steal their identity. Some even feared physical harm from other WoW players, who would now be able to identify and locate them. Finally, others felt that that using real names would undercut the fantasy elements of WoW. Three days after creating the

"what's new" companies >

policy, because of overwhelming complaints about the new policy, Activision-Blizzard reacted again by announcing that users would be allowed to use anonymous names after all.[36]

Companies like ScubaToys.com that respond quickly to customer letters of complaint (i.e., reactive customer monitoring) are viewed much more favorably than companies that are slow to respond or never respond.[37] In particular, studies have shown that when a company's follow-up letter thanks the customer for writing; offers a sincere, specific response to the complaint (not a form letter, but an explanation of how the problem will be handled); and contains a small gift, coupons, or a refund to make up for the problem, customers are much more likely to purchase products or services again from that company.[38]

Companies that *don't* respond promptly to customer complaints are instead likely to find customer rants and tirades posted publicly on places like www.planetfeedback.com. Customers hope that posting complaints on these sites will force someone to address their problems. It worked for Lena West. The day after she posted a complaint against Budget Rent-a-Car, she received an email containing an apology and a promise to resolve her problem.[39]

Proactive monitoring of customers means identifying and addressing customer needs, trends, and issues *before* they occur. Although it's commonly believed that attracting high rollers who bet huge amounts of money is the key to profitability in the gaming industry, **Harrah's** casinos determined that 80 percent of its revenues and 100 percent of its profits come from "low rollers," the 30 percent of its customers who only spend $100 to $500 per visit. Harrah's calls them "avid experience players" because of the regularity with which they gamble. The trick to attracting and keeping these customers is to identify and address their needs, which Harrah's does through its electronic "Total Rewards" program cards that these frequent gamblers insert into slot machines or hand to blackjack table attendants whenever they place a bet. Thanks to the data obtained from those cards, Harrah's can identify what different customers need to keep them coming back to Harrah's, rather than to other casinos. Linda Maranees, a regular customer, says, "Harrah's is savvy." Because she plays the slot machines, Harrah's will offer her cash rewards—which she can then put into slot machines. By contrast, Harrah's figured out that Tina Montgomery will bet more or visit more often if offered a free or "comped" hotel room. Why? Because her husband, who doesn't gamble, "stays in the room" when she goes to the casino.[40] How well does this work? By identifying and meeting customers' needs, Harrah's now gets 43 percent of its customers' gambling business now, compared to 36 percent before its Total Rewards program.[41]

< **"what's new" companies**

3.2 Competitor Component

Competitors are companies in the same industry that sell similar products or services to customers. Ford, Toyota, Honda, Nissan, Hyundai, and Kia all compete for automobile customers. NBC, ABC, CBS, and Fox (along with hundreds of cable channels) compete for TV viewers' attention. McDonald's, Burger King, Wendy's, Hardee's, Chick-fil-A, and a host of others compete for fast-food customers' dollars. Often the difference between business success and failure comes down to whether your company is doing a better job of satisfying customer wants and needs than the competition. Consequently, companies need to keep close track of what their competitors are doing. To do this, managers perform **competitive analysis**, which involves deciding who your competitors are, anticipating competitors' moves, and determining competitors' strengths and weaknesses.

Surprisingly, managers often do a poor job of identifying potential competitors, because they tend to focus on only two or three well-known competitors with similar

competitors companies in the same industry that sell similar products or services to customers.

competitive analysis a process for monitoring the competition that involves identifying competition, anticipating their moves, and determining their strengths and weaknesses.

mgmt:trends

No Summer Break for Cable

How do you gain more viewers in the hyper-competitive television market? Many cable companies have found that the answer is to take advantage of the season. Over-the-air broadcast networks (ABC, CBS, NBC, Fox) tend to premier their best shows in the fall while showing re-runs or lesser-known, newer shows in the summer. Cable networks are taking advantage by using the summer to debut new shows like *Rizzoli & Isles* on TNT, *Covert Affairs* on USA, and *Ice Road Truckers* on the History Channel. The strategy is a smashing success, as the ten largest cable networks have increased viewership by 5 percent from the previous year.[42]

goals and resources.[43] Historically, Coke and Pepsi spent more time keeping track of each other than they spent on other competitors, but when they each started losing ground to start-up energy drinks, bottled water, and fruit juices, both giants began to buy businesses to help them compete in these growing markets.[44] Likewise, Hoover Dirt Devil, and, more recently, Oreck competed fiercely in the market for vacuum cleaners. Because these companies produced relatively similar vacuum cleaners, they mostly competed on price. When Dyson entered the market with its radically different vacuum that developed and maintained significantly more suction power, the company garnered 20 percent market share within its first months on the shelves.[45] Only then did Hoover and Dirt Devil design their own bagless vacuums.

Another mistake managers may make when analyzing the competition is to underestimate potential competitors' capabilities. When this happens, managers don't take the steps they should to continue to improve their products or services. The result can be significant decreases in both market share and profits. For nearly a decade, traditional phone companies ignored the threat to their business from VoIP (Voice over Internet Protocol). Early on, software products like Cool Talk, Internet Phone, and Web Phone made it possible to make inexpensive long-distance phone calls using VoIP. Aside from the software, the only requirements were an Internet service provider and a computer that had a sound card, speakers, and a microphone. The sound quality was only as good as AM radio, but people who were used to poor-quality sound on their cell phones didn't care because the calls were so much cheaper.[46]

Today, because phone companies themselves were slow to adopt VoIP capabilities, they're facing a rash of new, unexpected VoIP competitors, all of which have slashed prices and taken market share using high-speed Internet service. For example, Comcast, a cable-TV provider that also offers high-speed Internet service, gains ten phone subscribers—at the expense of phone companies like Verizon and AT&T—for every cable TV subscriber that it loses.[47] VoIP is also threatening the phone companies' wireless services, which now account for most of their profits. When their cell phones are connected to a Wi-Fi hotspot, consumers can use Skype or TruPhone software to make VoIP-based telephone calls. For example, iPhone users can avoid cell phone charges by using Skype to make free phone calls to other Skype users on computers or cell phones.[48] Furthermore, calls to landline phones, including international calls, cost only a few cents per minute. With international cell phone traffic growing 16 percent per year, VoIP-based international calls originating from cell phones represent another threat to traditional phone companies. Vonage, a VoIP service that typically charges $25 to $35 a month for online phone service, gives

Facebook users free VoIP calls to any of their Facebook friends. And if any of those Facebook friends are international, it costs nothing to make an international call.[49]

The ultimate threat to the phone companies and cable companies comes from a VoIP product, the **Ooma** Telo. About the size of a small dinner plate, it plugs into your network router and then your phone. Plug in the power, and voila, at a one-time cost of roughly $200, you have phone service without a monthly phone bill.[50] With the average landline costing about $35 a month, Ooma pays for itself in just over six months, and then saves nearly $900 in monthly phone bills in just the first three years of use. Ooma does charge about $40 to port your current phone number to your Ooma account. And for just $10 a month for its Premier benefits, you get a second line or phone number, three-way conferencing, the ability to send voice mails to your email account, call screening, and much more. But, even at $10 a month, the total savings are still $300 per year. Even Vonage, which charges $25 to $35 a month for VoIP phone service and has been taking business away from the phone companies and cable companies, could lose business to Ooma.

< **"what's new" companies**

3.3 Supplier Component

Suppliers are companies that provide material, human, financial, and informational resources to other companies. U.S. Steel buys iron ore from suppliers to make steel products. When IBM sells a mainframe computer, it also provides support staff, engineers, and other technical consultants to the company that bought the computer. If you're shopping for desks, chairs, and office supplies, chances are Office Depot will be glad to help your business open a revolving charge account to pay for your purchases. When a clothing manufacturer has spent $100,000 to purchase new high-pressure "water drills" to cut shirt and pants patterns to precise sizes, the water drill manufacturer, as part of the purchase, will usually train the workers on the machinery.

A key factor influencing the impact and quality of the relationship between companies and their suppliers is how dependent they are on each other.[51] **Supplier dependence** is the degree to which a company relies on that supplier because of the importance of the supplier's product to the company and the difficulty of finding other sources for that product. Chinese mining companies, for example, provide 97 percent of rare-earth materials like samarium, scandium, and yttrium, which are used to manufacture TV screens, mobile phones, fiber optics, and electric motors.[52] When China announced it was cutting exports of rare-earth materials, Sojitz, which imports rare-earth materials to Japan for companies like Hitachi, estimated that Japanese companies would face shortages of 10,000 tons a year. "The only real solution to the problem is to buy new mining rights overseas," according to Toru Okabe, an engineering professor at the University of Tokyo. But, he says, "Mines outside of China don't have cost-competitiveness. If China begins to flood the market with cheap supplies again, they wouldn't stand the competition."[53]

suppliers companies that provide material, human, financial, and informational resources to other companies.

supplier dependence the degree to which a company relies on a supplier because of the importance of the supplier's product to the company and the difficulty of finding other sources of that product.

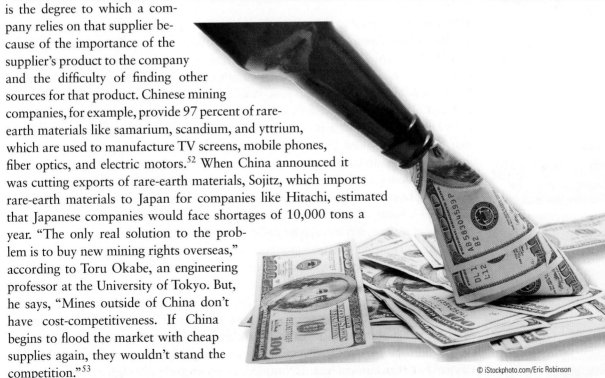

© iStockphoto.com/Eric Robinson

Buyer dependence is the degree to which a supplier relies on a buyer because of the importance of that buyer to the supplier's sales and the difficulty of finding other buyers of its products. For example, when InBev purchased Anheuser-Busch and renamed itself AB InBev, it became the world's largest brewer, controlling over 25 percent of global beer sales. This gave AB InBev tremendous bargaining power over its suppliers. One of the ways in which it leveraged that bargaining power was to tell its suppliers, who provide everything from malt to hops to yeast, that it would pay them for their product shipments 120 days after being invoiced. With existing contracts providing payment 30 days after being invoiced, that meant that AB InBev's suppliers would have to wait an extra three months to be paid. Delaying payments gives AB InBev an additional $1.2 billion in cash flow per year, but it did so at the expense of its suppliers. According to Elisavet Kinsey, who is commercial and procurement director at MaltEurop, one of the world's largest malt producers, those changes were simply "unacceptable."[54] There was little, however, that most AB InBev suppliers could do about this change.

As the rare-earth materials and AB InBev examples show, a high degree of buyer or seller dependence can lead to **opportunistic behavior**, in which one party benefits at the expense of the other. Although opportunistic behavior between buyers and suppliers will never be completely eliminated, many companies believe that both buyers and suppliers can benefit by improving the buyer–supplier relationship.[55]

In contrast to opportunistic behavior, **relationship behavior** focuses on establishing a mutually beneficial, long-term relationship between buyers and suppliers.[56] Toyota is well-known for developing positive long-term relationships with its key suppliers. Donald Esmond, who runs Toyota's U.S. division, says, "I think what they [suppliers] appreciate . . . is we don't go in and say, 'Reduce the costs by 6 percent; if you don't, somebody else is going to get the business.' We go in and say we want to come in and help you [figure out] where you can save costs so we can reduce our overall price. So it's a different approach."[57]

3.4 Industry Regulation Component

Whereas the political and legal component of the general environment affects all businesses, the **industry regulation** component consists of regulations and rules that govern the practices and procedures of specific industries, businesses, and professions. If your neighbor decides to make a little extra money selling homemade baked goods and sells you two apple pies, your neighbor could be fined. Why? In most states, it is illegal to sell food from your home. State regulations typically require a food business to obtain a license and a state certificate of inspection that indicates that the food is stored properly; insects have not infested the premises; ovens are state approved; electrical wiring, lighting, and smoke detectors are up to code; and so on.[58] Likewise, the auto industry is subject to CAFE (Corporate Average Fuel Economy) regulations that currently require cars and sport utility vehicles (SUVs) to average 27.5 and 22.5 miles per gallon (mpg), respectively.[59] Both cars and SUVs, however, must average 35 mpg by 2020.[60]

Regulatory agencies affect businesses by creating and enforcing rules and regulations to protect consumers, workers, or society as a whole. For example, the U.S. Department of Agriculture (USDA) and the Food and Drug Administration (FDA) regulate the safety of seafood (as well as meat and poultry) through the science-based Hazard Analysis and Critical Control Points program. Seafood processors are required to identify hazards (toxins, chemicals, pesticides, and decomposition) that could cause the fish they process to be unsafe. They must also establish critical control points to control hazards both inside and outside their fish-processing plants

buyer dependence the degree to which a supplier relies on a buyer because of the importance of that buyer to the supplier and the difficulty of finding other buyers for its products.

opportunistic behavior a transaction in which one party in the relationship benefits at the expense of the other.

relationship behavior the establishment of mutually beneficial, long-term exchanges between buyers and suppliers.

industry regulation regulations and rules that govern the business practices and procedures of specific industries, businesses, and professions.

doing the right thing

The Language of Bribery

In many foreign countries, bribery is an accepted, and even expected, part of doing business, even though there are laws that are meant to prevent illegal gifts and payments. Because of these laws, those who expect bribes often hide behind jargon or slang so that they can disguise the true nature of the exchange of money. In Italy, for example, a bribe might be called a *spintarella*, "a little push," while it might be called *fakelaki*, "a little purse," in Greece. An offer of a bribe might often be described as something to eat or drink—a *pot-de-vin* ("glass of wine") in France, a *mordida* ("a bite") in Spain, or a *finjaan 'ahwa* ("a cup of coffee") in Syria. In Russia, someone might ask for a bribe by suggesting that "we need to come to agreement." So how can companies navigate this confusing jumble of foreign slang? James Tillen and Sonia Delman, of the international law firm Miller & Chevalier Chartered, give the following suggestions:

» Incorporate local dialects, slang, and customs into compliance policies and training programs.

» Use role-play exercises with locally relevant language and customs in anticorruption training sessions.

» Instruct employees to clarify any dubious payment requests.

» Include colloquial bribery terms as "red flags" in internal audit modules.[61]

and then establish monitoring, corrective action, and verification procedures to certify that the fish they process is safe to consume.[62]

The nearly 100 federal agencies and regulatory commissions can affect almost any kind of business. For example, earlier in the chapter we described how the toy industry spent $200 million to increase the safety of its products after 20 million unsafe toys produced in China were recalled because of the presence of harmful chemicals. In addition to the voluntary recall by toy retailers and manufacturers, new federal regulations embodied in the Consumer Product Safety Improvement Act of 2008 ban phthalates from children's products and now require products to be tested for the presence of phthalates before they are sold.[63]

Exhibit 3.5 lists some of the most influential federal agencies and commissions, as well as their responsibilities and their websites. Overall, the number and cost of federal regulations has nearly tripled in the last 25 years. Today, for every $1 the federal government spends creating regulations, businesses spend $45 to comply with them.[64] In addition to federal regulations, businesses are also subject to state, county, and city regulations. Complying with all of these regulations costs businesses an estimated $1.1 trillion per year, or $5,633 per employee.[65] Surveys indicate that managers rank dealing with government regulation as one of the most demanding and frustrating parts of their jobs.[66]

3.5 Advocacy Groups

Advocacy groups are groups of concerned citizens who band together to try to influence the business practices of specific industries, businesses, and professions. The members of a group generally share the same point of view on a particular issue. For example, environmental advocacy groups might try to get manufacturers to

advocacy groups concerned citizens who band together to try to influence the business practices of specific industries, businesses, and professions.

Exhibit 3.5   Federal Regulatory Agencies and Commissions

Federal Agency	Regulatory Responsibilities
Consumer Product Safety Commission http://www.cpsc.gov	Reduces risk of injuries and deaths associated with consumer products, sets product safety standards, enforces product recalls, and provides consumer education
Department of Labor http://www.dol.gov	Collects employment statistics and administers labor laws concerning safe working conditions, minimum hourly wages and overtime pay, employment discrimination, and unemployment insurance
Environmental Protection Agency ttp://www.epa.gov	Reduces and controls pollution through research, monitoring, standard setting, and enforcement activities
Equal Employment Opportunity Commission http://www.eeoc.gov	Promotes fair hiring and promotion practices
Federal Communications Commission http://www.fcc.gov	Regulates interstate and international communications by radio, television, wire, satellite, and cable
Federal Reserve System http://www.federalreserve.gov	As nation's central bank, controls interest rates and money supply, and monitors the U.S. banking system to produce a growing economy with stable prices
Federal Trade Commission http://www.ftc.gov	Restricts unfair methods of business competition and misleading advertising, and enforces consumer protection laws
Food and Drug Administration http://www.fda.gov	Protects nation's health by making sure food, drugs, and cosmetics are safe
National Labor Relations Board http://www.nlrb.gov	Monitors union elections and stops companies from engaging in unfair labor practices
Occupational Safety & Health Administration http://www.osha.gov	Issues and enforces standards to protect the lives and health of workers
Securities and Exchange Commission http://www.sec.gov	Protects investors in the bond and stock markets, guarantees access to information on publicly traded securities, and regulates firms that sell securities or give investment advice

© Cengage Learning 2013

reduce smokestack pollution emissions. Unlike the industry regulation component of the specific environment, advocacy groups cannot force organizations to change their practices. Nevertheless, they can use a number of techniques to try to influence companies, including public communications, media advocacy, Web pages, blogs, and product boycotts.

The **public communications** approach relies on *voluntary* participation by the news media and the advertising industry to send out an advocacy group's message. For example, a public service campaign to encourage people to quit smoking ran the following ads in newspapers and magazines throughout Europe: a photo showing the foot of a young person with a toe tag (indicating the person was dead), with the caption "Smokers die younger"; a picture showing clean lungs next to brown- and black-stained lungs, with the caption "Smoking causes fatal lung cancer"; and a photo of a baby in an intensive care unit hooked up to a respirator, with the caption "Smoking when pregnant harms your baby."[67]

Media advocacy is much more aggressive than the public communications approach. A **media advocacy** approach typically involves framing the group's concerns as public issues (affecting everyone); exposing questionable, exploitative, or unethical practices; and creating controversy that is likely to receive extensive news coverage. In one of its latest protests, called "McCruelty: I'm Hatin' It," PETA (People for the Ethical Treatment of Animals) is protesting that McDonald's, which uses 290 million chickens a year, tolerates suppliers using inhumane killing methods—hanging the birds upside down, stunning them in water that carries an electrical current, and then

public communications an advocacy group tactic that relies on voluntary participation by the news media and the advertising industry to get the advocacy group's message out.

media advocacy an advocacy group tactic that involves framing issues as public issues; exposing questionable, exploitative, or unethical practices; and forcing media coverage by buying media time or creating controversy that is likely to receive extensive news coverage.

cutting their throats. PETA wants McDonald's suppliers to use gas to kill the birds, which it believes is more humane. Paul Shapiro, who heads the Humane Society's factory farming initiative, said, "It causes less suffering than the conventional method, which is archaic and inhumane." However, Marie Wheatley, president of the American Humane Association, disagrees, saying, "There is not definite proof either is more humane. Both technologies are acceptable in minimizing pain and suffering."[68] A McDonald's spokesperson said the company is committed to "humane treatment of animals by our suppliers in every part of the world where we do business."[69]

A **product boycott** is a tactic in which an advocacy group actively tries to persuade consumers not to purchase a company's product or service. When an explosion on one of British Petroleum's (BP) oil rigs in April 2010 caused massive amounts of oil to leak into the Gulf of Mexico, many American consumers expressed outrage by boycotting BP gas. Protesters created "Boycott BP" websites and Facebook groups, staged protests at BP service stations, and distributed bumper stickers that said, "Anyone But BP." Tyson Slocum, director of Public Citizen, an advocacy group, said, "These are symbolic acts taken by people who are outraged and frustrated. But this is a fitting response because, after all, BP over the years has spent millions promoting this image of being a green, environmentally friendly company. It was all for show. Boycotting their brand is the best way to counter that kind of charade."[70]

Specific Environment The specific environment is made up of five components: customers, competitors, suppliers, industry regulation, and advocacy groups. Companies can monitor customers' needs by identifying customer problems after they occur or by anticipating problems before they occur. Because they tend to focus on well-known competitors, managers often underestimate their competition or do a poor job of identifying future competitors. Suppliers and buyers are dependent on each other, and that dependence sometimes leads to opportunistic behavior, in which one benefits at the expense of the other. Regulatory agencies affect businesses by creating rules and then enforcing them. Overall, the level of industry regulation has nearly tripled in the last 25 years. Advocacy groups cannot regulate organizations' practices. Nevertheless, through public communications, media advocacy, and product boycotts, they try to convince companies to change their practices.

Review 3

4 Making Sense of Changing Environments

In Chapter 1, you learned that managers are responsible for making sense of their business environments. As our discussions of the general and specific environments have indicated, however, making sense of business environments is not an easy task. Because external environments can be dynamic, confusing, and complex, managers use a three-step process to make sense of the changes in their external environments: **4.1 environmental scanning, 4.2 interpreting environmental factors**, and **4.3 acting on threats and opportunities**.

4.1 Environmental Scanning

Environmental scanning involves searching the environment for important events or issues that might affect an organization. Managers scan the environment to stay up-to-date on important factors in their industry. The American Hospital Association,

product boycott an advocacy group tactic that involves protesting a company's actions by persuading consumers not to purchase its product or service.

environmental scanning searching the environment for important events or issues that might affect an organization.

for instance, publishes an "Environmental Scan" annually to help hospital and health system managers understand the trends and market forces that have a "high probability of affecting the healthcare field." In its latest environmental scan, it indicated that 60 percent of large employers now offer incentives to encourage wellness and healthy behaviors among employees; direct-to-consumer genetic testing will expand as costs continue to drop; it may become increasingly difficult to get access to primary care because retirements among primary care physicians outnumber graduates from medical schools; 66 percent of Americans are overweight and that obesity may soon cause more deaths than tobacco, which is the leading preventable cause of death; and a growing number of physicians will choose to be employed by hospitals rather than go into private practice.[71]

"what's new" companies > Managers also scan their environments to reduce uncertainty. Recently, **Gatorade** created a "Mission Control Center," a room filled with computer monitors and marketing experts, resembling a NASA control center, that constantly monitors social-media networks. The monitors display constantly updated visuals that provide real-time information on what people are saying about Gatorade, its competitors, and even sports nutrition in general, within social media networks. This allows Gatorade's marketing team to track how consumers are reacting to its ads and to make quick adjustments based on those reactions. After releasing a campaign called "Gatorade Has Evolved," Mission Control discovered that the ad's song, by David Banner, was so popular that within 24 hours the company produced and released a full-length version of the song. With such a speedy response that responded to consumers' desires, Gatorade has been able to increase engagement with its product education by 250 percent.[72]

"what's new" companies > Organizational strategies also affect environmental scanning. In other words, managers pay close attention to trends and events that are directly related to their company's ability to compete in the marketplace.[73] **Knights Apparel**, a manufacturer of collegiate-licensed clothing, based in South Carolina, recognized that its customers were increasingly concerned about buying clothes produced in "sweatshops" in developing countries where workers were paid as little as $100 per month. Instead of the legally required minimum wage of $147 a month, Knights' wages of $500 a month are based on the actual cost of living in the Dominican Republic. Although costs have increased by 20 percent, or 80 cents per T-shirt, the company has not increased its prices. CEO Joseph Bozich said, "We're pricing the product such that we're not asking the retailer or the consumer to sacrifice in order to support it."[74] Knights' hope is that this policy will make its product more desirable than those of its competitors, Nike and Adidas. Kellie A. McElhaney, a professor of corporate social responsibility at University of California–Berkeley said, "A lot of college students would much rather pay for a brand that shows workers are treated well." Knights has already received lucrative deals with Duke University, Barnes & Noble, and Follett's, a college textbook store chain.[75]

Finally, environmental scanning is important because it contributes to organizational performance. Environmental scanning helps managers detect environmental changes and problems before they become organizational crises.[76] Furthermore, companies whose CEOs do more environmental scanning have higher profits.[77] CEOs in better-performing firms scan their firm's environments more frequently and scan more key factors in their environments in more depth and detail than do CEOs in poorer-performing firms.[78]

4.2 Interpreting Environmental Factors

After scanning, managers determine what environmental events and issues mean to the organization. Typically, managers view environmental events and issues as either threats or opportunities. When managers interpret environmental events as threats, they take steps to protect the company from further harm. For example, now that Internet phone service (VoIP) has emerged as a threat, traditional phone companies have responded by spending billions to expand their fiber-optic networks so that they can offer phone (using VoIP), Internet service, and TV packages just like those the cable and satellite companies offer. For example, when this was being written, Comcast was losing 233,000 cable TV subscribers per quarter, while U-Verse, AT&T's digital TV service, and FiOS, Verizon's digital TV service, were adding 264,00 and 303,000 subscribers, respectively, during the same period.[79]

By contrast, when managers interpret environmental events as opportunities, they consider strategic alternatives for taking advantage of those events to improve company performance. Apple is known for recognizing opportunities and capitalizing on them. The market for high-end "smart" phones, full-featured mobile phones that also function as a handheld personal computer, is growing roughly 2 percent per year. Because of opportunities in this market, Apple developed its own smartphone—the iPhone. CEO Steve Jobs announced the release more than six months in advance, to generate hype, stimulate demand, and dampen sales of competitors. The iPhone features a wider screen, intuitive touch-screen controls, and the ability to use faster Wi-Fi networks so that users can email, surf the web, and communicate with Bluetooth-enabled devices—plus, of course, download and play iTunes music. Apple sold 21 million iPhones in its first 18 months on the market, far exceeding its goal of 10 million. Likewise, another sign of Apple's success with the iPhone is that the one-billionth iPhone application was downloaded just nine months after Apple opened its App Store for the iPhone and iPod Touch.[80]

© AP Images/PRNewsFoto/Apple

4.3 Acting on Threats and Opportunities

After scanning for information on environmental events and issues and interpreting them as threats or opportunities, managers have to decide how to respond to these environmental factors. Deciding what to do under conditions of uncertainty is always difficult. Managers can never be completely confident that they have all the information they need or that they correctly understand the information they have.

Because it is impossible to comprehend all the factors and changes, managers often rely on simplified models of external environments, called cognitive maps. **Cognitive maps** summarize the perceived relationships between environmental factors and possible organizational actions. For example, the cognitive map shown in Exhibit 3.6 represents a small clothing-store owner's interpretation of her business environment. The map shows three kinds of variables. The first variables, shown as rectangles, are environmental factors, such as a Walmart or a large mall 20 minutes away. The second variables, shown in ovals, are potential actions that the store owner might take, such as a low-cost strategy; a good-value, good-service strategy; or a "large selection of the latest fashions" strategy. The third variables, shown as trapezoids, are company strengths, such as low employee turnover, and weaknesses, such as small size.

The plus and minus signs on the map indicate whether the manager believes there is a positive or negative relationship between variables. For example, the manager believes that a low-cost strategy won't work because Walmart and Target are nearby. Offering a large selection of the latest fashions would not work either—not with the

cognitive maps graphic depictions of how managers believe environmental factors relate to possible organizational actions.

Exhibit 3.6 Cognitive Maps

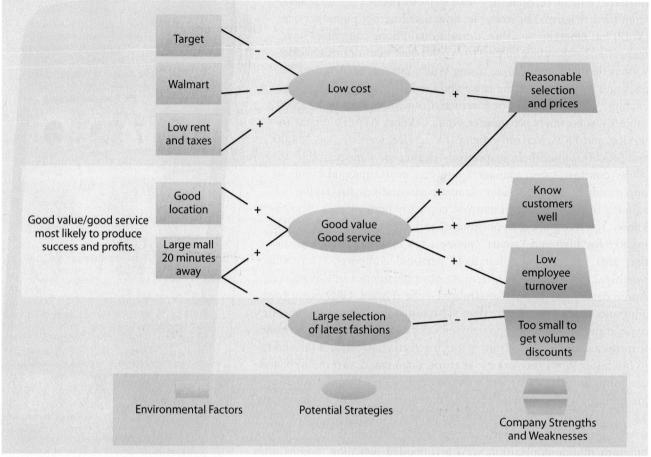

© Cengage Learning 2013

small size of the store and that large nearby mall. However, the manager believes that a good-value, good-service strategy would lead to success and profits because of the store's low employee turnover, good knowledge of customers, reasonable selection of clothes at reasonable prices, and good location.

In the end, managers must complete all three steps—environmental scanning, interpreting environmental factors, and acting on threats and opportunities—to make sense of changing external environments. Environmental scanning helps managers more accurately interpret their environments and take actions that improve company performance. Through scanning, managers keep tabs on what competitors are doing, identify market trends, and stay alert to current events that affect their company's operations. Armed with the environmental information they have gathered, managers can then minimize the impact of threats and turn opportunities into increased profits.

Review 4

Making Sense of Changing Environments   Managers use a three-step process to make sense of external environments: environmental scanning, interpreting information, and acting on threats and opportunities. Managers scan their environments based on their organizational strategies, their need for up-to-date information, and their need to reduce uncertainty. When managers identify environmental events as threats, they take steps to protect the company from harm. When managers identify environmental events as opportunities, they formulate alternatives for taking advantage of them to improve company performance. Using cognitive maps can help managers visually summarize the relationships between environmental factors and the actions they might take to deal with them.

Internal Environments

We have been looking at trends and events outside of companies that have the potential to affect them. By contrast, the **internal environment** consists of the trends and events *within* an organization that affect the management, employees, and organizational culture. Internal environments are important because they affect what people think, feel, and do at work.

Earlier in the chapter, you learned that innovative new products such as the iPod, iPhone, and Xbox 360, as well as aggressive cost cutting in the booming market for high-definition TVs (i.e., Sony's external environment), had hurt Sony's market share and profitability. Sony's problems, however, were directly linked to its hypercompetitive culture, where people in different parts of the company did not communicate with each other and where designing innovative, high-priced products no matter the cost was seen as the most important contribution to the company.

Now, thanks to programs such as "Sony United," which encourage Sony employees in different divisions and locations to work with each other, Sony's culture has begun to change. One example of that change is Sony's Webbie HD, a basic high-definition digital camcorder that sells for under $200, for recording video to post on the Internet. In contrast to its old culture, where the Webbie would have been designed by Tokyo engineers and produced in Sony factories, the idea for the Webbie came from Sony's American marketing team and is produced by a contract manufacturer in China.[81] Likewise, Sony's Mexican engineers worked with its U.S. marketing team to design Sony's new, inexpensive Bravia high-definition TV for the cost-competitive U.S. market. The Bravia sold so well at Walmart that Best Buy asked for Bravias in its stores.[82]

The key component in internal environments is **organizational culture**, or the set of key values, beliefs, and attitudes shared by members of the organization.

> ## After reading the next section, you should be able to
>
> 5. Explain how organizational cultures are created and how they can help companies be successful.

5 Organizational Cultures: Creation, Success, and Change

Let's take a closer look at **5.1 how organizational cultures are created and maintained, 5.2 the characteristics of successful organizational cultures,** and **5.3 how companies can accomplish the difficult task of changing organizational cultures.**

5.1 Creation and Maintenance of Organizational Cultures

A primary source of organizational culture is the company founder. Founders like Thomas J. Watson, Sr. (IBM), Sam Walton (Walmart), and Bill Gates (Microsoft) create organizations in their own images and imprint them with their beliefs, attitudes, and values. For example, Thomas J. Watson proclaimed that IBM's three basic beliefs were the pursuit of excellence, customer service, and showing respect for the individual, meaning company employees. Microsoft employees share founder Bill

internal environment the events and trends inside an organization that affect management, employees, and organizational culture.

organizational culture the values, beliefs, and attitudes shared by organizational members.

Gates' determination to stay ahead of software competitors. Says a Microsoft vice president, "No matter how good your product, you are only 18 months away from failure."[83] Although company founders are instrumental in the creation of organizational cultures, eventually founders retire, die, or choose to leave their companies. When the founders are gone, how are their values, attitudes, and beliefs sustained in the organizational culture? Answer: stories and heroes.

Organizational members tell **organizational stories** to make sense of organizational events and changes and to emphasize culturally consistent assumptions, decisions, and actions.[84] At Walmart, stories abound about founder Sam Walton's thriftiness as he strove to make Walmart the low-cost retailer that it is today.

> *In those days, we would go on buying trips with Sam, and we'd all stay, as much as we could, in one room or two. I remember one time in Chicago when we stayed eight of us to a room. And the room wasn't very big to begin with. You might say we were on a pretty restricted budget. (Gary Reinboth, one of Walmart's first store managers)[85]*

Sam Walton's thriftiness still permeates Walmart today. Everyone, including top executives and the CEO, flies coach rather than business or first class. When employees travel on business, it's still the norm to share rooms (though two to a room, not eight!) at inexpensive motels like Motel 6 and Super 8 instead of Holiday Inns. Likewise, Walmart will reimburse only up to $15 per meal on business travel, which is half to one-third the reimbursement rate at similar-sized companies (remember, Walmart is one of the largest companies in the world). At one of its annual meetings, former CEO Lee Scott reinforced Sam Walton's beliefs by exhorting Walmart employees to bring back and use the free pencils and pens from their travels. Most people in the audience didn't think he was kidding, and he probably wasn't.[86]

A second way in which organizational culture is sustained is by recognizing and celebrating heroes. By definition, **organizational heroes** are organizational people admired for their qualities and achievements within the organization. **AxleTech International** in Troy, Michigan, is a global manufacturer and supplier of axles, axle components, brakes, and aftermarket parts for specialty trucks, military vehicles, and off-highway machines used in construction, material handling, forestry, mining, and agriculture. When one of its largest, multimillion-dollar customers phoned on a Thursday night to call in a special order of parts urgently needed by Monday, engineer Richard Clisch took charge. Over the next three days, he contacted suppliers on different continents to make sure critical parts were flown overnight to AxleTech's factory, flew to the customer's plant in New York to double check that additional parts weren't needed, and slept just 30 minutes over a four-day span to heroically deliver the order on time.[87]

5.2 Successful Organizational Cultures

Preliminary research shows that organizational culture is related to organizational success. As shown in Exhibit 3.7, cultures based on adaptability, involvement, a clear mission, and consistency can help companies achieve higher sales growth, return on assets, profits, quality, and employee satisfaction.[88]

Adaptability is the ability to notice and respond to changes in the organization's environment. Cultures need to reinforce important values and behaviors, but a culture becomes dysfunctional if it prevents change. One of the surest ways to do that is to discourage open discussion and disagreement. Zappos.com is an online retailer that is founded on one principle—make customers happy. To help new employees adapt to a culture based on superior customer service, all new employees,

When the founders are gone, how are their values, attitudes, and beliefs sustained in the organizational culture?

"what's new" companies >

organizational stories stories told by organizational members to make sense of organizational events and changes and to emphasize culturally consistent assumptions, decisions, and actions.

organizational heroes people celebrated for their qualities and achievements within an organization.

whether website designers or box loaders or corporate lawyers, are required to attend the company's four-week training program for customer service representatives. New hires even spend two weeks taking phone calls from customers so that they can have firsthand experience in providing customers with the best possible service.[89]

In cultures that promote higher levels of *employee involvement* in decision making, employees feel a greater sense of ownership and responsibility. Employee involvement has been a hallmark of Genencor since its creation as a joint venture between Genentech and Corning in 1982. Genencor designs its human resources programs by regularly polling employees about which benefits they enjoy and which they would like the company to offer. Most dramatically, when Genencor built its headquarters, it gave its employees a say in the design. Scientists requested that the labs be placed along the building's exterior so they could receive natural light. "I've worked in labs without windows," says staff scientist Fiona Harding, "and seeing the sun makes the time spent in the lab much more pleasant." The building also features a "main street," where employees congregate to collaborate and interact throughout the day. CEO Jean-Jacques Bienaime believes that these employee-driven design features lead to a more stimulating workplace. "If you want employees to be productive, you have to create a nurturing environment and let them be creative," he says. Such a commitment to employee involvement in decision making is definitely paying off for the company. Its turnover rate was less than 4 percent (the national industry average is 18.5%), and its employees generate approximately $60,000 more revenue per employee than its largest competitor, Novozymes.[90]

Company mission is the business's purpose or reason for existing. In organizational cultures with a clear company mission, the organization's strategic purpose and direction are apparent to everyone in the company. When managers are uncertain about their business environments, the mission helps guide the discussions, decisions, and behavior of the people in the company. **Novo Nordisk**, a pharmaceutical company based in Denmark, has one clear goal: to cure diabetes. Everything it does as an organization—from research and innovation, to marketing, to its social responsibility—is geared toward revolutionizing the way diabetes is treated and prevented. Novo Nordisk's mission is about improving the lives of its customers.[91]

Specific mission statements strengthen organizational cultures by letting everyone know why the company is in business, what really matters (i.e., the company's values), and how those values can be used to guide daily actions and behaviors.[92] For example, Google's emphasizes its core business and its values, that is, what really matters, in a document called, "Ten things we know to be true," (www.google.com/corporate/tenthings.html).

The first item in that document is "Focus on the user and all else will follow." Google follows these criteria to make sure that its website and services benefit the people who use them: "The interface is clear and simple. Pages load instantly. Placement in search results is never sold to anyone. Advertising on the site must offer relevant content and not be a distraction." These criteria guide the daily actions and behavior of Google's employees as they improve and create Google's products and services.

Exhibit 3.7
Successful Organizational Cultures

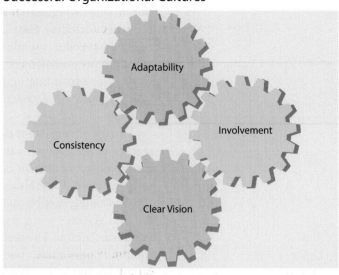

Source: D. R. Denison & A. K. Mishra, "Toward a Theory of Organizational Culture and Effectiveness," *Organization Science* 6 (1995): 204–233.

< **"what's new" companies**

company mission a company's purpose or reason for existing.

The second item, "It's best to do one thing really, really well," makes clear what business Google is in, and that's search. Google explains it this way, "Our dedication to improving search has also allowed us to apply what we've learned to new products, including Gmail, Google Desktop, and Google Maps. As we continue to build new products while making search better, our hope is to bring the power of search to previously unexplored areas, and to help users access and use even more of the ever-expanding information in their lives." You will learn more about mission statements (i.e., purpose statements) in Chapter 5 on planning and decision making.

Finally, in **consistent organizational cultures**, the company actively defines and teaches organizational values, beliefs, and attitudes. At Zappos, an online retailer, maintaining a consistent organizational culture begins with the hiring process. One of the reasons Tony Hsieh, now CEO of Zappos.com, sold his start-up company, LinkExchange, was because, "the company culture just went completely downhill." AsLinkExchange grew, managers hired people based on their skills alone and ignored the culture. The result: The company was staffed by employees who weren't excited or passionate about the work they were doing. When Hsieh joined Zappos, he and his employees developed a list of ten core values (for instance, "Embrace and Drive Change" and "Be Passionate and Determined") that gave everyone at the company shared values and a common corporate language. Then, to avoid the mistakes he made at LinkExchange, Hsieh made sure that Zappos' culture played a significant role in hiring decisions. As a result, prospective hires go through two rounds of interviews. Says Hsieh, "The hiring manager and his or her team will interview for the standard fit within the team, relevant experience, technical ability and so on. But then our H.R. department does a separate set of interviews purely for culture fit. They actually have questions for each and every one of the core values."[93]

Having a consistent or strong organizational culture doesn't guarantee good company performance. When core beliefs are widely shared and strongly held, it is very difficult to bring about needed change. Consequently, companies with strong cultures tend to perform poorly when they need to adapt to dramatic changes in their external environments. Their consistency sometimes prevents them from adapting to those changes.[94] Indeed, McDonald's saw its sales and profits decline in the late 1990s as customer eating patterns began to change. To rescue falling performance, the company introduced its "Plan to Win," which focused on the five elements that drive its business: people, products, place, price, and promotion. McDonald's developed hospitality and multilingual computer-training programs and expanded its menu to include more healthful and snack-oriented selections. Over 5,000 McDonald's restaurants were remodeled in a three-year period and now feature warmer lighting, upbeat music, flat-screen TVs, and Wi-Fi networks. And the company's promotional message, "I'm lovin' it," went from being derided by advertising executives to one of the most recognizable jingles in any market. Now seven years into the plan, McDonald's achieved 68 consecutive months of positive sales (its longest streak in 25 years), reached record annual revenues of more than $23 billion, and returned record cash dividends to its stockholders.[95]

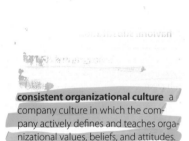

consistent organizational culture a company culture in which the company actively defines and teaches organizational values, beliefs, and attitudes.

© TEH ENG KOON/AFP/Getty Images/Newscom

mgmt:trends

New Places for Creativity

A change of scenery could be just what your company needs to rejuvenate creativity. Instead of renting out hotels or conference centers, managers at Duke Energy decided to hold corporate meetings at the offices of other companies. The decision was motivated, at first, by the recession, because it was thousands of dollars cheaper to meet in offices instead of hotels. But managers soon found that employees picked up ideas from other companies, were inspired by seeing different processes, learned from the expertise of others, and were energized by vibrant atmospheres. All of this led to a resurgence of innovative and creative thinking.[96]

© iStockphoto.com/Kirsty Pargeter

5.3 Changing Organizational Cultures

As shown in Exhibit 3.8, organizational cultures exist on three levels.[97] On the first, or surface, level are the reflections of an organization's culture that can be seen and observed, such as symbolic artifacts (for example, dress codes and office layouts) and workers' and managers' behaviors. Next, just below the surface, are the values and beliefs expressed by people in the company. You can't see these values and beliefs, but they become clear if you carefully listen to what people say and observe how decisions are made or explained. Finally, unconsciously held assumptions and beliefs about the company are buried deep below the surface. These are the unwritten views and rules that are so strongly held and so widely shared that they are rarely discussed or even thought about unless someone attempts to change them or unknowingly violates them. Changing such assumptions and beliefs can be very difficult. Instead, managers should focus on the parts of the organizational culture they can control. These include observable surface-level items, such as workers' behaviors and symbolic artifacts, and expressed values and beliefs, which can be influenced through employee selection. Let's see how these can be used to change organizational cultures.

One way of changing a corporate culture is to use behavioral addition or behavioral substitution to establish new patterns of behavior among managers and employees. **Behavioral addition** is the process of having managers and employees perform a new behavior, while **behavioral substitution** is having managers and employees perform a new behavior in place of another behavior. The key in both instances is to choose behaviors that are central to and symbolic of the old culture you're changing and the new culture that you want to create. When Mike Ullman became the CEO of JCPenney, he thought the company's culture was stuck in the nineteenth century (when the company was started). Employees called each other "Mr." and "Mrs."; casual attire was unacceptable even on Fridays; and any elaborate decoration of office cubicles was reported to a team of office police charged with enforcing corporate décor guidelines. Ullman

behavioral addition the process of having managers and employees perform new behaviors that are central to and symbolic of the new organizational culture that a company wants to create.

behavioral substitution the process of having managers and employees perform new behaviors central to the "new" organizational culture in place of behaviors that were central to the "old" organizational culture.

Exhibit 3.8 Three Levels of Organizational Culture

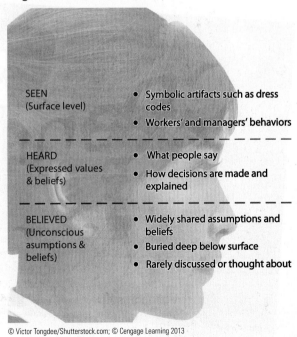

SEEN (Surface level)	• Symbolic artifacts such as dress codes • Workers' and managers' behaviors
HEARD (Expressed values & beliefs)	• What people say • How decisions are made and explained
BELIEVED (Unconscious assumptions & beliefs)	• Widely shared assumptions and beliefs • Buried deep below surface • Rarely discussed or thought about

© Victor Tongdee/Shutterstock.com; © Cengage Learning 2013

quickly determined that the company's stringent code of conduct was, among other things, keeping it from recruiting the talent it needed. Mike Theilmann, the human resources officer, drafted a list of what he called "quick hits," small changes that would have a big impact on the culture. The first of Theilmann's initiatives was a campaign titled "Just Call Me Mike," which he hoped would cure employees of the entrenched practice of calling executives and managers "Mr." and "Mrs." Three JCPenney officers are named Mike, along with nearly 400 other employees at headquarters. Theilmann created posters containing photos of the three executive Mikes along with a list of all the advantages of being on a first-name basis. Top of the list? "First names create a friendly place to shop and work."[98]

Another way in which managers can begin to change corporate culture is to change the **visible artifacts** of their old culture, such as the office design and layout, company dress code, and recipients (or nonrecipients) of company benefits and perks like stock options, personal parking spaces, or the private company dining room. To help anchor the internal culture change at JCPenney, Ullman issued new name badges to all 150,000 JCPenney employees. First names appeared in a large typeface; last names were printed much smaller. He also disbanded the office police, declared that suitable work attire was business casual, and sold or donated most of the 300 pieces in the company's art collection. (He replaced them with pictures of Penney's employees and other company-oriented art.) Most strikingly, Ullman updated founder James Cash Penney's code of conduct and replaced it with one that allows all employees—not just management—to receive the company's traditional Honor, Confidence, Service, Cooperation award for employee loyalty.[99]

Cultures can also be changed by hiring and selecting people with values and beliefs consistent with the company's desired culture. *Selection* is the process of gathering information about job applicants to decide who should be offered a job. As discussed in Chapter 11 on human resources, most selection instruments measure whether job applicants have the knowledge, skills, and abilities needed to succeed in their jobs. But companies are increasingly testing job applicants to determine how they fit with the company's desired culture (i.e., values and beliefs). Management consultant Ram Charan says, "A poor job match is not only harmful to the individual but also to the company."[100] At **Partners + Napier**, an advertising agency, the three most important values are courage, ingenuity, and family. So how do these values carry over into the hiring process? According to CEO Sharon Napier, the ideal candidate is curious, willing to try new things, and wants to learn about the products he or she is working on. According to Napier, "If you don't really want to know how something works, if you don't read a lot, then you're not a very curious person. And in our business you really have to be. If I'm going to put you on an account like Kodak, I want you to learn how to make a photo book. . . . if you're not interested in digging in, then that'll say a lot about you."[101]

The second step is to ensure that applicants fit with the culture by using selection tests, instruments, and exercises to measure these values and beliefs in job applicants. (See Chapter 11

visible artifacts visible signs of an organization's culture, such as the office design and layout, company dress code, and company benefits and perks, like stock options, personal parking spaces, or the private company dining room.

"what's new" companies >

HELLO
my name is
Mike

© AP Images/Dima Gavrysh

for a complete review of applicant and managerial selection.) At Southwest Airlines, humor and a good attitude are two of the most important requirements in its new hires. Cofounder and former CEO and board chair Herb Kelleher says, "What's important is that a customer should get off the airplane feeling: 'I didn't just get from A to B. I had one of the most pleasant experiences I ever had and I'll be back for that reason.'"[102] For instance, a flight attendant on a flight from Houston to Dallas addresses passengers over the speaker system, saying, "Could y'all lean in a little toward the center aisle, please?" Met with confused looks from passengers, he continues, "Just a bit, please. That's it. No, the other way, sir. Thanks. You see, the pilot has to pull out of this space here, and he needs to be able to check the rearview mirrors." On another Southwest plane, Yvonne Masters jokingly introduced her fellow flight attendants as her "former husband and his new girlfriend."[103] Southwest passenger Mark Rafferty said his favorite Southwest flight attendant joke was when "they told everyone on the plane's left side, toward the terminal, to put their faces in the window and smile so our competitors can see what a full flight looks like."[104] Corny, yes, but the humor is exactly what Southwest and its customers want, and the airline gets it by hiring people consistent with its hard-working, fun-loving culture. Says Kelleher, "We draft great attitudes. If you don't have a good attitude, we don't want you, no matter how skilled you are. We can change skill level through training. We can't change attitude."[105]

Corporate cultures are very difficult to change. Consequently, there is no guarantee that any one approach—changing visible cultural artifacts, using behavioral substitution, or hiring people with values consistent with a company's desired culture—will change a company's organizational culture. The best results are obtained by combining these methods. Together, these are some of the best tools managers have for changing culture because they send the clear message to managers and employees that "the accepted way of doing things" has changed.

Organizational Cultures: Creation, Success, and Change   Organizational culture is the set of key values, beliefs, and attitudes shared by organizational members. Organizational cultures are often created by company founders and then sustained through the telling of organizational stories and the celebration of organizational heroes. Adaptable cultures that promote employee involvement, make clear the organization's strategic purpose and direction, and actively define and teach organizational values and beliefs can help companies achieve higher sales growth, return on assets, profits, quality, and employee satisfaction. Organizational cultures exist on three levels: the surface level, where cultural artifacts and behaviors can be observed; just below the surface, where values and beliefs are expressed; and deep below the surface, where unconsciously held assumptions and beliefs exist. Managers can begin to change company cultures by focusing on the top two levels and using behavioral substitution and behavioral addition, changing visible artifacts, and selecting job applicants with values and beliefs consistent with the desired company culture.

Review 5

SELF-ASSESSMENT

Check Your Tolerance For Ambiguity

Think of the difference between playing chess (where you can see all the pieces and anticipate attacks and plan counterattacks) and playing poker (where no one knows anyone else's hand, and you have to make guesses based on your interpretation of opponents' betting patterns). In chess, there is little ambiguity, whereas in poker there is tremendous ambiguity.

Although many people liken business to a game of chess, probably because of the strategic aspects of the game, business is actually more like poker. The business environment is complex and uncertain, and managers never *really* know all the cards the opposition is holding. Managers must learn to adapt to environmental shifts and new developments—sometimes on a daily basis. For some managers, however, this can be a challenging task because everyone has a different comfort level when it comes to ambiguity. For some, not knowing all the details can be a source of significant stress, whereas for others uncertainty can be energizing.

As a manager, you will need to develop an appropriate tolerance for ambiguity. For example, being stressed out every time interest rates change can be counterproductive, but completely ignoring the economic environment can be detrimental to your company's performance.

Complete the following questionnaire to get a sense of your tolerance for ambiguity.[106] Indicate the extent to which you agree with the statements using the following scale:

1 Strongly disagree

2 Moderately disagree

3 Slightly disagree

4 Neutral

5 Slightly agree

6 Moderately agree

7 Strongly agree

1. I don't tolerate ambiguous situations well.
   1   (2)   3   4   5   6   7

2. I find it difficult to respond when faced with an unexpected event.
   1   (2)   3   4   5   6   7

3. I don't think new situations are any more threatening than familiar situations.
   1   2   3   4   5   (6)   7

4. I am drawn to situations that can be interpreted in more than one way.
   1   2   3   4   (5)   6   7

5. I would rather avoid solving problems that must be viewed from several different perspectives.
   1   (2)   3   4   5   6   7

6. I try to avoid situations that are ambiguous.
   (1)   2   3   4   5   6   7

7. I am good at managing unpredictable situations.
   1   2   3   4   5   (6)   7

8. I prefer familiar situations to new ones.
   1   2   3   4   5   (6)   7

9. Problems that cannot be considered from just one point of view are a little threatening.
   1   2   (3)   4   5   6   7

10. I avoid situations that are too complicated for me to easily understand.
    1   (2)   3   4   5   6   7

11. I am tolerant of ambiguous situations.
    1   2   3   4   5   (6)   7

12. I enjoy tackling problems that are complex enough to be ambiguous.
    1   2   3   (4)   5   6   7

13. I try to avoid problems that don't seem to have only one "best" solution.
    1   2   3   (4)   5   6   7

14. I often find myself looking for something new rather than trying to hold things constant in my life.
    1   2   3   4   (5)   6   7

15. I generally prefer novelty over familiarity.
    1   (2)   3   4   5   6   7

16. I dislike ambiguous situations.
    1   (2)   3   4   5   6   7

17. Some problems are so complex that just trying to understand them is fun.

    1   2   3   4   5   6   ⑦

18. I have little trouble coping with unexpected events.

    ①   2   3   4   5   6   7

19. I pursue problem situations that are so complex some people call them "mind-boggling."

    1   2   3   4   5   6   ⑦

20. I find it hard to make a choice when the outcome is uncertain.

    1   2   3   ④   5   6   7

21. I enjoy an occasional surprise.

    1   2   3   4   ⑤   6   7

22. I prefer a situation in which there is some ambiguity.

    1   2   3   4   ⑤   6   7

Scoring

Determine your score by entering your response to each survey item below, as follows. In blanks that say *regular score*, simply enter your response for that item. If your response was a 6, place a 6 in the *regular score* blank. In blanks that say *reverse score*, subtract your response from 8 and enter the result. So if your response was a 6, place a 2 (8 − 6 = 2) in the *reverse score* blank. Add up your total score.

1. regular score   _____

2. regular score   _____

3. reverse score   _____

4. reverse score   _____

5. regular score   _____

6. regular score   _____

7. reverse score   _____

8. regular score   _____

9. regular score   _____

10. regular score   _____

11. regular score   _____

12. reverse score   _____

13. regular score   _____

14. reverse score   _____

15. reverse score   _____

16. regular score   _____

17. reverse score   _____

18. reverse score   _____

19. reverse score   _____

20. regular score   _____

21. reverse score   _____

22. reverse score   _____

    TOTAL = _____

You can find the interpretation for your score at academic.cengage.com/management/Williams.

MANAGEMENT DECISION

No Paved Roads?[107]

"Wow, what a great opportunity!" you thought to yourself after a meeting with your supervisor. After just two short years at your global shipping firm, you've been offered a great promotion, a chance to head up your company's first venture overseas, a sorting and shipping facility in India. You're thrilled at the chance to learn about a new culture and meet different people, but most of all, by the opportunity to produce stunning results for your company by tapping into a rising technological titan that has some of the best minds in the world.

But as you think about how exciting it will be to be the boss in India, you recall the first time you went to visit there and how it seemed utterly impossible to get around conveniently. It was almost like everywhere you went, you had to fight through a mass of cars and people on the pot hole–riddled streets, all fighting for space and maybe a little bit of exhaust-free air. Why, the trip from the airport to your hotel, just barely ten miles, took more than two hours! During monsoon season, all of the potholes would fill with water, making the streets into a small maze of ponds. "How long," you wonder, "would it take for my employees to get to work every morning? To get our trucks to the facility? How long will my drivers have to sit in traffic? Will they be able to handle next-day shipments?"

The Indian government is certainly aware of the problems with the country's infrastructure. In fact, the government has pledged to spend $500 billion by 2012, and $1 trillion by 2017, to improve the country's roads, bridges, rails, and airports. But, as you learn from some research, even all that money may not be enough to make a difference, because the real source of India's infrastructure problems are a lack of civil engineers. Most Indian students opt to study business, computer science, or information technology to take advantage of the growing number of tech firms that are outsourcing to India. Even those trained in civil engineering mostly end up working in tech companies, which pay two or three times more than civil design firms.

The realization slowly sinks in that this is the environment that you will be working in—a place full of skilled people but plagued with terrible roads, traffic, and long travel hours. And your initial excitement at the opportunity slowly melds into anxiety.

Questions

1. Given the external environmental conditions presented by the state of Indian infrastructure, would you choose to open a new facility there? Why or why not?
2. Should your company take action to help improve infrastructure? Or, should it just look for another place to do business?

MANAGEMENT TEAM DECISION

Making a New Culture[108]

Home Depot stores used to be known for customer service. A host of friendly employees would help customers navigate a huge inventory, find exactly what they needed, and even provide detailed instruction. Those days seem long gone, though. Under the leadership of the former CEO, the company shifted its focus away from customer service to reducing inventory and cutting costs. Stores that once had an employee in nearly every aisle are now being manned by just a handful, even during the busiest times. Customers who were used to getting helpful, personal attention can no longer find even a cashier, much less someone can answer their questions on how to use a reciprocating saw.

Marvin Ellison, promoted to CEO in 2008, saw the disastrous results of Home Depot's lack of attention to customers. In the last three months of 2009, the company lost $54 million. To make matters worse, the company's reputation took tremendous hits. For many years, it routinely ranked near the bottom of the University of Michigan's American Customer Satisfaction Index, which measures consumers' evaluations of all major retailers. Even after Home Depot recovered in these rankings slightly, it still lagged far behind competitors like Lowe's and Ace. He had to listen to countless stories of how consumers would drive an extra 30 minutes, even an hour, to avoid going to Home Depot.

To turn things around, Marvin Ellison has committed to a new company vision—a culture that is dedicated to meeting three goals—clean warehouses, stocked shelves, and top customer services. He wants employees to set aside a portion of their shift to do nothing else but take care of customers. He wants to revise evaluations so that employees' performance is reviewed primarily on the basis of customer service. He wants to give financial incentives to employees who provide great service. He wants to reduce the number of messages that stores and employees get from headquarters so that they can focus on customers. In short, he wants to restore Home Depot's reputation for providing the very best in customer service.

Ellison has appointed you to a management team in charge of setting up a training and evaluating program that will get the entire company focused on his vision of customer service. You and your team face the difficult task of changing the entire company's culture so that the entire organization is focused on the customer. How will you do it?

For this Management Team Decision, form a group of three or four with other students, to act as the management team, and answer the questions below.

Questions

1. What kind of training and evaluation program would you institute to change Home Depot's culture?
2. Recall from the text that there are three levels of organizational culture. What kind of changes would you make to address each level?
3. How could an analysis of the company's external environment help in establishing a new customer-based culture?

PRACTICE BEING A MANAGER

Navigating Different Organizational Cultures

Effective managers recognize that organizational culture is an important, often critical, element of organizational health and performance. But recognizing and understanding culture, especially its less visible aspects, is often quite challenging. This exercise will give you some practice in recognizing cultural differences and the challenges and opportunities that managers face as they work with diverse cultures. Suppose that major music recording company Sony BMG has announced plans to hire several college students to form a team that will invest in the "next big things in music." The selected students will be paid $50,000 per year for working part-time. Sony BMG will also allocate up to $10 million for hiring artists, producing records, and so on, based on the team's recommendations.

The new team has been dubbed the Top Wave Team (TWT). If TWT's recommendations are fruitful, the company will sign each member of the team to $150,000 full-time contracts. The company also plans to keep the team together and to give members bonuses and promotions based on their group performance.

Your class has been chosen as the representative college class. The music company is now asking you to form affinity groups by musical preferences in your class (e.g., a Country Music group, an Urban and Hip-Hop group). Each group will nominate one of its members to receive the first $50,000 internship as a TWT team member at Sony BMG. The new TWT group will meet and discuss initial plans and investment recommendations, and then your class will discuss the process and outcomes.

Step 1: Choose your musical affinity. In the class session before this exercise, your professor will ask you to submit a survey form or sheet of paper with your name and your preferred musical genre or identity.

Identify yourself with one of the following musical genres based on (a) preference or affinity ("I prefer this music") and (b) knowledge and understanding ("Of all types of music, I know the most about _____ music/musicians"):

1. Rock
2. Country
3. Religious and Spiritual
4. Urban and Hip-Hop
5. Rap
6. Jazz and R&B
7. Pop and Mainstream
8. Classical
9. Folk and Bluegrass

Your professor will review your submitted preferences and organize affinity groups for the next class session.

Step 2: Organize into groups. Your professor will organize you by musical affinity. If your class is heavily concentrated in one or a few of the musical genres, you may be asked to further divide into smaller groups by subcategories (such as Rock—Heavy Metal and Rock—Popular or Hit).

Step 3: Prepare your recommendations. In groups, discuss what is important about your type of music and what investments the TWT team should make. Keep in mind that the investments made by the TWT team could have a big impact on the future of your favorite music. Recommend a dollar amount or percentage of the $10 million that your representative ought to secure for investment in your genre.

Each group should then select one of its members to receive the internship from Sony BMG and represent the group on the TWT team.

Step 4: Discuss recommendations before the class. Nominees from the musical affinity groups should discuss their recommendations before the class. Those not on the TWT should observe the process and take notes on what happens in this meeting.

Step 5: Hold the team meeting. Your professor will allocate a short time for the initial meeting of the TWT. It may occur before or during the class meeting. After the TWT reaches agreement on how it might allocate its investments by genre (or by some alternative approach), reaches impasse, or reaches the time limit, your professor will call an end to the TWT meeting.

Step 6: Debrief and discuss. As a class, discuss the process and outcomes of this exercise. Consider the following questions and/or others posed by your professor:

- Did you sense some cultural affinity with others who shared your musical tastes? Why or why not?

- What expectations might be associated with choosing someone to "represent" a group on a team such as the TWT?

- What tensions and challenges might face each member of the TWT in a real-life setting of serving on a group that represents various cultures?

DEVELOP YOUR CAREER POTENTIAL

Dealing with the Press

In this age of 24-hour cable news channels, tabloid news shows, and aggressive local and national news reporters intent on exposing corporate wrongdoing, one of the most important skills for a manager to learn is how to deal effectively with the press.[109] Test your ability to deal effectively with the press by putting yourself in the following situations. To make the situation more realistic, read the scenario and then give yourself two minutes to write a response to each question.

Rats Take over Manhattan Taco Bell

The release of Internet footage showed large rats running across the floors, over tables, and climbing onto countertops of a Manhattan Taco Bell. What is most surprising is that the day before the television crew filmed the rats through the restaurant window, New York City health inspectors had given the restaurant a passing grade! The broadcast prompted parent company Yum! Brands to temporarily close that and several other Taco Bell stores owned by franchisee ADF Companies. Based in New Jersey, ADF owns over 350 fast-food franchises in several states.

A TV reporter from Channel 5 has arrived with his camera crew at the Taco Bell you manage in Brooklyn. It's lunchtime, the restaurant is bustling, and the reporter walks right in with his crew and puts you on the spot, asking you whether you will grant a short interview and let him ask questions of a few of your patrons. When you agree, he starts right in with these questions:

1. "Yesterday's filming of rats at an ADF-owned Taco Bell has caused consumers to question the cleanliness of the restaurants where they eat. This restaurant is also owned by ADF Companies. Do you also have problems with rodents?"

2. "Recent outbreaks of E. coli at other Taco Bells in the Northeast were finally attributed to contaminated lettuce, so Taco Bell changed suppliers." [To the cameraman:] "Get the camera in close here [camera zooms into the kitchen area, the slop sink, and the hand-washing station] because I want our viewers to see the kitchen." [Back to you:] "How can consumers be sure that contamination occurred at the produce supplier and not inside filthy restaurants?"

3. "The health inspectors gave a passing grade to the rat-infested Taco Bell just a day before television crews filmed the rats running all over the restaurant. That doesn't instill our viewers with great confidence in the system. Would you be willing to let our camera crews accompany the health inspector during a full inspection of your restaurant so that viewers can see what an inspection entails?"

END NOTES

[1]J. Ball, "Currents—Power Shift: Climate Change: Garbage Gets Fresh Look as Source of Energy," *The Wall Street Journal*, May 15, 2009, A9; J. Fahey, "Waste Not," *Forbes Asia*, July 2010, 46; M. Gunther, "Waste Management's New Direction," *Fortune*, December 6, 2010, 103–108; A. Robinson & D. Schroeder, "Greener and Cheaper: The Conventional Wisdom Is That a Company's Costs Rise as Its Environmental Impact Falls; Think Again," *The Wall Street Journal*, March 23, 2009, R4; "2010 Sustainability Report," Waste Management, accessed February 6, 2011, from www.wm.com/sustainability/pdfs/2010_Sustainability_Report.pdf; "Municipal Solid Waste Generation, Recycling, and Disposal in the United States: Facts and Figures for 2008,"

U.S. Environmental Protection Agency, accessed February 14, 2011, from www.epa.gov/osw/nonhaz/municipal/pubs/msw2008rpt.pdf; and "Zero Waste," Wal-Mart*Corporate, accessed February 15, 2011, from http://walmartstores.com/Sustainability/7762.aspx.

[2]Y. Kane, "Sony CEO Urges Managers to 'Get Mad'; Conference Told That Company Needs to Be More Innovative, Bold," *The Wall Street Journal*, May 23, 2008, B8.

[3]"Industry Profile: Food Distributors," *First Research*, January 24, 2011, accessed February 2, 2011, from www.firstresearch.com/Industry.

[4]B. Fritz, "Once-Hot Nintendo Wii Now Struggling for Sales," *The Los Angeles Times*, November 30, 2010.

[5]N. Wingfield, "Microsoft Net Slips, but Sales Rise as Kinect Proves Popular," *The Wall Street Journal*, January 28, 2011, accessed February 2, 2011, from http://online.wsj.com/article/SB10001424052748704268104576108402196920910.html.

[6]Y. I. Kane & D. Wakabayashi, "Microsoft Puts Gaming Plans in Motion," *The Wall Street Journal*, June 13 2010, accessed June 15, 2010, from http://online.wsj.com/article/SB10001424052748703685404575307082443489528.html?mod=WSJ_hp_editorsPicks_3; and C. Morris, "Video Games Under the Gun," *CNBC*, June 14, 2010, accessed June 15, 2010, from www.cnbc.com/id/37685274/.

[7]E. Romanelli & M. L. Tushman, "Organizational Transformation as Punctuated Equilibrium: An Empirical Test," *Academy of Management Journal* 37 (1994): 1141–1166.

[8]H. Banks, "A Sixties Industry in a Nineties Economy," *Forbes*, May 9, 1994, 107–112.

[9]L. Cowan, "Cheap Fuel Should Carry Many Airlines to More Record Profits for 1st Quarter," *The Wall Street Journal*, April 4, 1998, B17A.

[10]"Annual Revenues and Earnings: U.S. Airlines—All Services," Air Transport Association, accessed January 15, 2005, from www.airlines.org; S. Carey, "Carrier Makes Deeper Cuts as It Seeks Federal Backing Needed to Exit Chapter 11," *The Wall Street Journal*, November 27, 2002, A3; S. Carey, "UAL Will Lay Off 1,500 Workers as Part of Cost-Cutting Strategy," *The Wall Street Journal*, January 6, 2003, A3; D. Carty, "Oral Testimony of Mr. Donald J. Carty, Chairman and CEO, American Airlines: United States Senate, Committee on Commerce, Science, and Transportation," accessed January 9, 2004, from www.amrcorp.com; and S. McCartney, M. Trottman, & S. Carey, "Northwest, Continental, America West Post Losses As Delta Cuts Jobs," *The Wall Street Journal*, November 18, 2002, B4.

[11]"Airlines Still in Upheaval, 5 Years after 9/11," *CNNMoney.com*, September 8, 2006, accessed July 25, 2008, from http://money.cnn.com/2006/09/08/news/companies/airlines_sept11/?postversion=2006090813&eref=yahoo.

[12]B. Jones, "The Changing Dairy Industry," Department of Agricultural & Applied Economics & Center for Dairy Profitability, accessed July 25, 2008, from www.aae.wisc.edu/jones/Presentations/Wisc&TotalDairyTrends.pdf.

[13]B. Stone, "Revenue at Craigslist is said to Top $100 Million," *The New York Times*, June 9, 2009, accessed August 1, 2010, from www.nytimes.com/2009/06/10/technology/internet/10craig.html?_r=1&ref=craigslist.

[14]J. Falls, "What the Wall Street Journal Has, Few Will Match," *Social Media Explorer*, October 30, 2009, accessed August 1, 2010, from www.socialmediaexplorer.com/2009/10/30/what-the-wall-street-journal-has-few-will-match/.

[15]"Samsung Invests $2.1B in LCD Line," *Electronic News*, March 7, 2005; "LG Phillips Develops World's Largest LCD Panel Measuring 100 Inches," NewLaunches.com, March 7, 2006, accessed July 25, 2008, from www.newlaunches.com/archives/lgphilips_develops_worlds_largest_lcd_panel_measuring_100_inches.php; H. Ryoo, "Samsung to Invest $1 Billion in New LCD Production Line," *eWeek*, April 1, 2003, accessed July 25, 2008, from www.eweek.com/c/a/Past-News/Samsung-to-Invest-1-Billion-in-New-LCDProduction-Line; "Samsung Develops World's Largest (820) Full HDTV TFT-LCD," accessed July 25, 2008, from www.samsung.com/us/business/semiconductor/newsView.do?news_id=638; E. Ramstad, "I Want My Flat TV Now!" *The Wall Street Journal*, May 27, 2004, B1; and P. Watt, "LCD Factories Expand," *PC-World*, accessed July 24, 2008, from http://blogs.pcworld.com/staffblog/archives/003369.html.

[16]E. Fyrwald, "The King of Water," interview by G. Colvin, *Fortune*, July 5, 2010, 52–59.

[17]N. Casey, "Tainted Toys Get Another Turn; After Last Year's Recalls, Spin Master and Mega Brands Try Again with New Look," *The Wall Street Journal*, October 31, 2008, B1.

[18]R. Norton, "Where Is This Economy Really Heading?" *Fortune*, August 7, 1995, 54–56.

[19]"CEO Confidence Survey," *The Conference Board*, 9 April 2009, accessed April 27, 2009, from www.conference-board.org.

[20]"Despite Recession, U.S. Small Business Confidence Index Increases Six Points; Small Business Research Board Study Finds Increase in Key Indicators," *U.S. Business Confidence*, February 23, 2009, accessed April 27, 2009, from www.ipasbrb.net.

[21]A. Tsotsis, "Kindle Books Overtake Paperback Books to Become Amazon's Most Popular Format," *TechCrunch*, January 27, 2011, available online at www.techcrunch.com/2011/01/27/kindle-books-overtake-paperback-books-to-become-amazons-most-popular-format/.

[22]T. Tsai & G. Fowler, "Business Technology: Race Heats Up to Supply E-Reader Screens," *The Wall Street Journal*, December 29, 2009, B1.

[23]J. Fletcher, "Extreme Nesting," *The Wall Street Journal*, January 7, 2000, W1.

[24]B. Sackett, "A Shopper for All Seasons; The Workplace Concierge Taking Care of Business," *The Washington Times*, November 30, 2007, C08.

[25]J. Cuneo, "10 Perks We Love," *Inc.*, June 2010, 94–95.

[26]"The Civil Rights Act of 1991," U.S. Equal Employment Opportunity Commission, available online at www.eeoc.gov/policy/cra91.html.

[27]"Compliance Assistance—Family and Medical Leave Act (FMLA),"

U.S. Department of Labor: Employment Standards Administration Wage and Hour Division, accessed July 25, 2005, from www.dol.gov/compliance/laws/comp-fmla.htm [accessed 25 July 2005].

[28]R. J. Bies & T. R. Tyler, "The Litigation Mentality in Organizations: A Test of Alternative Psychological Explanations," *Organization Science* 4 (1993): 352–366.

[29]M. Orey, "Fear of Firing," *Businessweek*, 23 April 2007, 52–62.

[30]S. Gardner, G. Gomes, & J. Morgan, "Wrongful Termination and the Expanding Public Policy Exception: Implications and Advice," *SAM Advanced Management Journal* 65 (2000): 38.

[31]Orey, "Fear of Firing."

[32]Ibid.

[33]"Toyota Settles Accelerator Pedal-Related Accident Suit," *The Wall Street Journal,* September 19, 2010, accessed February 3, 2011, from http://online.wsj.com/article/SB10001424052748703555660457550169380 5105922.html.

[34]"Products Liability Law: An Overview," Legal Information Institute, accessed March 12, 2009, from http://topics.law.cornell.edu/wex/products_liability.

[35]Gerdel, "Liability Suits."

[36]C. Morris, "Activision Battles 'Trolls', Backs Down on Privacy Fears," *CNBC.com*, July 9, 2010, accessed July 10, 2010, from www.cnbc.com/id/38171990/.

[37]R. Johnston & S. Mehra, "Best-Practice Complaint Management," *Academy of Management Experience* 16 (November 2002): 145–154.

[38]D. Smart & C. Martin, "Manufacturer Responsiveness to Consumer Correspondence: An Empirical Investigation of Consumer Perceptions," *Journal of Consumer Affairs* 26 (1992): 104.

[39]H. Appelman, "I Scream, You Scream: Consumers Vent over the Net," *The New York Times*, March 4, 2001.

[40]C. Binkley, "Lucky Numbers: Casino Chain Mines Data on Its Gamblers, and Strikes Pay Dirt—'Secret Recipe'

Lets Harrah's Target Its Low-Rollers At the Individual Level—A Free-Meal 'Intervention,'" *The Wall Street Journal*, May 4, 2000. "Harrah's Hits Customer Loyalty Jackpot: SAS Identifies Customers with Highest Potential to Return," *SAS Customer Success*, accessed February 4, 2011, from www.sas.com.

[41]T. Mullaney, "Harrah's," *Businessweek* (November 24, 2003): 94.

[42]Brian Stelter, "With Summer, Big Cable Channels Keep Getting Bigger," *The New York Times*, August 15, 2010, accessed December 15, 2010, from www.nytimes.com/2010/08/16/business/media/16cable.html.

[43]S. A. Zahra & S. S. Chaples, "Blind Spots in Competitive Analysis," *Academy of Management Executive* 7 (1993): 7–28.

[44]"The Cola Wars: Over a Century of Cola Slogans, Commercials, Blunders, and Coups," available at www.geocities.com/colacentury/.

[45]M. Frazier, "You Suck: Dyson, Hoover and Oreck Trade Accusations in Court, on TV as Brit Upstart Leaves Rivals in Dust," *Advertising Age*, July 25, 2005, 1.

[46]J. M. Moran, "Getting Closer Together—Videophones Don't Deliver TV Quality Sound, Visuals, but They're Improving," *Seattle Times*, March 15, 1998.

[47]D. Searcey, "Cable's Picture Gets Fuzzier; Market Leader Comcast's Stock Is Hit as Phone Companies Make Gains," *The Wall Street Journal*, November 8, 2007, B3.

[48]E. Fowler & A. Sharma, "Skype to Launch iPhone Software—Net-Calling Unit of eBay to Compete More Directly with Wireless Carriers," *The Wall Street Journal*, March 30, 2009, B2.

[49]Ryan Kim, "Vonage Call App Uses Facebook, No Minutes," SFGate.com, August 6, 2010, accessed October 12, 2010, from http://articles.sfgate.com/2010-08-06/business/22205815_1_facebook-call-phone-rings.

[50]R. Broida, "Replace Your Landline with $199 Ooma Telo," *The Cheapskate*, July 12, 2010, accessed February 5, 2011, from www.cnet.com/8301-13845_3-20010241-58.html.

[51]K. G. Provan, "Embeddedness, Interdependence, and Opportunism in Organizational Supplier-Buyer Networks," *Journal of Management* 19 (1993): 841–856.

[52]B. Preuschoff & P. McGroarty, "Rare Earth Shortages Hit Germany," *The Wall Street Journal*, October 26, 2010, accessed February 10, 2011, from http://online.wsj.com/article/SB10001424052702303341904575576162454449250.html.

[53]Y. Hayashi & J. Areddy, "Japan Scrambles for Rare Earth—Tokyo Seeks to Sidestep Reliance on Uncertain Supplies From China; Issue a Priority Elsewhere, Too," *The Wall Street Journal,*" October 25, 2010, A10.

[54]M. Dalton, "AB InBev Suppliers Feel Squeeze," *The Wall Street Journal*, April 17, 2009, B2.

[55]D. Birch, "Staying on Good Terms," *Supply Management*, April 12, 2001, 36.

[56]S. Parker & C. Axtell, "Seeing Another Viewpoint: Antecedents and Outcomes of Employee Perspective Taking," *Academy of Management Journal* 44 (2001): 1085–1100; and B. K. Pilling, L. A. Crosby, & D. W. Jackson, "Relational Bonds in Industrial Exchange: An Experimental Test of the Transaction Cost Economic Framework," *Journal of Business Research* 30 (1994): 237–251.

[57]"Carmakers Eye Economy with Unease," *USA Today*, May 24, 2004, B.06.

[58]"Title 25 Health Services Part 1: Texas Department of Health Chapter 229, Food and Drug Subchapter U, Permitting Retail Food Establishments," Texas Department of Health, accessed February 11, 2003, from www.tdh.state.tx.us/bfds/retail/permittingrules.html.

[59]M. Horn, "Sinning in an SUV," *U.S. News & World Report*, December 16, 2002, 10; and CAFE Overview: Frequently Asked Questions, accessed March 12, 2009, from www.nhtsa.dot.gov/cars/rules/cafe/overview.htm.

[60]P. Fairley, "The New CAFE Standards," *ABC News*, January 15, 2008, accessed May 10, 2009, from http://abcnews.go.com.

[61]James G. Tillen & Sonia M. Delman "A Bribe by Any Other Name"

Forbes.com. 28 May 2010, accessed December 10, 2010, from www .forbes.com/2010/05/28/bribery-slang-jargon-leadership-managing-compliance_2.html.

[62]"Seafood HACCP," U.S. Food and Drug Administration Center for Food Safety & Applied Nutrition, accessed March 12, 2009, www.cfsan.fda. gov/~comm/haccpsea.html.

[63]N. Casey & M. Trottman, "Toys Containing Banned Plastics Still on Market; Restrictions on Phthalates Don't Take Effect Until '09; Fears of Reproductive Defects," *The Wall Street Journal*, October 23, 2008, D1.

[64]S. Dudley, "The Coming Shift in Regulation," *Regulation*, October 1, 2002.

[65]S. Dudley, "Regulation and Small Business Competitive," *Federal Document Clearing House*, Congressional Testimony, Prepared Remarks for the House Committee on Small Business Subcommittee on Regulatory Reform and Oversight, May 20, 2004.

[66]H. Morley, "Bush Orders Cut in Regulations—Change Will Cut Red Tape for Small Businesses," *Knight-Ridder Tribune*, August 17, 2002.

[67]"EU's Aggressive Anti-Smoking Campaign," *Creative Bits*, http:// creativebits.org/eus_agressive_anti-smoking_campaign, January 17, 2005.

[68]M. Hughlett, "PETA Targets McDonald's over Slaughter of Chickens," *The Chicago Tribune*, February 16, 2009, accessed May 10, 2009, from www.Chicagotribune.com.

[69]S. Simon & J. Jargon, "PETA Ads to Target McDonald's," *The Wall Street Journal,* May 1, 2009, B7.

[70]Rich Blake, "Boycotting BP: Who Gets Hurt?" ABCNews. com. Jun 2 2010, accessed February 5, 2011, from http://abcnews. go.com/Business/bp-boycotts-spreading-frustration-oil-spill-boils/ story?id=10800309.

[71]"AHA Environmental Scan 2010," American Hospital Association, accessed February 5, 2010, from www.hhnmag.com/hhnmag_app/gate-Fold/pages/SEPTEMBER09.jsp.

[72]B. Bold, "Gatorade Takes Social Media Seriously with 'Mission Control Center,'" *The Wall*, June 17, 2010, accessed August 5, 2010, from www.wallblog.co.uk/2010/06/17/gatorade-takes-social-media-seriously-with-mission-control-center/.

[73]D. F. Jennings & J. R. Lumpkin, "Insights between Environmental Scanning Activities and Porter's Generic Strategies: An Empirical Analysis," *Journal of Management* 4 (1992): 791–803.

[74]S. Greenhouse, "Factory Defines Sweatshop Label, but Can It Thrive?" *The New York Times*, July 18, 2010, BU1.

[75]Ibid.

[76]E. Jackson & J. E. Dutton, "Discerning Threats and Opportunities," *Administrative Science Quarterly* 33 (1988): 370–387.

[77]B. Thomas, S. M. Clark, & D. A. Gioia, "Strategic Sensemaking and Organizational Performance: Linkages among Scanning, Interpretation, Action, and Outcomes," *Academy of Management Journal* 36 (1993): 239–270.

[78]R. Daft, J. Sormunen, & D. Parks, "Chief Executive Scanning, Environmental Characteristics, and Company Performance: An Empirical Study," *Strategic Management Journal* 9 (1988): 123–139; V. Garg, B. Walters, & R. Priem, "Chief Executive Scanning Emphases, Environmental Dynamism, and Manufacturing Firm Performance," *Strategic Management Journal* 24 (2003): 725–744; and D. Miller & P. H. Friesen, "Strategy-Making and Environment: The Third Link," *Strategic Management Journal* 4 (1983): 221–235.

[79]A. Sharma, "AT&T, Verizon Make Different Calls," *The Wall Street Journal*, January 29, 2009, B1; and N. Worden & V. Kumar, "Earnings: Comcast Feels the Strain of Economic Slump," *The Wall Street Journal*, February 19, 2009, B7.

[80]D. Ionescu, "Update: Apple Hits 1 Billion App Store Downloads," *PC World*, April 24, 2009, accessed May 10, 2009, from www.pcworld.com/ article/163785/update_apple_hits_1_billion_app_store_downloads.html.

[81]D. Wakabayashi & C. Lawton, "Sony Turns Focus to Low-Cost Video Camera," *The Wall Street Journal*, April 16, 2009, B9.

[82]Y. Kane, "Sony's Newest Display Is a Culture Shift," *The Wall Street Journal*, May 8, 2008, B1.

[83]P. Elmer-DeWitt, "Mine, All Mine; Bill Gates Wants a Piece of Everybody's Action, but Can He Get It?" *Time*, June 5, 1995.

[84]D. M. Boje, "The Storytelling Organization: A Study of Story Performance in an Office-Supply Firm," *Administrative Science Quarterly* 36 (1991): 106–126.

[85]S. Walton & J. Huey, *Sam Walton: Made in America* (New York: Doubleday, 1992).

[86]D. Rushe, "Wal-Martians," *Sunday Times* (London), June 10, 2001, 5.

[87]E. Thornton, "Perform or Perish," *Businessweek*, November 5, 2007, 38–45.

[88]D. R. Denison & A. K. Mishra, "Toward a Theory of Organizational Culture and Effectiveness," *Organization Science* 6 (1995): 204–223.

[89]S. Rosenbaum, "The Happiness Culture: Zappos Isn't a Company—It's a Mission," *Fast Company*, June 6, 2010, accessed August 5, 2010, from www.fastcompany.com/1657030/the-happiness-culture-zappos-isn-t-a-company-it-s-a-mission.

[90]F. Haley, "Mutual Benefit: How Does Genencor Maintain Its Incredibly Loyal Workforce? By Involving Its Employees in Almost Everything," *Fast Company*, October 2004, 98–100.

[91]"Changing Diabetes," Norvo Nordisk, August 4, 2010, from http:// changingdiabetes.novonordisk.com/.

[92]S. Yearout, G. Miles, & R. Koonce, "Multi-Level Visioning," *Training & Development*, March 1, 2001, 31.

[93]T. Hsieh, "Corner Office: On a Scale of 1 to 10, How Weird Are You?" interview by A. Bryant, *The New York Times*, January 9, 2010, accessed June 1, 2010, from www.nytimes.com/2010/01/10/ business/10corner.html.

[94]A. Zuckerman, "Strong Corporate Cultures and Firm Performance: Are There Trade-offs?" *Academy of Management Executive*, November 2002, 158–160.

[95]*McDonald's Summary Annual Report 2005*, 2–4; and D. Stires, "McDonald's Keeps Right on Cooking," *Fortune*, May 17, 2004, 102.

[96]Dana Mattioli, "New Room, New Vantage Point," *The Wall Street Journal*, March 8, 2010, B7.

[97]E. Schein, *Organizational Culture and Leadership*, 2nd ed. (San Francisco: Jossey-Bass, 1992).

[98]E. Byron, "'Call Me Mike!'—To Attract and Keep Talent, JCPenney CEO Loosens Up Once-Formal Workplace," *The Wall Street Journal*, March 27, 2006, B1.

[99]Ibid.

[100]C. Daniels, "Does This Man Need a Shrink? Companies Are Using Psychological Testing to Screen Candidates for Top Jobs," *Fortune*, February 5, 2001, 205.

[101]Adam Bryant, "On Her Team, It's All About Bench Strength," *The New York Times*, May 8, 2010, accessed November 11, 2011, from www

.nytimes.com/2010/05/09/business/09corner.html.

[102]S. Chakravarty, "Hit 'Em Hardest with the Mostest (Southwest Airlines' Management)," *Forbes*, September 16, 1991, 48.

[103]R. Suskind, "Humor Has Returned to Southwest Airlines after 9/11 Hiatus," *The Wall Street Journal*, January 13, 2003, A1.

[104]Ibid.

[105]K. Godsey, "Slow Climb to New Heights; Combine Strict Discipline with Goofy Antics and Make Billions," *Success*, October 1, 1996, 20.

[106]D. L. McCain, "The MSTAT-I: A New Measure of an Individual's Tolerance for Ambiguity," *Educational and Psychological Measurement*, 53 (1993): 183–190.

[107]Vikas Bajaj, "A High-Tech Titan Plagued by Potholes," *The New York Times*, August 25, 2010, accessed September 9, 2010, from

www.nytimes.com/2010/08/26/business/global/26engineer.html.

[108]The American Customer Satisfaction Index: www.theacsi.org/; and Jena McGregor "Putting Home Depot's House in Order." *Businessweek*, May 18, 2009, 54.

[109]K. Maher, "For Some Co-Workers, Bringing Fido to Office Has Become Pet Peeve," *The Wall Street Journal*, January 12, 2005, B1; "Making the Office Pet Friendly," *Plant Sites & Parks*, February 2001, 11; S. Linstedt, "Pets at Work Is Gnawing Subject for Many Buffalo, N.Y., Firms," *Buffalo News*, September 30, 2002; M. M. Perotin, "Some Fort Worth, Texas–Area Employers Allow Pets at Work," *Fort Worth Star-Telegram*, August 12, 2002; P. Lopes Harris, "Firms Begin to Ban Pets at Work," *San Jose Mercury News*, January 2, 2001; and J. Saranow, "Anybody Want to Take a Nap? Fun Perks Didn't End with the Dot-Com Bust—They Just Changed," *The Wall Street Journal*, January 25, 2005, R5.

© iStockphoto.com/Oner Döngel

BIZ FLIX

Charlie Wilson's War

"Good-Time" Charlie Wilson (Tom Hanks) is a Democratic Congressman from East Texas with a reputation for partying, drinking, and womanizing. When Afghanistan rebels against the Soviet troop invasion in the 1980s, Wilson becomes the unlikely champion of the Afghan cause through his role in two major congressional committees that deal with foreign policy and covert operations. Julia Roberts plays the Houston socialite and conservative political activist Joanne Herring, who urges Wilson to help the rebels. Wilson's covert dealings with the rebels have some unforeseen and long-reaching effects, however. In this clip from the beginning of the movie, Charlie Wilson is at work in the Capitol Building, on his way to chambers where he's about to cast a vote.

© GreenLight

What to Watch for and Ask Yourself

1. This chapter discussed organizational culture as having three levels of visibility. Visible artifacts are at the first level and are the easiest to see. Which visible artifacts did you observe in this sequence?

2. Values appear at the next level of organizational culture. You can infer a culture's values from the behavior of organizational members. Which values appear in this sequence?

3. Organizational members will unconsciously behave according to the basic assumptions of an organization's culture. You also infer these from observed behavior. Which basic assumptions appear in this sequence?

MANAGEMENT WORKPLACE

Camp Bow Wow: The Environment and Corporate Culture

In ten years, Camp Bow Wow has grown from a single kennel in Denver, Colorado, to a $40 million business, with more than 150 locations. The transition from a small family business to a national chain, however, required a shift from a family-based culture to a business- and performance-based culture. A key element of of Camp Bow Wow's culture is the staff's deep emotional connection with animals. The connection is immediately apparent at corporate headquarters, where offices are bustling with employees and pets alike. According to founder Heidi Ganahal, "What we do is focus on what's important to us, and that's the animals."

© Cengage Learning

Discussion Questions

1. What aspects of Camp Bow Wow's corporate culture reflect the surface level of the organizational culture? What aspects reflect the values and beliefs? What aspects reflect the unconsciously held assumptions and beliefs?

2. Why did Camp Bow Wow have to change its culture when it became a national franchise?

3. What impact does Heidi Ganahl's personal story have on employees at Camp Bow Wow?

CHAPTER 4

Ethics and Social Responsibility

Learning Outcomes

1. Discuss how the nature of management jobs creates the possibility for ethical abuses.

2. Identify common kinds of workplace deviance.

3. Describe the U.S. Sentencing Commission Guidelines for Organizations, and explain how they both encourage ethical behavior and punish unethical behavior by businesses.

4. Describe what influences ethical decision making.

5. Explain what practical steps managers can take to improve ethical decision making.

6. Explain to whom organizations are socially responsible.

7. Explain for what organizations are socially responsible.

8. Explain how organizations can choose to respond to societal demands for social responsibility.

9. Explain whether social responsibility hurts or helps an organization's economic performance.

what would **you do?**

American Express Headquarters, New York, New York[1]

With medical costs rising 10 to 15 percent per year, one of the members of your Board of Directors at **American Express** mentioned that some companies are now refusing to hire smokers and that the board should discuss this option at the next month's meeting. Nationwide, about 6,000 companies refuse to hire smokers. Weyco, an employee benefits company in Okemos, Michigan, requires all applicants to take a nicotine test. Weyco's CFO says, "We're not saying people can't smoke. We're just saying they can't smoke and work here. As an employee-benefits company, we need to take a leadership role in helping people understand the cost impact of smoking." The Cleveland Clinic, one of the top hospitals in the United States, doesn't hire smokers. Paul Terpeluk, the director of corporate and employee health, says that all applicants are tested for nicotine and that 250 people have lost job opportunities because they smoke. The Massachusetts Hospital Association also refuses to hire smokers. The company's CEO says, "Smoking is a personal choice, and as an employer I have a personal choice within the law about who we hire and who we don't."

As indicated by your board member, costs are driving the trend not to hire smokers. According to the U.S. Centers for Disease Control, a smoker costs about $4,000 more a year to employ because of increased health-care costs and lost productivity. Breaking that down, a smoker will have 50 percent higher absenteeism, and, when present, will work 39 fewer minutes per day because of smoke breaks, which leads to 1,817 lost hours of annual productivity. A smoker will have higher accident rates, cause $1,000 a year in property damage (from cigarette burns and smoke damage), and will cost up to $5,000 more a year for annual insurance premiums. John Banzhaf, executive director of an antismoking group in Washington, and a law professor at George Washington University, says, "Smoking is the biggest factor in controllable health-care costs."

Although few would disagree about the costs, others argue it is wrong not to hire smokers. Jay Whitehead, publisher of a magazine for human resources managers, says, "There is discrimination at many companies—and maybe even most companies—against people who smoke." Even if applicants aren't asked whether they smoke, it "doesn't mean that hiring managers turn off

© DANNY MOLOSHOK/Landov

study tips

Every chapter in this book contains diagrams and tables to illustrate the text material. One good way to study is to try to re-create the exhibit from scratch on your own. Draw a blank diagram, fill it in, and then check your work by comparing your worksheet with the original exhibit in the chapter.

© iStockphoto.com/Ivan Burmistrov

© iStockphoto.com/Alex Slobodkin

121

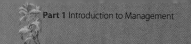

their sense of smell." Paul Sherer, a smoker who was fired less than a week after taking a new job, says, "Not hiring smokers affects millions of people and puts them in the same category as women able to bear children, that is, people who contribute to higher health-care costs. It's unfair." Law professor Don Garner believes that not hiring smokers is "an overreaction on the part of employers whose interest is cutting costs. If someone has the ability to do the job, he should get it. What you do in your home is your own business. . . . Not hiring smokers is 'respiratory apartheid.'"

Well, with the meeting just a month away, you've got to prepare for the Board of Directors' questions. For example, on what basis should the company decide whether to hire smokers? Should the decision be based on what's in the best interest of the firm, what the law allows, or what affirms and respects individual rights? The Board is interested in making good decisions for the company, but "doing the right thing" is also one of its core values. Next, is this an issue of ethics or social responsibility? Ethical decision making is concerned with doing right and avoiding wrong, whereas social responsibility is a business's obligation to pursue policies, make decisions, and take actions that benefit society. Finally, given that it so much cheaper not to hire smokers, the board will want to know whether refusing to hire smokers is a form of discrimination.

If you were in charge at American Express, what would you do?

The dilemma facing American Express, is an example of the tough decisions involving ethics and social responsibility that managers face. Unfortunately, no matter what you decide to do, someone or some group will be unhappy with the outcome. Managers don't have the luxury of choosing theoretically optimal, win–win solutions that are obviously desirable to everyone involved. In practice, solutions to ethics and social responsibility problems aren't optimal. Often, managers must be satisfied with a solution that just makes do or does the least harm. Rights and wrongs are rarely crystal clear to managers charged with doing the right thing. The business world is much messier than that.

We begin this chapter by examining ethical behavior in the workplace and explaining how unethical behavior can expose a business to penalties under the U.S. Sentencing Commission Guidelines for Organizations. Second, we examine the influences on ethical decision making and review practical steps managers can take to improve ethical decision making. We finish by considering to whom organizations are socially responsible, for what organizations are socially responsible, how organizations can respond to societal expectations for social responsibility, and whether social responsibility hurts or helps an organization's economic performance.

What Is Ethical and Unethical Workplace Behavior?

Ethics is the set of moral principles or values that defines right and wrong for a person or group. Unfortunately, numerous studies have consistently produced distressing results about the state of ethics in today's business world. A Society of Human Resources Management Survey found that only 27 percent of employees

ethics the set of moral principles or values that defines right and wrong for a person or group.

felt that their organization's leadership was ethical.[2] In a study of 1,324 randomly selected workers, managers, and executives across multiple industries, 48 percent of the respondents admitted to actually committing an unethical or illegal act in the past year! These acts included cheating on an expense account, discriminating against coworkers, forging signatures, paying or accepting kickbacks, and looking the other way when environmental laws were broken.[3] Clearly, with widely publicized corporate scandals, such as when Bernie Madoff used a pyramid scheme to bilk investors out of $13 billion, and with companies losing an average of 7 percent of their annual revenues to corporate fraud, business ethics is a serious and widespread problem.[4]

© TIMOTHY A. CLARY/AFP/Getty Images

Other studies contain good news. When people believe their work environment is ethical, they are six times more likely to stay with that company than if they believe they work in an unethical environment.[5] One study asked 570 white-collar workers which of 28 qualities were important in company leaders. The results? Honesty (24%) and integrity/morals/ethics (16%) ranked by far the highest. (Caring/compassion was third at 7%).[6] According to Eduardo Castro-Wright, vice chairman of Walmart Stores, "There's nothing that destroys credibility more than not being able to look someone in the eye and have them know that they can trust you."[7] In short, much needs to be done to make workplaces more ethical, but—and this is very important—most managers and employees want this to happen.

After reading the next three sections, you should be able to

1. *Discuss how the nature of management jobs creates the possibility for ethical abuses.*
2. *Identify common kinds of workplace deviance.*
3. *Describe the U.S. Sentencing Commission Guidelines for Organizations, and explain how they both encourage ethical behavior and punish unethical behavior by businesses.*

1 Ethics and the Nature of Management Jobs

Ethical behavior follows accepted principles of right and wrong. By contrast, unethical management behavior occurs when managers personally violate accepted principles of right and wrong—for example, by lying about company profits or knowingly producing an unsafe product—or encourage others to do so. Because of the nature of their jobs, managers can be tempted to engage in unethical managerial behavior in four areas: authority and power, handling information, influencing the behavior of others, and setting goals.

The *authority and power* inherent in some management positions can tempt managers to engage in unethical practices. Because they often control company resources, there is a risk that some managers will cross the line from legitimate use to personal use of these resources. For example, treating a client to dinner is a common and legitimate business practice in many companies. But what about treating

ethical behavior behavior that conforms to a society's accepted principles of right and wrong.

a client to a ski trip? Taking the company jet to attend a business meeting in San Diego is legitimate. But how about using the jet to come home to Chicago by way of Honolulu? Human resources can be misused as well. For example, unless it's in an employee's job description, using an employee to do personal chores, like picking up the manager's dry cleaning, is unethical behavior. Even worse, though, is using one's managerial authority and power for direct personal gain as some managers have done by using corporate funds to pay for extravagant personal parties, lavish home decorating, jewelry, or expensive works of art.

Handling information is another area in which managers must be careful to behave ethically. Information is a key part of management work, because managers collect it, analyze it, act on it, and disseminate it. In doing so, they are expected to be truthful and, when necessary, to keep confidential information confidential. Leaking company secrets to competitors, doctoring the numbers, wrongfully withholding information, and lying are some of the ways managers may misuse information entrusted to them. Satyam Computer is a leading Indian outsourcing and software company that serves more than a third of the *Fortune* 500 companies and the U.S. government. After years of "doctoring" the books, chairman and cofounder Ramalinga Raju finally admitted that he overstated profits and revenues and created a fake cash balance of $1 billion in hopes of making the company appear more successful than it was so it could attract more business and investment.[8]

Managers must also be careful to behave ethically in the way they *influence the behavior of others*, especially those they supervise. Managerial work gives managers significant power to influence others. If managers tell employees to perform unethical acts (or face punishment), such as faking the numbers to get results, they are abusing their managerial power. This is sometimes called the "move it or lose it" syndrome. "Move it or lose it" managers tell employees, "Do it. You're paid to do it. If you can't do it, we'll find somebody who can."[9] A study of 400 managers found that the "move it or lose it" syndrome even affects top managers. Forty-seven percent of the corporate executives in this study said they would be willing to commit financial fraud by understating accounting write-offs that reduced company profits. Tulane University business professor Art Brief, who conducted the study, says, "People in subordinate roles will comply with their superiors even when that includes wrongdoing that goes against their individual moral code. I thought they would stick with their values, but most organizations are structured to produce obedience."[10]

Although managers can influence their employees' behavior through direct order, they can also do so more indirectly through the *goals they set*. If managers set unrealistic goals, the pressure to perform and achieve those goals can influence employees to engage in unethical business behaviors, especially if they are just short of meeting their goals or a deadline.[11] Pressure to engage in unethical business practices was intense at **Galleon Group**, a hedge fund where stock traders were pushed to get illegal inside information about the performance of companies that gave them an advantage in buying and selling stocks. For example, according to the Securities and Exchange Commission, Galleon paid an analyst at a San Francisco investment firm who illegally told them, before public statements were released, what Google's quarterly profits would be. Once, when Google's profits unexpectedly decreased, Galleon shorted the stock, that is, bet that Google's stock would decrease in price, and earned $9 million on the trade. Galleon's aggressive investment goals led its senior managers and traders to berate, punish, and fire analysts who couldn't produce inside information. A former Galleon trader said, "Get an edge or you're gone." So far, 19 of the 26 defendants associated with Galleon's insider trading scandal have pled guilty.[12]

"what's new" companies >

Ethics and the Nature of Management Jobs   Ethics is the set of moral principles or values that define right and wrong. Ethical behavior occurs when managers follow those principles and values. Because they set the standard for others in the workplace, managers can model ethical behavior by using resources for company business and not for personal gain. Furthermore, managers can encourage ethical behavior by handling information in a confidential and honest fashion, not using their authority to influence others to engage in unethical behavior, and setting reasonable rather than unreasonable goals.

Review 1

2 Workplace Deviance

Depending on which study you look at, one-third to three-quarters of all employees admit that they have stolen from their employers, committed computer fraud, embezzled funds, vandalized company property, sabotaged company projects, faked injuries to receive workers' compensation benefits or insurance, or been "sick" from work when they weren't really sick. Experts estimate that unethical behaviors like these, which researchers call *workplace deviance*, may cost companies as much as $1 trillion a year, or roughly 7 percent of their revenues.[13] **Workplace deviance** is unethical behavior that violates organizational norms about right and wrong. As Exhibit 4.1 shows, workplace deviance can be categorized by how deviant the behavior is, from minor to serious, and by the target of the deviant behavior, either the organization or particular people in the workplace.[14] One kind of workplace deviance, called **production deviance**, hurts the quality and quantity of work produced.

Exhibit 4.1   Types of Workplace Deviance

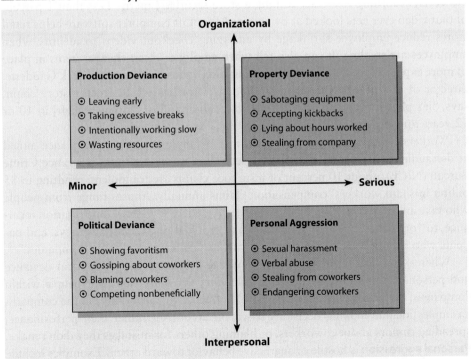

Source: "A Typology of Deviant Workplace Behaviors" (Figure), S. L. Robinson & R. J. Bennett, *Academy of Management Journal*, 1995, vol. 38. Reproduced with permission of Academy of Management (NY) in the formats Textbook and Other Book via Copyright Clearance Center.

workplace deviance unethical behavior that violates organizational norms about right and wrong.

production deviance unethical behavior that hurts the quality and quantity of work produced.

Examples include leaving early, taking excessively long work breaks, intentionally working slower, or wasting resources.

Property deviance is unethical behavior aimed at company property or products. Examples include sabotaging, stealing, damaging equipment or products, and overcharging for services and then pocketing the difference. For example, Karin Wilson, who owns the Page and Palette bookstore in Fairhope, Alaska, found that her bookkeeper was using the bookstore's company credit card to pay off her personal credit card and also writing checks to herself instead of paying publishers. In all, Wilson estimates that her bookkeeper made off with $150,000.[15] Employee stealing is more widespread than you'd think. A survey of 24 large retailers employing 2.3 million workers found that 1 out of 28 employees were caught stealing each year.[16] Likewise, 58 percent of office workers acknowledge taking company property for personal use, according to a survey conducted for Lawyers.com.[17]

Sometimes, property deviance involves the sabotage of company property. Vitek Boden worked for an information technology company that installed a computer system for Maroochy Shire sewage control, a local waste management company in Australia. After he applied for a job at Maroochy and was turned down, he used his technology skills and inside information (from installing their computer system) to release millions of gallons of raw sewage into local parks and rivers and a nearby hotel.[18] Boden, who admitted to conducting the "electronic revenge attacks," was sentenced to two years in jail.

Theft of company merchandise by employees, called **employee shrinkage**, is another common form of property deviance. Employee shrinkage costs U.S. retailers more than $19.5 billion a year, and employees steal more merchandise (47%) than shoplifters (32%).[19] "Sweethearting" occurs when employees discount or don't ring up merchandise their family or friends bring to the cash register. In "dumpster diving," employees unload trucks, stash merchandise in a dumpster, and then retrieve it after work.[20]

To prevent employee theft, most retail stores have cameras above checkout lanes. However, according to Malay Kundu, a store security expert, "Less than 1 percent of that video ever gets looked at by anyone." StopLift computer software helps retail stores reduce employee shrinkage by analyzing checkout videos to identify when employees are stealing. It can also tell when employees scan cheaper items in place of more expensive items, or when they scan three items but bag four. Mark Gaudette, director of loss prevention for Big Y Foods, a northeast U.S. grocery store chain, says, "It's probably the first breakthrough technology [for employee theft] in 10 or 12 years for our world."[21]

Workers' compensation fraud is another example of property deviance aimed at defrauding and hurting a company. According to the National Insurance Crime Bureau (NICB), about 10 percent of insurance claims are fraudulent, resulting in $5 billion in sham workers' compensation claims annually. Abuses range from people who fake an injury while on the job in order to collect workers' compensation insurance, to "organized criminal conspiracies of crooked physicians, attorneys, and patients who submit false and exaggerated medical claims to insurance companies."[22]

Whereas production and property deviance harm companies, political deviance and personal aggression are unethical behaviors that hurt particular people within companies. **Political deviance** is using one's influence to harm others in the company. Examples include making decisions based on favoritism rather than performance, spreading rumors about coworkers, or blaming others for mistakes they didn't make. **Personal aggression** is hostile or aggressive behavior toward others. Examples include sexual harassment, verbal abuse, stealing from coworkers, or personally threatening coworkers. One of the fastest-growing kinds of personal aggression is workplace violence. For example, an employee at Hartford Distributors, a beer distributorship in

property deviance unethical behavior aimed at the organization's property or products.

employee shrinkage employee theft of company merchandise.

political deviance using one's influence to harm others in the company.

personal aggression hostile or aggressive behavior toward others.

Hartford, Connecticut, was suspected of stealing beer. When he was called in for a disciplinary meeting and fired, he shot and killed eight workers and himself as he was being escorted from the building.[23] Violence in the workplace, however, isn't committed only by disgruntled employees. A man broke into headquarters of Discovery Channel armed with guns and explosives, taking multiple hostages before SWAT officers killed him. In an online message posted before the incident, he wrote that he hated the cable channel for broadcasting reality shows that encourage population growth, and that its environmental programming did little to help save the planet.[24]

More than 2 million Americans are victims of some form of workplace violence each year. According to a U.S. Bureau of Labor Statistics (BLS) survey of 7.4 million U.S. companies, 5.4 percent of all employees suffered an incident of workplace violence each year.[25] Between 525 and 1,000 people are actually killed at work each year.[26] Of those, 450 to 550 are typically homicides.[27] Store owners and company managers are killed most often, although many victims, as might be expected, are police officers, security guards, or taxi drivers.[28] For more information on workplace violence, see the BLS website, www.bls.gov/iif/osh_wpvs.htm.

Workplace Deviance   Workplace deviance is behavior that violates important organizational norms about right and wrong and harms the organization or its workers. Production deviance and property deviance harm the company, whereas political deviance and personal aggression harm individuals within the company.

Review 2

---

3 U.S. Sentencing Commission Guidelines for Organizations

A male supervisor is sexually harassing female coworkers. A sales representative offers a $10,000 kickback to persuade an indecisive customer to do business with his company. A company president secretly meets with the CEO of her biggest competitor, and they agree not to compete in markets where the other has already established customers. Each of these behaviors is clearly unethical (and in these cases also illegal). Historically, if management was unaware of such activities, the company could not be held responsible for them. Since 1991, however, when the U.S. Sentencing Commission Guidelines for Organizations were established, companies can be prosecuted and punished *even if management didn't know about the unethical behavior.* Penalties can be substantial, with maximum fines approaching a whopping $300 million.[29] An amendment made in 2004 outlines much stricter ethics training requirements and emphasizes creating a legal and ethical company culture.[30]

Let's examine **3.1 to whom the guidelines apply and what they cover** and **3.2 how, according to the guidelines, an organization can be punished for the unethical behavior of its managers and employees.**

3.1 Who, What, and Why?

Nearly all businesses are covered by the U.S. Sentencing Commission's guidelines. This includes nonprofits, partnerships, labor unions, unincorporated organizations and associations, incorporated organizations, and even pension funds, trusts, and joint stock companies. If your organization can be characterized as a business (remember, nonprofits count, too), then it is subject to the guidelines.[31]

The guidelines cover offenses defined by federal laws such as invasion of privacy, price fixing, fraud, customs violations, antitrust violations, civil rights violations, theft, money laundering, conflicts of interest, embezzlement, dealing in stolen goods, copyright infringements, extortion, and more. But it's not enough merely to stay within the law. The purpose of the guidelines is not just to punish companies *after* they or their employees break the law, but rather to encourage companies to take proactive steps that will discourage or prevent white-collar crime *before* it happens. The guidelines also give companies an incentive to cooperate with and disclose illegal activities to federal authorities.[32]

3.2 Determining the Punishment

The guidelines impose smaller fines on companies that take proactive steps to encourage ethical behavior or voluntarily disclose illegal activities to federal authorities. Essentially, the law uses a carrot-and-stick approach. The stick is the threat of heavy fines that can total millions of dollars. The carrot is a greatly reduced fine, but only if the company has started an effective compliance program (discussed below) to encourage ethical behavior *before* the illegal activity occurs.[33] The method used to determine a company's punishment illustrates the importance of establishing a compliance program, as illustrated in Exhibit 4.2.

The first step is to compute the *base fine* by determining what *level of offense* has occurred. The level of the offense (i.e., its seriousness) varies depending on the kind of crime, the loss incurred by the victims, and how much planning went into the crime. For example, simple fraud is a level 6 offense (there are 38 levels in all). But if the victims of that fraud lost more than $5 million, that level 6 offense becomes a level 22 offense. Moreover, anything beyond minimal planning to commit the fraud results in an increase of two levels to a level 24 offense. How much difference would this make to a company? As Exhibit 4.2 shows, crimes at or below level 6 incur a base fine of $5,000, whereas the base fine for level 24 is $2.1 million, a difference of $2.095 million! The base fine for level 38, the top-level offense, is a hefty $72.5 million.

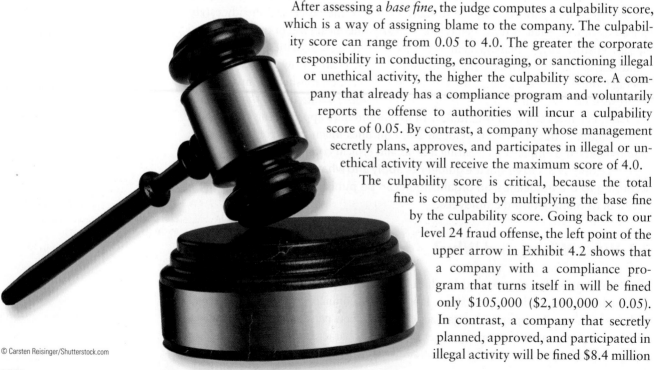

After assessing a *base fine*, the judge computes a culpability score, which is a way of assigning blame to the company. The culpability score can range from 0.05 to 4.0. The greater the corporate responsibility in conducting, encouraging, or sanctioning illegal or unethical activity, the higher the culpability score. A company that already has a compliance program and voluntarily reports the offense to authorities will incur a culpability score of 0.05. By contrast, a company whose management secretly plans, approves, and participates in illegal or unethical activity will receive the maximum score of 4.0.

The culpability score is critical, because the total fine is computed by multiplying the base fine by the culpability score. Going back to our level 24 fraud offense, the left point of the upper arrow in Exhibit 4.2 shows that a company with a compliance program that turns itself in will be fined only $105,000 ($2,100,000 × 0.05). In contrast, a company that secretly planned, approved, and participated in illegal activity will be fined $8.4 million

Exhibit 4.2   Offense Levels, Base Fines, Culpability Scores, and Possible Total Fines under the U.S. Sentencing Commission Guidelines for Organizations

Offense Level	Base Fine	Culpability Score					
		0.05	0.5	1.0	2.0	3.0	4.0
6 or less	$ 5,000	$ 250	$ 2,500	$ 5,000	$ 10,000	$ 15,000	$ 20,000
7	7,500	375	3,750	7,500	15,000	22,500	30,000
8	10,000	500	5,000	10,000	20,000	30,000	40,000
9	15,000	750	7,500	15,000	30,000	45,000	60,000
10	20,000	1,000	10,000	20,000	40,000	60,000	80,000
11	30,000	1,500	15,000	30,000	60,000	90,000	120,000
12	40,000	2,000	20,000	40,000	80,000	120,000	160,000
13	60,000	3,000	30,000	60,000	120,000	180,000	240,000
14	85,000	4,250	42,500	85,000	170,000	255,000	340,000
15	125,000	6,250	62,500	125,000	250,000	375,000	500,000
16	175,000	8,750	87,500	175,000	350,000	525,000	700,000
17	250,000	12,500	125,000	250,000	500,000	750,000	1,000,000
18	350,000	17,500	175,000	350,000	700,000	1,050,000	1,400,000
19	500,000	25,000	250,000	500,000	1,000,000	1,500,000	2,000,000
20	650,000	32,500	325,000	650,000	1,300,000	1,950,000	2,600,000
21	910,000	45,500	455,000	910,000	1,820,000	2,730,000	3,640,000
22	1,200,000	60,000	600,000	1,200,000	2,400,000	3,600,000	4,800,000
23	1,600,000	80,000	800,000	1,600,000	3,200,000	4,800,000	6,400,000
24	2,100,000	105,000	1,050,000	2,100,000	4,200,000	6,300,000	8,400,000
25	2,800,000	140,000	1,400,000	2,800,000	5,600,000	8,400,000	11,200,000
26	3,700,000	185,000	1,850,000	3,700,000	7,400,000	11,100,000	14,800,000
27	4,800,000	240,000	2,400,000	4,800,000	9,600,000	14,400,000	19,200,000
28	6,300,000	315,000	3,150,000	6,300,000	12,600,000	18,900,000	25,200,000
29	8,100,000	405,000	4,050,000	8,100,000	16,200,000	24,300,000	32,400,000
30	10,500,000	525,000	5,250,000	10,500,000	21,000,000	31,500,000	42,000,000
31	13,500,000	675,000	6,750,000	13,500,000	27,000,000	40,500,000	54,000,000
32	17,500,000	875,000	8,750,000	17,500,000	35,000,000	52,500,000	70,000,000
34	28,500,000	1,425,000	14,250,000	28,500,000	57,000,000	85,500,000	114,000,000
35	36,000,000	1,800,000	18,000,000	36,000,000	72,000,000	108,000,000	144,000,000
36	45,500,000	2,275,000	22,750,000	45,500,000	91,000,000	136,500,000	182,000,000
37	57,500,000	2,875,000	28,750,000	57,500,000	115,000,000	172,500,000	230,000,000
38 or more	72,500,000	3,625,000	36,250,000	72,500,000	145,000,000	217,500,000	290,000,000

Source: "Chapter Eight—Part C—Fines," 2004 Federal Sentencing Guidelines, available at www.ussc.gov/guidelines/2010_guidelines/index.cfm.

($2,100,000 × 4.0), as shown by the right point of the upper arrow. The difference is even greater for level 38 offenses. As shown by the left point of the bottom arrow, a company with a compliance program and a 0.05 culpability score is fined only $3.625 million, whereas a company with the maximum 4.0 culpability score is fined a whopping $290 million, as indicated by the right point of the bottom arrow. These differences clearly show the importance of having a compliance program in place.

Exhibit 4.3 Compliance Program Steps for the U.S. Sentencing Guidelines for Organizations

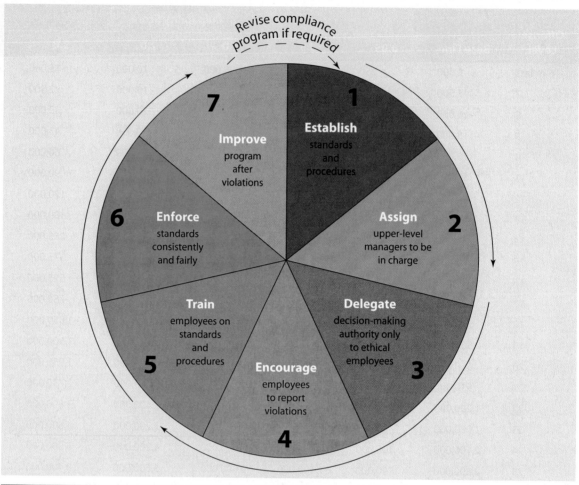

Source: D. R. Dalton, M. B. Metzger, & J. W. Hill, "The 'New' U.S. Sentencing Commission Guidelines: A Wake-up Call for Corporate America," *Academy of Management Executive* 8 (1994): 7–16.

Over the last decade, 1,494 companies have been charged under the U.S. Sentencing Guidelines. Seventy-six percent of those charged were fined, with the average fine exceeding $2 million. Company fines are on average 20 times larger now than before the implementation of the guidelines in 1991.[34]

Fortunately, for companies that want to avoid paying these stiff fines, the U.S. Sentencing Guidelines clearly spell out the seven necessary components of an effective compliance program.[35] Exhibit 4.3 lists those components. Caremark International, a managed-care service provider in Delaware, pleaded guilty to criminal charges related to its physician contracts and improper patient referrals. When it was sued by shareholders for negligence and poor management, the Delaware court dismissed the case, ruling that the company's ethics compliance program, built on the components described in Exhibit 4.3, was a good-faith attempt to monitor employees and that the company did not knowingly allow illegal and unethical behavior to occur. The court went on to rule that a compliance program based on the U.S. Sentencing Guidelines was enough to shield the company from liability.[36]

For more information, see "An Overview of the Organizational Sentencing Guidelines" at www.ussc.gov/Guidelines/Organizational_Guidelines/ORGOVERVIEW.pdf and "Sentencing Guidelines Educational Materials" at www.ussc.gov/Education_and_Training/Guidelines_Educational_Materials/index.cfm.

Review 3

U.S. Sentencing Commission Guidelines for Organizations Under the U.S. Sentencing Commission Guidelines, companies can be prosecuted and fined up to $300 million for employees' illegal actions. Fines are computed by multiplying the base fine by a culpability score, which ranges from 0.05 to 4.0. Companies that establish compliance programs to encourage ethical behavior can reduce their culpability scores and their fines. Companies without compliance programs can face much heavier fines than companies with established programs. Compliance programs must establish standards and procedures, be run by top managers, encourage hiring and promotion of honest and ethical people, encourage employees to report violations, educate employees about compliance, punish violators, and find ways to improve the program after violations occur.

How Do You Make Ethical Decisions?

On a cold morning in the midst of a winter storm, schools were closed and most people had decided to stay home from work. Nevertheless, Richard Addessi had already showered, shaved, and dressed to go to work. He kissed his wife Joan goodbye, but before he could get to his car, he fell dead on the garage floor of a sudden heart attack. Addessi was four months short of his 30-year anniversary with the company. Having begun work at IBM at the age of 18, he was just 48 years old.[37]

You're the vice president in charge of benefits at IBM. Given that he was only four months short of full retirement, do you award full retirement benefits to Richard Addessi's wife and daughters? If the answer is "yes," they will receive his full retirement benefits of $1,800 a month and free lifetime medical coverage. If you say no, his widow and two daughters will receive only $340 a month. They will also have to pay $473 a month to continue their current medical coverage. As the VP in charge of benefits at IBM, what would be the ethical thing for you to do?

After reading the next two sections, you should be able to

4. Describe what influences ethical decision making.

5. Explain what practical steps managers can take to improve ethical decision making.

4 Influences on Ethical Decision Making

Although some ethical issues are easily solved, many do not have clearly right or wrong answers. So, what did IBM decide to do? Because Richard Addessi had not completed 30 full years with the company, IBM officials felt they had no choice but to give Joan Addessi and her two daughters the smaller, partial retirement benefits. Do you think IBM's decision was ethical? Probably many of you don't. You may wonder how the company could be so heartless as to deny Richard Addessi's family the full benefits to which you believe they were entitled. Yet others might argue that IBM did the ethical thing by strictly following the rules laid out in its pension benefit

plan. After all, being fair means applying the same rules to everyone. Although the answers are rarely clear, managers do need to have a clear sense of how to arrive at an answer in order to manage this ethical ambiguity. The ethical answers that managers choose depend on **4.1 the ethical intensity of the decision, 4.2 the moral development of the manager**, and **4.3 the ethical principles used to solve the problem.**

4.1 Ethical Intensity of the Decision

Managers don't treat all ethical decisions the same. The manager who has to decide whether to deny or extend full benefits to Joan Addessi and her family is going to treat that decision much more seriously than the decision of how to deal with an assistant who has been taking paper home for personal use. These decisions differ in their **ethical intensity,** or the degree of concern people have about an ethical issue. When addressing an issue of high ethical intensity, managers are more aware of the impact their decision will have on others. They are more likely to view the decision as an ethical or moral decision rather than as an economic decision. They are also more likely to worry about doing the right thing.

Six factors must be taken into account when determining the ethical intensity of an action. These include:

> magnitude of consequences
> social consensus
> probability of effect
> temporal immediacy
> proximity of effect
> concentration of effect.[38]

Magnitude of consequences is the total harm or benefit derived from an ethical decision. The more people who are harmed or the greater the harm to those people, the larger the consequences. **Social consensus** is agreement on whether behavior is bad or good. **Probability of effect** is the chance that something will happen and then result in harm to others. If we combine these factors, we can see the effect they can have on ethical intensity. For example, if there is *clear agreement* (social consensus) that a managerial decision or action is *certain* (probability of effect) to have *large negative consequences* (magnitude of consequences) in some way, then people will be highly concerned about that managerial decision or action, and ethical intensity will be high.

Temporal immediacy is the time between an act and the consequences the act produces. Temporal immediacy is stronger if a manager has to lay off workers next week as opposed to three months from now. **Proximity of effect** is the social, psychological, cultural, or physical distance of a decision maker from those affected by his or her decisions. Thus, proximity of effect is greater when a manager lays off employees he knows than when he lays off employees that he doesn't know. Finally, whereas the magnitude of consequences is the total effect across all people, **concentration of effect** is how much an act affects the average person. Temporarily laying off 100 employees for 10 months without pay is a greater concentration of effect than temporarily laying off 1,000 employees for one month.

Which of these six factors has the most impact on ethical intensity? Studies indicate that managers are much more likely to view decisions as ethical issues when the magnitude of consequences (total harm) is high and there is a social consensus (agreement) that a behavior or action is bad.[39] Many people will likely feel IBM was

ethical intensity the degree of concern people have about an ethical issue.

magnitude of consequences the total harm or benefit derived from an ethical decision.

social consensus agreement on whether behavior is bad or good.

probability of effect the chance that something will happen and then harm others.

temporal immediacy the time between an act and the consequences the act produces.

proximity of effect the social, psychological, cultural, or physical distance between a decision maker and those affected by his or her decisions.

concentration of effect the total harm or benefit that an act produces on the average person.

wrong to deny full benefits to Joan Addessi. Why? IBM's decision met five of the six characteristics of ethical intensity. The difference in benefits, more than $23,000 per year, was likely to have serious and immediate consequences for the family, especially in terms of their monthly benefits ($1,800 and free medical coverage if full benefits were awarded versus $340 a month and medical care that costs $473 per month if they weren't). We can closely identify with Joan Addessi and her daughters as opposed to IBM's faceless, nameless corporate identity. The exception, as we will discuss below, is social consensus. Not everyone will agree that IBM's decision was unethical. The judgment also depends on your level of moral development and which ethical principles you use to decide.

4.2 Moral Development

A friend of yours has given you the latest version of Microsoft Office. She stuffed the software disks in your backpack with a note saying that you should install it on your computer and get it back to her in a couple of days. You're tempted. The Office package costs about $280, which you don't have. Besides, all of your friends have the same version of Microsoft Office, and they didn't pay for it either. Copying the software to your hard drive without buying your own copy clearly violates copyright laws. But no one would find out. Even if someone does, Microsoft probably isn't going to come after you. Microsoft goes after the big fish—companies that illegally copy and distribute software to their workers and pirates that illegally sell cheap unauthorized copies.[40] Your computer has booted up, and you've got your mouse in one hand and the installation disk in the other. What are you going to do?

In part, according to psychologist Lawrence Kohlberg, your decision will be based on your level of moral development. Kohlberg identified three phases of moral development, with two stages in each phase (see Exhibit 4.4).[41] At the **preconventional level of moral development**, people decide based on selfish reasons. For example, if you are in Stage 1, the punishment and obedience stage, your primary concern will be to avoid trouble for yourself. So you won't copy the software because you are afraid of being caught and punished. Yet, in Stage 2, the instrumental exchange stage, you worry less about punishment and more about doing things that directly advance your wants and needs. So you copy the software.

People at the **conventional level of moral development** make decisions that conform to societal expectations. In other words, they look outside themselves to others for guidance on ethical issues. In Stage 3, the "good boy, nice girl" stage, you normally do what the other "good boys" and "nice girls" are doing. If everyone else is illegally copying software, you will too. But if they aren't, you won't either. In the law and order stage, Stage 4, you again look for external guidance and do whatever the law permits, so you won't copy the software.

People at the **postconventional level of moral development** use internalized ethical principles to solve ethical dilemmas. In Stage 5, the social contract stage, you will refuse to copy the software because, as a whole, society is better off when the rights of others—in this case, the rights of software authors and manufacturers—are not violated. In Stage 6, the universal principle stage, you might or might not copy the software, depending on your principles of right and wrong. Moreover, you will stick to your principles even

preconventional level of moral development the first level of moral development, in which people make decisions based on selfish reasons.

conventional level of moral development the second level of moral development, in which people make decisions that conform to societal expectations.

postconventional level of moral development the third level of moral development, in which people make decisions based on internalized principles.

Exhibit 4.4 Kohlberg's Stages of Moral Development

Stage 1	Stage 2	Stage 3	Stage 4	Stage 5	Stage 6
Punishment and Obedience	Instrumental Exchange	Good Boy, Nice Girl	Law and Order	Social Contract	Universal Principle
Preconventional		Conventional		Postconventional	
Selfish		Societal Expectations		Internalized Principles	

Source: W. Davidson III & D. Worrell, "Influencing Managers to Change Unpopular Corporate Behavior through Boycotts and Divestitures," *Business & Society* 34 (1995): 171–196.

if your decision conflicts with the law (Stage 4) or what others believe is best for society (Stage 5). For example, those with socialist or communist beliefs would probably choose to copy the software because they believe goods and services should be owned by society rather than by individuals and corporations. (For information about the dos, don'ts, and legal issues concerning software piracy, see the Software & Information Industry Association's website at www.siia.net/piracy/default.asp.)

Kohlberg believed that people would progress sequentially from earlier stages to later stages as they became more educated and mature. But only 20 percent of adults ever reach the postconventional stage of moral development, where internal principles guide their decisions. Most adults are in the conventional stage of moral development in which they look outside themselves to others for guidance on ethical issues. This means that most people in the workplace look to and need leadership when it comes to ethical decision making.[42]

4.3 Principles of Ethical Decision Making

Beyond an issue's ethical intensity and a manager's level of moral maturity, the particular ethical principles that managers use will also affect how they solve ethical dilemmas. Unfortunately, there is no one ideal principle to use in making ethical business decisions.

According to professor LaRue Hosmer, a number of different ethical principles can be used to make business decisions: long-term self-interest, personal virtue, religious injunctions, government requirements, utilitarian benefits, individual rights, and distributive justice.[43] All of these ethical principles encourage managers and employees to take others' interests into account when making ethical decisions. At the same time, however, these principles can lead to very different ethical actions, as we can see by using these principles to decide whether to award full benefits to Joan Addessi and her children.

According to the **principle of long-term self-interest**, you should never take any action that is not in your or your organization's long-term self-interest. Although this sounds as if the principle promotes selfishness, it doesn't. What we do to maximize our long-term interests (save more, spend less, exercise every day, watch what we eat) is often very different from what we do to maximize short-term interests (max out our credit cards, be couch potatoes, eat whatever we want). At any given time, IBM has nearly 1,000 employees who are just months away from retirement. Thus, because of the costs involved, it serves IBM's long-term interest to pay full benefits only after employees have put in 30 full years.

The **principle of personal virtue** holds that you should never do anything that is not honest, open, and truthful and that you would not be glad to see reported in the newspapers or on TV. Using the principle of personal virtue, IBM might have quietly awarded Joan Addessi her husband's full benefits. Had it done so, it could have avoided the publication of an embarrassing *Wall Street Journal* article on this topic.

The **principle of religious injunctions** holds that you should never take an action that is unkind or that harms a sense of community, such as the positive feelings that come from working together to accomplish a commonly accepted goal. Using this principle, IBM would have been concerned foremost with compassion and kindness, and it would have awarded full benefits to Joan Addessi.

According to the **principle of government requirements**, the law represents the minimal moral standards of society, so you should never take any action that violates the law. Using this principle, IBM would deny full benefits to Joan Addessi because her husband did not work for the company for 30 years. Indeed, making exceptions would violate the federal Employee Retirement Income Security Act of 1974.

principle of long-term self-interest an ethical principle that holds that you should never take any action that is not in your or your organization's long-term self-interest.

principle of personal virtue an ethical principle that holds that you should never do anything that is not honest, open, and truthful and that you would not be glad to see reported in the newspapers or on TV.

principle of religious injunctions an ethical principle that holds that you should never take any action that is not kind and that does not build a sense of community.

principle of government requirements an ethical principle that holds that you should never take any action that violates the law, for the law represents the minimal moral standard.

The **principle of utilitarian benefits** states that you should never take an action that does not result in greater good for society. In short, you should do whatever creates the greatest good for the greatest number. At first, this principle seems to suggest that IBM should award full benefits to Joan Addessi. If IBM did this with any regularity, however, the costs would be enormous, profits would shrink, and IBM would have to cut its stock dividend, harming countless shareholders, many of whom rely on IBM dividends for retirement income. In this case, the principle does not lead to a clear choice.

The **principle of individual rights** holds that you should never take an action that infringes on others' agreed-upon rights. Using this principle, IBM would deny Joan Addessi full benefits. If it carefully followed the rules specified in its pension plan and granted Mrs. Addessi due process, meaning the right to appeal the decision, then IBM would not be violating her rights. In fact, it could be argued that providing full benefits to Mrs. Addessi would violate the rights of employees who had to wait 30 full years to receive full benefits.

Finally, under the **principle of distributive justice**, you should never take any action that harms the least fortunate among us in some way. This principle is designed to protect the poor, the uneducated, and the unemployed. Although Joan Addessi could probably find a job, it's unlikely that she could easily find one that would support her and her daughters in the manner to which they were accustomed after 20 years as a stay-at-home mom. Using the principle of distributive justice, IBM would award her full benefits.

As mentioned at the beginning of this chapter, one of the "real-world" aspects of ethical decisions is that no matter *what* you decide, someone or some group will be unhappy. This corollary is also true: No matter *how* you decide, someone or some group will be unhappy and will argue that you should have used a different principle or weighed concerns differently. Consequently, although all of these ethical principles encourage managers to balance others' needs against their own, they can also lead to very different ethical actions. So even when managers strive to be ethical, there are often no clear answers when it comes to doing the right thing.

principle of utilitarian benefits an ethical principle that holds that you should never take any action that does not result in greater good for society.

principle of individual rights an ethical principle that holds that you should never take any action that infringes on others' agreed-upon rights.

principle of distributive justice an ethical principle that holds that you should never take any action that harms the least fortunate among us: the poor, the uneducated, the unemployed.

Influences on Ethical Decision Making Three factors influence ethical decisions: the ethical intensity of the decision, the moral development of the decision maker, and the ethical principles used to solve the problem. Ethical intensity is strong when decisions have large, certain, immediate consequences and when we are physically or psychologically close to those affected by the decision. There are three levels of moral maturity, each with two stages. At the preconventional level, decisions are made for selfish reasons. At the conventional level, decisions conform to societal expectations. At the postconventional level, internalized principles are used to make ethical decisions. Finally, managers can use a number of different principles when making ethical decisions: self-interest, personal virtue, religious injunctions, government requirements, utilitarian benefits, individual rights, and distributive justice.

Review 4

5 Practical Steps to Ethical Decision Making

Managers can encourage more ethical decision making in their organizations by **5.1 carefully selecting and hiring ethical employees, 5.2 establishing a specific code of ethics, 5.3 training employees to make ethical decisions,** and **5.4 creating an ethical climate**.

5.1 Selecting and Hiring Ethical Employees

If you found a wallet containing $1,000, would you return the money? Informal studies typically show that 57 to 80 percent of people would, and that women and people in small towns are more likely to return the money.[44] As an employer, you can increase your chances of hiring an honest person who would return the wallet with the money if you give job applicants integrity tests. **Overt integrity tests** estimate job applicants' honesty by asking them directly what they think or feel about theft or about punishment of unethical behaviors.[45] For example, an employer might ask an applicant, "Would you ever consider buying something from somebody if you knew the person had stolen the item?" or "Don't most people steal from their companies?" Surprisingly, unethical people will usually answer "yes" to such questions, because they believe that the world is basically dishonest and that dishonest behavior is normal.[46]

Personality-based integrity tests indirectly estimate job applicants' honesty by measuring psychological traits such as dependability and conscientiousness. For example, prison inmates serving time for white-collar crimes (counterfeiting, embezzlement, and fraud) scored much lower than a comparison group of middle-level managers on scales measuring reliability, dependability, honesty, conscientiousness, and abiding by rules.[47] These results show that companies can selectively hire and promote people who will be more ethical.[48] For more on integrity testing, see the What Really Works feature in this chapter.

5.2 Codes of Ethics

Today, almost all large corporations have an ethics code in place. Exhibit 4.5 displays the ethical code of conduct for Caterpillar Incorporated, a large manufacturing company with corporate offices headquartered in Peoria, Illinois. Even if a company has a code of ethics like this, two things must still happen if those codes are to encourage ethical decision making and behavior.[49] First, a company must communicate its code to others both inside and outside the company. With the click of a computer mouse, anyone inside or outside Caterpillar can obtain detailed information about the company's core values, specific ethical business practices, and much more.

Second, in addition to having an ethics code with general guidelines like "do unto others as you would have others do unto you," management must also develop practical ethical standards and procedures specific to the company's line of business. Visitors to **Nortel's** website can download a comprehensive document, the "Code of Business Conduct," that establishes specific ethical standards on topics ranging from bribes and kickbacks to expense vouchers and illegal copying of software. For example, most businesspeople believe that it is wrong to take bribes or other gifts from a company that wants your business. Therefore, one of Nortel's ethical guidelines is "Directly or indirectly offering or receiving any gift or entertainment that might be perceived to improperly influence a business interaction violates our commitment to maintaining objectivity and transparency in our relationships." And just to be sure there's no confusion over what constitutes a gift, the guidelines spell things out explicitly: "Certain types of gifts may not be given to or received from persons doing business or seeking to do business with Nortel: Cash, gift certificates, or any other cash equivalent; Stock, stock options, or 'friends and family stock'; Discounts not generally available to the public."[50] Specific codes of ethics such as this make it much easier for employees to decide what to do when they want to do the right thing.

"what's new"
companies >

overt integrity tests a written test that estimates job applicants' honesty by directly asking them what they think or feel about theft or about punishment of unethical behaviors.

personality-based integrity tests a written test that indirectly estimates job applicants' honesty by measuring psychological traits, such as dependability and conscientiousness.

Exhibit 4.5 Ethical Code of Conduct for Caterpillar

Integrity—The Power of Honesty

We put Integrity into action when...

We Are Honest and Act with Integrity

We Avoid and Manage Conflict and Potential Conflicts of Interest

We Compete Fairly

We Ensure Accuracy and Completeness of our Financial Reports and Accounting Records

We Are Fair, Honest and Open in Our Communication

We Handle "Inside Information" Appropriately and Lawfully

We Refuse to Make Improper Payments

Excellence—The Power of Quality

We put Excellence in action when...

We Establish a Work Environment that Supports Excellence

We Select, Place and Evaluate Employees Based on Their Qualifications and Performance

We Provide Employees with Opportunities to Develop

We Accept Nothing But the Best Quality in Our Products and Services

We Focus on Delivering the Highest Value to Our Customers, Always with a Sense of Urgency

We See Risk as Something to be Managed, and as Potential Opportunity

We Take an "Enterprise Point of View"

Teamwork—The Power of Working Together

We put Teamwork into action when...

We Treat Others with Respect and Do Not Tolerate Intimidation or Harassment

We Treat People Fairly and Prohibit Discrimination

We Foster an Inclusive Environment

We Conduct Business Worldwide with Consistent Global Standards

We Collaborate with Key Entities and Organizations Outside Our Company

We Build Outstanding Relationships with Our Dealers and Distribution Channel Members

We View Our Suppliers as Our Business Allies

Commitment—The Power of Responsibility

We put Commitment into action when...

We Take Personal Responsibility

We Protect the Health and Safety of Others and Ourselves

We Protect Our Hard Assets, Our Brands and Our Other Intellectual Property

We Safeguard Our Confidential Information

We Use Electronic Communications Technology Responsibly and Professionally

We Recognize and Respect Personal Privacy

We Support Environmental Responsibility Through Sustainable Development

We Are Proactive Members of Our Communities

We Make Responsible Ownership and Investment Decisions

We Participate in Public Matters in an Appropriate Manner

Source: "Caterpillar's Worldwide Code of Conduct," Caterpillar, accessed April 20, 2011, from www.cat.com/code-of-conduct. Reprinted courtesy of Caterpillar, Inc.

5.3 Ethics Training

In addition to establishing ethical standards for the company, managers must sponsor and be involved in ethics and compliance training in order to create an ethical company culture.[51] The first objective of ethics training is to develop employees' awareness of ethics.[52] This means helping employees recognize which issues are ethical issues and then avoid rationalizing unethical behavior by thinking, "This isn't really illegal or immoral" or "No one will ever find out." Several companies have created board games to improve awareness of ethical issues.[53] Other ethics training tools, like the Kew Gardens Principles, examine how ethical decisions can be made in specific scenarios. The Kew Gardens Principles were based on the study of a murder in Kew Gardens, New York, in which witnesses to the attack failed to intervene or seek help. Researchers developed a series of four decision-making factors that are used to help employees determine how they should respond to problems and ethical situations, even when the problems were not of their own doing. These principles are:

1. Need—When the need is greater, you have a greater responsibility to act.
2. Proximity—How close are you to the problem? Proximity is not just physical; it can also apply to relationships.
3. Capability—You can be expected to intervene only insofar as you are able to.
4. Last Resort—If no one else is able to help, it becomes much more important for you to intervene.[54]

The second objective for ethics training programs is to achieve credibility with employees. Not surprisingly, employees can be highly suspicious of management's reasons for offering ethics training. Some companies have hurt the credibility of their ethics programs by having outside instructors and consultants conduct the classes.[55] Employees often complain that outside instructors and consultants are teaching theory that has nothing to do with their jobs and the practical dilemmas they actually face on a daily basis. Russ Berland, the Ethics Compliance Officer at **BearingPoint**, a management and technology consulting firm, addressed the credibility issue by asking employees, "What [ethics] situations make you feel squishy?" and "What have you seen in the field that gave you pause?" The resulting topics were so dramatic—managers making sexual passes at subordinates, consultants misrepresenting their technical expertise to get jobs, and inappropriately billing clients for expenses—that they decided to bring them to life in a series of ten videos taped over a weekend. The videos feature a fictional technology consulting firm called "Aggrieve," whose motto is "Aggrieve says yes when everyone else says no." Unlike most ethics training content, which can be dry and uninteresting, the Aggrieve videos resonated with BearingPoint employees. Reactions ranged from "This is the best training I've ever had," to "I worked for a Kevin [the boss depicted in the videos]." The ten videos, which debuted on ten consecutive Mondays, were so popular that thousands of employees began viewing them early on Fridays when they were posted to the company server.[56]

Ethics training becomes even more credible when top managers teach the initial ethics classes to their subordinates who in turn teach their subordinates.[57] Michael Hoffman, executive director for the Center for Business Ethics at Bentley College, says that having managers teach ethics courses greatly reinforces the seriousness with which employees treat ethics in the workplace.[58] Unfortunately, though, 25 percent of large companies don't require top managers to attend, much less teach, ethics training.[59] The good news is that this scenario is changing thanks to the 2004 amendment to the Sentencing Guidelines. Indeed, a recent survey shows that board

"what's new" companies >

Exhibit 4.6 A Basic Model of Ethical Decision Making

1. **Identify the problem.** What makes it an ethical problem? Think in terms of rights, obligations, fairness, relationships, and integrity. How would you define the problem if you stood on the other side of the fence?

2. **Identify the constituents.** Who has been hurt? Who could be hurt? Who could be helped? Are they willing players, or are they victims? Can you negotiate with them?

3. **Diagnose the situation.** How did it happen in the first place? What could have prevented it? Is it going to get worse or better? Can the damage now be undone?

4. **Analyze your options.** Imagine the range of possibilities. Limit yourself to the two or three most manageable. What are the likely outcomes of each? What are the likely costs? Look to the company mission statement or code of ethics for guidance.

5. **Make your choice.** What is your intention in making this decision? How does it compare with the probable results? Can you discuss the problem with the affected parties before you act? Could you disclose without qualm your decision to your boss, the CEO, the board of directors, your family, or society as a whole?

6. **Act.** Do what you have to do. Don't be afraid to admit errors. Be as bold in confronting a problem as you were in causing it.

Source: L. A. Berger, "Train All Employees to Solve Ethical Dilemmas," *Best's Review—Life-Health Insurance Edition* 95 (1995): 70–80. Used with permission.

involvement in ethics and compliance programs jumped from 21 percent in 1987 to 96 percent in 2005.[60]

The third objective of ethics training is to teach employees a practical model of ethical decision making. A basic model should help them think about the consequences their choices will have on others and consider how they will choose among different solutions. Exhibit 4.6 presents a basic model of ethical decision making.

5.4 Ethical Climate

Organizational culture is key to fostering ethical decision making. The 2009 National Business Ethics Survey reported that only 39 percent of employees who work at companies with a strong ethical culture (where core beliefs are widely shared and strongly held) have observed others engaging in unethical behavior, whereas 76 percent of those who work in organizations with weak ethical cultures (where core beliefs are not widely shared or strongly held) have observed others engage in unethical behavior. Employees in strong ethical cultures are also more likely to report violations, because they expect that management wants them reported and won't retaliate against them for doing so.[61]

We learned in Chapter 3 that leadership is an important factor in creating an organizational culture. So, it's no surprise that in study after study, when researchers ask, "What is the most important influence on your ethical behavior at work?" the answer comes back, "My manager." The first step in establishing an ethical climate is for managers, especially top managers, to act ethically themselves.

A second step in establishing an ethical climate is for top management to be active in and committed to the company ethics program.[62] Top managers who consistently talk about the importance of ethics and back up that talk by participating in their companies' ethics programs send the clear message that ethics matter. Business writer Dayton Fandray says, "You can have ethics offices and officers and training programs and reporting systems, but if the CEO doesn't seem to care, it's all just a sham. It's not surprising to find that the companies that really do care about ethics make a point of including senior management in all of their ethics and compliance programs."[63]

A third step is to put in place a reporting system that encourages managers and employees to report potential ethics violations. **Whistleblowing,** that is, reporting others' ethics violations, is a difficult step for most people to take.[64] Potential whistleblowers often fear that they, and not the ethics violators, will be punished.[65] Managers

whistleblowing reporting others' ethics violations to management or legal authorities.

© iStockphoto.com/Hans Martens

what really works
Integrity Tests

Under the 1991 and 2004 U.S. Sentencing Commission Guidelines, unethical employee behavior can lead to multimillion-dollar fines for corporations, and fraudulent behavior of executives can lead to criminal prosecution. Moreover, workplace deviance like stealing, fraud, and vandalism costs companies an estimated $660 billion a year. One way to reduce workplace deviance and the chances of a large fine for unethical employee behavior is to use overt and personality-based integrity tests to screen job applicants.

One hundred eighty-one studies, with a combined total of 576,460 study participants, have examined how well integrity tests can predict job performance and various kinds of workplace deviance. These studies show that not only can integrity tests help companies reduce workplace deviance, but they also provide the added bonus of helping companies hire workers who are better performers in their jobs.

Workplace Deviance (Counterproductive Behaviors)

Compared with job applicants who score poorly, there is an 82 percent chance that job applicants who score well on overt integrity tests will participate in less illegal activity, unethical behavior, drug abuse, or workplace violence.

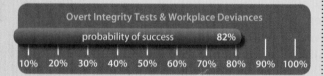

Personality-based integrity tests also do a good job of predicting who will engage in workplace deviance. Compared with job applicants who score poorly, there is a 68 percent chance that job applicants who score well on personality-based integrity tests will

participate in less illegal activity, unethical behavior, excessive absences, drug abuse, or workplace violence.

Job Performance

In addition to reducing unethical behavior and workplace deviance, integrity tests can help companies hire better performers. Compared with employees who score poorly, there is a 69 percent chance that employees who score well on overt integrity tests will be better performers.

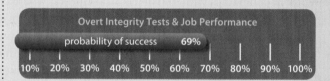

The figures are nearly identical for personality-based integrity tests. Compared with those who score poorly, there is a 70 percent chance that employees who score well on personality-based integrity tests will be better at their jobs.

Theft

Although integrity tests can help companies decrease most kinds of workplace deviance and increase employees' job performance, they have a smaller effect on a specific kind of workplace deviance: theft. Compared with employees who score poorly, there is a 57 percent chance that employees who score well on overt integrity tests will be less likely to steal. No theft data were available to assess personality-based integrity tests.

Faking and Coaching on Integrity Tests

Although overt and personality-based integrity tests do a very good job of helping companies hire people of higher integrity, it is possible to improve scores on these tests through coaching and faking. In coaching, job applicants are taught the underlying rationale of an integrity test or given specific directions for improving their integrity scores. Faking occurs when applicants simply try to "beat the test" or try to fake a good

impression. Unfortunately for the companies that use integrity tests, both strategies work.

On average, coaching can improve scores on overt integrity tests by an astounding 1.5 standard deviations and on personality-based integrity tests by a meaningful 0.36 standard deviation. This would be the equivalent of increasing your total SAT score by 150 and 36 points, respectively (the SAT has a mean of 500 and a standard deviation of 100). Likewise, on average, faking can improve scores on overt integrity tests by an impressive 1.02 standard deviations and on personality-based integrity tests by a meaningful 0.59 standard deviation. Again, this would be the equivalent of increasing your SAT score by 102 and 59 points, respectively.

Companies that want to avoid coaching and faking effects must maintain tight security over integrity tests so that applicants have little information regarding them, periodically check the validity of the tests to make sure they're accurately predicting workplace deviance and job performance, or periodically switch tests if they suspect that test security has been compromised.[66]

who have been interviewed about whistleblowing have said, "In every organization, someone's been screwed for standing up." "If anything, I figured that by taking a strong stand I might get myself in trouble. People might look at me as a goody two-shoes. Someone might try to force me out." Matthew Lee, a former vice president at **Lehman Brothers**, was troubled when he discovered that the firm was moving $50 billion off its balance sheet in an attempt to hide steep losses, which would eventually lead to the firm's collapse. When Lee raised concerns about the false accounting practices to the board of directors and the accounting firm doing the auditing, Ernst & Young, he was fired.[67]

Today, many federal and state laws protect the rights of whistleblowers (see www.whistleblowers.org for more information). In particular, the Sarbanes-Oxley Act of 2002 makes it a serious crime for publicly owned companies to retaliate in any way against corporate whistleblowers. Managers who punish whistleblowers can be imprisoned for up to ten years. Some companies, including defense contractor Northrop Grumman, have made it easier for whistleblowers to report possible violations by establishing anonymous, toll-free corporate ethics hot lines. Nortel, the telecommunications company, even publicizes which of its ethics hot lines don't have caller ID. At Ernst & Young, a "Big Four" accounting firm, phone- and web-based complaints are routed to EthicsPoint, an independent contractor who forwards them to appropriate E&Y managers or legal counsel.[68] The Sarbanes-Oxley Act requires all publicly held companies to establish anonymous hot lines to encourage reporting of unethical and illegal behaviors, so it's not surprising that a recent survey found that 91 percent of companies have an anonymous reporting system whereby employees can report observed misconduct.[69]

< **"what's new" companies**

141

"what's new" >
companies

Despite such provisions, it is not easy to be a whistleblower. The factor that does the most to discourage whistleblowers from reporting problems is lack of company action on their complaints.[70] Thus, the final step in developing an ethical climate is for management to fairly and consistently punish those who violate the company's code of ethics. When a loss prevention agent at **Macy's** department store in Fresno, California, observed an employee stuffing merchandise under his clothes, she called the local police. At his home, they found $400,000 of new Macy's merchandise, which he had been selling on eBay and Craigslist. Confronted with the stolen goods, he told police that he'd been stealing from Macy's for four years. Ironically, he was caught just two weeks before his retirement.[71] Amazingly, though, not all companies fire ethics violators. In fact, 8 percent of surveyed companies admit that they would promote top performers even if they violated ethical standards.[72]

Review 5

Practical Steps to Ethical Decision Making   Employers can increase their chances of hiring ethical employees by administering overt integrity tests and personality-based integrity tests to all job applicants. Most large companies now have corporate codes of ethics. To affect ethical decision making, these codes must be known both inside and outside the organization. In addition to offering general rules, ethics codes must also provide specific, practical advice. Ethics training seeks to increase employees' awareness of ethical issues, make ethics a serious and credible factor in organizational decisions, and teach employees a practical model of ethical decision making. The most important factors in creating an ethical business climate are the personal examples set by company managers, involvement of management in the company ethics program, a reporting system that encourages whistleblowers to report potential ethics violations, and fair but consistent punishment of violators.

What Is Social Responsibility?

Social responsibility is a business's obligation to pursue policies, make decisions, and take actions that benefit society.[73] Unfortunately, because there are strong disagreements over to whom and for what in society organizations are responsible, it can be difficult for managers to know what is or will be perceived as socially responsible corporate behavior. In a recent McKinsey & Co. study of 1,144 top global executives, 79 percent predicted that at least some responsibility for dealing with future social and political issues would fall on corporations, but only 3 percent said they themselves do a good job of dealing with these issues.[74] So what should managers and corporations do to be socially responsible?

Some say that corporations need to give more to nonprofit organizations. In fact, despite the economic slowdown, annual corporate giving to charities has increased to $14.1 billion in cash and in-kind gifts.[75] Checkbook philanthropy, however, isn't enough these days, says Susan Puflea, senior vice president and director of GolinHarris Change.[76] Companies, she says, also need to be socially responsible as they conduct their businesses. Consider some examples. A number of leading banks have decided to limit the financing that they provide to companies undertaking environmentally hazardous energy projects. Wells Fargo, Bank of America, Morgan Stanley, and Citibank announced they will stop financing companies that search for coal by blasting off mountain tops (and depositing the remains in the rivers and valleys below). HSBC, a London based bank, announced that it will no longer

social responsibility a business's obligation to pursue policies, make decisions, and take actions that benefit society.

finance palm oil production, which is blamed for massive deforestation in developing countries.[77] Andrew Paterno and Michael Wallstein, who operate 12 Burger King restaurants in New Jersey, recently announced plans to install speed bumps in their drive-thru lanes to produce electricity. Using new technology, the speed bumps collect the energy from cars moving over them and convert it to electricity. It's estimated that the traffic going through one restaurant's drive-thru lane could power more than 500,000 homes per day.[78]

© Kristoffer Tripplaar/Alamy

But Wells Fargo, Bank of America, Morgan Stanley, and Citibank and HSBC weren't socially responsible just out of the goodness of their hearts; they changed their lending policies because of the risk to their business reputations. Likewise, installing speed bumps at Burger King restaurants to create electricity from kinetic energy certainly sounds socially responsible, but installing that equipment would save, if not earn, those restaurants substantial financial returns. These two examples illustrate the challenges and different motivations of acting in a socially responsible manner: balancing the needs of different groups in the face of limited resources and/or constraints.

After reading the next four sections, you should be able to explain

6. *To whom organizations are socially responsible.*

7. *For what organizations are socially responsible.*

8. *How organizations can choose to respond to societal demands for social responsibility.*

9. *Whether social responsibility hurts or helps an organization's economic performance.*

6 To Whom Are Organizations Socially Responsible?

There are two perspectives regarding to whom organizations are socially responsible: the shareholder model and the stakeholder model. According to the late Nobel Prize–winning economist Milton Friedman, the only social responsibility that organizations have is to satisfy their owners, that is, company shareholders. This view—called the **shareholder model**—holds that the only social responsibility that businesses have is to maximize profits. By maximizing profit, the firm maximizes shareholder wealth and satisfaction. More specifically, as profits rise, the company stock owned by shareholders generally increases in value.

Friedman argued that it is socially irresponsible for companies to divert time, money, and attention from maximizing profits to social causes and charitable organizations. The first problem, he believed, is that organizations cannot act effectively

shareholder model a view of social responsibility that holds that an organization's overriding goal should be profit maximization for the benefit of shareholders.

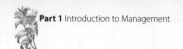

doing the right thing

Greenwashing

Many companies brag about how they care about the environment, whether it's car companies touting their fuel-efficient vehicles or computer makers talking about how they recycle electronic components. Most consumers, however, don't believe that companies are committed to being green. According to a Harris Interactive poll, just 16 percent of consumers believe that most companies are committed to improving the environment by practicing sustainable business or offering environmentally responsible products. Forty-eight percent of consumers believed that "some" companies are committed to that goal, whereas 24 percent believe that only a few companies are so committed. So what can managers do? Ron Loch, vice president for greentech and sustainability at Gibbs & Soell, says, "As long as companies are transparent in their communications and don't overstate the social and environmental impact of their efforts, they can avoid being painted with the greenwash brush. It gets back to the need of really taking inventory of what is happening throughout the organization and then weaving that into a compelling, credible and defensible narrative." So do the right thing—don't talk about "being green" just to get consumers' attention. Make sure that the message you send out to consumers reflects the social responsibility commitments that your company has made.[79]

as moral agents for all company shareholders. Although shareholders are likely to agree on investment issues concerning a company, it's highly unlikely that they have common views on what social causes a company should or should not support.

For instance, most *Fortune* 500 companies have corporate foundations that support nonprofit organizations. But even corporate leaders can't agree on what causes or nonprofit organizations should be supported. Honda works with the Detroit Symphony Orchestra to provide poor students instruments and music instruction.[80] Walmart and the Walmart Foundation have made a $2 billion commitment toward hunger relief in the United States through 2015.[81] Verizon Communications supports numerous programs to prevent and respond to domestic violence.[82] One could easily ask why Walmart doesn't support music instruction, or why Honda doesn't support domestic violence prevention. Thus, rather than act as moral agents, Friedman argued, companies should maximize profits for shareholders. Shareholders can then use their time and increased wealth to contribute to the social causes, charities, or institutions they want, rather than those that companies want.

The second major problem, Friedman said, is that the time, money, and attention diverted to social causes undermine market efficiency.[83] In competitive markets, companies compete for raw materials, talented workers, customers, and investment funds. A company that spends money on social causes will have less money to purchase quality materials or to hire talented workers who can produce a valuable product at a good price. If customers find the company's product less desirable, its sales and profits will fall. If profits fall, the company's stock price will decline, and the company will have difficulty attracting investment funds that could be used to fund long-term growth. In the end, Friedman argues, diverting the firm's money, time, and resources to social causes hurts customers, suppliers, employees, and shareholders. Russell Roberts, an economist at George Mason University, agrees, saying, "Doesn't it make more sense to have companies do what they do best, make

Exhibit 4.7
Stakeholder Model of Corporate Social Responsibility

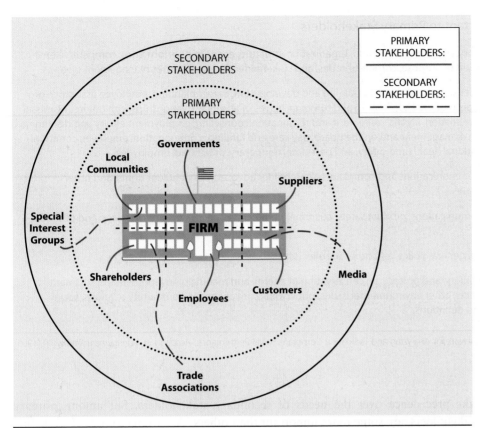

Source: "The Stakeholder Theory of the Corporation: Concepts, Evidence and Implications" (Figure), T. Donaldson & L. E. Preston, *Academy of Management Review*, 1995, vol. 20. Reproduced by permission of Academy of Management (NY) in the formats Textbook and Other Book via Copyright Clearance Center.

good products at fair prices, and then let consumers use the savings for the charity of their choice?"[84]

By contrast, under the **stakeholder model**, management's most important responsibility is the firm's long-term survival (not just maximizing profits), which is achieved by satisfying the interests of multiple corporate stakeholders (not just shareholders).[85] PepsiCo CEO Indra Nooyi says that because stakeholders are multifaceted, with different interests, a company operating under the stakeholder model has to redefine "profit." She says, "[we] have to make sure our new P&L (profit & loss statement) actually says revenue, less costs of goods sold, less costs to society— and that's your real profit."[86]

Stakeholders are persons or groups with a legitimate interest in a company.[87] Because stakeholders are interested in and affected by the organization's actions, they have a "stake" in what those actions are. Consequently, stakeholder groups may try to influence the firm to act in their own interests. Exhibit 4.7 shows the various stakeholder groups that the organization must satisfy to assure its long-term survival. Being responsible to multiple stakeholders raises two basic questions. First, how does a company identify organizational stakeholders? Second, how does a company balance the needs of different stakeholders? Distinguishing between primary and secondary stakeholders can help answer these questions.[88]

Some stakeholders are more important to the firm's survival than others. **Primary stakeholders** are groups on which the organization depends for its long-term survival; they include shareholders, employees, customers, suppliers, governments, and local communities. When managers are struggling to balance the needs of different stakeholders, the stakeholder model suggests that the needs of primary stakeholders

stakeholder model a theory of corporate responsibility that holds that management's most important responsibility, long-term survival, is achieved by satisfying the interests of multiple corporate stakeholders.

stakeholders persons or groups with a "stake" or legitimate interest in a company's actions.

primary stakeholders any group on which an organization relies for its long-term survival.

Exhibit 4.8 Issues Important to Primary Stakeholders

Company	Company history, industry background, organization structure, economic performance, competitive environment, mission or purpose, corporate codes, and stakeholder and social issues management systems.
Employees	Benefits, compensation and rewards, training and development, career planning, employee assistance programs, health promotion, absenteeism and turnover, leaves of absence, relationships with unions, dismissal and appeal, termination, layoffs, retirement and termination counseling, employment equity and discrimination, women in management and on the board, day care and family accommodation, employee communication, occupational health and safety, and part-time, temporary, or contract employees.
Shareholders	Shareholder communications and complaints, shareholder advocacy, shareholder rights, and other shareholder issues.
Customers	Customer communications, product safety, customer complaints, special customer services, and other customer issues.
Suppliers	Relative power, general policy, and other supplier issues.
Public Stakeholders	Public health, safety, and protection, conservation of energy and materials, environmental assessment of capital projects, other environmental issues, public policy involvement, community relations, social investment and donations.

Source: M. B. E. Clarkson, "A Stakeholder Framework for Analyzing and Evaluating Corporate Social Performance," *Academy of Management Review* 20 (1995): 92–117.

take precedence over the needs of secondary stakeholders. But among primary stakeholders, are some more important than others? According to the life-cycle theory of organizations, the answer is "yes." Organizations' needs change as they go through the life-cycle stages of formation/start-up, growth, maturity, and decline or transition. At each stage, different primary stakeholders will be critical to organizational well-being, and their concerns and issues will take precedence over those of other primary stakeholders.[89] In practice, though, CEOs typically give somewhat higher priority to shareholders, employees, and customers than to suppliers, governments, and local communities, no matter what stage of the life cycle a company is in.[90] Exhibit 4.8 lists issues that organizations will probably have to address to keep their primary stakeholders satisfied.

Addressing the concerns of primary stakeholders is important because if a stakeholder group becomes dissatisfied and terminates its relationship with the company, the company could be seriously harmed or go out of business. Few shoppers buy food without looking at the nutritional label. In a few years, Walmart shoppers will be able to consult a similar label to determine which products are environmentally friendly. By creating an environmental index that describes the total environmental impact of a product, from creation to shipping, to recycling, Walmart is addressing the environmental concerns of primary stakeholders, customers. Walmart not only expects the index to affect which products its customers buy; it is already telling its suppliers that products with higher environmental scores will receive preferential shelf space in its stores, which could dramatically affect product sales. The index debuts in 2013, but right now only 10 percent of Walmart's suppliers have done the independent research to determine their products' scores.[91]

Secondary stakeholders, such as the media and special interest groups, can influence or be influenced by the company. Unlike the primary stakeholders, however, they do not engage in regular transactions with the company and are not critical to its long-term survival. Meeting the needs of primary stakeholders is therefore usually more important than meeting the needs of secondary stakeholders. Nevertheless, secondary stakeholders are still important because they can affect public perceptions and opinions about socially responsible behavior.

secondary stakeholders any group that can influence or be influenced by a company and can affect public perceptions about the company's socially responsible behavior.

For instance, PETA, People for the Ethical Treatment of Animals, is calling for a total boycott of Australia's $2.2 billion wool industry. With an aggressive ad campaign entitled "Did your sweater cause a bloody butt?" PETA wants Australia's 55,000 sheep farmers to stop the practice of mulesing, which it considers cruel. Mulesing removes skin folds from a sheep's rear end, usually without anesthesia, to prevent blowfly egg infestations that turn into flesh-eating maggots. PETA has convinced 30 leading fashion retailers, such as Benetton, Abercrombie & Fitch, Timberland, H&M, and Hugo Boss, to stop using Australian wool. PETA spokesperson Matt Prescott says, "Approaching companies with big names and deep pockets is the best way to drive change."[92] Craig Johnston, an Australian farmer with 6,000 merino sheep, says, "We don't mules to be cruel, we do it because it's the best husbandry practice available. Once a sheep suffers flystrike you are at a loss to do anything."[93] Still, as a result of PETA's pressure, Australian Wool Innovation, the industry's trade group, is sponsoring research to develop alternatives to mulesing.[94]

So, to whom are organizations socially responsible? Many commentators, especially economists and financial analysts, continue to argue that organizations are responsible only to shareholders. Increasingly, however, top managers have come to believe that they and their companies must be socially responsible to their stakeholders. This view has gained adherents since the Great Depression, when General Electric first identified shareholders, employees, customers, and the general public as its stakeholders. In 1947, Johnson & Johnson listed customers, employees, managers, and shareholders as its stakeholders; and in 1950, Sears Roebuck announced that its most important stakeholders were "customers, employees, community, and stockholders."[95] Today, surveys show that as many as 80 percent of top-level managers believe that it is unethical to focus just on shareholders. Twenty-nine states have changed their laws to allow company boards of directors to consider the needs of employees, creditors, suppliers, customers, and local communities, as well as those of shareholders.[96] Although there is not complete agreement, a majority of opinion makers would argue that companies must be socially responsible to their stakeholders.

To Whom Are Organizations Socially Responsible? Social responsibility is a business's obligation to benefit society. To whom are organizations socially responsible? According to the shareholder model, the only social responsibility that organizations have is to maximize shareholder wealth by maximizing company profits. According to the stakeholder model, companies must satisfy the needs and interests of multiple corporate stakeholders, not just shareholders. However, the needs of primary stakeholders, on which the organization relies for its existence, take precedence over those of secondary stakeholders.

Review 6

7 For What Are Organizations Socially Responsible?

If organizations are to be socially responsible to stakeholders, what are they to be socially responsible *for*? As Exhibit 4.9 illustrates, companies can best benefit their stakeholders by fulfilling their economic, legal, ethical, and discretionary responsibilities.[97] Economic and legal responsibilities are at the bottom of the pyramid, because they play a larger part in a company's social responsibility than do ethical and discretionary responsibilities. However, the relative importance of these various responsibilities depends on society's expectations of corporate social responsibility

Exhibit 4.9
Social Responsibilities

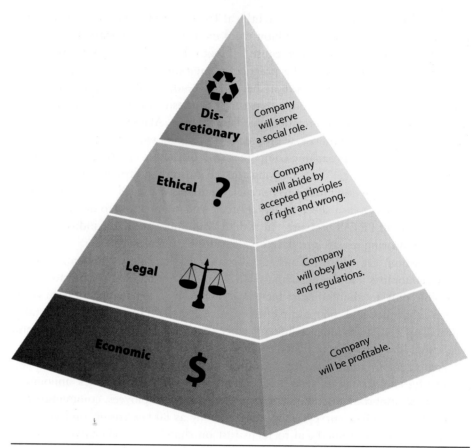

Source: Republished with permission of Academy of Management, P.O. Box 3020, Briar Cliff Manor, NY, 10510-8020, "A Three-Dimensional Conceptual Model of Corporate Performance," *Academy of Management Review*, 1978, vol. 4. Reproduced by permission of the publisher via Copyright Clearance Center, Inc.

at a particular point in time.[98] A century ago, society expected businesses to meet their economic and legal responsibilities and little else. Today, when society judges whether businesses are socially responsible, ethical and discretionary responsibilities are considerably more important than they used to be.

Historically, **economic responsibility**, or making a profit by producing a product or service valued by society, has been a business's most basic social responsibility. Organizations that don't meet their financial and economic expectations come under tremendous pressure. For example, company boards are quick these days to fire CEOs. Typically, all it takes is two or three bad quarters in a row. Owen Van Natta, CEO of MySpace, was fired after just eight months on the job. When he started, MySpace had 64 percent of social networking traffic compared to 29 percent for Facebook. When he was fired, Facebook had 68 percent and MySpace had 28 percent.[99] William Rollnick, who became acting chairman of Mattel after the company fired its previous CEO, says, "There's zero forgiveness. You screw up and you're dead."[100] On an annual basis, roughly 4 percent of the CEOS of large companies are fired.[101] Nearly one-third of all CEOs are eventually fired because of their inability to successfully change their companies.[102] In fact, CEOs are three times more likely to be fired today than they were two decades ago.

Legal responsibility is a company's social responsibility to obey society's laws and regulations as it tries to meet its economic responsibilities. For instance, companies award stock options so that managers and employees are rewarded when the company does well. Stock options give you the right to purchase shares of stock at a set price. Let's say that on June 1, the company awards you the right (or option) to buy 100 shares of stock, which, on that day, sells for $10 a share. If the stock price

economic responsibility a company's social responsibility to make a profit by producing a valued product or service.

legal responsibility a company's social responsibility to obey society's laws and regulations.

falls below $10, the options are worthless. But, if the stock price rises above $10, the options have value. Specifically, if the stock price rises to $15 a share, you can exercise your options by paying the company $1,000 (100 shares at $10 a share). But because the stock is selling for $15, you can sell your 100 shares for $1,500 and make $500. But what if you could go back in time to, say, January 1, when the stock was selling for $5? You'd make $1,000 instead of $500. It would be unethical and illegal, however, to "backdate" your options to when the stock sold for a lower price. Doing so would illegally increase the value of your options. But that's exactly what the president and chief operating officer did at Monster Worldwide (which runs Monster.com). By improperly backdating his options, he earned an additional $24 million.[103] At Monster, however, backdating was condoned by the CEO, who routinely backdated options for members of the management team.[104]

Ethical responsibility is a company's social responsibility not to violate accepted principles of right and wrong when conducting its business. Cyrus Hassankola has been "going out of business" for nearly two decades. Swiss-educated, but from Iran, he entered the Oriental rug business in Zurich. Because there were so many shops, he advertised that his was "going out of business." The store stayed open several more months and made huge amounts of money. He then opened and closed four more rug stores after running highly profitable "going out of business" sales. After moving to the United States, Hassankola replicated this strategy in five states, until, weary of traveling, he opened a store in Dallas and officially named it "Going Out of Business," with the hope that it would pull in customers on a regular basis. It's not illegal in Texas to name your store "Going Out of Business," but you are required to get a license for going out of business sales. The larger issue, however, is that most people would agree it's the wrong thing to do. David Beasley of Dallas's Better Business Bureau says, "I understand the desire to stay in business. But you can't do it by going out of business."[105] So, Hassankola's store is now the "Cyrus Rug Gallery," which has a "Liquidation Sale" banner out front. Because different stakeholders may disagree about what is or is not ethical, meeting ethical responsibilities is more difficult than meeting economic or legal responsibilities.

Discretionary responsibilities pertain to the social roles that businesses play in society beyond their economic, legal, and ethical responsibilities. After a massive earthquake in Haiti killed 220,000 people and destroyed the homes of 1.9 million more, companies came to aid by partnering with and supporting humanitarian agencies. UPS; TNT, a Dutch express parcel company; and Agility, a global sourcing and supply chain company, combined their efforts to deliver 2,000 metric tons of food and 15,000 metric tons of supplies per day! Likewise, Digicel, the largest mobile telecom company in the Caribbean, used its mobile network to instantly transfer funds to 2 million Haitians whose local banks had been destroyed in the quake. Finally, Google created a specially made missing persons database that helped families and the authorities learn what had happened to their loved ones.[106] Discretionary responsibilities such as these are voluntary. Companies are not considered unethical if they don't perform them. Today, however, corporate stakeholders expect companies to do much more than in the past to meet their discretionary responsibilities.

ethical responsibility a company's social responsibility not to violate accepted principles of right and wrong when conducting its business.

discretionary responsibilities the social roles that a company fulfills beyond its economic, legal, and ethical responsibilities.

© iStockphoto.com/Ken Brown

149

8 Responses to Demands for Social Responsibility

Social responsiveness refers to a company's strategy to respond to stakeholders' economic, legal, ethical, or discretionary expectations concerning social responsibility. A social responsibility problem exists whenever company actions do not meet stakeholder expectations. One model of social responsiveness, shown in Exhibit 4.10, identifies four strategies for responding to social responsibility problems: reactive, defensive, accommodative, and proactive. These strategies differ in the extent to which the company is willing to act to meet or exceed society's expectations.

A company using a **reactive strategy** will do less than society expects. It may deny responsibility for a problem or fight any suggestions that the company should solve a problem. Shortly after Apple introduced the iPhone 4, consumers started complaining about poor signal quality and dropped calls. The problem, created by a design that wrapped the antenna around the edge of the phone, led *Consumer Reports* to recommend that consumers "not buy" the phone. With widespread media attention and customers threatening class-action lawsuits, Apple's response was to deny the problem, telling customers they were holding the phone wrong (i.e., touching the lower, left corner of the phone). CEO Steve Jobs told one consumer who emailed him to "Just avoid holding it in that way." When complaints grew, Apple reported that the problem wasn't actually a weak signal, but a software problem that incorrectly displayed just one or two signal bars on the phone. Finally, after even more protests and the threat of government intervention, Apple announced that it would give every user a plastic case that would solve the problem. Even then, Steve Jobs continued to insist that only 55 percent of all iPhones had a problem, and that phones from competitors like Nokia, HTC, and Blackberry had the same issues.[107]

By contrast, a company using a **defensive strategy** would admit responsibility for a problem but would do the least required to meet societal expectations. Documents from a pending lawsuit against **Dell** suggest that the company shipped at least 11.8 million computers that had faulty electrical components and capacitors that broke and leaked fluid. As customer complaints mounted, Dell blamed the problems on the way customers were using the computers, for example, telling the University of Texas that it overworked the computers by having them perform complex math calculations. When an internal study helped Dell identify the

social responsiveness refers to a company's strategy to respond to stakeholders' economic, legal, ethical, or discretionary expectations concerning social responsibility.

reactive strategy a social responsiveness strategy in which a company does less than society expects.

defensive strategy a social responsiveness strategy in which a company admits responsibility for a problem but does the least required to meet societal expectations.

"what's new" companies >

Exhibit 4.10 Social Responsiveness

Reactive	Defensive	Accommodative	Proactive
Fight all the way	Do only what is required	Be progressive	Lead the industry
Withdrawal	Public Relations Approach	Legal Approach	Bargaining	Problem Solving

DO NOTHING ⟵──────────────⟶ DO MUCH

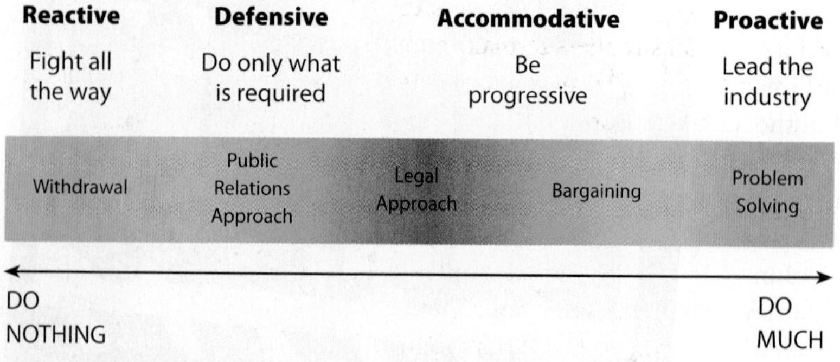

Source: A. B. Carroll, "A Three-Dimensional Conceptual Model of Corporate Performance," *Academy of Management Review* 4 (1979): 497–505.

mgmt:trends

Most companies are trying to make their products "green" by encouraging consumers to recycle the packaging. The snack-food manufacturer Frito-Lay has taken things one step further by offering the world's first 100 percent fully compostable bag. Its SunChips products now come in a bag made from plant-based polylactic acid. According to Frito-Lay, the bag will "fully break down in just 14 weeks when placed in a hot, active compost bin or pile." Although consumers can take the bag to a composting facility, Frito-Lay also provides detailed instructions on how they can start their own compost piles, making it easier to reduce waste.[108]

problem, instead of alerting customers or initiating a recall (an accommodative strategy), Dell continued to try to cover up the problem. One internal memo to salespeople said, "Don't bring this to customer's attention proactively." And, in many cases, Dell actually repaired the broken computers with more of the same faulty components. Ira Winkler, who was a computer analyst for the National Security Agency, said, "They were fixing bad computers with bad computers and were misleading customers at the same time." Although Dell took a $300 million charge to fix the computers, and has extended warranties for some customers, it has still not issued a general recall, which means that many customers may not be aware that they had purchased faulty computers. Dell's strategy throughout this process has been defensive.[109]

A company using an **accommodative strategy** will accept responsibility for a problem and take a progressive approach by doing all that could be expected to solve the problem. Unilever, one of the world's largest consumer product companies, annually buys 1.5 million tons of palm oil to be used in margarine, ice cream, soap, and shampoo. Greenpeace protestors dressed as orangutans and climbed to the top of the company's headquarters in London to draw attention to the palm oil suppliers, who they claimed were destroying palm forests in Indonesia and Malaysia. Emulating an award-winning Dove soap commercial, "Evolution," Greenpeace then produced a short video entitled "Dove Onslaught(er)," which attributed the use of palm oil in Unilever's Dove soap to deforestation of palm forests (see both on YouTube.com).[110] Unilever accepted responsibility for the problem, stating, "[F]ollowing a public challenge from Greenpeace, we formalized our commitment to draw all our palm oil from certified sustainable sources by 2015. We also agreed to support a moratorium on any further deforestation in South-East Asia."[111] Unilever also formed a coalition of 50 companies and nonprofits to influence palm oil growers, introduced resolutions at the Roundtable on Sustainable Palm Oil to encourage palm oil growers to change their foresting practices, began audits of their palm oil suppliers to make sure their practices were consistent with its new recommendations, and began working with Greenpeace and other groups to promote change in the industry.

Finally, a company using a **proactive strategy** will anticipate responsibility for a problem before it occurs, do more than expected to address the problem, and lead the industry in its approach. Two decades ago, **Merck**, a pharmaceutical company, began giving away its drug for river blindness, which thrives and spreads easily along fertile riverbanks in Africa and Latin America. River blindness affects 37 million people worldwide and could infect up to 100 million others.[112] Merck's drug program is the largest, on-going medical donation program in history. Since 1987, Merck has given away 530 million treatments at a cost of $3.75 billion. The World

accommodative strategy a social responsiveness strategy in which a company accepts responsibility for a problem and does all that society expects to solve that problem.

proactive strategy a social responsiveness strategy in which a company anticipates responsibility for a problem before it occurs and does more than society expects to address the problem.

< **"what's new" companies**

Health Organization now believes that, thanks to Merck's contributions, river blindness is on the verge of being completely eliminated in Africa.[113]

Review 8

Responses to Demands for Social Responsibility Social responsiveness is a company's response to stakeholders' demands for socially responsible behavior. There are four social responsiveness strategies. When a company uses a reactive strategy, it denies responsibility for a problem. When it uses a defensive strategy, it takes responsibility for a problem but does the minimum required to solve it. When a company uses an accommodative strategy, it accepts responsibility for problems and does all that society expects to solve them. Finally, when a company uses a proactive strategy, it does much more than expected to solve social responsibility problems.

9 Social Responsibility and Economic Performance

One question that managers often ask is, "Does it pay to be socially responsible?" In previous editions of this textbook, the answer was "no," as early research indicated that there was not an inherent relationship between social responsibility and economic performance.[114] Recent research, however, leads to different conclusions. There is no trade-off between being socially responsible and economic performance.[115] And there is a small, positive relationship between being socially responsible and economic performance that strengthens with corporate reputation.[116] Let's explore what each of these results means.

First, managers don't need to choose between being socially responsible and maximizing economic performance.[117] Being socially responsible usually won't make a business less profitable. What this suggests is that the costs of being socially responsible—and those costs can be high, especially early on—can be offset by a better product or corporate reputation, which results in stronger sales or higher profit margins.

"what's new" companies >

For example, **Honda**, which introduced the first hybrid car in North America, has long been an industry leader in fuel efficiency and environmentally friendly technology. So when it decided to enter the private plane market with the new Honda Jet, it took the same approach, using lightweight composite materials, instead of metal alloys, in the plane's body, and working closely with General Electric to design an efficient, lightweight, powerful engine that, when mounted—in a unique design—above the wings, further reduced fuel consumption. However, these features not only help the Honda Jet use less fuel, they make the Honda Jet lighter and faster than competitors. The unique engine and wing design gives it more interior space, reduces cabin noise, and makes it cheaper to operate. And although it seats a pilot and just four passengers, the cost of flying the Honda Jet will be no more expensive on a per mile basis than the common Canadair CRJ-200 regional jet, which transports 40 to 50 passengers. Honda believes that its socially responsible design is the key to making the Honda Jet profitable.[118]

© Kyodo/Landov

Second, it usually *does* pay to be socially responsible, and that relationship becomes stronger particularly when a company or its products have a strong reputation for social responsibility.[119] For example, GE, long one of the most admired and profitable corporations in the world, was one of the first and largest *Fortune 500* companies to make a strategic commitment to providing environmentally friendly products and service. CEO Jeffrey Immelt wants GE to "develop and drive the technologies of the future that will protect and clean our environment."[120] Is Immelt doing this because of personal beliefs? He says no. "It's no great thrill for me to do this stuff. ... I never put it in right versus wrong terms." GE calls its strategy "ecoimagination," which it says is "helping to solve the world's biggest environmental challenges while driving profitable growth for GE." Says Immelt, "We invest in the basic strategies that we think are going to fit into [ecoimagination], but make money for our investors at the same time."[121] In just five years, GE has increased the number of ecoimagination products from 17 to 80. As a result, it now sells more than $17 billion of such products and services each year, with annual revenue growth increasing by double digits.[122]

Finally, even if there is generally a small positive relationship between social responsibility and economic performance that becomes stronger when a company or its products have a positive reputation for social responsibility, and even if there is no trade-off between being socially responsible and economic performance, there is no guarantee that socially responsible companies will be profitable. Simply put, socially responsible companies experience the same ups and downs in economic performance that traditional businesses do. A good example is Ben & Jerry's, the ice cream company. Ben & Jerry's started in 1978, when founders Ben Cohen and Jerry Greenfield sent away for a $5 course on how to make ice cream. Ben & Jerry's is as famous for its commitment to social responsibility as for its super premium ice cream. The company donates 7.5 percent of its pretax profits to support AIDS patients, homeless people, and the environment.[123] Moreover, customers buy Ben & Jerry's ice cream because it tastes great *and* because they want to support a socially responsible company. As Ben Cohen says, "We see ourselves as somewhat of a social service agency and somewhat of an ice cream company."[124] But—and this is a big "but"—despite its outstanding reputation as a socially responsible company, Ben & Jerry's consistently had financial troubles after going public (selling shares of stock to the public) 15 years ago. In fact, its financial problems became so severe that Ben and Jerry sold the company to British-based Unilever.[125] Being socially responsible may be the right thing to do, and is usually associated with increased profits, but it doesn't guarantee business success.

Social Responsibility and Economic Performance Does it pay to be socially responsible? Studies show that there is generally no trade-off between social responsibility and economic performance. In most circumstances, there is generally a small positive relationship between social responsibility and economic performance that becomes stronger when a company or its products have a positive reputation. Social responsibility, however, does not guarantee profitability, as socially responsible companies experience the same ups and downs as other companies.

Review 9

SELF-ASSESSMENT

An Ethical Baseline

Most people think they are ethical, particularly when the right thing to do is seemingly obvious. But as you read in the chapter, 75 percent of the respondents in a nationwide survey indicated that they had witnessed unethical behavior at work. In another study across multiple industries, 48 percent of the respondents admitted to actually committing an unethical or illegal

KEY TERMS

act in the past year! And recall that with so many ways to approach ethical decision making, ethical choices are not always cut-and-dried. To give you an idea of your ethical perspective, take this assessment.[126]

Answer each of the questions using the following scale:

1 Strongly agree

2 Agree

3 Not sure

4 Disagree

5 Strongly disagree

1. Did you ever think about taking money from where you worked, but didn't go through with it?
   1   2   3   ④   5

2. Have you ever borrowed something from work without telling anyone?
   1   2   ③   4   5

3. There are times I've been provoked into a fistfight.
   1   2   3   ④   5

4. Is it okay to get around the law if you don't break it?
   1   2   3   ④   5

5. I've had fellow employees show me how to take things from where I work.
   1   2   3   4   ⑤

6. I will usually take someone up on a dare.
   1   2   3   4   ⑤

7. I've always driven insured vehicles.
   ①   2   3   4   5

8. If you were sent an extra item with an order, would you send it back?
   1   2   3   ④   5

9. Would you say everyone is a little dishonest?
   1   ②   3   4   5

10. Most supervisors treat their employees fairly.
    1   2   ③   4   5

11. I worry about getting hurt at work.
    1   2   3   4   ⑤

12. People say that I'm a workaholic.
    1   2   3   4   ⑤

13. I like to plan things carefully ahead of time.
    ①   2   3   4   5

14. Have you found a way a dishonest person in your job could take things from work?
    1   2   3   4   ⑤

15. I often act quickly without stopping to think things through.
    1   ②   3   4   5

16. It doesn't bother me what other people think.
    1   ②   3   4   5

17. I have friends who are a little dishonest.
    1   2   •3   ④   5

18. I am not a thrill seeker.
    1   2   3   4   ⑤

19. I have had my driver's license revoked.
    1   2   3   4   ⑤

20. Are you too honest to steal?
    1   ②   3   4   5

21. Do most employees take small items from work?
    1   2   3   ④   5

22. Do most employees get along well with their supervisors?
    1   2   ③   4   5

23. I'm lucky to avoid having accidents.
    1   2   ③   4   5

24. I always finish what I start.

    1   2   3   ④   5

25. I make sure everything is in its place before leaving home.

    ①   2   3   4   5

Scoring

Determine your average score for each category by entering your response to each survey item below, as follows. In blanks that say *regular score*, simply enter your response for that item. If your response was a 4, place a 4 in the *regular score* blank. In blanks that say *reverse score*, subtract your response from 6 and enter the result. So if your response was a 4, place a 2 $(6 - 4 = 2)$ in the *reverse score* blank. Total your scores; then compute your average score for each section.

Antisocial Behavior

1. regular score   _____
2. regular score   _____
3. regular score   _____
4. regular score   _____
5. regular score   _____
6. regular score   _____
7. reverse score   _____
8. reverse score   _____
14. regular score   _____
15. regular score   _____

16. regular score   _____
17. regular score   _____
18. reverse score   _____
19. regular score   _____
20. reverse score   _____

    TOTAL = _____ ÷ 15 = _____ (your average for Antisocial Behavior)

Orderliness/Diligence

12. regular score   _____
13. regular score   _____
24. regular score   _____
25. regular score   _____

    TOTAL = _____ ÷ 4 = _____ (your average for Orderliness/Diligence)

Positive Outlook

9. reverse score   _____
10. regular score   _____
11. reverse score   _____
21. reverse score   _____
22. regular score   _____
23. regular score   _____

    TOTAL = _____ ÷ 6 = _____ (your average for Positive Outlook)

You can find the interpretation for your scores at www.cengagebrain.com.

MANAGEMENT DECISION

Responding to Tragedy[127]

On April 5, 2010, an explosion at the Upper Big Branch coal mine in Montcoal, West Virginia, killed 29 workers. Over the next several weeks and days, as nationwide attention turned to this tragedy, it was discovered that the mine's operating company, Massey Energy, was cited for numerous safety and regulatory violations. One month prior to the accident, the mine was written up more than 50 times, with 12 of those notices relating to an excessive buildup of coal dust and methane, conditions that can cause explosions like the one that occurred. The very day of the explosion, federal regulators identified two more safety violations, a failure to have updated maps of escape routes in case of an accident and a failure to outfit miners with required communication and tracking equipment that would help them stay in contact with aboveground employees. All told, officials found 1,342 safety violations at Upper Big Branch from 2005 to April 2009. And according to these investigators, miners at Upper Big Branch lost more time to work-site accidents than any other mine in the country.

In spite of the large number of violations, Massey continues to insist that they are committed to safety. On its website, the company proclaims "Safety is the top priority for every Massey member. . . . We work hard to instill a zero-tolerance policy and commitment from all members, whether they work at corporate headquarters or in the mines, to make safety the number one priority—every day." However, the company's reactions to regulators' citations have generally been resistant and confrontational. According to government records, Massey has contested or appealed a good portion of the violations it has received since 2005. By doing so, it has been able to avoid paying the fines and making the safety changes required by regulators.

The question for you, as a manager at Massey Energy is this: How will you address your company's ethical responsibility? Will you continue to insist that the company is doing everything it can for safety, even as the number of violations skyrockets? Will you insist that all safety violations be addressed immediately and that unsafe mines be closed until they pass inspections, at the cost of hundreds of millions of dollars? What steps could you take to insure that your company is an industry leader in safety, while also remaining profitable?

Questions

1. How would you describe Massey's current approach to its ethical and social responsibility?
2. Which approach to social responsibility would you recommend that Massey take in the future?
3. How might the temporary closure of dangerous mines and the investment of funds into new safety systems be an economic stimulus for Massey?

MANAGEMENT TEAM DECISION

Environment and Business in St. Tropez[128]

There are few places in the world like St. Tropez, a city on the French Riviera—pristine, isolated beaches, perfect weather nearly all year round, and a string of ultra-luxurious hotels that host celebrities from all over the world, everyone from the Hilton sisters to Bono. But if the mayor of St. Tropez has his way, this ultimate vacation spot will soon look a lot different.

Mayor Roland Bruno's administration is highly concerned that the hotels, and all of their beachfront facilities, present a serious environmental threat. They want to protect rare plant species that grow in the sands, and prevent dunes from being worn down by constant foot traffic. According to the mayor's chief of staff, "We all want to be here for the long term. That's why we need to make sure there's a sustainable equilibrium between the environment and the community." Under the mayor's plan, the amount of beaches allowed for business use would decrease by 10 percent, and an entire section of the popular Pampelonne area would be closed off to protect wildlife. Additionally, all beaches would be closed by September 1, instead of October, as is usually the case, to reduce the number of people who travel to and through the beaches.

Many local hotel owners are up in arms about these proposals. One owner likened closing the beaches of the city to cutting the top off the Eiffel Tower. Others argue that closing the Pampelonne area is really intended to bring in large, multinational vacation companies to replace the small, locally owned resorts. As Carole Balligand, the head of a local business group says, "This would mean the total destruction of everything that has been here for nearly half a century."

The owner of your hotel has called a meeting of the management staff to draw up a response to the mayor's plan. Although all of you are in agreement that protecting the environment is important, your hotel happens to sit on one of the plots that is scheduled to be closed by the mayor's plan. Is there a way that your company can find a way to balance environmental concerns with the need to stay in business?

For this management team decision, form a group with three to five other students and consider the questions below.

Questions

1. How would you respond to the mayor's plan? Would you support its concern to protect the environment even if it meant the closure of your hotel? Would you oppose it and risk being perceived as uninterested in fulfilling social responsibility?
2. Can you come up with a scenario where the hotel could stay in business and still address the mayor office's environmental concerns?
3. In cases such as this, how would you justify the decision to fulfill the responsibility and face certain loss? How would you justify the decision to ignore the responsibility for the sake of staying in business?

PRACTICE BEING A MANAGER

Discerning Unethical Behavior

Applying ethical judgment in an organizational setting can be challenging. This exercise offers you the opportunity to consider how you might approach such a situation as a manager in an investment firm.

Read the scenario and prepare your responses to the individual (homework) questions in advance of discussing this exercise in class.

Scenario

Imagine that you are a newly hired portfolio manager at Excalibur Funds. Although you're new to this job, you have eight years' experience in the mutual fund business. You left a larger and more established mutual fund company to join Excalibur because of its reputation as a bright, up-and-coming investment company, a place where someone like yourself could participate in building a new and dynamic investment company.

Your new fund, the Pioneer Fund, is a growth-oriented fund investing in small companies. Typically, the majority of the fund's stock investments is in high-technology companies. Pioneer is moving up fast in its peer group, and if the fund continues to perform well, you stand a good chance of being the manager recognized when it breaks into the top tier of performance.

One of the features that attracted you to this job is the opportunity to work with a seasoned group of traders, analysts, and staff professionals. The Pioneer Fund staff has averaged 10 percent turnover over the past five years, unusual in an industry where turnover commonly reaches 60 to 80 percent. After a month of working with your new team, however, you have noticed some troubling patterns. First, you felt that some of your staff were delaying or stonewalling you on several occasions when you requested more detailed information on particular trades. It took too long to get the information, and when you did receive it, the information looked a little *too* neat and well organized. Second, the analysts have seemed guarded regarding their interaction with some of the technology companies in which the Pioneer Fund invests. On more than one occasion, you've noticed analysts quickly ending phone calls when you entered the office or minimizing computer screens when you walk by their desks. Finally, the group just seems a bit too *nice* when you are around. The investment business is often hectic and stressful. Shouting matches over investment decisions are not uncommon, and grumbling is a second language. But all you get are smiles and charm.

So here you are at your desk on a Saturday evening, finishing off the last of a pot of coffee and planning for Monday morning. One thing is clear—you must begin to scratch below the surface of the Pioneer Fund team. Your gut tells you that something is wrong here, perhaps very wrong. For all you know, you may be sitting on the next big investment scandal. Your head tells you that you have no hard evidence of unethical or illegal behavior and that you'd better tread carefully. If your gut is wrong and you run around making hasty accusations, you may lose what appears to be a very talented investment team.

What steps should you take starting Monday morning?

Preparing for Class Discussion

Complete the following steps individually in preparation for class discussion. Write your responses to the questions in each step.

Step 1: Understand the situation and key considerations. What considerations would be important to you in developing a plan of action in this situation? What resources might you draw upon to determine whether or not particular actions are unethical and/or illegal?

Step 2: Develop a plan of action. What steps would you follow in this scenario? What factors should you consider in planning your timing of these steps?

Step 3: Anticipate response(s). How might the Pioneer Fund employees respond to your plan of action? Develop a few scenarios.

Small Group and Class Discussion

Your professor will assign you to a small discussion group. Your group should discuss the following questions and be prepared to share your thoughts with the class:

1. What are the most difficult aspects of responding to a murky situation—those situations in which

you sense the presence of unethical and/or illegal behavior but haven't seen unequivocal proof of wrongdoing?

2. What are the risks of waiting for unequivocal proof before beginning to take action? What are the risks of acting decisively based on your "gut" sense of a situation?

3. What is different about acting ethically/responsibly within an organizational environment/culture like that of the Pioneer Fund versus acting ethically/responsibly as an individual? What are the particular challenges and dynamics associated with ethical and responsible behavior in an organization?

DEVELOP YOUR CAREER POTENTIAL

Examining Nonprofits

It is only the farmer who faithfully plants seeds in the Spring, who reaps a harvest in the Autumn.
—B. C. Forbes, founder of *Forbes* magazine

These assignments will help develop your present and future capabilities as a manager. Because stakeholders increasingly expect companies to do more to fulfill their discretionary responsibilities, chances are you and your company will be expected to support your community in some significant way. To begin learning about community needs and corporate social responsibility, visit a local charity or nonprofit organization of your choosing, perhaps a hospital, the Red Cross, Goodwill, Planned Parenthood, a soup kitchen, or a homeless shelter. Talk to the people who work or volunteer there. Gather the information you need to answer the following questions.

Questions

1. What is the organization's mission?
2. Whom does the organization serve, and how does it serve them?
3. What percentage of the organization's donations is used for administrative purposes? What percentage is used to directly benefit those served by the organization? What is the ratio of volunteers to paid workers?
4. What job or task does a typical volunteer perform for the organization? How much time does a typical volunteer give to the organization each week? For what types of jobs does the organization need more volunteers?
5. How does the business community support the organization?
6. Why are you interested in the activities of this organization?

END NOTES

[1]S. Azfzal, "Smokers Need Not Apply: Is Hiring Ban Trend of the Future?" *The Christian Science Monitor*, November 17, 2010, accessed March 4, 2011, from www.csmonitor.com/Business/2010/1117/Smokers-need-not-apply-Is-hiring-ban-trend-of-the-future; M. Hennessy, "Right to Smoke?" *CFO* (February 2006): 54; M. Janofsky, "Ban on Employees Who Smoke Faces Challenges of Bias," *The New York Times*, April 28, 1994, A1; M. Lecker, "The Smoking Penalty: Distributive Justice or Smokism?" *Journal of Business Ethics* 84 (2009): 47–64; K. Maher, "Companies Are Closing Doors On Job Applicants Who Smoke," *The Wall Street Journal*, December 21, 2004, B6; and A. Sulzberger,

"Hospitals Shift Smoking Bans to Smoker Ban," *The New York Times*, 10 February 2011, accessed March 4, 2011, from www.nytimes.com/2011/02/11/us/11smoking.html?_r=1&hp.

[2]J. Schramm, "Perceptions on Ethics," *HR Magazine* 49 (November 2004): 176.

[3]M. Jackson, "Workplace Cheating Rampant, Half of Employees Surveyed Admit They Take Unethical Actions," *Peoria Journal Star*, April 5, 1997.

[4]C. Bray, "The Madoff Fraud: Madoff Lawyer Says 12 Years Fair— Sentencing Set for Monday; 'Death Threats and Anti-Semitic Emails' Cited," *The Wall Street Journal*, June 24, 2009, C3;

and L. Rappaport, "Economic Hard Times Produce a Rise in Fraud," *The Wall Street Journal*, April 15, 2009, C4.

[5]C. Smith, "The Ethical Workplace," *Association Management* 52 (2000): 70–73.

[6]D. Jones, "More Workers Do Now Than Before Recent Big Scandals," *USA Today*, February 12, 2003, B7.

[7]Adam Bryant, "In a Word, He Wants Simplicity," *The New York Times*, May 23, 2009, accessed August 15, 2011, from www.nytimes.com/2009/05/24/business/24corner.html?_r=2&pagewanted=1.

[8]R. Guha & R. Krishna, "Corporate News: India Charges Satyam's

Founder, Eight Others," *The Wall Street Journal*, April 8, 2009, B4.

[9]M. Bordwin, "Don't Ask Employees to Do Your Dirty Work," *Management Review*, 1 (October 1995).

[10]C. Hymowitz, "Managers Must Respond to Employee Concerns about Honest Business," *The Wall Street Journal*, February 19, 2002, B1.

[11]M. Schweitzer, L. Ordonez, & B. Douma, "Goal Setting As a Motivator of Unethical Behavior," *Academy of Management Journal* 47 (2004): 422–432.

[12]S. Pulliam & M. Rothfield, "Plea Deals Ramp up Pressure in Galleon, *The Wall Street Journal*, January 27, 2011, C1; and G. Zuckerman, D. Clark, & S. Pulliam, "Colleagues Finger Billionaire—Galleon Founder Pushed Hard for Stock-Trading Tips; 'Get an Edge or You're Gone,'" *The Wall Street Journal*, October 19, 2009, A1.

[13]Association of Certified Fraud Examiners, "2008 Report to the Nation on Occupational Fraud and Abuse," accessed July 15, 2008, from www.acfe.com/resources/publications.asp?copy=rttn; K. Gibson, "Excuses, Excuses: Moral Slippage in the Workplace," *Business Horizons* 43, no. 6 (2000): 65; and S. L. Robinson & R. J. Bennett, "A Typology of Deviant Workplace Behaviors: A Multidimensional Scaling Study," *Academy of Management Journal* 38 (1995): 555–572.

[14]Association of Certified Fraud Examiners, "2008 Report to the Nation on Occupational Fraud and Abuse"; K. Gibson, "Excuses, Excuses: Moral Slippage in the Workplace"; and S. L. Robinson & R. J. Bennett, "A Typology of Deviant Workplace Behaviors."

[15]S. Covel, "Building Your Business: Today's Topic: Dealing With Dishonesty," *The Wall Street Journal*, February 19, 2009, B5.

[16]S. Needleman, "Businesses Say Theft by Their Workers Is Up—Companies Find That Trusted Employees Often Commit the Crimes, and They Believe the Recession Is to Blame," *The Wall Street Journal*, December 11, 2008, B8.

[17]J. Norman, "Cultivating a Culture of Honesty," *The Orange County Register*, October 23, 2006.

[18]G. Richards, "When the Sewage Hits the Fan," *Engineering & Technology*, 22 (May 2009): 47.

[19]K. Grannis, "Retail Losses Hit $41.6 Billion Last Year, According to National Retail Security Survey," *National Retail Federation*, June 11, 2007, accessed July 12, 2010, from www.nrf.com/modules.php?name=News&op=viewlive&sp_id=318.

[20]M. Pressler, "Cost and Robbers; Shoplifting and Employee Thievery Add Dollars to Price Tag," *The Washington Post*, February 16, 2003, H05.

[21]I. Sherr, "U.S. Retailers Continue Struggle with Employee Theft," *Reuters*, accessed February 19, 2011, from www.reuters.com/article/2009/07/10/us-usa-crime-retail-idUS-TRE56957N20090710, 0 July 2009.

[22]S. Miller, "Despite Workers' Comp Relief, Fraud Still Costly," Society for Human Resource Management, accessed March 13, 2009, from www.shrm.org.

[23]Emily Friedman & Ned Potter, "Gunman Opens Fire at Hartford Beer Distributorship, Kills 8 Before Shooting Himself," ABCNews.com, August 3, 2010, accessed February 19, 2011, from http://abcnews.go.com/US/shooting-connecticut-beer-distributor-shooter-driver-disciplinary-hearing/story?id=11313457.

[24]D. Dishneau & S. Brumfield, "Gunman Shot as Discover Hostages Planned Escape," *Yahoo! News*, September 2, 2010, accessed February 19, 2011, from http://news.yahoo.com/s/ap/us_discovery_channel_gunman.

[25]L. Middlebrooks & P. C. Vreeland, "Many U.S. Employers Aren't Doing Enough to Address Workplace Violence," *Alabama Employment Law Letter*, December 2006.

[26]J. Merchant & J. Lundell, "Workplace Violence: A Report to the Nation," University of Iowa Injury Prevention Center, accessed July 15, 2008, from www.public-health.uiowa.edu/iprc/NATION.PDF.

[27]Bureau of Labor Statistics, "Economic News Release: Census of Fatal Occupational Injuries Summary, 2009," U.S. Department of Labor, August 19, 2010, accessed February 19, 2011, from www.bls.gov/iif/oshcfoi1.htm.

[28]M. P. Coco, Jr., "The New War Zone: The Workplace," *SAM Advanced Management Journal* 63, no. 1 (1998): 15; and M. G. Harvey & R. A. Cosier, "Homicides in the Workplace: Crisis or False Alarm?" *Business Horizons* 38, no. 10 (1995): 11.

[29]D. Palmer & A. Zakhem, "Bridging the Gap between Theory and Practice: Using the 1991 Federal Sentencing Guidelines as a Paradigm for Ethics Training," *Journal of Business Ethics* 29, no. 1/2 (2001): 77–84.

[30]Tyler, "Do the Right Thing."

[31]D. R. Dalton, M. B. Metzger, & J. W. Hill, "The 'New' U.S. Sentencing Commission Guidelines: A Wake-Up Call for Corporate America," *Academy of Management Executive* 8 (1994): 7–16.

[32]B. Ettore, "Crime and Punishment: A Hard Look at White-Collar Crime," *Management Review* 83 (1994): 10–16.

[33]F. Robinson & C. C. Pauze, "What Is a Board's Liability for Not Adopting a Compliance Program?" *Healthcare FinancialManagement* 51, no. 9 (1997): 64.

[34]D. Murphy, "The Federal Sentencing Guidelines for Organizations: A Decade of Promoting Compliance and Ethics," *Iowa Law Review* 87 (2002): 697–719.

[35]Robinson & Pauze, "What Is a Board's Liability?"

[36]B. Schwartz, "The Nuts and Bolts of an Effective Compliance Program," *HR Focus* 74, no. 8 (1997): 13–15.

[37]L. A. Hays, "A Matter of Time: Widow Sues IBM over Death Benefits," *The Wall Street Journal*, July 6, 1995, A1.

[38]T. M. Jones, "Ethical Decision Making by Individuals in Organizations: An Issue-Contingent Model," *Academy of Management Review* 16 (1991): 366–395.

[39]S. Morris & R. McDonald, "The Role of Moral Intensity in Moral Judgments: An Empirical Investigation," *Journal of Business Ethics* 14 (1995): 715–726; and B. Flannery

& D. May, "Environmental Ethical Decision Making in the U.S. Metal-Finishing Industry," *Academy of Management Journal* 43 (2000): 642–662.

[40]L. Chao, "China Court Issues Rare Piracy Penalty to Windows Copycats," *The Wall Street Journal*, August 22, 2009, A9.

[41]L. Kohlberg, "Stage and Sequence: The Cognitive-Developmental Approach to Socialization," in *Handbook of Socialization Theory and Research*, ed. D. A. Goslin (Chicago: Rand McNally, 1969); and L. Trevino, "Moral Reasoning and Business Ethics: Implications for Research, Education, and Management," *Journal of Business Ethics* 11 (1992): 445–459.

[42]L. Trevino & M. Brown, "Managing to be Ethical: Debunking Five Business Ethics Myths," *Academy of Management Executive* 18 (May 2004): 69–81.

[43]L. T. Hosmer, "Trust: The Connecting Link between Organizational Theory and Philosophical Ethics," *Academy of Management Review* 20 (1995): 379–403.

[44]R. K. Bennett, "How Honest Are We?" *Reader's Digest* (December 1995): 49–55; L. Callaway, "On the Wallet Watch—Honesty's Not Big Apple's Policy," *New York Post*, July 31, 2000, 41; A. Golab, "Results of Honesty Test: Mostly 'Finders, Keepers,'" *Chicago Sun-Times*, March 12, 1999, 3; and D. Zlomislic, "We Left 20 Wallets around the GTA. Most Came Back," *Toronto Star*, April 25, 2009, accessed August 29, 2009, www.thestar.com.

[45]M. R. Cunningham, D. T. Wong, & A. P. Barbee, "Self-Presentation Dynamics on Overt Integrity Tests: Experimental Studies of the Reid Report," *Journal of Applied Psychology* 79 (1994): 643–658; and J. Wanek, P. Sackett, & D. Ones, "Toward an Understanding of Integrity Test Similarities and Differences: An Item-Level Analysis of Seven Tests," *Personnel Psychology* 56 (Winter 2003): 873–894.

[46]H. J. Bernardin, "Validity of an Honesty Test in Predicting Theft among Convenience Store Employees," *Academy of Management Journal* 36 (1993): 1097–1108.

[47]J. M. Collins & F. L. Schmidt, "Personality, Integrity, and White Collar Crime: A Construct Validity Study," *Personnel Psychology* (1993): 295–311.

[48]W. C. Borman, M. A. Hanson, & J. W. Hedge, "Personnel Selection," *Annual Review of Psychology* 48 (1997).

[49]P. E. Murphy, "Corporate Ethics Statements: Current Status and Future Prospects," *Journal of Business Ethics* 14 (1995): 727–740.

[50]"Code of Business Conduct" Nortel, accessed February 25, 2011, from www.nortel.com/corporate/community/ethics/collateral/nn104800-110309.pdf.

[51]"More Corporate Boards Involved in Ethics Programs; Ethics Training Becoming Standard Practice," *PR Newswire*, October 16, 2006.

[52]S. J. Harrington, "What Corporate America Is Teaching about Ethics," *Academy of Management Executive* 5 (1991): 21–30.

[53]L. A. Berger, "Train All Employees to Solve Ethical Dilemmas," *Best's Review—Life-Health Insurance Edition* 95 (1995): 70–80.

[54]D. Schmidt, "Ethics Can Be Taught," *Inc.*, June 24, 2008, accessed July 10, 2010, from www.inc.com/leadership-blog/2008/06/ethics_can_be_taught_1.html.

[55]L. Trevino, G. Weaver, D. Gibson, & B. Toffler, "Managing Ethics and Legal Compliance: What Works and What Hurts," *California Management Review* 41, no. 2 (1999): 131–151.

[56]D. Heath & C. Heath, "The Power of Razzle-Dazzle," *Fast Company*, December 2009, 69–70.

[57]Trevino et al., "Managing Ethics and Legal Compliance."

[58]White, "Theory & Practice: What Would You Do?"

[59]A. Countryman, "Leadership Key Ingredient in Ethics Recipe, Experts Say," *Chicago Tribune*, December 1, 2002, Business 1.

[60]"More Corporate Boards Involved in Ethics Programs," *PR Newswire*.

[61]Supplemental Research Brief, "2009 National Business Ethics Survey: The Importance of Ethical Culture," Ethics Resource Center, June 2010, accessed February 25, 2011, from www.ethics.org/files/u5/CultureSup4.pdf.

[62]G. Weaver & L. Trevino, "Integrated and Decoupled Corporate Social Performance: Management Commitments, External Pressures, and Corporate Ethics Practices," *Academy of Management Journal* 42 (1999): 539–552; and L. Trevino, G. Weaver, D. Gibson, & B. Toffler, "Managing Ethics and Legal Compliance: What Works and What Hurts," *California Management Review* 41, no. 2 (1999): 131–151.

[63]J. Salopek, "Do the Right Thing," *Training & Development* 55 (July 2001): 38–44.

[64]M. Gundlach, S. Douglas, & M. Martinko, "The Decision to Blow the Whistle: A Social Information Processing Framework," *Academy of Management Executive* 17 (2003): 107–123.

[65]M. Schwartz, "Business Ethics: Time to Blow the Whistle?" *Globe & Mail*, March 5, 1998, B2.

[66]G. Alliger & S. Dwight, "A Meta-Analytic Investigation of the Susceptibility of Integrity Tests to Faking and Coaching," *Educational and Psychological Measurement* 60 (2000): 59–72; and D. S. Ones, C. Viswesvaran, & F. L. Schmidt "Comprehensive Meta-Analysis of Integrity Test Validities: Findings and Implications for Personnel Selection and Theories of Job Performance," *Journal of Applied Psychology* 78 (1993): 679–703; and "2004 Report to the Nation on Occupational Fraud and Abuse."

[67]M. Corkery, "Lehman Whistle-Blower's Fate: Fired," *The Wall Street Journal*, March 15, 2010, accessed August 5, 2010, http://online.wsj.com/article/NA_WSJ_PUB:SB10001424052748704588404575124134271085018.html.

[68]"About EY/Ethics," Ernst & Young, accessed August 29, 2009, from https://secure.ethicspoint.com/domain/media/en/gui/6483/index.html.

[69]"More Corporate Boards Involved in Ethics Programs," *PR Newswire*.

[70]M. P. Miceli & J. P. Near, "Whistle-blowing: Reaping the Benefits," *Academy of Management Executive* 8 (1994): 65–72.

[71]A. Ritchie, "Just Days before Retiring, Macy's Employee Caught Red-Handed," KPMH Fox 26, 3 October 2009, accessed February 25, 2011, from www.kmph.com/Global/story. asp?S=11250987.

[72]M. Master & E. Heresniak, "The Disconnect in Ethics Training," *Across the Board* 39 (September 2002): 51–52.

[73]H. R. Bower, *Social Responsibilities of the Businessman* (New York: Harper & Row, 1953).

[74]"Beyond the Green Corporation," *Businessweek*, January 29, 2007.

[75]M. Nichols, "Corrected: Amid recession, U.S. companies Boost Non-Cash Giving," *Reuters*, 27 October 2010, accessed February 25, 2010, www.reuters.com/article/2010/10/27/ us-philanthropy-corporations-idUS-TRE69Q0I020101027.

[76]Z. Zuno, "Americans Send the Message: Get Down to Business on Corporate Citizenship: Ben & Jerry's, Target, Patagonia, SC Johnson and Gerber Top the 4th GolinHarris Corporate Citizenship Index in Rating of 152 Brands by 5,000 Americans," *Business Wire*, December 6, 2006.

[77]Tom Zeller, Jr. ,"Banks Grow Wary of Environmental Risks," *The New York Times*, August 30, 2010, accessed October 11, 2010, from www. nytimes.com/2010/08/31/business/ energy-environment/31coal.html.

[78]T. Hurst, "Burger King to Harness Kinetic Energy from Speed Bumps," CleanTechnica.com, July 7, 2009, accessed February 25, 2011, from http://cleantechnica.com/2009/07/07/ burger-king-to-harness-kinetic-energyfrom-speed-bumps/.

[79]Mark Dolliver, "Thumbs Down on Corporate Green Efforts," Adweek.com, August 31, 2010, accessed October 10, 2010, from www. adweek.com/aw/content_display/ news/client/e3i84260d4301c885f-91b2cd8a712f323cf.

[80]"Honda Partnership With the Detroit Symphony Orchestra," Honda, accessed February 25, 2011, http:// corporate.honda.com/america/events. aspx?id=dso.

[81]"Current Focus on Hunger Relief," The Wal-Mart Foundation: Creating Opportunities so People Can Live Better, accessed February 25, 2011, from http://walmartstores.com/CommunityGiving/203.aspx.

[82]"Domestic Violence," Verizon Communications, accessed February 25, 2011, from http://foundation.verizon. com/core/domestic.shtml.

[83]S. L. Wartick & P. L. Cochran, "The Evolution of the Corporate Social Performance Model," *Academy of Management Review* 10 (1985): 758–769.

[84]Nocera, "The Paradox of Businesses as Do-Gooders," *The New York Times*, C1.

[85]S. Waddock, C. Bodwell, & S. Graves, "Responsibility: The New Business Imperative," *Academy of Management Executive* 16 (2002): 132–148.

[86]"PepsiCo CEO: Redefine Profit and Loss" Marketplace, January 29, 2010, accessed February 25, 2010, from http://marketplace.publicradio .org/display/web/2010/01/29/ pm-davos-pepsi-ceo-q/.

[87]T. Donaldson & L. E. Preston, "The Stakeholder Theory of the Corporation: Concepts, Evidence, and Implications," *Academy of Management Review* 20 (1995): 65–91.

[88]M. B. E. Clarkson, "A Stakeholder Framework for Analyzing and Evaluating Corporate Social Performance," *Academy of Management Review* 20 (1995): 92–117.

[89]I. M. Jawahar & G. McLaughlin, "Toward a Descriptive Stakeholder Theory: An Organizational Life Cycle Approach," *Academy of Management Review* 26 (2001): 397–414.

[90]B. Agle, R. Mitchell, & J. Sonnenfeld, "Who Matters to CEOs? An Investigation of Stakeholder Attributes and Salience, Corporate Performance, and CEO Values," *Academy of Management Journal* 42 (1999): 507–525.

[91]K. Rockwood, "Walmart Shoppers: Clean-up in Aisle Nine," *Fast Company*, February 2010, 30–32.

[92]K. Capell, "The Wool Industry Gets Bloodied," *Businessweek*, July 14, 2008, 40.

[93]S. Williams & J. Melocco, "Telling the Real Yarn," *The Daily Telegraph* (Australia), June 14, 2008, 115.

[94]"Australian Wool Innovation's Road Map for Flystrike Control and Prevention," Australian Wool Innovation, accessed February 26, 2011, from http:// images.wool.com/pub/AWI0595_Flystrike_Road_Map_Leaflet_271109.pdf.

[95]L. E. Preston, "Stakeholder Management and Corporate Performance," *Journal of Behavioral Economics* 19 (1990): 361–375.

[96]E. W. Orts, "Beyond Shareholders: Interpreting Corporate Constituency Statutes," *George Washington Law Review* 61 (1992): 14–135.

[97]A. B. Carroll, "A Three-Dimensional Conceptual Model of Corporate Performance," *Academy of Management Review* 4 (1979): 497–505.

[98]A. B. Carroll, "A Three-Dimensional Conceptual Model of Corporate Performance."

[99]Mercedes Bunz, "What Ended Owen Van Natta's Short Reign at MySpace?" guardian.co.uk., February 11, 2010, accessed August 12, 2010, from www. guardian.co.uk/media/pda/2010/ feb/11/myspace-murdoch).

[100]J. Lublin & M. Murrary, "CEOs Leave Faster Than Ever Before as Boards, Investors Lose Patience," *The Wall Street Journal Interactive*, October 27, 2000.

[101]J. Lublin, "CEO Firings On the Rise As Downturn Gains Steam," *The Wall Street Journal*, January 13, 2009, B1.

[102]D. Woodruff, "Europe Shows More CEOs the Door," *The Wall Street Journal*, July 1, 2002.

[103]C. Bray, "Ex-Monster President Found Guilty in Backdating Case," May 13, 2009, *The Wall Street Journal*, C4.

[104]J. Bandler, "McKelvey Admits Monster Backdating; Ex-CEO to Repay Millions but Avoids Jail Due to Illness," *The Wall Street Journal*, January 24, 2008, B4.

[105]B. Newman, "In Texas, There's No Business Like 'Going Out of Business'—Owner Alters Rug Shop's Controversial Name But the Haggling Goes On and On," *The Wall Street Journal*, June 24, 2009, A1.

[106]R. Greenhill, "The Corporate Response to Haiti," *The Wall Street Journal*, July 17, 2010, A11.

[107]Brian X. Chen, "Apple's Answer to Antennagate: Free iPhone 4 Cases," *Wired*, July 16, 2010, accessed September 4, 2010, from www.wired.com/gadgetlab/2010/07/iphone-4/; Mark Hachman, "Apple's Jobs: You're Holding the iPhone 4 Wrong," PC Magazine, June 25, 2010, accessed September 4, 2010, from www.pcmag.com/article2/0,2817,2365705,00.asp; and Miguel Helft, "Apple Acknowledges Flaw in iPhone Signal Meter," *The New York Times*, July 2, 2010, accessed September 4, 2010, from www.nytimes.com/2010/07/03/technology/03apple.html?src=un&feedurl=http://json8.nytimes.com/pages/technology/index.jsonp.

[108]"Why Make a Better Bag?" accessed December 12, 2010, from www.sunchips.com/resources/pdf/sunchips_bags.pdf.

[109]A. Vance, "In Faulty-Computer Suit, Window to Dell Decline," *The New York Times*, June 28, 2010, accessed June 28, 2010, from www.nytimes.com/2010/06/29/technology/29dell.html?pagewanted=1&hp.

[110]A. Patrick, "After Protests, Unilever Does About-Face On Palm Oil," *The Wall Street Journal*, May 2, 2008, B1.

[111]"Sustainable Palm Oil," Unilever, accessed August 30, 2009, from www.unilever.com/sustainability/environment/agriculture/palmoil/.

[112]"FACT Sheet—Merck Mectizan® Donation Program—River Blindness (Onchocerciasis)," Merck, accessed February 26, 2011, www.merck.com/cr/docs/River%20Blindness%20Fact%20Sheet.pdf.

[113]A. Weintraub, "Will Pfizer's Giveaway Drugs Polish its Public Image?" *Businessweek*, August 3, 2009, 13.

[114]A. McWilliams & D. Siegel, "Corporate Social Responsibility: A Theory of the Firm Perspective," *Academy of Management Review* 26, no.1 (2001): 117–127; H. Haines, "Noah Joins Ranks of Socially Responsible Funds,"

Dow Jones News Service, October 13, 1995. A meta-analysis of 41 different studies also found no relationship between corporate social responsibility and profitability. Though not reported in the meta-analysis, when confidence intervals are placed around its average sample-weighted correlation of 0.06, the lower confidence interval includes zero, leading to the conclusion that there is no relationship between corporate social responsibility and profitability. See M. Orlitzky, "Does Firm Size Confound the Relationship between Corporate Social Responsibility and Firm Performance?" *Journal of Business Ethics* 33 (2001): 167–180; and S. Ambec & P. Lanoie, "Does It Pay to Be Green? A Systematic Overview," *Academy of Management Perspectives*, 22 (2008): 45–62.

[115]M. Orlitzky, "Payoffs to Social and Environmental Performance," *Journal of Investing* 14 (2005): 48–51.

[116]M. Orlitzky, F. Schmidt, & S. Rynes, "Corporate Social and Financial Performance: A Meta-analysis," *Organization Studies* 24 (2003): 403–441.

[117]Orlitzky, "Payoffs to Social and Environmental Performance."

[118]G. Reynolds, "Can Honda Bring Corporate-Style Jet Travel to the Masses?" *Popular Mechanics*, March 4, 2010, accessed September 5, 2010, from www.popularmechanics.com/technology/aviation/news/Honda Jet_air_travel.

[119]Orlitzky, Schmidt, & Rynes, "Corporate Social and Financial Performance."

[120]A. Murray & A. Strassel, "Environment (A Special Report); Ahead of the Pack: GE's Jeffrey Immelt on Why It's Business, Not Personal," *The Wall Street Journal*, March 24, 2008, R3.

[121]K. Kranhold, "Greener Postures: GE's Environment Push Hits Business Realities; CEO's Quest to Reduce Emissions Irks Clients; The Battle of the Bulbs," *The Wall Street Journal*, September 14, 2007, A1.

[122]"Ecoimagination Is GE," 2008 Ecoimagination Annual Report, accessed August 20, 2009 from http://ge.ecoimagination.com.

[123]D. Kadlec & B. Van Voorst, "The New World of Giving: Companies Are Doing More Good, and Demanding More Back," *Time*, May 5, 1997, 62.

[124]P. Carlin, "Will Rapid Growth Stunt Corporate Do-Gooders?" *Business & Society Review* (Spring 1995), 36–43.

[125]K. Brown, "Chilling at Ben & Jerry's: Cleaner, Greener," *The Wall Street Journal*, April 15, 2004, B1.

[126]J. E. Wanek, P. R. Sackett, & D. S. Ones, "Towards an Understanding of Integrity Test Similarities and Differences: An Item-Level Analysis of Seven Tests," *Personnel Psychology* 56 (2003): 873–894.

[127]Michael Cooper & Ian Urbina, "Mine Operator Escape Extra Oversight after Warning," *The New York Times*, April 9, 2010, accessed September 3, 2010, www.nytimes.com/2010/04/10/us/10westvirginia.html?hp; Steven Mufson, Jerry Markon, & Ed O'Keefe, "West Virginia Mine Has Been Cited for Myriad Safety Violations," *The Washington Post*, April 7, 2010, accessed September 4, 2010, from www.washingtonpost.com/wp-dyn/content/article/2010/04/05/AR2010040503877.html; "Safety," Massey Energy Company, accessed September 4, 2010, from www.masseyenergyco.com/safety/index.shtml; and Ian Urbina & Bernie Becker, "As Rescue Efforts Continue for Miners, Officials Press for Answers," *The New York Times*, April 8, 2010, accessed September 4, 2010, from www.nytimes.com/2010/04/08/us/08westvirginia.html.

[128]Liz Alderman, "Environment and Business Clash in Saint-Tropez," *The New York Times*, August 15, 2010, accessed October 12, 2010, from www.nytimes.com/2010/08/16/business/global/16iht-beach.html.

BIZ FLIX

Emperor's Club

William Hundert (Kevin Kline), a professor at Saint Benedict's preparatory school, believes in teaching his students about living a principled life as well as teaching them his beloved classical literature. Hundert's principled ways are challenged, however, by a new student, Sedgewick Bell (Emile Hirsch). Bell's behavior during the 73rd annual Julius Caesar competition causes Hundert to suspect that Bell leads a less than principled life. Years later, Hundert is the honored guest of his former student Sedgewick Bell (Joel Gretsch) at Bell's estate and competes in a reenactment of the Julius Caesar competition. Bell nearly wins the competition, but when Hundert notices that Bell is wearing an earpiece and is cheating with an assistant's help, he gives him a question he knows he cannot answer. This scene is an edited portion of the competition reenactment.

© GreenLight

What to Watch for and Ask Yourself

1. Based on the clip, what ethical principles do you think most inform William Hundert's thinking?

2. Describe Sedgewick Bell's level of moral development.

MANAGEMENT WORKPLACE

Theo Chocolate: Managing Ethics and Social Responsibility

Joe Whinney exudes a sense of mission in everything he does. After a trip to cacao farms in Central America, Whinney decided to build the first organic fair trade chocolate factory in the United States. By building the first sustainable chocolate maker in the nation, Whinney hoped to help solve social and environmental issues by operating a profitable and ethical business. While Theo Chocolate is finding good success in the organic foods industry, perhaps the most exciting thing for "Theonistas" is that the company is being hailed as a voice for change. Employees say they have gained a loyal following for their efforts in the developing world, and business success has opened up new opportunities for sharing their vision of a better world.

© Cengage Learning

Discussion Questions

1. Which of the four strategies for responding to social responsibility best reflects Theo Chocolate?

2. How does Theo Chocolate's business practices reflect the stakeholder model of social responsibility?

3. What would happen if fair trade goals conflicted with a company's primary responsibility to be profitable?

Chapter 5
Planning and Decision Making

This chapter examines the benefits and pitfalls of planning, making plans work, and the different plans used in organizations. You'll also learn the steps and limitations of rational decision making and review various group decision techniques.

DuPont

Chapter 6
Organizational Strategy

This chapter examines how managers use strategies to obtain a sustainable competitive advantage. Then you learn the strategy-making process and how companies answer these questions: What business should we be in? How should we compete in this industry? How should we compete against a particular firm?

DisneyLand

Chapter 7
Innovation and Change

This chapter reviews the issues associated with organizational innovation. The first part of this chapter shows you why innovation matters and how to manage innovation to create and sustain a competitive advantage. In the second part of the chapter, you will learn about organizational change and about the risk of not changing.

3M

Chapter 8
Global Management

In this chapter, we examine the impact of global business on U.S. firms and review the basic rules and agreements that govern global trade. You'll learn how and when companies go global. And you'll read how companies decide where to expand globally and confront issues like business climates and cultural differences.

Groupon

CHAPTER 5

Planning
and Decision
Making

Learning Outcomes

1. Discuss the benefits and pitfalls of planning.
2. Describe how to make a plan that works.
3. Discuss how companies can use plans at all management levels, from top to bottom.
4. Explain the steps and limits to rational decision making.
5. Explain how group decisions and group decision-making techniques can improve decision making.

what would **you do?**

DuPont Headquarters, Wilmington, Delaware[1]

The DuPont company got its start when Eleuthère Irénée du Pont de Nemours fled France's revolution to come to America, where, in 1802, he built a mill on the Brandywine River in Wilmington, Delaware, to produce blasting powder used in guns and artillery. In 1902, E.I. du Pont's great-grandson, Pierre S. du Pont, along with two cousins, bought out other family members and began transforming DuPont into the world's leading chemical company. In its second century, DuPont Corporation would go on to develop Freon for refrigerators and air conditioners; nylon, which is used in everything from women's hose to car tires; Lucite, a ubiquitous clear plastic used in baths, furniture, car lights, and phone screens; Teflon, famous for its nonstick properties in cookware and coatings; Dacron, a wash-and-wear, wrinkle-free polyester; Lycra, the stretchy, clingy fabric used in activewear and swimwear; Nome, a fire-resistant fiber used by firefighters, race car drivers, and to reduce heat in motors and electrical equipment; Corona, a high-end countertop used in homes and offices; and Kevlar, the "bulletproof" material used in body armor worn by police and soldiers, in helmets, and for vehicle protection.

You became DuPont's CEO right as "the world fell apart" at the height of the world financial crisis. Fortunately, you had early warning from sharply declining sales in DuPont's titanium dioxide division, which makes white pigment used in paints, sunscreen, and food coloring. Sales trends there can be counted on to indicate what will happen next in the general economy, so you and your leadership team began working with the heads of all of DuPont's divisions to make contingency plans in case sales dropped by 5 percent, 10 percent, 20 percent, or more. Many DuPont managers thought you were crazy, until the downturn hit. It was difficult, but with plans to cut 6,500 employees at the ready, you were prepared when sales dropped by 20 percent at the end of the year. But when that wasn't enough, salaried and professional employees were asked to voluntarily take unpaid time off and an additional 2,000 jobs were eliminated. In all, these moves reduced expenses by a billion dollars a year. But one place you refused to cut was DuPont's research budget, which remained at $1.4 billion per year.

One of the ways in which the Board of Directors measures company performance is by comparing DuPont's total stock returns to 19 peer companies. Over the last quarter century, DuPont has regularly ended up in the bottom third of the list. This makes clear that you have one overriding goal: to restore DuPont's prestige, performance, and competitiveness. The question, of course, is how? Before deciding, there are some big questions to consider. First, given sustained weak performance over the last quarter century, do you need to step back and consider DuPont's purpose, that is, the reason that you're in business? After transitioning from blasting powder to chemicals, DuPont's

"what's new" companies

DuPont
Nike
InterContinental Hotels
Hooker Furniture Corporation
Ocean Spray Cranberries
Kimberly-Clark
Arm & Hammer
USA Today
Kindermusik International
Imperial Sugar

< **"what's new" companies**

study tips ⊗

Try to explain the key concepts of this chapter to a friend or family member who is not taking the class with you. This will help you identify which areas you need to review.

167

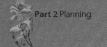

slogan became, "Better things for better living . . . through chemistry." Is it time, again, to reconsider what DuPont is all about? Or, instead of an intense focus on DuPont's purpose, would it make more sense to make lots of plans and lots of bets so that "a thousand flowers can bloom"? In other words, would it be better to keep options open by making small, simultaneous investments in many alternative plans? Then, when one or a few of these plans emerge as likely winners, you invest even more in these plans while discontinuing or reducing investment in the others. Finally, planning is a double-edged sword. If done right, it brings about tremendous increases in individual and organizational performance. But if done wrong, it can have just the opposite effect and harm individual and organizational performance. With that in mind, what kind of goals should you set for the company? Should you focus on finances, product development, or people? And should you have an overriding goal, or should you have separate goals for different parts of the company?

If you were the CEO at DuPont, what would you do?

Even inexperienced managers know that planning and decision making are central parts of their jobs. Figure out what the problem is. Generate potential solutions or plans. Pick the best one. Make it work. Experienced managers, however, know how hard it really is to make good plans and decisions. One seasoned manager says: "I think the biggest surprises are the problems. Maybe I had never seen it before. Maybe I was protected by my management when I was in sales. Maybe I had delusions of grandeur, I don't know. I just know how disillusioning and frustrating it is to be hit with problems and conflicts all day and not be able to solve them very cleanly."[2]

This chapter begins by examining the benefits and pitfalls of planning. Next, you will learn how to make a plan that works. Then you will look at the different kinds of plans that are used from the top to the bottom in most companies. In the second part of the chapter, we discuss the steps of rational decision making and consider its limitations. We finish the chapter by discussing how managers can use groups and group decision techniques to improve decisions.

What Is Planning?

"what's new" companies >

Planning, as defined in Chapter 1, is choosing a goal and developing a method or strategy to achieve that goal. For example, CEO Mark Parker announced that **Nike** aims to increase sales by more than 40 percent in five years, from $19 billion to $27 billion, by growing its retail and apparel business. To do that, Nike has reduced the number of styles it offers, the types of materials it uses, and the number of vendors it works with, so it can focus production, sales, and marketing efforts on top-selling items such as T-shirts, track jackets, and its Pro line of performance gear. Nike will

After reading the next three sections, you should be able to

1. *Discuss the benefits and pitfalls of planning.*
2. *Describe how to make a plan that works.*
3. *Discuss how companies can use plans at all management levels, from top to bottom.*

© david pearson/Alamy

spend $500 million to $600 million to open 300 more Nike-branded retail stores—ranging from all-inclusive stores that offer the entire Nike line to sports-specific stores specializing in running, soccer, or action sports, to brand-specific stores for Converse. It will also grow its "shops in shops," that is, Nike-specific retail sections that it operates in Foot Locker, Dick's Sporting Goods, and Finish Line.[3]

1 Benefits and Pitfalls of Planning

Are you one of those naturally organized people who always makes a daily to-do list, writes everything down so you won't forget, and never misses a deadline because you keep track of everything with your handy time-management notebook, iPhone, or PC? Or are you one of those flexible, creative, go-with-the-flow people who dislikes planning and organizing because it restricts your freedom, energy, and performance? Some people are natural planners. They love it and can see only its benefits. Others dislike planning and can see only its disadvantages. It turns out that *both* views have real value.

Planning has advantages and disadvantages. Let's learn about **1.1 the benefits** and **1.2 the pitfalls of planning.**

1.1 Benefits of Planning

Planning offers several important benefits: intensified effort, persistence, direction, and creation of task strategies.[4] First, as shown in Exhibit 5.1, managers and employees put forth greater effort when following a plan. Take two workers; instruct one to "do your best" to increase production, and instruct the other to achieve a 2 percent

Exhibit 5.1
Benefits of Planning

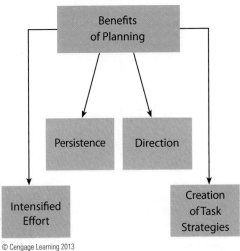

© Cengage Learning 2013

169

increase in production each month. Research shows that the one with the specific plan will work harder.[5]

Second, planning leads to persistence, that is, working hard for long periods. In fact, planning encourages persistence even when there may be little chance of short-term success.[6] McDonald's founder Ray Kroc, a keen believer in the power of persistence, had this quotation from President Calvin Coolidge hung in all of his executives' offices: "Nothing in the world can take the place of persistence. Talent will not; nothing is more common than unsuccessful men with talent. Genius will not; unrewarded genius is almost a proverb. Education will not; the world is full of educated derelicts. Persistence and determination alone are omnipotent."[7]

The third benefit of planning is direction. Plans encourage managers and employees to direct their persistent efforts *toward* activities that help accomplish their goals and *away* from activities that don't.[8] For example, a large insurance company wanted to improve the performance evaluation feedback its managers gave employees. To help the managers improve, company trainers taught them 43 effective performance feedback behaviors, such as, "I will give my subordinate a clear understanding of the results I expect him or her to achieve" and "During the performance appraisal interview, I will be very supportive, stressing good points before discussing needed improvement." During the training, managers were instructed to choose just 12 behaviors (out of the 43) on which they wanted to make the most improvement. When subordinates rated their managers on the 43 behaviors, it became clear that no matter which 12 behaviors different managers chose to concentrate on, they improved only on those 12 behaviors. Thus, plans direct behavior toward activities that lead to goal accomplishment and away from those that don't.

The fourth benefit of planning is that it encourages the development of task strategies. In other words, planning not only encourages people to work hard for extended periods and to engage in behaviors directly related to goal accomplishment, it also encourages them to think of better ways to do their jobs. Finally, perhaps the most compelling benefit of planning is that it has been proved to work for both companies and individuals. On average, companies with plans have larger profits and grow much faster than companies that don't.[9] The same holds true for individual managers and employees: There is no better way to improve the performance of the people who work in a company than to have them set goals and develop strategies for achieving those goals.

Exhibit 5.2
Pitfalls of Planning

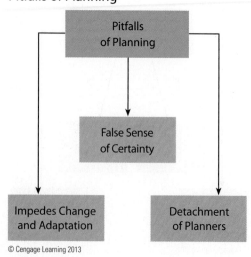

© Cengage Learning 2013

1.2 Pitfalls of Planning

Despite the significant benefits associated with planning, it is not a cure-all. Plans won't fix all organizational problems. In fact, many management authors and consultants believe that planning can harm companies in several ways.[10] As shown in Exhibit 5.2, the first pitfall of planning is that it can impede change and prevent or slow needed adaptation. Sometimes companies become so committed to achieving the goals set forth in their plans, or on following the strategies and tactics spelled out in them, that they fail to see that their plans aren't working or that their goals need to change. When it came to producing environmentally sound cars, General Motors missed its initial opportunity because its culture was "wedded to big cars and horsepower." Whereas Toyota formed its "green group" in the mid-1990s—which led to the development of the Prius, its popular electric hybrid—GM killed its electric car program, which produced the EV-1, to focus on selling highly profitable SUVs (sport utility vehicles). GM restarted work on hybrid cars in 2006. But, because of GM's late start, the new Chevy Volt, a battery-powered car that combines the use of off-peak electricity for overnight recharging of the batteries with daytime recharging by a small gas engine, faces stiff competition from other electric or plug-in hybrid vehicles, such as the Nissan Leaf, the Toyota Rav4 EV, the Mini-E from Mini Cooper, electric versions of the Ford Transit Connect and Focus, as well as offerings from the start-up companies Fisker and Tesla.[11]

The second pitfall is that planning can create a false sense of certainty. Planners sometimes feel that they know exactly what the future holds for their competitors, their suppliers, and their companies. However, all plans are based on assumptions: "The price of gasoline will increase by 4 percent per year"; "Exports will continue to rise." For plans to work, the assumptions on which they are based must hold true. If the assumptions turn out to be false, then the plans based on them are likely to fail.

The third potential pitfall of planning is the detachment of planners. In theory, strategic planners and top-level managers are supposed to focus on the big picture and not concern themselves with the details of implementation (i.e., carrying out the plan). According to management professor Henry Mintzberg, detachment leads planners to plan for things they don't understand.[12] Plans are meant to be guidelines for action, not abstract theories. Consequently, planners need to be familiar with the daily details of their businesses if they are to produce plans that can work.

Andrew Cosslett, CEO of **InterContinental Hotels** in London, describes one of his earliest experiences working as a sales representative for Wall's Ice Cream, a subsidiary of Unilever, which is based in London. Cosslett's supervisors passed to him a sales plan crafted by upper management that involved making sales calls on roughly 600 shops. Speaking to the detachment of planners, Coslett says, "The biggest thing I remember from those days … was how much of what comes out of corporate offices is of absolutely no purpose, and how far removed some people are from the front line. I was out there expected to sell this ice cream in the middle of winter in Liverpool. It was pretty tough, and I was in there trying to sell these two-pound ice cream cakes because head office said that's what we had to sell."[13]

If you doubt that the details are important to good execution of a plan, imagine that you're about to have coronary bypass surgery to replace four clogged arteries. You can have either an experienced surgeon or a first-year medical intern perform the procedure. The intern is a fully qualified M.D. who clearly understands the theory and the plan behind bypass surgery but has never performed such an operation. As you lie on the operating table, who is the last person you'd like to see as the anesthesia kicks in: the first-year intern who knows the plan but has never done a bypass or the experienced surgeon who has followed the plan hundreds of times? Planning works better when the people developing the plan are not detached from the process of executing the plan.

< **"what's new" companies**

Benefits and Pitfalls of Planning   Planning involves choosing a goal and developing a method to achieve that goal. Planning is one of the best ways to improve organizational and individual performance. It encourages people to work harder (intensified effort), work hard for extended periods (persistence), engage in behaviors directly related to goal accomplishment (directed behavior), and think of better ways to do their jobs (task strategies). Most importantly, companies that plan have larger profits and faster growth than companies that don't plan. However, planning also has three potential pitfalls. Companies that are overly committed to their plans may be slow to adapt to changes in their environment. Planning is based on assumptions about the future, and when those assumptions are wrong, the plans are likely to fail. Finally, planning can fail when planners are detached from the implementation of plans.

Review 1

2 How to Make a Plan That Works

Planning is a double-edged sword. If done right, planning brings about tremendous increases in individual and organizational performance. If planning is done wrong, however, it can have just the opposite effect and harm individual and organizational performance.

In this section, you will learn how to make a plan that works. As depicted in Exhibit 5.3, planning consists of **2.1 setting goals, 2.2 developing commitment to the goals, 2.3 developing effective action plans, 2.4 tracking progress toward goal achievement,** and **2.5 maintaining flexibility in planning.**

2.1 Setting Goals

The first step in planning is to set goals. To direct behavior and increase effort, goals need to be specific and challenging.[14] For example, deciding to "increase sales this year" won't direct and energize workers as much as deciding to "increase North American sales by 4 percent in the next six months." Likewise, deciding to "drop a few pounds" won't motivate you as much as deciding to "lose 15 pounds." Specific, challenging goals provide a target for which to aim and a standard against which to measure success.

One way of writing effective goals for yourself, your job, or your company is to use the SMART guidelines. **SMART goals** are **S**pecific, **M**easurable, **A**ttainable, **R**ealistic, and **T**imely.[15] Let's take a look at Nissan's zero-emissions program, which led to the electric car Leaf, to see how it might measure up to the SMART guidelines for goals.

First, is the goal *Specific?* Yes, because "zero emissions" tells us that Nissan isn't just looking to *reduce* emissions but to eliminate them. And "all-electric" rules out gas-electric hybrids like those produced by competitors. In addition to being specific, the goal is also *Measurable* because Nissan has put a number on the emissions—namely zero. Whether the goal is *Attainable* or not depends on whether the all-electric car performs as expected. Nissan has been researching lithium-ion battery technology for almost 20 years and claims to have developed a battery that can power a car up to 100 miles and recharge in just eight hours. Current trends in government regulation and consumer preferences toward more environmentally friendly vehicles and increasing gasoline prices suggests that an all-electric car is *Realistic* from a business standpoint, but that can't be determined until the Leaf is available to consumers. Finally, the goal is *Timely* because Nissan's goal was to roll out the Leaf in Japan and the United States in 2010, which it achieved, and then to the rest of the world by 2012.[16]

> **SMART goals** goals that are **S**pecific, **M**easurable, **A**ttainable, **R**ealistic, and **T**imely.

Exhibit 5.3 How to Make a Plan That Works

| 1 Set goals | 2 Develop commitment | 3 Develop effective action plans ☑ Who ☑ What ☑ When ☑ How | 4 Track progress toward goal achievement | 5 Maintain flexibility |

Revise existing plan or Begin planning process anew

© Cengage Learning 2013

2.2 Developing Commitment to Goals

Just because a company sets a goal doesn't mean that people will try to accomplish it. If workers don't care about a goal, that goal won't encourage them to work harder or smarter. Thus, the second step in planning is to develop commitment to goals.[17]

Goal commitment is the determination to achieve a goal. Commitment to achieve a goal is not automatic. Managers and workers must choose to commit themselves to a goal. Edwin Locke, professor emeritus of management at the University of Maryland and the foremost expert on how, why, and when goals work, tells a story about an overweight friend who lost 75 pounds. Locke says, "I asked him how he did it, knowing how hard it was for most people to lose so much weight." His friend responded, "Actually, it was quite simple. I simply decided that I *really wanted* to do it."[18] Put another way, goal commitment is really wanting to achieve a goal.

So how can managers bring about goal commitment? The most popular approach is to set goals participatively. Rather than assigning goals to workers ("Johnson, you've got till Tuesday of next week to redesign the flux capacitor so it gives us 10 percent more output"), managers and employees choose goals together. The goals are more likely to be realistic and attainable if employees participate in setting them. Another technique for gaining commitment to a goal is to make the goal public. For example, college students who publicly communicated their semester grade goals ("This semester, I'm shooting for a 3.5") to significant others (usually a parent or sibling) were much more committed to achieving their grades than those who did not. More important, those students earned grades that were nearly a half-grade higher than the grades of students who did not tell others about their grade goals. So, one way to increase commitment to goals is to go public by having individuals or work units tell others about their goals. Still another way to increase goal commitment is to obtain top management's support. Top management can show support for a plan or program by providing funds, speaking publicly about the plan, or participating in the plan itself.

2.3 Developing Effective Action Plans

The third step in planning is to develop effective action plans. An **action plan** lists the specific steps (how), people (who), resources (what), and time period (when) for accomplishing a goal. Coming out of bankruptcy, corporate reorganization, and a government bailout, Chrysler presented a detailed plan for returning to profitability. First, it established a time period (*when*) by presenting an outline of what the company would do over the next five years. Second, it clearly identified *who* is behind the company's new strategic plan. CEO Sergio Machionne spearheaded a "painful and difficult" process of assessing Chrysler's strengths and weakness, where "no stone [was] unturned." Third, Chrysler's plan explained *how* it would return to profitability by detailing a thorough makeover of its core brands Jeep, Chrysler, and Dodge. Under this plan, some older models will be redesigned and repackaged, whereas other models that have not sold well will be eliminated (such as the Jeep Commander and Chrysler Sebring). As for the resources (*what*), Chrysler's plan calls for extensive collaboration and borrowing from Italian automaker Fiat (which has a 20 percent stake in Chrysler). Not only will Chrysler sell the Fiat 500, a subcompact city car that has been extremely popular in Europe, but it will also borrow Fiat's technological and design innovations to offer fuel-efficient, stylish vehicles that will attract a new segment of U.S. consumers.[19]

2.4 Tracking Progress

The fourth step in planning is to track progress toward goal achievement. There are two accepted methods of tracking progress. The first is to set proximal goals and distal goals. **Proximal goals** are short-term goals or subgoals, whereas **distal goals** are long-term or primary goals.[20] The idea behind setting proximal goals is that

goal commitment the determination to achieve a goal.

action plan the specific steps, people, and resources needed to accomplish a goal.

proximal goals short-term goals or subgoals.

distal goals long-term or primary goals.

Sergio Machionne spearheaded a "painful and difficult" process of assessing Chrysler's strengths and weakness, where "no stone [was] unturned."

achieving them may be more motivating and rewarding than waiting to reach far-off distal goals. In a research study, Massachusetts Institute of Technology students were given a complex proofreading assignment. They were paid 10 cents for each error they found but were penalized $1 a day for turning in their work late. One group of students was given a single deadline—a distal goal—and told to turn in all of their work three weeks from the start of the study. A second group of students was given weekly deadlines—proximal goals—and told to turn in one-third of their work each week. A third group of students was allowed to set their own deadlines; they set their own proximal goals. The single-deadline students (those with no proximal goals, just a distal goal) were the worst performers: They turned in their work 12 days late and corrected only 70 errors. The students who were assigned weekly goals (proximal goals) were the best performers: They turned in their work only a half-day late and corrected 136 errors. Next best were the students who set their own proximal goals: They turned in their work 6.5 days late and corrected 104 errors.[21] The lesson for managers is clear. If you want people to do a better job of tracking the quality and timeliness of their work, use proximal goals to set multiple deadlines.[22]

The second method of tracking progress is to gather and provide performance feedback. Regular, frequent performance feedback allows workers and managers to track their progress toward goal achievement and make adjustments in effort, direction, and strategies.[23] Exhibit 5.4 shows the impact of feedback on safety behavior at a large bakery company with a worker safety record that was two and a half times worse than the industry average. During the baseline period, workers in the wrapping department, who measure and mix ingredients, roll the bread dough, and put it into baking pans, performed their jobs safely about 70 percent of the time (see 1 in Exhibit 5.4). The baseline safety record for workers in the makeup department, who bag and seal baked bread and assemble, pack, and tape cardboard cartons for shipping, was somewhat better at 78 percent (see 2). The company then gave workers 30 minutes of safety training, set a goal of 90 percent safe behavior, and then provided daily feedback (such as a chart similar to that in Exhibit 5.4). Performance improved dramatically. During the intervention period, safely performed behaviors rose to an average of 95.8 percent for wrapping workers (see 3) and 99.3 percent

Exhibit 5.4 Effects of Goal Setting, Training, and Feedback on Safe Behavior in a Bread Factory

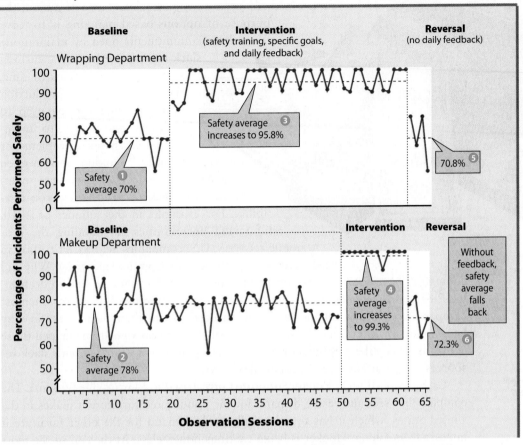

Source: From "A Behavioral Approach to Occupational Safety: Pinpointing and Reinforcing Safe Performance in a Food Manufacturing Plant," J. Komaki. K. D. Barwick, & L. R. Scott, *Journal of Applied Psychology,* 1978, vol. 63 (1978): 464–445. Copyright © 1978 by the American Psychological Association.

for workers in the makeup department (see 4), and never fell below 83 percent. Thus, the combination of training, a challenging goal, and feedback led to a dramatic increase in performance. The importance of feedback alone can be seen in the reversal stage, when the company quit posting daily feedback on safe behavior. Without daily feedback, the percentage of safely performed behavior returned to baseline levels—70.8 percent for the wrapping department (see 5) and 72.3 percent for the makeup department (see 6). For planning to be effective, workers need both a specific, challenging goal and regular feedback to track their progress. Indeed, additional research indicates that the effectiveness of goal setting can be doubled by the addition of feedback.[24]

2.5 Maintaining Flexibility

Because action plans are sometimes poorly conceived and goals sometimes turn out not to be achievable, the last step in developing an effective plan is to maintain flexibility. One method of maintaining flexibility while planning is to adopt an options-based approach.[25] The goal of **options-based planning** is to keep options open by making small, simultaneous investments in many alternative plans. Then, when one or a few of these plans emerge as likely winners, you invest even more in these plans while discontinuing or reducing investment in the others.

options-based planning maintaining planning flexibility by making small, simultaneous investments in many alternative plans.

© mmaxer/Shutterstock.com

In part, options-based planning is the opposite of traditional planning. Whereas the purpose of an action plan is to commit people and resources to a particular course of action, the purpose of options-based planning is to leave those commitments open by maintaining **slack resources**, that is, a cushion of resources, such as extra time, people, money, or production capacity, that can be used to address and adapt to unanticipated changes, problems, or opportunities.[26] Holding options open gives you choices. And choices, combined with slack resources, give you flexibility. For example, in the summer of 2010, still facing uncertainties surrounding the economic recovery, U.S. companies held $1.84 trillion in cash reserves, up 26 percent from a year earlier. Why did companies have so much cash on hand, much more than they needed to do business? Because when credit markets dried up at the beginning of the recession, most companies could not get the loans they needed to run their businesses. So why keep so much cash on hand? Maintaining substantial cash positions helped those companies keep their options open. And having options, combined with slack resources (i.e., that extra cash), equals flexibility.[27]

"what's new" companies >

Cash has piled up at **Hooker Furniture Corp.**, based in Martinsville, Virginia. The company has seen increasing demand for the upholstered furniture it makes in the United States, which it has found usually leads demand for the other furniture it imports from China. Hooker is being cautious nonetheless. At the end of the most recent quarter, it had $38.7 million in cash and other highly liquid assets on its balance sheet, up from $26.2 million a year earlier. "We're a fairly conservative company, and keeping our powder dry makes sense to us," said Hooker Chief Financial Officer E. Larry Ryder. Mr. Ryder says he sees the cash as a sort of insurance fund to make sure he can buy the raw materials and other inventory he will need to meet demand if business picks up.[28]

slack resources a cushion of extra resources that can be used with options-based planning to adapt to unanticipated change, problems, or opportunities.

learning-based planning learning better ways of achieving goals by continually testing, changing, and improving plans and strategies.

Another method of maintaining flexibility while planning is to take a learning-based approach. Traditional planning assumes that initial action plans are correct and will lead to success. By contrast, **learning-based planning** assumes that action plans need to be continually tested, changed, and improved as companies learn better ways of achieving goals.[29] At 76 million people, baby boomers, born between 1946 and 1964, represent the largest and wealthiest demographic in business history. But with the first boomers now turning 65, companies that have *not* traditionally targeted elderly consumers have to test, change, and improve their products and services to adapt to older customers. But with boomers, those changes come with one critical caveat: Don't suggest those changes have anything to do with aging!

"what's new" companies >

Ken Romanzi, chief operating officer at **Ocean Spray Cranberries, Inc.**, which has prospered by selling to health-conscious boomers, says, "We don't do anything to remind boomers that they are getting older." So what adjustments have companies

"what's new" companies >

made as they learned about aging boomers' preferences? **Kimberly-Clark** spent two years redesigning its Depend products, making them look more like gender-specific underwear than adult diapers. Mark Cammarota, who manages the Depends brand, says, "Past generations were more accepting that they had a condition, and this was the product that they have to wear. The boomers don't have that attitude. They

"what's new" companies >

demand and expect more." Likewise, **Arm & Hammer** learned that older customers struggled to read the lettering on its cat-litter packaging, so it increased the font size by 20 percent and made sure there were bright contrasts between the lettering and the background colors.[30]

How to Make a Plan That Works There are five steps to making a plan that works: (1) Set SMART goals, or goals that are **S**pecific, **M**easurable, **A**ttainable, **R**ealistic, and **T**imely. (2) Develop commitment to the goals from the people who contribute to goal achievement. Managers can increase workers' goal commitment by encouraging worker participation in goal setting, making goals public, and getting top management to show support for workers' goals. (3) Develop action plans for goal accomplishment. (4) Track progress toward goal achievement by setting both proximal and distal goals and by providing workers with regular performance feedback. (5) Maintain flexibility. Keeping options open through options-based planning and seeking continuous improvement through learning-based planning help organizations maintain flexibility as they plan.

Review 2

3 Planning from Top to Bottom

Planning works best when the goals and action plans at the bottom and middle of the organization support the goals and action plans at the top of the organization. In other words, planning works best when everybody pulls in the same direction. Exhibit 5.5 illustrates this planning continuity, beginning at the top with a clear definition of the company purpose and ending at the bottom with the execution of operational plans.

Let's see how **3.1 top managers create the organization's purpose statement and strategic objective, 3.2 middle managers develop tactical plans and use management by objectives to motivate employee efforts toward the overall purpose and strategic objective, and 3.3 first-level managers use operational, single-use, and standing plans to implement the tactical plans.**

Exhibit 5.5   Planning from Top to Bottom

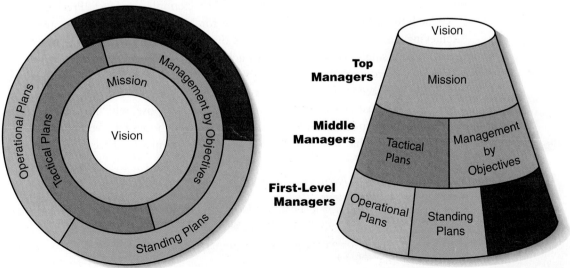

© Cengage Learning 2013

177

Exhibit 5.6 Time Lines for Strategic, Tactical, and Operational Plans

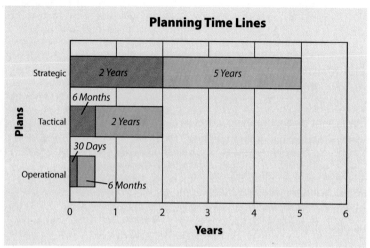

Planning Time Lines

© Cengage Learning 2013

3.1 Starting at the Top

As shown in Exhibit 5.6, top management is responsible for developing long-term **strategic plans** that make clear how the company will serve customers and position itself against competitors in the next two to five years. Zappos, the online shoe retailer recently purchased by Amazon, is working on a five-year plan to expand beyond shoes into other markets, particularly beauty care. Zappos' goal is to grow its beauty section from $1 million in sales last year to $75 million in five years.[31] (The strategic planning and management process is examined in its entirety in Chapter 6.) Strategic planning begins with the creation of an organizational purpose.

A **purpose statement**, which is often referred to as an organizational mission or vision, is a statement of a company's purpose or reason for existing.[32] Purpose statements should be brief—no more than two sentences. They should also be enduring, inspirational, clear, and consistent with widely shared company beliefs and values. An excellent example of a well-crafted purpose statement is that of Avon, the cosmetics company, shown in Exhibit 5.7. It guides everyone in the organization and provides a focal point for the delivery of beauty products and services to the customer, women around the world. The purpose is the same whether Avon is selling lipstick to women in India, shampoo packets to women in the Amazon, or jewelry to women in the United States. Despite these regional differences in specific strategy, the overall goal—understanding the needs of women globally—does not change. Furthermore, Avon's purpose is clear, inspirational, and consistent with Avon's company values and the principles that guide the company, also shown in Exhibit 5.7. Other examples of organizational purposes that have been particularly effective include Walt Disney Company's "to make people happy" and Schlage Lock Company's "to make the world more secure."[33]

The **strategic objective**, which flows from the purpose, is a more specific goal that unifies company-wide efforts, stretches and challenges the organization, and possesses a finish line and a time frame.[34] For example, in 1961, President John F. Kennedy established a strategic objective for NASA with this simple statement: "Achieving the goal, before this decade is out, of landing a man on the moon and returning him safely to earth."[35] NASA achieved this strategic objective on July 20, 1969, when astronaut Neil Armstrong walked on the moon. Once the strategic objective has been accomplished, a new one should be chosen. However, the new strategic objective must grow out of the organization's purpose, which does not change significantly over time. Consider, for example, NASA's hopes to accomplish its latest strategic goal, or what it calls its "exploration systems mission directorate," between

strategic plans overall company plans that clarify how the company will serve customers and position itself against competitors over the next two to five years.

purpose statement a statement of a company's purpose or reason for existing.

strategic objective a more specific goal that unifies company-wide efforts, stretches and challenges the organization, and possesses a finish line and a time frame.

Exhibit 5.7 Avon's Vision and Values

The Avon Vision	To be the company that best understands and satisfies the product, service and self-fulfillment needs of women—globally.
The Five Values of Avon	TRUST, RESPECT, BELIEF, HUMILITY, INTEGRITY.

Source: avoncompany.com/aboutavon/history/values.html.

mgmt:facts

Clean Hands = No Regret?

Your management team recently had to make the difficult choice of cutting 10 percent of the workforce. It was a hard decision, but it would help prevent the permanent closure of the company. Many of the managers, however, are feeling pretty guilty. What to do? Maybe they should wash their hands. Recent research shows that the act of washing hands might help people feel less regret about decisions. In one study, people were given a choice of two jars of jam. One group was allowed to wash their hands with an antiseptic wipe, whereas the other group was only allowed to look at the wipe. Although the group that did not wipe their hands rated the jam they chose 24 percent higher than what they did not choose, the group that did wipe their hands preferred their choice by only a statistically insignificant amount.[36]

2015 and 2020. NASA's strategic goal is to "return to the moon, where we will build a sustainable long term human presence."[37] NASA further explains its strategic goal by saying, "As the space shuttle approaches retirement and the International Space Station nears completion, NASA is building the next fleet of vehicles to bring astronauts back to the moon, and possibly to Mars and beyond."

3.2 Bending in the Middle

Middle management is responsible for developing and carrying out tactical plans to accomplish the organization's strategic objective. **Tactical plans** specify how a company will use resources, budgets, and people to accomplish specific goals related to its strategic objective for the next five years. Whereas strategic plans and objectives are used to focus company efforts over the next two to five years, tactical plans and objectives are used to direct behavior, efforts, and attention over the next six months to two years. Like nearly every other newspaper, **USA Today** has experienced severe losses over the past few years. With subscriptions down by 14 percent, nearly double the industry-wide average, it lost its status as the nation's number one newspaper to *The Wall Street Journal*. Gannett, its parent company, also posted losses of $1.34 billion. To return

> **tactical plans** plans created and implemented by middle managers that specify how the company will use resources, budgets, and people over the next six months to two years to accomplish specific goals within its mission.

< **"what's new" companies**

179

to profitability, *USA Today* announced that it would de-emphasize print media and focus on delivering digital content to computers and mobile devices. As part of this shift, the newspaper announced a tactical plan to eliminate 9 percent of its staff, spin off the sports division into its own division, and reorganize the newsroom from its traditional four content sections, News, Sports, Money, and Leisure, to Your Life, Travel, Breaking News, Investigative, and National.[38]

Management by objectives is a management technique often used to develop and carry out tactical plans. **Management by objectives (MBO)** is a four-step process in which managers and their employees (1) discuss possible goals; (2) collectively select goals that are challenging, attainable, and consistent with the company's overall goals; (3) jointly develop tactical plans that lead to the accomplishment of tactical goals and objectives; and (4) meet regularly to review progress toward accomplishment of those goals. At **Kindermusik International**, a music education publisher, all 50 employees attend weekly one-hour meetings to review the company's weekly goals and financial results. Half-day review sessions are held each quarter to review results against quarterly and annual goals and to discuss how to cut costs and increase revenues. Because they regularly review and discuss goal progress, employees were sensitive to reducing costs, so they proposed replacing the company's five-day sales convention, which costs about $50,000, with a series of year-round virtual meetings with sales managers, sales representatives, and customers. CEO Michael Dougherty said, "If you'd asked me, I would have said, 'We've always done the convention.' But the folks who are closer to the event and closer to the customers know that there were other and better ways to achieve the same goal."[39]

> **"what's new" companies** >

3.3 Finishing at the Bottom

Lower-level managers are responsible for developing and carrying out **operational plans**, which are the day-to-day plans for producing or delivering the organization's products and services. Operational plans direct the behavior, efforts, and priorities of operative employees for periods ranging from 30 days to six months. There are three kinds of operational plans: single-use plans, standing plans, and budgets.

Single-use plans deal with unique, one-time-only events. Just eight days after John Sheptor became CEO of **Imperial Sugar**, one of the company's factories in Georgia exploded, killing 14 employees and injuring many more. To deal with the catastrophe, Sheptor quickly put together a plan for identifying missing and injured workers, and establishing a command center to communicate with employees' families, the media, and local government officials.[40]

Unlike single-use plans that are created, carried out once, and then never used again, **standing plans** save managers time because once the plans are created, they can be used repeatedly to handle frequently recurring events. If you encounter a problem that you've seen before, someone in your company has probably written a standing plan that explains how to address it. Using this plan, rather than reinventing the wheel, will save you time. There are three kinds of standing plans: policies, procedures, and rules and regulations.

Policies indicate the general course of action that company managers should take in response to a particular event or situation. A well-written policy will also specify why the policy exists and what outcome the policy is intended to produce. All companies have travel policies with expense guidelines on how much employees can spend on airline tickets (coach, rather than business class or first class), hotel rooms, cars, or meals. Many companies require employees to book their travel using company-provided travel websites that automatically enforce those guidelines. New travel software, however, can generate automated emails to employees that encourage them to

> **"what's new" companies** >

management by objectives (MBO) a four-step process in which managers and employees discuss and select goals, develop tactical plans, and meet regularly to review progress toward goal accomplishment.

operational plans day-to-day plans, developed and implemented by lower-level managers, for producing or delivering the organization's products and services over a 30-day to six-month period.

single-use plans plans that cover unique, one-time-only events.

standing plans plans used repeatedly to handle frequently recurring events.

policies a standing plan that indicates the general course of action that should be taken in response to a particular event or situation.

what really works
Management by Objectives

For years, both managers and management researchers have wondered how much of an effect planning has on organizational performance, or indeed if it has any effect at all. Although proponents argued that planning encourages workers to work hard, persist in their efforts, engage in behaviors directly related to goal accomplishment, and develop better strategies for achieving goals, opponents argued that planning impedes organizational change and adaptation, creates the illusion of managerial control, and artificially separates thinkers and doers.

Now, however, the results from 70 different organizations strongly support the effectiveness of management by objectives (i.e., short-term planning).

Management by Objectives (MBO)

Management by objectives is a process in which managers and subordinates at all levels in a company sit down together to jointly set goals, share information, and discuss strategies that could lead to goal achievement, and then regularly meet to review progress toward accomplishing those goals. Thus, MBO is based on goals, participation, and feedback. On average, companies that effectively use MBO outproduce those that don't use MBO by an incredible 44.6 percent. And in companies where top management is committed to MBO—that is, where objective setting begins at the top—the average increase in performance is an even more astounding 56.5 percent. By contrast, when top management does not participate in or support MBO, the average increase in productivity is only 6.1 percent. In all, there is a 97 percent chance that companies that use

MBO will outperform those that don't! Thus, MBO can make a very big difference to the companies that use it.[41]

When done right, MBO is an extremely effective method of tactical planning. Still, MBO is not without disadvantages.[42] Some MBO programs involve excessive paperwork, requiring managers to file annual statements of plans and objectives, plus quarterly or semiannual written reviews assessing goal progress. Today, however, electronic and web-based management systems and software make it easier for managers and employees to set goals, link them to the organization's strategic direction, and continuously track and evaluate their progress.[43]

Another difficulty is that managers are frequently reluctant to give employees feedback about their performance. A third disadvantage is that managers and employees sometimes have difficulty agreeing on goals. And when employees are forced to accept goals that they don't want, goal commitment and employee effort suffer. Last, because MBO focuses on quantitative, easily measured goals, employees may neglect important but unmeasured parts of their jobs. In other words, if your job performance is judged only by whether you reduce costs by 3 percent or raise revenues by 5 percent, then you are unlikely to give high priority to the unmeasured but still important parts of your job, such as mentoring new employees or sharing knowledge and skills with coworkers.

purchase their airline tickets early relative to their travel dates. Typically, the earlier the purchase, the lower the cost. At American Honda, this early purchase travel policy is reinforced by travel expense tracking software that sends emails to employees and their bosses pointing out that a $1,000 ticket purchased by the employee could have been purchased for $800 a week earlier. Charles Franklin, Honda's corporate travel manager, says the policy matters, because with 40,000 annual trips made by American Honda employees, $100 less per trip would save the company $4 million a year.[44]

Procedures are more specific than policies because they indicate the series of steps that should be taken in response to a particular event. A manufacturer's procedure for handling defective products might include the following steps:

> » **Step 1:** Rejected material is locked in a secure area with "reject" documentation attached.
> » **Step 2:** Material Review Board (MRB) identifies the defect and how far outside the standard the rejected products are.
> » **Step 3:** MRB determines the disposition of the defective product as either scrap or rework.
> » **Step 4:** Scrap is either discarded or recycled, and rework is sent back through the production line to be fixed.
> » **Step 5:** If delays in delivery will result, MRB member notifies customer.[45]

procedures a standing plan that indicates the specific steps that should be taken in response to a particular event.

rules and regulations standing plans that describe how a particular action should be performed, or what must happen or not happen in response to a particular event.

budgeting quantitative planning through which managers decide how to allocate available money to best accomplish company goals.

Rules and regulations are even more specific than procedures because they specify what must happen or not happen. They describe precisely how a particular action should be performed. For instance, many companies have rules and regulations forbidding managers from writing job reference letters for employees who have worked at their firms, because a negative reference may prompt a former employee to sue for defamation of character.[46]

After single-use plans and standing plans, budgets are the third kind of operational plan. **Budgeting** is quantitative planning because it forces managers to decide how to allocate available money to best accomplish company goals. According to Jan King, author of *Business Plans to Game Plans*, "Money sends a clear message about your priorities. Budgets act as a language for communicating your goals to others." Exhibit 5.8 shows the operating budget outlays for the U.S. federal government. Together, social programs (Social Security and income security, or welfare) and health-care programs (Medicare and health) account for nearly 60 percent of the federal budget. Budgeting is a critical management task, one that most managers could do better. For more detailed information about budgeting, see *Essential Managers: Managing Budgets* by Stephen Brookson, or *Budgeting Basics & Beyond: A Complete Step-by-Step Guide for Nonfinancial Managers* by Jae K. Shim and Joel G. Siegel. Both books are written for budget beginners.

Exhibit 5.8 2009 U.S. Federal Government Budget Outlays

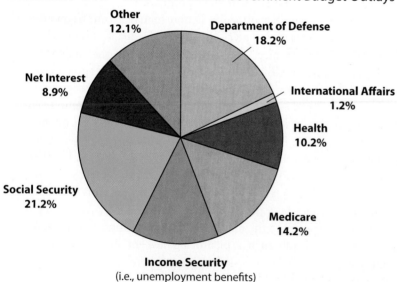

Source: "Table B-89. Federal Receipts and Outlays, by Major Category, and Surplus or Deficit, Fiscal Years 1940–2009," 2009 Economic Report of the President: 2009 Report Spreadsheet Tables, accessed March 5, 2011, from www.gpoaccess.gov/eop/2009/B80.xls.

Planning from Top to Bottom   Proper planning requires that the goals at the bottom and middle of the organization support the objectives at the top of the organization. Top management develops strategic plans that indicate how a company will serve customers and position itself against competitors over a period of two to five years. Middle managers use techniques like management by objectives to develop tactical plans that direct behavior, efforts, and priorities over the next six months to two years. Finally, lower-level managers develop operational plans that guide daily activities in producing or delivering an organization's products and services. Operational plans typically span periods ranging from 30 days to six months. There are three kinds of operational plans: single-use plans, standing plans (policies, procedures, and rules and regulations), and budgets.

What Is Rational Decision Making?

Imagine that your boss asks you for a recommendation on outfitting the sales force, many of whom travel regularly, with new computers. She asks you to prepare a report that details the problems the sales team has been having with its computers and summarizes both current and future needs. You need to come up with at least five plans or options for getting computers to help members of the sales team do their job as efficiently as possible, no matter where they are. When your boss delegates this "computer problem," what she really wants from you is a rational decision. **Decision making** is the process of choosing a solution from available alternatives.[47] **Rational decision making** is a systematic process in which managers define problems, evaluate alternatives, and choose optimal solutions that provide maximum benefits to their organizations. Thus, your boss expects you to define and analyze the computer problem and explore alternatives. Furthermore, your solution has to be optimal, because the department is going to live with the computer equipment you recommend for the next three years.

After reading the next two sections, you should be able to

4. *Explain the steps and limits to rational decision making.*

5. *Explain how group decisions and group decision-making techniques can improve decision making.*

4 Steps and Limits to Rational Decision Making

Exhibit 5.9 shows the six steps of the rational decision-making process.

Let's learn more about each of these steps: **4.1 define the problem, 4.2 identify decision criteria, 4.3 weight the criteria, 4.4 generate alternative courses of action, 4.5 evaluate each alternative,** and **4.6 compute the optimal decision.** Then we'll consider **4.7 limits to rational decision making.**

decision making the process of choosing a solution from available alternatives.

rational decision making a systematic process of defining problems, evaluating alternatives, and choosing optimal solutions.

Exhibit 5.9

Steps of the Rational Decision-Making Process

1 Define the Problem

2 Identify Decision Criteria

3 Weight the Criteria

4 Generate Alternative Courses of Action

5 Evaluate Each Alternative

6 Compute the Optimal Decision

© Cengage Learning 2013

problem a gap between a desired state and an existing state.

4.1 Define the Problem

The first step in decision making is identifying and defining the problem. A **problem** exists when there is a gap between a desired state (what is wanted) and an existing state (the situation you are actually facing). For instance, women want to look good and be comfortable in properly fitted clothes. But because the garment industry's size standards are outdated (collected 60 years ago on a small group of Caucasian women in their 20s) or ignored, fit varies tremendously. A size 8 in one brand will be a size 10 in another. As a result, women who can't find well-fitting clothes leave stores without purchasing or are forced to buy poorly fitted clothes that are returned to the store or discarded after several wearings. Either way, the result is the same: Clothing manufacturers have a problem because dissatisfied customers won't buy their brands in the future.[48]

The presence of a gap between an existing state and a desired state (such as selling clothes that should fit, but don't) is no guarantee that managers will make decisions to solve problems. Three things must occur for this to happen.[49] First, managers have to be aware of the gap. They have to know there is a problem before they can begin solving it. For example, after noticing that people were spending more money on their pets, a new dog food company created an expensive, high-quality dog food. To emphasize its quality, the dog food was sold in cans and bags with gold labels, red letters, and detailed information about its benefits and nutrients. Yet the product did not sell very well, and the company went out of business in less than a year. Its founders didn't understand why. When they asked a manager at a competing dog food company what their biggest mistake had been, the answer was, "Simple. You didn't have a picture of a dog on the package."[50] This problem would have been easy to solve if management had only been aware of it.

Being aware of a problem isn't enough to begin the decision-making process. Managers also have to be motivated to reduce the gap between a desired and an existing state. During the latest recession, Starbucks closed nearly a 1,000 stores and laid off over 25,000 employees, to cut expenses by $100 million, to restore profits. But, it wasn't until McDonald's rolled out a national advertising campaign for its lower-priced McCafé mochas, lattes, and cappuccinos that Starbucks was finally motivated to cut product prices. CEO Howard Schultz said, "We know customers are looking for meaningful value, not just a lower price. In the coming days we're going to arm our consumers and partners with the facts about Starbucks coffee."[51] Those facts include lowering the price of basic drinks, such as a "grande" iced coffee, by 45 cents, to less than $2. With profits down 77 percent and same-store sales down 8 percent, and with McDonald's now selling specialty coffee drinks for $3 or less, Starbucks was motivated to take steps to keep customers who might be tempted by McDonald's lower prices.

Finally, it's not enough to be aware of a problem and be motivated to solve it. Managers must also have the knowledge, skills, abilities, and resources to fix the problem. Product designer Cricket Lee tried to solve the sizing problem in the women's clothing industry by developing Fitlogic, a sizing standard that takes account of body types and is not intimidating for larger women. Said Lee, "My intention is to standardize fit. This is what women in America want."[52] Although relatively unknown, Lee has convinced QVC (a home shopping TV network), Nordstroms, Macy's, and Jones Apparel to license Fitlogic to help women with different body shapes buy better-fitting clothes. With 84 percent of women experiencing fit problems, and poor fit accounting for nearly 40 percent of returned clothes, Lee has clearly identified a widespread problem. Other retailers, such as Banana Republic and Chico's FAS, are taking note by creating their own specialized sizing systems, as Banana Republic does by assigning different names to pants with different fits.[53]

4.2 Identify Decision Criteria

Decision criteria are the standards used to guide judgments and decisions. Typically, the more criteria a potential solution meets, the better that solution will be. Let's return to the employee who was given the responsibility for making a rational decision about the office computer setup. What general factors would be important when purchasing computers for the office? Reliability, price, warranty, on-site service, and compatibility with existing software, printers, and computers would all be important, but you must also consider the technical details. What specific factors would you want the office computers to have? Well, with technology changing so quickly, you'll probably want to buy computers with as much capability and flexibility as you can afford. Today, for the first time, laptops now account for over 50 percent of the market.[54] Business laptops come in four distinct model types. There are budget models that are good for routine office work but are usually saddled with a slower processor; workhorse models that are not lightweight but have all the features; slim models for traveling that usually require an external drive to read/write to a DVD/CD; and tablet models like Apple's iPad.[55] What will the users really need? Will they need to burn CDs and DVDs or just read them? How much memory and hard drive space will the users need? Should you pay extra for durability, file encryption, larger screens, and extra-large batteries? Answering questions like these will help you identify the criteria that will guide the purchase of the new equipment.

4.3 Weight the Criteria

After identifying decision criteria, the next step is deciding which criteria are more or less important. Although there are numerous mathematical models for weighting decision criteria, all require the decision maker to provide an initial ranking of the criteria. Some use **absolute comparisons**, in which each criterion is compared with a standard or ranked on its own merits. For example, *Consumer Reports* uses this checklist when it rates and recommends new cars: predicted reliability, previous owners' satisfaction, predicted depreciation (the price you could expect if you sold the car), ability to avoid an accident, fuel economy, crash protection, acceleration, ride, and front seat comfort.[56]

Different individuals will rank these criteria differently, depending on what they value or require in a car. Exhibit 5.10 shows the absolute weights that someone buying a car might use. Because these weights are absolute, each criterion is judged

decision criteria the standards used to guide judgments and decisions.

absolute comparisons a process in which each decision criterion is compared to a standard or ranked on its own merits.

Exhibit 5.10 Absolute Weighting of Decision Criteria for a Car Purchase

Highlighted numbers indicate how important the particular criterion is to a hypothetical car buyer. Your rankings might be very different.

	CU	NVI	SI	I	CI
1. Predicted reliability	1	2	3	4	**5**
2. Owner satisfaction	1	**2**	3	4	5
3. Predicted depreciation	**1**	2	3	4	5
4. Avoiding accidents	1	2	3	**4**	5
5. Fuel economy	1	2	3	4	**5**
6. Crash protection	1	2	3	**4**	5
7. Acceleration	**1**	2	3	4	5
8. Ride	1	2	**3**	4	5
9. Front seat comfort	1	2	3	4	**5**

Note: CU: completely unimportant; NVI: not very important; SI: somewhat important; I: important; CI: critically important

© Cengage Learning 2013

on its own importance, using a five-point scale, with "5" representing "critically important" and "1" representing "completely unimportant." In this instance, predicted reliability, fuel economy, and front seat comfort were rated most important, and acceleration and predicted depreciation were rated least important.

Another method uses **relative comparisons**, in which each criterion is compared directly with every other criterion.[57] Exhibit 5.11 shows six criteria that someone might use when buying a house. Moving down the first column of Exhibit 5.11, we see that the time of the daily commute has been rated less important (–1) than school system quality; more important (+1) than having an inground pool, sunroom, or a quiet street; and just as important as the house being brand new (0). Total weights, which are obtained by summing the scores in each column, indicate that the daily commute and school system quality are the most important factors to this home buyer, while an in ground pool, sun room, and a quiet street are the least important. So with relative comparison, criteria are directly compared with each other.

relative comparisons a process in which each decision criterion is compared directly with every other criterion.

Exhibit 5.11 Relative Comparison of Home Characteristics

Home Characteristics	DC	SSQ	IP	SR	QS	NBH
Daily commute (DC)		+1	–1	–1	–1	0
School system quality (SSQ)	–1		–1	–1	–1	–1
Inground pool (IP)	+1	+1		0	0	+1
Sun room (SR)	+1	+1	0		0	0
Quiet street (QS)	+1	+1	0	0		0
Newly built house (NBH)	0	+1	–1	0	0	
Total weight	+2	+5	–3	–2	–2	0

© Cengage Learning 2013

4.4 Generate Alternative Courses of Action

After identifying and weighting the criteria that will guide the decision-making process, the next step is to identify possible courses of action that could solve the problem. In general, at this step the idea is to generate as many alternatives as possible. Let's assume that you're trying to select a city in Europe to be the location of a major office. After meeting with your staff, you generate a list of possible alternatives: Amsterdam, Netherlands; Barcelona or Madrid, Spain; Berlin or Frankfurt, Germany; Brussels, Belgium; London, England; Milan, Italy; Paris, France; and Zurich, Switzerland.

4.5 Evaluate Each Alternative

The next step is to systematically evaluate each alternative against each criterion. Because of the amount of information that must be collected, this step can take much longer and be much more expensive than other steps in the decision-making process. When selecting a European city for your office, you could contact economic development offices in each city, systematically interview businesspeople or executives who operate there, retrieve and use published government data on each location, or rely on published studies such as Cushman & Wakefield's *European Cities Monitor*, which conducts an annual survey of more than 500 senior European executives who rate 34 European cities on 12 business-related criteria.[58]

No matter how you gather the information, once you have it, the key is to systematically use that information to evaluate each alternative against each criterion. Exhibit 5.12 shows how each of the ten cities on your staff's list fared on each of the 12 criteria (higher scores are better), from qualified staff to freedom from pollution. Although London has the most qualified staff, the best access to markets and telecommunications, and is the easiest city to travel to and from, it is also one of the most polluted and expensive cities on the list. Paris offers excellent access to markets and clients, but if your staff is multilingual, Amsterdam may be a better choice.

4.6 Compute the Optimal Decision

The final step in the decision-making process is to compute the optimal decision by determining the optimal value of each alternative. This is done by multiplying the rating for each criterion (Step 4.5) by the weight for that criterion (Step 4.3), and then summing those scores for each alternative course of action that you generated (Step 4.4). For example, the 500 executives participating in Cushman & Wakefield's survey of the best European cities for business rated the 12 decision criteria in terms of importance, as shown in the first column of Exhibit 5.12. Access to quality staff, markets, telecommunication, and easy travel to and from the city were the four most important factors, and quality of life and freedom from pollution were the least important factors. To calculate the optimal value for Paris, its score in each category is multiplied by the weight for each category (0.60×0.79 in the qualified staff category, for example). Then all of these scores are added together to produce the optimal value, as follows:

$$(0.60 \times 0.79) + \_(0.59 \times 1.11) + \_(0.54 \times 0.79) + \_$$
$$(0.53 \times 1.39) + \_(0.40 \times 0.21) + \_(0.27 \times 0.26) + \_$$
$$(0.27 \times 0.57) + \_(0.26 \times 0.31) + \_(0.25 \times 1.10) + \_$$
$$(0.24 \times 0.45) + \_(0.21 \times 0.61) + \_(0.18 \times 0.16) = \_3.22$$

Because London has a weighted average of 4.27 compared to 3.22 for Paris and 2.29 for Frankfurt, London clearly ranks as the best location for your company's new European office because of its large number of qualified staff; easy access to markets; outstanding ease of travel to, from, and within the city; excellent telecommunications; and top-notch business climate.

Exhibit 5.12   Criteria Ratings Used to Determine the Best Locations in Europe for a New Office

	WEIGHTS	Amsterdam	Barcelona	Berlin	Brussels	Frankfurt	London	Madrid	Milan	Paris	Zurich
QUALIFIED STAFF	57%	.35	.30	.40	.44	.58	1.32	.30	.33	.78	.41
ACCESS TO MARKETS	60%	.39	.30	.28	.54	.71	1.36	41	.38	1.18	.24
TRAVEL TO/ FROM CITY	52%	.66	.26	.19	.55	1.19	1.74	.30	.23	1.42	.27
TELECOMMUNI-CATIONS	50%	.32	.21	.33	.40	.58	1.22	.24	.20	.80	.34
BUSINESS CLIMATE	32%	.34	.40	.36	.35	.11	.51	.52	.11	.20	.51
COST OF STAFF	35%	.16	.73	.27	.19	.05	.15	.60	.21	.11	.07
COST & VALUE OF OFFICE SPACE	31%	.28	.57	.52	.44	.26	.18	.48	.17	.20	.18
AVAILABLE OFFICE SPACE	30%	.26	.46	.63	.42	.45	.55	.58	.21	.39	.25
TRAVEL WITHIN CITY	22%	.34	.45	.53	.34	.41	1.09	.38	.19	1.19	.38
LANGUAGES SPOKEN	24%	1.00	.22	.34	1.13	.53	1.41	.21	.17	.50	.66
QUALITY OF LIFE	16%	.30 .41	1.21	.24	.38	.14	.39	.61	.26	.67	.55
FREEDOM FROM POLLUTION	13%	.44	.44	.17	.18	.12	.06	.16	.03	.10	.94
WEIGHTED AVERAGE SCORE		1.68	1.69	1.48	1.93	2.20	4.17	1.63	.99	3.07	1.36
RANKING		6	5	8	4	3	1	7	10	2	9

Source: "European Cities Monitor," Cushman & Wakefield Healy & Baker, available at www.cushmanwakefield.com/cwglobal/docviewer/European%20Cities%20Monitor.pdf?id=ca1500006&repositoryKey=CoreReposityr&itemDesc=document.

4.7 Limits to Rational Decision Making

In general, managers who diligently complete all six steps of the rational decision-making model will make better decisions than those who don't. So when they can, managers should try to follow the steps in the rational decision-making model, especially for big decisions with long-range consequences.

It's highly doubtful, however, that rational decision making can always help managers choose *optimal* solutions that provide *maximum* benefits to their organizations. The terms *optimal* and *maximum* suggest that rational decision making leads to perfect or near-perfect decisions. Of course, for managers to make perfect decisions, they have to operate in perfect worlds with no real-world constraints. In an optimal world, the manager who asked you to develop a computer strategy for the sales team would be able to clearly define which salespeople needed budget laptops, slim laptops, workhorse laptops, or tablet laptops, and simply ensure that all team members received exactly what they needed to do their jobs effectively. You would not be constrained by price or time as you develop solutions. Furthermore, without any constraints, the manager could identify and weight an extensive list of decision criteria, generate a complete list of possible solutions, and then test and evaluate each computer against each decision criterion. Finally, the manager would have the necessary experience and knowledge with computers to easily make sense of all these sophisticated tests and information. Of course, it never works like that in the real world. Managers face time and money constraints. They often don't have time to make extensive lists of decision criteria. And they often don't have the resources to test all possible solutions against all possible criteria.

The rational decision-making model describes the way decisions *should* be made. In other words, decision makers wanting to make optimal decisions *should not* have to face time and cost constraints. They *should* have unlimited resources and time to generate and test all alternative solutions against all decision criteria. And they *should* be willing to recommend any decision that produces optimal benefits for the company, even if that decision would harm their own jobs or departments. Of course, very few managers actually make rational decisions the way they *should*. The way in which managers actually make decisions is more accurately described as bounded (or limited) rationality. **Bounded rationality** means that managers try to take a rational approach to decision making but are restricted by real-world constraints, incomplete and imperfect information, and their own limited decision-making capabilities.

In theory, fully rational decision makers **maximize** decisions by choosing the optimal solution. In practice, however, limited resources along with attention, memory, and expertise problems make it nearly impossible for managers to maximize decisions. Consequently, most managers don't maximize—they satisfice. Whereas maximizing is choosing the best alternative, **satisficing** is choosing a "good-enough" alternative. With 24 decision criteria, 50 alternative computers to choose from, two computer labs with hundreds of thousands of dollars of equipment, and unlimited time and money, the manager could test all alternatives against all decision criteria and choose the perfect computer. In reality, however, the manager's limited time, money, and expertise mean that only a few alternatives will be assessed against a few decision criteria. In practice, the manager will visit two or three computer or electronic stores, read a couple of recent computer reviews, and get bids from Dell, Lenovo, and Hewlett-Packard as well as some online superstores like CDW or PC Connection. The decision will be complete when the manager finds a good-enough laptop that meets a few decision criteria.

bounded rationality a decision-making process restricted in the real world by limited resources, incomplete and imperfect information, and managers' limited decision-making capabilities.

maximize choosing the best alternative.

satisficing choosing a "good enough" alternative.

Steps and Limits to Rational Decision Making Rational decision making is a six-step process in which managers define problems, evaluate alternatives, and compute optimal solutions. The first step is identifying and defining the problem. Problems exist where there is a gap between desired and existing states. Managers won't begin the decision-making process unless they are aware of the gap, motivated to reduce it, and possess the necessary resources to fix it. The second step is defining the decision criteria that are used when judging alternatives. In Step 3, an absolute or relative comparison process is used to rate the importance of the decision criteria. Step 4 involves generating as many alternative courses of action (i.e., solutions) as possible. Potential solutions are assessed in Step 5 by systematically gathering information and evaluating each alternative against each criterion. In Step 6, criterion ratings and weights are used to compute the optimal value for each alternative course of action. Rational managers then choose the alternative with the highest optimal value.

The rational decision-making model describes how decisions should be made in an ideal world without limits. However, bounded rationality recognizes that in the real world,

Review 4

managers' limited resources, incomplete and imperfect information, and limited decision-making capabilities restrict their decision-making processes. These limitations often prevent managers from being rational decision makers.

5 Using Groups to Improve Decision Making

According to a study reported in *Fortune* magazine, 91 percent of U.S. companies use teams and groups to solve specific problems (i.e., make decisions).[59] Why so many? Because when done properly, group decision making can lead to much better decisions than those typically made by individuals. In fact, numerous studies show that groups consistently outperform individuals on complex tasks.

Let's explore the **5.1 advantages and pitfalls of group decision making** and see how the following group decision-making methods—**5.2 structured conflict, 5.3 the nominal group technique, 5.4 the Delphi technique, 5.5 the stepladder technique,** and **5.6 electronic brainstorming**—can be used to improve decision making.

5.1 Advantages and Pitfalls of Group Decision Making

Groups can do a much better job than individuals in two important steps of the decision-making process: defining the problem and generating alternative solutions. There are four reasons for this. First, groups are able to view problems from multiple perspectives because group members usually possess different knowledge, skills, abilities, and experiences. Being able to view problems from different perspectives, in turn, can help groups perform better on complex tasks and make better decisions than individuals.[60]

© iStockphoto.com/Pixdeluxe

Second, groups can find and access much more information than individuals alone. At 1-800-GOT-JUNK?, a national chain of over 200 locations that provides efficient, timely junk removal, applicants are not interviewed by one person at a time. Instead, each applicant is interviewed by a group of eight people with eight different areas of expertise. Together they assess the candidate immediately following the interview. CEO Brian Scudamore believes there is wisdom in crowds, and relying on groups to conduct interviews has helped his company maintain a remarkably low employee turnover rate of only 1.4 percent.[61]

Third, the increased knowledge and information available to groups make it easier for them to generate more alternative solutions. Studies show that generating lots of alternative solutions is critical to improving the quality of decisions. Finally, if groups are involved in the decision-making process, group members will be more committed to making chosen solutions work.

Although groups can do a better job of defining problems and generating alternative solutions, group decision making is subject to some pitfalls that can quickly erase these gains. One possible pitfall is groupthink. **Groupthink** occurs in highly cohesive groups when group members feel intense pressure to agree with each other so that the group can approve a proposed solution.[62] Because groupthink leads to consideration of a limited number of solutions and restricts discussion of any considered solutions, it usually results in poor decisions. Groupthink is most likely to occur under the following conditions:

> » The group is insulated from others with different perspectives.
> » The group leader begins by expressing a strong preference for a particular decision.
> » The group has no established procedure for systematically defining problems and exploring alternatives.
> » Group members have similar backgrounds and experiences.63

Groupthink may be one of the key reasons behind the failure of Lehman Brothers in 2008, one of Wall Street's largest and most storied investment banks, and the second largest bankruptcy of all time. Lehman Brothers was highly leveraged, which means most of the money it had invested was borrowed money. This is a highly risky strategy. Imagine walking into a casino with $100 in your pocket. But before sitting down at the blackjack table, you take out a $4,000 cash advance on a credit card. Now, instead of making small bets, you can make huge ones. If you win, that big bet brings huge payoffs. But if you lose, which is more likely, you owe $4,000 plus the interest on that loan.

Well, Lehman Brothers was highly leveraged, and they began to lose. But instead of getting out and limiting their losses—which is what you'd expect a firm of financial professionals to do—they kept right on betting. Why? In part, groupthink. Lehman's risk management staff kept telling top management that it was too highly leveraged and that economic conditions could quickly lead to huge losses, but Lehman's leadership wouldn't listen. Lawrence McDonald, a Lehman's brother executive, said that when CEO Dick Fuld was warned by the company's fixed-income manager that huge losses were likely, Fuld "decided to bully him, to belittle him publicly."[64] Likewise, two years earlier, when Lehman's top risk management officer, Madelyn Antoncic, started sounding alarms, Fuld excluded her and ignored her reports from big decisions, and then fired her for her dissenting views.

A second potential problem with group decision making is that it takes considerable time. Reconciling schedules so that group members can meet takes time. Furthermore, it's a rare group that consistently holds productive task-oriented meetings to effectively work through the decision process. Some of the most common complaints about meetings (and thus group decision making) are that the meeting's purpose is unclear, participants are unprepared, critical people are absent or late, conversation doesn't stay focused on the problem, and no one follows up on the decisions that were made. Teresa Taylor, the chief operations officer at Qwest, avoids many of these problems by opening every meeting with the question "Do we all know why we're here?" Surprisingly, she often finds that many people can't answer the question—they just show up to a meeting because they've been invited. Taylor will clarify the purpose of the meeting even further by asking, "Are we making decisions? Are you going to ask me for something at the end?" In doing so, she helps participants focus their attention. Once the purpose is identified, Taylor will even allow people to leave the meeting if they feel like they don't need to be there.[65]

A third possible pitfall to group decision making is that sometimes one or two people, perhaps the boss or a strong-willed, vocal group member, can dominate group

groupthink a barrier to good decision making caused by pressure within the group for members to agree with each other.

discussions and limit the group's consideration of different problem definitions and alternative solutions. And unlike individual decisions where people feel personally responsible for making a good choice, another potential problem is that group members may not feel accountable for the decisions made and actions taken by the group.

Although these pitfalls can lead to poor decision making, this doesn't mean that managers should avoid using groups to make decisions. When done properly, group decision making can lead to much better decisions. The pitfalls of group decision making are not inevitable. Managers can overcome most of them by using the various techniques described next.

5.2 Structured Conflict

Most people view conflict negatively. Yet the right kind of conflict can lead to much better group decision making. **C-type conflict**, or "**cognitive conflict**," focuses on problem and issue-related differences of opinion.[66] In c-type conflict, group members disagree because their different experiences and expertise lead them to view the problem and its potential solutions differently. C-type conflict is also characterized by a willingness to examine, compare, and reconcile those differences to produce the best possible solution. Alteon Websystems, now a division of Nortel Networks, makes critical use of c-type conflict. Top manager Dominic Orr described Alteon's c-type conflict this way:

> People arrive with a proposal or a solution—and with the facts to support it. After an idea is presented, we open the floor to objective, and often withering, critiques. And if the idea collapses under scrutiny, we move on to another: no hard feelings. We're judging the idea, not the person. At the same time, we don't really try to regulate emotions. Passionate conflict means that we're getting somewhere, not that the discussion is out of control. But one person does act as referee—by asking basic questions like "Is this good for the customer?" or "Does it keep our time-to-market advantage intact?" By focusing relentlessly on the facts, we're able to see the strengths and weaknesses of an idea clearly and quickly.[67]

By contrast, **a-type conflict**, meaning "**affective conflict**," refers to the emotional reactions that can occur when disagreements become personal rather than professional. A-type conflict often results in hostility, anger, resentment, distrust, cynicism, and apathy. Unlike c-type conflict, a-type conflict undermines team effectiveness by preventing teams from engaging in the activities characteristic of c-type conflict that are critical to team effectiveness. Examples of a-type conflict statements are "your idea," "our idea," "my department," "you don't know what you are talking about," or "you don't understand our situation." Rather than focusing on issues and ideas, these statements focus on individuals.[68]

Two methods of introducing structured c-type conflict into the group decision-making process are devil's advocacy and dialectical inquiry. The **devil's advocacy** approach can be used to create c-type conflict by assigning an individual or a subgroup the role of critic. The following five steps establish a devil's advocacy program:

c-type conflict (cognitive conflict) disagreement that focuses on problem- and issue-related differences of opinion

a-type conflict (affective conflict) disagreement that focuses on individuals or personal issues.

devil's advocacy a decision-making method in which an individual or a subgroup is assigned the role of a critic.

1. Generate a potential solution.
2. Assign a devil's advocate to criticize and question the solution.
3. Present the critique of the potential solution to key decision makers.
4. Gather additional relevant information.
5. Decide whether to use, change, or not use the originally proposed solution.[69]

Dialectical inquiry creates c-type conflict by forcing decision makers to state the assumptions of a proposed solution (a thesis) and then generate a solution that is the opposite (antithesis) of the proposed solution. The following are the five steps of the dialectical inquiry process:

1. Generate a potential solution.
2. Identify the assumptions underlying the potential solution.
3. Generate a conflicting counterproposal based on the opposite assumptions.
4. Have advocates of each position present their arguments and engage in a debate in front of key decision makers.
5. Decide whether to use, change, or not use the originally proposed solution.[70]

BMW uses dialectical inquiry in its design process, typically creating six internal design teams to compete against each other to design a new car. After a front-runner or leading design emerges from one of the teams, another team is assigned to design a car that is diametrically opposed to the leading design (Step 3 of the dialectical inquiry method).[71]

When properly used, both the devil's advocacy and dialectical inquiry approaches introduce c-type conflict into the decision-making process. Contrary to the common belief that conflict is bad, studies show that these methods lead not only to less a-type conflict but also improved decision quality and greater acceptance of decisions once they have been made.[72] See the What Really Works feature for more information on both techniques.

5.3 Nominal Group Technique

Nominal means "in name only." Accordingly, the **nominal group technique** received its name because it begins with a quiet time in which group members independently write down as many problem definitions and alternative solutions as possible. In other words, the nominal group technique begins by having group members act as individuals. After the quiet time, the group leader asks each member to share one idea at a time with the group. As they are read aloud, ideas are posted on flip charts or wallboards for all to see. This step continues until all ideas have been shared. In the next step, the group discusses the advantages and disadvantages of the ideas. The nominal group technique closes with a second quiet time in which group members independently rank the ideas presented. Group members then read their rankings aloud, and the idea with the highest average rank is selected.[73]

The nominal group technique improves group decision making by decreasing a-type conflict. But it also restricts c-type conflict. Consequently, the nominal group technique typically produces poorer decisions than the devil's advocacy and dialectical inquiry approaches. Nonetheless, more than 80 studies have found that nominal groups produce better ideas than those produced by traditional groups.[74]

5.4 Delphi Technique

In the **Delphi technique,** the members of a panel of experts respond to questions and to each other until reaching agreement on an issue. The first step is to assemble a panel of experts. Unlike other approaches to group decision making, however, it isn't necessary to bring the panel members together in one place. Because the Delphi technique does not require the experts to leave their offices or disrupt their schedules,

dialectical inquiry a decision-making method in which decision makers state the assumptions of a proposed solution (a thesis) and generate a solution that is the opposite (antithesis) of that solution.

nominal group technique a decision-making method that begins and ends by having group members quietly write down and evaluate ideas to be shared with the group.

Delphi technique a decision-making method in which members of a panel of experts respond to questions and to each other until reaching agreement on an issue.

doing the right thing

Dos and Don'ts of Conference Calls

Conference calls are a great way to hold meetings. They are an easy way to get people to "check in" no matter where they are, but there are also many challenges for making them effective and efficient. It can be hard to hear what other people are saying. Some people might be watching TV or surfing the web instead of paying attention. Some people aren't used to talking on the phone with more than one person and can end up talking over each other. David Lavenda, vice president of Mainsoft, offers up ten tips for making good conference calls.

1. Keep statements short and ask for frequent feedback.
2. Don't use slides if you can avoid it, since reading slides with text is boring, and you can't control what people are looking at.
3. If you must show slides, don't send them ahead of time.
4. Send out an agenda ahead of time and stick to it.
5. Use video if possible. Skype or webcams provide visual cues that help people stay engaged, and off the video games.
6. Let the participants know if you are recording the call.
7. Start on time.
8. Make sure the moderator dials in early.
9. Don't dial in from a mobile phone.
10. Set limits on call duration.[75]

they are more likely to participate. For example, a colleague and I were asked by a local government agency to use a Delphi technique to assess the "ten most important steps for small businesses." The first step is to assemble the group. We assembled a panel of local top-level managers and CEOs.

The second step is to create a questionnaire consisting of a series of open-ended questions for the group. We asked our panel of experts to answer questions like these: "What is the most common mistake made by small-business owners?" "Right now, what do you think is the biggest threat to the survival of most small businesses?" "If you had one piece of advice to give to the owner of a small business, what would it be?"

In the third step, the group members' written responses are analyzed, summarized, and fed back to the group for reactions until the members reach agreement. In our Delphi study, it took about a month to get the panel members' written responses to the first three questions. Then we summarized their responses in a brief report (no more than two pages). We sent the summary to the panel members and asked them to explain why they agreed or disagreed with the conclusions from the first round of questions. Asking group members why they agree or disagree is important because it helps uncover their unstated assumptions and beliefs. Again, this process of summarizing panel feedback and obtaining reactions to that feedback continues until the panel members reach agreement. For our study, it took just one more round for the panel members to reach a consensus. In all, it took approximately three and a half months to complete our Delphi study.

Exhibit 5.13   Stepladder Technique for Group Decision Making

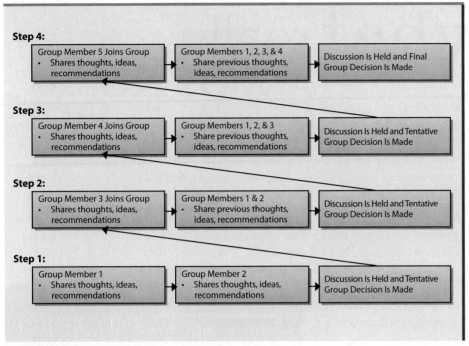

© Cengage Learning 2013

5.5 Stepladder Technique

The stepladder technique improves group decision making by ensuring that each member's contributions are independent and are considered and discussed by the group. As shown in Exhibit 5.13, the **stepladder technique** begins with discussion between two group members who share their thoughts, ideas, and recommendations before jointly making a tentative decision. Other group members are added to the discussion one at a time at each step, like a stepladder. The existing group members take the time to listen to and understand each new member's thoughts, ideas, and recommendations. Then they share the ideas and suggestions they had already considered. The group discusses the new and old ideas together and makes a tentative decision. This process (new member's ideas are heard, group shares previous ideas and suggestions, discussion is held, tentative group decision is made) continues until each group member's ideas have been discussed.

For the stepladder technique to work, group members must have enough time to consider the problem or decision on their own, present their ideas to the group, and thoroughly discuss all ideas and alternatives with the group at each step. Rushing through a step destroys the advantages of this technique. Also, groups must make sure that subsequent group members are completely unaware of previous discussions and suggestions. This will ensure that each member who joins the group brings truly independent thoughts and suggestions, thus greatly increasing the chances of making better decisions. All members must be present before a final decision is made.

One study found that groups using the stepladder technique produced significantly better decisions than did traditional groups in which all group members are present for the entire discussion. Moreover, the stepladder groups performed better than the best individual member of their group 56 percent of the time, whereas traditional groups outperformed the best individual member of their group only 13 percent of the time.[76] Besides better performance, groups using the stepladder technique also generated more ideas and were more satisfied with the decision-making process. This

stepladder technique a decision-making method in which group members are added to a group discussion one at a time (like a stepladder). The existing group members listen to each new member's thoughts, ideas, and recommendations; then the group shares the ideas and suggestions that it had already considered, discusses the new and old ideas, and makes a decision.

© iStockphoto.com/Hans Martens

what really works

Devil's Advocacy, Dialectical Inquiry, and Considering Negative Consequences

Ninety percent of the decisions managers face are well-structured problems that recur frequently under conditions of certainty. For example, for most retailers a customer's request for a refund on a returned item without a receipt is a well-structured problem. It happens every day (recurs frequently), and it's easy to determine whether a customer has a receipt (condition of certainty).

Well-structured problems are solved with programmed decisions, in which a policy, procedure, or rule clearly specifies how to solve the problem. Thus, there's no mystery about what to do when someone shows up without a receipt: Allow the item to be exchanged for one of similar value, but don't give a refund.

In some sense, programmed decisions really aren't decisions, because anyone with experience knows what to do. No thought is required. What keeps managers up at night is the other 10 percent of problems. Ill-structured problems that are novel (no one's seen them before) and exist under conditions of uncertainty are solved with nonprogrammed decisions. Nonprogrammed decisions do not involve standard methods of resolution. Every time managers make a nonprogrammed decision, they have to figure out a new way of handling a new problem. That's what makes the decisions so tough.

Both the devil's advocacy and dialectical inquiry approaches to decision making, along with a related approach, considering negative consequences, can be used to improve nonprogrammed decision making. All three work because they force decision makers to identify and criticize the assumptions underlying the nonprogrammed decisions that they hope will solve ill-structured problems.

Devil's Advocacy

There is a 58 percent chance that decision makers who use the devil's advocacy approach to criticize and question their solutions will produce decisions that are better than decisions based on the advice of experts.

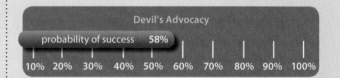

Dialectical Inquiry

There is a 55 percent chance that decision makers who use the dialectical inquiry approach to criticize and question their solutions will produce decisions that are better than decisions based on the advice of experts.

Note that each technique has been compared with decisions obtained by following experts' advice. So, although these probabilities of success, 55 percent and 58 percent, seem small, they very likely understate the effects of both techniques. In other words, the probabilities of better decisions would have been much larger if both techniques had been compared with unstructured decision-making processes.

Group Decision Making and Considering Negative Consequences

Considering negative consequences, such as with a devil's advocate or via critical inquiry, means pointing out the potential disadvantages of proposed solutions. There is an 86 percent chance that groups that consider negative consequences will produce better decisions than those that don't.[77]

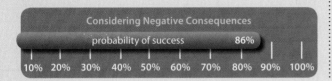

Considering Negative Consequences

probability of success   86%

10% 20% 30% 40% 50% 60% 70% 80% 90% 100%

Managers should not use the Delphi technique for common decisions. Because it is a time-consuming, labor-intensive, and expensive process, the Delphi technique is best reserved for important long-term issues and problems. Nonetheless, the judgments and conclusions obtained from it are typically better than those you would get from one expert.

technique also works particularly well with audio conferencing, in which geographically dispersed group members make decisions via a telephone conference call.[78]

5.6 Electronic Brainstorming

Brainstorming, in which group members build on others' ideas, is a technique for generating a large number of alternative solutions. Brainstorming has four rules:

1. The more ideas, the better.
2. All ideas are acceptable, no matter how wild or crazy they might seem.
3. Other group members' ideas should be used to come up with even more ideas.
4. Criticism or evaluation of ideas is not allowed.

Although brainstorming is great fun and can help managers generate a large number of alternative solutions, it does have a number of disadvantages. Fortunately, **electronic brainstorming,** in which group members use computers to communicate and generate alternative solutions, overcomes the disadvantages associated with face-to-face brainstorming.[79]

The first disadvantage that electronic brainstorming overcomes is **production blocking,** which occurs when you have an idea but have to wait to share it because someone else is already presenting an idea to the group. During this short delay, you may forget your idea or decide that it really wasn't worth sharing. Production blocking doesn't happen with electronic brainstorming. All group members are seated at computers, so everyone can type in ideas whenever they occur. There's no waiting your turn to be heard by the group.

The second disadvantage that electronic brainstorming overcomes is **evaluation apprehension,** that is, being afraid of what others will think of your ideas. With electronic brainstorming, all ideas are anonymous. When you type in an idea and hit the Enter key to share it with the group, group members see only the idea. Furthermore, many brainstorming software programs also protect anonymity by displaying ideas in random order. So if you laugh maniacally when you type "Cut top management's pay by 50 percent!" and then hit the Enter key, it won't show up immediately on everyone's screen. This makes it doubly difficult to determine who is responsible for which comments.

In the typical layout for electronic brainstorming, all participants sit in front of computers around a U-shaped table. This configuration allows them to see their computer screens, the other participants, a large main screen, and a meeting leader or facilitator. Exhibit 5.14 shows what the typical electronic brainstorming group member will see on his or her computer screen. Step 1 in electronic brainstorming is to anonymously generate as many ideas as possible. Groups commonly generate 100 ideas in

brainstorming a decision-making method in which group members build on each others' ideas to generate as many alternative solutions as possible.

electronic brainstorming a decision-making method in which group members use computers to build on each others' ideas and generate as many alternative solutions as possible.

production blocking a disadvantage of face-to-face brainstorming in which a group member must wait to share an idea because another member is presenting an idea.

evaluation apprehension fear of what others will think of your ideas.

Exhibit 5.14 What You See on the Computer During Electronic Brainstorming

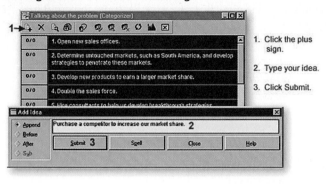

Source: Developing Consensus with GroupSystems. © 2002 GroupSystems.com

a half-hour period. Step 2 is to edit the generated ideas, categorize them, and eliminate redundancies. Step 3 is to rank the categorized ideas in terms of quality. Step 4, the last step, has three parts: Generate a series of action steps, decide the best order for accomplishing these steps, and identify who is responsible for each step. All four steps are accomplished with computers and electronic brainstorming software.[80]

Studies show that electronic brainstorming is much more productive than face-to-face brainstorming. Four-person electronic brainstorming groups produce 25 to 50 percent more ideas than four-person regular brainstorming groups, and 12-person electronic brainstorming groups produce 200 percent more ideas than regular groups of the same size! In fact, because production blocking (having to wait your turn) is not a problem for electronic brainstorming, the number and quality of ideas generally increase with group size.[81]

Even though it works much better than traditional brainstorming, electronic brainstorming has disadvantages, too. An obvious problem is the expense of computers, networks, software, and other equipment. As these costs continue to drop, however, electronic brainstorming will become cheaper.

Another problem is that the anonymity of ideas may bother people who are used to having their ideas accepted by virtue of their position (i.e., the boss). On the other hand, one CEO said, "Because the process is anonymous, the sky's the limit in terms of what you can say, and as a result it is more thought-provoking. As a CEO, you'll probably discover things you might not want to hear but need to be aware of."[82]

A third disadvantage is that outgoing individuals who are more comfortable expressing themselves verbally may find it difficult to express themselves in writing. Finally, the most obvious problem is that participants have to be able to type. Those who can't type, or who type slowly, may be easily frustrated and find themselves at a disadvantage to experienced typists. For example, one meeting facilitator was informed that an especially fast typist was pretending to be more than one person. Says the facilitator, "He'd type 'Oh, I agree' and then 'Ditto, ditto' or 'What a great idea,' all in quick succession, using different variations of uppercase and lowercase letters and punctuation. He tried to make it seem like a lot of people were concurring, but it was just him." Eventually, the person sitting next to him got suspicious and began watching his screen.[83]

Review 5

Using Groups to Improve Decision Making When groups view problems from multiple perspectives, use more information, have a diversity of knowledge and experience, and become committed to solutions they help choose, they can produce better solutions than individual decision makers. However, group decisions can suffer from these disadvantages: groupthink, slowness, discussions dominated by just a few individuals, and unfelt responsibility for decisions. Group decisions work best when group members encourage c-type conflict. However, group decisions don't work as well when groups become mired in a-type conflict. The devil's advocacy and dialectical inquiry approaches improve group decisions because they bring structured c-type conflict into the decision-making process. By contrast, the nominal group technique and the Delphi technique both improve decision making by reducing a-type conflict through limited interactions between group members. The stepladder technique improves group decision making by adding each group member's independent contributions to the discussion one at a time. Finally, because it overcomes the problems of production blocking and evaluation apprehension, electronic brainstorming is a more effective method of generating alternatives than face-to-face brainstorming.

SELF-ASSESSMENT

Self-Management

A key part of planning is setting goals and tracking progress toward their achievement. As a manager, you will be involved in some type of planning in an organization. But the planning process is also used in a personal context, where it is called self-management. Self-management involves setting goals for yourself, developing a method or strategy to achieve them, and then carrying it out. For some people, self-management comes naturally. Everyone seems to know someone who is highly organized, self-motivated, and disciplined. That someone may even be you. If that someone is not you, however, then you will need to develop your self-management skills as a means to becoming a better manager.

A part of planning, and therefore management, is setting goals and tracking progress toward goal achievement.[84] Answer each of the questions using the following scale:

1   Strongly disagree
2   Disagree
3   Not sure
4   Agree
5   Strongly agree

1. I regularly set goals for myself.
    1   2   3   4   ⑤

2. I keep track of how well I've been doing.
    1   2   3   4   ⑤

3. I generally keep the resolutions that I make.
    1   2   3   4   ⑤

4. I often seek feedback about my performance.
    1   2   3   4   ⑤

5. I am able to focus on positive aspects of my work.
    1   2   3   ④   5

6. I'll sometimes deny myself something until I've set my goals.
    1   ②   3   4   5

7. I use a to-do list to plan my activities.
    1   2   ③   4   5

8. I have trouble working without supervision.
    ①   2   3   4   5

9. When I set my mind on some goal, I persevere until it's accomplished.
    1   2   3   ④   5

KEY TERMS

absolute comparisons 185
action plan 173
a-type conflict (affective conflict) 192
bounded rationality 189
brainstorming 197
budgeting 182
c-type conflict (cognitive conflict) 192
decision criteria 185
decision making 183
Delphi technique 193
devil's advocacy 192
dialectical inquiry 193
distal goals 173
electronic brainstorming 197
evaluation apprehension 197
goal commitment 173
groupthink 191
learning-based planning 176
management by objectives (MBO) 180

maximize 189
nominal group technique 193
operational plans 180
options-based planning 175
policies 180
problem 184
procedures 182
production blocking 197
proximal goals 173
purpose statement 178
rational decision making 183
relative comparisons 186
rules and regulations 182
satisficing 189
single-use plans 180
slack resources 176
SMART goals 172
standing plans 180
stepladder technique 195
strategic objective 178
strategic plans 178
tactical plans 179

10. I'm a self-starter.
    1   2   3   4   (5)

11. I make lists of things I need to do.
    1   2   3   (4)   5

12. I'm good at time management.
    1   2   3   4   (5)

13. I'm usually confident that I can reach my goals.
    1   2   3   (4)   5

14. I am careful about how I manage my time.
    1   2   3   4   (5)

15. I always plan my day.
    1   2   (3)   4   5

16. I often find I spend my time on trivial things and put off doing what's really important.
    1   2   (3)   4   5

17. Unless someone pushes me a bit, I have trouble getting motivated.
    1   (2)   3   4   5

18. I reward myself when I meet my goals.
    1   2   3   (4)   5

19. I tend to dwell on unpleasant aspects of the things I need to do.
    1   2   (3)   4   5

20. I tend to deal with life as it comes rather than to try to plan things.
    1   2   (3)   4   5

21. I generally try to find a place to work where I'll be free from interruptions.
    1   2   3   (4)   5

22. I'm pretty disorganized.
    (1)   2   3   4   5

23. The goals I set are quite specific.
    1   2   3   (4)   5

24. Distractions often interfere with my performance.
    1   (2)   3   4   5

25. I sometimes give myself a treat if I've done something well.
    1   2   3   (4)   5

26. I am able to focus on positive aspects of my activities.
    1   2   3   (4)   5

27. I use notes or other prompts to remind myself of schedules and deadlines.
    1   2   3   4   (5)

28. I seem to waste a lot of time.
    1   (2)   3   4   5

29. I use a day planner or other aids to keep track of schedules and deadlines.
    1   2   (3)   4   5

30. I often think about how I can improve my performance.
    1   2   3   4   (5)

31. I tend to lose track of the goals I've set for myself.
    1   (2)   3   4   5

32. I tend to set difficult goals for myself.
    1   2   (3)   4   5

33. I plan things for weeks in advance.
    1   2   3   4   (5)

34. I try to make a visible commitment to my goals.
    1   2   3   (4)   5

35. I set aside blocks of time for important activities.
    1   2   (3)   4   5

Scoring

Determine your score by entering your response to each survey item, as follows. In blanks that say *regular score*, simply enter your response for that item. If your response was a 4, place a 4 in the *regular score* blank. In blanks that say *reverse score*, subtract your response from 6 and enter the result. So if your response was a 4, place a 2 (6 – 4 = 2) in the *reverse score* blank. Add up your total score.

1. regular score   _____
2. regular score   _____
3. regular score   _____
4. regular score   _____
5. regular score   _____
6. regular score   _____
7. regular score   _____
8. reverse score   _____
9. regular score   _____
10. regular score   _____
11. regular score   _____
12. regular score   _____
13. regular score   _____
14. regular score   _____
15. regular score   _____
16. reverse score   _____
17. reverse score   _____
18. regular score   _____
19. reverse score   _____
20. reverse score   _____
21. regular score   _____
22. reverse score   _____

23. regular score	_____	31. reverse score	_____
24. reverse score	_____	32. regular score	_____
25. regular score	_____	33. regular score	_____
26. regular score	_____	34. regular score	_____
27. regular score	_____	35. regular score	_____
28. reverse score	_____	TOTAL = _____	
29. regular score	_____		
30. regular score	_____		

You can find the interpretation for your score at academic.cengage.com/management/Williams.

MANAGEMENT DECISION

What Should We Call It?[85]

Your jobs as a marketing manager at GM certainly has been challenging. Through government bailouts, bankruptcy, and a thorough reorganization, you've had the unenviable job of trying to persuade the buying public that your cars are still high-quality, high-value products. Some of your campaigns went off better than others—who can forget the disastrous ad campaign that tried to convince married women to buy more pickup trucks? But with exciting new models coming out of factories and a renewed sense of determination from senior executives, you're quite excited about getting the word out about how great GM cars are.

One particular day, you get a phone call from your supervisor, asking you to help solve a little problem. It turns out that GM wants to offer an industry-leading warranty on its Opel- and Vauxhall-branded cars that it sells in Europe. The warranty would cover any issues, except for accidental damage, for 100,000 miles, with no limitations on date. Managers are even exploring ways for the warranty to be fully transferrable so that people who buy a used car will be protected by the warranty.

"Sounds like a great way to sell cars," you tell your boss, "so what do you need me for?" The problem, he tells you, is that some executives in the company want to market the warranty as a "lifetime warranty." How

is it that a warranty with a mileage limit qualified as "lifetime"? According to GM research, drivers in Britain only drive about 8,200 miles a year, meaning that the 100,000 mile limit would last for 12 years. Plus, they've found that 95% of car owners in Britain don't use their cars for more than ten years. So, they argue, even though the warranty has a limit, it's essentially a "lifetime" warranty because most owners will never use their cars long enough.

Being the ace manager that you are, your supervisor has asked you to make the decision as to whether GM should go ahead with labeling the warranty as "lifetime." The phrase "lifetime warranty" certainly has a nice ring to it, and your head is full of great ideas about how to take advantage of it to sell more cars. At the same time, you wonder whether, and maybe even when, consumers will get angry about being misled. Is it really a lifetime warranty if it comes with an expiration date? What to do . . .?

Questions

1. What recommendation would you make as to how to label the warranty in marketing campaigns? Why?
2. In making the decision, how could you benefit from the various group decision-making techniques described in the chapter? Which might be most effective for the decision you face?

MANAGEMENT TEAM DECISION

To Pay or Not to Pay?[86]

Toyota used to sit on top of the world. It basked in the reputation of building high-quality cars efficiently. It enjoyed unprecedented growth, even surpassing

General Motors as the largest car manufacturer in the world. But all of that came tumbling down with reports that cars were accelerating out of control, careening down highways, and putting everyone's lives

in danger. There was even a recording of a 911 call from an off-duty policeman who lost control of his car and died in the ensuing crash. Toyota responded with a recall of historic proportions—nearly 8 million cars in the United States and 1.8 million in Europe. It even suspended sales of brand new models, including the best-selling Camry and Corolla, until the vehicles could be repaired. But still, there was confusion about what was causing the problems—was it the floor mats, the braking system, the software controlling the engine, or something else? Conspiracy theorists argued that Toyota had no clue what was causing the sudden acceleration and that their recall was basically worthless.

By early 2009, your company was in a situation it had not faced for decades—its sales had dropped by 16 percent. Even General Motors, the bankrupt General Motors, which looked like it could do nothing right for many years, grew 8 percent during the same time. According to some journalists, the recall cost Toyota more than $2 billion. But by March 2010, things seemed to be on the rebound. Sales picked up dramatically, 35 percent from the previous year, and 88 percent from the previous month. Customers were once again buying Toyotas and putting their confidence in its ability to produce reliable cars.

But just as things seemed to be rosy again, Transportation Secretary Ray LaHood announced plans to levy a fine of $16.4 million against your company. The money itself isn't necessarily a problem. Even with losses, Toyota still made $1.8 billion in the fourth quarter of 2009. The fine would be less than 1 percent of what you earned in just three months. So why not just "take the medicine" as it were, pay the fine,

and move on from the whole mess? Because the fine comes attached with a statement that Toyota "knowingly hid" safety problems in order to avoid a costly recall. According to LaHood, "We now have proof that Toyota failed to live up to its legal obligations. Worse yet, they knowingly hid a dangerous defect for months from U.S. officials and did not take action to protect millions of drivers and their families."

So what will you choose to do? You could just pay the fine and admit fault, but if you do, the company's reputation for quality will take a perhaps fatal blow. You wouldn't just be admitting that you made a mistake, but that you deliberately lied about it in order to keep making money. What's more, an admission of covering up would give great support to the hundreds of lawsuits that claim Toyota committed consumer fraud. How much money would those settlements cost? You could, of course, just contest the fine and the admission. But, your company's reputation is already fragile, and fighting the government (and potentially losing) may make things even worse.

Form a group with three or four other students and discuss what decision you would make as a Toyota management team by answering the following questions.

Questions

1. What is your recommendation for how Toyota should approach this situation?
2. What are the decision criteria that should be used in this situation, and how should they be weighted?
3. Under what conditions do you think it is acceptable for Toyota to settle for a "good enough" decision?

PRACTICE BEING A MANAGER

Effective planning and decision making are crucial to the success of organizations. Your success as a manager will be determined in large part by your planning and decision-making capabilities. This exercise highlights some well-tested tools for strengthening your planning and decision-making skills.

Individual Preparation

Step 1: Identify your "best company." Suppose that you are going to develop a plan that will result in your being hired to work for the single *best company* possible. "Best company" has not been defined for you,

so you must determine what this might mean. Identify your "best company," and make your plan. You need to consider such aspects as building the right academic and work profile, marketing yourself to the company, and interviewing effectively. Carefully record both your plan and the steps that you took to develop it. In class, you will be asked to share this information with a small discussion group.

Small Group Discussion

Step 2: Discuss your plan. Taking turns, individually share your plan with the members of your discussion group. Members should listen carefully, ask questions, and make notes regarding the similarities and differences of individual plans.

Step 3: Create a brochure. Now suppose that your group has been asked to develop a brochure for distribution in college career centers. The brochure will be titled "Getting a Job with Your Dream Company."

Using what you have learned from sharing your individual plans, work as a group to develop a sketch/outline of this brochure.

Class Discussion

Step 4: As a class, discuss the following questions:

- Did you follow the rational decision-making process in identifying your best company and creating your plan for landing a job with this company? Why or why not?

- What role might bounded rationality have played in your individual and/or team decision-making process?

- Does planning increase the likelihood of success in being hired by a great company? Why or why not?

- If you were an editor assigned the project of developing the brochure "Getting a Job with Your Dream Company," would you be more likely to give the assignment to (1) a qualified individual or (2) a qualified group? Considering your recent experiences in this exercise, what are the trade-offs of each approach (individual versus group decision making)?

DEVELOP YOUR CAREER POTENTIAL

What Do You Want to Be When You Grow Up?

What do you want to be when you grow up?[87] Still not sure? Ask around. You're not alone. Chances are, your friends and relatives aren't certain either. Sure, they may have jobs and careers, but you're likely to find that, professionally, many of them don't want to be where they are today. Sometimes people's interests change, or they may burn out. And some people are unhappy with their current job or career because they weren't in the right one to begin with.

Getting the job and career you want is not easy. It takes time, effort, and persistence. And even though you will probably follow multiple career paths in your life, your career-planning process will be easier (and more effective) if you take the time to develop a personal career plan.

Begin by answering the following questions. (*Hint:* Treat this seriously. If you do it effectively, this plan could guide your career decisions for the next five to seven years.)

1. Describe your strengths and weaknesses. Don't just rely on your opinions of your abilities. Ask your parents, relatives, friends, and employers what they think too. Encourage them to be honest and then be prepared to hear some things that you may not want to hear. Remember, though, this information can help you pick the right job or career.

2. Write an advertisement for the job you want to have five years from now. Be specific. Describe the company, title, responsibilities, required education and experience, salary, and benefits. Use employment ads in the Sunday job listings as inspiration.

3. Create a detailed plan to obtain this job. In the short term, what classes do you need to take? Should you change your major? Do you need a business major or minor or maybe a minor in a foreign language? What kind of summer work experience will move you closer to getting the job you want five years from now? What job do you need to get right out of college to obtain the work experience you need? Create a specific plan for each of the five years in your career plan, keeping in mind that the plans for later years are likely to change. The value in planning is that it forces you to think about what you want and the steps you can take now to help achieve those goals.

4. Decide when you will monitor and evaluate the progress you're making with your plan. Career experts suggest that every six months is about right. Pick two dates and write them in your schedule. Furthermore, right now, before you forget, set five specific, challenging goals that you need to accomplish in the next six months in order to achieve your career plans.

END NOTES

[1]C. Loomis & D. Burke, "Can Ellen Kullman Make DuPont Great Again?" *Fortune*, May 3, 2010, 156–163; and M. Reisch, "Leading DuPont: After a Difficult First Year as CEO, Ellen Kullman Sets the Stage for Growth," *Chemical & Engineering News*, April 12, 2010, 10–13.

[2]L. A. Hill, *Becoming a Manager: Master a New Identity* (Boston: Harvard Business School Press, 1992).

[3]Jennifer Ernst Beaudry "Inside Nike's $27B Plans," *Women's Wear Daily*, May 12, 2010, accessed June 30, 2010, from www.wwd.com/footwear-news/inside-nikes-27b-plans-3067422; and Andria Cheng, "Nike Sets Growth Goal of $27 Billion Sales in 5 Years," Marketwatch, May 5, 2010, accessed June 30, 2010, from www.marketwatch.com/story/nike-growth-goal-27-billion-in-sales-in-5-years-2010-05-05.

[4]E. A. Locke & G. P. Latham, *A Theory of Goal Setting & Task Performance* (Englewood Cliffs, NJ: Prentice Hall, 1990).

[5]M. E. Tubbs, "Goal-Setting: A Meta-Analytic Examination of the Empirical Evidence," *Journal of Applied Psychology* 71 (1986): 474–483.

[6]J. Bavelas & E. S. Lee, "Effect of Goal Level on Performance: A Trade-Off of Quantity and Quality," *Canadian Journal of Psychology* 32 (1978): 219–240.

[7]D. Turner, "Ability, Aspirations Fine, but Persistence Is What Gets Results," *Seattle Times*, February 13, 2005, accessed March 5, 2011, from http://community.seattletimes.nwsource.com/archive/?date=20030215&slug=dale15m.

[8]Harvard Management Update, "Learn by 'Failing Forward,'" *Globe & Mail*, October 31, 2000, B17.

[9]C. C. Miller, "Strategic Planning and Firm Performance: A Synthesis of More Than Two Decades of Research," *Academy of Management Performance* 37 (1994): 1649–1665.

[10]H. Mintzberg, "Rethinking Strategic Planning: Part I: Pitfalls and Fallacies," *Long Range Planning* 27 (1994): 12–21, and "Part II: New Roles for Planners," 22–30; and H. Mintzberg, "The Pitfalls of Strategic Planning," *California Management Review* 36 (1993): 32–47.

[11]J. Stoll, "GM Sees Brighter Future," *The Wall Street Journal*, January 18, 2008, A3; D. Welch, "Live Green or Die," *Businessweek*, May 26, 2008, 36–41; L. Greenemeier, "GM's Chevy Volt to Hit the Streets of San Francisco and Washington, D.C.," *60-Second Science Blog*, February 5, 2009, accessed November 30, 2010, from www.scientificamerican.com/blog/post.cfm?id=chevy-volt-to-hit-the-streets-of-sa-2009-02-05; and "Electric Vehicles Expected in the Next Two Years (Photos)," CNET, July 16, 2010, accessed August 15, 2010, from http://news.cnet.com/2300-11128_3-10004136.html?tag=mncol.

[12]Mintzberg, "The Pitfalls of Strategic Planning."

[13]A. Cosslett, "Corner Office: Where Are You When the Going Gets Tough?" interview by A. Bryant, *The New York Times*, April 2, 2010, accessed August 11, 2010, from www.nytimes.com/2010/04/04/business/04corner.html?_r=1.

[14]Locke & Latham, *A Theory of Goal Setting & Task Performance*.

[15]A. King, B. Oliver, B. Sloop, & K. Vaverek, *Planning & Goal Setting for Improved Performance: Participant's Guide* (Cincinnati, OH: Thomson Executive Press, 1995).

[16]A. Taylor III, "Here Comes the Electric Nissan," *Fortune*, March 1, 2010, 90–98.

[17]C. Loomis, J. Schlosser, J. Sung, M. Boyle, & P. Neering, "The 15% Delusion: Brash Predictions about Earnings Growth Often Lead to Missed Targets, Battered Stock, and Creative Accounting—and That's When Times Are Good," *Fortune*, February 5, 2001, 102; H. Paster, "Manager's Journal: Be Prepared," *The Wall Street Journal*, September 24, 2001, A24; P. Sellers, "The New Breed: The Latest Crop of CEOs Is Disciplined, Deferential, Even a Bit Dull," *Fortune*, November 18, 2002, 66; and H. Klein & M. Wesson, "Goal and Commitment and the Goal-Setting Process: Conceptual Clarification and Empirical Synthesis," *Journal of Applied Psychology* 84 (1999): 885–896.

[18]Locke & Latham, *A Theory of Goal Setting & Task Performance*.

[19]K. Linbaugh & N.E. Boudette, "Fiat Models to Drive Chrysler," *The Wall Street Journal*, October 27, 2009, accessed September 1, 2010, from http://online.wsj.com/article/SB125659536562909009.html?mg=com-wsj; and B. Vlasic & N. Bunkley, "Party's Over: A New Tone for Chrysler," *The New York Times*, November 4, 2009, accessed September 1, 2010, from www.nytimes.com/2009/11/05/business/05auto.html.

[20]A. Bandura & D. H. Schunk, "Cultivating Competence, Self-Efficacy, and Intrinsic Interest through Proximal Self-Motivation," *Journal of Personality & Social Psychology* 41 (1981): 586–598.

[21]D. Ariely & K. Wertenboch, "Procrastination, Deadlines, and Performance: Self-Control by Precommitment," *Psychological Science* 13 (2002): 219–224.

[22]N. Carr, "Curbing the Procrastination Instinct," *Harvard Business Review* (October 2001): 26.

[23]Locke & Latham, *A Theory of Goal Setting & Task Performance*.

[24]M. J. Neubert, "The Value of Feedback and Goal Setting over Goal Setting Alone and Potential Moderators of This Effect: A Meta-Analysis," *Human Performance* 11 (1998): 321–335.

[25]E. H. Bowman & D. Hurry, "Strategy through the Option Lens: An Integrated View of Resource Investments and the Incremental-Choice Process," *Academy of Management Review* 18 (1993): 760–782.

[26]M. Lawson, "In Praise of Slack: Time Is of the Essence," *Academy of Management Executive* 15 (2000): 125–135.

27 J. Lahart, "U.S. Firms Build Up Record Cash Piles," *The Wall Street Journal*, June 10, 2010, accessed June 11, 2010, from http://online.wsj.com/article/SB1000142405274870431 21045752986525679882 46.html?mod=WSJ_hps_LEFTWhatsNews.

28 Ibid.

29 N. A. Wishart, J. J. Elam, & D. Robey, "Redrawing the Portrait of a Learning Organization: Inside Knight-Ridder, Inc.," *Academy of Management Executive* 10 (1996): 7–20.

30 E. Byron, "From Diapers to 'Depends': Marketers Discreetly Retool for Aging Boomers," *The Wall Street Journal*, February 5, 2011, accessed March 5, 2011, from http://online.wsj.com/article/SB10001424052748704040 136045761043942090629 96.html.

31 R. Brown, "Zappos Eyes 5-Year Goal of $75M Beauty Biz," *Women's Wear Daily*, April 9, 2010, 10.

32 J. C. Collins & J. I. Porras, "Organizational Vision and Visionary Organizations," *California Management Review* (Fall 1991): 30–52.

33 R. Brown, "Zappos Eyes 5-Year Goal of $75M Beauty Biz."

34 J. C. Collins & J. I. Porras, "Organizational Vision and Visionary Organizations," *California Management Review* (Fall 1991): 30–52; and J. A. Pearce II, "The Company Mission as a Strategic Goal," *Sloan Management Review* (Spring 1982): 15–24. Collins and Porras define an organization's mission: "A mission is a clear and compelling goal that serves to unify an organization's efforts. An effective mission must stretch and challenge the organization, yet be achievable." However, many others define mission as an organization's purpose. In this edition, to be more specific and avoid confusion, we used Collins and Porras's term *purpose statement*, meaning a clear statement of an organization's purpose or reason for existence. Furthermore, we continued to use Collins and Porras's definition of a mission (i.e., "a clear and compelling goal . . .,") but instead call it "the strategic objective."

35 "President Bush Announces New Vision for Space Exploration Program," The White House, accessed April 17, 2005, from www.whitehouse.gov/news/releases/2004/01/20040114-1.html.

36 "Clean Hands Appear to Calm the Mind," *The Wall Street Journal*, May 18, 2010, accessed August 10, 2010, from http://online.wsj.com/article/SB1 0001424052748703460404575244823148621434.html.

37 "NASA's Exploration Systems Mission Directorate," Exploration: NASA's Plans to Explore the Moon, Mars, and Beyond, accessed May 29, 2009, from www.nasa.gov.

38 Greg Bensinger, "Gannett's USA Today to Cut 130 Jobs, Shuffles Management Posts," Bloomberg.com, August 27, 2010, from http://www.bloomberg.com/news/2010-08-27/gannett-s-usa-today-to-cut-130-jobs-restructure-as-circulation-declines.html; and Michael Liedtke, "USA Today Shaking up Staff in 'Radical' Overhaul," Associated Press, August 27, 2010, from www.google.com/hostednews/ap/article/ALeqM5j5qqSYmjDdJs6syeIugPf5J-50p9AD9HS2JJG0.

39 L. Lorberf, "Running the Show—An Open Book: When Companies Share Their Financial Data with Employees, the Results Can Be Dramatic," *The Wall Street Journal*, February 23, 2009, R8.

40 "The Issue: Coping with Catastrophe," *Bloomberg Businessweek*, November 20, 2009, accessed January 10, 2010, from www.businessweek.com/managing/content/nov2009/ca20091120_038561.htm.

41 R. Rodgers & J. E. Hunter, "Impact of Management by Objectives on Organizational Productivity," *Journal of Applied Psychology* 76 (1991): 322–336.

42 E. Marlow & R. Schilhavy, "Expectation Issues in Management by Objectives Programs," *Industrial Management* 33, no. 4 (1991): 29.

43 "Web MBO Teams with Deloitte & Touche to Deliver Innovative Web-Based 'Management-by-Objectives and Performance Management' Solutions," *PR Newswire*, June 19, 2001.

44 S. McCartney, "Is Your Boss Spying on Your Upgrades?" *The Wall Street Journal*, August 12, 2008, D1.

45 Adapted from quality procedure at G&G Manufacturing, Cincinnati, Ohio.

46 N. Humphrey, "References a Tricky Issue for Both Sides," *Nashville Business Journal* 11 (May 8, 1995): 1A.

47 K. R. MacCrimmon, R. N. Taylor, & E. A. Locke, "Decision Making and Problem Solving," in *Handbook of Industrial & Organizational Psychology*, ed. M. D. Dunnette (Chicago: Rand McNally, 1976), 1397–1453.

48 A. Zimmerman, "Cricket Lee Takes on the Fashion Industry," *The Wall Street Journal*, March 17, 2008, R1.

49 MacCrimmon, Taylor, & Locke, "Decision Making and Problem Solving."

50 G. Kress, "The Role of Interpretation in the Decision Process," *Industrial Management* 37 (1995): 10–14.

51 J. Jargon, "As Profit Cools, Starbucks Plans Price Campaign," *The Wall Street Journal*, April 30, 2009, B3.

52 Zimmerman, "Cricket Lee Takes on the Fashion Industry."

53 Ibid.

54 "Notebook Shipments Surpass Desktops in the U.S. Market for the First Time, According to IDC," BusinessWire, accessed May 30, 2009, from www.businesswire.com/news/home/20081028005575/en/Notebook-Shipments-Surpass-Desktops-U.S.-Market-Time, October 28, 2008.

55 *Consumer Reports Buying Guide 2006*, 129–131.

56 "New-Vehicle Ratings Comparison by Car Category," ConsumerReports.org, accessed February 29, 2005, from www.consumerreports.org/cro/cars/index.htm.

57 P. Djang, "Selecting Personal Computers," *Journal of Research on Computing in Education* 25 (1993): 327.

58 "European Cities Monitor 2007 Reveals That London Has Increased Its Lead over Paris . . .," Cushman & Wakefield, October 9, 2007, accessed March 5, 2011, from www.cushwake.com/cwglobal/jsp/newsDetail.jsp?Country=GB&Language=EN&repId=c12300059p.

59 B. Dumaine, "The Trouble with Teams," *Fortune*, September 5, 1994, 86–92.

60 L. Pelled, K. Eisenhardt, & K. Xin, "Exploring the Black Box: An Analysis of Work Group Diversity, Conflict, and Performance," *Administrative Science Quarterly* 44, no. 1 (March 1, 1999): 1.

[61]B. Scudamore, "Gather Round! For a Group Interview," *Inc.* (August 2006): 94.

[62]I. L. Janis, *Groupthink* (Boston: Houghton Mifflin, 1983).

[63]C. P. Neck & C. C. Manz, "From Groupthink to Teamthink: Toward the Creation of Constructive Thought Patterns in Self-Managing Work Teams," *Human Relations* 47 (1994): 929–952; and J. Schwartz & M. L. Wald, "'Groupthink' Is 30 Years Old, and Still Going Strong," *The New York Times*, March 9, 2003, 5.

[64]R. Wartzman, "10 Management Lessons from Lehman's Demise," *Businessweek Online*, September 21, 2009, 13.

[65]"Everything on One Calendar, Please," *The New York Times*, December 26, 2009, accessed January 2, 2010, from www.nytimes.com/2009/12/27/business/27corner.html?pagewanted=all.

[66]A. Mason, W. A. Hochwarter, & K. R. Thompson, "Conflict: An Important Dimension in Successful Management Teams," *Organizational Dynamics* 24 (1995): 20.

[67]C. Olofson, "So Many Decisions, So Little Time: What's Your Problem?" *Fast Company*, October 1, 1999, 62.

[68]Ibid.

[69]R. Cosier & C. R. Schwenk, "Agreement and Thinking Alike: Ingredients for Poor Decisions," *Academy of Management Executive* 4 (1990): 69–74.

[70]Ibid.

[71]B. Breen, "BMW: Driven by Design," *Fast Company*, September 1, 2002, 123.

[72]K. Jenn & E. Mannix, "The Dynamic Nature of Conflict: A Longitudinal Study of Intragroup Conflict and Group Performance," *Academy of Management Journal* 44, no. 2 (2001): 238–251; and R. L. Priem, D. A. Harrison, & N. K. Muir, "Structured Conflict and Consensus Outcomes in Group Decision Making," *Journal of Management* 21 (1995): 691–710.

[73]A. Van De Ven & A. L. Delbecq, "Nominal versus Interacting Group Processes for Committee Decision Making Effectiveness," *Academy of Management Journal* 14 (1971): 203–212.

[74]A. R. Dennis & J. S. Valicich, "Group, Sub-Group, and Nominal Group Idea Generation: New Rules for a New Media?" *Journal of Management* 20 (1994): 723–736.

[75]David Lavenda, "10 Rules for Effective Conference Calls" *Fast Company*, May 23, 2010, available online at http://www.fastcompany.com/1651164/10-rules-for-effective-conference-calls.

[76]S. G. Rogelberg, J. L. Barnes-Farrell, & C. A. Lowe, "The Stepladder Technique: An Alternative Group Structure Facilitating Effective Group Decision Making," *Journal of Applied Psychology* 77 (1992): 730–737; and S. G. Rogelberg & M. S. O'Connor, "Extending the Stepladder Technique: An Examination of the Self-Paced Stepladder Groups," *Group Dynamics: Theory, Research, & Practice* 2 (1998): 82–91.

[77]C. R. Schwenk, "Effects of Devil's Advocacy and Dialectical Inquiry on Decision Making: A Meta-Analysis," *Organizational Behavior & Human Decision Performance* 47 (1990): 161–176; and M. Orlitzky & R. Hirokawa, "To Err Is Human, to Correct for It Divine: A Meta-Analysis of Research Testing the Functional Theory of Group Decision-Making Effectiveness," *Small Group Research* 32, no. 3 (June 2001): 313–341.

[78]S. Rogelberg, M. O'Connor, & M. Sedergurg, "Using the Stepladder Technique to Facilitate the Performance of Audioconferencing Groups," *Journal of Applied Psychology* 87 (2002): 994–1000.

[79]R. B. Gallupe, W. H. Cooper, M. L. Grise, & L. M. Bastianutti, "Blocking Electronic Brainstorms," *Journal of Applied Psychology* 79 (1994): 77–86.

[80]R. B. Gallupe & W. H. Cooper, "Brainstorming Electronically," *Sloan Management Review* (Fall 1993): 27–36.

[81]Ibid.

[82]G. Kay, "Effective Meetings through Electronic Brainstorming," *Management Quarterly* 35 (1995): 15.

[83]A. LaPlante, "90s Style Brainstorming," *Forbes ASAP*, October 25, 1993, 44.

[84]R.J. Aldag & L. W. Kuzuhara, *Mastering Management Skills: A Manager's Toolkit* (Mason, OH: Thomson South-Western, 2005), 172–173.

[85]John Reed, "GM Woos Europe with 'Lifetime Warranty,'" *Financial Times*, August 5, 2010, accessed October 10, 2010, from www.ft.com/cms/s/0/e4caae36-a0b7-11df-badd-00144feabdc0.html.

[86]Ashby Jones, "The Toyota Fine: The $16M Might Not Be Toyota's Biggest Problem," *The Wall Street Journal*, April 7, 2010, accessed June 20, 2010, from http://blogs.wsj.com/law/2010/04/07/the-toyota-fine-the-16m-might-not-be-toyotas-biggest-problem/; Micheline Maynard & Hiroko Tabuchi, "Toyota Sees Sales Rebounding," *The New York Times*, March 30, 2010, accessed June 20, 2010, from www.nytimes.com/2010/03/31/business/global/31toyota.html; and "Sizing up the Damage," *Marketwatch*, January 29, 2010, accessed June 20, 2010, from www.marketwatch.com/story/toyota-faces-grim-january-sales-2010-01-29; and "Toyota Car Recall May Cost $2bn," *BBC*, accessed June 20, 2010, from http://news.bbc.co.uk/2/hi/business/8493414.stm.

[87]"20 Hot Job Tracks," *U.S. News & World Report*, October 30, 1995, 98–104; C. Boivie, "Planning for the Future . . . Your Future," *Journal of Systems Management* 44 (1993): 25–27; J. Connelly, "How to Choose Your Next Career," *Fortune*, February 6, 1995, 145–146; and P. Sherrid, "A 12-Hour Test of My Personality," *U.S. News & World Report*, October 31, 1994, 109.

© iStockphoto.com/Oner Döngel

BIZ FLIX

Inside Man

The 2006 crime thriller *Inside Man* features Denzel Washington as a tough New York Police Department hostage negotiator. He finds himself in a high-stakes cat-and-mouse game with a clever bank robber (Clive Owen), who confuses and outwits the police at every turn. Bank robber Dalton Russell is holding 50 people hostage in the vault of the Manhattan Trust Bank building, and Detective Frazier is determined to get them out alive, but the movie's tagline—"It looked like the perfect bank robbery. But you can't judge a crime by its cover"—tells us this there is more going on than seems to be. In this scene, Captain John Darius (Willem Dafoe) updates Detective Frazier on what is happening inside the bank.

© GreenLight

What to Watch for and Ask Yourself

1. Does this scene show strategic or tactical planning?
2. What pieces of the planning type does it specifically show? Give examples from the scene.
3. Do you expect this plan to succeed? Why or why not?

MANAGEMENT WORKPLACE

Plant Fantasies: Managerial Decision Making

Teresa Carleo, owner of Plant Fantasies, is the gardener for such well-known New York City properties as the Trump Organization, John Jay College, and Jack Resnick & Sons. In landscaping, success often boils down to big decisions over little details. Although some decisions involve plant colors and types, others involve complex negotiation with people, such as when Plant Fantasies builds designs created by outside landscape architects. Despite Carleo's confidence in her own decision making, the Plant Fantasies owner understands the benefits of empowering others. But regardless of who makes decisions, Carleo expects all her employees to share her high standards for quality.

© Cengage Learning

Discussion Questions

1. Did Plant Fantasies owner Teresa Carleo follow the rational decision-making process to launch Plant Fantasies? Explain.
2. List an example of a programmed decision at Plant Fantasies. Identify a nonprogrammed decision at Plant Fantasies.

CHAPTER 6

Organizational Strategy

Learning Outcomes

1. Specify the components of sustainable competitive advantage, and explain why it is important.
2. Describe the steps involved in the strategy-making process.
3. Explain the different kinds of corporate-level strategies.
4. Describe the different kinds of industry-level strategies.
5. Explain the components and kinds of firm-level strategies.

what would you do?

Walt Disney Company Headquarters, Burbank, California[1]

Over two decades, your predecessor and boss at the Walt Disney Company, CEO Michael Eisner, accomplished much, starting the Disney Channel, the Disney Stores, and Disneyland Paris, and acquiring ABC television, Starwave Web services (from Microsoft cofounder Paul Allan), and Infoseek (an early Web search engine). But his strong personality and critical management style created conflict with shareholders, creative partners, and board members, including Roy Disney, nephew of founder Walt Disney.

One of your first moves as Disney's new CEO was repairing relationships with Pixar Studios and its then CEO Steve Jobs. Pixar produced computer-animated movies for Disney to distribute and market. Disney also had the right to produce sequels to Pixar Films, such as *Toy Story*, without Pixar's involvement. Jobs argued, however, that Pixar should have total financial and creative control over its films. When Disney CEO Michael Eisner disagreed, relations broke down, with Pixar seeking other partners. On becoming CEO, you approached Jobs about Disney buying Pixar for $7 billion. More important than the price, however, was promising Jobs and Pixar's leadership, President Ed Catmull and creative guru John Lasseter, total creative control of Pixar's films *and* Disney's storied but struggling animation unit. Said Jobs, "I wasn't sure I could get Ed and John to come to Disney unless they had that control."

Although Pixar and Disney animation thrived under the new arrangement, Disney still had a number of critical strategic problems to address. Disney was "too old" and suffering from brand fatigue as its classic but aging characters, Mickey Mouse (created in 1928) and Winnie-the-Pooh (licensed by Disney in 1961), accounted for 80 percent of consumer sales. On the other hand, Disney was also "too young" and suffering from "age compression," meaning it appealed only to young children and not preteens, who gravitated to Nickelodeon, and certainly not to teens at all. Finally, despite its legendary animated films, over time Disney products had developed a reputation for low-quality production, poor acting, and weak scripts. Movies "High School Musical 3: Senior Year," "Beverly Hills Chihuahua," "Bolt," "Confessions of a Shopaholic," "Race to Witch Mountain," and "Bedtime Stories" disappointed audiences and failed to meet financial goals. As you told your board of directors, "It's not the marketplace, it's our slate [of TV shows and movies]."

With many of Disney's brands and products clearly suffering, you face a basic decision: Should Disney grow, stabilize, or retrench? Disney is an entertainment conglomerate with Walt Disney Studios (films), parks and resorts (including Disney Cruise lines and vacations), consumer products (i.e., toys, clothing, books, magazines, and

study tips

Pick up a copy of *The Wall Street Journal* and read several articles. List the strategy issues facing the companies you read about. Fresh examples of management topics can be found every day in the business press.

merchandise), and media networks such as TV (ABC, ESPN, Disney Channels, ABC Family), radio, and the Disney Interactive Media Group (online, mobile, and video games and products). If Disney should grow, where? Like Pixar, is another strategic acquisition necessary? If so, who? If stability, how do you improve quality to keep doing what Disney has been doing, but even better? Finally, retrenchment would mean shrinking Disney's size and scope. If you were to do this, what divisions would you shrink or sell?

Next, given the number of different entertainment areas that Disney has, what business is it really in? Is Disney a content business, creating characters and stories? Or is it a technology/distribution business that simply needs to find ways to buy content wherever it can, for example, by buying Pixar and then delivering that content in ways that customers want (i.e., DVDs, cable channels, iTunes, Netflix, social media, Internet TV, etc.)?

Finally, from a strategic perspective, how should Disney's different entertainment areas be managed? Should there be one grand strategy (i.e., growth, stability, retrenchment) that every division follows, or should each division have a focused strategy for its own market and customers? Likewise, how much discretion should division managers have to set and execute their strategies, or should that be controlled and approved centrally by the strategic planning department at Disney headquarters?

If you were CEO at Disney, what would you do?

In Chapter 5, you learned that *strategic plans* are overall plans that clarify how a company intends to serve customers and position itself against competitors over the next two to five years.

This chapter begins with an in-depth look at how managers create and use strategies to obtain a sustainable competitive advantage, or, in Disney's case, to get their competitive advantage back. Then you learn the three steps of the strategy-making process. Next, you learn about corporate-level strategies that help managers answer the question "What business or businesses should we be in?" You then examine the industry-level competitive strategies that help managers determine how to compete successfully within a particular line of business. The chapter finishes with a review of the firm-level strategies of direct competition and entrepreneurship.

Basics of Organizational Strategy

Less than a decade ago, Apple Computer was not in the music business. And then it released the iPod, which quickly set the standard for all other digital music devices. Designed around a 1.8-inch-diameter hard drive, the iPod boasted low battery consumption and enough memory to hold literally thousands of songs in an easy-to-use product smaller than a deck of cards, designed with unparalleled style. Because Apple used existing and readily available technology to make the iPod, Sony, Samsung, Dell, Creative, and Microsoft moved quickly to produce their own MP3 players.

As the market has matured over the past several years, competitors have increasingly tried to steal—or at least minimize—Apple's competitive advantage by adding unique features to their MP3 players. Sony's new S Series Walkman includes touchscreen navigation, built-in noise cancellation, the ability to surf the Internet via Wi-Fi, to view pictures and videos, and to store—and listen to at your convenience—FM radio and Web-based radio shows.

SanDisk, best known as a maker of flash memory, has been competing with Apple for about six years. Its latest model, the Fuze +, is similar to the iPod in terms of audio and video capabilities. It even lets owners listen to FM radio. However, it lacks the touch-screen controls and the tens of thousands of apps that are available on an iPod touch. Microsoft's Zune HD 64 has touch-screen controls, HD radio (similar to the quality of satellite radio), and HD output, which lets you hook up your Zune to a high-def TV. It even allows you to download music and videos directly from your Zune to your computer. Even with this competition, Apple still holds a commanding 73.8 percent of the digital music player market, with Sansa at 7.2 percent and Microsoft at 1.1 percent.[2]

How can a company like Apple, which dominates a particular industry, maintain its competitive advantage as strong, well-financed competitors enter the market? What steps can Apple and other companies take to better manage their strategy-making process?

After reading the next two sections, you should be able to

1. *Specify the components of sustainable competitive advantage and explain why it is important.*
2. *Describe the steps involved in the strategy-making process.*

1 Sustainable Competitive Advantage

Resources are the assets, capabilities, processes, employee time, information, and knowledge that an organization controls. Firms use their resources to improve organizational effectiveness and efficiency. Resources are critical to organizational strategy because they can help companies create and sustain an advantage over competitors.[3]

Organizations can achieve a **competitive advantage** by using their resources to provide greater value for customers than competitors can. For example, the iPod's competitive advantage came partly from its simple, attractive design relative to its price. But Apple's most important advantage was the iTunes store. Although Apple was not the first to introduce an online music store, it negotiated agreements with nearly all of the major record labels to distribute their songs from a central online library, giving iTunes an inventory unmatched by its competitors. The user-friendly site also linked seamlessly with free software that customers could use to organize and manage their digital music libraries, and iTunes quickly became the premier platform for music downloading. [4]

The goal of most organizational strategies is to create and then sustain a competitive advantage. A competitive advantage becomes a **sustainable competitive advantage** when other companies cannot duplicate the value a firm is providing to customers. Sustainable competitive advantage is *not* the same as a long-lasting competitive advantage, though companies obviously want a competitive advantage to last a long time. Instead, a competitive advantage is *sustained* if competitors have tried unsuccessfully to duplicate the advantage and have, for the moment, stopped trying to duplicate it. It's the corporate equivalent of your competitors saying, "We

resources the assets, capabilities, processes, employee time, information, and knowledge that an organization uses to improve its effectiveness and efficiency, create and sustain competitive advantage, and fulfill a need or solve a problem.

competitive advantage providing greater value for customers than competitors can.

sustainable competitive advantage a competitive advantage that other companies have tried unsuccessfully to duplicate and have, for the moment, stopped trying to duplicate.

Exhibit 6.1 Four Requirements for Sustainable Competitive Advantage

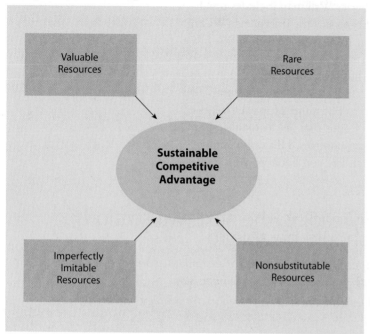

© Cengage Learning 2013

give up. You win. We can't do what you do, and we're not even going to try to do it anymore." As Exhibit 6.1 shows, four conditions must be met if a firm's resources are to be used to achieve a sustainable competitive advantage. The resources must be valuable, rare, imperfectly imitable, *and* nonsubstitutable.

Valuable resources allow companies to improve their efficiency and effectiveness. Unfortunately, changes in customer demand and preferences, competitors' actions, and technology can make once-valuable resources much less valuable. Throughout the 1980s, Sony controlled the portable music market with its ubiquitous Sony Walkman, which has sold over 230 million units worldwide since its introduction in 1979. For many years, Sony had the technology to produce a higher quality of music than other portable devices on the market. Sony leveraged the capabilities of its engineers and inventors (more resources) to make incremental changes to the Walkman that were not matched by the competition, that is, until the MP3 player came along. With the introduction of Apple's iPod to the market, Sony's Walkman lost nearly all its value. Sony finally changed the Walkman to a portable digital device and created its own online music store (Connect), which did not match the simplicity or availability of songs at the iTunes store.[5] When Connect proved unprofitable, Sony shut it down.[6]

For sustained competitive advantage, valuable resources must also be rare resources. Think about it: How can a company sustain a competitive advantage if all of its competitors have similar resources and capabilities? Consequently, **rare resources**, resources that are not controlled or possessed by many competing firms, are necessary to sustain a competitive advantage. When Apple introduced the iPod, no other portable music player on the market used existing hard-drive technology in its design. The iPod gained an immediate advantage over competitors because it was able to satisfy the desire of consumers to carry large numbers of songs in a portable device, something the newer MP3 systems and older single CD players could not do. The technology that powered the iPod, however, was readily available, so competitors were able to quickly imitate and, for short periods, exceed the iPod's basic storage capacity. As competitors began introducing their iPod look-alikes, Apple responded by replacing the original mechanical control wheel with an easier-to-use solid-state touch wheel and then doubled the hard-drive storage so that it was larger than those in competitors' devices.

Once again, Apple used its design talents (resources) to gain an advantage over the competition. One of Apple's truly rare resources is its ability to reconfigure existing technology into a package that is easy to use, elegantly designed, and therefore highly desired by customers. Another example of this capability is the iPod Touch, of which Apple has sold 45 million.[7] The iPod Touch can do nearly everything an iPhone can—run apps, browse the web, and use touch-screen controls—save for making phone calls and taking pictures. But, with apps like Skype, iPod Touch owners will even be able to make phone calls as long as they have a Wi-Fi connection to the Internet.[8] The newest version of the iPod touch has two cameras, one in the back that can shoot high-definition video and one on the front that lets users run FaceTime, a video chat application.[9]

valuable resource a resource that allows companies to improve efficiency and effectiveness.

rare resource a resource that is not controlled or possessed by many competing firms.

As this example shows, valuable and rare resources can create temporary competitive advantage. For sustained competitive advantage, however, other firms must be unable to imitate or find substitutes for those valuable, rare resources. **Imperfectly imitable resources** are those resources that are impossible or extremely costly or difficult to duplicate. For example, despite numerous attempts by competitors to imitate it, iTunes has retained its competitive lock on the music download business. Because it capitalized on Apple's reputation for developing customer-friendly software, the library of music, movies, and podcasts on iTunes is still two to three times larger than those of other music download sites.

Because the company initially developed a closed system for its iTunes and iPod, it was difficult for consumers to download music from sources other than Apple's iTunes store. But for many customers, who wouldn't even consider another brand, this was not a problem. Kelly Moore, a sales representative for a Texas software company, takes her pink iPod mini everywhere she goes and keeps it synchronized with her iBook laptop. She says, "Once I find something I like, I don't switch brands."[10] She's not alone. As of this writing, sales at the iTunes store total over 11.7 billion songs, 450 million TV shows, and 10 billion applications.[11] No other competitor comes close to those numbers.

Valuable, rare, imperfectly imitable resources can produce sustainable competitive advantage only if they are also **nonsubstitutable resources**, meaning that no other resources can replace them and produce similar value or competitive advantage. The industry has tried to produce equivalent substitutes for iTunes, but competitors have had to experiment with different business models in order to get customers to accept them. For example, eMusic is a club retailer, like Costco or Sam's Club, which sells music downloads to club members for 25 percent to 50 percent less than iTunes and Amazon.com. At Microsoft's Zune Marketplace, customers can purchase songs, albums, and videos just like on iTunes, but the Zune Pass subscription allows you to download and stream every bit of music on the Zune Marketplace onto multiple devices, such as your Zune MP3 player or your PC, Windows Phone, or Xbox 360. In addition to straight subscription models, some companies experimented with price. Where iTunes charges 69 cents, 99 cents, or $1.29 per song, period, Amazon's online store typically charges 99 cents per song but has a large collection of 25,000+ songs for which it only charges 69 cents. Amazon is also aggressive with album prices, offering 100 albums a day for $5, and bestselling albums for $7.99. In response to competitors' experimentation, Apple went to the variable pricing mentioned above, 69 cents, 99 cents, or $1.29 cents per song, and also removed digital rights management, which restricted the extent to which users could copy their music from one device to another.[12] It will take years to find out whether these new means of purchase will constitute an effective substitute to iTunes.[13]

In summary, Apple has reaped the rewards of a first-mover advantage from its interdependent iPod and iTunes. The company's history of developing customer-friendly software, the innovative capabilities of the iPod, the simple pay-as-you-go sales model of iTunes, and the unmatched list of music and movies available for download provide customers with a service that has been valuable, rare, relatively nonsubstitutable, and, in the past, imperfectly imitable. Past success is, however, no guarantee of future success: Apple must continually change and develop its offerings or risk being unseated by a more nimble competitor whose products are more relevant and have higher perceived value to the consumer.

imperfectly imitable resource a resource that is impossible or extremely costly or difficult for other firms to duplicate.

nonsubstitutable resource a resource that produces value or competitive advantage and has no equivalent substitutes or replacements.

© Francisco Martinez/Alamy

Review 1

2 Strategy-Making Process

To create a sustainable competitive advantage, a company must have a strategy.[14] Exhibit 6.2 displays the three steps of the strategy-making process: **2.1 assess the need for strategic change, 2.2 conduct a situational analysis**, and then **2.3 choose strategic alternatives**. Let's examine each of these steps in more detail.

2.1 Assessing the Need for Strategic Change

competitive inertia a reluctance to change strategies or competitive practices that have been successful in the past.

"what's new" companies >

The external business environment is much more turbulent than it used to be. With customers' needs constantly growing and changing, and with competitors working harder, faster, and smarter to meet those needs, the first step in creating a strategy is determining the need for strategic change. In other words, the company should determine whether it needs to change its strategy to sustain a competitive advantage.[15]

Determining the need for strategic change might seem easy to do, but it's really not. There's a great deal of uncertainty in strategic business environments. Furthermore, top-level managers are often slow to recognize the need for strategic change, especially at successful companies that have created and sustained competitive advantages. Because they are acutely aware of the strategies that made their companies successful, they continue to rely on those strategies, even as the competition changes. In other words, success often leads to **competitive inertia**—a reluctance to change strategies or competitive practices that have been successful in the past.

Carrefour, the French retail giant that invented hypermarket stores (combination grocery and department stores under one roof) half a century ago, is a prime example of a company suffering from competitive inertia. Carrefour, which grew to be the second largest retail chain in the world behind Walmart, has lost market share in its hypermarket stores for five straight years.[16] Carrefour's "quality for all" approach, which focused on high-quality goods and food, relied on frequent price increases to keep profits strong. European customers, however, realized they could get cheaper prices and better service at

Exhibit 6.2   Three Steps of the Strategy-Making Process

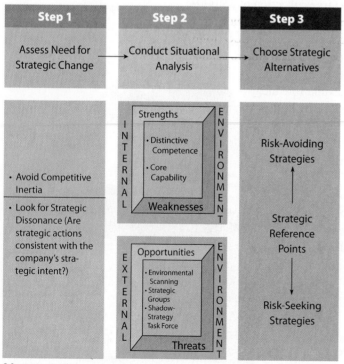

specialized stores, such as electronics stores. And, unlike Carrefour, specialized stores were also quicker to get in and out of and didn't require far drives to the edge of towns and cities (where most Carrefour stores are located). Why did Carrefour stick with this losing strategy for so long? According to new CEO Lars Olofsson, none of Carrefour's executives had ever worked outside of the company. Said Olofsson, "Carrefour never had a top manager coming from elsewhere."[17] Oloffson, who came to Carrefour as an outsider, has attacked Carrefour's competitive inertia by replacing the entire top management team with outsiders from other companies. He's also declared that Carrefour will follow a low price strategy that relies on selling its own house brands rather than those of other companies. Says Oloffson, "What's very important is price image. If I'm the No. 1 preferred retailer . . . I'm the most likely to be the most profitable."[18]

Besides being aware of the dangers of competitive inertia, what can managers do to improve the speed and accuracy with which they determine the need for strategic change? One method is to actively look for signs of strategic dissonance. **Strategic dissonance** is a discrepancy between a company's intended strategy and the strategic actions managers take when actually implementing that strategy.[19] For example, by emphasizing efficiency, lean inventory, and continuous improvement, and even allowing factory workers to stop the assembly line when they spotted problems, Toyota produced the highest quality cars in the world. But starting in 2008, widespread problems with stuck gas pedals, defective brakes, sludge-ruined engines, and SUVs prone to roll over led to the recall of 8 million Toyotas. How did this happen at a company famed for its quality?[20] Instead of maintaining its focus on quality, which was its long-term strategy, Toyota combined aggressive cost cutting with aggressive expansion, adding 17 new production plants worldwide while cutting annual spending by $2.2 billion. These strategic actions were at direct odds with the previous emphasis on quality. CEO Akio Toyoda, grandson of Toyota's founder, agreed, saying, "I fear the pace at which we have grown may be too quick. Priorities became confused, and we were not able to stop, think, and make improvements as much as were able to before."[21]

Note, however, that strategic dissonance is not the same thing as when a strategy does not produce the results that it's supposed to. For example, while eBay is the leading auction site on the Internet, its strategy the last few years has been to compete in online retailing (there were thousands of eBay stores selling new goods of all kinds), which put it in direct competition with Amazon.com. Because eBay's sales have been dropping while Amazon's sales have been increasing, eBay CEO John Donahoe indicated that eBay is abandoning online retailing and returning to selling used and overstock goods via online auctions.[22] So, in this instance, eBay was executing a strategy that didn't work. This would have been strategic dissonance only if eBay had not actually been implementing its strategy of being a full online retailer. Either way, however, the strategy is not working and strategic change is needed.

2.2 Situational Analysis

A situational analysis can also help managers determine the need for strategic change. A **situational analysis**, also called a **SWOT analysis** for *strengths*, *weaknesses*, *opportunities*, and *threats*, is an assessment of the strengths and weaknesses in an organization's internal environment and the opportunities and threats in its external environment.[23] Ideally, as shown in Step 2 of Exhibit 6.1, a SWOT analysis helps a company determine how to increase internal strengths and minimize internal weaknesses while maximizing external opportunities and minimizing external threats.

When Memorial Hospital of Fremont, Ohio, decided that the process it used to order all the necessary medical and administrative supplies was out of control, managers asked all the departments to work together to conduct a SWOT analysis. The

strategic dissonance a discrepancy between a company's intended strategy and the strategic actions managers take when implementing that strategy.

situational (SWOT) analysis an assessment of the strengths and weaknesses in an organization's internal environment and the opportunities and threats in its external environment.

process helped the hospital identify its strengths, such as the experience of the materials management group, and its weaknesses, which included allowing anyone in the organization to order anything he or she wanted from any vendor. Departments outlined opportunities to dramatically improve the quality and flow of supplies while controlling costs and determined that one of the biggest threats was expired medical supplies. Using the SWOT analysis as a map, the hospital began requiring all vendors to register when they entered the building, wear a visitor's badge while on hospital premises, and process all orders through the central purchasing department. Soon, the hospital staff developed the right mix of products and product inventories required for each area of the hospital and at the same time dramatically reduced the number of staff involved in purchasing and stocking supplies. Over two years, the hospital saved more than $1 million, and administrators won praise from hospital departments for their ability to improve services.[24]

As this example illustrates, a SWOT analysis can be used to evaluate entire companies or individual operations within an organization. All companies' competitive advantages can erode over time if internal strengths eventually become weaknesses. Consequently, an analysis of an organization's internal environment, that is, a company's strengths and weaknesses, often begins with an assessment of its distinctive competencies and core capabilities. A **distinctive competence** is something that a company can make, do, or perform better than its competitors. For example, *Consumer Reports* magazine consistently ranks Honda and Subaru cars as tops in quality and reliability.[25] Similarly, *PC Magazine* readers ranked Apple's desktop and laptop computers best in terms of service and reliability.[26]

Whereas distinctive competencies are tangible—for example, a product or service is faster, cheaper, or better—the core capabilities that produce distinctive competencies are not. **Core capabilities** are the less visible, internal decision-making routines, problem-solving processes, and organizational cultures that determine how efficiently inputs can be turned into outputs. Distinctive competencies cannot be sustained for long without superior core capabilities. Offering gourmet, environmentally conscious food products at a low cost is the distinctive competence of Trader Joe's. One can find ten kinds of hummus and every kind of dried fruit imaginable. Most of the products sold at Trader Joe's have no artificial colors, artificial flavors, or preservatives. The core capabilities the company uses to execute this strategy are to buy in large quantities and to find great, new products for its stores. In terms of buying in large quantities, Trader Joe's accomplishes this by selling fewer varieties of each product.

distinctive competence what a company can make, do, or perform better than its competitors.

core capabilities the internal decision-making routines, problem-solving processes, and organizational cultures that determine how efficiently inputs can be turned into outputs.

mgmt:trends

Fuel-Sipping Trucks

For more than 50 years, American car companies have found success by emphasizing power and brawn—big cars with big engines that could go fast and carry a huge load. But with rising fuel prices and growing awareness of global warming, Ford is betting on a new strategy. For the first time ever, Ford will offer a fuel-efficient V-6 engine in its entire lineup of F-150 trucks, which has been the best-selling vehicle in the United States for nearly 30 years. In fact, Ford will offer more V-6 engines with the truck than V-8 engines, which dominate the truck market. By offering a more fuel-efficient engine, Ford is hoping to protect its most profitable product line from further increases in gasoline prices.[27]

© iStockphoto.com/Kirsty Pargeter

For instance, while a typical grocery store will sell 40 different kinds of peanut butter, Trader Joe's sells just ten, which means that it's more likely to sell out of each kind quicker. That, in turn, means that suppliers sell higher volumes of their products to Trader Joe's for much lower prices. The key to making that work, however, is for Trader's Joe's customers to know its products are very good. A former employee put it this way, if customers are "going to get behind only one jar of Greek olives, then they're sure as heck going to make sure it's the most fabu-

© Francis Specker/Bloomberg via Getty Images

lous jar of Greek olives they can find for the price."[28] Unlike most grocery chains that rely on trade shows for their research, Trader Joe's core capability is sending its four best buyers, also known as product developers, all around the world in search of new, high-quality, great-tasting products. As a result, its travel expenses are much higher than its competitors, but with great results, as its stores feature 15 or more new products each week, bringing curious customers back to find out what's new. [29]

After examining internal strengths and weaknesses, the second part of a situational analysis is to look outside the company and assess the opportunities and threats in the external environment. In Chapter 3, you learned that *environmental scanning* involves searching the environment for important events or issues that might affect the organization, such as pricing trends or new products and technology. In a situational analysis, however, managers use environmental scanning to identify specific opportunities and threats that can either improve or harm the company's ability to sustain its competitive advantage. Identification of strategic groups and formation of shadow-strategy task forces are two ways to do this.

Strategic groups are not groups that actually work together. They are companies—usually competitors—that managers closely follow. More specifically, a **strategic group** is a group of other companies within an industry against which top managers compare, evaluate, and benchmark their company's strategic threats and opportunities.[30] (*Benchmarking* involves identifying outstanding practices, processes, and standards at other companies and adapting them to your own company.) Typically, managers include companies as part of their strategic group if they compete directly with those companies for customers or if those companies use strategies similar to theirs. The U.S. home improvement industry has annual sales in excess of $290 billion.[31] It's likely that the managers at Home Depot, the largest U.S. home improvement and hardware retailer, assess strategic threats and opportunities by comparing their company to a strategic group consisting of the other major home improvement supply companies. Exhibit 6.3 shows the number of stores, the size of the typical new store, and the overall geographic distribution (states, countries) of Home Depot stores compared with Lowe's, 84 Lumber, and Ace Hardware.

In fact, when scanning the environment for strategic threats and opportunities, managers tend to categorize the different companies in their industries as core,

strategic group a group of companies within an industry against which top managers compare, evaluate, and benchmark strategic threats and opportunities.

Exhibit 6.3   Strategic Groups for Home Depot

	No. of Stores	No. of States	Countries	Size of Modern Store (sq. ft)
Home Depot	2,248	50	4	130,000
Lowe's	1,725	50	2	117,000
Ace Hardware	4,600	50	70	10,000 to 14,000
84 Lumber	265	35	1	33,000

© Cengage Learning 2013

secondary, and transient firms.[32] **Core firms** are the central companies in a strategic group. Home Depot operates 2,248 stores covering all 50 states, Puerto Rico, the U.S. Virgin Islands, Mexico, Canada, and China. The company has 321,000 employees and annual revenue of over $68 billion. By comparison, Lowe's has more than 1,725 stores and 234,000 employees in 50 states and 12 provinces in Canada, stocks more than 40,000 products in each store, and has annual revenues of more than $48.8 billion.[33] Clearly, Lowe's is the closest competitor to Home Depot and is the core firm in Home Depot's strategic group. Even though Ace Hardware has more stores (4,600) than Home Depot and appears to be a bigger multinational player (70 different countries), Ace's franchise structure and small, individualized stores (10,000 to 14,000 square feet, with each store laid out differently with a different mix of products) keeps it from being a core firm in Home Depot's strategic group.[34] Likewise, Home Depot's management probably doesn't include Aubuchon Hardware in its core strategic group, because Aubuchon has only 125 stores in New England and upstate New York.[35]

When most managers scan their environments for strategic threats and opportunities, they concentrate on the strategic actions of core firms, not unrelated firms like Aubuchon. Where does a firm like Ace Hardware fit in? The company has made significant efforts to position itself as a more helpful version of Home Depot. Ace's Vision 21 strategic plan aims to make franchisees the leaders in Ace's unique convenience-store approach to selling hardware. Ace operates stores in over 70 countries and has moved aggressively over the past decade to improve its supply chain operation. But, as we noted above, Ace's franchise structure and small, individualized stores keep it from being a core firm in Home Depot's strategic group.[36]

Secondary firms are firms that use strategies related to but somewhat different from those of core firms. 84 Lumber has 265 stores in 35 states, but even though its stores are open to the public, the company focuses on supplying professional contractors, to whom it sells 95 percent of its products. Without the wide variety of products on the shelves or assistance available to the average consumer, people without expertise in building or remodeling probably don't find 84 Lumber stores very accessible. Home Depot would most likely classify 84 Lumber as a secondary firm in its strategic group analysis.[37] Managers need to be aware of the potential threats and opportunities posed by secondary firms, but they usually spend more time assessing the threats and opportunities associated with core firms.

Transient firms are companies whose strategies are changing from one strategic position to another. Ace Hardware is moving directly toward Home Depot's primary market. To compete more effectively with Home Depot and Lowe's, Ace recently increased the capacity of its warehouse operation, which now carries more than 65,000 products and makes them available to all Ace stores. In other words, Ace Hardware is trying to become one of Home Depot's core competitors. Likewise, True Value Hardware has expanded to 5,000 stores in 54 countries.[38] But rather than compete on the basis of assortment, True Value is attempting to compete with Home Depot and Lowe's on price and fast delivery. Because the strategies of transient firms are changing, managers may not know what to think about these firms and may overlook or misjudge the potential threats and opportunities posed by transient firms.

Because top managers tend to limit their attention to the core firms in their strategic group, some companies have started using shadow-strategy task forces to more aggressively scan their environments for strategic threats and opportunities.

core firms the central companies in a strategic group.

secondary firms the firms in a strategic group that follow strategies related to but somewhat different from those of the core firms.

transient firms the firms in a strategic group whose strategies are changing from one strategic position to another.

A **shadow-strategy task force** actively seeks out its own company's weaknesses and then, thinking like a competitor, determines how other companies could exploit them for competitive advantage.[39] To make sure that the task force challenges conventional thinking, its members should be independent-minded, come from a variety of company functions and levels, and have the access and authority to question the company's current strategic actions and intent. For example, when Starbucks CEO Howard Schultz became concerned that the company had drifted from its small company roots into a soul-less mega-corporation (and with 17,000 stores in 50,000 countries and $11 billion in annual revenues, how could it not?), he formed a shadow-strategy task force with a key group of employees. Schultz asked them, "If you were going to open a store to compete with Starbucks, how would you do it?" He gave them a budget and told them to come back when they were finished. Their answer was 15th Ave. Coffee & Tea in Seattle, Washington. Modeled after local coffee houses, 15th Avenue Coffee & Tea will sell wine and beer, host music and poetry readings, and use manual rather than automated espresso machines. Likewise, all of the baked goods and food will be local. Schultz hopes to have Starbucks regain some of its lost authenticity by learning from 15th Avenue Coffee & Tea.[40] Starbucks customer Dana Godfrey agrees, saying, "I really liked the ambience; it's not as loud as most of your Starbucks. It just feels more European."[41]

In short, a situational analysis has two basic parts. The first is to examine internal strengths and weaknesses by focusing on distinctive competencies and core capabilities. The second is to examine external opportunities and threats by focusing on environmental scanning, strategic groups, and shadow-strategy task forces.

2.3 Choosing Strategic Alternatives

After determining the need for strategic change and conducting a situational analysis, the last step in the strategy-making process is to choose strategic alternatives that will help the company create or maintain a sustainable competitive advantage. According to strategic reference point theory, managers choose between two basic alternative strategies. They can choose a conservative, *risk-avoiding strategy* that aims to protect an existing competitive advantage. Or they can choose an aggressive, *risk-seeking strategy* that aims to extend or create a sustainable competitive advantage. Menards is a hardware store chain with 40,000 employees and 210 locations throughout the Midwest.[42] When hardware giant Home Depot entered the Midwest, Menards faced a basic choice: Avoid risk by continuing with the strategy it had in place before Home Depot's arrival, or seek risk by trying to further its competitive advantage against Home Depot, which is six times its size. Some of its competitors decided to fold. Kmart closed all of its Builders Square hardware stores when Home Depot came to Minneapolis. Handy Andy liquidated its 74 stores when Home Depot came to the Midwest. But Menards decided to fight, spending millions to open 35 new stores at the same time that Home Depot was opening 44 of its own.[43]

The choice to seek risk or avoid risk typically depends on whether top management views the company as falling above or below strategic reference points. **Strategic reference points** are the targets that managers use to measure whether their firm has developed the core competencies that it needs to achieve a sustainable competitive advantage. If a hotel chain decides to compete by providing superior quality and service, then top management will track the success of this strategy through customer surveys or published hotel ratings such as those provided by the prestigious Mobil Travel Guide. If a hotel chain decides to compete on price, it will regularly conduct market surveys to check the prices of other hotels. The competitors' prices are the hotel managers' strategic reference points against which to compare their own pricing strategy.

shadow-strategy task force a committee within a company that analyzes the company's own weaknesses to determine how competitors could exploit them for competitive advantage.

strategic reference points the strategic targets managers use to measure whether a firm has developed the core competencies it needs to achieve a sustainable competitive advantage.

Exhibit 6.4
Strategic Reference Points

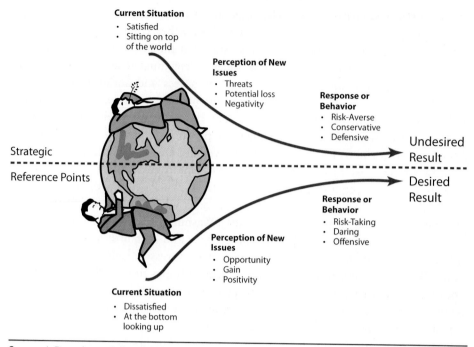

Source: A. Fiegenbaum, S. Hart, & D. Schendel, "Strategic Reference Point Theory," *Strategic Management Journal* 17 (1996): 219–235.

If competitors can consistently underprice them, then the managers need to determine whether their staff and resources have the core competencies to compete on price.

As shown in Exhibit 6.4, when a company is performing above or better than its strategic reference points, top management will typically be satisfied with the company's strategy. Ironically, this satisfaction tends to make top management conservative and risk averse. Because the company already has a sustainable competitive advantage, the worst thing that could happen would be to lose it, so new issues or changes in the company's external environments are viewed as threats. By contrast, when a company is performing below or worse than its strategic reference points, top management will typically be dissatisfied with the company's strategy. In this instance, managers are much more likely to choose a daring, risk-taking strategy. If the current strategy is producing substandard results, the company has nothing to lose by switching to risky new strategies in the hopes that it can create a sustainable competitive advantage. Managers of companies in this situation view new issues or changes in external environments as opportunities for potential gain.

Strategic reference point theory is not deterministic, however. Managers are not predestined to choose risk-averse or risk-seeking strategies for their companies. Indeed, one of the most important elements of the theory is that managers *can* influence the strategies chosen by their company by *actively changing and adjusting* the strategic reference points they use to judge strategic performance. If a company has become complacent after consistently surpassing its strategic reference points, then top management can change from a risk-averse to a risk-taking orientation by raising the standards of performance (i.e., the strategic reference points). This is just what happened at Menards.

Instead of being satisfied with merely protecting its existing stores (a risk-averse strategy), founder John Menard changed the strategic reference points the company had been using to assess strategic performance. To encourage a daring, offensive-minded strategy that would allow the company to open nearly as many new stores as Home Depot, he determined that Menards would have to beat Home Depot on not one or two, but four, strategic reference points: price, products, sales per square foot, and "friendly accessibility." The strategy appears to be succeeding. In terms

what really works

Strategy Making for Firms, Big and Small

Companies create strategies that produce sustainable competitive advantage by using the strategy-making process (assessing the need for strategic change, conducting a situational analysis, and choosing strategic alternatives). For years, it had been thought that strategy making was something that only large firms could do well. It was believed that small firms did not have the time, knowledge, or staff to do a good job of strategy making. However, two meta-analyses indicate that strategy making can improve the profits, sales growth, and return on investment of both big *and* small firms.

Strategy Making for Big Firms

There is a 72 percent chance that big companies that engage in the strategy-making process will be more profitable than big companies that don't. Not only does strategy making improve profits. but it also helps companies grow. Specifically, there is a 75 percent chance that big companies that engage in the strategy-making process will have greater sales and earnings growth than big companies that don't. Thus, in practical terms, the strategy-making process can make a significant difference in a big company's profits and growth.

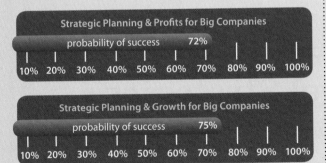

Strategy Making for Small Firms

Strategy making can also improve the performance of small firms. There is a 61 percent chance that small

firms that engage in the strategy-making process will have more sales growth than small firms that don't. Likewise, there is a 62 percent chance that small firms that engage in the strategy-making process will have a larger return on investment than small companies that don't. Thus, in practical terms, the strategy-making process can make a significant difference in a small company's profits and growth too.

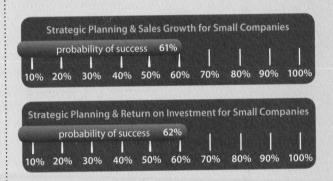

External Growth Through Acquisitions

One way to grow a company is through external growth, or buying other companies (see Section 3.1 on portfolio strategy). However, researchers have long debated whether buying other companies actually adds value to the acquiring company. A meta-analysis based on 103 studies and a sample of 25,205 companies indicates that, on average, acquiring other companies actually *hurts* the value of the acquiring firm. In other words, there is only a 45 percent chance that growing a company through external acquisitions will work![44]

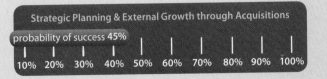

of price, market research indicates that a 100-item shopping cart of goods is consistently cheaper at Menards. In terms of products, Menards sells 50,000 products per store, the same as Home Depot. In terms of sales per square foot, Menards ($407 per square foot) outsells Home Depot ($300 per square foot).[45] Finally, unlike Home Depot's warehouse-like stores, Menards' stores are built to resemble grocery stores. Shiny tiled floors, wide aisles, and easy-to-reach products all make Menards a "friendlier" place for shoppers. And now with Lowe's, the second-largest hardware store chain in the nation, also entering its markets, Menards has added a fifth strategic reference point: store size. At 225,000 square feet, most new Menards stores are more than double the size of Home Depot's stores and 100,000 square feet larger than Lowe's biggest stores.[46] John Caulfield, who wrote a book about Home Depot and the hardware business, says, "Menards is clearly throwing the gauntlet down at Lowe's. They're saying, 'If you come into Chicago, here is what you're going to face.'"[47]

So even when (perhaps *especially* when) companies have achieved a sustainable competitive advantage, top managers must adjust or change strategic reference points to challenge themselves and their employees to develop new core competencies for the future. In the long run, effective organizations will frequently revise their strategic reference points to better focus managers' attention on the new challenges and opportunities that occur in their ever-changing business environments.

Review 2

Strategy-Making Process   The first step in the strategy-making process is determining whether a strategy needs to be changed to sustain a competitive advantage. Because uncertainty and competitive inertia make this difficult to determine, managers can improve the speed and accuracy of this step by looking for differences between top management's intended strategy and the strategy actually implemented by lower-level managers (i.e., looking for strategic dissonance). The second step is to conduct a situational analysis that examines internal strengths and weaknesses (distinctive competencies and core capabilities), as well as external threats and opportunities (environmental scanning, strategic groups, and shadow-strategy task forces). In the third step of the strategy-making process, strategic reference point theory suggests that when companies are performing better than their strategic reference points, top management will typically choose a risk-averse strategy. When performance is below strategic reference points, it is more likely to choose risk-seeking strategies. Importantly, however, managers can influence the choice of strategic alternatives by actively changing and adjusting the strategic reference points they use to judge strategic performance.

Corporate-, Industry-, and Firm-Level Strategies

To formulate effective strategies, companies must be able to answer these three basic questions:

> » What business are we in?
> » How should we compete in this industry?
> » Who are our competitors, and how should we respond to them?

These simple but powerful questions are at the heart of corporate-, industry-, and firm-level strategies.

3 Corporate-Level Strategies

Corporate-level strategy is the overall organizational strategy that addresses the question "What business or businesses are we in or should we be in?"

Consumers Union (CU), which publishes *Consumer Reports* magazine and ConsumerReports.org, provides unbiased reviews for products ranging from treadmills to TVs, to breakfast cereals, to cars. To maintain its independent, unbiased status, it doesn't take free samples, doesn't take advertising in its magazine or on its website, and doesn't permit its ratings and rankings to be used in product advertising. This means, for example, that unlike most auto magazines and websites, which rely on auto companies to loan them cars during testing, CU buys *every* car it tests. CU's mission, or the reason it is in business, is to "work for a fair, just, and safe marketplace for all consumers and to empower consumers to protect themselves." As CEO Jim Guest describes it, "From our perspective, we test [products], and we report good, bad, or indifferent. We are all about products." So when its auto tests determined that the Lexus GX460 SUV was prone to rollovers in quick turns, *Consumer Reports* didn't hesitate to hit the GX460 with a "Don't Buy" recommendation. It did the same thing when Apple's iPhone4 signal reception dropped dramatically just by holding the phone. *Consumer Reports'* results are so influential that both companies reacted immediately to fix those problems so that the "Don't Buy" recommendations could be removed after further testing.[48]

Exhibit 6.5 shows the two major approaches to corporate-level strategy that companies use to decide which businesses they should be in: **3.1 portfolio strategy** and **3.2 grand strategies**.

After reading the next three sections, you should be able to

3. Explain the different kinds of corporate-level strategies.
4. Describe the different kinds of industry-level strategies.
5. Explain the components and kinds of firm-level strategies.

< **"what's new" companies**

corporate-level strategy the overall organizational strategy that addresses the question "What business or businesses are we in or should we be in?"

diversification a strategy for reducing risk by buying a variety of items (stocks or, in the case of a corporation, types of businesses) so that the failure of one stock or one business does not doom the entire portfolio.

3.1 Portfolio Strategy

One of the standard strategies for stock market investors is **diversification**, or owning stocks in a variety of companies in different industries. The purpose of this strategy is to reduce risk in the overall stock portfolio (the entire collection of stocks). The basic idea is simple: If you invest in ten companies in ten different industries, you won't lose your entire investment if one company performs poorly. Furthermore, because they're in different industries, one company's losses are likely to be offset by another company's gains. Portfolio strategy is based on these same ideas. We'll start by taking a look at the theory and ideas behind portfolio strategy and then proceed with a critical review that suggests that some of the key ideas behind portfolio strategy are *not* supported.

Exhibit 6.5   Corporate-Level Strategies

Portfolio Strategy	Grand Strategies
• Acquisitions, unrelated diversification, related diversification, single businesses	• Growth
• Boston Consulting Group matrix	• Stability
• Stars	• Retrenchment/recovery
• Question marks	
• Cash cows	
• Dogs	

© Cengage Learning 2013

Portfolio strategy is a corporate-level strategy that minimizes risk by diversifying investment among various businesses or product lines.[49] Just as a diversification strategy guides an investor who invests in a variety of stocks, portfolio strategy guides the strategic decisions of corporations that compete in a variety of businesses. For example, portfolio strategy could be used to guide the strategy of a company like 3M, which makes 55,000 products for six different business sectors: consumers and offices (Post-its, Scotch tape); display and graphics (for computers, cell phones, PDAs, TVs); electronics and communications (flexible circuits used in printers and electronic displays); health care (medical, surgical, dental, and personal-care products); industrial and transportation (tapes, adhesives, supply chain software, products and components for the manufacture, repair, and maintenance of autos, aircraft, boats, and other vehicles); safety, security, and protection services (glass safety, fire protection, respiratory products); and transportation.[50] Similarly, portfolio strategy could be used by Johnson & Johnson, which has 250 divisions making health-care products for the pharmaceutical, medical device and diagnostic, consumer, and health-care-professionals markets.[51]

Just as investors consider the mix of stocks in their stock portfolio when deciding which stocks to buy or sell, managers following portfolio strategy try to acquire companies that fit well with the rest of their corporate portfolio and to sell those that don't. After Verizon revised its strategy to focus on its cell phone and FiOS (superfast optical Internet, TV, and phone services for homes and businesses) divisions, it sold local phone businesses that provide phone service in rural areas and small towns across 14 states to Frontier Communications for $8.6 billion and then reinvested the proceeds in its core businesses. John Killian, Verizon's chief financial officer, said, "These are good properties, but they're much more rural in nature, and they really don't fit with the strategy we have for FiOS and broadband."[52] Portfolio strategy provides the following guidelines to help companies make these difficult decisions.

First, according to portfolio strategy, the more businesses in which a corporation competes, the smaller its overall chances of failing. Think of a corporation as a stool and its businesses as the legs of the stool. The more legs or businesses added to the stool, the less likely it is to tip over. Using this analogy, portfolio strategy reduces 3M's risk of failing because the corporation's survival depends on essentially six different business sectors. Managers employing portfolio strategy can either develop new businesses internally or look for **acquisitions**, that is, other companies to buy. Either way, the goal is to add legs to the stool.

Second, beyond adding new businesses to the corporate portfolio, portfolio strategy predicts that companies can reduce risk even more through **unrelated diversification**—creating or acquiring companies in completely unrelated businesses (more on the accuracy of this prediction later). According to portfolio strategy, when businesses are unrelated, losses in one business or industry should have minimal effect on the performance of other companies in the corporate portfolio. One of the best examples of unrelated diversification is Samsung of Korea. Samsung has businesses in electronics (computer memory chips, computer and telecommunication equipment, color TV displays, glass bulbs, corporate IT service providers, high-speed optical network service providers); machinery and heavy industries (shipbuilding, construction, airplane engine manufacturing, fiber optics, semiconductors); chemicals (engineering plastics and specialty chemicals); financial services (life and accident insurance, credit cards, installment financing, and financial securities and trusts); and other areas ranging from engineering consulting to hotels and home security products and services.[53] Because most internally grown businesses tend to be related to existing products or services, portfolio strategy suggests that acquiring new businesses is the preferred method of unrelated diversification.[54]

portfolio strategy a corporate-level strategy that minimizes risk by diversifying investment among various businesses or product lines.

acquisition the purchase of a company by another company.

unrelated diversification creating or acquiring companies in completely unrelated businesses.

Third, investing the profits and cash flows from mature, slow-growth businesses into newer, faster-growing businesses can reduce long-term risk. The best-known portfolio strategy for guiding investment in a corporation's businesses is the Boston Consulting Group (BCG) matrix.[55] The **BCG matrix** is a portfolio strategy that managers use to categorize their corporation's businesses by growth rate and relative market share, helping them decide how to invest corporate funds. The matrix, shown in Exhibit 6.6, separates businesses into four categories based on how fast the market is growing (high growth or low growth) and the size of the business's share of that market (small or large). **Stars** are companies that have a large share of a fast-growing market. To take advantage of a star's fast-growing market and its strength in that market (large share), the corporation must invest substantially in it. The investment is usually worthwhile, however, because many stars produce sizable future profits. **Question marks** are companies that have a small share of a fast-growing market. If the corporation invests in these companies, they may eventually become stars, but their relative weakness in the market (small share) makes investing in question marks more risky than investing in stars. **Cash cows** are companies that have a large share of a slow-growing market. Companies in this situation are often highly profitable, hence the name "cash cow." Finally, **dogs** are companies that have a small share of a slow-growing market. As the name suggests, having a small share of a slow-growth market is often not profitable.

Because the idea is to redirect investment from slow-growing to fast-growing companies, the BCG matrix starts by recommending that while the substantial cash flows from cash cows last, they should be reinvested in stars (see 1 in Exhibit 6.6) to help them grow even faster and obtain even more market share. Using this strategy, current profits help produce future profits. Over time, as their market growth slows, some stars may turn into cash cows (see 2). Cash flows should also be directed to some question marks (see 3). Though riskier than stars, question marks have great potential because of their fast-growing market. Managers must decide which question marks are most likely to turn into stars (and therefore warrant further investment) and which ones are too risky and should be sold. Over time, managers hope some question marks will become stars as their small markets become large ones (see 4). Finally, because dogs lose money, the corporation should "find them new owners" or "take them to the pound." In other words, dogs should either be sold to other companies or closed down and liquidated for their assets (see 5).

Although the BCG matrix and other forms of portfolio strategy are relatively popular among managers, portfolio strategy has some drawbacks. The most significant? Contrary to the predictions of portfolio strategy, the evidence suggests that acquiring unrelated businesses is *not* useful. As shown in Exhibit 6.7 there is a U-shaped relationship between diversification and risk. The left side of the curve shows that single businesses with no diversification are extremely risky (if the single business fails, the entire business fails). So, in part, the portfolio strategy of diversifying is correct—competing in a variety of different businesses can lower risk. However, portfolio strategy is partly wrong, too—the right side of the curve shows that conglomerates

Exhibit 6.6 Boston Consulting Group Matrix

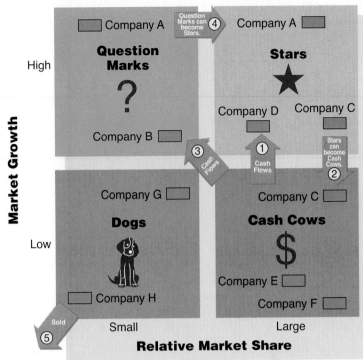

© Cengage Learning 2013

BCG matrix a portfolio strategy, developed by the Boston Consulting Group, that categorizes a corporation's businesses by growth rate and relative market share, and helps managers decide how to invest corporate funds.

star a company with a large share of a fast-growing market.

question mark a company with a small share of a fast-growing market.

cash cow a company with a large share of a slow-growing market.

dog a company with a small share of a slow-growing market.

Exhibit 6.7 U-Shaped Relationship
Between Diversification and Risk

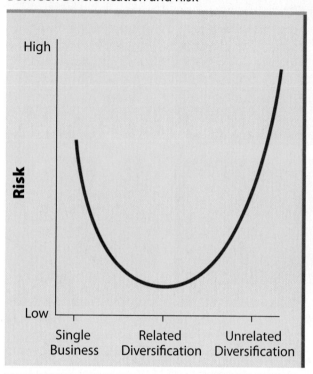

composed of completely unrelated businesses are even riskier than single, undiversified businesses.[56]

A second set of problems with portfolio strategy has to do with the dysfunctional consequences that can occur when companies are categorized as stars, cash cows, question marks, or dogs. Contrary to expectations, the BCG matrix often yields incorrect judgments about a company's potential. In other words, managers using the BCG matrix aren't very good at accurately determining which companies should be categorized as stars, cash cows, questions marks, or dogs. The most common mistake is simply miscategorizing highly profitable companies as dogs.[57] In part, this is because the BCG relies on past performance (previous market share and previous market growth), which is a notoriously poor predictor of future company performance. More worrisome, however, is research that indicates that the BCG matrix actually makes managers worse at judging the future profitability of a business. A study conducted in six countries over five years gave managers and business students clear information about the current and future profits (i.e., slow or fast growth) of three companies and asked them to select the one that would be most successful in the future. Although not labeled this way, one company was clearly a star, another was a dog, and the last was a cash cow. Just exposing people to the ideas in the BCG matrix led them to incorrectly categorize less profitable businesses as the most successful businesses 64 percent of the time, while actually *using* the BCG matrix led to making the same mistake 87 percent of the time.[58]

Furthermore, using the BCG matrix can also weaken the strongest performer in the corporate portfolio, the cash cow. As funds are redirected from cash cows to stars, corporate managers essentially take away the resources needed to take advantage of the cash cow's new business opportunities. As a result, the cash cow becomes less aggressive in seeking new business or in defending its present business. For example, Procter & Gamble's Tide, the laundry detergent that P&G brought to market in 1946, is clearly a cash cow, accounting for $3.5 billion in worldwide revenues. In addition to Tide, P&G has 23 other brands, such as Bounty paper towels, Crest toothpaste, Gillette razors, and Pampers diapers, each of which exceed $1 billion in annual sales. Out of 250 brands company-wide, those 23 $1 billion+ brands account for nearly 70 percent of P&G's sales and 75 percent of its profits.[59] A few years ago, however, in a bid to bring new products to market, the company was diverting up to half a billion dollars a year from cash cows like Tide to promote potential product blockbusters (i.e., stars) such as Febreze, a spray that eliminates odors; Dryel, which dry-cleans clothes at home; Fit, a spray that kills bacteria on fruits and vegetables; and Impress, a high-tech plastic wrap.[60] P&G ultimately reversed the diversion of funds when the potential blockbusters did not find much success, and the company refocused on its biggest brands (its cash cows).[61] Indeed, of the stars listed above, Febreze, Dryel, Fit, and Impress, only Febreze has become a $1 billion brand, and much of that has been achieved by cross-branding Febreze with existing P&G products, like Tide and Gain detergents, and Bounce and Downy fabric softeners.[62] Finally, labeling a top performer as a cash cow can harm employee morale. Cash-cow employees realize that they have inferior status and that instead of working for themselves, they are now working to fund the growth of stars and question marks.

Exhibit 6.8 Portfolio Strategy: Problems and Recommendations

Problems with Portfolio Strategy	Recommendations for Making Portfolio Strategy Work
Unrelated diversification does not reduce risk.	Don't be so quick to sell dogs or question marks. Instead, management should commit to the markets in which it competes by strengthening core capabilities.
Present performance is used to predict future performance.	Put your "eggs in similar (not different) baskets" by acquiring companies in related businesses.
Assessments of a business's growth potential are often inaccurate.	Acquire companies with complementary core capabilities.
Cash cows fail to aggressively pursue opportunities and defend themselves from threats.	Encourage collaboration and cooperation between related firms and businesses within the company.
Being labeled a "cash cow" can hurt employee morale.	"Date before you marry." Work with a business before deciding to acquire it.
Companies often overpay to acquire stars.	When in doubt, don't acquire new businesses. Mergers and acquisitions are inherently risky and difficult to make work. Only acquire firms that can help create or extend a sustainable competitive advantage.
Acquiring firms often treat acquired stars as "conquered foes." Key stars' managers, who once controlled their own destiny, often leave because they are now treated as relatively unimportant middle managers.	

Source: M. Lubatkin, "Value-Creating Mergers: Fact or Folklore?" *Academy of Management Executive* 2 (1998): 295–302; M. Lubatkin & S. Chatterjee, "Extending Modern Portfolio Theory into the Domain of Corporate Diversification: Does It Apply?" *Academy of Management Journal* 37 (1994): 109–136; and M. H. Lubatkin & P. J. Lane, "Psst . . . The Merger Mavens Still Have It Wrong!" *Academy of Management Executive* 10 (1996): 21–39.

So, what kind of portfolio strategy does the best job of helping managers decide which companies to buy or sell? The U-shaped curve in Exhibit 6.7 indicates that, contrary to the predictions of portfolio strategy, the best approach is probably **related diversification**, in which the different business units share similar products, manufacturing, marketing, technology, or cultures. The key to related diversification is to acquire or create new companies with core capabilities that complement the core capabilities of businesses already in the corporate portfolio. Hormel Foods is an example of related diversification in the food business. The company both manufactures and markets a variety of foods, from deli meats to salsa, to the infamous SPAM.

We began this section with the example of 3M and its 55,000 products sold in over seven different business sectors. Although seemingly different, most of 3M's product divisions are based in some fashion on its distinctive competencies in adhesives and tape (e.g., wet or dry sandpaper, Post-it notes, Scotchgard fabric protector, transdermal skin patches, and reflective material used in traffic signs). Furthermore, all of 3M's divisions share its strong corporate culture that promotes and encourages risk taking and innovation. In sum, in contrast to a single, undiversified business or unrelated diversification, related diversification reduces risk because the different businesses can work as a team, relying on each other for needed experience, expertise, and support. Exhibit 6.8 details the problems associated with portfolio strategy and recommends ways that managers can increase their chances of success through related diversification.

3.2 Grand Strategies

A **grand strategy** is a broad strategic plan used to help an organization achieve its strategic goals.[63] Grand strategies guide the strategic alternatives that managers of

related diversification creating or acquiring companies that share similar products, manufacturing, marketing, technology, or cultures.

grand strategy a broad corporate-level strategic plan used to achieve strategic goals and guide the strategic alternatives that managers of individual businesses or subunits may use.

© AP Images/PRNewsFoto/PepsiCo

"what's new"
companies >

"what's new"
companies >

individual businesses or subunits may use in deciding what businesses they should be in. There are three kinds of grand strategies: growth, stability, and retrenchment/recovery.

The purpose of a **growth strategy** is to increase profits, revenues, market share, or the number of places (stores, offices, locations) in which the company does business. Companies can grow in several ways. They can grow externally by merging with or acquiring other companies in the same or different businesses. Some of the largest mergers and acquisitions of recent years include Roche acquiring Genentech (pharmaceuticals), Pfizer acquiring Wyeth (pharmaceuticals), Mars acquiring Wrigley (gum and candy), and InBev acquiring Anheuser-Busch (beer and alcoholic beverages).

Another way to grow is internally, directly expanding the company's existing business or creating and growing new businesses. After Coca-Cola spent $4.1 billion to acquire Glaceau Vitaminwater, a group of vitamin-enhanced, flavored, noncarbonated drinks, PepsiCo realized that its **SoBe** line of beverages, which offer similar products, would face much stiffer competition. To spur growth and get into more stores, PepsiCo cut prices to $1.18 a bottle. It started a new marketing campaign, which included a new bottle design and celebrity endorsements, to reconnect with target customers (15- to 30-year-olds). And it offered a no-calorie version of its drinks to cater to growing consumer concerns about obesity. As a result, SoBe's market share doubled to 3.8 percent, and sales of its leading product, Lifewater, a variety of fruit-flavored, vitamin-enhanced, zero-calorie drinks, are up 85 percent.[64]

The purpose of a **stability strategy** is to continue doing what the company has been doing, just doing it better. Companies following a stability strategy try to improve the way in which they sell the same products or services to the same customers. Since its inception in 1938, **REI** has never strayed from its focus on the outdoors. Its Mountain Safety Research division designs and makes mountaineering equipment, clothing, and camping products. REI Adventures offers adventure travel packages (e.g., kayaking, climbing, and backpacking) with hand-picked local guides on all seven continents. Finally, in addition to its website, REI has 80 stores in 27 states, selling high-quality outdoor gear, clothing, and footwear.[65] And today, with 3.5 million members whose membership entitles them to discounts and expert advice, REI is one of the largest retail co-ops in the world. Companies often choose a stability strategy when their external environment doesn't change much or after they have struggled with periods of explosive growth.

The purpose of a **retrenchment strategy** is to turn around very poor company performance by shrinking the size or scope of the business or, if a company is in multiple businesses, by closing or shutting down different lines of the business. The first step of a typical retrenchment strategy might include making significant cost reductions; laying off employees; closing poorly performing stores, offices, or manufacturing plants; or closing or selling entire lines of products or services.[66] After Sears saw its earnings drop from $800 million to a loss of $50 million over the course of 18 months, it reduced administrative expenses by $168 million by cutting jobs at headquarters and distribution centers and by consolidating its Kenmore, Craftsman, and Diehard brands into one division. It also reduced inventory, particularly in appliances, by substantially cutting prices, decreasing the value of on-hand inventory

growth strategy a strategy that focuses on increasing profits, revenues, market share, or the number of places in which the company does business.

stability strategy a strategy that focuses on improving the way in which the company sells the same products or services to the same customers.

retrenchment strategy a strategy that focuses on turning around very poor company performance by shrinking the size or scope of the business.

doing the right thing

Accentuate the Positive

During an economic downturn, it is hard for managers and employees to stay positive. If it's not the threat of lay-offs, it's the near-constant barrage of news about how entire industries are struggling to stay afloat. Research shows, however, that optimism in the workplace helps companies grow even during difficult times. By measuring workplace engagement with questions like "Does your boss support you?" and "Do you have a best friend at work?" researchers found that increased employee engagement led to increased company performance. Best Buy, the electronics retailer, found in one of its stores that for every 2 percent increase in employee engagement, there was a $100,000 increase in annual sales. So, in down times, do the right thing—resist the urge to spread bad news and don't let a pessimistic culture develop. Instead, accentuate the positive, be optimistic, and make sure that your employees feel supported, rewarded, and engaged at work. Not only will they be happier, but their performance will likely be better too.[67]

from $10.3 billion to $9.5 billion. So, despite sales dropping by 7 percent, Sears' retrenchment strategy returned it to profitability a year later.[68]

After cutting costs and reducing a business's size or scope, the second step in a retrenchment strategy is recovery. **Recovery** consists of the strategic actions that a company takes to return to a growth strategy. This two-step process of cutting and recovery is analogous to pruning roses. Prior to each growing season, roses should be cut back to two-thirds their normal size. Pruning doesn't damage the roses; it makes them stronger and more likely to produce beautiful, fragrant flowers. The retrenchment-and-recovery process is similar. Cost reductions, layoffs, and plant closings are sometimes necessary to restore companies to good health. In the early days of online shopping, **Priceline.com** started out with a bang, offering a "name your own price" service on everything from airplane tickets to groceries. The business quickly collapsed, however, as consumers realized they didn't want to save $50 flying from New York to Los Angeles with a five-hour layover in Dallas. The company's stock plummeted from $974 to just $7, and it was on the verge of collapse. CEO Jeffrey Boyd has led a dramatic recovery by shifting strategy. Instead of airplane tickets and groceries, Priceline's focus is now on hotels. By partnering with major hotel chains, and acquiring discount travel websites in Europe and Asia, Priceline partners with 100,000 hotels in 90 countries that appeal to a wide range of consumers. Furthermore, international bookings account for 61 percent of its revenues, nearly twice that of Expedia (34%) and 4.4 times Orbitz (14%). Thanks to the new emphasis on hotels, the company was recently ranked number 1 on *Bloomberg Businessweek*'s list of 50 best performing stocks on the S&P 500 index; its market valuation is estimated at $8.8 billion; and annual growth is estimated to approach 20 percent.[69]

Like pruning, those cuts are intended to allow companies to eventually return to a successful growth strategy (i.e., recovery). When company performance drops significantly, a strategy of retrenchment and recovery may help the company return to a successful growth strategy.

< **"what's new" companies**

recovery the strategic actions taken after retrenchment to return to a growth strategy.

Review 3

Corporate-Level Strategies Corporate-level strategies, such as portfolio strategy and grand strategies, help managers determine what businesses they should be in. Portfolio strategy focuses on lowering business risk by being in multiple, unrelated businesses and by investing the cash flows from slow-growth businesses into faster-growing businesses. One portfolio strategy, the BCG matrix, suggests that cash flows from cash cows should be reinvested in stars and in carefully chosen question marks. Dogs should be sold or liquidated. Portfolio strategy has several problems, however. Acquiring unrelated businesses actually increases risk rather than lowering it. The BCG matrix is often wrong when predicting companies' futures (as dogs or cash cows, for example). And redirecting cash flows can seriously weaken cash cows. The most successful way to use the portfolio approach to corporate strategy is to reduce risk through related diversification.

The three kinds of grand strategies are growth, stability, and retrenchment/recovery. Companies can grow externally by merging with or acquiring other companies, or they can grow internally through direct expansion or creating new businesses. Companies choose a stability strategy—selling the same products or services to the same customers—when their external environment changes very little or after they have dealt with periods of explosive growth. Retrenchment strategy, shrinking the size or scope of a business, is used to turn around poor performance. If retrenchment works, it is often followed by a recovery strategy that focuses on growing the business again.

4 Industry-Level Strategies

Industry-level strategy addresses the question "How should we compete in this industry?"

Let's find out more about industry-level strategies, shown in Exhibit 6.9, by discussing **4.1 the five industry forces that determine overall levels of competition in an industry**, as well as **4.2 the positioning strategies** and **4.3 adaptive strategies that companies can use to achieve sustained competitive advantage and above-average profits**.

4.1 Five Industry Forces

According to Harvard professor Michael Porter, five industry forces determine an industry's overall attractiveness and potential for long-term profitability. These include the character of the rivalry, the threat of new entrants, the threat of substitute products or services, the bargaining power of suppliers, and the bargaining

Exhibit 6.9 Industry-Level Strategies

Five Industry Forces	Positioning Strategies	Adaptive Strategies
Character of the rivalry	Cost leadership	Defenders
Threat of new entrants	Differentiation	Prospectors
Threat of substitute products or services	Focus	Analyzers
Bargaining power of suppliers		Reactors
Bargaining power of buyers		

© Cengage Learning 2013

industry-level strategy a corporate strategy that addresses the question "How should we compete in this industry?"

power of buyers. The stronger these forces, the less attractive the industry becomes to corporate investors, because it is more difficult for companies to be profitable. Porter's industry forces are illustrated in Exhibit 6.10. Let's examine how these forces are bringing changes to several kinds of industries.

Character of the rivalry is a measure of the intensity of competitive behavior among companies in an industry. Is the competition among firms aggressive and cutthroat, or do competitors focus more on serving customers than on attacking each other? Both industry attractiveness and profitability decrease when rivalry is cutthroat. For example, selling cars is a highly competitive business. Pick up a local newspaper on Friday, Saturday, or Sunday morning, and you'll find dozens of pages of car advertising ("Anniversary Sale-A-Bration," "Ford March Savings!" and "$99 Down, You Choose!"). In fact, competition in new car sales is so intense that if it weren't for used-car sales, repair work, and replacement parts, many auto dealers would actually lose money.

The **threat of new entrants** is a measure of the degree to which barriers to entry make it easy or difficult for new companies to get started in an industry. If new companies can enter the industry easily, then competition will increase, and prices and profits will fall. For example, **Unilever PLC** is bringing its Magnum premium ice-cream bars to the United States. Introduced in the United Kingdom in 1987, the Magnum is the top-selling ice-cream bar in the world, accounting for 6.8 percent of the global market. Although Michael Polk, president of Unilever's global food division, believes that the Magnum will double the market for "super-premium ice-cream novelties" in the United States, which accounts for 4 percent of the $9.3 billion U.S. ice-cream market, the introduction of the Magnum is bad news for Dove and Häagen Dazs' ice cream bars, which have dominated this market in the United States.[70] On the other hand, if there are sufficient barriers to entry, such as large capital requirements to buy expensive equipment or plant facilities, or the need for specialized knowledge, then competition will be weaker, and prices and profits will generally be higher. For instance, high costs make it very difficult to enter the natural gas business. Anadarko Petroleum has discovered three immense natural gas sites off the coast of Mozambique, which are estimated to yield 6 to 8 trillion cubic feet of gas. At a minimum, it will take $2 billion and six years, two for planning and four for construction, before any gas can be extracted and shipped to customers.[71]

The **threat of substitute products or services** is a measure of the ease with which customers can find substitutes for an industry's products or services. If customers can easily find substitute products or services, the competition will be greater and profits will be lower. If there are few or no substitutes, competition will be weaker and profits will be higher. Generic medicines are some of the best-known examples of substitute products. Under U.S. patent law, a company that develops a drug has exclusive rights to produce and market that drug for 20 years. Prices and profits are generally high during this period if the drug sells well. After 20 years, however, the patent will expire, and any pharmaceutical company can manufacture and sell the same drug. When this happens, drug prices drop substantially, and the company that developed the drug typically sees its revenues drop sharply. Over the next few years, Astro Zeneca will lose patent protection for Crestor (which lowers cholesterol) and

Exhibit 6.10 Porter's Five Industry Forces

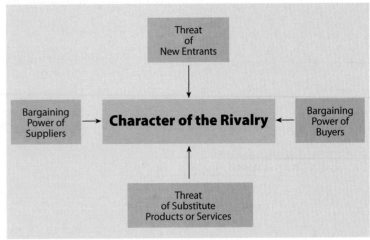

< **"what's new" companies**

character of the rivalry a measure of the intensity of competitive behavior between companies in an industry.

threat of new entrants a measure of the degree to which barriers to entry make it easy or difficult for new companies to get started in an industry.

threat of substitute products or services a measure of the ease with which customers can find substitutes for an industry's products or services.

Symbicort (for asthma). Other companies that have drugs with expiring patents include Eli Lilly and Zyprexa (for schizophrenia); Forest Laboratories and Lexapro (for depression); and Pfizer and Lipitor (for cholesterol), Aricept (for Alzheimer's), and Xalatan (for glaucoma).[72]

Bargaining power of suppliers is a measure of the influence that suppliers of parts, materials, and services to firms in an industry have on the prices of these inputs. When companies can buy parts, materials, and services from numerous suppliers, the companies will be able to bargain with the suppliers to keep prices low. On the other hand, if there are few suppliers, or if a company is dependent on a supplier with specialized skills and knowledge, then the suppliers will have the bargaining power to *"what's new" companies* > dictate price levels. With 60 percent of the global market, **Hitachi Automotive Systems** dominates the production and supply of automotive airflow sensors that measure how much air has been drawn into an engine so that the proper amount of fuel is injected into the engine's cylinder. Car engines can't run correctly without this device. Only two other companies, Siemens AG and Robert Bosch GmbH, make them, but not for all automakers. So when Japan's catastrophic earthquake damaged Hitachi's Japanese factories, GM, Toyota, and PSA Peugeot-Citroen had to shut down production because no other suppliers produced the airflow sensors needed for their cars.[73]

Bargaining power of buyers is a measure of the influence that customers have on the firm's prices. If a company sells a popular product or service to multiple buyers, then the company has more power to set prices. By contrast, if a company is dependent on just a few high-volume buyers, those buyers will typically have enough *"what's new" companies* > bargaining power to dictate prices. **Costco**, a membership warehouse chain, and the third largest retailer in the United States, focuses on offering extremely low prices. Oftentimes, when it believes that a supplier charges too much for a product, it simply stops carrying it. So when Coca-Cola wanted to raise prices aggressively, Costco stopped selling Coca-Cola products. According to a message on Costco's website, "At this time, Coca-Cola has not provided Costco with competitive pricing so that we may pass along the value our members deserve." After three weeks of negotiations, Coca-Cola lowered its prices, and its products were back on Costco shelves.[74]

4.2 Positioning Strategies

After analyzing industry forces, the next step in industry-level strategy is to protect your company from the negative effects of industry-wide competition and to create a sustainable competitive advantage. According to Michael Porter, there are three positioning strategies: cost leadership, differentiation, and focus.

Cost leadership means producing a product or service of acceptable quality at consistently lower production costs than competitors so that the firm can offer the product or service at the lowest price in the industry. Cost leadership protects companies from industry forces by deterring new entrants, who will have to match low costs and prices. Cost leadership also forces down the prices of substitute products and services, attracts bargain-seeking buyers, and increases bargaining power with suppliers, who have to keep their prices low if they want to do business with the cost leader. **Supervalu Inc.**, which owns and runs Albertsons, Acme Markets, and Jewel-Osco stores, is the fourth largest U.S. grocer, with $40 billion in annual revenues. With 1,100 stores, Supervalu uses 1.5 billion plastic and paper bags a year. At 2 cents for a plastic bag and 5 cents for a paper bag, it spends over $35 million a year on grocery bags! Supervalu spokesman Mike Siemienas says, "We're in a very competitive industry. Anything we can do to lower our expenses will help us keep our prices as fair as possible."[75] So it has implemented an extensive training program—with the slogan, "When you're done, add one."—to teach its baggers how to efficiently put

bargaining power of suppliers a measure of the influence that suppliers of parts, materials, and services to firms in an industry have on the prices of these inputs.

bargaining power of buyers a measure of the influence that customers have on a firm's prices.

cost leadership the positioning strategy of producing a product or service of acceptable quality at consistently lower production costs than competitors can, so that the firm can offer the product or service at the lowest price in the industry.

"what's new" companies >

more in each bag. Over the last 18 months, the average number of items per bag has increased by 5 percent, saving the company about $5 million a year. To emphasize the importance of cutting costs, store managers participate in a monthly conference call that reviews the number of bags used at each store and region. Finally, all cashiers and baggers are required to take a 41-question quiz on bagging, which the company is considering administering on a weekly basis.

Differentiation means making your product or service sufficiently different from competitors' offerings so that customers are willing to pay a premium price for the extra value or performance that it provides. Differentiation protects companies from industry forces by reducing the threat of substitute products. It also protects companies by making it easier to retain customers and more difficult for new entrants trying to attract new customers. The starting price of the hybrid cars is $22,000 for a Toyota Prius, $26,000 for a Honda Civic, and $28,000 for a Ford Fusion. With these lower-priced options, why would anyone spend $40,000 on a Chevy Volt hybrid? With its innovative gas-electric hybrid engine, the Volt is the most fuel-efficient car in the U.S. market. It rechargeable battery-powered engine—plug it in and it's recharged in four hours—can take you 40 miles before the gas-powered engine kicks in. So, commuters who drive less than 40 miles a day will never need to buy gas. For those with longer commutes, the combination of battery power and the small gas engine could give typical commuters somewhere between 75 and 230 miles per gallon.[76] So although Chevy has differentiated the Volt from traditional hybrids with its plug-in rechargeable engine and its high price, the question is will this differentiation strategy work? Will consumers be willing to pay $12,000 to $18,000 more for a hybrid that gets two to five times the gas mileage of typical hybrids?

With a **focus strategy**, a company uses either cost leadership or differentiation to produce a specialized product or service for a limited, specially targeted group of customers in a particular geographic region or market segment. Focus strategies typically work in market niches that competitors have overlooked or have difficulty serving. From newspapers to magazines, to books, the publishing industry finds falling sales, reduced revenues, and no clear idea what to do about it. One area in publishing, however, is growing $100 million a year, nearly 8 percent per year on average. It appeals to a small segment of readers and accounts for just 14 percent of all books sold. But this book segment is the top-performing category on *The New York Times, USA Today,* and *Publishers Weekly* best-seller lists. Can you guess what it is? Romance novels. Yes, sales of romance novels are growing for publishers like Avon Romance (owned by HarperCollins Publishers) by appealing to targeted groups of readers interested in NASCAR, quilting, transgender, knitting, military, and paranormal (think vampires and werewolves). Indeed, on the day this was written, the Avon Romance website was featuring *Vampire Mine*, by Kerrelyn Sparks, *Sex and the Single Vampire* by Katie MacAlister, *A Tale of Two Vikings* by Sandra Hill, and *How I Met my Countess* by Elizabeth Boyle. One of the most popular subject areas, according to sales figures, is Mennonite and Amish-themed romances. A highly anticipated novel, for example, tells the story of a young woman whose parents have died in a horse-drawn-carriage accident and who meets a suitor who will test the limits of her Amish faith. So, although most people don't read romance novels, catering to those who do with micro-themed books (i.e., a focus strategy) is one of the few successful strategies in publishing today.[77]

4.3 Adaptive Strategies

Adaptive strategies are another set of industry-level strategies. Whereas the aim of positioning strategies is to minimize the effects of industry competition and build a

differentiation the positioning strategy of providing a product or service that is sufficiently different from competitors' offerings that customers are willing to pay a premium price for it.

focus strategy the positioning strategy of using cost leadership or differentiation to produce a specialized product or service for a limited, specially targeted group of customers in a particular geographic region or market segment.

sustainable competitive advantage, the purpose of adaptive strategies is to choose an industry-level strategy that is best suited to changes in the organization's external environment. There are four kinds of adaptive strategies: defenders, prospectors, analyzers, and reactors.[78]

Defenders seek moderate, steady growth by offering a limited range of products and services to a well-defined set of customers. In other words, defenders aggressively "defend" their current strategic position by doing the best job they can to hold on to customers in a particular market segment. **Broadview Security**, formerly known as Brink's Home Security, is the best in the home security market at keeping customers. Homeowners will select a home security company to install their security system and then typically sign a three-year contract with the same company to provide security service, which includes 24-hour monitoring for break-ins and/or fire. At the end of that three-year contract, most consumers will shop around for the best deal. It's at that point that many customers are lost. But not at Broadview, where on average customers end up staying for 12 years. Broadview's defender strategy is even more impressive because they only target customers with good credit records. Ian Zaffino, a business analyst at Oppenheimer Funds, says Broadview "isn't really into adding [subscribers] for the heck of it. They are concerned with adding high-quality subs [subscribers]."[79] As a result, the company has zero debt. With nearly 70 million U.S. homes lacking security systems, Broadview's goal is to achieve steady, moderate growth by adding 60,000 to 80,000 subscribers a year.

Prospectors seek fast growth by searching for new market opportunities, encouraging risk taking, and being the first to bring innovative new products to market. Prospectors are analogous to gold miners who "prospect" for gold nuggets (i.e., new products) in hopes that the nuggets will lead them to a rich deposit of gold (i.e., fast growth). 3M has long been known for its innovative products, particularly in the areas of adhesives. Since 1904, it has invented sandpaper; masking, cellophane, electrical, and Scotch tapes; the first commercially available audiotapes and videotapes; and its most famous invention, Post-it notes. Lately, 3M has invented a film that increases the brightness of LCD displays on laptop computers; developed a digital system for construction companies to detect underground telecommunication, gas, water, sewer, or electrical lines without digging; and created a pheromone spray that, by preventing harmful insects from mating, will protect apple, walnut, tomato, cranberry, and grape crops. For more on 3M's innovative products, see the 3M innovation archive (http://solutions.3m.com/wps/portal/3M/en_WW/History/3M/Company/century-innovation/.)

Analyzers are a blend of the defender and prospector strategies. They seek moderate, steady growth *and* limited opportunities for fast growth. Analyzers are rarely first to market with new products or services. Instead, they try to simultaneously minimize risk and maximize profits by following or imitating the proven successes of prospectors. In Sister Bay, Wisconsin, goats eat the grass on sod-covered roof of Al Johnson's Swedish Restaurant. When a friend gave him a goat as a gag gift in 1973, someone took the gag one step further by putting the goat on the roof. When customers thronged to the restaurant to see the goat, Johnson heeded his father's words, "Lars, you have something very valuable here," and registered a "Goats on the Roof" trademark.[80] But any time you have a good business idea, you can expect imitators. For instance, there is a Goats on the Roof Coffee Shop in Northumberland, England; The Old Country Market in Coombs, British Columbia, which advertises itself as the "Home of the Goats on the Roof"; and the Tiger Mountain Market in Rabun County, Georgia, which has had goats on its lawn-covered roof since 2007. Al Johnson's "Goats on the Roof" trademark only covers U.S. businesses, so only Tiger Mountain Market pays Johnson a licensing fee to continue using goats on his roof to market his company.

"what's new" companies >

defenders companies using an adaptive strategy aimed at defending strategic positions by seeking moderate, steady growth and by offering a limited range of high-quality products and services to a well-defined set of customer.

prospectors companies using an adaptive strategy that seeks fast growth by searching for new market opportunities, encouraging risk taking, and being the first to bring innovative new products to market.

analyzers companies using an adaptive strategy that seeks to minimize risk and maximize profits by following or imitating the proven successes of prospectors.

All three of these imitators, however, are clearly following an analyzer strategy by imitating Al Johnson and his goats.

Finally, unlike defenders, prospectors, or analyzers, **reactors** do not follow a consistent strategy. Rather than anticipating and preparing for external opportunities and threats, reactors tend to "react" to changes in their external environment after they occur. Not surprisingly, reactors tend to be poorer performers than defenders, prospectors, or analyzers. A reactor approach is inherently unstable, and firms that fall into this mode of operation must change their approach or face almost certain failure. Hard Rock Café International has 125 restaurants and ten hotels around the world. When it spent $400 million in Myrtle Beach, South Carolina, to create the Hard Rock Café Park, a rock and roll–based theme park with monster rides (like the Led Zeppelin roller coaster, which blared the band's "Whole Lotta Love"), there was every expectation that success would follow. But bankruptcy occurred after just

© Magone/Shutterstock.com

one season because the park's managers did not anticipate or prepare for the basic challenges they would face in this resort town. Economist Don Schunk said, "There was just sort of this assumption that all they had to do was throw the Hard Rock name around and people would figure it out on their own."[81] In a town famous for its beautiful and *free* beach, admission was $50 per customer. Moreover, park managers didn't coordinate their limited promotions with nearby hotels or local tourism officials. Paul Ruben, who edits *Park World*, the trade industry magazine for the amusement park industry said, "You want to draw families, theme the park as storybook land or fairytale land. I don't think the Hard Rock name is necessarily the best route for an amusement park."[82]

reactors companies using an adaptive strategy of not following a consistent strategy, but instead reacting to changes in the external environment after they occur.

Industry-Level Strategies Industry-level strategies focus on how companies choose to compete in their industry. Five industry forces determine an industry's overall attractiveness to corporate investors and its potential for long-term profitability. Together, a high level of new entrants, substitute products or services, bargaining power of suppliers, bargaining power of buyers, and rivalry among competitors combine to increase competition and decrease profits. Three positioning strategies can help companies protect themselves from the negative effects of industry-wide competition. Under a cost leadership strategy, firms try to keep production costs low so that they can sell products at prices lower than competitors can. Differentiation is a strategy aimed at making a product or service sufficiently different from competitors' products that it can command a premium price. Using a focus strategy, firms seek to produce a specialized product or service for a limited, specially targeted group of customers. The four adaptive strategies help companies adapt to changes in the external environment. Defenders want to "defend" their current strategic positions. Prospectors look for new market opportunities by bringing innovative new products to market. Analyzers minimize risk by following the proven successes of prospectors. Reactors do not follow a consistent strategy, but instead react to changes in their external environment after they occur.

Review 4

5 Firm-Level Strategies

Microsoft brings out its Xbox 360 video-game console; Sony counters with its PlayStation 3. Sprint Nextel drops prices and increases monthly cell phone minutes; Verizon strikes back with better reception and even lower prices and more minutes. FedEx, the overnight delivery company, buys Kinko's copying and printing stores and turns them into FedEx Kinko's Office and Print Centers to provide a convenient place for businesspeople to drop off and pick up packages; UPS buys Mail Boxes, Etc. and turns its outlets into UPS Stores for exactly the same purpose. Starbucks Coffee opens a store, and nearby locally run coffeehouses respond by improving service, increasing portions, and holding the line on prices. Attack and respond, respond and attack. **Firm-level strategy** addresses the question "How should we compete against a particular firm?"

Let's find out more about the firm-level strategies (direct competition between companies) shown in Exhibit 6.11 by reading about **5.1 the basics of direct competition, 5.2 the strategic moves involved in direct competition between companies,** and **5.3 entrepreneurship and intrapreneurship.**

5.1 Direct Competition

Although Porter's five industry forces indicate the overall level of competition in an industry, most companies do not compete directly with all the firms in their industry. For example, McDonald's and Red Lobster are both in the restaurant business, but no one would characterize them as competitors. McDonald's offers low-cost, convenient fast food in a seat-yourself restaurant, whereas Red Lobster offers mid-priced, sit-down seafood dinners complete with servers and a bar.

Instead of competing with an industry, most firms compete directly with just a few companies within it. **Direct competition** is the rivalry between two companies offering similar products and services that acknowledge each other as rivals and take offensive and defensive positions as they act and react to each other's strategic actions.[83] Two factors determine the extent to which firms will be in direct competition with each other: market commonality and resource similarity. **Market commonality** is the degree to which two companies have overlapping products, services, or customers in multiple markets. The more markets in which there is product, service, or customer overlap, the more intense the direct competition between the two companies. **Resource similarity** is the extent to which a competitor has similar amounts and kinds of resources, that is, similar assets, capabilities, processes, information, and knowledge used to create and sustain an advantage over competitors. From a competitive standpoint, resource similarity means that your direct competitors can probably match the strategic actions that your company takes.

Exhibit 6.12 shows how market commonality and resource similarity interact to determine when and where companies are in direct competition.[84] The overlapping area in each quadrant (between the triangle and the rectangle, or between the

firm-level strategy a corporate strategy that addresses the question "How should we compete against a particular firm?"

direct competition the rivalry between two companies that offer similar products and services, acknowledge each other as rivals, and act and react to each other's strategic actions.

market commonality the degree to which two companies have overlapping products, services, or customers in multiple markets.

resource similarity the extent to which a competitor has similar amounts and kinds of resources.

Exhibit 6.11 Firm-Level Strategies (Direct Competition)

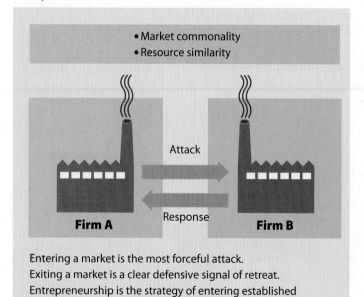

Entering a market is the most forceful attack.
Exiting a market is a clear defensive signal of retreat.
Entrepreneurship is the strategy of entering established markets or developing new markets.

© Cengage Learning 2013

differently colored rectangles) depicts market commonality. The larger the overlap, the greater the market commonality. Shapes depict resource similarity, with rectangles representing one set of competitive resources and triangles representing another. Quadrant I shows two companies in direct competition because they have similar resources at their disposal and a high degree of market commonality. These companies try to sell similar products and services to similar customers. McDonald's and Burger King would clearly fit here as direct competitors.

In Quadrant II, the overlapping parts of the triangle and rectangle show two companies going after similar customers with some similar products or services, but doing so with different competitive resources. McDonald's and Wendy's restaurants would fit here. Wendy's is after the same lunchtime and dinner crowds that McDonald's is. Nevertheless, with its more expensive hamburgers, fries, shakes, and salads,

Wendy's is less of a direct competitor to McDonald's than Burger King is. For example, Wendy's Garden Sensation salads (using fancy lettuce varieties, grape tomatoes, and mandarin oranges) bring in customers who would have eaten at more expensive casual dining restaurants like Applebee's.[85] A representative from Wendy's says, "We believe you win customers by consistently offering a better product at a strong, everyday value."[86]

In Quadrant III, the very small overlap shows two companies with different competitive resources and little market commonality. McDonald's and Luby's cafeterias fit here. Although both are in the fast-food business, there's almost no overlap in terms of products and customers. Luby's sells baked chicken, turkey, roasts, meat loaf, and vegetables, none of which are available at McDonald's. Furthermore, Luby's customers aren't likely to eat at McDonald's. In fact, Luby's is not really competing with other fast-food restaurants, but with eating at home. Company surveys show that close to half of its customers would have eaten at home, not at another restaurant, if they hadn't come to Luby's.[87]

Finally, in Quadrant IV, the small overlap between the two rectangles shows that McDonald's and Subway compete with similar resources but with little market commonality. In terms of resources, sales at McDonald's are much larger, but Subway has grown substantially in the last decade and now has 33,749 stores worldwide, compared to 32,737 worldwide at McDonald's (just 14,027 in the United States).[88] Although Subway and McDonald's compete, they aren't direct competitors in terms of market commonality in the way that McDonald's and Burger King are, because Subway, unlike McDonald's, sells itself as a provider of healthy fast food. Thus, the overlap is much smaller in Quadrant IV than in Quadrant I. With its advertising featuring "Jared," who lost 245 pounds eating at Subway, the detailed nutritional information available in its stores, and its close relationship with the American Heart Association, Subway's goal "is to emphasize that the Subway brand represents all that is good about health and well-being."[89] And although fast-food customers tend to eat at both restaurants, Subway's customers are twice as loyal as McDonald's customers, most likely because of Subway's healthier food.[90]

Exhibit 6.12 A Framework of Direct Competition

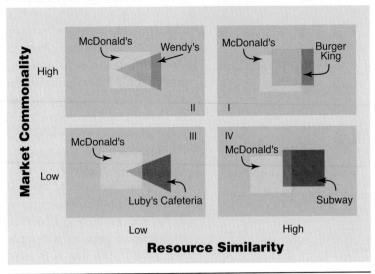

Source: From M. Chen, "Competitor Analysis and Interfirm Rivalry: Toward a Theoretical Integration," *Academy of Management Review* 21 (1996): 21–39. Reproduced by permission of Academy of Management (NY) in the formats Textbook and Other Book via Copyright Clearance Center.

5.2 Strategic Moves of Direct Competition

Whereas corporate-level strategies help managers decide what business to be in and industry-level strategies help them determine how to compete within an industry, firm-level strategies help managers determine when, where, and what strategic actions should be taken against a direct competitor. Firms in direct competition can make two basic strategic moves: attack and response. These moves occur all the time in virtually every industry, but they are most noticeable in industries where multiple large competitors are pursuing customers in the same market space.

An **attack** is a competitive move designed to reduce a rival's market share or profits. For example, the two leaders in the e-reader market, Amazon and Barnes & Noble, had both priced their devices at $259. However, Barnes & Noble attacked Amazon's Kindle e-reader by aggressively cutting the price on its Nook e-reader to $199.[91] A **response** is a countermove, prompted by a rival's attack, that is designed to defend or improve a company's market share or profit. There are two kinds of responses.[92] The first is to match or mirror your competitor's move. This is what Amazon did when it cut the price on its Kindle e-reader to $189, undercutting the price of Barnes & Noble's Nook by $10.[93] The second kind of response, however, is to respond along a different dimension from your competitor's move or attack. For example, instead of cutting the price of its Kobo e-reader, Borders responded to its two competitors' price cuts by offering a $20 Borders gift card with the purchase of each Kobo.[94]

Market commonality and resource similarity determine the likelihood of an attack or response, that is, whether a company is likely to attack a direct competitor or to strike back with a strong response when attacked. When market commonality is large and companies have overlapping products, services, or customers in multiple markets, there is less motivation to attack and more motivation to respond to an attack. The reason for this is straightforward: When firms are direct competitors in a large number of markets, they have a great deal at stake. So when Barnes & Noble launched an aggressive price war, Amazon had no choice but to respond by cutting its own prices. With competing products like the Kobo and new e-readers from Acer and Sony, the e-reader space was already becoming crowded before an outside threat (Apple's iPad) forced Amazon and Barnes & Noble to quickly cut prices. The iPad's threat to Barnes & Noble's Nook and Amazon's Kindle became clear when Apple CEO Steve Jobs announced that iPad users had purchased over 5 million e-books in the two months since its release (that's roughly 2.5 books per iPad). Indeed, soon after the introduction of the iPad, Amazon introduced a lighter, thinner, faster, and cheaper (just $139) Kindle with a better screen and twice as much storage capability (up to 3,500 books).[95] Although Kindle sales tripled after dropping the price from $259 to $189, cutting the price to $139 boosted sales to 8 million Kindles per year.[96] Moreover, iPad sales have not dented Kindle book sales. Indeed, 40 percent of e-book sales for iPads have come through Amazon's Kindle store (Amazon has a Kindle app for the iPad and other devices) compared to just 29 percent through Apple's iBookstore.[97] Finally, although 53 percent of Kindle owners use their device to read books on a daily basis, only 25 percent of iPad users do so.[98] For now, the Kindle appears to be more than holding its own against competitors.

Whereas market commonality affects the likelihood of an attack or a response to an attack, resource similarity largely affects response capability, that is, how quickly and forcefully a company can respond to an attack. When resource similarity is strong, the responding firm will generally be able to match the strategic moves of the attacking firm. Consequently, a firm is less likely to attack firms with similar levels of

attack a competitive move designed to reduce a rival's market share or profits.

response a competitive countermove, prompted by a rival's attack, to defend or improve a company's market share or profit.

resources because it is unlikely to gain any sustained advantage when the responding firms strike back. On the other hand, if one firm is substantially stronger than another (i.e., there is low resource similarity), then a competitive attack is more likely to produce sustained competitive advantage.

With over 32,737 stores to Burger King's 12,174 stores and much greater financial resources, McDonald's hoped a price war would inflict serious financial damage on Burger King while suffering minimal financial damage itself. It put eight items on a new $1 value menu, including two sandwiches, the Big N' Tasty and the McChicken, which usually sold for $1.99.[99] This strategy worked to some extent. Although Burger King already sold 11 menu items for 99 cents, it wasn't willing or able to cut the price of its bestselling Whopper sandwiches to 99 cents (from $1.99). Basically admitting that it couldn't afford to match McDonald's price cuts on more expensive sandwiches, a Burger King spokesperson insisted, "McDonald's can't sell those sandwiches at $1 without losing money. It isn't sustainable." Thanks to its much larger financial resources, McDonald's had the funds to outlast Burger King in the price war. As often happens, though, the price war ended up hurting both companies' profits.[100] McDonald's ended the price war when it became clear that lower prices didn't draw more customers to its restaurants.

In general, the more moves (i.e., attacks) a company initiates against direct competitors, and the greater a company's tendency to respond when attacked, the better its performance. More specifically, attackers and early responders (companies that are quick to launch a retaliatory attack) tend to gain market share and profits at the expense of late responders. This is not to suggest that a full-attack strategy always works best. In fact, attacks can provoke harsh retaliatory responses. When it first came on the market, Sony's PlayStation 3 (PS3) cost $599, but it came with an 80-GB hard drive and a then-rare Blu-ray disc player. Sales lagged. However, Nintendo's Wii game console cost $249 and Microsoft's Xbox 360 game console cost $400. So Sony cut the price of the 80-GB PS3 to $499 and introduced a 40-GB PS3 for $399.[101] Microsoft responded over the next four years by cutting the price of an Xbox 360 with a 20-GB hard drive from $349 to $299, cutting the price of an Xbox 360 with a 60-GB hard drive from $349 to $299, and cutting a 120-GB Xbox 360 from $399 to $299.[102] Today, with a 320-GB PS3 costing $400 and a 160-GB PS3 costing $300, Sony is now priced more competitively with 250-GB Xbox 360, which costs $300. As a result, global sales of the PS3 now total 43.4 million units compared to the Xbox 360's 42.9 million.[103] Microsoft responded to the PS3's increased sales with the introduction of the Xbox Kinect, a motion-sensing device that allows you to play games without controllers. With Kinect proving enormously popular—sales of 8 million units in the first six months—Microsoft hopes to increase Xbox 360 sales at the expense of the PS3.[104] Consequently, when deciding when, where, and what strategic actions to take against a direct competitor, managers should always consider the possibility of retaliation.

5.3 Entrepreneurship and Intrapreneurship: Entering New Markets

As the Amazon.com and Barnes & Noble, McDonald's and Burger King, and PS3 and Xbox 360 examples illustrate, attacks and responses can include smaller, more tactical moves like price cuts, specially advertised sales or promotions, or improvements in service. On a larger scale, they can also involve resource-intensive strategic moves such as expanding service and production facilities, introducing new products or services within the firm's existing business, or entering a completely new line of business for the first time.

Of these, *market entries* and *market exits* are probably the most important kinds of attacks and responses. Entering a market is perhaps the most forceful attack or response because it sends the clear signal that the company is committed to gaining or defending market share and profits at a direct competitor's expense. By contrast, exiting a market is an equally clear defensive signal that your company is retreating.[105]

Because **entrepreneurship** is the process of entering new or established markets with new goods or services, entrepreneurship is also a firm-level strategy. In fact, the basic strategic act of entrepreneurship is new entry, or creating a new business from a brand-new start-up firm. The insurance company **Asurion Corporation** estimates that 30 million mobile phones are lost every year. Though there are services that help people find phones once they are lost, two companies have created a new market by introducing products that help consumers not to lose their phones in the first place. The Zomm is a "wireless leash," a small disc-shaped device that connects to a mobile phone through Bluetooth. When the distance between it and phone increases, the disc begins to vibrate and flash; when the distance exceeds 30 feet, it emits a sharp alarm to let you know that you've left your phone behind nearby. The Phone Halo, in addition to emitting a warning sound like the Zomm, will also send a lost-phone notification through email and Twitter to a designated list of contacts.[106]

Established firms can be entrepreneurial too, by entering new or established markets with new goods or services. When existing companies are entrepreneurial, it's called **intrapreneurship**.[107] Chances are that you've purchased private-label goods, such as Walmart's Sam's Choice Cola instead of brands like Coke or Pepsi. Private-label goods can be as much as 20 percent of a retailer's business. Electronics retailer Best Buy is being intrapraneurial by developing its own private-label line of electronics goods. At first, it simply sold the same electronics products, such as Blu-ray DVD players, that you could get at Walmart and Radio Shack (because they were made by the same Chinese suppliers). Now, however, using the terabytes of customer satisfaction data gathered in its stores and a team of engineers, it is designing private-label electronics goods that are different from the products already in its stores. For instance, after its store data indicated that a large share of DVD players were purchased for children, it designed a spill-resistant model with rubber edges. Best Buy now sells hundreds of products under its own brands, including Insignia and Dynex TVs, Rocketfish video cables, and Geek Squad flash drives.[108]

Whereas the *goal* of an intrapreneurial strategy is new entry, the *process* of carrying out an intrapreneurial strategy depends on the ability of the company's founders or existing managers to foster an entrepreneurial orientation (remember, intrapreneurship is entrepreneurship in an existing organization). An **entrepreneurial orientation** is the set of processes, practices, and decision-making

"what's new" companies >

entrepreneurship the process of entering new or established markets with new goods or services.

intrapreneurship entrepreneurship within an existing organization.

entrepreneurial orientation the set of processes, practices, and decision-making activities that lead to new entry, characterized by five dimensions: risk taking, autonomy, innovativeness, proactiveness, and competitive aggressiveness.

© AP Images/Paul Sakuma

activities that lead to new entry. Five key dimensions characterize an entrepreneurial orientation:[109]

> » **Risk taking.** Entrepreneurial firms are willing to take some risks by making large resource commitments that may result in costly failure. Another way to conceptualize risk taking is to think of it as a managerial preference for bold rather than cautious acts.
>
> » **Autonomy.** If a firm wants to successfully develop new products or services to enter new markets, it must foster creativity among employees. To be creative, employees need the freedom and control to develop a new idea into a new product or service opportunity without interference from others. In other words, they need autonomy.
>
> » **Innovativeness.** Entrepreneurial firms also foster innovativeness by supporting new ideas, experimentation, and creative processes that might produce new products, services, or technological processes.
>
> » **Proactiveness.** Entrepreneurial firms have the ability to anticipate future problems, needs, or changes by developing new products or services that may not be related to their current business, by introducing new products or services before the competition does, and by dropping products or services that are declining (and likely to be replaced by new products or services).[110]
>
> » **Competitive aggressiveness.** Because new entrants are more likely to fail than existing firms are, they must be aggressive if they want to succeed. A new firm often must be willing to use unconventional methods to directly challenge competitors for their customers and market share.

Without these five key characteristics, an entrepreneurial orientation is unlikely to be created, and an intrapreneurial strategy is unlikely to succeed.

Firm-Level Strategies   Firm-level strategies are concerned with direct competition between firms. Market commonality and resource similarity determine whether firms are in direct competition and thus likely to attack each other or respond to each other's attacks. In general, the more markets in which there is product, service, or customer overlap, and the greater the resource similarity between two firms, the more intense the direct competition between them. When firms are direct competitors in a large number of markets, attacks are less likely because responding firms are highly motivated to quickly and forcefully defend their profits and market share. By contrast, resource similarity affects response capability, meaning how quickly and forcefully a company responds to an attack. When resource similarity is strong, attacks are much less likely to produce a sustained advantage, because the responding firm is capable of striking back with equal force.

Market entries and exits are the most important kinds of attacks and responses. Entering a new market is a clear offensive signal, whereas exiting a market is a clear signal that a company is retreating. Market entry is perhaps the most forceful attack or response because it sends the clear signal that the company is committed to gaining or defending market share and profits at a direct competitor's expense. In general, attackers and early responders gain market share and profits at the expense of late responders. Attacks must be carefully planned and carried out, however, because they can provoke harsh retaliatory responses.

Finally, the basic strategic act of entrepreneurship is new entry. To carry out an entrepreneurial strategy, a company must create an entrepreneurial orientation by encouraging risk taking, autonomy, innovativeness, proactiveness, and competitive aggressiveness.

Review 5

SELF-ASSESSMENT

Strategy Questionnaire

Generally speaking, a strategy is a plan of action that is designed to help you achieve a goal. Strategies are not limited to grand plans that help you accomplish grand goals. You probably use strategies every day in simple ways. For example, think of a route you regularly drive. Do you know how fast (or slow) you need to go to catch all the lights on green? Or where to swerve to avoid a pothole? Or even when to take a side street to shave a few minutes off your commute? Speeding up for one block in order to catch the green lights at the next five intersections is a strategy. Strategy, then, involves thinking about how you are going to accomplish what you set out (i.e., have planned) to do.

This assessment will provide some baseline information on attitudes you might have that will relate to your management skills.[111] Answer each of the questions as either "True" or "False." Try not to spend too much time on any one item, and be sure to answer all the questions.

1. I get satisfaction from competing with others.
2. It's usually not important to me to be the best.
3. Competition destroys friendships.
4. Games with no clear-cut winners are boring.
5. I am a competitive individual.
6. I will do almost anything to avoid an argument.
7. I try to avoid competing with others.
8. I would like to be on a debating team.
9. I often remain quiet rather than risk hurting another person.
10. I find competitive situations unpleasant.
11. I try to avoid arguments.
12. In general, I will go along with the group rather than create conflict.
13. I don't like competing against other people.
14. I don't like games that are winner-take-all.
15. I dread competing against other people.
16. I enjoy competing against an opponent.
17. When I play a game, I like to keep score.
18. I often try to outperform others.
19. I like competition.
20. I don't enjoy challenging others even when I think they are wrong.

To determine your score, count the number of responses marked "True" and enter it here ___3___. You can find the interpretation for your score at www.cengagebrain.com.

MANAGEMENT DECISION

Dealing with Competition[112]

You are an executive at Pepsi, and you've just made what feels like a great decision. For many years, various health and children's groups have been calling for reductions of high-calorie and high-fat foods in U.S. schools. Even if schools provided nutritious, fresh, and healthy food, they argued, it was no competition for the salty and sugary treats available in vending machines. These groups even had First Lady Michelle Obama lead a nationwide campaign.

In response, you've made a monumental decision, the first by any soft-drink producer—to remove full-calorie beverages from all schools in over 200 countries by 2012. Your decision is being hailed by numerous organizations, from the World Heart Federation and the American Heart Association to the William J. Clinton Foundation. Not only do they credit your company for taking an important first step in the fight against childhood obesity, but they also celebrate your willingness to take initiative instead of waiting for government regulations.

Some of your colleagues, however, are not in a celebratory mood. Though your company has received some great publicity, they've read numerous reports that Coca-Cola will take a different course. Although all soft-drink producers agreed not to sell full-calorie products in primary/elementary schools, Coca-Cola recently revised its sales policy to allow sales in schools if parents or school officials request it. What is more, Coca-Cola has decided that it will continue to sell full-calorie beverage to secondary schools, as

they argue that parents and school officials "should have the right to choose what is best for their schools."

Your colleagues worry that Coca-Cola's policy could give them a huge competitive advantage. Even though Pepsi will still have a presence in primary and secondary schools, their offerings will be limited to low-calorie diet drinks, bottled water, low-fat milk, and juice with no added sugar. These products may have to compete with Coca-Cola's lineup of full-calorie, sugar-loaded drinks. There doesn't seem to be much doubt about what the students will choose. After all, if students opted for diet drinks or water in the first place, the sale of full-calorie drinks would not have turned into a public health issue.

Your colleagues fear that Pepsi's commitment to public health will give Coca-Cola an insurmountable competitive edge. So late in one business day, a group of colleagues come to your office. "You're the one that came up with this great plan," they say. "How are we going to respond?"

Questions

1. Using Porter's Five Industry Forces, map the soft-drink industry.
2. What are the risks and opportunities of the strategies followed by Pepsi? Of Coca-Cola?
3. How would you respond to Coca-Cola's change in sales policy? How would you ensure Pepsi's board that this response will allow you to remain competitive and profitable?

MANAGEMENT TEAM DECISION

A New Strategy for India?[113]

During the most recent management meeting at Nokia's Asian headquarters, you heard about a small company called Micromax that is one of the fastest-growing cell phone companies in India. The company started as a pay phone provider but quickly branched into mobile phones. In just a few short years, it's been able to sell 1 million handsets per year, grabbing 4 percent of the Indian market. And much of this growth is coming at Nokia's expense, which has

seen its market share in India dip from 64 percent to 52 percent.

One of the keys to Micromax's success has been its strategy of creating phones that cater specifically to the Indian market. Its first phone, which featured a small screen and a huge battery and could run for five days, was inspired when Micromax executives saw a long line of people waiting to use a man's car battery to charge their cell phones. A popular current model is inspired by Bollywood films and features

ornate costume jewelry. One of the reasons that Micromax is so popular is that most of its handsets allow consumers to access multiple accounts, either by hosting two phone numbers or allowing for very easy switching of SIM cards (small cards that identify a particular user on the network). And because these phones are targeted toward a market where Internet and 3G coverage is still sporadic, most of Micromax's phones lack Wi-Fi, 3G, or GPS, features that are critical to a phone's success in the United States or Europe.

All of this runs counter to Nokia's strategy, which has been to make phones for a worldwide market, meaning that it sells what is basically the same phone in Midland, Texas, as in Mumbai, and to emphasize the quality of its products. In fact, each phone spends 18 months in development, as it is tested for quality and durability.

But as your market share in the rapidly growing Indian market continues to spiral downward, some in the company wonder if maybe a change in strategy is needed. Instead of offering high-priced, high-tech phones that are similar to what it sells in the rest of the world, they wonder whether the company shouldn't try to duplicate what Micromax is doing and sell phones that are more suited to Indian consumer tastes.

Form a group with three or four other students, and discuss how you would approach this issue as Nokia's management team by answering the following questions.

Questions

1. What do you think would be a more effective strategy for Nokia to respond to Micromax—to differentiate itself from Micromax or replicate what it is doing?
2. How could a shadow-strategy task force help Nokia identify the best way to proceed?
3. What strategies might Nokia use to get a better sense of what Indian consumers want and to meet those desires?

PRACTICE BEING A MANAGER

Most Likely to Succeed

Organizational strategy is aimed at achieving sustainable competitive advantage over rivals in a particular market. This exercise will offer you the opportunity to consider how companies in the restaurant industry might develop a strategy and attempt to gain sustainable competitive advantage.

For purposes of this exercise, your professor will organize your class into small teams. Each team will be competing for the title of "Most Likely to Succeed." One team will be designated as judges for this competition.

Step 1 (15 minutes): Develop a concept for a new restaurant business. You may choose to develop your concept as a local, regional, or national company—but in all cases, you must plan to open a restaurant in your local area. Your concept should include the following: (1) a name for your restaurant/chain; (2) a description of your menu, layout, and any other distinguishing features; and (3) likely direct competitors of your new concept. Prepare an informal presentation of not more than two minutes.

Step 2 (20 minutes): Present the concepts. Each team will make an informal two-minute presentation of the restaurant concepts.

Step 3 (5 minutes): Judge the presentations. Judges will confer and reach a decision regarding the top concepts on the basis of "Most Likely to Succeed." Judges should apply the sustainable competitive advantage concept/factors in making their selections. While the judges are conferring, each team should discuss and evaluate the concepts presented by the competing teams. Teams should apply the tools and concepts in this chapter in evaluating these concepts.

Step 4: Discuss as a class.

- What are the challenges of achieving sustainable competitive advantage in the restaurant business? Consider cases of failure and success in your local market—what factors seemed to play a role in determining success or failure?
- What *strategic groups*, or clusters of direct competitors (e.g., fast-food burgers), were identified in the team presentations? Which

strategic groups might be tougher to enter in your local area? Which might be easier to enter?

- Do major restaurant chains have a built-in sustainable competitive advantage over local competition in your area? If you think so, what

is the source of this advantage, and is it more pronounced in some strategic groups than in others (e.g., greater in tacos than in fine dining)? If not, what strategies have the "locals" used to successfully compete with larger restaurant chains?

DEVELOP YOUR CAREER POTENTIAL

An Individual SWOT Analysis

To maintain and sustain a competitive advantage, companies continue to analyze their overall strategy in light of their current situation.[114] In doing so, they often use a SWOT analysis, which focuses on the strengths and weaknesses in the firm's internal environment and the opportunities and threats present in the firm's external environment. One way to gain experience in conducting a SWOT analysis is to perform one on yourself—in other words, conduct a personal SWOT analysis.

Assume you have just completed your college education and are ready to apply for a job as a manager of a small- to medium-sized facility. Perform a personal SWOT analysis to determine whether your current situation matches your overall strategy. Identifying your strengths will probably be the easiest step in the analysis. They will most likely be the skills, abilities, experience, and knowledge that help differentiate you from your competitors. Take care to be realistic and honest in analyzing your strengths and weaknesses.

One way to identify both strengths and weaknesses is to look at previous job evaluation comments and talk to former and present employers and coworkers. Their comments will typically focus on objective strengths and weaknesses that you have exhibited on the job. You may also gather information about your strengths and weaknesses by analyzing your personal interests and learning more about your personality type. Most college placement offices have software to help students identify their interests and personality types and then match that information to certain career paths. This type of assessment can help ensure that you do not choose a career path that is incongruent with your personality and interests.

Probably the hardest portion of the personal SWOT analysis will be the identification of your weaknesses. As humans, we are often reluctant to focus on our deficiencies; nonetheless, being aware of potential weaknesses can help us reduce them or improve upon them. Because you are preparing for

a career in management, you should research what skills, abilities, knowledge, and experience are needed to be a successful manager. Comparing your personal strengths against those needed as a manager can help you identify potential weaknesses. Once you identify weaknesses, develop a plan to overcome them. Remember that most annual evaluations will include both strengths and weaknesses, so don't forget to include them in your analysis.

You can identify opportunities now by looking at employment possibilities for entry-level managers. In this part of the analysis, it helps to match your personal strengths with opportunities. For example, if you have experience in manufacturing, you may initially choose to apply only to manufacturing-type businesses.

The last step of the analysis involves identifying potential threats. Threats are barriers that can prevent you from obtaining your goals. Threats may include events such as an economic recession that reduces the number of job openings for entry-level managers. By knowing what the barriers are and by assembling proactive plans to help deal with them, you can reduce the possibility of your strategy becoming ineffective.

Focusing on a personal SWOT analysis can be a practical way to prepare for an actual company analysis, and it also allows you to learn more about yourself and your long-term plans.

Questions

1. In light of the SWOT analysis, what plans might you propose for yourself that will help you maximize your strengths, exploit your opportunities, and minimize your weaknesses and threats? Write three SMART goals (remember Chapter 5) that will help you implement your plans.
2. How might this assignment prepare you for both your academic and your professional career?

END NOTES

[1] D. Fonda, L. Locke, J. Ressner, & R. Corliss, "When Woody Met Mickey," *Time*, February 6, 2006, 46–47; R. Grover, "How Bob Iger Unchained Disney," *Businessweek*, February 5, 2007, 74–79; M. Marr, "Better Mousetrap: In Shakeup, Disney Rethinks How It Reaches Audiences; Iger Seeks High-Tech Delivery Of Movies, TV Shows; Theater Owners Worry; 'Housewives' on a Handheld," *The Wall Street Journal*, October 1, 2005, A1; R. Siklos, "Q&A, The Iger Difference," *Fortune*, April 28, 2008, 90–94; R. Siklos, "Bob Iger Rocks Disney," *Fortune*, January 19, 2009, 80–86; and T. Stanley, "Iger Needs Superpowers for Quick Fix at Disney," *Advertising Age*, March 21, 2005, 33–34.

[2] James Delahunty, "iPod Market Share at 73.8%, 225 Million iPods Sold, More Games for Touch Than PSP & NDS: Apple," AfterDawn.com., September 9, 2009, accessed April 9, 2011, from www.afterdawn.com/news/article .cfm/2009/09/09/ipod_market_share_ at_73_8_percent_225_million_ipods_ sold_more_games_for_touch_than_ psp_nds_apple.

[3] J. Barney, "Firm Resources and Sustained Competitive Advantage," *Journal of Management* 17 (1991): 99–120; and J. Barney, "Looking Inside for Competitive Advantage," *Academy of Management Executive* 9 (1995): 49–61.

[4] J. Snell, "Apple's Home Run," *Macworld* (November 2006): 7.

[5] J. DArcy & T. Davies, "The Walkman at 20," *Maclean's*, August 30, 1999, 10; and K. Hall, "Sony's iPod Assault Is No Threat to Apple."

[6] E. Smith, "Sony to Take Over Music Partnership; and Firm Raises Its Bet on Ailing Industry; Bertelsmann Exits," *The Wall Street Journal*, August 6, 2008, B1.

[7] E. Slivka, "Total iPod Touch Sales Estimated at Over 45 Million," *MacRumors.com*, September 6, 2010, accessed March 29, 2011, from www.macrumors .com/2010/09/06/total-ipod-touch-sales-estimated-at-over-45-million/.

[8] K. Boehret, "The Mossberg Solution: IPod to Reach Out and Touch Someone," *The Wall Street Journal*, April 29, 2009, B11.

[9] Jesus Diaz, "The Complete Guide to the New iPod Touch," Gizmodo, September 1, 2010, accessed April 9, 2011 from http://gizmodo.com/5627599/the-complete-guide-to-the-new-ipod-touch.

[10] Athavaley & Guth, "How the Zune Is Faring So Far with Consumers," D7.

[11] L. Rao, "iTunes Downloads: 100M Movies, 450M TV Episodes, 35M Books, 11.7B Songs," TechCrunch, September 1, 2010, accessed March 28, 2011, from http://techcrunch.com/ 2010/09/01/itunes-downloads-100-million-movies-35-million-books-11-7-billion-songs/; and S. Sande, "App Store Could Surpass Total iTunes Music Sales by March," *TUAW The Unofficial Apple Weblog*, January 17, 2011, accessed March 28, 2011, from www.tuaw.com/2011/01/17/app-store-could-surpass-total-itunes-music-sales-by-march/.

[12] E. Smith & Y. Kane, "Apple Changes Tune on Music Pricing," *The Wall Street Journal*, January 7, 2009, B1.

[13] R. Levine, "Napster's Ghost Rises," *Fortune*, March 6, 2006, 30; and "30 Products for 30 Years," *MacWorld* (June 2006): 15–16.

[14] S. Hart & C. Banbury, "How Strategy-Making Processes Can Make a Difference," *Strategic Management Journal* 15 (1994): 251–269.

[15] R. A. Burgelman, "Fading Memories: A Process Theory of Strategic Business Exit in Dynamic Environments," *Administrative Science Quarterly* 39 (1994): 24–56; and R. A. Burgelman & A. S. Grove, "Strategic Dissonance," *California Management Review* 38 (Winter 1996): 8–28.

[16] C. Passariello, "Carrefour's Makeover Plan: Become IKEA of Groceries," *The Wall Street Journal*, September 16, 2010, B1.

[17] C. Passariello, "Olofsson's Fight Against the Status Quo at Carrefour," *The Wall Street Journal*, September 16, 2010, accessed March 29, 2011, from http://online.wsj.com/article/SB10001 42405274870374350457549381306 5751290.html.

[18] C. Passariello, "Carrefour's Makeover Plan."

[19] Burgelman & Grove, "Strategic Dissonance."

[20] Bill Saporito, "Behind the Troubles at Toyota," *Time*, February 11, 2010, accessed September 23, 2010, from www.time.com/time/magazine/article/0,9171,1963744,00.html.

[21] A. Ohnsman, J. Green, & K. Inoue, "Toyota Recall Crisis Said to Lie in Cost Cuts, Growth Ambitions," *Bloomberg Businessweek*, February 26, 2010, accessed March 30, 2011, from www.businessweek.com/news/ 2010-02-26/toyota-woes-said-to-lie-in-cost-cuts-growth-targets-update1- .html.

[22] G. Fowler, "EBay Retreats in Web Retailing—Company Will Return to Its Roots as Internet Flea Market, Put Focus on PayPal," *The Wall Street Journal*, March 12, 2009, A1.

[23] A. Fiegenbaum, S. Hart, & D. Schendel, "Strategic Reference Point Theory," *Strategic Management Journal* 17 (1996): 219–235.

[24] "Most and Least Reliable Brands," *Consumer Reports*, accessed July 29, 2008, from www.consumerreports.org/ cro/money/resource-center/most-and-least-reliable-brands-5-07/cars/0507_ brands_cars_1.htm.

[25] "Automaker Report Cards," *Consumer Reports*, April 2011, accessed April 5, 2011, from www.consumer-reports.org/cro/cars/new-cars/buy-ing-advice/who-makes-the-best-cars/ automaker-report-cards/index.htm.

[26] B. Gottesman, "The Tech Brands You Trust Most," *PC Magazine*, October 2011, 30–43.

[27] Joseph B. White, "Ford's New Pickup Line: Like My Tough V-6?" *The Wall Street Journal*, August 18, 2010, accessed November 20, 2010, from http://online.wsj.com/article/SB 10001424052748704554104575435 343519425512.html.

[28]B. Kowitt, "Inside Trader Joe's," *Fortune*, September 6, 2010, 86–96.

[29]C. Palmieri, "Inside Tesco's New U.S. Stores," *Businessweek Online*, December 4, 2007, accessed 9 April 2011, from www.businessweek.com/globalbiz/content/dec2007/gb2007123_870617_page_2.htm; "Unique Products, Reasonable Prices Spell Success for Trader Joe's," *The Food Institute Report* 81 (March 3, 2008): 4; and "Trader Joe's: Why the Hype?" *Bulletin* (Bend, Oregon), March 27, 2008.

[30]A. Fiegenbaum & H. Thomas, "Strategic Groups as Reference Groups: Theory, Modeling and Empirical Examination of Industry and Competitive Strategy," *Strategic Management Journal* 16 (1995): 461–476.

[31]"Continued Weaknesses in Housing and the Overall Economy Are Now Foreseen to Result in Three Consecutive Years of Market Declines," *Home Improvement Research Institute*, accessed June 5, 2009, from www.hiri.org.

[32]R. K. Reger & A. S. Huff, "Strategic Groups: A Cognitive Perspective," *Strategic Management Journal* 14 (1993): 103–124.

[33]"U.S. Store Count by State," Home Depot, accessed April 5, 2011, from http://ir.homedepot.com/phoenix.zhtml?c=63646&p=irol-factsFaq; and "Frequently Asked Questions," Lowes, accessed April 5, 2011, from http://media.lowes.com.

[34]"Frequently Asked Questions," Ace Hardware, accessed April 6, 2011, from www.acehardware.com/corp/index.jsp?page=faq.

[35]"About Aubuchon Hardware," Aubuchon Hardware, accessed April 6, 2011, from www.hardwarestore.com/about-aubuchon-hardware.aspx.

[36]Ace Hardware FAQ, accessed July 29, 2008, from www.acehardware.com/corp/index.jsp?page=faq.

[37]84 Lumber, accessed July 29, 2008, www.84lumber.com.

[38]"Company Overview: A Clear Direction for Growth and Success," True Value, accessed April 6 2011, from http://truevaluecompany.com/about_true_value/company-overview.asp.

[39]W. B. Werther, Jr., & J. L. Kerr, "The Shifting Sands of Competitive Advantage," *Business Horizons* (May–June 1995): 11–17.

[40]S. Berfeld, "Starbucks: Howard Schultz vs. Howard Schultz," *Businessweek*, August 6, 2009, accessed April 6, 2011, from www.businessweek.com/magazine/content/09_33/b4143028813542.htm.

[41]P. Oppmann, "I Spy a 'Stealth Starbucks,'" CNN Living, January 6, 2010, http://articles.cnn.com/2010-01-06/living/i.spy.stealth.starbucks_1_coffee-giant-coffee-shop-stores?_s=PM:LIVING.

[42]"Menard, Inc.," *Hoover's Company Profiles*, May 8, 2003.

[43]J. Samuelson, "Tough Guy Billionaire," *Forbes*, February 24, 1997, 64–66.

[44]Hart & Banbury, "How Strategy-Making Processes Can Make a Difference"; C. C. Miller & L. B. Cardinal, "Strategic Planning and Firm Performance: A Synthesis of More Than Two Decades of Research," *Academy of Management Journal* 37 (1994): 1649–1665; D. King, D. Dalton, C. Daily, & J. Covin, "Meta-Analyses of Post-Acquisition Performance: Indications of Unidentified Moderators," *Strategic Management Journal* 25 (2004): 187–200; and C. R. Schwenk, "Effects of Formal Strategic Planning on Financial Performance in Small Firms: A Meta Analysis," *Entrepreneurship Theory & Practice* (Spring 1993): 53–64.

[45]S. Bucksot, C. Jensen, & D. Tratensek, "Where Are We Headed?" *2005 Market Measure: The Industry's Annual Report*, www.nrha.org/MM2004.pdf, March 6, 2005.

[46]H. Murphy, "Menard's Tool in Retail Battle: Gigantic Stores," *Crain's Chicago Business*, August 12, 2002, 3.

[47]Ibid.

[48]D. Leonard, "Who's Afraid of Steve Jobs?" *Bloomberg Businessweek*, July 26–August 1, 2010, 58–63.

[49]M. Lubatkin, "Value-Creating Mergers: Fact or Folklore?" *Academy of Management Executive* 2 (1988): 295–302; M. Lubatkin & S. Chatterjee, "Extending Modern Portfolio Theory into the Domain of Corporate Diversification: Does It Apply?" *Academy of Management Journal* 37 (1994): 109–136; and M. H. Lubatkin & P. J. Lane, "Psst . . . The Merger Mavens Still Have It Wrong!" *Academy of Management Executive* 10 (1996): 21–39.

[50]"Who We Are," 3M, accessed April 7, 2009, from http://solutions.3m.com/wps/portal/3M/en_US/about-3M/information/about/us/.

[51]"Our Company," Johnson & Johnson, accessed April 7, 2009, from www.jnj.com/connect/about-jnj/?flash=true.

[52]A. Sharma, "Verizon Sells Phone Lines in 14 States to Frontier," *The Wall Street Journal*, May 14, 2009, B1.

[53]"About Samsung," Samsung, accessed July 29, 2008, from www.samsung.com/us/aboutsamsung/index.html.

[54]"Affiliated Companies," Samsung, April 7, 2011, from www.samsung.com/hk_en/aboutsamsung/samsunggroup/affiliatedcompanies/SAMSUNG-Group_AffiliatedCompanies.html.

[55]www.bcg.com/this_is_BCG/bcg_history/bcg_history_2005.html; and www.wikipedia.org/wiki/Boston_Consulting_Group_Matrix.

[56]D. Hambrick, I. MacMillan, & D. Day, "Strategic Attributes and Performance in the BCG Matrix—A PIMS-based Analysis of Industrial Product Businesses," *Academy of Management Journal* 25 (1982): 510–531.

[57]J. Armstrong & R. Brodie, "Effects of Portfolio Planning Methods on Decision Making: Experimental Results," *International Journal of Research in Marketing* 11 (1994): 73–84.

[58]K. Brooker, "Plugging the Leaks at P&G: A First-Year Report Card for CEO Durk Jager," *Fortune*, February 21, 2000, 44; and "R&D's Formula for Success," Procter & Gamble, accessed March 17, 2009, from www.pg.com/science/rd_formula_success.shtml.

[59]J. McCracken & E. Byron, "P&G Considers Booting Some Brands," *The Wall Street Journal*, October 29, 2009, B1.

[60]P. Sellers, "P&G: Teaching an Old Dog New Tricks," *Fortune*, May 31, 2004, 166.

[61]E. Byron, "P&G Rekindles an Old Flame: New Febreze Candles Aim to Extend Product Line; Is Growth a

Burning Issue?" *The Wall Street Journal*, June 5, 2007, B6.

[62]E. Byron, "Febreze Joins P&G's $1 Billion Club," *The Wall Street Journal*, March 9, 2011, B1.

[63]J. A. Pearce II, "Selecting among Alternative Grand Strategies," *California Management Review* (Spring 1982): 23–31.

[64]"How PepsiCo Reversed Its SoBe Water Brand," *Bloomberg Businessweek*, June 28–July 4, 2010, 15–16.

[65]"About REI," *REI*, accessed June 7, 2009, from www.rei.com/aboutrei/about_rei.html; and "Recreational Equipment, Inc.," Hoover, accessed June 7, 2009, from www.hoovers.com/company/Recreational_Equipment_Inc/hcxjji-1.html.

[66]J. A. Pearce II, "Retrenchment Remains the Foundation of Business Turnaround," *Strategic Management Journal* 15 (1994): 407–417.

[67]Michelle Conlin, "Is Optimism a Competitive Advantage," *Bloomberg Businessweek*, August 13, 2009, accessed February 1, 2011, from www.businessweek.com/magazine/content/09_34/b4144052828198.htm.

[68]M. Bustillo, "Corporate News: Sears Swings to a Profit and Secures New Credit," *The Wall Street Journal*, May 22, 2009, B3; G. McWilliams, "Corporate News: Sears, Like Consumers, Cuts Back; Jobs, Budgets Pared as Retailer Preserves Financial Strength," *The Wall Street Journal*, May 6, 2008, B5; K. Talley & D. Kardos, "Corporate News: Sears Turns in Loss as Sales Drop 5.8%; Costco's Net Rises 32% as Consumers Shop for Bulk Bargains," *The Wall Street Journal*, May 30, 2008, B3; and P. Eavis, "Sears Looks in Dire Shape," *The Wall Street Journal,* May 30, 2008, C14.

[69]"50 Top Performers," *Bloomberg Businessweek*, June 21–27 2010, 56–58.

[70]Paul Sonne, "Unilever Brings Out Is Magnum, Escalating a U.S. Ice Cream War," *The Wall Street Journal*, March 18, 2011, B5.

[71]D. Winning, "Anadarko Considers Mozambique Gas Site," *The Wall Street Journal*, November 30, 2010, accessed April 8, 2011, from http://online.wsj.com/article/SB1000142405 2748704584804575645190168232732.html.

[72]"10 Pharmaceutical Stocks and Their Patent Expiration Drugs," *Seeking Alpha*, April 7, 2008, accessed June 7, 2009, from http://www.seekingalpha.com/article/71375-10-pharmaceutical-stocks-and-their-patent-expiration-drugs.

[73]M. Ramsey & S. Moffett, "Japan Parts Shortage Hits Auto Makers—Hard-to-Find Electronic Component Made by Hitachi Causes U.S., European Production Cutbacks by GM and Peugeot," *The Wall Street Journal*, March 24, 2011, B1.

[74]Emily Fredrix & Sarah Skidmore, "Costco Nixes Coke Products Over Pricing Dispute," ABCNews.com, November 17, 2009, from http://abcnews.go.com/Business/wireStory?id=9103485; and "Update1—Costco to Resume Stocking Coca-Cola drinks," Reuters.com, December 10, 2009, from www.reuters.com/article/idUSN1020190520091210.

[75]I. Brat, "At Supervalue, Cost Cuts are in the Bag," *The Wall Street Journal*, March 23, 2011, B1.

[76]"2011 Chevrolet Volt Review," Edmunds.com, accessed September 21, 2010, from www.edmunds.com/chevrolet/volt/2011/review.html.

[77]S. Morgan, "Getting Dirty in Dutch Country," *Bloomberg Businessweek*, July 26–August 1, 2010, 69–71.

[78]R. E. Miles & C. C. Snow, *Organizational Strategy, Structure, & Process* (New York: McGraw-Hill, 1978); S. Zahra & J. A. Pearce, "Research Evidence on the Miles-Snow Typology," *Journal of Management* 16 (1990): 751–768; and W. L. James & K. J. Hatten, "Further Evidence on the Validity of the Self Typing Paragraph Approach: Miles and Snow Strategic Archetypes in Banking," *Strategic Management Journal* 16 (1995): 161–168.

[79]D. Benoit, "Losing Its Brink's Name, Broadview Feels Secure—Home-Alarm Company, Spun Off From Parent, Looks to Expand Stable Customer Base During Transition," *The Wall Street Journal*, July 22, 2009, page no. n/a.

[80]J. Scheck & S. Woo, "Lars Johnson as Goats on his Roof and a Stable of Lawyers to Prove It," *The Wall Street Journal*, September 17, 2010, A1.

[81]R. Feintzeig, "Amusement Park Is Given a Second Chance to Thrill—With or Without the Hard Rock Name, New Owners Hope to Draw Tourists to the Myrtle Beach, S.C., Attraction," *The Wall Street Journal*, March 18, 2009.

[82]Ibid.

[83]M. Chen, "Competitor Analysis and Interfirm Rivalry: Toward a Theoretical Integration," *Academy of Management Review* 21 (1996): 100–134; and J. C. Baum & H. J. Korn, "Competitive Dynamics of Interfirm Rivalry," *Academy of Management Journal* 39 (1996): 255–291.

[84]Ibid.

[85]S. Leung, "Wendy's Sees Green in Salad Offerings—More Sophistication, Ethnic Flavors Appeal to Women, Crucial to Building Market Share," *The Wall Street Journal*, April 24, 2003, B2.

[86]M. Stopa, "Wendy's New-Fashioned Growth: Buy Hardee's," *Crain's Detroit Business*, October 21, 1996.

[87]L. Lavelle, "The Chickens Come Home to Roost, and Boston Market Is Prepared to Expand," *The Record*, October 6, 1996.

[88]J. Jargon, "Subway Runs Past McDonald's Chain," *The Wall Street Journal*, March 8, 2011, accessed April 9, 2011 from http://online.wsj.com/article/SB1000142405274870338670457618643217746405 2.html; "2010 Annual Report," McDonald's, accessed April 9, 2011, from www.aboutmcdonalds.com/etc/medialib/aboutMcDonalds/investor_relations3.Par.56096.File.dat/2010.

[89]"Frequently Asked Questions," Subway Restaurants, accessed March 18, 2009, from www.subway.com/subwayroot/AboutSubway/subwayFaqs.aspx.

[90]S. Leung, "Fast-Food Firms' Big Budgets Don't Buy Consumer Loyalty," *The Wall Street Journal*, July 24, 2003, B4.

[91]B. Stone, "In Price War, E-Readers Go Below $200," *The New York Times*, June 21, 2010, accessed July 2, 2010, from www.nytimes.com/2010/06/22/technology/22reader.html?_r=2.

[92]D. Ketchen, Jr., C. Snow, & V. Street, "Improving Firm Performance by Matching Strategic Decision-Making Processes to Competitive Dynamics," *Academy of Management Executive* 18 (2004): 29–43.

[93]B. Stone, "In Price War, E-Readers Go Below $200."

[94]H. McCracken, "E-Reader Price Wars: You Out There, Sony?" *PC World*, June 23, 2010, accessed July 2, 2010, from www.pcworld.com/article/199628/ereader_price_wars_you_out_there_sony.html?tk=hp_new.

[95]B. Stone, "In Price War, E-Readers Go Below $200"; H. McCracken, "E-Reader Price Wars: You Out There, Sony?"; and S. Canaves & C. Kok, "Acer, Sony Rev E-Reader Race," *The Wall Street Journal*, May 27, 2010, accessed July 2, 2010, from http://online.wsj.com/article/SB10001424052748704269204575270251614597606.html?KEYWORDS=ereader+price+war.

[96]J. Galante & P. Burrows, "Amazon.com Kindle Sales Are Said to Exceed Estimates," *Bloomberg Businessweek*, December 23, 2010, accessed April 9, 2011, from www.businessweek.com/news/2010-12-23/amazon-com-kindle-sales-are-said-to-exceed-estimates.html.

[97]J. Milliot, "Amazon Ups Its Edge," *Publishers Weekly*, January 24, 2011, 5–6.

[98]"Kindle Users Read More Often than iPad Users," *Bookseller*, December 10, 2010, 30.

[99]G. Marcial, "How Wendy's Stayed Out of the Fire," *Businessweek*, December 9, 2002, 138.

[100]S. Matthews, "Financial: Salads Help McD Post First U.S. Sales Gain in 14 Months," *Chicago Sun-Times*, May 14, 2003, 69.

[101]Y. Kane, "Sony Price Cut Helps Its PS3 Gain Traction; Move Boosts Sales of Game Consoles in Time for Holidays," *The Wall Street Journal*, November 26, 2007, B4.

[102]D. Wakabayashi, "Hope Fades for PS3 as a Comeback Player—In Battle of the Game Consoles, Nintendo Wii and Microsoft Xbox Widen Leads over Sony's PlayStation," *The Wall Street Journal*, December 29, 2008, B1; N. Wingfield, "Microsoft Cuts Xbox to $199," *The Wall Street Journal*, September 4, 2008, B9; and N. Wingfield, "Microsoft to Cut Xbox 360 Pro Price," *The Wall Street Journal*, July 11 2008, B6.

[103]B. Strauss, "PS3 Surpasses Xbox 360 in Worldwide Sales," *Business Insider*, March 31, 2011, accessed April 9, 2011, from www.businessinsider.com/ps3-surpasses-xbox-360-in-worldwide-sales-2011-3.

[104]A. Ostrow, "Microsoft Kinect Sales Surpass 8 Million," Mashable.com, January 5, 2011, accessed April 9, 2011, from http://mashable.com/2011/01/05/kinect-sales/.

[105]Baum & Korn, "Competitive Dynamics of Interfirm Rivalry."

[106]Rich Jaroslovsky "Lost Phone Panic Breeds Gadgets to Find Them," *Bloomberg Businessweek*, September 2, 2010, accessed September 10, 2010, from www.bloomberg.com/news/2010-09-02/lost-phone-panic-breeds-gadgets-to-find-them-rich-jaroslovsky.html.

[107]B. Antoncic & R. D. Hisrich, "Intrapreneurship: Construct Refinement and Cross-Cultural Validation," *Journal of Business Venturing* 16 (2001): 495–527.

[108]M. Bustillo & C. Lawton, "Best Buy Expands Private-Label Brands," *The Wall Street Journal*, April 27, 2009, B1.

[109]G. T. Lumpkin & G. G. Dess, "Clarifying the Entrepreneurial Orientation Construct and Linking It to Performance," *Academy of Management Review* 21 (1996): 135–172.

[110]N. Venkatraman, "Strategic Orientation of Business Enterprises: The Construct, Dimensionality, and Measurement," *Management Science* 35 (1989): 942–962.

[111]J. M. Houston & R. D. Smither, "The Nature of Competitiveness: The Development and Validation of the Competitiveness Index," *Educational and Psychological Measurement* 52 (1992): 407–418.

[112]Betsy McKay. "Soft-Drink Sales Drop in Schools, Group Says," *The Wall Street Journal*, March 8, 2010, B3; and "Pepsi Says No to Soda Sales at Schools," *The Wall Street Journal*, March 17, 2010, D3.

[113]Mehul Srivastava, "India's Mobile Phone Hitmaker," *Bloomberg Businessweek*, August 12, 2010, accessed December 12, 2010, from www.businessweek.com/magazine/content/10_34/b4192036523358.htm.

[114]P. Buhler, "Managing Your Career: No Longer Your Company's Responsibility," *Supervision*, May 1997.

reel to real

© iStockphoto.com/Oner Döngel

BIZ FLIX

Field of Dreams

© GreenLight

In the classic 1989 film *Field of Dreams*, Ray Kinsella (Kevin Costner) hears a voice, while working in his Iowa cornfield, that says, "If you build it, he will come." Ray concludes that "he" is legendary "Shoeless Joe" Jackson (Ray Liotta), a 1919 Chicago White Sox player suspended for rigging the 1919 World Series. With the support of his wife Annie (Amy Madigan), Ray jeopardizes his farm by plowing under a cornfield and creating a modern baseball diamond in its place. Shoeless Joe soon arrives, followed by the rest of the suspended players. This charming fantasy film, based on W. P. Kinsella's novel *Shoeless Joe*, shows the rewards of pursuing a dream. In this clip, Ray's brother-in-law Mark (Timothy Busfield) insists that they will have to start farming on the field again if they're going to make enough money to avoid foreclosure on their property, but Ray's daughter Karin (Gaby Hoffman) suggests another idea.

What to Watch for and Ask Yourself

1. If you were Ray, what would you do in this situation? Would you be more likely to take Mark's advice or Karin's?

2. If Ray decides to do what his daughter Karin suggests with the field, could you call that an example of entrepreneurship? Intrapreneurship?

3. What are the risks Ray faces if he acts on Karin's suggestion?

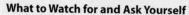

MANAGEMENT WORKPLACE

Theo Chocolate: Strategy Formulation and Execution

When Theo Chocolate first started its production, the company offered an exotic line of dark-chocolate and milk-chocolate bars and truffles. These early treats had unusual names such as the 3400 Phinney Bar, and they were wrapped in artistic watercolor packaging with whimsical cover designs. Though the chocolate was well received by critics and organic food enthusiasts, it was not popular with mainstream consumers. Founder Joe Whinney began working on a new strategy, creating classic milk chocolate bars as a gateway product that would attract consumers more easily. The end result is that Theo now offers two distinct product lines for two different market segments—a Classic line of milk-chocolate bars for mainstream customers, and Fantasy Flavors for more adventurous eaters.

© Cengage Learning

Discussion Questions

1. Evaluate Theo's new strategy in light of the company's strengths, weaknesses, opportunities, and threats.

2. Using the BCG Matrix, explain Theo's decision to offer a classic line of chocolate bars after having limited success with Fantasy Flavor chocolates.

3. Which of the three competitive strategies—differentiation, cost leadership, or focus—do you think is right for Theo Chocolate? Explain.

CHAPTER 7

Innovation
and Change

Learning Outcomes

1. Explain why innovation matters to companies.

2. Discuss the different methods that managers can use to effectively manage innovation in their organizations.

3. Discuss why not changing can lead to organizational decline.

4. Discuss the different methods that managers can use to better manage change as it occurs.

what would **you do?**

3M Headquarters, Minneapolis, MN[1]

With 40,000 global patents and patent applications, 3M, maker of Post-it notes, reflective materials (Scotch lite), and 55,000 products in numerous industries (displays and graphics, electronics and communications, health care, safety and security, transportation, manufacturing, office products, and home and leisure), has long been one of the most innovative companies in the world. 3M codified its focus on innovation into a specific goal, "30/5," which meant that 30 percent of its sales each year must come from products no more than five years old. The logic was simple but powerful. Each year, five-year-old products become six years old and would not be counted toward the 30 percent of sales. Thus, the 30/5 goal encouraged everyone at 3M to be on the lookout for and open to new ideas and products. Furthermore, 3M allowed its engineers and scientists to spend 5 percent of their time, roughly two hours per week, doing whatever they wanted as long as it was related to innovation and new product development.

And it worked, for a while. A decade ago, the Boston Consulting Group, one of the premier consulting companies in the world, ranked 3M as *the* most innovative company in the world. In subsequent years, it dropped to second, third, and then seventh. Today, 3M doesn't even crack the top 50. Dev Patnaik, of Jump Associates, an innovation consulting firm, says, "People have kind of forgotten about those guys [3M]. When was the last time you saw something innovative or experimental coming out of there?" So, what happened?

When your predecessor became CEO ten years ago, he found a struggling, inefficient, oversized company in need of change. He cut costs by laying off 8,000 people. Marketing, and research and development funds, which had been allocated to divisions independent of performance (all divisions got the same increase each year), were now distributed based on past performance and growth potential. Perform poorly, and your funds would shrink the next year. Likewise, with U.S. sales stagnating and Asia sales rising, management decreased headcount, hiring, and capital expenditures in the United States, while significantly increasing all three in fast-growing Asian markets. Six Sigma processes, popularized at Motorola and GE, were introduced to analyze how things got done, to remove unnecessary steps, and to change procedures that caused defects. Thousands of 3M

"what's new" companies

3M
Memorial Hospital
Pixar Studios
West Paw Design
Sysco
Troy Lee Designs
Summit Entertainment
Research In Motion
The Associated Press
Ryla Teleservices
Kaiser Permanente

< **"what's new" companies**

study tips

On a separate sheet, write the titles of the exhibits in this chapter. Then, with your book closed, try to reproduce the diagrams exactly as they are in the text.

Write a short description of what each diagram depicts; then open your book to check your work.

managers and employees became trained as Six Sigma "black belts" and returned to their divisions and departments to root out inefficiencies, reduce production times, and decrease waste and product errors. And it worked incredibly well, in part. Costs and capital spending dropped, while profits surged 35 percent to record levels. But, product innovation, as compared to the 30/5 goal sank dramatically, as only 21 percent of profits were generated by products that were no more than five years old.

So, what should 3M do? From inception, 3M has been an innovator, bringing a stream of new products and services to market, creating value for customers, sustainable advantage over competitors, and sizable returns for investors. Thanks to your predecessor, 3M has lower costs, is highly efficient, and much more profitable. But it no longer ranks among the most innovative firms in the world. In fact, the use of Six Sigma procedures appears to be inversely related to product innovation. If that's the case, should 3M continue to focus on using Six Sigma procedures to reduce costs and increase efficiencies, or should it strive again to encourage its scientists and managers to focus on innovation? Which will make 3M more competitive in the long run?

When people think of innovation, they tend to think of game-changing advances that render current products obsolete, for example, comparing the iPhone to text-based "smartphones." Innovation, however, also occurs with lots of incremental changes over time. What are the advantages and disadvantages for 3M of each approach, and when and where would each be more likely to work? Finally, some companies innovate from within by successfully implementing creative ideas in their products or services. Sometimes, though, innovation is acquired by purchasing other companies that have made innovative advances. For example, although Google is generally rated as one of the most innovative companies in the world, most people have forgotten that Google bought YouTube to combine its search expertise with YouTube's online video capabilities. Over time, how much should companies like 3M rely on acquisitions for innovation? Should 3M acquire half, one-third, 10 percent, or 5 percent of its new products through acquisitions? What makes the most sense and why?

If you were in charge at 3M, what would you do?

We begin this chapter by reviewing the issues associated with organizational innovation, the problem facing 3M. Organizational innovation is the successful implementation of creative ideas in an organization.[2] **Creativity**, which is a form of organizational innovation, is the production of novel and useful ideas.[3] In the first part of this chapter, you will learn why innovation matters and how to manage innovation to create and sustain a competitive advantage. In the second part, you will learn about **organizational change**, which is a difference in the form, quality, or condition of an organization over time.[4] You will also learn about the risk of not changing and the ways in which companies can manage change.

Organizational Innovation

creativity the production of novel and useful ideas.

organizational change a difference in the form, quality, or condition of an organization over time.

Sometimes the solution to a problem causes another problem. Jernhusen AB, a Swedish property-administration firm, is building a new 13-story office and retail building near Stockholm's Central Station. How should the company heat it? Problem number two: How should it get rid of excess heat in the train station, generated by the 250,000 people who pass through it every day? As Karl Sundholm, representative of

Jernhusen, puts it, "All people produce heat, and that heat is in fact fairly difficult to get rid of. Instead of opening windows and letting all that heat go to waste we want to harness it through the ventilation system."[5] The innovative solution to both problems? Convert the heat in the station to hot water and pump it through the heating system of the new building, using pipes that connect the building to the station. Sundholm estimates the system will cost about 300,000 kronor (32,000 euros; US$47,000) to install, and it is likely to reduce energy consumption by 15 percent. Per Berggren, Jernhusen's managing director, notes, "It's more like thinking out of the box, being environmentally smart."[6]

After reading the next two sections on organizational innovation, you should be able to

1. *Explain why innovation matters to companies.*
2. *Discuss the different methods that managers can use to effectively manage innovation in their organizations.*

Organizational innovation is the successful implementation of creative ideas, like using the heat generated by train terminal passengers to heat a train terminal.[7]

1 Why Innovation Matters

When was the last time you used a record player to listen to music, tuned up your car, baked cookies from scratch, or manually changed the channel on your TV? Because of product innovations and advances in technology, it's hard to remember, isn't it? In fact, since compact discs began replacing vinyl record albums almost three decades ago, many of you may *never* have played a record album. And your little brothers and sisters may never have played music from a CD! Lots of people used to tune up their own cars because it was easy, quick, and cheap. Change the points, spark plugs, and distributor cap, and your car was good for another six months or 12,000 miles. Today, with advanced technology and computerized components, tuning up a car is far too complex for most people. Hardly anybody makes cookies from scratch anymore, either. Millions of kids think that baking cookies means adding water to a powdered mix or getting premade cookie dough out of the refrigerator. As for manually changing the channels on your TV, you may have done that recently, but only because you couldn't find the remote.

We can only guess what changes technological innovations will bring in the next 20 years. Will we carry computers in our pockets? Today's iPhones, BlackBerries, and Android phones are a step in that direction. Will solar power and wind power get cheap and efficient enough so that your home has a stand-alone power source off the main electrical grid? And will HD TVs, now the standard, be replaced by lifelike HD holographic pictures (think of R2D2 projecting Princess Leia in *Star Wars*) that project lifelike 3D images?[8] Who knows? The only thing we do know about the next 20 years is that innovation will continue to change our lives. For a fuller appreciation of how technological innovation has changed our lives, see Exhibit 7.1.

Let's begin our discussion of innovation by learning about **1.1 technology cycles** and **1.2 innovation streams.**

1.1 Technology Cycles

In Chapter 3, you learned that technology consists of the knowledge, tools, and techniques used to transform inputs (raw materials and information) into outputs (products and services). A **technology cycle** begins with the birth of a new technology and

organizational innovation the successful implementation of creative ideas in organizations.

technology cycle a cycle that begins with the "birth" of a new technology and ends when that technology reaches its limits and is replaced by a newer, substantially better technology.

Exhibit 7.1 Technical Innovation Since 1900

There's no better way to understand how technology has repeatedly and deeply changed modern life than to read a decade-by-decade list of innovations since 1900. The first time through the list, simply appreciate the amount of change that has occurred. The second time through, look at each invention and ask yourself two questions: What brand-new business or industry was created by this innovation? And what old business or industry was made obsolete by this innovation?

1900–1910
- electric typewriter
- air conditioner
- airplane
- reinforced concrete skyscraper
- vacuum tube
- plastic
- chemotherapy
- electric washing machine

1911–1920
- artificial kidney
- mammography
- 35mm camera
- zipper
- sonar
- tank
- Band-Aid
- submachine gun

1921–1930
- self-winding watch
- TB vaccine
- frozen food
- commercial fax service
- talking movies
- black and white television
- penicillin
- jet engine
- supermarket

1931–1940
- defibrillator
- radar
- Kodachrome film
- helicopter
- nylon
- ballpoint pen
- first working computer
- fluorescent lighting
- color television

1941–1950
- aerosol can
- nuclear reactor
- atomic bomb
- first modern herbicide
- microwave oven
- bikini
- disposable diaper
- ENIAC computer
- mobile phone
- transistor
- credit card

1951–1960
- Salk's polio vaccine
- DNA's structure deciphered
- oral contraceptive
- solar power
- Tylenol
- *Sputnik*
- integrated circuit
- breast implants

1961–1970
- measles vaccine
- navigation satellite
- miniskirt
- video recorder
- soft contact lenses
- coronary bypass
- handheld calculator
- computer mouse
- Arpanet (prototype Internet)
- bar-code scanner
- lunar landing

1971–1980
- compact disc
- Pong (first computer game)
- word processor
- gene splicing
- Post-it note
- Ethernet (computer network)
- laser printer
- personal computer
- VHS video recording

- fiber optics
- linked ATMs
- magnetic resonance imaging

1981–1990
- MS-DOS
- space shuttle
- clone of IBM personal computer
- cell phone network
- computer virus
- camcorder
- human embryo transfer
- CD-ROM
- Windows software
- 3-D video game
- disposable contact lenses
- Doppler radar
- RU-486 (abortion pill)
- global positioning system (GPS) by satellite
- stealth bomber
- World Wide Web

1991–2000
- baboon-human liver transplant
- Taxol (cancer drug)
- mapping of the male chromosome
- Pentium processor
- Channel tunnel opens
- HIV protease inhibitor
- gene for obesity discovered
- Java (computer language)
- MP3s
- cloning of an adult mammal

2001–Today
- mapping of human genome
- first cloning of human embryo
- inexpensive global positioning tracking/mapping/guidance systems
- Abiocor artificial heart

Source: T. Gideonse, "Decade by Decade: A Rich Century of Better Mousetraps," *Newsweek Special Issue: The Power of Invention*, Winter 1997–1998, 12–15.

ends when that technology reaches its limits and dies as it is replaced by a newer, substantially better technology.[9] For example, technology cycles occurred when air-conditioners supplanted fans, when Henry Ford's Model T replaced horse-drawn carriages, when planes replaced trains as a means of cross-country travel, when vaccines that prevented diseases replaced medicines designed to treat them, and when battery-powered wristwatches replaced mechanically powered, stem-wound wristwatches.

From Gutenberg's invention of the printing press in the 1400s to the rapid advance of the Internet, studies of hundreds of technological innovations have shown that nearly all technology cycles follow the typical **S-curve pattern of innovation**, shown in Exhibit 7.2.[10] Early in a technology cycle, there is still much to learn, so progress is slow, as depicted by point A on the S-curve. The flat slope indicates that increased effort (in terms of money or research and development) brings only small improvements in technological performance.

Intel's technology cycles have followed this pattern. Intel spends billions to develop new computer chips and to build new production facilities to produce them. Intel has found that the technology cycle for its integrated circuits is about three years. In each three-year cycle, Intel introduces a new chip, improves the chip by making it a little bit faster each year, and then replaces that chip at the end of the cycle with a brand-new, different chip that is substantially faster than the old chip. At first, though, the billions Intel spends typically produce only small improvements in performance. For instance, Intel's first 60-megahertz (MHz) Pentium processors ran at a speed of 51 based on the iComp Index, as shown in Exhibit 7.3. (The iComp Index is a benchmark test for measuring relative computer speed. For example, a computer with an iComp score of 200 is twice as fast as a computer with an iComp score of 100.) Six months later, Intel's new 75-MHz Pentium was only slightly faster, with an iComp speed of 67.

Fortunately, as the new technology matures, researchers figure out how to get better performance from it. This is represented by point B of the S-curve in Exhibit 7.2. The steeper slope indicates that small amounts of effort will result in significant increases in performance. Again, Intel's technology cycles have followed this pattern. After six months to a year with a new chip design, Intel's engineering and production people typically figure out how to make the new chips much faster than they were initially. Despite slow progress at point A in the first six months, Intel soon rolled out 100-MHz, 120-MHz, 133-MHz, 150-MHz, and 166-MHz Pentium chips that, based on the iComp Index, were 76 percent, 96 percent, 117 percent, 124 percent, and 149 percent faster than the original 60-MHz speed (see Exhibit 7.3).

Exhibit 7.2
S-Curves and Technological Innovation

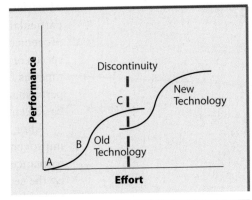

Source: R. N. Foster, *Innovation: The Attacker's Advantage* (New York: Summit, 1986).

S-curve pattern of innovation a pattern of technological innovation characterized by slow initial progress, then rapid progress, and then slow progress again as a technology matures and reaches its limits.

Exhibit 7.3 iComp Index 2.0 Comparing the Relative Performance of Different Intel Microprocessors

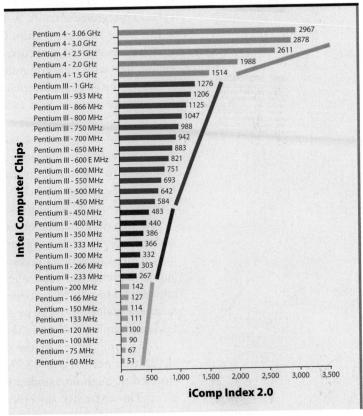

Sources: "Intel iComp (Full List)," Ideas International, available at www.ideasinternational.com, May 16, 2002; "Benchmark Resources: iComp Index 3.0," Intel, October 13, 2001, accessed May 4, 2011, from http://developer.intel.com; and "PC CPU Benchmarks, News, Process and Reviews," *CPU Scorecard*, March 17, 2003, accessed May 4, 2011, from www.cpuscorecard.com.

At point C in Exhibit 7.2, the flat slope again indicates that further efforts to develop this particular technology will result in only small increases in performance. More importantly, however, point C indicates that the performance limits of that particular technology are being reached. In other words, additional significant improvements in performance are highly unlikely. Exhibit 7.3 shows that with iComp speeds of 127 and 142, Intel's 166-MHz and 200-MHz Pentiums were 2.49 and 2.78 times as fast as its original 60-MHz Pentiums. Yet, despite these impressive gains in performance, Intel was unable to make its Pentium chips run any faster because the basic Pentium design had reached its limits.

After a technology has reached its limits at the top of the S-curve, significant improvements in performance usually come from radical new designs or new performance-enhancing materials. In Exhibit 7.2, that new technology is represented by the second S-curve. The changeover or discontinuity between the old and new technologies is represented by the dotted line. At first, the old and new technologies will likely coexist. Eventually, however, the new technology will replace the old technology. When that happens, the old technology cycle will be complete, and a new one will have started.

The changeover between Intel's Pentium processors, the old technology, and its Pentium II processors, the new technology (despite their similar names, these chips used significantly different technologies), took approximately one year. Exhibit 7.3 shows this changeover or discontinuity between the two technologies. With an iComp speed of 267, the first Pentium II (233 MHz) was 88 percent faster than the last and fastest 200-MHz Pentium processor. And because their design and performance were significantly different from (and faster than) Pentium II chips, Intel's Pentium III chips represented the beginning of yet another S-curve technology cycle in integrated circuits. A 450-MHz Pentium III chip was 21 percent faster than a 450-MHz Pentium II chip. Over time, improving existing technology (tweaking the performance of the current technology cycle), combined with replacing old technology with new technology cycles (the Pentium 4 replacing the Pentium III replacing the Pentium II replacing the Pentium), has increased the speed of Pentium computer processors by a factor of 58 in just 17 years, and all computer processors by a factor of 300! Of course, Intel has continued to improve the speed and capability of its processors. For example, today's super powerful 64-bit processors, which provide instantaneous processing and results, have 592 million transistors compared to 3.1 million transistors for 1990s 32-bit processors, 275,000 transistors for the earliest 1980s 32-bit processors, or just 4,500 transistors for the 8-bit processors, which began personal computing in the 1970s.[11]

Though the evolution of Intel's Pentium chips has been used to illustrate S-curves and technology cycles, it's important to note that technology cycles and technological innovation don't necessarily involve faster computer chips or cleaner-burning automobile engines. Remember, *technology* is simply the knowledge, tools, and techniques used to transform inputs into outputs. So a technology cycle occurs whenever there are major advances or changes in the *knowledge, tools*, and *techniques* of a field or discipline, whatever they may be.

For example, one of the most important technology cycles in the history of civilization occurred in 1859, when 1,300 miles of central sewer line were constructed throughout London to carry human waste to the sea more than 11 miles away. This extensive sewer system replaced the widespread practice of dumping raw sewage directly into streets, where people walked through it and where it drained into public wells that supplied drinking water. Though the relationship between raw sewage and cholera wasn't known at the time, preventing waste run-off from contaminating water supplies stopped the spread of that disease, which had killed millions of people for centuries in cities throughout the world.[12] Safe water supplies immediately translated into better health and longer life expectancies. Indeed, the water you drink today is safe thanks to this technological breakthrough.

Likewise, today, while most cities could benefit from commuter rail transportation systems, the cost is prohibitive relative to the benefits except in the most highly populated cities, like Boston, New York, or Washington, D.C. Even aboveground light rail systems, which are supposed to be less expensive, cost $5 million a mile because of the cost of laying electrical rail to power the system. This is why the self-powered rail cars made by US Rail Car are so innovative. Unlike typical passenger trains that are pulled by a locomotive, US Rail's single-deck (94 passengers) and double-deck (188 passengers) cars are self-propelled by two built-in diesel engines and can pull up to two other passenger cars. As a result, passenger loads are 18 percent higher, fuel costs are half of normal passenger car systems, and pollution is reduced by 72 percent. And because they are engineered to use existing rail lines, no new rail has to be laid. Furthermore, they're 75 percent less expensive than light rail because the self-propelled cars avoid the cost of electrifying each mile of track to run the system. The only cost is new stations and parking lots. Finally, initial capital outlays are small because cities don't have to buy an entire fleet of locomotives and passenger cars to start a new rail system. If initial ridership is light, simply buy one or two self-propelled cars and have them pull one or two passenger cars. As ridership slowly grows, add more self-propelled cars.[13]

So, when you think about technology cycles, don't automatically think "high technology." Instead, broaden your perspective by considering advances or changes in any kind of knowledge, tools, and techniques.

Single-level DMU Because US Rail's cars are self-propelled by two built-in diesel engines and can pull up to two other passenger cars, they don't require expensive electrical rail systems or locomotive engines.

1.2 Innovation Streams

In Chapter 6, you learned that organizations can create *competitive advantage* for themselves if they have a *distinctive competence* that allows them to make, do, or perform something better than their competitors. A competitive advantage becomes sustainable if other companies cannot duplicate the benefits obtained from that distinctive competence. Technological innovation, however, can enable competitors to duplicate the benefits obtained from a company's distinctive advantage. It can also quickly turn a company's competitive advantage into a competitive disadvantage.

For more than 110 years, Eastman Kodak was the dominant producer of photographic film worldwide. Retailers often dedicated an entire aisle to the yellow and red boxes containing Kodak film in a variety of speeds and exposures, for all types of cameras. The Kodak brand was associated with quality, availability, and value, and consumers purchased rolls of film by the billions. That is, until Kodak invented the digital camera (U.S. patent number 4,131,919). But Kodak itself was unprepared for the rapid acceptance of its new technology, and its managers watched film quickly become obsolete for the majority of camera users. Technological innovation turned Kodak's competitive advantage into a competitive disadvantage. This technology shift has had a significant impact on Kodak, which reduced its film operation to a quarter of its former size by laying off over 27,000 employees. In a further nod to its declining film sales, Kodak stopped production of its Kodachrome film line,

Exhibit 7.4 Innovation Streams: Technology Cycles over Time

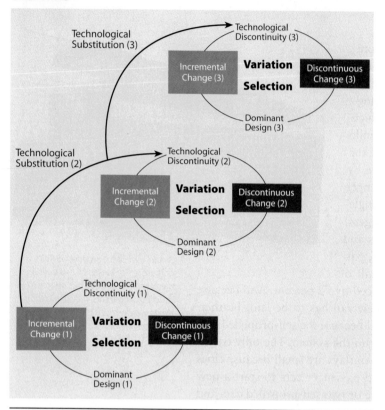

Source: Adapted from M. L. Tushman, P. C. Anderson, & C. O'Reilly, "Technology Cycles, Innovation Streams, and Ambidextrous Organizations," in *Managing Strategic Innovation and Change*, M. L. Tushman & P. Anderson, eds., (1997), 3–23. © 1997 by Oxford University Press, Inc. Used by permission of Oxford University Press, Inc.

which included film for stills and slides, as well as movies.[14] To adjust to the new marketplace, Kodak has been bolstering investments in its digital camera division; the chemicals, paper, and kiosks used for picture printing; and consumer inkjet printers (to print photographs) and fast digital inkjet printers for commercial uses.[15]

As the Kodak example shows, companies that want to sustain a competitive advantage must understand and protect themselves from the strategic threats of innovation. Over the long run, the best way for a company to do that is to create a stream of its own innovative ideas and products year after year. Consequently, we define **innovation streams** as patterns of innovation over time that can create sustainable competitive advantage.[16] Exhibit 7.4 shows a typical innovation consisting of a series of technology cycles. Recall that a technology cycle begins with a new technology and ends when that technology is replaced by a newer, substantially better technology. The innovation stream in Exhibit 7.4 shows three such technology cycles.

An innovation stream begins with a **technological discontinuity**, in which a scientific advance or a unique combination of existing technologies creates a significant breakthrough in performance or function. For example, minimally invasive techniques are revolutionizing brain surgery. When Douglas Baptist had a golf ball–sized tumor, his surgeon cut a tiny opening through his eyebrow, removed the tumor, and sewed up the opening, leaving practically no trace of the operation. Previously, his skull would have been sawed open. Dr. John Mangiardi, who did the procedure, says, "We used to have to shave off half the head. We don't do that anymore."[17] Today, surgeons use endoscopes (tiny cameras with lights attached to mini surgical tools) and MRI and CT scans (which create 3-D maps of the brain) to remove brain tumors with precision and little physical trauma. Further advances in technology are now being used to remove brain tumors via an endoscope inserted through the patient's nose. Dr. Carl Snyderman, of the University of Pittsburgh Medical Center, says, "We go into the center of a tumor and take it out in small little pieces and take these little pieces out through the nose one at a time."[18] As a result of these advances, the cost and length of hospital stays associated with these surgeries have been cut in half.

Technological discontinuities are followed by a **discontinuous change**, which is characterized by technological substitution and design competition. **Technological substitution** occurs when customers purchase new technologies to replace older technologies. It used to be that if you wanted to watch a movie at home, you would drive to a video store, hope that they had a copy of the movie you wanted, wait in line, and then take it home. Founded in 1985, and eventually growing to 3,000 locations, Blockbuster controlled a majority of the videotape rental market. However, a series of technological changes began revolutionizing the business. Compared to larger, heavier videotapes, smaller DVDs allowed Netflix, founded in 1997, to mail movies and TV shows to its online subscribers. Instead of driving to the video

innovation streams patterns of innovation over time that can create sustainable competitive advantage.

technological discontinuity the phase of an innovation stream in which a scientific advance or unique combination of existing technologies creates a significant breakthrough in performance or function.

discontinuous change the phase of a technology cycle characterized by technological substitution and design competition.

technological substitution the purchase of new technologies to replace older ones.

store, those subscribers selected what they wanted to see from Netflix's website and then received and returned their movies by mail. Today, with numerous on-demand streaming services offered by cable, phone, and Internet companies, all you have to do is just sit back on the couch, hit a few buttons on the remote control, and in seconds the movie you want is ready to watch on your TV. Not surprisingly, video-rental store sales declined rapidly. Movie Gallery, the second largest video rental chain, shut its doors for good in early 2010, while Blockbuster, the former leader, declared bankruptcy as it struggles to deal with $1 billion in debt.[19]

Discontinuous change is also characterized by **design competition**, in which the old technology and several different new technologies compete to establish a new technological standard or dominant design. Because of large investments in old technology, and because the new and old technologies are often incompatible with each other, companies and consumers are reluctant to switch to a different technology during a design competition. Indeed, the telegraph was so widely used as a means of communication in the late 1800s that at first almost no one understood why telephones would be a better way to communicate. It's hard to envision today, with everyone constantly checking cell phones for email, texts, tweets, and voice mail, but as Edwin Schlossberg explains in his book *Interactive Excellence*, "People could not imagine why they would want or need to talk immediately to someone who was across town or, even more absurdly, in another town. Although people could write letters to one another, and some could send telegraph messages, the idea of sending one's voice to another place and then instantly hearing another voice in return was simply not a model that existed in people's experience. They also did not think it was worth the money to accelerate sending or hearing a message."[20] In addition, during design competition, the older technology usually improves significantly in response to the competitive threat from the new technologies; this response also slows the changeover from older to newer technologies.

Discontinuous change is followed by the emergence of a **dominant design**, which becomes the new accepted market standard for technology.[21] Dominant designs emerge in several ways. One is critical mass, meaning that a particular technology can become the dominant design simply because most people use it. This happened in the design competition between Toshiba's HD DVD technology and Sony's Blu-ray technology for dominance in establishing a new standard format for high-definition home video. Toshiba lost the design competition because Warner Bros., which had been using both technologies, decided to go exclusively with Blu-ray. At the time of Warner's announcement, Blu-ray held 64 percent of the market, compared to 36 percent for HD DVD.[22] Retailers soon joined Warner Bros. in announcing their intentions to sell only Blu-ray equipment and videos.

The best technology doesn't always become the dominant design, because a number of other factors come into play. For instance, a design can become dominant if it solves a practical problem. The QWERTY keyboard (named for the top left line of letters) became the dominant design for typewriters because it slowed typists who, by typing too fast, caused mechanical typewriter keys to jam. Though computers can easily be switched to the DVORAK keyboard layout, which doubles typing speed and cuts typing errors in half, QWERTY lives on as the standard keyboard. In this instance, the QWERTY keyboard solved a problem that, with computers, is no longer relevant. Yet it remains the dominant design not because it is the best technology, but because most people learned to type that way and continue to use it.

Dominant designs can also emerge through independent standards bodies. The International Telecommunication Union (ITU) (www.itu.ch) is an independent organization that establishes standards for the communications industry. The ITU was founded in Paris in 1865, because European countries all had different telegraph systems that could not communicate with each other. Messages crossing borders had

design competition competition between old and new technologies to establish a new technological standard or dominant design.

dominant design a new technological design or process that becomes the accepted market standard.

to be transcribed from one country's system before they could be coded and delivered on another. After three months of negotiations, 20 countries signed the International Telegraph Convention, which standardized equipment and instructions, enabling telegraph messages to flow seamlessly from country to country. Today, as in 1865, various standards are proposed, discussed, negotiated, and changed until agreement is reached on a final set of standards that communication industries (Internet, telephony, satellites, radio) will follow worldwide. For example, because most cell phones have different charger interfaces (i.e., plugs) and electrical requirements, you've probably had to buy new chargers—one for home, one for work, and one for your car—each time you got a new cell phone. That's now a thing of the past, as the ITU has adopted a micro-USB standard (look at the connector that plugs into your digital camera) that can be used with any phone. This new standard will not only make it easy to borrow someone else's charger when you leave yours at home, it will also prevent consumers from throwing away 51,000 tons of obsolete chargers each year (that worked with their old phones, but not their new ones). The new chargers are also much more energy efficient.[23]

No matter how it happens, the emergence of a dominant design is a key event in an innovation stream. First, the emergence of a dominant design indicates that there are winners and losers. Technological innovation is both competence enhancing and competence destroying. Companies that bet on the now-dominant design usually prosper. By contrast, when companies bet on the wrong design or the old technology, they may experience **technological lockout**, which occurs when a new dominant design (i.e., a significantly better technology) prevents a company from competitively selling its products or makes it difficult to do so.[24]

For example, as mentioned above, Toshiba has stopped producing HD DVD players because a critical mass of consumers and technology adopted Blu-ray technology, which became the dominant design. Toshiba will continue to make spare parts for existing machines and may apply the technology to downloading videos online. But it will shift its business strategy to other sectors such as flash drives, which are beginning to replace hard drives in computers.[25] In fact, more companies are likely to go out of business in a time of discontinuous change and changing standards than in an economic recession or slowdown.

Second, the emergence of a dominant design signals a shift from design experimentation and competition to **incremental change**, a phase in which companies innovate by lowering the cost and improving the functioning and performance of the dominant design. For example, manufacturing efficiencies enable Intel to cut the cost of its chips by one-half to two-thirds during a technology cycle, while doubling or tripling their speed. This focus on improving the dominant design continues until the next technological discontinuity occurs.

© WIKTOR DABKOWSKI/dpa/Landov

The International Telecommunications Union helped establish a standard format for cell phone chargers.

technological lockout the inability of a company to competitively sell its products because it relied on old technology or a nondominant design.

incremental change the phase of a technology cycle in which companies innovate by lowering costs and improving the functioning and performance of the dominant technological design.

Review 1

Why Innovation Matters Technology cycles typically follow an S-curve pattern of innovation. Early in the cycle, technological progress is slow and improvements in technological performance are small. As a technology matures, however, performance improves quickly. Finally, as the limits of a technology are reached, only small improvements occur. At this point, significant improvements in performance must come from new technologies.

The best way to protect a competitive advantage is to create a stream of innovative ideas and products. Innovation streams begin with technological discontinuities that create significant breakthroughs in performance or function. Technological discontinuities are followed by discontinuous change, in which customers purchase new technologies (technological substitution) and companies compete to establish the new dominant design (design competition). Dominant designs emerge because of critical mass, because they solve a practical problem, or because of the negotiations of independent standards bodies. Because technological innovation is both competence enhancing and competence destroying, companies that bet on the wrong design often struggle (technological lockout), whereas companies that bet on the eventual dominant design usually prosper. Emergence of a dominant design leads to a focus on incremental change, lowering costs, and making small, but steady improvements in the dominant design. This focus continues until the next technological discontinuity occurs.

2 Managing Innovation

One consequence of technology cycles and innovation streams is that managers must be equally good at managing innovation in two very different circumstances. First, during discontinuous change, companies must find a way to anticipate and survive the technological changes that can suddenly transform industry leaders into losers and industry unknowns into powerhouses. Companies that can't manage innovation following technological discontinuities risk quick organizational decline and dissolution. Second, after a new dominant design emerges following discontinuous change, companies must manage the very different process of incremental improvement and innovation. Companies that can't manage incremental innovation slowly deteriorate as they fall farther behind industry leaders.

Unfortunately, what works well when managing innovation during discontinuous change doesn't work well when managing innovation during periods of incremental change (and vice versa). Consequently, to successfully manage innovation streams, companies need to be good at three things: **2.1 managing sources of innovation, 2.2 managing innovation during discontinuous change**, and **2.3 managing innovation during incremental change.**

2.1 Managing Sources of Innovation

Innovation comes from great ideas. So a starting point for managing innovation is to manage the sources of innovation, that is, where new ideas come from. One place that new ideas originate is with brilliant inventors. Do you know who invented the telephone, the light bulb, a way to collect and store electricity, air conditioning, radio, television, automobiles, the jet engine, computers, and the Internet? These innovations were created by Alexander Graham Bell, Thomas Edison, Pieter van Musschenbroek, Willis Carrier, Guglielmo Marconi, John Baird and Philo T. Farnsworth, Gottlieb Daimler and Wilhelm Maybach, Sir Frank Whittle, Charles Babbage, and Vint Cerf and Robert Kahn, respectively. These innovators and their innovations forever changed the course of modern life. But only a few companies have the likes of an Edison, Marconi, or Bell working for them. Given that great thinkers and inventors are in short supply, what might companies do to ensure a steady flow of good ideas?

Well, when we say that innovation begins with great ideas, we're really saying that innovation begins with creativity. As we defined it at the beginning of this chapter, creativity is the production of novel and useful ideas.[26] Although companies can't

Exhibit 7.5 Components of Creative Work Environments

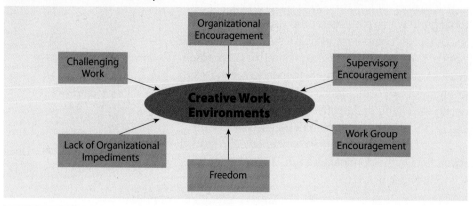

Source: T. M. Amabile, R. Conti, H. Coon, J. Lazenby, & M. Herron, "Assessing the Work Environment for Creativity," *Academy of Management Journal* 39 (1996): 1154–1184.

command employees to be creative ("You *will* be more creative!"), they can jump-start innovation by building **creative work environments**, in which workers perceive that creative thoughts and ideas are welcomed and valued. As Exhibit 7.5 shows, creative work environments have six components that encourage creativity: challenging work, organizational encouragement, supervisory encouragement, work group encouragement, freedom, and

a lack of organizational impediments.[27] Leaders at the Tata Group, a conglomerate based in India that produces everything from coffee to cars, encourage every employee to think and act like an innovator. The company allows every employee to use 10 percent of the work week for personal projects, whether it's to learn a new skill, develop an idea, or pursue a personal interest. The company also launched IdeaMax, a social-networking site on which employees can submit creative ideas and critique others' ideas. Through this support, Tata hopes to develop a creative environment by encouraging employees at all levels to share ideas to foster what it calls "a culture of creative dissatisfaction with the status quo."[28]

Work is *challenging* when it requires effort, demands attention and focus, and is perceived as important to others in the organization. According to researcher Mihaly Csikszentmihalyi (pronounced "ME-high-ee CHICK-sent-me-high-ee"), challenging work promotes creativity because it creates a rewarding psychological experience known as "flow." **Flow** is a psychological state of effortlessness, in which you become completely absorbed in what you're doing and time seems to fly. When flow occurs, who you are and what you're doing become one. Csikszentmihalyi first encountered flow when studying artists: "What struck me by looking at artists at work was their tremendous focus on the work, this enormous involvement, this forgetting of time and body. It wasn't justified by expectation of rewards, like, 'Aha, I'm going to sell this painting.'"[29] Csikszentmihalyi has found that chess players, rock climbers, dancers, surgeons, and athletes regularly experience flow, too. A key part of creating flow experiences, and thus creative work environments, is to achieve a balance between skills and task challenge. Workers become bored when they can do more than is required of them and anxious when their skills aren't sufficient to accomplish a task. When skills and task challenge are balanced, however, flow and creativity can occur.

A creative work environment requires three kinds of encouragement: organizational, supervisory, and work group encouragement. *Organizational encouragement* of creativity occurs when management encourages risk taking and new ideas, supports and fairly evaluates new ideas, rewards and recognizes creativity, and encourages the sharing of new ideas throughout different parts of the company. *Supervisory encouragement* of creativity occurs when supervisors provide clear goals, encourage open interaction with subordinates, and actively support development teams' work and ideas. *Work group encouragement* occurs when group members have diverse experience, education, and backgrounds, and the group fosters mutual openness to ideas; positive, constructive challenge to ideas; and shared commitment to ideas. For further discussion of these factors, see Chapter 10 on managing teams.

creative work environments workplace cultures in which workers perceive that new ideas are welcomed, valued, and encouraged.

flow a psychological state of effortlessness in which you become completely absorbed in what you're doing and time seems to pass quickly.

CEO Philip Newbold uses organizational and supervisory encouragement to spur creativity at **Memorial Hospital** in South Bend, Indiana. Memorial spends 1 percent of revenues each year, upwards of $700,000, to test and implement new ideas. Likewise, Newbold's "good try" rewards, such as four free weeks of housecleaning at employees' homes, are given for promising ideas that failed. Why reward failed ideas? Because employees will be more creative if they realize that they won't be punished if their ideas don't work. Finally, Newbold created the Innovation Café, a refurbished deli across the street from the hospital. The Café doesn't offer food, but serves up an inviting environment where employees work together to share and develop creative ideas.[30]

> **"what's new" companies**

Freedom means having autonomy over one's day-to-day work and a sense of ownership and control over one's ideas. Numerous studies have indicated that creative ideas thrive under conditions of freedom. At Dunkin' Donuts, members of the Culinary Innovation Team are given the freedom to explore new areas, whether it's testing 28 varieties of shortening or spending three months researching new potato products.[31] Likewise, the Tata Group established IdeaMax, an in-house social media network, that lets employees propose, comment, and vote on ideas, some 12,000 of which have been proposed within the last year.[32]

To foster creativity, companies may also have to *remove impediments* to creativity from their work environments. Internal conflict and power struggles, rigid management structures, and a conservative bias toward the status quo can all discourage creativity. They create the perception that others in the organization will decide which ideas are acceptable and deserve support. In Hollywood, "creative interference," where noncreative managers, such as marketing, accounting, or financial executives, influence key decisions about storylines or actors, is a common impediment to creativity. At **Pixar Studios** (now owned by Disney), however, creative interference is minimized because each film project is "filmmaker led." In other words, when Pixar's producers and directors made *The Incredibles*, *Finding Nemo*, and the *Toy Story* series of films, they knew that company management, rules, and procedures would not get in the way of producing great films. In fact, at Pixar, it's just the opposite. According to Ed Catmull, Pixar cofounder and president of Pixar and Disney Animation Studios, "During production, we leave the operating decisions to the film's leaders, and we don't second-guess or micromanage them. Indeed, even when a production runs into a problem, we do everything possible to provide support without undermining their authority."[33]

> **"what's new" companies**

doing the right thing

Don't Steal Ideas

Stealing ideas is never a good idea. By taking credit for other people's great work, you're disregarding the efforts that they put into thinking of and developing the next great idea that will fuel your company's success. But did you know that stealing ideas is also bad for the entire organization? When you steal ideas from others, it actually squelches the creative powers in your company. After all, if someone else is just going to take credit for all of your creative work and get all of the benefits, then what's the point? Why even bother thinking of anything innovative? So do the right thing, and don't steal others' ideas. It will help keep the creative juices flowing.[34]

Exhibit 7.6 Comparing the Experiential and Compression Approaches to Managing Innovation

	Experiential Approach to Innovation: Managing Innovation during Discontinuous Change	**Compression Approach to Innovation: Managing Innovation during Incremental Change**

Environment	Highly uncertain
	    discontinuous change—technological substitution and design competition
		Certain
		    incremental change—established technology (i.e., dominant design)

Goals	Speed Significant improvements in performance Establishment of new dominant design	Speed Lower costs Incremental improvements in performance of dominant design
Approach	Build something new, different, and substantially better	Compress time and steps needed to bring about small improvements
Steps	Design iterations Testing Milestones Multifunctional teams Powerful leaders	Planning Supplier involvement Shortening the time of individual steps Overlapping steps Multifunctional teams

© Cengage Learning 2013

2.2 Experiential Approach: Managing Innovation during Discontinuous Change

experiential approach to innovation an approach to innovation that assumes a highly uncertain environment and uses intuition, flexible options, and hands-on experience to reduce uncertainty and accelerate learning and understanding.

A study of 72 product-development projects (i.e., innovation) in 36 computer companies across the United States, Europe, and Asia sheds light on how to manage innovation. Companies that succeeded in periods of discontinuous change (characterized by technological substitution and design competition, as described earlier) typically followed an experiential approach to innovation.[35] The **experiential approach to innovation** assumes that innovation is occurring within a highly uncertain environment and that the key to fast product innovation is to use intuition, flexible options, and hands-on experience to reduce uncertainty and accelerate learning and understanding. As Exhibit 7.6 shows, the experiential approach to innovation has five aspects: design iterations, testing, milestones, multifunctional teams, and powerful leaders.[36]

An iteration is a repetition. So a **design iteration** is a cycle of repetition in which a company tests a prototype of a new product or service, improves on the design, and then builds and tests the improved product or service prototype. A **product prototype** is a full-scale working model that is being tested for design, function, and reliability. **Testing** is a systematic comparison of different product designs or design iterations. Companies that want to create a new dominant design following a technological discontinuity quickly build, test, improve, and retest a series of different product prototypes. Rickster Powell has jumped from an airplane 20,000 times in order to test parachute designs for sporting and military uses.[37] Powell explains how it works: "When . . . the chief parachute designer . . . comes up with a new design and we're going to test it for the first time [and are] not sure whether it will fly or not, I put on a skydiving rig which is composed of [an] emergency backup parachute as well as a main parachute, and then the parachute to be tested will go on the front. So that's in case there's a real problem with it, [such as] it doesn't fly, [or] it's unstable, then I can get rid of that parachute and still be in a normal skydiving situation with a main parachute and a reserve parachute."[38] He and a partner strap cameras to their bodies to film the chute's

Jupiter/Brand X

deployment, which enables the manufacturers to look for problems. Not all parachute design iterations end up working as planned. In fact, only 9 out of 50 designs he's tested have actually been produced.

By trying a number of very different designs or making successive improvements and changes in the same design, frequent design iterations reduce uncertainty and improve understanding. Simply put, the more prototypes you build, the more likely you are to learn what works and what doesn't. Also, when designers and engineers build a number of prototypes, they are less likely to fall in love with a particular prototype. Instead, they'll be more concerned with improving the product or technology as much as they can. Testing speeds up and improves the innovation process too. When two very different design prototypes are tested against each other, or the new design iteration is tested against the previous iteration, product design strengths and weaknesses quickly become apparent. Likewise, testing uncovers errors early in the design process, when they are easiest to correct. Finally, testing accelerates learning and understanding by forcing engineers and product designers to examine hard data about product performance. When there's hard evidence that prototypes are testing well, the confidence of the design team grows. Also, personal conflict between design team members is less likely when testing focuses on hard measurements and facts rather than personal hunches and preferences.

Milestones are formal project review points used to assess progress and performance. For example, a company that has put itself on a 12-month schedule to complete a project might schedule milestones at the 3-month, 6-month, and 9-month points on the schedule. At Pixar and Disney Animation Studios, there are 14 steps involved in creating a full-length animated film, from pitching story ideas, to drawing story boards, to actors recording character voices, to using "digital light" (the equivalent of stage lighting) to light each scene in the movie. When it comes time to animate each scene in the movie, Pixar's animation team is always on a short, tight schedule. As a result, the film director uses daily milestones to review progress and keep the film on budget and on schedule. Ed Catmull, president of Pixar and Disney Animation Studios, explains that at the end of each day's work, the artists performing the computerized animation will "show work in an incomplete state to the whole animation crew, and although the director makes decisions, everyone is encouraged to comment." The benefits from these reviews, what Pixar calls "dailies," are tremendous. Says Catmul, "First, once people get over the embarrassment of showing work still in progress, they become more creative. Second, the director or creative leads guiding the review process can communicate important points to the entire crew at the same time. Third, people learn from and inspire each other; a highly creative piece of animation will spark others to raise their game. Finally, there are no surprises at the end: When you're done, you're done. People's overwhelming desire to make sure their work is "good" before they show it to others increases the possibility that their finished version won't be what the director wants. The dailies process avoids such wasted efforts."[39]

By making people regularly assess what they're doing, how well they're performing, and whether they need to take corrective action, milestones provide structure to the general chaos that follows technological discontinuities. Milestones also shorten the innovation process by creating a sense of urgency that keeps everyone on task. Finally, milestones are beneficial for innovation because meeting regular milestones builds momentum by giving people a sense of accomplishment.

Multifunctional teams are work teams composed of people from different departments. Multifunctional teams accelerate learning and understanding by mixing and integrating technical, marketing, and manufacturing activities. By involving all key departments in development from the start, multifunctional teams speed innovation through early identification of new ideas or problems that would typically not have been generated or addressed until much later.

design iteration a cycle of repetition in which a company tests a prototype of a new product or service, improves on that design, and then builds and tests the improved prototype.

product prototype a full-scale working model that is being tested for design, function, and reliability.

testing the systematic comparison of different product designs or design iterations.

milestones formal project review points used to assess progress and performance.

multifunctional teams work teams composed of people from different departments.

mgmt:trends

Reverse Innovation

For most companies involved in global business, innovation flows "downward." That is, a product or service is created in a developed economy, such as the United States, and then adapted for sale in emerging economies. So, for example, Kentucky Fried Chicken first established itself as a fast-food chain in the United States and then expanded internationally. General Electric, however, has created an innovation in innovation, so to speak. In what the company calls "reverse innovation," new products are first developed in emerging economies and then adapted for and distributed to developed countries. For example, GE's researchers in India created a handheld electrocardiogram device (a machine that records heart activity), while GE teams in China came up with a portable ultrasound scanner that is slightly larger than an iPod. Both devices were developed to meet the needs of local doctors who needed affordable, light, and portable diagnostic tools that they could take to service patients in rural areas. However, both devices also help GE offer lower prices than its competitors in the United States and other developed markets. According to Vijay Govindarajan and Chris Trimble, professors at Dartmouth University, reverse innovation allows GE to expand into emerging economies and prevent competitors from selling similar products. Rethinking the direction of innovation has allowed GE to be more competitive at home and abroad.[40]

© iStockphoto.com/Kirsty Pargeter

"what's new" companies >

After the five-person research and development team at **West Paw Design**, a manufacturer of pet toys and accessories, struggled to come up with new products, production manager Seth Partain held a company-wide design contest to generate ideas. Partain had two key requirements. First, everyone in the company, from janitors to the president had to participate. Second, people would be randomly placed in teams by having their names pulled out of a fishbowl. Why randomly? Because company leaders wanted to use multifunctional teams that mixed people and ideas from all areas of the organization. The Eco Bed, which won the latest contest, was designed by a salesperson who noticed that retail stores were looking for eco-friendly products, a seamstress who suggested using material made from recycled plastic bottles, and several warehouse workers. The Eco Bed was a hit, and the company now offers it in two designs.[41]

Powerful leaders provide the vision, discipline, and motivation to keep the innovation process focused, on time, and on target. Powerful leaders are able to get resources when they are needed, are typically more experienced, have high status in the company, and are held directly responsible for the products' success or failure. On average, powerful leaders can get innovation-related projects done nine months faster than leaders with little power or influence.

One such powerful leader was Phil Martens, the former head of Ford's product development. With a year to go before introduction and Ford's hybrid Escape months behind schedule, he told the team, "We are going to deliver on time. ... Anything you need you'll get."[42] Martens said, "You could have heard a pin drop." But he followed this declaration by strongly supporting the team. Except for daily inquiries from above, he promised no interruptions or interference from anyone— even top management. When the team members needed something, they got it without waiting. When language differences created problems with the Japanese company that made the hybrid's batteries, "a Ford battery expert fluent in Japanese was dispatched to Japan within 24 hours."[43] Martens said, "I allowed them to be entrepreneurial, and they doubled their productivity." Mary Ann Wright, the launch manager charged with making sure the project stayed on schedule, said, "The same people who had been coming into my office saying, 'I don't know how we're going to get there,' were saying within weeks and months, 'My God, we can get there.'"[44]

2.3 Compression Approach: Managing Innovation during Incremental Change

Whereas the experiential approach is used to manage innovation in highly uncertain environments during periods of discontinuous change, the compression approach is used to manage innovation in more certain environments during periods of incremental change, as shown in Exhibit 7.6. Whereas the goals of the experiential approach are significant improvements in performance and the establishment of a *new* dominant design, the goals of the compression approach are lower costs and incremental improvements in the performance and function of the *existing* dominant design.

The general strategies in each approach are different too. With the experiential approach, the general strategy is to build something new, different, and substantially better. Because there's so much uncertainty—no one knows which technology will become the market leader—companies adopt a winner-take-all approach by trying to create the market-leading, dominant design. With the compression approach, the general strategy is to compress the time and steps needed to bring about small, consistent improvements in performance and functionality. Because a dominant technology design already exists, the general strategy is to continue improving the existing technology as rapidly as possible.

In short, a **compression approach to innovation** assumes that innovation is a predictable process, that incremental innovation can be planned using a series of steps, and that compressing the time it takes to complete those steps can speed up innovation. As Exhibit 7.6 shows, the compression approach to innovation has five aspects: planning, supplier involvement, shortening the time of individual steps, overlapping steps, and multifunctional teams.[45]

In Chapter 5, *planning* was defined as choosing a goal and a method or strategy to achieve that goal. When *planning for incremental innovation*, the goal is to squeeze or compress development time as much as possible, and the general strategy is to create a series of planned steps to accomplish that goal. Planning for incremental innovation helps avoid unnecessary steps and enables developers to sequence steps in the right order to avoid wasted time and delays between steps. Planning also reduces misunderstandings and improves coordination.

Most planning for incremental innovation is based on the idea of generational change. **Generational change** occurs when incremental improvements are made to a dominant technological design such that the improved version of the technology is fully backward compatible with the older version.[46] Software is backward compatible if a new version of the software will work with files created by older versions. One of the expected and important features of gaming machines like the PlayStation 3, Xbox 360, and Nintendo Wii is their ability to play games purchased for earlier machines. In fact, the latest Game Boy can play games released more than 20 years ago. Backward compatibility is an important component of ensuring the success of new technology. When developing its PlayStation 3 (PS3), Sony decided to reduce the game machine's backward compatibility with its predecessor, the PlayStation 2

compression approach to innovation an approach to innovation that assumes that incremental innovation can be planned using a series of steps and that compressing those steps can speed innovation.

generational change change based on incremental improvements to a dominant technological design such that the improved technology is fully backward compatible with the older technology.

(PS2), because of production costs. Making the PS3 units fully compatible would have required including separate high-end technology chips for PS2 games and for PS3 games, which would have significantly added to the costs of the new unit. Designers opted instead to load software into the PS3 chip that would allow the new system to play older games. But not all PS2 games worked with the software, and often when PS2 games were played on the PS3 machines, the screens would freeze or the system would lock up. Adding to that frustration, dedicated PS3 games were not rolled out as quickly as expected. As you can imagine, Sony paid the price in reduced sales and angry consumers.[47]

Because the compression approach assumes that innovation can follow a series of preplanned steps, one of the ways to shorten development time is *supplier involvement*. Delegating some of the preplanned steps in the innovation process to outside suppliers reduces the amount of work that internal development teams must do. Plus, suppliers provide an alternative source of ideas and expertise that can lead to better designs. **Sysco**, the largest foodservice distributor in North America, not only supplies restaurants and chefs with the ingredients they need but also helps them find ways to improve their business through a free consulting business called Business Review. In this program, Sysco employees help restaurateurs select and use ingredients to maximize profitability, design menus so that the most profitable items catch customers' attentions, and train waitstaff to provide excellent customer service. For example, Everett Sanderson, a Houston restaurateur, approached Sysco with a problem: his cooks were throwing away 25 percent of salmon fillets because they kept sticking to the pans. Sysco chef Neil Doherty solved Sanderson's problem by recommending that he use a vegetable/olive oil mix. Not only did the product prevent salmon from sticking, preventing huge amounts of loss, it was also cheaper than other cooking oils that Sanderson had previously used.[48] In general, the earlier suppliers are involved, the quicker they catch and prevent future problems, such as unrealistic designs or mismatched product specifications.

> **"what's new" companies** >

Another way to shorten development time is simply to *shorten the time of individual steps* in the innovation process. A common way to do that is through computer-aided design (CAD). CAD speeds up the design process by allowing designers and engineers to make and test design changes using computer models rather than physically testing expensive prototypes. CAD also speeds innovation by making it easy to see how design changes affect engineering, purchasing, and production. For example, 3-D design software reduces the time and cost involved in creating new products. In the past, when Jeff David, the product manager at **Troy Lee Designs**, wanted to create a new sports helmet, he would have to sketch out a rough concept, mold it in clay, and then ship the mold to a factory in Asia that would produce the prototype. Revisions required physical changes to the prototype, or even a new mold, which would then be sent back to Asia. This process of shipping molds and prototypes slowed development, which could take up to two years before a product was ready for market. After investing in CAD modeling software, David can create digital 3-D models of the helmet on his computer, to exact specifications. And with the click of his mouse, he can instantly send the new design specifications to his Asian factory. By using CAD software, David estimates that production time has been cut by six months, while costs have come down 35 percent.[49]

> **"what's new" companies** >

> **"what's new" companies** >

In a sequential design process, each step must be completed before the next step begins. But sometimes multiple development steps can be performed at the same time. *Overlapping steps* shorten the development process by reducing delays or waiting time between steps. **Summit Entertainment** used overlapping steps to great success in producing the *Twilight* movie franchise. Although it used the same actors and screenwriter throughout the series, by using new directors and production crews for each film, Summit was able to begin

© iStockphoto.com/Jason Lugo

mgmt:facts

What's In a Name? (A Lot!)

The success or failure of an innovative, revolutionary product isn't always a function of the product itself. Sometimes, success for new products depends on what you call it. As psychologists have found, when people encounter something unfamiliar, they try to make sense of it by connecting it to something familiar. So, when companies introduce the "next great thing," their success or failure often depends on how they connect to what people already know. For instance, in the 1890s, automobile companies helped consumers understand their revolutionary new product by calling them "horseless carriages." When digital photography was still in its infancy, Lexar Media helped consumers understand what memory cards were by calling them "digital film." So, as your company searches for the next game-changing product, you may want to use your creativity not just to create the product, but also to decide on its name.[50]

production on each film while the previous film was in post-production. This allowed the studio to release films at regular intervals in order to capitalize on the surprising success of the first film in a timely manner.[51]

Managing Innovation To successfully manage innovation streams, companies must manage the sources of innovation and learn to manage innovation during both discontinuous and incremental change. Because innovation begins with creativity, companies can manage the sources of innovation by supporting a creative work environment in which creative thoughts and ideas are encouraged. Creative work environments provide challenging work; offer organizational, supervisory, and work group encouragement; allow significant freedom; and remove organizational impediments to creativity.

Companies that succeed in periods of discontinuous change typically follow an experiential approach to innovation. The experiential approach assumes that intuition, flexible options, and hands-on experience can reduce uncertainty and accelerate learning and understanding. This approach involves frequent design iterations, frequent testing, regular milestones, creation of multifunctional teams, and use of powerful leaders to guide the innovation process. A compression approach to innovation works best during periods of incremental change. This approach assumes that innovation can be planned using a series of steps and that compressing the time it takes to complete those steps can speed up innovation. The five aspects of the compression approach are planning (generational change), supplier involvement, shortening the time of individual steps (computer-aided design), overlapping steps, and multifunctional teams.

Review 2

Organizational Change

Five years ago, sales of BlackBerry phones, made by Canadian-based **Research in Motion (RIM)**, dominated corporate and consumer markets, and were growing faster than any other cell phone maker. And while RIM still has 16 percent of the world market for smartphones, with the surging sales and growth of Apple's iPhones and

< **"what's new" companies**

© iStockphoto.com/Kirsty Pargeter

Google's Android phones, neither of which was in the market five years ago, no one, based on RIM's recent moves, expects RIM's sales and market share to do anything but continue dropping. Sales of the BlackBerry Torch, RIM's answer to the iPhone and Android phones, have been disappointing. Likewise, so have sales of BlackBerry apps on the online BlackBerry app store. Although there are nearly 370,000 apps available for the iPhone and 260,000 available for Android phones, only 26,000 apps are available for BlackBerries.[52] Also, unlike its competitors' app stores, which are simple to use, buying and installing BlackBerry apps is often cumbersome, requiring multiple download, installation, and payment steps. App developers also find writing apps for BlackBerry phones frustrating. Andrew Stein, director of mobile business development for PopCap Games, which sells popular games like *Bejeweled* and *Plants vs. Zombies*, says, "RIM today is not really on our radar."[53] While RIM has responded by courting app developers, simplifying its app website, cutting phone prices, and by giving away its enterprise server software (needed to link BlackBerry phones to corporate email servers) to small companies, company leadership might be better served to figure out why, after spending 6.8 percent of sales on research, or $1.35 billion a year, the company can't come up with competitive products.[54]

Some industry analysts are now calling RIM "Research in Slow Motion," because the company has been unable to change its business quickly enough to stop the erosion of its sales and market share. Indeed, most businesses operate in a constantly changing environment. Recognizing and adapting to internal and external changes can mean the difference between continued success and going out of business. Companies that fail to change run the risk of organizational decline. Although RIM is financially strong, the fear is that its recent inability to change may eventually lead to its demise.

After reading the next two sections on organizational change, you should be able to

3. *Discuss why not changing can lead to organizational decline.*

4. *Discuss the different methods that managers can use to better manage change as it occurs.*

3 Organizational Decline: The Risk of *Not* Changing

Businesses operate in a constantly changing environment. Recognizing and adapting to internal and external changes can mean the difference between continued success and going out of business. Companies that fail to change run the risk of organizational decline.[55] **Organizational decline** occurs when companies don't anticipate, recognize, neutralize, or adapt to the internal or external pressures that threaten their survival. In other words, decline occurs when organizations don't recognize the need for change. General Motors' loss of market share in the automobile industry (from 52% to 22%) is an example of organizational decline.[56] There are five stages of organizational decline: blinded, inaction, faulty action, crisis, and dissolution.

In the *blinded stage*, decline begins because key managers fail to recognize the internal or external changes that will harm their organizations. This blindness may be due to a simple lack of awareness about changes or an inability to understand their significance. It may also come from the overconfidence that can develop when a company has been successful. Blinded by its status as the world's largest car maker, General Motors was confident that with its enormous marketing and research and

organizational decline a large decrease in organizational performance that occurs when companies don't anticipate, recognize, neutralize, or adapt to the internal or external pressures that threaten their survival.

development budget, it could afford to offer many options for its customers. Its strategy of offering consumers 70 different car models across eight separate brands was based on the strategy chosen by its legendary chairman, Alfred P. Sloan, to offer a "car for every purse and purpose."[57] Gerald Meyers, the former CEO of American Motors Corporation (which was purchased by Chrysler), said, "Nobody else could cover the whole range of the marketplace like GM, not Ford, not Chrysler."[58] But the reasons for GM's success eventually became the reasons for its failure. According to Meyers, strategies and approaches that had once made GM innovative and progressive "became a millstone on the whole company." GM's management failed to see the trend toward smaller, more reliable, more fuel-efficient vehicles built by its Japanese-based rivals, Honda, Toyota, and Nissan, which together eventually built more than a dozen auto assembly facilities in the United States as their market share grew and GM's declined.

In the *inaction stage*, as organizational performance problems become more visible, management may recognize the need to change but still take no action. The managers may be waiting to see whether the problems will correct themselves. Or they may find it difficult to change the practices and policies that previously led to success. Possibly, too, they wrongly assume that they can easily correct the problems, so they don't feel the situation is urgent. Indeed, just ten months before declaring bankruptcy, then CEO Rick Wagoner said, "What exposes us to failure now is not our product lineup, or our business plan, or our long-term strategy," suggesting that the slowdown in the economy was the sole reason for GM's problems.[59] But even before then, GM's engineers and managers, if they had taken action, would have been well ahead of their competitors. For example, GM's engineers were designing minivans a decade before Chrysler brought the first minivan to market. Likewise, GM began work on hybrid car technology in the early 1990s, well ahead of Toyota, which has now sold over 600,000 Prius hybrid cars. However, GM never followed through. Former GM CEO Robert Stempel said, "I'm furious. GM had the [hybrid] technology. The lead was there. I know it."[60]

In the *faulty action stage*, faced with rising costs and decreasing profits and market share, management will announce belt-tightening plans designed to cut costs, increase efficiency, and restore profits. In other words, rather than recognizing the need for fundamental changes, managers assume that if they just run a tighter ship, company performance will return to previous levels. General Motors fit this pattern, too. Rather than reexamine the basic need for change, GM's management focused on cost cutting. But even that didn't take hold immediately. After losing $8.65 billion in 2005, 4 years before declaring bankruptcy, GM continued to invest billions in its small car brands, like Saturn, hoping to turn sales around. Only when GM reported a $15.5 billion loss 2 years later did it make the commitment to cut $10 billion in expenses by killing its Oldsmobile brand, closing unneeded assembly plants, and laying off workers.[61] Still, killing off other brands was, according to then CEO Wagoner, "not a thoughtful discussion."[62] Furthermore, he declared, speculations about bankruptcy "don't help anything and are completely inaccurate." Unfortunately for GM, cost-cutting moves were too little, too late, particularly with the company burning cash at the rate of a billion dollars a month.

In the *crisis stage*, bankruptcy or dissolution (breaking up the company and selling its parts) is likely to occur unless the company completely reorganizes the way it does business. At this point, however, companies typically lack the resources to fully change how they run their businesses. Cutbacks and layoffs will have reduced the level of talent among employees. Furthermore, talented managers who were savvy enough to see the crisis coming will have found jobs with other companies, often with competitors. Because of rising costs and lower sales, cash is tight, and lenders and suppliers are unlikely to extend further loans or credit to ease the cash crunch.

The cash crunch, together with an inability to raise capital, prompted General Motors to approach Congress for a bailout. GM then burned through $20 billion in government-provided funds *before* filing for bankruptcy, at which point it received another $30 billion in government funding.[63]

In the *dissolution stage*, after failing to make the changes needed to sustain the organization, the company is dissolved through bankruptcy proceedings or by selling assets in order to pay suppliers, banks, and creditors. GM's bankruptcy on June 1, 2009, was the second largest in history. Rather than a dissolution, which would have closed the company, GM's bankruptcy was a reorganization intended to lower costs and help the company become profitable again. At the time of the filing, GM had 235,000 employees (91,000 in the United States) to which it was paying $476 million a month in salaries and benefits. At this point in organizational decline, a new CEO may be brought in to oversee the closing of stores, offices, and manufacturing facilities, the final layoff of managers and employees, and the sale of assets. Indeed, CEO Rick Wagoner was replaced by a new CEO, Frederick Henderson, who, unlike Wagoner, acknowledged that bankruptcy was possible. Henderson began an aggressive cost-cutting plan to lay off nearly 30,000 factory workers and 10,000 white-collar employees and close 17 factories and parts centers.[64]

It is important to note that decline is reversible at each of the first four stages, and that not all companies in decline reach final dissolution. Two years after filing for bankruptcy and aggressively cutting costs, stabilizing market share, and using innovative production techniques, GM had its best year since 1999 in 2010 by earning $4.7 billion and awarding each of its 45,000 union workers a record $4,200 in profit sharing.[65]

Review 3

Organizational Decline: The Risk of *Not* Changing   The five-stage process of organizational decline begins when organizations don't recognize the need for change. In the blinded stage, managers fail to recognize the changes that threaten their organization's survival. In the inaction stage, management recognizes the need to change but doesn't act, hoping that the problems will correct themselves. In the faulty action stage, management focuses on cost cutting and efficiency rather than facing up to the fundamental changes needed to ensure survival. In the crisis stage, failure is likely unless fundamental reorganization occurs. Finally, in the dissolution stage, the company is dissolved through bankruptcy proceedings; by selling assets to pay creditors; or through the closing of stores, offices, and facilities. If companies recognize the need to change early enough, however, dissolution may be avoided.

4 Managing Change

According to social psychologist Kurt Lewin, change is a function of the forces that promote change and the opposing forces that slow or resist change.[66] **Change forces** lead to differences in the form, quality, or condition of an organization over time. By contrast, **resistance forces** support the status quo, that is, the existing conditions in an organization. Change is difficult under any circumstances. In a study of heart bypass patients, doctors told participants straightforwardly to change their eating and health habits or they would die. Unbelievably, a full 90 percent of participants did *not* change their habits at all![67] This fierce resistance to change also applies to organizations.

Resistance to change is caused by self-interest, misunderstanding and distrust, and a general intolerance for change.[68] People resist change out of *self-interest* because they fear that change will cost or deprive them of something they value. Resistance

change forces forces that produce differences in the form, quality, or condition of an organization over time.

resistance forces forces that support the existing state of conditions in organizations.

resistance to change opposition to change resulting from self-interest, misunderstanding and distrust, or a general intolerance for change.

might stem from a fear that the changes will result in a loss of pay, power, responsibility, or even perhaps one's job. **The Associated Press**, a news agency employing over 10,000 journalists worldwide, recently changed its policy on employees' use of social media. According to the policy, any material on an employee's Facebook site, even messages from friends, must conform to AP standards concerning decency and political neutrality. The policy states, "Monitor your [Facebook] profile page to make sure material posted by others doesn't violate AP standards: any such material should be deleted." AP reporters resisted the change in policy not only because of the potential violation of free speech rights, but also because they could be suspended or fired for what other people post on their Facebook page.[69]

< **"what's new" companies**

People also resist change because of *misunderstanding and distrust*; they don't understand the change or the reasons for it, or they distrust the people—typically management—behind the change. Resistance isn't always visible at first. In fact, some of the strongest resisters may initially support the changes in public, nodding and smiling their agreement, but then ignore the changes in private and do their jobs as they always have. Management consultant Michael Hammer calls this deadly form of resistance the "Kiss of Yes."[70]

Resistance may also come from a generally low tolerance for change. Some people are simply less capable of handling change than others. People with a *low tolerance for change* feel threatened by the uncertainty associated with change and worry that they won't be able to learn the new skills and behaviors needed to successfully negotiate change in their companies.

Because resistance to change is inevitable, successful change efforts require careful management. In this section, you will learn about **4.1 managing resistance to change**, **4.2 what not to do when leading organizational change**, and **4.3 different change tools and techniques.**

4.1 Managing Resistance to Change

According to Kurt Lewin, managing organizational change is a basic process of unfreezing, change intervention, and refreezing. **Unfreezing** is getting the people affected by change to believe that change is needed. During the **change intervention** itself, workers and managers change their behavior and work practices. **Refreezing** is supporting and reinforcing the new changes so that they stick.

Resistance to change is an example of frozen behavior. Given the choice between changing and not changing, most people would rather not change. Because resistance to change is natural and inevitable, managers need to unfreeze resistance to change to create successful change programs. The following methods can be used to manage resistance to change: education and communication, participation, negotiation, top-management support, and coercion.[71]

When resistance to change is based on insufficient, incorrect, or misleading information, managers should *educate* employees about the need for change and *communicate* change-related information to them. Managers must also supply the information and funding or other support employees need to make changes. For example, resistance to change can be particularly strong when one company buys another company. This is because one company in the merger usually has a higher status due to its size, or higher profitability, or the fact that it is the acquiring company. These status differences are important to managers and employees, particularly if they're in the lower-status company, who worry about retaining their jobs or influence after the merger. That fear or concern can greatly increase resistance to change.[72] When the leadership of AT&T's Credit Corporation bought the company from its parent corporation, AT&T, legal considerations restricted the amount

unfreezing getting the people affected by change to believe that change is needed.

change intervention the process used to get workers and managers to change their behavior and work practices.

refreezing supporting and reinforcing new changes so that they "stick."

Employees are less likely to resist change if they are allowed to discuss and agree on who will do what after change occurs.

and kind of information that could be shared. Management addressed the issue by establishing a toll-free 800 number for employees to call to review all the up-to-date information that could be shared with them. Furthermore, daily and weekly updates were also shared in company meetings, emails, and electronic bulletin boards. "As the divestiture process took longer than expected, the 800 line featured ATTCC's CEO talking about the change, explaining what he was personally experiencing and how he and his family were dealing with it."[73]

Another way to reduce resistance to change is to have those affected by the change *participate in planning and implementing the change process*. Employees who participate have a better understanding of the change and the need for it. Furthermore, employee concerns about change can be addressed as they occur if employees participate in the planning and implementation process. The San Diego Zoo and Wild Animal Park took innovative steps in order to reposition itself as a leader in conservation. A core element of the planning was input from the zoo's staff, as the strategy team invited employees from all departments to provide insights on what they felt the zoo did well and what it could do better. Through this process, the zoo enacted a plan that would highlight its internal resources and capabilities through an expansion of its consulting business, the use of facilities to display sustainable technology and products, and hosting events that would highlight the knowledge of zoo scientists.[74]

Employees are also less likely to resist change if they are allowed *to discuss and agree on who will do what* after change occurs. When DEGW, an architectural firm, was working with the Canadian Broadcasting Company to determine how to redesign its 1.5 million square foot headquarters in Toronto, it couldn't get company teams, leaders, and real estate managers to agree on what the redesigned space should look like. So, out of frustration, it created a board game called "The Sandbox," in which the goal is to create an ideal work environment within a set space. When playing the game, employees must talk about and make decisions regarding furniture and desk configurations, office privacy, noise, lounge and public spaces. A finalized design usually emerges after three two-hour game sessions. Game developer Scott Francisco says, "We needed a vehicle to pinpoint the priorities of the company. The Sandbox allowed us to address underperforming space by tapping into the knowledge and skills of staff at all levels, turning an intractable problem into a creative outcome." "It's designed to elicit interest and engagement."[75] The Sandbox works so well at generating discussions and leading to consensus that DEGW uses it worldwide with its clients.

Resistance to change also decreases when change efforts receive *significant managerial support*. Managers must do more than talk about the importance of change, though. They must provide the training, resources, and autonomy needed to make change happen. In the tele-marketing industry, the work is stressful and repetitive, and there's little career upside. Not surprisingly, 43 percent of call center workers quit their jobs each year. **Ryla Teleservices**, however, has a much lower rate of turnover, 27 percent, because of its caring environment and the training it invests

Exhibit 7.7 What to Do When Employees Resist Change

UNFREEZING	
• Share reasons	Share the reasons for change with employees.
• Empathize	Be empathetic to the difficulties that change will create for managers and employees.
• Communicate	Communicate the details simply, clearly, extensively, verbally, and in writing.
CHANGE	
• Explain benefits	Explain the benefits, "what's in it for them."
• Champion	Identify a highly respected manager to manage the change effort.
• Seek input	Allow the people who will be affected by change to express their needs and offer their input.
• Choose timing	Don't begin change at a bad time, for example, during the busiest part of the year or month.
• Maintain security	If possible, maintain employees' job security to minimize fear of change.
• Offer training	Offer training to ensure that employees are both confident and competent to handle new requirements.
• Pace yourself	Change at a manageable pace. Don't rush.

Source: G. J. Iskat & J. Liebowitz, "What to Do When Employees Resist Change," *Supervision*, August 1, 1996.

in its workers. Found Mark Wilson says, "The industry has a bad stereotype of sweatshops and high turnover. We're proving you can overcome that if you take a creative approach."[76] While Ryla's employees appreciate this approach, Wilson has learned that call center workers used to working for stricter telemarketing companies haven't always believed the company's management philosophy. For example, after a new employee training session, one of Ryla's trainers heard an employee complain about having to work the day after Thanksgiving. On learning this, Wilson was disappointed that employees didn't raise the issue directly with him. So he went to the training center and asked, "Does anybody have a problem with the holiday schedule?" When someone responded that they'd never been asked to work the day after Thanksgiving, Wilson, on the spot, gave everyone the day off. He says, "I had to prove to them that an open-door policy can make an impact."

Finally, resistance to change can be managed through **coercion**, or the use of formal power and authority to force others to change. Because of the intense negative reactions it can create (e.g., fear, stress, resentment, sabotage of company products), coercion should be used only when a crisis exists or when all other attempts to reduce resistance to change have failed. Exhibit 7.7 summarizes some additional suggestions for what managers can do when employees resist change.

4.2 What *Not* to Do When Leading Change

So far, you've learned about the basic change process (unfreezing, change, refreezing) and managing resistance to change. Harvard Business School professor John Kotter argues that knowing what *not* to do is just as important as knowing what to do when it comes to achieving successful organizational change.[77]

coercion the use of formal power and authority to force others to change.

Exhibit 7.8 Errors Managers Make When Leading Change

UNFREEZING
1. Not establishing a great enough sense of urgency.
2. Not creating a powerful enough guiding coalition.

CHANGE
3. Lacking a vision.
4. Undercommunicating the vision by a factor of 10.
5. Not removing obstacles to the new vision.
6. Not systematically planning for and creating short-term wins.

REFREEZING
7. Declaring victory too soon.
8. Not anchoring changes in the corporation's culture.

Source: J. P. Kotter, "Leading Change: Why Transformation Efforts Fail," *Harvard Business Review* 73, no. 2 (March–April 1995): 59.

Exhibit 7.8 shows the most common errors that managers make when they lead change. The first two errors occur during the unfreezing phase, when managers try to get the people affected by change to believe that change is really needed. The first and potentially most serious error is *not establishing a great enough sense of urgency*. Indeed, Kotter estimates that more than half of all change efforts fail because the people affected are not convinced that change is necessary. People will feel a greater sense of urgency if a leader in the company makes a public, candid assessment of the company's problems and weaknesses. Celestica, Inc., located in Toronto, Canada, is an electronics manufacturing services company that produces complex printed circuit assemblies, such as PC motherboards and networking cards, flat-screen TVs, and Xbox video game systems for Microsoft. When Craig Muhlhauser took over as president and CEO, Celestica, Inc., was losing money and market share. Muhlhauser went to work right away. He informed employees that the company couldn't survive if it didn't change. Within his first 30 days as CEO, he reduced staff by 35 percent, moved new people into important positions, and had everyone in the company's attention.[78]

The second mistake that occurs in the unfreezing process is *not creating a powerful enough coalition*. Change often starts with one or two people. But change has to be supported by a critical and growing group of people to build enough momentum to change an entire department, division, or company. Besides top management, Kotter recommends that key employees, managers, board members, customers, and even union leaders be members of a *core change coalition* that guides and supports organizational change. "In a turnaround, there are three kinds of employees," said Muhlhauser—those on your side, those on the fence, and those who will never buy in. The latter have to be let go and those on the fence should be persuaded to contribute or leave. Says Muhlhauser, "We have to make change, change is difficult and as we make change, it is important to realize that there are people who are going to resist that change. In talking to those people, the objective is to move everybody into the column of supporters. But that is probably unachievable."[79] It's also important to strengthen this core change coalition's resolve by periodically bringing its members together for off-site retreats.

The next four errors that managers make occur during the change phase, when a change intervention is used to try to get workers and managers to change their behavior and work practices. *Lacking a vision* for change is a significant error at this point. As you learned in Chapter 5, a *vision* (defined as a *purpose statement* in Chapter 5) is a statement of a company's purpose or reason for existing. A vision for change makes clear where a company or department is headed and why the change is occurring. Change efforts that lack vision tend to be confused, chaotic, and contradictory. By contrast, change efforts guided by visions are clear and easy to understand and can be effectively explained in five minutes or less. Procter & Gamble's beauty and grooming division accounts for one-third of P&G's global sales. But with beauty sales down 4 percent and grooming sales down 7 percent, division chief Ed Shirley has introduced a clear vision for changing the division. Said Shirley, "Our principal beauty focus has been winning with women, yet we're not broadly serving male consumers' needs outside of Gillette and fine fragrances."[80] The change, he said, "will require a cultural shift" as well as a change in the organizational structure based on gender, rather than products, "to better serve 'Him and Her.'"[81]

Undercommunicating the vision by a factor of 10 is another mistake in the change phase. According to Kotter, companies mistakenly hold just one meeting to announce the vision. Or, if the new vision receives heavy emphasis in executive speeches or company newsletters, senior management then undercuts the vision by behaving in ways contrary to it. Successful communication of the vision requires that top managers link everything the company does to the new vision and that they "walk the talk" by behaving in ways consistent with the vision. Furthermore, even companies that begin change with a clear vision sometimes make the mistake of *not removing obstacles to the new vision*. They leave formidable barriers to change in place by failing to redesign jobs, pay plans, and technology to support the new way of doing things. One of Celestica's key obstacles was efficiently and effectively managing its supply chain; it worked with 4,000 suppliers around the world. The complexity of this supply chain network and the costs of uncoordinated transportation and shipping reduced the speed with which it could meet customer orders and made it difficult to keep costs low. Muhlhauser and his management team removed this obstacle by implementing Liveshare, an information system that gave it and its suppliers real-time data on sales, production, inventory, and shipping for all of its products. For example, if Best Buy wanted to buy more units of a hot-selling video game, it used to have to contact Celestica via phone, email, or fax to see how quickly the order could be delivered. But now with Liveshare, it can see live, up-to-date numbers indicating how many of those video games are rolling off Celestica's production lines or are now on trucks in route to Best Buy trucking depots.[82]

Another error in the change phase is *not systematically planning for and creating short-term wins*. Most people don't have the discipline and patience to wait 2 years to see if the new change effort works. Change is threatening and uncomfortable, so people need to see an immediate payoff if they are to continue to support it. Kotter recommends that managers create short-term wins by actively picking people and projects that are likely to work extremely well early in the change process. Celestica's Craig Muhlhauser understood the important of short-term wins. Said Muhlhauser, "My approach was to look at the first 30 days, then at the first 3 months, then at the first 12 months and then I took a look at the 3 years. In a turnaround, you have to take hold very quickly. You have to show relatively quick hits [i.e., short-term wins]—to show your turnaround strategy is working—and then you deal with a multitude of issues in a very focused way that will allow you to continue to show improvement."[83]

The last two errors that managers make occur during the refreezing phase, when attempts are made to support and reinforce changes so that they stick. *Declaring victory too soon* is a tempting mistake in the refreezing phase. Managers typically declare victory right after the first large-scale success in the change process. Declaring success too early has the same effect as draining the gasoline out of a car: It stops change efforts dead in their tracks. With success declared, supporters of the change process stop pushing to make change happen. After all, why push when success has been achieved? Rather than declaring victory, managers should use the momentum from short-term wins to push for even bigger or faster changes. This maintains urgency and prevents change supporters from slacking off before the changes are frozen into the company's culture.

The last mistake that managers make is *not anchoring changes in the corporation's culture*. An *organization's culture* is the set of key values, beliefs, and attitudes shared by organizational members that determines the accepted way of doing things in a company. As you learned in Chapter 3, changing cultures is extremely difficult and slow. According to Kotter, two things help anchor changes in a corporation's culture. The first is directly showing people that the changes have actually improved

performance. At Celestica, this was demonstrated by the quick increase in quarterly profits, which led to a 60 percent increase in its stock price.[84] The second is to make sure that the people who get promoted fit the new culture. If they don't, it's a clear sign that the changes were only temporary. To anchor this change, Muhlhauser created a culture of meritocracy that rewarded managers and employees for their contributions. The rewards have come in the form of promotions, pay increases, and huge bonuses. Customer satisfaction has improved. With the increasing demand for consumer products, such as smartphones, employees are excited about the prospects for Celestica. "We've got some new programs in the pipeline so we're optimistic about our ability to compete in and win in that market," said Muhlhauser.[85]

4.3 Change Tools and Techniques

Imagine that your boss came to you and said, "All right, genius, you wanted it. You're in charge of turning around the division." Where would you begin? How would you encourage change-resistant managers to change? What would you do to include others in the change process? How would you get the change process off to a quick start? Finally, what approach would you use to promote long-term effectiveness and performance? Results-driven change, the General Electric workout, transition management teams, and organizational development are different change tools and techniques that can be used to address these issues.

One of the reasons that organizational change efforts fail is that they are activity-oriented rather than results-oriented. In other words, they focus primarily on changing company procedures, management philosophy, or employee behavior. Typically, there is much buildup and preparation as consultants are brought in, presentations are made, books are read, and employees and managers are trained. There's a tremendous emphasis on doing things the new way. But, with all the focus on "doing," almost no attention is paid to *results*, to seeing if all this activity has actually made a difference.

By contrast, **results-driven change** supplants the emphasis on activity with a laserlike focus on quickly measuring and improving results.[86] Top managers at Hyundai knew that if they were to compete successfully against the likes of Honda and Toyota, they would have to improve the quality of their cars substantially. So top managers guided the company's results-driven change process by, first, increasing the number of quality teams from 100 to 865. Then, all employees were required to attend seminars on quality improvement and use the results of industry quality studies, like those published annually by J. D. Power and Associates, as their benchmark. Hyundai then measured the effects of the focus on quality. Before the change, a new Hyundai averaged 23.4 initial quality problems; after the results-driven change efforts, that number dropped to 9.6.[87] Today, according to J. D. Power and Associates Hyundai ranks seventh overall out of 33 automakers in initial car quality behind Porsche, Acura, Mercedes-Benz, and Lexus, Ford, and Honda.[88] Another advantage of results-driven change is that managers introduce changes in procedures, philosophy, or behavior only if they are likely to improve measured performance. In other words, managers and workers actually test to see if changes make a difference. Consistent with this approach, Hyundai invested $30 million in a test center where cars could be subjected to a sequence of extremely harsh conditions for as long as they could withstand them, allowing engineers to pinpoint defects and fix the problems.[89]

A third advantage of results-driven change is that quick, visible improvements motivate employees to continue to make additional changes to improve measured performance. A few years into Hyundai's change process, Chrysler and Mitsubishi Motors announced they would use Hyundai-designed four-cylinder engines in

results-driven change change created quickly by focusing on the measurement and improvement of results.

280

their small and midsized cars, reinforcing the quality strides that Hyundai had made.[90] As a result of the superb quality of its cars, Hyundai's global sales actually rose 5 percent during the recession when nearly every other auto manufacturer, including Toyota and Honda, saw their sales drop 25 to 35 percent.[91] Today, less than a decade after it took steps to address the quality of its cars, Hyundai is the fifth largest auto manufacturer in the world.[92] As seen at Hyundai, the quick successes associated with results-driven change can be particularly effective at reducing resistance to change. Exhibit 7.9 describes the basic steps of results-driven change.

The **General Electric workout** is a special kind of results-driven change. The "workout" involves a 3-day meeting that brings together managers and employees from different levels and parts of an organization to quickly generate and act on solutions to specific business problems.[93] On the first morning, the boss discusses the agenda and targets specific business problems that the group will solve. Then, the boss leaves and an outside facilitator breaks the group (typically 30 to 40 people) into five or six teams and helps them spend the next day and a half discussing and debating solutions.

One day three, in what GE calls a "town meeting," the teams present specific solutions to their boss, who has been gone since day one. As each team's spokesperson makes specific suggestions, the boss has only three options: agree on the spot, say no, or ask for more information so that a decision can be made by a specific, agreed-on date. GE boss Armand Lauzon sweated his way through a town meeting. To encourage him to say yes, his workers set up the meeting room to put pressure on Lauzon. He says, "I was wringing wet within half an hour. They had 108 proposals, I had about a minute to say yes or no to each one, and I couldn't make eye contact with my boss without turning around, which would show everyone in the room that I was chicken."[94] In the end, Lauzon agreed to all but eight suggestions. Furthermore, once those decisions were made, no one at GE was allowed to overrule them.

While the GE workout clearly speeds up change, it may also fragment change if different managers approve conflicting suggestions in separate town meetings across a company. By contrast, a transition management team provides a way to coordinate change throughout an organization. A **transition management team (TMT)** is a team of eight to twelve people whose full-time job is to manage and coordinate a company's change process.[95] One member of the TMT is assigned to anticipate and manage the emotions and behaviors related to resistance to change. Despite their importance, many companies overlook the impact that negative emotions and resistant behaviors can have on the change process. TMT members report to the CEO every day, decide which change projects are approved and funded, select and evaluate the people in charge of different change projects, and make sure that different change projects complement one another.

Premier Diagnostic Health Services (PDHS), based in Vancouver, British Columbia, Canada, uses PET-CT (Positron Emission Tomography—Computed Tomography) scanning devices in the diagnostic imaging clinics it operates. PDHS currently operates several clinics in China's larger cities like Beijing, Shanghai, and Guangzhou, but estimates that there are 70 more cities of 1 million to 15 million people that will need new diagnostic imaging clinics. PDHS formed a transition team consisting of the CEO, CFO, president/CEO of its China operations, and two new managers hired

Exhibit 7.9 Results-Driven Change Programs

- Management should create measurable, short-term goals to improve performance.

- Management should use action steps only if they are likely to improve measured performance.

- Management should stress the importance of immediate improvements.

- Consultants and staffers should help managers and employees achieve quick improvements in performance.

- Managers and employees should test action steps to see if they actually yield improvements. Action steps that don't should be discarded.

- It takes few resources to get results-driven change started.

Source: R. H. Schaffer & H. A. Thomson, J.D., "Successful Change Programs Begin with Results," *Harvard Business Review on Change* (Boston: Harvard Business School Press, 1998), 189–213.

General Electric workout a three-day meeting in which managers and employees from different levels and parts of an organization quickly generate and act on solutions to specific business problems.

transition management team (TMT) a team of 8 to 12 people whose full-time job is to manage and coordinate a company's change process.

Exhibit 7.10 Primary Responsibilities of Transition Management Teams

1. Establish a context for change and provide guidance.
2. Stimulate conversation.
3. Provide appropriate resources.
4. Coordinate and align projects.
5. Ensure congruence of messages, activities, policies, and behaviors.
6. Provide opportunities for joint creation.
7. Anticipate, identify, and address people problems.
8. Prepare the critical mass.

Source: J. D. Duck, "Managing Change: The Art of Balancing," *Harvard Business Review on Change* (Boston: Harvard Business School Press, 1998), 55–81.

by the company, because it was dissatisfied with the pace of progress in China. According to a company press release, "the [Transition Management] Team is charged with accelerating the Company's rate of growth and . . . working to ensure that the required plans and resources, both human and financial, are in place. . . . The Team will focus on plans that are results-oriented."[96]

It is also important to say what a TMT is *not*. A TMT is not an extra layer of management further separating upper management from lower managers and employees. A TMT is not a steering committee that creates plans for others to carry out. Instead, the members of the TMT are fully involved with making change happen on a daily basis. Furthermore, it's not the TMT's job to determine how and why the company will change. That responsibility belongs to the CEO and upper management. Finally, a TMT is not permanent. Once the company has successfully changed, the TMT is disbanded. Exhibit 7.10 lists the primary responsibilities of TMTs.

organizational development a philosophy and collection of planned change interventions designed to improve an organization's long-term health and performance.

change agent the person formally in charge of guiding a change effort.

Organizational development is a philosophy and collection of planned change interventions designed to improve an organization's long-term health and performance. Organizational development takes a long-range approach to change; assumes that top-management support is necessary for change to succeed; creates change by educating workers and managers to change ideas, beliefs, and behaviors so that problems can be solved in new ways; and emphasizes employee participation in diagnosing, solving, and evaluating problems.[97] As shown in Exhibit 7.11, organizational development interventions begin with the recognition of a problem. Then, the company designates a **change agent** to be formally in charge of guiding the change effort. This person can be someone from the company or a professional

Exhibit 7.11 General Steps for Organizational Development Interventions

1. **Entry**	A problem is discovered and the need for change becomes apparent. A search begins for someone to deal with the problem and facilitate change.
2. **Startup**	A change agent enters the picture and works to clarify the problem and gain commitment to a change effort.
3. **Assessment & feedback**	The change agent gathers information about the problem and provides feedback about it to decision makers and those affected by it.
4. **Action planning**	The change agent works with decision makers to develop an action plan.
5. **Intervention**	The action plan, or organizational development intervention, is carried out.
6. **Evaluation**	The change agent helps decision makers assess the effectiveness of the intervention.
7. **Adoption**	Organizational members accept ownership and responsibility for the change, which is then carried out through the entire organization.
8. **Separation**	The change agent leaves the organization after first ensuring that the change intervention will continue to work.

Source: W. J. Rothwell, R. Sullivan, & G. M. McLean, *Practicing Organizational Development: A Guide for Consultants* (San Diego: Pfeiffer & Co., 1995).

consultant. The change agent clarifies the problem, gathers information, works with decision makers to create and implement an action plan, helps to evaluate the plan's effectiveness, implements the plan throughout the company, and then leaves (if from outside the company) after making sure the change intervention will continue to work.

Chris McCarthy is a change agent by another name. **Kaiser Permanente**, one of the largest health-care systems in California, calls him an "innovation specialist." His job is to figure out how to make changes in Kaiser Permanente's hospitals that bring about better service and happier employees. He does this by observing nurses, doctors, and patients, and then taking notes and photos to document who did what, who said what, and what went right or wrong. McCarthy interviews hospital staff to learn what they like about their jobs and hear their thoughts about the care their patients receive. Ultimately, his job is to sense and define problems and then propose ways to solve them. For instance, it was McCarthy's idea to start KP MedRite to reduce medication error rates, such as giving patients the wrong dose or the wrong medication. Through observation, McCarthy observed that, "One nurse trying to give one medication to one person was interrupted 17 times during a single medication pass." So after considering hundreds of ideas, the KP MedRite team recommended that nurses dispensing medications wear yellow sashes to signal they were not to be disturbed or interrupted. This change project cost $470,000 to develop and deliver in Kaiser Permanent's hospitals, but so far it has reduced the costs associated with medication errors by $965,000.[98]

Organizational development interventions are aimed at changing large systems, small groups, or people.[99] More specifically, the purpose of *large system interventions* is to change the character and performance of an organization, business unit, or department. *Small group intervention* focuses on assessing how a group functions and helping it work more effectively to accomplish its goals. *Person-focused intervention* is intended to increase interpersonal effectiveness by helping people become aware of their attitudes and behaviors and acquire new skills and knowledge. Exhibit 7.12 describes the most frequently used organizational development interventions for large systems, small groups, and people. For additional information about changing systems, groups, and people, see the "What Really Works" feature.

< *"what's new" companies*

Exhibit 7.12   Different Kinds of Organizational Development Interventions

LARGE SYSTEM INTERVENTIONS	
Sociotechnical systems	An intervention designed to improve how well employees use and adjust to the work technology used in an organization.
Survey feedback	An intervention that uses surveys to collect information from the members, reports the results of that survey to the members, and then uses those results to develop action plans for improvement.
SMALL GROUP INTERVENTIONS	
Team building	An intervention designed to increase the cohesion and cooperation of work group members.
Unit goal setting	An intervention designed to help a work group establish short- and long-term goals.
PERSON-FOCUSED INTERVENTIONS	
Counseling/coaching	An intervention designed so that a formal helper or coach listens to managers or employees and advises them on how to deal with work or interpersonal problems.
Training	An intervention designed to provide individuals with the knowledge, skills, or attitudes they need to become more effective at their jobs.

Source: W. J. Rothwell, R. Sullivan, & G. M. McLean, *Practicing Organizational Development: A Guide for Consultants* (San Diego: Pfeiffer & Co., 1995).

what really works

Change the Work Setting or Change the People? Do Both!

Let's assume that you believe that your company needs to change. Congratulations! Just recognizing the need for change puts you ahead of 80 percent of the companies in your industry. But now that you've recognized the need for change, how do you make change happen? Should you focus on changing the work setting or the behavior of the people who work in that setting? It's a classic chicken-or-egg type of question. Which would you do?

A recent meta-analysis based on 52 studies and a combined total of 29,611 study participants indicated that it's probably best to do both!

Changing the Work Setting

An organizational work setting has four parts: organizing arrangements (control and reward systems, organizational structure), social factors (people, culture, patterns of interaction), technology (how inputs are transformed into outputs), and the physical setting (the actual physical space in which people work). Overall, there is a 55 percent chance that organizational change efforts will successfully bring changes to a company's work setting. Although the odds are 55–45 in your favor, this is a much lower probability of success than you've seen with the management techniques discussed in other chapters. This simply reflects how strong resistance to change is in most companies.

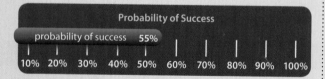

Changing the People

Changing people means changing individual work behavior. The idea is powerful. Change the decisions

people make. Change the activities they perform. Change the information they share with others. And change the initiatives they take on their own. Change these individual behaviors and collectively you change the entire company. Overall, there is a 57 percent chance that organizational change efforts will successfully change people's individual work behavior. If you're wondering why the odds aren't higher, consider how difficult it is to change personal behavior. It's incredibly difficult to quit smoking, change your diet, or maintain a daily exercise program. Not surprisingly, changing personal behavior at work is also difficult. Viewed in this context, a 57 percent chance of success is a notable achievement.

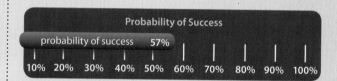

Changing Individual Behavior and Organizational Performance

The point of changing individual behavior is to improve organizational performance (increase profits, market share, and productivity, and lower costs). Overall, there is a 76 percent chance that changes in individual behavior will produce changes in organizational outcomes. So, if you want to improve your company's profits, market share, or productivity, focus on changing the way that your people behave at work.[100]

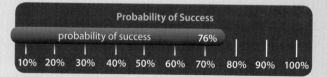

Managing Change The basic change process involves unfreezing, change, and refreezing. Resistance to change, which stems from self-interest, misunderstanding and distrust, and a general intolerance for change, can be managed through education and communication, participation, negotiation, top-management support, and coercion. Knowing what *not* to do is as important as knowing what to do to achieve successful change. Managers should avoid these errors when leading change: not establishing urgency, not creating a guiding coalition, lacking a vision, undercommunicating the vision, not removing obstacles to the vision, not creating short-term wins, declaring victory too soon, and not anchoring changes in the corporation's culture.

Finally, managers can use a number of change techniques. Results-driven change and the GE workout reduce resistance to change by getting change efforts off to a fast start. Transition management teams, which manage a company's change process, coordinate change efforts throughout an organization. Organizational development is a collection of planned change interventions (large system, small group, person-focused), guided by a change agent, that are designed to improve an organization's long-term health and performance.

Review 4

SELF-ASSESSMENT

Mind Benders

Innovation is a key to corporate success. Companies that innovate and embrace the changes in their business environment tend to outperform those that stand still. Even so, innovative companies don't simply rely on the creativity of their own workforce. They often contract with outside providers to generate new ideas for everything from operations to new products. In other words, innovative companies fill gaps in their own creativity by looking outside the organization.

As a manager, you will benefit from understanding how you are creative (not *whether* you are creative). And just as important as your own creativity is your attitude toward creative endeavors.

This assessment will provide some baseline information you can use as you develop your managerial skills.[101] Indicate the extent to which each of the following statements is true of either your actual behavior or your intentions at work. That is, describe the way you are or the way you intend to be on the job. Use this scale for your responses:

1 Almost never true
2 Seldom true
3 Not applicable
4 Often true
5 Almost always true

1. I openly discuss with my supervisor how to get ahead.

   1   2   3   4   ⑤

KEY TERMS

change agent 282
change forces 274
change intervention 275
coercion 277
compression approach to
    innovation 269
creative work
    environments 264
creativity 254
design competition 261
design iteration 266
discontinuous change 260
dominant design 261
experiential approach to
    innovation 266
flow 264
General Electric workout 281
generational change 269
incremental change 262
innovation streams 260
milestones 267

multifunctional teams 267
organizational change 254
organizational decline 272
organizational
    development 282
organizational
    innovation 255
product prototype 266
refreezing 275
resistance forces 274
resistance to change 274
results-driven change 280
S-curve pattern of
    innovation 257
technological
    discontinuity 260
technological lockout 262
technological substitution 260
technology cycle 255
testing 266
transition management team
    (TMT) 281
unfreezing 275

2. I try new ideas and approaches to problems.
1   2   3   4   (5)

3. I take things or situations apart to find out how they work.
1   2   3   4   (3)

4. I welcome uncertainty and unusual circumstances related to my tasks.
1   2   3   4   (5)

5. I negotiate my salary openly with my supervisor.
1   2   3   4   (5)

6. I can be counted on to find a new use for existing methods or equipment.
1   2   3   (4)   5

7. Among my colleagues and coworkers, I will be the first or nearly the first to try out a new idea or method.
1   2   3   (4)   5

8. I take the opportunity to translate communications from other departments for my work group.
1   2   3   4   (5)

9. I demonstrate originality.
1   2   3   (4)   5

10. I will work on a problem that has caused others great difficulty.
1   2   (3)   4   5

11. I provide critical input toward a new solution.
1   2   3   (4)   5

12. I provide written evaluations of proposed ideas.
1   2   3   (4)   (5)

13. I develop contacts with experts outside my firm.
1   2   3   (4)   5

14. I use personal contacts to maneuver into choice work assignments.
1   2   3   (4)   5

15. I make time to pursue my own pet ideas or projects.
1   2   (3)   4   5

16. I set aside resources for the pursuit of a risky project.
1   2   3   (4)   5

17. I tolerate people who depart from organizational routine.
1   2   3   (4)   5

18. I speak out in staff meetings.
1   2   3   (4)   5

19. I work in teams to try to solve complex problems.
1   2   (3)   4   5

20. If my coworkers are asked, they will say I am a wit.
1   2   (3)   4   5

TOTAL = 73

You can find an interpretation of your score at academic.cengage.com/management/Williams.

MANAGEMENT DECISION

Innovation Copycats[102]

Until a few years ago, your company, Vibram, was known for making soles for hiking boots. It's the only thing your company did for over 75 years. But one day, a member of your design team came up with a quirky idea—running shoes that look like gloves for your feet. The prototype he showed you was thin, lightweight, and kind of funny looking, since it had individual sections for each toe. As the designer explained to you, the shoe would give the wearer the feeling of running barefoot, while protecting his or her feet from dirt and cuts. Seemingly overnight, the shoe, called FiveFingers, became a sensation. It was praised by professional athletes, amateur runners, journalists, and even the Harvard Medical School. Scientists wrote about how your shoes promoted a "barefoot" running-style that produces less stress on the joints and increased leg,

ankle, and foot strength. And consumers could not get enough. Sales for the current year are expected to top $50 million, up from $11 million in the previous year. To meet demand, Vibram had to double their warehouse space and expand from one factory to five.

Not all is rosy with Vibram, however. First of all, it faces stiff competition from some of the biggest names in the athletic apparel industry, as Nike, New Balance, and others are planning to release a similar product. But even more worrisome are counterfeiters. Over the past few months, you've discovered more than 200 websites that sell fake versions of the FiveFingers shoes. And these websites aren't just selling shoes that sort of look like yours—they're almost exact copies. They have the same styles, colors, logo, and box design. They have a return label that looks just like yours, and has your company's address on it! When consumers want to return the fakes, they end up in your offices, and customers want you to refund them for shoes they bought from a counterfeiter.

Your company, of course, wants to fight back against the counterfeiters. Not only do the fake shoes reduce your sales, but they could also hurt your reputation of producing high-quality products. But fighting counterfeiters is expensive. You have to hire and send inspectors to China, where most of the factories producing copies of your shoes are located. And for every fake website you find, it costs $2,500 to get the World Intellectual Property Organization to shut it down. How should your respond to companies that take advantage of a product that your company worked so hard to design and create?

Questions

1. As a manager, would you recommend that Vibram keep paying the costs associated with fighting counterfeiters? Why or why not?
2. Some Vibram employees might be discouraged by counterfeiters, feeling that the innovations they worked hard to create are being stolen too quickly. How would you nurture the creative environment at Vibram in spite of counterfeiters?

MANAGEMENT TEAM DECISION

Face the Future[103]

Times don't seem to be much better to be in the oil business. Sure, there have been some bumps in the road the past few years—the tragic oil spill in the Gulf of Mexico and unstable prices and supply due to political situations. But there's one piece of news that makes all those obstacles easier to deal with—profits are up, and not just a little bit either. Profits are positively soaring. Exxon announced that its earnings for the most recent quarter were up 69 percent from the previous year, to $10.65 billion. Royal Dutch Shell posted an increase of 30 percent to $6.29 billion, even while experiencing a 2.5 percent decrease in production, and Occidental Petroleum's earnings jumped 46 percent to $1.55 billion.

Times certainly seem to be great, but there are many executives in your company who are pushing for big changes. Sure, they argue, revenues and earnings and profits are sky-high right now. But what about the future? Consumers and governments around the world are growing more concerned about oil—about how it impacts the environment and about whether there will be enough to meet fuel demands. In response to these concerns, there has been much research and development dedicated to alternative fuel vehicles, from all-electric cars like the Nissan Leaf, to gas-electric hybrids like the Chevy Volt or hydrogen-powered cars like the Honda FCX Clarity. And consumers have responded quite favorably. In just four short months, GM sold over 2,000 Volts and Nissan sold over 1,000 Leafs. What's even a more encouraging sign is that nearly 20,000 customers have already paid a deposit to be put on a waiting list for the Leaf, and almost 54,000 are on the Volt waiting list.

The executives pushing for change point to these figures as a sign that the auto industry will soon experience a dramatic shift. They're arguing that the age of the gasoline engine (along with gas stations and gas companies) will soon be over, replaced by a more environmentally friendly method of fueling cars. In their view, the company should act now, and quickly, to take advantage of this shift by investing in a nation-wide network of electric charging stations, where consumers recharge their all-electric or plug-in hybrid cars. That way, when gas-engine technology is eventually surpassed, your company will be in prime position to provide recharging infrastructure to the entire country.

There are others in the company, however, who doubt that this is the right step to take. Although they recognize that gas engines may not last forever, they're not convinced that it's a technology in decline. They recognize as well that sales of electric cars and hybrids are on the rise, but these are still microscopic compared to the 11.5 million conventional cars sold in the United States or the 18 million sold in China last year. They are also concerned that all-electric cars are just one choice among many alternative fuels; there are also hydrogen-powered cars, natural gas–powered cars, biofuels, and who knows what else will be developed in the future. Their great worry is that the company will spend huge amounts of time and money to develop a recharging network only to have another alternative fuel rise as the dominant design.

So what should the company do? Should it look to the future right now, even as its earnings from oil are near record highs? Or should it stay the course?

For this Management Team Decision, form a group with three or four other students and answer the questions on next page.

Questions

1. What is your recommendation for how the company should proceed? Should it take action on developing an alternative fuel network or wait until a dominant design arises?

2. What are the advantages and disadvantages of choosing a technology format before a dominant design arises?

3. What steps could the company take to help ensure that electric engines become the dominant design?

PRACTICE BEING A MANAGER

Supporting Creativity

Successfully managing innovation is challenging. Companies must find ways to support creativity and invention, while screening their investments in support of innovation. This exercise will give you an opportunity to experience a bit of the organizational dynamic regarding innovation and investment.

Step 1: Assign roles. Your professor will assign you to a pair or small group and give your team a role as either "Inventors" or "Investors." Regardless of role, assume that you work for a large clothing and accessories company that targets college students. Your company makes some traditional clothing and gear (such as backpacks and folios) but also prides itself on developing new and innovative products. And recently there has been some interest in considering new services that the company might offer to the college market, things like event or trip planning.

Step 2: Work with your partner(s) on the following tasks, depending on your assigned role. *Inventors:* Brainstorm and work to develop a new product or service concept. Be prepared to explain your concept to those inside the company who screen ideas and recommend investments.

Investors: Discuss and agree upon some criteria that your company should use to screen new-product and service concepts and to identify which ones to recommend to senior management. Be prepared to listen to one or more concept presentations, ask questions, and then use your criteria to evaluate the concept(s).

Step 3: Pair up. As instructed by your professor, Inventor and Investor groups should pair up. Inventors will now present their new concept, and investors will ask questions and then use their criteria to rate the concept.

Step 4: Change roles. As time allows, your professor will rotate Inventor and Investor pairings through a few rounds of concept presentation and investor evaluation.

Step 5: Debrief. Return to your original Inventor or Investor pair or group, and discuss your experiences in this role play. What are some of the challenges of playing this role? What was it like to interact with the "other side" of the presentation/evaluation process?

Step 6: Discuss challenges. As a class, discuss the challenges likely faced by companies as they try to successfully manage innovation. Some items for discussion might include:

1. What is the impact of an "evaluation/rating" on the creative process?

2. Do you think that "inventor units" (such as product development and R&D) and "investor units" (finance) often clash over new-product investment decisions? Why or why not?

3. What role might organizational culture (and subculture) play in the innovation and investment processes?

4. How might managers support healthy innovation and wise investment?

DEVELOP YOUR CAREER POTENTIAL

Spark Your Own Creativity

Creativity is a vital part of every organization—and not just the whiz-bang, multimillion-dollar type of creativity.[104] Even banal tasks can benefit from a new

approach: An office assistant may think creatively about how to manage the company's filing system or figure out a simple way to keep track of who is in and out of the office. A Chicago company called

Inventables has developed innovation kits—boxes containing disparate items to spark creativity—which it sells to clients like Procter & Gamble and Motorola four times a year. The idea is that designers and engineers will be inspired by tinkering with the contents of the kits.

You don't need Inventables to become inspired, however. Nor do you have to wait for your company to develop a creative work environment before you can become creative. You can spark your own creativity and think "outside the box" on your own. Eureka! Ranch, a Cincinnati-based innovation consultancy company, uses toys to help adults remember how to be imaginative, and its long client list of *Fortune 500* companies is a testament to founder Doug Hall's methods. Another company, MindWare, specializes in educational activities and toys that can help adults regain access to their imaginations. Just looking through its catalog of erector sets, science sets, puzzle books, strategy games, and tangrams may be enough to get your juices flowing.

Activities

1. Visit www.eurekaranch.com and search for the audio clip of what the company does and how it does it. Listen to the clip. What do you think of the three dimensions of creativity?

2. At the Eureka! Ranch website, find the page on Brain Brew. What is Brain Brew Radio? Is it available in your area? If it is, consider listening to it once a month to hear the creative ideas that people across the country are working on.

3. Visit www.mindwareonline.com and peruse some of the products the company sells. Which products do you find most appealing? If it's in your budget, order one of the items as a tool to help you develop and refine your creative side.

END NOTES

[1] "The 50 Most Innovative Companies 2010," *Bloomberg Businessweek*, accessed May 4, 2011, from www.businessweek.com/interactive_reports/innovative_companies_2010.html; M. Arndt & D. Brady, "3M's Rising Star," *Businessweek*, April 12, 2004, 62–74; M. Gunther, M. Adamo, & B. Feldman, "3M'S Innovation Revival," Fortune, September 27, 2010, 73–76; and B. Hindo, "3M: Struggle between Efficiency and Creativity," *Businessweek Online*, September 17, 2007, 36.

[2] T. M. Amabile, R. Conti, H. Coon, J. Lazenby, & M. Herron, "Assessing the Work Environment for Creativity," *Academy of Management Journal 39* (1996): 1154–1184.

[3] Ibid.

[4] A. H. Van de Ven & M. S. Poole, "Explaining Development and Change in Organizations," *Academy of Management Review* 20 (1995): 510–540.

[5] "Swedes to Use Body Heat to Warm Offices," ABC News, accessed September 17, 2008, from http://abcnews.go.com/International/wireStory?id=410819; E. Yerger, "Company in Sweden Uses Body Heat to Warm Office Building," *Unusual Things*, accessed September 17, 2008, from www.popfi.com/2008/01/14/company-to-use-body-heat-to-warmoffice-building-2; and D. Chazan, "Office Block Warmed by Body Heat," BBC News, accessed September 17, 2008, from http://news.bbc.co.uk/2/hi/science/nature/7233123.stm.

[6] Ibid.

[7] Amabile et al., "Assessing the Work Environment for Creativity."

[8] S. McBride, "Thinking About Tomorrow: How We Watch Movies and TV," *The Wall Street Journal*, January 28, 2008, R1.

[9] P. Anderson & M. L. Tushman, "Managing Through Cycles of Technological Change," *Research/Technology Management* (May–June 1991): 26–31.

[10] R. N. Foster, *Innovation: The Attacker's Advantage* (New York: Summit, 1986).

[11] "The Silicon Engine: A Timeline of Semiconductors in Computers," Computer History Museum, accessed April 22, 2011, from www.computerhistory.org/semiconductor/.

[12] J. Burke, *The Day the Universe Changed* (Boston: Little, Brown, 1985).

[13] A. Otis, "The Impetus for Vermont Buying Colorado Railcar DMU's," *TrainRiders/Northeast*, January 1, 2007, accessed November 11, 2009, from www.railivemont.org/passenger/the-colorado-railcar-dmu-purchase/new-dmus-the-impitus-for-their-purchase.html; and www.usrailcar.com.

[14] R. Tomsho, "Kodak to Take Kodachrome Away," *The Wall Street Journal*, June 23, 2009, B1.

[15] "Industry Snapshot," *Time*, 5 December 2005, 110; W. Symonds, "Kodak: Is This the Darkest Hour?" *Businessweek Online*, 8 August 2006, 3; W. Bulkeley, "Kodak CEO Bets Big on Printers—Perez Says Cash Is Sufficient As Camera Icon Tries to Crack Inkjet Market," *The Wall Street Journal*, 8 July 2009, B6.

[16] M. L. Tushman, P. C. Anderson, & C. O'Reilly, "Technology Cycles, Innovation Streams, and Ambidextrous Organizations: Organization Renewal Through Innovation Streams and Strategic Change," in *Managing Strategic Innovation and Change*, M. L. Tushman & P. Anderson, eds. (New York: Oxford Press, 1997), 3–23.

[17]P. Landers, "Brain Surgery Made Simple—New Less-Invasive Procedures Reduce Pain, Recovery Time; Sending in the Tiny Robots," *The Wall Street Journal*, October 31, 2002, D1.

[18]"Breakthrough Brain Surgery: Neurosurgeons Can Now Remove Brain Cancer Endoscopically," *ScienceDaily*, 1 August 2005, accessed November 8, 2009, from www.sciencedaily.com.

[19]David Lieberman, "Blockbuster Files for Chapter 11 Bankruptcy, Will Reorganize," *USA Today*, September 23, 2010, accessed May 4, 2011, from. http://www.usatoday.com/money/media/2010-09-23-blockbuster23_ST_N.htm

[20]E. Schlossberg, *Interactive Excellence: Defining and Developing New Standards for the Twenty-First Century* (New York: Ballantine, 1998).

[21]W. Abernathy & J. Utterback, "Patterns of Industrial Innovation," *Technology Review* 2 (1978): 40–47.

[22]"Blu Capabilities Still Up in the Air," *Home Media Magazine*.

[23]"Universal Phone Charger Approved," BBC News, October 23, 2009, accessed November 8, 2009, from http://news.bbc.co.uk/2/hi/8323018.stm.

[24]M. Schilling, "Technological Lockout: An Integrative Model of the Economic and Strategic Factors Driving Technology Success and Failure," *Academy of Management Review* 23 (1998): 267–284; and M. Schilling, "Technology Success and Failure in Winner-Take-All Markets: The Impact of Learning Orientation, Timing, and Network Externalities," *Academy of Management Journal* 45 (2002): 387–398.

[25]S. McBride & Y. I. Kane, "As Toshiba Surrenders: What's Next for DVDs?" *The Wall Street Journal*, February 18, 2008, accessed October 2, 2008, from http://online.wsj.com/article/SB120321618700574049.html?mod=MKTW; and Y. I. Kane, "Toshiba Regroups After Losing DVD War," *The Wall Street Journal*, February 20, 2008, accessed October 2, 2008, from http://online.wsj.com/article/SB120342115442976687.html?mod=googlenews.

[26]Amabile et al., "Assessing the Work Environment for Creativity."

[27]Ibid.

[28]J. Scanlon, "How to Build a Culture of Innovation," *Bloomberg Businessweek*, August 19, 2009, accessed August 9, 2010, from www.businessweek.com/innovate/content/aug2009/id20090819_070601.htm.

[29]M. Csikszentmihalyi, *Flow: The Psychology of Optimal Experience* (New York: Harper & Row, 1990).

[30]J. S. Lublin "A CEO's Recipe for Fresh Ideas" *The Wall Street Journal*, September 2, 2008, accessed October 15, 2009, from http://online.wsj.com/article/SB122030336412088091.html.

[31]B. Kowitt, "Dunkin' Brands' Kitchen Crew," *Fortune*, May 24, 2010, 72–74.

[32]Scanlon, "How to Build a Culture of Innovation."

[33]E. Catmull, "How Pixar Fosters Collective Creativity," *Harvard Business Review*, September 2008, 64–72.

[34]Shelley Carson, "Plagiarism and Its Effect on Creative Work," *Psychology Today*, October 16, 2010, accessed 4 May 2011 from http://www.psychologytoday.com/blog/life-art/201010/plagiarism-and-its-effect-creative-work.

[35]K. M. Eisenhardt, "Accelerating Adaptive Processes: Product Innovation in the Global Computer Industry," *Administrative Science Quarterly* 40 (1995): 84–110.

[36]Ibid.

[37]E. Masamitsu, "This Is My Job: Parachute Tester," *Popular Mechanics* 185 (June 2008): 174.

[38]L. Hansen, "A High-Flying Career: Testing Parachutes," NPR, July 6, 2008, accessed November 8, 2009, from www.npr.org/templates/story/story.php?storyId=92267958.

[39]E. Catmull, "How Pixar Fosters Collective Creativity."

[40]K. Shwiff, "GE CEO Touts 'Reverse Innovation' Model," *The Wall Street Journal*, September 23, 2009, accessed 4 May 2011 from http://online.wsj.com/article/NA_WSJ_PUB:SB125364544835231531.html.

[41]Nadine Heintz, "Managing: Unleashing Employee Creativity," *Inc.*, June 1, 2009, accessed 4 May 2011 from www.inc.com/magazine/20090601/managing-unleashing-employee-creativity.html.

[42]C. Salter, "Ford's Escape Route," *Fast Company*, October 1, 2004, 106.

[43]Ibid.

[44]Ibid.

[45]L. Kraar, "25 Who Help the U.S. Win: Innovators Everywhere Are Generating Ideas to Make America a Stronger Competitor. They Range from a Boss Who Demands the Impossible to a Mathematician with a Mop," *Fortune*, March 22, 1991.

[46]M. W. Lawless & P. C. Anderson, "Generational Technological Change: Effects of Innovation and Local Rivalry on Performance," *Academy of Management Journal* 39 (1996): 1185–1217.

[47]B. Kuchera, "Sony Confirms 40GB PS3 for Europe, Removes Backwards Compatibility," *Ars Technica*, October 5, 2007, accessed 20 August 2011 from http://arstechnica.com/gaming/news/2007/10/sony-confirms-40gb-ps3-for-europe-removes-all-backwards-compatibility.ars.

[48]C. Palmeri, "Sysco's Hands-On Way of Keeping Restaurants Going," *Bloomberg Businessweek*, May 7, 2009, accessed August 6, 2010, from www.businessweek.com/magazine/content/09_20/b4131052577089.htm?chan=magazine+channel_what's+next.

[49]Emily Maltby, "Affordable 3-D Arrives," *The Wall Street Journal*, July 29, 2010, B7.

[50]Mary Tripsas, "It's Brand New, but Make It Sound Familiar," *The New York Times*, October 3, 2009, accessed January 3, 2010,, from www.nytimes.com/2009/10/04/business/04proto.html.

[51]J. Rich, "Twilight Exclusive: Chris Weitz Will Not Direct Third Film, 'Eclipse,'" *Hollywood Insider*, February 21, 2009, accessed July 23, 2010, from http://hollywoodinsider.ew.com/2009/02/21/twilight-chris/; G. McIntyre, "On the Set: 'New Moon' on the Rise," *The Los Angeles Times*, July 19, 2009, accessed July 23, 2010, from www.latimes.com/entertainment/news/la-ca-newmoon19-2009jul19,0,3312678,full.story; N. Sperling, "It's Official: Bill Condon Will Direct Twilight's Final Chapter

'Breaking Dawn,'" *Hollywood Insider*, April 28, 2010, accessed July 23, 2010, from http://hollywoodinsider.ew.com/2010/04/28/bill-condon-will-direct-twilights-final-chapter-breaking-dawn/.

[52]"No. of Apps: Apple vs. BlackBerry vs. Windows!" Gadget Fan Site, April 4, 2011, accessed April 23, 2011, from http://gadgetfansite.com/no-of-apps-apple-vs-android-vs-blackberry-vs-windows.html.

[53]P. Dvorak, "Digital Media: RIM Tries Harder on Apps—BlackBerry Maker Hopes New Tools Lure Customers From iPhone, Other Devices," *The Wall Street Journal*, October 15, 2010, B5.

[54]S. Weinberg, "Corporate News: BlackBerry Gets Squeezed by Rivals," *The Wall Street Journal*, September 17, 2010, B3. By contrast, Apple, which leads the industry innovative products, spends just 2.7 percent of sales on research. M. Peers, "RIM: Less Research = More Motion," *The Wall Street Journal*, March 30, 2011, C16.

[55]P. Strebel, "Choosing the Right Change Path," *California Management Review* (Winter 1994): 29–51.

[56]P. Ingrassia, "How GM Lost Its Way," *The Wall Street Journal*, June 2, 2009, A21.

[57]M. Maynard, "At GM, Innovation Sacrificed to Profits," *The New York Times*, November 7, 2008, accessed January 10, 2009, from www.nytimes.com/2008/12/06/business/06motors.html?fta=y&pagewanted=all.

[58]J. Stoll, K. Helliker, & N. Boudette, "A Saga of Decline and Denial," *The Wall Street Journal*, June 2, 2009, A1.

[59]Maynard, "At GM, Innovation Sacrificed to Profits."

[60]Ibid.

[61]Stoll, Helliker, & Boudette, "A Saga of Decline and Denial."

[62]Ibid.

[63]J. McCracken, "The GM Bankruptcy: Filings Reveal Depth of Problems," *The Wall Street Journal*, June 2, 2009, A13.

[64]N. King, Jr., & S. Terlep, "GM Collapses Into Government's Arms—Second-Largest Industrial Bankruptcy in History; Obama Defends Intervention as CEO Asks Public for 'Another Chance'," *The Wall Street Journal*, June 2, 2009, A1; S. Terlep & M. Beauette, "Corporate News: GM Adds Plants in Louisiana to List of Closings," *The Wall Street Journal*, June 25, 2009, B3; and S. Terlep, "Corporate News: GM to Eliminate More Jobs as It Accelerates Downsizing," *The Wall Street Journal*, June 24, 2009, B2.

[65]S. Terlep, "GM Rebounds With Best Year Since 1999," *The Wall Street Journal*, February 25, 2011, B1.

[66]K. Lewin, *Field Theory in Social Science: Selected Theoretical Papers* (New York: Harper & Brothers, 1951).

[67]A. Deutschman, "Making Change: Why Is It So Darn Hard to Change Our Ways?" *Fast Company*, May 2005, 52–62.

[68]Lewin, *Field Theory in Social Science*.

[69]D. Kravets, "AP Issues Strict Facebook, Twitter Guidelines to Staff," *Wired.com*, June 23, 2009, accessed August 8, 2010, from www.wired.com/threatlevel/2009/06/facebookfollow/.

[70]A. B. Fisher, "Making Change Stick," *Fortune*, April 17, 1995, 121.

[71]J. P. Kotter & L. A. Schlesinger, "Choosing Strategies for Change," *Harvard Business Review* (March–April 1979): 106–114.

[72]S. Giessner, G. Viki, T. Otten, S. Terry, & D. Tauber, "The Challenge of Merging: Merger Patterns, Premerger Status, and Merger Support," *Personality and Social Psychology Bulletin* 32, no. 3 (2006): 339–352.

[73]J. Cotter, "How Employee Involvement Creates Successful Mergers," The Real Deal, May 12, 2009, accessed April 23, 2011, from http://cottertherealdeal.blogspot.com/2009/05/how-employee-involvement-creates.html.

[74]J. Scanlon, "San Diego Zoo's Newest Exhibit: Innovation," *Businessweek*, October 14, 2009, accessed 4 May 2011, from www.businessweek.com/innovate/content/oct2009/id20091014_325112.htm.

[75]H. Schwarz, "A Game Can Change the Office," TFM Facility Blog, July 16, 2008, accessed April 23, 2011, from www.todaysfacilitymanager.com/facilityblog/2008/07/a-game-can-change-the-office.html.

[76]S. Covel, "Small Business Link: Telemarketer Bucks High Turnover Trend; Communication, Promotions and Financial Perks Help Employees Stay Loyal," *The Wall Street Journal*, November 19, 2007, B6.

[77]J. P. Kotter, "Leading Change: Why Transformation Efforts Fail," *Harvard Business Review* 73 (March–April 1995): 59.

[78]G. Pitts, "A Classic Turnaround—With Some Twists," *The Globe and Mail*, July 7, 2008, B1.

[79]Ibid.

[80]E. Byron, "P&G Makes a Bigger Play for Men," *The Wall Street Journal*, April 29, 2009.

[81]Ibid.

[82]P. Engardio & J. McGregor, "Lean and Mean Gets Extreme," *Businessweek*, March 23, 2009, 60.

[83]Pitts, "A Classic Turnaround."

[84]R. Carrick, "Rising from the Stock Market Rubble," *The Globe and Mail (Canada)*, June 21, 2008, B15; and W. Dabrowski, "Celestica Buoyed by Smartphone Market Potential: Electronics Maker's CEO Optimistic about Ability to 'Compete and Win' Despite Fall in Profit, Revenue," *The Toronto Star*, April 24, 2009, B04.

[85]Ibid.

[86]S. Cramm, "A Change of Hearts," *CIO*, April 1, 2003, accessed May 20, 2003, from www.cio.com/archive/040103/hs_leadership.html.

[87]M. Ihlwan, L. Armstrong, & M. Eidam, "Hyundai: Kissing Clunkers Goodbye," *Businessweek*, May 17, 2004, 46.

[88]J.D. Power and Associates, "J.D. Power and Associates Reports: Domestic Brands Surpass Imports in Initial Quality for the First Time in IQS History," Autoblog, June 17, 2010, accessed April 23, 2011, from www.autoblog.com/2010/06/17/jd-power-2010-initial-quality-study-domestics-lead-imports/.

[89]P. Ingrassia, "Why Hyundai Is an American Hit," *The Wall Street Journal*, September 14, 2009, A13.

[90]Ibid.

[91]M. Ihlwan, L. Armstrong, & M. Eidam, "Hyundai: Kissing Clunkers Goodbye," *Businessweek*, May 17, 2004, 46.

[92]K. Choi, "Hyundai Targets 10% Growth in Auto Sales," *The Wall Street Journal Online*, January 3, 2011, no page number available.

[93]R. N. Ashkenas & T. D. Jick, "From Dialogue to Action in GE WorkOut: Developmental Learning in a Change Process," in W. A. Pasmore and R. W. Woodman (eds.), *Research in Organizational Change and Development*, vol. 6 (Greenwich, CT: JAI Press, 1992), 267–287.

[94]T. Stewart, "GE Keeps Those Ideas Coming," *Fortune*, August 12, 1991, 40.

[95]J. D. Duck, "Managing Change: The Art of Balancing," *Harvard Business Review on Change* (Boston: Harvard Business School Press, 1998), 55–81.

[96]Premier Diagnostic Health Services, "PDH Announces the Formation of a Transition Management Team," Market Wire, February 14, 2011, accessed April 23, 2011, from www.marketwire.com/press-release/PDH-Announces-the-Formation-of-a-Transition-Management-Team-CNSX-PDH-1395677.htm.

[97]W. J. Rothwell, R. Sullivan, & G. M. McLean, *Practicing Organizational Development: A Guide for Consultants* (San Diego, CA: Pfeiffer & Co., 1995).

[98]Lew McCreary, "Kaiser Permanente's Innovation on the Front Line," *Harvard Business Review* 88 (September 2010): 92, 94–97, 126.

[99]Rothwell, Sullivan, & McLean, *Practicing Organizational Development*.

[100]P. J. Robertson, D. R. Roberts, & J. I. Porras, "Dynamics of Planned Organizational Change: Assessing Empirical Support for a Theoretical Model," *Academy of Management Journal* 36 (1993): 619–634.

[101]J. E. Ettlie & R. D. O'Keefe, "Innovative Attitudes, Values, and Intentions in Organizations," *Journal of Management Studies* 19 (1982): 163–182.

[102]Jennifer Alsever, "Barefoot Shoes Try to Outrace the Black Market," CNNMoney.com., August 13, 2010, accessed http://money.cnn.com/2010/08/13/smallbusiness/vibram_fivefingers/index.htm.

[103]Nevin Batiwalla, "Nissan's Leaf Sales Spike in April," *Nashville Business Journal*, May 3, 2011, accessed May 9, 2011, from www.bizjournals.com/nashville/news/2011/05/03/nissan-leaf-sales-spike.html; "China 2010 Auto Sales Reach 18 Million, Extend Lead," *Bloomberg Businessweek*, January 10, 2011, accessed May 9, 2011, from www.bloomberg.com/news/2011-01-10/china-2010-auto-sales-reach-18-million-extend-lead-update1-.html; Craig Trudell "U.S. Auto Sales Probably Rose, Completed 2010 Rebound," *Bloomberg Businessweek*, January 3, 2011, accessed May 9, 2011, from www.bloomberg.com/news/2011-01-03/u-s-auto-sales-may-match-2010-high-complete-first-annual-gain-in-5-years.html; GM Volt Wait List Data, accessed May 9, 2011, from http://gm-volt.com/wait-list-data/; Isabel Ordonez, "Exxon, Shell Profits Soar On Higher Oil Prices," *The Wall Street Journal*, April 29, 2011, accessed May 9, 2011, from http://online.wsj.com/article/SB10001424052748704330404576291350999515650.html; and "Sales Update: Nissan Leaf Hits 573, Chevy Volt at 493 in April," Autoblog.com, May 3, 2011, accessed May 9, 2011, from www.autoblog.com/2011/05/03/sales-update-nissan-leaf-hits-573-chevy-volt-at-493-in-april/.

[104]Julie Schlosser, "Inside-the-Box Thinking," *Fortune*, November 1, 2004, 54; and www.mindwareonline.com; www.eurekaranch.com.

BIZ FLIX

Field of Dreams

In the classic 1989 film *Field of Dreams*, Ray Kinsella (Kevin Costner), while working in his Iowa cornfield, hears a voice that says, "If you build it, he will come." Ray concludes that "he" is legendary "Shoeless Joe" Jackson (Ray Liotta), a 1919 Chicago White Sox player suspended for rigging the 1919 World Series. With the support of his wife Annie (Amy Madigan), Ray jeopardizes his farm by plowing under a cornfield and creating a modern baseball diamond in its place. Shoeless Joe soon arrives, followed by the rest of the suspended players. This charming fantasy film, based on W. P. Kinsellas' novel *Shoeless Joe*, shows the rewards of pursuing a dream. In this clip, Ray's brother-in-law Mark (Timothy Busfield) insists that they will have to start farming on the field again if they're going to make enough money to avoid foreclosure on their property, but Ray's daughter Karin (Gaby Hoffman) suggests another idea.

© GreenLight

What to Watch for and Ask Yourself

1. When someone suggests an idea to you that you don't completely understand, how open are you to considering it?
2. Which character is the most resistant to the idea of changing the farm into a ball field? Why?
3. Which characters demonstrate the most creativity and vision?

MANAGEMENT WORKPLACE

Holden Outerwear: Managing Change and Innovation

Founded in 2002 by professional snowboarder Mikey LeBlanc, Holden Outerwear has given traditional baggy outerwear a complete style make-over. Unlike ski-apparel brands that focus on utility at the expense of looking good, Holden pants and jackets possess features that are inspired by runway brands like Marc Jacobs and G-Star, as Holden is always looking to bring new elements of style to the slopes. Holden has the attention of everyone in its industry. Retailers wait anxiously to see LeBlanc's newest collections, and competitors from Burton and Salomon to Bonfire and Walmart borrow heavily from Holden's collections. LeBlanc doesn't worry too much about the rampant plagiarism that goes on in his industry. As he sees it, imitation is the highest form of flattery. Plus, Holden's business is based on finding the next big thing. When it comes to style, Holden is the leader, never the follower.

© Cengage Learning

Discussion Questions

1. Identify the type of change that Holden's leaders are managing on a daily basis.
2. What resistance has Holden encountered while introducing innovative garment designs? How was it able to overcome that resistance?

CHAPTER 8

Global Management

Learning Outcomes

1. Discuss the impact of global business and the trade rules and agreements that govern it.
2. Explain why companies choose to standardize or adapt their business procedures.
3. Explain the different ways that companies can organize to do business globally.
4. Explain how to find a favorable business climate.
5. Discuss the importance of identifying and adapting to cultural differences.
6. Explain how to successfully prepare workers for international assignments.

what would you do?

Groupon Headquarters, Chicago, Illinois[1]

From 400 subscribers and 30 daily deals in 30 cities in December 2008 to 35 million subscribers and 900 daily deals in 550 markets today, **Groupon** got to $1 billion in sales faster than any other company. Starbucks CEO Howard Schultz, who was an eBay board member and is now a Groupon investor and board member, said, "Starbucks and eBay were standing still compared to what is happening with Groupon. I candidly haven't witnessed anything quite like this. They have cracked the code on a very significant opportunity." Eric Lefkofsky, who chairs Groupon's board said, "The numbers got crazy a long time ago, and they keep getting crazier." So, what is propelling Groupon's astronomical growth? How does it work?

Groupon sends a daily email to its 35 million subscribers offering a discount to a restaurant, museum, store, or service provider in their city. This "coupon" becomes a "groupon" because the company offering the discount specifies how many people (i.e., a group) must buy before the deal "tips." For example, a local restaurant may require 100 people to buy. If only 90 do, then no one gets the discount. Daily deals go viral as those who buy send the discount to others who might be interested. When the deal tips (and 95% do), the company and Groupon split the revenue.

Why would companies sign up, especially since half of the money goes to Groupon? Nearly all of Groupon's clients are local companies, which have few cost effective ways of advertising. Radio, newspapers, and online advertising all require upfront payment (whether they work or not). By contrast, local companies pay Groupon only after the daily deal attracts enough customers to be successful. Another problem with traditional ads is that they are broadcast to a wide group of people, many of whom have little interest in what's being advertised. The viral nature of Groupon's coupons, however, along with tailoring deals based on subscribers' ages, interests, and discretionary dollars, lets companies target Groupon's daily deals to customers who are more likely to buy. Groupon's CEO, Andrew Mason, said, "We think the Internet has the potential to change the way people discover and buy from local businesses.

Because there are few barriers to entry and the basic web platform is easy to copy, Groupon's

study tips

Review your class notes. Do they give you enough information? Do they give you the right information? If not, visit your campus study center to learn how to take good notes.

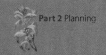

record growth and 80 percent U.S. market share has attracted start-up competitors like Living Social, Tippr, Bloomspot, Scoutmob, and BuyWithMe, along with offerings from Google, Facebook, and Walmart. Globally, Groupon's business has been copied in 50 countries. China alone has 1,000 Groupon-type businesses, including one that has copied Groupon's website down to the www.groupon.com. Likewise, Taobao, which is part of Alibaba Group Holdings, one of China's largest Internet companies, has a group buying service call "Ju Hua Suan," which translates to "Group Bargain."

So although Groupon has grown to $1 billion in sales faster than any other company, competitors threaten to take much of that business, especially in international markets, which Groupon is just starting to enter. As Groupon goes global, should it adapt its business to different cultures? For example, it relies on a large Chicago-based sales force to build and retain business with merchants, and 70 comedy writers to write ad copy. Similarly, who should make key decisions—managers at headquarters or managers in each country? In short, should Groupon run its business the same way all around the world? How should Groupon expand internationally? Should it license its web services to businesses in each area, form a strategic alliance with key foreign business partners (it rejected Google's $6 billion offer in the United States), or should it completely own and control each Groupon business throughout the world? Finally, deciding where to go global is always important, but with so many foreign markets already heavy with competitors, the question for Groupon isn't where to expand, but how to expand successfully in so many different places at the same time.

If you were in charge at Groupon, what would you do?

Groupon's challenge regarding international expansion is an example of the central issue in global business: How can you be sure that the way you run your business in one country is the right way to run that business in another? This chapter discusses how organizations answer that question. We start by examining global business in two ways: first by exploring its impact on U.S. businesses and then by reviewing the basic rules and agreements that govern global trade. Next, we examine how and when companies go global by examining the trade-off between consistency and adaptation and by discussing how to organize a global company. Finally, we look at how companies decide where to expand globally. Here, we consider how to find the best business climate, how to adapt to cultural differences, and how to prepare employees for international assignments.

What Is Global Business?

global business the buying and selling of goods and services by people from different countries.

Business is the buying and selling of goods or services. Buying this textbook was a business transaction. So was selling your first car. So was getting paid for babysitting or for mowing lawns. **Global business** is the buying and selling of goods and services by people from different countries. The Timex watch that I wore while I was writing this chapter was purchased at a Walmart in Texas. But because it was made in the Philippines, I participated in global business when I wrote Walmart a check. Walmart, for its part, had already

After reading the next section, you should be able to

1. *Discuss the impact of global business and the trade rules and agreements that govern it.*

paid Timex, which had paid the company that employs the Filipino managers and workers who made my watch. Of course, there is more to global business than buying imported products at Walmart.

1 Global Business, Trade Rules, and Trade Agreements

If you want a simple demonstration of the impact of global business, look at the tag on your shirt, the inside of your shoes, and the inside of your cell phone (take out your battery). Chances are all of these items were made in different places around the world. As I write this, my shirt, shoes, and cell phone were made in Thailand, China, and Korea. Where were yours made?

Let's learn more about **1.1 the impact of global business, 1.2 how tariff and non-tariff trade barriers have historically restricted global business, 1.3 how today global and regional trade agreements are reducing those trade barriers worldwide, and 1.4 how consumers are responding to those changes in trade rules and agreements.**

1.1 The Impact of Global Business

Thomas Friedman, author and columnist for *TheNew York Times*, observed global business in action when he visited **Infosys,** a consulting and information technology company, in India:

I guess the eureka moment came on a visit to the campus of Infosys Technologies, one of the crown jewels of the Indian outsourcing and software industry. Nandan Nilekani, the Infosys CEO, was showing me his global videoconference room, pointing with pride to a wall-size flat-screen TV, which he said was the biggest in Asia. Infosys, he explained, could hold a virtual meeting of the key players from its entire global supply chain for any project at any time on that supersize screen. So its American designers could be on the screen speaking with their Indian software writers and their Asian manufacturers all at once. That's what globalization is all about today, Nilekani said. Above the screen there were eight clocks that pretty well summed up the Infosys workday: 24/7/365. The clocks were labeled United States West, United States East, G.M.T. [Greenwich Mean Time], India, Singapore, Hong Kong, Japan, Australia.[2]

< *"what's new" companies*

Infosys does global business by selling products and services worldwide with managers and employees from different continents working together as seamlessly as if they were next door to each other. But Infosys isn't unique. There are thousands of other multinational companies just like it.

Multinational corporations are corporations that own businesses in two or more countries. In 1970, more than half of the world's 7,000 multinational corporations were headquartered in just two countries: the United States and the United Kingdom. Today, there are 82,000 multinational corporations, more than 11 times as many as in 1970, and only 2,418, or 2.9 percent, are based in the United States.[3] Today, 58,783 multinationals, or 71.6 percent, are based in other developed countries (e.g., Germany, Italy, Canada, and Japan), whereas 21,425, or 26.1 percent, are based in developing countries (e.g., Colombia, South Africa, and other developing countries). So, today multinational companies can be found by the thousands all over the world!

multinational corporation a corporation that owns businesses in two or more countries.

Exhibit 8.1 Direct Foreign Investment in the United States

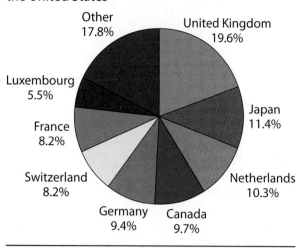

Source: M. Ibarra-Caton, "Direct Investment Positions for 2009: Country and Industry Detail," Bureau of Economic Analysis, July 2010, accessed May 7, 2010, from www.bea.gov/scb/pdf/2010/07%20July/0710_dip.pdf.

"what's new" >
companies

direct foreign investment a method of investment in which a company builds a new business or buys an existing business in a foreign country.

trade barriers government-imposed regulations that increase the cost and restrict the number of imported goods.

protectionism a government's use of trade barriers to shield domestic companies and their workers from foreign competition.

Exhibit 8.2 U.S. Direct Foreign Investment Abroad

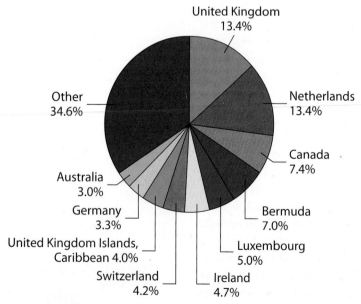

Source: M. Ibarra-Caton, "Direct Investment Positions for 2009: Country and Industry Detail," Bureau of Economic Analysis, July 2010, accessed May 7, 2010, from www.bea.gov/scb/pdf/2010/07%20July/0710_dip.pdf.

Another way to appreciate the impact of global business is by considering direct foreign investment. **Direct foreign investment** occurs when a company builds a new business or buys an existing business in a foreign country. **Nokia-Siemens Networks**, operated jointly by Finland-based Nokia and Germany-based Siemens, made a direct foreign investment in the United States when it paid $1.2 billion to buy Motorola's network equipment business, to add new customers in Japan and North America.[4] Of course, companies from many other countries also own businesses in the United States. As Exhibit 8.1 shows, companies from the United Kingdom, Japan, the Netherlands, Canada, Germany, Switzerland, France, and Luxembourg have the largest direct foreign investment in the United States. Overall, foreign companies invest more than $2.3 trillion a year to do business in the United States.

But direct foreign investment in the United States is only half the picture. U.S. companies also have made large direct foreign investments in countries throughout the world. For example, Hershey Co., a Pennsylvania-based candy company, purchased Barry Callebaut AG's Van Houten consumer chocolate business in Asia, allowing Hershey, which gets most of its growth from North America, to expand internationally.[5] As Exhibit 8.2 shows, U.S. companies have made their largest direct foreign investments in the United Kingdom, the Netherlands, and Canada. Overall, U.S. companies invest more than $3.5 trillion a year to do business in other countries.

So, whether foreign companies invest in the United States or U.S. companies invest abroad, direct foreign investment is an increasingly important and common method of conducting global business.

1.2 Trade Barriers

Although today's consumers usually don't care where the products they buy come from (more on this in Section 1.4), national governments have traditionally preferred that consumers buy domestically made products in hopes that such purchases would increase the number of domestic businesses and workers. Indeed, governments have done much more than hope that you will buy from domestic companies. Historically, governments have actively used **trade barriers** to make it much more expensive or difficult (or sometimes impossible) for consumers to buy or consume imported goods. For example, the Chinese government adds a 105 percent tariff to the price of chickens imported from the United States. The U.S. government, in turn, imposes a 35 percent tariff on tires imported from China.[6] By establishing these restrictions and taxes, the Chinese and U.S. governments are engaging in **protectionism**, which is the use of trade barriers to protect local companies and their workers from foreign competition.

Governments have used two general kinds of trade barriers: tariff and nontariff barriers. A **tariff** is a direct tax on imported goods. Tariffs increase the cost of imported goods relative to that of domestic goods. For example, the U.S. import tax on trucks is 25 percent. This means that U.S. buyers must pay $25,000 for a $20,000 imported truck, with the $5,000 tariff going to the U.S. government. As a result, fewer than 10,000 pickup trucks are imported by the United States each year.[7] **Nontariff barriers** are nontax methods of increasing the cost or reducing the volume of imported goods. There are five types of nontariff barriers: quotas, voluntary export restraints, government import standards, government subsidies, and customs valuation/classification. Because there are so many different kinds of nontariff barriers, they can be an even more potent method of shielding domestic industries from foreign competition.

Quotas are specific limits on the number or volume of imported products. For example, China only allows 20 foreign films to be released in Chinese movie theaters each year.[8] Like quotas, **voluntary export restraints** limit the amount of a product that can be imported annually. The difference is that the exporting country rather than the importing country imposes restraints. Usually, however, the "voluntary" offer to limit exports occurs because the importing country has implicitly threatened to impose quotas. For example, to protect South African textile manufacturers from cheap and plentiful Chinese textile products, the South African government convinced China to "voluntarily" restrict the textiles it exports to South Africa each year.[9] According to the World Trade Organization (see the discussion in Section 1.3), however, voluntary export restraints are illegal and should not be used to restrict imports.[10]

© ImagineChina via AP Images

In theory, **government import standards** are established to protect the health and safety of citizens. In reality, such standards are often used to restrict or ban imported goods. For example, Taiwan restricts both the age and type of beef that can be imported from the United States. According to Taiwanese government and health officials, this is to prevent the spread of mad cow disease among Taiwanese cattle, and protect Taiwanese consumers from developing Creutzfeldt-Jakob disease. However, the ban, which essentially blocks any U.S. beef from entering Taiwan, is being used to protect the Taiwanese beef industry. Kie-Duck Park, of South Korea's independent Sejong Institute, agreed, saying, "We [in Asia] see the agricultural industry as a kind of strategic industry, and people want to keep that industry safe."[11]

Many nations also use **subsidies**, such as long-term, low-interest loans, cash grants, and tax deferments, to develop and protect companies in special industries. Not surprisingly, businesses complain about unfair trade practices when foreign companies receive government subsidies. Indeed, the World Trade Organization has ruled what Boeing had been arguing for years, namely, that Airbus, the largest airplane manufacturer in the world, illegally benefited from European government subsidies in the form of no- or low-interest loans. According to the WTO, if Airbus had not received $15 billion in European government subsidies, it "would not have been possible for Airbus to have launched all of these models, as originally designed and at the times it did," and that some of its planes, "could not have been launched . . . without significantly higher costs."[12] The European Union has filed a similar charge with the WTO, alleging that Boeing has benefitted from $20 billion in tax breaks and military contracts from the U.S. government.

tariff a direct tax on imported goods.

nontariff barriers nontax methods of increasing the cost or reducing the volume of imported goods.

quota a limit on the number or volume of imported products.

voluntary export restraints voluntarily imposed limits on the number or volume of products exported to a particular country.

government import standard a standard ostensibly established to protect the health and safety of citizens but, in reality, often used to restrict imports.

subsidies government loans, grants, and tax deferments given to domestic companies to protect them from foreign competition.

The last type of nontariff barrier is **customs classification**. As products are imported into a country, they are examined by customs agents, who must decide which of nearly 9,000 categories they should be classified into (see the Official Harmonized Tariff Schedule of the United States at www.usitc.gov/tata/hts/index.htm for more information). Classification is important because the category assigned by customs agents can greatly affect the size of the tariff and whether the item is subject to import quotas. For example, the U.S. Customs Service has several customs classifications for imported shoes. Tariffs on imported leather or "nonrubber" shoes are about 10 percent, whereas tariffs on imported rubber shoes, such as athletic footwear or waterproof shoes, range from 20 to 84 percent. (See www.usitc.gov for full information on tariffs.) The difference is large enough that some importers try to make their rubber shoes look like leather in hopes of receiving the nonrubber customs classification and lower tariff.

1.3 Trade Agreements

Thanks to the trade barriers described above, buying imported goods has often been much more expensive and difficult than buying domestic goods. During the 1990s, however, the regulations governing global trade were transformed. The most significant change was that 124 countries agreed to adopt the Uruguay Round of the **General Agreement on Tariffs and Trade (GATT)**. GATT, which existed from 1947 to 1995, was an agreement to regulate trade among (eventually) more than 120 countries, the purpose of which was "substantial reduction of tariffs and other trade barriers and the elimination of preferences."[13] GATT members engaged in eight rounds of trade negotiations, with the Uruguay Round signed in 1994 and going into effect in 1995. Although GATT itself was replaced by the **World Trade Organization (WTO)** in 1995, the changes that it made continue to encourage international trade. Today, the WTO and its member countries are negotiating what's known as the Doha Round, which seeks to advance trade opportunities for developing countries in areas ranging from agriculture to services, to intellectual property rights.

The WTO, headquartered in Geneva, Switzerland, administers trade agreements, provides a forum for trade negotiations, handles trade disputes, monitors national trade policies, and offers technical assistance and training for developing countries for its 153 member countries. Through tremendous decreases in tariff and nontariff barriers, the Uruguay round of GATT made it much easier and cheaper for consumers in all countries to buy foreign products. First, tariffs were cut 40 percent on average worldwide by 2005. Second, tariffs were eliminated in ten specific industries: beer, alcohol, construction equipment, farm machinery, furniture, medical equipment, paper, pharmaceuticals, steel, and toys. Third, stricter limits were put on government subsidies. For example, the Uruguay round of GATT put limits on how much national governments can subsidize private research in electronic and high-technology industries (see the discussion of subsidies in Section 1.2). Fourth, the Uruguay round of GATT established protections for intellectual property, such as trademarks, patents, and copyrights.

Protection of intellectual property has become an increasingly important issue in global trade because of widespread product piracy. For example, according to the International Federation of the Phonographic Industry, which represents the global recording industry, 95 percent of all music downloads violate copyrights.[14] Likewise, according to the International Data Corporation, an IT marketing firm, 40 percent of all software used in the world is pirated, costing companies $51 billion in lost sales.[15] Product piracy is also costly to the movie industry, as movie studios,

customs classification a classification assigned to imported products by government officials that affects the size of the tariff and imposition of import quotas.

General Agreement on Tariffs and Trade (GATT) a worldwide trade agreement that reduced and eliminated tariffs, limited government subsidies, and established protections for intellectual property.

World Trade Organization (WTO) the successor to GATT; the only international organization dealing with the global rules of trade between nations. Its main function is to ensure that trade flows as smoothly, predictably, and freely as possible.

distributors, and theaters, as well as video/DVD distributors lose $18 billion each year to pirates.[16]

Finally, trade disputes between countries now are fully settled by arbitration panels from the WTO. In the past, countries could use their veto power to cancel a panel's decision. For instance, the French government routinely vetoed rulings that its large cash grants to French farmers constituted unfair subsidies. Now, however, countries that are members of the WTO no longer have veto power. Thus, WTO rulings are complete and final. For more information, go to the WTO's website at www.wto.org. Exhibit 8.3 provides a brief overview of the WTO and its functions.

Exhibit 8.3 The World Trade Organization

☑ **FACT FILE**

WORLD TRADE ORGANIZATION

Location: Geneva, Switzerland
Established: January 1, 1995
Created by: Uruguay Round negotiations (1986–1994)
Membership: 153 countries on July 23, 2008
Budget: 194 million Swiss francs for 2010
Secretariat staff: 637
Head: Pascal Lamy (Director-General)

Functions:
- Administering WTO trade agreements
- Forum for trade negotiations
- Handling trade disputes
- Monitoring national trade policies
- Technical assistance and training for developing countries
- Cooperation with other international organizations

Source: Accessed May 8, 2011, from www.wto.org/english/thewto_e/whatis_e/whatis_e.htm.

The second major development that has reduced trade barriers has been the creation of **regional trading zones**, or zones in which tariff and nontariff barriers are reduced or eliminated for countries within the trading zone. The largest and most important trading zones are in Europe (the Maastricht Treaty), North America (the North American Free Trade Agreement, or NAFTA), Central America (Central America Free Trade Agreement, or CAFTA-DR), South America (Union of South American Nations, or USAN), and Asia (the Association of Southeast Asian Nations, or ASEAN, and Asia-Pacific Economic Cooperation, or APEC). The map in Exhibit 8.4 shows the extent to which free trade agreements govern global trade.

In 1992, Belgium, Denmark, France, Germany, Greece, Ireland, Italy, Luxembourg, the Netherlands, Portugal, Spain, and the United Kingdom adopted the **Maastricht Treaty of Europe**. The purpose of this treaty was to transform their 12 different economies and 12 currencies into one common economic market, called the European Union (EU), with one common currency. Austria, Finland, and Sweden joined the EU in 1995, followed by Cyprus, the Czech Republic, Estonia, Hungary, Latvia, Lithuania, Malta, Poland, Slovakia, and Slovenia in 2004, and Bulgaria and Romania in 2007, bringing the total membership to 27 countries.[17] Croatia, Macedonia, Iceland, Montenegro and Turkey have applied and are being considered for membership.[18] On January 1, 2002, a single common currency, the euro, went into circulation in 12 of the EU's members (Austria, Belgium, Finland, France, Germany, Greece, Ireland, Italy, Luxembourg, the Netherlands, Portugal, and Spain).

Prior to the treaty, trucks carrying products were stopped and inspected by customs agents at each border. Furthermore, because the required paperwork, tariffs, and government product specifications could be radically different in each country, companies often had to file 12 different sets of paperwork, pay 12 different tariffs, produce 12 different versions of their basic product to meet various government specifications, and exchange money in 12 different currencies. Likewise, open business travel from state to state, which we take for granted in the United States, was complicated by inspections at each border crossing. If you lived in Germany but worked in Luxembourg, your car was stopped and your passport was inspected twice every day as you traveled to and from work. Also, every business transaction required a currency exchange, for example, from German deutsche marks to Italian

regional trading zones areas in which tariff and nontariff barriers on trade between countries are reduced or eliminated.

Maastricht Treaty of Europe a regional trade agreement between most European countries.

Exhibit 8.4 Global Map of Regional Trade Agreements

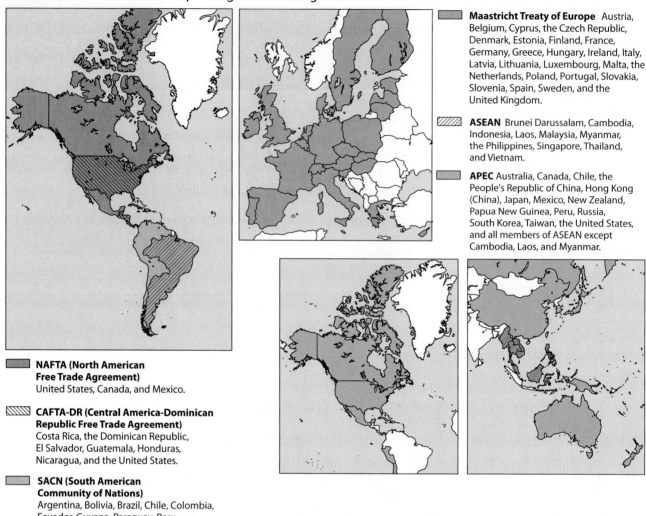

Maastricht Treaty of Europe Austria, Belgium, Cyprus, the Czech Republic, Denmark, Estonia, Finland, France, Germany, Greece, Hungary, Ireland, Italy, Latvia, Lithuania, Luxembourg, Malta, the Netherlands, Poland, Portugal, Slovakia, Slovenia, Spain, Sweden, and the United Kingdom.

ASEAN Brunei Darussalam, Cambodia, Indonesia, Laos, Malaysia, Myanmar, the Philippines, Singapore, Thailand, and Vietnam.

APEC Australia, Canada, Chile, the People's Republic of China, Hong Kong (China), Japan, Mexico, New Zealand, Papua New Guinea, Peru, Russia, South Korea, Taiwan, the United States, and all members of ASEAN except Cambodia, Laos, and Myanmar.

NAFTA (North American Free Trade Agreement)
United States, Canada, and Mexico.

CAFTA-DR (Central America-Dominican Republic Free Trade Agreement)
Costa Rica, the Dominican Republic, El Salvador, Guatemala, Honduras, Nicaragua, and the United States.

SACN (South American Community of Nations)
Argentina, Bolivia, Brazil, Chile, Colombia, Ecuador, Guyana, Paraguay, Peru, Suriname, Uruguay, and Venezuela.

Mercosur
Argentina, Brazil, Paraguay, and Uruguay.

© Cengage Learning 2013

lira, or from French francs to Dutch guilders. Imagine all of this happening to millions of trucks, cars, and businesspeople each day, and you can begin to appreciate the difficulty and cost of conducting business across Europe before the Maastricht Treaty. For more information about the Maastricht Treaty, the EU, and Europe's new common currency, the euro, see http://europa.eu/abc/12lessons/index_en.htm.

NAFTA, the **North American Free Trade Agreement** between the United States, Canada, and Mexico, went into effect on January 1, 1994. More than any other regional trade agreement, NAFTA has liberalized trade between countries so that businesses can plan for one market (North America) rather than for three separate markets (the United States, Canada, and Mexico). One of NAFTA's most important achievements was to eliminate most product tariffs *and* prevent the three countries from increasing existing tariffs or introducing new ones. Overall, Mexican and Canadian exports to the United States are up 247 percent since NAFTA went into effect. U.S. exports to Mexico and Canada are up 171 percent too, growing twice as fast as U.S. exports to any other part of the world.[19] In fact, Mexico and Canada now account for 40 percent of all U.S. exports.[20] For more information about NAFTA, see

North American Free Trade Agreement (NAFTA) a regional trade agreement between the United States, Canada, and Mexico.

the Office of NAFTA & Inter-American Affairs at www.ustr.gov/trade-agreements/free-trade-agreements/north-american-free-trade-agreement-nafta.

CAFTA-DR, the new **Central America Free Trade Agreement** between the United States, the Dominican Republic, and the Central American countries of Costa Rica, El Salvador, Guatemala, Honduras, Nicaragua, and the Dominican Republic went into effect in August 2005. With a combined population of 48.2 million, the CAFTA-DR countries together are the seventh largest U.S. export market in the world and the third-largest U.S. export market in Latin America, after Mexico and Brazil. U.S. companies export more than $26.3 billion in goods each year to the CAFTA-DR countries.[21] Furthermore, U.S. exports to CAFTA-DR countries, which are increasing at 16 percent per year, are by far the fastest-growing export market for U.S. companies.[22] For more information about CAFTA-DR, see www.fas.usda.gov/itp/CAFTA/cafta.asp.

On May 23, 2008, 12 South American countries signed the **Union of South American Nations (UNASUR)** Constitutive Treaty, which united the former Mercosur (Argentina, Brazil, Paraguay, Uruguay, and Venezuela) and Andean Community (Bolivia, Colombia, Ecuador, and Peru) alliances along with Guyana, Suriname, and Chile. UNASUR aims to create a unified South America by permitting free movement between nations, creating a common infrastructure that includes an interoceanic highway, and establishing the region as a single market by eliminating all tariffs by 2019. UNASUR is one of the largest trading zones in the world, encompassing 361 million people in South America with a combined gross domestic product of nearly $973 billion.[23] For more about UNASUR see www.comunidadandina.org/ingles/sudamerican.htm.

ASEAN, the **Association of Southeast Asian Nations,** and **APEC,** the **Asia-Pacific Economic Cooperation,** are the two largest and most important regional trading groups in Asia. ASEAN is a trade agreement between Brunei Darussalam, Cambodia, Indonesia, Lao PDR, Malaysia, Myanmar, the Philippines, Singapore, Thailand, and Vietnam, which form a market of more than 591 million people. U.S. trade with ASEAN countries exceeds $161 billion a year.[24] In fact, the United States is ASEAN's fourth largest trading partner (China is its largest), and ASEAN'S member nations constitute the fifth largest trading partner of the United States ASEAN. An ASEAN free trade area will begin in 2015 for the six original countries (Brunei Darussalam, Indonesia, Malaysia, the Philippines, Singapore, and Thailand) and in 2018 for the newer member countries (Cambodia, Lao PDR, Myanmar, and Vietnam).[25] For more information about ASEAN, see www.aseansec.org.

APEC is a broad agreement that includes Australia, Canada, Chile, the People's Republic of China, Hong Kong, Japan, Mexico, New Zealand, Papua New Guinea, Peru, Russia, South Korea, Taiwan, the United States, and all the members of ASEAN except Cambodia, Lao PDR, and Myanmar. APEC's 21 member countries contain 2.75 billion people, account for 44 percent of all global trade, and have a combined gross domestic product of over $34 trillion.[26] APEC countries began reducing trade barriers in 2000, though all the reductions will not be completely phased in until 2020.[27] For more information about APEC, see www.apec.org.

1.4 Consumers, Trade Barriers, and Trade Agreements

In Tokyo, a 12-ounce Coke costs $1.49.[28] A cup of regular coffee costs $10.19 in Moscow, $6.77 in Paris, and $6.62 in Athens.[29] In the United States, each of these items costs about a dollar.[30] A Big Mac from McDonald's costs an average of $3.71 in the United States, $4.18 in Canada, and $6.78 in Switzerland. Although not all products are more expensive in other countries (in some, they are cheaper;

Central America Free Trade Agreement (CAFTA-DR) a regional trade agreement between Costa Rica, the Dominican Republic, El Salvador, Guatemala, Honduras, Nicaragua, and the United States.

Union of South American Nations (UNASUR) Definition to come

Association of Southeast Asian Nations (ASEAN) a regional trade agreement between Brunei Darussalam, Cambodia, Indonesia, Laos, Malaysia, Myanmar, the Philippines, Singapore, Thailand, and Vietnam.

Asia-Pacific Economic Cooperation (APEC) a regional trade agreement between Australia, Canada, Chile, the People's Republic of China, Hong Kong, Japan, Mexico, New Zealand, Papua New Guinea, Peru, Russia, South Korea, Taiwan, the United States, and all the members of ASEAN except Cambodia, Laos, and Myanmar.

© Eriko Sugita/Reuters/Landov

One of the most widely known methods of comparing the purchasing power of nations is the Big Mac Index, compiled yearly by The Economist. *In Japan, a Big Mac costs the equivalent of $3.91.*

for example, a Big Mac averages $2.18 in China and $2.79 in South Africa), international studies find that American consumers get much more for their money than consumers in the rest of the world.[31] For example, the average worker earns nearly $65,430 a year in Switzerland, $84,640 in Norway, $38,080 in Japan, and $46,360 in America.[32] Yet, after adjusting these incomes for how much they can buy, the Swiss income is equivalent to just $47,100, the Norwegian income to $55,420, and the Japanese income to $33,440.[33] This is the same as saying that $1 of income can buy you only 72 cents worth of goods in Switzerland, 65 cents in Norway, and 88 cents' worth in Japan. In other words, Americans can buy much more with their incomes than those in other countries can.

One reason that Americans get more for their money is that the U.S. marketplace is the most competitive in the world and has been one of the easiest for foreign companies to enter.[34] Although some U.S. industries, such as textiles, have been heavily protected from foreign competition by trade barriers, for the most part, American consumers (and businesses) have had plentiful choices among American-made and foreign-made products. More important, the high level of competition between foreign and domestic companies that creates these choices helps keep prices low in the United States. Furthermore, it is precisely the lack of choice and the low level of competition that keep prices higher in countries that have not been as open to foreign companies and products. For example, Japanese trade barriers are estimated to cost Japanese consumers more than $100 billion a year. In fact, Japanese trade barriers amount to a 51 percent tax on food for the average Japanese family.[35]

So why do trade barriers and free trade agreements matter to consumers? They're important because free trade agreements increase choices, competition, and purchasing power and thus decrease what people pay for food, clothing, necessities, and luxuries. Accordingly, today's consumers rarely care where their products and services come from. Mark Sneed, president of Phillips Foods, which imports blue crabs from its Asian processing factories at one-third the cost of crab caught and processed in the United States, says, "I've never once had a customer ask me if we served domestic or imported crabs, just like they never ask if we have foreign shrimp."[36] Among Chinese consumers, six of the ten most popular brands—Nokia, Nike, Apple, KFC, Sony, and Coca-Cola—aren't Chinese.[37] Likewise, prices for American pecans, which have dropped for years, are now double what they were two years ago because Chinese consumers are willing to pay nearly $7 a pound for them. And despite those higher prices, China imported 83 million pounds of U.S. pecans this year and now accounts for 28 percent of the world pecan market today compared to just 1 percent in 2005.[38] Peter Germano, a New York jeweler who sells diamonds, says people don't care where the diamonds are from; they "just want to know which is cheaper."[39] And why do trade barriers and free trade agreements matter to managers? The reason, as you're about to read, is that while free trade agreements create new business opportunities, they also intensify competition, and addressing that competition is a manager's job.

Review 1

Global Business, Trade Rules, and Trade Agreements Today, there are more than 79,000 multinational corporations worldwide; just 3.1 percent are based in the United States. Global business affects the United States in two ways: through direct foreign investment in the United States by foreign companies and through U.S. companies' investment in business in other countries. United States direct foreign investment throughout the world typically amounts to about $2.8 trillion per year, whereas direct foreign investment by foreign companies in the United States amounts to $2.1 trillion per year. Historically, tariffs and nontariff trade barriers, such as quotas, voluntary export restraints, government import standards, government subsidies, and customs classifications, have made buying foreign goods much harder or more expensive than buying domestically produced products. In recent years, however, worldwide trade agreements such as GATT, along with regional trading agreements like the Maastricht Treaty of Europe, NAFTA, CAFTA-DR, USAN, ASEAN, and APEC, have substantially reduced tariff and nontariff barriers to international trade. Companies have responded by investing in growing markets in Asia, Eastern Europe, and Latin America. Consumers have responded by purchasing products based on value, rather than geography.

How to Go Global?

Once a company has decided that it *will* go global, it must decide *how* to go global. For example, if you decide to sell in Singapore, should you try to find a local business partner who speaks the language, knows the laws, and understands the customs and norms of Singapore's culture? Or should you simply export your products from your home country? What do you do if you are also entering Eastern Europe, perhaps starting in Hungary? Should you use the same approach in Hungary that you used in Singapore?

After reading the next two sections, you should be able to

2. *Explain why companies choose to standardize or adapt their business procedures.*

3. *Explain the different ways that companies can organize to do business globally.*

2 Consistency or Adaptation?

In this section, we return to a key issue: How can you be sure that the way you run your business in one country is the right way to run that business in another? In other words, how can you strike the right balance between global consistency and local adaptation?

Global consistency means that a multinational company with offices, manufacturing plants, and distribution facilities in different countries uses the same rules, guidelines, policies, and procedures to run those offices, plants, and facilities. Managers at company headquarters value global consistency because it simplifies decisions. By contrast, a company following a policy of **local adaptation** modifies its standard operating procedures to adapt to differences in foreign customers, governments, and regulatory agencies. Local adaptation is typically preferred by local managers who are charged with making the international business successful in their countries.

If companies lean too much toward global consistency, they run the risk of using management procedures poorly suited to particular countries' markets, cultures, and employees (i.e., a lack of local adaptation). For instance, Swedish-based **H&M** is the third largest clothing retailer, with stores in 37 countries. Much of its success is due to the fact that all of its stores carry the same products all over the world. However, this also limits the areas in which H&M can do business. Because most of its clothes are designed for climates that are similar to Sweden, in other words, long

global consistency when a multinational company has offices, manufacturing plants, and distribution facilities in different countries and runs them all using the same rules, guidelines, policies, and procedures.

local adaptation modifying rules, guidelines, policies, and procedures to adapt to differences in foreign customers, governments, and regulatory agencies.

< "what's new" companies

cold winters and short summers, H&M has been unable to enter markets that have drastically different climates. Thus, although H&M has stores in Toledo, Ohio, it has only a minimal presence in Los Angeles, and no presence at all in Dallas, Texas. If it is to continue to grow, H&M must adapt its product selection to warmer climates.[40]

If, however, companies focus too much on local adaptation, they run the risk of losing the cost effectiveness and productivity that result from using standardized rules and procedures throughout the world. Consider the case of **Tupperware** in India. Since it first entered India in 1996, Tupperware has grown by nearly 30 percent each year. In fact, Tupperware is acknowledged as a major contributor in the doubling of the Indian kitchenware market in just five years. Much of the company's success is due to adapting and changing its product line to suit local food habits. For example, Indian households have traditionally stored their leftovers in metal, rather than plastic, containers. So Tupperware had to convince Indian consumers that plastic containers were better than metal. Likewise, one of Tupperware's best-selling products worldwide is a square bread container, perfect for storing slices from bread loaves. In India, however, Tupperware created a new round bread container that could store *roti* and *chapati*, round flatbreads that are integral to Indian cuisine. Finally, in order to reduce prices and compete effectively with local businesses, Tupperware built a new factory in the city of Dehradun, India.[41]

> **"what's new"**
> **companies** >

Review 2

Consistency or Adaptation? Global business requires a balance between global consistency and local adaptation. Global consistency means using the same rules, guidelines, policies, and procedures in each location. Managers at company headquarters like global consistency because it simplifies decisions. Local adaptation means adapting standard procedures to individual markets. Local managers prefer a policy of local adaptation because it gives them more control. Not all businesses need the same combinations of global consistency and local adaptation. Some thrive by emphasizing global consistency and ignoring local adaptation. Others succeed by ignoring global consistency and emphasizing local adaptation.

3 Forms for Global Business

Besides determining whether to adapt organizational policies and procedures, a company must also determine how to organize itself for successful entry into foreign markets. Historically, companies have generally followed the *phase model of globalization*, in which a company makes the transition from a domestic company to a global company in the following sequential phases: **3.1 exporting, 3.2 cooperative contracts, 3.3 strategic alliances,** and **3.4 wholly owned affiliates.** At each step, the company grows much larger, uses those resources to enter more global markets, is less dependent on home country sales, and is more committed in its orientation to global business. Some companies, however, do not follow the phase model of globalization.[42] Some skip phases on their way to becoming more global and less domestic. Others don't follow the phase model at all. These are known as **3.5 global new ventures.** This section reviews these forms of global business.[43]

3.1 Exporting

exporting selling domestically produced products to customers in foreign countries.

When companies produce products in their home countries and sell those products to customers in foreign countries, they are **exporting.** Located about 90 minutes from Shanghai, the city of Honghe is one of China's largest sweater producers. Half of its 100,000 citizens work in over 100 factories that generate $650 million a year by producing and exporting 200 million sweaters annually.[44] A-Power Energy Generation Systems, a Chinese alternative energy company, runs a production and assembly plant in Nevada. Although the facility produces wind turbines that are sold in the United States, A-Power also exports wind turbines from Nevada to Mexico, Canada, and Central and South America.[45]

Exporting as a form of global business offers many advantages. It makes the company less dependent on sales in its home market and provides a greater degree of control over research, design, and production decisions. Caterpillar's CEO, Jim Owens, says "[we try] to educate our employees on the importance of exports to us. We exported $10 billion worth of product last year, and many jobs in our U.S. Facilities are very much geared to export markets."[46]

Do you know who this year's winner of *American Idol* was? *Idol* has been America's No. 1 television show for nearly a decade, so chances are you or someone you know does. But did you know that there are 42 other versions of *American Idol* (which is modeled after *Pop* Idol in Britain) around the world? And did you know that Fremantle Media, which owns and exports those different versions of *American Idol*, produces global versions of, *Family Feud* (48 countries), *The Price Is Right* (30 countries), and *Got Talent* (27 countries)?[47] What makes this work in so many different countries is Fremantle Media's tight control of production. CEO Tony Cohen says, "It's not just about the licensing of formats but the brilliance with which you execute it. You've got to do it well. These things have been through evolution and are pretty well perfect. You can't tamper with it; we're very possessive about that." In all of these different countries says Cohen, "We do all the merchandising, all the telephony, there's an Idol camp—a summer camp where you can learn all aspects of performing . . . . There have been Idol cars in Belgium and Holland, Idol-branded perfume in multiple territories. People really like it."[48]

Though advantageous in a number of ways, exporting also has its disadvantages. The primary disadvantage is that many exported goods are subject to tariff and nontariff barriers that can substantially increase their final cost to consumers. A second disadvantage is that transportation costs can significantly increase the price of an exported product. For example, when the price of crude oil was approaching $150 a barrel, manufacturers who made everything from batteries to sofas to industrial parts started bringing manufacturing production from overseas back to North America. Jeff Rubin, chief economist at CIBC World Markets in Toronto, said, "In a world of triple-digit oil prices, distance cost money."[49] Claude Hayes, president of the retail heating division at the DESA LLC, said at the time, "my cost of getting a shipping container here from China just keeps going up—and I don't see any end in sight." Yet a third disadvantage of exporting: Companies that export depend on foreign importers for product distribution. If, for example, the foreign importer makes a mistake on the paperwork that accompanies a shipment of imported goods, those goods can be returned to the foreign manufacturer at the manufacturer's expense.

3.2 Cooperative Contracts

When an organization wants to expand its business globally without making a large financial commitment to do so, it may sign a **cooperative contract** with a foreign business owner who pays the company a fee for the right to conduct that business in his or her country. There are two kinds of cooperative contracts: licensing and franchising.

Under a **licensing** agreement, a domestic company, the *licensor*, receives royalty payments for allowing another company, the *licensee*, to produce its product, sell its

cooperative contract an agreement in which a foreign business owner pays a company a fee for the right to conduct that business in his or her country.

licensing an agreement in which a domestic company, the licensor, receives royalty payments for allowing another company, the licensee, to produce the licensor's product, sell its service, or use its brand name in a specified foreign market.

doing the right thing

Fair and Safe Working Conditions in Foreign Factories

Requiring workers to work 15-hour days or to work seven days a week with no overtime pay, beating them for arriving late, requiring them to apply toxic materials with their bare hands, charging them excessive fees for food and lodging—these are just a few of the workplace violations found in the overseas factories that make shoes, clothes, bicycles, and other goods for large U.S. and multinational companies. The Fair Labor Association, which inspects overseas factories for Adidas-Salomon, Levi Strauss, Liz Claiborne, Nike, Reebok, Polo Ralph Lauren, and others, recommends the following workplace standards for foreign factories:

» Make sure there is no forced labor or child labor; no physical, sexual, psychological, or verbal abuse or harassment; and no discrimination.

» Provide a safe and healthy working environment to prevent accidents.

» Respect the right of employees to freedom of association and collective bargaining. Compensate employees fairly by paying the legally required minimum wage or the prevailing industry wage, whichever is higher.

» Provide legally required benefits. Employees should not be required to work more than 48 hours per week and 12 hours of overtime (for which they should receive additional pay), and they should have at least one day off per week.

Do the right thing. Investigate and monitor the working conditions of overseas factories where the goods sold by your company are made. Insist that improvements be made. Find another supplier if they aren't.[50]

service, or use its brand name in a particular foreign market. BioDelivery Sciences International (BDSI), a pharmaceutical company in North Carolina, reached a licensing agreement with TTY Biopharm, a Taiwanese drug company. TTY Biopharm paid BDSI a $1.3 million licensing fee in exchange for the right to manufacture and sell BDSI's Onsolis painkilling drug for cancer patients in Taiwan.[51]

One of the most important advantages of licensing is that it allows companies to earn additional profits without investing more money. As foreign sales increase, the royalties paid to the licensor by the foreign licensee increase. Moreover, the licensee, not the licensor, invests in production equipment and facilities to produce the product. Licensing also helps companies avoid tariff and nontariff barriers. Because the licensee manufactures the product within the foreign country, tariff and nontariff barriers don't apply. Royal Philips Electronics, a Dutch consumer electronic company, has signed a licensing agreement with India-based Videocon Industries to make Philips TVs "as per specifications and standards maintained by Philips globally." The agreement gives Philips entry into the growing Indian TV market, which is dominated by Samsung, LG, and Panasonic. Alok Shende, with Ascentius, a technology research firm, commented, "It is a win–win situation for both companies as Videocon, with a low cost base and large manufacturing facilities, gets access to a global brand."[52]

The biggest disadvantage associated with licensing is that the licensor gives up control over the quality of the product or service sold by the foreign licensee. Unless the licensing agreement contains specific restrictions, the licensee controls the entire business from production to marketing, to final sales. Many licensors include inspection clauses in their license contracts, but closely monitoring product or service quality from thousands of miles away can be difficult. An additional disadvantage is that licensees can eventually become competitors, especially when a licensing agreement includes access to important technology or proprietary business knowledge.

A **franchise** is a collection of networked firms in which the manufacturer or marketer of a product or service, the *franchisor*, licenses the entire business to another person or organization, the *franchisee*. For the price of an initial franchise fee plus royalties, franchisors provide franchisees with training, assistance with marketing and advertising, and an exclusive right to conduct business in a particular location. Most franchise fees run between $5,000 and $35,000. Franchisees pay McDonald's, one of the largest franchisors in the world, an initial franchise fee of $45,000. Another $950,900 to $1,797,700 is needed beyond that to pay for food inventory, kitchen equipment, construction, landscaping, and other expenses (the cost varies per country). Although franchisees typically borrow part of this cost from a bank, McDonald's requires franchisees to put down 40 percent in cash for the initial investment.[53] Because typical royalties range from 2 to 12.5 percent of gross sales, franchisors are well rewarded for the help they provide to franchisees. More than 400 U.S. companies franchise their businesses to foreign franchise partners.

Overall, franchising is a fast way to enter foreign markets. Over the last 20 years, U.S. franchisors have more than doubled their number of global franchises, for a total of more than 100,000 global franchise units. Because it gives the franchisor additional cash flows from franchisee fees and royalties, franchising can be a good strategy when a company's domestic sales have slowed. **Yum! Brands**, which owns and runs Pizza Hut, Taco Bell, KFC (formerly Kentucky Fried Chicken), A&W Restaurants, and Long John Silver's, is accepting very few new franchises in the United States because the U.S. market is saturated with fast-food outlets. However, Yum! is growing thanks to expansion in other countries. Over the last three years, Yum! closed 240 U.S. restaurants while opening 1,080 international restaurants.[54] Similarly, Wendy's/Arby's Group signed an agreement with Wenrus Restaurant Group of Moscow to open 180 Arby's/Wendy's in Russia, and an agreement with a private operator to open 24 restaurants in the Caribbean. Great Steak and Potato Company entered into an agreement with Pastelerías Servicios Corporativos SA de CV to open 30 restaurants in Mexico.[55]

Despite franchising's many advantages, franchisors face a loss of control when they sell businesses to franchisees who are thousands of miles away. Franchising specialist Cheryl Scott says, "One franchisor I know was wondering why the royalties coming from India were so small when he knew the shop was always packed. It was because the franchisee wasn't putting all of the sales through the cash register."[56]

Although there are exceptions, franchising success may be somewhat culture bound. Because most global franchisors begin by franchising their businesses in similar countries or regions (Canada is by far the first choice for American companies taking their first step into global franchising), and because 65 percent of franchisors make absolutely no change in their business for overseas franchisees, that success may not generalize to cultures with different lifestyles, values, preferences, and technological infrastructures. Customizing menus to local tastes is one of the primary ways that fast-food companies can succeed in international markets. When Taco Bell went to India, its menu was adapted to Indian tastes and included potato tacos and burritos filled with paneer, an Indian cheese. It also hired employees to explain burritos, tacos, and quesadillas to customers.

< **"what's new" companies**

franchise a collection of networked firms in which the manufacturer or marketer of a product or service, the franchisor, licenses the entire business to another person or organization, the franchisee.

309

KFC succeeds in China by selling congee (rice porridge) and a chicken wrap inspired by Peking duck. Pizza Hut sells Asian-inspired products like a salmon roll seasoned with lemon and a seafood pizza with crab sticks, green pepper, and pineapple.[57]

3.3 Strategic Alliances

"what's new" companies >

Companies forming **strategic alliances** combine key resources, costs, risks, technology, and people. **Garmin**, which produces satellite navigation devices, and Volvo Penta, which makes leisure and commercial boat engines and propulsion systems, have formed a strategic alliance to jointly develop and market marine instrumentation, navigation, and communication equipment.[58] The most common strategic alliance is a **joint venture**, which occurs when two existing companies collaborate to form a third company. The two founding companies remain intact and unchanged except that together they now own the newly created joint venture.

One of the advantages of global joint ventures is that, like licensing and franchising, they help companies avoid tariff and nontariff barriers to entry. Another advantage is that companies participating in a joint venture bear only part of the costs and the risks of that business. Many companies find this attractive because of the expense of entering foreign markets or developing new products. For example, Italian automaker Fiat established a joint venture with Russian automaker OAO Sollers to produce 500,000 cars a year. Under the agreement, OAO Sollers will produce nine Fiat models, including Jeep SUVs (Jeep is owned by Fiat), and market them in Russia and other countries. For Fiat, which has struggled in foreign markets, the joint venture provides an opportunity to establish a larger presence in the growing Russian market.[59]

Global joint ventures can be especially advantageous to smaller local partners who link up with larger, more experienced foreign firms that can bring advanced management, resources, and business skills to the joint venture. For example, Daimler AG, the Germany-based automaker, recently agreed to a joint venture with China-based Beiqi Foton Motor Company to manufacture and sell large trucks in China. While Daimler will benefit from establishing a presence in China's quickly growing market, Beiqi Foton will benefit from having access to Daimler's expertise in diesel engines and exhaust systems.[60]

Global joint ventures are not without problems, though. Because companies share costs and risks with their joint venture partners, they must also share profits. Managing global joint ventures can also be difficult because they represent a merging of four cultures: the country and the organizational cultures of the first partner, and the country and the organizational cultures of the second partner. Often, to be fair to all involved, each partner in the global joint venture will have equal ownership and power. But this can result in power struggles and a lack of leadership. Because of these problems, companies forming global joint ventures should carefully develop detailed contracts that specify the obligations of each party. Toshiba, which participated in its first global joint ventures in the early 1900s by making light bulb filaments with General Electric, treats joint ventures like a marriage of the two companies and views the contract as a prenuptial agreement. The joint venture contract specifies how much each company will invest, what its rights and responsibilities are, and what it is entitled to if the joint venture does not work out. These steps are important because the rate of failure for global joint ventures is estimated to be as high as 70 percent.[61]

When companies involved in global joint ventures don't carefully specify the obligations of each party, difficulties can occur. Danone, one of the world's largest food companies, and Hangzhour Wahaha Group, the largest beverage maker in China, entered into an agreement that created 40 separate joint ventures, producing

strategic alliance an agreement in which companies combine key resources, costs, risk, technology, and people.

joint venture a strategic alliance in which two existing companies collaborate to form a third, independent company.

and marketing everything from children's clothes to soft drinks, to frozen vegetables. Although many of their joint venture companies were successful, the relationship between the two companies disintegrated when Danone discovered that Wahaha was using its brand name on products that were not produced from their agreed-on joint ventures. In effect, Wahaha used Danone's product knowledge to create separate product lines that competed with products from their joint venture. In the end, all of the JVs were dissolved, and Danone lost its sales presence in China, which represented 10 percent of its total worldwide sales.[62]

3.4 Wholly Owned Affiliates (Build or Buy)

Approximately one-third of multinational companies enter foreign markets through wholly owned affiliates. Unlike licensing arrangements, franchises, or joint ventures, **wholly owned affiliates** are 100 percent owned by the parent company. Haier America, which has a refrigerator factory in Camden, South Carolina, is a wholly owned affiliate of the Haier Group based in Qingdao, China, which sells and markets a wide range of household goods like refrigerators, air conditioners, and MP3 players.[63] Likewise, to take advantage of the high growth in Chinese markets, Caterpillar has built a new 350,000-square-foot wholly owned subsidiary in Suzhou, China, that produces wheel loaders (which have large metal buckets used to scoop up dirt and rocks or other materials during construction).[64]

The primary advantage of wholly owned businesses is that the parent company receives all of the profits and has complete control over the foreign facilities. The biggest disadvantage is the expense of building new operations or buying existing businesses. Although the payoff can be enormous if wholly owned affiliates succeed, the losses can be immense if they fail, because the parent company assumes all of the risk.

Deutsche Telekom, the largest telecommunications company in Europe, established a presence in the United States through its affiliate T-Mobile USA. Though never a market leader, T-Mobile had decent performance for almost a decade, sometimes even outperforming Deutsche Telekom's other European divisions. More recently, however, T-Mobile has slumped badly. When AT&T, and later Verizon, began selling the extremely popular iPhone, T-Mobile began losing customers almost immediately. In 2010 alone, the company lost 390,000 fixed-contract customers, and it has a churn rate (the percent of customers not renewing their contracts) of 3.2 percent, tops in the industry and more than double the rate of the closest competitor. These struggles in the United States contributed to a 37 percent drop in profits for Deutsche Telekom, which in turn led Deutsche Telekom to sell T-Mobile USA to AT&T for $39 billion.[65]

3.5 Global New Ventures

Companies used to evolve slowly from small operations selling in their home markets to large businesses selling to foreign markets. Furthermore, as companies went global, they usually followed the phase model of globalization. Recently, however, three trends have combined to allow companies to skip the phase model when going global. First, quick, reliable air travel can transport people to nearly any point in the world within one day. Second, low-cost communication technologies, such as email, teleconferencing, phone conferencing, and the Internet, make it easier to communicate with global customers, suppliers, managers, and employees. Third, there is now a critical mass of businesspeople with extensive personal experience in all aspects of global business.[66] This combination of developments has made it possible to start companies that are global from inception. With sales, employees, and financing in

wholly owned affiliates foreign offices, facilities, and manufacturing plants that are 100 percent owned by the parent company.

different countries, **global new ventures** are companies that are founded with an active global strategy.[67]

Although there are several different kinds of global new ventures, all share two common factors. First, the company founders successfully develop and communicate the company's global vision from inception. Second, rather than going global one country at a time, new global ventures bring a product or service to market in several foreign markets at the same time. Founded by longtime airline executives Steven Udvar-Hazy and John L. Plueger, **Air Lease Corporation** is a company that provides aircraft to commercial airlines through lease agreements. Although based in Los Angeles, its mission is to provide equipment and financing to airlines all over the world. CEO Udvar-Hazy says, "We look forward to working with the leading global airlines as they modernize their fleets." Within a year of start-up, Air Lease expects to have a fleet of over 100 commercial jets leased to airlines throughout the world.[68]

"what's new" companies >

Review 3

Forms for Global Business   The phase model of globalization says that as companies move from a domestic to a global orientation, they use these organizational forms in sequence: exporting, cooperative contracts (licensing and franchising), strategic alliances, and wholly owned affiliates. Yet not all companies follow the phase model. For example, global new ventures are global from their inception.

Where to Go Global?

Deciding where to go global is just as important as deciding how your company will go global.

4 Finding the Best Business Climate

After reading the next three sections, you should be able to

4. *Explain how to find a favorable business climate.*

5. *Discuss the importance of identifying and adapting to cultural differences.*

6. *Explain how to successfully prepare workers for international assignments.*

When deciding where to go global, companies try to find countries or regions with promising business climates.

An attractive global business climate **4.1 positions the company for easy access to growing markets, 4.2 is an effective but cost-efficient place to build an office or manufacturing facility, and 4.3 minimizes the political risk to the company.**

4.1 Growing Markets

The most important factor in an attractive business climate is access to a growing market. For example, no product is known and purchased by as many people throughout the world as Coca-Cola. Yet even Coke, which is available in over 200 countries, still has tremendous potential for further global growth. Coca-Cola gets 78 percent of its sales outside of North America, and emerging markets, where it has seen its fastest growth, now account for half of Coke's sales worldwide.[69]

global new ventures new companies that are founded with an active global strategy and have sales, employees, and financing in different countries.

Exhibit 8.5 How Consumption of Coca-Cola Varies with Purchasing Power Around the World

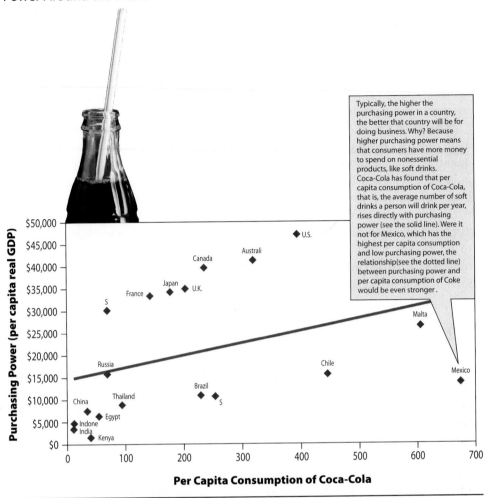

Typically, the higher the purchasing power in a country, the better that country will be for doing business. Why? Because higher purchasing power means that consumers have more money to spend on nonessential products, like soft drinks. Coca-Cola has found that per capita consumption of Coca-Cola, that is, the average number of soft drinks a person will drink per year, rises directly with purchasing power (see the solid line). Were it not for Mexico, which has the highest per capita consumption and low purchasing power, the relationship (see the dotted line) between purchasing power and per capita consumption of Coke would be even stronger.

Sources: "Per Capita Consumption of Company Beverage Products," The Coca-Cola Company, available online at www.thecoca-colacompany.com/ourcompany/ar/pdf/2010-per-capita-consumption.pdf; and "Country Comparison: GDP—per Capita (PPP)," The World Factbook, available online at https://www.cia.gov/library/publications/the-world-factbook/rankorder/2004rank.html.

Two factors help companies determine the growth potential of foreign markets: purchasing power and foreign competitors. **Purchasing power** is measured by comparing the relative cost of a standard set of goods and services in different countries. Earlier in the chapter, we noted that a Coke costs $1.49 cents in Tokyo. Because a 12-ounce Coke costs only about 75 cents in the United States, the average American would have more purchasing power than the average Japanese. Purchasing power is growing in countries like India, and China, which have low average levels of income. This is because basic living expenses such as food, shelter, and transportation are very inexpensive in those countries, so consumers still have money to spend after paying for necessities, especially as salaries increase thanks to demand from international trade.

Consequently, countries with high and growing levels of purchasing power are good choices for companies looking for attractive global markets. As Exhibit 8.5 shows, Coke has found that the per capita consumption of Coca-Cola, or the number of Cokes a person drinks per year, rises directly with purchasing power. For example, in China, Brazil, and Australia, where the average person earns, respectively, $7,400, $10,900, and $41,300 annually, the number of Coca-Cola soft drinks consumed per year increases, respectively, from 34 to 229 to 319. The more purchasing

purchasing power the relative cost of a standard set of goods and services in different countries.

313

power people have, the more likely they are to purchase soft drinks. And the Coca-Cola Company expects strong growth to continue in these markets, stating in its 2010 Annual Report, "To measure our growth potential, we look to our per capita consumption—the average number of 8-ounce servings of our beverages consumed each year in a given market. It is predicted that by the year 2020, the world will have nearly 1 billion more people whose disposable incomes will afford them choices and opportunities unthinkable a generation ago. We must discover innovative ways to connect with our traditional consumer base and this emerging global middle class— by creating new products and packaging formats for all lifestyles and occasions."[70]

The second part of assessing the growth potential of global markets involves analyzing the degree of global competition, which is determined by the number and quality of companies that already compete in a foreign market. For example, Marcopolo Brazil's biggest bus maker, with $1.1 billion in annual sales, focuses on selling buses in emerging-market countries like Argentina, Mexico, Colombia, and South Africa, where there's strong demand and little competition. Embraer, Brazil's leading airplane manufacturer, gets one-third of its sales from emerging markets (compared to 1% in 2005). Unlike Marcopolo, however, Embraer is seeing increased competition from Russia's Sukhio and the Commercial Aircraft Corporation of China for sales in these markets.[71]

4.2 Choosing an Office/Manufacturing Location

Companies do not have to establish an office or manufacturing location in each country they enter. They can license, franchise, or export to foreign markets, or they can serve a larger region from one country. But there are many reasons why a company might choose to establish a location in a foreign country. Some foreign offices are established through global mergers and acquisitions, and some are established because of a commitment to grow in a new market. Brembo SpA, based in Milan, Italy, which makes high performance brakes for the Cadillac CTS-v and Corvette ZR1, is opening its U.S. headquarters and research and development facility in Detroit. Brembo Managing Director Alberto Bombassei said, "We want to transfer part of our research and development operations to the United States because we want to invest to boost our market share with new products."[72] Other companies seek a tax haven (although this is more difficult for American companies due to legal concerns), want to reflect their customer base, or strive to create a global brand. Although a company must be legally incorporated in one place, some companies have anywhere from 9 to 23 global hubs and don't regard any one as more central than another.[73]

The criteria for choosing an office or manufacturing location are different from the criteria for entering a foreign market. Rather than focusing on costs alone, companies should consider both qualitative and quantitative factors. Two key qualitative factors are workforce quality and company strategy. Workforce quality is important because it is often difficult to find workers with the specific skills, abilities, and experience that a company needs to run its business. Workforce quality is one reason that many companies doing business in Europe locate their customer call centers in the Netherlands. As shown in Exhibit 8.6, workers in the Netherlands are the most linguistically gifted in Europe, with 73 percent speaking two languages, 44 percent speaking three languages, and 12 percent speaking more than three. Of course, with employees who speak several languages, call centers located in the Netherlands can handle calls from more countries and generally employ 30 to 50 percent fewer employees than those located in other parts of Europe. Another advantage of locating a call center in the Netherlands is that 60 percent of call center workers have university or advanced degrees in technology or management.[74]

A company's strategy is also important when choosing a location. For example, a company pursuing a low-cost strategy may need plentiful raw materials, low-cost transportation, and low-cost labor. A company pursuing a differentiation strategy (typically a higher-priced, better product or service) may need access to high-quality materials and a highly skilled and educated workforce.

Quantitative factors such as the kind of facility being built, tariff and nontariff barriers, ex-

Exhibit 8.6 Quality of the Netherlands Workforce for Call Center Jobs

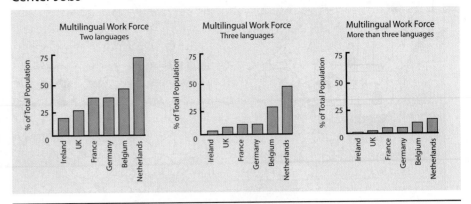

Sources: "Customer Care in the Netherlands," The Netherlands Foreign Investment Agency, accessed February 13, 2007, from www.nfia.com/customer_care.html; and "Customer Care Centers," *Netherlands Foreign Investment Agency Information Manual,* accessed February 13, 2007, from www.nfia.com/downloads/customercare.htm.

change rates, and transportation and labor costs should also be considered when choosing an office or manufacturing location. A real estate specialist in company location decisions explains how things change with different types of facility: "If it's an assembly plant, a company might be inclined to look for incentives that would subsidize its hiring. With a distribution facility, an adequate transportation network will likely be critical. A corporate headquarters will need a good communications network, a multilingual labor force, and easy access by air. On the other hand, a research and development operation will require proximity to a high-tech infrastructure and access to good universities."[75] Companies rely on studies such as Cushman & Wakefield's annually published "European Cities Monitor" to compare business climates throughout Europe.[76] Similar studies are available for other parts of the world. Exhibit 8.7 offers a quick overview of the best cities for business, based on a variety of criteria. This information is a good starting point if your company is trying to decide where to put an international office or manufacturing plant.

4.3 Minimizing Political Risk

When managers think about political risk in global business, they envision burning factories and riots in the streets. Although political events such as these receive dramatic and extended coverage from the media, the political risks that most companies face usually are not covered as breaking stories on Fox News or CNN. Nonetheless, the negative consequences of ordinary political risk can be just as devastating to companies that fail to identify and minimize that risk.[77]

When conducting global business, companies should attempt to identify two types of political risk: political uncertainty and policy uncertainty.[78] **Political uncertainty** is associated with the risk of major changes in political regimes that can result from war, revolution, death of political leaders, social unrest, or other influential events. **Policy uncertainty** refers to the risk associated with changes in laws and government policies that directly affect the way foreign companies conduct business.

Policy uncertainty is the most common—and perhaps most frustrating—form of political risk in global business, especially when changes in laws and government policies directly undercut sizable investments made by foreign companies. BlackBerry smart phones, made by the Canadian-based Research In Motion (RIM),

political uncertainty the risk of major changes in political regimes that can result from war, revolution, death of political leaders, social unrest, or other influential events.

policy uncertainty the risk associated with changes in laws and government policies that directly affect the way foreign companies conduct business.

Exhibit 8.7 World's Best Cities for Business

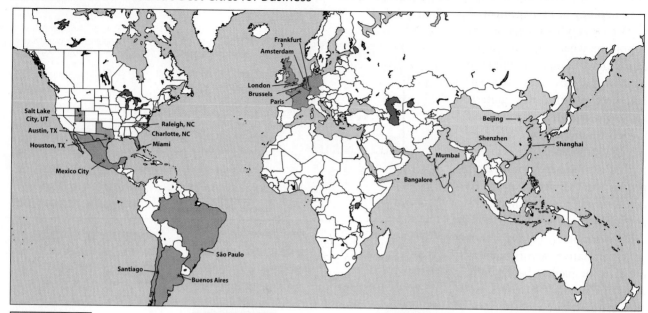

North America	Latin America	Europe	Asia Pacific
1. Washington D.C.	1. Miami	1. London	1. Hong Kong
2. Omaha	2. Santiago	2. Paris	2. Shanghai
3. Boston	3. Sao Paolo	3. Frankfurt	3. Singapore
4. Des Moines	4. Mexico City	4. Brussels	4. Kuala Lumpur
5. Minneapolis-St. Paul	5. Rio de Janeiro	5. Barcelona	5. Beijing

Sources: R. Britt, "America's Best Cities for Business in 2011," Yahoo! Real Estate (Market Watch), December 20, 2010, accessed May 11, 2011, from http://realestate.yahoo.com/promo/americas-best-cities-for-business-in-2011.html; "European Cities Monitor," Cushman & Wakefield, accessed May 11, 2011, from www.europeancitiesmonitor.eu/wp-content/uploads/2010/10/ECM-2010-Full-Version.pdf; "Ranking 2010: The Best Cities for Doing Business in Latin America," América Economía, accessed May 11, 2011, from http://rankings.americaeconomia.com/2010/mejoresciudades/las-15-mejores-rio-de-janeiro.php; and "Asian Cities Monitor," Cushman & Wakefield, accessed May 11, 2011, from https://www.cushwake.com/cwglobal/docviewer/Research_Report_Asia_Pacific_Cities_Monitor_2008sec_EN.pdf?id=c13800215p&repositoryKey=CoreRepository&itemDesc=document&cid=c11900014p&crep=Core&cdesc=binaryPubContent&Country=Asia&Language=EN&just_logged_in=1.

doing the right thing

Obey the Laws

In 1997, the member countries of the Organisation for Economic Co-operation and Development adopted the OECD Anti-Bribery Convention. Each country that ratified the convention (38 in total, covering the world's largest economies) agreed to enact and enforce legislation that makes it illegal to bribe a foreign business or government official. The convention has required a number of countries to create new laws against bribery or enhance laws that were already written. In a recent survey, however, the anti-corruption agency Transparency International reveals that more than half of OECD convention members are failing to enforce antibribery laws. This puts more pressure on you, as a manager. Even though your competitors may use bribes to try to get ahead, do the right thing and stay within the boundaries of the law.[79]

are extraordinarily popular in Saudi Arabia because they offer secure, encrypted, electronic communication. Saudi Arabia's Communication and Information Technology Commission, however, worries that RIM's encryption systems will prevent security officials from monitoring terrorist groups that use BlackBerries for communication. As a result, the Saudi government announced that BlackBerry phones would be prohibited. Because of this policy change, RIM was suddenly at risk of losing 750,000 users. After intense negotiations, RIM Research agreed to install computer servers giving the Saudi government unencrypted access to monitor user communications and activities.[80]

Several strategies can be used to minimize or adapt to the political risk inherent in global business. An *avoidance strategy* is used when the political risks associated with a foreign country or region are viewed as too great. If firms are already invested in high-risk areas, they may divest or sell their businesses. If they have not yet invested, they will likely postpone their investment until the risk shrinks. For example, fewer companies are investing in Mexico because battles between drug cartels have resulted in over 31,000 murders in the last four years. Ron DeFeo, CEO of Terex, which makes heavy equipment and construction cranes, said, "We won't put a factory in Mexico until some of this violence gets addressed. We just can't put our people at risk."[81]

Exhibit 8.8 shows the long-term political stability for various countries in the Middle East (higher scores indicate less political risk). The following factors, which were used to compile these ratings, indicate greater political risk: government instability, poor socioeconomic conditions, internal or external conflict, military involvement in politics, religious and ethnic tensions, high foreign debt as a percentage of gross domestic product, exchange rate instability, and high inflation.[82] An avoidance strategy would likely be used for the riskiest countries shown in Exhibit 8.8, such as Iran and Jordan, but might not be needed for the less risky countries, such as Israel or Oman. Risk conditions and factors change, so be sure to make risk decisions with the latest available information from resources such as the PRS Group, www.prsgroup.com, which supplies information about political risk to 80 percent of the *Fortune* 500 companies.

Control is an active strategy to prevent or reduce political risks. Firms using a control strategy lobby foreign governments or international trade agencies to change laws, regulations, or trade barriers that hurt their business in that country. Emerson Electric Co. had virtually no business for its InSinkErator garbage disposals in Europe during the 1990s. The company lobbied European governments to convince them of the environmentally friendly impact of a waste disposer compared to other methods of getting rid of food waste, such as composting, which involves garbage trucks, and landfills that

BlackBerries would have been banned in Saudi Arabia unless Research In Motion had gave the Saudi government unencrypted access to monitor BlackBerry users' communications and activities.

Exhibit 8.8 Long-Term Political Stability in the Middle East

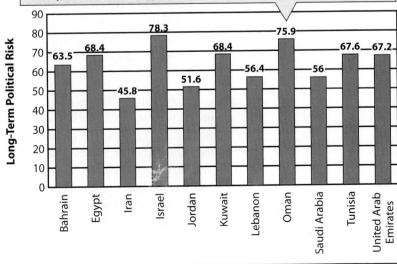

Higher scores indicate *less* long-term political risk, which is calculated by estimating government instability, socioeconomic conditions, internal or external conflict, military involvement in politics, religious and ethnic tensions, foreign debt as a percent of gross domestic product, exchange rate instability, and whether there is high inflation.

Country	Long-Term Political Risk
Bahrain	63.5
Egypt	68.4
Iran	45.8
Israel	78.3
Jordan	51.6
Kuwait	68.4
Lebanon	56.4
Oman	75.9
Saudi Arabia	56
Tunisia	67.6
United Arab Emirates	67.2

Source: Terry Alexander, *UAE Business Forecast Report*, 2011 3rd Quarter, 7–12.

emit methane gases. By contrast, garbage disposals are the cheapest method to dispose of food waste because they enable water-treatment plants to turn methane (that comes through the sewer system) into power and decrease the carbon footprint by reducing the amount of waste transported by trucks. Partially as a result of its lobbying, Emerson now sells over 100,000 disposals each year in Europe.[83]

Another method for dealing with political risk is *cooperation*, which involves using joint ventures and collaborative contracts, such as franchising and licensing. Although cooperation does not eliminate the political risk of doing business in a country, it can limit the risk associated with foreign ownership of a business. For example, a German company forming a joint venture with a Chinese company to do business in China may structure the joint venture contract so that the Chinese company owns 51 percent or more of the joint venture. Doing so qualifies the joint venture as a Chinese company and exempts it from Chinese laws that apply to foreign-owned businesses. However, cooperation cannot always protect against *policy risk* if a foreign government changes its laws and policies to directly affect the way foreign companies conduct business.

Review 4

Finding the Best Business Climate The first step in deciding where to take your company global is finding an attractive business climate. Look for a growing market where consumers have strong purchasing power and foreign competitors are weak. When locating an office or manufacturing facility, consider both qualitative and quantitative factors. In assessing political risk, be sure to examine political uncertainty and policy uncertainty. If the location you choose has considerable political risk, you can avoid it, try to control the risk, or use a cooperation strategy.

5 Becoming Aware of Cultural Differences

Some of the more interesting and amusing aspects of global business are the unexpected confrontations that people have with cultural differences, "the way they do things over there." *Wall Street Journal* columnist Geoffrey Fowler relates the following story from Hong Kong, where he works:

> *I was riding the elevator a few weeks ago with a Chinese colleague here in the Journal's Asian headquarters. I smiled and said, "Hi." She responded, "You've gained weight." I might have been appalled, but at least three other Chinese coworkers also have told me I'm fat. I probably should cut back on the pork dumplings.*[84]

Uttered in the United States, such comments would be considered rude. Fowler indicates that in China, however, where people openly talk about people's weight, body shapes, and salaries, such comments are probably just friendliness. Likewise, the Chinese colleagues of American Jennifer Gallo, who works in Beijing, have commented on her clothing ("very nice, could be European"), her muscle tone ("flabby"), and her likeliness to bear children ("certain to have many boys").[85] So what does Fowler say when his friendly Chinese colleagues tell him he's fat? "There's so much good food here."

National culture is the set of shared values and beliefs that affects the perceptions, decisions, and behavior of the people from a particular country. The first step in dealing with culture is to recognize that there are meaningful differences. Professor Geert

national culture the set of shared values and beliefs that affects the perceptions, decisions, and behavior of the people from a particular country.

Exhibit 8.9   Hofstede's Five Cultural Dimensions

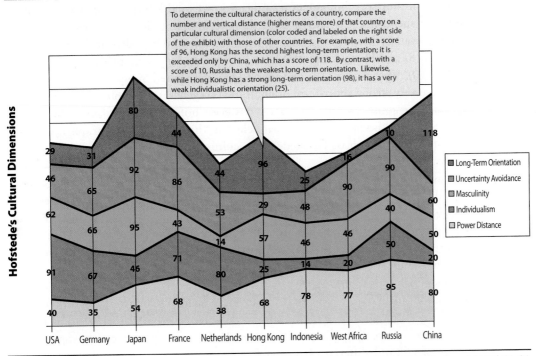

To determine the cultural characteristics of a country, compare the number and vertical distance (higher means more) of that country on a particular cultural dimension (color coded and labeled on the right side of the exhibit) with those of other countries. For example, with a score of 96, Hong Kong has the second highest long-term orientation; it is exceeded only by China, which has a score of 118. By contrast, with a score of 10, Russia has the weakest long-term orientation. Likewise, while Hong Kong has a strong long-term orientation (98), it has a very weak individualistic orientation (25).

- Long-Term Orientation
- Uncertainty Avoidance
- Masculinity
- Individualism
- Power Distance

Source: G. H. Hofstede, "Cultural Constraints in Management Theories," *Academy of Management Executive 7*, no. 1 (1993): 81–94.

Hofstede spent 20 years studying cultural differences in 53 different countries. His research shows that there are five consistent cultural dimensions across countries: power distance, individualism, masculinity, uncertainty avoidance, and short-term versus long-term orientation.[86]

Power distance is the extent to which people in a country accept that power is distributed unequally in society and organizations. In countries where power distance is weak, such as Denmark and Sweden, employees don't like their organization or their boss to have power over them or tell them what to do. They want to have a say in decisions that affect them. As Exhibit 8.9 shows, Russia and China, with scores of 95 and 80, respectively, are much stronger in power distance than Germany (35), the Netherlands (38), and the United States (40).

Individualism is the degree to which societies believe that individuals should be self-sufficient. In individualistic societies, employees put loyalty to themselves first and loyalty to their company and work group second. In Exhibit 8.9, the United States (91), the Netherlands (80), France (71), and Germany (67) are the strongest in individualism, whereas Indonesia (14), West Africa (20), and China (20) are the weakest.

Masculinity and *femininity* capture the difference between highly assertive and highly nurturing cultures. Masculine cultures emphasize assertiveness, competition, material success, and achievement, whereas feminine cultures emphasize the importance of relationships, modesty, caring for the weak, and quality of life. In Exhibit 8.9, Japan (95), Germany (66), and the United States (62) have the most masculine orientations, whereas the Netherlands (14) has the most feminine orientation.

The cultural difference of *uncertainty avoidance* is the degree to which people in a country are uncomfortable with unstructured, ambiguous, unpredictable situations. In countries with strong uncertainty avoidance, like Greece and Portugal, people tend to be aggressive and emotional and seek security rather than uncertainty. In Exhibit 8.9, Japan (92), France (86), West Africa (90), and Russia (90) are strongest in uncertainty avoidance, whereas Hong Kong (29) is the weakest.

Short-term/long-term orientation addresses whether cultures are oriented to the present and seek immediate gratification or to the future and defer gratification. Not surprisingly, countries with short-term orientations are consumer driven, whereas countries with long-term orientations are savings driven. In Exhibit 8.9, China (118) and Hong Kong (96) have very strong long-term orientations, whereas Russia (10), West Africa (16), Indonesia (25), the United States (29), and Germany (31) have very strong short-term orientations. To generate a graphical comparison of two different country's cultures, go to www.geert-hofstede.com/hofstede_dimensions .php. Select a "home culture"; then select a "host culture." A graph comparing the countries on each of Hofstede's five cultural differences will automatically be generated.

Cultural differences affect perceptions, understanding, and behavior. Recognizing cultural differences is critical to succeeding in global business. Nevertheless, as Hofstede pointed out, descriptions of cultural differences are based on averages—the average level of uncertainty avoidance in Portugal, the average level of power distance in Argentina, and so forth. Accordingly, says Hofstede, "If you are going to spend time with a Japanese colleague, you shouldn't assume that overall cultural statements about Japanese society automatically apply to this person."[87] Similarly, cultural beliefs may differ significantly from one part of a country to another.[88]

After becoming aware of cultural differences, the second step is deciding how to adapt your company to those differences. Unfortunately, studies investigating the effects of cultural differences on management practices point more to difficulties than to easy solutions. One problem is that different cultures will probably perceive management policies and practices differently. For example, blue-collar workers in France and Argentina, all of whom performed the same factory jobs for the same multinational company, perceived its company-wide safety policy differently.[89] French workers perceived that safety wasn't very important to the company, but Argentine workers thought that it was. The fact that something as simple as a safety policy can be perceived differently across cultures shows just how difficult it can be to standardize management practices across different countries and cultures.

Another difficulty is that cultural values are changing, albeit slowly, in many parts of the world. The fall of communism in Eastern Europe and the former Soviet Union and the broad economic reforms in China have produced sweeping changes on two continents in the last two decades. Thanks to increased global trade resulting from free trade agreements, major economic transformations are also under way in India, China, Central America, and South America. Consequently, when trying to adapt management practices to cultural differences, companies must ensure that they are not basing their adaptations on outdated and incorrect assumptions about a country's culture.

Review 5

Becoming Aware of Cultural Differences National culture is the set of shared values and beliefs that affects the perceptions, decisions, and behavior of the people from a particular country. The first step in dealing with culture is to recognize meaningful differences such as power distance, individualism, masculinity, uncertainty avoidance, and short-term/long-term orientation. Cultural differences should be carefully interpreted because they are based on averages, not individuals. Adapting managerial practices to cultural differences is difficult because policies and practices can be perceived differently in different cultures. Another difficulty is that cultural values may be changing in many parts of the world. Consequently, when companies try to adapt management practices to cultural differences, they need to be sure that they are not using outdated assumptions about a country's culture.

6 Preparing for an International Assignment

Tom Bonkenburg is Director of European Operations for St. Onge Company, a supply-chain consulting firm in York, Pennsylvania. Bonkenburg went to Moscow for a first-time meeting with the director of a Russian firm with which his company hoped to do business. He said that when he met the Russian director, "I gave my best smile, handshake and friendly joke . . . only to be met with a dreary and unhappy look." Afterward, though, he received a friendly email from the Russian director, indicating that the meeting had been very positive. Subsequently, Bonkenburg learned that Russians save smiling and friendliness for personal meetings and are expected to be serious at business meetings. Says, Bonkenburg, "He was working as hard to impress me as I was to impress him."[90]

If you become an **expatriate**, someone who lives and works outside his or her native country, chances are you'll run into cultural surprises like Tom Bonkenburg did. The difficulty of adjusting to language, cultural, and social differences is the primary reason for expatriate failure in overseas assignments. For example, although there have recently been disagreements among researchers about these numbers, it is probably safe to say that 5 to 20 percent of American expatriates sent abroad by their companies will return to the United States before they have successfully completed their assignments.[91] Of those who do complete their international assignments, about one-third are judged by their companies to be no better than marginally effective.[92] Because the average cost of sending an employee on a three-year international assignment is $1 million, failure in those assignments can be extraordinarily expensive.[93]

The chances for a successful international assignment can be increased through **6.1 language and cross-cultural training** and **6.2 consideration of spouse, family, and dual-career issues.**

6.1 Language and Cross-Cultural Training

Pre-departure language and cross-cultural training can reduce the uncertainty that expatriates feel, the misunderstandings that take place between expatriates and natives, and the inappropriate behaviors that expatriates unknowingly commit when they travel to a foreign country. Indeed, simple things like using a phone, locating a public toilet, asking for directions, finding out how much things cost, exchanging greetings, or understanding what people want can become tremendously complex when expatriates don't know a foreign language or a country's customs and cultures. In his book *Blunders in International Business*, David Ricks tells the story of an American manager working in the South Pacific who, by hiring too many local workers from one native group, unknowingly upset the balance of power in the island's traditional status system. The islanders met on their own and quickly worked out a solution to the problem. After concluding their meeting at 3 A.M., they calmly went to the manager's home to discuss their solution with him (time was not important in their culture). But because the American didn't speak their language and didn't understand why they had shown up en masse outside his home at 3 A.M., he called in the Marines, who were stationed nearby, to disperse what he thought was a riot.

Expatriates who receive pre-departure language and cross-cultural training make faster adjustments to foreign cultures and perform better on their international assignments.[94] Unfortunately, only a third of the managers who go on international assignments are offered any kind of pre-departure training, and only half of those

expatriate someone who lives and works outside his or her native country.

© Paddy Eckersley/Photolibrary

actually participate in the training![95] Suzanne Bernard, director of international mobility at Bombadier Aerospace in Canada, says, "We always offer cross-cultural training, but it's very seldom used by executives leaving in a rush at the last minute."[96] This is somewhat surprising given the failure rates for expatriates and the high cost of those failures. Furthermore, with the exception of some language courses, pre-departure training is not particularly expensive or difficult to provide. Three methods can be used to prepare workers for international assignments: documentary training, cultural simulations, and field experiences.

Documentary training focuses on identifying specific critical differences between cultures. For example, when 60 workers at Axcelis Technologies in Beverly, Massachusetts, were preparing to do business in India, they learned that while Americans make eye contact and shake hands firmly when greeting others, Indians, as a sign of respect, do just the opposite, avoiding eye contact and shaking hands limply.[97]

After learning specific critical differences through documentary training, trainees can then participate in *cultural simulations*, in which they practice adapting to cultural differences. EMC, a global provider of information storage solutions, uses cultural simulations to train its people. In its early days, EMC was largely based in the United States, but with research labs, offices, and customers on every continent, cross-cultural interactions are a daily part of business. EMC's cultural simulations use photos, and audio and video clips to present real world situations. EMC employees must decide what to do and then learn what happened as a result of their choices. Whether it's interacting with customers or dealing with EMC employees from other countries, at every step they have the opportunity to learn good and bad methods of responding to cultural differences. EMC requires its worldwide workforce of 40,500 people to regularly use the cultural simulations. Louise Korver-Swanson, EMC's global head of executive development said, "This is about ensuring that we're truly a global company. We need everyone in the organization to be tuned in."[98]

Finally, *field simulation* training, a technique made popular by the U.S. Peace Corps, places trainees in an ethnic neighborhood for three to four hours to talk to residents about cultural differences. For example, a U.S. electronics manufacturer prepared workers for assignments in South Korea by having trainees explore a nearby South Korean neighborhood and talk to shopkeepers and people on the street about South Korean politics, family orientation, and day-to-day living practices.

6.2 Spouse, Family, and Dual-Career Issues

When William Hines was sent by his employer, Lincoln Electric Company, to its facility at Torreon, Mexico, the company had only one other employee there at the time, so there was no one to help Hines and his wife, Meg Sondey, make the adjustment to the local community. As a result, Hines's wife, Meg, found herself dealing with all sorts of issues on her own—finding housing, taking care of immigration issues, and getting a driver's license. She describes the experience "like jumping into

mgmt:facts

Wanted: International Experience

Working as an expat has always had an appeal to those who love experiencing other cultures. And, it's helped companies find a place in markets all over the world. Research has found, however, that overseas experience also makes for better managers. A research study at Northwestern's Kellogg School of Management found that 60 percent of students who lived abroad were able to solve a creative thinking problem, compared to just 42 percent of students who did not live abroad. In another study, conducted at Sorbonne University in Paris, researchers showed students three words and were asked to come up with another word that linked all of them. Those who studied abroad were able to give more correct answers than those who did not. So what's a great way to develop great managers? Send them overseas![99]

a cold lake. It's uncomfortable, frightening, everything is on hyper alert because it is so different."[100]

Not all international assignments are as difficult for expatriates and their families, but the evidence clearly shows that how well an expatriate's spouse and family adjust to the foreign culture is the most important factor in determining the success or failure of an international assignment.[101] Barry Kozloff of Selection Research International says, "The cost of sending a family on a foreign assignment is around $1 million and their failure to adjust is an enormous loss."[102] Unfortunately, despite its importance, there has been little systematic research on what does and does not help expatriates' families successfully adapt. A number of companies, however, have found that adaptability screening and intercultural training for families can lead to more successful overseas adjustment.

Adaptability screening is used to assess how well managers and their families are likely to adjust to foreign cultures. For example, Prudential Relocation Management's international division has developed an "Overseas Assignment Inventory" (OAI) to assess a spouse and family's open-mindedness, respect for others' beliefs, sense of humor, and marital communication. The OAI was initially used to help the U.S. Peace Corps, the U.S. Navy, and The Canadian International Development Agency, select people who could adapt well in foreign cultures. Success there led to its use in helping companies assess whether managers and their spouses were good candidates for international assignments.[103] Likewise, Pennsylvania-based AMP, a worldwide producer of electrical connectors, conducts extensive psychological screening on expatriates and their spouses when making international assignments. But adaptability screening does not just involve a company assessing an employee; it can also involve an employee screening international assignments for desirability. Because more employees are becoming aware of the costs of international assignments (spouses having to give up or change jobs, children having to change schools, everyone having to learn a new language), some companies are willing to pay for a pre-assignment trip so the employee and his or her spouse can investigate the country *before* accepting the international assignment.[104]

Only 40 percent of expatriates' families receive language and cross-cultural training, yet such training is just as important for the families of expatriates as for

what really works
Cross-Cultural Training

Most expatriates will tell you that cross-cultural training helped them adjust to foreign cultures. Such anecdotal data, however, are not as convincing as systematic studies. Twenty-one studies, with a combined total of 1,611 participants, have examined whether cross-cultural training affects the self-development, relationships, perceptions, adjustment, and job performance of expatriates. Overall, they show that cross-cultural training works extremely well in most instances.

Self-Development

When you first arrive in another country, you must learn how to make decisions that you took for granted in your home country: how to get to work, how to get to the grocery, how to pay your bills, and so on. If you've generally been confident about yourself and your abilities, an overseas assignment can challenge that sense of self. Cross-cultural training helps expatriates deal with these and other challenges. Expatriates who receive cross-cultural training are 79 percent more likely to report healthy psychological well-being and self-development than those who don't receive training.

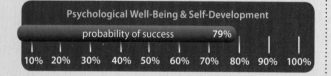

Fostering Relationships

One of the most important aspects of an overseas assignment is establishing and maintaining relationships with host nationals. If you're in Brazil, you need to make friends with Brazilians. Many expatriates, however, make the mistake of making friends only with

other expatriates from their home country. In effect, they become social isolates in a foreign country. They work and live there, but as much as they can, they speak their native language, eat their native foods, and socialize with other expatriates from their home country. Cross-cultural training makes a big difference in whether expatriates establish relationships with host nationals. Expatriates who receive cross-cultural training are 74 percent more likely to establish such relationships.

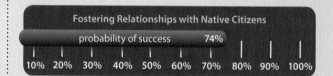

Accurate Perceptions of Culture

Another characteristic of successful expatriates is that they understand the cultural norms and practices of the host country. For example, many Americans do not understand the famous pictures of Japanese troops turning their backs to American military commanders on V-J Day, when Japan surrendered to the United States at the end of World War II. Americans viewed this as a lack of respect, when, in fact, in Japan turning one's back in this way is a sign of respect. Cross-cultural training makes a big difference in the accuracy of perceptions concerning host country norms and practices. Expatriates who receive cross-cultural training are 74 percent more likely to have accurate perceptions.

Rapid Adjustment

New employees are most likely to quit in the first six months because this initial period requires the most adjustment: learning new names, new faces, new procedures, and new information. It's tough. Of course, expatriates have a much harder time adjusting to their new jobs because they are also learning new languages, new foods, new customs, and often new lifestyles. Expatriates who receive cross-cultural training are 74 percent more likely to make a rapid adjustment to a foreign country.

Job Performance

It's good that cross-cultural training improves self-development, fosters relationships, improves the

accuracy of perceptions, and helps expatriates make rapid adjustments to foreign cultures. From an organizational standpoint, however, the ultimate test of cross-cultural training is whether it improves expatriates' job performance. The evidence shows that cross-cultural training makes a significant difference in expatriates' job performance, although the difference is not quite as large as for the other factors. Nonetheless, it is estimated that cross-cultural training for 100 managers could bring about $390,000 worth of benefits to a company, or nearly $4,000 per manager. This is an outstanding return on investment, especially when you consider the high rate of failure for expatriates. Expatriates who have received cross-cultural training are 71 percent more likely to have better on-the-job performance than those who did not receive cross-cultural training.[105]

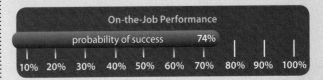

the expatriates themselves.[106] In fact, it may be more important because, unlike expatriates, whose professional jobs often shield them from the full force of a country's culture, spouses and children are fully immersed in foreign neighborhoods and schools. Households must be run, shopping must be done, and bills must be paid. Unfortunately, expatriate spouse Laurel Larsen, despite two hours of Chinese lessons a week, hasn't learned enough of the language to communicate with the family's babysitter. She has to phone her husband, who became fluent in Chinese in his teens, to translate. Expatriates' children must deal with different cultural beliefs and practices, too. Although the Larsens' three daughters love the private, international school that they attend, they still have had difficulty adapting to, from their perspective, the incredible differences in inner China. Six-year-old Emma taped this poem to her parents' nightstand: "Amarica is my place! I love Amarica. It was fun. It was so fun. I miss it."[107] In addition to helping families prepare for the cultural differences they will encounter, language and cross-cultural training can help reduce uncertainty about how to act and decrease misunderstandings between expatriates and their families and locals.

Preparing for an International Assignment Many expatriates return prematurely from international assignments because of poor performance. However, premature return is much less likely to happen if employees receive language and cross-cultural training, such as documentary training, cultural simulations, or field experiences, before going on assignment. Adjustment of expatriates' spouses and families, which is the most important determinant of success in international assignments, can be improved through adaptability screening and intercultural training.

Review 6

SELF-ASSESSMENT

Are You Nation-Minded or World-Minded?

Attitudes about global business are as varied as managers are numerous. It seems that the business press can always find someone who is for globalization and someone who is against it. But regardless of your opinion on the subject, managers will increasingly confront issues related to the globalization of the business environment. It is probable that, as a manager, you will need to develop global sensibilities (if you don't already have them). Understanding your own cultural perspective is the first step in doing so.

This assessment has three parts: Step 1, complete the questionnaire shown below; Step 2, determine your score; Step 3, develop a plan to increase your global managerial potential.[108]

Step 1: Use the 6-point rating scale to complete the 32-question inventory shown below.

1 Strongly disagree

2 Disagree

3 Mildly disagree

4 Mildly agree

5 Agree

6 Strongly agree

1. Our country should have the right to prohibit certain racial and religious groups from entering it to live.

     1   2   3   4   5   6

2. Immigrants should not be permitted to come into our country if they compete with our own workers.

     1   2   3   4   5   6

3. It would set a dangerous precedent if every person in the world had equal rights that were guaranteed by an international charter.

     1   2   3   4   5   6

4. All prices for exported food and manufactured goods should be set by an international trade committee.

     1   2   3   4   5   6

5. Our country is probably no better than many others.

     1   2   3   4   5   6

6. Race prejudice may be a good thing for us because it keeps many undesirable foreigners from coming into this country.

     1   2   3   4   5   6

7. It would be a mistake for us to encourage certain racial groups to become well educated because they might use their knowledge against us.

     1   2   3   4   5   6

8. We should be willing to fight for our country without questioning whether it is right or wrong.

     1   2   3   4   5   6

9. Foreigners are particularly obnoxious because of their religious beliefs.

     1   2   3   4   5   6

10. Immigration should be controlled by a global organization rather than by each country on its own.

      1   2   3   4   5   6

11. We ought to have a world government to guarantee the welfare of all nations irrespective of the rights of any one.

      1   2   3   4   5   6

12. Our country should not cooperate in any global trade agreements that attempt to better world economic conditions at our expense.

      1   2   3   4   5   6

KEY TERMS

Asia-Pacific Economic Cooperation (APEC) 303
Association of Southeast Asian Nations (ASEAN) 303
Central America Free Trade Agreement (CAFTA-DR) 303
cooperative contract 307
customs classification 300
direct foreign investment 298
expatriate 321
exporting 306
franchise 309
General Agreement on Tariffs and Trade (GATT) 300
global business 296
global consistency 305
global new ventures 312
government import standard 299
joint venture 310
licensing 307
local adaptation 305

Maastricht Treaty of Europe 301
multinational corporation 297
national culture 318
nontariff barriers 299
North American Free Trade Agreement (NAFTA) 302
policy uncertainty 315
political uncertainty 315
protectionism 298
purchasing power 313
quota 299
regional trading zones 301
strategic alliance 310
subsidies 299
tariff 299
trade barriers 298
Union of South American Nations (UNASUR) 303
voluntary export restraints 299
wholly owned affiliates 311
World Trade Organization (WTO) 300

13. It would be better to be a citizen of the world than of any particular country.

    1 2 3 4 5 6

14. Our responsibility to people of other races ought to be as great as our responsibility to people of our own race.

    1 2 3 4 5 6

15. A global committee on education should have full control over what is taught in all countries about history and politics.

    1 2 3 4 5 6

16. Our country should refuse to cooperate in a total disarmament program even if some other nations agree to it.

    1 2 3 4 5 6

17. It would be dangerous for our country to make international agreements with nations whose religious beliefs are antagonistic to ours.

    1 2 3 4 5 6

18. Any healthy individual, regardless of race or religion, should be allowed to live wherever he or she wants to in the world.

    1 2 3 4 5 6

19. Our country should not participate in any global organization that requires that we give up any of our national rights or freedom of action.

    1 2 3 4 5 6

20. If necessary, we ought to be willing to lower our standard of living to cooperate with other countries in getting an equal standard for every person in the world.

    1 2 3 4 5 6

21. We should strive for loyalty to our country before we can afford to consider world brotherhood.

    1 2 3 4 5 6

22. Some races ought to be considered naturally less intelligent than ours.

    1 2 3 4 5 6

23. Our schools should teach the history of the whole world rather than of our own country.

    1 2 3 4 5 6

24. A global police force ought to be the only group in the world allowed to have armaments.

    1 2 3 4 5 6

25. It would be dangerous for us to guarantee by international agreement that every person in the world should have complete religious freedom.

    1 2 3 4 5 6

26. Our country should permit the immigration of foreign peoples, even if it lowers our standard of living.

    1 2 3 4 5 6

27. All national governments ought to be abolished and replaced by one central world government.

    1 2 3 4 5 6

28. It would not be wise for us to agree that working conditions in all countries should be subject to international control.

    1 2 3 4 5 6

29. Patriotism should be a primary aim of education so that our children will believe our country is the best in the world.

    1 2 3 4 5 6

30. It would be a good idea if all the races were to intermarry until there was only one race in the world.

    1 2 3 4 5 6

31. We should teach our children to uphold the welfare of all people everywhere, even though it may be against the best interests of our own country.

    1 2 3 4 5 6

32. War should never be justifiable, even if it is the only way to protect our national rights and honor.

    1 2 3 4 5 6

Step 2: Determine your score by entering your response to each survey item below, as follows. In blanks that say *regular score*, simply enter your response for that item. If your response was a 4, place a 4 in the *regular score* blank. In blanks that say *reverse score*, subtract your response from 7 and enter the result. So if your response was a 4, place a 3 (7 − 4 = 3) in the *reverse score* blank.

1. reverse score ————
2. reverse score ————
3. reverse score ————
4. regular score ————
5. regular score ————
6. reverse score ————
7. reverse score ————
8. reverse score ————
9. reverse score ————
10. regular score ————
11. regular score ————
12. reverse score ————
13. regular score ————
14. regular score ————
15. regular score ————
16. reverse score ————
17. reverse score ————

18. regular score	_____		28. reverse score	_____
19. reverse score	_____		29. reverse score	_____
20. regular score	_____		30. regular score	_____
21. reverse score	_____		31. regular score	_____
22. reverse score	_____		32. regular score	_____
23. regular score	_____			
24. regular score	_____			
25. reverse score	_____			
26. regular score	_____			
27. regular score	_____			

Scoring

Total your scores from items 1–16 _____

Total your scores from items 17–32 _____

Add together to compute TOTAL _____

MANAGEMENT DECISION

Cultural Backlash in India[109]

As you look at the latest quarterly earnings report of your clothing and accessories company, you think to yourself "You are a genius!" It was your idea to move manufacturing to India last year, and it was your idea to partner with a local retail chain to get your products to Indian consumers. So even though your U.S. sales fell 5 percent, much in part due to the recession, your company's profits actually rose 35 percent, thanks to all the money you made in India. Almost every day, you walk through the city and you see young, affluent Indians wearing your jeans, clutching your purses, donning your sunglasses, and you are unbelievably glad that you decided to come into this dynamic, fast-growing market that really likes Western fashion styles.

There are many people, however, who aren't so fond of your styles, and of Western culture in general. Various religious and political conservative groups have recently been protesting the growing influence of Western culture in India, sometimes in quite violent ways. During a recent Valentine's Day, a group of men publicly beat young couples who were holding hands or having a romantic dinner. In another city, a group of people attacked women who were at bars and dance clubs. And just the other day, you saw a crowd of people throwing your jeans, purses, and sunglasses into a big bonfire as a statement against Western fashion. Even businesses are getting into the anti-American sentiment; a local beverage company announced that they would take on the popularity of Coke and Pepsi by selling a beverage based on cow urine, which is considered a holy, medicinal drink by Hindus.

When you came up with the idea of expanding into India, you certainly didn't think that you would find yourself in the middle of a cultural clash. "I'm just here to sell jeans," you think, "not to tell people how to live." But clearly, many people view companies like yours as a threat to their culture and heritage.

Questions

1. How would you, as the manager of this company, deal with the risk associated with doing business in countries that feel threatened by American culture?
2. How might your company use an alliance with local companies to adapt to local concerns about American culture?

MANAGEMENT TEAM DECISION

A Different Way to Go Global[110]

Exporting, cooperative contracts, licensing, franchising, joint ventures, wholly owned affiliates, global new ventures … as a management team wanting to take your business to the next level, you have a smorgasbord of options available to you. But in addition to these traditional options, there is another angle you can take, one that is becoming increasingly popular among start-up companies like yours: social entrepreneurship. Social entrepreneurs use business skills to solve social problems. You and the members of your team, just out of your MBA programs, are excited about the business and want to grow it and make money. But you are also passionate about making a difference when it comes to problems like homelessness in the United States or AIDS in Africa.

As your team discusses how and where to go global, you think about the problems you'd like to address and you look to role models to help you brainstorm and plan. You read about how Pfizer—a pharmaceutical giant, not a start-up—started a program to offer free medicines to recently unemployed Americans. Other companies are doing the same in Africa. Peet's Coffee & Tea has been working recently to develop the economic well-being of coffee farmers in Kenya, Rwanda, Tanzania, and Uganda by teaching them to grow better-quality coffee that Peet's can market to its customers in coffee-loving developed economies. As much as your team wants to help others in need, you also recognize that doing good can't come at the expense of the bottom line. In fact, Peet's Coffee's effort is currently run by a nonprofit and hasn't started making Peet's any money yet. You know that the success of such ventures is untested, but your team is also aware that any effort at going global involves some type of risk. Thinking it through, you ask yourselves what's in

it for companies who undertake social entrepreneurship—and what might be in it for you? Pfizer adopted this program to create customer loyalty, exchanging a brick (something it has) for a jade (something even more valuable and harder to come by). Customers who drink Peet's care about where their coffee comes from and about its quality, so Peet's establishes relationships with African farmers partly in response to customer demand and to build its brand.

With all of this in mind, it's your team's task to figure out how you can balance your interest in doing business on a global scale with your interest in making a difference in the world.

Questions

1. What are the advantages of social entrepreneurship as a way to approach doing business in developing economies outside the United States? What are the disadvantages?
2. How might you combine social entrepreneurship with traditional options for going global?
3. Can establishing a multinational corporation or a joint venture serve the principles of social entrepreneurship? Would some options lend themselves better to social entrepreneurship than others? What might such a business venture look like?

PRACTICE BEING A MANAGER

Hometown Culture

One of the major dilemmas in global management concerns the degree to which a multinational firm should adapt its business practices to particular locations and cultures versus the degree to which it should maintain consistency across all its operations. In general, firms prefer consistency because it streamlines operations and may result in global economies of scale. At the same time, multinational firms cannot gloss over differences without running the risk of losing a particular market to more responsive (local) competition. In this exercise, you will interpret your "hometown" culture for a large multinational company.

Suppose that a large multinational equipment company (based outside your country of origin) is planning to open a major production facility and retail dealership in your hometown. This company has hired you as a consultant to help it successfully establish operations in your hometown.

Step 1: Describe your hometown. Write a brief sketch (one or two pages, using bullet points, will suffice) in which you describe the important cultural features of your hometown, including such aspects as language, dress, courtesy and customs, and attitudes toward "foreignness" and newcomers. Try as much as possible to capture aspects of the location and culture of your hometown that would be important for newcomers to recognize and respect.

Step 2: Form a team. Your professor will assign you to small discussion groups of three to five students.

Step 3: Share your description. Take turns in your discussion groups introducing yourselves, identifying your hometown, and sharing the highlights of your brief sketch of your hometown. Listen for similarities and differences across your hometowns.

Step 4: Make recommendations. As a group, agree on some recommendations to the multinational company.

Assume that the company is planning to enter all of your hometowns simultaneously. To what degree might the company use a consistent (same) approach in entering your hometowns? Is one or more of your hometowns likely to require a foreign multinational to make more particular adaptations?

Step 5: Share findings with class. Each group should share its list of hometowns and its recommendations with the class.

Step 6: Consider challenges. As a class, discuss the challenges of entering global markets, particularly in regard to achieving the appropriate mix of consistency and adaptation.

DEVELOP YOUR CAREER POTENTIAL

Building Cultural Bridges Inside American Business

All savvy managers seem to be familiar with the Japanese custom of exchanging business cards, the French custom of the two-hour lunch, and the South American custom of getting to know potential business partners on a personal level before discussing business.[111] But how many managers are aware of the cultural differences that exist within the United States? For example, how many Manhattanites know that in some parts of the country, businesses close down on the first day of hunting season?

Political rhetoric often refers to "two Americas" and the differences between the heartland and the coasts, but many other oppositional geographic pairings also represent different sets of cultural norms. Some other obvious examples are North–South, East–West, and the more general urban–rural. How many businesspeople know how to be effective in all these American cultures? Much has been made of the political and cultural implications of these divides, but not enough attention has been paid to what it means for business.

Cultural differences were addressed in Chapter 3 and will be again in Chapter 15. In the context of this chapter, however, it is important to note that many of the issues related to global management are applicable in any geographic context. Deciding whether to locate a firm in Alabama versus Oregon requires the same due diligence as deciding between Madrid and Madagascar. Managers need to assess the best business climate, identify and adapt to cultural differences, and prepare workers who will be transferred to the new location.

Activities

1. Think of yourself as a member of a particular geographic cultural group. (In the United States, we are conditioned to think of cultural groups based on ethnicity and race, but for this exercise, think in terms of location.) What are the characteristics of this group?

2. Once you have an outline of your geographic culture, try to identify the group most opposite to your own. For example, if you consider yourself a New Yorker, you may think of a Mississippian or a Californian.

3. Research regional and local periodicals to learn about the norms in the other culture. You might also talk with a friend who attends college in a different region or state to get a more personal understanding of norms in other parts of the country. List some of the norms in the other location, and compare them with the norms in your area of the country.

END NOTES

[1] L. Chao, "Taobao to Launch Local Deals on Group-Buying Website," *The Wall Street Journal*, February 23, 2011, accessed May 15, 2011, from http://online .wsj.com/article/SB100014240527870 3775704576161340839989996.html; B. Stone & D. MacMillan, "Groupon's $6 Billion Snub," *Bloomberg Businessweek*, December 13, 2010, 6–7; B. Stone & D. MacMillan, "Are Four Words Worth $25 Billion?" *Bloomberg Businessweek*, March 21, 2011, 70–75; and R. Underwood, "Groupon versus the World," Inc., October 2010, 116–118; and B. Weiss, "The Weekend Interview with Andrew Mason: Groupon's $6 Billion Gambler," *The Wall Street Journal*, December 18, 2010, A15.

[2] T. Friedman, "It's a Flat World, After All," *The New York Times*, April 3, 2005, 33.

[3] "Annex table A.I.8. Number of parent corporations and foreign affiliates, by region and economy, latest available year (Number)," World Investment Report 2009, United Nations

Conference on Trade & Development, accessed May 7, 2011, www.unctad.org/en/docs/wir2009_en.pdf.

[4]T. Virki, "Nokia Siemens buys Motorola network ops for $1.2 billion," Reuters, July 19, 2010, accessed July 23, 2010, from www.reuters.com/article/idUSTRE66I24P20100719.

[5]A. Cordeiro, "Hershey to Expand in Asia," *The Wall Street Journal*, March 12, 2009, B5.

[6]E. L. Andrews, "U.S. Adds Tariffs on Chinese Tires," *The Wall Street Journal*, September 11, 2009, accessed June 9, 2010, from www.nytimes.com/2009/09/12/business/global/12tires.html?_r=1&scp=1&sq=tariff&st=cse; and M. Kitchen, "China to Set Anti-Dumping Measures on U.S. Chicken," Market Watch, February 5, 2010, accessed August 3, 2010, from www.marketwatch.com/story/china-to-set-anti-dumping-measures-on-us-chicken-2010-02-05.

[7]G. Williams III, "News on the Road Column," *San Antonio Express-News*, March 3, 2006.

[8]K. Bradsher, "W.T.O. Rules Against China's Limits on Imports," *The New York Times*, August 12, 2009, accessed June 9, 2010, from www.nytimes.com/2009/08/13/business/global/13trade.html?scp=3&sq=trade%20quota&st=cse.

[9]R. Geldenhuys, "China Import Quotas Illegal under WTO Law?" Floor, Inc. Attorneys, September 18, 2006, accessed May 13, 2011 from www.tradelaw.co.za/news/article.asp?newsID_101.

[10]"Understanding the WTO," *World Trade Organization*, accessed August 5, 2008, from www.wto.org/english/thewto_e/whatis_e/tif_e/agrm9_e.htm.

[11]J. Adams, "Taiwan Curbs U.S. Beef Imports in Latest Asia Trade Frictions," *The Christian Science Monitor*, January 5, 2010, accessed July 23, 2010, from www.csmonitor.com/World/Asia-Pacific/2010/0105/Taiwan-curbs-US-beef-imports-in-latest-Asia-trade-frictions.

[12]C. Drew, "In Ruling, W.T.O. Faults Europe over Aid to Airbus," *The New York Times*, June 30, 2010, accessed July 23, 2010, from www.nytimes.com/2010/07/01/business/global/01wto.html.

[13]"GATT/WTO," Duke Law: Library & Technology, accessed June 12, 2009, from www.law.duke.edu/lib/researchguides/gatt.html.

[14]P. Sonne & M. Colchester, "France, the U.K. Take Aim at Digital Pirates," *The Wall Street Journal*, April 15, 2010, accessed June 9, 2010, from http://online.wsj.com/article/SB100014240527023046040420457518182075061494.html.

[15]John E. Dunn, "Pirate Software Costs $51 Billion, Says Survey," ComputerworldUK, September 16, 2010, accessed October 6, 2010, from www.computerworlduk.com/news/it-business/3239830/pirate-software-costs-51-billion-says-survey/.

[16]G. Fowler, "Estimates of Copyright Piracy Losses Vary Widely," *The Wall Street Journal*, June 2, 2006, A13.

[17]"The History of the European Union," *Europa—The European Union Online*, accessed August 6, 2008, from http://europa.eu/abc/european_countries/index_en.htm; and "Member States of the EU," Europa: The EU at a Glance, accessed May 8, 2011, from http://europa.eu/abc/european_countries/candidate_countries/index_en.htm.

[18]"Candidate Countries," Europa: The EU at a Glance, accessed May 8, 2011, from http://europa.eu/abc/european_countries/candidate_countries/index_en.htm.

[19]"Testimony of Under Secretary of Commerce for International Trade Grant D. Aldona: The Impact of NAFTA on the United States Economy," Senate Foreign Relations Committee, Subcommittee on International Economic Policy, Export & Trade Promotion, February 7, 2007.

[20]"Top U.S. Export Markets: Free Trade Agreement and Country Fact Sheets," International Trade Administration, U.S. Department of Commerce, 2009, accessed May 8, 2011, from http://trade.gov/publications/pdfs/top-us-export-markets-2009.pdf.

[21]"CAFTA-DR (Dominican Republic-Central America FTA)," Office of the United States Trade Representative, accessed June 13, 2008, from www.ustr.gov/trade-agreements/free-trade-agreements/cafta-dr-dominican-republic-central-america-fta.

[22]"US Trade with the CAFTA-DR Countries," Office of the United States Trade Representative (July 2007), accessed August 6, 2008, from www.ustr.gov/assets/Trade_Agreements/Bilateral/CAFTA/Briefing_Book/asset_upload_file601_13191.pdf.

[23]UNASUR, Union of South American Nations, accessed May 8, 2011, from www.comunidadandina.org/ingles/sudamerican.htm.

[24]"Selected Basic ASEAN Indicators, 2011," *Association of Southeast Nations*, February 15, 2011, accessed May 8, 2011, from www.aseansec.org/stat/Table1.pdf.

[25]"Selected Basic ASEAN Indicators, 2005," Association of Southeast Nations, accessed August 6, 2008, from www.aseansec.org/stat/Table1.pdf; "Top Ten ASEAN Trade Partner Countries/Regions, 2005," Association of Southeast Nations, accessed August 6, 2008, from www.aseansec.org/Stat/Table20.pdf; "ASEAN Free Trade Area (AFTA)," Association of Southeast Nations, accessed August 6, 2008, www.aseansec.org/12021.htm.

[26]"Frequently Asked Questions (FAQs)" *Asia—PacificEconomic Cooperation*, accessed May 8, 2011, from www.apec.org/FAQ.aspx.

[27]"Member Economies," Asia Pacific Economic Cooperation, accessed August 6, 2008, from www.apec.org/apec/member_economies/key_websites.html; "Frequently Asked Questions (FAQs)," Asia-Pacific Economic Cooperation, accessed August 6, 2008, from www.apec.org/apec/tools/faqs.html.

[28]www.tokyoprices.com/category/food-prices/.

[29]Z. Greenburg, "World's Most Expensive Cups of Coffee," *Forbes*, July 24, 2008, accessed June 13, 2009, from www.forbes.com/2008/07/23/cities-coffee-expensive-forbeslife-cx_zg_0724expensivecoffee.html.

[30]Z. Greenburg, "Moscow Tops Most Expensive Cup of Coffee List," *Forbes* on MSNBC.com, August 13, 2008, from www.msnbc.msn.com/id/26062313/ns/business-forbescom/t/moscow-tops-most-expensive-cup-coffee-list/.

[31]"The Big Mac Index: An Indigestible Problem," *The Economist*, October 14, 2010, accessed May 8, 2011, from www.economist.com/node/17257797?story_id=17257797.

[32]Ibid.

[33]"2009 GNI per capita, PPP (current international $)," The World Bank, accessed May 8, 2011, from http://data.worldbank.org/indicator/NY.GNP.PCAP.PP.CD/countries; and "2009 GNI per Capita, Atlas Method (current US$)," The World Bank, accessed May 8, 2011, from http://data.worldbank.org/indicator/NY.GNP.PCAP.CD/countries.

[34]"The Global Competitiveness Report: 2008–2009," World Economic Forum, accessed June 14, 2009, from www.weforum.org/documents/GCR0809/index.html.

[35]"Freer Trade Cuts the Cost of Living," *World Trade Organization*, accessed August 6, 2008, from www.wto.org/english/thewto_e/whatis_e/10ben_e/10b04_e.htm.

[36]B. Thevenot, "Clawing for Survival, Louisiana's Crab Processors Are Being Pinched by Low Prices and Foreign Competition," *New Orleans Times-Picayune*, October 6, 1999, A1.

[37]N. O'Leary, "Most Popular Brands in China are Imported," *AdWeek*, April 18, 2011, 47.

[38]D. Wessel, "Shell Shock: Chinese Demand Reshapes U.S. Pecan Business," *The Wall Street Journal*, April 18, 2011, accessed May 8, 2011, from http://online.wsj.com/article/SB10001424052748704076804576180774248237738.html.

[39]L. Grant, "More United States Diamond Buyers Turn to Canada: Gem Seekers Want to Avoid Stones at Center of Conflicts," *USA Today*, July 17, 2001, B2.

[40]Elizabeth Holmes, "How H&M Keeps Its Cool," *The Wall Street Journal*, May 10, 2010, accessed September 9, 2010, from http://online.wsj.com/article/SB10001424052748703338004575230493697911432.html?mod=dist_smartbrief.

[41]A. Singh and S. Shankar, "Tupperware Parties Help Reshape India's Kitchens," Bloomberg.com, July 13 2010, accessed July 23, 2010, from www.Businessweek.com/globalbiz/content/jul2010/gb20100713_165186.htm; and A. Singh & S. Shankar, "Tupperware Story Throws up Some Success Mantras for Indian Market," *The Economic Times*, June 11, 2010, accessed July 23, 2010, from http://economictimes.indiatimes.com/Features/Corporate-Dossier/Tupperware-story-throws-up-some-success-mantras-for-Indian-market/articleshow/6034418.cms?curpg=1.

[42]A. Sundaram & J. S. Black, "The Environment and Internal-Organization of Multinational Enterprises," *Academy of Management Review* 17 (1992): 729–757.

[43]H. S. James, Jr., & M. Weidenbaum, *When Businesses Cross International Borders: Strategic Alliances & Their Alternatives* (Westport, CT: Praeger Publishers, 1993).

[44]J. T. Areddy, "China's Export Machine Threatened by Rising Costs," *The Wall Street Journal*, June 30, 2008, A1.

[45]W. Sedgwick, "Nevada Lands First Chinese Wind Turbine Factory in US," Greentechnologydaily.com, March 11, 2010, accessed August 8, 2010, from www.greentechnologydaily.com/solar-wind/661-nevada-lands-first-chinese-wind-turbine-factory-in-us.

[46]I. Brat & B. Gruley, "Boss Talk: Global Trade Galvanizes Caterpillar; Maker of Heavy Equipment Thrives Under CEO Owens, Fervent Free-Trade Advocate," *The Wall Street Journal*, February 26, 2007, B1.

[47]"Fast Facts about FremantleMedia," FremantleMedia, accessed May 9, 2011, from www.fremantlemedia.com/About_Us/Fast_Facts_About_Us.aspx.

[48]A. Davidson, "TV Boss with the X Factor," *The Sunday Times*, September 23, 2007, Business 9.

[49]T. Aeppel, "Oil Shocker: Stung by Soaring Transportation Cost: Factories Bring Jobs Home Again," *The Wall Street Journal*, June 13, 2008, A1.

[50]"Workplace Code of Conduct," Fair Labor Association, accessed May 12, 2003, from www.fairlabor.org//fla/go.asp?u=/pub/mp&Page=FLACodeConduct; and A. Bernstein, M. Shari, and E. Malkin, "A World of Sweatshops," *Businessweek*, November 6, 2000, 84.

[51]Frank Vinulan "BDSI Strikes $1.3 Million Licensing Deal for Onsolis Cancer Patch in Taiwan," *Triangle Business Journal*, October 7, 2010, accessed October 7, 2010, from www.bizjournals.com/triangle/stories/2010/10/04/daily41.html?q=licensing.

[52]Kenan Machado, "Videocon to Make, Sell Philips' TV Sets in India," *The Wall Street Journal* (Online), April 19, 2010, accessed May 9, 2011, from http://online.wsj.com/article/SB100014240527487046719045751936708822088824.html.

[53]"New Restaurants," McDonald's, accessed March 18, 2009, from www.aboutmcdonalds.com/mcd/franchising/us_franchising/purchasing_your_franchise/new_restaurants.html.

[54]"Yum! Financial Data: Restaurant Counts," Yum!, accessed May 9, 2011, http://www.yum.com/investors/restcounts.asp.

[55]Alan J. Liddle, "U.S. Chains Ramp up Growth Abroad," *Nation's Restaurant News*, August 12, 2010, accessed May 9, 2010, from www.nrn.com/article/us-chains-ramp-growth-abroad.

[56]K. Le Mesurier, "Overseas and Overwhelmed," *BRW*, January 25, 2007, 51.

[57]Kathy Chu, "Fast-Food Chains in Asia Cater Menus to Customers," *USA Today*, September 7, 2010, accessed October 8, 2010, from www.usatoday.com/money/world/2010-09-07-asiatastes07_ST_N.htm; and Steven Stern "Fast-Food Chains Adapt to Local Tastes," CNN, April 8, 2010, accessed October 8, 2010, from http://articles.cnn.com/2010-04-08/living/fast.food_1_taco-bell-burger-burritos-and-quesadillas?_s=PM:LIVING.

[58]Press Release, "Garmin and Volvo Penta Form Strategic Alliance to Create Marine Instrumentation, Navigation and Communication Equipment," Garmin, February 18, 2011, accessed May 9, 2011, from http://garmin.blogs.com/my_weblog/2011/02/garmin-and-volvo-penta-form-strategic-alliance-to-create-marine-instrumentation-navigation-and-commu.html.

[59]A. Ustinova and S. G. Forden, "Fiat, Sollers Form $3.3 Billion Russian Car Venture," *Bloomberg Businessweek*, February 11, 2010, accessed July 23, 2010, from www.Businessweek.com/news/2010-02-11/fiat-sollers-will-set-up-2-4-billion-euro-russian-car-venture.html.

[60]C. Rauwald, "Daimler, Beiqi Foton Ink Deal On China Truck Joint Venture," *The Wall Street Journal*, July 16,

2010, accessed September 10, 2010, from http://online.wsj.com/article/SB10001424052748704682604575370061075262570.html.

[61]B. R. Schlender, "How Toshiba Makes Alliances Work," *Fortune*, October 4, 1993, 116–120; and "Joint Ventures," *Encyclopedia of Business*, 2nd ed., accessed August 6, 2008, from www.referenceforbusiness.com/encyclopedia/Int-Jun/Joint-Ventures.html#WHY_JOINT_VENTURES_FAIL.

[62]Ulrich Wassmer, Pierre Dussauge, & Marcel Planellas, "How to Manage Alliances Better Than One at a Time," *MIT Sloan Management Review*, April 1, 2010, accessed October 8, 2010 (subscription required), from http://sloanreview.mit.edu/the-magazine/articles/2010/spring/51305/how-to-manage-alliances-better-than-one-at-a-time/; and J. Areddy, "Danone Pulls Out of Disputed China Venture," *The Wall Street Journal*, October 1, 2009, B1.

[63]S. Prasso, "American Made ... Chinese Owned," *Fortune*, May 24, 2010, 87; "About Haier," Haier.com, accessed August 8, 2010, from www.haieramerica.com/en/aboutus/?sessid=6bad9187383748176bddd8a3e6cf55c9.

[64]"Caterpillar in China: Suzhou," Caterpillar in China, accessed May 9, 2011, from http://china.cat.com/cda/components/fullArticle?m=315897&x=7&id=1629442.

[65]"Deutsche Telekom Profit down 37 Percent to $696 Million," *Yahoo! News*, May 6, 2011, accessed May 14, 2011, from http://news.yahoo.com/s/ap/20110506/ap_on_bi_ge/eu_germany_earns_deutsche_telekom_1; and Kevin J. O'Brien, "How the iPhone Led to the Sale of T-Mobile USA," *The New York Times*, March 21, 2011, accessed May 14, 2011, from http://dealbook.nytimes.com/2011/03/21/how-the-iphone-led-to-the-sale-of-t-mobile-usa/.

[66]W. Hordes, J. A. Clancy, & J. Baddaley, "A Primer for Global Start-Ups," *Academy of Management Executive*, May 1995, 7–11.

[67]Pavlos, J. Johnson, J. Slow, & S. Young, "Micromultinationals: New Types of Firms for the Global Competitive Landscape," *European Management Journal* 21, no. 2 (April 2003): 164; B. M. Oviatt & P. P. McDougall, "Toward a Theory of International New Ventures," *Journal of International Business Studies* (Spring 1994): 45–64; and S. Zahra, "A Theory of International New Ventures: A Decade of Research," *Journal of International Business Studies* (January 2005): 20–28.

[68]Newswire, "Air Lease Corporation, the New Global Aviation Venture, Is Ready for Take-Off with Substantial Financing and a Top-Flight Senior Management Team," *PR Newswire*, July 15, 2010, accessed July 23, 2010, from www.prnewswire.com/news-releases/air-lease-corporation-the-new-global-aviation-venture-is-ready-for-take-off-with-substantial-financing-and-a-top-flight-senior-management-team-98529409.html.

[69]"2010 Annual Report," The Coca-Cola Company, accessed May 11, 2011, from www.thecoca-cola-company.com/ourcompany/ar/pdf/TCCC_2010_Annual_Review.pdf.

[70]"2010 Annual Report," The Coca-Cola Company.

[71]S. Kennedy, M. Bristow, & S. Adam, "There's a New Silk Road, and It Doesn't Lead to the U.S.," *Bloomberg Businessweek*, August 9–15, 2010, 13–14.

[72]J. Clark, "Italy's Brembo Looks to Increase U.S. Market Share," *The Wall Street Journal*, June 24, 2010, accessed May 11, 2011, http://online.wsj.com/article/SB10001424052748704911704575326590322494762.html.

[73]P. Dvorak, "Why Multiple Headquarters Multiply," *The Wall Street Journal*, November 19, 2007, B1; and J. L. Yang, "Making Mergers Work," *Fortunei* (November 26, 2007): 42.

[74]"Customer Care in the Netherlands," The Netherlands Foreign Investment Agency, accessed February 13, 2007, from www.nfia.com/customer_care.html.

[75]"Foreign Corrupt Business Practices Act," U.S. Department of Justice, accessed May 10, 2003, from www.usdoj.gov/criminal/fraud/fcpa.

[76]A. Snyder, "European Expansion: How to Shop Around," *Management Review* (November 1, 1993): 16.

[77]J. Oetzel, R. Bettis, & M. Zenner, "How Risky Are They?" *Journal of World Business* 36, no. 2 (Summer 2001): 128–145.

[78]K. D. Miller, "A Framework for Integrated Risk Management in International Business," *Journal of International Business Studies*, 2nd Quarter 1992, 311.

[79]Vanessa Kortekaas, "OECD Nations 'Failing to Enforce Anti-Bribery Rules,'" *Financial Times*, October 26, 2010, accessed 13 May 2011X, from www.ft.com/cms/s/0/06704206-e0e3-11df-87da-00144feabdc0.html#axzz1DNqVGvkv

[80]Abdullah Al-Shihri "Blackberry-Saudi Arabia to Share User Data in Deal That Could Set Precedent," *The Huffington Post*, August 7, 2010, accessed October 15, 2010, from www.huffingtonpost.com/2010/08/07/blackberrysaudi-arabia-de_n_674621.html.

[81]N. Casey & J. Hagerty, "Companies Shun Violent Mexico, Wall Street Journal, 17 December 2010, B1.

[82]"Chapter 1: Political Outlook," *UAE Business Forecast Report*, 2007 1st Quarter, 5–10.

[83]I. Brat, "Going Global by Going Green," *The Wall Street Journal*, February 26, 2008, B1.

[84]G. Fowler, "In China's Offices, Foreign Colleagues Might Get an Earful," *The Wall Street Journal*, 13 February 2007, B1.

[85]Ibid.

[86]G. Hofstede, "The Cultural Relativity of the Quality of Life Concept," *Academy of Management Review* 9 (1984): 389–398; G. Hofstede, "The Cultural Relativity of Organizational Practices and Theories," *Journal of International Business Studies*, Fall 1983, 75–89; G. Hofstede, "The Interaction between National and Organizational Value Systems," *Journal of Management Studies*, July 1985, 347–357; and M. Hoppe, "An Interview with Geert Hofstede," *Academy of Management Executive*, February 2004, 75–79.

[87]R. Hodgetts, "A Conversation with Geert Hofstede," *Organizational Dynamics*, Spring 1993, 53–61.

[88]T. Lenartowicz & K. Roth, "Does Subculture within a Country Matter? A Cross-Cultural Study of Motivational Domains and Business Performance in Brazil," *Journal of International Business Studies* 32 (2001): 305–325.

[89]M. Janssens, J. M. Brett, & F. J. Smith, "Confirmatory Cross-Cultural Research: Testing the Viability of a Corporation-Wide Safety Policy," *Academy of Management Journal* 38 (1995): 364–382.

[90]E. Maltby, "Expanding Abroad? Avoid Cultural Gaffes—Entrepreneurs Looking Overseas Often Neglect to Learn Local Business Etiquette; In Britain, a 'Scheme' Carries No Taint," *The Wall Street Journal*, January 19, 2010, B5.

[91]J. S. Black, M. Mendenhall, & G. Oddou, "Toward a Comprehensive Model of International Adjustment: An Integration of Multiple Theoretical Perspectives," *Academy of Management Review* 16 (1991): 291–317; R. L. Tung, "American Expatriates Abroad: From Neophytes to Cosmopolitans," *Columbia Journal of World Business*, 22 June 1998, 125; A. Harzing, "The Persistent Myth of High Expatriate Failure Rates," *International Journal of Human Resource Management* 6 (1995): 457–475; A. Harzing, "Are Our Referencing Errors Undermining Our Scholarship and Credibility? The Case of Expatriate Failure Rates," *Journal of Organizational Behavior* 23 (2002): 127–148; and N. Forster, "The Persistent Myth of High Expatriate Failure Rates: A Reappraisal," *International Journal of Human Resource Management* 8 (1997): 414–433.

[92]J. Black, "The Right Way to Manage Expats," *Harvard Business Review* 77 (March–April 1999): 52; and C. Joinson, "No Returns," *HR Magazine*, November 1, 2002, 70.

[93]C. Joinson, "No Returns."

[94]J. S. Black & M. Mendenhall, "Cross-Cultural Training Effectiveness: A Review and Theoretical Framework for Future Research," *Academy of Management Review* 15 (1990): 113–136.

[95]K. Essick, "Executive Education: Transferees Prep for Life, Work in Far-Flung Lands," *The Wall Street Journal*, November 12, 2004, A6.

[96]Ibid.

[97]P. W. Tam, "Culture Course— 'Awareness Training' Helps U.S. Workers Better Know Their Counterparts in India," *The Wall Street Journal*, May 25, 2004, B1.

[98]S. Hamm, "Aperian: Helping Companies Bridge Cultures," *Businessweek*, September 8, 2008, 16.

[99]William W. Maddux, Adam D. Galinsky, & Carmit T. Tadmor, "Be a Better Manager: Live Abroad" *Harvard Business Review*, September 9, 2010, accessed November 20, 20-10, from http://hbr.org/2010/09/be-a-better-manager-live-abroad/ar/1.

[100]T. Mohn, "The Dislocated Americans," *The New York Times*, December 1, 2008, accessed July 23, 2010, from www.nytimes.com/2008/12/02/business/worldbusiness/02expat.html?ref=americans_abroad.

[101]W. Arthur, Jr., & W. Bennett, Jr., "The International Assignee: The Relative Importance of Factors Perceived to Contribute to Success," *Personnel Psychology* 48 (1995): 99–114; and B. Cheng, "Home Truths about Foreign Postings; To Make an Overseas Assignment Work, Employers Need More Than an Eager Exec with a Suitcase. They Must Also Motivate the Staffer's Spouse," *Businessweek Online*, accessed March 20, 2009, from www.Businessweek.com/careers/content/jul2002/ca20020715_9110.htm.

[102]M. Netz, "It's Not Judging—It's Assessing: The Truth about Candidate Assessments," *NRRE Magazine*, March 2004, accessed August 8, 2008, from http://rismedia.com/wp/2004-03-03/its-not-judgingits-assessing.

[103]"OAI: Overseas Assignment Inventory," Prudential Real Estate and Relocation Services Intercultural Group, accessed May 11, 2011, from www.performanceprograms.com/userfiles/image/Cross%20Culture/OAI_Fact_Sheet.pdf.

[104]S. P. Deshpande & C. Viswesvaran, "Is Cross-Cultural Training of Expatriate Managers Effective? A Meta-Analysis," *International Journal of Intercultural Relations* 16, no. 3 (1992): 295–310.

[105]R. Donkin, "Recruitment: Overseas Gravy Train May Be Running Out of Steam—Preparing Expatriate Packages Is Challenging the

Expertise of Human Resource Management," *Financial Times*, November 30, 1994, 10.

[106]Eschbach, G. Parker, & P. Stoeberl, "American Repatriate Employees' Retrospective Assessments of the Effects of Cross-Cultural Training on Their Adaptation to International Assignments," *International Journal of Human Resource Management* 12 (2001): 270–287; and "Culture Training: How to Prepare Your Expatriate Employees for Cross- Cultural Work Environments," *Managing Training & Development*, February 1, 2005.

[107]J. Areddy, "Deep Inside China, American Family Struggles to Cope."

[108]R. W. Boatler, "Study Abroad: Impact on Student Worldmindedness," *Journal of Teaching in International Business* 2, no. 2 (1990): 13–17; R. W. Boatler, "Worldminded Attitude Change in a Study Abroad Program: Contact and Content Issues," *Journal of Teaching in International Business* 3, no. 4 (1992): 59–68; H. Lancaster, "Learning to Manage in a Global Workplace (You're on Your Own)," *The Wall Street Journal*, June 2, 1998, B1; and D. L. Sampson & H. P. Smith, "A Scale to Measure Worldminded Attitudes," *Journal of Social Psychology* 45 (1957): 99–106.

[109]Mehul Srivastava, "Business Caught in Middle of India's Culture War," *Bloomberg Businessweek*, February 18, 2009, accessed September 10, 2010, from www.Businessweek.com/globalbiz/content/feb2009/gb20090218_783926_page_2.htm.

[110]I. Bodner, "Social Entrepreneurship," *Fast Company*, June 2, 2009, accessed June 12, 2009, from www.fastcompany.com/1723694/social-entrepreneurship-and-the-common-brand; K. Krippendorff, "A Prescription For Doing Good—Pfizer's New Ethonomic Treatment Plan," *Fast Company*, June 34, 2009, accessed June 12, 2008, from www.fastcompany.com/blog/kaihan-krippendorff/outthinker-mavericks-out-innovate-competition/prescription-doing-good-pfize; and S. Hamm, "Into Africa: Capitalism from the Ground Up," *Businessweek*, May 4, 2009, 60–61.

[111]A. Hanft, "Passport to America," *Inc.*, October 2004, 14.

© iStockphoto.com/Oner Döngel

BIZ FLIX

Lost in Translation

The 2003 film *Lost in Translation*, based on Sofia Coppola's Academy Award–winning screenplay, stars Scarlett Johansson as a recent college graduate and newlywed named Charlotte. She visits Tokyo with her husband, a photographer on assignment in the city, who leaves her alone to navigate her way through a country whose culture and language she doesn't understand. When she meets Bob Harris (Bill Murray), an actor who is there to shoot a whiskey commercial and pocket a quick $2 million for it, they forge an unlikely friendship. This clip is an edited composite taken from different scenes in the movie. It shows us what Japan looks like through Charlotte's eyes as she explores it on her own and tries to make sense of what she sees.

© GreenLight

What to Watch for and Ask Yourself

1. Imagine you have just arrived in Japan, and you are experiencing what Charlotte is for the first time. Do you understand everything you see?

2. If you were managing a company that had operations in foreign countries, how important do you think it would be to experience new places and learn about different cultures the way Charlotte does?

3. How might it change the way you did business in those countries if you had actually been to them?

4. Does Charlotte seem to be culturally sensitive or insensitive?

MANAGEMENT WORKPLACE

Holden Outerwear: Managing in a Global Environment

Like so many other American brands, Holden apparel is made in China. Although the company would like to manufacture in the United States, government regulations, labor costs, and high corporate tax rates are too heavy a burden. Availability of materials is another factor, as many of the pieces that Holden needs, like buttons, snaps, and fabrics, would still have to be brought in from Asia even if the garment was made in the United States. In addition, garment making requires skilled laborers, and founder Mikey LeBlanc says that the United States lacks a manufacturing base to do the job. For any company that sources materials and labor overseas, shipping is a vital, ongoing concern. In the early years, LeBlanc used nearly a dozen shippers to transport garments from China to the United States. To increase efficiency and reduce costs, LeBlanc found a way to coordinate shipping through a single distribution hub in China, so that just two companies now handle all of Holden's shipping.

© Cengage Learning

Discussion Questions

1. Which stage of globalization characterizes Holden Outerwear's international involvement?

2. Identify Holden's primary approach to entering the international market. What are the benefits of this entry strategy?

3. What are the challenges of international management for leaders at Holden?

Organizing

Chapter 9
Designing Adaptive Organizations

This chapter shows you the traditional organizational structure approach to organizational design (the vertical and horizontal configuration of departments, authority, and jobs within a company), as well as how contemporary organizations are redesigning their processes to better transform inputs into outputs.

Eli Lilly

Chapter 10
Managing Teams

Chapter 10 reviews the advantages and disadvantages of teams and explores when companies should use them. You'll also read about the different types of work teams and the characteristics common to all teams, and learn practical steps to managing teams—team goals and priorities, and organizing, training, and compensating teams.

Cessna

Chapter 11
Managing Human Resource Systems

This chapter covers the key aspects of human resource systems: determining your human resource needs; finding qualified employees; developing the knowledge, skills, and abilities of the workforce; implementing effective compensation practices; and effectively managing separation.

Nick's Pizza & Pub

Chapter 12
Managing Individuals and a Diverse Workforce

In this chapter, you'll learn what diversity is and why it matters. We'll go over surface-level diversity (how age, gender, race/ethnicity, and disabilities affect people at work) and deep-level diversity (how core personality differences influence behavior and attitudes). You will also learn how diversity can be managed.

Circuit Court, Macomb County, Michigan

CHAPTER 9

Designing Adaptive Organizations

Learning Outcomes

1. Describe the departmentalization approach to organizational structure.
2. Explain organizational authority.
3. Discuss the different methods for job design.
4. Explain the methods that companies are using to redesign internal organizational processes (i.e., intraorganizational processes).
5. Describe the methods that companies are using to redesign external organizational processes (i.e., interorganizational processes).

what would **you do?**

Eli Lilly Headquarters, Indianapolis, Indiana[1]

Tick-tock. After being named Lilly's new CEO, you sent each top executive a digital clock counting down the time to October 23, 2011, the day that Lilly's 20-year patent runs out on Zyprexa, a schizophrenia drug that generates $5 billion a year in revenue. On that day, **Eli Lilly** loses the exclusive right to sell Zyprexa, and other drug manufacturers will begin selling generic versions for much lower prices. Lilly has seven other major drugs that will fall off the "patent cliff" in the next seven years, and stands to lose 75 percent of its annual revenue if it doesn't generate new "blockbuster" drugs. Like a Hollywood studio, Lilly needs to keep coming up with "blockbusters" in order to sustain profitability and market share. Hence, the message inscribed on the clocks, "Do what we do," that is, discover and develop new drugs at Lilly. Tick-tock.

Lilly isn't the only pharmaceutical company in this situation. Over the next three years, the entire industry will see half of its revenues fall off patent as three dozen major drugs become eligible to be sold as generics. When that happens, the company that held the patent typically sees sales of that drug drop by 80 percent. Pfizer will lose an estimated $13 billion a year when Lipitor, the top-selling statin, a cholesterol-lowering drug, loses its patent. By 2012, Merck will lose patent protection on its three top-selling drugs, Fosamax (osteoporosis), Singulair (asthma), and Cozaar (blood pressure), which account for 44 percent of its sales.

Unfortunately, Lilly has been here before, when its patent expired on Prozac, a drug for depression, taken daily by 40 million people. Then-CEO Sidney Taurel said, "The situation we had in the mid-1990s, of having 35 percent of our sales dependent on Prozac, won't repeat itself." Taurel took steps to energize Lilly's drug development by increasing the research and development (R&D) budget by 30 percent, hiring 700 new scientists, and instructing Lilly's 7,000 researchers to focus on drugs that could produce 500 million dollars a year in sales. This time, however, expanding headcount and increasing R&D budgets aren't options. With the potential loss of so much revenue, you had to lower costs. Accordingly, you laid off 5,500 workers and cut $1 billion in annual expenses. Less Funtleyder, an analyst at Miller Tabak & Co. in New York, said, "It's been another tough year for Big Pharma [cutting 37,000 jobs]. Lilly is not in this boat alone, by any means. But they probably have the biggest immediate challenge, because their patent cliff is so steep."

With those short-term steps behind you, the long-term challenge is to grow Lilly's drug pipeline? But how? You need to encourage faster, less expensive innovation, which is never easy.

"what's new" companies

Eli Lilly
Microsoft
Boston Scientific
Scharffen Berger Chocolate Maker
Southwest Airlines
Justin.tv
UBS AG

< **"what's new" companies**

Eli Lilly and Company Lilly Corporate Center

© AP Images/Darron Cumming

study tips

Try the exercise with a variety of company types, and then see whether the companies you used have organizational information on their websites. Practicing building organizational structures will help you better understand the different elements covered in the chapter.

Think about your favorite company and imagine how you think it could be organized. Draw an organizational structure that you think makes sense for the business and the industry it's in.

© iStockphoto.com/Alex Slobodkin

© iStockphoto.com/Ivan Burmistrov

Some think that large budgets, centralized approval for allocating research dollars, and siloed research (where few know and understand what others in the company are working on) stifle innovation and slow the decision-making process. If that's the case, what might Lilly do internally to restructure itself to improve communication in product development teams and speed up the entire drug development process? Also, if the traditional company structure used by pharmaceutical firms, typically functional, product, or matrix structures, haven't been successful at encouraging drug development, are there nontraditional organizational structures that Lilly could use to do so that can also help to speed development and lower costs? Finally, to what extent should Lilly outsource parts of its drug development process to outside vendors and companies? Because you risk creating new competitors with your own dollars when you outsource, a general guideline is to only outsource noncore business activities. But when you're a pharmaceutical firm, drug development is the core of your business. Is there a way for Lilly to effectively outsource drug development that gets around those risks? Tick-tock. Tick-tock. The clock is running.

If you were Lilly's CEO, what would you do?

No one builds a house without first looking at the design. Put a window there. Take out a wall here. Soon you've got the design you want. Only then do you start building. These days, the design of a company is just as important as the design of a house. Even successful companies, such as Lilly, must constantly examine their organizational design.

This chapter begins by reviewing the traditional organizational structure approach to organizational design. **Organizational structure** is the vertical and horizontal configuration of departments, authority, and jobs within a company. Organizational structure is concerned with questions such as "Who reports to whom?" and "Who does what?" and "Where is the work done?" For example, Sony Corporation of America is headed by Chairman and CEO Howard Stringer, who is based in New York City. But Sony has a number of divisions to handle different sectors of the company's business, each headed by its own president or CEO. PlayStations are developed and managed in Foster City, California, by Sony Computer Entertainment, which is part of the Consumer Products and Services Group.[2] Sony camcorders, home theater

Exhibit 9.1 Sony's Organizational Structure

CEO

Sony Ericsson Mobile Communications

Consumer Products & Services Group
- Home Entertainment Business Group
- Personal Imaging & Sound Business Group
- VAIO & Mobile Business Group
- Sony Network Entertainment
- Sony Computer Entertainment

Professional, Device & Solutions Group
- Professional Solutions Group
- Semiconductor Business Group
- Device Solutions Business Group

Sony DADC

Sony Music Entertainment

Sony Pictures Entertainment

Sony Financial Holdings Group

Common Platforms
- Global Sales & Marketing Platform
- Manufacturing, Logistics, Procurement and CS Platform
- R&D Platform
- Common Software Platform

Headquarters

Source: "Sony Group Organizational Chart Summary," Sony, April 1, 2011, accessed May 15, 2011, from www.sony.net/SonyInfo/CorporateInfo/Data/organization.html.

equipment, LCD screens, VAIO computers, Blu-ray players, and the Walkman are handled in San Diego by Sony Electronics. The Spider-Man films, *Jeopardy!* and *Seinfeld* were brought to you by Sony Pictures, a division of Sony Entertainment in Culver City, California, and the music of Justin Timberlake, Pink, Shakira, and Avril Lavigne comes courtesy of Sony Music Entertainment in New York City.[3] Companies like Sony use organizational structure to set up departments and relationships among employees in order to make business happen. You can see Sony's organizational structure in Exhibit 9.1. In the first half of the chapter, you will learn about the traditional vertical and horizontal approaches to organizational structure, including departmentalization, organizational authority, and job design.

In the second half of the chapter, you will learn how contemporary organizations are becoming more adaptive by redesigning their internal and external processes. An **organizational process** is the collection of activities that transform inputs into outputs that customers value.[4] Organizational process asks, "How do things get done?" For example, **Microsoft** uses basic internal and external processes, shown in Exhibit 9.2, to write computer software. The process starts when Microsoft gets feedback from customers through Internet newsgroups, email, phone calls, or letters. This information helps Microsoft understand customers' needs and problems, and identify important software issues and needed changes and functions. Microsoft then rewrites the software, testing it internally at the company and then externally through its beta testing process, in which customers who volunteer or are selected by Microsoft give the company extensive feedback. The feedback is then used to make improvements to the software. The beta testing process may take as long as a year and involve thousands of knowledgeable people. After final corrections are made to the software, the company distributes and sells it to customers. They start the process again by giving Microsoft more feedback. Indeed, Microsoft's advertising campaign for the kickoff of Windows 7, which was developed through extensive beta testing, was "I'm a PC, and Windows 7 was my idea."

This process view of Microsoft, which focuses on how things get done, is very different from the hierarchical view of Sony, which focuses on accountability, responsibility, and positions within the chain of command. In the second half of the chapter, you will learn how companies use reengineering, empowerment, and behavioral informality to redesign their internal organizational processes. The chapter ends with a discussion about the ways in which companies are redesigning their external processes, that is, how they are changing to improve their interactions with those outside the company. In that discussion, you will explore the basics of modular and virtual organizations.

organizational structure the vertical and horizontal configuration of departments, authority, and jobs within a company.

organizational process the collection of activities that transform inputs into outputs that customers value.

< **"what's new" companies**

Exhibit 9.2 Process View of Microsoft's Organization

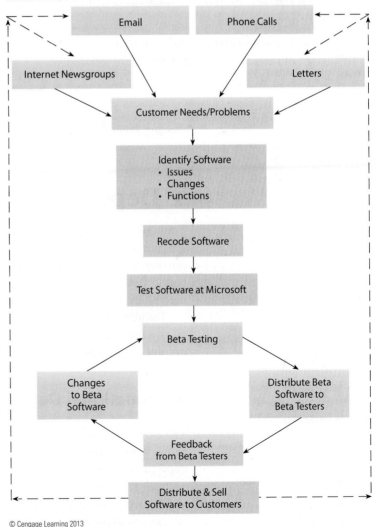

© Cengage Learning 2013

Designing Organizational Structures

"what's new"
companies > With 15,700 patents, 13,000 products, and 17 manufacturing facilities worldwide, **Boston Scientific** is one of the largest medical device companies in the world. To improve company performance, Boston Scientific changed its organizational structure to focus on four product areas: the cardiology, rhythm and vascular group (for treating coronary artery disease, irregular heart rhythms, and vascular blockages), the endoscopy division (for treating the digestive system and the lungs), the urology and women's health division (for treating kidney and bladder stones, as well as incontinence), and the neuromodulation division (for treating chronic pain). Furthermore, the headquarters for international business will be eliminated. The presidents of the Japan, Europe, and the newly formed Emerging Markets Group (India, China, Brazil, Russia, Eastern Europe, and parts of the Middle East, Asia, and Latin America) will instead report directly to the CEO. "The actions we are announcing today will provide the organizational structure and leadership needed to execute our strategic plan and fulfill the enormous promise of this company," said Ray Elliott, president and CEO of Boston Scientific.[5]

Why would a large company like Boston Scientific, with 25,000 employees and $7.8 billion in annual revenues, completely restructure its organizational design? What does it expect to gain from this change?

After reading the next three sections, you'll have a better understanding of the importance of organizational structure because you should be able to

1. *Describe the departmentalization approach to organizational structure.*
2. *Explain organizational authority.*
3. *Discuss the different methods for job design.*

1 Departmentalization

Traditionally, organizational structures have been based on some form of departmentalization. **Departmentalization** is a method of subdividing work and workers into separate organizational units that take responsibility for completing particular tasks.[6] Bayer, a Germany-based company, has separate departments or divisions for health care, crop science, material science, and services.[7]

Traditionally, organizational structures have been created by departmentalizing work according to five methods: **1.1 functional, 1.2 product, 1.3 customer, 1.4 geographic,** and **1.5 matrix.**

1.1 Functional Departmentalization

departmentalization subdividing work and workers into separate organizational units responsible for completing particular tasks.

functional departmentalization organizing work and workers into separate units responsible for particular business functions or areas of expertise.

The most common organizational structure is functional departmentalization. Companies tend to use this structure when they are small or just starting out. **Functional departmentalization** organizes work and workers into separate units responsible for particular business functions or areas of expertise. A common functional structure might have individuals organized into accounting, sales, marketing, production, and human resources departments.

Not all functionally departmentalized companies have the same functions. The insurance company and the advertising agency shown in Exhibit 9.3 both have sales, accounting, human resources, and information systems departments, as indicated by the green boxes. The blue and khaki boxes indicate the functions that are different. As would be expected, the insurance company has separate departments for life, auto, home, and health insurance. The advertising agency has departments for artwork, creative work, print advertising, and Internet advertising. So the functional departments in a company that uses functional structure depend in part on the business or industry a company is in.

Functional departmentalization has some advantages. First, it allows work to be done by highly qualified specialists. Although the accountants in the accounting department take responsibility for producing accurate revenue and expense figures, the engineers in research and development can focus their efforts on designing a product that is reliable and simple to manufacture. Second, it lowers costs by reducing duplication. When the engineers in research and development come up with a fantastic new product, they don't have to worry about creating an aggressive advertising campaign to sell it. That task belongs to the advertising experts and sales representatives in marketing. Third, with everyone in the same department having similar work experience or training, communication and coordination are less problematic for departmental managers.

At the same time, functional departmentalization has a number of disadvantages. To start, cross-department coordination can be difficult. Managers and employees are often more interested in doing what's right for their function than in doing what's right for the entire organization. A good example is the traditional conflict between marketing and manufacturing. Marketing typically pushes for spending more money to make more products with more capabilities to meet customer needs. By contrast, manufacturing pushes for fewer products with simpler designs so that manufacturing facilities can ship finished products on time and keep costs within expense budgets. As companies grow, functional departmentalization may also lead to slower decision making and produce managers and workers with narrow experience and expertise.

Exhibit 9.3
Functional Departmentalization

© Cengage Learning 2013

1.2 Product Departmentalization

Product departmentalization organizes work and workers into separate units responsible for producing particular products or services. Exhibit 9.4 shows the product departmentalization structure used by United Technologies Corporation (UTC), which is organized along six different product lines: Carrier (heating, ventilating, and air conditioning), Hamilton Sundstrand (aircraft electrical power generation and distribution systems), Otis (design, manufacture, installation, maintenance, and servicing of elevators and escalators), Pratt & Whitney (commercial and military jet aircraft engines), Sikorsky (military and commercial helicopters), and UTC Fire & Security (fire safety and security products and services).[8]

One of the advantages of product departmentalization is that, like functional departmentalization, it allows managers and workers to specialize in one area of expertise. Unlike the narrow expertise and experiences in functional departmentalization, however, managers and workers develop a broader set of experiences and expertise related to an entire product line. Likewise, product departmentalization

product departmentalization organizing work and workers into separate units responsible for producing particular products or services.

343

Exhibit 9.4 Product Departmentalization: United Technologies

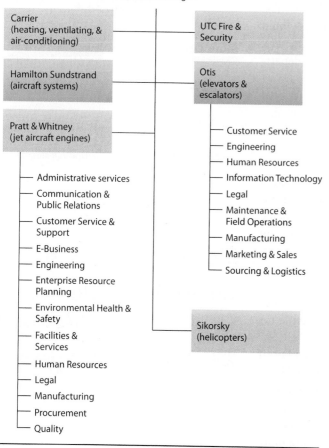

United Technologies

Carrier (heating, ventilating, & air-conditioning)

Hamilton Sundstrand (aircraft systems)

Pratt & Whitney (jet aircraft engines)

- Administrative services
- Communication & Public Relations
- Customer Service & Support
- E-Business
- Engineering
- Enterprise Resource Planning
- Environmental Health & Safety
- Facilities & Services
- Human Resources
- Legal
- Manufacturing
- Procurement
- Quality

UTC Fire & Security

Otis (elevators & escalators)

- Customer Service
- Engineering
- Human Resources
- Information Technology
- Legal
- Maintenance & Field Operations
- Manufacturing
- Marketing & Sales
- Sourcing & Logistics

Sikorsky (helicopters)

Source: Accessed 30 August, 2011, from http://utc.com/About+UTC/Company+Reports/2010+Annual+report+English.

makes it easier for top managers to assess work-unit performance. Because of the clear separation of their six different product divisions, United Technologies' top managers can easily compare the performance of the Otis elevators division and the Pratt & Whitney aircraft engines division. The divisions had similar revenues—almost $11.8 billion for Otis and $12.6 billion for Pratt & Whitney—but Otis had a profit of $2.4 billion (a 20.3% profit margin) compared with just $1.8 billion (a 14.3% profit margin) for Pratt & Whitney.[9] Finally, decision making should be faster because managers and workers are responsible for the entire product line rather than for separate functional departments; in other words, there are fewer conflicts compared to functional departmentalization.

The primary disadvantage of product departmentalization is duplication. You can see in Exhibit 9.4 that UTC's Otis elevators and Pratt & Whitney divisions both have customer service, engineering, human resources, legal, manufacturing, and procurement (similar to sourcing and logistics) departments. Duplication like this often results in higher costs. If United Technologies were instead organized by function, one lawyer could handle matters related to both elevators and aircraft engines rather than working on only one or the other.

A second disadvantage is the challenge of coordinating across the different product departments. United Technologies would probably have difficulty standardizing its policies and procedures in product departments as different as the Carrier (heating, ventilating, and air-conditioning) and Sikorsky (military and commercial helicopters) divisions.

1.3 Customer Departmentalization

Customer departmentalization organizes work and workers into separate units responsible for particular kinds of customers. For example, as Exhibit 9.5 shows, Swisscom AG, Switzerland's leading telecommunications provider, is organized into departments by type of customer: residential customers (fixed line and voice, mobile and voice, broadband Internet, and digital TV); small- and medium-sized businesses (fixed line and voice, mobile line and voice, Internet and data services, and maintenance and operation of IT infrastructure); larger corporations (fixed-line voice and data, mobile-line voice and data, Internet and data services, and maintenance and operation of IT infrastructure); and network

The S-92 helicopter built by UTC's Sikorsky helicopter division.

© Reuters/Sikorsky/Landov

Exhibit 9.5
Customer
Departmentalization:
Swisscom AG

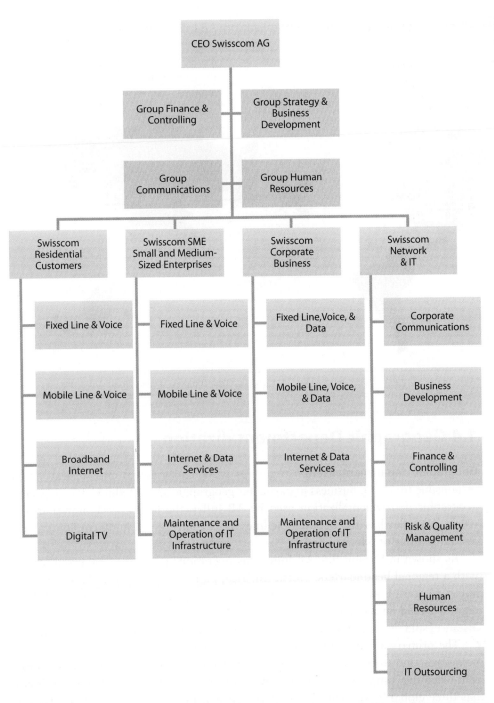

Source: "Overview," Sprint, accessed May 1, 2005, from www.sprint.com/sprint/fastfacts/overview/index.html.

and IT customers (corporate communications, business development, finance and controlling, risk and quality management, human resources, IT outsourcing).[10]

The primary advantage of customer departmentalization is that it focuses the organization on customer needs rather than on products or business functions. Furthermore, creating separate departments to serve specific kinds of customers allows companies to specialize and adapt their products and services to customer needs and problems. The primary disadvantage of customer departmentalization is that, like product departmentalization, it leads to duplication of resources. It can be difficult to achieve coordination across different customer departments, as is also the case with product departmentalization. Finally, the emphasis on meeting customers' needs may lead workers to make decisions that please customers but hurt the business.

customer departmentalization organizing work and workers into separate units responsible for particular kinds of customers.

345

Exhibit 9.6 Geographic Compartmentalization: AB InBev Company

Source: http://www.ab-inbev.com/go/investors/overview/anheuser_busch_inbev_company_profile.cfm.

1.4 Geographic Departmentalization

Geographic departmentalization organizes work and workers into separate units responsible for doing business in particular geographic areas. Exhibit 9.6 shows the geographic departmentalization used by AB InBev, the largest beer brewer in the world. AB InBev has 133 brewing facilities in 23 countries, 114,000 employees, and annual revenue of $36.3 billion.[11]

As shown in Exhibit 9.6, AB InBev has operations in six regional groups, each with a regional headquarters: North America, Latin America North, Latin America South, Western Europe, Central and Eastern Europe, and Asia Pacific. Each of these regions would be a sizable company by itself. The smallest region, Asia Pacific, for instance, sold 50.3 million hectoliters of beer for annual revenue of $292 million.

The primary advantage of geographic departmentalization is that it helps companies respond to the demands of different markets. This can be especially important when the company sells in different countries. For example, although AB InBev has three global brands (Budweiser, Stella Artois, and Beck's) sold worldwide) and two (Hoegaarden and Leffe) sold in multiple countries, most of its brands are local. You'll find the Antarctica and Bohemia brands in Brazil, the Bell-Vue and Jupiler brands in Belgium, and the Sibirskaya Korona and T. Tolstiak brands in Russia.[12]

Another advantage is that geographic departmentalization can reduce costs by locating unique organizational resources closer to customers. For instance, it is cheaper in the long run for AB InBev to build bottling plants in each region than to, for example, transport beer to Belgium, where it has four beverage plants, after it has been brewed and bottled in Russia, where it has 10 beverage plants.[13]

The primary disadvantage of geographic departmentalization is that it can lead to duplication of resources. For example, while it may be necessary to adapt products and marketing to different geographic locations, it's doubtful that AB InBev needs significantly different inventory tracking systems from location to location. Also, even more than with the other forms of departmentalization, it can be difficult

geographic departmentalization
organizing work and workers into separate units responsible for doing business in particular geographic areas.

Exhibit 9.7 Matrix Departmentalization: Procter & Gamble

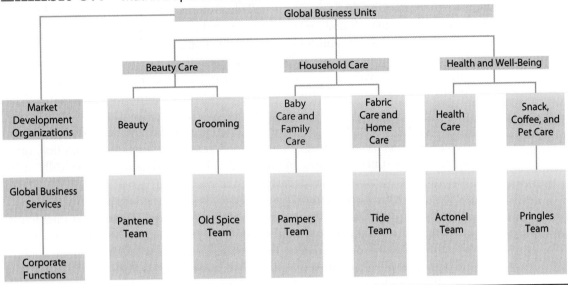

Source: "Corporate Structure: Strength in Structure," P&G, accessed May 17, 2011, from www.pg.com/en_US/company/global_structure _operations/corporate_structure.shtml.

to coordinate departments that are literally thousands of miles from each other and whose managers have very limited contact with each other.

1.5 Matrix Departmentalization

Matrix departmentalization is a hybrid structure in which two or more forms of departmentalization are used together. The most common matrix combines the product and functional forms of departmentalization, but other forms may also be used. Exhibit 9.7 shows the matrix structure used by Procter & Gamble, which has 127,000 employees working in 80 different countries.[14] Across the top of Exhibit 9.7, you can see that the company uses a product unit structure where it groups its billion-dollar brands into three global business units, each of which has two segments: beauty care (beauty and grooming), household care (baby care and family care plus fabric care and home care), and health and well-being (health care and snacks, coffee, and pet care). Global business units are responsible for product initiatives or upgrades, which are typically launched simultaneously with a worldwide marketing campaign. The left side of the figure, however, shows that the company is also using a functional structure based on three functions: market development, which makes sure that a product is adapted to and sells well within a particular region in the world (market development regions include North America, Asia/India/Australia, Northeast Asia, Greater China, Central-Eastern Europe/Middle East Africa, Western Europe, and Latin America); global business services, which enable the company to operate efficiently, work effectively with business partners, and increase employee productivity; and corporate functions, which provide global business units with the functional business assistance (i.e., finance, accounting, human resources, information technology, etc.) they need.[15]

The boxes in the figure represent the matrix structure, created by the combination of the product and functional structures. For example, the Pantene Team (Pantene is a set of hair care products within the beauty segment of the beauty care global business unit) would work with market development to adapt and sell Pantene products worldwide, use global business services to work with suppliers and keep costs down, and then rely on corporate functions for assistance in hiring

matrix departmentalization a hybrid organizational structure in which two or more forms of departmentalization, most often product and functional, are used together.

employees, billing customers, and paying suppliers. Similar matrix combinations are shown for P&G's Old Spice, Pampers, Tide, Actonel, and Pringles teams within each of the six segments found under its three global business units.

Several things distinguish matrix departmentalization from the other traditional forms of departmentalization.[16] First, most employees report to two bosses, one from each core part of the matrix. For example, in Exhibit 9.7 a manager on the Pampers team responsible for marketing would report to a boss in the baby care and family care segment of the household care global business unit as well as to a manager in the market development function. Second, by virtue of their hybrid design, matrix structures lead to much more cross-functional interaction than other forms of departmentalization. In fact, although matrix workers are typically members of only one functional department (based on their work experience and expertise), they are also commonly members of several ongoing project, product, or customer groups. Third, because of the high level of cross-functional interaction, matrix departmentalization requires significant coordination between managers in the different parts of the matrix. In particular, managers have the complex job of tracking and managing the multiple demands (project, product, customer, or functional) on employees' time.

The primary advantage of matrix departmentalization is that it allows companies to manage in an efficient manner large, complex tasks like researching, developing, and marketing pharmaceuticals or carrying out complex global businesses. Efficiency comes from avoiding duplication. For example, rather than having an entire marketing function for each project, the company simply assigns and reassigns workers from the marketing department (or market development at P&G) as they are needed at various stages of product completion. More specifically, an employee from a department may simultaneously be part of five different ongoing projects but may be actively completing work on only a few projects at a time. Another advantage is the pool of resources available to carry out large, complex tasks. Because of the ability to quickly pull in expert help from all the functional areas of the company, matrix project managers have a much more diverse set of expertise and experience at their disposal than managers in the other forms of departmentalization.

The primary disadvantage of matrix departmentalization is the high level of coordination required to manage the complexity involved in running large, ongoing projects at various levels of completion. Matrix structures are notorious for confusion and conflict between project bosses in different parts of the matrix. When Yahoo! founder Jerry Yang was trying to convince Carol Bartz, formerly CEO at Autodesk, to become CEO at Yahoo!, she asked him to draw a picture of the organizational structure. Bartz, who is now Yahoo!'s CEO, said, "It was like a Catholic school kid diagramming a sentence, where the lines sloppily crisscrossed and it was clear no one was in charge."[17]

Disagreements or misunderstandings about schedules, budgets, available resources, and the availability of employees with particular functional expertise are common in matrix structures. At Yahoo!, this manifested itself in slow decision making because multiple executives and divisions had overlapping responsibility for similar products and services. For example, Flickr (a Yahoo! website), Yahoo! Photos, Yahoo! Media Group, and the search unit's video service all shared responsibility for web-based photo and video services. The result, said then CEO Carol Bartz, is that "you'd be amazed at how complicated some things are here." The solution, according to Autodesk CEO Carl Bass, is, "They need one person in charge to coordinate what they do."[18] Another disadvantage is that matrix structures require much more management skill than the other forms of departmentalization.

Because of these problems, many matrix structures evolve from a **simple matrix**, in which managers in different parts of the matrix negotiate conflicts and resources

simple matrix a form of matrix departmentalization in which managers in different parts of the matrix negotiate conflicts and resources.

directly, to a **complex matrix**, in which specialized matrix managers and departments are added to the organizational structure. In a complex matrix, managers from different parts of the matrix might report to the same matrix manager, who helps them sort out conflicts and problems.

Sometimes, however, even these steps aren't enough to alleviate the problems that can occur in matrix structures. Europe-based Unilever is the maker and marketer of such well-known products as Dove soap, Vaseline Intensive Care lotions, Hellman's mayonnaise, I Can't Believe It's Not Butter, Lipton teas, Wishbone salad dressings, Skippy peanut butter, and Lawry's seasonings. Unilever was run using a complex matrix structure. The company even had dual headquarters in Rotterdam, the Netherlands, and London, England. The confusion and conflict associated with having two sets of management located in two headquarters were so great that Unilever has now switched to just one CEO and one headquarters. In addition, the company has moved to a simpler organizational structure based on geography, with three regional chiefs (in Europe, the Americas, and Asia/Africa) plus two global divisions (foods and soaps).[19] Patrick Cescau, the new CEO, says, "We have recognized the need for greater clarity of leadership and we are moving to a simpler leadership structure that will provide a sharper operational focus."[20] In short, because everyone now reports to just one boss, "we have clarified who calls the shots," says Cescau.

Departmentalization The five traditional departmental structures are functional, product, customer, geographic, and matrix. Functional departmentalization is based on the different business functions or expertise used to run a business. Product departmentalization is organized according to the different products or services a company sells. Customer departmentalization focuses its divisions on the different kinds of customers a company has. Geographic departmentalization is based on the different geographic areas or markets in which the company does business. Matrix departmentalization is a hybrid form that combines two or more forms of departmentalization, the most common being the product and functional forms. There is no single best departmental structure. Each structure has advantages and disadvantages.

Review 1

---

2 Organizational Authority

The second part of traditional organizational structures is authority. **Authority** is the right to give commands, take action, and make decisions to achieve organizational objectives.[21] Traditionally, organizational authority has been characterized by the following dimensions: **2.1 chain of command, 2.2 line versus staff authority, 2.3 delegation of authority,** and **2.4 degree of centralization.**

2.1 Chain of Command

Turn back a few pages to Sony's organizational chart in Exhibit 9.1. If you place your finger on any position in the chart, say, VAIO & Mobile Business Group (under Consumer Products & Services Group), you can trace a line upward to the company's CEO, Howard Stringer. This line, which vertically connects every job in the company to higher levels of management, represents the chain of command. The **chain of command** is the vertical line of authority that clarifies who reports to whom throughout the organization. People higher in the chain of command have the right, *if they so choose*, to give commands, take action, and make decisions concerning

complex matrix a form of matrix departmentalization in which managers in different parts of the matrix report to matrix managers, who help them sort out conflicts and problems.

authority the right to give commands, take action, and make decisions to achieve organizational objectives.

chain of command the vertical line of authority that clarifies who reports to whom throughout the organization.

activities occurring anywhere below them in the chain. In the following discussion about delegation and decentralization, you will learn that managers don't always choose to exercise their authority directly.[22]

One of the key assumptions underlying the chain of command is **unity of command**, which means that workers should report to just one boss.[23] In practical terms, this means that only one person can be in charge at a time. Matrix organizations, in which employees have two bosses (or two headquarters, as in the Unilever example you just read about), automatically violate this principle. This is one of the primary reasons that matrix organizations are difficult to manage. Unity of command serves an important purpose: to prevent the confusion that might arise when an employee receives conflicting commands from two different bosses. Robert Steinberg and John Scharffenberger founded **Scharffen Berger Chocolate Maker**, a producer of high-end, gourmet chocolate. Early on, they served as coleaders, which hurt company performance. Subordinates weren't sure who reported to whom. And because there wasn't one clear vision of how the company would operate, employees were often confused about priorities and goals. As Scharffenberger described it, "Peter Kocaurek [a maintenance manager] could ask me a question and [then ask] Robert the same question and take the answer he wanted. When you're formulating [a business], it's one thing, and when you're operating [a business], it's another." Having two bosses slowed the company. Eventually, though, Scharffenberger eventually bought out his partner. With a single person in charge, the company took off, with revenues reaching $10 million in just a few years. Eventually, the company proved so successful that it was sold to Hershey for $50 million.[24]

"what's new" companies >

2.2 Line versus Staff Authority

A second dimension of authority is the distinction between line and staff authority. **Line authority** is the right to command immediate subordinates in the chain of command. For example, Sony CEO Howard Stringer has line authority over the head of Sony's Professional, Device & Solutions Group, which includes Sony's Semiconductor Business Group. Stringer can issue orders to that division president and expect them to be carried out. In turn, the head of Sony Professional, Device & Solutions can issue orders to his subordinates and expect them to be carried out. **Staff authority** is the right to *advise*, but not command, others who are not subordinates in the chain of command. For example, a manager in human resources at Sony might advise the manager in charge of Sony's Home Entertainment Business Group on a hiring decision but cannot order him or her to hire a certain applicant.

The terms *line* and *staff* are also used to describe different functions within the organization. A **line function** is an activity that contributes directly to creating or selling the company's products. So, for example, activities that take place within the manufacturing and marketing departments would be considered line functions. A **staff function**, such as accounting, human resources, or legal services, does not contribute directly to creating or selling the company's products, but instead supports

unity of command a management principle that workers should report to just one boss.

line authority the right to command immediate subordinates in the chain of command.

staff authority the right to advise, but not command, others who are not subordinates in the chain of command.

line function an activity that contributes directly to creating or selling the company's products.

staff function an activity that does not contribute directly to creating or selling the company's products, but instead supports line activities.

line activities. For example, marketing managers might consult with the legal staff to make sure the wording of a particular advertisement is legal.

2.3 Delegation of Authority

Managers can exercise their authority directly by completing tasks themselves, or they can choose to pass on some of their authority to subordinates. **Delegation of authority** is the assignment of direct authority and responsibility to a subordinate to complete tasks for which the manager is normally responsible.

When a manager delegates work, three transfers occur, as illustrated in Exhibit 9.8. First, the manager transfers full responsibility for the assignment to the subordinate. At Apple, when you've been delegated to a certain task, you become the DRI, or the "directly responsible individual." As a former Apple employee explains, "Any effective meeting at Apple will have an action list. Next to each action item will be the DRI," who of course, is responsible for completing that delegated responsibility. Furthermore, when you're trying to figure out who to contact to get something done in Apple's corporate structure, people simply ask, "Who's the DRI on that?"[25]

Many managers, however, find giving up full responsibility somewhat difficult. Consultant David Nadler says, "There is a savior complex that says, 'I'm the only one' who can lead this company effectively."[26] One reason it is difficult for some managers to delegate is that they often fear that the task won't be done as well as if they did it themselves. However, one CEO says, "If you can delegate a task to somebody who can do it 75 percent to 80 percent as well as you can today, you delegate it immediately." Why? The reason is that many tasks don't need to be done perfectly; they just need to be *done*. And delegating tasks that someone else can do frees managers to assume other important responsibilities. Delegating authority can generate a related problem: micromanaging. Sometimes managers delegate, only to interfere later with how the employee is performing the task. But delegating full responsibility means that the employee—not the manager—is now completely responsible for task completion. Good managers need to trust their subordinates to do the job.

The second transfer that occurs with delegation is that the manager gives the subordinate full authority over the budget, resources, and personnel needed to do the job. To do the job effectively, subordinates must have the same tools and information at their disposal that managers had when they were responsible for the same task. In other words, for delegation to work, delegated authority must be commensurate with delegated responsibility. After numerous product recalls tarnished its reputation for building the most reliable cars in the world, Toyota created a North American Quality Advisory Panel to determine how to significantly improve product quality. And to make sure it has the budget, resources, and personnel it needs, the Panel will have direct lines of communication to CEO Akio Toyoda, "an unlimited budget to pursue its mandate," and "will be able to commission any additional outside reviews it deems necessary."[27]

The third transfer that occurs with delegation is the transfer of accountability. The subordinate now has the authority and responsibility to do the job and, in return, is accountable for getting the job done. In other words, managers delegate their managerial authority and responsibility to subordinates in exchange for results. *Forbes* magazine columnist John Rutledge calls delegation "MBB," Management by Belly Button. He says, "The belly button is the person whose belly you point your finger at when you want to know how the work is proceeding, that is, the

Exhibit 9.8
Delegation: Responsibility, Authority, and Accountability

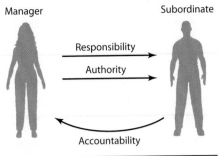

Manager   Subordinate

Responsibility

Authority

Accountability

Source: C. D. Pringle, D. F. Jennings, & J. G. Longenecker, *Managing Organizations: Functions and Behaviors* © 1990. Adapted by permission of Pearson Education, Inc., Upper Saddle River, NJ.

delegation of authority the assignment of direct authority and responsibility to a subordinate to complete tasks for which the manager is normally responsible.

Exhibit 9.9   How to Be a More Effective Delegator

1. **Trust your staff to do a good job.** Recognize that others have the talent and ability to complete projects.

2. **Avoid seeking perfection.** Establish a standard of quality and provide a time frame for reaching it.

3. **Give effective job instructions.** Make sure employees have enough information to complete the job successfully.

4. **Know your true interests.** Delegation is difficult for some people who actually prefer doing the work themselves rather than managing it.

5. **Follow up on progress.** Build in checkpoints to help identify potential problems.

6. **Praise the efforts of your staff**

7. **Don't wait to the last minute to delegate.** Avoid crisis management by routinely delegating work.

8. **Ask questions, expect answers, and assist employees** to help them complete the work assignments as expected.

9. **Provide the resources** you would expect if you were doing an assignment yourself.

10. **Delegate to the lowest possible level** to make the best possible use of organizational resources, energy, and knowledge.

Source: S. B. Wilton, "Are You an Effective Delegator?" *Female Executive,* November 1, 1994, 19.

person who will actually be accountable for each step. . . . The belly button is not a scapegoat—a person to blame later when things go wrong. He or she is the person who makes sure that things go right."[28] Exhibit 9.9 gives some tips on how to be an effective delegator.

2.4 Degree of Centralization

If you've ever called a company's toll-free number with a complaint or a special request and been told by the customer service representative, "I'll have to ask my manager" or "I'm not authorized to do that," you know that centralization of authority exists in that company. **Centralization of authority** is the location of most authority at the upper levels of the organization. In a centralized organization, managers make most decisions, even the relatively small ones. That's why the customer service representative you called couldn't make a decision without first asking the manager.

If you are lucky, however, you may have talked to a customer service representative at another company who said, "I can take care of that for you right now." In other words, the person was able to handle your problem without any input from or consultation with company management. **Decentralization** is the location of a significant amount of authority in the lower levels of the organization. An organization is decentralized if it has a high degree of delegation at all levels. In a decentralized organization, workers closest to problems are authorized to make the decisions necessary to solve the problems on their own.

Decentralization has a number of advantages. It develops employee capabilities throughout the company and leads to faster decision making and more satisfied customers and employees. Furthermore, a study of 1,000 large companies found that companies with a high degree of decentralization outperformed those with a low degree of decentralization in terms of return on assets (6.9% vs. 4.7%), return on investment (14.6% vs. 9.0%), return on equity (22.8% vs. 16.6%), and return on sales (10.3% vs. 6.3%). Surprisingly, the same study found that few large companies actually are decentralized. Specifically, only 31 percent of employees in these 1,000 companies were responsible for recommending improvements to management. Overall, just 10 percent of employees received the training and information needed to support a truly decentralized approach to management.[29]

With results like these, the key question is no longer *whether* companies should decentralize, but *where* they should decentralize. One rule of thumb is to stay centralized where standardization is important and to decentralize where standardization is unimportant. **Standardization** is solving problems by consistently applying the same rules, procedures, and processes. As its name suggests, Air Products & Chemicals serves global customers by selling gases (from argon to hydrogen, to nitrogen, to specialty gases), gas equipment and services, and related chemical products. As it grew over the last decade through acquisitions, its information technology (IT) department inherited 14 different databases, five different corporate networks,

centralization of authority the location of most authority at the upper levels of the organization.

decentralization the location of a significant amount of authority in the lower levels of the organization.

standardization solving problems by consistently applying the same rules, procedures, and processes.

and, of course, different kinds of servers, personal computers, and handheld devices. Not surprisingly, with so many different platforms to support, IT costs were rising 5 percent to 10 percent per year. So senior IT managers devised a "standardization index" to track and reduce the number of IT platforms the company was supporting. IT Manager Ron Crane said, "From day one, the business understood that standardizing would save them 3 percent to 7 percent annually."[30] After 5 years of planning and tracking via the standardization index, the company now has only two kinds of databases, one company network, one family of servers, and just four PC options. As a result, instead of rising, IT costs have been reduced by $3 million to $5 million a year.

Organizational Authority Organizational authority is determined by the chain of command, line versus staff authority, delegation, and the degree of centralization in a company. The chain of command vertically connects every job in the company to higher levels of management and makes clear who reports to whom. Managers have line authority to command employees below them in the chain of command but have only staff, or advisory, authority over employees not below them in the chain of command. Managers delegate authority by transferring to subordinates the authority and responsibility needed to do a task; in exchange, subordinates become accountable for task completion. In centralized companies, most authority to make decisions lies with managers in the upper levels of the company. In decentralized companies, much of the authority is delegated to the workers closest to problems, workers who can then make the decisions necessary for solving the problems themselves. Centralization works best for tasks that require standardized decision making. When standardization isn't important, decentralization can lead to faster decisions, greater employee and customer satisfaction, and significantly better financial performance.

Review 2

---

3 Job Design

Imagine that McDonald's decided to pay $75,000 a year to its drive-through window cashiers. That's $75,000 for saying, "Welcome to McDonald's. May I have your order please?" Would you take the job? Sure you would. Work a couple of years; make a hundred and fifty grand. Why not? Let's assume, however, that to get this salary, you have to be a full-time McDonald's drive-through window cashier for the next 10 years. Would you still take the job? Just imagine, 40 to 60 times an hour, you'd repeat the same basic process:

1. "Welcome to McDonald's. May I have your order please?"
2. Listen to the order. Repeat it for accuracy. State the total cost. "Please drive to the second window."
3. Take the money. Make change.
4. Give customers drinks, straws, and napkins.
5. Give customers food.
6. "Thank you for coming to McDonald's."

Could you stand to do the same simple tasks an average of 50 times per hour, 400 times per day, 2,000 times per week, 8,000 times per month? Few can. Fast-food

workers rarely stay on the job more than six months. Indeed, McDonald's and other fast-food restaurants have well over 100 percent employee turnover each year.[31]

In this next section, you will learn about **job design**—the number, kind, and variety of tasks that individual workers perform in doing their jobs. You will learn **3.1 why companies continue to use specialized jobs like the McDonald's drive-through job** and **3.2 how job rotation, job enlargement, job enrichment,** and **3.3 the job characteristics model** are being used to overcome the problems associated with job specialization.

3.1 Job Specialization

Job specialization occurs when a job is composed of a small part of a larger task or process. Specialized jobs are characterized by simple, easy-to-learn steps, low variety, and high repetition, like the McDonald's drive-through window job just described. One of the clear disadvantages of specialized jobs is that, being so easy to learn, they quickly become boring. This, in turn, can lead to low job satisfaction and high absenteeism and employee turnover, all of which are very costly to organizations.

Why, then, do companies continue to create and use specialized jobs? The primary reason is that specialized jobs are very economical. As we learned from Frederick W. Taylor and Frank and Lillian Gilbreth in Chapter 2, once a job has been specialized, it takes little time to learn and master. Consequently, when experienced workers quit or are absent, the company can replace them with new employees and lose little productivity. For example, next time you're at McDonald's, notice the pictures of the food on the cash registers. These pictures make it easy for McDonald's trainees to quickly learn to take orders. Likewise, to simplify and speed operations, the drink dispensers behind the counter are set to automatically fill drink cups. Put a medium cup below the dispenser. Punch the medium drink button. The soft-drink machine then fills the cup to within a half-inch of the top, while that same worker goes to get your fries. At McDonald's, every task has been simplified in this way. Because the work is designed to be simple, wages can remain low because it isn't necessary to pay high salaries to attract highly experienced, educated, or trained workers.

3.2 Job Rotation, Enlargement, and Enrichment

Because of the efficiency of specialized jobs, companies are often reluctant to eliminate them. Consequently, job redesign efforts have focused on modifying jobs to keep the benefits of specialized jobs while reducing their obvious costs and disadvantages. Three methods—job rotation, job enlargement, and job enrichment—have been used to try to improve specialized jobs.[32]

In factory work or even some office jobs, many workers perform the same task all day long. If you attach side mirrors in an auto factory, you probably complete this task 45 to 60 times an hour. If you work as the cashier at a grocery store, you check out a different customer every two to three minutes. And if you work as an office receptionist, you may answer and direct phone calls up to 200 times an hour. **Job rotation** attempts to overcome the disadvantages of job specialization by periodically moving workers from one specialized job to another to give them more variety and the opportunity to use different skills. For example, an office receptionist who does nothing but answer phones could be systematically rotated to a different job, such as typing, filing, or data entry, every day or two. Likewise, the "mirror attacher" in the automobile plant might attach mirrors in the first half of the work shift and

job design the number, kind, and variety of tasks that individual workers perform in doing their jobs.

job specialization a job composed of a small part of a larger task or process.

job rotation periodically moving workers from one specialized job to another to give them more variety and the opportunity to use different skills.

then install bumpers during the second half. Because employees simply switch from one specialized job to another, job rotation allows companies to retain the economic benefits of specialized work. At the same time, the greater variety of tasks makes the work less boring and more satisfying for workers. With $8 billion in sales, and a ranking in the *Fortune* 500, Trader Joes is one of the fastest growing retailers in the United States. A big factor in its success is how it treats employees. Trader Joes pays the highest salaries in retail, with full-time entry-level employees making $40,000–$60,000. Furthermore, Joes gives its workers multiple tasks and responsibilities. By contrast, at most grocery stores, you're hired to do a job, for example, cashier. But because of job rotation at Trader Joes, there are no designated cashiers, baggers, or stockers. Performing multiple tasks not only prevents boredom, it also familiarizes employees with how the entire store operates.[33]

Another way to counter the disadvantages of specialization is to enlarge the job. **Job enlargement** increases the number of different tasks that a worker performs within one particular job. Instead of being assigned just one task, workers with enlarged jobs are given several tasks to perform. For example, an enlarged "mirror attacher" job might include attaching the mirror, checking to see that the mirror's power adjustment controls work, and then cleaning the mirror's surface. Though job enlargement increases variety, many workers report feeling more stress when their jobs are enlarged. Consequently, many workers view enlarged jobs as simply more work, especially if they are not given additional time to complete the additional tasks.

Job enrichment attempts to overcome the deficiencies in specialized work by increasing the number of tasks *and* by giving workers the authority and control to make meaningful decisions about their work.[34] At AES, an independent power company that sells electricity to public utilities and steam (for power) to industrial organizations, workers are given an extraordinary level of authority and control. For example, with his hands still blackened after unloading coal from a barge, employee Jeff Hatch calls a broker to determine which Treasury bills the company should buy to maximize the short-term return on its available cash. Hatch asks his broker, "What kind of rate can you give me for $10 million at 30 days?" When the broker tells him, "6.09 percent," he responds, "But I just got a 6.13 percent quote from Chase."[35] Indeed, ordinary plant technicians at AES are given budgets worth several million dollars and are trusted to purchase everything from mops to gas turbines. In

job enlargement increasing the number of different tasks that a worker performs within one particular job.

job enrichment increasing the number of tasks in a particular job and giving workers the authority and control to make meaningful decisions about their work.

mgmt:trends

Go Small or Go Home

What's the best way for an organization to grow? No doubt, most people would answer this question by talking about expansion, opening more stores, selling more products, or offering more services. But a number of retail companies have found that it's easier to grow by going small. Anchor Blue, a clothing retailer in California, recently remodeled its store by abandoning half of its original floor space. The smaller spaces allow Anchor Blue to reduce excess inventory, cut labor costs, save on rent, and therefore run the store more efficiently. In its smaller form, the store's foot traffic is up 7 percent and its sales are up 23 percent. This goes to show that sometimes, the best way to grow is to shrink.[36]

© iStockphoto.com/Kirsty Pargeter

most companies, such tasks would be entrusted only to managers, but former CEO Dennis Bakke says, "The more you increase individual responsibility, the better the chances for incremental improvements in operations." Paul Burdick, an engineer entrusted with the ability to purchase billions of dollars of coal, agrees, adding, "You're given a lot of leeway and a lot of rope. You can use it to climb or you can hang yourself."[37]

3.3 Job Characteristics Model

In contrast to job rotation, job enlargement, and job enrichment, which focus on providing variety in job tasks, the **job characteristics model (JCM)** is an approach to job redesign that seeks to formulate jobs in ways that motivate workers and lead to positive work outcomes.[38]

As shown in Exhibit 9.10, the primary goal of the model is to create jobs that result in positive personal and work outcomes, such as internal work motivation, satisfaction with one's job, and work effectiveness. Of these, the central concern of the JCM is internal motivation. **Internal motivation** is motivation that comes from the job itself rather than from outside rewards such as a raise or praise from the boss. If workers feel that performing the job well is itself rewarding, then the job has internal motivation. Statements such as "I get a nice sense of accomplishment" or "I feel good about myself and what I'm producing" are examples of internal motivation.

Moving to the left in Exhibit 9.10, you can see that the JCM specifies three critical psychological states that must occur for work to be internally motivating. First, workers must *experience the work as meaningful*; that is, they must view their job as being important. Second, they must *experience responsibility for work outcomes*—they must feel personally responsible for the work being done well. Third, workers must have *knowledge of results*; that is, they must know how well they are performing their jobs. All three critical psychological states must occur for work to be internally motivating.

Exhibit 9.10 Job Characteristics Model

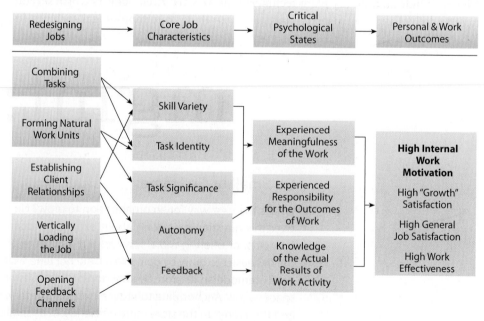

job characteristics model (JCM) an approach to job redesign that seeks to formulate jobs in ways that motivate workers and lead to positive work outcomes.

internal motivation motivation that comes from the job itself rather than from outside rewards.

Source: J. R. Hackman & G. R. Oldham, *Work Redesign* (Reading, MA: Addison-Wesley, 1980). Reprinted by permission of Addison-Wesley Longman.

Let's return to our grocery store cashier. Cashiers usually have knowledge of results. When you're slow, your checkout line grows long. If you make a mistake, customers point it out: "No, I think that's on sale for $2.99, not $3.99." Likewise, cashiers experience responsibility for work outcomes. At the end of the day, the register is totaled and the money is counted. Ideally, the money matches the total sales in the register. If the money in the till is less than what's recorded in the register, most stores make the cashier pay the difference. Consequently, most cashiers are very careful to avoid being caught short at the end of the day. Nonetheless, despite knowing the results and experiencing responsibility for work outcomes, most grocery store cashiers (at least where I shop) aren't internally motivated because they don't experience the work as meaningful. With scanners, it takes little skill to learn or do the job. Anyone can do it. In addition, cashiers have few decisions to make, and the job is highly repetitive.

What kinds of jobs produce the three critical psychological states? Moving another step to the left in Exhibit 9.10, you can see that these psychological states arise from jobs that are strong on five core job characteristics: skill variety, task identity, task significance, autonomy, and feedback. **Skill variety** is the number of different activities performed in a job. **Task identity** is the degree to which a job, from beginning to end, requires completion of a whole and identifiable piece of work. **Task significance** is the degree to which a job is perceived to have a substantial impact on others inside or outside the organization. **Autonomy** is the degree to which a job gives workers the discretion, freedom, and independence to decide how and when to accomplish the work. Finally, **feedback** is the amount of information the job provides to workers about their work performance.

To illustrate how the core job characteristics work together, let's use them to assess more thoroughly why the McDonald's drive-through window job is not particularly satisfying or motivating. To start, skill variety is low. Except for the size of an order or special requests ("no onions"), the process is the same for each customer. At best, task identity is moderate. Although you take the order, handle the money, and deliver the food, others are responsible for a larger part of the process—preparing the food. Task identity will be even lower if the McDonald's has two drive-through windows, because each drive-through window worker will have an even more specialized task. The first is limited to taking the order and making change, whereas the second just delivers the food.

Task significance, the impact you have on others, is probably low. Autonomy is also very low: McDonald's has strict rules about dress, cleanliness, and procedures. But the job does provide immediate feedback such as positive and negative customer comments, car horns honking, the amount of time it takes to process orders, and the number of cars in the drive-through. With the exception of feedback, the low levels of the core job characteristics show why the drive-through window job is not internally motivating for many workers.

What can managers do when jobs aren't internally motivating? The far left column of Exhibit 9.10 lists five job redesign techniques that managers can use to strengthen a job's core characteristics. *Combining tasks* increases skill variety and task identity by joining separate, specialized tasks into larger work modules. For example, some trucking firms are now requiring truck drivers to load their rigs as well as drive them. The hope is that involving drivers in loading will ensure that trucks are properly loaded, thus reducing damage claims.

© Tim Boyle/Getty Images

This two-window drive-through in Monroe, Washington, is typical of McDonald's (and other fast-food restaurants) around the country. But even though this way of organizing the work is extremely efficient, it can be less than stimulating for employees.

skill variety the number of different activities performed in a job.

task identity the degree to which a job, from beginning to end, requires the completion of a whole and identifiable piece of work.

task significance the degree to which a job is perceived to have a substantial impact on others inside or outside the organization.

autonomy the degree to which a job gives workers the discretion, freedom, and independence to decide how and when to accomplish the job.

feedback the amount of information the job provides to workers about their work performance.

© iStockphoto.com/Hans Martens

what really works

The Job Characteristics Model: Making Jobs More Interesting and Motivating

Think of the worst job you ever had. Was it factory work where you repeated the same task every few minutes? Was it an office job requiring a lot of meaningless paperwork? Or was it a job so specialized that it took no effort or thinking whatsoever to do?

The job characteristics model reviewed in this chapter suggests that workers will be more motivated or satisfied with their work if their jobs have greater task identity, task significance, skill variety, autonomy, and feedback. Eighty-four studies, with a combined total of 22,472 participants, found that, on average, these core job characteristics make jobs more satisfying for most workers. In addition, jobs rich with the five core job characteristics are especially satisfying for workers who possess an individual characteristic called *growth need strength*. Read on to see how well the JCM really increases job satisfaction and reduces workplace absenteeism.

Job Satisfaction

There is a 66 percent chance that workers will be more satisfied with their work when their jobs have task identity, the chance to complete an entire job from beginning to end, than when they don't.

On average, there is a 69 percent chance that workers will be more satisfied with their work when their jobs have task significance—a substantial impact on others—than when they don't.

On average, there is a 70 percent chance that workers will be more satisfied with their work when their jobs have skill variety—a variety of activities, skills, and talents—than when they don't.

On average, there is a 73 percent chance that workers will be more satisfied with their work when their jobs have autonomy—the discretion to decide how and when to accomplish the work—than when they don't.

On average, there is a 70 percent chance that workers will be more satisfied with their work when their jobs provide feedback—information about their work performance—than when they don't.

These statistics indicate that, on average, the JCM has, at worst, a 66 percent chance of improving workers' job satisfaction. In all, this is impressive evidence that the model works. In general, you can expect these results when redesigning jobs based on the model.

We can be more accurate about the effects of the JCM, however, if we split workers into two groups: those with high growth need strength and those with low growth need strength. *Growth need strength* is the need or desire to achieve personal growth and development through one's job. Workers high in growth need strength respond well to jobs designed according to the JCM because they enjoy work that challenges them and allows them to learn new skills and knowledge. In fact, there is an 84 percent chance that workers with high growth need strength will be more satisfied with their work when their jobs are redesigned according to the JCM.

By comparison, because they aren't as interested in being challenged or learning new things at work, there is only a 69 percent chance that workers low in growth need strength will be satisfied with jobs that have been redesigned according to the principles of the JCM. This is still a favorable percentage, but it is weaker than the 84 percent chance of job satisfaction that occurs for workers high in growth need strength.

Workplace Absenteeism

Although not shown in the job characteristics model displayed in Exhibit 9.10, workplace absenteeism is an important personal or work outcome affected by a job's core characteristics. In general, the "richer" your job is with task identity, task significance, skill variety, autonomy, and feedback, the more likely you are to show up for work every day.

Workers are 63 percent more likely to attend work when their jobs have task identity than when they don't.

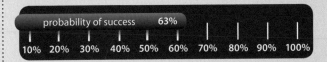

Workers are 68 percent more likely to attend work when their jobs have task significance than when they don't.

Workers are 72 percent more likely to attend work when their jobs have skill variety than when they don't.

Workers are 74 percent more likely to attend work when their jobs have autonomy than when they don't.

Workers are 72 percent more likely to attend work when their jobs provide feedback than when they don't.[39]

Work can be formed into *natural work units* by arranging tasks according to logical or meaningful groups. Although many trucking companies randomly assign drivers to trucks, some have begun assigning drivers to particular geographic locations (e.g., the Northeast or Southwest) or to truckloads that require special driving skill (e.g., oversized loads or hazardous chemicals). Forming natural work units increases task identity and task significance.

Establishing client relationships increases skill variety, autonomy, and feedback by giving employees direct contact with clients and customers. In some companies, truck drivers are expected to establish business relationships with their regular customers. When something goes wrong with a shipment, customers are told to call drivers directly.

Vertical loading means pushing some managerial authority down to workers. For truck drivers, this means that they have the same authority as managers to resolve

customer problems. In some companies, if a late shipment causes problems for a customer, the driver has the authority to fully refund the cost of that shipment, without first obtaining management's approval.

The last job redesign technique offered by the model, *opening feedback channels*, means finding additional ways to give employees direct, frequent feedback about their job performance. For example, with advances in electronics, many truck drivers get instantaneous data as to whether they're on schedule and driving their rigs in a fuel-efficient manner. Likewise, the increased contact with customers also means that many drivers now receive monthly data on customer satisfaction. For additional information on the JCM, see this chapter's What Really Works feature.

Review 3

Job Design Companies use specialized jobs because they are economical and easy to learn and don't require highly paid workers. But specialized jobs aren't motivating or particularly satisfying for employees. Companies have used job rotation, job enlargement, job enrichment, and the job characteristics model to make specialized jobs more interesting and motivating. With job rotation, workers move from one specialized job to another. Job enlargement simply increases the number of different tasks within a particular job. Job enrichment increases the number of tasks in a job and gives workers authority and control over their work. The goal of the job characteristics model is to make jobs intrinsically motivating. For this to happen, jobs must be strong on five core job characteristics (skill variety, task identity, task significance, autonomy, and feedback), and workers must experience three critical psychological states (knowledge of results, responsibility for work outcomes, and meaningful work). If jobs aren't internally motivating, they can be redesigned by combining tasks, forming natural work units, establishing client relationships, vertical loading, and opening feedback channels.

---

mechanistic organization an organization characterized by specialized jobs and responsibilities; precisely defined, unchanging roles; and a rigid chain of command based on centralized authority and vertical communication.

organic organization an organization characterized by broadly defined jobs and responsibility; loosely defined, frequently changing roles; and decentralized authority and horizontal communication based on task knowledge.

Designing Organizational Processes

More than 40 years ago, Tom Burns and G. M. Stalker described how two kinds of organizational designs, mechanistic and organic, are appropriate for different kinds of organizational environments.[40] **Mechanistic organizations** are characterized by specialized jobs and responsibilities; precisely defined, unchanging roles; and a rigid chain of command based on centralized authority and vertical communication. This type of organization works best in stable, unchanging business environments. By contrast, **organic organizations** are characterized by broadly defined jobs and responsibility; loosely defined, frequently changing roles; and decentralized authority and horizontal communication based on task knowledge. This type of organization works best in dynamic, changing business environments.

The organizational design techniques described in the first half of this

After reading the next two sections, you should be able to

4. *Explain the methods that companies are using to redesign internal organizational processes (i.e., intraorganizational processes).*

5. *Describe the methods that companies are using to redesign external organizational processes (i.e., interorganizational processes).*

chapter—departmentalization, authority, and job design—are better suited for mechanistic organizations and the stable business environments that were more prevalent before 1980. By contrast, the organizational design techniques discussed next, in the second part of the chapter, are more appropriate for organic organizations and the increasingly dynamic environments in which today's businesses compete. The key difference between these approaches is that mechanistic organizational designs focus on organizational structure, whereas organic organizational designs are concerned with organizational process, or the collection of activities that transform inputs into outputs valued by customers.

4 Intraorganizational Processes

An **intraorganizational process** is the collection of activities that take place within an organization to transform inputs into outputs that customers value. The steps involved in an automobile insurance claim are a good example of an intraorganizational process:

1. Document the loss (the accident).
2. Assign an appraiser to determine the dollar amount of damage.
3. Make an appointment to inspect the vehicle.
4. Inspect the vehicle.
5. Write an appraisal and get the repair shop to agree to the damage estimate.
6. Pay for the repair work.
7. Return the repaired car to the customer.

Let's take a look at how companies are using **4.1 reengineering, 4.2 empowerment,** and **4.3 behavioral informality** to redesign intraorganizational processes like these.

4.1 Reengineering

In their best-selling book *Reengineering the Corporation*, Michael Hammer and James Champy define **reengineering** as "the *fundamental* rethinking and *radical* redesign of business *processes* to achieve *dramatic* improvements in critical, contemporary measures of performance, such as cost, quality, service and speed."[41] Hammer and Champy further explained the four key words shown in italics in this definition. The first key word is *fundamental*. When reengineering organizational designs, managers must ask themselves, "Why do we do what we do?" and "Why do we do it the way we do?" The usual answer is "Because that's the way we've always done it." The second key word is *radical*. Reengineering is about significant change, about starting over by throwing out the old ways of getting work done. The third key word is *processes*. Hammer and Champy noted that "most business people are not process oriented; they are focused on tasks, on jobs, on people, on structures, but not on processes." The fourth key word is *dramatic*. Reengineering is about achieving quantum improvements in company performance.

An example from IBM Credit's operation illustrates how work can be reengineered.[42] IBM Credit lends businesses money to buy IBM computers. Previously, the loan process began when an IBM salesperson called the home office to obtain credit approval for a customer's purchase. The first department involved in the

intraorganizational process the collection of activities that take place within an organization to transform inputs into outputs that customers value.

reengineering fundamental rethinking and radical redesign of business processes to achieve dramatic improvements in critical measures of performance, such as cost, quality, service, and speed.

process took the credit information over the phone from the salesperson and recorded it on the credit form. The credit form was sent to the credit checking department, then to the pricing department (where the interest rate was determined), and on through a total of five departments. In all, it took the five departments six days to approve or deny the customer's loan. Of course, this delay cost IBM business. Some customers got their loans elsewhere. Others, frustrated by the wait, simply canceled their orders.

Finally, two IBM managers decided to walk a loan straight through each of the departments involved in the process. At each step, they asked the workers to stop what they were doing and immediately process their loan application. They were shocked by what they found. From start to finish, the entire process took just 90 minutes! The six-day turnaround time was almost entirely due to delays in handing off the work from one department to another. The solution: IBM redesigned the process so that one person, not five people in five separate departments, now handles the entire loan approval process without any handoffs. The results were indeed dramatic. Reengineering the credit process reduced approval time from six days to four hours and allowed IBM Credit to increase the number of loans it handled by a factor of 100! Likewise, reengineering helped Schneider National, a trucking company, reduce the time it took to bid for trucking jobs from two weeks to two days.[43]

Reengineering changes an organization's orientation from vertical to horizontal. Instead of taking orders from upper management, lower- and middle-level managers and workers take orders from a customer who is at the beginning and end of each process. Instead of running independent functional departments, managers and workers in different departments take ownership of cross-functional processes. Instead of simplifying work so that it becomes increasingly specialized, reengineering complicates work by giving workers increased autonomy and responsibility for complete processes.

In essence, reengineering changes work by changing **task interdependence**, the extent to which collective action is required to complete an entire piece of work. As shown in Exhibit 9.11, there are three kinds of task interdependence.[44] In **pooled interdependence**, each job or department contributes to the whole independently. In **sequential interdependence**, work must be performed in succession, as one group's or job's outputs become the inputs for the next group or job. Finally, in **reciprocal interdependence**, different jobs or groups work together in a back-and-forth manner to complete the process. By reducing the handoffs between different jobs or groups, reengineering decreases sequential interdependence. Likewise, reengineering decreases pooled interdependence by redesigning work so that formerly independent jobs or departments now work together to complete processes. Finally, reengineering increases reciprocal interdependence by making groups or individuals responsible for larger, more complete processes in which several steps may be accomplished at the same time.

As an organizational design tool, reengineering promises big rewards, but it has also come under severe criticism. The most serious complaint is that because it allows a few workers to do the work formerly done by many, reengineering is simply a corporate code word for cost cutting and worker layoffs.[45] For this reason, detractors claim that reengineering hurts morale and performance. Even though ordering times were reduced from three weeks to three days, Levi Strauss ended an $850 million reengineering project because of the fear and turmoil it created in the company's workforce. One low point occurred when Levi management, encouraged by its reengineering consultants, told 4,000 workers that they would have to "reapply

task interdependence the extent to which collective action is required to complete an entire piece of work.

pooled interdependence work completed by having each job or department independently contribute to the whole.

sequential interdependence work completed in succession, with one group's or job's outputs becoming the inputs for the next group or job.

reciprocal interdependence work completed by different jobs or groups working together in a back-and-forth manner.

Exhibit 9.11
Reengineering and Task Interdependence

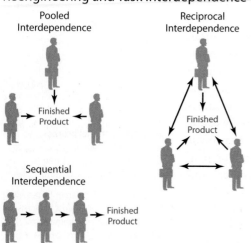

© Cengage Learning 2013

for their jobs" as the company shifted from its traditional vertical structure to a process-based form of organizing. Thomas Kasten, Levi Strauss's vice president for reengineering and customer service, says, "We felt the pressure building up [over reengineering efforts], and we were worried about the business."[46] Today, even reengineering gurus Hammer and Champy admit that roughly 70 percent of all reengineering projects fail because of the effects on people in the workplace. Says Hammer, "I wasn't smart enough about that [the people issues]. I was reflecting my engineering background and was insufficiently appreciative of the human dimension. I've [now] learned that's critical."[47]

4.2 Empowerment

Another way of redesigning intraorganizational processes is through empowerment. **Empowering workers** means permanently passing decision-making authority and responsibility from managers to workers. For workers to be fully empowered, companies must give them the information and resources they need to make and carry out good decisions and then reward them for taking individual initiative.[48] Unfortunately, this doesn't happen often enough. As Michael Schrage, author and MIT researcher, wrote:

> A warehouse employee can see on the intranet that a shipment is late but has no authority to accelerate its delivery. A project manager knows—and can mathematically demonstrate—that a seemingly minor spec change will bust both her budget and her schedule. The spec must be changed anyway. An airline reservations agent tells the Executive Platinum Premier frequent flier that first class appears wide open for an upgrade. However, the airline's yield management software won't permit any upgrades until just four hours before the flight, frequent fliers (and reservations) be damned. In all these cases, the employee has access to valuable information. Each one possesses the "knowledge" to do the job better. But the knowledge and information are irrelevant and useless. Knowledge isn't power; the ability to act on knowledge is power.[49]

When workers are given the proper information and resources and are allowed to make good decisions, they experience strong feelings of empowerment. **Empowerment** is a feeling of intrinsic motivation, in which workers perceive their work to have meaning and perceive themselves to be competent, have an impact, and be capable of self-determination.[50] Work has meaning when it is consistent with personal standards and beliefs. Workers feel competent when they believe they can perform an activity with skill. The belief that they are having an impact comes from a feeling that they can affect work outcomes. A feeling of self-determination arises from workers' belief that they have the autonomy to choose how best to do their work.

Empowerment can lead to changes in organizational processes because meaning, competence, impact, and self-determination produce empowered employees who take active rather than passive roles in their work. At **Southwest Airlines**, every employee, from pilots to baggage handlers, is trained to follow a simple philosophy: "Treat others how you'd like to be treated." According to spokeswoman Brandy King, the company deals with customer-relations issues proactively, which means that employees are given freedom to address customers' needs even before they make a complaint. Recently, a man needed to get from Los Angeles to Denver so that he could see his two-year-old grandson who was about to be taken off life support.

When workers are given the proper information and resources and are allowed to make good decisions, they experience strong feelings of empowerment.

empowering workers permanently passing decision-making authority and responsibility from managers to workers by giving them the information and resources they need to make and carry out good decisions.

empowerment feelings of intrinsic motivation, in which workers perceive their work to have impact and meaning and perceive themselves to be competent and capable of self-determination.

< **"what's new" companies**

Though he arrived at the airport two hours early, long lines at security made him late for his flight. He ran through the terminal in his socks, trying to catch his flight, but got to the gate 12 minutes late. At the gate, one of the agents asked him "Are you Mark Dickinson? . . . We're holding the plane for you." As it turns out, the pilot found about Dickinson's situation from the agent who sold the ticket and decided to hold the plane at the gate until he was ready to go.[51]

4.3 Behavioral Informality

How would you describe the atmosphere in the office where you last worked? Was it a formal, by-the-book, follow-the-rules, address-each-other-by-last-names atmosphere? Or was it more informal, with an emphasis on results rather than rules, casual business dress rather than suits, and first names rather than last names and titles? Or was it somewhere in between?

Behavioral informality (or formality) is a third influence on intraorganizational processes. **Behavioral informality** refers to workplace atmospheres characterized by spontaneity, casualness, and interpersonal familiarity. By contrast, **behavioral formality** refers to workplace atmospheres characterized by routine and regimen, specific rules about how to behave, and impersonal detachment. As Exhibit 9.12 shows, behavioral formality and informality are characterized by four factors: language

behavioral informality a workplace atmosphere characterized by spontaneity, casualness, and interpersonal familiarity.

behavioral formality a workplace atmosphere characterized by routine and regimen, specific rules about how to behave, and impersonal detachment.

Exhibit 9.12 Differences Between Formal and Informal Workplaces

	Formal	Informal
LANGUAGE USAGE	Fully articulated speech ("What are you doing?") Grammatically complete phrasing ("Would you like some coffee?") Use of formal word choices ("Would you care to dine?") Use of honorifics ("Ms.," "Sir," "Dr.") Elimination of "I" and "you" ("It is requested that . . .")	Phonological slurring ("Whatcha doin'?") Use of elliptical expressions ("Coffee?") Use of colloquial and slang expressions ("Wanna grab a bite to eat?") Use of the vivid present ("So I come down the stairs, and she says . . .") First name, in-group names ("Mac," "Bud")
CONVERSATIONAL TURN TAKING AND TOPIC SELECTION	Turn taking well regulated Few interruptions or overlaps Few changes of topic Generally serious topics	Turn taking relatively unregulated Many interruptions or overlaps Many shifts of topic possible Joking or conversational levity possible
EMOTIONAL AND PROXEMIC GESTURES	Sober facial demeanor Much interpersonal distance No touching; postural attention	Greater latitude of emotional expression Small interpersonal distance Touching, postural relaxation allowed
PHYSICAL AND CONTEXTUAL CUES	Formal clothing, shoes, etc. Central focus of attention Symmetric arrangement of chairs/furniture Artifacts related to official status Hushed atmosphere, little background noise	Informal clothing, shoes, etc. Decentralized, multiple centers of attention possible Asymmetric arrangement of chairs/furniture Informal trappings: flowers, art, food, soft furniture Background noise acceptable

Source: "The Role of Behavioral Formality and Informality in the Enactment of Bureaucratic versus Organic Organizations," *Academy of Management Review* 20 (1995): 831–872. Reproduced by permission of Academy of Management, PO Box 3020, Briar Cliff Manor NY, 10510-8020. via Copyright Clearance Center.

usage, conversational turn taking and topic selection, emotional and proxemic gestures, and physical and contextual cues. Let's examine each in more detail.[52]

Compared with formal work atmospheres, the language in informal workplaces is often slurred ("Whatcha doin'?"), elliptical ("Coffee?" versus "Would you like some coffee?"), and filled with slang terms and vivid descriptions. People use first names and perhaps nicknames to address each other, rather than Mr., Ms., Dr., or other formal titles. When it comes to conversations in informal workplaces, people jump right in when they have something to say (known as unregulated turn taking); conversations shift from topic to topic, many of which are unrelated to business; and joking and laughter are common. From joy to disappointment, people show much more emotion in informal workplaces. Relaxed behavior, such as putting your feet on your desk or congregating in hallways for impromptu discussions, is more common too. In terms of physical and contextual cues, informal workplaces de-emphasize differences in hierarchical status or rank to encourage more frequent interaction between organizational members. Consequently, to make their organizations feel less formal, many companies have eliminated such management perks as executive dining rooms, reserved parking spaces, and large corner offices separated from most workers by virtue of their location on a higher floor of the company building (the higher the floor, the greater one's status). Justin Kan, the CEO of **Justin.tv**, a site that hosts live streaming videos, doesn't have a private office and likes to run an informal workplace. When the bulk of his daily tasks are focused on engineering, he will move his desk to sit with the other engineers. When he needs to focus more on the business side of things, he will move his desk over to that side of the office. If employees ever want to meet with him privately, instead of sequestering in some private room, Kan will suggest that they take a walk around the block or maybe go to a café around the corner.[53]

< **"what's new" companies**

Casual dress policies and open office systems are two of the most popular methods for increasing behavioral informality. In fact, a survey conducted by the Society for Human Resource Management indicates that casual dress policies (no suits, ties, jackets, dresses, or formal clothing required) are extremely popular.[54] Today, 84 percent of companies have some form of casual dress code, up from 63 percent 11 years ago and 24 percent 16 years ago.[55] Similarly, 42 percent of all companies permit casual dress at least one day a week, compared with 17 percent 7 years ago. Moreover, 33 percent of companies permit casual dress every day of the week, up from 20 percent 9 years ago.

Still, companies such as retailer Target have instituted formal dress codes that ban business casual based on the idea that a more professional workplace will lead to better results.[56] Similarly, **UBS AG**, a Swiss bank, created and tested a 43-page dress code regarding professional business dress. In particular, UBS required employees to wear blue, navy blue, or dark gray suits, which "symbolize competence, formalism, and sobriety." UBS spokesman Jean-Raphael Fontannaz said, "The goal is for clients to immediately know that they are at UBS when they are entering the bank."[57]

< **"what's new" companies**

However, according to John Challenger, chief executive of Challenger, Gray & Christmas, a Chicago-based outplacement company, "no study shows that productivity goes up with better dress."[58] Indeed, casual dress appears to improve employee attitudes. Colin Stanbridge, the chief executive of London's Chamber of Commerce, says, "People tend to work at their best when they feel most comfortable. And today I think the vast majority of people feel at their most comfortable when wearing casual dress."[59] In fact, 85 percent of human resources directors believe that casual dress can improve office morale, and 79 percent say that employees are very satisfied with casual dress codes.[60] Moreover, nearly two-thirds of the human resources directors believe that casual dress policies are an important tool for attracting qualified

Open offices encourage communication and interaction throughout an organization, but they have their drawbacks as well. In fact, sales of taller cube walls, like the ones shown here, are increasing, while sales of traditional four-foot walls are decreasing.

employees in tight labor markets. Michael Losey, president of the Society for Human Resource Management, concludes that "for the majority of corporations and industries, allowing casual dress can have clear advantages at virtually no cost."[61]

Although casual dress increases behavioral informality by having managers and workers at all levels dress in a more relaxed manner, open office systems increase behavioral informality by significantly increasing the level of communication and interaction among employees. By definition, **open office systems** try to increase interaction by removing physical barriers that separate workers. One characteristic of open office systems is that they have much more shared space than private space. **Shared spaces** are areas used by and open to all employees. Cubicles with low-to-the-ground partitions (used by 75% of office workers); offices with no doors or with glass walls; collections of comfortable furniture that encourage people to congregate; and common areas with tables and chairs that encourage people to meet, work, or eat together are examples of shared space.[62] In contrast, **private spaces**, such as private offices with doors, are used by and open to just one employee.

The advantage of an open office with extensive shared space is that it dramatically increases the amount of unplanned, spontaneous, and chance communication among employees.[63] People are much more likely to plan meetings and work together when numerous collaboration spaces with conference tables, white boards, and computers are readily available. With no office walls, inviting common areas, and different departments mixed together in large open spaces, spontaneous communication occurs more often. For instance, people whose office cubicles are directly adjacent to main walk ways or office atriums report 60 percent more face-to-face communication. Similarly, workers with informal meeting spaces (such as open lounges, or team work rooms) within 75 feet of their desks report 102 percent more face-to-face communication.[64]

As these numbers show, open office systems increase chance encounters by making it much more likely that people from different departments or areas will run into each other. When Sigma-Aladrich, a biotechnology firm, built a new office with a three-story open staircase at the center of the building, the main goal, according to Keld Sorensen, director of research and development, was to increase "interaction."[65] The open staircase, which is complemented by benches and expansive landings on each story (so people would sit and talk) has led to 156 percent more chance encounters than at the old building, which had elevators and an enclosed stairwell. Indeed, soon after the move to the new office, two scientists from opposite sides of the building ran into each other on the stairs, stopped to talk, and ended up generating a significant new reagent for scientific testing.

Not everyone is enthusiastic about open offices, however. For example, Ingrid Tischer, who sits in a cubicle next to the kitchen in her office, says she can't help being distracted by others' conversations, and frequently joins in. Because of the location of her cubicle, "I know things about my colleagues' lives, and they know things about mine."[66] In fact, cubicle dwellers are interrupted by "noise, visual distractions, and chatty visitors" up to 21 times a day. And, because it takes about three minutes each time to refocus on what they were doing, cubicle workers can lose an hour a day to these interruptions. Attorney Phillip Fisher says,[67] "I honestly don't know how people can concentrate in a cubicle." For this reason, Sun Microsystems

open office systems offices in which the physical barriers that separate workers have been removed in order to increase communication and interaction.

shared spaces spaces used by and open to all employees.

private spaces spaces used by and open to just one employee.

and Microsoft give their employees private offices. William Agnello, Sun's vice president of real estate and the workplace, says, "We have researched the heck out of this. Our studies show that, for our engineers, there are just too many distractions and interruptions."[68] Microsoft's John Pinette agrees: "Private offices allow our employees to concentrate on their work and to avoid unnecessary distractions—[which is] obviously critical when you're doing something that requires as much focus as developing software does."[69]

Indeed, because there is so much shared space and so little private space, companies with open systems have to take steps to give employees privacy when they need to concentrate on individual work. One step is simply to use taller cubicles. Indeed, Herman Miller, a manufacturer of office furniture and systems, has seen sales of its 62-inch-high cubicle panels increase by 18 percent while sales of its 46-inch-high panels have dropped by 19 percent. Another approach is to install white-noise machines to prevent voices and other noises from disrupting others.[70] Dynasound, which makes sound-masking machines that use white noise to make conversations difficult to hear, has seen sales increase by 141 percent.[71] Yet another approach is to make conference rooms available. In contrast to traditional offices, where such rooms are used for meetings, many employees in open systems reserve conference rooms when they need private time to work. Another possibility is to turn a cubicle into a more private space. When Mark Saunders, of Glaxo-SmithKline Consumer Healthcare, moved from a private office to a cubicle at the end of a busy hallway, he "felt sensory overload." To make it easier for him to concentrate, the company's office design team created a nylon screen that can be placed around his cubicle to block out visual distractions.[72] If your office doesn't provide such screens, you can always fork out $15.00 for the Cube-a-Door, a free-standing cardboard partition stamped with the words "Work in Progress. Do Not Disturb," that will serve as a "door" to your cubicle when you need to screen out interruptions.[73]

Don't Scavenge That Office If Somebody Is Still in It

It's like road kill in the animal kingdom. As soon as the word gets out that someone is leaving the company, coworkers start scheming to scavenge the office leftovers—chairs, computer monitors, filing cabinets, even staplers. "This issue is practically everywhere," says Mary Wong, president of a human resources consulting company. "Professionals—anyone you and I would normally consider to be very adult—turn into children" over the prospect of picking an empty office clean of its "goodies." Sometimes—and this is where it gets disrespectful—office scavengers move in even before the employee, who's often been laid off, has left. Ethics consultant Steve Lawler tells the story of a laid-off manager who, just hours after hearing the bad news, was already getting requests for the expensive Herman Miller Aeron chair in which he was still sitting. Office scavenging is a strange and predictable aspect of office life. It happens everywhere. But if you're going to scavenge, and you probably will, do the right thing by maintaining the dignity of departing coworkers: Wait until the office is empty before you strike.[74]

Review 4

Intraorganizational Processes Today, companies are using reengineering, empowerment, and behavioral informality to change their intraorganizational processes. Through fundamental rethinking and radical redesign of business processes, reengineering changes an organization's orientation from vertical to horizontal. Reengineering changes work processes by decreasing sequential and pooled interdependence and by increasing reciprocal interdependence. Reengineering promises dramatic increases in productivity and customer satisfaction, but it has been criticized as simply an excuse to cut costs and lay off workers.

Empowering workers means taking decision-making authority and responsibility from managers and giving it to workers. Empowered workers develop feelings of competence and self-determination and believe that their work has meaning and impact. Workplaces characterized by behavioral informality are spontaneous and casual. The formality or informality of a workplace depends on four factors: language usage, conversational turn taking and topic selection, emotional and proxemic gestures, and physical and contextual cues. Casual dress policies and open office systems are two of the most popular methods for increasing behavioral informality.

5 Interorganizational Processes

An **interorganizational process** is a collection of activities that occur *among companies* to transform inputs into outputs that customers value. In other words, many companies work together to create a product or service that keeps customers happy. From soundtracks to staging, to locations, to post-production and marketing, dozens of different firms worked with Warner Bros. Pictures to create the last two films in the *Harry Potter* movies series, *Harry Potter and the Deathly Hallows*, parts 1 and 2. Part 1 was filmed at Leavesden Film Studios, owned by Warner Brothers and located in Hertfordshire, England. Part 2 was filmed at Pinewood Studios, also located in England. The visual effects of both movies were handled by two companies, Double Negative, which won an Oscar for its special effects work in *Inception*, and Framestore, which won an Oscar for its work on *The Golden Compass*. The music for both films was composed by Alexander Desplat and performed by the London Symphony Orchestra.[75]

In this section, you'll explore interorganizational processes by learning about **5.1 modular organizations** and **5.2 virtual organizations**.[76]

5.1 Modular Organizations

Stephen Roach, chief economist for investment bank Morgan Stanley, says that companies increasingly want to take "functions that aren't central to their core competency," and outsource them.[77] Except for the core business activities that they can perform better, faster, and cheaper than others, **modular organizations** outsource all remaining business activities to outside companies, suppliers, specialists, or consultants. The term *modular* is used because the business activities purchased from outside companies can be added and dropped as needed, much like adding pieces to a three-dimensional puzzle. Exhibit 9.13 depicts a modular organization in which the company has chosen to keep training, human resources, sales, product design, manufacturing, customer service, research and development, and information technology as core business activities but has outsourced the noncore activities of product distribution, web page design, advertising, payroll, accounting, and packaging.

interorganizational process a collection of activities that take place among companies to transform inputs into outputs that customers value.

modular organization an organization that outsources noncore business activities to outside companies, suppliers, specialists, or consultants.

Modular organizations have several advantages. First, because modular organizations pay for outsourced labor, expertise, or manufacturing capabilities only when needed, they can cost significantly less to run than traditional organizations. For example, most of the design and marketing work for Apple's iPad 2 is run out of company headquarters in Cupertino, California. Most of the components for the device, however, are outsourced to other companies. Two South Korean companies, LG and Samsung, make the iPad 2's LCD panels, whereas the touch panel that goes on top of the screen comes from TPK and Wintek, both based in China. The chips that control Wi-Fi, Bluetooth, and GPS connections are sourced from Broadcom, headquartered in Irvine, California, whereas final assembly of the product is handled by Foxconn, a Taiwanese company that operates production facilities in China.[78] To obtain these advantages, however, modular organizations need reliable partners—vendors and suppliers with whom they can work closely and can trust.

Modular organizations have disadvantages too. The primary disadvantage is the loss of control that occurs when key business activities are outsourced to other companies. Also, companies may reduce their competitive advantage in two ways if they mistakenly outsource a core business activity. First, as a result of competitive and technological change, the noncore business activities a company has outsourced may suddenly become the basis for competitive advantage. Second, related to that point, suppliers to whom work is outsourced can sometimes become competitors.

Exhibit 9.13 Modular Organization

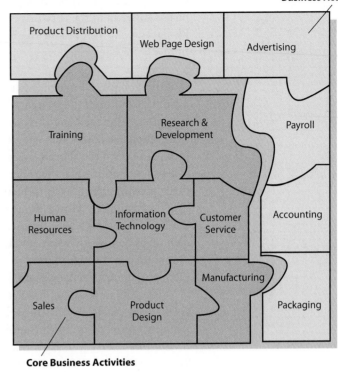

© Cengage Learning 2013

5.2 Virtual Organizations

In contrast to modular organizations in which the interorganizational process revolves around a central company, a **virtual organization** is part of a network in which many companies share skills, costs, capabilities, markets, and customers with each other. Exhibit 9.14 shows a virtual organization in which, for "today," the parts of a virtual company consist of product design, purchasing, manufacturing, advertising, and information technology. Unlike modular organizations, in which the outside organizations are tightly linked to one central company, virtual organizations work with some companies in the network alliance, but not with all. So, whereas a puzzle with various pieces is a fitting metaphor for a modular organization, a potluck dinner is an appropriate metaphor for a virtual organization. All participants bring their finest food dish but eat only what they want.

Another difference is that the working relationships between modular organizations and outside companies tend to be more stable and longer lasting than the shorter, often temporary relationships found among the virtual companies in a network alliance. The composition

virtual organization an organization that is part of a network in which many companies share skills, costs, capabilities, markets, and customers to collectively solve customer problems or provide specific products or services.

Exhibit 9.14 Virtual Organization

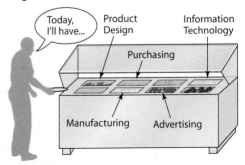

© Cengage Learning 2013

of a virtual organization is always changing. The combination of network partners that a virtual corporation has at any one time depends on the expertise needed to solve a particular problem or provide a specific product or service. This is why the businessperson in the network organization shown in Exhibit 9.14 is saying, "Today, I'll have . . . ." Tomorrow, the business could want something completely different. In this sense, the term *virtual organization* means the organization that exists "at the moment."

For example, 21 carton manufacturers have formed a network of virtual organizations called the Independent Carton Group (ICG).[79] The original network, which brought five independent carton companies together, was designed so that each of the five companies could help each other in case a catastrophe occurred at one of their production facilities. For instance, if an ICG company ever experienced a catastrophe at a production facility, the other four members of the ICG would be there to temporarily provide alternative production arrangements so the affected company wouldn't lose its customers. However, as the group grew, they realized they could trade off manufacturing capacities with each other to better serve customers' needs, so they combined their efforts to provide carton packaging in 16 different industries, from automotive to biotech to food to electronics. ICG customers benefit from competitive pricing, uninterrupted supplies, and group purchasing power.

Virtual organizations have a number of advantages. They let companies share costs. Inspired by the ICG model, 15 regional ink manufacturers, blenders, and distributors formed the Print Suppliers Group to grow their businesses and combine orders for paint supplies to take advantage of volume purchasing discounts. John Toigo, president of Grand Rapids Printing Ink, says, "Combining our purchasing allows us a much better price point,"[80] Marlon Tusche, vice president of sales and marketing for Pertech Printing Inks, agrees: "By working together, our purchasing power is much stronger, plus we can share our knowledge, which makes us stronger technically."[81]

And because members of virtual organizations can quickly combine their efforts to meet customers' needs, they are fast and flexible. Although member companies of ICG are highly specialized, as a collective, ICG is able to bid for larger and complex orders and then assign the work to a smaller group of member companies that have the expertise required to meet customer specifications. "We are able to deliver what the customer wants in a timely manner at a good price," said Andrew Willie, executive director of the ICG group.[82] Finally, because each member of the network alliance is the best at what it does, virtual organizations should in theory provide better products and services in all respects.

As with modular organizations, a disadvantage of virtual organizations is that once work has been outsourced, it can be difficult to control the quality of work done by network partners. The greatest disadvantage, however, is that tremendous managerial skills are required to make a network of independent organizations work well together, especially because their relationships tend to be short and based on a single task or project.

Virtual organizations are using two methods to solve this problem. The first is to use a *broker*. In traditional, hierarchical organizations, managers plan, organize, and control. But with the horizontal, interorganizational processes that characterize virtual organizations, the job of a broker is to create and assemble the knowledge, skills, and resources from different companies for outside parties, such as customers.[83] The second way to make networks of virtual organizations more manageable is to use a *virtual organization agreement* that, somewhat like a contract, specifies the schedules, responsibilities, costs, payouts, and liabilities for participating organizations.[84] For more information on how a virtual organizations works, see www.independentcartongroup.com.

Interorganizational Processes Organizations are using modular and virtual organizations to change interorganizational processes. Because modular organizations outsource all noncore activities to other businesses, they are less expensive to run than traditional companies. However, modular organizations require extremely close relationships with suppliers, may result in a loss of control, and could create new competitors if the wrong business activities are outsourced. Virtual organizations participate in a network in which they share skills, costs, capabilities, markets, and customers. As customer problems, products, or services change, the combination of virtual organizations that work together changes. Virtual organizations can reduce costs, respond quickly, and, if they can successfully coordinate their efforts, produce outstanding products and service.

Review 5

SELF-ASSESSMENT

Flexibility and Structure

Every organization needs some degree of flexibility and standardization. In other words, companies need to have enough flexibility in their organizations to respond to changes in their business environment, but firms also must have certain structures in place to ensure smooth operations. For example, if someone gets hurt on company property, clear procedures about what to do in the case of an accident help managers respond quickly and confidently. But being overly committed to following rules can hamstring an organization and keep it from growing. As a manager, you will probably encounter both types of situations, and to respond appropriately, you will need to have an idea of how comfortable you are in a formal environment versus a more loosely structured workplace. Every organization needs some degree of flexibility to adapt to new situations and some degree of standardization to make routine tasks and decisions as efficient and effective as possible.[85] In this assessment, indicate the extent to which you agree or disagree with the following statements. Use this scale for your responses:

1 Strongly disagree

2 Disagree

3 Slightly disagree

4 Neutral

5 Slightly agree

6 Agree

7 Strongly agree

KEY TERMS

authority 349
autonomy 357
behavioral formality 364
behavioral informality 364
centralization of authority 352
chain of command 349
complex matrix 349
customer departmentalization 344
decentralization 352
delegation of authority 351
departmentalization 342
empowering workers 363
empowerment 363
feedback 357
functional departmentalization 342
geographic departmentalization 346
internal motivation 356
interorganizational process 368
intraorganizational process 361
job characteristics model (JCM) 356
job design 354
job enlargement 355
job enrichment 355
job rotation 354

job specialization 354
line authority 350
line function 350
matrix departmentalization 347
mechanistic organization 360
modular organization 368
open office systems 366
organic organization 360
organizational process 341
organizational structure 340
pooled interdependence 362
private spaces 366
product departmentalization 343
reciprocal interdependence 362
reengineering 361
sequential interdependence 362
shared spaces 366
simple matrix 348
skill variety 357
staff authority 350
staff function 350
standardization 352
task identity 357
task interdependence 362
task significance 357
unity of command 350
virtual organization 369

1. If a written rule does not cover some situation, we make up informal rules for doing things as we go along.

   1   2   3   4   5   6   7

2. I feel that I am my own boss in most matters.

   1   2   3   4   5   6   7

3. There are many things in my business that are not covered by some formal procedure.

   1   2   3   4   5   6   7

4. A person can make his or her own decisions without checking with somebody else.

   1   2   3   4   5   6   7

5. Usually, my contact with my company and its representatives involves doing things "by the rule book."

   1   2   3   4   5   6   7

6. How things are done here is left up to the person doing the work.

   1   2   3   4   5   6   7

7. Contacts with my company and its representatives are on a formal, preplanned basis.

   1   2   3   4   5   6   7

8. People here are allowed to do almost anything as they please.

   1   2   3   4   5   6   7

9. I ignore the rules and reach informal agreements to handle some situations.

   1   2   3   4   5   6   7

10. Most people here make their own rules on the job.

    1   2   3   4   5   6   7

11. When rules and procedures exist in my company, they are usually written agreements.

    1   2   3   4   5   6   7

12. The employees are constantly being checked on for rule violations.

    1   2   3   4   5   6   7

13. People here feel as though they are constantly being watched, to see that they obey all the rules.

    1   2   3   4   5   6   7

Scoring

Determine your score by entering your response to each survey item, as follows. In blanks that say *regular score*, simply enter your response for that item. If your response was a 6, place a 6 in the *regular* score blank. In blanks that say *reverse score*, subtract your response from 8 and enter the result. So if your response was a 6, place a 2 ($8 - 6 = 2$) in the *reverse score* blank.

1. reverse score ___
2. reverse score ___
3. reverse score ___
4. reverse score ___
5. regular score ___
6. reverse score ___
7. regular score ___
8. reverse score ___
9. reverse score ___
10. reverse score ___
11. regular score ___
12. regular score ___
13. regular score ___

   TOTAL = ___

You can see where you fall on the formality continuum and find the interpretation of your score at: www.cengagebrain.com.

MANAGEMENT DECISION

Dressing Up (or Down) for Work[86]

Does it matter what people wear to the office? You've never thought about that question before. When you first started at your architectural firm—more than 40 years ago now—everyone dressed formally. And it wasn't just to the office; you remember when families dressed to their best to go to the movies, go out to dinner, or take an airplane flight. When you look around your office lately, it's quite a different scene.

There are interns wearing T-shirts and jeans and mail clerks wearing flip-flops. There are folks sitting at their desks wearing short and sneakers. Even most of your managers take advantage of the business casual look, preferring polos and khakis to the three-piece suit that you wear every day.

In the past, on most issues, you've given the employees whatever they wanted, so long as they produced good work. You always tried to keep them satisfied and happy in order to create a dynamic, creative environment that produced stunning, innovative building designs. You wonder, however, if things have gotten a bit too casual. It seemed okay when men in your office wore a jacket and pants with no tie. But really—a T-shirt and jeans? A sweatshirt? A dress that basically looks like a muumuu? And it seems that the casual clothing has led to a casual atmosphere. Sometimes, you walk into the office, see all the people milling around, chatting, laughing, and it looks more like social hour than a place of business.

Apparently, other business owners and managers have similar concerns. According to research data, the number of companies that are allowing business casual throughout the week actually fell. Even the number of companies that are allowing casual Fridays fell by 5 percent. UBS, a Swiss bank, is taking things one step further. Not only did it institute a dress code, it gives every employee a 43-page guidebook that is filled with fashion and grooming tips. The guide even prescribes how employees should apply makeup, how often they should get their hair cut, and how to avoid having bad breath (*Hint:* no onions or garlic!). Is it time to make a switch back? True, it's not as if an architect needs to wear a suit and tie to do her work well. But at the same time, you'd like to remind your employees that the office needs to be about more than comfort and fun.

Questions

1. What are the advantages and disadvantages of having an informal workplace? What are the advantages and disadvantages of having a formal work place?

2. As the manager of this firm, would you institute a formal dress code?

MANAGEMENT TEAM DECISION

China—The Future of General Motors?[87]

It's been a rough ride for General Motors. In 2008, GM's remarkable run of 77 years as the world's largest automaker came to a crashing halt. In 2009, after a decade of mismanagement and declining sales, the company declared bankruptcy and needed a massive government bailout and thorough reorganization to stay afloat. During that time, more than 2000 dealers were closed for good, and almost 23,000 employees were released. There is some hope that the new, streamlined GM, featuring new models, will regain its once-dominant position in the US auto market. However, it is becoming increasingly clear that GM's future may lie in China.

In 2009, there were 13.6 million cars sold in China, an increase of 46 percent from 2008, and nearly 3 million more cars than were sold in the United States at the same time. In 1977, there were just 1 million cars in China; as of 2008, there were 51 million, and it's conservatively expected that the Chinese auto market will grow 10 percent to 15 percent every year. Unlike in the United States, GM hasn't been stuck on the sidelines in China. It sold 1.83 million cars in 2009, an increase of 67 percent over the previous year, and has a solid record of 15 consecutive months in which its sales have grown by double digits. By 2015, GM hopes to sell 3 million cars per year in China. This would not only make GM the largest auto seller in China, but it would make China GM's largest and most lucrative market.

Currently, GM operates in China as part of a joint venture with the SAIC Motor Corporation. Through the partnership, GM owns a minority stake in two companies, SAIC-GM-Wuling and Shanghai General Motors. Increasingly, however, you've heard your GM colleagues argue that new organizational design is needed, one that will give the company a stronger presence in China, and decrease its dependence on the U.S. market. A group of these managers has come to you to seek out your opinion on how GM can organize to best take advantage of shifting conditions in the global auto market.

Questions

1. The text describes a number of different approaches concerning organizational structure. Which do you think would be ideal for GM's success in China? Which of the structures would help GM expand to other foreign markets?

2. What are the advantages and disadvantages of promoting decentralization in GM's operations in China?

PRACTICE BEING A MANAGER

Work Dynamics

Effective organization is vital to the accomplishment of company objectives. Two critical aspects of effective organization are departmentalization and the design of jobs. In this role-play exercise, you will have the opportunity to experience some of the work dynamics surrounding the grouping of workers and the design of jobs.

Step 1: Form work groups. Your professor will form groups and give you a role assignment.

Step 2: Review your role. Read your role assignment carefully, and prepare to begin working per your role assignment.

Step 3 (10–20 minutes): Begin acting. When your professor directs you to begin, you should start working as assigned by your role.

Step 4: Compile your results. Total your results by work group, and compare across the teams.

Step 5: Debrief as a class. Discuss the results as a class. What factors seemed to play a role in the efficiency and effectiveness of the work groups? What role did organization and job design play? If this were an actual organizational work group, what might you do to improve performance and worker satisfaction?

DEVELOP YOUR CAREER POTENTIAL

"Work" in Someone Else's Shoes

Why is learning to see things from someone else's perspective one of the most difficult things to do in today's workplace? Sometimes, the inability to see things as others see them has to do with the people involved. Inexperience, ignorance, and selfishness can all play a role. In most organizations, however, the inability to see things from someone else's perspective results from the jobs themselves, not the people who do them. Because jobs limit who we talk to, what we talk about, what we think about, and what we care about at work, it should not be a surprise that people who perform different jobs have very different views about each other and the workplace.

For example, at Southwest Airlines the pilots who fly the planes and the ground crews who unload, load, and refuel them had little appreciation for each other. The ground crews felt that the pilots treated them like second-class citizens. The pilots couldn't understand why the ground crews weren't doing more to get their planes out of the gates and in the air as fast as possible. To improve understanding and help them see things from each other's perspective, Southwest created a program called Cutting Edge, in which the captains and ground crews learned a lot about each other's jobs. For example, the pilots brought the ground crews into their cockpits and showed them the detailed processes they were required to follow to get planes ready for departure. The pilots, on the other hand, gained appreciation and understanding by actually working as members of Southwest's ground crews. After several days of demanding ground crew work, Southwest pilot Captain Mark Boyter said:

I remember one time when I was working the ramp [as a member of a ground crew] in Los Angeles. I was dead tired. I had flown that morning and had a couple of legs in, so I got out of my uniform and jumped into my ramp clothes. That afternoon was very hot. It was in the 80s—I can't imagine how they do it on a 120-degree day in Phoenix. I was tired and hungry and hadn't had a break. Then I saw this pilot sitting up there in the cockpit eating his frozen yogurt. I said to myself, "Man, I'd like to be up there now." Then I caught myself. I'm up there every day. Now, I know that pilot has been up since 3:00 in the morning. I know that he's been flying an airplane since 6:00 AM. I know it's 3:00 in the afternoon and he hasn't had a chance to get off and have a meal yet today. I know all that, and yet, the yogurt still looks really good to me. Then I thought, "How can a ramp agent [on the ground crew] in Los Angeles who works his butt off for two or three years, working double shifts two or three times a week, understand this?" It hit me that there's a big gap in understanding here.[88]

The misunderstandings between Southwest's pilots and ground crews are not unique. All organizations experience them. Nurses and doctors, teachers and students, and managers and employees all have difficulty seeing things from each other's perspective. As Southwest's Cutting Edge program shows, however, you can minimize differences and build understanding by "working" in someone else's shoes.

Questions

1. Describe the job-related differences or tensions where you work. Who is involved? What jobs do they do? Explain why the job-related differences or tensions exist.

2. Because the best way to see things from someone else's perspective is to "work" in his or her shoes, see whether you can spend a day, a morning, or even two hours performing one of these jobs. If that's not possible, spend some time carefully observing the jobs and then interview several people who perform them. Describe your boss's reaction to this request. Was he or she supportive? Why or why not?

3. Answer the following questions after you have worked the job or conducted your interviews. What most surprised you about this job? What was easiest? What was hardest? Explain. Now that you've had the chance to see things as others see them, what do you think would happen, good or bad, from letting other people in your organization work in someone else's shoes? Explain.

Fun Trivia

The Original Mechanical Turk

The original Mechanical Turk was an eighteenth-century chess-playing automaton that purportedly could beat anyone at chess. The Turk was a mannequin, but the machine concealed a human chess master who would actuate the Turk with mechanical controls. The Turk beat many statesman and luminaries, including Napoleon Bonaparte and Benjamin Franklin. Read more in Tom Standage's book *The Mechanical Turk*.

END NOTES

[1] M. Arndt, "Eli Lilly: Life after Prozac," *Businessweek*, July 23, 2001, 80–82; P. Loftus, "Patent Expirations Loom for Lilly," *The Wall Street Journal*, August 12, 2009, no page number available; P. Loftus, "Corporate News: Lilly Set to Cut Jobs as Patents Expire," *The Wall Street Journal*, September 15, 2009, B3; P. Loftus, "Boss Talk: With Patents Expiring, Eli Lilly Retools," *The Wall Street Journal*, July 6, 2010, B5; B. Martinez & J. Goldstein, "Big Pharma Faces Grim Prognosis; Industry Fails to Find New Drugs to Replace Wonders Like Lipitor," *The Wall Street Journal*, December 6, 2007, A1; J. Russell, "Cuts at Lilly Yield Painful Progress," *Indianapolis Star*, October 2, 2010, A1; and A. Weintrub & M. Tirrell, "Eli Lilly's Drug Assembly Line," *Businessweek*, March 8, 2010, 56–57.

[2] "Sony Group Organizational Chart Summary," Sony, April 1, 2011, accessed May 15, 2011, from www.sony.net/SonyInfo/CorporateInfo/Data/organization.html.

[3] "Corporate Fact Sheet," Sony Pictures, accessed May 15, 2011, from www.sonypictures.com/corp/corporatefact.html; and "Facts and Figures," Sony Music, accessed May 15, 2011, from www.sonymusic.com/page/facts-and-figures.

[4] M. Hammer & J. Champy, *Reengineering the Corporation: A Manifesto for Business Revolution* (New York: Harper & Row, 1993).

[5] "Boston Scientific Announces Management Changes and Restructuring Initiatives," *Boston Scientific*, February 10, 2010, accessed May 15, 2011, from http://bostonscientific.mediaroom.com/index.php?s=43&item=895.

[6] J. G. March & H. A. Simon, *Organizations* (New York: John Wiley & Sons, 1958).

[7] "Bayer Group: Profile and Organization," Bayer AG, accessed March 20, 2009, from www.bayer.com/bayer-group/profileand-organization/page2351.htm.

[8] "Company Overview: 2010 " UTC, accessed May 15, 2010, from www.utc.com/StaticFiles/UTC/StaticFiles/utc_overview.pdf.

[9] "Company Overview: 2010," UTC, accessed May 15, 2010, from www.utc.com/StaticFiles/UTC/StaticFiles/utc_overview.pdf.

[10] "Company Structure," Swisscom AG, accessed May 15, 2011, from www.swisscom.ch/GHQ/content/Portraet/Unternehmen/Unternehmensstruktur/?lang=en.

[11] "About AB InBev: In a Few Facts," AB InBev, accessed May 16, 2011, from www.ab-inbev.com/go/about_abinbev/our_company/in_a_few_facts.cfm.

[12] "Our Top 10 Markets," AB InBev, accessed May 16, 2011, from https://docs.google.com/viewer?url=http://www.ab-inbev.com/pdf/AB_InBev_AR10_OurTopTenMarkets.pdf.

[13] "Anheuser Busch InBev in Russia Key Facts & Figures," AB InBev, accessed May 16, 2011, from https://

docs.google.com/viewer?url=http://www.ab-inbev.com/pdf/factsheets/Russia2010.pdf; and "Anheuser Busch InBev in Belgium Key Facts & Figures," AB InBev, accessed May 16, 2011, from www.ab-inbev.com/pdf/factsheets/Belgium2010.pdf.

[14] "Who We Are," P&G, accessed November 14, 2009, from www.pg.com.

[15] "Corporate Info: Corporate Structure—Four Pillars," Procter & Gamble, accessed March 20, 2009, from www.pg.com/jobs/corporate_structure/four_pillars.jhtml; and "P&G Management," Procter & Gamble, accessed March 20, 2009, from www.pg.com/news/management/bios_photos.jhtml.

[16] L. R. Burns, "Adoption and Abandonment of Matrix Management Programs: Effects of Organizational Characteristics and Interorganizational Networks," *Academy of Management Journal* 36 (1993): 106–138.

[17] J. Fortt, "Yahoo's Taskmaster," April 27, 2009, 80–84.

[18] Ibid.

[19] D. Ball, "Unilever Shakes Up Its Management to Spur Growth," *The Wall Street Journal*, February 11, 2005, A2.

[20] "Unilever Streamlines Its Leadership Structure," Unilever, October 2, 2005, accessed March 20, 2009, from www.unilever.com/mediacentre/pressreleases/2005/Unileverstreamlinesitsleadershipstructure.aspx.

[21] H. Fayol, *General and Industrial Management*, trans. C. Storrs (London: Pitman Publishing, 1949).

[22] M. Weber, *The Theory of Social and Economic Organization*, trans. and ed. A. M. Henderson and T. Parsons (New York: Free Press, 1947).

[23] Fayol, *General and Industrial Management*.

[24] "John Scharffenberger, "The Tastemaker," Inc.com, May 1, 2009, accessed October 25, 2010, from www.inc.com/magazine/20090501/john-scharffenberger-the-tastemaker.html.

[25] A. Lashinsky, "Inside Apple, From Steve Jobs Down to the Janitor: How America's Most Successful—And Most Secretive—Bib Company Really Works," *Fortune*, May 23, 2011, 125–134.

[26] R. Guth, "Gates–Ballmer Clash Shaped Microsoft's Coming Handover," *The Wall Street Journal*, June 5, 2008, A1.

[27] Frank Filipponio, "Former U.S. Sec. of Transportation to lead Toyota Quality Advisory Panel," Autoblog.com March 4, 2010, accessed October 10, 2010, from www.autoblog.com/2010/03/04/former-u-s-sec-of-transportation-to-lead-toyota-qualit/.

[28] J. Rutledge, "Management by Belly Button," *Forbes*, November 4, 1996, 64.

[29] E. E. Lawler, S. A. Mohrman, & G. E. Ledford, *Creating High Performance Organizations: Practices and Results of Employee Involvement and Quality Management in Fortune 1000 Companies* (San Francisco: Jossey-Bass, 1995).

[30] R. Swanborg, "The Ideal Standardization," *CIO*, October 1, 2009, 19.

[31] S. Curry, "Retention Getters," *Incentive*, 1 April 2005.

[32] R. W. Griffin, *Task Design* (Glenview, IL: Scott, Foresman, 1982).

[33] Beth Kowitt, "Inside the secret world of Trader Joe's," *Fortune*, August 23, 2010, accessed October 10, 2010, http://money.cnn.com/2010/08/20/news/companies/inside_trader_joes_full_version.fortune/index.htm.

[34] F. Herzberg, *Work and the Nature of Man* (Cleveland, OH: World Press, 1966).

[35] A. Markels, "Team Approach: A Power Producer Is Intent on Giving Power to Its People—Groups of AES Employees Do Complex Tasks Ranging from Hiring to Investing—Making Sure Work Is 'Fun,'" *The Wall Street Journal*, July 3, 1995, A1.

[36] Stephanie Clifford, "In These Lean Days, Even Stores Shrink," *The New York Times*, November 9, 2010, accessed October 10, 2010, from www.nytimes.com/2010/11/10/business/10small.html.

[37] Ibid.

[38] R. Hackman & G. R. Oldham, *Work Redesign* (Reading, MA: Addison-Wesley, 1980).

[39] Y. Fried & G. R. Ferris, "The Validity of the Job Characteristics Model: A Review and Meta-Analysis," *Personnel Psychology* 40 (1987): 287–322; and B. T. Loher, R. A. Noe, N. L. Moeller, & M. P. Fitzgerald, "A Meta-Analysis

of the Relation of Job Characteristics to Job Satisfaction," *Journal of Applied Psychology* 70 (1985): 280–289.

[40] T. Burns & G. M. Stalker, *The Management of Innovation* (London: Tavistock, 1961).

[41] Hammer & Champy, *Reengineering the Corporation*.

[42] Ibid.

[43] C. Tuna, "Remembrances: Champion of 'Re-Engineering' Saved Companies, Challenged Thinking," *The Wall Street Journal*, September 6, 2008, A12.

[44] J. D. Thompson, *Organizations in Action* (New York: McGraw-Hill, 1967).

[45] D. Pink, "Who Has the Next Big Idea?" *Fast Company*, September 1, 2001, 108.

[46] J. B. White, "'Next Big Thing': Re-Engineering Gurus Take Steps to Remodel Their Stalling Vehicles," *The Wall Street Journal Interactive*, November 26, 1996.

[47] C. Tuna, "Remembrances: Champion of 'Re-Engineering' Saved Companies, Challenged Thinking," *The Wall Street Journal*, September 6, 2008, A12.

[48] G. M. Spreitzer, "Individual Empowerment in the Workplace: Dimensions, Measurement, and Validation," *Academy of Management Journal* 38 (1995): 1442–1465.

[49] M. Schrage, "I Know What You Mean. And I Can't Do Anything about It," *Fortune*, April 2, 2001, 186.

[50] K. W. Thomas & B. A. Velthouse, "Cognitive Elements of Empowerment," *Academy of Management Review* 15 (1990): 666–681.

[51] Deb Stanley, "Southwest Holds Plane for Grandfather of Slain Boy," The Denver Channel.com, January 13, 2011, accessed February 3, 2011, from www.thedenverchannel.com/news/26483696/detail.html.

[52] A. Morand, "The Role of Behavioral Formality and Informality in the Enactment of Bureaucratic versus Organic Organizations," *Academy of Management Review* 20 (1995): 831–872.

[53] "The Way I Work: Justin Kan of Justin.tv," *Inc.*, July 1, 2010, accessed

October 20, 2010, from www.inc
.com/magazine/20100701/the-way-i-
work-justin-kan-of-justintv.html.

[54]L. Munoz, "The Suit Is Back—Or Is
It? As Dot-Coms Die, So Should Busi-
ness Casual. But the Numbers Don't
Lie," *Fortune*, June 25, 2001, 202; and
F. Swoboda, "Casual Dress Becomes
the Rule," *Las Vegas Review-Journal*,
March 3, 1996.

[55]A. C. Lu-Lien Tan, "Business Attire:
The Office Coverup," *The Wall Street
Journal*, August 5, 2006, P1.

[56]Ibid.

[57]E. Berton, "Dress to Impress, UBS
Tells Its Staff," *The Wall Street Journal*, December 15, 2010, C1.

[58]"Casual Office Attire Going, Going...,"
USA Today, January 1, 2005, 8; and
J. Fassnacht, "Pendulum Swings Away
from Casual Attire in the Workplace,"
Reading (PA) Eagle, October 18,
2004.

[59]"Suits Lose Appeal as Casual Dress
Rules in London Offices," *Evening
Standard* (London), October 19, 2004.

[60]"SHRM Online Poll Results," Society for Human Resource Management, www.shrm.org/poll/results.asp?
Question#89, 21 May 2003.

[61]K. McCullough, "Analysis: More
Companies Allowing Employees to
Dress Down, Which Makes Productivity
Go Up," *Money Club*, March 26, 1996.

[62]W. Bounds, "Phone Calls Are Public
Affairs for Open-Plan Office Dwellers," *The Wall Street Journal*, July 10,
2002, B1.

[63]"Designing the Ever-Changing
Workplace," *Architectural Record*
(September 1995): 32–37.

[64]J. Stryker, "In Open Workplaces,
Traffic and Head Count Matters,"
Harvard Business Review (December
2009): v87, 24.

[65]A. Frangos, "Property Report: See
You on the Way Up! Office Stairs Get
'Aspirational,'" *The Wall Street Jour-
nal*, May 19, 2004, B1.

[66]J. Sandberg, "Cookies, Gossip,
Cubes: It's a Wonder Any Work Gets
Done at the Office," *The Wall Street
Journal*, April 28, 2004, B1.

[67]Ibid.

[68]. L. Gallagher, "At Work: Get Out of
My Face: Open Offices Were Hailed as
the Answer to Hierarchical, Rigid Organizations. Employees Would Rather
Have Privacy," *Forbes*, October 18,
1999, 105.

[69]K. A. Edelman, "Take Down the
Walls!" *Across the Board*, March 1,
1997.

[70]S. Hwang, "Cubicle Culture: Office
Vultures Circle Still-Warm Desks Left
Empty by Layoffs," *The Wall Street
Journal*, August 14, 2002, B1.

[71]M. Rich, "Shut Up So We Can Do
Our Jobs!—Fed Up Workers Try to
Muffle Chitchat, Conference Calls and
Other Open-Office Din," *The Wall
Street Journal*, August 29, 2001, B1.

[72]D. Mattioli, "Job Fears Make Offices
All Ears—Human-Resources Officials
Say Rise in Employee Eavesdropping
Fans Rumors," *The Wall Street Jour-
nal*, January 20, 2009, B7.

[73]J. Gannon, "Glaxo SmithKline,
Alcoa, Marconi, PNC Open Up Of-
fice Environments," *Pittsburgh Post-
Gazette*, February 9, 2003.

[74]Accessed November 15, 2009, from
www.cube-a-door.com.

[75]"Harry Potter," Wikipedia, accessed May 18, 2011, from http://
en.wikipedia.org/wiki/Harry_
Potter_and_the_Deathly_Hallows_
(film)#Production.

[76]G. G. Dess, A. M. A. Rasheed, K. J.
McLaughlin, & R. L. Priem, "The New
Corporate Architecture," *Academy of
Management Executive* 9 (1995): 7–18.

[77]W. Bulkeley, "New IBM Jobs Can
Mean Fewer Jobs Elsewhere," *The Wall
Street Journal*, March 8, 2004, B1.

[78]Daniel Eran Diliger, "Report Details iPad 2 Components, 5 Million
unit supply," Apple Insider, www
.appleinsider.com/articles/11/
01/30/report_details_ipad_2_
components_5_million_unit_supply.
html.

[79]"About the ICG," Independent Carton Group, accessed May 18, 2011,
from www.independentcartongroup.
com/about.htm.

[80]D. Savastano, "Print Suppliers
Group Is Coming into Its Own," *Ink
World*, March 2006, 50–52.

[81]Ibid.

[82]About the Independent Carton
Group," Independent Carton Group,
accessed November 15, 2009, from
http://independentcartongroup.com.

[83]C. C. Snow, R. E. Miles, & H. J.
Coleman, Jr., "Managing 21st Century
Network Organizations," *Organiza-
tional Dynamics*, Winter 1992, 5–20.

[84]J. H. Sheridan, "The Agile Web:
A Model for the Future?" *Industry
Week*, March 4, 1996, 31.

[85]G. Bruner, K. James, & P. Hensel,
Marketing Scales Handbook (Chicago: American Marketing Association, 2001), vol. 3 931–934.

[86]Elena Berton, "Dress to Impress,
UBS Tells Staff," *The Wall Street Journal*, December 14, 2010, accessed
January 4, 2011, from http://online.
wsj.com/article/SB10001424052748
704694004576019783931381042.
html?mod=googlenews_wsj; Philip
Walzer "Businesses Take Casual Attitude toward Attire," The *Virginian-
Pilot*, December 5, 2010, accessed
January 4, 2011, from http://hamp-
tonroads.com/2010/12/businesses-
take-casual-attitude-toward-attire.

[87]"China Ends U.S's Reign as Largest
Auto Market," *Bloomberg News*, January 11, 2010, accessed November 15,
201, from www.bloomberg.com/apps/
news?pid=20601087&sid=aE.x_r_
l9NZE; "GM's China Sales Exceed U.S.
for Third Straight Month," *Businessweek*, April 2, 2010, accessed November 15, 2010, from www.Businessweek.
com/news/2010-04-02/gm-sales-gain-
in-china-on-government-stimulus-up-
date1-.html; and Ester Fung, "GM Sees
Chain Sales Exceeding 3 Mln Units
in 2015," *The Wall Street Journal*,
April 12, 2010, accessed November
15, 2010, from http://online.wsj.com/
article/BT-CO-20100412-701317.
html?mod=WSJ_World_MIDDLE-
HeadlinesAsia.

[88]K. Freiberg & J. Freiberg, *Nuts!
Southwest Airlines' Crazy Recipe for
Business and Personal Success* (Austin,
TX: Bard, 1996).

reel to real

© iStockphoto.com/Oner Döngel

BIZ FLIX

Rendition

"What if someone you love … just disappeared?" This is the question posed by the 2007 dramatic thriller *Rendition*. Anwar El-Ibrahimi (Omar Metwally) boards a flight in South Africa but never arrives home to his family in the States. His pregnant wife Isabella (Reese Witherspoon) doesn't know that he has been named as a suspected terrorist and sent to a secret detention facility in North Africa, where he is tortured and interrogated. Eventually, CIA analyst Douglas Freeman (Jake Gyllenhaal), who has overseen the interrogation, becomes convinced of El-Ibrahimi's innocence, but he is ordered to continue with the detention. In this scene, Senator Hawkins (Alan Arkin) is talking to congressional aide Alan Smith (Peter Sarsgaard) about the situation and explaining why they think there may be a connection between the terrorists and El-Ibrahimi.

© GreenLight

What to Watch for and Ask Yourself

1. How would you describe the workplace atmosphere in this scene? Would you say it demonstrates behavioral informality or formality?

2. Do you think the scene shows line authority or staff authority between these two men?

3. What kind of feedback is Alan Smith getting from Senator Hawkins? Is it primarily positive or negative?

MANAGEMENT WORKPLACE

Modern Shed: Designing Adaptive Organizations

Modern Shed, based in Seattle, builds paneled dwellings for use as studio spaces, home offices, pool houses, project sheds, guesthouses, and more. Like the sheds, the company is built to be adaptive, scalable, and suited to the needs of the environment. Modern Shed counts only 12 to 14 full time employees. But at times, its output rivals that of a large builder, thanks to collaboration with outside sales reps and a dealer network comprised of 35 independent contractors. According to Smith, the logical process of building sheds from smaller scale structures to larger ones is a metaphor for how modern organizations should be built. "You can use the analogy for organizations and people as well as structures," Smith states. "If you go too big you don't understand it; you have to start small."

© Cengage Learning

Discussion Questions

1. Describe how Modern Shed functions as a modular organization.

2. What are the advantages and disadvantages of Modern Shed's organizational structure?

CHAPTER 10

Managing
Teams

Learning Outcomes

1. Explain the good and bad of using teams.

2. Recognize and understand the different kinds of teams.

3. Understand the general characteristics of work teams.

4. Explain how to enhance work team effectiveness.

what would **you do?**

Cessna Headquarters, Wichita, Kansas[1]

The words "Cessna Skyhawk" have special meaning for anyone who has ever wanted to learn to fly. At 27 feet long and 8 feet tall, with a 36-foot wingspan, a 140 mph cruising speed, and room for two adults and their luggage, more people have learned to fly with a Cessna Skyhawk than with any other plane in aviation history. In fact, the Cessna Skyhawk is the best-selling plane of all time. Clyde Cessna built his first plane in 1911, and Cessna became a storied name in aviation. Cessna built 750 gliders for the army in World War II, introduced the Skyhawk in 1956, produced the first turbo-charged and cabin-pressurized single-engine planes in the 1960s, delivered its first business jet in the 1970s, topped $1 billion in sales in the 1980s, and then, in one of the worst downturns in the history of aviation business, nearly went out of business over the next decade and a half.

Sales of general aviation aircraft, which had topped out at 17,000 planes per year, dropped to 12,000 planes within a year, and over the next decade finally hit rock bottom at 928 planes for the entire industry. During the same time, Cessna's sales of piston-engine planes, like the Skyhawk, dropped from 8,000 per year to just 600. Cessna was forced to lay off 75 percent of the employees at its piston-engine plane factories (Cessna also makes business jets and larger planes) and eventually stopped making piston-engine planes altogether. However, after the economy improved and the U.S. government approved the General Aviation Revitalization Act (barring product liability lawsuits on any plane over 18 years old), Cessna decided to start building its legendary Skyhawks again.

This is where you come in. With nearly 20 years in the company, your first job with Cessna was teaching Cessna dealers how to service and maintain single-engine planes. But now, with profits flowing again and the company's legal risk greatly reduced thanks to the Revitalization Act, you've been made the vice-president of Cessna's "new" single-engine business. It's your job to rebuild this part of the business from the ground up. And because pilots tend to remain loyal to the kind of airplane on which they learned to fly, much depends on your success or failure. If you can rebuild Cessna's single-engine business, the pilots who learn to fly on today's Cessna Skyhawks will be buying Cessna business jets 20 years from now.

One of the advantages of starting completely over is that you get to design the entire production facility, from its location, to the new workers, to the suppliers, everything is up for grabs. For instance, Cessna does most of its production in Wichita, Kansas. But since it left the single-engine plane business, Wichita mostly produces a small number of highly customized jets each year, just the opposite of your business, which is a high number of standardized, single-engine planes. So, given the differences, you locate the new single-engine plane factory in Independence, Kansas, two hours

< **"what's new" companies**

study tips

Make up a crossword puzzle using the key terms in this chapter. Writing the clues will help you remember the definition and the context of each concept.

Make photocopies for exam time and for your study group.

away by car, and only 40 minutes away in one of Cessna's small planes. Along with a new location, you're debating taking a new approach to manufacturing planes by using production teams. This decision may strike some colleagues as radical, particularly at conservative-minded Cessna where, one of your fellow managers admitted, "we probably got into a mode of doing things for the future based on how we'd always done things in the past." But the more you think about it, the more you are convinced that it is the right decision. Instead of using a standard production line where each worker does just one task, you are thinking about using teams to assemble Skyhawks and other single-engine planes. In an incredible departure from the engineering-based standards in which the motions of every worker on the assembly line are studied for time, cost, and efficiency implications, production teams would be completely responsible for assembling the planes and for costs and quality.

You expect to see several benefits from a team-based approach, increased customer satisfaction from improved product quality, faster, more efficient production, and higher employee job satisfaction. A few things worry you, however. Despite all of their promise, teams and teamwork are also prone to significant disadvantages. They're expensive to implement. They require significant training. And they only work about a third of the time they're used. So, despite their promise, you can't ignore the reality that using teams would be quite risky for Cessna.

Still, you can't help thinking that teams could pay off and that there might be ways for you to minimize the risk of failure. For example, because the plant will be in a new location, Independence, Kansas, you get to start with a brand new workforce. What kinds of people should you hire for teamwork? What kinds of skills and experience will they need to succeed in a team environment? If you decide to take the plunge and use teams, how much authority and responsibility should you give them? Should they be limited to just advising management, or should you make them totally responsible for quality, costs, and productivity? Finally, while you're considering using teams on the assembly line, are there other places in which you might use teams? Not all teams are alike. Maybe there are other places in which teams could contribute to the success of Cessna's "new" single-engine plane-manufacturing facility?

If you were in charge of Cessna's "new" single-engine factory, what would you do?

Ninety-one percent of organizations are significantly improving their effectiveness by using work teams.[2] Procter & Gamble and Cummins Engine began using teams in 1962 and 1973, respectively. Boeing, Caterpillar, Champion International, Ford Motor Company, 3M, and General Electric established work teams in the mid- to late 1980s. Today, most companies use teams to tackle a variety of issues.[3] "Teams are ubiquitous. Whether we are talking about software development, Olympic hockey, disease outbreak response, or urban warfare, teams represent the critical unit that 'gets things done' in today's world."[4]

We begin this chapter by reviewing the advantages and disadvantages of teams and exploring when companies should use teams instead of more traditional approaches. Next, we discuss the different types of work teams and the characteristics that all teams share. The chapter ends by focusing on the practical steps to managing teams: team goals and priorities, and organizing, training, and compensating teams.

Why Work Teams?

Work teams consist of a small number of people with complementary skills who hold themselves mutually accountable for pursuing a common purpose, achieving performance goals, and improving interdependent work processes.[5] By this definition, computer programmers working on separate projects in the same department of a company would not be considered a team. To be a team, the programmers would have to be interdependent and share responsibility and accountability for the quality and amount of computer code they produced.[6] Teams are becoming more important in many industries because they help organizations respond to specific problems and challenges. Though work teams are not the answer for every situation or organization, if the right teams are used properly and in the right settings, teams can dramatically improve company performance over more traditional management approaches while also instilling a sense of vitality in the workplace that is otherwise difficult to achieve.

After reading the next two sections, you should be able to

1. *Explain the good and bad of using teams.*
2. *Recognize and understand the different kinds of teams.*

1 The Good and Bad of Using Teams

Let's begin our discussion of teams by learning about **1.1 the advantages of teams**, **1.2 the disadvantages of teams**, and **1.3 when to use and not use teams**.

1.1 The Advantages of Teams

Companies are making greater use of teams because teams have been shown to improve customer satisfaction, product and service quality, speed and efficiency in product development, employee job satisfaction, and decision making.[7] For example, one survey indicated that 80 percent of companies with more than 100 employees use teams, and 90 percent of all U.S. employees work part of their day in a team.[8]

Teams help businesses increase *customer satisfaction* in several ways. One way is to create work teams that are trained to meet the needs of specific customers. For example, **Staff Management**, which hires temporary workers for companies, was asked by a leading online retailer to hire 10,000 people for the 2010 holiday season. Joan Davison Chief Operating Officer for Staff Management says, "Our clients increase their workforce by as much as 100 percent during the holiday season." Staff Management's hiring team used social media, such as Facebook, job fairs, and other hiring events to generate the applicants. Jerry Wimer, Vice President of Operations, said, "Staff Management as an organization is extremely proud of this dedicated team who sacrificed their time with family and friends over the busy holiday season serving our client. Many people, including hard-working recruiters and coaches, supervisors and safety managers, data entry clerks and directors from across the country, had a hand in helping this client succeed."[9]

Businesses also create problem-solving teams and employee involvement teams to study ways to improve overall customer satisfaction and make recommendations

< **"what's new" companies**

work team a small number of people with complementary skills who hold themselves mutually accountable for pursuing a common purpose, achieving performance goals, and improving interdependent work processes.

for improvements. Teams like these typically meet on a weekly or monthly basis. At one of its manufacturing facilities, Chrysler has turned to employee involvement teams to take responsibility for quality of the transmissions manufactured there. Each morning, the manufacturing teams meet in front of a white dry-erase "problems board," where team members write the problems they're seeing based on the quality data they've collected. Chrysler spokesperson Ed Saenz says, "The primary driver [for using teams] is trying to empower and support assemblers—doing far more listening and a lot less giving orders than we ever have. Team leaders are union members, not management or supervisors; they are empowered to lead teams with six to ten people per team. . . . we were asking them to take their brain and hang them on a hook at work. If you free people up and empower them, they bring the skills they have outside the plant to work. These are the people who know how to do the job and how to do it better."[10]

"what's new" companies >

Teams also help firms improve *product and service quality* in several ways.[11] In contrast to traditional organizational structures where management is responsible for organizational outcomes and performance, teams take direct responsibility for the quality of the products and service they produce and sell. **Oriental Trading Company (OTC)** sells party supplies, arts and crafts, toys and games, and teaching supplies on the Internet. Like most retail websites, OTC's customers can write comments about the products they buy. When customers complained about an Inflatable Solar System OTC sold, giving it two stars out of five, members of OTC's intradepartmental teams sprang to action. A team member from the quality department worked directly with the manufacturer to improve quality. Another from copy writing worked with a team member from merchandising to post new photos of the improved product along with a rewritten, more accurate product description. Other members of the team contacted dissatisfied customers to tell them that OTC had listened and had taken steps to address their concerns. Seven weeks after reading the first negative comment on its website, the new improved product was for sale on its website. Customers consistently rate the new version at four out of five stars.[12]

As you learned in Chapter 7, companies that are slow to innovate or integrate new features and technologies into their products are at a competitive disadvantage. Therefore, a third reason that teams are increasingly popular is that they can increase *speed and efficiency when designing and manufacturing products*.[13] Louis Vuitton, the French-based world-renowned fashion house, designs and makes some of the most expensive, best-selling purses, shoulder bags, tote bags, and luggage in the world. With many bags costing $1,000 or more, it might surprise you to learn that it used to take 30 craftspeople eight days to produce just one bag! This was because each worker completed just one task, such as cutting leather, gluing and sewing, or stitching the lining, and bottlenecks would form as the slower workers forced faster workers to wait for the next purse to come to them for work. Louis Vuitton fixed the problem by switching to teams of 6 to 12 workers who learned to complete four different production steps. Teams were then positioned in U-shaped workstations with sewing machines and assembly tables so that team members could pass bags back and forth without waiting. The result? It now takes just one day and 6 to 12 workers to produce a bag. Furthermore, because team members complete multiple tasks, teams can now work on different kinds of bags, which allows the company to switch production quickly to its best-selling items. Finally, with quality up significantly, returns of defective bags have dropped by two-thirds.[14]

Another reason for using teams is that teamwork often leads to increased *job satisfaction*.[15] One reason that teamwork can be more satisfying than traditional work is that it gives workers a chance to improve their skills. This is often accomplished through **cross-training**, in which team members are taught how to do all or most of the jobs performed by the other team members. The advantage for the organization

cross-training training team members to do all or most of the jobs performed by the other team members.

is that cross-training allows a team to function normally when one member is absent, quits, or is transferred. The advantage for workers is that cross-training broadens their skills and increases their capabilities while also making their work more varied and interesting.

A second reason that teamwork is satisfying is that work teams often receive proprietary business information that is available only to managers at most companies. For example, Whole Foods has an "open books, open door, open people" philosophy. Team members are given full access to their store's financial information and everyone's salaries, including those of the store manager and the CEO.[16] Each day, next to the time clock, Whole Foods employees can see the previous day's sales for each team as well as the sales on the same day from the previous year. Each week, team members can examine the same information, broken down by team, for all of the Whole Foods stores in their region. And each month, store managers review information on profitability, including sales, product costs, wages, and operating profits, with each team in the store. Because team members decide how much to spend, what to order, what things should cost, and how many team members should work each day, this information is critical to making teams work at Whole Foods.[17] Whole Foods creates an empowering work environment to honor one of its core values: "supporting team member excellence and happiness."[18]

Team members also gain job satisfaction from unique leadership responsibilities that are not typically available in traditional organizations. Orchestras are led by a conductor who is clearly in charge. Can you imagine an orchestra without a conductor? The award-winning, New York City–based Orpheus Chamber Orchestra doesn't have one. Instead, it has a concert master who is responsible for a performance. What is most interesting is that the concert master's role is rotated among different members of the orchestra. Although a typical concertmaster is a violinist, at Orpheus the position rotates around the various instruments of the orchestra. Flutist Susan Palma-Nidel says that assuming the concertmaster's role "has allowed me to discover strengths that I didn't know I had. Not only have I helped lead the group, but I've also been interviewed by the media—something I never thought I'd do. If I hadn't been forced to do those things, I'm not sure that I ever would have."[19] Furthermore, rotating leadership among team members can lead to more participation and cooperation in team decision making and improved team performance.[20]

Finally, teams share many of the advantages of group decision making discussed in Chapter 5. For instance, because team members possess different knowledge, skills, abilities, and experiences, a team is able to view problems from multiple perspectives. This diversity of viewpoints increases the odds that team decisions will solve the underlying causes of problems and not just address the symptoms. The increased knowledge and information available to teams also make it easier for them to generate more alternative solutions, a critical part of improving the quality of decisions. Because team members are involved in decision-making processes, they are also likely to be more committed to making those decisions work. In short, teams can do a much better job than individuals in two important steps of the decision-making process: defining the problem and generating alternative solutions. Exhibit 10.1 summarizes the advantages and disadvantages of teams. (The disadvantages are discussed in the next section.)

1.2 The Disadvantages of Teams

Although teams can significantly improve customer satisfaction, product and service quality, speed and efficiency in product development, employee job satisfaction, and decision making, using teams does not guarantee these positive outcomes. In fact,

Exhibit 10.1 Advantages and Disadvantages of Teams

ADVANTAGES 👍	DISADVANTAGES 👎
☺ Customer satisfaction	☹ Initially high employee turnover
☺ Product and service quality	☹ Social loafing
☺ Speed and efficiency in product development	☹ Disadvantages of group decision making (groupthink, inefficient meetings, domination by a minority, lack of accountability)
☺ Employee job satisfaction	
☺ Better decision making and problem solving (multiple perspectives, more alternative solutions, increased commitment to decisions)	

© Cengage Learning 2013

if you've ever participated in team projects in your classes, you're probably already aware of some of the problems inherent in work teams. Despite all of their promise, teams and teamwork are also prone to these significant disadvantages: initially high turnover, social loafing, and the problems associated with group decision making.

The first disadvantage of work teams is *initially high turnover*. Teams aren't for everyone, and some workers balk at the responsibility, effort, and learning required in team settings. When General Electric's Salisbury plant switched to teams, the turnover rate jumped from near zero to 14 percent. Plant manager Roger Gasaway says of teams and teamwork, "It's not all wonderful stuff."[21] Some people may quit because they object to the way team members closely scrutinize each other's job performance, particularly when teams are small. Randy Savage, who works for Eaton Corporation, a manufacturer of car and truck parts, said, "They say there are no bosses here, but if you screw up, you find one pretty fast." Beverly Reynolds, who quit Eaton's team-based system after nine months, says her coworkers "weren't standing watching me, but from afar, they were watching me." And even though her teammates were willing to help her improve her job performance, she concludes, "As it turns out, it just wasn't for me at all."[22]

Social loafing is another disadvantage of work teams. **Social loafing** occurs when workers withhold their efforts and fail to perform their share of the work.[23] A nineteenth-century French engineer named Maximilian Ringlemann first documented social loafing when he found that one person pulling on a rope alone exerted an average of 139 pounds of force on the rope. In groups of three, the average force dropped to 117 pounds per person. In groups of eight, the average dropped to just 68 pounds per person. Ringlemann concluded that the larger the team, the smaller the individual effort. In fact, social loafing is more likely to occur in larger groups where identifying and monitoring the efforts of individual team members can be difficult.[24] In other words, social loafers count on being able to blend into the background where their lack of effort isn't easily spotted. From team-based class projects, most students already know about social loafers, or "slackers," who contribute poor, little, or no work whatsoever. Not surprisingly, a study of 250 student teams found that the most talented students are typically the least satisfied with teamwork because of having to carry slackers and do a disproportionate share of their team's work.[25] Perceptions of fairness are negatively related to the extent of social loafing within teams.[26]

How prevalent is social loafing on teams? One study found that when team activities were not mandatory, only 25 percent of manufacturing workers volunteered to join problem-solving teams; 70 percent were quiet, passive supporters (that is,

social loafing behavior in which team members withhold their efforts and fail to perform their share of the work.

Exhibit 10.2 Factors That Encourage People to Withhold Effort in Teams

1. **The presence of someone with expertise.** Team members will withhold effort when another team member is highly qualified to make a decision or comment on an issue.

2. **The presentation of a compelling argument.** Team members will withhold effort if the arguments for a course of action are very persuasive or similar to their own thinking.

3. **The lack of confidence in one's ability to contribute.** Team members will withhold effort if they are unsure about their ability to contribute to discussions, activities, or decisions. This is especially so for high-profile decisions.

4. **An unimportant or meaningless decision.** Team members will withhold effort by mentally withdrawing or adopting a "who cares" attitude if decisions don't affect them or their units, or if they don't see a connection between their efforts and their team's successes or failures.

5. **A dysfunctional decision-making climate.** Team members will withhold effort if other team members are frustrated or indifferent or if a team is floundering or disorganized.

Source: P. W. Mulvey, J. F. Veiga, & P. M. Elsass, "When Teammates Raise a White Flag," *Academy of Management Executive* 10, no. 1 (1996): 40–49.

they didn't put forth effort); and 5 percent were actively opposed to these activities.[27] Another study found that on management teams, 56 percent of the managers, or more than half, withheld their effort in one way or another. Exhibit 10.2 lists the factors that encourage people to withhold effort in teams.

Finally, teams share many of the *disadvantages of group decision making* discussed in Chapter 5, such as groupthink. In *groupthink*, members of highly cohesive groups feel intense pressure not to disagree with each other so that the group can approve a proposed solution. Because groupthink restricts discussion and leads to consideration of a limited number of alternative solutions, it usually results in poor decisions. Also, team decision making takes considerable time, and team meetings can often be unproductive and inefficient. Another possible pitfall is *minority domination*, where just one or two people dominate team discussions, restricting consideration of different problem definitions and alternative solutions. Scott Jessup, formerly CEO of Marque Inc., an ambulance and hearse manufacturer, explains how his presence would regularly produce minority domination: "I think at times I stifle our best thinking. When a CEO wanders into a team meeting an entirely different dynamic takes place and everybody sits back and waits for the CEO to put forth pearls of wisdom."[28] Finally, team members may not feel accountable for the decisions and actions taken by the team.

1.3 When to Use Teams

As the two previous subsections made clear, teams have significant advantages *and* disadvantages. Therefore, the question is not whether to use teams, but *when* and *where* to use teams for maximum benefit and minimum cost. As Doug Johnson, associate director at the Center for Collaborative Organizations at the University of North Texas, puts it, "Teams are a means to an end, not an end in themselves. You have to ask yourself questions first. Does the work require interdependence? Will the team philosophy fit company strategy? Will management make a long-term commitment to this process?"[29] Exhibit 10.3 provides some additional guidelines on when to use or not use teams.[30]

First, teams should be used when there is a clear, engaging reason or purpose for using them. Too many companies use teams because they're popular or because the companies assume that teams can fix all problems. Teams are much more likely to succeed if they know why they exist and what they are supposed to accomplish, and more

© Doug Pensinger/Getty Images

Johan Bruynell understands the need for planning well in advance. Here, he's pictured with his team in Albuquerque, New Mexico, a full six months before the start of the Tour de France.

likely to fail if they don't. Johan Bruyneel has won the Tour de France nine times, not as a rider, but as a team director. Although Bruyneel has clearly worked with talented riders, no other team director has even come close to his record. What accounts for his teams' successes? Clear purposes and goals. Bruyneel understands that it takes a year to win the three-week Tour de France. So he plans out the entire year before the race, mixing in the right combination of training, racing, and rest. Then, for each of the nine members of his riding teams, he develops daily, weekly, monthly, and annual goals to prepare them to fulfill their team roles.[31] Jon Katzenbach, coauthor of The *Wisdom of Teams*, supports Bruyneel's approach, saying, "If groups want to achieve team performance, the most important factor is not the leader of the team; it is the clarity around the performance purpose for that group. The more clear and compelling that is, the more naturally those people will function as a team."[32]

Second, teams should be used when the job can't be done unless people work together. This typically means that teams are needed when tasks are complex, require multiple perspectives, or require repeated interaction with others to complete. For example, contrary to stories of legendary programmers who write software programs by themselves, Microsoft uses teams to write code because of the enormous complexity of today's software. Most software simply has too many options and features for one person (or even one team) to complete it all. Likewise, Microsoft uses teams because writing good software requires repeated interaction with others. Microsoft ensures this interaction by having its teams "check in" their computer

Exhibit 10.3 When to Use or Not Use Teams

🚦 USE TEAMS WHEN...	🛑 DON'T USE TEAMS WHEN...
✓ there is a clear, engaging reason or purpose.	✗ there isn't a clear, engaging reason or purpose.
✓ the job can't be done unless people work together.	✗ the job can be done by people working independently.
✓ rewards can be provided for teamwork and team performance.	✗ rewards are provided for individual effort and performance.
✓ ample resources are available.	✗ the necessary resources are not available.
✓ teams will have clear authority to manage and change how work gets done.	✗ management will continue to monitor and influence how work gets done.

Source: R. Wageman, "Critical Success Factors for Creating Superb Self-Managing Teams," *Organizational Dynamics* 26, no. 1 (1997): 49–61.

code every few days. The different pieces of code written by different teams are then compiled to create an updated working build or prototype of the software. The next day, all the teams and their members begin testing and debugging the new build. Over and over again, the computer code is compiled, sent back to the teams to be tested and improved, and then compiled and tested again.[33] The mistake that Microsoft made when developing Vista, its widely criticized operating system, was that the different development teams didn't share their plans with each other; that is, Microsoft didn't have enough repeated interaction between teams. So although each team's code tested cleanly on its own, conflicts and failure would occur when the different team codes were combined. Microsoft's Julie Larson-Green said, "That's where the conflicts started."[34] So when developing and testing Windows 7, Vista's replacement, Microsoft development teams shared their plans with each other and spent time listening and collaborating with engineers at computer manufacturers like HP and Dell. John Cook, HP's vice president of desktop marketing, said that Microsoft "had some brutally honest discussions with what our engineers and customers thought of Vista. . . . They listened and were much more humble."[35] In the end, the collaboration among teams and with computer manufacturers paid off in Windows 7 being faster, more reliable, and more flexible than Vista. Ian LeGrow, a Microsoft group program manager, said, "Instead of it being a plan owned by one team, our plan was a part of all the teams."[36]

If tasks are simple and don't require multiple perspectives or repeated interaction with others, however, teams should not be used.[37] Consultant Jeff Palfini says, "Managers confronted with a new task should always consider whether pulling together a team will be the most efficient way to complete the task. Sometimes it's faster and less complicated to parcel it out or delegate it to one or two people, especially if the task is fairly routine."[38]

Third, teams should be used when rewards can be provided for teamwork and team performance. Rewards that depend on team performance rather than individual performance are the key to rewarding team behaviors and efforts. You'll read more about team rewards later in the chapter, but for now it's enough to know that if the type of reward (individual vs. team) is not matched to the type of performance

mgmt:facts

Good Meetings

Meetings often feel like a necessary evil. Yes, they're important for communicating information, making key decisions, and formulating strategy. But they also never start on time, run on forever, and make you feel like you could've left two hours earlier. So how can you have better meetings? Glenn Parker, author of *Meeting Excellence: 33 Tools to Lead Meetings That Get Results*, offers up three basic suggestions. First, make sure that there is a purpose to the meeting. A meeting shouldn't be held just because you haven't had one in a while. You should make sure that there is a clear reason for the meeting. Second, make sure the people who will attend the meeting know what its purpose is so that they can prepare ahead of time. Even if you've established a really clear goal for the meeting, it will do no good if no one else knows what it is. Finally, make sure that the right people are in the meeting. This means that all those who need to be in the meeting are actually there, and that those who don't need to be aren't.[39]

"what's new" >
companies

(individual vs. team), teams won't work. This was the case at **Savills**, a London-based global real estate advising and consulting firm. Director Mark Ridley realized that the company's incentive structure was encouraging individual, but not group effort. Says Ridley, "We were only rewarding one element of behavior—[individual] financial performance. It was difficult to get someone in Scotland to pass work to Birmingham or to get someone in London to help in Scotland." While the old system was based on 81 different profit and loss statements and only rewarded individuals, the new reward system is based on individual performance plus the performance of their overall division, their local team, and their contributions to the team, such as cross-selling with other Savills' salespeople. Behavior has already begun to change.[40] Systems that reward individual performance but hope for high team-level performance are sure to fail.[41]

Review 1

The Good and Bad of Using Teams   In many industries, teams are growing in importance because they help organizations respond to specific problems and challenges. Teams have been shown to increase customer satisfaction (specific customer teams), product and service quality (direct responsibility), speed and efficiency in product development (overlapping development phases), and employee job satisfaction (cross-training, unique opportunities, and leadership responsibilities). Although teams can produce significant improvements in these areas, using teams does not guarantee these positive outcomes. Teams and teamwork have the disadvantages of initially high turnover and social loafing (especially in large groups). Teams also share many of the advantages (multiple perspectives, generation of more alternatives, and more commitment) and disadvantages (groupthink, time consuming, poorly run meetings, domination by a few team members, and weak accountability) of group decision making. Finally, teams should be used for a clear purpose, when the work requires that people work together, when rewards can be provided for both teamwork and team performance, when ample resources can be provided, and when teams can be given clear authority over their work.

2 Kinds of Teams

Companies use different kinds of teams for different purposes. Google uses teams to innovate and develop new products as well as tweak and improve its search algorithms and functions.[42] JCPenney uses teams to execute its "door to floor" strategy, which aims to get the right merchandise to the right store at the right time so that Penney's customers find what they want when they want it.[43] At the Spinal Cord and Traumatic Brain Injury Unit at the Burke Rehabilitation Hospital in White Plains, New York, nurses work in teams to treat patients with spinal stenosis, a narrowing of the spinal cord which produces intense pain.[44]

Let's continue our discussion of teams by learning about the different kinds of teams that companies like Google and JCPenney use to make themselves more competitive. We look first at **2.1 how teams differ in terms of autonomy, which is the key dimension that makes one team different from another**, and then at **2.2 some special kinds of teams**.

2.1 Autonomy, the Key Dimension

Teams can be classified in a number of ways, such as permanent or temporary, or functional or cross-functional. However, studies indicate that the amount of

Exhibit 10.4 Team Authority Continuum

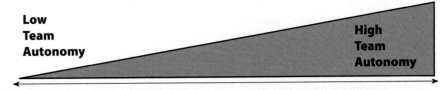

RESPONSIBILITIES	TRADITIONAL WORK GROUPS	EMPLOYEE INVOLVEMENT GROUPS	SEMI-AUTONOMOUS WORK GROUPS	SELF-MANAGING TEAMS	SELF-DESIGNING TEAMS
Control Design of					
Team					✓
Tasks					✓
Membership					✓
All Production/Service Tasks					
Make Decisions				✓	✓
Solve Problems				✓	✓
Major Production/Service Tasks					
Make Decisions			✓	✓	✓
Solve Problems			✓	✓	✓
Receive Information			✓	✓	✓
Give Advice/Make Suggestions		✓	✓	✓	✓
Execute Task	✓	✓	✓	✓	✓

Sources: R. D. Banker, J. M. Field, R. G. Schroeder, & K. K. Sinha, "Impact of Work Teams on Manufacturing Performance: A Longitudinal Field Study," *Academy of Management Journal* 39 (1996): 867–890; and J. R. Hackman, "The Psychology of Self-Management in Organizations," in *Psychology and Work: Productivity, Change, and Employment*, M. S. Pallak & R. Perlof, eds. (Washington, DC: American Psychological Association), 85–136.

autonomy possessed by a team is the key difference among teams.[45] *Autonomy* is the degree to which workers have the discretion, freedom, and independence to decide how and when to accomplish their jobs. Exhibit 10.4 shows how five kinds of teams differ in terms of autonomy. Moving left to right across the autonomy continuum at the top of the exhibit, traditional work groups and employee involvement groups have the least autonomy; semiautonomous work groups have more autonomy; and, finally, self-managing teams and self-designing teams have the most autonomy. Moving from bottom to top along the left side of the exhibit, note that the number of responsibilities given to each kind of team increases directly with its autonomy. Let's review each of these kinds of teams and their autonomy and responsibilities in more detail.

The smallest amount of autonomy is found in **traditional work groups,** where two or more people work together to achieve a shared goal. In these groups, workers are responsible for doing the work or "executing the task," but they do not have direct responsibility or control over their work. Workers report to managers, who are responsible for their performance and have the authority to hire and fire them, make job assignments, and control resources. For instance, suppose that an

traditional work group a group composed of two or more people who work together to achieve a shared goal.

experienced worker blatantly refuses to do his share of the work, saying, "I've done my time. Let the younger employees do the work." In a team with high autonomy, the responsibility of getting this employee to put forth his fair share of effort would belong to his teammates. But, in a traditional work group, that responsibility belongs to the boss or supervisor. The supervisor in this situation calmly confronted the employee and told him, "We need your talent, [and] your knowledge of these machines. But if you won't work, you'll have to go elsewhere." Within days, the employee's behavior improved.[46]

Employee involvement teams, which have somewhat more autonomy, meet on company time on a weekly or monthly basis to provide advice or make suggestions to management concerning specific issues such as plant safety, customer relations, or product quality.[47] Though they offer advice and suggestions, they do not have the authority to make decisions. Membership on these teams is often voluntary, but members may be selected because of their expertise. The idea behind employee involvement teams is that the people closest to the problem or situation are best able to recommend solutions. At **Eichstaedt**, a San Francisco–based accounting firm, employee involvement teams serve as developmental opportunities for junior accountants. For example, Cynthia Bonavia led the "rewards" team charged with studying employee perceptions of the firm's rewards and benefits system, nonmonetary rewards, work/life balance, and employee satisfaction. Likewise, Tracy Hom led a team that studied how to improve employee mentoring. Said Hom, we learned "The No. 1 thing they wanted was more feedback on job performance. We then had to figure out what it would entail to implement a formal mentoring program and how to keep tabs on the mentoring relationships to find out if they were working."[48]

Semiautonomous work groups not only provide advice and suggestions to management but also have the authority to make decisions and solve problems related to the major tasks required to produce a product or service. Semiautonomous groups regularly receive information about budgets, work quality and performance, and competitors' products. Furthermore, members of semiautonomous work groups are typically cross-trained in a number of different skills and tasks. In short, semiautonomous work groups give employees the authority to make decisions that are typically made by supervisors and managers.

That authority is not complete, however. Managers still play a role, though one that is much reduced compared with traditional work groups, in supporting the work of semiautonomous work groups. The role a manager plays on a team usually evolves over time. "It may start with helping to transition problem-solving responsibilities to the team, filling miscellaneous requests for the team, and doing ad hoc tasks," says Steven Hitchcock, president of Axis Performance Advisors in Portland, Oregon. Later, the team may develop into a mini-enterprise and the former manager becomes externally focused—sort of an account manager for the customer. Managers have to adjust what they do based on the sophistication of the team.[49] A lot of what managers of semiautonomous work groups do is ask good questions, provide resources, and facilitate performance of group goals.

Self-managing teams differ from semiautonomous work groups in that team members manage and control *all* of the major tasks *directly related* to production of a product or service without first getting approval from management. This includes managing and controlling the acquisition of materials, making a product or providing a service, and ensuring timely delivery. At a **Bandag** tire re-tread factory in Iowa, the self-managing teams in Plant 4 were entirely responsible for decision making, resolving internal and external conflicts, evaluating team member performance and providing feedback, recognizing good performance, running team meetings, deciding who needed what kind of training, and then selecting team members to rotate through three key team leadership roles. Plant 4, which used to lose money, is now

"what's new" >
companies

employee involvement team team that provides advice or makes suggestions to management concerning specific issues.

semiautonomous work group a group that has the authority to make decisions and solve problems related to the major tasks of producing a product or service.

self-managing team a team that manages and controls all of the major tasks of producing a product or service.

"what's new" >
companies

solidly profitable thanks to a 50 percent improvement in efficiency produced by its self-managed teams.[50] The use of self-directed teams has significantly increased productivity at a number of other companies, increasing quality by 12 percent at AT&T, reducing errors by 13 percent at FedEx, and helping 3M increase production by 300 percent at one of its manufacturing plants.[51] Seventy-two percent of *Fortune* 1,000 companies have at least one self-managing team, up from 28 percent in 1987.[52]

Self-designing teams have all the characteristics of self-managing teams, but they can also control and change the design of the teams themselves, the tasks they do and how and when they do them, and the membership of the teams. ICU Medical in San Clemente, California, makes devices such as the Click Lock, which prevents medical workers from getting stuck with needles and IV systems from accidentally becoming disconnected. At the company, which is organized around self-designing teams, any worker can—on his or her own—form any team to address any problem. The teams set meetings, assign tasks, and determine deadlines. For example, Dom Romstead, who planned production schedules in manufacturing facilities, watched a forklift slowly move parts back and forth between a warehouse and a molding machine. Frustrated with the inefficiency of the process, he talked with coworkers and started a team to examine the entire manufacturing process related to the company's best-selling product. After six months of study, the team, which included two of his superiors, the director of manufacturing and the head of logistics, reduced the number of manufacturing steps from 36 to 27, saving the company $500,000 a year. Ben Rosen, a management professor at the University of North Carolina, said of ICU Medical, "It's rare that a company says, 'Go form your own team and go address this issue.'"[53]

2.2 Special Kinds of Teams

Companies are also increasingly using several other kinds of teams that can't easily be categorized in terms of autonomy: cross-functional teams, virtual teams, and project teams. Depending on how these teams are designed, they can be either low- or high-autonomy teams.

Cross-functional teams are intentionally composed of employees from different functional areas of the organization.[54] Because their members have different functional backgrounds, education, and experience, cross-functional teams usually attack problems from multiple perspectives and generate more ideas and alternative solutions, all of which are especially important when trying to innovate or do creative problem solving.[55] Cross-functional teams can be used almost anywhere in an organization and are often used in conjunction with matrix and product organizational structures (see Chapter 9). They can also be used either with part-time or temporary team assignments or with full-time, long-term teams. General Electric used a cross-functional team to design a set of stainless steel, high-end kitchen appliances, called the Café Series, which look like they belong in a restaurant kitchen but are for serious cooks who love entertaining at home. Marketing staffers came up with the concept. Industrial and technical designers made the refrigerators, stoves, dishwashers, and ovens resemble restaurant kitchen appliances. And, together, the designers and marketing staff studied consumers who tried the prototype appliances in GE's test kitchens.[56]

Virtual teams are groups of geographically and/or organizationally dispersed coworkers who use a combination of telecommunications and information technologies to accomplish an organizational task.[57] Christopher Rice, CEO of BlessingWhite, a global consulting firm, indicates that virtual teams are common. Said Rice, "In

self-designing team a team that has the characteristics of self-managing teams but also controls team design, work tasks, and team membership.

cross-functional team a team composed of employees from different functional areas of the organization.

virtual team a team composed of geographically and/or organizationally dispersed coworkers who use telecommunication and information technologies to accomplish an organizational task.

With virtual teams, employees can work with each other regardless of physical location, time zone, or organizational affiliation.

© Jon Feingersh/Blend Images/Photolibrary

three-quarters of large organizations, team members are dispersed across different locations and time zones . . . but relatively few organizations address the frustrations and difficulties that arise with managing such teams."[58]

Members of virtual teams rarely meet face-to-face; instead, they use email, videoconferencing, and group communication software. _Charter_, the magazine of the Institute of Chartered Accountants in Australia, describes the prevalence of virtual teams in Sydney's local cafés: "Dateline: 4pm at a Surry Hills café in Sydney. The lunch crowd has long gone but the room is bustling, a sea of laptops, vibrating BlackBerrys and iPhones. While a few arty locals chatter and sip lattes, most clientele are glued to their screens, sporting headsets and in fully engaged work mode. . . . You will find this growing modern workforce prolifically sprouting in every industrialized groove of the globe. Most of them are logged in to a morning meeting in Dubai, going over a spreadsheet with a colleague lunching in Singapore, or waiting for London to wake up."[59]

The principal advantage of virtual teams is their flexibility. Employees can work with each other, regardless of physical location, time zone, or organizational affiliation.[60] Because the team members don't meet in a physical location, virtual teams also find it much easier to include other key stakeholders such as suppliers and customers. Plus, virtual teams have certain efficiency advantages over traditional team structures. Because the teammates do not meet face-to-face, a virtual team typically requires a smaller time commitment than a traditional team does. Moreover, employees can fulfill the responsibilities of their virtual team membership from the comfort of their own offices without the travel time or downtime typically required for face-to-face meetings.[61]

A drawback of virtual teams is that the team members must learn to express themselves in new contexts.[62] The give-and-take that naturally occurs in face-to-face meetings is more difficult to achieve through video conferencing or other methods of virtual teaming. Billie Williamson, a partner at Ernst & Young, one of the "Big Four" accounting firms that has been managing virtual teams for a decade, says, "Listen carefully to every team member on phone calls. You don't have the benefit of face-to-face interactions (although videoconferencing can help). I focus on how the person is speaking. Is the person excited? Bored? Is the choice of words overly careful? Is there a quality in the speaker's voice that would make a private conversation advisable? It's important to listen to everything, particularly any silences. Silence can mean consent, or it can mean the person you're not hearing from disagrees with the team's strategy or is disengaged. You need to hear from everyone to make sure the team is moving forward together. If I sense that a team member is lacking engagement— not responding, not participating, or missing deadlines—I call as soon as possible after the meeting to find out what's going on. And I always send an email after each meeting to document and confirm discussions, conclusions, and next steps."[63] Consistent with this example, several studies have shown that physical proximity enhances information processing.[64] Therefore, some companies bring virtual team

Exhibit 10.5   Tips for Managing Successful Virtual Teams

- Select people who are self-starters and strong communicators.

- Keep the team focused by establishing clear, specific goals and by explaining the consequences and importance of meeting these goals.

- Provide frequent feedback so that team members can measure their progress.

- Keep team interactions upbeat and action-oriented by expressing appreciation for good work and completed tasks.

- "Personalize" the virtual team by periodically bringing team members together and by encouraging team members to share information with each other about their personal lives. This is especially important when the virtual team first forms.

- Improve communication through increased telephone calls, e-mails, and Internet messaging and videoconference sessions.

- Periodically ask team members how well the team is working and what can be done to improve performance.

- Empower virtual teams so they have the discretion, freedom, and independence to decide how and when to accomplish their jobs.

Sources: W. F. Cascio, "Managing a Virtual Workplace," *Academy of Management Executive* 14 (2000): 81–90; B. Kirkman, B. Rosen, P. Tesluk, & C. Gibson, "The Impact of Team Empowerment on Virtual Team Performance: The Moderating Role of Face-to-Face Interaction," *Academy of Management Journal* 47 (2004): 175–192; S. Furst, M. Reeves, B. Rosen, & R. Blackburn, "Managing the Life Cycle of Virtual Teams," *Academy of Management Executive* (May 2004): 6–20; and C. Solomon, "Managing Virtual Teams," *Workforce* 80 (June 2001), 60.

members together on a regular basis to try to minimize these problems. Again, Ernst & Young's Billie Williamson says, "'Virtual' should not mean you never meet. With international teams, I visit each country's team once a year. With Ernst & Young's Americas Inclusiveness team [which she manages], . . . we all get together annually. In the current economy, it might not be possible to meet as often as you would like. But you need to step up the frequency of communication. Check in more often, and make sure people understand what's going on."[65] Exhibit 10.5 provides a number of tips for successfully managing virtual teams.

Project teams are created to complete specific, one-time projects or tasks within a limited time.[66] Project teams are often used to develop new products, significantly improve existing products, roll out new information systems, or build new factories or offices. The project team is typically led by a project manager who has the overall responsibility for planning, staffing, and managing the team, which usually includes employees from different functional areas. Effective project teams demand both individual and collective responsibility.[67] One advantage of project teams is that drawing employees from different functional areas can reduce or eliminate communication barriers. In turn, as long as team members feel free to express their ideas, thoughts, and concerns, free-flowing communication encourages cooperation among separate departments and typically speeds up the design process.[68] BMW, the German automaker, wanted to create an eco-friendly car that would appeal to urban drivers. And although the car would have to be small and light, it would also have to have the performance and luxury of a BMW. So, BMW created Project i, a special team of 15 people, including engineers, exterior specialists, and interior designers, to create prototypes, field test systems, and design the final product—the Multi City Vehicle, or MCV—which it hopes to release in 2013.[69]

Another advantage of project teams is their flexibility. When projects are finished, project team members either move on to the next project or return to their functional units. For example, publication of this book required designers, editors, page compositors, and Web designers, among others. When the task was finished, these people applied their skills to other textbook projects. Because of this flexibility, project teams are often used with the matrix organizational designs discussed in Chapter 9.

project team a team created to complete specific, one-time projects or tasks within a limited time.

Review 2

Kinds of Teams Companies use different kinds of teams to make themselves more competitive. Autonomy is the key dimension that makes teams different. Traditional work groups (which execute tasks) and employee involvement groups (which make suggestions) have the lowest levels of autonomy. Semiautonomous work groups (which control major direct tasks) have more autonomy, whereas self-managing teams (which control all direct tasks) and self-designing teams (which control membership and how tasks are done) have the highest levels of autonomy. Cross-functional, virtual, and project teams are common but are not easily categorized in terms of autonomy. Cross-functional teams combine employees from different functional areas to help teams attack problems from multiple perspectives and generate more ideas and solutions. Virtual teams use telecommunications and information technologies to bring coworkers together, regardless of physical location or time zone. Virtual teams reduce travel and work time, but communication may suffer because team members don't work face-to-face. Finally, project teams are used for specific, one-time projects or tasks that must be completed within a limited time. Project teams reduce communication barriers and promote flexibility; teams and team members are reassigned to their department or new projects as old projects are completed.

Managing Work Teams

"Why did I ever let you talk me into teams? They're nothing but trouble."[70] Lots of managers have this reaction after making the move to teams. Many don't realize that this reaction is normal, both for them and for workers. In fact, such a reaction is characteristic of the *storming* stage of team development (discussed in Section 3.5). Managers who are familiar with these stages and with the other important characteristics of teams will be better prepared to manage the predictable changes that occur when companies make the switch to team-based structures.

After reading the next two sections, you should be able to

3. *Understand the general characteristics of work teams.*
4. *Explain how to enhance work team effectiveness.*

3 Work Team Characteristics

Understanding the characteristics of work teams is essential for making teams an effective part of an organization. Therefore, in this section you'll learn about **3.1 team norms, 3.2 team cohesiveness, 3.3 team size, 3.4 team conflict**, and **3.5 the stages of team development**.

3.1 Team Norms

Over time, teams develop **norms,** which are informally agreed-on standards that regulate team behavior.[71] Norms are valuable because they let team members know what is expected of them. Although leading Orbis International, a nonprofit organization in which a Boeing DC-10, converted to a "Flying Eye Hospital," transports volunteer doctors and nurses to treat eye disease throughout the world, Jilly Stephens noticed a problem with punctuality. She said, "When I first got to the field, you would have the nurses, engineers, whoever, waiting, and you would maybe have one [person] who just couldn't drag himself out of bed and everybody's waiting." So she

norms informally agreed-on standards that regulate team behavior.

simply decided that there would be a new norm for the team: We leave on time . . . "If they aren't there [on time], the bus leaves. You get to the airport yourself. If we were in Tunisia, that meant finding a bike and cycling across the desert to get to the airport." Says Stephens, "We saw behaviors change fairly rapidly."[72]

Studies indicate that norms are one of the most powerful influences on work behavior because they regulate the everyday actions that allow teams to function effectively. Team norms are often associated with positive outcomes such as stronger organizational commitment, more trust in management, and stronger job and organizational satisfaction.[73] Effective work teams develop norms about the quality and timeliness of job performance, absenteeism, safety, and honest expression of ideas and opinions. Surgeon Atul Gawande, author of *The Checklist Manifesto*, says that with 6,000 drugs, 4,000 medical procedures, and doctors and nurses specializing in hundreds of medical subfields, "The complexity of what we [in modern medicine] have to deliver on exceeds our abilities as experts partly because the volume of knowledge has exceeded what training can possibly provide."[74] So, in his operating rooms, Gawande and his surgical teams use and review checklists to make sure each small but critical step is completed. Before anesthesia, the nurse and anesthetist will determine whether the site of the surgery is marked, whether the anesthesia machine and medication check have been completed, and whether the patient has a difficult airway or is at risk of aspiration (vomiting into their airway). Likewise, before the first incision takes place, all team members will be asked to introduce themselves and the roles they'll be performing, and the surgeon will be asked to state where the incision will be made and what kind of critical, non-routine steps might be taken if things don't go as planned.[75] The review checklists are a powerful way of making sure that each member of the surgical team does what they're supposed to, that is, following agreed-on standards of behavior or norms.

Norms can also influence team behavior in negative ways. For example, most people would agree that damaging organizational property; saying or doing something to hurt someone at work; intentionally doing one's work badly, incorrectly, or slowly; griping about coworkers; deliberately bending or breaking rules; or doing something to harm the company or boss are negative behaviors. A study of workers from 34 teams in 20 different organizations found that teams with negative norms strongly influenced their team members to engage in these negative behaviors. In fact, the longer individuals were members of a team with negative norms, and the more frequently they interacted with their teammates, the more likely they were to perform negative behaviors. Because team norms typically develop early in the life of a team, these results indicate how important it is for teams to establish positive norms from the outset.[76]

3.2 Team Cohesiveness

Cohesiveness is another important characteristic of work teams. **Cohesiveness** is the extent to which team members are attracted to a team and motivated to remain in

cohesiveness the extent to which team members are attracted to a team and motivated to remain in it.

it.[77] Burlington Northern Santa Fe Railway's intermodal team, which was charged with finding efficient ways to combine transportation through trucks and trains, was a particularly cohesive team. Dave Burns, a member of that team, says, "In my mind, the key word to this team was 'shared.' We shared everything. There was a complete openness among us. And the biggest thing that we shared was an objective and a strategy that we had put together jointly. That was our benchmark every day. Were we doing things in support of *our* plan?"[78] The same was true of the team that came up with MasterCard's endearing "Priceless" ad campaigns. Each ad in the series features a list of ordinary transactions and the dollar amounts associated with those

© iStockphoto.com/Hans Martens

what really works

Cohesion and Team Performance

Have you ever worked in a really cohesive group where everyone liked and enjoyed each other and was glad to be part of the group? It's great. By contrast, have you ever worked in a group where everyone really disliked each other and was unhappy to be part of the group? It's terrible. Anyone who has had either of these experiences can appreciate how important group cohesion is and the effect it can have on team performance. Indeed, 46 studies based on 1,279 groups confirm that cohesion does matter.

Team Performance

On average, there is a 66 percent chance that cohesive teams will outperform less cohesive teams.

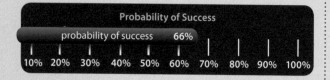

Team Performance with Interdependent Tasks

Teams work best for interdependent tasks that require people to work together to get the job done. When teams perform interdependent tasks, there is a 73 percent chance that cohesive teams will outperform less cohesive teams.

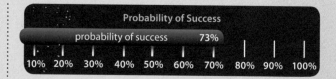

Team Performance with Independent Tasks

Teams generally are not suited for independent tasks that people can accomplish by themselves. When teams perform independent tasks, there is only a 60 percent chance that cohesive teams will outperform less cohesive teams.

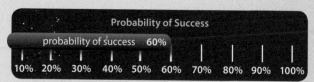

Some caution is warranted in interpreting these results. For example, there is always the possibility that a team could become so cohesive that its team goals become more important than organizational goals. Also, teams sometimes unite around negative goals and norms that are harmful rather than helpful to organizations. Nonetheless, there is also room for even more optimism about cohesive teams. Teams that are cohesive *and* committed to the goals they are asked to achieve should have an even higher probability of success than the numbers shown here.[79]

purchases. The final item in the series, however, is always pitched as "priceless." Joyce Thomas, a member of the team that conceived of and created those ads, says, "We were very comfortable working together, so we debated everything freely."[80]

The level of cohesiveness in a group is important for several reasons. To start, cohesive groups have a better chance of retaining their members. As a result, cohesive groups typically experience lower turnover.[81] In addition, team cohesiveness promotes cooperative behavior, generosity, and a willingness on the part of team members to assist each other.[82] When team cohesiveness is high, team members are more motivated to contribute to the team because they want to gain the approval of other team members. For these reasons and others, studies have clearly established that cohesive teams consistently perform better.[83] Furthermore, cohesive teams quickly achieve high levels of performance. By contrast, teams low in cohesion take much longer to reach the same levels of performance.[84]

What can be done to promote team cohesiveness? First, make sure that all team members are present at team meetings and activities. Team cohesiveness suffers when members are allowed to withdraw from the team and miss team meetings and events.[85] Second, create additional opportunities for teammates to work together by rearranging work schedules and creating common workspaces. When task interdependence is high and team members have lots of chances to work together, team cohesiveness tends to increase.[86] Third, engaging in nonwork activities as a team can help build cohesion. At **Priority Designs**, a product design consulting firm in Columbus, Ohio, owner Paul Kolada tried picnics and trips to state parks to build cohesion in the small, 50-person firm. Then, on a lark, he entered the firm in a derby car race sponsored by the Industrial Designers Society of America. The race requires teams to build (to preset and strictly enforced specifications) a fast, easy rolling, aerodynamic car that rolls down a hill propelled only by the weight of the car and its driver. The firm's engineers and designers loved the process of building the car and began staying late to use the track the company installed to test their derby cars. Kolada says, "There's an incredible fire and spark when you're doing something" other than business. And even though it costs the firm $10,000 in lost billable time, he's certain that the cohesiveness it creates is worth it. Says Kolada, "When we go into employee reviews, people will say it's so important."[87] Finally, companies build team cohesiveness by making employees feel that they are part of a organization.

< **"what's new" companies**

3.3 Team Size

The relationship between team size and performance appears to be curvilinear. Very small or very large teams may not perform as well as moderately sized teams. For most teams, the right size is somewhere between six and nine members.[88] A team of this size is small enough for the team members to get to know each other and for each member to have an opportunity to contribute in a meaningful way to the success of the team. At the same time, the team is also large enough to take advantage of team members' diverse skills, knowledge, and perspectives. It is also easier to instill a sense of responsibility and mutual accountability in teams of this size.[89]

When teams get too large, team members find it difficult to get to know one another, and the team may splinter into smaller subgroups. When this occurs, subgroups sometimes argue and disagree, weakening overall team cohesion. As teams grow, there is also a greater chance of *minority domination*, where just a few team members dominate team discussions. Even if minority domination doesn't occur, larger groups may not have time for all team members to share their input. And when team members feel that their contributions are unimportant or not needed, the result is less involvement, effort, and accountability to the team.[90] Large teams also face logistical

problems such as finding an appropriate time or place to meet. Finally, the incidence of social loafing, discussed earlier in the chapter, is much higher in large teams.

Just as team performance can suffer when a team is too large, it can also be negatively affected when a team is too small. Teams with just a few people may lack the diversity of skills and knowledge found in larger teams. Also, teams that are too small are unlikely to gain the advantages of team decision making (multiple perspectives, generating more ideas and alternative solutions, and stronger commitment) found in larger teams.

What signs indicate that a team's size needs to be changed? If decisions are taking too long, the team has difficulty making decisions or taking action, a few members dominate the team, or the commitment or efforts of team members are weak, chances are the team is too big. In contrast, if a team is having difficulty coming up with ideas or generating solutions, or the team does not have the expertise to address a specific problem, chances are the team is too small.

3.4 Team Conflict

Conflict and disagreement are inevitable in most teams. But this shouldn't surprise anyone. From time to time, people who work together are going to disagree about what and how things get done. What causes conflict in teams? Although almost anything can lead to conflict—casual remarks that unintentionally offend a team member or fighting over scarce resources—the primary cause of team conflict is disagreement over team goals and priorities.[91] Other common causes of team conflict include disagreements over task-related issues, interpersonal incompatibilities, and simple fatigue.

Though most people view conflict negatively, the key to dealing with team conflict is not avoiding it, but rather making sure that the team experiences the right kind of conflict. In Chapter 5, you learned about *c-type conflict*, or *cognitive conflict*, which focuses on problem-related differences of opinion, and *a-type conflict*, or *affective conflict*, which refers to the emotional reactions that can occur when disagreements become personal rather than professional.[92] Cognitive conflict is strongly associated with improvements in team performance, whereas affective conflict is strongly associated with decreases in team performance.[93] Why does this happen? With cognitive conflict, team members disagree because their different experiences and expertise lead them to different views of the problem and solutions. Indeed, managers who participated on teams that emphasized cognitive conflict described their teammates as "smart," "team players," and "best in the business." They described their teams as "open," "fun," and "productive." One manager summed up the positive attitude that team members had about cognitive conflict by saying, "We scream a lot, then laugh, and then resolve the issue."[94] Thus, cognitive conflict is also characterized by a willingness to examine, compare, and reconcile differences to produce the best possible solution.

By contrast, affective conflict often results in hostility, anger, resentment, distrust, cynicism, and apathy. Managers who participated on teams that experienced affective conflict described their teammates as "manipulative," "secretive," "burned out," and "political."[95] Not surprisingly, affective conflict can make people uncomfortable and cause them to withdraw and decrease their commitment to a team.[96] Affective conflict also lowers the satisfaction of team members, may lead to personal hostility between coworkers, and can decrease team cohesiveness.[97] So, unlike cognitive conflict, affective conflict undermines team performance by preventing teams from engaging in the kinds of activities that are critical to team effectiveness.

So, what can managers do to manage team conflict? First, they need to realize that emphasizing cognitive conflict alone won't be enough. Studies show that cognitive and affective conflicts often occur together in a given team activity! Sincere attempts to reach agreement on a difficult issue can quickly deteriorate from cognitive to affective conflict if the discussion turns personal and tempers and emotions flare. Although cognitive conflict is clearly the better approach to take, efforts to engage in cognitive conflict should be managed well and checked before they deteriorate and the team becomes unproductive.

Can teams disagree and still get along? Fortunately, they can. In an attempt to study this issue, researchers examined team conflict in 12 high-tech companies. In four of the companies, work teams used cognitive conflict to address work problems but did so in a way that minimized the occurrence of affective conflict.

Affective conflict results in hostility, anger, resentment, distrust, cynicism, and apathy.

There are several ways teams can have a good fight; the steps are shown in Exhibit 10.6.[98] First, work with more, rather than less, information. If data are plentiful, objective, and up-to-date, teams will focus on issues, not personalities. Second, develop multiple alternatives to enrich debate. Focusing on multiple solutions diffuses conflict by getting the team to keep searching for a better solution. Positions and opinions are naturally more flexible with five alternatives than with just two. Third, establish common goals. Remember, most team conflict arises from disagreements over team goals and priorities. Therefore, common goals encourage collaboration and minimize conflict over a team's purpose. Steve Jobs, former CEO of Apple, explained it this way: "It's okay to spend a lot of time arguing about which route to take to San Francisco when everyone wants to end up there, but a lot of time gets wasted in such arguments if one person wants to go to San Francisco and another secretly wants to go to San Diego."[99] Fourth, inject humor into the workplace. Humor relieves tension, builds cohesion, and just makes being in teams fun. Fifth, maintain a balance of power by involving as many people as possible in the decision process. And sixth, resolve issues without forcing a consensus. Consensus means that everyone must agree before decisions are finalized. Effectively, requiring consensus gives everyone on the team veto power. Nothing gets done until everyone agrees, which, of course, is nearly impossible. As a result, insisting on consensus usually promotes affective rather than cognitive conflict. If team members can't agree after constructively discussing their options, it's better to have the team leader

Exhibit 10.6
How Teams Can Have a Good Fight

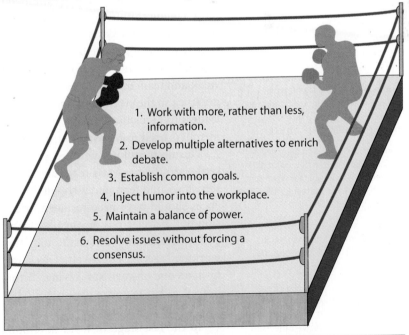

1. Work with more, rather than less, information.
2. Develop multiple alternatives to enrich debate.
3. Establish common goals.
4. Inject humor into the workplace.
5. Maintain a balance of power.
6. Resolve issues without forcing a consensus.

Source: K. M. Eisenhardt, J. L. Kahwajy, & L. J. Bourgeois III, "How Management Teams Can Have a Good Fight," *Harvard Business Management Review* 75, no. 4 (July–August 1997): 77–85.

Exhibit 10.7
Stages of Team Development

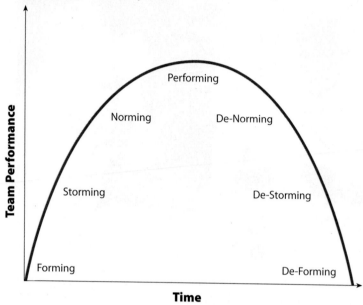

Sources: J. F. McGrew, J. G. Bilotta, & J. M. Deeney, "Software Team Formation and Decay: Extending the Standard Model for Small Groups," *Small Group Research* 30, no. 2 (1999): 209–234; and B. W. Tuckman, "Development Sequence in Small Groups," *Psychological Bulletin* 63, no. 6 (1965); 384–399.

make the final choice. Most team members can accept the team leader's choice if they've been thoroughly involved in the decision process.

3.5 Stages of Team Development

As teams develop and grow, they pass through four stages of development. As shown in Exhibit 10.7, those stages are forming, storming, norming, and performing.[100] Although not every team passes through each of these stages, teams that do tend to be better performers.[101] This holds true even for teams composed of seasoned executives. After a period of time, however, if a team is not managed well, its performance may start to deteriorate as the team begins a process of decline and progresses through the stages of de-norming, de-storming, and de-forming.[102]

Forming is the initial stage of team development. This is the getting-acquainted stage in which team members first meet each other, form initial impressions, and try to get a sense of what it will be like to be part of the team. Some of the first team norms will be established during this stage as team members begin to find out what behaviors will and won't be accepted by the team. During this stage, team leaders should allow time for team members to get to know each other, set early ground rules, and begin to set up a preliminary team structure.

Conflicts and disagreements often characterize the second stage of team development, **storming**. As team members begin working together, different personalities and work styles may clash. Team members become more assertive at this stage and more willing to state opinions. This is also the stage when team members jockey for position and try to establish a favorable role for themselves on the team. In addition, team members are likely to disagree about what the group should do and how it should do it. Team performance is still relatively low, given that team cohesion is weak and team members are still reluctant to support each other. Because teams that get stuck in the storming stage are almost always ineffective, it is important for team leaders to focus the team on team goals and on improving team performance. Team members need to be particularly patient and tolerant with each other in this stage.

During **norming**, the third stage of team development, team members begin to settle into their roles as team members. Positive team norms will have developed by this stage, and teammates should know what to expect from each other. Petty differences should have been resolved, friendships will have developed, and group cohesion will be relatively strong. At this point, team members will have accepted team goals, be operating as a unit, and, as indicated by the increase in performance, be working together effectively. This stage can be very short and is often characterized by someone on the team saying, "I think things are finally coming together." Note, however, that teams may also cycle back and forth between storming and norming several times before finally settling into norming.

In the last stage of team development, **performing**, performance improves because the team has finally matured into an effective, fully functioning team. At this point, members should be fully committed to the team and think of themselves as

forming the first stage of team development, in which team members meet each other, form initial impressions, and begin to establish team norms.

storming the second stage of development, characterized by conflict and disagreement, in which team members disagree over what the team should do and how it should do it.

norming the third stage of team development, in which team members begin to settle into their roles, group cohesion grows, and positive team norms develop.

performing the fourth and final stage of team development, in which performance improves because the team has matured into an effective, fully functioning team.

members of a team and not just employees. Team members often become intensely loyal to one another at this stage and feel mutual accountability for team successes and failures. Trivial disagreements, which can take time and energy away from the work of the team, should be rare. At this stage, teams get a lot of work done, and it is fun to be a team member.

The team should not become complacent, however. Without effective management, its performance may begin to decline as the team passes through the stages of de-norming, de-storming, and de-forming.[103] Indeed, John Puckett, manufacturing vice president for circuit-board manufacturer XEL Communications, says, "The books all say you start in this state of chaos and march through these various stages, and you end up in this state of ultimate self-direction, where everything is going just great. They never tell you it can go back in the other direction, sometimes just as quickly."[104]

In **de-norming**, which is a reversal of the norming stage, team performance begins to decline as the size, scope, goal, or members of the team change. With new members joining the group, older members may become defensive as established ways of doing things are questioned and challenged. Expression of ideas and opinions becomes less open. New members change team norms by actively rejecting or passively neglecting previously established team roles and behaviors.

In **de-storming**, which is a reversal of the storming phase, the team's comfort level decreases. Team cohesion weakens as more group members resist conforming to team norms and quit participating in team activities. Angry emotions flare as the group explodes in conflict and moves into the final stage of de-forming.

In **de-forming**, which is a reversal of the forming stage, team members position themselves to gain control of pieces of the team. Team members begin to avoid each other and isolate themselves from team leaders. Team performance rapidly declines as the members quit caring about even minimal requirements of team performance.

If teams are actively managed, decline is not inevitable. However, managers need to recognize that the forces at work in the de-norming, de-storming, and de-forming stages represent a powerful, disruptive, and real threat to teams that have finally made it to the performing stage. Getting to the performing stage is half the battle. Staying there is the second half.

de-norming a reversal of the norming stage, in which team performance begins to decline as the size, scope, goal, or members of the team change.

de-storming a reversal of the storming phase, in which the team's comfort level decreases, team cohesion weakens, and angry emotions and conflict may flare.

de-forming a reversal of the forming stage, in which team members position themselves to control pieces of the team, avoid each other, and isolate themselves from team leaders.

Work Team Characteristics The most important characteristics of work teams are team norms, cohesiveness, size, conflict, and development. Norms let team members know what is expected of them and can influence team behavior in positive and negative ways. Positive team norms are associated with organizational commitment, trust, and job satisfaction. Team cohesiveness helps teams retain members, promotes cooperative behavior, increases motivation, and facilitates team performance. Attending team meetings and activities, creating opportunities to work together, and engaging in nonwork activities can increase cohesiveness. Team size has a curvilinear relationship with team performance: Teams that are very small or very large do not perform as well as moderate-sized teams of six to nine members. Teams of this size are cohesive and small enough for team members to get to know each other and contribute in a meaningful way but are large enough to take advantage of team members' diverse skills, knowledge, and perspectives. Conflict and disagreement are inevitable in most teams. The key to dealing with team conflict is to maximize cognitive conflict, which focuses on issue-related differences, and minimize affective conflict, the emotional reactions that occur when disagreements become personal rather than professional. As teams develop and grow, they pass through four stages of development: forming, storming, norming, and performing. After a period of time, however, if a team is not managed well, its performance may decline as the team regresses through the stages of de-norming, de-storming, and de-forming.

Review 3

4 Enhancing Work Team Effectiveness

Making teams work is a challenging and difficult process. Nonetheless, companies can increase the likelihood that teams will succeed by carefully managing **4.1 the setting of team goals and priorities** and **4.2 how work team members are selected, 4.3 trained**, and **4.4 compensated**.[105]

4.1 Setting Team Goals and Priorities

In Chapter 5, you learned that having specific, measurable, attainable, realistic, and timely (SMART) goals is one of the most effective means for improving individual job performance. Fortunately, team goals also improve team performance. In fact, team goals lead to much higher team performance 93 percent of the time.[106] For example, Best Buy, the electronic retailer, put together four groups of salespeople, all in their 20s and early 30s, and had them live together in a Los Angeles apartment for 10 weeks. Jeremy Sevush, a sales floor supervisor, said, "My friends joked and said I was joining 'Real World: Best Buy Edition.'" Their goal—to generate quick, easy-to-start business ideas for Best Buy. Because they had a clear goal and limited time, everyone was focused. Said Sevush, "Living together and knowing we only had 10 weeks sped up our team-building process. We voluntarily worked longer hours, talking about business models while making spaghetti." And it worked. Sevush and his team came up with Best Buy Studio, web-design consulting for small businesses. It was up and running just a few weeks after moving out of the apartments.[107]

Why is setting *specific* team goals so critical to team success? One reason is that increasing a team's performance is inherently more complex than just increasing one individual's job performance. For instance, consider that any team is likely to involve at least four different kinds of goals: each member's goal for the team, each member's goal for himself or herself on the team, the team's goal for each member, and the team's goal for itself.[108] In other words, without a specific goal for the team itself (the last of the four goals listed), team members may head off in all directions at once pursuing these other goals. Consequently, setting a specific goal *for the team* clarifies team priorities by providing a clear focus and purpose.

Challenging team goals affect how hard team members work. In particular, they greatly reduce the incidence of social loafing. When faced with difficult goals, team members necessarily expect everyone to contribute. Consequently, they are much more likely to notice and complain if a teammate isn't doing his or her share. In fact, when teammates know each other well, when team goals are specific, when team communication is good, and when teams are rewarded for team performance (discussed below), there is only a 1 in 16 chance that teammates will be social loafers.[109]

What can companies and teams do to ensure that team goals lead to superior team performance? One increasingly popular approach is to give teams stretch goals. *Stretch goals* are extremely ambitious goals that workers don't know how to reach.[110] Hyundai recently set a goal of having its entire product line average 50 miles per gallon or better by 2025, an improvement of nearly 60 percent over current ratings. Although John Krafcik, a spokesmen for Hyundai, recognized the difficulty of the goal—"We don't know precisely how to get there right now"—he reaffirmed the company's commitment to setting high ambitions, stating, "We want to help set the trajectory for the industry."[111]

Four things must occur for stretch goals to effectively motivate teams.[112] First, teams must have a high degree of autonomy or control over how they achieve their

doing the right thing

The Rights and Wrongs of Socializing

Looking for a way to bring your team members closer together? There may be nothing better than a team outing. Whether it's dinner on a Friday night or a weekend retreat to Niagara Falls, a group outing is a great way to develop cohesiveness and interpersonal skills within a team. There are, however, certain situations to avoid. For example, you may not want to go to a bar for drinks if a team member is a recovering alcoholic. You may not want to schedule an event too late at night, or too far away, if some team members have young children at home. So do the right thing—make sure you get to know your team members and their unique circumstances so that you can plan team activities that everyone can participate in and enjoy.[113]

goals. At CSX's railroad division, top management challenged the new management team at its Cumberland, Maryland, office to increase productivity by 16 percent. The goal was specific and challenging: Ship the same amount of coal each month, but do it with 4,200 railcars instead of 5,000 railcars. The local team, consisting of five new managers, quickly figured out that trains were spending too much time sitting idly in the rail yards. Finance director Peter Mills says, "We'd look out our office windows at the tracks and wonder, 'Why aren't the cars moving?'" The problem? Headquarters wouldn't let the trains run until they had 160 full railcars to pull, but amassing that many cars could take nearly a week. Because the local management team had the autonomy to pay for the extra crews to run the trains more frequently, it started running trains with as few as 78 cars. Now, coal cars never wait more than a day to be transported to customers, and rail productivity has skyrocketed.[114]

Second, teams must be empowered with control resources, such as budgets, workspaces, computers, or whatever else they need to do their jobs. Steve Kerr, Goldman Sachs' chief learning officer, says, "We have a moral obligation to try to give people the tools to meet tough goals. I think it's totally wrong if you don't give employees the tools to succeed, then punish them when they fail."[115]

Third, teams need structural accommodation. **Structural accommodation** means giving teams the ability to change organizational structures, policies, and practices if doing so helps them meet their stretch goals. Needing to increase the speed with which it bring new drugs to market, GlaxoSmithKline, one of the world's largest pharmaceutical firms, divided thousands of its researchers into small groups of 20 to 60 scientists, called discovery performance units (DPUs). DPUs, which control their budgets, have three to five years to show results. Critically, Glaxo gave them the ability to change policies that get in their way. For example, Chemist David Wilson, who is a member of Glaxo's EpiNova DPU, was discussing experimental drugs with fellow researchers, over coffee. They couldn't figure out how the drugs affected a special enzyme and decided to conduct tests. But Glaxo didn't have anyone who could do the testing. So instead of getting approval from Glaxo, Wilson went straight to Kevin Lee, who runs EpiNova, to let him know they needed to hire someone to do the work. Two days later an outside firm began the testing. Said Wilson, "[that] wouldn't have happened in the past."[116]

structural accommodation the ability to change organizational structures, policies, and practices in order to meet stretch goals.

Finally, teams need bureaucratic immunity. **Bureaucratic immunity** means that teams no longer have to go through the frustratingly slow process of multilevel reviews and sign-offs to get management approval before making changes. Once granted bureaucratic immunity, teams are immune from the influence of various organizational groups and are accountable only to top management. Therefore, teams can act quickly, and even experiment, with little fear of failure. Richard Branson, founder of the Virgin Group, Ltd., encourages all of his companies to provide top-notch customer service, and that doesn't happen without teamwork. Says Branson, "Delivering good customer service requires that a frontline worker receive supportive assistance from an entire network of co-workers. . . . And when it comes to helping a customer, the chain of assistance is only as strong as its weakest link." Branson tells a story about a Virgin America airline customer who, when not picked up by the airline's limo service, rushed to the airport via a cab, hoping not to miss his flight. At the airport, the Virgin Atlantic agent helping him not only escorted him through security so he could get to his gate on time, she also refunded his taxi fare out of her pocket. When she asked her boss for reimbursement, he asked for the taxi receipt. When she explained, "There was no time for that," he responded "No receipt, no reimbursement." Branson goes on to explain that because of this exceptional act of customer service, her boss should have granted her bureaucratic immunity from the rules requiring her to turn in a receipt. Said Branson, "Happily, the story came to the airport manager's attention and he quickly took steps to redress the imbalance between company procedures and customer service. He advised the finance team that he'd approved the cash shortfall, while the supervisor got a quick refresher on how important we at Virgin think it is to catch people doing something right."[117]

4.2 Selecting People for Teamwork

University of Southern California management professor Edward Lawler says, "People are very naive about how easy it is to create a team. Teams are the Ferraris of work design. They're high performance but high maintenance and expensive."[118] It's almost impossible to have an effective work team without carefully selecting people who are suited for teamwork or for working on a particular team. A focus on teamwork (individualism–collectivism), team level, and team diversity can help companies choose the right team members.[119]

Are you more comfortable working alone or with others? If you strongly prefer to work alone, you may not be well suited for teamwork. Indeed, studies show that job satisfaction is higher in teams when team members prefer working with others.[120] An indirect way to measure someone's *preference for teamwork* is to assess the person's degree of individualism or collectivism. **Individualism–collectivism** is the degree to which a person believes that people should be self-sufficient and that loyalty to one's self is more important than loyalty to one's team or company.[121] *Individualists*, who put their own welfare and interests first, generally prefer independent tasks in which they work alone. In contrast, *collectivists*, who put group or team interests ahead of self-interests, generally prefer interdependent tasks in which they work with others. Collectivists would also rather cooperate than compete and are fearful of disappointing team members or of being ostracized from teams. Given these differences, it makes sense to select team members who are collectivists rather than individualists. Indeed, many companies use individualism–collectivism as an initial screening device for team members.

Although many people think of golf as the ultimate individual game, team play, where individual players work together, can be found at the highest level of the professional game in the Ryder Cup, where, for eight decades, European and American

bureaucratic immunity the ability to make changes without first getting approval from managers or other parts of an organization.

individualism–collectivism the degree to which a person believes that people should be self-sufficient and that loyalty to one's self is more important than loyalty to team or company.

Exhibit 10.8 The Team Player Inventory

	STRONGLY DISAGREE				STRONGLY AGREE
1. I enjoy working on team/group projects.	1	2	3	4	5
2. Team/group project work easily allows others to not pull their weight.	1	2	3	4	5
3. Work that is done as a team/group is better than the work done individually.	1	2	3	4	5
4. I do my best work alone rather than in a team/group.	1	2	3	4	5
5. Team/group work is overrated in terms of the actual results produced.	1	2	3	4	5
6. Working in a team/group gets me to think more creatively.	1	2	3	4	5
7. Teams/groups are used too often, when individual work would be more effective.	1	2	3	4	5
8. My own work is enhanced when I am in a team/group situation.	1	2	3	4	5
9. My experiences working in team/group situations have been primarily negative.	1	2	3	4	5
10. More solutions/ideas are generated when working in a team/group situation than when working alone.	1	2	3	4	5

Reverse score items 2, 4, 5, 7, and 9. Then add the scores for items 1 to 10. Higher scores indicate a preference for teamwork, whereas lower total scores indicate a preference for individual work.

Source: T. J. B. Kline, "The Team Player Inventory: Reliability and Validity of a Measure of Predisposition Toward Organizational Team-Working Environments," *Journal for Specialists in Group Work* 24, no. 1 (1999): 102–112.

players have squared off every other year in team-based competition. Olin Browne, a professional golfer who served as assistant captain for the American team, said, "Working together for the common good is not normally a function for us out on the PGA Tour. We play as individuals."[122] But instead of selecting players based on their golf records alone (i.e., individualism), Browne and U.S. coach Paul Azinger selected players based on their ability to fit into the overall U.S. team of 12 players and into smaller "pods" of four players (i.e., collectivism). The advantage of this collectivist approach to an individual game like golf, said Browne, is that "the pods [of four people each] allowed the players, without any formal training, to feed off each other and help each other and to manage all the different things that come up in a pressure-cooker situation like the Ryder Cup. In the larger 12-man group, some guys with quieter personalities might have [otherwise] been lost in the shuffle. Some of the rookies might have been [otherwise] too intimidated to speak out."[123] If team diversity is desired, however, individualists may also be appropriate, as discussed below. To determine your preference for teamwork, take the Team Player Inventory shown in Exhibit 10.8.

Team level is the average level of ability, experience, personality, or any other factor on a team. For example, a high level of team experience means that a team has particularly experienced team members. This does not mean that every member of the team has considerable experience, but that enough team members do to significantly raise the average level of experience on the team. Team level is used to guide selection of teammates when teams need a particular set of skills or capabilities to do their jobs well. For example, at GE's Aerospace Engines manufacturing plant in Durham, North Carolina, only applicants who have an FAA-certified mechanic's license are considered for hire. Following that, all applicants are tested in 11 different areas, only one of which involved technical skills. Keith McKee, who works at the plant, says, "You have to be above the bar in all 11 of the areas: helping skills,

team level the average level of ability, experience, personality, or any other factor on a team.

team skills, communication skills, diversity, flexibility, coaching ability, work ethic, and so forth. Even if just one thing out of the 11 knocks you down, you don't come to work here."[124]

Whereas team level represents the average level or capability on a team, **team diversity** represents the variances or differences in ability, experience, personality, or any other factor on a team.[125] From a practical perspective, why is team diversity important? Professor John Hollenbeck explains, "Imagine if you put all the extroverts together. Everyone is talking, but nobody is listening. [By contrast,] with a team of [nothing but] introverts, you can hear the clock ticking on the wall."[126] Not only do strong teams have talented members (that is, a high team level), but those talented members are also different in terms of ability, experience, or personality.

Faced with slowdowns in the manufacture of its new 787 Dreamliner passenger jet, Jim Albaugh, who runs Boeing's Commercial Airplanes division, decided that the team charged with bringing the Dreamliner to market lacked diversity. They were too inexperienced. So Albaugh tapped eight retired executives to create a Senior Advisory Group to work with Boeing's engineers and project managers. Said Albaugh, "They've got some strong views." They recommended reducing Boeing's reliance on outsourced parts, given that suppliers were unable to produce high-quality parts on schedule. Boeing then brought many of the outsourced jobs back in-house and sent Boeing engineers to monitor its suppliers' quality and progress. John Roundhill, an engineer and former vice president of product strategy and development, who retired a decade ago, said, "The response [from Boeing's current managers and engineers] has been overwhelmingly positive, and the temptation is to work too much. But we know it's their day now, our day has passed."[127] As in this example, team diversity is often used to guide the selection of team members when teams must complete a wide range of different tasks or when tasks are particularly complex.

Once the right team has been put together in terms of individualism–collectivism, team level, and team diversity, it's important to keep the team together as long as practically possible. Interesting research by the National Transportation Safety Board shows that 73 percent of serious mistakes made by jet cockpit crews are made the very first day that a crew flies together as a team and that 44 percent of serious mistakes occur on their very first flight together that day (pilot teams fly two to three flights per day). Moreover, research has shown that fatigued pilot crews who have worked together before make significantly fewer errors than rested crews who have never worked together.[128] Their experience working together helps them overcome their fatigue and outperform new teams that have not worked together before. So, once you've created effective teams, keep them together as long as possible.

4.3 Team Training

After selecting the right people for teamwork, you need to train them. To be successful, teams need significant training, particularly in interpersonal skills, decision-making and problem-solving skills, conflict resolution skills, and technical training. Organizations that create work teams *often underestimate the amount of training* required to make teams effective. This mistake occurs frequently in successful organizations where managers assume that if employees can work effectively on their own, they can work effectively in teams. In reality, companies that successfully use teams provide thousands of hours of training to make sure that teams work. Stacy Myers, a consultant who helps companies implement teams, says, "When we help

team diversity the variances or differences in ability, experience, personality, or any other factor on a team.

companies move to teams, we also require that employees take basic quality and business knowledge classes as well. Teams must know how their work affects the company, and how their success will be measured."[129]

Most commonly, members of work teams receive training in interpersonal skills. **Interpersonal skills** such as listening, communicating, questioning, and providing feedback enable people to have effective working relationships with others. Consultant Peter Grazier, founder of Teambuilding Inc., says, "Teams have told us that if they had to do it over again they would have more of the people skills upfront. They don't struggle with the technical stuff. They tend to struggle with the people skills."[130] Because of teams' autonomy and responsibility, many companies also give team members training in *decision-making and problem-solving skills* to help them do a better job of cutting

© iStockphoto.com/studiovision

costs and improving quality and customer service. Many organizations also teach teams *conflict resolution skills*. Teambuilding Inc.'s Grazier explains that, "The diversity of values and personalities makes a team powerful, but it can be the greatest source of conflict. If you're a detail person and I'm not, and we get on a team, you might say that we need more analysis on a problem before making a decision, [while I] may want to make a decision [right away]. But, if I've been trained in problem-solving and conflict resolution, then I look at your detail [focus] as something that is needed in a team because it's a shortcoming of mine."[131] Taine Moufarrige, executive director of Servcorp, a global company hosting serviced and virtual offices for about 12,000 clients, agrees. Says Moufarrige, "It's not just about disagreements, it's about working through problems, managing differences of opinion, and that's vital for moving forward."[132]

Firms must also provide team members with the *technical training* they need to do their jobs, particularly if they are being cross-trained to perform all of the different jobs on the team. Before teams were created at Milwaukee Mutual Insurance, separate employees performed the tasks of rating, underwriting, and processing insurance policies. After extensive cross-training, however, each team member can now do all three jobs.[133] Cross-training is less appropriate for teams of highly skilled workers. For instance, it is unlikely that a group of engineers, computer programmers, and systems analysts would be cross-trained for each other's jobs.

Team leaders need training too, as they often feel unprepared for their new duties. New team leaders face myriad problems, ranging from confusion about their new roles as team leaders (compared with their old jobs as managers or employees) to not knowing where to go for help when their teams have problems. Exhibit 10.9 lists the top ten problems team leaders face. The solution is extensive training. Overall, does team training work? One recent study found that across a wide variety of setting, tasks, team types, and 2,650 teams in different organizations, team training was positively related to team performance outcomes.[134]

interpersonal skills skills, such as listening, communicating, questioning, and providing feedback, that enable people to have effective working relationships with others.

Exhibit 10.9 Top Ten Problems Reported by Team Leaders

1. Confusion about their new roles and about what they should be doing differently.

2. Feeling they've lost control.

3. Not knowing what it means to coach or empower.

4. Having personal doubts about whether the team concept will really work.

5. Uncertainty about how to deal with employees' doubts about the team concept.

6. Confusion about when a team is ready for more responsibility.

7. Confusion about how to share responsibility and accountability with the team.

8. Concern about promotional opportunities, especially about whether the "team leader" title carries any prestige.

9. Uncertainty about the strategic aspects of the leader's role as the team matures.

10. Not knowing where to turn for help with team problems, as few, if any, of their organization's leaders have led teams.

Source: B. Filipczak, M. Hequet, C. Lee, M. Picard, & D. Stamps, "More Trouble with Teams," *Training*, October 1996, 21.

4.4 Team Compensation and Recognition

Compensating teams correctly is very difficult. For instance, one survey found that only 37 percent of companies were satisfied with their team compensation plans and even fewer, just 10 percent, reported being "very positive."[135] One of the problems, according to Susan Mohrman of the Center for Effective Organizations at the University of Southern California, is that "there is a very strong set of beliefs in most organizations that people should be paid for how well they do. So when people first get put into team-based organizations, they really balk at being paid for how well the team does. It sounds illogical to them. It sounds like their individuality and their sense of self-worth are being threatened."[136] Consequently, companies need to carefully choose a team compensation plan and then fully explain how teams will be rewarded. One basic requirement for team compensation to work is that the level of rewards (individual vs. team) must match the level of performance (individual vs. team).

Employees can be compensated for team participation and accomplishments in three ways: skill-based pay, gainsharing, and nonfinancial rewards. **Skill-based pay** programs pay employees for learning additional skills or knowledge.[137] These programs encourage employees to acquire the additional skills they will need to perform multiple jobs within a team and to share knowledge with others within their work groups.[138] For example, at the **Patience and Nicholson (P&N)** drill bit factory in Kaiapoi, New Zealand, workers produce 50,000 drill bits a day for export to Australia, Taiwan, Thailand, and other locations primarily in Asia. P&N uses a skill-based pay system. As employees learn how to run the various machines required to produce drill bits, their pay increases. According to operations manager Rick Smith, workers who are dedicated to learning can increase their pay by $6 an hour over the course of three or four years.[139]

In **gainsharing** programs, companies share the financial value of performance gains, such as productivity increases, cost savings, or quality improvements, with their workers.[140] Walk into any **Nucor Corporation** plant, and nearly every production worker can tell you within a tenth of a percent what his team's weekly bonus will be at that point. Team size ranges from 12 to 20, and each team includes

"what's new" companies >

skill-based pay compensation system that pays employees for learning additional skills or knowledge.

gainsharing a compensation system in which companies share the financial value of performance gains, such as productivity, cost savings, or quality, with their workers.

"what's new" companies >

Exhibit 10.10   Managers' Preferences for Team-Based Pay

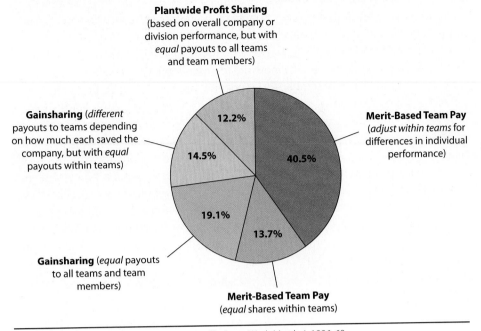

Plantwide Profit Sharing
(based on overall company or
division performance, but with
equal payouts to all teams
and team members)

Gainsharing (*different*
payouts to teams depending
on how much each saved the
company, but with *equal*
payouts within teams)

Merit-Based Team Pay
(*adjust within teams* for
differences in individual
performance)

12.2%

14.5%

40.5%

19.1%

13.7%

Gainsharing (*equal* payouts
to all teams and team
members)

Merit-Based Team Pay
(*equal* shares within teams)

Source: J. H. Sheridan, "'YES' to Team Incentives," *Industry Week*, March 4, 1996, 63.

production workers, maintenance workers and supervisors. "People expect a complicated [incentive] plan, but our plan is really simple: quality tons out the door and pay weekly," says Dan Krug, manager of HR and organizational development at Nucor in Charlotte, North Carolina. With bonuses included, the typical Nucor steel mill worker makes $72,000 a year.[141] *Nonfinancial rewards* are another way to reward teams for their performance. These rewards, which can range from vacations to T-shirts, plaques, and coffee mugs, are especially effective when coupled with management recognition, such as awards, certificates, and praise.[142] Nonfinancial awards tend to be most effective when teams or team-based interventions, such as total quality management (see Chapter 18), are first introduced.[143]

Which team compensation plan should your company use? In general, skill-based pay is most effective for self-managing and self-directing teams performing complex tasks. In these situations, the more each team member knows and can do, the better the whole team performs. By contrast, gainsharing works best in relatively stable environments where employees can focus on improving the productivity, cost savings, or quality of their current work system.

Finally, given the level of dissatisfaction with most team compensation systems, what compensation plans would today's managers like to use with the teams in their companies? As shown in Exhibit 10.10, 40.5 percent of managers would directly link merit-pay increases to team performance but allow adjustments within teams for differences in individual performance. By contrast, 13.7 percent would also link merit-based increases directly to team performance but give each team member an equal share of the team's merit-based reward. And 19.1 percent would use gainsharing plans based on quality, delivery, productivity, or cost reduction and then provide equal payouts to all teams and team members. Another 14.5 percent would also use gainsharing, but they would vary the team gainsharing award, depending on how much money the team saved the company. Payouts would still be equally distributed within teams. Finally, 12.2 percent of managers would opt for plant-wide profit-sharing plans tied to overall company or division performance.[144] In this case, there would be no payout distinctions between or within teams.

Review 4

Enhancing Work Team Effectiveness   Companies can make teams more effective by setting team goals and managing how team members are selected, trained, and compensated. Team goals provide a clear focus and purpose, reduce the incidence of social loafing, and lead to higher team performance 93 percent of the time. Extremely difficult stretch goals can be used to motivate teams as long as teams have autonomy, control over resources, structural accommodation, and bureaucratic immunity. Not everyone is suited for teamwork. When selecting team members, companies should select people who have a preference for teamwork (individualism-collectivism) and should consider team level (average ability on a team) and team diversity (different abilities on a team). Organizations that successfully use teams provide thousands of hours of training to make sure that teams work. The most common types of team training are for interpersonal skills, decision-making and problem-solving skills, conflict resolution, technical training to help team members learn multiple jobs (i.e., cross-training), and training for team leaders. Employees can be compensated for team participation and accomplishments in three ways: skill-based pay, gainsharing, and nonfinancial rewards.

SELF-ASSESSMENT

Working in Groups

From sports to school, to work, to civic involvement, working in teams is increasingly part of our experience. Even though teams are frequently used to get work done, people still have widely varying opinions of their value. Think of your own situation. When a professor divides the class into groups to complete a project, do you respond with an inward smile or a heavy sigh? Do you enjoy team projects, or would you rather just do your own work? The following 20-question survey assesses your thoughts about working in teams.[145] Indicate the extent to which you agree with each of the following statements. Try not to spend too much time on any one item, and be sure to answer all the questions. Use this scale for your responses:

1   Strongly disagree

2   Disagree

3   Slightly disagree

4   Neutral

5   Slightly agree

6   Agree

7   Strongly agree

1. Only those who depend on themselves get ahead in life.

   1   2   3   4   5   6   7

2. To be superior, a person must stand alone.

   1   2   3   4   5   6   7

3. If you want something done right, you've got to do it yourself.

   1   2   3   4   5   6   7

KEY TERMS

bureaucratic immunity 406
cohesiveness 397
cross-functional team 393
cross-training 384
de-forming 403
de-norming 403
de-storming 403
employee involvement team 392
forming 402
gainsharing 410
individualism–collectivism 406
interpersonal skills 409
norming 402

norms 396
performing 402
project team 395
self-designing team 393
self-managing team 392
semiautonomous work group 392
skill-based pay 410
social loafing 386
storming 402
structural accommodation 405
team diversity 408
team level 407
traditional work group 391
virtual team 393
work team 383

4. What happens to me is my own doing.

   1   2   3   4   5   6   7

5. In the long run, the only person you can count on is yourself.

   1   2   3   4   5   6   7

6. Winning is everything.

   1   2   3   4   5   6   7

7. I feel that winning is important in both work and games.

   1   2   3   4   5   6   7

8. Success is the most important thing in life.

   1   2   3   4   5   6   7

9. It annoys me when other people perform better than I do.

   1   2   3   4   5   6   7

10. Doing your best isn't enough; it is important to win.

   1   2   3   4   5   6   7

11. I prefer to work with others in a group rather than working alone.

   1   2   3   4   5   6   7

12. Given the choice, I would rather do a job where I can work alone than do a job where I have to work with others in a group.

   1   2   3   4   5   6   7

13. Working with a group is better than working alone.

   1   2   3   4   5   6   7

14. People should be made aware that if they are going to be part of a group, then they are sometimes going to have to do things they don't want to do.

   1   2   3   4   5   6   7

15. People who belong to a group should realize that they're not always going to get what they personally want.

   1   2   3   4   5   6   7

16. People in a group should realize that they sometimes are going to have to make sacrifices for the sake of the group as a whole.

   1   2   3   4   5   6   7

17. People in a group should be willing to make sacrifices for the sake of the group's well-being.

   1   2   3   4   5   6   7

18. A group is more productive when its members do what they want to do rather than what the group wants them to do.

   1   2   3   4   5   6   7

19. A group is most efficient when its members do what they think is best rather than doing what the group wants them to do.

   1   2   3   4   5   6   7

20. A group is more productive when its members follow their own interests and desires.

   1   2   3   4   5   6   7

Scoring

Determine your score by entering your response to each survey item below, as follows. In blanks that say *regular score*, simply enter your response for that item. If your response was a 3, place a 3 in the *regular score* blank. In blanks that say *reverse score*, subtract your response from 8 and enter the result. So if your response was a 3, place a 5 (8 – 3 = 5) in the *reverse score* blank.

1. reverse score   ————

2. reverse score   ————

3. reverse score   ————

4. reverse score   ————

5. reverse score   ————

6. reverse score   ————

7. reverse score   ————

8. reverse score   ————

9. reverse score   ————

10. reverse score   ————

11. regular score   ————

12. reverse score   ————

13. regular score   ————

14. regular score   ————

15. regular score   ————

16. regular score   ————

17. regular score   ————

18. reverse score   ————

19. reverse score   ————

20. reverse score   ————

    TOTAL = ———

You can find the interpretation of your score at www.cengagebrain.com.

MANAGEMENT DECISION

Should I Hit The Recruiting Trail?

Your life as a college basketball coach used to be fairly easy, because it was based on just one principle—get the most talented players. A few months every year, you and your army of assistants and scouts would comb the country, looking high and low for the best players and convincing them that your program was where they belonged. And even if recruiting didn't go your way one year, you could expect that that the players you did get would be a part of your program for three or four years.

Well, times have certainly changed. You still have to go recruiting, but the allure of playing big-time college basketball for four years has faded. At first, your players started leaving for the NBA before they graduated, some as early as their sophomore years. And then, elite high school players decided that they didn't need to go to college at all, going straight into the pros. To try and revitalize the college game, the NBA passed the "one and done" rule in 2005, requiring that its players be one year removed from high school graduation. But this made your job even tougher—even though the best high school players came to play for you, they only stayed one season. This left your program with little continuity and stability. What's worse, you were left with little margin of error; if you didn't recruit well each and every year, your team would be quickly passed by the competition.

There have been a number of basketball programs that have found success using a completely different approach to team building. Rather than aiming for top

talent that might be at school for two years, if lucky, coaches at smaller, lesser-known schools, often called the "mid-majors," recruit lesser-known, complementary, role-players who have little ambition for the pros and will likely be a part of the team for four years. And even though these coaches won't be working with the next Michael Jordan, many have created cohesive teams that have had great success. Gonzaga University has made the NCAA tournament every year since 1999, and Xavier University has reached the "dance" every year since 2001. George Mason reached the "Final Four" in 2006, and Butler University made it all the way to the championship game in 2010 and then repeated that improbable run in 2011. It's not just that these teams are lucky. They're the product of an approach to team building that emphasizes cohesion, cooperation, and commitment to the team.

So, which approach to team building do you think would be the best for your program and, more importantly, your sanity? Will you continue to look for as many superstars as you can, knowing that they may not stay around too long? Or are you willing to pay more attention to complementary role players?

Questions

1. What are advantages and disadvantages of each type of team?
2. If you were to decide on the superstar-player approach, how would you deal with the instability within your organization?

MANAGEMENT TEAM DECISION

Getting Along

Nine months ago, the executives running your design firm decided to start using teams. Before that, all of the work was done on an individual basis. Ron the marketing guy would run some consumer surveys to try to identify new fads. He would pass this information on to the Susie in the art department, who would come up with some sketches of new products based on the surveys. She would then pass this on to production,

where Maury would look at the sketches and see what kind of materials would have to be ordered so that Sharon could have a chance to work up some prototypes. Finally, about five months later, Marcus in sales would have some samples that he could take around to potential customers. But after switching to one team where all these people could work together and share their ideas at each step of the process, that time was cut down to just six weeks.

The executives of your company were thrilled with these results, and no doubt they patted themselves on the back for coming up with the brilliant idea of using teams. There is, though, just one thing that they didn't take into consideration—the team members hate each other! Marcus thinks that Ron talks too much and dominates every single team meeting. Maury, who hates sports, thinks that Susie wastes all of her time following the University of Michigan football team. Susie, meanwhile, hates it that Sharon won't stop it with stories about her kids. As for Marcus, nobody can quite figure him out, but almost everyone on the team thinks that he is bigoted.

With all of these negative emotions floating around, your project team has become stagnant. The meetings are uncomfortable, to say the least, and the interaction between the members has become toxic. It's been virtually impossible to get people to share ideas, reflect on others' ideas, or even just look each other in the eyes. Most meetings, it's plainly obvious that the only reason people are in the meetings is because they have to be.

A few weeks ago, Ron and Maury went to senior managers and asked what they would need to do to not have to work in teams anymore. The managers, in turn, told them to tell everyone else that, in effect, they were stuck with what they got. The managers are unwilling to give up the gains in productivity and speed, so the team is just going to have to learn how to work together.

So here you sit, a dysfunctional team, with a directive from your bosses to learn how to get along. How do you do it?

Questions

1. In your opinion, do the interpersonal conflicts in this group make it impossible for team members to work together?

2. What are some ways that this group can decrease their interpersonal conflicts and increase its cohesiveness?

PRACTICE BEING A MANAGER

Campus Improvement

Teamwork is vital to the success of organizations. And this makes creating high-performance teams an important management challenge. In this exercise, you will work with fellow students to brainstorm the creation of a high-performing team. Pay particular attention to the assumptions that you and your peers bring to this process regarding what works and what doesn't work in creating a high-performance team. At the conclusion of the exercise, you will have an opportunity to discuss the theory and common assumptions regarding effective team building.

Step 1: Get into groups. Your professor will organize small groups.

Step 2: Review the situation. Assume that your group has been handpicked by the president of your college or university to work for one semester as a "campus improvement" team. At the end of the year, you will submit your recommendations to the president and the board of your institution. These leaders have assured you that they will make every effort to implement your recommendations.

Step 3: Develop a plan. Brainstorm to develop a plan for working as a team to achieve the objective of delivering a set of quality recommendations to the president and the board. You should consider the following in developing your plan:

- Working well together as a team

- Establishing criteria for "quality recommendations" (such as representing the various important constituencies and interests on campus)

- Outlining steps, areas and types of work, and assignments for each member that are most likely to take full advantage of the capabilities and resources in your team

Step 4: Discuss your plans as a class. Is this the sort of project that is well suited to using a work team? Why or why not? How might work team characteristics such as norms, cohesiveness, and team size play a role in this team effort? What conflicts might be likely down the road, and at what stage of the process are these conflicts most likely to occur?

DEVELOP YOUR CAREER POTENTIAL

Evaluate Your Team Skills

Step 1: Answer the following questions the way that you think *other members of your team* would if they were describing your actions.[146] Use this scale for your responses:

1 Almost never
2 Seldom
3 Sometimes
4 Usually
5 Almost always

I. Honor Team Values and Agreements

As a team member, I

_____ a. show appreciation for other team members' ideas.

_____ b. help other team members cope with change.

_____ c. encourage others to use their strengths.

_____ d. help the team develop a productive relationship with other teams.

_____ e. willingly assume a leadership role when needed.

Total for Section I: _____

II. Promote Team Development

As a team member, I

_____ a. volunteer for all types of tasks, including the hard ones.

_____ b. help orient and train new team members.

_____ c. help organize and run effective meetings.

_____ d. help examine how we are doing as a team and make any necessary changes in the way we work together.

_____ e. help identify milestones and mini-successes to celebrate.

Total for Section II: _____

III. Help Make Team Decisions

As a team member, I

_____ a. analyze what a decision entails.

_____ b. ensure that the team selects and includes the appropriate people in the decision process.

_____ c. clearly state my concerns.

_____ d. search for common ground when team members have different views.

_____ e. actively support the team's decisions.

Total for Section III: _____

IV. Coordinate and Carry Out Team Tasks

As a team member, I

_____ a. help identify the information, skills, and resources necessary to accomplish team tasks.

_____ b. help formulate and agree on a plan to meet performance goals.

_____ c. stay abreast of what is happening in other parts of the organization and bring that information to the team.

_____ d. find innovative ways to meet the needs of the team and of others in the organization.

_____ e. maintain a win–win outlook in all dealings with other teams.

Total for Section IV: _____

V. Handle Difficult Issues with the Team

As a team member, I

_____ a. bring team issues and problems to the team's attention.

_____ b. encourage others on the team to state their views.

_____ c. help build trust among team members by speaking openly about the team's problems.

_____ d. give specific, constructive, and timely feedback to others.

_____ e. admit when I have made a mistake.

Total for Section V: _____

Step 2: Transfer the section totals to this table:

Category

Total Score

Honor team values and agreements _____

Promote team development _____

Help make team decisions _____

Coordinate and carry out team tasks _____

Handle difficult issues with the team _____

Interpreting Scores

- A score of 20 or above in any activity indicates an area of strength.
- A score of below 20 in any activity indicates an area that needs more attention.

Questions to Ask Yourself

Looking at your scores, what areas are strengths? How can you maintain these strengths? What areas are weaknesses? What steps can you take to turn these areas into strengths?

END NOTES

[1]"You. Happy. You. Learning to Fly," Cessna. [Online], accessed May 22, 2011, from www.cessna.com/learn-to-fly.html; T. Greenwood, M. Bradford, & B. Greene, "Becoming A Lean Enterprise: A Tale of Two Firms," *Strategic Finance*, November 1, 2002, 32; B. Milligan, "Cessna Uses Baldrige Process to Identify Best Suppliers," *Purchasing*, April 6, 2000, 75; J. Morgan, "Cessna Charts a Supply Chain Flight Strategy," *Purchasing*, September 7, 2000, 42; J. Morgan, "Cross-Functional Buying: Why Teams Are Hot," *Purchasing*, April 5, 2001, 27; J. Morgan, "Cessna Aims To Drive SCM to Its Very Core: Here Are 21 Steps and Tools It's Using to Make This Happen," *Purchasing*, June 6, 2002, 31; P. Siekman, "Cessna Tackles Lean Manufacturing," *Fortune*, May 1, 2000, I222 B+; and P. Siekman, "The Snap-Together Business Jet; Bombardier's New Recipe: A Dozen Big Pieces, Four Days To Assemble Them, and It's Ready To Fly," *Fortune*, January 21, 2002, 104A.

[2]B. Dumaine, "The Trouble with Teams," *Fortune*, September 5, 1994, 86–92.

[3]K. C. Stag, E. Salas, & S. M. Fiore, "Best Practices in Cross Training Teams," in *Workforce Cross Training Handbook*, D. A. Nembhard, ed. (Boca Raton, FL: CRC Press), 156–175.

[4]M. Marks, "The Science of Team Effectiveness," *Psychological Science in the Public Interest* (December 2006): pi–i.

[5]J. R. Katzenbach & D. K. Smith, *The Wisdom of Teams* (Boston: Harvard Business School Press, 1993).

[6]S. G. Cohen & D. E. Bailey, "What Makes Teams Work: Group

Effectiveness Research from the Shop Floor to the Executive Suite," *Journal of Management* 23, no. 3 (1997): 239–290.

[7]S. E. Gross, *Compensation for Teams* (New York: American Management Association, 1995); B. L. Kirkman & B. Rosen, "Beyond Self-Management: Antecedents and Consequences of Team Empowerment," *Academy of Management Journal* 42 (1999): 58–74; G. Stalk & T. M. Hout, *Competing against Time: How Time-Based Competition Is Reshaping Global Markets* (New York: Free Press, 1990); and S. C. Wheelwright & K. B. Clark, *Revolutionizing New Product Development* (New York: Free Press, 1992).

[8]Mohamed, J. E. McGrath, A. T. Florey, & S. W. Vanderstoep, "Time Matters in Team Performance: Effects of Member Familiarity, Entrainment, and Task Discontinuity on Speed and Quality," *Personnel Psychology* 56, no. 3 (August 2003): 633–669.

[9]PRWeb, "Staff Management|SMX Named a Finalist in the 2011 American Business Awards," *Yahoo! News*, May 18, 2011, accessed May 21, 2011, from http://news.yahoo.com/s/prweb/20110518/bs_prweb/prweb8455166_2; and "Staff Management's Expertise in Large-Scale Seasonal Hiring Projects Featured in Several Major Online Publications," Staff Management, December 10, 2010, accessed May 21, 2011, from www.staffmanagement.com/News-Story/Staff-Management-Expertise-Large-Scale-Hiring.aspx.

[10]D. Zatz, "Empowered Work Teams at Chrysler: Responsibility Replaces Inspectors," AllPar, accessed May 21, 2011, from www.allpar.com/corporate/empowered-work-teams.html.

[11]R. D. Banker, J. M. Field, R. G. Schroeder, & K. K. Sinha, "Impact of Work Teams on Manufacturing Performance: A Longitudinal Field Study," *Academy of Management Journal* 39 (1996): 867–890.

[12]"Entire Organization Rallies to Improve Product Ratings, Sales," Bazaarvoice, accessed May 21, 2011, from www.bazaarvoice.com/resources/case-studies/entire-organization-rallies-improve-product-ratings-sales.

[13]Stalk & Hout, *Competing against Time.*

[14]C. Passariello, "Brand-New Bag: Louis Vuitton Tries Modern Methods on Factory Lines; For Craftsmen, Multitasking Replaces Specialization; Inspiration from Japan; 'What Do Our Clients Want?'" *The Wall Street Journal*, October 9, 2006, A1.

[15]J. L. Cordery, W. S. Mueller, & L. M. Smith, "Attitudinal and Behavioral Effects of Autonomous Group Working: A Longitudinal Field Study," *Academy of Management Journal* 34 (1991): 464–476; and T. D. Wall, N. J. Kemp, P. R. Jackson, & C. W. Clegg, "Outcomes of Autonomous Workgroups: A Long-Term Field Experiment," *Academy of Management Journal* 29 (1986): 280–304.

[16]"Declaration of Interdependence," Whole Foods Market, accessed August 12, 2008, from www.wholefoodsmarket.com/company/declaration.html.

[17]Fishman, "The Anarchist's Cookbook."

[18]"Whole Foods Market Soars to Number 5 Spot on *Fortune*'s '100 Best Companies to Work For' List,"

Whole Foods, accessed March 20, 2009, from www.wholefoodsmarket.com/pressroom/2007/01/09/whole-foods-market-soars-to-number-5-spot-on-fortunes-100-best-companies-to-work-for-list/.

[19]R. Lieber, "Leadership Ensemble: How Do the Musicians of Orpheus Get to Carnegie Hall? They Practice—Not Just Their Music, but a Radical Approach to Leadership That Has Become a Compelling Metaphor for Business," *Fast Company*, May 1, 2000, 286.

[20]A. Erez, J. Lepine, & H. Elms, "Effects of Rotated Leadership and Peer Evaluation on the Functioning and Effectiveness of Self-Managed Teams: A Quasi-Experiment," *Personnel Psychology* 55, no. 4 (2002): 929.

[21]J. Hoerr, "The Payoff from Teamwork—The Gains in Quality Are Substantial—So Why Isn't It Spreading Faster?" *Businessweek*, July 10, 1989, 56.

[22]T. Aeppel, "Missing the Boss: Not All Workers Find Idea of Empowerment As Neat As It Sounds—Some Hate Fixing Machines, Apologizing for Errors, Disciplining Teammates—Rah-Rah Types Do the Best," *The Wall Street Journal*, September 8, 1997, A1.

[23]R. Liden, S. Wayne, R. Jaworski, and N. Bennett, "Social Loafing: A Field Investigation," *Journal of Management* 30 (2004): 285–304.

[24]J. George, "Extrinsic and Intrinsic Origins of Perceived Social Loafing in Organizations," *Academy of Management Journal* 35 (1992): 191–202.

[25]T. T. Baldwin, M. D. Bedell, & J. L. Johnson, "The Social Fabric of a Team-Based M.B.A. Program: Network Effects on Student Satisfaction and Performance," *Academy of Management Journal* 40 (1997): 1369–1397.

[26]K. H. Price, D. A. Harrison, & J. H. Gavin, "Withholding Inputs in Team Contexts: Member Composition, Interaction Processes, Evaluation Structure and Social Loafing," *Journal of Applied Psychology* 91(6) (2006): 1375–1384.

[27]Hoerr, "The Payoff from Teamwork."

[28]P. Strozniak, "Teams at Work," Industry Week.com, accessed May 21, 2011, from www.teambuildinginc.com/article_teamsatwork.htm.

[29]C. Joinson, "Teams at Work," *HR Magazine*, May 1, 1999, 30.

[30]R. Wageman, "Critical Success Factors for Creating Superb Self-Managing Teams," *Organizational Dynamics* 26, no. 1 (1997): 49–61.

[31]R. Karlgaard, "Leadership Lessons from the Tour de France," *Forbes*, July 31, 2009, accessed November 16, 2009, from www.forbes.com/2009/07/31/karlgaard-leadership-sports-intelligent-technology-sports.html.

[32]Wageman, "Critical Success Factors for Creating Superb Self-Managing Teams."

[33]M. A. Cusumano, "How Microsoft Makes Large Teams Work Like Small Teams," *Sloan Management Review* 39, no. 1 (Fall 1997): 9–20.

[34]N. Wingfield, "Tech Journal: To Rebuild Windows, Microsoft Razed Walls Three-Year Effort to Create Latest Version Meant Close Collaboration Among Workers to Avoid Vista's Woes," *The Wall Street Journal*, October 20, 2009, B9.

[35]Ibid.

[36]Ibid.

[37]Harrison et al., "Time Matters."

[38]J. Palfini, "Forget What You Learned in Grade School: Five Teamwork Myths," BNET: The CBS Interactive Business Network, August 1, 2007, www.bnet.com/blog/teamwork/forget-what-you-learned-in-grade-school-five-teamwork-myths/103.

[39]Josh Spiro, "How to Run an Effective Meeting," *Inc.*, August 4, 2010, accessed July 19, 2010, from www.inc.com/guides/2010/08/how-to-run-effective-meeting.html.

[40]Says Ridley, "People Are Hunting [i.e., Selling] in Packs Together." No author, "Ridley's Reforms Reward Team Effort," *Estates Gazette*, March 20, 2010, 35.

[41]M. Bolch, "Rewarding the Team: Make Sure Team-Oriented Compensation Plans Are Designed Carefully," *HR Magazine*, February 2007, 52(2).

[42]J. Vascellaro, "Google Searches for Ways to Keep Big Ideas at Home—Giant Speeds Access to Bosses in Effort to Transform More Projects into Products," *The Wall Street Journal*, June 18, 2009, B1.

[43]"'Mission Almost Complete,'" JLife: JC Penney Associates Winning Together," September 2009, accessed May 21, 2011, http://jcpenney.net/jlife/2009/09/Door_to_floor.html.

[44]P. Potempa, "Nurses Use Teamwork to Care for Spinal Stenosis Patients," Nurse.com, October 19, 2009, accessed May 21, 2011, from http://news.nurse.com/article/20091019/NJ02/110190003.

[45]Kirkman & Rosen, "Beyond Self-Management: Antecedents and Consequences of Team Empowerment."

[46]K. Kelly, "Managing Workers Is Tough Enough in Theory. When Human Nature Enters the Picture, It's Worse," *Businessweek*, October 21, 1996, 32.

[47]S. Easton & G. Porter, "Selecting the Right Team Structure to Work in Your Organization," in *Handbook of Best Practices for Teams*, vol. 1, G. M. Parker, ed. (Amherst, MA: Irwin, 1996).

[48]C. Kauffman, "Employee Involvement: A New Blueprint for Success," *Journal of Accountancy* 209 (2010): 46–49.

[49]R. M. Yandrick, "A Team Effort: The Promise of Teams Isn't Achieved without Attention to Skills and Training," *HR Magazine*, June 2001, 46(6).

[50]D. O'Connell & D. Heriein, "The Marvel of Plant 4: Bandag's Journey of Self-Direction," *People & Strategy* 32 (2009): 34–41.

[51]R. Williams, "Self-Directed Work Teams: A Competitive Advantage."

[52]R. M. Yandrick, "A Team Effort: The Promise of Teams Isn't Achieved without Attention to Skills and Training."

[53]E. White, "How a Company Made Everyone a Team Player," *The Wall Street Journal*, August 13, 2007, B1.

[54]R. J. Recardo, D. Wade, C. A. Mention, & J. Jolly, *Teams* (Houston: Gulf Publishing Co., 1996).

[55]D. R. Denison, S. L. Hart, & J. A. Kahn, "From Chimneys to Cross-Functional Teams: Developing and Validating a Diagnostic Model," *Academy of Management Journal* 39, no. 4 (1996): 1005–1023.

[56]P. Kotler, R. Wolcott, & S. Chandrasekhar, "Product Development—

Playing Well with Others: How to Improve the Relationship between the Marketing and R&D Departments—and Increase the Chance of Coming Up with Successful New Products," *The Wall Street Journal*, June 22, 2009, R5.

[57]A. M. Townsend, S. M. DeMarie, & A. R. Hendrickson, "Virtual Teams: Technology and the Workplace of the Future," *Academy of Management Executive* 13, no. 3 (1998): 17–29.

[58]K. Butler, "Virtual Reality: Most Teams Work Remotely, Increasing Need for Different Processes," *Employee Benefit News*, February 1, 2008.

[59]N. Apostolou, "Making Virtual Teams a Reality," *Charter* 81, no. 8 (2010): 52–53.

[60]Wellins, Byham, & Dixon, *Inside Teams*.

[61]Townsend, DeMarie, & Hendrickson, "Virtual Teams."

[62]W. F. Cascio, "Managing a Virtual Workplace," *Academy of Management Executive* 14 (2000): 81–90.

[63]B. Williamson, "Managing at a Distance," *Businessweek*, July 27, 2009, 64.

[64]R. Katz, "The Effects of Group Longevity on Project Communication and Performance," *Administrative Science Quarterly* 27 (1982): 245–282.

[65]B. Williamson, "Managing at a Distance."

[66]D. Mankin, S. G. Cohen, & T. K. Bikson, *Teams and Technology: Fulfilling the Promise of the New Organization* (Boston: Harvard Business School Press, 1996).

[67]A. P. Ammeter & J. M. Dukerich, "Leadership, Team Building, and Team Member Characteristics in High Performance Project Teams," *Engineering Management* 14, no. 4 (December 2002): 3–11.

[68]K. Lovelace, D. Shapiro, & L. Weingart, "Maximizing Cross-Functional New Product Teams' Innovativeness and Constraint Adherence: A Conflict Communications Perspective," *Academy of Management Journal* 44 (2001): 779–793.

[69]Phil Patton, "Envisioning a Small Electric BMW for the World's Very Big Cities," *The New York Times*, July 1, 2010, accessed August 15, 2010, from www.nytimes.com/2010/07/04/automobiles/04MEGACITY.html?_r=1&ref=automobiles.

[70]L. Holpp & H. P. Phillips, "When Is a Team Its Own Worst Enemy?" *Training*, September 1, 1995, 71.

[71]S. Asche, "Opinions and Social Pressure," *Scientific American* 193 (1995): 31–35.

[72]J. Stephens, "Corner Office: Rah-Rah Isn't for Everyone," interview by A. Bryant, *The New York Times*, April 9, 2010, accessed June 11, 2010, from www.nytimes.com/2010/04/11/business/11corner.html?pagewanted=2.

[73]S. G. Cohen, G. E. Ledford, & G. M. Spreitzer, "A Predictive Model of Self-Managing Work Team Effectiveness," *Human Relations* 49, no. 5 (1996): 643–676.

[74]R. Collett, "How to Improve Product Development Productivity—Lessons from the Checklist Manifesto," The EE Compendium: The Home of Electronic Engineering and Embedded Systems Programming, accessed May 22, 2011, from http://ee.cleversoul.com/news/lessons-from-the-checklist-manifesto.html.

[75]"Surgical Safety Checklist," World Health Organization, accessed May 22, 2011, from www.projectcheck.org/uploads/1/0/9/0/1090835/surgical_safety_checklist_production.pdf. While this seems simple, checklists are remarkably effective in reducing surgical errors. M. Semel. S. Resch, A. Haynes, L. Funk, A. Bader, W. Berry, T. Weiser, & A. Gawande, "Adopting A Surgical Safety Checklist Could Save Money And Improve The Quality of Care in US Hospitals," *Health Affairs* 29, no. 9 (2010): 1593–1599.

[76]M. Fischetti, "'Team Doctors, Report To ER': Is Your Team Headed for Intensive Care? Our Specialists Offer Prescriptions for the Five Illnesses That Can Afflict Even the Best Teams," *Fast Company*, February 1, 1998, 170.

[77]K. Bettenhausen & J. K. Murnighan, "The Emergence of Norms in Competitive Decision-Making Groups," *Administrative Science Quarterly* 30 (1985): 350–372.

[78]M. E. Shaw, *Group Dynamics* (New York: McGraw-Hill, 1981).

[79]E. Levenson, "The Power of an Idea," *Fortune*, June 12, 2006, 131.

[80]Katzenback & Smith, *The Wisdom of Teams*.

[81]S. E. Jackson, "The Consequences of Diversity in Multidisciplinary Work Teams," in *Handbook of Work Group Psychology*, M. A. West, ed. (Chichester, UK: Wiley, 1996).

[82]A. M. Isen & R. A. Baron, "Positive Affect as a Factor in Organizational Behavior," in *Research in Organizational Behavior* 13, L. L. Cummings & B. M. Staw, eds. (Greenwich, CT: JAI Press, 1991): 1–53.

[83]C. R. Evans & K. L. Dion, "Group Cohesion and Performance: A Meta Analysis," *Small Group Research* 22, no. 2 (1991): 175–186.

[84]R. Stankiewicsz, "The Effectiveness of Research Groups in Six Countries," in *Scientific Productivity*, F. M. Andrews, ed. (Cambridge: Cambridge University Press, 1979), 191–221.

[85]F. Rees, *Teamwork from Start to Finish* (San Francisco: Jossey-Bass, 1997).

[86]S. M. Gully, D. S. Devine, & D. J. Whitney, "A Meta-Analysis of Cohesion and Performance: Effects of Level of Analysis and Task Interdependence," *Small Group Research* 26, no. 4 (1995): 497–520.

[87]Gully, Devine, & Whitney, "A Meta- Analysis of Cohesion and Performance."

[88]S. Covel, "Small Business Link: Games, Outings Keep Workers Connected," *The Wall Street Journal*, November 19, 2011, B6.

[89]F. Tschan & M. V. Cranach, "Group Task Structure, Processes and Outcomes," in *Handbook of Work Group Psychology*, M. A. West, ed. (Chichester, UK: Wiley, 1996).

[90]D. E. Yeatts & C. Hyten, *High Performance Self-Managed Teams* (Thousand Oaks, CA: Sage Publications, 1998); and H. M. Guttman & R. S. Hawkes, "New Rules for Strategic Development," *Journal of Business Strategy* 25, no. 1 (2004): 34–39.

[91]Ibid; J. Colquitt, R. Noe, & C. Jackson, "Justice in Teams: Antecedents and Consequences of Procedural Justice Climate," *Personnel Psychology*, April 1, 2002, 83.

[92]D. S. Kezsbom, "Re-Opening Pandora's Box: Sources of Project Team Conflict in the '90s," *Industrial Engineering* 24, no. 5 (1992): 54–59.

[93]A. C. Amason, W. A. Hochwarter, & K. R. Thompson, "Conflict: An Important Dimension in Successful Management Teams," *Organizational Dynamics* 24 (1995): 20.

[94]A. C. Amason, "Distinguishing the Effects of Functional and Dysfunctional Conflict on Strategic Decision Making: Resolving a Paradox for Top Management Teams," *Academy of Management Journal* 39, no. 1 (1996): 123–148.

[95]K. M. Eisenhardt, J. L. Kahwajy, & L. J. Bourgeois III, "How Management Teams Can Have a Good Fight," *Harvard Business Review* 75, no. 4 (July–August 1997): 77–85.

[96]Ibid.

[97]C. Nemeth & P. Owens, "Making Work Groups More Effective: The Value of Minority Dissent," in *Handbook of Work Group Psychology*, M. A. West, ed. (Chichester, UK: Wiley, 1996).

[98]J. M. Levin & R. L. Moreland, "Progress in Small Group Research," *Annual Review of Psychology* 9 (1990): 72–78; and S. E. Jackson, "Team Composition in Organizational Settings: Issues in Managing a Diverse Work Force," in *Group Processes and Productivity*, S. Worchel, W. Wood, & J. Simpson, eds. (Beverly Hills, CA: Sage, 1992).

[99]Eisenhardt, Kahwajy, & Bourgeois, "How Management Teams Can Have a Good Fight."

[100]Ibid.

[101]B. W. Tuckman, "Development Sequence in Small Groups," *Psychological Bulletin* 63, no. 6 (1965): 384–399.

[102]J. F. McGrew, J. G. Bilotta, & J. M. Deeney, "Software Team Formation and Decay: Extending the Standard Model for Small Groups," *Small Group Research* 30, no. 2 (1999): 209–234.

[103]Ibid.

[104]J. Case, "What the Experts Forgot to Mention: Management Teams Create New Difficulties, but Succeed for XEL Communication," *Inc.*, September 1, 1993, 66.

[105]J. R. Hackman, "The Psychology of Self- Management in Organizations," in *Psychology and Work: Productivity, Change, and Employment*, M. S. Pallak & R. Perloff, eds. (Washington, DC: American Psychological Association, 1986), 85–136.

[106]A. O 'Leary-Kelly, J. J. Martocchio, & D. D. Frink, "A Review of the Influence of Group Goals on Group Performance," *Academy of Management Journal* 37, no. 5 (1994): 1285–1301.

[107]R. Jana, "Real Life Imitates Real World," *Businessweek*, March 23, 2009, 42.

[108]A. Zander, "The Origins and Consequences of Group Goals," in *Retrospections on Social Psychology*, L. Festinger, ed. (New York: Oxford University Press, 1980), 205–235.

[109]M. Erez & A. Somech, "Is Group Productivity Loss the Rule or the Exception? Effects of Culture and Group-Based Motivation," *Academy of Management Journal* 39, no. 6 (1996): 1513–1537.

[110]S. Sherman, "Stretch Goals: The Dark Side of Asking for Miracles," *Fortune*, November 13, 1995.

[111]Nick Bunkley, "Hyundai Says Its Cars Will Average 50 M.P.G. by 2025," *The New York Times*, Wheels Blog, August 4, 2010, accessed May 11, 2011, from http://wheels.blogs.nytimes.com/2010/08/04/hyundai-says-its-cars-will-average-50-m-p-g-by-2025/.

[112]K. R. Thompson, W. A. Hochwarter, & N. J. Mathys, "Stretch Targets: What Makes Them Effective?" *Academy of Management Executive* 11, no. 3 (1997): 48–60.

[113]"7 Ways to Socialize With Your Employees (Without Getting in Trouble)," *Inc.*, August 11, 2010, accessed August 19, 2-010, from www.inc.com/guides/2010/08/7-ways-to-socialize-with-your-employees.html.

[114]S. Tully, "Why to Go for Stretch Targets," *Fortune*, November 14, 1994, 145.

[115]Sherman, "Stretch Goals."

[116]J. Whalen, "Glaxo Tries Biotech Model to Spur Drug Innovations," *The Wall Street Journal (Online)*, July 1, 2010, accessed May 22, 2011, from http://online.wsj.com/article/SB100014240527487045692045753285809211336768.html.

[117]Richard Branson, "Teamwork Is Key to Good Service," Livemint.com, June 19, 2010, accessed September 20, 2010, from www.livemint.com/2010/07/19230138/Teamwork-is-key-to-good-servic.html.

[118]Dumaine, "The Trouble with Teams."

[119]G. A. Neuman, S. H. Wagner, & N. D. Christiansen, "The Relationship between Work-Team Personality Composition and the Job Performance of Teams," *Group & Organization Management* 24, no. 1 (1999): 28–45.

[120]M. A. Campion, G. J. Medsker, & A. C. Higgs, "Relations between Work Group Characteristics and Effectiveness: Implications for Designing Effective Work Groups," *Personnel Psychology* 46, no. 4 (1993): 823–850.

[121]B. L. Kirkman & D. L. Shapiro, "The Impact of Cultural Values on Employee Resistance to Teams: Toward a Model of Globalized Self-Managing Work Team Effectiveness," *Academy of Management Review* 22, no. 3 (1997): 730–757.

[122]J. Newport, "Golf Journal: Team USA's Management Victory; Ryder Cup Captain Paul Azinger Used a Group-Dynamic Philosophy with Lessons for Golf and Beyond," *The Wall Street Journal*, September 27, 2008, W9.

[123]Ibid.

[124]C. Fishman, "Engines of Democracy: The General Electric Plant in Durham, North Carolina Builds Some of the World's Most Powerful Jet Engines. But the Plant's Real Power Lies in the Lessons That It Teaches about the Future of Work and about Workplace Democracy," *Fast Company*, October 1, 1999, 174.

[125]J. Bunderson & K. Sutcliffe, "Comparing Alternative Conceptualizations of Functional Diversity in Management Teams: Process and Performance Effects," *Academy of Management Journal* 45 (2002): 875–893.

[126]J. Barbian, "Getting to Know You," *Training*, June 2001, 60–63.

[127]P. Sanders, "Boeing Brings in Old Hands, Gets an Earful," *The Wall Street Journal*, July 19, 2010. B1.

[128]J. Hackman, "New Rules for Team Building—The Times Are Changing—and So Are the Guidelines for Maximizing Team Performance," *Optimize*, July 1, 2002, 50.

[129]Joinson, "Teams at Work."

[130]P. Strozniak, "Teams at Work," Industry Week.com, accessed May 21, 2011, from www.teambuildinginc.com/article_teamsatwork.htm.

[131]Ibid.

[132]P. Nicholas, "It's All about Flight of Fight," Weekend Australian, March 14, 2009, 1.

[133]Wellins, Byham, & Dixon, *Inside Teams*.

[134]E. Salas, D. DiazGranados, C. Klein, C. Burke, K. Stagl, G. Goodwin, & S. Halpin, "Does Team Training Improve Team Performance? A Meta-Analysis," *Human Factors* 50, no. 6 (2008): 903–933.

[135]S. Caudron, "Tie Individual Pay to Team Success," *Personnel Journal* 73, no. 10 (October 1994): 40.

[136]Ibid.

[137]Gross, *Compensation for Teams*.

[138]G. Ledford, "Three Case Studies on Skill-Based Pay: An Overview," *Compensation & Benefits Review* 23, no. 2 (1991): 11–24.

[139]T. Law, "Where Loyalty is Rewarded," *The Press*, September 29, 2008, Business Day 4.

[140]J. R. Schuster & P. K. Zingheim, *The New Pay: Linking Employee and Organizational Performance* (New York: Lexington Books, 1992).

[141]M. Bolch, "Rewarding the Team.

[142]Cohen and Bailey, "What Makes Teams Work."

[143]R. Allen & R. Kilmann, "Aligning Reward Practices in Support of Total Quality Management," *Business Horizons* 44 (May 2001): 77–85.

[144]J. H. Sheridan, "'Yes' to Team Incentives," *Industry Week*, March 4, 1996, 63.

[145]J. A. Wagner, "Studies of Individualism-Collectivism: Effects on Cooperation in Groups," *Academy of Management Journal* 38, no. 1 (1995): 152–172.

[146]M. A. West, ed., *Handbook of Work Group Psychology* (Chichester, UK: Wiley, 1996).

BIZ FLIX

Failure to Launch

In the 2006 romantic comedy *Failure to Launch*, Matthew McConaughey plays Tripp, a 35-year-old confirmed bachelor who lives a great life in a nice house—his parents'. Whenever a woman starts getting too serious about him, Tripp brings them home to see his childhood bedroom. It's his surefire way of getting rid of clingy girlfriends without ever having to break up with them. His mother Sue (Kathy Bates) and father Al (Terry Bradshaw) are desperate to get Tripp out of the house, so they hire Paula (Sarah Jessica Parker), who specializes in detaching grown children from their families. In this scene, Paula's quirky roommate Kit (Zooey Deschanel) enlists Tripp's friend Ace (Justin Bartha) in getting rid of a bird that has been making too much noise outside her window.

© GreenLight

What to Watch for and Ask Yourself

1. Do you think Kit and Ace make a good team? How well do they work together to first shoot the bird and then save it?

2. Is there a clear leader? Who is making most of the decisions in this scene?

3. Is there any evidence of team conflict?

MANAGEMENT WORKPLACE

Holden Outerwear: Leading Teams

At Holden Outerwear, it's all about teamwork. Founder Mikey LeBlanc believes that teamwork is critical to the company's position as an innovation leader. Holden's use of teams is something that emerged out of necessity. For much of the company's brief history, managers worked independently on design projects. But as the company grew, LeBlanc needed more designers, and he began looking to outside freelancers for help. Nikki Brush, a design and development manager at Holden, remembers when she was first brought on as a freelancer. Today she is a full time manager at the company. The switch from freelancer to in-house manager has been positive for Nikki Brush, although her role on the team has changed. Even so, she is happier working inside the firm. Not only does she now know where Holden is going, but she helps set the course.

© Cengage Learning

Discussion Questions

1. What type of team did Nikki Brush participate in when she was a freelancer? What type of team does she participate in as a full-time employee at Holden?

2. What are the advantages and disadvantages of using teams at Holden? What can managers do to help avoid the disadvantages?

3. What steps do the leaders of Holden take to insure that their workgroups have high levels of cohesion?

CHAPTER 11

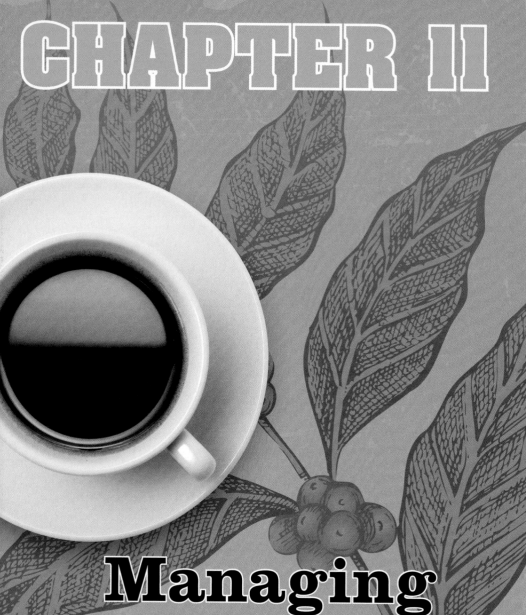

Managing Human Resources

Learning Outcomes

1. Describe the basic steps involved in human resource planning.
2. Explain how different employment laws affect human resource practice.
3. Explain how companies use recruiting to find qualified job applicants.
4. Describe the selection techniques and procedures that companies use when deciding which applicants should receive job offers.
5. Describe how to determine training needs and select the appropriate training methods.
6. Discuss how to use performance appraisal to give meaningful performance feedback.
7. Describe basic compensation strategies and explain how they affect human resource practice.
8. Discuss the four kinds of employee separations: termination, downsizing, retirements, and turnover.

what would **you do?**

Nick's Pizza & Pub, Crystal Lake, Illinois[1]

Your start in the pizza business came in the eighth grade, when your father opened the Village Pizza restaurant. After graduation, you entered the construction business, building homes for more than a decade. But, then, something drew you back. So, you took the family recipes and started your own restaurant, Nick's Pizza & Pub (far enough away to avoid competing with Dad).

Your goal was simple: to build a fun, family restaurant. Nick's Pizza & Pubs—there are now two—have 26-foot high, floor-to-ceiling stone fireplaces, stuffed bears and moose, "antler chandeliers," huge aquariums separating the bar and the restaurant, and wood everywhere—oak floors and huge beams recycled from century-old barns. And they're huge, each seating 320 guests. On a Friday night, 1,500 customers will eat at Nick's, most waiting an hour for their tables, while having a drink and eating free peanuts at the bar. Those 1,500 customers will eat 600 pizzas, and carry-out customers order another 200. Why do they come? Beyond the great pizza, they come for the value. A medium cheese pizza is $11; soft drinks are $1.75, with free refills; and the popular Italian beef sandwich is under $6.00. Nick's is really affordable, especially for a sit-down restaurant.

With things going so well, you decided to open three more restaurants in the next five years. Unfortunately, the recession changed your plans. Guest counts dropped by 20 percent, or 100,000 people per year, decreasing revenues by nearly $1 million. On top of that, your managers were having difficulty controlling costs. Each week, they conducted a physical count, comparing food inventories (tomato sauce, flour, cheese, beef, liquor, etc.) to the previous week, and then adjusted for this week's sales. But beverage and food costs were still above goal, 22 percent of revenues for beverages and 20 percent of revenues for food. The problem, as you discovered, was your management, all hired externally because of their extensive experience at established well-known restaurant chains. Their idea of leadership, learned in the "command and control" cultures of other restaurants, was telling people what to do. So, they had someone else put in the inventory numbers, and when the numbers came out wrong, they didn't dig deeper or ask questions to discover why.

In the end, with costs up, revenues down, and lending standards tightening, the bank didn't approve the new construction loans. So rather than expanding, your immediate challenge is to fix and grow the two Nick's restaurants that you've got. Frustrated with your managers, you gave responsibility for reducing costs to a 24-year-old who had worked for you since she was 16. She fixed the problem in four weeks by discussing the problem with the kitchen, wait, and bar staffs, who suggested immediate solutions to reduce costs.

"what's new" companies

Nick's Pizza & Pub
Dorner Manufacturing Company
ATK
MTI
Massey Energy Company
First Student
ABM Industries
Dairy Farmers of America
RedStream Technology
Apex Companies
Finish Line
Dealer.com
Installation & Service Technologies

< **"what's new" companies**

study tips

Check your work by reading the actual review paragraphs on pages 431, 437, 442, 453, 457, 462, 467, and 471.

Use the chapter outline on the preceding page as a study tool. After reading the whole chapter, return to the list and write a summary of each item.

Sensing that she was onto something, you pulled together the staffs in both restaurants to make a financial presentation that showed in detail how and where Nick's was earning revenue and incurring expenses. After answering their questions, you asked for their help on three key issues: pay, hiring, and training. Of course, everyone wants to be paid more, but with costs being an issue, are there ways to pay people more but link those increases to the company's profitability and workers doing their jobs better and staying with the company longer? If so, how? Next, because hiring talented workers is key in the restaurant business, how should Nick's redesign its interview and selection process to do a better job of finding and keeping the best kitchen, wait, and bar staff? What is it about interviews that doesn't work and should be abandoned? If so, what should be done instead, and why? Finally, at most restaurants, training is simply shadowing experienced workers to see what they do. So, what could be done at Nick's to improve training that would help them do their jobs better and to continue learning and improving over time?

If you were in charge at Nick's, what would you do?

Human resource management (HRM), or the process of finding, developing, and keeping the right people to form a qualified workforce, is one of the most difficult and important of all management tasks. This chapter is organized around the four parts of the human resource management process shown in Exhibit 11.1: determining human resource needs and attracting, developing, and keeping a qualified workforce.

This chapter will walk you through the steps of the HRM process. The chapter begins by reviewing how human resource planning determines human resource needs, such as the kind and number of employees a company requires to meet its strategic plans and objectives. Next, we explore how companies use recruiting and selection techniques to attract and hire qualified employees to fulfill those needs. The third part of the chapter discusses how training and performance appraisal can develop the knowledge, skills, and abilities of the workforce. The chapter concludes with a review of compensation and employee separation; that is, how companies can keep their best workers through effective compensation practices and how they can manage the separation process when employees leave the organization.

human resource management (HRM) the process of finding, developing, and keeping the right people to form a qualified workforce.

Determining Human Resource Needs

After reading the next two sections, you should be able to

1. *Describe the basic steps involved in human resource planning.*
2. *Explain how different employment laws affect human resource practice.*

Should we hire more workers? What should we pay our current employees to slow employee turnover? What kinds of training do our new employees need to be prepared to do a good job, and what's the best way to deliver that training? In other words, what are our human resource needs, and what's the best way to address them? The human resource management process, shown in Exhibit 11.1, can provide answers to these questions.

We can see how the HRM process works by examining what Google is doing to make sure that it has the talent it needs to stay competitive. First, with its expanding set of product offerings, from Google Apps to Google Docs to Google Checkout, Google has a growing need for software engineers. Second, Google finds itself competing with Apple and Facebook to hire those engineers, who according to venture capitalist Marc Andreessen, "Can easily have 10 job offers." With tech job openings up 62 percent and with 4,600 tech jobs open in Silicon Valley, competition to hire the best people is intense. Third, after hiring top engineers, Google still needs to work hard to keep them. Indeed, because of the competition for talent, Google gave all of its employees a 10 percent raise and a $1,000 bonus. But that hasn't stopped people from leaving, as more than 200 Google employees now work at Facebook. When Facebook offered one of Google's software engineers a job, Google countered the offer with a 15 percent raise, a $500,000 cash bonus to stay one year, and four times the stock benefits. But the engineer still left. How important is this issue to Google? According to Patrick Pichette, Google's chief financial officer, "We strongly believe that the difference between the winners and the losers in our industry will be to a large extent determined by who can continue to attract and retain the very best people." Employee recruiter Paul Daversa agrees, saying, "Google is an attraction and training ground for incredible talent. The question is: Can Google replace talent as fast as it's losing it?"[2]

For Google, the HRM process shown in Exhibit 11.1 comes full circle, as attracting, developing, and then keeping qualified software engineers affect its human resource needs.

Exhibit 11.1
The Human Resource Management Process

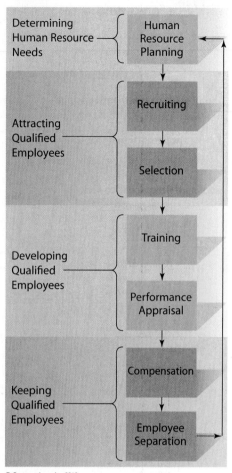

© Cengage Learning 2013

1 Human Resource Planning

Human resource planning (HRP) is the process of using an organization's goals and strategy to forecast its human resource needs in terms of attracting, developing, and keeping a qualified workforce.[3] Why is HRP important? Companies that don't use HRP or that do it poorly may end up with either a surplus of employees that has to be corrected with layoffs or a shortage of employees that leads to increased overtime costs and an inability to meet demand for the company's product or service.

Let's explore human resource planning by examining how to **1.1 forecast the demand and supply of human resources** and **1.2 use human resource information systems to improve those forecasts**.

1.1 Forecasting Demand and Supply

Workforce forecasting is the process of predicting the number and kind of workers with specific skills and abilities that an organization will need in the future.[4] There are two kinds of workforce forecasts: internal and external forecasts; and there are three kinds of forecasting methods: direct managerial input, best guess, and statistical/ historical ratios.

human resource planning (HRP) using an organization's goals and strategy to forecast the organization's human resource needs in terms of attracting, developing, and keeping a qualified workforce.

workforce forecasting the process of predicting the number and kind of workers with specific skills and abilities that an organization will need in the future.

Exhibit 11.2
Internal and External Factors That Influence Workforce Forecasting

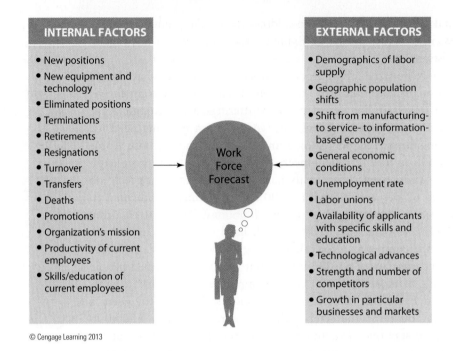

INTERNAL FACTORS

- New positions
- New equipment and technology
- Eliminated positions
- Terminations
- Retirements
- Resignations
- Turnover
- Transfers
- Deaths
- Promotions
- Organization's mission
- Productivity of current employees
- Skills/education of current employees

Work Force Forecast

EXTERNAL FACTORS

- Demographics of labor supply
- Geographic population shifts
- Shift from manufacturing- to service- to information-based economy
- General economic conditions
- Unemployment rate
- Labor unions
- Availability of applicants with specific skills and education
- Technological advances
- Strength and number of competitors
- Growth in particular businesses and markets

© Cengage Learning 2013

Internal forecasts are projections about factors within the organization that affect the supply and demand for human resources. These factors include the financial performance of the organization; its productivity; its mission; changes in technology or the way the work is performed; and terminations, promotions, transfers, retirements, resignations, and deaths of current employees. For example, after years of declining market share, losses, and layoffs, Ford Motor Company earned a record profit of $6.6 billion (up 141 percent from the previous year), cut its debt in half (from $33.6 billion to $14.5 billion), and increased sales and market share significantly. Based on this success and projections of strong future sales, Ford announced that it is hiring 7,000 new workers, most of whom will work in its assembly plants.[5] Exhibit 11.2 provides a more complete list of factors that influence internal forecasts.

External forecasts are projections about factors outside the organization that affect the supply of and demand for human resources. These factors include the labor supply for specific types of workers, the economy (unemployment rate), labor unions, demographics of the labor force (e.g., proportion of labor force in various age groups), geographic movement of the labor force, strength of competitors, and growth in particular businesses and markets. For example, when the economy

"what's new" companies >

went into recession, **Dorner Manufacturing Corporation**, which makes conveyor machines, saw its business slow dramatically and asked all its employees, including owners and top executives, to take a one-week layoff per quarter. Karen Wolf, Dorner's human resource manager said, "Because it was an 'equal' hit for all employees, everyone bought into the plan."[6] She explained, "Since we have approximately 170 employees, we will save a significant amount of salary costs."[7] After the short layoffs, the company will catch employees up on their health and life insurance and other benefits. Exhibit 11.2 provides a more complete list of factors that influence external forecasts.

Three kinds of forecasting methods—direct managerial input, best guess, and statistical/historical ratios—are often used to predict the number and kind of workers with specific skills and abilities that an organization will need in the future.[8] The most common forecasting method, *direct managerial input*, is based on straightforward projections of cash flows, expenses, or financial measures such as return on capital. Though financial indicators are relatively quick to calculate and can help managers determine how many workers might be needed, they don't help managers decide which critical skills new employees should possess.

The *best-guess* forecasting method is based on managers' assessment of current head count plus a best guess of how internal factors and external factors will affect that head count. A recent survey reported that managers typically overestimate future staffing levels needed to achieve business goals. The survey also found that organizations are more accurate when it comes to forecasting employment increases than when forecasting employment decreases.[9]

Finally, the *statistical/historical ratios* forecasting method uses statistical methods such as multiple regression in combination with historical data to predict the number and kind of workers a company should hire. For example, a manager might run a regression analysis using data from the last two years. In this analysis, the number of employees that need to be hired is the dependent (predicted) variable, and the number of items manufactured, number of clients, average increase in sales, and similar factors are the independent (predictor) variables. The regression analysis produces a simple equation that indicates how many more employees should be added for each increase in independent variables such as items manufactured or increased sales. This approach takes advantage of existing data and can be much more accurate than best-guess predictions, but only if a company's internal and external environments have not changed significantly.

ATK, a defense and aerospace company, uses a variety of sophisticated statistical tools to predict its workforce needs. Whereas a company like McDonald's has thousands of employees working in a small number of routine jobs, ATK has thousands of employees working in thousands of specialized jobs, few like any of the others. So at ATK, if an employee leaves, there's often no one in the company who can step up and fill that opening right away. As a result, ATK uses regression analysis to calculate the "flight risk" of each of its professional employees by examining trends for the future supply and demand for particular jobs. If someone is considered "high risk," the company might assign a junior engineer to begin working with that employee, or study salary and compensation levels to be prepared in case the employee comes in with a job offer from another employer. Carl Willis, ATK's vice president of human resources believes that workforce forecasting will save the firm hundreds of thousands of dollars in reduced replacement costs.[10]

< **"what's new"
companies**

human resource information system (HRIS) a computerized system for gathering, analyzing, storing, and disseminating information related to the HRM process.

1.2 Human Resource Information Systems

Human resource information systems (HRISs) are computerized systems for gathering, analyzing, storing, and disseminating information related to attracting, developing, and keeping a qualified workforce.[11] Exhibit 11.3 shows some of the data that are commonly used in HRISs, such as personal and educational information, company employment history, performance appraisal information, work history, and promotions.

Human resource information systems can be used for transaction processing, employee self-service, and decision support. For HRISs, *transaction*

Exhibit 11.3 Common Data Categories in Human Resource Information Systems

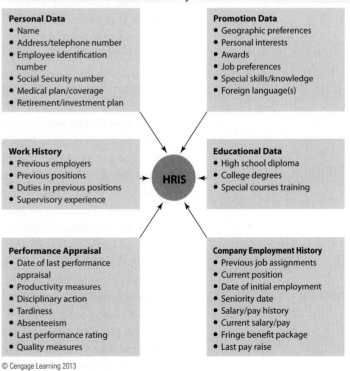

Personal Data
- Name
- Address/telephone number
- Employee identification number
- Social Security number
- Medical plan/coverage
- Retirement/investment plan

Promotion Data
- Geographic preferences
- Personal interests
- Awards
- Job preferences
- Special skills/knowledge
- Foreign language(s)

Work History
- Previous employers
- Previous positions
- Duties in previous positions
- Supervisory experience

Educational Data
- High school diploma
- College degrees
- Special courses training

HRIS

Performance Appraisal
- Date of last performance appraisal
- Productivity measures
- Disciplinary action
- Tardiness
- Absenteeism
- Last performance rating
- Quality measures

Company Employment History
- Previous job assignments
- Current position
- Date of initial employment
- Seniority date
- Salary/pay history
- Current salary/pay
- Fringe benefit package
- Last pay raise

© Cengage Learning 2013

processing usually involves employee payroll checks, taxes, and benefit deductions. For example, when ER One, a Michigan-based company that provides physicians and other clinicians for hospital emergency rooms, was small, it used paper files and different computer spreadsheets and databases to keep track of compensation and benefits for its employees. But now that the company has 180 employees in seven different locations, it uses an HRIS to keep track of everything. This system quickly provides accurate, up-to-date information about employee compensation and benefits, and can be easily accessed from any of the company's locations, says Pat Brainard, the company's director of human resources.[12] HRISs can also reduce administrative costs by preparing certain routine reports, such as the EEOC (Equal Employment Opportunity Commission) or OSHA (Occupational Safety and Health Administration) reports that are required of many companies.

Though typically used to give managers and HR staffers access to human resource data, today's secure web-based HRISs also give employees immediate, 24-hour *self-service* access to personal data such as benefits and retirement packages. By entering a username and a password, employees can access and change their medical insurance plan, adjust the mix of investments in their 401(k) retirement plan, or check on the status of medical or child-care reimbursements. Hewitt Associates is a global HR consulting and benefits outsourcing firm that provides its customers with secure access to HR data and applications using web-services technology, 24/7. Customers (i.e., employees of client organizations) can access and change their current health-care enrollment, check on their retirement benefits, and reallocate their 401(k) investments.[13]

In addition to gathering and storing information, HRISs also help managers by serving as decision support systems for critical HR decisions.[14] In Chapter 17, you will learn that *decision support systems (DSSs)* help managers understand problems and potential solutions by acquiring and analyzing information with sophisticated models and tools. For example, a human resources decision support system helped a senior vice president of sales determine that 25 percent of his salespeople accounted for 60 percent of his company's revenue. He was surprised, however, to learn that top salespeople were leaving the company at a 67 percent annual rate of turnover. By contrast, the lowest 25 percent of his salespeople were leaving at a rate of 7 percent. To fix the problem, the company established a minimum sales goal that had to be met for salespeople to keep their base salaries. Six months later, 80 percent of the poor performing salespeople had left. The company used the money it saved to fund bonuses for its best salespeople, reducing their quit rate to 31 percent and increasing company sales by $800 million a year.[15]

In terms of decision support systems, while it's common for companies to use HRISs to do key word résumé screening (looking for key word matches), companies have just begun to use interactive voice response (IVR) systems, similar to those used by your credit card company's 800 support number (i.e., "please state your 16-digit card number followed by the # sign"), to "interview" applicants by phone. Applicants are asked a series of prerecorded questions and the IVR records their verbal responses, which can be played back or searched for specific responses. For example, to reduce employee theft, retail companies will ask applicants about prior incidents of workplace theft, bribery, gambling, or drug or alcohol use. Darrel Knight, whose company, **MTI**, makes IVR systems, says, surprisingly, many people answer "yes" to such questions. Says Knight, "You can also tell a lot about the person by the delay between when the question is asked and when he starts his response, and that's not something you get from a website. You get more human feedback."[16]

"what's new" companies >

An HRIS can also be used effectively to screen *internal applicants* on particular qualifications, to match the qualifications of external applicants against those of internal applicants, to compare salaries within and between departments, and to review and change employees' salaries instantaneously without lengthy paperwork. In short, today's HRISs can help managers make any number of critical human resource decisions.

Human Resource Planning   Human resource planning (HRP) uses organizational goals and strategies to determine what needs to be done to attract, develop, and keep a qualified workforce. Workforce forecasts are used to predict the number and kind of workers with specific skills and abilities that an organization needs. Workforce forecasts consider both internal and external factors that affect the supply of and demand for workers and can be formulated using three kinds of forecasting methods: direct managerial input, best guess, and statistical/historical ratios. Computerized human resource information systems improve HRP by gathering, analyzing, storing, and disseminating information (personal, educational, work history, performance, and promotions) related to human resource management activities. Human resource information systems can be used for transaction processing (payroll checks and routine reports), employee self-service (24-hour web access allowing instant changes to benefit and retirement packages), and decision support for human resource decisions (analyzing résumés, background screening, and pre-employment testing).

Review 1

2 Employment Legislation

Since their inception, Hooters restaurants have hired only female servers. Moreover, consistent with the company's marketing theme, the servers wear short nylon shorts and cutoff T-shirts that show their midriffs. The Equal Employment Opportunity Commission (EEOC) began an investigation of Hooters when a Chicago man filed a sex-based discrimination charge. The man alleged that he had applied for a server's job at a Hooters restaurant and was rejected because of his sex. The dispute between Hooters and the EEOC quickly gained national attention. One sarcastic letter to the EEOC printed in *Fortune* magazine read as follows:

> *Dear EEOC:*
>
> *Hi! I just wanted to thank you for investigating those Hooters restaurants, where the waitresses wear those shorty shorts and midriffy T-shirts. I think it's a great idea that you have decided to make Hooters hire men as—how do you say it?—waitpersons. Gee, I never knew so many men wanted to be waitpersons at Hooters. No reason to let them sue on their own either. You're right, the government needs to take the lead on this one.[17]*

This letter characterized public sentiment at the time. Given its backlog of 100,000 job discrimination cases, many wondered if the EEOC didn't have better things to do with its scarce resources.

Three years after the initial complaint, the EEOC ruled that Hooters had violated antidiscrimination laws and offered to settle the case if the company would agree to pay $22 million to the EEOC for distribution to male victims of the "Hooters Girl" hiring policy, establish a scholarship fund to enhance opportunities or education for men, and provide sensitivity training to teach Hooters' employees how to be more sensitive to men's needs. Hooters responded with a $1 million publicity campaign criticizing the EEOC's investigation. Billboards featuring "Vince," a man dressed in a Hooters Girl uniform and blond wig, sprang up all over the country. Hooters customers were given postcards to send complaints to the EEOC. Of course, Hooters

Should Hooter's give men the same opportunity as women to work as waitstaff?

paid the postage. As a result of the publicity campaign, restaurant sales increased by 10 percent. Soon thereafter, the EEOC announced that it would not pursue discriminatory hiring charges against Hooters.[18] Nonetheless, the company ended up paying $3.75 million to settle a class-action suit brought by seven men who claimed that their inability to get a job at Hooters violated federal law.[19] Under the settlement, Hooters maintained its women-only policy for server jobs but had to create additional support jobs, such as hosts and bartenders, that would also be open to men. The story doesn't end there, however, as a male applicant who wants to be a Hooters waitperson has sued Hooters, seeking to overturn the prior settlement, which would allow him to be only a host or bartender.[20]

As the Hooters example illustrates, the human resource planning process occurs in a very complicated legal environment. Let's explore employment legislation by reviewing **2.1 the major federal employment laws that affect human resource practice, 2.2 how the concept of adverse impact is related to employment discrimination**, and **2.3 the laws regarding sexual harassment in the workplace**.

2.1 Federal Employment Laws

Exhibit 11.4 lists the major federal employment laws and their websites, where you can find more detailed information. Except for the Family and Medical Leave Act and the Uniformed Services Employment and Reemployment Rights Act, which are administrated by the Department of Labor (www.dol.gov), all of these laws are administered by the EEOC (www.eeoc.gov). The general effect of this body of law, which is still evolving through court decisions, is that employers may not discriminate in employment decisions on the basis of sex, age, religion, color, national origin, race, or disability. The intent is to make these factors irrelevant in employment decisions. Stated another way, employment decisions should be based on factors that are "job related," "reasonably necessary," or a "business necessity" for successful job performance. The only time that sex, age, religion, and the like can be used to make employment decisions is when they are considered a bona fide occupational qualification.[21] Title VII of the 1964 Civil Rights Act says that it is legal to hire and employ someone on the basis of sex, religion, or national origin when there is a **bona fide occupational qualification (BFOQ)** that is "reasonably necessary to the normal operation of that particular business." A Baptist church hiring a new minister can reasonably specify that being a Baptist rather than a Catholic or Presbyterian is a BFOQ for the position. However, it's unlikely that the church could specify race or national origin as a BFOQ. In general, the courts and the EEOC take a hard look when a business claims that sex,

bona fide occupational qualification (BFOQ) an exception in employment law that permits sex, age, religion, and the like to be used when making employment decisions, but only if they are "reasonably necessary to the normal operation of that particular business." BFOQs are strictly monitored by the Equal Employment Opportunity Commission.

Exhibit 11.4 Summary of Major Federal Employment Laws

Equal Pay Act of 1963	http://www.eeoc.gov/laws/statutes/epa.cfm	Prohibits unequal pay for males and females doing substantially similar work.
Civil Rights Act of 1964	http://www.eeoc.gov/laws/statutes/titlevii.cfm	Prohibits discrimination on the basis of race, color, religion, sex, or national origin.
Age Discrimination in Employment Act of 1967	http://www.eeoc.gov/laws/statutes/adea.cfm	Prohibits discrimination in employment decisions against persons age 40 and over.
Pregnancy Discrimination Act of 1978	http://www.eeoc.gov/laws/statutes/pregnancy.cfm	Prohibits discrimination in employment against pregnant women.
Americans with Disabilities Act of 1990	http://www.eeoc.gov/laws/statutes/ada.cfm	Prohibits discrimination on the basis of physical or mental disabilities.
Civil Rights Act of 1991	http://www.eeoc.gov/laws/statutes/cra-1991.cfm	Strengthened the provisions of the Civil Rights Act of 1964 by providing for jury trials and punitive damages.
Family and Medical Leave Act of 1993	http://www.dol.gov/dol/topic/benefits-leave/fmla.htm	Permits workers to take up to 12 weeks of unpaid leave for pregnancy and/or birth of a new child, adoption or foster care of a new child, illness of an immediate family member, or personal medical leave.
Uniformed Services Employment and Reemployment Rights Act of 1994	http://www.osc.gov/userra.htm	Prohibits discrimination against those serving in the Armed Forces Reserve, the National Guard, or other uniformed services; guarantees that civilian employers will hold and then restore civilian jobs and benefits for those who have completed uniformed service.

© Cengage Learning 2013

age, religion, color, national origin, race, or disability is a BFOQ. For instance, the EEOC disagreed with Hooters' claim that it was "in the business of providing vicarious sexual recreation" and that "female sexuality is a bona fide occupational qualification."[22]

It is important to understand, however, that these laws apply to the entire HRM process and not just to selection decisions (e.g., hiring or promotion). These laws also cover all training and development activities, performance appraisals, terminations, and compensation decisions. Employers who use sex, age, race, or religion to make employment-related decisions when those factors are unrelated to an applicant's or employee's ability to perform a job may face charges of discrimination from employee lawsuits or the EEOC. **Massey Energy Company**, the fourth largest coal company in the United States, bought a shuttered mine from Horizon Natural Resources. When it reopened the mine and began hiring previous employees, it reportedly refused to hire anyone over the age of 40. After a group of more than 200 miners sued, Massey settled the age discrimination suit for $8.75 million.[23] Boeing, the jet plane manufacturer, paid $72.5 million to settle a similar lawsuit brought by a group of its female employees who claimed they were denied overtime, training, or transfers.[24]

< **"what's new" companies**

In addition to the laws presented in Exhibit 11.4, there are two other important sets of federal laws: labor laws and laws and regulations governing safety standards. Labor laws regulate the interaction between management and labor unions that represent groups of employees. These laws guarantee employees the right to form and

join unions of their own choosing. For more information about labor laws, see the National Labor Relations Board at www.nlrb.gov.

The Occupational Safety and Health Act (OSHA) requires that employers provide employees with a workplace that is "free from recognized hazards that are causing or are likely to cause death or serious physical harm." This law is administered by the Occupational Safety and Health Administration (which, like the act, is referred to as OSHA). OSHA sets safety and health standards for employers and conducts inspections to determine whether those standards are being met. Employers who do not meet OSHA standards may be fined.[25] For example, OSHA fined British Petroleum $23.8 million after a refinery explosion in Texas City, Texas, killed 15 workers and injured 180 employees.[26] OSHA announced the fine for "egregious, willful violations" of safety standards that led to the fatal explosion.[27] The U.S. Chemical Safety and Hazard Investigation Board, a government agency that investigates major workplace accidents, accused BP of knowing about "widespread safety problems" prior to the accident, which it said was the result of "drastic cost-cutting at the Texas refinery, where maintenance and infrastructure deteriorated over time, setting the stage for the disaster."[28] For more information about OSHA, see www.osha.gov.

2.2 Adverse Impact and Employment Discrimination

The EEOC has investigatory, enforcement, and informational responsibilities. Therefore, it investigates charges of discrimination, enforces the employment discrimination laws in federal court, and publishes guidelines that organizations can use to ensure they are in compliance with the law. One of the most important guidelines, jointly issued by the EEOC, the Department of Labor, the U.S. Justice Department, and the federal Office of Personnel Management, is the *Uniform Guidelines on Employee Selection Procedures*, which can be read in their entirety at www.ipacweb.org/files/ug.pdf. These guidelines define two important criteria, disparate treatment and adverse impact, which are used in determining whether companies have engaged in discriminatory hiring and promotion practices.

Disparate treatment, which is *intentional* discrimination, occurs when people, despite being qualified, are *intentionally* not given the same hiring, promotion, or membership opportunities as other employees because of their race, color, age, sex, ethnic group, national origin, or religious beliefs.[29] For example, Green Bay Dressed Beef, a meat-processing company, paid $1.65 million to settle a disparate treatment lawsuit in which it was accused of purposefully discriminating against 970 female applicants in hiring decisions.[30] Likewise, the University of Kentucky paid a $125,000 settlement for religious discrimination to Martin Gaskell, a professor of astronomy, when inter-departmental emails revealed that he was not hired because of his evangelical Christian beliefs.[31]

Legally, a key element of discrimination lawsuits is establishing motive, meaning that the employer intended to discriminate. If no motive can be established, then a claim of disparate treatment may actually be a case of adverse impact. **Adverse impact**, which is *unintentional* discrimination, occurs when members of a particular race, sex, or ethnic group are *unintentionally* harmed or disadvantaged because they are hired, promoted, or trained (or any other employment decision) at substantially lower rates than others. The courts and federal agencies use the **four-fifths (or 80 percent) rule** to determine whether adverse impact has occurred. Adverse impact occurs if the decision rate for a protected group of people is less than four-fifths (or 80%) of the decision rate for a nonprotected group (usually white males). So, if 100 white applicants and 100 black applicants apply for entry-level jobs, and 60 white applicants

disparate treatment intentional discrimination that occurs when people are purposely not given the same hiring, promotion, or membership opportunities because of their race, color, sex, age, ethnic group, national origin, or religious beliefs.

adverse impact unintentional discrimination that occurs when members of a particular race, sex, or ethnic group are unintentionally harmed or disadvantaged because they are hired, promoted, or trained (or any other employment decision) at substantially lower rates than others.

four-fifths (or 80 percent) rule a rule of thumb used by the courts and the EEOC to determine whether there is evidence of adverse impact. A violation of this rule occurs when the selection rate for a protected group is less than 80 percent or four-fifths of the selection rate for a nonprotected group.

are hired (60/100 = 60%), but only 20 black applicants are hired (20/100 = 20%), adverse impact has occurred (0.20/0.60 = 0.33). The criterion for the four-fifths rule in this situation is 0.48 (0.60 × 0.80 = 0.48). Because 0.33 is less than 0.48, the four-fifths rule has been violated.

Violation of the four-fifths rule is not an automatic indication of discrimination, however. If an employer can demonstrate that a selection procedure or test is valid, meaning that the test accurately predicts job performance or that the test is job related because it assesses applicants on specific tasks actually used in the job, then the organization may continue to use the test. If validity cannot be established, however, then a violation of the four-fifths rule may likely result in a lawsuit brought by employees, job applicants, or the EEOC itself.

The City of New Haven, Connecticut, hired an experienced testing firm to develop a set of fair tests to select the best candidates for promotion to 8 lieutenant's jobs and 7 captain's positions in its Fire Department. Thirty-four of the 77 people who took the *lieutenant's* selection *test* passed, 25 of whom were white, 6 were black, and 3 were Hispanic. Under the city's guidelines, only the 10 top candidates could be offered positions for the 8 lieutenant's jobs. All were white. Of the 41 people who took the *captain's selection test*, 22 passed, 16 of whom were white, 3 were black, and 3 were Hispanic. Again, under the city's guidelines, only the top 9 candidates could be offered positions for the 7 captain's jobs. This time, 7 were white and 2 were Hispanic. These results, in which black and Hispanic applicants appeared to be disadvantaged, were exactly what the city was hoping to avoid. After contentious public hearings, the City's board split its vote 2–2 on whether to use the test results to make promotion decisions. The split vote automatically decertified the test results, which meant that the city would not use the test scores to make promotion decisions.

In a 5–4 decision, the U.S. Supreme Court ruled that the city violated Title VII of the 1964 Civil Rights Act, whose purpose is "to promote hiring on the basis of job qualifications, rather than on the basis of race or color." Justice Kennedy, writing for the court's majority, said, "Whatever the City's ultimate aim—however well intentioned or benevolent it might have seemed—the City made its employment decision because of race. The City rejected the test results solely because the higher scoring candidates were white." Kennedy went on to say that the City's action of tossing the test results amounted to a "de facto quota system." This practice, he said, would allow "an employer to discard test results (or other employment practices) with the intent of obtaining the employer's preferred racial balance." Therefore, the court ruled that because the tests were valid and job related, the test scores should have been used to decide who should be promoted to lieutenant or captain.[32]

2.3 Sexual Harassment

According to the EEOC, **sexual harassment** is a form of discrimination in which unwelcome sexual advances, requests for sexual favors, or other verbal or physical conduct of a sexual nature occurs. From a legal perspective, there are two kinds of sexual harassment, quid pro quo and hostile work environment.[33]

Quid pro quo sexual harassment occurs when employment outcomes, such as hiring, promotion, or simply keeping one's job, depend on whether an individual submits to being sexually harassed. For example, in a quid pro quo sexual harassment lawsuit against **First Student**, a company that provides school bus transportation, four females alleged that a supervisor made elicit comments about their bodies and what he wanted to do to them. He was also alleged to have touched a female worker's breasts, exposed himself, and then rubbed himself against her. When his sexual advances were refused, he punished the women by cutting their work hours,

sexual harassment a form of discrimination in which unwelcome sexual advances, requests for sexual favors, or other verbal or physical conduct of a sexual nature occurs while performing one's job.

quid pro quo sexual harassment a form of sexual harassment in which employment outcomes, such as hiring, promotion, or simply keeping one's job, depend on whether an individual submits to sexual harassment.

< **"what's new" companies**

while promising longer hours to the other women if they would do what he asked. This made it a quid pro quo case by linking sexual acts to economic outcomes.[34]

A **hostile work environment** occurs when unwelcome and demeaning sexually related behavior creates an intimidating, hostile, and offensive work environment. In contrast to quid pro quo cases, a hostile work environment may not result in economic injury. However, it can lead to psychological injury from a stressful work environment. **ABM Industries**, a building maintenance company, agreed to pay $5.8 million for creating a sexually hostile work environment for 21 female janitors. The EEOC had charged that male employees exposed themselves and that the women were subject to unwelcome sexual advances. Moreover, when the women complained to management, they were ignored. One of the women said, "I asked for help and they wouldn't help me. Instead my supervisor would laugh at me even more."[35]

"what's new" >
companies

What common mistakes do managers make when it comes to sexual harassment laws?[36] First, many assume that the victim and harasser must be of opposite sexes. According to the courts, they do not. Sexual harassment can also occur between people of the same sex. Second, managers often assume that sexual harassment can occur only between coworkers or between supervisors and subordinates. Not so. Agents of employers, such as consultants, and even nonemployees can be sexual harassers. The key is not employee status, but whether the harassment takes place while company business is being conducted. Third, it is often assumed that only people who have themselves been harassed can file complaints or lawsuits. In fact, especially in hostile work environments, anyone affected by offensive conduct can file a complaint or lawsuit.

Finally, what should companies do to make sure that sexual harassment laws are followed and not violated?[37] First, respond immediately when sexual harassment is reported. A quick response encourages victims of sexual harassment to report problems to management rather than to lawyers or the EEOC. Furthermore, a quick and fair investigation may serve as a deterrent to future harassment. A lawyer for the EEOC says, "Worse than having no sexual harassment policy is a policy that is not followed. It's merely window dressing. You wind up with destroyed morale when people who come forward are ignored, ridiculed, retaliated against, or nothing happens to the harasser."[38] Next, take the time to write a clear, understandable sexual harassment policy that is strongly worded, gives specific examples of what constitutes sexual harassment, spells outs sanctions and punishments, and is widely publicized within the company. This lets potential harassers and victims know what will not be tolerated and how the firm will deal with harassment should it occur.

hostile work environment a form of sexual harassment in which unwelcome and demeaning sexually related behavior creates an intimidating and offensive work environment.

Next, establish clear reporting procedures that indicate how, where, and to whom incidents of sexual harassment can be reported. The best procedures ensure that a complaint will receive a quick response, that impartial parties will handle the complaint, and that the privacy of the accused and accuser will be protected. At DuPont, Avon, and Texas Industries, employees can call a confidential hotline 24 hours a day, 365 days a year.[39]

Finally, managers should also be aware that most states and many cities or local governments have their own employment-related laws and enforcement agencies. So compliance with federal law is often not enough. In fact, organizations can be in full compliance with federal law and at the same time be in violation of state or local sexual harassment laws.

© iStockphoto.com/Andrew Johnson

At DuPont, Avon, and Texas Industries, employees can call a confidential hotline 24 hours a day, 365 days a year, to report sexual harassment.

Employment Legislation   Human resource management is subject to the following major federal employment laws: Equal Pay Act, Civil Rights Acts of 1964 and 1991, Age Discrimination in Employment Act, Pregnancy Discrimination Act, Americans with Disabilities Act, Family and Medical Leave Act, and Uniformed Services Employment and Reemployment Rights Act. Human resource management is also subject to review by these federal agencies: Equal Employment Opportunity Commission, Department of Labor, Occupational Safety and Health Administration, and National Labor Relations Board. In general, these laws state that sex, age, religion, color, national origin, race, disability, and pregnancy may not be considered in employment decisions unless these factors reasonably qualify as BFOQs. Two important criteria, disparate treatment (intentional discrimination) and adverse impact (unintentional discrimination), are used to decide whether companies have wrongly discriminated against someone. Motive is a key part of determining disparate treatment; the courts and federal enforcement agencies use the four-fifths rule to determine whether adverse impact has occurred. The two kinds of sexual harassment are quid pro quo and hostile work environment. Managers often wrongly assume that the victim and harasser must be of the opposite sex, that sexual harassment can occur only between coworkers or between supervisors and their employees, and that only people who have themselves been harassed can file complaints or lawsuits. To ensure compliance with sexual harassment laws, companies should respond immediately when harassment is reported; write a clear, understandable sexual harassment policy; establish clear reporting procedures; and be aware of and follow city and state laws concerning sexual harassment.

Review 2

Finding Qualified Workers

Despite the highest average wages in the country, Australia's mining companies are finding it nearly impossible to find the workers they need. David Knox, CEO of Santos, Ltd., an oil and gas exploration and production company, said, "One of the real challenges in Australia is continuing to get a really high-quality, high-skilled labor force."[40] With some estimating that the industry needs as many as 70,000 to 100,000 more skilled workers, Australian mining companies have had to go as far as London, Berlin, Amsterdam, and India to find and recruit applicants. Similar shortages occur in dairy farming. Ed Schoen, who runs a 180-cow farm and is on the board of the **Dairy Farmers of America**, said, "We need a stable supply of labor. The dairy industry's survival depends on it . . . worrying about workers is another level of stress we don't need."[41] As these examples illustrate, finding qualified workers can be an increasingly difficult task. But finding qualified applicants is just the first step. Deciding which applicants to hire is the second. Gail Hyland-Savage, CEO of real estate and marketing firm Michaelson, Connor & Boul, says, "Staffing is absolutely critical to the success of every company. To be competitive in today's economy, companies

< **"what's new" companies**

After reading the next two sections, you should be able to

3. *Explain how companies use recruiting to find qualified job applicants.*

4. *Describe the selection techniques and procedures that companies use when deciding which applicants should receive job offers.*

need the best people to create ideas and execute them for the organization. Without a competent and talented workforce, organizations will stagnate and eventually perish. The right employees are the most important resources of companies today."[42]

3 Recruiting

Recruiting is the process of developing a pool of qualified job applicants. Let's examine **3.1 what job analysis is and how it is used in recruiting, 3.2 how companies use internal recruiting,** and **3.3 external recruiting to find qualified job applicants.**

3.1 Job Analysis and Recruiting

Job analysis is a "purposeful, systematic process for collecting information on the important work-related aspects of a job."[43] A job analysis typically collects four kinds of information:

> » Work activities such as what workers do and how, when, and why they do it.
> » The tools and equipment used to do the job.
> » The context in which the job is performed, such as the actual working conditions or schedule.
> » The personnel requirements for performing the job, meaning the knowledge, skills, and abilities needed to do a job well.[44]

Job analysis information can be collected by having job incumbents and/or supervisors complete questionnaires about their jobs or by direct observation, interviews, or filming employees as they perform their jobs.

Job descriptions and job specifications are two of the most important results of a job analysis. A **job description** is a written description of the basic tasks, duties, and responsibilities required of an employee holding a particular job. **Job specifications**, which are often included as a separate section of a job description, are a summary of the qualifications needed to successfully perform the job. Exhibit 11.5 shows a job description and the job specifications for a helicopter pilot for the city of Little Rock, Arkansas.

Because a job analysis specifies what a job entails as well as the knowledge, skills, and abilities that are needed to do the job well, companies must complete a job analysis *before* beginning to recruit job applicants. Exhibit 11.6 shows that job analysis, job descriptions, and job specifications are the foundation on which all critical human resource activities are built. They are used during recruiting and selection to match applicant qualifications with the requirements of the job. Sioux Logan, of **RedStream Technology**, an IT staffing company, uses job descriptions to sort through the hundreds of applicants she gets for each job. She explains that when she narrows the pool to the best applicants, "I [will] resend the job description first by email [because] a lot of times people apply for many jobs without reading the whole job description." She does this to make sure they really want the job. Then she uses the subsequent email exchanges to judge applicants' professionalism and writing skills. By having applicants read and respond to the job description, Logan is giving them the opportunity to make the case to her that they are a good match for the job. The exchange of emails also allows her to evaluate the applicants' writing skills and professionalism, giving her one more way to make sure she's got the right person for the job.[45]

recruiting the process of developing a pool of qualified job applicants.

job analysis a purposeful, systematic process for collecting information on the important work-related aspects of a job.

job description a written description of the basic tasks, duties, and responsibilities required of an employee holding a particular job.

job specifications a written summary of the qualifications needed to successfully perform a particular job.

"what's new" companies >

Exhibit 11.5 Job Description and Job Specifications for a Helicopter Pilot for the City of Little Rock, Arkansas

DESCRIPTION FOR HELICOPTER PILOT

To provide assistance for air searches, river rescues, high-rise building rescues, and other assignments, by providing air survey and aviation response. Pilots a rotary-wing aircraft, serving as pilot or copilot, to assist in air searches, river rescues, high-rise building rescues, and other assignments. Ensures that aircraft is properly outfitted for each assignment (equipment, rigging tools, supplies, etc.). Performs preflight inspection of aircraft; checks rotors, fuel, lubricants, controls, etc. Prepares written reports on assignments; maintains flight logs. Obtains weather reports; determines to proceed with assignments given forecasted weather conditions. Operates a radio to maintain contact with and to report information to airport personnel and police department personnel.

JOB SPECIFICATIONS FOR HELICOPTER PILOT

Must possess a valid Commercial Pilot's License for rotary-wing aircraft before employment and maintain licensure for the duration of employment in this position. Must have considerable knowledge of Federal Aviation Administration (FAA) laws and regulations, rotary-wing aircraft operating procedures, air traffic safety, flying procedures and navigational techniques, and FAA and police radio operation and procedures. Must have some knowledge of preventive maintenance methods, repair practices, safety requirements, and inspection procedures. Must have skill in the operation of a rotary-wing aircraft and radio equipment and the ability to conduct safety inspections of aircraft, to maintain aircraft maintenance logs and prepare reports, to detect and identify aircraft malfunction symptoms, to detect and recognize ground conditions and characteristics (utility line breaks, river currents, etc.), to read maps and air navigation charts, and to communicate effectively, both orally and in writing. Must have completed high school; at least one thousand hours of flight time experience in piloting rotary-wing aircraft; OR any equivalent combination of experience and training that provides the required knowledge, skills, and abilities.

Source: "Job Description: Helicopter Pilot," City of Little Rock, Arkansas, www.littlerock.org, May 31, 2003.

Job descriptions are also used throughout the staffing process to ensure that selection devices and the decisions based on these devices are job related. For example, the questions asked in an interview should be based on the most important work activities identified by a job analysis. Likewise, during performance appraisals, employees should be evaluated in areas that a job analysis has identified as the most important in a job.

Job analyses, job descriptions, and job specifications also help companies meet the legal requirement that their human resource decisions be job related. To be judged *job related*, recruitment, selection, training, performance appraisals, and employee separations must be valid and be directly related to the important aspects of the job as identified by a careful job analysis. In fact, in *Griggs v. Duke Power Co.* and *Albemarle Paper Co. v. Moody*, the U.S. Supreme Court stated that companies should use job analyses to help establish the job relatedness of their human resource procedures.[46] The EEOC's *Uniform Guidelines on Employee Selection Procedures* also recommend that companies base their human resource procedures on job analysis.

3.2 Internal Recruiting

Internal recruiting is the process of developing a pool of qualified job applicants from people who already work in the company. Internal recruiting, sometimes called "promotion from within," improves employee commitment, morale, and motivation. Recruiting current employees also reduces recruitment start-up time and costs, and because employees are already familiar with the company's culture and procedures, they are more likely to succeed in new jobs. Internal recruitment "provides a higher level of

internal recruiting the process of developing a pool of qualified job applicants from people who already work in the company.

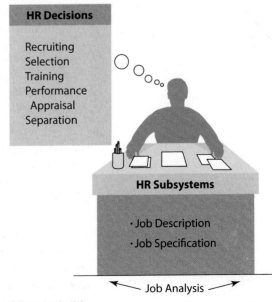

Exhibit 11.6
Importance of Job Analysis to Human Resource Management

HR Decisions

Recruiting
Selection
Training
Performance
 Appraisal
Separation

HR Subsystems

· Job Description
· Job Specification

← Job Analysis →

© Cengage Learning 2013

employee satisfaction, so certainly it can be a retention driver," says Maureen Henson, vice president of human resources at Henry Ford Bi-County Hospital in Warren, Michigan. Internal applicants represent a "known commodity," relieving some of the risk of making a bad hiring decision.[47] Job posting and career paths are two methods of internal recruiting.

Job posting is a procedure for advertising job openings within the company to existing employees. A job description and requirements are typically posted on a bulletin board, in a company newsletter, or in an internal computerized job bank that is accessible only to employees. Shawna Swanson, an employment litigation partner with Fenwick & West in San Francisco, recommends making the internal and external processes the same, rather than having two separate paths, such as posting internally first for a period of time and then advertising externally.[48] Job posting helps organizations discover hidden talent, allows employees to take responsibility for career planning, and makes it easier for companies to retain talented workers who are dissatisfied in their current jobs and would otherwise leave the company.[49] Tim Reynolds, corporate director of talent and organization development at Whirlpool, the appliance manufacturer, said, "If employees aren't given the opportunity to move within their own company, then they'll get out in the marketplace to get new experiences. As long as they're developing where they are, there's no need to go someplace else."[50] Indeed, a study of 70 large global companies found that organizations which formalize internal recruiting and job posting have a lower average rate of turnover, 11 percent, compared to companies that don't, which average 15 percent turnover.[51]

A *career path* is a planned sequence of jobs through which employees may advance within an organization. For example, 30 years ago, Procter & Gamble CEO Bob McDonald started out as a brand assistant. He then moved up to assistant brand manager and brand manager. From there, he became an associate advertising manager, and then a product manager before taking on various regional management positions. McDonald then became vice president and then president of P&G's Northeast Asia division. He then served as Vice Chairman of Global Operations and COO before finally stepping in as CEO of the world's largest consumer-products company.[52]

3.3 External Recruiting

External recruiting is the process of developing a pool of qualified job applicants from outside the company. For example, Walmart has traditionally promoted from within for store manager jobs. However, the company was unable to keep up with its growth. So Walmart created an external recruiting program to find store managers from the ranks of junior military officers returning from Iraq and Afghanistan who typically led 30 to 40 soldiers. According to Jennifer Seidner, senior recruiting manager at Walmart, this allowed the company to "[b]ring in world-class leadership talent that was already trained and ready to go. And then we could teach them retail, because we know that pretty well." The focus on veterans—company outsiders—is now a critical part of Walmart's recruiting strategy in all parts of the company.[53]

External recruitment methods include advertising (newspapers, magazines, direct mail, radio, or television), employee referrals (asking current employees to recommend possible job applicants), walk-ins (people who apply on their own), outside organizations (universities, technical/trade schools, professional societies), employment services (state or private employment agencies, temporary help agencies, and professional search firms), special events (career conferences or job fairs), and Internet job sites. Which external recruiting method should you use? Studies show that employee referrals, walk-ins, newspaper advertisements, and state employment

external recruiting the process of developing a pool of qualified job applicants from outside the company.

agencies tend to be used most frequently for office/clerical and production/service employees. By contrast, newspaper advertisements and college/university recruiting are used most frequently for professional/technical employees. When recruiting managers, organizations tend to rely most heavily on newspaper advertisements, employee referrals, and search firms.[54]

In the last decade, the biggest change in external recruiting has been the increased use of the Internet. Some companies now recruit applicants through Internet job sites such as Monster.com, HotJobs.com, Hire.com, and CareerBuilder.com. Companies can post job openings for 30 days on one of these sites for about half the cost of running an advertisement just once in a Sunday newspaper. Plus, Internet job listings generate nine times as many résumés as one ad in the Sunday newspaper.[55] And because these sites attract so many applicants and offer so many services, companies save by finding qualified applicants without having to use more expensive recruitment and search firms, which typically charge one-third or more of a new hire's salary.[56]

Some companies have even begun using search-engine ads, where, for example, a recruiting advertisement will be found on websites next to key words like "accountant" or "nurse." These ads can be restricted by zip codes so that a company looking for an accountant in Indianapolis doesn't have ads shown to potential applicants in Los Angeles. Because they only pay when the recruiting ads are clicked on, search-engine ads can be even cheaper than job websites. And for some companies, they also attract more applicants. Baylor Health Care System, a large health-care company in Dallas, found that search-engine ads generated 5,250 applicants at a cost of $4 per applicant, job websites generated 3,125 applicants at a cost of $30 each, and newspaper and magazine ads generated just 215 applicants at a cost of $750 per applicant. Eileen Bouthillet, Baylor's director of human resources communications, said, "Before we were throwing darts at a dart board trying to see what might stick. Now we have a very targeted strategy and a point of comparison so we can make wise decisions on where we spend our money."[57]

Despite their many benefits, however, job websites have a significant drawback: Companies may receive hundreds, if not thousands, of applications from *unqualified* applicants. The sheer volume increases the importance of proper screening and selection. When **Apex Companies**, an environmental consulting firm, was hiring an industrial hygienist, a position that pays $47,000 a year and requires specialized training certification, it received 150 applicants, three times as many as normal. But only five were qualified for the position. Carolyn Henn, Apex's head of hiring, said, "We've always been looking for a needle in a haystack. There's still only one needle, but the haystack has gotten a lot bigger than it was before."[58] For example, Subway accepts applications for part-time work at its 34,605 restaurants in 98 countries at its website (www.mysubwaycareer.com). In fact, 60 percent of the people hired via the Internet have applied at a company website.

Today, between 82 percent and 92 percent of companies use the Internet to fill job openings. In fact, Internet recruiting is now second to newspaper advertising in terms of the number of applicants it generates.[59] And with the addition of the ".jobs" Internet top-level domain (for example, www.ibm.jobs for jobs at IBM), more and more companies will use their websites to attract, recruit, and screen job applicants.[60] That's because job seekers tend to visit company websites *before* looking

< **"what's new" companies**

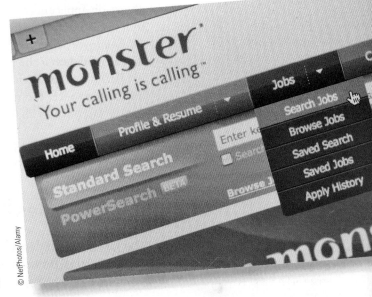

© NetPhotos/Alamy

for a job through more general sites. In fact, 95 percent of *Fortune* 500 companies have career portals on their corporate websites.[61] A recent survey conducted by SHRM indicates that companies that leverage the .jobs domain have more effective recruiting practices across a range of areas and that the domain provides job seekers with a simple, fast, and convenient destination when job hunting.[62]

Review 3

Recruiting   Recruiting is the process of finding qualified job applicants. The first step in recruiting is to conduct a job analysis to collect information about the important work-related aspects of the job. The job analysis is then used to write a job description of basic tasks, duties, and responsibilities and to write job specifications indicating the knowledge, skills, and abilities needed to perform the job. Job analyses, descriptions, and specifications help companies meet the legal requirement that their human resource decisions be job related. Internal recruiting, or finding qualified job applicants from inside the company, can be done through job posting and career paths. External recruiting, or finding qualified job applicants from outside the company, is done through advertising, employee referrals, walk-ins, outside organizations, employment services, special events, and Internet job sites. The Internet is a particularly promising method of external recruiting because of its low cost, wide reach, and ability to communicate and receive unlimited information.

4 Selection

Once the recruitment process has produced a pool of qualified applicants, the selection process is used to determine which applicants have the best chance of performing well on the job. At Boston Consulting Group (BCG), one of the world's premiere consulting firms, a team of three recruiters examine resumes from 30 universities. Mel Wolfgang, a partner who heads Americas recruiting for BCG, says, "We look for well-rounded individuals whose interests and life experiences suggest that they would adapt well. We look for evidence that they have led and been empathic with a team or challenging situations." Only six applicants are chosen for a 40-minute interview with two BCG consultants. From there, three applicants go on to second-round interviews with four BCG partners. After consulting with the consultants and partners who conducted interviews, the hiring manager makes the final decision.[63]

As this example illustrates, **selection** is the process of gathering information about job applicants to decide who should be offered a job. To make sure that selection decisions are accurate and legally defensible, the EEOC's *Uniform Guidelines on Employee Selection Procedures* recommend that all selection procedures be validated. **Validation** is the process of determining how well a selection test or procedure predicts future job performance. The better or more accurate the prediction of future job performance, the more valid a test is said to be. See the What Really Works feature later in this chapter for more on the validity of common selection tests and procedures.

Let's examine common selection procedures such as **4.1 application forms and résumés, 4.2 references and background checks, 4.3 selection tests,** and **4.4 interviews.**

4.1 Application Forms and Résumés

The first selection devices that most job applicants encounter when they seek a job are application forms and résumés. Both contain similar information about an applicant, such as name, address, job and educational history, and so forth. Though an

selection the process of gathering information about job applicants to decide who should be offered a job.

validation the process of determining how well a selection test or procedure predicts future job performance. The better or more accurate the prediction of future job performance, the more valid a test is said to be.

Exhibit 11.7 Topics That Employers Should Avoid in Application Forms, Interviews, or Other Parts of the Selection Process

1. *Children.* Don't ask applicants if they have children, plan to have them, or have or need child care. Questions about children can unintentionally single out women.

2. *Age.* Because of the Age Discrimination in Employment Act, employers cannot ask job applicants their age during the hiring process. Since most people graduate high school at the age of 18, even asking for high school graduation dates could violate the law.

3. *Disabilities.* Don't ask if applicants have physical or mental disabilities. According to the Americans with Disabilities Act, disabilities (and reasonable accommodations for them) cannot be discussed until a job offer has been made.

4. *Physical characteristics.* Don't ask for information about height, weight, or other physical characteristics. Questions about weight could be construed as leading to discrimination toward overweight people, who studies show are less likely to be hired in general.

5. *Name.* Yes, you can ask an applicant's name, but you cannot ask a female applicant for her maiden name because it indicates marital status. Asking for a maiden name could also lead to charges that the organization was trying to establish a candidate's ethnic background.

6. *Citizenship.* Asking applicants about citizenship could lead to claims of discrimination on the basis of national origin. However, according to the Immigration Reform and Control Act, companies may ask applicants if they have a legal right to work in the United States.

7. *Lawsuits.* Applicants may not be asked if they have ever filed a lawsuit against an employer. Federal and state laws prevent this to protect whistleblowers from retaliation by future employers.

8. *Arrest records.* Applicants cannot be asked about their arrest records. Arrests don't have legal standing. However, applicants can be asked whether they have been convicted of a crime.

9. *Smoking.* Applicants cannot be asked if they smoke. Smokers might be able to claim that they weren't hired because of fears of higher absenteeism and medical costs. However, they can be asked if they are aware of company policies that restrict smoking at work.

10. *AIDS/HIV.* Applicants can't be asked about AIDS, HIV, or any other medical condition. Questions of this nature would violate the Americans with Disabilities Act, as well as federal and state civil rights laws.

Source: J. S. Pouliot, "Topics to Avoid with Applicants," *Nation's Business* 80, no. 7 (1992): 57.

organization's application form often asks for information already provided by the applicant's résumé, most organizations prefer to collect this information in their own format for entry into a human resource information system.

Employment laws apply to application forms just as they do to all selection devices. Application forms may ask applicants only for valid, job-related information. Nonetheless, application forms commonly ask applicants for non-job-related information such as marital status, maiden name, age, or date of high school graduation. Indeed, one study found that 73 percent of organizations had application forms that violated at least one federal or state law.[64] Exhibit 11.7 lists the kinds of information that companies may *not* request in application forms, during job interviews, or in any other part of the selection process. Courts will assume that you consider all of the information you request of applicants even if you actually don't. Be sure to ask only those questions that directly relate to the candidate's ability and motivation to perform the job.

Companies should also be aware that employment laws in other countries may differ from U.S. laws. For instance, employers in France may ask applicants for non-job-related personal information such as their age or the number of children. And most French employers expect applicants to include a picture with their résumé.[65] Consequently, companies should closely examine their application forms, interview questions, and other selection procedures for compliance with the law wherever they do business.

Résumés also pose problems for companies, but in a different way. Accu-Screen Inc. has kept records for 14 years on résumé falsification data and reports that approximately 43 percent of résumés and job applications contain false information. According to a study conducted by J.J. Keller & Associates, Inc., the nation's leading provider of risk and regulatory management solutions, 55 percent of human resource professionals have discovered lies on résumés or applications when conducting pre-employment background or reference checks.[66] Therefore, managers should verify the information collected via résumés and application forms by comparing it with additional information collected during interviews and other stages of the selection process, such as references and background checks, which are discussed next.

4.2 References and Background Checks

Nearly all companies ask an applicant to provide **employment references**, such as previous employers or coworkers, whom they can contact to learn more about the candidate. **Background checks** are used to verify the truthfulness and accuracy of information that applicants provide about themselves and to uncover negative, job-related background information not provided by applicants. Background checks are conducted by contacting "educational institutions, prior employers, court records, police and governmental agencies, and other informational sources, either by telephone, mail, remote computer access, or through in-person investigations."[67]

Unfortunately, previous employers are increasingly reluctant to provide references or background check information for fear of being sued by previous employees for defamation.[68] If former employers provide potential employers with unsubstantiated information that damages applicants' chances of being hired, applicants can (and do) sue for defamation. As a result, 54 percent of employers will not provide information about previous employees.[69] Many provide only dates of employment, positions held, and date of separation.

When previous employers decline to provide meaningful references or background information, they put other employers at risk of *negligent hiring* lawsuits, in which an employer is held liable for the actions of an employee who would not have been hired if the employer had conducted a thorough reference search and background check.[70] A Chicago family sued McDonald's for negligent hiring when an employee, a playground equipment cleaner, exposed himself to their 10-year old daughter. The employee later pled guilty to sexual exploitation of a child. According to the lawsuit, McDonalds did not perform a background check on the employee, which would have revealed that he had previously been arrested for public indecency and criminal sexual abuse.[71]

With previous employers generally unwilling to give full, candid references and with negligent hiring lawsuits awaiting companies that don't get such references and background information, what can companies do? They can conduct criminal record checks, especially if the job for which the person is applying involves money, drugs, control over valuable goods, or access to the elderly or children, people with disabilities, or people's homes.[72] According to the Society for Human Resource Management, 96 percent of companies conduct background checks and 80 percent of companies go further and conduct criminal record checks.[73] Now that companies provide criminal record checks for $10 an applicant, pulling data from 3,100 court systems nationwide, there's no excuse not to check. Louis DeFalco, corporate director of safety, security and investigations at ABC Fine Wine & Spirits, which has 175 stores in Florida, makes the case for criminal record checks: "If I have a guy with four arrests and bad credit versus someone who has never been in trouble in his life, who am I going to hire? It's not rocket science."[74]

employment references sources such as previous employers or coworkers who can provide job-related information about job candidates.

background checks procedures used to verify the truthfulness and accuracy of information that applicants provide about themselves and to uncover negative, job-related background information not provided by applicants.

Another option is to use public networking sites like www.linkedin.com to identify and contact the colleagues, customers, and suppliers who are "linked" or connected to job applicants. LinkedIn's CEO Dan Nye says that the company called 23 of his LinkedIn connections without his knowledge before offering him a face-to-face interview. With the growing use and popularity of social networking websites, Nye says such practices are "fair game." One downside to this approach is that it could unintentionally alert an applicant's current employer that they're seeking another job. As a result, says Chuck Wardell, managing director at Korn/Ferry International, an executive recruitment firm, "You have to be careful referencing people who have jobs because you might blow them out of their jobs."[75]

After doing a background check, dig deeper for more information. Ask references to provide references. Voca Corporation, based in Columbus, Ohio, has 2,500 employees, in six states, who care for people with mental retardation and developmental disabilities. Hilary Franklin, director of human resources, says she not only checks references but also asks the references to provide references and then asks those references for still others. She says, "As you get two or three times removed, you get more detailed, honest information."[76]

So be sure to ask applicants to sign a waiver that permits you to check references, run a background check, or contact anyone else with knowledge of their work performance or history. Likewise, ask applicants whether there is anything they would like the company to know or whether they expect you to hear anything unusual when contacting references.[77] This in itself is often enough to get applicants to share information they typically withhold. When you've finished checking, keep the findings confidential to minimize the chances of a defamation charge. Always document all reference and background checks, noting who was called and what information was obtained. Document everything, not just information you received. To reduce the likelihood that negligent hiring lawsuits will succeed, it's particularly important to document even which companies and people refused to share reference check and background information.

Finally, consider hiring private investigators to conduct background checks, which can often uncover information missed by traditional background checks. For example, while traditional background checks should be able to verify applicants' academic credentials, a private investigator hired by *The Wall Street Journal* found that 7 out of 358 senior executives at publicly traded firms had falsified claims regarding the college degrees they had earned. For example, Ronald Zarallela, former CEO of Bausch & Lomb, claimed to have earned an MBA from New York University, though he never completed the program. Dave Edmondson, former CEO of Radio Shack, said that he earned a degree in psychology from Pacific Coast Baptist College (California), even though the school didn't have a psychology program.[78] Although these are just two examples, remember that traditional background checks didn't uncover the false academic credentials discovered by a private investigator.

4.3 Selection Tests

We're all aware that some people do well in jobs, whereas other people do poorly, but how do you determine into which category an applicant falls? Selection tests give organizational decision makers a chance to know who will likely do well in a job and who won't. The basic idea behind selection testing is to have applicants take a test that measures something directly or indirectly related to doing well on the job. The selection tests discussed here are specific ability tests, cognitive ability tests, biographical data, personality tests, work sample tests, and assessment centers.

Exhibit 11.8 Clerical Test Items Similar to Those Found on the Minnesota Clerical Test

NUMBERS/LETTERS		SAME	
1. 3468251	3467251	Yes	No
2. 4681371	4681371	Yes	No
3. 7218510	7218520	Yes	No
4. ZXYAZAB	ZXYAZAB	Yes	No
5. ALZYXMN	ALZYXNM	Yes	No
6. PRQZYMN	PRQZYMN	Yes	No

Source: N. W. Schmitt & R. J. Klimoski, *Research Methods in Human Resource Management* (Mason, OH: South-Western, 1991). Used with permission.

Specific ability tests measure the extent to which an applicant possesses the particular kind of ability needed to do a job well. Specific ability tests are also called **aptitude tests** because they measure aptitude for doing a particular task well. For example, if you took the SAT to get into college, then you've taken the aptly named Scholastic Aptitude Test, which is one of the best predictors of how well students will do in college (i.e., scholastic performance). Specific ability tests also exist for mechanical, clerical, sales, and physical work. For example, clerical workers have to be good at accurately reading and scanning numbers as they type or enter data. Exhibit 11.8 shows items similar to the Minnesota Clerical Test, in which applicants have only a short time to determine whether the two columns of numbers and letters are identical. Applicants who are good at this are likely to do well as clerical or data entry workers.

Cognitive ability tests measure the extent to which applicants have abilities in perceptual speed, verbal comprehension, numerical aptitude, general reasoning, and spatial aptitude. In other words, these tests indicate how quickly and how well people understand words, numbers, logic, and spatial dimensions. Whereas specific ability tests predict job performance in only particular types of jobs, cognitive ability tests accurately predict job performance in almost all kinds of jobs.[79] Why is this so? The reason is that people with strong cognitive or mental abilities are usually good at learning new things, processing complex information, solving problems, and making decisions, and these abilities are important in almost all jobs.[80] In fact, cognitive ability tests are almost always the best predictors of job performance. Consequently, if you were allowed to use just one selection test, a cognitive ability test would be the one to use.[81] (In practice, though, companies use a battery of different tests because doing so leads to much more accurate selection decisions.)

Biographical data, or **biodata**, are extensive surveys that ask applicants questions about their personal backgrounds and life experiences. The basic idea behind biodata is that past behavior (personal background and life experience) is the best predictor of future behavior. For example, during World War II, the U.S. Air Force had to test tens of thousands of men without flying experience to determine who was likely to be a good pilot. Because flight training took several months and was very expensive, quickly selecting the right people for training was important. After examining extensive biodata, it found that one of the best predictors of success in flight school was whether students had ever built model airplanes that actually flew. This one biodata item was almost as good a predictor as the entire set of selection tests that the Air Force was using at the time.[82]

Most biodata questionnaires have over 100 items that gather information about habits and attitudes, health, interpersonal relations, money, what it was like growing up in your family (parents, siblings, childhood years, teen years), personal habits, current home (spouse, children), hobbies, education and training, values, preferences, and work.[83] In general, biodata are very good predictors of future job performance, especially in entry-level jobs.

You may have noticed that some of the information requested in biodata surveys also appears in Exhibit 11.7 as topics employers should avoid in applications, interviews, or other parts of the selection process. This information can be requested in biodata questionnaires provided that the company can demonstrate that the information is job related (i.e., valid) and does not result in adverse impact against protected groups of job applicants. Biodata surveys should be validated and tested for adverse impact before they are used to make selection decisions.[84]

specific ability tests (aptitude tests) tests that measure the extent to which an applicant possesses the particular kind of ability needed to do a job well.

cognitive ability tests tests that measure the extent to which applicants have abilities in perceptual speed, verbal comprehension, numerical aptitude, general reasoning, and spatial aptitude.

biographical data (biodata) extensive surveys that ask applicants questions about their personal backgrounds and life experiences.

doing the right thing

Don't Use Psychics, Lie Detectors, or Handwriting Analysis to Make HR Decisions

The Coronado Bay Resort in San Diego hired a psychic to work with its 18-member management team as a way of "moving the managers to the next step." Seventy-five percent of the organizations in France and Switzerland use handwriting analysis for hiring and promotion decisions. In the past, employers in the United States regularly used polygraphs (lie detectors) for pre-employment screening. What do these methods have in common? Companies use them, but they don't work. For example, there is no scientific evidence that handwriting analysis works, yet managers continue to use it. Lie detectors are no more accurate than a coin flip in screening out unethical employees. Fortunately, the Employee Polygraph Protection Act now prevents organizations from using polygraphs for hiring and promotion decisions. As for psychics at work—well, enough said. So, when you're hiring and promoting people, do the right thing. Stay away from fads. Use the reliable, valid, scientifically proven selection and assessment procedures discussed here to hire the right workers and promote the right people into management.[85]

Personality is the relatively stable set of behaviors, attitudes, and emotions displayed over time that makes people different from each other. **Personality tests** measure the extent to which applicants possess different kinds of job-related personality dimensions. In Chapter 12, you will learn that there are five major personality dimensions (the Big Five)—extroversion, emotional stability, agreeableness, conscientiousness, and openness to experience—related to work behavior.[86] Of these, only conscientiousness, the degree to which someone is organized, hardworking, responsible, persevering, thorough, and achievement oriented, predicts job performance across a wide variety of jobs.[87] Conscientiousness works especially well in combination with cognitive ability tests, allowing companies to select applicants who are organized, hardworking, responsible, and smart!

Work sample tests, also called *performance tests*, require applicants to perform tasks that are actually done on the job. So, unlike specific ability, cognitive ability, biographical data, and personality tests, which are indirect predictors of job performance, work sample tests directly measure job applicants' capability to do the job. For example, a computer-based work sample test has applicants assume the role of a real estate agent who must decide how to interact with virtual clients in a game-like scenario. As in real life, the clients can be frustrating, confusing, demanding, or indecisive. In one situation, the wife loves the virtual house but the husband hates it. The applicants, just like actual real estate agents, must demonstrate what they would do in these realistic situations.[88] This work sample simulation gives real estate companies direct evidence of whether applicants can do the job if they are hired. Work sample tests are generally very good at predicting future job performance; however, they can be expensive to administer and can be used for only one kind of job. For example, an auto dealership could not use a work sample test for mechanics as a selection test for sales representatives.

Assessment centers use a series of job-specific simulations that are graded by multiple trained observers to determine applicants' ability to perform managerial

personality tests tests that measure the extent to which applicants possess different kinds of job-related personality dimensions.

work sample tests tests that require applicants to perform tasks that are actually done on the job.

assessment centers a series of managerial simulations, graded by trained observers, that are used to determine applicants' capability for managerial work.

447

Exhibit 11.9   In-Basket Item for an Assessment Center for Store Managers

```
February 28
Sam & Dave's Discount Warehouse
Orange, California


Dear Store Manager,


Last week, my children and I were shopping in your store.
After doing our grocery shopping, we stopped in the
electronics department and asked the clerk, whose name
is Donald Block, to help us find a copy of the latest
version of the Madden NFL video game. Mr. Block was rude,
unhelpful, and told us to find it for ourselves as he
was busy.


I've been a loyal customer for over six years and expect
you to immediately do something about Mr.Block's
behavior. If you don't, I'll start doing my shopping
somewhere else.


Sincerely,
Margaret Quinlan
```

Source: Adapted from N. W. Schmitt & R. J. Klimoski, *Research Methods in Human Resource Management* (Mason, OH: South-Western, 1991). Used with permission.

work. Unlike the previously described selection tests that are commonly used for specific jobs or entry-level jobs, assessment centers are most often used to select applicants who have high potential to be good managers. Assessment centers often last two to five days and require participants to complete a number of tests and exercises that simulate managerial work.

Some of the more common assessment center exercises are in-basket exercises, role-plays, small-group presentations, and leaderless group discussions. An *in-basket exercise* is a paper-and-pencil test in which an applicant is given a manager's in-basket, containing memos, phone messages, organizational policies, and other communications normally received by and available to managers. Applicants have a limited time to read through the in-basket, prioritize the items, and decide how to deal with each item. Experienced managers then score the applicants' decisions and recommendations. Exhibit 11.9 shows an item that could be used in an assessment center for evaluating applicants for a job as a store manager.

In a *leaderless group discussion*, another common assessment center exercise, a group of six applicants is given approximately two hours to solve a problem, but no one is put in charge (hence the name *leaderless* group discussion). Trained observers watch and score each participant on the extent to which he or she facilitates discussion, listens, leads, persuades, and works well with others.

Are tests perfect predictors of job performance? No, they aren't. Some people who do well on selection tests will do poorly in their jobs. Likewise, some people who do poorly on selection tests (and therefore weren't hired) would have been very good performers. Nonetheless, valid tests will minimize selection errors (hiring people who should not have been hired and not hiring people who should have been hired), while maximizing correct selection decisions (hiring people who should have been hired and not hiring people who should not have been hired). In short, tests increase the chances that you'll hire the right person for the job, that is, someone who turns out to be a good performer. So, although tests aren't perfect, almost nothing predicts future job performance as well as the selection tests discussed here. For more on how well selection tests increase the odds of hiring the right person for the job, see the What Really Works feature.

4.4 Interviews

Sharon Ball, director of recruiting and administration for Epitec Group, has interviewed all kinds of mistake-prone job candidates: one with food on his sweater, another with breath that "smelled like bile," one who reeked of marijuana, and one who stopped the interview to talk on his cell phone for five minutes. Only the applicant with bad breath was hired. She says, "Nice guy. We had to pump him full of Tic Tacs."[89] In **interviews**, company representatives ask job applicants job-related questions to determine whether they are qualified for the job. Interviews are probably the most frequently used and relied on selection device. There are several basic kinds of interviews: unstructured, structured, and semistructured.

interviews a selection tool in which company representatives ask job applicants job-related questions to determine whether they are qualified for the job.

what really works

Using Selection Tests to Hire Good Workers

Hiring new employees is always something of a gamble. When you say, "We'd like to offer you the job," you never know how it's going to turn out. Nonetheless, the selection tests discussed in this chapter can go a long way toward taking the gambling aspect out of the hiring process. Indeed, more than 1,000 studies based on over 100,000 study participants strongly indicate that selection tests can give employers a much better than average (50–50) chance of hiring the right workers. If you had odds like these working for you in Las Vegas, you'd make so much money the casinos wouldn't let you in the door.

Cognitive Ability Tests

There is a 76 percent chance that applicants who do well on cognitive ability tests will be much better performers in their jobs than applicants who do not do well on such tests.

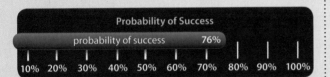

Work Sample Tests

There is a 77 percent chance that applicants who do well on work sample tests will be much better performers in their jobs than applicants who do not do well on such tests.

Assessment Centers

There is a 69 percent chance that applicants who do well on assessment center exercises will be much better managers than applicants who do not do well on such exercises.

Structured Interviews

There is a 76 percent chance that applicants who do well in structured interviews will be much better performers in their jobs than applicants who do not do well in such interviews.

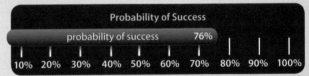

Cognitive Ability—Work Sample Tests

When deciding whom to hire, most companies use a number of tests to make even more accurate selection decisions. There is an 82 percent chance that applicants who do well on a combination of cognitive ability tests and work sample tests will be much better performers in their jobs than applicants who do not do well on both tests.

© Cengage Learning 2013

(continued)

Cognitive Ability—Integrity Tests

There is an 83 percent chance that applicants who do well on a combination of cognitive ability tests and integrity tests (see Chapter 4 for a discussion of integrity tests) will be much better performers in their jobs than applicants who do not do well on both tests.

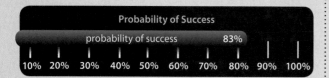

Probability of Success
probability of success 83%
10% 20% 30% 40% 50% 60% 70% 80% 90% 100%

Cognitive Ability—Structured Interviews

There is an 82 percent chance that applicants who do well on a combination of cognitive ability tests and structured interviews will be much better performers in their jobs than applicants who do not do well on both tests.[90]

Probability of Success
probability of success 82%
10% 20% 30% 40% 50% 60% 70% 80% 90% 100%

In **unstructured interviews,** interviewers are free to ask applicants anything they want, and studies show that they do. Because interviewers often disagree about which questions should be asked during interviews, different interviewers tend to ask applicants very different questions.[91] Furthermore, individual interviewers even seem to have a tough time asking the same questions from one interview to the next. This high level of variety can make things difficult. As a result, although unstructured interviews do predict job performance with some success, they are about half as accurate as structured interviews at predicting which job applicants should be hired.[92]

By contrast, with **structured interviews,** standardized interview questions are prepared ahead of time so that all applicants are asked the same job-related questions.[93] Four kinds of questions are typically asked in structured interviews:

unstructured interviews interviews in which interviewers are free to ask the applicants anything they want.

structured interviews interviews in which all applicants are asked the same set of standardized questions, usually including situational, behavioral, background, and job-knowledge questions.

» Situational questions ask applicants how they would respond in a hypothetical situation ("What would you do if . . . ?"). These questions are more appropriate for hiring new graduates, who are unlikely to have encountered real-work situations because of their limited work experience.

>> Behavioral questions ask applicants what they did in previous jobs that were similar to the job for which they are applying ("In your previous jobs, tell me about . . . ."). These questions are more appropriate for hiring experienced individuals.

>> Background questions ask applicants about their work experience, education, and other qualifications ("Tell me about the training you received at . . . .").

>> Job-knowledge questions ask applicants to demonstrate their job knowledge (e.g., nurses might be asked, "Give me an example of a time when one of your patients had a severe reaction to a medication. How did you handle it?").[94]

The primary advantage of structured interviews is that comparing applicants is much easier because they are all asked the same questions. Structuring interviews also ensures that interviewers ask only for important, job-related information. Not only are the accuracy, usefulness, and validity of the interview improved, but the chances that interviewers will ask questions about topics that violate employment laws are reduced (go back to Exhibit 11.7 for a list of these topics). **Finish Line**, an athletic footwear retailer with 660 stores in 47 states, taught their managers how to conduct structured interviews. Mike Marchetti, Finish Line's executive vice president of store operations, said this training "gives our managers a more structured way in which to go through the interview and hiring process. As a result, we've been able to teach our associates to be better interviewers." Plus, more accurate screening has produced better employee fit. As a result, retention has increased 10 percent, and

< *"what's new" companies*

mgmt:facts

Job Interview Myths

Going into a job interview, you might think that your interviewers have done all the necessary prep work. They have a long list of questions that they'll use to find out about your intellect and character. They're willing to give 100 percent attention to finding the best person for the job. And, you hope, they'll be really excited for the chance to have a first meeting with the newest member of their team. You might think all these things, but chances are good that you'll be wrong, because your interviewers may in fact not have done much preparation at all. Here are ten other myths that you should know about before heading in to a job interview.

1. The interviewer is prepared.
2. Most interviewers have been trained to conduct thorough job interviews.
3. It's only polite to accept an interviewer's offer of a refreshment.
4. Interviewers expect you to hand over references' contact information right away.
5. There's a right answer to every question an interviewer asks.
6. You should always keep your answers short.
7. If you've got great qualifications, your appearance doesn't matter.
8. When asked where you see yourself in five years, you should show tremendous ambition.
9. If the company invites you to an interview, that means the job is still open.
10. The most qualified person gets the job.[95]

© iStockphoto.com/Kirsty Pargeter

Exhibit 11.10 Guidelines for Conducting Effective Structural Interviews

Interview Stage | **What to Do**

Planning the Interview

- Identify and define the knowledge, skills, abilities, and other (KSAO) characteristics needed for successful job performance.
- For each essential KSAO, develop key behavioral questions that will elicit examples of past accomplishments, activities, and performance.
- For each KSAO, develop a list of things to look for in the applicant's responses to key questions.

Conducting the Interview

- Create a relaxed, nonstressful interview atmosphere.
- Review the applicant's application form, résumé, and other information.
- Allocate enough time to complete the interview without interruption.
- Put the applicant at ease; don't jump right into heavy questioning.
- Tell the applicant what to expect. Explain the interview process.
- Obtain job-related information from the applicant by asking those questions prepared for each KSAO.
- Describe the job and the organization to the applicant. Applicants need adequate information to make a selection decision about the organization.

After the Interview

- Immediately after the interview, review your notes and make sure they are complete.
- Evaluate the applicant on each essential KSAO.
- Determine each applicant's probability of success and make a hiring decision.

Source: B. M. Farrell, "The Art and Science of Employment Interviews," *Personnel Journal* 65 (1986): 91–94.

attendance, measured by the average number of days that employees show up for work, has increased by 5 percent. Importantly, says Marchetti, "People who stay longer are better at driving sales."[96]

Semistructured interviews lie between structured and unstructured interviews. A major part of the semistructured interview (perhaps as much as 80%) is based on structured questions, but some time is set aside for unstructured interviewing to allow the interviewer to probe into ambiguous or missing information uncovered during the structured portion of the interview.

How well do interviews predict future job performance? Contrary to what you've probably heard, recent evidence indicates that even unstructured interviews do a fairly good job.[97] When conducted properly, however, structured interviews can lead to much more accurate hiring decisions than unstructured interviews. In some cases, the validity of structured interviews can rival that of cognitive ability tests.

But even more important, because interviews are especially good at assessing applicants' interpersonal skills, they work particularly well with cognitive ability tests. Combining the two—using structured interviews together with cognitive ability tests to identify smart people who work well in conjunction with others—leads to even better selection decisions than using either alone.[98] Exhibit 11.10 provides a set of guidelines for conducting effective structured employment interviews.

Selection Selection is the process of gathering information about job applicants to decide who should be offered a job. Accurate selection procedures are valid, are legally defendable, and improve organizational performance. Application forms and résumés are the most common selection devices. Because many application forms request illegal, non-job-related information, and as many as one-third of job applicants falsify information on résumés, these procedures are often of little value in making hiring decisions. References and background checks can also be problematic, given that previous employers are reluctant to provide such information for fear of being sued for defamation. Unfortunately, without this information, other employers are at risk of negligent hiring lawsuits. Selection tests generally do the best job of predicting applicants' future job performance. In general, cognitive ability tests, work sample tests, biographical data, and assessment centers are the most valid tests, followed by personality tests and specific ability tests, which are still good predictors. Selection tests aren't perfect predictors of job performance, but almost nothing predicts future job performance as well as selection tests. The three kinds of job interviews are unstructured, structured, and semistructured interviews. Of these, structured interviews work best because they ensure that all applicants are consistently asked the same situational, behavioral, background, or job-knowledge questions, in the same order.

Review 4

Developing Qualified Workers

According to a recent survey by Mercer Human Resource Consulting, 49 percent of companies are increasing their training budgets. For instance, Hewlett-Packard recently increased its training budget to a whopping $300 million.[99] What is driving the infusion of dollars into training and development budgets of companies? Companies like HP recognize that it is more cost-efficient and competitive to develop talent from within rather than compete for talent on the open market.[100] In addition, according to the American Society for Training and Development, a typical investment in training increases productivity by an average of 17 percent, reduces employee turnover, and makes companies more profitable.[101]

Giving employees the knowledge and skills they need to improve their performance is just the first step in developing employees, however. The second step—and not enough companies do this—is giving employees formal feedback about their actual job performance. A CEO of a large telecommunications company hired an outside consultant to assess and coach (provide feedback to) the company's top 50 managers. To the CEO's surprise, 75 percent of those managers indicated that the feedback they received from the consultant regarding their strengths and weaknesses was the only substantial feedback they had received about their performance in the last five years. On a more positive note, as a result of that feedback, two-thirds of the managers then took positive steps to improve their skills, knowledge, and job performance and expressed a clear desire for more feedback, especially from their boss, the CEO.[102]

After reading the next two sections, you should be able to

5. *Describe how to determine training needs and select the appropriate training methods.*

6. *Discuss how to use performance appraisal to give meaningful performance feedback.*

So, in today's competitive business environment, even top managers understand the importance of formal performance feedback to their growth and development.

5 Training

Training means providing opportunities for employees to develop the job-specific skills, experience, and knowledge they need to do their jobs or improve their performance. American companies spend more than $60 billion a year on training. To make sure those training dollars are well spent, companies need to **5.1 determine specific training needs, 5.2 select appropriate training methods**, and **5.3 evaluate training**.

5.1 Determining Training Needs

Needs assessment is the process of identifying and prioritizing the learning needs of employees. Needs assessments can be conducted by identifying performance deficiencies, listening to customer complaints, surveying employees and managers, or formally testing employees' skills and knowledge. The Work Keys method created by American College Testing (maker of the ACT test used for college admissions) in Iowa City, Iowa, is a needs assessment tool used for 7,000 different jobs by more than 1,400 companies nationwide.[103] Work Keys is a series of tests that can be used to determine employees' knowledge and skill levels in communication (listening, reading for information, and writing), problem solving (applied mathematics, applied technology, locating information, and observation), and interpersonal skills (teamwork). As shown in Step 1 of Exhibit 11.11, a needs assessment using Work Keys begins with a job analysis (what ACT calls "job profiling") to determine the knowledge and skill levels required to perform a job successfully. Step 1 shows that a worker needs a skill level of 4 in reading for information, a 5 in applied mathematics, a 3 in applied technology, and a 4 in teamwork (skill levels range from 1 to 6) to do

training developing the skills, experience, and knowledge employees need to perform their jobs or improve their performance.

needs assessment the process of identifying and prioritizing the learning needs of employees.

Exhibit 11.11   Work Keys Needs Assessment for a Manufacturing Job

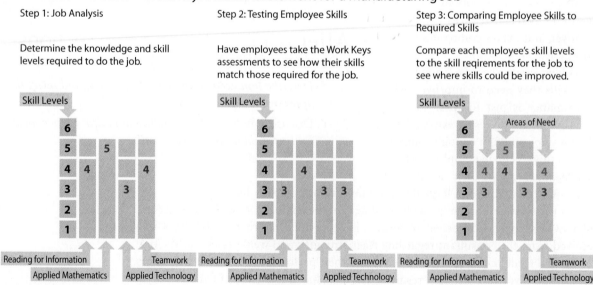

Source: "Work Keys for Business: The System in Action," *ACT: Information for Life's Transitions,* May 31, 2002, available at www.act.org/workkeys/index .html http://www.act.org/workkeys/index.html, 31 May 3002. Copyright 1999 by ACT, Inc.

well in a manufacturing job. Following the job analysis, employees are tested to see how well their skills match those required for the job, as shown in Step 2 of Exhibit 11.11. Then, as shown in Step 3 of the exhibit, employees' skill levels are compared with the requirements for the job. The greater the difference between an employee's skill levels and those required, the greater the need for training. Based on the Work Keys needs assessment, this employee needs some training in reading for information, applied mathematics, and teamwork.

Note that training should never be conducted without first performing a needs assessment. Sometimes, training isn't needed at all or isn't needed for all employees. Because the needs assessment shown in Exhibit 11.11 indicates that the employee's applied technology skills match those required for the job, it would be a waste of time and money to send this employee for training in that area. Unfortunately, however, many organizations simply require all employees to attend training whether they need to or not. As a result, employees who are not interested or don't need the training may react negatively during or after training. Likewise, employees who should be sent for training, but aren't, may also react negatively. Consequently, a needs assessment is an important tool for deciding who should or should not attend training. In fact, employment law restricts employers from discriminating on the basis of age, sex, race, color, religion, national origin, or disability when selecting training participants. Just like hiring decisions, the selection of training participants should be based on job-related information.

5.2 Training Methods

Assume that you're a training director for a major oil company and that you're in charge of making sure all employees know how to respond effectively in case of an oil spill.[104] Exhibit 11.12 lists a number of training methods you could use: films and videos, lectures, planned readings, case studies, coaching and mentoring, group discussions, on-the-job training, role-playing, simulations and games, vestibule training, and computer-based learning. Which method would be best?

To choose the best method, you should consider a number of factors, such as the number of people to be trained, the cost of training, and the objectives of the training. For instance, if the training objective is to impart information or knowledge to trainees, then you should use films and videos, lectures, and planned readings. In our example, trainees might read a manual or attend a lecture about how to protect a shoreline to keep it from being affected by the spill.

If developing analytical and problem-solving skills is the objective, then use case studies, coaching and mentoring, and group discussions. In our example, trainees might view a video documenting how a team handled exposure to hazardous substances, talk with first responders, and discuss what they would do in a similar situation.

If practicing, learning, or changing job behaviors is the objective, then use on-the-job training, role-playing, simulations and games, and vestibule training. In our example, trainees might participate in a mock shoreline cleanup to learn what to do in the event oil comes to shore. This simulation could take place on an actual shoreline or on a video game–like virtual shoreline.

If training is supposed to meet more than one of these objectives, then your best choice may be to combine one of the previous methods with computer-based training. When UPS found that 30 percent of its driver candidates were not passing its traditional classroom-based training program, it introduced Integrad, a new training system that emphasizes hands-on learning. A key element of this system is "Clarksville," a simulated town in which the driver operates a virtual truck and has to deal with simulations of real-world situations like kids playing in the street and

Exhibit 11.12 Training Objectives and Methods

Training Objective	Training Method
Impart Information and Knowledge	• **Films and videos.** Films and videos share information, illustrate problems and solutions, and effectively hold trainees' attention. • **Lectures.** Trainees listen to instructors' oral presentations. • **Planned readings.** Trainees read about concepts or ideas before attending training.
Develop Analytical and Problem-Solving Skills	• **Case studies.** Cases are analyzed and discussed in small groups. The cases present a specific problem or decision, and trainees develop methods for solving the problem or making the decision. • **Coaching and mentoring.** Coaching and mentoring of trainees by managers involves informal advice, suggestions, and guidance. This method is helpful for reinforcing other kinds of training and for trainees who benefit from support and personal encouragement. • **Group discussions.** Small groups of trainees actively discuss specific topics. The instructor may perform the role of discussion leader.
Practice, Learn, or Change Job Behaviors	• **On-the-job training (OJT).** New employees are assigned to experienced employees. The trainee learns by watching the experienced employee perform the job and eventually by working alongside the experienced employee. Gradually, the trainee is left on his or her own to perform the job. • **Role-playing.** Trainees assume job-related roles and practice new behaviors by acting out what they would do in job-related situations. • **Simulations and games.** Experiential exercises place trainees in realistic job-related situations and give them the opportunity to experience a job-related condition in a relatively low-cost setting. The trainee benefits from "hands-on experience" before actually performing the job where mistakes may be more costly. • **Vestibule training.** Procedures and equipment similar to those used in the actual job are set up in a special area called a vestibule. The trainee is then taught how to perform the job at his or her own pace without disrupting the actual flow of work, making costly mistakes, or exposing the trainee and others to dangerous conditions.
Impart Information and Knowledge; Develop Analytical and Problem-Solving Skills; and Practice, Learn, or Change Job Behaviors	• **Computer-based learning.** Interactive videos, software, CD-ROMs, personal computers, teleconferencing, and the Internet may be combined to present multimedia-based training.

Source: A. Fowler, "How to Decide on Training Methods," *People Management* 25, no. 1 (1995): 36.

customers confusing UPS with other delivery services. Since switching to Integrad, UPS has seen the failure rate of its trainees drop to just 10 percent.[105]

These days, many companies are adopting Internet training, or "e-learning." E-learning can offer several advantages. Because employees don't need to leave their jobs, travel costs are greatly reduced. Also, because employees can take training modules when it is convenient (i.e., they don't have to fall behind at their jobs to attend weeklong training courses), workplace productivity should increase and employee stress should decrease. And, if a company's technology infrastructure can support it, e-learning can be much faster than traditional training methods. The training department of **Dealer.com**, a company that designs and manages car dealer websites to drive customer traffic to auto showrooms, spent 14 months creating UFuel, the company's online training system. UFuel (for "fuel your own growth") allows employees to become certified on Dealer.com's products and services, and to take more than 100 other courses from Web design to Microsoft Office, all from the comfort of their desks. UFuel also helps new hires learn about the company's history, culture, and policies. And, to make sure that its employees understand their customers, car dealers, UFuel has a dealership simulation that presents its employees with common

"what's new" companies >

problems and situations facing dealerships. Matt Murray, the director of training says, "We want them to see the world through the customer's eyes."[106]

There are, however, several disadvantages to e-learning. First, despite its increasing popularity, it's not always the appropriate training method. E-learning can be a good way to impart information, but it isn't always as effective for changing job behaviors or developing problem-solving and analytical skills. Second, e-learning requires a significant investment in computers and high-speed Internet and network connections for all employees. Finally, though e-learning can be faster, many employees find it so boring and unengaging that they may choose to do their jobs rather than complete e-learning courses when sitting alone at their desks. E-learning may become more interesting, however, as more companies incorporate gamelike features such as avatars and competition into their e-learning courses. Sun Microsystems uses video games to teach employees about its core values and principles. Every employee plays through either "Rise of the Shadow Specters" or "Dawn of the Shadow Specters," which are set on a fictional planet home to a society that is based on Sun's core principles. In the games, employees control a group of lost colonists who must inhabit the planet Solaris and create an information network that spans the entire universe so that the colonists never get lost again. As Karie Willyerd, chief learning officer of Sun, describes it, the games make "what otherwise might be dry material more palatable and exciting."[107]

5.3 Evaluating Training

After selecting a training method and conducting the training, the last step is to evaluate the training. Training can be evaluated in four ways: on *reactions* (how satisfied trainees were with the program), on *learning* (how much employees improved their knowledge or skills), on *behavior* (how much employees actually changed their on-the-job behavior because of training), or on *results* (how much training improved job performance, such as increased sales or quality, or decreased costs).[108] In general, training provides meaningful benefits for most companies if it is done well. For example, a study by the American Society for Training and Development shows that a training budget as small as $680 per employee can increase a company's total return on investment by 6 percent.[109]

Training Training is used to give employees the job-specific skills, experience, and knowledge they need to do their jobs or improve their job performance. To make sure training dollars are well spent, companies need to determine specific training needs, select appropriate training methods, and then evaluate the training. Needs assessments can be conducted by identifying performance deficiencies, listening to customer complaints, surveying employees and managers, or formally testing employees' skills and knowledge. Selection of an appropriate training method depends on a number of factors, including the number of people to be trained, the cost of training, and the objectives of the training. If the objective is to impart information or knowledge, then films and videos, lectures, and planned readings should be used. If developing analytical and problem-solving skills is the objective, then case studies, coaching and mentoring, and group discussions should be used. If practicing, learning, or changing job behaviors is the objective, then on-the-job training, role-playing, simulations and games, and vestibule training should be used. If training is supposed to meet more than one of these objectives, then it may be best to combine one of the previous methods with computer-based training. Training can be evaluated on reactions, learning, behavior, or results.

Review 5

6 Performance Appraisal

Performance appraisal is the process of assessing how well employees are doing their jobs. Most employees and managers intensely dislike the performance appraisal process. Yahoo!'s former CEO Carol Barts said, "If I had my way, I wouldn't do annual reviews. I think the annual review process is so antiquated. I almost would rather ask each employee to tell us if they've had a meaningful conversation with their manager this quarter. Yes or no. And if they say no, they ought to have one."[110]

Unfortunately, attitudes like this are all too common. In fact, 70 percent of employees are dissatisfied with the performance appraisal process in their companies. Likewise, according to the Society for Human Resource Management, 90 percent of human resource managers are dissatisfied with the performance appraisal systems used by their companies.[111]

Performance appraisals are used for four broad purposes: making administrative decisions (e.g., pay increase, promotion, retention), providing feedback for employee development (e.g., performance feedback, developing career plans), evaluating human resource programs (e.g., validating selection systems), and for documentation purposes (e.g., documenting performance ratings and decisions based on those ratings).[112]

Let's explore how companies can avoid some of these problems with performance appraisals by **6.1 accurately measuring job performance** and **6.2 effectively sharing performance feedback with employees**.

performance appraisal the process of assessing how well employees are doing their jobs.

6.1 Accurately Measuring Job Performance

Workers often have strong doubts about the accuracy of their performance appraisals—and they may be right. For example, it's widely known that assessors are prone to errors when rating worker performance. Three of the most common rating errors are central tendency, halo, and leniency. *Central tendency error* occurs when assessors rate all workers as average or in the middle of the scale. *Halo error* occurs when assessors rate all workers as performing at the same level (good, bad, or average) in all parts of their jobs. *Leniency error* occurs when assessors rate all workers as performing particularly well. One of the reasons managers make these errors is that they often don't spend enough time gathering or reviewing performance data. Winston Connor, the former vice president of human resources at Huntsman Chemical, says, "Most of the time, it's just a ritual that managers go through. They pull out last year's review, update it and do it quickly."[113] What can be done to minimize rating errors and improve the accuracy with which job performance is measured? In general, two approaches have been used: improving performance appraisal measures themselves and training performance raters to be more accurate.

One of the ways companies try to improve performance appraisal measures is to use as many

© Image Source /Jupiterimages

objective performance measures as possible. **Objective performance measures** are measures of performance that are easily and directly counted or quantified. Common objective performance measures include output, scrap, waste, sales, customer complaints, and rejection rates.

But when objective performance measures aren't available (and frequently they aren't), subjective performance measures have to be used instead. **Subjective performance measures** require that someone judge or assess a worker's performance. The most common kind of subjective performance measure is the graphic rating scale (GRS) shown in Exhibit 11.13. Graphic rating scales are most widely used because they are easy to construct, but they are very susceptible to rating errors.

A popular alternative to graphic rating scales is the **behavior observation scale (BOS).** BOS requires raters to rate the frequency with which workers perform specific behaviors representative of the job dimensions that are critical to successful job performance. Exhibit 11.13 shows a BOS for two important job dimensions for a retail salesperson: customer service and money handling. Notice that each dimension lists several specific behaviors characteristic of a worker who excels in that dimension of job performance. (Normally, the scale would list 7 to 12 items per dimension, not 3, as in the exhibit.) Notice also that the behaviors are good behaviors, meaning they indicate good performance, and the rater is asked to judge how frequently an employee engaged in those good behaviors. The logic behind the BOS is that better performers engage in good behaviors more often.

Not only do BOSs work well for rating critical dimensions of performance, but studies also show that managers strongly prefer BOSs for giving performance feedback; accurately differentiating between poor, average, and good workers; identifying training needs; and accurately measuring performance. And in response to the statement "If I were defending a company, this rating format would be an asset to my case," attorneys strongly preferred BOSs over other kinds of subjective performance appraisal scales.[114]

The second approach to improving the measurement of workers' job performance is **rater training.** The most effective is frame-of-reference training, in which a group of trainees learn how to do performance appraisals by watching a videotape of an employee at work. Next, they evaluate the performance of the person in the

Exhibit 11.13 Subjective Performance Appraisal Scales

Graphic Rating Scale

Example 1:

	Very Poor	Poor	Average	Good	Very Good
1. Quality of work performed is	1	2	3	4	5

Example 2:

	Very Poor (20% errors)	Poor (15% errors)	Average (10% errors)	Good (5% errors)	Very Good (less than 5% errors)
2. Quality of work performed is	1	2	3	4	5

Behavioral Observation Scale

Dimension: Customer Service

	Almost Never				Almost Always
1. Greets customers with a smile and a "hello."	1	2	3	4	5
2. Calls other stores to help customers find merchandise that is not in stock.	1	2	3	4	5
3. Promptly handles customer concerns and complaints.	1	2	3	4	5

Dimension: Money Handling

	Almost Never				Almost Always
1. Accurately makes change from customer transactions.	1	2	3	4	5
2. Accounts balance at the end of the day, no shortages or surpluses.	1	2	3	4	5
3. Accurately records transactions in computer system.	1	2	3	4	5

© Cengage Learning 2013

objective performance measures measures of job performance that are easily and directly counted or quantified.

subjective performance measures measures of job performance that require someone to judge or assess a worker's performance.

behavior observation scale (BOS) rating scales that indicate the frequency with which workers perform specific behaviors that are representative of the job dimensions critical to successful job performance.

rater training training performance appraisal raters in how to avoid rating errors and increase rating accuracy.

videotape. A trainer (an expert in the subject matter) then shares his or her evaluations, and trainees' evaluations are compared with the expert's. The expert then explains the rationales behind his or her evaluations. This process is repeated until the difference in evaluations given by trainees and evaluations by the expert are minimized. The underlying logic behind the frame-of-reference training is that by adopting the frame of reference used by an expert, trainees will be able to accurately observe, judge, and use the scale to evaluate performance of others.[115]

6.2 Sharing Performance Feedback

After gathering accurate performance data, the next step is to share performance feedback with employees. Unfortunately, even when performance appraisal ratings are accurate, the appraisal process often breaks down at the feedback stage. Employees become defensive and dislike hearing any negative assessments of their work, no matter how small. Managers become defensive too and dislike giving appraisal feedback as much as employees dislike receiving it. One manager says, "I myself don't go as far as those who say performance reviews are inherently destructive and ought to be abolished, but I agree that the typical annual-review process does nothing but harm. It creates divisions. It undermines morale. It makes people angry, jealous, and cynical. It unleashes a whole lot of negative energy, and the organization gets nothing in return."[116]

What can be done to overcome the inherent difficulties in performance appraisal feedback sessions? Because performance appraisal ratings have traditionally been the judgments of just one person, the boss, one possibility is to use **360-degree feedback**. In this approach, feedback comes from four sources: the boss, subordinates, peers and coworkers, and the employees themselves. The data, which are obtained anonymously (except for the boss's), are compiled into a feedback report comparing the employee's self-ratings with those of the boss, subordinates, and peers and coworkers. Usually, a consultant or human resource specialist discusses the results with the employee. The advantage of 360-degree programs is that negative feedback ("You don't listen") is often more credible when it comes from several people. For example, one boss who received 360-degree feedback thought he was a great writer, so he regularly criticized and corrected his subordinates' reports. Though the subordinates had never discussed this among themselves, they all complained about it in the 360-degree feedback and asked that he stop rewriting their reports. After receiving the feedback, he apologized and stopped.[117]

A word of caution, though: About half of the companies using 360-degree feedback for performance appraisal now use the feedback only for developmental purposes. They found that sometimes when raises and promotions were on the line, peers and subordinates would give high ratings in order to get high ratings from others. Ed Smiley, a manager who works for a manufacturer, says they stopped using 360-degree feedback at his company because of too much "mutual back scratching." Said Smiley, "What you don't get is true feedback."[118] Conversely, in some situations employees distorted ratings to harm competitors or help people they liked. A senior manager at a New York City marketing company agrees, saying that 360-degree feedback "also allows people to vent their frustrations and anger on bosses and colleagues in an insensitive way."[119] On the other hand, studies clearly show that ratees prefer to receive feedback from multiple raters, so 360-degree feedback is likely to continue to grow in popularity.[120]

Herbert Meyer, who has been studying performance appraisal feedback for more than 30 years, recommends a list of topics to discuss in performance appraisal

360-degree feedback a performance appraisal process in which feedback is obtained from the boss, subordinates, peers and coworkers, and the employees themselves.

Exhibit 11.14
What to Discuss in a
Performance Appraisal
Feedback Session

- ✔ Overall progress—an analysis of accomplishments and shortcomings.

- ✔ Problems encountered in meeting job requirements.

- ✔ Opportunities to improve performance.

- ✔ Long-range plans and opportunities— for the job and for the individual's career.

- ✔ General discussion of possible plans and goals for the coming year.

Source: H. H. Meyer, "A Solution to the Performance Appraisal Feedback Enigma," *Academy of Management Executive* 5, no. 1 (1991): 68–76.

feedback sessions (see Exhibit 11.14).[121] Furthermore, managers can do three different things to make performance reviews more comfortable and productive. First, they should separate developmental feedback, which is designed to improve future performance, from administrative feedback, which is used as a reward for past performance, such as for raises. When managers give developmental feedback, they're acting as coaches, but when they give administrative feedback, they're acting as judges. These roles, coaches and judges, are clearly incompatible. As coaches, managers encourage, point out opportunities for growth and improvement, and employees are typically open and receptive to feedback. But as judges, managers are evaluative, and employees are typically defensive and closed to feedback.

Second, Meyer suggests that performance appraisal feedback sessions be based on self-appraisals, in which employees carefully assess their own strengths, weaknesses, successes, and failures in writing. Because employees play an active role in the review of their performance, managers can be coaches rather than judges. Also, because the focus is on future goals and development, both employees and managers are likely to be more satisfied with the process and more committed to future plans and changes. And because the focus is on development and not administrative assessment, studies show that self-appraisals lead to more candid self-assessments than traditional supervisory reviews.[122]

Finally, what people do with the performance feedback they receive really matters. A study of 1,361 senior managers found that managers who reviewed their 360-degree feedback with an executive coach (hired by the company) were more likely to set specific goals for improvement, ask their bosses for ways to improve, and subsequently improve their performance.[123]

A five-year study of 252 managers found that their performance improved dramatically if they met with their subordinates to discuss their 360-degree feedback ("You don't listen") and how they were going to address it ("I'll restate what others have said before stating my opinion"). Performance was dramatically lower for managers who never discussed their 360-degree feedback with subordinates and for managers who did not routinely do so (some managers did not review their 360-degree feedback with subordinates each year of the study). Why is discussing 360-degree feedback with subordinates so effective? These discussions help managers understand their weaknesses better, force them to develop a plan to improve,

and demonstrate to the subordinates the managers' public commitment to improving.[124] In short, it helps to have people discuss their performance feedback with others, but it particularly helps to have them discuss their feedback with the people who provided it. This is why HCL Technologies, an outsourcer of technology services, not only has employees rate their bosses, but also posts each managers' ratings on the company intranet for everyone to see, in order to hold top managers accountable.[125]

It is clear that organizations, and specifically managers, must take the task of providing feedback seriously. Recent studies have reported that employees' satisfaction with feedback they receive influences not only their job satisfaction but also their future performance.[126] An employee's satisfaction with feedback is influenced by his or her perceptions of how well the manager knows the employee's job, the extent to which evaluations were based on job-related factors, whether the feedback process included goal setting, and whether the manager provided insights on how to improve future performance.[127]

Review 6

Performance Appraisal Most employees and managers intensely dislike the performance appraisal process. Some of the problems associated with appraisals can be avoided, however, by accurately measuring job performance and effectively sharing performance feedback with employees. Organizations should develop good performance appraisal scales and preferably use behavior observation scales (BOSs). They should train raters to accurately evaluate performance, perhaps by providing frame-of-reference training. They should impress upon managers the value of providing feedback in a clear, consistent, and fair manner and of setting goals and monitoring progress toward those goals.

One way to overcome the inherent difficulties in performance appraisal feedback is to provide 360-degree feedback, in which feedback is obtained from four sources: the boss, subordinates, peers and coworkers, and the employees themselves. Feedback tends to be more credible if it is heard from several sources. Finally, especially for managers, it's helpful to have people discuss the feedback they received with executive coaches or the people who provided it.

(Keeping Qualified Workers

At Penske Automotive Group, which has 300 car dealerships worldwide, 8 percent of CEO Roger Penske's bonus is tied to keeping employee turnover below 31 percent. Pep Boys, a car parts retail chain, does the same, making 10 percent of its middle managers' pay contingent on low employee turnover. Likewise, ExlService Holdings, an India-based outsourcing company, links 30 percent of its lower-level managers' pay to employee turnover. Why link managers' pay to employee turnover? According to Tony Pordon, senior vice president at Penske Automotive, "We believe that employee turnover is a symptom of bigger

After reading the next two sections, you should be able to

7. *Describe basic compensation strategies and explain how they affect human resource practice.*

8. *Discuss the four kinds of employee separations: termination, downsizing, retirements, and turnover.*

problems at the dealership level."[128] Mark Royal, a consultant for the Hay Group, which specializes in employee compensation, further explains that linking managers' pay to turnover, "is a recognition, on the one hand, of people as a driver of business success. It also reflects a recognition that turnover is costly."[129]

7 Compensation

Compensation includes both the financial and the nonfinancial rewards that organizations give employees in exchange for their work. Let's learn more about compensation by examining the **7.1 compensation decisions that managers must make** and **7.2 the role that employment benefits play in compensating today's employees**.

7.1 Compensation Decisions

As Exhibit 11.15 shows, there are four basic kinds of compensation decisions: pay level, pay variability, pay structure, and employment benefits. We'll discuss employment benefits in the next subsection.[130]

Pay-level decisions are decisions about whether to pay workers at a level that is below, above, or at current market wages. Companies use job evaluation to set their pay structures. **Job evaluation** determines the worth of each job by determining the market value of the knowledge, skills, and requirements needed to perform it. After conducting a job evaluation, most companies try to pay the going rate, meaning the current market wage. There are always companies, however, whose financial situation causes them to pay considerably less than current market wages. Although a director of a child-care center in Vermont may make up to $25 an hour, its teachers make only $9–$11 an hour.[131] According to the American Federation of Teachers, the average annual wage for early child-care workers is $18,820, and hourly wages have increased only 39 cents in the last 25 years.[132]

Some companies choose to pay above-average wages to attract and keep employees. *Above-market wages* can attract a larger, more qualified pool of job applicants, increase the rate of job acceptance, decrease the time it takes to fill positions, and increase the time that employees stay.[133] One of the best known examples of the power of above-market wages was Henry Ford, founder of Ford Motor, who doubled the pay of his workers in 1914 from $2.50 to $5 a day. Ford did this to combat an astronomical 380 percent rate of turnover, which forced him to hire 52,000 people a year to staff the company's 13,600 assembly jobs. But after he doubled wages, Ford was able to attract a much more qualified, reliable pool of job applicants. Employee turnover fell to 16 percent, and despite higher wages, Ford saw overall costs

compensation the financial and nonfinancial rewards that organizations give employees in exchange for their work.

job evaluation a process that determines the worth of each job in a company by evaluating the market value of the knowledge, skills, and requirements needed to perform it.

Exhibit 11.15 Kinds of Compensation Decisions

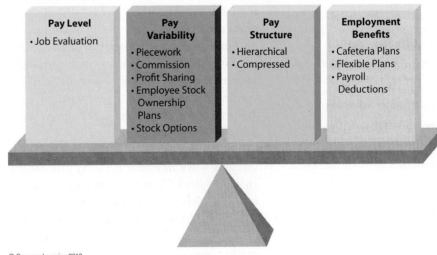

Pay Level	Pay Variability	Pay Structure	Employment Benefits
• Job Evaluation	• Piecework • Commission • Profit Sharing • Employee Stock Ownership Plans • Stock Options	• Hierarchical • Compressed	• Cafeteria Plans • Flexible Plans • Payroll Deductions

© Cengage Learning 2013

© Big Cheese Photo/Jupiterimages

drop dramatically. With productivity sky-rocketing, he was able to cut the price of Ford's Model T car by 10 percent a year for three straight years. And with more people able to buy Model T's, Ford's profit doubled. Ford concluded that doubling wages "was one of the finest cost-cutting moves we ever made."[134]

Pay-variability decisions concern the extent to which employees' pay varies with individual and organizational performance. Linking pay to performance is intended to increase employee motivation, effort, and job performance. Piecework, sales commissions, profit sharing, employee stock ownership plans, and stock options are common pay-variability options. For instance, under **piecework** pay plans, employees are paid a set rate for each item produced up to some standard (e.g., 35 cents per item produced for output up to 100 units per day). Once productivity exceeds the standard, employees are paid a set amount for each unit of output over the standard (e.g., 45 cents for each unit above 100 units). Under a sales **commission** plan, salespeople are paid a percentage of the purchase price of items they sell. The more they sell, the more they earn. At **Installation & Service Technologies**, which sells point-of-sales (high-tech cash registers) systems, a salesperson's pay is determined in large part by how much they sell. Each member of the sales staff receives a small base salary (about 35% of total pay) and a commission based on how much gross profit they make on sales—17 percent for $1 to $50,000, 24 percent for $50,001 to $100,000, and 30 percent over $100,000. Plus, every time a salesperson reaches a new profit level, they receive an extra $1,000.[135]

Because pay plans such as piecework and commissions are based on individual performance, they can reduce the incentive that people have to work together. Therefore, companies also use group incentives (discussed in Chapter 10) and organizational incentives, such as profit sharing, employee stock ownership plans, and stock options, to encourage teamwork and cooperation.

With **profit sharing**, employees receive a portion of the organization's profits over and above their regular compensation. After posting a surprise $2.7 billion profit for 2009—its first in four years—Ford announced it would be issuing profit-sharing checks of about $450 to each of its hourly workers.[136]

Employee stock ownership plans (ESOPs) compensate employees by awarding them shares of the company stock in addition to their regular compensation. Joe Hernandez, a 41-year-old migrant worker at McKay Nursery in Waterloo, Wisconsin, makes $20,000 a year working from April to November. But Joe also gets 20 percent to 25 percent in company stock. So far, he's accumulated more than $80,000 through the company ESOP.[137]

Stock options give employees the right to purchase shares of stock at a set price. Options work like this: Let's say you are awarded the right (or option) to buy 100 shares of stock from the company for $5 a share. If the company's stock price rises to $15 a share, you can exercise your options, sell the stock for $15 a share, and come out with $1,000. When you exercise your options, you pay the company $500 (100 shares at $5 a share), but, because the stock is selling for $15 in the stock market, you can sell your 100 shares for $1,500 and make $1,000. Of course, as

"what's new" > **companies**

piecework a compensation system in which employees are paid a set rate for each item they produce.

commission a compensation system in which employees earn a percentage of each sale they make.

profit sharing a compensation system in which a company pays a percentage of its profits to employees in addition to their regular compensation.

employee stock ownership plan (ESOP) a compensation system that awards employees shares of company stock in addition to their regular compensation.

stock options a compensation system that gives employees the right to purchase shares of stock at a set price, even if the value of the stock increases above that price.

the company's profits and share values increase, stock options become even more valuable to employees. Stock options have no value, however, if the company's stock falls below the option "grant price," the price at which the options have been issued to you. The options you have on 100 shares of stock with a grant price of $5 aren't going to do you a lot of good if the company's stock is worth $2.50. Proponents of stock options argue that this gives employees and managers a strong incentive to work hard to make the company successful. If they do, the company's profits and stock price increase, and their stock options increase in value. If they don't, profits stagnate or turn into losses, and their stock options decrease in value or become worthless. To learn more about ESOPs and stock options, see the National Center for Employee Ownership (www.nceo.org).

The incentive has to be more than just a piece of paper, however. At Van Meter Industrial, based in Cedar Rapids, Iowa, some employees didn't know what stock was, let alone care about their ESOP program. One even said, "Why don't you just give me a couple hundred bucks for beer and cigarettes [instead]?"[138] So the company created an employee committee to educate their coworkers about how the ESOP program works, meeting with workers in small groups where it's safe to ask questions, and emphasizing, for example, that the company contributes the equivalent of 9.5 weeks of their pay into each employee ESOP each year. Also, employees reaching their six-month anniversary are given a jacket with the words "I am in" written on it to emphasize that they're now part of the ESOP. As a result of these efforts, Van Meter Industrial's workers now take a strong interest in what they can do to save the company money on a daily basis because, as the company becomes more profitable, the value of their ESOP shares rises. Although Van Meter's stock value was barely keeping up with inflation before this program, it increased 78 percent after the program was implemented.[139]

Pay-structure decisions are concerned with internal pay distributions, meaning the extent to which people in the company receive very different levels of pay.[140] With *hierarchical pay structures*, there are big differences from one pay level to another. The highest pay levels are for people near the top of the pay distribution. The basic idea behind hierarchical pay structures is that large differences in pay between jobs or organizational levels should motivate people to work harder to obtain those higher-paying jobs. Many publicly owned companies have hierarchical pay structures, paying huge salaries to their top managers and CEOs. For example, the average CEO now makes 319 times as much as the average worker, down from 525 times the pay of the average worker just ten years ago. But with CEO pay packages averaging $9.25 million per year ($4,625 per hour) and average workers earning just $41,340 ($20.67 per hour), the difference is still huge and can have a significant detrimental impact on employee morale.[141]

By contrast, *compressed pay structures* typically have fewer pay levels and smaller differences in pay between levels. Pay is less dispersed and more similar across jobs in the company. The basic idea behind compressed pay structures is that similar pay levels should lead to higher levels of cooperation, feelings of fairness and a common purpose, and better group and team performance.

So should companies choose hierarchical or compressed pay structures? The evidence isn't straightforward, but studies seem to indicate that there are significant problems with the hierarchical approach. The most damaging finding is that there appears to be little link between organizational performance and the pay of top managers.[142] Furthermore, studies of professional athletes indicate that hierarchical pay structures (e.g., paying superstars 40 to 50 times as much as the lowest-paid athlete on the team) hurt the performance of teams and individual players.[143] Likewise, managers are twice as likely to quit their jobs when their companies have very strong hierarchical pay structures (i.e., when they're paid dramatically less than the

people above them).[144] For now, it seems that hierarchical pay structures work best for independent work, where it's easy to determine the contributions of individual performers and little coordination with others is needed to get the job done. In other words, hierarchical pay structures work best when clear links can be drawn between individual performance and individual rewards. By contrast, compressed pay structures, in which everyone receives similar pay, seem to work best for interdependent work, which requires employees to work together. Some companies are pursuing a middle ground: combining hierarchical and compressed pay structures by giving ordinary workers the chance to earn more through ESOPs, stock options, and profit sharing.

7.2 Employment Benefits

Employment benefits include virtually any kind of compensation other than direct wages paid to employees.[145] Three employee benefits are mandated by law: Social Security, workers' compensation insurance, and unemployment insurance. To attract and retain a good workforce, however, most organizations offer a wide variety of benefits, including retirement plans and pensions, paid holidays, paid vacations, sick leave, health insurance, life insurance, dental care, eye care, day-care facilities, paid personal days, legal assistance, physical fitness facilities, educational assistance, and discounts on company products and services. Although the cost of employee benefits varies by company and by industry, according to the Bureau of Labor Statistics, on average, benefits cost organizations about 29.3 percent of their payroll.[146] Managers should understand that although benefits are unlikely to improve employee motivation and performance, they do affect job satisfaction, employee decisions about staying or leaving the company, and the company's attractiveness to job applicants.[147] One way that organizations make their benefit plans more attractive is by offering **cafeteria benefit plans** or **flexible benefit plans**, which allow employees to choose which benefits they receive, up to a certain dollar value.[148] Many cafeteria or flexible benefit plans start with a core of benefits, such as health insurance and life insurance, that are available to all employees. Then employees are allowed to select the other benefits that best fit their needs, up to a predetermined dollar amount. Some organizations allow employees to choose from several packages of benefits. The packages are of equivalent value but offer a different mix of benefits. For example, older employees may prefer more benefit dollars spent on retirement plans, whereas younger employees may prefer additional vacation days.

Pretax payroll deductions, which enable employees to pay for expenses such as medical care, day care, and commuting out of pretax dollars, are one of the more popular benefits options because they provide significant tax savings for employees and organizations. Nevertheless, only 18 percent of eligible employees participate in their company's pretax payroll deduction plan. The problem, as employee Kate Morrison explained, has been that "by the time you filled out the paperwork and mailed it off and they processed it, it could take up to 45 days to get your money back [from your pretax account]."[149] Some companies have solved these problems by giving employees a debit card attached to their pretax spending accounts that they can use to pay expenses directly, thereby avoiding the paperwork and the wait for reimbursement. So-called prepaid debit cards can double or triple the rate of participation in pretax payroll deductions.[150] The drawback to flexible benefit plans has been the high cost of administering them. With advances in information processing technology and HRISs, however, the cost has begun to drop in recent years.

employment benefits a method of rewarding employees that includes virtually any kind of compensation other than wages or salaries.

cafeteria benefit plans (flexible benefit plans) plans that allow employees to choose which benefits they receive, up to a certain dollar value.

Compensation Compensation includes both the financial and the nonfinancial rewards that organizations give employees in exchange for their work. There are four basic kinds of compensation decisions: pay level, pay variability, pay structure, and employment benefits. Pay-level decisions determine whether workers will receive wages below, above, or at current market levels. Pay-variability decisions concern the extent to which pay varies with individual and organizational performance. Piecework, sales commissions, profit sharing, employee stock ownership plans, and stock options are common pay-variability options. Pay-structure decisions concern the extent to which people in the company receive very different levels of pay. Hierarchical pay structures work best for independent work, whereas compressed pay structures work best for interdependent work.

Employee benefits include virtually any kind of compensation other than direct wages paid to employees. Flexible or cafeteria benefit plans offer employees a wide variety of benefits, improve job satisfaction, increase the chances that employees will stay with companies, and make organizations more attractive to job applicants. The cost of administering flexible benefit plans has begun to drop in recent years.

Review 7

8 Employee Separations

Employee separation is a broad term covering the loss of an employee for any reason. *Involuntary separation* occurs when employers terminate or lay off employees. *Voluntary separation* occurs when employees quit or retire. Because employee separations affect recruiting, selection, training, and compensation, organizations should forecast the number of employees they expect to lose through terminations, layoffs, turnover, or retirements when doing human resource planning.

Let's explore employee separation by examining **8.1 terminations, 8.2 downsizing, 8.3 retirements**, and **8.4 turnover**.

8.1 Terminating Employees

The words "You're fired!" may have never been directed at you, but lots of people hear them, as more than 400,000 people a year get fired from their jobs. Getting fired is a terrible thing, but many managers make it even worse by bungling the firing process, needlessly provoking the person who was fired and unintentionally inviting lawsuits. Manager Craig Silverman had to fire the head of a company that his organization had just acquired. He was specifically instructed to invite her to a meeting, which would require her to travel halfway across the country, and then fire her immediately on arrival. He said, "I literally had to tell the car service to wait. I don't think it ever entered [her] mind that [she] would be terminated."[151] A computer systems engineer was fired on "Take Your Daughter to Work Day," with his 8-year-old daughter sitting next to him in the human resource manager's office. He and his daughter were both escorted from the building.[152] Four hundred employees at the Fort Worth headquarters of RadioShack got the following email message: "The workforce reduction notification is currently in progress. Unfortunately your position is one that has been eliminated."[153] How would you feel if you had been fired in one of these ways? Though firing is never pleasant (and managers hate firings nearly as much as employees do), managers can do several things to minimize the problems inherent in firing employees.

employee separation the voluntary or involuntary loss of an employee.

To start, in most situations, firing should not be the first option. Instead, employees should be given a chance to change their behavior. When problems arise, employees should have ample warning and must be specifically informed as to the nature and seriousness of the trouble they're in. After being notified, they should be given sufficient time to change their behavior. Mitch McLeod, owner of Arcos Inc., a software company based in Columbus, Ohio, was frustrated with his best software engineer, who always showed up late to work with bizarre excuses, such as his cat hid his car keys. McLeod could have fired him but instead decided to switch his schedule so that he could start later in the day. With the later start time, the engineer was never late again. And because McLeod worked with him and gave him the chance to change, he was able to keep a top performer.[154]

If problems continue, the employees should again be counseled about their job performance, what could be done to improve it, and the possible consequences if things don't change (such as a written reprimand, suspension without pay, or firing). Sometimes this is enough to solve the problem. If the problem isn't corrected after several rounds of warnings and discussions, however, the employee may be terminated.[155]

Second, employees should be fired only for a good reason. Employers used to hire and fire employees under the legal principle of employment at will, which allowed them to fire employees for a good reason, a bad reason, or no reason at all. (Employees could also quit for a good reason, a bad reason, or no reason whenever they desired.) As employees began contesting their firings in court, however, the principle of wrongful discharge emerged. **Wrongful discharge** is a legal doctrine that requires employers to have a job-related reason to terminate employees. In other words, like other major human resource decisions, termination decisions should be made on the basis of job-related factors such as violating company rules or consistently poor performance. And with former employees winning 68 percent of wrongful discharge cases and the average wrongful termination award at $532,000 and climbing, managers should record the job-related reasons for the termination, document specific instances of rule violations or continued poor performance, and keep notes and documents from the counseling sessions held with employees.[156]

Finally, to reduce the chances of a wrongful discharge suit, employees should always be fired in private. State the reason for discharge, but don't go into detail or engage in a lengthy discussion with the employee. Make every attempt to be as kind and respectful as possible when informing someone that he or she is being fired. It is permissible and sometimes a good idea to have a witness present. This person should be from human resources or part of the employee's chain of command, such as the supervisor's boss. Company security may be nearby but should not be in the room unless the employee has made direct threats toward others. Finally, managers should be careful not to publicly criticize the employee who has just been fired, as this can also lead to a wrongful discharge lawsuit. In general, unless someone has a "business reason to know" why an employee was fired, the reasons and details related to the firing should remain confidential.[157]

8.2 Downsizing

Downsizing is the planned elimination of jobs in a company. Whether it's because of cost cutting, declining market share, previous overaggressive hiring and growth, or outsourcing, companies typically eliminate 1 million to 1.9 million jobs a year.[158] Two-thirds of companies that downsize will downsize a second time within a year. For example, after laying off 1,520 employees in December and almost 1,000 employees 10 months earlier, Yahoo!, which saw its profits drop by 78 percent,

wrongful discharge a legal doctrine that requires employers to have a job-related reason to terminate employees.

downsizing the planned elimination of jobs in a company.

announced plans to cut 5 percent of its remaining workforce.[159] General Motors announced it would cut 4,000 white-collar jobs with an overall goal of eliminating 10,000 of its 73,000 salaried positions worldwide. When complete, GM will employ 23,500 white-collar workers, half the number it had a decade ago.[160]

Does downsizing work? In theory, downsizing is supposed to lead to higher productivity and profits, better stock performance, and increased organizational flexibility. However, numerous studies demonstrate that it doesn't. For instance, a 15-year study of downsizing found that downsizing 10 percent of a company's workforce produced only a 1.5 percent decrease in costs; that firms that downsized increased their stock price by only 4.7 percent over 3 years, compared with 34.3 percent for firms that didn't; and that profitability and productivity were generally not improved by downsizing.[161] Downsizing can also result in the loss of skilled workers who would be expensive to replace when the company grows again.[162] These results make it clear that the best strategy is to conduct effective human resource planning and avoid downsizing altogether. Indeed, downsizing should always be a last resort.

If companies do find themselves in financial or strategic situations where downsizing is required for survival, however, they should train managers in how to break the news to downsized employees, have senior managers explain in detail why downsizing is necessary, and time the announcement so that employees hear it from the company and not from other sources, such as TV or newspaper reports.[163] Finally, companies should do everything they can to help downsized employees find other jobs. One of the best ways to do this is to use **outplacement services** that provide employment counseling for employees faced with downsizing. Outplacement services often include advice and training in preparing résumés, getting ready for job interviews, and even identifying job opportunities in other companies. Fifty-five percent of companies provide outplacement services for laid-off employees, 76 percent provide extended health coverage, and 45 percent offer extended access to employee assistance programs.[164] Exhibit 11.16 provides additional guidelines for conducting layoffs.

Companies also need to pay attention to the survivors, the employees remaining after layoffs have occurred. University of Pennsylvania management professor Peter Cappelli says that survivors "may feel like they could just as easily be the next person laid off."[165] Lori Stewart Coletti, director of client services at Elaine Construction, a Newton, Massachusetts–based firm, said, "The general feeling is, 'Could I be next?' That's the level of uncertainty that you really have to combat."[166] The key to working with layoff survivors, according to Barry Nickerson, president of Dallas-based Marlow Industries, which downsized from 800 to 200 employees, is "Communicate.

Exhibit 11.16 Guidelines for Conducting Layoffs

1. Provide clear reasons and explanations for the layoffs.

2. To avoid laying off employees with critical or irreplaceable skills, knowledge, and expertise, get input from human resources, the legal department, and several levels of management.

3. Train managers in how to tell employees that they are being laid off (stay calm; make the meeting short; explain why, but don't be personal; and provide information about immediate concerns, such as benefits, job search, and collecting personal goods).

4. Give employees the bad news early in the day, and try to avoid laying off employees just before holidays.

5. Provide outplacement services and counseling to help laid-off employees find new jobs.

6. Communicate with survivors to explain how the company and their jobs will change.

Source: M. Boyle, "The Not-So-Fine Art of the Layoff," *Fortune*, March 19, 2001, 209.

outplacement services employment-counseling services offered to employees who are losing their jobs because of downsizing.

doing the right thing

More on Downsizing

What is an employee's greatest fear when a company struggles? The answer, of course, is losing his or her job. And for good reason, because whether it's been because of poor strategy or a shrinking economy, when companies struggle to stay afloat, they cut jobs in order to save on costs. However, a growing body of research shows that downsizing hurts companies more than it helps. Companies that downsize have negative stock returns, reduced profitability, and reduced productivity. There are also negative effects on the remaining employees. Most of the talented people who the company wants to keep end up leaving for other jobs, while those who remain have lower morale, lower productivity, decreased engagement, and increased distrust of management. Downsizing even hurts the broader economy—when people lose jobs, they spend less, leading to decreased overall demand on goods and services, which weakens other companies. So yes, times are tough, and companies have to find ways to tighten the belt. But do the right thing—downsizing just may end up hurting, not helping, your company, so make it a last option.[167]

Communicate. Communicate." Nickerson says, "Every time we had a change we had a meeting to explain exactly what we were doing. We were very open with our employees about where we were financially. We would explain exactly the current status and where we were."[168]

8.3 Retirement

Early retirement incentive programs (ERIPs) offer financial benefits to employees to encourage them to retire early. Companies use ERIPs to reduce the number of employees in the organization; lower costs by eliminating positions after employees retire; lower costs by replacing high-paid retirees with lower-paid, less-experienced employees; or to create openings and job opportunities for people inside the company. For example, the state of Wyoming offered its employees a lump-sum bonus, additional insurance benefits, and increased monthly retirement payments to encourage early retirement. Its ERIP must have been fairly attractive, because 56 percent of the state employees eligible for early retirement accepted. Thirty percent of the 437 positions vacated by the early retirees remained empty, saving the state $23.2 million over the first 46 months of the program and a projected $65 million over eight years. After accounting for the costs of the increased early retirement benefits, the predicted savings came to more than $148,000 per retiree.[169]

Although ERIPs can save companies money, they can pose a big problem for managers if they fail to accurately predict which employees—the good performers or the poor performers—and how many will retire early. Consultant Ron Nicol says, "The thing that doesn't work is just asking for volunteers. You get the wrong volunteers. Some of your best people will feel they can get a job anywhere. Or you have people who are close to retirement and are a real asset to the company."[170] When Progress Energy, in Raleigh, North Carolina, identified 450 jobs it wanted to eliminate with an ERIP, it carefully shared the list of jobs with employees, indicated that layoffs would follow if not enough people took early retirement, and then held 80 meetings

early retirement incentive programs (ERIPs) programs that offer financial benefits to employees to encourage them to retire early.

with employees to answer questions. Despite this care, an extra 1,000 employees, for a total of 1,450, took the ERIP offer and applied for early retirement![171]

Because of the problems associated with ERIPs, many companies are now offering **phased retirement**, in which employees transition to retirement by working reduced hours over a period of time before completely retiring. The advantage for employees is that they have more free time but continue to earn salaries and benefits without changing companies or careers. The advantage for companies is that it allows them to reduce salaries and hiring and training costs and retain experienced, valuable workers.[172]

8.4 Employee Turnover

Employee turnover is the loss of employees who voluntarily choose to leave the company. In general, most companies try to keep the rate of employee turnover low to reduce recruiting, hiring, training, and replacement costs. Not all kinds of employee turnover are bad for organizations, however. In fact, some turnover can actually be good. **Functional turnover** is the loss of poor-performing employees who choose to leave the organization.[173] Functional turnover gives the organization a chance to replace poor performers with better workers. In fact, one study found that simply replacing poor-performing leavers with average workers would increase the revenues produced by retail salespeople in an upscale department store by $112,000 per person per year.[174] By contrast, **dysfunctional turnover**, the loss of high performers who choose to leave, is a costly loss to the organization.

Employee turnover should be carefully analyzed to determine whether good or poor performers are choosing to leave the organization. If the company is losing too many high performers, managers should determine the reasons and find ways to reduce the loss of valuable employees. The company may have to raise salary levels, offer enhanced benefits, or improve working conditions to retain skilled workers. One of the best ways to influence functional and dysfunctional turnover is to link pay directly to performance. A study of four sales forces found that when pay was strongly linked to performance via sales commissions and bonuses, poor performers were much more likely to leave (i.e., functional turnover). By contrast, poor performers were much more likely to stay when paid large, guaranteed monthly salaries and small sales commissions and bonuses.[175]

phased retirement employees transition to retirement by working reduced hours over a period of time before completing retiring.

employee turnover loss of employees who voluntarily choose to leave the company.

functional turnover loss of poor-performing employees who voluntarily choose to leave a company.

dysfunctional turnover loss of high-performing employees who voluntarily choose to leave a company.

Employee Separations Employee separation is the loss of an employee; separation can occur voluntarily or involuntarily. Before firing or terminating employees, managers should give employees a chance to improve. If firing becomes necessary, it should be done because of job-related factors, such as violating company rules or consistently performing poorly. Downsizing is supposed to lead to higher productivity and profits, better stock performance, and increased organizational flexibility, but studies show that it doesn't. The best strategy is to downsize only as a last resort. Companies that do downsize should offer outplacement services to help employees find other jobs. Companies use early retirement incentive programs to reduce the number of employees in the organization, lower costs, and create openings and job opportunities for people inside the company. The biggest problem with ERIPs is accurately predicting who and how many will accept early retirement. Companies generally try to keep the rate of employee turnover low to reduce costs. Functional turnover can be good for organizations, however, because it offers the chance to replace poor performers with better workers. Managers should analyze employee turnover to determine who is resigning and take steps to reduce the loss of good performers.

Review 8

SELF-ASSESSMENT

Interview Anxiety

How would you feel if you got a call to interview for your dream job? Excited? Nervous? Or downright panicked? It's not uncommon to get butterflies in your stomach at the prospect of a job interview, but some candidates have more than weak knees and sweaty palms. Complete the assessment below by indicating the extent to which you agree with each of the following statements.[176] Your score will be a baseline as you begin working on the skills you'll need during your job hunt. Try not to spend too much time on any one item, and be sure to answer all the questions. Use this scale for your responses:

1 Strongly disagree
2 Disagree
3 Neutral
4 Agree
5 Strongly agree

1. I become so apprehensive in job interviews that I am unable to express my thoughts clearly.
    1   2   3   4   5

2. I often feel uneasy about my appearance when I am being interviewed for a job.
    1   2   3   4   5

3. While taking a job interview, I become concerned that the interviewer will perceive me as socially awkward.
    1   2   3   4   5

4. In job interviews, I get very nervous about whether my performance is good enough.
    1   2   3   4   5

5. During job interviews, my hands shake.
    1   2   3   4   5

6. I get so anxious while taking job interviews that I have trouble answering questions that I know.
    1   2   3   4   5

7. Before a job interview, I am so nervous that I spend an excessive amount of time on my appearance.
    1   2   3   4   5

8. I become very uptight about having to socially interact with a job interviewer.
    1   2   3   4   5

9. I am overwhelmed by thoughts of doing poorly when I am in job interview situations.
    1   2   3   4   5

10. My heartbeat is faster than usual during job interviews.
    1   2   3   4   5

11. During job interviews, I often can't think of a thing to say.
    1   2   3   4   5

12. In job interviews, I worry that the interviewer will focus on what I consider to be my least attractive physical features.
    1   2   3   4   5

KEY TERMS

360-degree feedback 460
adverse impact 434
assessment centers 447
background checks 444
behavior observation scale (BOS) 459
biographical data 446
bona fide occupational qualification (BFOQ) 432
cafeteria benefit plans 466
cognitive ability tests 446
commission 464
compensation 463
disparate treatment 434
downsizing 468
dysfunctional turnover 471
early retirement incentive programs (ERIPs) 470
employee separation 467
employee stock ownership plan (ESOP) 464
employee turnover 471
employment benefits 466
employment references 444
external recruiting 440
four-fifths (or 80 percent) rule 434
functional turnover 471
hostile work environment 436
human resource information system (HRIS) 429
human resource management (HRM) 426

human resource planning (HRP) 427
internal recruiting 439
interviews 448
job analysis 438
job description 438
job evaluation 463
job specifications 438
needs assessment 454
objective performance measures 459
outplacement services 469
performance appraisal 458
personality tests 447
phased retirement 471
piecework 464
profit sharing 464
quid pro quo sexual harassment 435
rater training 459
recruiting 438
selection 442
sexual harassment 435
specific ability tests 446
stock options 464
structured interviews 450
subjective performance measures 459
training 454
unstructured interviews 450
validation 442
workforce forecasting 427
work sample tests 447
wrongful discharge 468

13. I get afraid about what kind of personal impression I am making on job interviews.
    1   2   3   4   5

14. I worry that my job interview performance will be lower than that of other applicants.
    1   2   3   4   5

15. It is hard for me to avoid fidgeting during a job interview.
    1   2   3   4   5

16. I feel that my verbal communication skills are strong.
    1   2   3   4   5

17. If I do not look my absolute best in a job interview, I find it very hard to be relaxed.
    1   2   3   4   5

18. During a job interview, I worry that my actions will not be considered socially appropriate.
    1   2   3   4   5

19. During a job interview, I am so troubled by thoughts of failing that my performance is reduced.
    1   2   3   4   5

20. Job interviews often make me perspire (e.g., sweaty palms and underarms).
    1   2   3   4   5

21. During job interviews, I find it hard to understand what the interviewer is asking me.
    1   2   3   4   5

22. I feel uneasy if my hair is not perfect when I walk into a job interview.
    1   2   3   4   5

23. I worry about whether job interviewers will like me as a person.
    1   2   3   4   5

24. During a job interview, I worry about what will happen if I don't get the job.
    1   2   3   4   5

25. My mouth gets very dry during job interviews.
    1   2   3   4   5

26. I find it easy to communicate my personal accomplishments during a job interview.
    1   2   3   4   5

27. During a job interview, I worry about whether I have dressed appropriately.
    1   2   3   4   5

28. When meeting a job interviewer, I worry that my handshake will not be correct.
    1   2   3   4   5

29. While taking a job interview, I worry about whether I am a good candidate for the job.
    1   2   3   4   5

30. I often feel sick to my stomach when I am interviewed for a job.
    1   2   3   4   5

Scoring

Reverse your score on items 16 and 26. That is, if you wrote in a "5," change it to a "1" and vice versa; if you wrote in a "4," change it to a "2" and vice versa.

TOTAL = _____

You can find the interpretation of your score at: www.cengagebrain.com.

MANAGEMENT DECISION

To Facebook or Not to Facebook

For the past six months, you've been heading a hiring committee in charge of hiring a new division manager. It's been a grueling process—filtering through thousands of applications, seemingly endless meetings and discussions debating people's qualifications, so many interviews in different cities that it's hard to remember whom you met and where, and even more debates about who should be flown to your headquarters for a day of final interviews.

But it's almost all over now. After so many interviews and meetings and discussions, the committee has settled on a candidate that everyone thinks is ideal

for the job—Ivy-league educated, lots of management experience, a great personality, driven to succeed, willing to learn. . . . He was near the top of your list when you began this process six months ago, and here he is now, in first place at the finish line.

You head into the last hiring committee meeting with lots of relief. Not only are you happy that you found the right person for the job, but you're really glad that this meeting is just going be a formality. No more debates or arguments about applicants' work experiences, education, or hobbies. Just walk on in, take a quick vote, and then make a call with the job offer.

But as you walk into the committee meeting, there's a strange vibe. Some people look quite worried, whereas others are just angry. When you ask what's going on, one of the committee members responds that in the past few days, she added the final candidate as a friend on Facebook, and what she found on his profile was quite disturbing. There were several photos of him passed out on the sidewalk after drinking too much. Other photos showed him smoking marijuana at a friend's apartment. Another photo shows him wearing a Nazi costume for what you assume is a Halloween party. And there's the language—almost all of his posts are filled with obscenities.

After seeing all of this, half the committee wants to go with another candidate. They can't imagine that this is the kind of person they want leading your company's most important division. The other half of the committee thinks it's not a big deal at all. They believe that how he spends his personal time has absolutely no reflection on his ability to manage, and they're angry that committee members would try to use it against him.

So here you are, faced with a split (and angry) committee. They're looking to you to make break the deadlock—should we hire this guy or move on to someone else?

Questions

1. What decision would you make? Would you hire this person or reopen the search?
2. In your opinion, are companies justified in using an applicant's Facebook or Twitter accounts when considering them for a job?
3. Do you believe that a company should be concerned with how a potential employee spends his or her personal time?

MANAGEMENT TEAM DECISION

Training for Great Service

At one time or another, almost every retailer claims that their first and only priority is to make the customer happy. Few, however, can duplicate what Nordstrom does. For the Seattle-based upscale retailer, "the customer is always right" is not just a promotional motto, but a way of life that guides the organization. The entire company is directed toward one goal—catering to the needs of customers. Sales associates are given incredible freedom to do what is needed to make customers happy—refunding a purchase made years ago, personally delivering items to airports and hotels for busy customers, and even lending out jewelry for a customer who was attending a party. The importance of making a customer even extends into store inventory, as managers try to stock every conceivable size, color, and variant of an item so that customers will always find what they are looking for. And in the rare instance that they can't, employees will call other Nordstrom stores, or even competitor stores, to track it down.

This emphasis on customer service has even spawned an urban legend. The story goes that many years ago, a man walked into a Nordstrom store in Alaska (or Seattle) with two snow tires. Nordstrom, of course, doesn't sell tires (snow or otherwise); the man had bought them from a tire store that had recently closed, the site of which was taken over by Nordstrom. Nonetheless, the man took the tires to a counter, said that he was unhappy with them, and asked for a full refund. The sales associate, eager to please the customer, gave it to him.

As the HR team of Nordstrom, you face a particular challenge—you need to create a team that is not only skilled for the job, but has the personality, attitude, and motivation to provide consistently superior customer service. Form a group with three or four other students and discuss how you would approach staffing and training issues at Nordstrom by answering the following questions.

Questions

1. Can a friendly, customer-oriented attitude be developed in a person? Can Nordstrom "train" employees to prioritize making customers happy, or is it purely a matter of personality?
2. What kind of selection tools would you use to find people who would fit Nordstrom's culture of customer service?
3. What kind of training programs would help new employees learn what is expected of them at Nordstrom?

PRACTICE BEING A MANAGER

Legal Recruiting

Managing human resources in today's complex business and legal environment is not easy. Not only must companies hire the creative and hard-working employees who will fuel growth and competitive advantage but they must be careful to do so legally and ethically. Unfair discrimination in any HR process will result in poor placement, turnover, and legal woes. This exercise will give you some practice in navigating the challenges of legal and effective recruitment and selection of employees.

Step 1: Get into groups. Your professor will assign you to groups of four or five students. One student will be given the role of HR attorney for the applicants, two students the role of nursing shift (day/night) managers at Montclair Hospital, and the remaining student(s) will be assigned the role of senior hospital administrator at Montclair Hospital.

Scenario: Montclair Hospital needs to hire new nurses. In fact, the hospital is in a bit of a crisis. Three nurses were recently fired for using drugs while on duty. In the ensuing publicity, a journalist uncovered that two of these nurses were convicted felons. As if these problems were not enough, nurse turnover is up 20 percent this year over last, and productivity of the remaining staff is substandard. Absences are also up lately, particularly those related to child-care or elder-care issues.

Both the day and the night nursing shift managers need to hire some quality nurses—and fast. Hospital administrators have made it abundantly clear that they do not want a repeat of the headline "Felons and Drug Users among Montclair Nursing Staff." Your compensation and benefits are competitive, and, with the exception of the recent news coverage, your hospital enjoys a strong reputation. The nursing labor market is tight (there are fewer nurses than openings), and most new hires are recent nursing school graduates.

Nursing shift managers need to work together to develop a plan to achieve the following:

1. Hire top-flight nurses to fill vacancies left by recent firings and resignations.

2. Stem the turnover of quality nurses already employed by Montclair.

3. Reduce absenteeism, especially unplanned "emergency" absences that wreak havoc with planning the work of an upcoming shift.

Step 2a: Outline a plan. The day and the night nursing shift managers should work together to sketch out a plan for making progress on the three concerns of Montclair Hospital administration (hiring, turnover, absenteeism). Some elements of this plan might include the following:

- Deciding where and how to recruit top nursing candidates

- Screening applicants to reduce risks of turnover, criminal/behavioral problems, and disruptive absenteeism

- Dealing with the turnover, absenteeism, and productivity problems of existing nursing staff

Step 2b: Review the plan. Students in the roles of hospital administrator and HR attorney should listen to the nursing managers as they sketch out their plans. Do not offer comments unless one of the managers asks you for your input. Take careful notes regarding what you hear, with particular attention to concerns and questions. Those in the HR attorney role should consider what you hear from the perspective of both potential applicants (and litigants) and Montclair Hospital (defense of HR practices).

Are the nursing managers developing a plan likely to successfully address the three concerns related to hiring, turnover, and absenteeism? Why or why not? Do you hear anything that might raise a legal concern (such as inappropriate interview questions, possible discrimination)?

Step 3: Debrief as a class. Students should open with comments from each perspective: (1) HR attorneys, (2) hospital administrators, and (3) nursing shift managers. What are some of the specific concerns or questions that arose in your mind as you played your particular role? What are some of the tensions that face the managers and administrators in this situation? How might the HR system of a hospital be improved? Why might nurses represent a particularly challenging set of HR concerns?

360-Degree Feedback

Whereas most performance appraisal ratings have traditionally come from just one person, the boss, 360-degree feedback is obtained from four sources: the boss, subordinates, peers and coworkers, and the

employees themselves. In this assignment, you will be gathering 360-degree feedback from people whom you work with or from a team or group that you're a member of for a class.

Here are some guidelines for obtaining your 360-degree feedback:

- *Carefully select respondents.* One of the keys to good 360-degree feedback is getting feedback from the right people. In general, the people you ask for feedback should interact with you on a regular basis and should have the chance to regularly observe your behavior. Also, be sure to get a representative sample of opinions from a similar number of coworkers and subordinates (assuming you have some).

- *Get a large enough number of responses.* In addition to your boss, you should have a minimum of three peers and three subordinates giving you feedback. Five or six respondents in each of those categories are even better.

- *Ensure confidentiality.* Respondents are much more likely to be honest if they know that their comments are confidential and anonymous. So, when you ask respondents for feedback, have them return their comments to someone other than yourself. This person, your "feedback facilitator," will remove the names and any other information that would identify who made particular comments.

- *Explain how the 360-degree feedback will be used.* In this case, explain that the feedback is for a class assignment, that the results will be used for your own personal growth and development, and that the feedback they give you will not affect your grade or formal assessment at work.

- *Ask respondents to make their feedback as specific as possible.* For instance, "bad attitude" isn't very good feedback. "Won't listen to others' suggestions" is much better because it would let you know how to improve your behavior. Have your respondents use the feedback form below to provide your feedback.

Here's what you need to turn in for this assignment:

1. The names and relationships (boss, peers, subordinates, classmates, teammates) of those whom you've asked for feedback

2. The name of the person you've asked to be your feedback facilitator

3. Copies of all written feedback that was returned to you

4. A one-page summary of the written feedback

5. A one-page description of your specific goals and action plans for responding to the feedback you received

DEVELOP YOUR CAREER POTENTIAL

360-Degree Feedback Form

As part of a class assignment, I, _____, am collecting feedback from you about my performance. What you say or write will not affect my grade. The purpose of this assignment is for me to receive honest feedback from the people I work with in order to identify the things I'm doing well and the things that I need to improve. So please be honest and direct in your evaluation.

When you have completed this feedback form, please return it to _____. He or she has been selected as my feedback facilitator and is responsible for ensuring that your confidentiality and anonymity are maintained. After all feedback forms have been returned to _____, he or she will make sure that your particular responses cannot be identified. Only then will the feedback be shared with me.

Please provide the following feedback.

Continue doing …

Describe three things that _____ is doing that are a positive part of his or her performance and that you want him or her to continue doing.

1.

2.

3.

Start doing …

Describe three things that _____ needs to start doing that would significantly improve his or her performance.

1.

2.

3.

Please make your feedback as specific and behavioral as possible. For instance, "needs to adjust attitude" isn't very good feedback. "Needs to begin listening to others' suggestions" is much better because the person now knows exactly how to change his or her behavior. So please be specific. Also, please write more than one sentence per comment. This will help the feedback recipient better understand your comments.

END NOTES

[1] B. Burlingham, "Lessons From a Blue-Collar Millionaire," *Inc.*, February 2010, 56–63; N. Sarillo, "How to Tap Your Staff for Brilliant Ideas," Owner, Nick's Pizza & Pub, Crystal Lake, Ill., May 24, 2011, accessed May 26, 2011, from www.bnet.com/blog/smb/how-to-tap-your-staff-for-brilliant-ideas/4628?tag=sec-river2; and K. Springen, "Building A Perfect Pizzeria; How a Construction Worker from Chicago Built His $9 Million Pizza Business—One Weathered Beam at a Time," *Newsweek*, July 6, 2005, accessed May 26, 2011, from www.newsweek.com/2005/07/05/building-a-perfect-pizzeria.html.

[2] J. Guynn, "War Heats Up for Top Silicon Valley Talent," *The Los Angeles Times*, November 10, 2010, accessed May 23, 2011, from http://articles.latimes.com/2010/nov/10/business/la-fi-silicon-pay-war-20101111.

[3] B. Schneider & N. Schmitt, *Staffing Organizations*, 2nd ed. (Glenview, IL: Scott, Foresman & Co., 1986).

[4] D. M. Atwater, "Workforce Forecasting," *Human Resource Planning* 18, no. 4 (1995): 50.

[5] Nick Bunkley, "Ford Plans to Hire More than 7,000 Workers," *The New York Times*, January 10, 2011, from www.nytimes.com/2011/01/11/business/11ford.html.

[6] K. Wolf, "Dorner Mfg Corp's Layoff Strategy. SHRM Economic Stimulus Prize Winner and Their Case Studies," *Society for Human Resource Management*, February 1, 2009, accessed October 2, 2009, from www.shrm.org/about/awards/Pages/econstudies.aspx.

[7] Ibid.

[8] Atwater, "Workforce Forecasting"; D. Ward, "Workforce Demand Forecasting Techniques," *Human Resource Planning* 19, no. 1 (1996): 54.

[9] S. M. Director & J. Schramm, "Staffing Research: Estimating Future Staffing Levels: Implications for HR Strategy," Society for Human Resource Management, accessed March 23, 2009, from www.shrm.org/Research/Articles/Articles/Documents/06-0596_StaffMgmtInsert_Fall06.pdf&pli=1.

[10] E. Frauenheim, "Personnel Precision," *Workforce Management* 90, v11 (2011): 22–26.

[11] A. J. Walker, "The Analytical Element Is Important to an HRIS," *Personnel Administrator* 28 (1983): 33–35, 85.

[12] L. Thornburg, "Case Study: HRIS Implementation: EROne Chooses HROffice," *Society for Human Resource Management*, accessed March 23, 2009, from www.capacityplus.org/hris/hris-toolkit/tools/step_solution.html.

[13] C. Allen, "Enabling Faster HRIS Integration," Society for Human Resource Management, accessed March 23, 2009, from www.shrm.org/hrdisciplines/technology/Articles/Pages/CMS_006591.aspx.

[14] R. Zeidner, "Watson Wyatt: Employers Use Technology to Drive Employee Behavior Changes," *Society of Human Resource Management*, February 26, 2008, accessed March 23, 2009, from www.shrm.org/hrdisciplines/technology/Articles/Pages/UseTechnologyDriveBehavior.aspx.

[15] D. Hilbert, "The Newest Analytical Technologies Make the Future for HR," *Employment Relations* 36, no. 1 (2009): 1–7.

[16] L. Klie, "For the Best Hires, Retailers Hire Speech," *Speech Technology Magazine* 14, no. 3 (2009): 28–32.

[17] S. Bing, "The Feds Make a Pass at Hooters," *Fortune*, January 15, 1996, 82.

[18] J. Helyar, "Hooters: A Case Study," *Fortune*, September 1, 2003, 140.

[19] A. Samuels, "Pushing Hot Buttons and Wings," *St. Petersburg (FL) Times*, March 10, 2003, 1A.

[20] J. Casale, R. Ceniceros, & M. Hofmann, "Hooters Wannabe Resists Girls-Only Policy," *Business Insurance* 43, no. 4 (2009), 23.

[21] P. S. Greenlaw & J. P. Kohl, "Employer 'Business' and 'Job' Defenses in Civil Rights Actions," *Public Personnel Management* 23, no. 4 (1994): 573.

[22] Associated Press, "Hooters Settles Suit, Won't Hire Waiters," *Denver Post*, October 1, 1997, A11.

[23] "Massey Settles Age Discrimination Suit for $8.75 Million," Cleveland.com., October 30, 2009, accessed September 5, 2010, from www.cleveland.com/business/index.ssf/2009/10/massey_settles_age_discriminat.html.

[24]B. Morris, K. Bonamici, S. Kaufman, & P. Neering, "How Corporate America Is Betraying Women," *Fortune*, January 10, 2005, 64.

[25]J. L. Ledvinka, *Federal Regulation of Personnel and Human Resource Management* (Boston: Kent Publishing Co., 1982), 137–198.

[26]C. Cummins, "BP's Accident Put Its Celebrated CEO on the Hot Seat," *The Wall Street Journal*, June 16, 2006, B1.

[27]N. Adams, "Marketplace Report: BP Oil Fined for Lax Safety," National Pubic Radio, September 23, 2005, accessed March 23, 2009, from www.npr.org.

[28]A. Smith, "BP Faces Disaster Report from Baker Panel," CNNMoney.com, January 17, 2007, accessed March 23, 2009, from http://money.cnn.com/2007/01/15/news/companies/bp/index.htm.

[29]Greenlaw & Kohl, "Employer 'Business' and 'Job' Defenses in Civil Rights Actions."

[30]D. Ramde, "Wis. Plan Settles Discrimination Case for $1.65m," *Bloomberg Businessweek*, February 4, 2011, accessed March 4, 2011, from www.businessweek.com/ap/financialnews/D9L60CP00.htm.

[31]Martin Cothran, "Gaskell Case Shows UK Does Not Value Diversity," *Lexington Herald Leader*, January 24, 2011, accessed March 4, 2011, from www.kentucky.com/2011/01/24/1609118/gaskell-case-shows-uk-does-not.html#more.

[32]*Ricci v. DeStefano et al.*, U.S. Supreme Court, June 29, 2009.

[33]W. Peirce, C. A. Smolinski, & B. Rosen, "Why Sexual Harassment Complaints Fall on Deaf Ears," *Academy of Management Executive* 12, no. 3 (1998): 41–54.

[34]Ryan Gray, "First Student to Pay $150K to Settle Sexual Harassment, Retaliation Suit," *School Transportation News*, February 4, 2011, accessed May 23, 2011, from www.stnonline.com/home/latest-news/3104-eeoc-orders-first-student-to-pay-150k-to-settle-sexual-harassment-retaliation-suit.

[35]Brian Watt, "ABM Industries Settles Sexual Harassment Suit with Female Janitorial Workers," SCPR.org, September 2, 2010, www.scpr.org/news/2010/09/02/abm-industries-agrees-settle-sexual-harassment-sui/.

[36]"Facts about Sexual Harassment," U.S. Equal Employment Opportunity Commission, accessed March 23, 2009, www.eeoc.gov/facts/fs-sex.html.

[37]Peirce, Smolinski, & Rosen, "Why Sexual Harassment Complaints Fall on Deaf Ears."

[38]Ibid.

[39]E. Larson, "The Economic Costs of Sexual Harassment," *The Freeman* 46, August 1996, accessed August 13, 2008, from www.fee.org/publications/the-freeman/article.asp?aid= 4114.

[40]C. Koons, "Australia's Recovering Mining Industry Struggles to Fill Jobs," *The Wall Street Journal*, September 21, 2009, A15.

[41]M. Jordan, "Dairy Farms Run Low on Labor—Even in Recession, U.S. Job Candidates Are Scarce; Milk Producers Relying on Immigrants Worry About a Crackdown," *The Wall Street Journal*, July 30, 2009, A13; and L. Landro, "Staff Shortages in Labs May Put Patients at Risk," *The Wall Street Journal*, May 13, 2009, D1.

[42]G. Hyland-Savage, "General Management Perspective on Staffing: The Staffing Commandments," in *On Staffing*, N. C. Bukholder, P. J. Edwards, Jr., & L. Sartain, eds. (Hoboken, NJ: Wiley, 2004), 280.

[43]R. D. Gatewood & H. S. Field, *Human Resource Selection* (Fort Worth, TX: Dryden Press, 1998).

[44]Ibid.

[45]Gene Marks, "How to Surf the Resume Tsunami," *Forbes*. July 16, 2010, accessed August 23, 2010, from www.forbes.com/2010/07/16/hiring-jobs-small-business-entrepreneurs-human-resources-gene-marks.html.

[46]*Griggs v. Duke Power Co.*, 401 U.S. 424, 436 (1971); *Albemarle Paper Co. v. Moody*, 422 U.S. 405 (1975).

[47]L. Grensing-Pophal, "Internal Selections," *HR Magazine* 51, no. 12 (2006), accessed March 4, 2011, from www.shrm.org/Publications/hrmagazine/EditorialContent/Pages/1206agenda_empstaff.aspx.

[48]Ibid.

[49]J. A. Breaugh, *Recruitment: Science and Practice* (Boston: PWSKent, 1992).

[50]L. Klaff, "New Internal Hiring Systems Reduce Cost and Boost Morale," *Workforce Management* 83 (March 2004): 76–79.

[51]Ibid.

[52]"Executive Team: Bob McDonald, Biography," Procter & Gamble, January 2010, accessed July 27, 2010, from www.pg.com/en_US/downloads/company/executive_team/bios/pg_executive_bio_bob_mcdonald.pdf.

[53]B. O'Keefe, "Battle-Tested: How a Decade of War Has Created … A New Generation of Elite Business Leaders," *Fortune*, March 22, 2010, 108-111.

[54]J. Breaugh and M. Starke, "Research on Employee Recruitment: So Many Studies, So Many Remaining Questions," *Journal of Management* 26 (2000): 405–434.

[55]"Internet Recruitment Report," NAS Insights, accessed August 14, 2008, from www.nasrecruitment.com/talenttips/NASinsights/InternetRecruitingReport06.pdf.

[56]K. Maher, "Corporations Cut Middlemen and Do Their Own Recruiting," *The Wall Street Journal*, January 14, 2003, B10.

[57]S. Needleman, "Theory & Practice: Recruiters Use Search Engines to Lure Job Hunters—Cash-Strapped Companies Save with Search Ads, Scale Back on Rival Media Like Job Boards and Newspapers," *The Wall Street Journal*, March 9, 2009, B4.

[58]Mark Whitehouse, "Some Firms Struggle to Hire Despite High Unemployment," *The Wall Street Journal*, August 9, 2010, accessed March 4, 2011, from http://online.wsj.com/article/SB10001424052748704895004575395491314812452.html.

[59]"Research Demonstrates the Success of Internet Recruiting," *HR Focus*, April 2003, 7.

[60]"New Jobs Suffix Approved for Worldwide Recruiting/Hiring," *Human Resource Department Management Report*, May 2005, 9.

[61]E. Agnvall, "Recruiting by Ones and Zeros," Society for Human Resource

Management, accessed March 4, 2011, from www.shrm.org/hrtx/library_/nonIC/CMS_014953.asp; and D. Robb, "Career Portals Boost Online Recruiting," *HR Magazine* (April 2004), Society for Human Resource Management, www.shrm.org/Publications/hrmagazine/EditorialContent/Pages/0901hrtech.aspx.

[62]S. Fegley, "2007 Advances in E-Recruiting: Leveraging the .jobs Domain," a survey report published by the Society for Human Resource Management, 2007.

[63]Sarah E. Needleman, "Lifting the Curtain on the Hiring Process," *The Wall Street Journal*, January 26, 2010, accessed March 4, 2011, from http://online.wsj.com/article/SB10001424052748703808090457502525507893551 56.html.

[64]C. Camden & B. Wallace, "Job Application Forms: A Hazardous Employment Practice," *Personnel Administrator* 28 (1983): 31–32.

[65]J. Kennedy, "Europeans Expect Different Type of Résumé," *The Chicago Sun-Times*, June 3, 1999, 73.

[66]T. Minton-Eversole, "Background Screens Even More Crucial during Economic Slump," Society of Human Resource Management, 30 July 2008, accessed March 4, 2011, from www.**shrm**.org/ema/library_published/nonIC/CMS_026257.asp.

[67]S. Adler, "Verifying a Job Candidate's Background: The State of Practice in a Vital Human Resources Activity," *Review of Business* 15, no. 2 (1993/1994): 3–8.

[68]W. Woska, "Legal Issues for HR Professionals: Reference Checking/Background Investigations," *Public Personnel Management* 36 (Spring 2007): 79–89.

[69]"More Than 70 Percent of HR Professionals Say Reference Checking Is Effective in Identifying Poor Performers," Society for Human Resource Management, accessed February 3, 2005, www.shrm.org/press_published/CMS_011240.asp.

[70]P. Babcock, "Spotting Lies: The High Cost of Careless Hiring," *HR Magazine* 48, no. 10 (October 2003), accessed November 5, 2009, from http://findarticles.com/p/articles/mi_m3495/is_10_48/ai_109136217/.

[71]"Suit: McDonald' Employee Exposed Himself to Girl at Eatery," CBSChicago.com, December 29, 2010, accessed February 23, 2011, from http://chicago.cbslocal.com/2010/12/29/suit-mcdonalds-employee-exposed-himself-to-girl-at-eatery/.

[72]M. Le, T. Nguyen, & B. Kleiner, "Legal Counsel: Don't Be Sued for Negligent Hiring," *Nonprofit World*, May 1, 2003, 14–15.

[73]"Why It's Critical to Set a Policy on Background Checks for New Hires," *Managing Accounts Payable*, September 2004, 6; and J. Schramm, "Future Focus: Background Checking," *HR Magazine* (January 2005), page not available.

[74]D. Belkin, "More Job Seekers Scramble to Erase Their Criminal Past," *The Wall Street Journal*, November 11, 2009, A1.

[75]A. Athavaley, "Job References You Can't Control," *The Wall Street Journal*, September 27, 2007, D1.

[76]M. P. Cronin, "This Is a Test," *Inc.* (August 1993): 64–69.

[77]C. Cohen, "Reference Checks," *CA Magazine* (November 2004): 41.

[78]Rachel Zupek, "Infamous Resume Lies," Msn.com, July 7, 2010, accessed March 4, 2011, from http://msn.careerbuilder.com/Article/MSN-1154-Cover-Letters-Resumes-Infamous-R%C3%A9sum%C3%A9-Lies/.

[79]J. Hunter, "Cognitive Ability, Cognitive Aptitudes, Job Knowledge, and Job Performance," *Journal of Vocational Behavior* 29 (1986): 340–362.

[80]F. L. Schmidt, "The Role of General Cognitive Ability and Job Performance: Why There Cannot be a Debate," *Human Performance* 15 (2002): 187–210.

[81]K. Murphy, "Can Conflicting Perspectives on the Role of *g* in Personnel Selection Be Resolved?" *Human Performance* 15 (2002): 173–186.

[82]E. E. Cureton, "Comment," in *Research Conference on the Use of Autobiographical Data as Psychological Predictors*, E. R. Henry, ed. (Greensboro, NC: The Richardson Foundation, 1965), 13.

[83]J. R. Glennon, L. E. Albright, & W. A. Owens, *A Catalog of Life History Items* (Greensboro, NC: The Richardson Foundation, 1966).

[84]Gatewood and Field, *Human Resource Selection*.

[85]G. Dean, "The Bottom Line: Effect Size," in *The Write Stuff: Evaluations of Graphology—The Study of Handwriting Analysis*, B. Beyerstein & D. Beyerstein, eds. (Buffalo, NY: Prometheus Books, 1992); K. Dunham, "Career Journal: The Jungle, Seeing the Future," *The Wall Street Journal*, May 15, 2001, B12; J. Kurtz & W. Wells, "The Employee Polygraph Protection Act: The End of Lie Detector Use in Employment Decisions?" *Journal of Small Business Management* 27, no. 4 (1989): 76–80; B. Leonard, "Reading Employees," *HR Magazine* (April 1999): 67; S. Lilienfeld, J. Wood, & H. Garb, "The Scientific Status of Projective Techniques," *Psychological Science in the Public Interest* 1 (2000): 27–66; and E. Neter & G. Ben-Shakhar, "The Predictive Validity of Graphological Inferences: A Meta-Analytic Approach," *Personality & Individual Differences* 10 (1989): 737–745.

[86]J. M. Digman, "Personality Structure: Emergence of the Five-Factor Model," *Annual Review of Psychology* 41 (1990): 417–440; and M. R. Barrick & M. K. Mount, "The Big Five Personality Dimensions and Job Performance: A Meta-Analysis," *Personnel Psychology* 44 (1991): 1–26.

[87]N. Schmitt, "Beyond the Big Five: Increases in Understanding and Practical Utility," *Human Performance* 17 (2004): 347–357.

[88]I. Kotlyar & K. Ades, "HR Technology: Assessment Technology Can Help Match the Best Applicant to the Right Job," *HR Magazine* (May 1, 2002): 97.

[89]K. Maher, "The Jungle: Focus on Recruitment, Pay and Getting Ahead," *The Wall Street Journal*, November 19, 2002, B8.

[90]J. Cortina, N. Goldstein, S. Payne, K. Davison, & S. Gilliland, "The Incremental Validity of Interview Scores Over and Above Cognitive Ability and Conscientiousness Scores," *Personnel Psychology* 53, no. 2 (2000): 325–351; and F. L. Schmidt & J. E. Hunter, "The Validity and Utility of Selection Methods in Personnel Psychology:

Practical and Theoretical Implications of 85 Years of Research Findings," *Psychological Bulletin* 124, no. 2 (1998): 262–274.

[91]M. S. Taylor & J. A. Sniezek, "The College Recruitment Interview: Topical Content and Applicant Reactions," *Journal of Occupational Psychology* 57 (1984): 157–168.

[92]M. Harris, "Reconsidering the Employment Interview: A Review of Recent Literature and Suggestions for Future Research," *Personnel Psychology* (Winter 1989): 691–726.

[93]Taylor & Sniezek, "The College Recruitment Interview."

[94]R. Burnett, C. Fan, S. J. Motowidlo, & T. DeGroot, "Interview Notes and Validity," *Personnel Psychology* 51, (1998): 375–396; and M. A. Campion, D. K. Palmer, & J. E. Campion, "A Review of Structure in the Selection Interview," *Personnel Psychology* 50, no. 3 (1997): 655–702.

[95]Anne Fisher, "Top 10 Myths about Job Interviews," CNNMoney.com, November 18, 2010, accessed December 21, 2010, from http://money.cnn.com/2010/11/18/news/economy/top_10_job_interview_myths.fortune/index.htm.

[96]"Finish Line Increases Employee Retention, Improves Manager Productivity, and Drives Sales Performance," Kronos, accessed May 24, 2011, from www.kronos.com/Case-Study/FinishLine.aspx.

[97]T. Judge, "The Employment Interview: A Review of Recent Research and Recommendations for Future Research," *Human Resource Management Review* 10, no. 4 (2000): 383–406.

[98]Cortina, Goldstein, Payne, Davison, & Gilliland, "The Incremental Validity of Interview Scores."

[99]K. Tyler, "Training Revs Up," *HR Magazine* (April 2005), Society for Human Resource Management, accessed March 23, 2009, from www.shrm.org/Publications/hrmagazine/EditorialContent/Pages/0405tyler.aspx.

[100]Ibid.

[101]S. Livingston, T. W. Gerdel, M. Hill, B. Yerak, C. Melvin, & B. Lubinger, "Ohio's Strongest Companies All

Agree That Training Is Vital to Their Success," *The Cleveland Plain Dealer*, May 21, 1997, 30S.

[102]G. Kesler, "Why the Leadership Bench Never Gets Deeper: Ten Insights about Executive Talent Development," *Human Resource Planning*, January 1, 2002, 32.

[103]"Frequently Asked Questions," WorkKeys, accessed March 23, 2009, from www.act.org/workkeys/overview/faq.html#skills.

[104]The Oil Spill Training Company, accessed August 14, 2008, from http://oilspilltraining.com/home/index.asp.

[105]Jennifer Levitz, "UPS Thinks Out of the Box on Driver Training," *The Wall Street Journal*, April 6, 2010, accessed June 10, 2010, from http://online.wsj.com/article/SB10001424052702303912104575164573823418844.html.

[106]Leigh Buchanan, "Training: Auto Didacts," *Inc.*, June 8, 2010, accessed August 12, 2010, from www.inc.com/top-workplaces/2010/articles/online-employee-training.html.

[107]Dave Zielinski, "Training Games," SHRM, March 1, 2010, accessed March 12, 2010, from www.shrm.org/Publications/hrmagazine/EditorialContent/2010/0310/Pages/0310tech.aspx.

[108]D. L. Kirkpatrick, "Four Steps to Measuring Training Effectiveness," *Personnel Administrator* 28 (1983): 19–25.

[109]L. Bassi, J. Ludwig, D. McMurrer, & M. Van Buren, "Profiting from Learning: Do Firms' Investments in Education and Training Pay Off?" American Society for Training and Development, accessed August 14, 2008, from www.astd.org/NR/rdonlyres/91956A5E-6E57-44DDAE5D-FCFFCDC11C3F/0/ASTD_Profiting_From_Learning.pdf.

[110]C. Bartz, "Corner Office: Imagining a World of No Annual Reviews," interview by A. Bryant, *The New York Times*, October 17, 2009, accessed July 30, 2010, from www.nytimes.com/2009/10/18/business/18corner.html?_r=1.

[111]D. Murphy, "Are Performance Appraisals Worse Than a Waste of Time? Book Derides Unintended

Consequences," *The San Francisco Chronicle*, September 8, 2001, W1.

[112]K. R. Murphy & J. N. Cleveland, *Understanding Performance Appraisal: Social, Organizational and Goal-Based Perspectives* (Thousand Oaks, CA: Sage, 1995).

[113]T. D. Schellhardt, "Annual Agony: It's Time to Evaluate Your Work, and All Involved Are Groaning," *The Wall Street Journal*, November 19, 1996, A1.

[114]U. J. Wiersma & G. P. Latham, "The Practicality of Behavioral Observation Scales, Behavioral Expectation Scales, and Trait Scales," *Personnel Psychology* 39 (1986): 619–628; and U. J. Wiersma, P. T. Van Den Berg, & G. P. Latham, "Dutch Reactions to Behavioral Observation, Behavioral Expectation, and Trait Scales," *Group & Organization Management* 20 (1995): 297–309.

[115]D. J. Schleicher, D. V. Day, B. T. Mayes, & R. E. Riggio, "A New Frame for Frame-of-Reference Training: Enhancing the Construct Validity of Assessment Centers," *Journal of Applied Psychology* (August 2002): 735–746.

[116]Stack, "The Curse of the Annual Performance Review."

[117]B. O'Reilly, "360-Degree Feedback Can Change Your Life," *Fortune*, October 17, 1994, 93.

[118]J. Sandberg, "Performance Reviews Need Some Work, Don't Meet Potential," *The Wall Street Journal*, November 20, 2007, B1.

[119]C. Hymowitz, "Do '360' Job Reviews by Colleagues Promote Honesty or Insults?" *The Wall Street Journal*, December 12, 2000, B1.

[120]D. A. Waldman, L. E. Atwater, & D. Antonioni, "Has 360 Feedback Gone Amok?" *Academy of Management Executive* 12, no. 2 (1998): 86–94.

[121]H. H. Meyer, "A Solution to the Performance Appraisal Feedback Enigma," *Academy of Management Executive* 5, no. 1 (1991): 68–76; G. C. Thornton, "Psychometric Properties of Self-Appraisals of Job Performance," *Personnel Psychology* 33 (1980): 263–271.

[122]G. C. Thornton, "Psychometric Properties of Self-Appraisals of Job Performance," *Personnel Psychology* 33 (1980): 263–271.

[123]J. Smither, M. London, R. Flautt, Y. Vargas, & I. Kucine, "Can Working with an Executive Coach Improve Multisource Feedback Ratings over Time? A Quasi-Experimental Field Study," *Personnel Psychology* (Spring 2003): 21–43.

[124]A. Walker & J. Smither, "A Five-Year Study of Upward Feedback: What Managers Do with Their Results Matters," *Personnel Psychology* (Summer 1999): 393–422.

[125]J. McGregor, "The Employee Is Always Right," *Businessweek*, November 8, 2007, accessed August 14, 2008, from www.businessweek.com/globalbiz/content/nov2007/gb2007118_541063.htm.

[126]I. M. Jawahar, "Correlates of Satisfaction with Performance Appraisal Feedback," *Journal of Labor Research* 26 (2006): 213–236.

[127]Ibid.

[128]C. Tuna, "In Some Offices, Keeping Workers Earns a Bonus; More Firms Like Penske Tie Top Managers' Pay to Employee Retention," *The Wall Street Journal*, June 30, 2008, B6.

[129]Ibid.

[130]G. T. Milkovich & J. M. Newman, *Compensation*, 4th ed. (Homewood, IL: Irwin, 1993).

[131]J. A. Livingston, "Child Care Wages and Benefits Study," Child Care Resource, August 2, 2006, accessed August 14, 2008, from www.childcareresource.org/home_announce/cc%20wages%20and%20benefits%20report.final.augst.2006.pdf.

[132]"A Worthy Wage?" *American Federation of Teachers*, 1 May 2008, accessed August 14, 2008, from www.aft.org/news/download/AFT-Worthy-Wage-Day2008-Ad.pdf.

[133]M. L. Williams & G. F. Dreher, "Compensation System Attributes and Applicant Pool Characteristics," *Academy of Management Journal* 35, no. 3 (1992): 571–595.

[134]D. Lee, "The Supply-Side Lesson of Henry Ford," Investors.com, September 20, 2010, accessed May 24, 2011, from www.investors.com/NewsAndAnalysis/Article/547855/201009201845/The-Supply-Side-Lesson-Of-Henry-Ford.aspx.

[135]Steve Cooper & Colleen Debaise, "Best Ways to Pay Your Sales Staff," *Bloomberg Businessweek*, June 5, 2009, accessed September 6, 2010, from www.businessweek.com/magazine/content/09_66/s0906028668952.htm.

[136]N. Bunkley, "Ford Profit Comes as Toyota Hits a Bump," *The Wall Street Journal*, January 28, 2010, accessed June 15, 2010, from www.nytimes.com/2010/01/29/business/29ford.html?scp=3&sq=profit-sharing&st=cse.

[137]J. Kaufman, "Sharing the Wealth: At McKay Nursery, Migrant Workers Get a Chance to Own Part of the Company," *The Wall Street Journal*, April 9, 1998, R10.

[138]L. S. Covel, "How to Get Workers to Think and Act Like Owners," *The Wall Street Journal*, February 7, 2008, B6.

[139]Ibid.

[140]M. Bloom, "The Performance Effects of Pay Dispersion on Individuals and Organizations," *Academy of Management Journal* 42, no. 1 (1999): 25–40.

[141]"Trends in CEO Pay," AFL-CIO, accessed August 11, 2011, from www.aflcio.org/corporatewatch/paywatch/pay/index.cfm; and "Employer Costs for Employee Compensation," *Economic News Release*, Bureau of Labor Statistics, June 9 2010, accessed August 11, 2010, from www.bls.gov/news.release/ecec.nr0.htm.

[142]W. Grossman & R. E. Hoskisson, "CEO Pay at the Crossroads of Wall Street and Main: Toward the Strategic Design of Executive Compensation," *Academy of Management Executive* 12, no. 1 (1998): 43–57.

[143]Bloom, "The Performance Effects of Pay Dispersion."

[144]M. Bloom & J. Michel, "The Relationships among Organizational Context, Pay Dispersion, and Managerial Turnover," *Academy of Management Journal* 45 (2002): 33–42.

[145]J. S. Rosenbloom, "The Environment of Employee Benefit Plans," in *The Handbook of Employee Benefits*, J. S. Rosenbloom, ed. (Chicago: Irwin, 1996), 3–13.

[146]"Employer Costs for Employee Compensation Summary," Bureau of Labor Statistics, accessed March 11, 2011, from www.bls.gov/news.release/ecec.nr0.htm.

[147]A. E. Barber, R. B. Dunham, & R. A. Formisano, "The Impact of Flexible Benefits on Employee Satisfaction: A Field Study," *Personnel Psychology* 45 (1992): 55–75; B. Heshizer, "The Impact of Flexible Benefits on Job Satisfaction and Turnover Intentions," *Benefits Quarterly* 4 (1994): 84–90; and D. M. Cable & T. A. Judge, "Pay Preferences and Job Search Decisions: A Person-Organization Fit Perspective," *Personnel Psychology* 47 (1994): 317–348.

[148]B. T. Beam & J. J. McFadden, *Employee Benefits* (Chicago: Dearborn Financial Publishing, 1996).

[149]R. Lieber, "Employers Offer New Pretax Perk: Debit Cards Allow Instant Access to Accounts for Medical Fees and Commuting Expenses," *The Wall Street Journal*, September 2, 2003, D1.

[150]L. Sheperd, "Prepaid Benefit Cards Poised for Growth," *Employee Benefit News*, June 15, 2008, 46–49.

[151]S. Needleman, "Bad Firings Can Hurt Firm's Reputation," *The Wall Street Journal*, July 8, 2008, D4.

[152]A. Rupe, "Horrors from the Bad-Firing File," *Workforce Management*, November 2003, 16.

[153]"400 at RadioShack Are Told by E-Mail: You're Outta Here," Associated Press, August 31, 2006, accessed March 11, 2011, from http://seattletimes.nwsource.com/html/businesstechnology/2003236874_radioshack31.html.

[154]Sarah E. Needleman, "'The Cat Hid My Car Keys'—Excuses Workers Make," *The Wall Street Journal*, May 14, 2010, accessed September 5, 2010, from http://online.wsj.com/article/NA_WSJ_PUB:SB10001424052748703339304575240770333031745.html.

[155]P. Michal-Johnson, *Saying Good-Bye: A Manager's Guide to Employee Dismissal* (Glenview, IL: Scott, Foresman & Co., 1985).

[156]M. Bordwin, "Employment Law: Beware of Time Bombs and Shark-Infested Waters," *HR Focus*, April 1, 1995, 19; and D. Jones, "Fired Workers Fight Back … and Win; Laws,

Juries Shift Protection to Terminated Employees," *USA Today*, April 2, 1998, B1.

157T. Bland, "Fire at Will, Repent at Leisure," *Security Management* 44 (May 2000): 64.

158"Mass Layoffs in December 2007 and Annual Totals for 2007," Bureau of Labor Statistics News, January 24, 2008, accessed August 15, 2008, from www.bls.gov/news.release/archives/mmls_01242008.pdf.

159S. Shankland, "Yahoo Plans Layoff after Profit Plunges," cnet.com, April 21, 2009, accessed October 10, 2009, from http://news.cnet.com/8301-1023_3-10224390-93.html.

160S. Terlep and J. Stoll, "GM to Eliminate More Jobs as It Accelerates Downsizing," *The Wall Street Journal*, June 24, 2009, B2.

161J. R. Morris, W. F. Cascio, & C. E. Young, "Downsizing after All These Years: Questions and Answers about Who Did It, How Many Did It, and Who Benefited from It," *Organizational Dynamics* 27, no. 3 (1999): 78–87.

162K. Maher, "Hiring Freezes Cushion New Layoffs," *The Wall Street Journal,* January 24, 2008, A13.

163K. E. Mishra, G. M. Spreitzer, and A. K. Mishra, "Preserving Employee Morale during Downsizing," *Sloan Management Review* 39, no. 2 (1998): 83–95.

164K. Frieswick, "Until We Meet Again?" *CFO*, October 1, 2001, 41.

165J. Hilsenrath, "Adventures in Cost Cutting," *The Wall Street Journal*, May 10, 2004, R1.

166M. Jackson, "Downsized, but Still in the Game: Keeping Up Morale Crucial after Job Cuts," *The Boston Globe*, January 11, 2009, G1.

167"Lay Off the Layoffs," *Newsweek*, February 5, 2010, accessed October 12, 2010, from www.newsweek.com/2010/02/04/lay-off-the-layoffs.html.

168J. Ackerman, "Helping Layoff Survivors Cope: Companies Strive to Keep Morale High," *The Boston Globe*, December 30, 2001, H1.

169D. Ferrari, "Designing and Evaluating Early Retirement Programs: The State of Wyoming Experience," *Government Finance Review* 15, no. 1 (1999): 29–31.

170Hilsenrath, "Adventures in Cost Cutting."

171J. Lublin & S. Thurm, "How Companies Calculate Odds in Buyout Offers," *The Wall Street Journal*, March 27, 2009, B1.

172M. Willett, "Early Retirement and Phased Retirement Programs for the Public Sector," *Benefits & Compensation Digest*, April 2005, 31.

173D. R. Dalton, W. D. Todor, & D. M. Krackhardt, "Turnover Overstated: The Functional Taxonomy," *Academy of Management Review* 7 (1982): 117–123.

174J. R. Hollenbeck & C. R. Williams, "Turnover Functionality versus Turnover Frequency: A Note on Work Attitudes and Organizational Effectiveness," *Journal of Applied Psychology* 71 (1986): 606–611.

175C. R. Williams, "Reward Contingency, Unemployment, and Functional Turnover," *Human Resource Management Review* 9 (1999): 549–576.

176J. McCarthy & R. Goffin, "Measuring Job Interview Anxiety: Beyond Weak Knees and Sweaty Palms," *Personnel Psychology* 54, no. 3 (2004): 31.

BIZ FLIX

Played

Thief-for-hire Ray Burns (Mick Rossi) just served eight years of prison time thanks to a crooked cop (Vinnie Jones). Now he's back on the streets and plans to settle the score. *Played* is a fast-moving crime thriller from 2006. The film is a gritty look inside London's criminal underground. In this clip from the movie, a shipment of heroin is arriving from Amsterdam, and they're making plans to pick it up. But first they need to assemble a team.

© GreenLight

What to Watch for and Ask Yourself

1. How would you write the job description for the recruits who will carry out the task discussed in this scene?

2. Would you say this is an example of internal or external recruiting?

3. Is compensation discussed?

MANAGEMENT WORKPLACE

Barcelona Restaurant Group: Managing Human Resources

At the Barcelona Restaurant Group, turnover among waitstaff is 60 percent to 70 percent. One way that Barcelona tries to reduce turnover is to select the right people, using a three-stage recruitment process. First, leaders conduct 20-minute interviews with dozens of candidates. Next, applicants are asked to spend $100 dollars at a Barcelona restaurant and write an essay about the event. The third step is "the trail," when job candidates command the floor, interact with waitstaff and customers, and demonstrate job skills. Approximately one-fourth of the candidates who go on a trail can expect to be hired. At the end of the day, according to Scott Lawton, people either possess the necessary intelligence and skills to run a restaurant or they don't. The industry doesn't have much time for learning curves, and the success or failure of any establishment depends on the performance of competent self-motivated employees.

© Cengage Learning

Discussion Questions

1. List the three main activities of human resource management (HRM), and identify which activity is examined at length in the video.

2. Of the various steps in Barcelona's employee selection process, the job interview is the most brief. Do you agree with the company's approach to interviewing? Why or why not?

3. Describe Barcelona's three-stage process for matching job applicants with its organizational objectives, and explain how each stage reveals the fit between job applicants and the needs of the restaurant.

CHAPTER 12

Managing Individuals and a Diverse Workforce

Learning Outcomes

1. Describe diversity and explain why it matters.

2. Understand the special challenges that the dimensions of surface-level diversity pose for managers.

3. Explain how the dimensions of deep-level diversity affect individual behavior and interactions in the workplace.

4. Explain the basic principles and practices that can be used to manage diversity.

what would **you do?**

Circuit Court, Macomb County, Michigan[1]

Hooters restaurants are known for spicy chicken wings, the Owl mascot (i.e., "Hooters"), and Hooters' girls, dressed in, as the company describes it, "white Hooters tank top, orange shorts, suntan hose, white socks, solid white shoes, brown Hooters pouch, name-tag and of course…a smile!" Hooters only hires female servers and readily admits that "the element of female sex appeal" is part of its business, but no more so, it argues, than the "socially acceptable" Dallas Cowboy Cheerleaders, Sports Illustrated swimsuit models, or Radio City Rockettes. Hooters states, "The 'nearly world famous' Hooters Girls are the cornerstone of the Hooters concept, and as part of their job, these all-American cheerleaders make promotional and charitable appearances in their respective communities. Hooters hires women who best fit the image of a Hooters Girl to work in this capacity." Hooters provides detailed guidelines on its website about hair, eyes, skin, makeup, and exercise. Consistent with maintaining the image of a Hooters Girl, all of its female waitstaff must attend image classes and pass an image quiz.

Hooters is being sued for discrimination by two waitresses from Roseville, Michigan: Cassandra Smith and Leeanne Convery. Smith received positive performance evaluations and was promoted to shift supervisor. But at her last evaluation, the 5'8" Smith says she was advised to lose weight and join a gym, despite dropping from 145 pounds, when hired, to her current 132.5 pounds. She says she was given 30 days to lose more weight, and when she didn't, was fired. Says Smith, "I had these two women from [Hooters headquarters in] Atlanta telling me I had 30 days to make an improvement, and I didn't know what I'm supposed to improve. I was proud of myself, working out the last months, losing 10 pounds to get ready for my summer body. For that (phone call) to happen, it was almost a slap in the face." Convery, who is 4'11" and weighs 115 pounds says she was also placed on weight probation and then fired, despite losing 15 lbs.

In a written statement, Hooters said, "No employee in Michigan has been asked to lose weight and … the company does not enforce any weight requirement." Company spokesperson Mike McNeil said, "We never mentioned weight. We never mentioned pounds. We never mentioned scales." But, he said, "We have an image to uphold. We've been upholding it for 27 years. Hopefully, we'll be doing it for another 27 years." Moreover, he said, "You're hired based on the image you have when you walk through the door."

As the judge in the case, you've got a number of key determinations to make. First, the women are basically arguing that being fired for being too heavy is akin to being fired because of their

© iStockphoto.com/Frances Twitty

study tips

In the margin next to each paragraph or section in the chapter, write the question that the section answers. For example, "What is the difference between surface- and deep-level diversity?" could go on page 492.

Once you have questions throughout the chapter, you can quiz yourself by using a blank piece of paper to cover the content. To check yourself, reveal each paragraph after you have answered the corresponding question.

© iStockphoto.com/Alex Slobodkin

© iStockphoto.com/Ivan Burmistrov

age, religion, sex, color, or national origin. In short, they say they're being discriminated against because of their weight. So, if Hooters fired them because they were too heavy, is that illegal under state and federal law? Second, Hooters will claim that the image of the Hooter Girl is central to their business and consequently allows them to discipline and fire waitresses for not maintaining that image. This is known as a bona fide occupational qualification (BFOQ). When a BFOQ is "reasonably necessary to the normal operation of that particular business," personnel decisions can be made on the basis of race, color, religion, sex, or national origin. Is the Hooter Girl image, and more specifically, the weight of a Hooter Girl, a BFOQ and thus a legally justifiable reason for Hooters' hiring, firing, and promotion decisions? Finally, Convery claims that since giving birth to her son, she has had problems maintaining her weight. In other words, having children changes a woman's physique, making it more difficult to return to one's pre-baby weight. If that's so, could she possibly have a legal case on the basis of the Americans with Disability Act?

If you were the judge in this case, what would you do?

Workplace diversity as we know it is changing. Exhibit 12.1 shows predictions from the U.S. Bureau of the Census of how the U.S. population will change over the next 40 years. The percentage of white, non-Hispanic Americans in the general population is expected to decline from 64.7 percent in 2010 to 46.3 percent by the year 2050, whereas the percentage of

Exhibit 12.1 Percentage of the Projected Population by Race and Hispanic Origin for the United States: 2010 to 2050

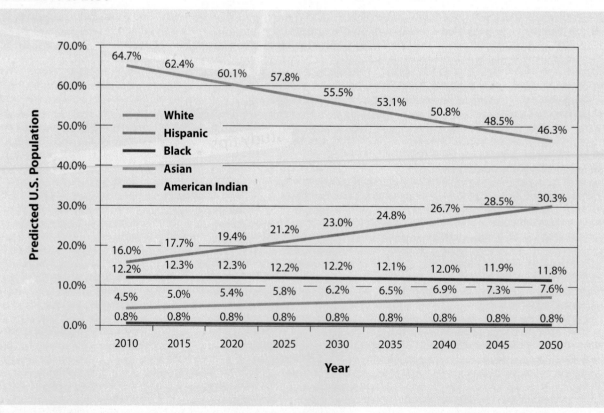

Source: U.S. Census Bureau, accessed May 27, 2011, from www.census.gov/population/www/projections/files/nation/summary/np2008-t6.xls.

black Americans will decrease from 12.2 percent to 11.8 percent. The percentage of Asians, meanwhile, will increase from 4.5 percent to 7.6 percent, whereas the proportion of Native Americans will hold steady (between 0.76% and 0.77%). The fastest-growing group by far, though, will be Hispanics, who are expected to increase from 16 percent of the total population in 2010 to 30.3 percent by 2050. Other significant changes have already occurred. For example, today women hold 46.5 percent of the jobs in the United States, up from 38.2 percent in 1970.[2] Furthermore, white males, who composed 63.9 percent of the workforce in 1950, hold just 38.2 percent of today's jobs.[3]

These rather dramatic changes have taken place in a relatively short time. And, as these trends clearly show, the workforce of the near future will be increasingly Hispanic, Asian American, African American, and female. It will also be older, as the average Baby Boomer approaches the age of 70 around 2020. Because many Boomers are likely to postpone retirement and work well into their 70s to offset predicted reductions in Social Security and Medicare benefits, the workforce may become even older than expected. For instance, between 1984 and 2014, 16- to 24-year-olds (21.1% to 13.7%), 25- to 34-year-olds (28.8% to 22.7%), and 35- to 44-year-olds (22% to 20.6%) will have become a smaller part of the U.S. labor force. By contrast, those 45 years and older (28.1% to 43.1%), 55 years and older (13.1% to 21.2%), and 65 years and older (2.6% to 5.4%) will all have become larger parts of the U.S. labor force.[4]

This chapter begins with a review of workforce diversity; we'll talk about what diversity is and why it matters. Next, you will learn about two basic dimensions of diversity: surface-level diversity (how age, sex, race/ethnicity, and mental and physical disabilities affect people at work) and deep-level diversity (how core personality differences influence behavior and attitudes). In the last section, you will learn how diversity can be managed. Here, you'll read about diversity paradigms, principles, and practices that help managers strengthen the diversity *and* the competitiveness of their organizations.

Diversity and Why It Matters

Diversity means variety. Therefore, **diversity** exists in organizations when there is a variety of demographic, cultural, and personal differences among the people who work there and the customers who do business there. For example, **Kayak.com** is a travel search engine that gives users data on the prices of airline tickets, rental cars, and hotels from hundreds of providers. The company fields phone calls and email from customers all over the world, so CEO Paul English hired German, Greek, Russian, Italian, French, and Indian employees to address the different needs, cultures, and languages represented in its customer base. As English puts it, "One of my missions is that we will be able to answer every customer call, in any language."[5]

By contrast, some companies lack diversity in their workforce, their customers, or both. Denny's restaurants paid $54.4 million to settle a class-action lawsuit alleging discriminatory treatment of black customers at its restaurants.[6] Verizon Communications paid $48.9 million to settle a lawsuit in which it was accused of discriminating

< **"what's new"** **companies**

After reading the next section, you should be able to

1. Describe diversity and explain why it matters.

diversity a variety of demographic, cultural, and personal differences among an organization's employees and customers.

Though it was once sued for discriminating against pregnant women and working mothers, Verizon changed its diversity practices and has been named to Working Mother *magazine's list of 100 best companies for working mothers for nine years running.*

against employees who were pregnant or on maternity leave.[7] And ICM, also known as International Creative Management, a talent agency that represents actors, speakers, and writers, paid $4.5 million to 150 TV show writers, all over the age of 40, who claimed they were discriminated against by ICM's agents.[8] In recent years, Tyson Foods, Coca-Cola, Los Alamos National Laboratory, Federal Express, Abercrombie & Fitch, and many other companies have settled class-action discrimination lawsuits.[9]

Today, however, Denny's, Edison International, Verizon, and Coca-Cola have made great improvements in their level of diversity. For example, minorities own nearly 40 percent of Denny's franchises and comprise 59 percent of its workers, 41 percent of its managers, and 44 percent of its board of directors. *Hispanic Business*, *Black Enterprise*, *Asian Enterprise*, *Family Digest*, and *Fortune* magazine have recognized Denny's for its progress on diversity.[10] Verizon, which was sued for discriminating against employees who were pregnant or on maternity leave, has been named, for nine straight years, to *Working Mother* magazine's list of best 100 companies for working mothers and been recognized by the National Association for Female Executives and the Women's Business Enterprise National Council as a top workplace for female managers and executives.[11]

1 Diversity: Differences That Matter

You'll begin your exploration of diversity by learning **1.1 that diversity is not affirmative action** and **1.2 how to build a business case for diversity**.

1.1 Diversity Is Not Affirmative Action

A common misconception is that workplace diversity and affirmative action are the same, yet these concepts differ in several critical ways, including their purpose, how they are practiced, and the reactions they produce. To start, **affirmative action** refers to purposeful steps taken by an organization to create employment opportunities for minorities and women.[12] By contrast, diversity exists in organizations when there is a variety of demographic, cultural, and personal differences among the people who work there and the customers who do business there. So one key difference is that affirmative action is more narrowly focused on demographics such as sex and race, whereas diversity has a broader focus that includes demographic, cultural, and personal differences.

A second difference is that affirmative action is a policy for actively creating diversity, but diversity can exist even if organizations don't take purposeful steps to create it. A local restaurant located near a university in a major city is likely to have a more diverse group of employees than one located in a small town. So, organizations can achieve diversity without affirmative action. Conversely, affirmative action does not guarantee diversity. An organization can create employment opportunities for women and minorities yet not have a diverse workforce.

A third important difference is that affirmative action is required by law for private employers with 50 or more employees while diversity is not. Affirmative action

affirmative action purposeful steps taken by an organization to create employment opportunities for minorities and women.

originated with Executive Order 11246 (http://www.dol.gov/ofccp/rregs/compliance/ca_11246.htm) but is also related to the1964 Civil Rights Act, which bans discrimination in voting, public places, federal government programs, federally supported public education, and employment. Title VII of the Civil Rights Act (www.eeoc.gov/laws/statutes/titlevii.cfm) requires that workers have equal employment opportunities when being hired or promoted. More specifically, Title VII prohibits companies from discriminating on the basis of race, color, religion, sex, or national origin. Title VII also created the Equal Employment Opportunity Commission, or EEOC (www.eeoc.gov), to administer these laws. By contrast, there is no federal law or agency to oversee diversity. Organizations that pursue diversity goals and programs do so voluntarily. "Until recently, the commitment many companies had to diversity was fundamentally based on moral, ethical and compliance reasons," says Rudy Mendez, vice president for diversity and inclusion at McDonald's. "But now that we can add business impact, diversity executives are being given a much bigger role."[13]

Fourth, affirmative action programs and diversity programs also have different purposes. The purpose of affirmative action programs is to compensate for past discrimination, which was widespread when legislation was introduced in the 1960s; to prevent ongoing discrimination; and to provide equal opportunities to all, regardless of race, color, religion, sex, or national origin. Organizations that fail to uphold these laws may be required to

> » hire, promote, or give back pay to those not hired or promoted;
> » reinstate those who were wrongly terminated;
> » pay attorneys' fees and court costs for those who bring charges against them; or
> » take other actions that make individuals whole by returning them to the condition or place they would have been had it not been for discrimination.[14]

Consequently, affirmative action is basically a punitive approach.[15] By contrast, as shown in Exhibit 12.2, the general purpose of diversity programs is to create a positive work environment where no one is advantaged or disadvantaged, where "we" is everyone, where everyone can do his or her best work, where differences are respected and not ignored, and where everyone feels comfortable.[16] So, unlike affirmative action, which punishes companies for not achieving specific sex and race ratios in their workforces, diversity programs seek to benefit both organizations and their employees by encouraging organizations to value all kinds of differences.

Despite the overall success of affirmative action in making workplaces much fairer than they used to be, many people argue that some affirmative action programs unconstitutionally offer preferential treatment to females and minorities at the expense of other employees, a view accepted by some courts.[17] The American Civil Rights Institute successfully campaigned to ban race- and sex-based affirmative action in college admissions, government hiring, and government contracting programs in California (1996), Washington (1998), and Michigan (2006). Led by Ward Connerly, the Institute backed similar efforts in Arizona, Colorado, Missouri, Nebraska, and Oklahoma in 2008. Opponents to affirmative action like Connerly believe that affirmative action policies establish only surface-level diversity and, ironically, promote preferential treatment.[18]

Furthermore, research shows that people who have gotten a job or promotion as a result of affirmative action are frequently viewed as unqualified, even when clear evidence of their qualifications exists.[19] One woman said, "I won a major prize [in

Exhibit 12.2   General Purpose of Diversity Programs

To creat a positive work environment where
• No one is advantaged or disadvantaged.
• "We" is everyone.
• Everyone can do his or her best work.
• Differences are respected and not ignored.
• Everyone feels comfortable.

Source: T. Roosevelt, "From Affirmative Action to Affirming Diversity," *Harvard Business Review* 68, no. 2 (1990): 107–117.

my field], and some of the guys in my lab said it was because I was a woman. I'm certain they didn't choose me because I was a woman. But it gave some disgruntled guys who didn't get the prize a convenient excuse."[20] So, while affirmative action programs have created opportunities for minorities and women, those same minorities and women are frequently presumed to be unqualified when others believe they obtained their jobs as a result of affirmative action.

In summary, affirmative action and diversity are not the same thing. Not only are they fundamentally different, but they also differ in purpose, practice, and the reactions they produce.

1.2 Diversity Makes Good Business Sense

Those who support the idea of diversity in organizations often ignore its business aspects altogether, claiming instead that diversity is simply the right thing to do. Yet diversity actually makes good business sense in several ways: cost savings, attracting and retaining talent, and driving business growth.[21]

Diversity helps companies with *cost savings* by reducing turnover, decreasing absenteeism, and avoiding expensive lawsuits.[22] Because of lost productivity and the cost of recruiting and selecting new workers, companies lose substantial amounts of money when employees quit their jobs. In fact, turnover costs typically amount to more than 90 percent of employees' salaries. By this estimate, if an executive who makes $200,000 leaves, the organization will have to spend approximately $180,000 to find a replacement; even the lowest-paid hourly workers can cost the company as much as $10,000 when they quit. Because turnover rates for African Americans average 40 percent higher than for whites, and because women quit their jobs at twice the rate men do, companies that manage diverse workforces well can cut costs by reducing the turnover rates of these employees.[23] And with women absent from work 60 percent more often than men, primarily because of family responsibilities, diversity programs that address the needs of female workers can also reduce the substantial costs of absenteeism.

Diversity programs also save companies money by helping them avoid discrimination lawsuits, which have increased by a factor of 20 since 1970 and quadrupled just since 1995. In one survey conducted by the Society of Human Resource Management, 78 percent of respondents reported that diversity efforts helped them avoid lawsuits and litigation costs.[24] Indeed, because companies lose two-thirds of all discrimination cases that go to trial, the best strategy from a business perspective is not to be sued for discrimination at all. When companies lose, the average individual settlement amounts to more than $600,000.[25] And settlement costs can be substantially higher in class-action lawsuits, in which individuals join together to sue a company as a group. For example, Eastman Kodak paid $21.4 million to settle a class-action suit brought by African American workers who alleged that they were discriminated against in pay, promotions, and job assignments.[26] Novartis, a pharmaceutical company, agreed to $175 million to settle claims from female sales representatives who accused the company of routinely bypassing them for promotions, denying maternity leave requests, and harassing women for getting pregnant.[27] Finally, 17 TV networks and seven talent agencies paid $70 million to settle a class-action suit for age discrimination from 165 TV writers, all over the age of 40, who alleged that the companies refused to hire or represent them because of their age.[28]

In fact, the average class-action lawsuit costs companies $58.9 million for racial discrimination and $24.9 million for sex discrimination.[29] Moreover, just announcing that a publically owned company has been hit with an age discrimination lawsuit lowers the total value of its stock by an average of $40 million.[30]

Diversity also makes business sense by helping companies *attract and retain talented workers.*[31] Indeed, diversity-friendly companies tend to attract better *and* more diverse job applicants. Very simply, diversity begets more diversity. Companies that make *Fortune* magazine's list of the 50 best companies for minorities or are recognized by *Working Women* and *DiversityInc* magazines have already attracted a diverse and talented pool of job applicants. But after being recognized for their efforts, they subsequently experience big increases in both the quality and the diversity of people who apply for jobs. Research shows that companies with acclaimed diversity programs not only attract more talented workers but also have higher performance in the stock market.[32]

The third way that diversity makes business sense is by *driving business growth.* In the United States today, there are 40.5 million African Americans, 47.7 million Hispanic Americans, and 14.2 million Asian Americans with, respectively, $1.1 trillion, $1.2 trillion, and $459 billion in purchasing power.[33] Given the size of those markets, it shouldn't be surprising that a survey conducted by the Society for Human Resource Management found that tapping into "diverse customers and markets" was the No. 1 reason managers gave for implementing diversity programs.[34] Diversity, therefore, can help companies grow by improving their understanding of the marketplace. When companies have diverse workforces, they are better able to understand the needs of their increasingly diverse customer bases. **Turner Broadcasting**, which operates cable networks such as CNN, TNT, and the Cartoon Network, uses nine business resource groups (BRGs) to infuse the thoughts and views of diverse groups into the kinds of shows it develops. For example, the African American BRG helped Turner realize that there were few shows on TV focusing on black culture, families, or comedy. With their guidance, Turner gained new sponsors and reached new viewers by broadcasting critically acclaimed documentaries like *Black in America*, and *Latino in America* and minority-driven programming such as *Tyler Perry's House of Pain* and *Are We There Yet?* Likewise, Turner Parents, another BRG group, helped the Cartoon Network develop an online game for kids and advised CNN FitNation about ideas for shows on health issues for families and children.[35]

Diversity also helps companies grow through higher-quality problem solving. Though diverse groups initially have more difficulty working together than homogeneous groups, diverse groups eventually establish a rapport and do a better job of identifying problems and generating alternative solutions, the two most important steps in problem solving.[36] Ernest Drew, former CEO of Hoechst Celanese, a chemical company, recalls a company conference in which the top 125 managers, mostly white males, were joined by 50 lower-level employees, mostly minorities and women. Problem-solving teams were formed to discuss how the company's corporate culture affected business and how it could be changed. Half the teams were composed of white males, whereas the other half were of mixed sex and race. Drew says, "It was so obvious that the diverse teams had the broader solutions. They had ideas I hadn't even thought of. For the first time, we realized that diversity is a strength as it relates to problem solving. Before, we just thought of diversity as the total number of minorities and women in the company, like affirmative action. Now we knew we needed diversity at every level of the company where decisions are made."[37]

In short, "Diversity is no longer about counting heads; it's about making heads count," says Amy George, vice president of diversity and inclusion at Pepsico.[38] Harvard Business School professor David Thomas, agrees: "Where 10 or 20 years ago, companies were asking, 'Will we be diverse?' today they must ask, 'How should we use diversity as a resource to be more effective as a business?'"[39] Ernest Hicks, who directs Xerox's corporate diversity office, says, "Because we gain a competitive advantage by drawing on the experience, insight and creativity of a well-balanced, diverse workforce, diversity enables Xerox to attract talent from the broadest possible

< **"what's new" companies**

In the United States today, there are 40.5 million African Americans, 47.7 million Hispanic Americans, and 14.2 million Asian Americans with, respectively, $1.1 trillion, $1.2 trillion, and $459 billion in purchasing power.

pool of candidates. It creates more diverse work teams—facilitating diversity of thought and more innovative ideas—and it positions Xerox to attract a wider customer base and to address the needs of diverse customers."[40]

Review 1

Diversity: Differences That Matter Diversity exists in organizations when there are a variety of demographic, cultural, and personal differences among the people who work there and the customers who do business there. A common misconception is that workplace diversity and affirmative action are the same. But affirmative action is more narrowly focused on demographics, is required by law, and is used to punish companies that discriminate on the basis of race, color, religion, sex, or national origin. By contrast, diversity is broader in focus (going beyond demographics), voluntary, more positive in that it encourages companies to value all kinds of differences, and substantially less controversial than affirmative action. Thus, affirmative action and diversity differ in purpose, practice, and the reactions they produce. Diversity also makes good business sense in terms of cost savings (reducing turnover, decreasing absenteeism, and avoiding lawsuits), attracting and retaining talent, and driving business growth (improving marketplace understanding and promoting higher-quality problem solving).

Diversity and Individual Differences

A survey that asked managers "What is meant by diversity to decision-makers in your organization?" found that they most frequently mentioned race, culture, sex, national origin, age, religion, and regional origin.[41] When managers describe workers this way, they are focusing on surface-level diversity. **Surface-level diversity**, as illustrated in Exhibit 12.3, consists of differences that are immediately observable, typically unchangeable, and easy to measure.[42] In other words, independent observers can usually agree on dimensions of surface-level diversity, such as another person's age, sex, race/ethnicity, or physical capabilities.

Most people start by using surface-level diversity to categorize or stereotype other people. But those initial categorizations typically give way to deeper impressions formed from knowledge of others' behavior and psychological characteristics such as personality and attitudes.[43] When you think of others this way, you are focusing on deep-level diversity. **Deep-level diversity** consists of differences that are communicated through verbal and nonverbal behaviors and are learned only through extended interaction with others.[44] Examples of deep-level diversity include personality differences, attitudes, beliefs, and values. In other words, as people in diverse workplaces get to know each other, the initial focus on surface-level differences such as age, race/ ethnicity, sex, and physical capabilities is replaced by deeper, more complex knowledge of coworkers.

If managed properly, the shift from surface- to deep-level diversity can accomplish two things.[45] First, coming to know and understand each other better can result in reduced prejudice and conflict. Second, it can lead to stronger social integration. **Social integration** is the degree to which group members are psychologically attracted to working with each

surface-level diversity differences such as age, sex, race/ethnicity, and physical disabilities that are observable, typically unchangeable, and easy to measure.

deep-level diversity differences such as personality and attitudes that are communicated through verbal and nonverbal behaviors and are learned only through extended interaction with others.

social integration the degree to which group members are psychologically attracted to working with each other to accomplish a common objective.

After reading the next two sections, you should be able to

2. *Understand the special challenges that the dimensions of surface-level diversity pose for managers.*

3. *Explain how the dimensions of deep-level diversity affect individual behavior and interactions in the workplace.*

other to accomplish a common objective, or, as one manager put it, "working together to get the job done."

2 Surface-Level Diversity

Because age, sex, race/ethnicity, and disabilities are usually immediately observable, many managers and workers use these dimensions of surface-level diversity to form initial impressions and categorizations of coworkers, bosses, customers, or job applicants. Whether intentionally or not, sometimes those initial categorizations and impressions lead to decisions or behaviors that discriminate. Consequently, these dimensions of surface-level diversity pose special challenges for managers who are trying to create positive work environments where everyone feels comfortable and no one is advantaged or disadvantaged.

Let's learn more about those challenges and the ways that **2.1 age, 2.2 sex, 2.3 race/ethnicity, and 2.4 mental or physical disabilities can affect decisions and behaviors in organizations.**

2.1 Age

Age discrimination is treating people differently (e.g., in hiring and firing, promotion, and compensation decisions) because of their age. The victims of age discrimination are almost always older workers, and the discrimination is based on the assumption that "You can't teach an old dog new tricks." It's commonly believed that older workers can't learn how to use computers and technology; won't adapt to change; are sick more often; and, in general, are much more expensive to employ than younger workers. One manager explains his preference for younger workers over older workers this way: "The way I look at it, for $40,000 or $50,000, I can get a smart, raw kid right out of undergrad who's going to work seven days a week for me for the next two years. I'll train him the way I want him, he'll grow with me, and I'll pay him long-term options so I own him, for lack of a better word. He'll do exactly what I want—and if he doesn't, I'll fire him. . . . The alternative is to pay twice as much for some 40-year-old who does half the amount of work, has been trained improperly, and doesn't listen to what I say."[46] Unfortunately, attitudes like this are all too common.[47] According to the Society for Human Resource Management, 53 percent of 428 surveyed managers believed that older workers "didn't keep up with technology," and 28 percent said that older workers were "less flexible."[48] For example, when 57-year-old Sam Horgan, a former chief financial officer, was interviewing for a job, he was asked by a 30-something job interviewer, "Would you have trouble working with young bright people?"[49] It is also commonly assumed that older workers cost more, and some companies fear that older workers will require higher salaries and more health-care benefits.[50]

Not surprisingly, 80 percent of human resource managers surveyed by *Personnel Management* magazine said that age discrimination was a major problem in their organizations and, moreover, that older employees were not receiving the same training and promotional opportunities as younger workers.[51] Likewise, two-thirds of 10,000 people surveyed by AARP (American Association of Retired Persons) felt that they had been wrongly discharged from a job because of their age. In fact, a study by the Society for Human Resource Management found that 20 percent of all companies had been sued for age discrimination in the preceding five years.[52] Normally, somewhere between 17,000 and 23,000 age discrimination cases are filed with the EEOC each year (http://eeoc.gov/eeoc/statistics/enforcement/charges.cfm), and these

Exhibit 12.3
Surface- and Deep-Level Diversity

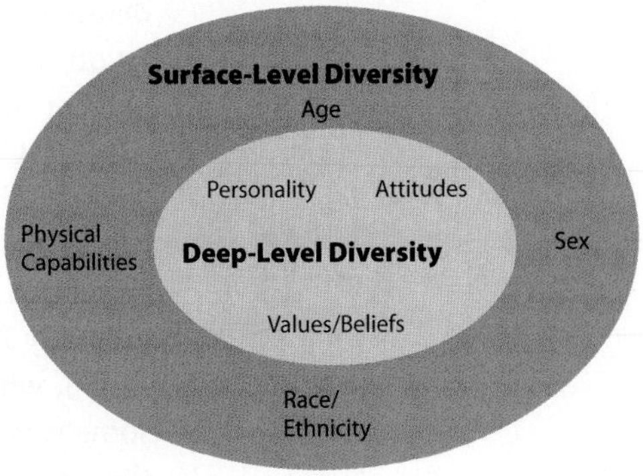

© Cengage Learning 2013

age discrimination treating people differently (e.g., in hiring and firing, promotion, and compensation decisions) because of their age.

493

numbers may increase given a U.S. Supreme Court ruling that employees may sue for age discrimination even if the discrimination was not intentional (see Chapter 11's discussion of disparate treatment and adverse impact).[53] In fact, the recent round of layoffs and organizational restructuring caused by the economic recession led to a 29 percent increase in the number of allegations of age-based discrimination filed with the EEOC.[54] And it takes older employees who are laid off much longer to find a job. A U.S. Labor Department study found that three years after an economic downturn, 65 percent to 69 percent of younger workers, ages 20 to 54, had found new jobs after being laid off. By contrast, just 56 percent of 55- to 64-year-olds had regained jobs, and only 24 percent of those 65 or older had found jobs.[55]

So, what's reality and what's myth? Do older employees actually cost more? In some ways, they do. The older people are and the longer they stay with a company, the more the company pays for salaries, pension plans, and vacation time. But older workers cost companies less too, because they show better judgment, care more about the quality of their work, and are less likely to quit, show up late, or be absent, the cost of which can be substantial.[56] A survey by Chicago outplacement firm Challenger, Gray & Christmas found that only 3 percent of employees age 50 and over changed jobs in any given year, compared with 10 percent of the entire workforce and 12 percent of workers ages 25 to 34. The study also found that although older workers make up about 14 percent of the workforce, they suffer only 10 percent of all workplace injuries and use fewer health-care benefits than younger workers with school-age children.[57] As for the widespread belief that job performance declines with age, the scientific evidence clearly refutes this stereotype. Performance does not decline with age, regardless of the type of job.[58]

What can companies do to reduce age discrimination?[59] To start, managers need to recognize that age discrimination is much more pervasive than they probably think. Whereas "old" used to mean mid-50s, in today's workplace, "old" is closer to 40. When 773 CEOs were asked, "At what age does a worker's productivity peak?" the average age they gave was 43. Thus, age discrimination may be affecting more workers because perceptions about age have changed. In addition, with the aging of the Baby Boomers, age discrimination is more likely to occur simply because there are millions more older workers than there used to be. And because studies show that interviewers rate younger job candidates as more qualified (even when they aren't), companies need to train managers and recruiters to make hiring and promotion decisions on the basis of qualifications, not age.

Companies also need to monitor the extent to which older workers receive training. The Bureau of Labor Statistics found that the number of training courses and number of hours spent in training drops dramatically after employees reach the age of 44.[60] Finally, companies need to ensure that younger and older workers interact with each other. One study found that younger workers generally hold positive views of older workers and that the more time they spent working with older coworkers, the more positive their attitudes became.[61]

> Performance does not decline with age, regardless of the type of job.

2.2 Sex

Sex discrimination occurs when people are treated differently because of their sex. Sex discrimination and racial/ethnic discrimination (discussed in the next section) are often associated with the so-called **glass ceiling**, the invisible barrier that prevents women and minorities from advancing to the top jobs in organizations.

To what extent do women face sex discrimination in the workplace? Almost every year, the EEOC receives between 23,000 and 28,000 charges of sex-based discrimination.[62] In some ways, there is much less sex discrimination than there used

sex discrimination treating people differently because of their sex.

glass ceiling the invisible barrier that prevents women and minorities from advancing to the top jobs in organizations.

to be. For example, whereas women held only 17 percent of managerial jobs in 1972, today they hold 40 percent of managerial jobs, 51.5 percent of managerial and professional jobs, and 46.8 percent of all jobs in the workplace.[63]

Likewise, women own 40 percent of all U.S. businesses. Whereas women owned 700,000 businesses in 1977 and 4.1 million businesses in 1987, today they own 10.1 million businesses generating $1.9 trillion in sales![64] Finally, though women still earn less than men on average, the differential is narrowing, as Exhibit 12.4 shows. Women earned 79.9 percent of what men did in 2008, up from 63 percent in 1979.[65]

Although progress is being made, sex discrimination continues to operate via the glass ceiling at higher levels in organizations, as shown in Exhibit 12.5. For instance, although the trends are going upward, women are the top earners in just 7.6 percent of companies in 2011.[66] Likewise, whereas there has been progress, only 14.4 percent of corporate officers (i.e., top management) were women, and the numbers are even lower for women of color. Indra K. Nooyi, PepsiCo's CEO; Andrea Jung, Avon's CEO; and Ursula Burns, Xerox's CEO, are the only women of color heading *Fortune* 500 companies.[67] Indeed, only 12 of the 500 largest companies in the United States have women CEOs. Likewise, four women are CEOs of *Fortune* 500 companies.[68] Similarly, only 15.72 percent of the members of corporate boards of directors are women.[69]

Is sex discrimination the sole reason for the slow rate at which women have been promoted to middle and upper levels of management and corporate boards? Some studies indicate that it's not.[70] In some instances, the slow progress appears to be due to career and job choices. Whereas men's career and job choices are often driven by the search for higher pay and advancement, women are more likely to choose jobs or careers that also give them a greater sense of accomplishment, more control over their work schedules, and easier movement in and out of the workplace.[71] For instance, 82 percent of women without children are interested in being promoted to the next level compared to 73 percent of women

Exhibit 12.4 Women's Earnings as a Percentage of Men's

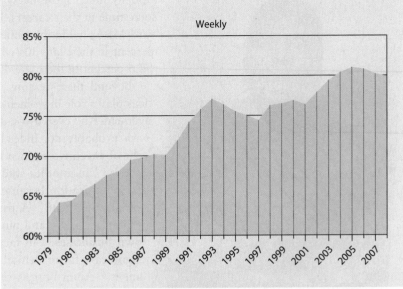

Source: "Women's Earnings as a Percentage of Men's," U.S. Department of Labor, Bureau of Labor Statistics, October 14, 2009, accessed November 7, 2009, from www.bls.gov/opub/ted/2009/ted_20091014_data.htm.

Exhibit 12.5 Women at *Fortune* 500 and 1000 Companies

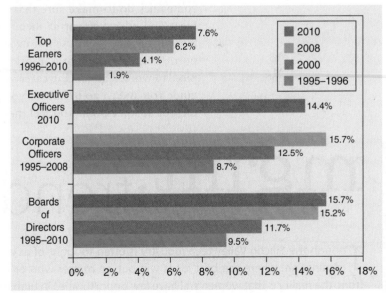

Board Directors: Rachel Soares, Jan Combopiano, Allyson Regis, Yelena, Shur, and Rosita Wong, 2010 Catalyst Census: Fortune 500 Women Board Directors (Catalyst, 2010); Catalyst, 2008 Catalyst Census of Women Board Directors of the Fortune 500 (2009); Catalyst, 2000 Catalyst Census of Women Board Directors of the Fortune 500 (2000); Catalyst, 1995 Catalyst Census of Women Board Directors of the Fortune 500 (1995). *Executive Officers and Top Earners:* Rachel Soares, Jan Combopiano, Allyson Regis, Yelena Shur, and Rosita Wong, 2010 Catalyst Census: Fortune 500 Women Executives (Catalyst, 2010). *Corporate Officers and Top Earners:* Catalyst, 2008 Catalyst Census of Women Corporate Officers and Top Earners of the Fortune 500 (2008); Catalyst, 2000 Catalyst Census of Women Corporate Officers and Top Earners of the Fortune 500 (2000); Catalyst, 1996 Catalyst Census of Women Corporate Officers and Top Earners of the Fortune 500 (1996).

Ursula Burns, the CEO of Xerox, is one of only three women of color heading Fortune 500 companies.

with two or more children.[72] As those numbers suggest, women are historically much more likely than men to prioritize family over work at some time in their careers. For example, 96 percent of 600 female Harvard MBAs held jobs while they were in their 20s. That dropped to 71 percent in their late 30s when they had children, but then increased to 82.5 percent in their late 40s as their children became older.[73]

Beyond these reasons, however, it's likely that sex discrimination does play a role in women's slow progress into the higher levels of management. And even if you don't think so, many of the women you work with probably do. Indeed, one study found that more than 90 percent of executive women believed that the glass ceiling had hurt their careers.[74] In another study, 80 percent of women said they left their last organization because the glass ceiling had limited their chances for advancement.[75] A third study indicated that the glass ceiling is prompting more and more women to leave companies to start their own businesses.[76] In fact, discrimination is believed to be the most significant factor behind the lack of women at top levels of management.[77] Anita Borg, a senior researcher at a *Fortune* 500 company, sums up the frustrations of many professional women when she says, "You run into subtle sexism every day. It's like water torture. It wears you down."[78] Very few professional women achieve the same status as their male counterparts even in advanced economies, such as the United States, Canada, the United Kingdom, and Japan.[79]

In a Catalyst study of *Fortune* 1000 organizations, about two-thirds of the executives and half of the CEOs surveyed identified the failure of senior leadership to assume accountability for women's advancement to be the key barrier preventing professional women from progressing to senior executive positions.[80] So, what can companies do to make sure that women have the same opportunities for development and advancement as men? One strategy is mentoring, or pairing promising female executives with senior executives from whom they can seek advice and support. A vice president at a utility company says, "I think it's the single most critical piece to women advancing career-wise. In my experience you need somebody to help guide you and ... go to bat for you."[81] In fact, 91 percent of female executives had a mentor at some point and feel their mentor was critical to their advancement.

mgmt:trends

Though the Silicon Valley tech industry is often thought of as a place free of discrimination, where the best ideas win out no matter who or where they come from, the reality is that women still have few opportunities in high tech. A recent survey showed that just 8 percent of venture capital–backed tech start-ups have been established by women. According to the National Center for Women and Information Technology, women make up just 6 percent of senior executives at the top 100 tech companies. And according to the National Venture Capital Association, just 14 percent of people who finance tech start-ups are women. One organization that is trying to change this scene is i/o Ventures, based in San Francisco. Partnering with Ariana Huffington, Donna Karan, and Sarah Brown, the venture capital fund is offering a $25,000 investment, along with free office space, to the winner of a contest that will identify the most promising female tech entrepreneur.[82]

Another strategy is to make sure that male-dominated social activities don't unintentionally exclude women. Nearly half (47%) of women in the workforce believe that "exclusion from informal networks" makes it more difficult to advance their careers. By contrast, just 18 percent of CEOs thought this was a problem.[83] One final strategy is to designate a go-to person other than their supervisors that women can talk to if they believe that they are being held back or discriminated against because of their sex. Make sure this person has the knowledge and authority to conduct a fair, confidential internal investigation.[84]

2.3 Race/Ethnicity

Racial and ethnic discrimination occurs when people are treated differently because of their race or ethnicity. To what extent is racial and ethnic discrimination a factor in the workplace? Every year, the EEOC receives between 26,000 and 35,000 charges of race discrimination, which is more than any other type of charge of discrimination.[85] However, it is true that since the passage of the 1964 Civil Rights Act and Title VII, there is much less racial and ethnic discrimination than there used to be. For example, 16 *Fortune* 500 firms had an African American or Hispanic CEO in 2011, whereas none did in 1988.[86] Nonetheless, strong racial and ethnic disparities still exist. For instance, whereas 12.2 percent of Americans are black, only 6.4 percent of managers and 2.8 percent of CEOs are black. Similarly, 16 percent of Americans are Hispanic, but only 7.6 percent are managers and 4.8 percent are CEOs. By contrast, Asians, who constitute 4.5 percent of the population, are better represented, holding 4.8 percent of management jobs and 4.4 percent of CEO jobs.

What accounts for the disparities between the percentages of minority groups in the general population and their smaller representation in management positions? Some studies have found that the disparities are due to preexisting differences in training, education, and skills. When African Americans, Hispanics, Asian Americans, and whites have similar skills, training, and education, they are much more likely to have similar jobs and salaries.[87]

Other studies, however, provide increasingly strong direct evidence of racial or ethnic discrimination in the workplace. For example, one study directly tested hiring discrimination by sending pairs of black and white males and pairs of Hispanic and non-Hispanic males to apply for the same jobs. Each pair had résumés with identical qualifications, and all were trained to present themselves in similar ways to minimize differences during interviews. The researchers found that the white males got three times as many job offers as the black males, and that the non-Hispanic males got three times as many offers as the Hispanic males.[88] Another study, which used similar methods to test hiring procedures at 149 different companies, found that whites received 10 percent more interviews than blacks. Half of the whites interviewed then received job offers, but only 11 percent of the blacks. And when job offers were made, blacks were much more likely to be offered lower-level positions, whereas whites were more likely to be offered jobs at higher levels than the jobs they had applied for.[89]

Critics of these studies point out that it's nearly impossible to train different applicants to give identical responses in job interviews and that differences in interviewing skills may have somehow accounted for the results. However, British researchers found similar kinds of discrimination just by sending letters of inquiry to prospective employers. As in the other studies, the letters were identical except for the applicant's race. Employers frequently responded to letters from Afro-Caribbean, Indian, or Pakistani applicants by indicating that the positions had been filled. By contrast, they often responded to white, Anglo-Saxon applicants by inviting them to face-to-face interviews. Similar results were found with Vietnamese and Greek applicants in

racial and ethnic discrimination treating people differently because of their race or ethnicity.

Australia.[90] In short, the evidence strongly indicates that there is strong and persistent racial and ethnic discrimination in the hiring processes of many organizations.

What can companies do to make sure that people of all racial and ethnic backgrounds have the same opportunities?[91] Start by looking at the numbers. Compare the hiring rates of whites with the hiring rates for racial and ethnic applicants. Do the same thing for promotions within the company. See whether nonwhite workers quit the company at higher rates than white workers. Also, survey employees to compare white and nonwhite employees' satisfaction with jobs, bosses, and the company as well as their perceptions concerning equal treatment. Next, if the numbers indicate racial or ethnic disparities, consider employing a private firm to test your hiring system by having applicants of different races with identical qualifications apply for jobs in your company.[92] Although disparities aren't proof of discrimination, it's much better to investigate hiring and promotion disparities yourself than to have the EEOC or a plaintiff's lawyer do it for you.

Another step companies can take is to eliminate unclear selection and promotion criteria. Vague criteria allow decision makers to focus on non-job-related characteristics that may unintentionally lead to employment discrimination. Instead, selection and promotion criteria should spell out the specific knowledge, skills, abilities, education, and experience needed to perform a job well. Finally, as explained in Chapter 11, "Managing Human Resources," it is also important to train managers and others who make hiring and promotion decisions.

2.4 Mental or Physical Disabilities

When Walgreens opened 14 new distribution centers, it designed them to accommodate people with disabilities. Each warehouse uses technology, such as touch-screen software with function keys that limits the amount of required typing and reading, photos of different animals that serve as visual reminders of where workers' stations are, and flashing lights that signal which trucks and staging areas need to be unloaded. Walgreens' goal was for people with disabilities to make up one-third of the staff, but its accommodation strategies (you'll learn more about this below) were so successful that 40 percent to 45 percent of its warehouses employees have disabilities. Angela Mackey, career outreach coordinator at Walgreens' Anderson, South Carolina distribution center, who has cerebral palsy, said, "Once you're given a chance, disability or not, you can prove yourself."[93]

According to the Americans with Disabilities Act (www.ada.gov), a **disability** is a mental or physical impairment that substantially limits one or more major life activities.[94] One in every five Americans, or more than 54 million people, has a disability.[95] **Disability discrimination** occurs when people are treated differently because of their disabilities. To what extent is disability discrimination a factor in the workplace? Although 79.7 percent of the overall U.S. population was employed in 2006, just 36.9 percent of people with disabilities had jobs. Individuals with sensory disabilities (46.4 percent), such as blindness or deafness, had the highest employment rates; those with self-care disabilities (16.7 percent), which inhibit their motor skills and their ability to care for their grooming needs, were the least represented in the workforce.[96] Furthermore, people with disabilities are disproportionately employed in low-status or part-time jobs, have little chance for advancement, and, on average, are twice as likely to live in poverty as people without disabilities.[97] Numerous studies also indicate that managers and the general public believe that discrimination against people with disabilities is common and widespread.[98]

What accounts for the disparities between the employment and income levels of people with and without disabilities? Contrary to popular opinion, it has nothing

disability a mental or physical impairment that substantially limits one or more major life activities.

disability discrimination treating people differently because of their disabilities.

to do with how well people with disabilities can do their jobs. Studies show that as long as companies make reasonable accommodations for disabilities (e.g., changing procedures or equipment), people with disabilities perform their jobs just as well as people without disabilities. Furthermore, they have better safety records and are not any more likely to be absent or quit their jobs.[99]

What can companies do to make sure that people with disabilities have the same opportunities as everyone else? Beyond educational efforts to address incorrect stereotypes and expectations, a good place to start is to commit to reasonable workplace accommodations such as changing work schedules,

Exhibit 12.6 Reasonable Accommodations for Workers with Disabilities

- Physical changes, such as installing a ramp or modifying a workspace or restroom.

- A quieter workspace or other changes that reduce noisy distractions for someone with a mental disability.

- Training and other written materials in an accessible format, such as in Braille, on audio tape, or on computer disk.

- TTYs for use with telephones by people who are deaf, and hardware and software that make computers accessible to people who have vision impairments or who have difficulty using their hands.

- Time off for someone who needs treatment for a disability.

Source: "American with Disabilities Act: A Guide for People with Disabilities Seeking Employment," U.S. Department of Justice, available at http://www.ada.gov/workta.htm/, October 2, 2003.

reassigning jobs, acquiring or modifying equipment, or providing assistance when needed. Accommodations for disabilities needn't be expensive. According to the Job Accommodation Network, 56 percent of accommodations don't cost anything at all, whereas those with costs are typically just $600.[100] IBM was recently ranked No. 1 in DiversityInc's survey of the Top 10 Companies for People with Disabilities. In addition to education and recruitment programs, IBM provides a wide range of accommodations for its disabled workers. Ramps and power doors are installed for employees who use wheelchairs. Captioning devices, sign language interpreters, and note takers are available for deaf employees. Software programs that read text on a computer screen, and audio transcripts of company publications, are available for the blind. IBM has also formed Accommodation Assessment Teams to consult with employees to continue identifying and resolving unmet accommodations.[101] For further information about reasonable accommodations, visit the Job Accommodation Network (http://askjan.org), which provides free help and has a database of 26,000 successful accommodations. Exhibit 12.6 provides a list of common, inexpensive accommodations that companies can make for workers with disabilities.

Some of the accommodations just described involve *assistive technology* that gives workers with disabilities the tools they need to overcome their disabilities. Providing workers with assistive technology is also an effective strategy to recruit, retain, and enhance the productivity of people with disabilities. According to the National Council on Disability, 92 percent of workers with disabilities who use assistive technology report that it helps them work faster and better, 81 percent indicate that it helps them work longer hours, and 67 percent say that it is critical to getting a job.[102] To learn about assistive technologies that can help workers with disabilities, see Abledata (www.abledata.com), which lists 25,000 products from 3,000 organizations, or the National Rehabilitation Information Center (www.naric.com), which provides information for specific disabilities.

Finally, companies should actively recruit qualified workers with disabilities. Numerous organizations, such as Mainstream, Kidder Resources, the American Council of the Blind (www.acb.org), the National Federation of the Blind (www.nfb.org), the National Association of the Deaf (www.nad.org), the Epilepsy Foundation (www.epilepsyfoundation.org), and the National Amputation Foundation (www.nationalamputation.org), actively work with employers to find jobs for qualified people with disabilities. Companies can also place advertisements in publications, such as *Careers and the Disabled*, that specifically target workers with disabilities.[103]

Review 2

Surface-Level Diversity Age, sex, race/ethnicity, and physical and mental disabilities are dimensions of surface-level diversity. Because those dimensions are (usually) easily observed, managers and workers tend to rely on them to form initial impressions and stereotypes. Sometimes this can lead to age, sex, racial/ethnic, or disability discrimination (i.e., treating people differently) in the workplace. In general, older workers, women, people of color or different national origins, and people with disabilities are less likely to be hired or promoted than white males. This disparity is often due to incorrect beliefs or stereotypes, such as "job performance declines with age," or "women aren't willing to travel on business," or "workers with disabilities aren't as competent as workers without disabilities." To reduce discrimination, companies can determine the hiring and promotion rates for different groups, train managers to make hiring and promotion decisions on the basis of specific criteria, and make sure that everyone has equal access to training, mentors, reasonable work accommodations, and assistive technology. Finally, companies need to designate a go-to person whom employees can talk to if they believe they have suffered discrimination.

3 Deep-Level Diversity

Have you ever taken an instant dislike to someone—perhaps because of the way the person talked, acted, or treated you—only to decide, after spending some time working or interacting with this person, that your initial impressions were wrong and that he or she wasn't so bad after all? If you've had this experience, then you understand the difference between surface and deep-level diversity.

As you learned in Section 2, people often use the dimensions of surface-level diversity to form initial impressions about others. Over time, however, as people have a chance to get to know each other, initial impressions based on age, sex, race/ethnicity, and mental or physical disabilities give way to deeper impressions based on behavior and psychological characteristics. When we think of others this way, we are focusing on deep-level diversity. *Deep-level diversity* represents differences that can be learned only through extended interaction with others. Examples of deep-level diversity include differences in personality, attitudes, beliefs, and values. In short, recognizing deep-level diversity requires getting to know and understand one another better. And that matters, because it can result in less prejudice, discrimination, and conflict in the workplace. These changes can then lead to better *social integration*, the degree to which organizational or group members are psychologically attracted to working with each other to accomplish a common objective.

Let's examine deep-level diversity by exploring **3.1 the "Big Five" dimensions of personality** and **3.2 other significant work-related aspects of personality**.

3.1 Big Five Dimensions of Personality

Stop for a second and think about your boss (or the boss you had in your last job). What words would you use to describe him or her? Is your boss introverted or extroverted? Emotionally stable or unstable? Agreeable or disagreeable? Organized or disorganized? Open or closed to new experiences? When you describe your boss or others in this way, what you're really doing is describing dispositions and personality.

A **disposition** is the tendency to respond to situations and events in a predetermined manner. **Personality** is the relatively stable set of behaviors, attitudes, and

disposition the tendency to respond to situations and events in a predetermined manner.

personality the relatively stable set of behaviors, attitudes, and emotions displayed over time that makes people different from each other.

emotions displayed over time that makes people different from each other.[104] For example, which of your aunts or uncles is a little offbeat, a little out of the ordinary? What was that aunt or uncle like when you were small? What is she or he like now? Chances are that she or he is pretty much the same wacky person. In other words, the person's core personality hasn't changed. For years, personality researchers studied hundreds of different ways to describe people's personalities. In the last decade, however, personality research conducted in different cultures, different settings, and different languages has shown that five basic dimensions of personality account for most of the differences in peoples' behaviors, attitudes, and emotions (or for why your boss is the way he or she is!). The *Big Five Personality Dimensions* are extroversion, emotional stability, agreeableness, conscientiousness, and openness to experience.[105]

Extroversion is the degree to which someone is active, assertive, gregarious, sociable, talkative, and energized by others. In contrast to extroverts, introverts are less active, prefer to be alone, and are shy, quiet, and reserved. For the best results in the workplace, introverts and extroverts should be correctly matched to their jobs. Can introverts be effective managers? Sixty-five percent of senior managers believe that introversion prevents people from being promoted to higher management levels. But research shows that both introverts and extroverts can be successful managers. Although extroverts may be more effective (and comfortable) in public roles, introverts are effective in one-on-one interactions and in involving others in decision making. Colgate-Palmolive's CEO, Ian Cook, says his listening skills helped him advance in the company. Says Cook, "I listen intently. I am extremely attentive to language and body cues." Subordinates can mistakenly view their boss's introversion as aloofness, particularly if they're quiet during meetings. When Campbell Soup CEO, Douglas Conant, was president of a division at Nabisco, "People were drawing [inaccurate] conclusions about my behavior." So, he shared with his coworkers and subordinates that it takes him time to formulate his thoughts and responses. Conant said that helped, and, "The more transparent I became, the more engaged people became."[106]

Emotional stability is the degree to which someone is not angry, depressed, anxious, emotional, insecure, or excitable. People who are emotionally stable respond well to stress. In other words, they can maintain a calm, problem-solving attitude in even the toughest situations (e.g., conflict, hostility, dangerous conditions, or extreme time pressures). By contrast, emotionally unstable people find it difficult to handle the most basic demands of their jobs under only moderately stressful situations and become distraught, tearful, self-doubting, and anxious. Emotional stability is particularly important for high-stress jobs such as police work, fire fighting, emergency medical treatment, piloting planes, or commanding rockets. A well-known incident in which a JetBlue flight attendant lost his cool when dealing with a rude passenger illustrates what can happen when emotional stability is lacking in stressful situations. Moments after a JetBlue flight from Pittsburgh landed at New York's John F. Kennedy International Airport, a passenger stood up to retrieve his bags from the overhead bin while the plane was still moving—before the crew gave permission. When flight attendant Steven Slater told the passenger to remain seated, he refused. Slater approached the passenger just as he was pulling his bag down, striking Slater in the head. When Slater asked for an apology, the passenger cursed at him. Slater responded by cursing the passenger over the plane's public address system microphone, grabbing two beers from the beverage cart, and activating the emergency chute, which he used to slide out of the plane, head to the parking lot, and go home. Slater lost his job because of his inability to remain emotionally stable in this situation.[107] As you learned in Chapter 1, emotional stability is also important for managers. Indeed, the No. 1 mistake managers make is intimidating, bullying, and being abrasive to the people who work for them.

extroversion the degree to which someone is active, assertive, gregarious, sociable, talkative, and energized by others.

emotional stability the degree to which someone is not angry, depressed, anxious, emotional, insecure, and excitable.

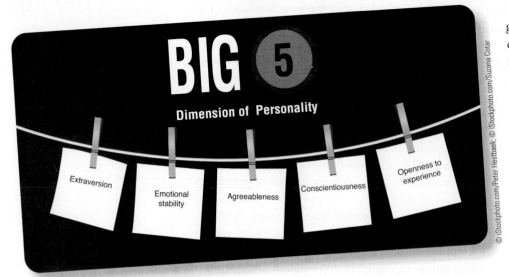

Agreeableness is the degree to which someone is cooperative, polite, flexible, forgiving, good-natured, tolerant, and trusting. Basically, agreeable people are easy to work with and be around, whereas disagreeable people are distrusting and difficult to work with and be around. A number of companies have made general attitude or agreeableness the most important factor in their hiring decisions. Small-business owner Roger Cook says, "Hire nice people. I'm looking for personal—not professional—traits. I want a good or nice person. I can teach the skills. I call their references and ask, 'Is he or she a nice person?' I take a close look at how applicants answer questions and carry themselves. Why nice people? Because they're trustworthy; they get along with other crew members: they are good with customers and they are usually hard workers."[108]

Conscientiousness is the degree to which someone is organized, hardworking, responsible, persevering, thorough, and achievement oriented. One management consultant wrote about his experiences with a conscientious employee: "He arrived at our first meeting with a typed copy of his daily schedule, a sheet bearing his home and office phone numbers, addresses, and his email address. At his request, we established a timetable for meetings for the next four months. He showed up on time every time, day planner in hand, and carefully listed tasks and due dates. He questioned me exhaustively if he didn't understand an assignment and returned on schedule with the completed work or with a clear explanation as to why it wasn't done."[109] Conscientious employees are also more likely to engage in positive behaviors, such as helping new employees, coworkers, and supervisors, and are less likely to engage in negative behaviors, such as verbally or physically abusing coworkers or stealing.[110]

Openness to experience is the degree to which someone is curious, broadminded, and open to new ideas, things, and experiences; is spontaneous; and has a high tolerance for ambiguity. Most companies need people who are strong in terms of openness to experience to fill certain positions, but for other positions, this dimension is less important. People in marketing, advertising, research, or other creative jobs need to be curious, open to new ideas, and spontaneous. By contrast, openness to experience is not particularly important to accountants, who need to apply stringent rules and formulas consistently to make sense out of complex financial information.

Which of the Big Five Personality Dimensions has the largest impact on behavior in organizations? The cumulative results of multiple studies indicate that conscientiousness is related to job performance across five different occupational groups (professionals, police, managers, sales, and skilled or semiskilled jobs).[111] In short, people "who are dependable, persistent, goal directed, and organized tend to be higher performers on virtually any job; viewed negatively, those who are careless, irresponsible, low achievement striving, and impulsive tend to be lower performers on virtually any job."[112] (See the What Really Works feature in this chapter for further explanation.) The results also indicate that extroversion is related to performance in jobs such as sales and management that involve significant interaction with others.

agreeableness the degree to which someone is cooperative, polite, flexible, forgiving, good-natured, tolerant, and trusting.

conscientiousness the degree to which someone is organized, hardworking, responsible, persevering, thorough, and achievement oriented.

openness to experience the degree to which someone is curious, broadminded, and open to new ideas, things, and experiences; is spontaneous; and has a high tolerance for ambiguity.

In people-intensive jobs like these, it helps to be sociable, assertive, and talkative and to have energy and be able to energize others. Finally, people who are extroverted and open to experience seem to do much better in training. Being curious and open to new experiences as well as sociable, assertive, talkative, and full of energy helps people perform better in learning situations.[113]

3.2 Work-Related Personality Dimensions

Does the way you keep your desk reveal something about your personality? Lots of people think so. For example, people with ultra-neat desks tend to believe that a desk buried under mounds of paper, food wrappers, and old magazines is a sign that its owner is lazy, disorganized, undependable, and a dreamer. On the other hand, people with messy desks believe that a spotless desk with everything in its place is a sign that its owner is impatient, critical, controlling, analytical, and a perfectionist. Who knows, maybe if your desk is somewhere between operating-room clean and the aftermath of a tornado, it is a sign that you have a good-natured, flexible, and fun-loving personality.[114] Although studies indicate that extroversion, emotional stability, agreeableness, conscientiousness, and openness to experience are the five basic dimensions of personality in any culture, setting, or language, research has also identified additional personality dimensions that directly affect workplace attitudes and behaviors. These additional personality dimensions are authoritarianism, Machiavellian tendencies, Type A/B personality, locus of control, and positive/negative affectivity.

Authoritarianism is the extent to which an individual believes there should be power and status differences within the organization.[115] Authoritarian employees are likely to prefer a direct leadership style in which the boss tells them exactly what to do. Although this sounds desirable, one disadvantage is that authoritarian employees may simply carry out their boss's orders without question, even when they know a better solution or are aware of problems. Also, authoritarian employees may not perform well on ambiguous tasks or for managers who encourage employees to use their own initiative and judgment.

Authoritarian leaders are highly demanding and expect employees to unquestioningly obey their orders. One such boss, a body builder who liked to show off his strength to managers by doing 25 push-ups at the start of meetings, used to call the vice president of marketing at all hours to scream about things that had gone wrong. A second bully boss, the CEO of a semiconductor network start-up, ridiculed employees publicly. "He'd pick up something I'd written and say, 'Who wrote this? A second grader? It's the stupidest thing I've ever read,'" says the firm's marketing vice president. Business executives who are too demanding or who ridicule and scream at employees undermine productivity, discourage innovation, and may cause a talent drain at their companies, says James Clifton, CEO of the Gallup Organization.[116]

People with **Machiavellian** personalities believe that virtually any type of behavior is acceptable if it helps satisfy needs or accomplish goals.[117] In other words, people with Machiavellian personalities believe that the ends justify the means. "High Machs" are generally more willing to use lies and deceit to get their way than are "low Machs," even in situations where the chances of being caught in a lie are high.[118] High Machs believe that most people are gullible and can be manipulated. High Machs are also more effective at persuading others than low Machs are and tend to be resistant to others' efforts to persuade them.[119] One reason high Machs are more effective at persuading others is that low Machs (i.e., most people) may be distracted by emotions or issues unrelated to winning. By contrast, high Machs are difficult to persuade because they ignore emotions and secondary issues and

authoritarianism the extent to which an individual believes there should be power and status differences within organizations.

Machiavellian the extent to which individuals believe that virtually any type of behavior is acceptable in trying to satisfy their needs or meet their goals.

© iStockphoto.com/Hans Martens

what really works

Conscientiousness: The Organized, Hardworking, Responsible Personality

Conscientious people are organized, hardworking, responsible, persevering, thorough, and achievement oriented. Who wouldn't want to hire people with these personality traits? Indeed, 92 studies across five occupational groups (professionals, police, managers, sales, and skilled/semiskilled jobs) with a combined total of 12,893 study participants indicated that, on average, conscientious people are inherently more motivated and are better at their jobs.

Motivational Effort

There is a 71 percent chance that conscientious workers will be more motivated and will work harder than less conscientious workers.

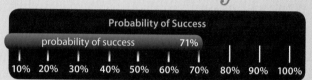

Job Performance

There is a 66 percent chance that conscientious workers will be better at their jobs than less conscientious workers.[120]

focus only on the things that move them closer to their goals. Also, because they are out for themselves and no one else, high Machs don't do well in work teams. High Machs often cause conflicts within teams and sometimes cause teams to break up. *The Wall Street Journal* offers this vivid description of high Machs: "They tend to be narcissistic, arrogant, manipulative, and goal-oriented. They trust no one and refuse to collaborate. They lack a capacity for empathy but are skilled at politics. Though they purposely disregard how they're coming off to colleagues or subordinates, they're often very good at sweet-talking bosses, who remain oblivious to their dastardly ways."[121] One study found that employees stuck with such manipulative bosses experienced more exhaustion, job tension, nervousness, depressed mood, and mistrust.[122]

The **Type A/B personality dimension** is the extent to which people tend toward impatience, hurriedness, competitiveness, and hostility.[123] **Type A personalities** try to complete as many tasks as possible in the shortest possible time and are hard-driving, competitive, impatient, perfectionistic, angry, and unable to relax.[124] Type As have a high need for achievement and are also likely to be aggressive, self-confident, dominant, and extroverted. By contrast, **Type B personalities** are easygoing, patient, and able to relax and engage in leisure activities. Unlike Type A personalities, they are neither highly competitive nor excessively driven to accomplishment.

What do we know about the Type A/B personality dimension and the workplace? Contrary to what you'd expect, Type As don't always outperform Type Bs on the job. Type As tend to perform better on tasks that demand quick decisions made at a rapid

Type A/B personality dimension the extent to which people tend toward impatience, hurriedness, competitiveness, and hostility.

Type A personality a person who tries to complete as many tasks as possible in the shortest possible time and is hard driving, competitive, impatient, perfectionistic, angry, and unable to relax.

Type B personality a person who is relaxed, easygoing, and able to engage in leisure activities without worrying about work.

work pace under time pressure, whereas Type Bs tend to perform better at tasks requiring well-thought-out decisions when there is little time pressure. And despite the characteristic Type A ambition to succeed, top managers are much more likely to have Type B personalities.[125] Ironically, the task complexity and psychological challenge inherent in management jobs actually work against many Type A managers by dramatically increasing their stress levels.[126] Type Bs, on the other hand, do a much better job of handling and responding to the stress of managerial jobs.

A study involving 6,148 people aged 14 to 102 conducted by a group of researchers and the U.S. National Institute of Aging found absolutely no connection between a hard-driving personality and heart disease, contrary to previous studies and conventional wisdom. This study clearly establishes that Type A personality in itself is not related to heart disease.[127] However, individuals who are Type A and also hostile and angry may be at risk of heart attack. For example, businessperson Matt Sicinski gets extremely hostile and angry when his coworkers miss deadlines or don't follow directions. Says Sicinski, "My feet get cold, and I get a throbbing in my head. I can feel every muscle in my body tense up." If he gets angry with someone on the phone, sometimes he presses the mute button so he can't be heard and begins "cursing somebody up one side and down the other."[128] How dangerous is angry, hostile behavior to your health? A long-term study at Duke University followed a group of lawyers for 25 years and found that those with higher hostility scores were 4.2 times as likely to have died over that period as those with low scores.[129] This does not bode well for Sicinski, who at age 30 already has dangerously high blood pressure, which he admits is not responding well to medications.

You do poorly on an exam. Quick: Whom do you blame—yourself or the professor? The answer to that question may, to some extent, indicate whether you have an internal or external locus of control. **Locus of control** is the degree to which people believe that their actions influence what happens to them. **Internal locus of control** is the belief that what happens to you is largely under your control. Students with an internal locus of control are more likely to hold themselves accountable for their exam performance ("I studied the wrong material" or "I didn't study enough"). Besides believing that what happens to them is largely under their control, internals are also easier to motivate (especially when rewards are linked to performance), more difficult to lead, more independent, and better able to handle complex information and solve complex problems.[130]

By contrast, an **external locus of control** is the belief that what happens to you is primarily due to factors beyond your control, such as luck, chance, or powerful people.[131] Students with an external locus of control are more likely to attribute their poor exam performance to luck ("If only it had been an essay exam instead of multiple choice"), chance ("I didn't get enough sleep"), or the professor (a powerful person). In general, externals are more compliant and conforming and therefore easier to lead than internals. For example, internals may question directives from their managers, whereas externals are likely to quietly accept them. Finally, internals are likely to perform better on complex tasks that require initiative and independent decision making, whereas externals tend to perform better on simple, repetitive tasks that are well structured.

Affectivity is the stable tendency to experience positive or negative moods and to react to things in a generally positive or negative way.[132] People with **positive affectivity** consistently notice and focus on the positive aspects of themselves and their environments. In other words, they seem to be in a good mood most of the time and are predisposed to being optimistic, cheerful, and cordial. By contrast, people with **negative affectivity** consistently notice and focus on the negative in themselves and their environments. They are frequently in bad moods, consistently expect the worst to happen, and are often irritated or pessimistic.

locus of control the degree to which individuals believe that their actions can influence what happens to them.

internal locus of control the belief that what happens to you is largely the result of your own actions.

external locus of control the belief that what happens to you is largely the result of factors beyond your control.

affectivity the stable tendency to experience positive or negative moods and to react to things in a generally positive or negative way.

positive affectivity a personality trait in which individuals tend to notice and focus on the positive aspects of themselves and their environments.

negative affectivity a personality trait in which individuals tend to notice and focus on the negative aspects of themselves and their environments.

How stable are the moods associated with positive and negative affectivity? A ten-year study by the National Institute of Aging found that even when people changed jobs or companies, the people who were the happiest at the beginning of the study were still the happiest at the end of the study ten years later.[133] Likewise, a much longer study found that high school counselors' ratings of student cheerfulness predicted how satisfied these people were with their jobs 30 years later.[134] Because dispositions toward positive or negative affectivity are long lasting and very stable, some companies have begun measuring affectivity during the hiring process. Indeed, a recent survey of 1,000 customers, conducted by Accenture, indicates that poor customer service drives nearly half of consumers to take their business elsewhere. Many experts agree that hiring people who are enthusiastic and have a positive outlook is important for providing world-class customer service.[135] Studies also show that employees with positive affectivity are absent less often, report feeling less stress, are less likely to be injured in workplace accidents, and are less likely to retaliate against management and the company when they believe that they have been treated unfairly.[136] In fact, research shows that people with a high level of negative affectivity are more likely to engage in counterproductive work behaviors, such as stealing, abusing other employees, and retaliating against management and the company.[137]

Affectivity is also important because of **mood linkage**, a phenomenon in which one worker's negative affectivity and bad moods can spread to others. Studies of nurses and accountants show a strong relationship between individual workers' moods and the moods of their coworkers.[138] Finally, people with positive affectivity are better decision makers, are rated as having much higher managerial potential, and are more successful in sales jobs.[139] Indeed, numerous studies show that happy individuals are successful across multiple domains, including marriage, friendship, income, work performance, and health.[140]

Review 3

Deep-Level Diversity Deep-level diversity matters because it can reduce prejudice, discrimination, and conflict, while increasing social integration. It consists of dispositional and personality differences that can be learned only through extended interaction with others. Research conducted in different cultures, settings, and languages indicates that there are five basic dimensions of personality: extroversion, emotional stability, agreeableness, conscientiousness, and openness to experience. Of these, conscientiousness is perhaps the most important to companies because conscientious workers tend to be better performers on virtually any job. Extroversion is also related to performance in jobs that require significant interaction with others. Studies also show that the personality dimensions of authoritarianism, Machiavellian tendencies, Type A/B personality, locus of control, and positive/negative affectivity are important in the workplace. These personality dimensions are related to honesty, trust, teamwork, persuasive abilities, job performance, decision making, stress, heart disease, adaptability, promotions, interpersonal skills, motivation, initiative, job satisfaction, absenteeism, accidents, retaliatory behavior, mood linkage, and management potential.

How Can Diversity Be Managed?

mood linkage a phenomenon in which one worker's negative affectivity and bad moods can spread to others.

"what's new" companies >

How much should companies change their standard business practices to accommodate the diversity of their workers? In San Mateo, California, Hani Khan, a storeroom worker for **Hollister**, a retail store selling California-style clothing, was fired for refusing to quit wearing a *hijab*, a head scarf warn by many Muslim women. When she was hired, her manager's only request was that she wear a white, navy blue, or gray scarf, consistent with Hollister's "look policy." Says Khan, "I was fine with that." Six months later, a district manager visiting her store noticed her scarf and notified the corporate human resources division. When HR asked her to stop wearing the hijab, she told them that "it was part of my religion, and that it is meant to promote modesty. Really, it's just a symbol, like a Jewish person wearing a yarmulke, or a Christian wearing a cross." Khan was removed from the store schedule. A week later, HR requested again that she not wear the hijab. When she refused, she was fired.[141]

Should Khan be allowed to wear a *hijab* consistent with her religious beliefs or was the company correct for insisting she abide by their dress code? What do you do when a talented top executive has a drinking problem that seems to affect his be-havior only at company business par-ties (for entertaining clients), where he has made inappropriate advances to-ward female employees? What do you do when, despite aggressive company policies against racial discrimination, employees continue to tell racial jokes and publicly post cartoons displaying racial humor? And because many peo-

After reading the next section, you should be able to

4. *Explain the basic principles and practices that can be used to manage diversity.*

ple confuse diversity with affirmative action, what do you do to make sure that your company's diversity practices and policies are viewed as benefiting all workers and not just some workers?

No doubt about it, questions like these make managing diversity one of the toughest challenges that managers face.[142] Nonetheless, there are steps companies can take to begin to address these issues.

4 Managing Diversity

As discussed earlier, diversity programs try to create a positive work environment where no one is advantaged or disadvantaged, where "we" is everyone, where ev-eryone can do his or her best work, where differences are respected and not ignored, and where everyone feels comfortable. Let's begin to address those goals by learn-ing about **4.1 different diversity paradigms, 4.2 diversity principles,** and **4.3 diversity training and practices.**

4.1 Diversity Paradigms

As shown in Exhibit 12.7, there are several different methods or paradigms for man-aging diversity: the discrimination and fairness paradigm, the access and legitimacy paradigm, and the learning and effectiveness paradigm.[143]

The *discrimination and fairness paradigm*, which is the most common method of approaching diversity, focuses on equal opportunity, fair treatment, recruitment of minorities, and strict compliance with the equal employment opportunity laws. Under this approach, success is usually measured by how well companies achieve recruitment, promotion, and retention goals for women, people of different racial/ ethnic backgrounds, or other underrepresented groups. According to a recent work-place diversity practices survey conducted by the Society of Human Resource Man-agement, 66 percent to 91 percent of companies use specialized strategies to recruit,

Exhibit 12.7 Paradigms for Managing Diversity

Diversity paradigm	Focus	Success measured by	Benefits	Limitations
Discrimination & Fairness	Equal opportunity Fair treatment Recruitment of minorities Strict compliance with laws	Recruitment, promotion, and retention goals for underrepresented groups	Fairer treatment Increased demographic diversity	Focus on surface-level diversity
Access & Legitimacy	Acceptance and celebration of differences	Diversity in company matches diversity of primary stakeholders	Establishes a clear business reason for diversity	Focus on surface-level diversity
Learning & Effectiveness	Integrating deep-level differences into organization	Valuing people on the basis of individual knowledge, skills, and abilities	Values common ground Distinction between individual and group differences Less conflict, backlash, and divisiveness Bringing different talents and perspectives together	Focus on deep-level diversity is more difficult to measure and quantify

© Cengage Learning 2013

> "If you don't measure something, it doesn't count. You measure your market share. You measure your profitability. The same should be true for diversity."

retain, and promote talented women and minorities. The percentages increase with company size, and companies of more than 500 employees are the most likely to use these strategies. Seventy-seven percent of companies with more than 500 employees systematically collect measurements on diversity-related practices.[144] One manager says, "If you don't measure something, it doesn't count. You measure your market share. You measure your profitability. The same should be true for diversity. There has to be some way of measuring whether you did, in fact, cast your net widely, and whether the company is better off today in terms of the experience of people of color than it was a few years ago. I measure my market share and my profitability. Why not this?"[145] The primary benefit of the discrimination and fairness paradigm is that it generally brings about fairer treatment of employees and increases demographic diversity. The primary limitation is that the focus of diversity remains on the surface-level diversity dimensions of sex, race, and ethnicity.[146]

The *access and legitimacy paradigm* focuses on the acceptance and celebration of differences to ensure that the diversity within the company matches the diversity found among primary stakeholders, such as customers, suppliers, and local communities. This is similar to the *business growth* advantage of diversity discussed earlier in the chapter. The basic idea behind this approach is to create a demographically diverse workforce that attracts a broader customer base. Consistent with this goal, Ed Adams, vice president of human resources for Enterprise Rent-a-Car, says, "We want people who speak the same language, literally and figuratively, as our customers. We don't set quotas. We say [to our managers], 'Reflect your local market.'"[147] The primary benefit of this approach is that it establishes a clear business reason for diversity. Like the discrimination and fairness paradigm, however, it focuses only on the surface-level diversity dimensions of sex, race, and ethnicity. Furthermore, employees who are assigned responsibility for customers and stakeholders on the basis of their sex, race, or ethnicity may eventually feel frustrated and exploited.

Whereas the discrimination and fairness paradigm focuses on assimilation (having a demographically representative workforce) and the access and legitimacy paradigm focuses on differentiation (having demographic differences inside the company match those of key customers and stakeholders), the *learning and effectiveness paradigm* focuses on integrating deep-level diversity differences, such as personality, attitudes, beliefs, and values, into the actual work of the organization. One sign that

Exhibit 12.8 Creating a Learning and Effectiveness Diversity Paradigm in an Organization

1. The leadership must understand that a diverse workforce will embody different perspectives and approaches to work, and must truly value variety of opinion and insight.

2. The leadership must recognize both the learning opportunities and the challenges that the expression of different perspectives presents for an organization.

3. The organizational culture must create an expectation of high standards of performance for everyone.

4. The organizational culture must stimulate personal development.

5. The organizational culture must encourage openness and a high tolerance for debate and support constructive conflict on work-related matters.

6. The culture must make workers feel valued.

7. The organization must have a well-articulated and widely understood mission. This keeps discussions about work differences from degenerating into debates about the validity of people's perspectives.

8. The organization must have a relatively egalitarian, nonbureaucratic structure.

Source: D. A. Thomas & R. J. Ely, "Making Differences Matter: A New Paradigm for Managing Diversity," *Harvard Business Review* 74 (September–October 1996): 79–90.

a company hasn't yet created a learning and effectiveness paradigm is that people withhold their opinions for fear of being seen as different. For example, although Helena Morrissey is the CEO of New Investment Management, a London firm that invests $71 billion for its clients, she admits to sometimes keeping her business opinions to herself for fear of being seen as "the annoying" woman at the table. She says, "At a recent meeting I wasn't comfortable with a controversial point and I spoke up, but I also had a different view on the next item on the agenda but instead of speaking up I held back." Says Morrissey, "I have been conscious of feeling that where I did have different views from the rest of the [all-male] group, I may be being perceived as the 'difficult woman' rather than being listened to for what I was saying," She felt this way despite there being "no evidence that the men were actually feeling that."[148]

Exhibit 12.8 shows the necessary preconditions for creating a learning and effectiveness diversity paradigm within an organization, one of which (no. 5) includes encouraging openness and a high tolerance for debate on work-related matters.

The learning and effectiveness paradigm is consistent with achieving organizational plurality. **Organizational plurality** is a work environment where (1) all members are empowered to contribute in a way that maximizes the benefits to the organization, customers, and themselves and (2) the individuality of each member is respected by not segmenting or polarizing people on the basis of their membership in a particular group.[149]

The learning and effectiveness diversity paradigm offers four benefits.[150] First, it values common ground. Dave Thomas of the Harvard Business School explains, "Like the fairness paradigm, it promotes equal opportunity for all individuals. And like the access paradigm, it acknowledges cultural differences among people and recognizes the value in those differences. Yet this new model for managing diversity lets the organization internalize differences among employees so that it learns and grows because of them. Indeed, with the model fully in place, members of the organization can say, 'We are all on the same team, with our differences—not despite them.'"[151]

Second, this paradigm makes a distinction between individual and group differences. When diversity focuses only on differences between groups, such as females versus males, large differences within groups are ignored.[152] For example, think of the women you know at work. Now, think for a second about what they have in common. After that, think about how they're different. If your situation is

organizational plurality a work environment where (1) all members are empowered to contribute in a way that maximizes the benefits to the organization, customers, and themselves, and (2) the individuality of each member is respected by not segmenting or polarizing people on the basis of their membership in a particular group.

© wavebreakmedia ltd/Shutterstock.com

typical, the list of differences should be just as long as the list of commonalties, if not longer. In short, managers can achieve a greater understanding of diversity and their employees by treating them as individuals and by realizing that not all African Americans, Hispanics, women, or white males want the same things at work.[153]

Third, because the focus is on individual differences, the learning and effectiveness paradigm is less likely to encounter the conflict, backlash, and divisiveness sometimes associated with diversity programs that focus only on group differences. Taylor Cox, one of the leading management writers on diversity, says, "We are concerned here with these more destructive forms of conflict which may be present with diverse workforces due to language barriers, cultural clash, or resentment by majority-group members of what they may perceive as preferential and unwarranted treatment of minority-group members."[154] And Ray Haines, a consultant who has helped companies deal with the aftermath of diversity programs that became divisive, says, "There's a large amount of backlash related to diversity training. It stirs up a lot of hostility, anguish, and resentment but doesn't give people tools to deal with [the backlash]. You have people come in and talk about their specific ax to grind."[155] Not all diversity programs are divisive or lead to conflict. But by focusing on individual rather than group differences, the learning and effectiveness paradigm helps to minimize these potential problems.

Finally, unlike the other diversity paradigms that simply focus on surface-level diversity, the learning and effectiveness paradigm focuses on bringing different talents and perspectives *together* (i.e., deep-level diversity) to make the best organizational decisions and to produce innovative, competitive products and services.

4.2 Diversity Principles

Diversity paradigms are general approaches or strategies for managing diversity. Whatever diversity paradigm a manager chooses, the diversity principles shown in Exhibit 12.9 will help managers do a better job of *managing company diversity programs*.[156]

Exhibit 12.9   Diversity Principles

1. Carefully and faithfully follow and enforce federal and state laws regarding equal employment opportunity.
2. Treat group differences as important, but not special.
3. Find the common ground.
4. Tailor opportunities to individuals, not groups.
5. Reexamine, but maintain, high standards.
6. Solicit negative as well as positive feedback.
7. Set high but realistic goals.

Source: L. S. Gottfredson, "Dilemmas in Developing Diversity Programs," in *Diversity in the Workplace,* S. S. Jackson & Associates, eds. (New York: Guilford Press, 1992).

Begin by *carefully and faithfully following and enforcing federal and state laws regarding equal opportunity employment.* Diversity programs can't and won't succeed if the company is being sued for discriminatory actions and behavior. Faithfully following the law will also reduce the time and expense associated with EEOC investigations or lawsuits. Start by learning more at the EEOC website (www.eeoc.gov). Following the law also means strictly and fairly enforcing company policies.

Treat group differences as important, but not special. Surface-level diversity dimensions such as age, sex, and race/ethnicity should be respected but should not be treated as more important than other kinds of differences (i.e., deep-level diversity). Remember, the shift from surface- to deep-level diversity helps people know and understand each other better, reduces prejudice and conflict, and leads to stronger social integration with people wanting to work together and get the job done. Also, *find the common ground.* Although respecting differences is important, it's just as important, especially with diverse workforces, to actively find ways for employees to see and share commonalties.

Tailor opportunities to individuals, not groups. Special programs for training, development, mentoring, or promotions should be based on individual strengths and weaknesses, not on group status. Instead of making mentoring available for just one group of workers, create mentoring opportunities for everyone who wants to be mentored. All programs at Pacific Enterprises, including Career Conversations forums, in which upper-level managers are publicly interviewed about themselves and how they got their jobs, are open to all employees.[157]

Maintain high standards. Companies have a legal and moral obligation to make sure that their hiring and promotion procedures and standards are fair to all. At the same time, in today's competitive markets, companies should not lower standards to promote diversity. This not only hurts the organizations but also feeds the stereotype that applicants who are hired or promoted in the name of affirmative action or diversity are less qualified. Chrysler's executive director of diversity Monica Emerson says, "As a diversity executive, I not only have to have solid business capabilities, I need to be very knowledgeable of the different businesses in my organization to align diversity initiatives to support the needs of the businesses. Maintaining high standards when making employment decisions and involving the top management and the board in diversity initiatives is critical to the success of workplace diversity parctices."[158]

Solicit negative as well as positive feedback. Diversity is one of the most difficult management issues. No company or manager gets it right from the start. Consequently, companies should aggressively seek positive and negative feedback about their diversity programs. One way to do that is to use a series of measurements to see whether progress is being made. Jaya Bohlmann, a vice president at **Sodexo**, a food services and facilities management company, says, "We measure our progress systematically, using an objective scorecard that ties 15 percent of managers' compensation and 25 percent of our executives' compensation to their success [to ensure that] we continue to attract, develop and retain a diverse and highly skilled workforce. We report on our diversity progress annually, posting the reports on our website."[159]

< **"what's new"**
companies

Set high but realistic goals. Just because diversity is difficult doesn't mean that organizations shouldn't try to accomplish as much as possible. The general purpose of diversity programs is to try to create a positive work environment where no one is advantaged or disadvantaged, where "we" is everyone, where everyone can do his or her best work, where differences are respected and not ignored, and where everyone feels comfortable. Even if progress is slow, companies should not shrink from these goals.

4.3 Diversity Training and Practices

Organizations use diversity training and several common diversity practices to manage diversity. There are two basic types of diversity training programs. **Awareness training** is designed to raise employees' awareness of diversity issues, such as those discussed in this chapter, and to get employees to challenge underlying assumptions or stereotypes they may have about others. As a starting point in awareness training, some companies have begun using the Implicit Association Test (IAT), which measures the extent to which people associate positive or negative thoughts (i.e., underlying assumptions or stereotypes) with blacks or whites, men or women, homosexuals or heterosexuals, young or old, or other groups. For example, test takers are shown black or white faces that they must instantly pair with various words. Response times (shorter responses generally indicate stronger associations) and the pattern of associations indicate the extent to which people are biased. Most people are, and strongly so. For example, 88 percent of whites have a more positive mental association toward whites than toward blacks, but, surprisingly, 48 percent of blacks show the same bias. Taking the IAT is a good way to increase awareness of diversity issues. To take the IAT and to learn more about the decade of research behind it, go to https://implicit.harvard.edu/implicit/.[160] By contrast, **skills-based diversity training** teaches employees the practical skills they need for managing a diverse workforce, skills such as flexibility and adaptability, negotiation, problem solving, and conflict resolution.[161]

Companies also use diversity audits, diversity pairing, and minority experiences for top executives to better manage diversity. **Diversity audits** are formal assessments that measure employee and management attitudes, investigate the extent to which people are advantaged or disadvantaged with respect to hiring and promotions, and review companies' diversity-related policies and procedures. Branch managers at Merrill Lynch's Global Private Client Group are annually assessed on how well they recruit, hire, and develop diverse job candidates. This includes comparing the revenue that different groups of brokers produce. Merrill's Dan Sontag, head of Merrill's Global Private Client Americas group, explains that if average revenue growth were 10 percent, but a branch manager's female and minority advisors grew revenues by 12 percent, then the branch manager would score well on this measure of diversity. He says, however, "In order to do that, you have to provide effective training and development programs to make sure that they grow in the role for the organization." That appears to be happening as female and diverse financial advisors' revenues are growing at twice the firm's average over the last three years.[162]

Earlier in the chapter you learned that *mentoring*, pairing a junior employee with a senior employee, is a common strategy for creating learning and promotional opportunities for women. Diversity pairing is a special kind of mentoring. In **diversity pairing**, people of different cultural backgrounds, sexes, or races/ethnicities are paired for mentoring. The hope is that stereotypical beliefs and attitudes will change as

awareness training training that is designed to raise employees' awareness of diversity issues and to challenge the underlying assumptions or stereotypes they may have about others.

skills-based diversity training training that teaches employees the practical skills they need for managing a diverse workforce, such as flexibility and adaptability, negotiation, problem solving, and conflict resolution.

diversity audits formal assessments that measure employee and management attitudes, investigate the extent to which people are advantaged or disadvantaged with respect to hiring and promotions, and review companies' diversity-related policies and procedures.

diversity pairing a mentoring program in which people of different cultural backgrounds, sexes, or races/ethnicities are paired together to get to know each other and change stereotypical beliefs and attitudes.

© Stephen Coburn/Shutterstock.com

people get to know each other as individuals.[163] Consultant Tom McGee, who has set up mentoring programs for numerous companies, supports diversity pairing, saying, "The assumption that people participating in diversity mentoring programs are looking for someone of the same race or gender has been proved wrong in many cases."[164]

For more than 20 years, Xerox has been fostering a culture where women and minorities are prepared and considered for top positions. CEO Ursula Burns, the first African American woman to lead a major U.S. company, worked as special assistant to Xerox's president of marketing and customer operations, Wayland Hicks. Reginald Brown, Jr., CEO of Brown Technology Group, who worked with Burns at Xerox, said, "These [appointments as special assistants] were jobs in the company that division presidents put their best people in. Most of them were white males, so to have an African American female in such a position of power, you knew early on she had great potential." Burns was then given a similar role with former Xerox CEO Paul A. Allaire. When Anne Mulcahy became CEO in 2001, Burns was gradually given control of day-to-day operations while Mulcahy repaired Xerox's financial position and customer service. David Thomas, a Harvard Business School professor, says because of steps (such as diversity pairing) to promote diversity at Xerox, "You have a culture where having women and people of color as candidates for powerful jobs has been going on for two decades."[165]

Finally, because top managers are still overwhelmingly white and male, a number of companies believe that it is worthwhile to *have top executives experience what it is like to be in the minority*. This can be done by having top managers go to places or events where nearly everyone else is of a different sex or racial/ethnic background. At Hoechst Celanese (which has now split into two companies), top managers would join two organizations in which they were a minority. For instance, the CEO, a white male, joined the board of Hampton University, a historically African American college, and Jobs for Progress, a Hispanic organization that helps people prepare for jobs. Commenting on his experiences, he said, "The only way to break out of comfort zones is to be exposed to other people. When we are, it becomes clear that all people are similar." A Hoechst vice president who joined three organizations in which he was in the minority said, "Joining these organizations has been more helpful to me than two weeks of diversity training."[166]

Managing Diversity   The three paradigms for managing diversity are the discrimination and fairness paradigm (equal opportunity, fair treatment, strict compliance with the law), the access and legitimacy paradigm (matching internal diversity to external diversity), and the learning and effectiveness paradigm (achieving organizational plurality by integrating deep-level diversity into the work of the organization). Unlike the other paradigms, which focus on surface-level differences, the learning and effectiveness program values common ground, distinguishes between individual and group differences, minimizes conflict and divisiveness, and focuses on bringing different talents and perspectives together. What principles can companies use when managing diversity? Follow and enforce federal and state laws regarding equal employment opportunity. Treat group differences as important, but not special. Find the common ground. Tailor opportunities to individuals, not groups. Reexamine, but maintain, high standards. Solicit negative as well as positive feedback. Set high but realistic goals. The two types of diversity training are awareness training and skills-based diversity training. Companies also manage diversity through diversity audits and diversity pairing and by having top executives experience what it is like to be in the minority.

Review 4

SELF-ASSESSMENT

Do You Know Your Mind?

Do you always speak your mind? Chances are that you probably don't—at least not always. In some cases, you may not even know your mind. Our conscious mind is not always aligned with our subconscious, and we may be motivated by deeply held beliefs that diverge from our image of who we are or want to be. Researchers at Harvard have developed a series of assessments to help you identify your implicit associations about a variety of topics, many related to the diversity issues you learned about in this chapter. Unlike the other assessments in this book, this one requires you to go online. Each Project Implicit test, which is also called an Implicit Association Test (IAT), takes about 10 minutes to complete. However, you'll find it worthwhile to complete all of the different IATs. The researchers ask that you complete the initial surveys so that they can further enrich their data, but you needn't worry about privacy issues. They are only interested in the raw data and not in who actually contributed it.

1. To begin, go to https://implicit.harvard.edu and click on "**Demonstration.**"

2. You will then be given a brief description of the project and prompted to "**Go to the demonstration tests.**" Click on that hot link.

3. The front page of the demonstration tests is a more detailed synopsis of the project and a disclaimer. Read the information, and then click on "**I wish to proceed.**"

4. You will then reach the list of all the tests: age, gender-science, race, presidents, sexuality, gender-career, Arab-Muslim, weight, religion, disability, Native, Asian, weapons, and skin tone. The tests most closely related to Chapter 12's content on diversity are age, race, sexuality, gender-career, weight, disability, Native, Asian, and skin tone. Each time you complete an IAT, return to the list to select the next relevant test for this course. We'll use the age IAT as the basis for these instructions. Once you get the hang of it, you will be able to move through the preliminaries on any of the IATs. To begin, click on "**Age IAT.**"

5. You will be directed to a page of technical information related to your computer settings. If you can see the green check mark, then click to begin. At the next page, click on "**Continue.**"

6. A survey of general information will pop up. The survey for each IAT is slightly different, except for the main demographic information at the bottom (age, race, etc.). Once you complete the survey, click on "**Proceed.**"

7. Read the instructions carefully. In essence, each time a certain word or image appears, you will need to either respond by typing an "e" or an "i." The words used are purposely set to be obviously good or bad. For example, few people would dispute that *evil* goes in the category labeled "bad," and *love* goes in the category labeled "good." Don't get caught up in semantics; just classify the terms as they are understood in the common language.

8. The test will ask you to classify the words and images several times, switching the words and images from the left hand to the right hand. That way, your right hand isn't always typing an "i" for good and your left an "e" for bad. Pay attention to the changes.

9. Once you have finished the IAT on a particular topic, you will receive a results page. Check with

KEY TERMS

affectivity 505
affirmative action 488
age discrimination 493
agreeableness 502
authoritarianism 503
awareness training 512
conscientiousness 502
deep-level diversity 492
disability 498
disability discrimination 498
disposition 500
diversity audits 512
diversity 487
diversity pairing 512
emotional stability 501
external locus of control 505
extroversion 501
glass ceiling 494

internal locus of control 505
locus of control 505
Machiavellian 503
mood linkage 506
negative affectivity 505
openness to experience 502
organizational plurality 509
personality 500
positive affectivity 505
racial and ethnic discrimination 497
sex discrimination 494
skills-based diversity training 512
social integration 492
surface-level diversity 492
Type A/B personality dimension 504
Type A personality 504
Type B personality 504

your professor if he or she wants you to print it out or keep track of results in any way. Your instructor may want to average class results.

After completing the IATs, think about your results. Do any surprise you, or were you aware that you were making the unconscious associations the software identified?

MANAGEMENT DECISION

Expanding Your Market[167]

This has to be one of the most depressing annual review meetings you've ever sat through. Sure, times have been tough before, but never like this. In the past year, your power-tools company has lost 37 percent market share. Sales have decreased by 64 percent. Profit is down almost 70 percent. You had to lay off one-third of your workforce. And worst of all, it doesn't look to be getting better anytime soon. Housing sales and construction are at an all-time low, meaning your best customers, contractors, have little work to do and even less money to spend on new tools.

"We have to increase sales!" you tell the rest of your management staff. They just stare back at you, of course, because everyone knows what needs to be done. They just don't know how to do it. How do you sell a product when demand is so low?

As everyone in the room ponders over this, an intern sitting in the back corner raises her hand and says, "Why don't we sell more to women?" She mentions that she's read of a number of companies that have found new success by reaching out to a more diverse customer base. Harley Davidson, for example, which has long been known primarily for motorcycles that appeal to older white men, was able to increase market share by appealing to women. It produced a new

motorcycle, the SuperLow, which has a lower seat, making it easier to get on, and weighs 150 pounds less than other Harleys. It hired supermodel Marisa Miller for an ad campaign specifically targeted to female riders. And it holds women-only events at dealerships where women can see up-close, personal demonstrations about a Harley's safety and features.

"And it doesn't have to be just women," she continues, "We can target a whole bunch of groups that we've never given much thought to before."

An enthusiastic energy courses through the room as people start discussing the potentials—new customers, more sales, higher revenues, and good times again! But the mood quickly dampens when you ask some questions: "How do we sell a reciprocating saw to women? Do we just slap some pink paint on it and expect customers to come flocking? How do we appeal to different kinds of customers without insulting them?"

Questions

1. What is an effective way for this company to increase the diversity of its customers?
2. What steps could you take to make sure that your marketing campaign targeted to women actually addresses their needs and wants without offending them?

MANAGEMENT TEAM DECISION

Negative Reactions to Affirmative Action

Ten years ago, your company made an organization-wide commitment to increase diversity. Every single employee, from entry level clerks to senior executives, attended a two-weeklong diversity training course. After that course, a group of employees and managers formed a committee that met each week to talk about how to make sure that their workplace was one that respected and appreciated everyone's uniqueness.

Senior managers also create a new item in the budget. They called it "social affairs," and it was a large pool of money that was to be used for holding group dinners, movie nights, weekend camping trips, and other social activities that were designed to help workers get to know each other better.

A controversial part of this plan to encourage diversity had to do with hiring. After one particular company-wide training session, the senior management

team came to the realization that the company lacked minorities. There were few African Americans, Latinos, or Asians among the employees, and even fewer women. Every single person on the senior management team was a Caucasian male, and there were only two minorities among 75 middle managers. After a series of conversations, the senior managers decided that the company would hire more minorities at all levels of the company and give them the support and training they would need to get promotions.

In just ten short years, the company looks radically different. More than 50 percent of all employees are minorities, and more than 30 percent of the managers are African American or Latino. Women now make up just less than 50 percent of middle management, and three women were recently promoted to senior level positions.

Although the senior management team is elated with these developments, not all employees agree. A group of Caucasian male employees have been complaining for several months that they are the victims of reverse discrimination. They complain that they've been passed over for promotions, even though they're the best qualified, in favor of minorities with lesser qualifications. They also argue that they receive far less training and coaching, that their performance reviews are much more critical, and that they receive pay raises and bonuses far less frequently than those of their nonwhite, non-male colleagues.

As a group of white male employees explains to your senior management team, it's not that they're against diversity. They want to do all they can to make this company a great place for diversity. But, they wonder, how does it help increase diversity if white men feel like they're being discriminated against for being white men? That's the question they want you to answer.

For this Management Team Decision, form a group with three or four other students and consider how you would respond to the group of white male employees, as the company's senior management team.

Questions

1. Do you believe that companies should adopt Affirmative Action to increase their diversity? Are there alternatives to Affirmative Action that a company can use to increase diversity?
2. Do you think that Affirmative Action is discriminatory toward white males? If so, is it an acceptable means of increasing diversity?

PRACTICE BEING A MANAGER

Culture, Subcultures, and You

Diversity may contribute a richness of perspective and understanding to a work group or organization. But to unlock these riches, it is essential that we develop tools for understanding individuals and cultures different from our own. Not all college students have experienced crossing a cultural boundary to live in another country. But most have encountered subcultures in the context of their middle or high school years. Teen subcultures are often quite pronounced and diverse. This exercise will offer practice in recognizing and understanding diversity.

Step 1: Get into groups. Your professor will organize you in small groups of three or four students.

Step 2: Identify teen subcultures. Think back to your middle school or high school experiences and identify some of the major subcultures you observed (Athletes, Toughs, and so on). Share descriptions of these subcultures with the members of your group.

Step 3: Conduct diversity training. Take turns training each other on what it would be like to be a member of one of the subcultures that you knew well. It is not necessary to have belonged to this subculture, but only to be able to recall it vividly. Teach your fellow group members what a young person would need to know to fit in with this subculture, including such dimensions as these:

- Clothing
- Manner of speech, common slang, or "code language"
- Music
- Value of the subculture to members; what it means to be "in" this group

Step 4: Discuss how teen subcultures are diverse. Discuss as a group the impact of teen subcultures on valuing diversity. In what ways do teen subcultures bond diverse people together (athletes of different races, e.g.), and help them to understand one another better?

In what ways do teen subcultures separate people into "cliques" or foster stereotyping ("us" vs. "them")?

Step 5: Debrief as a class. Based on your group discussions, what are the challenges for organizations that are seriously attempting to value diversity? What are the benefits to these organizations? How do organizations train people about cultural (and subcultural) differences without falling into stereotyping?

DEVELOP YOUR CAREER POTENTIAL

From Majority to Minority and Back Again

Do you know what it feels like to walk into a room where, because of your sex, race/ethnicity, religion, language, or some other dimension, you are intensely aware of being different from everyone else?[168] Some of you do. Most of you probably don't. And because most managers are white and male, it's a good bet that they don't know either. The experience can be unsettling, especially the first time it happens.

Some companies have begun broadening perspectives and understanding by having their managers join groups or attend events where they are different from everyone else. As you read in Section 4.3, at Hoechst Celanese, the CEO, a white male, joined the board of Hampton University, a historically African American college, and Jobs for Progress, a Hispanic organization that helps people prepare for jobs.

For more than 30 years, UPS has required its top managers to participate in community service programs in inner cities or poor rural areas. James Casey, UPS's founder, started the program in 1968, to expose his white male managers to diverse experiences, people, and communities. Casey also hoped that the experience would increase empathy, break down stereotypes, and encourage volunteer and community service. Today, managers with 10 to 30 years of experience are assigned to community service tasks in inner cities or rural areas. Don Wofford, who directs the program, says, "We choose managers on the fast track, people who'll be positioned to influence their workforce and the community for years to come." The managers spend two weeks doing community service, followed by a weekend at home and then two more weeks of community service. Wofford says, "This format gives them a chance to digest the experience—they tend to come back renewed after the break, with a new focus, sometimes even more bewildered, but still ready to go for it."

Your assignment is to attend an event, meeting, or activity where you are different from almost everyone else in terms of your sex, race/ethnicity, religion, language, or some other dimension. You can choose a church service, local community group, volunteer organization, or student group on campus. Ask your professor for ideas. You should probably contact the group beforehand to arrange your visit. Answer the following questions after your visit.

Questions

1. Describe the event, meeting, activity, or organization you visited.
2. How were you different from others in attendance? Describe what it was like to be different from everyone else.
3. In what ways was this experience actually similar to previous experiences that you've had? In other words, whereas question 2 focuses on differences, this question focuses on similarities and commonalties.
4. What did you learn from this experience?

END NOTES

[1]"About Hooters," Hooters, accessed May 30, 2011, from www.hooters.com/About.aspx; "Hourly Employment," Hooters, accessed May 30, 2011, from www.hooters.com/Hourly.aspx; A. Foley, "Hooters Loses Motion to Dismiss Suit Filed by Servers Fired over Weight," Mlive.com, August 24, 2010, accessed May 30, 2011, from www.mlive.com/news/detroit/index.ssf/2010/08/hooters_loses_motion_to_dismis.html; A. Lewis, "Al's Emporium: The Skinny on Hooters," *The Wall Street Journal*, August 29, 2010, B2; R. Ruehlen, "Hooters Official: 'It Matters What They Look Like,'" CandGnews.com, accessed May 30, 2011, from http://cgjournal.com/

Homepage-Articles/2010/06-02-2010/ Roseville-Hooters-lawsuit.asp; C. Selweski, "Hooters Waitress Files Lawsuit—Says She Lost Weight," *The New Haven Register*, May 25, 2010, accessed May 30, 2011, from www. nhregister.com/articles/2010/05/25/ news/doc4bfbe256a2ae2049162868. txt; and C. Smith, "Constructively Discharged or Discharge Constructed?" *Business Insurance*, May 31, 2010, 22.

[2]J. H. Boyett & J. T. Boyett, *Beyond Workforce 2000* (New York: Dutton, 1995); and "Quick Stats on Women Workers, 2008," United States Department of Labor," accessed November 4, 2009, from www.dol.gov/wb/stats/main.htm.

[3]Ibid.

[4]M. Toossi, "Labor Force Projections to 2014: Retiring Boomers," *Monthly Labor Review* (November 2005): 25–44.

[5]P. English, "The Way I Work: Paul English of Kayak," interview by L. Welch, Inc., February 1, 2010, accessed July 27, 2010, from www.inc.com/magazine/20100201/the-way-i-work-paul-english-of-kayak.html.

[6]R. S. Johnson, "The 50 Best Companies for Asians, Blacks, & Hispanics: Talent Comes in All Colors," Fortune, August 3, 1999, 94.

[7]"Verizon Communications Inc.: Company to Pay $48.9 Million in Settlement of Bias Lawsuit," *The Wall Street Journal*, June 6, 2006, accessed May 20, 2011, from www.wsj.com.

[8]L. Simmons, "ICM Smoothes out Age Wrinkle," *Hollywood Reporter*, August 20, 2008, 5–12.

[9]D. D. Stanford, "Coke's Diversity Case Closed: Report Says Progress Made," *Atlanta Journal Constitution*, December 2, 2006, 1C; "Racism Lawsuit against New York Manufacturer Settled for $1.25 Million," Associated Press Financial Wire, December 28, 2006, accessed May 20, 2011, from www.ap.org; "Payouts Delayed in Lawsuit Settlement with Los Alamos Lab," Associated Press State & Local Wire, November 27, 2006, accessed May 2011, from www.ap.org; and "Tyson Settles Discrimination Lawsuit for $871,000," *Financial Times*, November 7, 2006, available online at www.financialtimes.net.

[10]"Denny's Diversity Speaks," Denny's, accessed June 5, 2009, from www .dennysdiversity.com.

[11]"Verizon Named to Working Mother Magazine's List of 100 Best Companies, for Ninth Consecutive Year," Verizon, accessed November 5, 2009, from http://newscenter.verizon.com/press-releases/verizon/2009/verizon-named-to-working.html.

[12]Equal Employment Opportunity Commission, "Affirmative Action Appropriate under Title VII of the Civil Rights Act of 1964, As Amended. Chapter XIV—Equal Employment Opportunity Commission, Part 1608," accessed November 5, 2009, from www .access.gpo.gov/nara/cfr/waisidx_ 04/29cfr1608_04.html.

[13]R. Rodriguez, "Diversity Finds Its Place: More Organizations Are Dedicating Senior-Level Executives to Drive Diversity Initiatives for Bottom-Line Effect," *HR Magazine*, August 2006, Society for Human Resource Management, accessed March 24, 2009, from www.shrm.org.

[14]Equal Employment Opportunity Commission, "Federal Laws Prohibiting Job Discrimination: Questions and Answers," accessed August 21, 2008, from www.eeoc.gov/facts/qanda.html.

[15]A. P. Carnevale & S. C. Stone, *The American Mosaic: An In-Depth Report on the Future of Diversity at Work* (New York: McGraw-Hill, 1995).

[16]T. Roosevelt, "From Affirmative Action to Affirming Diversity," *Harvard Business Review* 68, no. 2 (1990): 107–117.

[17]A. M. Konrad & F. Linnehan, "Formalized HRM Structures: Coordinating Equal Employment Opportunity or Concealing Organizational Practices?" *Academy of Management Journal* 38, no. 3 (1995): 787–820; see, for example, *Hopwood v. Texas*, 78 F.3d 932 (5th Cir., March 18, 1996). The U.S. Supreme Court has upheld the principle of affirmative action but has struck down some specific programs.

[18]P. Schmidt, "5 More States May Curtail Affirmative Action," *The Chronicle of Higher Education*, October 19, 2007, A1.

[19]M. E. Heilman, C. J. Block, & P. Stathatos, "The Affirmative Action

Stigma of Incompetence: Effects of Performance Information Ambiguity," *Academy of Management Journal* 40, no. 3 (1997): 603–625.

[20]K. C. Cole, "Jury Out on Whether Affirmative Action Beneficiaries Face Stigma: Research Studies Arrive at Conflicting Conclusions," *The Los Angeles Times*, May 1, 1995, 18.

[21]E. Orenstein, "The Business Case for Diversity," *Financial Executive*, May 2005, 22–25; G. Robinson & K. Dechant, "Building a Business Case for Diversity," *Academy of Management Executive* 11, no. 3 (1997): 21–31.

[22]E. Esen, "2005 Workplace Diversity Practices: Survey Report," Society for Human Resource Management, accessed May 20, 2100, from www. shrm.org/Research/SurveyFindings/ Articles/Documents/05-0509Wk-plcDivPrcSR_FINAL_rev.pdf.

[23]Orenstein, "Business Case for Diversity."

[24]Esen, "2005 Workplace Diversity Practices."

[25]Orenstein, "Business Case for Diversity."

[26]Mike Dickinson, "Judge OKs Settlement of Class-Action Lawsuits against Kodak," *Rochester Business Journal*, September 3, 2010, accessed November 21, 2010, from www.rbj.net/article .asp?aID=185021.

[27]"Chad Bray, "Novartis Unit Settles Gender Suit for About $175 Million," *The Wall Street Journal*, July 14 2010, accessed November 21, 2010, from http://online.wsj.com/article/SB10001 42405274870339420457536753077 7045418.html

[28]"Age-Discrimination Case: TV Writers to Get $70M," *The Huffington Post*, January 22, 2010, accessed November 21, 2010, from www.huffingtonpost .com/2010/01/22/agediscrimination-case-tv_n_433843.html.

[29]M. Selmi, "The Price of Discrimination: The Nature of Class Action Employment Discrimination Litigation and Its Effects," *Texas Law Review*, April 1, 2003, 1249.

[30]N. Ursel & M. Armstrong-Stassen, "How Age Discrimination in Employment Affects Stockholders," *Journal of Labor Research* 27 (2006): 89–99.

[31]P. Wright & S. P. Ferris, "Competitiveness through Management of Diversity: Effects on Stock Price Valuation," *Academy of Management Journal* 38 (1995): 272–285.

[32]Ibid.

[33]D. Dodson, "Minority Groups' Share of $10 Trillion U.S. Consumer Market Is Growing Steadily, According to Annual Buying Power Study from Terry College's Selig Center for Economic Growth," Selig Center for Economic Growth, accessed November 6, 2009, from www.terry.uga.edu/news/releases/2007/minority_buying_power_report.html.

[34]E. Esen, "2005 Workplace Diversity Practices: Survey Report," (Society for Human Resource Management: Alexandria, VA, 2005); and L. E. Wynter, "Business & Race: Advocates Try to Tie Diversity to Profit," *The Wall Street Journal*, February 7, 1996, B1.

[35]Megan Angelo, "At TBS, Diversity Pays Its Own Way," *The New York Times*, May 28, 2010, accessed September 2, 2010, from www.nytimes.com/2010/05/30/arts/television/30tbs.html; and Alaina Love, "Diversity as a Strategic Advantage," *Bloomberg Businessweek*, May 14, 2010, accessed August 23, 2010, from www.businessweek.com/managing/content/may2010/ca20100513_748402.htm.

[36]W. W. Watson, K. Kumar, & L. K. Michaelsen, "Cultural Diversity's Impact on Interaction Process and Performance: Comparing Homogeneous and Diverse Task Groups," *Academy of Management Journal* 36 (1993): 590–602; K. A. Jehn, G. B. Northcraft, & M. A. Neale, "Why Differences Make a Difference: A Field Study of Diversity, Conflict, and Performance in Workgroups," *Administrative Science Quarterly* 44 (1999): 741–763; and E. Kearney, D. Gebert, & S. Voelpel, "When and How Diversity Benefits Teams: The Importance of Team Members' Need for Cognition," *Academy of Management Journal* 52 (2009): 581–598.

[37]F. Rice, "How to Make Diversity Pay," *Fortune*, August 8, 1994, 78.

[38]Rodriguez, "Diversity Finds Its Place."

[39]C. Hymowitz, "The New Diversity: In a Global Economy, It's No Longer about How Many Employees You Have in This Group and That Group; It's a Lot More Complicated—And if You Do It Right, A Lot More Effective," *The Wall Street Journal*, November 14, 2005, R1.

[40]"Diversity at Work: Public Relations Make a Difference for Global Giants," *Public Relations Society of America*, October 1, 2010, accessed June 1, 2011, from www.prsa.org/Intelligence/Tactics/Articles/view/8828/1021/Diversity_at_work_Public_relations_makes_a_differe.

[41]M. R. Carrell & E. E. Mann, "Defining Workplace Diversity Programs and Practices in Organizations," *Labor Law Journal* 44 (1993): 743–764.

[42]D. A. Harrison, K. H. Price, & M. P. Bell, "Beyond Relational Demography: Time and the Effects of Surface- and Deep-Level Diversity on Work Group Cohesion," *Academy of Management Journal* 41 (1998): 96–107.

[43]D. Harrison, K. Price, J. Gavin, & A. Florey, "Time, Teams, and Task Performance: Changing Effects of Surface- and Deep-Level Diversity on Group Functioning," *Academy of Management Journal* 45 (2002): 1029–1045.

[44]Harrison, Price, & Bell, "Beyond Relational Demography."

[45]Ibid.

[46]N. Munk, "Finished at Forty: In the New Economy, the Skills That Come with Age Count for Less and Less," *Fortune*, February 1, 1999, 50.

[47]K. Wrenn & T. Maurer, "Beliefs about Older Workers' Learning and Development Behavior in Relation to Beliefs about Malleability of Skills, Age-Related Decline, and Control," *Journal of Applied Social Psychology* 34 (February 2004): 223–242.

[48]J. Helyar & B. Cherry, "50 and Fired," *Fortune*, May 16, 2005, 78.

[49]Ibid.

[50]E. White, "The New Recruits: Older Workers," *The Wall Street Journal*, January 14, 2008, B3.

[51]S. E. Sullivan & E. A. Duplaga, "Recruiting and Retaining Older Workers for the Millennium," *Business Horizons* 40 (November 12, 1997): 65.

[52]Munk, "Finished at Forty."

[53]J. Bravin, "Court Expands Age Bias Claims for Work Force," *The Wall Street Journal*, March 31, 2005, B1.

[54]J. Levitz & P. Shishkin, "More Workers Cite Age Bias after Layoffs," *The Wall Street Journal*, March 11, 2009, D1.

[55]L. Wolgemuth, "When Age Bias Hinders the Job Hunt," *U.S. News & World Report*, October 1, 2009, 72.

[56]S. R. Rhodes, "Age-Related Differences in Work Attitudes and Behavior," *Psychological Bulletin* 92 (1983): 328–367.

[57]A. Fisher, "Wanted: Aging Baby-Boomers," *Fortune*, September 30, 1996, 204.

[58]G. M. McEvoy & W. F. Cascio, "Cumulative Evidence of the Relationship between Employee Age and Job Performance," *Journal of Applied Psychology* 74 (1989): 11–17.

[59]Sullivan & Duplaga, "Recruiting and Retaining Older Workers."

[60]T. Maurer & N. Rafuse, "Learning, Not Litigating: Managing Employee Development and Avoiding Claims of Age Discrimination," *Academy of Management Executive* 15, no. 4 (2001): 110–121.

[61]B. L. Hassell & P. L. Perrewe, "An Examination of Beliefs about Older Workers: Do Stereotypes Still Exist?" *Journal of Organizational Behavior* 16 (1995): 457–468.

[62]"Charge Statistics: FY 1997 through FY 2010," U.S. Equal Employment Opportunity Commission, accessed May 28, 2011, from http://eeoc.gov/eeoc/statistics/enforcement/charges.cfm.

[63]"Statistics & Data: Quick Stats on Women Workers, 2009," U.S. Department of Labor, www.dol.gov/wb/stats/main.htm; "Employment Status of the Civilian Noninstitutional Population by Age, Sex, and Race," 2010 Current Population Survey, Bureau of Labor Statistics, www.bls.gov/cps/cpsaat3.pdf.

[64]"Key Facts about Women-Owned Businesses, The Overall Picture: 2008-2009," Center for Women's Business Research, accessed May 28, 2011, from www.womensbusinessresearchcenter.org/research/keyfacts/.

[65]Women's Earnings as a Percentage of Men's, 2008," U.S. Department of Labor, Bureau of Labor Statistics, October 14, 2009, accessed May 28, 2011, from www.bls.gov/opub/ted/2009/ted_20091014_data.htm.

[66]"U.S. Women in Business," Catalyst, accessed May 28, 2011, from www.catalyst.org/publication/132/us-women-in-business.

[67]"Catalyst 2008 Census of the Fortune 500 Reveals Women Gained Little Ground Advancing to Business Leadership Positions," Catalyst, December 10, 2008, accessed November 7, 2009, from www.catalyst.org/press-release/141/catalyst-2008-census-of-the-fortune-500-reveals-women-gained-little-ground-advancing-to-business-leadership-positions; A. Joyce, "They Open More Doors for Women," *The Washington Post*, February 4 , 2007, F4; and "The 2007 Fortune 500: Women CEOs," *Fortune*, accessed August 21, 2008, from http://money.cnn.com/galleries/2007/fortune/0704/gallery.F500_womenCEOs.fortune/index.html [content no longer available online].

[68]"Women CEOs of the Fortune 1000: Fortune 500 (12 CEOs)," Catalyst, May 2011, accessed May 28, 2011, from www.catalyst.org/publication/322/women-ceos-of-the-fortune-1000.

[69]"Women on Boards: Global Board Seats Held by Women," Catalyst, May 2011, accessed May 28, 2011, from www.catalyst.org/publication/433/women-on-boards.

[70]M. Bertrand & K. Hallock, "The Gender Gap in Top Corporate Jobs," *Industrial & Labor Relations Review* 55 (2001): 3–21.

[71]J. R. Hollenbeck, D. R. Ilgen, C. Ostroff, & J. B. Vancouver, "Sex Differences in Occupational Choice, Pay, and Worth: A Supply-Side Approach to Understanding the Male-Female Wage Gap," *Personnel Psychology* 40 (1987): 715–744.

[72]S. Shellenbarger, "Does Having Kids Dull Career Opportunities?" WSJ Blogs: The Juggle, *The Wall Street Journal*, April 6, 2011, accessed May 28, 2011, from http://blogs.wsj.com/juggle/2011/04/06/does-having-kids-dull-job-ambition/.

[73]A. Chaker & H. Stout, "Second Chances: After Years Off, Women Struggle to Revive Careers," *The Wall Street Journal*, May 6, 2004, A1.

[74]Korn-Ferry International, 1993.

[75]Department of Industry, Labor and Human Relations, *Report of the Governor's Task Force on the Glass Ceiling Commission* (Madison, WI: State of Wisconsin, 1993).

[76]M. Fix, G. C. Galster, & R. J. Struyk, "An Overview of Auditing for Discrimination," in *Clear and Convincing Evidence: Measurement of Discrimination in America*, M. Fix and R. Struyk, eds. (Washington, DC: Urban Institute Press, 1993), 1–68.

[77]E. O. Wright & J. Baxter, "The Glass Ceiling Hypothesis: A Reply to Critics," *Gender & Society* 14 (2000): 814–821.

[78]S. Hamm, "Why Are Women So Invisible?" *Businessweek*, August 25, 1997, 136.

[79]D. Chenevert & M. Tremblay, "Managerial Career Success in Canadian Organizations: Is Gender a Determinant?" *International Journal of Human Resource Management* 13 (2002): 920–941; F. Neathey, S. Dench, & L. Thomas, "Monitoring Progress toward Pay Equality," Institute for Employment Studies report on behalf of the Equal Opportunities Commission 2003, www.eoc.org.uk [content no longer available online]; and S. Wellington, M. B. Kropf, & P. R. Gerkovich, "What's Holding Women Back?" *Harvard Business Review* 81 (2003): 82–111.

[80]Wellington et al., "What's Holding Women Back?"

[81]B. R. Ragins, B. Townsend, & M. Mattis, "Gender Gap in the Executive Suite: CEOs and Female Executives Report on Breaking the Glass Ceiling," *Academy of Management Executive* 12 (1998): 28–42.

[82]Jessica Guynn, "Wanted: Women as Technology Entrepreneurs," *Los Angeles Times*, August 11, 2010, accessed May 28, 2011, from http://latimesblogs.latimes.com/technology/2010/08/wanted-women-technology-entrepreneurs-1.html; and Claire Cain Miller, "Out of the Loop in Silicon Valley," *The New York Times*, April 17, 2010, accessed May 28, 2011, from www.nytimes.com/2010/04/18/technology/18women.html?_r=1.

[83]N. Lockwood, "The Glass Ceiling: Domestic and International Perspectives," *HR Magazine* (2004 Research Quarterly): 2–10.

[84]T. B. Foley, "Discrimination Lawsuits Are a Small-Business Nightmare: A Guide to Minimizing the Potential Damage," *The Wall Street Journal*, September 28, 1998, 15.

[85]"Charge Statistics FY 1997 through FY 2008," U.S. Equal Employment Opportunity Commission, accessed November 7, 2008, from www.eeoc.gov/stats/charges.html [content no longer available online].

[86]"African American CEOs of Fortune 500 Companies," BlackEntrepreneurProfile.com, May 29, 2011, accessed May 29, 2011, from www.blackentrepreneurprofile.com/fortune-500-ceos/; and R. Fortner, "Cracking the Plexi Glass Ceiling: 2010 Fortune 500 CEOs of Color," USA Rise Up, February 9, 2011, accessed May 29, 2011, from www.usariseup.com/eyes-enterprise/cracking-plexi-glass-ceiling-2010-fortune-500-ceos-color.

[87]D. A. Neal & W. R. Johnson, "The Role of Premarket Factors in Black-White Wage Differences," *Journal of Political Economy* 104, no. 5 (1996): 869–895.

[88]Fix, Galster, & Struyk, "An Overview of Auditing for Discrimination."

[89]M. Bendick, Jr., C. W. Jackson, & V. A. Reinoso, "Measuring Employment Discrimination through Controlled Experiments," in *African-Americans and Post-Industrial Labor Markets*, James B. Stewart, ed. (New Brunswick, NJ: Transaction Publishers, 1997), 77–100.

[90]P. B. Riach & J. Rich, "Measuring Discrimination by Direct Experimental Methods: Seeking Gunsmoke," *Journal of Post Keynesian Economics* 14, no. 2 (Winter 1991–1992): 143–150.

[91]A. P. Brief, R. T. Buttram, R. M. Reizenstein, & S. D. Pugh, "Beyond Good Intentions: The Next Steps toward Racial Equality in the American Workplace," *Academy of Management Executive* 11 (1997): 59–72.

[92]L. E. Wynter, "Business & Race: Federal Agencies, Spurred on by

Nonprofit Groups, Are Increasingly Embracing the Use of Undercover Investigators to Identify Discrimination in the Marketplace," *The Wall Street Journal*, July 1, 1998, B1.

[93]Jennifer Crossley Howard, "Walgreens Sets Global Example in Hiring Disabled," *Standard-Examiner*, November 2, 2010, accessed May 29, 2011, from www.standard.net/topics/business/2010/11/02/walgreens-sets-global-example-hiring-disabled.

[94]"ADA Questions and Answers," U.S. Department of Justice, May 2002, accessed March 24, 2009, from www.ada.gov.

[95]"Frequently Asked Questions," *Disability Statistics: Online Resource for U.S. Disability Statistics*, accessed August 21, 2008, from www.ilr.cornell.edu/edi/disabilitystatistics.

[96]"2007 Disability Status Report: United States," Rehabilitation Research and Training Center on Disability Demographics and Statistics, accessed November 7, 2009, from www.ilr.cornell.edu/edi/disabilitystatistics/statusreports.

[97]F. Bowe, "Adults with Disabilities: A Portrait," *President's Committee on Employment of People with Disabilities* (Washington, DC: GPO, 1992); and D. Braddock & L. Bachelder, *The Glass Ceiling and Persons with Disabilities*, Glass Ceiling Commission, U.S. Department of Labor (Washington, DC: GPO, 1994).

[98]Louis Harris & Associates, Inc., *Public Attitudes toward People with Disabilities* (Washington, DC: National Organization on Disability, 1991); and Louis Harris & Associates, Inc., *The ICD Survey II: Employing Disabled Americans* (New York: Louis Harris & Associates, Inc., 1987).

[99]R. Greenwood & V. A. Johnson, "Employer Perspectives on Workers with Disabilities," *Journal of Rehabilitation* 53 (1987): 37–45.

[100]"Work Accommodations: Low Cost, High Impact" U.S. Department of Labor's Office of Disability Employment Policy, accessed November 7, 2009, from www.jan.wvu.edu/media/LowCostHighImpact.doc.

[101]"Accessibility at IBM: An Integrated Approach" IBM.com. no date,

accessed August 10, 2010, from www-03.ibm.com/able/access_ibm/execbrief.html#recruiting; and "The DiversityInc Top 10 Companies for People with Disabilities," DiversityInc, May 6, 2010, accessed August 15, 2010, from http://diversityinc.com/content/1757/article/7554/.

[102]"Study on the Financing of Assistive Technology Devices and Services for Individuals with Disabilities: A Report to the President and the Congress of the United States," National Council on Disability, accessed August 21, 2008, from www.ncd.gov/publications/1993/Mar41993.

[103]Ibid.

[104]R. B. Cattell, "Personality Pinned Down," *Psychology Today* 7 (1973): 40–46; and C. S. Carver & M. F. Scheier, *Perspectives on Personality* (Boston: Allyn & Bacon, 1992).

[105]J. M. Digman, "Personality Structure: Emergence of the Five-Factor Model," *Annual Review of Psychology* 41 (1990): 417–440; and M. R. Barrick & M. K. Mount, "The Big Five Personality Dimensions and Job Performance: A Meta-Analysis," *Personnel Psychology* 44 (1991): 1–26.

[106]J. Lublin, "Introverted Execs Find Ways to Shine," *The Wall Street Journal*, April 14, 2011, accessed May 29, 2011, from http://online.wsj.com/article/SB10001424052748703983104576263053775879800.html.

[107]Andy Newman & Ray Rivera, "Fed-Up Flight Attendant Makes Sliding Exit," *The New York Times*, August 9, 2010, accessed May 28, 2011, from www.nytimes.com/2010/08/10/nyregion/10attendant.html.

[108]R. Cook, "The Changing 'Face' of Your Business: Finding Good People . . . and Keeping Them Motivated," *PRO Magazine* (March 2005): 43.

[109]O. Behling, "Employee Selection: Will Intelligence and Conscientiousness Do the Job?" *Academy of Management Executive* 12 (1998): 77–86.

[110]R. S. Dalal, "A Meta-Analysis of the Relationship between Organizational Citizenship Behavior and Counterproductive Work Behavior," *Journal of Applied Psychology*, 90 (2005): 1241–1255.

[111]Barrick & Mount, "The Big Five Personality Dimensions and Job

Performance"; M. K. Mount & M. R. Barrick, "The Big Five Personality Dimensions: Implications for Research and Practice in Human Resource Management," *Research in Personnel & Human Resources Management* 13 (1995): 153–200; M. K. Mount & M. R. Barrick, "Five Reasons Why the 'Big Five' Article Has Been Frequently Cited," *Personnel Psychology* 51 (1998): 849–857; and D. S. Ones, M. K. Mount, M. R. Barrick, & J. E. Hunter, "Personality and Job Performance: A Critique of the Tett, Jackson, and Rothstein (1991) Meta-Analysis," *Personnel Psychology* 47 (1994): 147–156.

[112]Mount & Barrick, "Five Reasons Why the 'Big Five' Article Has Been Frequently Cited."

[113]J. A. Lopez, "Talking Desks: Personality Types Revealed in State Workstations," *Arizona Republic*, January 7, 1996, D1.

[114]T. W. Adorno, E. Frenkel-Brunswik, D. J. Levinson, & R. N. Stanford, *The Authoritarian Personality* (New York: Harper & Row, 1950).

[115]Barrick & Mount, "The Big Five Personality Dimensions and Job Performance."

[116]C. Hymowitz, "In the Lead: Two Football Coaches Have a Lot to Teach Screaming Managers," *The Wall Street Journal*, January 29, 2007, B1.

[117]R. G. Vleeming, "Machiavellianism: A Preliminary Review," *Psychological Reports* 53 (1979): 295–310.

[118]F. L. Geis & T. H. Moon, "Machiavellianism and Deception," *Journal of Personality & Social Psychology* 41 (1981): 766–775.

[119]R. Christie & F. L. Geis, *Studies in Machiavellianism* (New York: Academic Press, 1970), 312.

[120]Mount & Barrick, "Five Reasons Why the 'Big Five' Article Has Been Frequently Cited."

[121]J. Zaslow, "Why Jerks Get Ahead: Being Obnoxious Often Pays Off in the Workplace," *The Wall Street Journal*, March 29, 2004, R6.

[122]B. Kallestad, "Florida State Research Shows Bad Managers' Effect on Workers," Associated Press State & Local Wire, January 1, 2007, accessed May 20, 2011, from www.ap.org.

[123]K. A. Matthews, "Psychological Perspectives on the Type A Behavior Pattern," *Psychological Bulletin* 91 (1982): 293–323.

[124]M. Friedman & R. H. Rosenman, *Type A Behavior and Your Heart* (New York: Fawcett Crest, 1974).

[125]M. Lee & R. Kanungo, *Management of Work and Personal Life* (New York: Praeger, 1984).

[126]J. Schaubroeck, D. C. Ganster, & B. E. Kemmerer, "Job Complexity, 'Type A' Behavior, and Cardiovascular Disorders," *Academy of Management Journal* 37 (1994): 37.

[127]"Cardiovascular Research: Type A Personality Is Not Linked to Heart Disease," *Science Letter*, September 19, 2006, 386.

[128]R. Winslow, "Choose Your Neurosis: Some Type-A Traits Are Riskier Than Others," *The Wall Street Journal*, October 22, 2003, D1.

[129]J. E. Bishop, "Health: Hostility, Distrust May Put Type A's at Coronary Risk," *The Wall Street Journal Interactive*, January 17, 1989, accessed May 20, 2011, from www.wsj.com.

[130]P. E. Spector, "Behavior in Organizations as a Function of Employee's Locus of Control," *Psychological Bulletin* 91 (1982): 482–497.

[131]J. B. Rotter, "Generalized Expectancies for Internal versus External Control of Reinforcement," *Psychological Monographs* 80 (1966): Whole No. 609; and J. B. Rotter, "Some Problems and Misconceptions Related to the Construct of Internal versus External Control of Reinforcement," *Journal of Consulting & Clinical Psychology* 43 (1975): 56–67.

[132]R. S. Lazarus, *Emotion and Adaptation* (New York: Oxford University Press, 1991).

[133]"The Secrets of Happiness," *Psychology Today* 25 (July 1992): 38.

[134]B. M. Staw, N. E. Bell, & J. A. Clausen, "The Dispositional Approach to Job Attitudes: A Lifetime Longitudinal Test," *Administrative Science Quarterly* 31 (1986): 56–77.

[135]"Accenture Survey: Poor Customer Service Drives Nearly Half of U.S. Consumers to Take Their Business Elsewhere," *Wireless News*, August 8, 2006, accessed May 20, 2011, from www.m2.com.

[136]A. M. Isen & R. A. Baron, "Positive Affect and Organizational Behavior," in *Research in Organizational Behavior*, 12th ed., B. M. Staw and L. L. Cummings, eds. (Greenwich, CT: JAI Press, 1990); J. M. George & A. P. Brief, "Feeling Good–Doing Good: A Conceptual Analysis of the Mood at Work—Organizational Spontaneity Relationships," *Psychological Bulletin* 112 (1992): 310–329; R. D. Iverson & P. J. Erwin, "Predicting Occupational Injury: The Role of Affectivity," *Journal of Occupational & Organizational Psychology* 70 (1997): 113–128; and D. P. Skarlicki, R. Folger, & P. Tesluk, "Personality as a Moderator in the Relationship between Fairness and Retaliation," *Academy of Management Journal* 42 (1999): 100–108.

[137]Dalal, "A Meta-Analysis."

[138]P. Totterdell, S. Kellett, K. Teuchmann, & R. B. Briner, "Evidence of Mood Linkage in Work Groups," *Journal of Personality & Social Psychology* 74 (1998): 1503–1515.

[139]M. E. P. Seligman & S. Schulman, "Explanatory Style as a Predictor of Productivity and Quitting among Life Insurance Sales Agents," *Journal of Personality & Social Psychology* 50 (1986): 832–838.

[140]L. Sonja, K. Laura, & E. Diener, "The Benefits of Frequent Positive Affect: Does Happiness Lead to Success?" *Psychological Bulletin* (November 2005): 803–855.

[141]David Knowles, "Store Fires Woman for Wearing Muslim Head Scarf," *AOL News*, February 26, 2010, accessed May 28, 2011, from www.aolnews.com/2010/02/26/store-fires-woman-for-wearing-muslim-head-scarf/.

[142]Staff, "The Diverse Work Force," *Inc.*, January 1993, 33.

[143]D. A. Thomas & R. J. Ely, "Making Differences Matter: A New Paradigm for Managing Diversity," *Harvard Business Review* 74 (September–October 1996): 79–90.

[144]Esen, "2005 Workplace Diversity Practices: Survey Report."

[145]D. A. Thomas & S. Wetlaufer, "A Question of Color: A Debate on Race in the U.S. Workplace," *Harvard Business Review* 75 (September–October 1997): 118–132.

[146]E. Esen, "2007 State of Workplace Diversity Management. A Survey Report by the Society for Human Resource Management," 2008.

[147]A. Fisher, "How You Can Do Better on Diversity," *Fortune*, November 15, 2004, 60.

[148]Javier Espinoza, "Working to Prove Benefits of More Women at the Top," *The Wall Street Journal*, February 27, 2011, accessed March 15, 2011, from http://online.wsj.com/article/SB10001424052748704150604576166483012821352.html.

[149]J. R. Norton & R. E. Fox, *The Change Equation: Capitalizing on Diversity for Effective Organizational Change* (Washington, DC: American Psychological Association, 1997).

[150]Ibid.

[151]Thomas & Ely, "Making Differences Matter."

[152]R. R. Thomas, Jr., *Beyond Race and Gender: Unleashing the Power of Your Total Workforce by Managing Diversity* (New York: AMACOM, 1991).

[153]Ibid.

[154]T. Cox, Jr., "The Multicultural Organization," *Academy of Management Executive* 5 (1991): 34–47.

[155]S. Lubove, "Damned If You Do, Damned If You Don't: Preference Programs Are on the Defensive in the Public Sector, but Plaintiffs' Attorneys and Bureaucrats Keep Diversity Inc. Thriving in Corporate America," *Forbes*, December 15, 1997, 122.

[156]L. S. Gottfredson, "Dilemmas in Developing Diversity Programs," in *Diversity in the Workplace*, S. E. Jackson & Associates, eds. (New York: Guilford Press, 1992).

[157]R. B. Lieber & L. Urresta, "Pacific Enterprises Keeping Talent: After Being Encouraged to Explore Jobs Elsewhere, Most Employees Stay Put," *Fortune*, August 3, 1998, 96.

[158]Rodriguez, "Diversity Finds Its Place."

[159]"Diversity at Work: Public Relations Makes a Difference for Global

Giants," Public Relations Tactics by Public Relations Society of America, October 1, 2010, accessed May 29, 2011, from www.prsa.org/Intelligence/Tactics/Articles/view/8828/1021/Diversity_at_work_Public_relations_makes_a_differe.

[160]A. Greenwald, B. Nosek, & M. Banaji, "Understanding and Using the Implicit Association Test: I. An Improved Scoring Algorithm," *Journal of Personality & Social Psychology* (August 2003): 197–206; and S. Vedantam, "See No Bias; Many Americans Believe They Are Not Prejudiced," *The Washington Post*, January 23, 2005, W12.

[161]Carnevale & Stone, *The American Mosaic.*

[162]D. Maxey, "CEO Compensation Survey (A Special Report); Compensation Carrot: Can Pay Policies Help Create a More Diverse Workplace? The Jury is Still Out," *The Wall Street Journal*, April 9, 2007, R4.

[163]R. Joplin & C. S. Daus, "Challenges of Leading a Diverse Workforce," *Academy of Management Executive* 11 (1997): 32–47.

[164]Fisher, "Ask Annie: Should People Choose Their Own Mentors?" *Fortune*, November 29, 2004, 72.

[165]N. Byrnes & R. O. Crocket, "An Historic Succession at Xerox", *Business Week*, June 8, 2009, 18–22.

[166]Rice, "How to Make Diversity Pay."

[167]Mark Clothier, "Why Harley is Showing Its Feminine Side," *Bloomberg Businessweek*, September 30, 2010, accessed November 21, 2010, from www.businessweek.com/magazine/content/10_41/b4198025711235.htm.

[168]M. Crowe, "UPS Managers Trained in the Real World to Deliver Results," *The Business Journal—San Jose*, September 21, 1998, 26; and Rice, "How to Make Diversity Pay."

reel to real

© GreenLight

BIZ FLIX

Because I Said So

In the 2007 romantic comedy *Because I Said So*, Daphne Wilder (Diane Keaton) is a meddling, overprotective, and divorced mother of three grown girls. Maggie and Mae (Lauren Graham and Piper Perabo) have already married and settled down. That leaves Milly (Mandy Moore) as the focus of Daphne's undivided attention. On the eve of her 60th birthday, Daphne decides to do everything she can to prevent Milly from making the same mistakes she did in life by finding her a nice, stable man to marry. She secretly places an ad in the online personals for her daughter, screens the applicants, and submits those she approves of to Milly. In this scene, Daphne tries to convince Milly to go out with Jason (Tom Everett Scott), who she believes would be good for her.

What to Watch for and Ask Yourself

1. Have you ever had someone meddle in your life the way Daphne does? How did it make you feel? Do you think this kind of behavior is justified if the person's intentions are good?

2. Which Big Five personality traits best describe Daphne? Give examples of behavior from the film scene to support your observations.

3. Which Big Five personality traits best describe Milly? Give examples of behavior from the film scene to support your observations.

MANAGEMENT WORKPLACE

Mitchell Gold + Bob Williams: Managing Diversity

© Cengage Learning

When Mitchell Gold and Bob Williams started their furniture company in 1989, they had a vision for how they wanted to run things. They would guarantee comfort, minimize costs, enact rigorous controls, and produce the styles they liked for their own homes. They had one other important goal: to foster a diverse workplace where employees could labor unburdened by stress, worry, or discrimination. The company has clear nondiscrimination policies, extensive diversity training, and insures that all employees receive the same benefits, regardless of race, gender, or religion. As employees have come to recognize, Mitchell Gold + Bob Williams is a diversity trendsetter. The company's founders envisioned a workplace where individuals felt safe and respected, and now, some 20 years later, the business is reaping rewards of diversity. With more than $100 million in annual sales, it's clear that people-focused business strategies are paying off.

Discussion Questions

1. What are advantages and disadvantages of diversity at Mitchell Gold + Bob Williams?

2. How does MG + BW's approach to diversity reflect the learning and effectiveness paradigm?

3. How might a commitment to diversity at MG + BW help managers with globalization?

Leading

PART 4

Chapter 13
Motivation

This chapter covers the basics of motivation—effort, needs, and intrinsic and extrinsic rewards. As we progress through the chapter, we build on that basic model of motivation by adding concepts of equity, expectancy, reinforcement, and goal-setting theories. There's also a summary of practical, theory-based actions that managers can take to motivate their workers.

SAS

Chapter 14
Leadership

This chapter discusses what leadership is, what characteristics are common of leaders, and what leaders do that makes them different from people who aren't leaders. We examine major contingency theories of leadership and review strategic leadership issues, such as charismatic and transformational leadership.

Apple

Chapter 15
Communication

This chapter examines perception in communication, the communication process, and the kinds of organizational communication. You'll also learn about effective one-on-one communication as well as techniques for organization wide communication.

Google

CHAPTER 13

Motivation

Learning Outcomes

1. Explain the basics of motivation.
2. Use equity theory to explain how employees' perceptions of fairness affect motivation.
3. Use expectancy theory to describe how workers' expectations about rewards, effort, and the link between rewards and performance influence motivation.
4. Explain how reinforcement theory works and how it can be used to motivate.
5. Describe the components of goal-setting theory and how managers can use them to motivate workers.
6. Discuss how the entire motivation model can be used to motivate workers.

what would **you do?**

SAS World Headquarters, Cary, North Carolina[1]

SAS (pronounced "sass"), which is short for Statistical Analysis System, began when it set out to create statistical software to help agricultural researchers who were studying the effects of soil, seeds, and the weather on crop yields. In 1970, researchers had to write new computer programs every time they analyzed data. SAS standardized that process and made it faster. Because the statistics faculty who wrote SAS needed to generate funds to cover the expiring grant money that paid their salaries, they started leasing SAS to universities and pharmaceutical companies. By 1976, they had 100 customers. However, it wasn't until the first SAS Users Conference later that year, when 300 people showed up, that they realized their business opportunity. As you tell people now, that was pretty much the "'aha' moment."

From website traffic, to credit cards replacing cash, to genome sequencing, to sentiment analysis (analyzing every tweet, blog, and discussion group comment about your company and its products), the amount of digital data that a company has to go through is increasing at exponential rates. As a result, 79 percent of Fortune 500 companies use SAS. Shell Oil uses it to analyze data to predict how long the pumps will run on its North Sea oil-drilling platforms. Kohl's department store maximizes profits by using SAS to analyze which products to mark down for sale. Credit card companies use SAS to reduce fraud by identifying unusual credit card purchases in real time. Finally, telecomm companies offer great deals to customers who, via SAS, they've determined are more likely to switch to competitors.

Although SAS has been profitable every year since inception, there are threats to its highly successful business model. First, says Gareth Doherty, an industry analyst, "Most organizations aren't in a position to be able to leverage some of the sophisticated applications that SAS offers because the No. 1 constraint when you're working with a tool this sophisticated is the user. If you don't have a rocket scientist sitting behind the desk, it doesn't matter what you have running on the desktop." Second, SAS products are expensive, starting at $1 million for industry specific products (i.e., banking or retail), followed by subscription renewals that are 20 percent to 30 percent of the purchase price. Although SAS spends 22 percent of its revenue on research and development each year, larger firms are buying business intelligence companies to compete directly with SAS. SAP paid $6.8 billion for Business Objects, and Oracle paid $3.3 billion for Hyperion. The largest threat may come, however, from IBM, which paid $4.9 billion for Cognos and $1.2 billion for SPSS. IBM combined those firms into its business analytics group, which will employ 200

"what's new" companies

37signals.com
S.C. Johnson
Amgen
Miller Brewing Company
Atlassian
Aflac
Family Dollar Stores
CrowdFlower
Fog Creek Software
Electric Boat
Single Source Systems

study tips

One way to make sure you understand the concepts in the chapter is to re-create the chapter outline from scratch.

scientists and 4,000 consultants and analysts. Industry analyst Bill Hostmann says, "It will be a dogfight. SAS has never faced a competitor like IBM. And I do think IBM sees SAS as a big, fatted cow."

With competition intensifying, SAS is shortening its product development cycle from 24 to 36 months to 12 to 18 months. Change like that can't be achieved without attracting and retaining a highly motivated workforce. That's increasingly difficult with tech job openings up 62 percent and a 22 percent average turnover rate in the software industry. That's why Google gave all of its employees a 10 percent raise and a $1,000 bonus. So, the first step in maintaining your competitiveness is figuring out what motivates people to join a SAS. Second, getting people to join SAS is one thing, but how do you get them to work hard and maximize their efforts? Should you be egalitarian and pay everyone the same, or should you closely link pay and performance? Finally, how do you get your most talented managers and software engineers to stay? Does SAS need to "go public" like its competitors and issue stock and stock options to its employees? Or are there other ways for SAS to reward people and remain competitive in the talent market?

If you were in charge at SAS, what would you do?

What makes people happiest and most productive at work? Is it money, benefits, opportunities for growth, interesting work, or something else altogether? And if people desire different things, how can a company keep everyone motivated? It takes insight and hard work to motivate workers to join the company, perform well, and then stay with the company. Indeed, when asked to name their biggest management challenge, nearly one-third of executives polled by Creative Group, a specialized staffing service in Menlo Park, California, cited "motivating employees."[2]

This chapter begins by reviewing the basics of motivation—effort, needs, and intrinsic and extrinsic rewards. We will start with a basic model of motivation and add to it as we progress through each section in the chapter. Next, we will explore how employees' equity perceptions and reward expectations affect their motivation. If you're familiar with the phrase "perception is reality," you're off to a good start in understanding the importance of perceptions and expectations in motivation. The third part of the chapter reviews the role that rewards and goals play in motivating employees. You'll see that finding the right combination of goals and rewards is much harder in practice than it looks. The chapter finishes with a summary of practical, theory-based actions that managers can take to motivate their workers.

What Is Motivation?

motivation the set of forces that initiates, directs, and makes people persist in their efforts to accomplish a goal.

Motivation is the set of forces that initiates, directs, and makes people persist in their efforts to accomplish a goal.[3] *Initiation of effort* is concerned with the choices that people make about how much effort to put forth in their jobs. ("Do I really knock myself out for these performance appraisals or just do a decent job?") *Direction of effort* is concerned with the choices that people make in deciding where to put forth effort

After reading the next section, you should be able to

1. *Explain the basics of motivation.*

in their jobs. ("I should be spending time with my high-dollar accounts instead of learning this new computer system!") *Persistence of effort* is concerned with the choices that people make about how long they will put forth effort in their jobs before reducing or eliminating those efforts. ("I'm only halfway through the project, and I'm exhausted. Do I plow through to the end, or just call it quits?") As Exhibit 13.1 shows, initiation, direction, and persistence are at the heart of motivation.

Exhibit 13.1 The Components of Motivation

© Cengage Learning 2013

1 Basics of Motivation

Jenny Miller manages 170 engineers who design and build computer systems for aircraft carrier flight decks. Despite long hours each week, they were at risk of not meeting a December 1 deadline for their project. So, with the overtime budget already spent, she asked for volunteers to work Friday, Saturday, or Sunday of Thanksgiving weekend, without pay or compensatory time off. Still, 20 engineers showed up, the deadline was met, and Miller thanked those who volunteered with $100 gift cards.[4]

At **37signals.com**, a Chicago software company, founder Jason Fried has avoided using promotions to reward his 30 employees. Says Fried, "We revere 'horizontal' ambition—in which employees who love what they do are encouraged to dig deeper, expand their knowledge, and become better at it. We always try to hire people who yearn to be master craftspeople, that is, designers who want to be great designers, not managers of designers; developers who want to master the art of programming, not management."[5]

< *"what's new" companies*

Would you be motivated to volunteer to work over a holiday weekend if it helped your company meet a key deadline? Which would motivate you more? The chance to become a master craftsperson or the opportunity for promotion and management responsibilities? Answering questions like these is at the heart of figuring out how best to motivate people at work.

Let's learn more about motivation by building a basic model of motivation out of **1.1 effort and performance, 1.2 need satisfaction, and 1.3 extrinsic and intrinsic rewards** and then discussing **1.4 how to motivate people with this basic model of motivation.**

1.1 Effort and Performance

When most people think of work motivation, they think that working hard (effort) should lead to a good job (performance). Exhibit 13.2 shows a basic model of work motivation and performance, displaying this process. The first thing to notice about Exhibit 13.2 is that this is a basic model of work motivation *and* performance. In practice, it's almost impossible to talk about one without mentioning the other. Not surprisingly, managers often assume motivation to be the only determinant of performance, saying things such as "Your performance was really terrible last quarter. What's the matter? Aren't you as motivated as you used to be?" In fact, motivation is just one of three

Exhibit 13.2
A Basic Model of Work Motivation and Performance

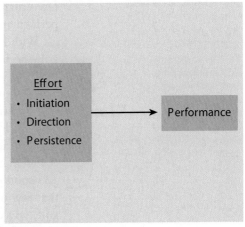

© Cengage Learning 2013

primary determinants of job performance. In industrial psychology, job performance is frequently represented by this equation:

$$\text{Job Performance} = \text{Motivation} \times \text{Ability} \times \text{Situational Constraints}$$

In this formula, *job performance* is how well someone performs the requirements of the job. *Motivation*, as defined previously, is effort, the degree to which someone works hard to do the job well. *Ability* is the degree to which workers possess the knowledge, skills, and talent needed to do a job well. And *situational constraints* are factors beyond the control of individual employees, such as tools, policies, and resources that have an effect on job performance. Because job performance is a multiplicative function of motivation times ability times situational constraints, job performance will suffer if any one of these components is weak.

To see how these components interact to determine performance, let's examine the unique case of Dan McLaughlin. On his 30th birthday, June 27, 2009, Dan quit his day job as a commercial photographer to become a professional golfer. The only problem was Dan had never played a round of golf. Yes, he'd been to a driving range several times, but that was it. Was Dan a gifted athlete? He had been a competitive tennis player, so he was athletic, but he didn't know a 9-iron from a sand wedge. In other words, when it came to golf, Dan had no ability, or, more specifically, no golf-specific knowledge, skills, or talent. He began fixing that, however, by convincing Christopher Smith, a top 100 golf instructor, to agree to coach him.[6]

As one of his first lessons, Coach Smith had Dan read the research of K. Anders Ericsson, a psychology professor at Florida State University. His research, popularized by author Malcolm Gladwell, indicates that sustained, concentrated effort, not natural talent, is what distinguishes the best performers in the world from the rest. According to Ericcson, if a person can dedicate 10,000 hours to something, he or she will become expert at it. Ericsson states, "There are no shortcuts. It will take you at least a decade to achieve expertise, and you will need to invest that time wisely, by engaging in 'deliberate' practice—practice that focuses on tasks beyond your current level of competence and comfort. You will need a well-informed coach not only to guide you through deliberate practice but also to help you learn how to coach yourself."[7]

For most people, finding 10,000 hours to master anything, the violin, a sport, or dance, is difficult. That's why elite performers typically start learning and practicing as youths. For an adult, finding 10,000 hours is nearly impossible. But Dan had quit his job, so he had time. Moreover, he had $100,000 in the bank (he's notoriously cheap and spends little), a live-in girlfriend (who *has* a job), and sponsors (who provided equipment and limited financial support). With all of that in place, Dan faced few situational constraints, that is, factors outside of his control that might limit his performance.

With few situational constraints, and a coach and sponsors to help him acquire golf-specific ability, the only thing left to determine was whether Dan McLaughlin was motivated. Well, he ran cross-country for a year in high school, but quit. In college, he studied physics and math for a year, but quit. After college, he took a job as a photojournalist for a newspaper for one year, and, yes, quit. So to convince everyone else—and himself—that he was serious, Dan committed to "The Dan Plan," which meant practicing golf for six hours a day, six days a week for six years.[8]

What are his odds of succeeding? With 27 million people who play golf and only 125 spots each year on the PGA tour, the odds look terrible. But when you consider that few of those 27 million will, like Dan, have put 10,000 hours into mastering golf, you can see why he just might have a chance. To see how he's performing, check TheDanPlan.com. And, remember, performance is a multiplicative function

Exhibit 13.3 Adding Need Satisfaction to the Model

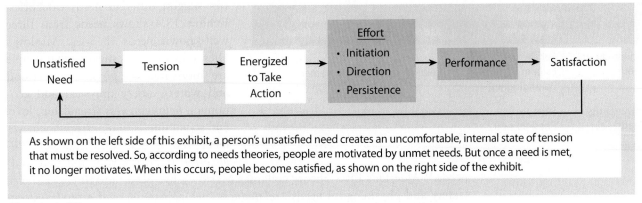

As shown on the left side of this exhibit, a person's unsatisfied need creates an uncomfortable, internal state of tension that must be resolved. So, according to needs theories, people are motivated by unmet needs. But once a need is met, it no longer motivates. When this occurs, people become satisfied, as shown on the right side of the exhibit.

© Cengage Learning 2013

of motivation times ability times situational constraints. Job performance declines when any one of those components is weak.

1.2 Need Satisfaction

In Exhibit 13.2, we started with a very basic model of motivation in which effort leads to job performance. But managers want to know, "What leads to effort?" and they will try almost anything they can to find the answer. Employees at **S.C. Johnson,** a manufacturer of cleaning products, can use a concierge service to mail packages, send flowers, pick up groceries, and even take their car in for an oil change. **Amgen,** a biotech company, gives its employees three weeks of paid vacation per year, as well as 17 paid holidays, nearly double other businesses. At Netflix, meanwhile, employees are given unlimited vacation days, and no one keeps track of how many days workers are in or out of the office. When employees of the **Miller Brewing Company** need a place to unwind after work, they can head to Fred's Pub, a bar, located in the company's facilities, that serves 20 different kinds of beer—for free.[9] As you can see, employers will do almost anything to motivate employees to put extra effort into their jobs.

Needs are the physical or psychological requirements that must be met to ensure survival and well-being.[10] As shown on the left side of Exhibit 13.3, a person's unmet need creates an uncomfortable, internal state of tension that must be resolved. For example, if you normally skip breakfast but then have to work through lunch, chances are you'll be so hungry by late afternoon that the only thing you'll be motivated to do is find something to eat. So, according to needs theories, people are motivated by unmet needs. But a need no longer motivates once it is met. When this occurs, people become satisfied, as shown on the right side of Exhibit 13.3.

Note: Throughout the chapter, as we build on this basic model, the parts of the model that we've already discussed will appear shaded in color. For example, because we've already discussed the effort → performance part of the model, those components are shown with a colored background. When we add new parts to the model, they will have a white background. Because we're adding need satisfaction to the model at this step, the need–satisfaction components of unsatisfied need, tension, energized to take action, and satisfaction are shown with a white background. This shading convention should make it easier to understand the work motivation model as we add to it in each section of the chapter.

Because people are motivated by unmet needs, managers must learn what those unmet needs are and address them. This is not always a straightforward task,

< *"what's new"*
companies

< *"what's new"*
companies

< *"what's new"*
companies

needs the physical or psychological requirements that must be met to ensure survival and well-being.

Exhibit 13.4 Needs Classification of Different Theories

	Maslow's Hierarchy	Alderfer's Erg	Mcclelland's Learned Needs
Higher-Order Needs	Self-Actualization Esteem Belongingness	Growth Relatedness	Power Achievement Affiliation
Lower-Order Needs	Safety Physiological	Existence	

© Cengage Learning 2013

however, because different needs theories suggest different needs categories. Exhibit 13.4 shows needs from three well-known needs theories. Maslow's Hierarchy of Needs suggests that people are motivated by *physiological* (food and water), *safety* (physical and economic), *belongingness* (friendship, love, and social interaction), *esteem* (achievement and recognition), and *self-actualization* (realizing your full potential) needs.[11] Alderfer's ERG Theory collapses Maslow's five needs into three: *existence* (safety and physiological needs), *relatedness* (belongingness), and *growth* (esteem and self-actualization).[12] McClelland's Learned Needs Theory suggests that people are motivated by the need for *affiliation* (to be liked and accepted), the need for *achievement* (to accomplish challenging goals), or the need for *power* (to influence others).[13]

Things become even more complicated when we consider the different predictions made by these theories. According to Maslow, needs are arranged in a hierarchy from low (physiological) to high (self-actualization). Within this hierarchy, people are motivated by their lowest unsatisfied need. As each need is met, they work their way up the hierarchy from physiological to self-actualization needs. By contrast, Alderfer says that people can be motivated by more than one need at a time. Furthermore, he suggests that people are just as likely to move down the needs hierarchy as up, particularly when they are unable to achieve satisfaction at the next higher need level. McClelland argues that the degree to which particular needs motivate varies tremendously from person to person, with some people being motivated primarily by achievement and others by power or affiliation. Moreover, McClelland says that needs are learned, not innate. For instance, studies show that children whose parents own a small business or hold a managerial position are much more likely to have a high need for achievement.[14]

So, with three different sets of needs and three very different ideas about how needs motivate, how do we provide a practical answer to managers who just want to know "What leads to effort?" Fortunately, the research evidence simplifies things a bit. To start, studies indicate that there are two basic kinds of needs categories.[15] As shown in Exhibit 13.4, *lower-order needs* are concerned with safety and with physiological and existence requirements, whereas *higher-order needs* are concerned with relationships (belongingness, relatedness, and affiliation); challenges and accomplishments (esteem, self-actualization, growth, and achievement); and influence (power). Studies generally show that higher-order needs will not motivate people as long as lower-order needs remain unsatisfied.[16]

For example, imagine that you graduated from college six months ago and are still looking for your first job. With money running short (you're probably living on your credit cards) and the possibility of having to move back in with your parents looming (if this doesn't motivate you, what will?), your basic needs for food, shelter, and security drive your thoughts, behavior, and choices at this point. But once you land that job, find a great place (of your own!) to live, and put some money in the bank, these basic needs should decrease in importance as you begin to think about making new friends and taking on challenging work assignments. In fact, once lower-order needs are satisfied, it's difficult for managers to predict which higher-order needs will motivate behavior.[17] Some people will be motivated by affiliation, whereas others will be motivated by growth or esteem. Also, the relative importance of the various needs may change over time, but not necessarily in any predictable

Exhibit 13.5 Adding Rewards to the Model

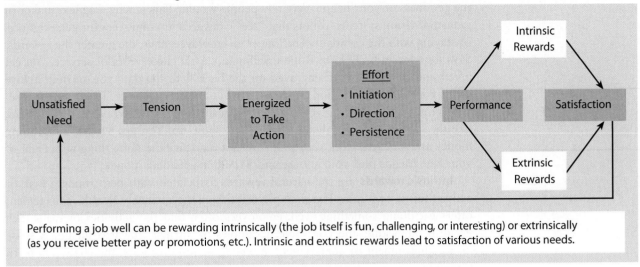

Performing a job well can be rewarding intrinsically (the job itself is fun, challenging, or interesting) or extrinsically (as you receive better pay or promotions, etc.). Intrinsic and extrinsic rewards lead to satisfaction of various needs.

© Cengage Learning 2013

pattern. So, what leads to effort? In part, needs do. After we discuss rewards in Subsection 1.3, in Subsection 1.4 we discuss how managers can use what we know from need–satisfaction theories to motivate workers.

1.3 Extrinsic and Intrinsic Rewards

No discussion of motivation would be complete without considering rewards. Let's add two kinds of rewards, extrinsic and intrinsic, to the model in Exhibit 13.5.[18]

Extrinsic rewards are tangible and visible to others and are given to employees contingent on the performance of specific tasks or behaviors.[19] External agents (managers, for example) determine and control the distribution, frequency, and amount of extrinsic rewards, such as pay, company stock, benefits, and promotions. For example, 80 percent of 1,000 large and medium-sized U.S. companies surveyed by Hewitt Associates, a consulting company based in Lincolnshire, Illinois, offer incentives or bonuses to reward employees.[20] The payout from Intel's employee incentive plan is determined by how well it meets financial targets. After an extraor-

extrinsic reward a reward that is tangible, visible to others, and given to employees contingent on the performance of specific tasks or behaviors.

dinarily strong quarter, when sales rose 28 percent and profit totaled $2.2 billion, Intel gave each employee $1,000 as a "Thank You Bonus." And with Intel's financial performance continuing to grow, employees received two more rounds of bonuses that, on average, gave employees an extra 23 days of pay, the largest bonuses in nearly a decade.[21]

Why do companies need extrinsic rewards? To get people to do things they wouldn't otherwise do. Companies use extrinsic rewards to motivate people to perform four basic behaviors: join the organization, regularly attend their jobs, perform their jobs well, and stay with the organization.[22] Think about it. Would you

© iStockphoto.com/Cristian Baitg

show up at work every day to do the best possible job that you could just out of the goodness of your heart? Very few people would. This is why Cognex, maker of industrial vision systems (robots that "see"), rewards its employees for perseverance, or staying with the company. The longer an employee stays, the greater the rewards. Says founder and CEO Dr. Robert Shillman, "After three years of service, you get a very nice-looking watch engraved on the back with the date you started. At five years, you get a gold pin and extra weekend vacation someplace. The 15-year perseverance award is a trip for you and your spouse to one of the wonders of the world, like the Great Wall of China. All you do is show up. You get $1,000 in spending money and an extra week vacation. After 20 years, it's the same thing with eight of your best friends plus your spouse and $1,500 in spending money."[23]

Intrinsic rewards are the natural rewards associated with performing a task or activity for its own sake. For example, aside from the external rewards management offers for doing something well, employees often find the activities or tasks they perform interesting and enjoyable. Examples of intrinsic rewards include a sense of accomplishment or achievement, a feeling of responsibility, the chance to learn something new or interact with others, or simply the fun that comes from performing an interesting, challenging, and engaging task. **Atlassian**, an Australian software company that develops collaboration tools for teams, uses intrinsic rewards during its quarterly "FedEx Days." Atlassian's Jesse Gibbs says that, "During FedEx days, Atlassian developers have 24 hours to build and deliver a working software prototype. They've produced a ton of cool features that eventually make it into shipping products (as well as producing a lot of empty beer bottles and pizza cartons). At the end, everyone presents their software in front of the company, and Atlassians vote for their favorite FedEx 'delivery.'"[24] The program produced so many valuable innovations that Atlassian expanded the policy, allowing employees to use 20 percent of the workweek on projects of their choice. A company spokesperson says, "Our hope is that 20% time gives engineers back dedicated slack time—of their own direction—to spend on product innovation, features, plug-ins, fixes or additions that *they* think are the most important."[25]

Which types of rewards are most important to workers in general? A number of surveys suggest that both extrinsic and intrinsic rewards are important. One survey found that the most important rewards were good benefits and health insurance, job security, a week or more of vacation (all extrinsic rewards), interesting work, the opportunity to learn new skills, and independent work situations (all intrinsic rewards). And employee preferences for intrinsic and extrinsic rewards appear to be relatively stable. Studies conducted over the last three decades have consistently found that employees are twice as likely to indicate that important and meaningful work matters more to them than what they are paid.[26] Indeed, when asked, "If you were to get enough money to live as comfortably as you would like for the rest of your life, would you continue to work or would you stop working?" Sixty-nine percent of American workers said they would keep working. Clearly, intrinsic rewards matter.[27]

1.4 Motivating with the Basics

So, given the basic model of work motivation in Exhibit 13.5, what practical steps can managers take to motivate employees to increase their effort?

As shown in Exhibit 13.6, *start by asking people what their needs are.* Dan Amos, the CEO of **Aflac**, which sells supplemental insurance, wanted to find out what could be done to prevent talented people from leaving the company for other jobs. So two decades ago, when he became CEO he asked—and that process of asking created

Exhibit 13.6   Motivating to Increase Effort

- Start by asking people what their needs are.

- Satisfy lower-order needs first.

- Expect people's needs to change.

- As needs change and lower-order needs are satisfied, create opportunities for employees to satisfy higher-order needs.

© Cengage Learning 2013

Aflac's annual employee company-wide survey. What he found was that instead of just more money, Aflac's employees, nearly 70 percent of whom are women, wanted more recognition for their work and on-site daycare. The survey also revealed that many women in the company struggled with balancing work and home responsibilities, so Amos set up a flexible scheduling program. By asking employees what they needed, Aflac has been able to keep its employee turnover rate close to zero. As Amos says, if you listen, "The survey never lies."[28] So, if you want to meet employees' needs, just ask.

Next, *satisfy lower-order needs first.* Because higher-order needs will not motivate people as long as lower-order needs remain unsatisfied, companies should satisfy lower-order needs first. In practice, this means providing the equipment, training, and knowledge to create a safe workplace free of physical risks, paying employees well enough to provide financial security, and offering a benefits package that will protect employees and their families through good medical coverage and health and disability insurance. Indeed, a survey based on a representative sample of Americans found that when people choose jobs or organizations, three of the four most important factors—starting pay/salary (62%), employee benefits (57%), and job security (47%)—are lower-order needs.[29] Consistent with the idea of satisfying lower-order needs first, a survey of 12,000 employees found that inadequate compensation is the No. 1 reason employees leave organizations.[30]

Third, managers should *expect people's needs to change.* As some needs are satisfied or situations change, what motivated people before may not motivate them now. Likewise, what motivates people to accept a job may not necessarily motivate them once they have the job. For instance, David Stum, president of the Loyalty Institute, says, "The [attractive] power of pay and benefits is only [strong] during the recruitment stage. After employees take the job, pay and benefits become entitlements to them. They think: 'Now that I work here, you owe me that.'"[31]

Managers should also expect needs to change as people mature.[32] For older employees, benefits are as important as pay, which is always ranked as more important by younger employees. Older employees also rank job security as more important than personal and family time, which is more important to younger employees.[33]

Finally, *as needs change and lower-order needs are satisfied, create opportunities for employees to satisfy higher-order needs.* Recall that intrinsic rewards such as accomplishment, achievement, learning something new, and interacting with others are the natural rewards associated with performing a task or activity for its own sake. And with the exception of influence (power), intrinsic rewards correspond very closely to higher-order needs that are concerned with relationships (belongingness, relatedness, and affiliation) and challenges and accomplishments (esteem, self-actualization, growth, and achievement). Therefore, one way for managers to meet employees' higher-order needs is to create opportunities for employees to experience intrinsic rewards by providing challenging work, encouraging employees to take greater responsibility for their work, and giving employees the freedom to pursue tasks and projects they find naturally interesting.

Review 1

Basics of Motivation *Motivation* is the set of forces that initiates, directs, and makes people persist in their efforts, over time, to accomplish a goal. Managers often assume motivation to be the only determinant of performance, but job performance is a multiplicative function of motivation times ability times situational constraints. If any one of these components is weak, job performance will suffer. Needs are the physical or psychological requirements that must be met to ensure survival and well-being. When needs are not met, people experience an internal state of tension. But once a particular need is met, it no longer motivates. When this occurs, people become satisfied and are then motivated by other unmet needs.

Different motivational theories, such as Maslow's Hierarchy of Needs (physiological, safety, belongingness, esteem, and self-actualization), Alderfer's ERG Theory (existence, relatedness, and growth), and McClelland's Learned Needs Theory (affiliation, achievement, and power), specify a number of different needs. However, studies show that there are only two general kinds of needs, lower-order needs and higher-order needs, and that higher-order needs will not motivate people as long as lower-order needs remain unsatisfied.

Both extrinsic and intrinsic rewards motivate people. Extrinsic rewards, which include pay, company stock, benefits, and promotions, are used to motivate people to join organizations and attend and perform their jobs. The basic model of motivation suggests that managers can motivate employees by asking them what their needs are, satisfying lower-order needs first, expecting people's needs to change, and satisfying higher-order needs through intrinsic rewards.

How Perceptions and Expectations Affect Motivation

When employees perceive that they will be unable to perform at a level necessary to obtain rewards, whether extrinsic or intrinsic, they are likely to be *demotivated*. Reward systems at many organizations are geared toward top performers and ignore the mid-level performers. Most banks, for instance, reward the top 10 percent of the sales force; other sales representatives, who don't believe they can generate enough sales to end up in the top category, simply give up. Stephen O'Malley, an independent consultant, says that one way to avoid this scenario is to create an open-ended incentive program that keeps the top-performer programs intact while offering awards for mid-level performers who surpass their annual sales goals by 10 percent.

After reading the next two sections, you should be able to

2. *Use equity theory to explain how employees' perceptions of fairness affect motivation.*

3. *Use expectancy theory to describe how workers' expectations about rewards, effort, and the link between rewards and performance influence motivation.*

This system, implemented at a large U.S.-based financial services institution, successfully influenced perceptions and expectations of mid-level performers, resulted in better performance from all employees, and increased revenue for the company.

Specifically, two-thirds of the company's mid-level performers qualified for rewards by collectively contributing almost 80 percent of the total sales growth and creating $14 million in incremental profit. The contributions of these mid-level performers as a group outpaced the growth of top performers by 16 percent. By influencing perceptions and expectations of the entire sales force, the company was able to achieve a 47 percent overall increase in sales growth, three times the industry average.[34]

2 Equity Theory

Finnish businessman Jaako Rytsola was out driving in his car one evening. "The road was wide and I was feeling good. It was nice to be driving when there was no one in sight." Unfortunately for Rytsola, he wasn't really alone. A police officer pulled him over and issued him a speeding ticket for driving 43 mph in a 25 mph zone. The cost of the ticket: $71,400! Janne Rajala, a college student, was also pulled over for driving 18 mph over the speed limit. However, Rajala's ticket cost him only $106. The $71,294 difference occurred because Finland bases traffic fines on the severity of the offense, which was identical in this case, *and* the income of the driver, which clearly wasn't. Similarly, a Swiss millionaire driving a red Ferrari Testarossa was caught going 85 mph through a small village, 35 mph over the limit, and was fined $290,000. As in Finland, the penalty was based on his wealth, which the court estimated at $22.7 million.[35] Finally, a Swedish driver was caught going 180 mph, 110 mph over the speed limit, and faces a $1 million fine.[36]

Is the method of determining speeding fines fair or unfair in Finland, Switzerland, and Sweden? Most Americans would argue that their approach is unfair, that fairness requires that fines be proportional to the offense and that everyone who breaks the law to the same degree should pay the same fine. By contrast, most Finns, Swedes, and Swiss believe that fines proportional to income are fair. Erkki Wuouma of Finland's Ministry of the Interior says, "This is a Nordic tradition. We have progressive taxation and progressive punishments. So the more you earn, the more you pay." Rytsola pays more because he is a high-earning Internet entrepreneur. Rajala pays less because he's a low-earning college student.[37]

Fairness, or what people perceive to be fair, is also a critical issue in organizations. **Equity theory** says that people will be motivated at work when they *perceive* that they are being treated fairly. In particular, equity theory stresses the importance of perceptions. So, regardless of the actual level of rewards people receive, they must also perceive that, relative to others, they are being treated fairly. For example, you learned in Chapter 11 that the average CEO now makes 319 times more than the average worker.[38] Furthermore, CEOs of companies listed in the Standard & Poor's 500 make an average of $9.25 million a year.[39] The ten highest-paid CEOs, however, led by Gregory Maffei of the Liberty Media Group who made $87.1 million, average $44 million a year.[40]

Many people believe that CEO pay is obscenely high and unfair. In order to keep CEO salaries in check, companies like Aflac have adopted "say-on-pay" policies that allow investors a vote on executive compensation packages.[41] Others believe that CEO pay is fair because the supply and demand for executive talent largely determine what CEOs are paid. They argue that if it were easier to find good CEOs, then CEOs would be paid much less. Finally, some companies have addressed the issue of fairness by closely tying their CEOs' compensation to company performance. According to Walt Riker, McDonald's vice president of corporate media relations, "Eighty-one percent of our CEO's compensation was tied to performance and creating long-term shareholder value." CEO Jim Skinner received a $1.4 million salary, but his bonus

equity theory a theory that states that people will be motivated when they perceive that they are being treated fairly.

was $11.5 million thanks to McDonald's financial performance, which provided shareholders a 16 percent return, tops among the companies in the Dow Jones Industrial Average. Compensation expert Paul Dorf said, "Clearly he [Skinner] has done the right things—cut costs, brought in new revenue streams and improved shareholder value. If the opposite happened, his salary would have been much lower."[42]

As explained below, equity theory doesn't focus on objective equity (i.e., that CEOs make 344 times more than blue-collar workers). Instead, equity theory says that equity, like beauty, is in the eye of the beholder.

Let's learn more about equity theory by examining **2.1 the components of equity theory, 2.2 how people react to perceived inequities,** and **2.3 how to motivate people using equity theory.**

2.1 Components of Equity Theory

The basic components of equity theory are inputs, outcomes, and referents. **Inputs** are the contributions employees make to the organization. They include education and training, intelligence, experience, effort, number of hours worked, and ability. **Outcomes** are what employees receive in exchange for their contributions to the organization. They include pay, fringe benefits, status symbols, and job titles and assignments. And because perceptions of equity depend on comparisons, **referents** are other people with whom people compare themselves to determine whether they have been treated fairly. The referent can be a single person (comparing yourself with a coworker), a generalized other (comparing yourself with "students in general," for example), or even yourself over time ("I was better off last year than I am this year"). Usually, people choose to compare themselves with referents who hold the same or similar jobs or who are otherwise similar in gender, race, age, tenure, or other characteristics.[43] For instance, by any objective measure, it's hard to argue that the best professional athletes, who make as much as $30 million a year (and no doubt more by the time you read this), are treated unfairly, given that the typical American earns $46,040 a year.[44] Nonetheless, most top athletes' contracts include escalator clauses specifying that if another top player at the same position (i.e., their referent) receives a larger contract, then their contract will automatically be increased to that amount.

According to the equity theory process shown in Exhibit 13.7, employees compare their outcomes (the rewards they receive from the organization) with their inputs (their contributions to the organization). This comparison of outcomes with inputs is called the **outcome/input (O/I) ratio.** After an internal comparison in which they compare their outcomes with their inputs, employees then make an external comparison in which they compare their O/I ratio with the O/I ratio of a referent.[45] When people perceive that their O/I ratio is equal to the referent's O/I ratio, they conclude that they are being treated fairly. But when people perceive that their O/I ratio is different from their referent's O/I ratio, they conclude that they have been treated inequitably or unfairly.

Inequity can take two forms, under-reward and over-reward. **Under-reward** occurs when a referent's O/I ratio is better than your O/I ratio. In other words, you are getting fewer outcomes relative to your inputs than the referent you compare yourself with is getting. When people perceive that they have been under-rewarded, they tend to experience anger or frustration. For example, when a manufacturing company received notice that some important contracts had been canceled, management cut employees' pay by 15 percent in one plant, but not in another. Just as equity theory predicts,

inputs in equity theory, the contributions employees make to the organization.

outcomes in equity theory, the rewards employees receive for their contributions to the organization.

referents in equity theory, others with whom people compare themselves to determine if they have been treated fairly.

outcome/input (O/I) ratio in equity theory, an employee's perception of how the rewards received from an organization compare with the employee's contributions to that organization.

under-reward a form of inequity in which you are getting fewer outcomes relative to inputs than your referent is getting.

Exhibit 13.7 Outcome/Input Ratios

$$\frac{\text{OUTCOMES}_{\text{SELF}}}{\text{INPUTS}_{\text{SELF}}} = \frac{\text{OUTCOMES}_{\text{REFERENT}}}{\text{INPUTS}_{\text{REFERENT}}}$$

© Cengage Learning 2013

theft doubled in the plant that received the pay cut. Likewise, employee turnover increased from 5 percent to 23 percent.[46]

By contrast, **over-reward** occurs when a referent's O/I ratio is worse than your O/I ratio. In this case, you are getting more outcomes relative to your inputs than your referent is. In theory, when people perceive that they have been over-rewarded, they experience guilt. But, not surprisingly, people have a very high tolerance for over-reward. It takes a tremendous amount of overpayment before people decide that their pay or benefits are more than they deserve.

2.2 How People React to Perceived Inequity

As a child do you ever remember calling for a do-over? Even as children, we have a strong desire for fairness, for being treated equitably. When this need isn't met, we are strongly motivated to find a way to restore equity and be fair, hence the do-over. Not surprisingly, equity is just as important at the office as it is on the playground.

So what happens when people perceive that they have been treated inequitably at work? Exhibit 13.8 shows that perceived inequity affects satisfaction. In the case of under-reward, this usually translates into frustration or anger; with over-reward, the reaction is guilt. These reactions lead to tension and a strong need to take action

over-reward a form of inequity in which you are getting more outcomes relative to inputs than your referent.

Exhibit 13.8 Adding Equity Theory to the Model

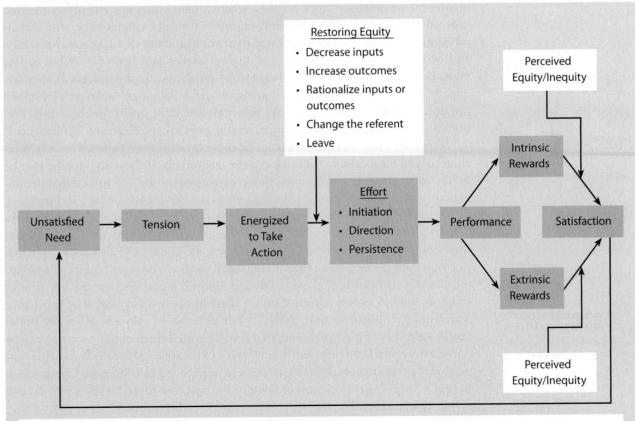

When people perceive that they have been treated inequitably at work because of the intrinsic or extrinsic rewards they receive relative to their efforts, they are dissatisfied (or frustrated or angry), because their needs aren't met. Those reactions lead to tension and a strong need to take action to restore equity in some way (as explained in the "Restoring Equity" box).

© Cengage Learning 2013

to restore equity in some way. At first, a slight inequity may not be strong enough to motivate an employee to take immediate action. If the inequity continues or there are multiple inequities, however, tension may build over time until a point of intolerance is reached, and the person is energized to take action.[47] For example, after being told he was going to be laid off, a data analyst for the Transportation Security Administration tried to install a computer virus in the U.S. Government's terrorism database, containing the critical "no-fly" list. The virus was intended to corrupt the database but was quickly discovered and neutralized.[48] Likewise, after being fired from a Texas advertising firm, an account executive convinced her boss to avoid embarrassment by letting her stay till the end of the week. She said, "Please don't change the locks and make a big show of it." The next morning, when the materials on her desk looked different, the company's IT manager became suspicious. The computer logs showed that four hours after being fired, she returned to the office to copy the entire client list, which she then emailed to herself to print at home.[49]

When people perceive that they have been treated unfairly, they may try to restore equity by reducing inputs, increasing outcomes, rationalizing inputs or outcomes, changing the referent, or simply leaving. We will discuss these possible responses in terms of the inequity associated with under-reward, which is much more common than the inequity associated with over-reward.

People who perceive that they have been under-rewarded may try to restore equity by *decreasing or withholding their inputs (that is, effort)*. Pilots at American Airlines took a 23 percent pay cut after 9/11 to help keep the airline out of bankruptcy. When American Airlines began doing well again, top managers collectively received a quarter-billion dollars in stock bonuses, whereas pilots and other employees received only small pay raises. When the pilots requested their old salaries back, with adjustments for inflation, American indicated that would amount to a 50 percent pay raise and cost the company $1.4 billion in higher salaries and benefits.[50] When airline pilots perceive that their pay and benefits are unfair (i.e., under-rewarded), they frequently protest by calling in sick or going on strike. Although American's pilots did not do so this time, about five years before this incident 2,400 American pilots reported in "sick" during a labor dispute, resulting in the cancellation of 1,100 flights.[51]

Increasing outcomes is another way people try to restore equity. This might include asking for a raise or pointing out the inequity to the boss and hoping that he or she takes care of it. Sometimes, however, employees may go to external organizations such as labor unions, federal agencies, or the courts for help in increasing outcomes to restore equity. For instance, the U.S. Department of Labor estimates that 10 percent of workers are not getting the extra overtime pay they deserve when they work more than 40 hours a week.[52] These are known as Fair Labor Standards Act violations. In fact, more than 30,000 such cases are brought each year, and employees win two-thirds of them.[53] Edward Harold, a partner with the law firm of Fisher & Phillips in New Orleans, says, "There has been an explosion of Fair Labor Standards Act litigation since 2002."[54] For example, employees of **Family Dollar Stores** sued the company, claiming that it had cheated them out of overtime pay by purposefully misclassifying hourly employees (who are eligible for overtime pay) as managers (who are not). The case ultimately went to the U.S. Supreme Court, which upheld a lower court's decision in favor of the workers. Over 1,400 employees will divide $35.6 million.[55]

Another method of restoring equity is to *rationalize or distort inputs or outcomes*. Instead of decreasing inputs or increasing outcomes, employees restore equity by making mental or emotional adjustments in their O/I ratios or the O/I ratios of their referents. For example, suppose that a company downsizes 10 percent of its workforce. It's likely that the survivors (the people who still have jobs) will be angry or frustrated with company management because of the layoffs. If alternative jobs are difficult to

"what's new" companies >

find, however, these survivors may rationalize or distort their O/I ratios and conclude, "Well, things could be worse. At least I still have my job." Rationalizing or distorting outcomes may be used when other ways to restore equity aren't available.

Changing the referent is another way of restoring equity. In this case, people compare themselves with someone other than the referent they had been using for previous O/I ratio comparisons. Because people usually choose to compare themselves with others who hold the same or similar jobs or who are otherwise similar (i.e., friends, family members, neighbors who work at other companies), they may change referents to restore equity when their personal situations change, such as a decrease in job status or pay.[56]

Finally, when none of these methods—reducing inputs, increasing outcomes, rationalizing inputs or outcomes, or changing referents—is possible or restores equity, *employees may* leave by quitting their jobs, transferring, or increasing absenteeism.[57] For example, attorneys and accountants at the Securities and Exchange Commission (SEC) quit their jobs at twice the rate of employees in other federal agencies. Why? One reason is that the SEC's attorneys and accountants are paid 40 percent less than their counterparts at other government agencies. Furthermore, they can get jobs in the private sector that pay $180,000 to $250,000 per year.[58]

2.3 Motivating with Equity Theory

What practical steps can managers take to use equity theory to motivate employees? As Exhibit 13.9 shows, they can *start by looking for and correcting major inequities*. Among other things, equity theory makes us aware that an employee's sense of fairness is based on subjective perceptions. What one employee considers grossly unfair may not affect another employee's perceptions of equity at all. Although these different perceptions make it difficult for managers to create conditions that satisfy all employees, it's critical that they do their best to take care of major inequities that can energize employees to take disruptive, costly, or harmful actions such as decreasing inputs or leaving. So, whenever possible, managers should look for and correct major inequities. At Burgerville, a 39-restaurant fast-food chain in Vancouver, Washington, annual employee turnover was 128 percent per year. The key inequity? Employees making $9 an hour couldn't afford health insurance for themselves and their families. Indeed, although Burgerville's health plan was cheap, at $42 a month for employees and $105 a month for families, it provided limited benefits and came with a $1,000 deductible. As a result, only 3 percent of employees were enrolled in it. Under Burgerville's revised health plan, employees who work at least 20 hours a week get full health insurance at a cost of just $15 a month for themselves and $90 a month for their families—in both instances, there's no deductible. Although the new plan was expensive, nearly doubling the company's health-care costs from $2.1 million to $4.1 million, the cost was easily offset by lower employee turnover, which dropped from 128 percent per year to 54 percent per year, and higher sales, which were up 11 percent. Furthermore, 98 percent of Burgerville's hourly employees and 97 percent of its salaried employees enrolled in the new health plan, compared to just 3 percent before.[59]

© iStockphoto.com/John Peacock

Second, managers can *reduce employees' inputs*. Increasing outcomes is often the first and only strategy that companies use to restore equity, yet reducing employee inputs is just as viable a strategy. In fact, with dual-career

Exhibit 13.9   Motivating with Equity Theory

- Look for and correct major inequities.
- Reduce employees' inputs.
- Make sure decision-making processes are fair.

© Cengage Learning 2013

couples working 50-hour weeks, more and more employees are looking for ways to reduce stress and restore a balance between work and family. Consequently, it may make sense to ask employees to do less, not more; to have them identify and eliminate the 20 percent of their jobs that doesn't increase productivity or add value for customers; and to eliminate company-imposed requirements that really aren't critical to the performance of managers, employees, or the company (for example., unnecessary meetings and reports). In addition to higher pay, more vacation time, concierge services, and town hall sessions, the "Big Four" accounting firms are trying to make the jobs of junior accountants more equitable by reducing the hours (that is, inputs) they must work. To shrink the workload, the firms are hiring more accountants, adding staff from other departments to help, and even turning away business that they lack the staff to handle. Bob Moritz, a senior partner at PriceWaterhouseCoopers, says, "The profession has recognized that we have a lot of stress in the system, and we're doing a lot of things [to fix it]."[60]

Finally, managers should *make sure decision-making processes are fair*. Equity theory focuses on **distributive justice**, the degree to which outcomes and rewards are fairly distributed or allocated. However, **procedural justice**, the fairness of the procedures used to make reward allocation decisions, is just as important.[61] Procedural justice matters because even when employees are unhappy with their outcomes (that is, low pay), they're much less likely to be unhappy with company management if they believe that the procedures used to allocate outcomes were fair. For example, employees who are laid off tend to be hostile toward their employer when they perceive that the procedures leading to the layoffs were unfair. By contrast, employees who perceive layoff procedures to be fair tend to continue to support and trust their employers.[62] Also, if employees perceive that their outcomes are unfair (that is, distributive injustice) but that the decisions and procedures leading to those outcomes were fair (that is, procedural justice), they are much more likely to seek constructive ways of restoring equity, such as discussing these matters with their manager. By contrast, if employees perceive both distributive and procedural injustice, they may resort to more destructive tactics, such as withholding effort, absenteeism, tardiness, or even sabotage and theft.[63]

distributive justice the perceived degree to which outcomes and rewards are fairly distributed or allocated.

procedural justice the perceived fairness of the process used to make reward allocation decisions.

doing the right thing

Find Out What Your Employees Want

A reward program can be a great way to motivate employees at work. A reward for great performance, record-setting sales, or beating a project deadline can assure employees that their efforts are recognized and appreciated. The question is, do you know what to give them? A recent survey by the International Association of Administrative Professionals and the consulting firm OfficeTeam shows that what employees want and what managers think they want are very different. In the survey, most managers thought that the best way to show appreciation to employees was with promotions or cash bonuses. On the other hand, most employees reported that what motivated them was a personal thank-you or a positive report to senior management. So as you look for ways to motivate your employees, do the right thing and take the time to listen. To them, a handwritten note that says, "Thanks for a great job" might be worth much more than a $50 coffee card.[64]

Interactional justice refers to the fairness of interpersonal treatment that individuals receive during the enactment of organizational procedures. Two elements central to perceptions of interactional justice are (1) whether the reasons underlying the resource allocation decisions are clearly, truthfully, and adequately explained to affected parties; and (2) whether those responsible for implementing the decision treat the affected individuals with dignity and respect.[65] Recent studies indicate that interactional justice perceptions are at least as important as perceptions of procedural justice and distributive justice.[66] In addition, most managers are likely to have more control over interactional justice perceptions than, for example, fairness of organizational procedures or reward allocations in organizations.

Equity Theory   The basic components of equity theory are inputs, outcomes, and referents. After an internal comparison in which employees compare their outcomes with their inputs, they then make an external comparison in which they compare their O/I ratio with the O/I ratio of a referent or a person who works in a similar job or is otherwise similar. When their O/I ratio is equal to the referent's O/I ratio, employees perceive that they are being treated fairly. But when their O/I ratio is different from their referent's O/I ratio, they perceive that they have been treated inequitably or unfairly.

There are two kinds of inequity, under-reward and over-reward. Under-reward occurs when a referent's O/I ratio is better than the employee's O/I ratio, and leads to anger or frustration. Over-reward occurs when a referent's O/I ratio is worse than the employee's O/I ratio and can lead to guilt, but only when the level of over-reward is extreme. When employees perceive that they have been treated inequitably (under-rewarded), they may try to restore equity by reducing inputs, increasing outcomes, rationalizing inputs or outcomes, changing the referent, or simply leaving.

Managers can use equity theory to motivate workers by looking for and correcting major inequities, reducing employees' inputs, and emphasizing procedural as well as distributive justice. Most importantly, they should treat workers in an interpersonally sensitive manner and work to make sure that organizational procedures are fair and are applied in a consistent manner.

Review 2

3 Expectancy Theory

How attractive do you find each of the following rewards?

» A company concierge service that will pick up your car from the mechanic and send someone to be at your house when the cable guy or repair person shows up

» A "7 to 7" travel policy stipulating that no one has to leave home for business travel before 7 A.M. on Mondays and that everyone should be home from business travel by 7 P.M. on Fridays

» The opportunity to telecommute so that you can feed your kids breakfast, pick them up after school, and tuck them into bed at night[67]

If you have kids, you might love the chance to telecommute; but if you don't, you may not be interested. If you don't travel much on business, you won't be interested in the "7 to 7" travel policy; but if you do, you'll probably love it. One of the hardest things about motivating people is that not everyone is attracted to the same rewards.

Expectancy theory says that people will be motivated to the extent to which they believe that their efforts will lead to good performance, that good performance will be rewarded, and that they will be offered attractive rewards.[68]

Let's learn more about expectancy theory by examining **3.1 the components of expectancy theory** and **3.2 how to use expectancy theory as a motivational tool.**

3.1 Components of Expectancy Theory

Expectancy theory holds that people make conscious choices about their motivation. The three factors that affect those choices are valence, expectancy, and instrumentality.

Valence is simply the attractiveness or desirability of various rewards or outcomes. Expectancy theory recognizes that the same reward or outcome—say, a promotion—will be highly attractive to some people, will be highly disliked by others, and will not make much difference one way or the other to still others. Accordingly, when people are deciding how much effort to put forth, expectancy theory says that they will consider the valence of all possible rewards and outcomes that they can receive from their jobs. The greater the sum of those valences, each of which can be positive, negative, or neutral, the more effort people will choose to put forth on the job.

"what's new" companies >

CrowdFlower, a San Francisco–based employment agency that breaks big projects into smaller tasks that can be completed by individual workers (i.e., "crowd-sourcing"), understands that different people are motivated by different rewards. So, when it assigns someone to a task, which can range from verifying search engine links to categorizing Twitter posts, it gives them the option of receiving payment in cash or virtual cash. Some employees choose real money, whereas others choose virtual money that can be spent in online games like Farmville, Mafia Wars, or TinierMe.com. Though the idea of working for virtual money may sound strange, Amanda Dorsey, one of CrowdFlower's workers, says, "Doing work for virtual currency is pretty much like any other form of putting forth an effort for a reward."[69]

Expectancy is the perceived relationship between effort and performance. When expectancies are strong, employees believe that their hard work and efforts will result in good performance, so they work harder. By contrast, when expectancies are weak, employees figure that no matter what they do or how hard they work, they won't be able to perform their jobs successfully, so they don't work as hard.

Instrumentality is the perceived relationship between performance and rewards. When instrumentality is strong, employees believe that improved performance will lead to better and more rewards, so they choose to work harder. When instrumentality is weak, employees don't believe that better performance will result in more or better rewards, so they choose not to work as hard.

Expectancy theory holds that for people to be highly motivated, all three variables—valence, expectancy, and instrumentality—must be high. Thus, expectancy theory can be represented by the following simple equation:

$$\text{Motivation} = \text{Valence} \times \text{Expectancy} \times \text{Instrumentality}$$

If any one of these variables (valence, expectancy, or instrumentality) declines, overall motivation will decline too.

Exhibit 13.10 incorporates the expectancy theory variables into our motivation model. Valence and instrumentality combine to affect employees' willingness to put forth effort (i.e., the degree to which they are energized to take action), whereas expectancy transforms intended effort ("I'm really going to work hard in this job") into actual effort. If you're offered rewards that you desire and you believe that you

expectancy theory the theory that people will be motivated to the extent to which they believe that their efforts will lead to good performance, that good performance will be rewarded, and that they will be offered attractive rewards.

valence the attractiveness or desirability of a reward or outcome.

expectancy the perceived relationship between effort and performance.

instrumentality the perceived relationship between performance and rewards.

Exhibit 13.10 Adding Expectancy Theory to the Model

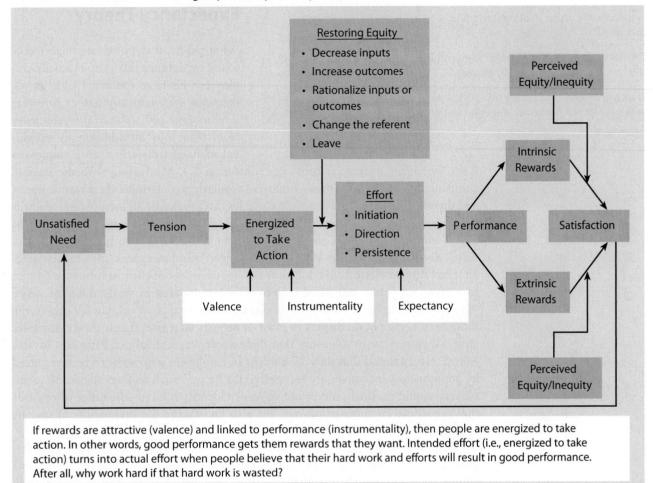

Restoring Equity
- Decrease inputs
- Increase outcomes
- Rationalize inputs or outcomes
- Change the referent
- Leave

If rewards are attractive (valence) and linked to performance (instrumentality), then people are energized to take action. In other words, good performance gets them rewards that they want. Intended effort (i.e., energized to take action) turns into actual effort when people believe that their hard work and efforts will result in good performance. After all, why work hard if that hard work is wasted?

© Cengage Learning 2013

will in fact receive these rewards for good performance, you're highly likely to be energized to take action. However, you're not likely to actually exert effort unless you also believe that you can do the job (i.e., that your efforts will lead to successful performance). Nucor Corporation, a steel products company, is the safest, highest-quality, lowest-cost, most productive and profitable steel company in the world. The Nucor performance management system integrates valence, expectancy, and instrumentality. First, Nucor offers a wide variety of rewards, including employee recognition programs, incentives and bonuses, and a no-layoff policy, so that all of its employees can receive highly valent rewards that they desire. Second, it manages expectancies through rigorous selection, orientation, and placement for new employees and through training and development opportunities for continuing employees. Finally, Nucor manages instrumentality by linking rewards to the specific results, behaviors, and values it wants to reward. For instance, manufacturing employees are paid weekly bonuses based on quality and quantity of steel produced by their work groups. This bonus averages 80 percent to 170 percent of base wages and has no cap. As long as quality and quantity increase, so does the bonus. Department managers earn annual incentive bonuses, as much as 100 percent of base salary, based on the return on investment of their manufacturing facility. Likewise, professional and staff employees, such as accountants, engineers, clerks, receptionists, and others, can earn bonuses up to 28 percent of salary. Every employee at Nucor knows exactly how rewards are determined and perceives a strong link between performance and pay.[70]

Exhibit 13.11 Motivating with Expectancy Theory

- Systematically gather information to find out what employees want from their jobs.

- Take specific steps to link rewards to individual performance in a way that is clear and understandable to employees.

- Empower employees to make decisions if management really wants them to believe that their hard work and effort will lead to good performance.

© Cengage Learning 2013

3.2 Motivating with Expectancy Theory

What practical steps can managers take to use expectancy theory to motivate employees? First, as Exhibit 13.11 shows, they can *systematically gather information to find out what employees want from their jobs*. In addition to individual managers directly asking employees what they want from their jobs (see Subsection 1.4, Motivating with the Basics), companies need to survey their employees regularly to determine their wants, needs, and dissatisfactions. Because people consider the valence of all the possible rewards and outcomes that they can receive from their jobs, regular identification of wants, needs, and dissatisfactions gives companies the chance to turn negatively valent rewards and outcomes into positively valent rewards and outcomes, thus raising overall motivation and effort. Mark Peterman, vice president of client solutions at Maritz Incentives, says that individual employees are motivated in vastly different ways: "For some, being honored in front of one's peers is a great award, but for others, the thought of being put on display in front of peers embarrasses them." And companies have a long way to go to ensure that their employees feel valued, Peterman says. A Maritz survey found that only 27 percent of employees who want to be recognized by nonmonetary incentives are recognized that way.[71] Such findings suggest that employers should routinely survey employees to identify not only the range of rewards that are valued by most employees but also understand the preferences of specific employees.

Second, managers can *take specific steps to link rewards to individual performance in a way that is clear and understandable to employees*. Unfortunately, most employees are extremely dissatisfied with the link between pay and performance in their organizations. In one study based on a representative sample, 80 percent of the employees surveyed wanted to be paid according to a different kind of pay system! Moreover, only 32 percent of employees were satisfied with how their annual pay raises were determined, and only 22 percent were happy with the way the starting salaries for their jobs were determined.[72]

One way to make sure that employees see the connection between pay and performance (see Chapter 11 for a discussion of compensation strategies) is for managers to publicize the way in which pay decisions are made. This is especially important given that only 41 percent of employees know how their pay increases are determined.[73] At **Fog Creek Software**, founder Joel Spolsky addresses this issue by using experience (years of full-time experience in your area), scope of responsibilities (Do you manage others, a department, a product or product line?), and programming skills (from new programmer to an expert critical to project success) to categorize each employee into one of nine different levels. Then, to make sure that the connection between pay and performance is clear, Fog Creek does two things. People with higher levels get more pay. And everyone at the same level gets the same pay. Spolsky says, "Once a year, my management team sits down, reviews every employee's work, and recalculates every employee's level." And if your responsibilities and experience and programming skills increase, your level and your pay do too.[74]

Finally, managers should *empower employees to make decisions if management really wants them to believe that their hard work and effort will lead to good performance*. If valent rewards are linked to good performance, people should be

"what's new" companies >

energized to take action. However, this works only if they also believe that their efforts will lead to good performance. One of the ways that managers destroy the expectancy that hard work and effort will lead to good performance is by restricting what employees can do or by ignoring employees' ideas. In Chapter 9, you learned that *empowerment* is a feeling of intrinsic motivation, in which workers perceive their work to have meaning and perceive themselves to be competent, have an impact, and be capable of self-determination.[75] So, if managers want workers to have strong expectancies, they should empower them to make decisions. Doing so will motivate employees to take active rather than passive roles in their work.

© iStockphoto.com/Troels Graugaard

Managers should empower employees to make decisions if management really wants them to believe that their hard word and effort will lead to good performance.

Expectancy Theory   Expectancy theory holds that three factors affect the conscious choices people make about their motivation: valence, expectancy, and instrumentality. Valence is simply the attractiveness or desirability of various rewards or outcomes. Expectancy is the perceived relationship between effort and performance. Instrumentality is the perceived relationship between performance and rewards. Expectancy theory holds that all three factors must be high in order for people to be highly motivated. If any one of these factors declines, overall motivation will decline too. Managers can use expectancy theory to motivate workers by systematically gathering information to find out what employees want from their jobs, by linking rewards to individual performance in a way that is clear and understandable to employees, and by empowering employees to make decisions, which will increase their expectancies that hard work and effort will lead to good performance.

Review 3

How Rewards and Goals Affect Motivation

When used properly, rewards motivate and energize employees. But when used incorrectly, they can demotivate, baffle, and even anger them. For example, consider the dot-com company that gave *every* employee a plaque for outstanding performance. Then it compounded that mistake (How can every employee be outstanding?) by firing one of those "outstanding" employees, James Finkel,

After reading the next three sections, you should be able to

4. *Explain how reinforcement theory works and how it can be used to motivate.*

5. *Describe the components of goal-setting theory and how managers can use them to motivate workers.*

6. *Discuss how the entire motivation model can be used to motivate workers.*

© iStockphoto.com/Stephen Rees

two weeks after awarding him his plaque. Says Finkel, "My reward for outstanding performance was getting canned. I left the plaque sitting on my desk."[76]

Goals are supposed to motivate employees. But leaders who focus blindly on meeting goals at all costs often find that they destroy motivation. For instance, a president of a technology company calls his vice president of sales daily and asks, "Did you make your numbers today?" Consultant Richard Hapburg, who works with the vice president who receives these daily calls, says that the VP should be focusing on long-term solutions that increase sales, but "he's under enormous pressure to meet certain sales and profit targets on a daily basis now." The clear danger to using goals in this way, says Hapburg, is "that it's hard to capture employees' hearts, and best efforts, with numbers alone."[77]

4 Reinforcement Theory

Reinforcement theory says that behavior is a function of its consequences, that behaviors followed by positive consequences (i.e., reinforced) will occur more frequently, and that behaviors either followed by negative consequences or not followed by positive consequences will occur less frequently.[78] For example, more and more hotels with "100 percent smoke-free policies" have increased fines (i.e., negative consequences) for customers who smoke in their rooms. Sheraton Hotels charges a $200 fine, Walt Disney World charges $500, and Swissotel Chicago raised its fine from $175 to $250. Swissotel's marketing director, Nicole Jachimiak, says, "$175 wasn't quite enough to get people to stop."[79] More specifically, **reinforcement** is the process of changing behavior by changing the consequences that follow behavior.[80]

Reinforcement has two parts: reinforcement contingencies and schedules of reinforcement. **Reinforcement contingencies** are the cause-and-effect relationships between the performance of specific behaviors and specific consequences. For example, if you get docked an hour's pay for being late to work, then a reinforcement contingency exists between a behavior (being late to work) and a consequence (losing an hour's pay). A **schedule of reinforcement** is the set of rules regarding reinforcement contingencies such as which behaviors will be reinforced, which consequences will follow those behaviors, and the schedule by which those consequences will be delivered.[81]

Exhibit 13.12 incorporates reinforcement contingencies and reinforcement schedules into our motivation model. First, notice that extrinsic rewards and the schedules of reinforcement used to deliver them are the primary method for creating reinforcement contingencies in organizations. In turn, those reinforcement contingencies directly affect valences (the attractiveness of rewards), instrumentality (the perceived link between rewards and performance), and effort (how hard employees will work).

Let's learn more about reinforcement theory by examining **4.1 the components of reinforcement theory, 4.2 the different schedules for delivering reinforcement,** and **4.3 how to motivate with reinforcement theory.**

4.1 Components of Reinforcement Theory

As just described, *reinforcement contingencies* are the cause-and-effect relationships between the performance of specific behaviors and specific consequences. There are four kinds of reinforcement contingencies: positive reinforcement, negative reinforcement, punishment, and extinction.

reinforcement theory the theory that behavior is a function of its consequences, that behaviors followed by positive consequences will occur more frequently, and that behaviors followed by negative consequences, or not followed by positive consequences, will occur less frequently.

reinforcement the process of changing behavior by changing the consequences that follow behavior.

reinforcement contingencies cause-and-effect relationships between the performance of specific behaviors and specific consequences.

schedule of reinforcement rules that specify which behaviors will be reinforced, which consequences will follow those behaviors, and the schedule by which those consequences will be delivered.

Exhibit 13.12 Adding Reinforcement Theory to the Model

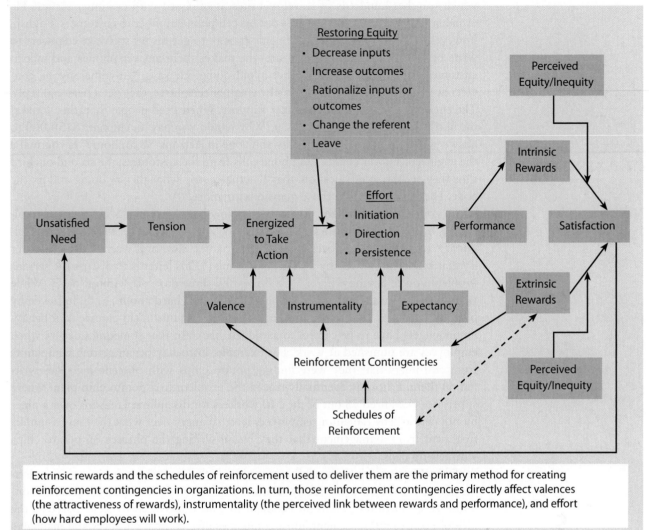

Extrinsic rewards and the schedules of reinforcement used to deliver them are the primary method for creating reinforcement contingencies in organizations. In turn, those reinforcement contingencies directly affect valences (the attractiveness of rewards), instrumentality (the perceived link between rewards and performance), and effort (how hard employees will work).

© Cengage Learning 2013

Positive reinforcement strengthens behavior (i.e., increases its frequency) by following behaviors with desirable consequences. Even though most consumers and businesses know that they should recycle the cans and plastic bottles their favorite beverages come in, few actually do—only 34 percent of all beverage containers and 25 percent of all plastic bottles are recycled. So Pepsi and Waste Management teamed up to create the "dream machine" point system to encourage consumers to recycle. Each bottle or can deposited into a dream machine is rewarded with points that can be used on coupons for shopping, entertainment, dining, travel, and personal services from vendors like Marriott, Domino's, and Blockbuster. Jeremy Cage, PepsiCo's dream machine project director says, "There's got to be something in it for people, both through material rewards and emotional rewards." Is the positive reinforcement working? Paul Ligon, Waste Management's managing director for "GreenOps," says that a pilot program at a Whole Foods store, customers would recycle an average of 10 bottles each visit, and "Then they walk in the door with their receipt and shop."[82]

Negative reinforcement strengthens behavior by withholding an unpleasant consequence when employees perform a specific behavior. Negative reinforcement is also called *avoidance learning*, because workers perform a behavior to *avoid* a

positive reinforcement reinforcement that strengthens behavior by following behaviors with desirable consequences.

negative reinforcement reinforcement that strengthens behavior by withholding an unpleasant consequence when employees perform a specific behavior.

negative consequence. Paul English, the cofounder of travel website, Kayak.com, which searches hundreds of travel websites, is obsessed with customer service. He even handles calls himself and gives out his cell phone number to customers. English, however, uses a negative reinforcement strategy to get his 60 software engineers to write better code for Kayak's website—he makes them answer phones and talk to customers—something they'd rather avoid doing. He says, "Anytime anyone contacts us with a question, whether it's by email or telephone, they get a personal reply. The engineers and I handle customer support. When I tell people that, they look at me like I'm smoking crack. They say, 'Why would you pay an engineer $150,000 to answer phones when you could pay someone in Arizona $8 an hour?' If you make the engineers answer emails and phone calls from the customers, the second or third time they get the same question, they'll actually stop what they're doing and fix the code. Then we don't have those questions anymore."[83]

By contrast, **punishment** weakens behavior (i.e., decreases its frequency) by following behaviors with undesirable consequences. For example, the standard disciplinary or punishment process in most companies is an oral warning ("Don't ever do that again"), followed by a written warning ("This letter is to discuss the serious problem you're having with ..."), followed by three days off without pay ("While you're at home not being paid, we want you to think hard about ... "), followed by being fired ("That was your last chance"). Though punishment can weaken behavior, managers have to be careful to avoid the backlash that sometimes occurs when employees are punished at work. For example, Frito-Lay began getting complaints from customers that they were finding potato chips with obscene messages written on them. Frito-Lay eventually traced the problem to a potato chip plant where supervisors had fired 58 out of the 210 workers for disciplinary reasons over a nine-month period. The remaining employees were so angry over what they saw as unfair treatment from management that they began writing the phrases on potato chips with felt-tip pens.[84]

Extinction is a reinforcement strategy in which a positive consequence is no longer allowed to follow a previously reinforced behavior. By removing the positive consequence, extinction weakens the behavior, making it less likely to occur. Based on the idea of positive reinforcement, most companies give company leaders and managers substantial financial rewards when the company performs well. Based on the idea of extinction, you would then expect that leaders and managers would not be rewarded (i.e., the positive consequence would be removed) when companies perform poorly. If companies really want pay to reinforce the right kinds of behaviors, then rewards have to be removed when company management doesn't produce successful performance. This occurred at Toyota which, after a devastating stretch of quality problems and recalls, saw a decade low in sales, market share decline for the first time in years, and a loss for the first time in more than 50 years. Because of this performance, Toyota cut the pay of CEO Akio Toyoda and his top managers by 10 percent. Toyoda and his senior managers also forfeited their bonuses for the second straight year.[85] By contrast, NYSE Euronext CEO Duncan Niederauer received a $4 million bonus, even as the company lost $738 million and its stock price dropped 69 percent.[86]

4.2 Schedules for Delivering Reinforcement

As mentioned earlier, a schedule of reinforcement is the set of rules regarding reinforcement contingencies such as which behaviors will be reinforced, which consequences will follow those behaviors, and the schedule by which those consequences will be delivered. There are two categories of reinforcement schedules: continuous and intermittent.

punishment reinforcement that weakens behavior by following behaviors with undesirable consequences.

extinction reinforcement in which a positive consequence is no longer allowed to follow a previously reinforced behavior, thus weakening the behavior.

Exhibit 13.13   Intermittent Reinforcement Schedules

	Intermittent Reinforcement Schedules	
	Fixed	**Variable**
INTERVAL (TIME)	Consequences follow behavior after a fixed time has elapsed.	Consequences follow behavior after different times, some shorter and some longer, that vary around a specific average time.
RATIO (BEHAVIOR)	Consequences follow a specific number of behaviors.	Consequences follow a different number of behaviors, sometimes more and sometimes less, that vary around a specified average number of behaviors.

© Cengage Learning 2013

With **continuous reinforcement schedules,** a consequence follows every instance of a behavior. For example, employees working on a piece-rate pay system earn money (consequence) for every part they manufacture (behavior). The more they produce, the more they earn. By contrast, with **intermittent reinforcement schedules,** consequences are delivered after a specified or average time has elapsed or after a specified or average number of behaviors has occurred. As Exhibit 13.13 shows, there are four types of intermittent reinforcement schedules. Two of these are based on time and are called *interval reinforcement schedules*; the other two, known as *ratio schedules,* are based on behaviors.

With **fixed interval reinforcement schedules,** consequences follow a behavior only after a fixed time has elapsed. For example, most people receive their paychecks on a fixed interval schedule (e.g., once or twice per month). As long as they work (behavior) during a specified pay period (interval), they get a paycheck (consequence). With **variable interval reinforcement schedules,** consequences follow a behavior after different times, some shorter and some longer, that vary around a specified average time. On a 90-day variable interval reinforcement schedule, you might receive a bonus after 80 days or perhaps after 100 days, but the average interval between performing your job well (behavior) and receiving your bonus (consequence) would be 90 days.

With **fixed ratio reinforcement schedules,** consequences are delivered following a specific number of behaviors. For example, a car salesperson might receive a $1,000 bonus after every ten sales. Therefore, a salesperson with only nine sales would not receive the bonus until he or she finally sold a tenth car.

With **variable ratio reinforcement schedules,** consequences are delivered following a different number of behaviors, sometimes more and sometimes less, that vary around a specified average number of behaviors. With a 10-car variable ratio reinforcement schedule, a salesperson might receive the bonus after 7 car sales, or after 12, 11, or 9 sales, but the average number of cars sold before receiving the bonus would be 10 cars.

Students often have trouble envisioning how these schedules can actually be used in work settings, so a couple of examples will help. In a study designed to increase employee attendance, employees participated in an innovative variable ratio schedule in which they drew a card from a deck of playing cards every day they came to work. At the end of each week, the employee with the best poker hand from those cards received a $20 bonus.[87] In another variable reinforcement system, **Electric Boat,** which builds nuclear submarines, uses a lottery that gives workers with good attendance a chance to win sizable rewards. Eligibility for the various rewards depends on the level of attendance. For example, 933 workers with two years of perfect attendance were placed in a lottery in which 20 of them would win $2,500. Likewise, 1,400

continuous reinforcement schedule a schedule that requires a consequence to be administered following every instance of a behavior.

intermittent reinforcement schedule a schedule in which consequences are delivered after a specified or average time has elapsed or after a specified or average number of behaviors has occurred.

fixed interval reinforcement schedule an intermittent schedule in which consequences follow a behavior only after a fixed time has elapsed.

variable interval reinforcement schedules an intermittent schedule in which the time between a behavior and the following consequences varies around a specified average.

fixed ratio reinforcement schedule an intermittent schedule in which consequences are delivered following a specific number of behaviors.

variable ratio reinforcement schedule an intermittent schedule in which consequences are delivered following a different number of behaviors, sometimes more and sometimes less, that vary around a specified average number of behaviors.

< **"what's new" companies**

mgmt:facts

When the Going Gets Tough …

It's easy to motivate employees when times are good. A fat bonus check, an extra week of vacation, a remodeled break room with leather sofas, free food, and a high-def TV—all of these things are a drop in the bucket when profits are high. But what about during the bad times? When sales are slow, when the economy of the entire world is struggling in historic proportions, how do you keep your employees motivated? John Ryan, president of the Center for Creative Leadership, says that three things need to happen if managers are to keep employees happy, motivated, and engaged. First is regular feedback. Managers should not wait for annual reviews, but give regular feedback to let employees know how they are doing and how they can improve. The second is coaching—managers should help employees look at circumstances from a new perspective in order to broaden their thinking and set good goals. Finally, managers must challenge themselves. Instead of just giving advice to others, the effective manager must be willing to receive feedback from others about his or her performance. What is more, managers should identify one or two areas in which they need to improve, so that they always work with the mindset of getting better.[88]

© iStockphoto.com/Kirsty Pargeter

workers with a year of perfect attendance were placed in a lottery where 75 would win $1,000, 50 would win $500, 25 would win prime parking spaces, and all would win a $25 gift certificate for the company store. Greg Angelini, who won a $1,000 prize, says, "I'm not a gambler, but it sure was nice to get that check right before Christmas. And it was just as nice that the powers that be noticed that I've had perfect attendance."[89] Electric Boat's lottery system is so rewarding that, on average, an amazing 41 percent of its workers have perfect attendance.

Which reinforcement schedules work best? In the past, the standard advice was to use continuous reinforcement when employees were learning new behaviors, because reinforcement after each success leads to faster learning. Likewise, the standard advice was to use intermittent reinforcement schedules to maintain behavior after it is learned, because intermittent rewards are supposed to make behavior much less subject to extinction.[90] Research shows, however, that except for interval-based systems, which usually produce weak results, the effectiveness of continuous reinforcement, fixed ratio, and variable ratio schedules differs very little.[91] In organizational settings, all three consistently produce large increases over noncontingent reward schedules. So managers should choose whichever of these three is easiest to use in their companies.

4.3 Motivating with Reinforcement Theory

What practical steps can managers take to use reinforcement theory to motivate employees? University of Nebraska business professor Fred Luthans, who has been studying the effects of reinforcement theory in organizations for more than a quarter of a century, says that there are five steps to motivating workers with reinforcement theory: *identify, measure, analyze, intervene,* and *evaluate* critical performance-related behaviors.[92]

Identify means singling out critical, observable, performance-related behaviors. These are the behaviors that are most important to successful job performance. In addition, they must also be easily observed so that they can be accurately measured. *Measure* means determining the baseline frequencies of these behaviors. In other words, find out how often workers perform them. *Analyze* means studying the causes and consequences of these behaviors. Analyzing the causes helps managers create the conditions that produce these critical behaviors, and analyzing the consequences helps them determine whether these behaviors produce the results that they want. *Intervene* means changing the organization by using positive and negative reinforcement to increase the frequency of these critical behaviors. *Evaluate* means assessing the extent to which the intervention actually changed workers' behavior. This is done by comparing behavior after the intervention to the original baseline of behavior before the intervention. For more on the effectiveness of reinforcement theory, see the What Really Works? feature in this chapter.

In addition to these five steps, managers should remember three other key things when motivating with reinforcement theory; these are listed in Exhibit 13.14. First, *Don't reinforce the wrong behaviors*. Although reinforcement theory sounds simple, it's actually very difficult to put into practice. One of the most common mistakes is accidentally reinforcing the wrong behaviors. Sometimes managers reinforce behaviors that they don't want! If you want to become a merit-based company, stop rewarding behavior that is not exceptional, says Dave Anderson, a management consultant. According to him, "the average car salesperson in the United States sells 10 cars per month, but many pay plans begin to pay bonuses at 7, 8, 9, or 10 cars. Under a typical plan, an employee who sells 8 cars gets a $200 bonus, another $250 for selling 2 additional cars, and $300 for selling 2 more cars. The total bonus for selling 12 cars in a month is $750." Anderson notes, "Based on national averages, such a pay plan financially rewards average and below-average results." Many of his clients have revised their system and only pay an $800 bonus to an employee *after* he or she has sold 12 cars, thus ending bonus payments for employees who sell fewer than the target amount of cars.[93] In this system, you pay more for better performance but don't fall into the trap of rewarding and endorsing the wrong things, rewarding below average performance.

Managers should also *correctly administer punishment at the appropriate time*. Many managers believe that punishment can change workers' behavior and help them improve their job performance. Furthermore, managers believe that fairly punishing workers also lets other workers know what is or isn't acceptable.[94] A danger of using punishment is that it can produce a backlash against managers and companies. But if administered properly, punishment can weaken the frequency of undesirable behaviors without creating a backlash.[95] To be effective, the punishment must be strong enough to stop the undesired behavior and must be administered objectively (same rules applied to everyone), impersonally (without emotion or anger), consistently and contingently (each time improper behavior occurs), and quickly (as soon as possible following the undesirable behavior). In addition, managers should clearly explain what the appropriate behavior is and why the employee is being punished. Employees typically respond well when punishment is administered this way.[96]

Finally, managers should *choose the simplest and most effective schedule of reinforcement*. When choosing a schedule of reinforcement, managers need to balance effectiveness against simplicity. In fact, the more complex the schedule

Exhibit 13.14 Motivating with Reinforcement Theory

- Identify, measure, analyze, intervene, and evaluate critical performance-related behaviors.

- Don't reinforce the wrong behaviors.

- Correctly administer punishment at the appropriate time.

- Choose the simplest and most effective schedule of reinforcement.

© Cengage Learning 2013

what really works
Financial, Nonfinancial, and Social Rewards

Throughout this chapter, we have been making the point that there is more to motivating people than money. But we haven't yet examined how well financial (money or prizes), nonfinancial (performance feedback), and social (recognition and attention) rewards motivate workers by themselves or in combination. However, the results of two meta-analyses, one with 19 studies based on more than 2,800 people (study 1) and another based on 72 studies and 13,301 people (study 2), clearly indicate that rewarding and reinforcing employees greatly improve motivation and performance, especially when combined.

Financial Rewards

On average, there is a 68 percent chance that employees whose behavior is reinforced with financial rewards will outperform employees whose behavior is not reinforced. This increases to 84 percent in manufacturing organizations but drops to 61 percent in service organizations.

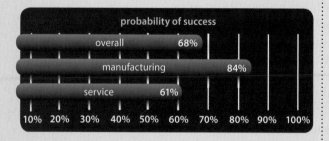

Nonfinancial Rewards

On average, there is a 58 percent chance that employees whose behavior is reinforced with nonfinancial rewards will outperform employees whose behavior is not reinforced. This increases to 87 percent in manufacturing organizations but drops to 54 percent in service organizations.

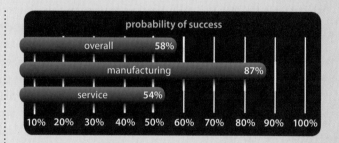

Social Rewards

On average, there is a 63 percent chance that employees whose behavior is reinforced with social rewards will outperform employees whose behavior is not reinforced.

Financial and Nonfinancial Rewards

On average, there is a 62 percent chance that employees whose behavior is reinforced with a combination of financial and nonfinancial rewards will outperform employees whose behavior is not reinforced.

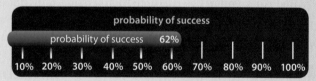

Financial and Social Rewards

On average, there is only a 52 percent chance that employees whose behavior is reinforced with a combination of financial and social rewards will outperform employees whose behavior is not reinforced.

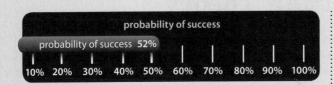

Nonfinancial and Social Rewards

On average, there is a 61 percent chance that employees whose behavior is reinforced with a combination of nonfinancial and social rewards will outperform employees whose behavior is not reinforced.

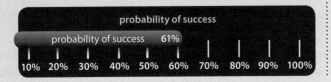

Financial, Nonfinancial, and Social Rewards

On average, there is a 90 percent chance that employees whose behavior is reinforced with a combination of financial, nonfinancial, and social rewards will outperform employees whose behavior is not reinforced.[97]

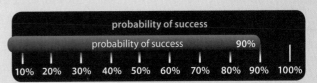

of reinforcement, the more likely it is to be misunderstood and resisted by managers and employees. For example, a forestry and logging company experimented with a unique variable ratio schedule. When tree-planters finished planting a bag of seedlings (about 1,000 seedlings per bag), they got to flip a coin. If they called the coin flip correctly (heads or tails), they were paid $4, double the regular rate of $2 per bag. If they called the coin flip incorrectly, they got nothing. The company began having problems when several workers and a manager, who was a part-time minister, claimed that the coin flip was a form of gambling. Then another worker found that the company was taking out too much money for taxes from workers' paychecks. Because the workers didn't really understand the reinforcement schedule, they blamed the payment plan associated with it and accused the company of trying to cheat them out of their money. After all of these problems, the researchers who implemented the variable ratio schedule concluded that "the results of this study may not be so much an indication of the relative effectiveness of different schedules of reinforcement as they are an indication of the types of problems that one encounters when applying these concepts in an industrial setting."[98] In short, choose the simplest, most effective schedule of reinforcement. Because continuous reinforcement, fixed ratio, and variable ratio schedules are about equally effective, continuous reinforcement schedules may be the best choice in many instances, by virtue of their simplicity.

Reinforcement Theory Reinforcement theory says that behavior is a function of its consequences. Reinforcement has two parts: reinforcement contingencies and schedules of reinforcement. The four kinds of reinforcement contingencies are positive reinforcement and negative reinforcement (which strengthen behavior), and punishment and extinction (which weaken behavior). There are two kinds of reinforcement schedules, continuous and intermittent; intermittent schedules, in turn, can be divided into fixed and variable interval schedules and fixed and variable ratio schedules. Managers can use reinforcement theory to motivate workers by following five steps (identify, measure, analyze, intervene, and evaluate critical performance-related behaviors); not reinforcing the wrong behaviors; correctly administering punishment at the appropriate time; and choosing a reinforcement schedule, such as continuous reinforcement, that balances simplicity and effectiveness.

Review 4

5 Goal-Setting Theory

**"what's new"
companies** >

The basic model of motivation with which we began this chapter showed that individuals feel tension after becoming aware of an unfulfilled need. Once they experience tension, they search for and select courses of action that they believe will eliminate this tension. In other words, they direct their behavior toward something. This something is a goal. A **goal** is a target, objective, or result that someone tries to accomplish. For instance, **Single Source Systems**, a software company in Fishers, Indiana, sets 15 annual goals, such as automating some of the software functions that it uses to write code. But, with 15 goals to accomplish, CEO Tony Petrucciani and his staff divided their efforts and attention in too many directions. Petrucciani said, "Nobody focused on any one thing" and they missed their revenue goal of $8.1 million by 11 percent. Now, Petrucciani only sets a few key goals each year. As a result, with a clearer focus, Single Source Systems met its revenue goal of $10 million last year.[99]

Goal-setting theory says that people will be motivated to the extent to which they accept specific, challenging goals and receive feedback that indicates their progress toward goal achievement. Let's learn more about goal setting by examining **5.1 the components of goal-setting theory** and **5.2 how to motivate with goal-setting theory.**

5.1 Components of Goal-Setting Theory

goal a target, objective, or result that someone tries to accomplish.

goal-setting theory the theory that people will be motivated to the extent to which they accept specific, challenging goals and receive feedback that indicates their progress toward goal achievement.

goal specificity the extent to which goals are detailed, exact, and unambiguous.

goal difficulty the extent to which a goal is hard or challenging to accomplish.

goal acceptance the extent to which people consciously understand and agree to goals.

performance feedback information about the quality or quantity of past performance that indicates whether progress is being made toward the accomplishment of a goal.

The basic components of goal-setting theory are goal specificity, goal difficulty, goal acceptance, and performance feedback.[100] **Goal specificity** is the extent to which goals are detailed, exact, and unambiguous. Specific goals, such as "I'm going to have a 3.0 average this semester," are more motivating than general goals, such as "I'm going to get better grades this semester."

Goal difficulty is the extent to which a goal is hard or challenging to accomplish. Difficult goals, such as "I'm going to have a 3.5 average and make the Dean's List this semester," are more motivating than easy goals, such as "I'm going to have a 2.0 average this semester."

Goal acceptance, which is similar to the idea of goal commitment discussed in Chapter 5, is the extent to which people consciously understand and agree to goals. Accepted goals, such as "I really want to get a 3.5 average this semester to show my parents how much I've improved," are more motivating than unaccepted goals, such as "My parents really want me to get a 3.5 average this semester, but there's so much more I'd rather do on campus than study!"

Performance feedback is information about the quality or quantity of past performance and indicates whether progress is being made toward the accomplishment of a goal. Performance feedback, such as "My prof said I need a 92 on the final to get an 'A' in that class," is more motivating than no feedback, "I have no idea what my grade is in that class." In short, goal-setting theory says that people will be motivated to the extent

© iStockphoto.com/huseyin harmandağlı

to which they accept specific, challenging goals and receive feedback that indicates their progress toward goal achievement.

How does goal setting work? To start, challenging goals focus employees' attention (i.e., direction of effort) on the critical aspects of their jobs and away from unimportant areas. Goals also energize behavior. When faced with unaccomplished goals, employees typically develop plans and strategies to reach those goals. Goals also create tension between the goal, which is the desired future state of affairs, and where the employee or company is now, meaning the current state of affairs. This tension can be satisfied only by achieving or abandoning the goal. Finally, goals influence persistence. Because goals only go away when they are accomplished, employees are more likely to persist in their efforts in the presence of goals. Exhibit 13.15 incorporates goals into the motivation model by showing how goals directly affect tension, effort, and the extent to which employees are energized to take action.

5.2 Motivating with Goal-Setting Theory

What practical steps can managers take to use goal-setting theory to motivate employees? Exhibit 13.16 lists three suggestions, beginning with *assign specific,*

Exhibit 13.15   Adding Goal-Setting Theory to the Model

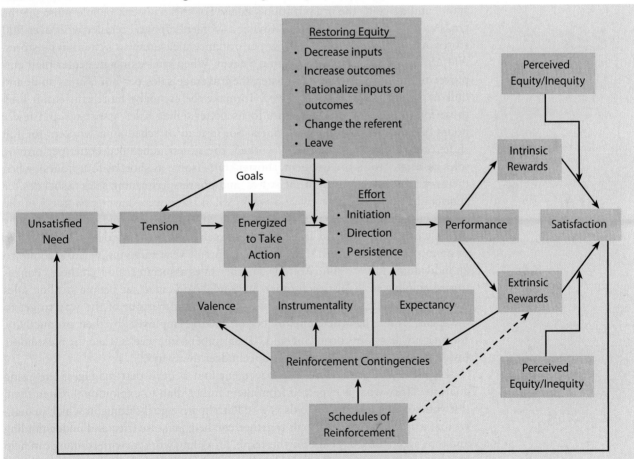

Goals create tension between the goal, which is the desired future state of affairs, and where the employee or company is now, meaning the current state of affairs. This tension can be satisfied only by achieving or abandoning the goal. Goals also energize behavior. When faced with unaccomplished goals, employees typically develop plans and strategies to reach those goals. Finally, goals influence persistence.

© Cengage Learning 2013

Exhibit 13.16 Motivating with Goal-Setting Theory

- Assign specific, challenging goals.

- Make sure workers truly accept organizational goals.

- Provide frequent, specific, performance-related feedback.

© Cengage Learning 2013

challenging goals. One of the simplest, most effective ways to motivate workers is to give them specific, challenging goals. For example, Valpak Direct Marketing Systems is a direct-mailing company that awards regional franchises to people with enough business experience and cash ($43,000 is usually enough for a small region). However, if you work for Valpak and meet the goal of $1.1 million in sales over three years, putting you among the top third of its best salespeople, the company lets you choose your reward: $50,000 toward the purchase of a small regional territory or $10,000 toward getting your MBA. Joe Bourdow, Valpak's president, said, "Sharp people coming out of school have choices, and so we're trying to give them a reason to at least consider us."[101] For more information on assigning specific, challenging goals, see the discussion in Chapter 5 on SMART goals.

Second, managers should *make sure workers truly accept organizational goals.* Specific, challenging goals won't motivate workers unless they really accept, understand, and agree to the organization's goals. For this to occur, people must see the goals as fair and reasonable. Ann Taylor, a women's apparel retailer with over 900 stores in 46 states, rolled out a new performance measurement system in its stores, ATLAS, Ann Taylor Labor Allocation System. When sales associates enter their employee numbers into the cash register, their average sales per hour, units sold, and dollars per transaction are displayed. To make the company more efficient, it used those metrics to assign more hours to its better-selling sales associates and fewer hours to poorer-performing associates. So, instead of scheduling workers for full shifts on the days on which they worked, the system scheduled better-performing sales associates for more frequent, shorter shifts (some as short as four hours), when there were more customers in the stores, and poorer-performing sales associates for shorter shifts, just once or twice a week, when there were fewer customers in the stores. This move, more than anything else, created frustration and resentment. Kelly Engle, who worked at Ann Taylor's Beavercreek, Ohio, store said, "There was a lot of animosity" toward ATLAS. "Computers aren't very forgiving when it comes to an individual's life."[102] Julie Abrams, another sales associate, said that these changes turned employees against each other. She said, "You could see people stealing sales from other people." They "were trying to get each other out of the way to get to the client." And when the company began ranking employees by their productivity, Abrams saw her hours drop. She said, "I remember some weeks when the most hours I was getting was just eight. It is hard to budget that way."[103]

Employees must also trust management and believe that managers are using goals to clarify what is expected from them rather than to exploit or threaten them ("If you don't achieve these goals . . . "). Participative goal setting, in which managers and employees generate goals together, can help increase trust and understanding and thus acceptance of goals. Furthermore, providing workers with training can help increase goal acceptance, particularly when workers don't believe they are capable of reaching the organization's goals.[104]

Finally, managers should *provide frequent, specific, performance-related feedback.* Once employees have accepted specific, challenging goals, they should receive frequent performance-related feedback so that they can track their progress toward goal completion. Feedback leads to stronger motivation and effort in three ways.[105]

Receiving specific feedback about the quality of their performance can encourage employees who don't have specific, challenging goals to set goals to improve their performance. Once people meet goals, performance feedback often encourages them to set higher, more difficult goals. And feedback lets people know whether they need to increase their efforts or change strategies in order to accomplish their goals.

For example, in an effort to improve worker safety on offshore oil-drilling platforms, an oil company generated a list of dangerous work behaviors by analyzing previous accident reports, reviewing industry safety manuals, and interviewing and observing workers. Following detailed safety training, each work crew set goals to engage in safe behaviors 100 percent of the time on each shift. To help workers track their improvement, management posted a weekly safety record in the galley of each rig so that the workers could see it when they gathered for meals and coffee breaks. Previously, employees were engaging in safe work behaviors just 76 percent of the time. After a year of goal setting (100% safe behavior on each shift) and weekly performance feedback at two oil rigs, however, workers behaved safely over 90 percent of the time. As a result, accident rates dropped from 21.1 percent to 6.1 percent at the first rig and from 14.2 percent to 12.1 percent at the second rig. By contrast, at a third oil rig, where training, goal setting, and feedback were not used, the total accident rate *increased* from 11.6 percent to 20.3 percent over the same time.[106] So, to motivate employees with goal-setting theory, make sure they receive frequent performance-related feedback so that they can track their progress toward goal completion.

A goal is a target, objective, or result that someone tries to accomplish. Goal-setting theory says that people will be motivated to the extent to which they accept specific, challenging goals and receive feedback that indicates their progress toward goal achievement. The basic components of goal-setting theory are goal specificity, goal difficulty, goal acceptance, and performance feedback. Goal specificity is the extent to which goals are detailed, exact, and unambiguous. Goal difficulty is the extent to which a goal is hard or challenging to accomplish. Goal acceptance is the extent to which people consciously understand and agree to goals. Performance feedback is information about the quality or quantity of past performance and indicates whether progress is being made toward the accomplishment of a goal. Managers can use goal-setting theory to motivate workers by assigning specific, challenging goals, making sure workers truly accept organizational goals, and providing frequent, specific, performance-related feedback.

Review 5

6 Motivating with the Integrated Model

We began this chapter by defining motivation as the set of forces that initiates, directs, and makes people persist in their efforts to accomplish a goal. We also asked the basic question that managers ask when they try to figure out how to motivate their workers: "What leads to effort?" Though the answer to that question is likely to be somewhat different for each employee, Exhibit 13.17 helps you begin to answer it by consolidating the practical advice from the theories reviewed in this chapter in one convenient location. So, if you're having difficulty figuring out why people aren't motivated where you work, Exhibit 13.17 provides a useful, theory-based starting point.

Exhibit 13.17 Motivating with the Integrated Model

MOTIVATING WITH . . .	MANAGERS SHOULD . . .
THE BASICS	• Ask people what their needs are. • Satisfy lower-order needs first. • Expect people's needs to change. • As needs change and lower-order needs are satisfied, create opportunities for employees to satisfy higher-order needs.
EQUITY THEORY	• Look for and correct major inequities. • Reduce employees' inputs. • Make sure decision-making processes are fair.
EXPECTANCY THEORY	• Systematically gather information to find out what employees want from their jobs. • Take specific steps to link rewards to individual performance in a way that is clear and understandable to employees. • Empower employees to make decisions if management really wants them to believe that their hard work and efforts will lead to good performance.
REINFORCEMENT THEORY	• Identify, measure, analyze, intervene, and evaluate critical performance-related behaviors. • Don't reinforce the wrong behaviors. • Correctly administer punishment at the appropriate time. • Choose the simplest and most effective schedule of reinforcement.
GOAL-SETTING THEORY	• Assign specific, challenging goals. • Make sure workers truly accept organizational goals. • Provide frequent, specific, performance-related feedback.

© Cengage Learning 2013

SELF-ASSESSMENT

What Do You Need?

What people want out of their jobs is as varied as the jobs themselves.[107] And as you would expect, need theories show why not everyone wants to be CEO. Take the example of the woman who is extremely organized and efficient in her job as an assistant. She is so effective that she is offered a promotion to management, but she turns it down flatly, saying that she has no interest in moving up the ladder, that she is happy doing what she does. What she needs from work clearly differs from the needs of the person who jumps at every opportunity to move up the corporate hierarchy. Not everyone needs or wants the same things from their jobs.[108] Indicate the extent to which you agree with each of the following statements. Try not to spend too much time on any one item, and be sure to answer all the questions. Use this scale for your responses:

1 Strongly disagree

2 Disagree

3 Slightly disagree

4 Neutral

5 Slightly agree

6 Agree

7 Strongly agree

1. I get enough money from my job to live comfortably.
   1 ② 3 4 5 6 7

2. Our benefits cover many of the areas they should.
   1 ② 3 4 5 6 7

3. My boss encourages people to make suggestions.
   1 2 3 4 5 6 ⑦

4. I can count on my coworkers to give me a hand when I need it.
   1 2 3 4 5 ⑥ 7

5. I always get the feeling of learning new things from my work.
   1 ② 3 4 5 6 7

6. I often think about how to improve my job performance.

   1   2   3   ④   5   6   7

7. My pay is adequate to provide for the basic things in life.

   1   2   3   4   ⑤   6   7

8. The benefit program here gives nearly all the security I want.

   1   ②   3   4   5   6   7

9. My boss takes account of my wishes and desires.

   1   2   3   ④   5   6   7

10. My coworkers will speak out in my favor if justified.

    1   2   3   ④   5   6   7

11. My job requires that a person use a wide range of abilities.

    1   2   3   4   5   6   ⑦

12. I will actively try to improve my job performance in the future.

    1   2   3   4   5   ⑥   7

13. Considering the work required, the pay is what it should be.

    ①   2   3   4   5   6   7

14. Compared to other places, our benefits are excellent.

    1   ②   3   4   5   6   7

15. My boss keeps me informed about what is happening in the company.

    1   2   ③   4   5   6   7

16. I can tell my coworkers how I honestly feel.

    1   2   ③   4   5   6   7

17. My job requires making one (or more) important decision(s) every day.

    1   2   3   4   ⑤   6   7

18. I intend to do a lot more at work in the future.

    1   2   3   ④   5   6   7

19. Compared to the rates for similar work, here, my pay is good.

    1   ②   3   4   5   6   7

20. The benefit program here is adequate.

    1   ②   3   4   5   6   7

21. My boss lets me know when I could improve my performance.

    1   2   3   ④   5   6   7

22. My coworkers welcome opinions different from their own.

    1   2   ③   4   5   6   7

23. I have the opportunity to do challenging things at work.

    1   2   ③   4   5   6   7

24. I will probably do my best to perform well on the job in the future.

    1   2   3   4   ⑤   6   7

Scoring

(A) Add together your scores for items 1, 2, 7, 8, 13, 14, 19, and 20: _18_

(B) Add together your scores for items 3, 4, 9, 10, 15, 16, 21, and 22: _38_

(C) Add together your scores for items 5, 6, 11, 12, 17, 18, 23, and 24: _33_

You can find the interpretation for your score at www.cengagebrain.com.

KEY TERMS

continuous reinforcement schedule 553
distributive justice 544
equity theory 539
expectancy 546
expectancy theory 546
extinction 552
extrinsic reward 535
fixed interval reinforcement schedule 553
fixed ratio reinforcement schedule 553
goal 558
goal acceptance 558
goal difficulty 558
goal-setting theory 558
goal specificity 558
inputs 540
instrumentality 546
intermittent reinforcement schedule 553
intrinsic reward 536
motivation 530
needs 533
negative reinforcement 551
outcome/input (O/I) ratio 540
outcomes 540
over-reward 541
performance feedback 558
positive reinforcement 551
procedural justice 544
punishment 552
referents 540
reinforcement 550
reinforcement contingencies 550
reinforcement theory 550
schedule of reinforcement 550
under-reward 540
valence 546
variable interval reinforcement schedules 553
variable ratio reinforcement schedule 553

MANAGEMENT DECISION

Why Won't They Take A Break?[109]

Five years ago, your company assigned you to a management position in its new research facility in South Korea. You were thrilled with the promotion, and grateful to your bosses, who recognized your skills and talents. At the same time, there was a lot to be nervous about—adjusting to a new culture and language, finding a school for your kids and a job for your wife, figuring out where to buy familiar groceries. But even with all the struggles, you've thoroughly enjoyed your time in Korea, as you got to learn new things from your employees and teach them new things from your experiences. In fact, you're quite surprised that you've had such little conflict with your Korean associates.

There is, however, one area that you could never quite get a handle on—vacation time. Like every other employee in the company, your employees were given three weeks of paid vacation per year. But, other than the occasional three-day weekend, they never took any time off. At first, you wondered if this was just unique to your company. But then, you saw statistics that showed that Koreans, on average, worked more than 2,300 hours per year, 600 more than the average American. Although these long hours show great organizational commitment, they have extremely negative effects. Overworked employees are more prone to stress and physical illness, and are less likely to be efficient or productive. Indeed, according to the Organization of Economic Cooperation and Development, an international group comprised of 30 of the world's largest economies, South Korea ranks near the bottom in terms of productivity.

Even the South Korean government has taken notice of the dangers of overwork. A few months ago, President Myung Bak Lee announced that all state employees would be required to take 16 days of vacation per year. You were quite happy to hear about this policy, and hopeful that it would influence the private sector. But you also wonder if there aren't other changes needed. From your conversations with Korean managers, you've learned that there is one big reason why Korean employees don't take vacation time—because their supervisors don't take vacation time. Even while requiring government employees to take 16 days off, President Lee himself has taken off only 4 days since his 2008 election. Jin-soo Kim, a director in the Ministry of Public Administration who wrote the 16-day policy, took no vacation time at all in 2008. Even you, the "enlightened" American, remember working through Lunar New Year's Day, one of the biggest holidays in Korea.

You desperately want your employees to take more time off. It's what's best for them, their families, and for the company's productivity and efficiency. What is the best way to motivate them to take a break?

Questions

1. Which motivation theories do you think would help communicate the importance of vacation time to your employees?
2. How would you convince your employees that working fewer hours, not more, is more beneficial for them and the company?

MANAGEMENT TEAM DECISION

Ready for Football?[110]

The CEO of your advertising firm recently put together your team, made up of managers, employees, and even interns, to solve a thorny issue—sports. Almost every Friday and Monday, she has noticed many employees at their desks, looking at their monitors quite intently. At first, she wanted to praise them for working so hard, but on closer inspection, she found that their attention was fixed on fantasy football. These folks,

dozens of them all over the office, weren't analyzing company data or working on new sales leads. Instead, they were looking for players to add to their fantasy teams or emailing other people in their league about making a trade.

Needless to say, the CEO was quite disheartened to see how preoccupied everyone was with sports. So, she assigned your team the task of putting together an office policy on this issue.

At first glance, the solution seems simple enough—just prohibit employees from playing fantasy sports during work hours. After all, whatever amount of time employees spend on playing or watching games is that much time they spend not working. A study by the outplacement firm Challenger, Gray & Christmas showed that lost productivity costs American companies around $1.5 billion during a football season.

But then again, perhaps the answer is not that simple. Another survey by Challenger, Gray & Christmas shows that fantasy football has little actual impact on productivity. In their survey, 100 Human Resources officers were asked to rate how big of a distraction fantasy football was on a scale of 1 to 10. The average response—just 3.42. What is more, an office-wide fantasy football league might actually help motivate workers. Letting employees indulge in a fantasy league may actually give them a mental break so that they are even more productive when their attention turns back to work. John Challenger argues that a company that allows employees to participate in fantasy football is likely to see long-benefits in morale, productivity, and employee retention.

So the question that your team faces is this: What do we do with fantasy sports? Should you keep letting employees partake of fantasy leagues during work hours, even though it's often frustrating to see workers do everything else but work? But if you prohibit fantasy sports leagues at work, do you really think that employees will spend their newly found time doing work, or will they just find another distraction? And if you do prohibit, how will you deal with the negative response from employees?

For this Management Team Decision, form a group with three to four other students and consider the questions below.

Questions

1. Do you think that allowing employees to play in fantasy leagues at work is a good motivational tool? Why or why not?
2. What would be an effective method to have employees stop playing fantasy games without destroying their morale or motivation?

PRACTICE BEING A MANAGER

The Makings of Motivation

Motivation is an invisible and powerful force. Strong motivation can drive individuals and organizations to remarkable heights of achievement. A loss of motivation can leave us dispirited and ineffective. One of the fundamental responsibilities of managers is to support healthy worker motivation. This exercise will allow you to practice designing support for worker motivation.

Step 1: Divide intro groups. Your professor will organize you in pairs or groups of three.

Step 2: Prepare interviews. Between this class session and the target date set by your professor, you and your partner(s) will each interview two individuals about motivation at work. You should brainstorm about possible types of work, interesting individuals, and so on, and then agree on each partner's list of interviewees/job holders.

Some considerations for brainstorming include jobs or types of work that you consider particularly interesting, appealing, or mysterious; jobs or types of work that you consider particularly uninteresting, dull, or monotonous (how does a person do that work day after day?); and self-employed or creative work (how do such workers manage their own motivation without a boss or supervisor?)

Step 3: Conduct interviews. Outside of class, students should complete their assigned interviews. Inform the potential interviewee that you are interested in talking about workplace motivation. Set a time that is convenient, and ensure that you arrive on time and prepared. Make the interview brief, with 15–20 minutes a good target. Go beyond 20 minutes only if the interviewee gives permission and the discussion is lively. Be sure to thank the interviewee for taking the time to visit with you.

Your instructor may give additional instructions for these interviews, and you should carefully follow these guidelines in conducting the interview.

Interview questions might include the following:

1. How would you describe your work? What are some of the things that you particularly like about your work?

2. We are currently studying the topic of motivation in one of my classes. What boosts your motivation at work? If you have ever experienced a period of low motivation, can you identify things that might have contributed to your losing steam in your work?

3. What kinds of rewards or incentives work best to motivate individuals and/or teams who do your type of work? What kinds of rewards or incentives don't work so well?

Step 4: Summarize your findings. Write a one-page paper summarizing your interview findings. Be prepared to compare notes with your partners and to contribute to class discussion.

Step 5: Debrief as a class. Pairs or small groups report their findings and discuss them as a class. What did you learn from your interviews? Did you notice common themes or issues across the interviews you conducted? Did you notice any striking differences across individuals or types of work? What are some possible implications of these interview findings for managers who are responsible for cultivating healthy motivation in a particular work setting?

DEVELOP YOUR CAREER POTENTIAL

Cut Your Costs, Not Your Morale

Management textbooks abound with discussions of the importance of honest and open communication when disseminating negative information to employees.[111] One study suggests that the best way to ruin morale and motivation is to spring bad news on employees without explaining the reasoning or rationale. Yet despite the need to maintain a high level of motivation and morale during a receding economy, many companies cut perks without communicating the need to their employees. During the high-tech boom at the end of the twentieth century, many companies implemented programs to increase productivity, motivation, and job satisfaction. Some of the perks provided were minor, such as free soft drinks, catered lunches, snacks, and tickets to events such as a baseball game or the opera. Other free perks were more extravagant, such as concierge services to run errands for employees, service their vehicles, and pick up their laundry. Some firms even provided their employees with in-house massages and annual Caribbean cruises. Obviously, cutting these non-value-added expenses can save tremendous money for a struggling firm. In fact, many firms cut out both the extravagant perks and the basics as a way to conserve much-needed cash. Cutting perks, however, doesn't have to be forever. Perks can be powerful motivational tools that companies can reintegrate into their performance reward systems.

For this assignment, consider your own budget and expenses in terms of revenue and perks. Imagine that like so many companies, you experience a cash crunch. Your revenue (income) shrinks 25 percent, so you must trim some fat from your budget.

Questions

1. First, you will need to review your expenditures. What "perks" have you built into your budget as a student? (Think pizza and beer.) Make a list of all your non-value-added expenses. This includes anything not directly related to your studies (like books, tuition, enrollment fees, pens, paper) or your fixed expenses (like rent, car payments, insurance).

2. If you experienced a 25 percent reduction in your income—as numerous firms did after the tech bubble burst—which perks would you eliminate? In addition, are there items that you previously considered necessities that you could cut out? An example would be selling your car (thereby eliminating car payments and related insurance) and taking public transportation or catching a ride with a friend. What about getting a roommate, moving into the dorms, or living with your parents?

3. Often employees develop a sense of entitlement about perks, and when the perks are trimmed, great dissatisfaction can result. Companies even lose employees when perks are cut. In this exercise, let's consider that cutting out your non-value-added (i.e., fun) expenditures may put a crimp in your social life. In fact, you may have trouble staying in the loop. What can you do to "retain" your

social friends as you cut down on your personal perks? Do you think that "retention" will even be an issue for you? Why or why not?

4. Once you have taken the axe to your perks, how can you reincorporate them into your budget, this time as motivational tools? Which perks would motivate you to have perfect attendance in class? To make an "A"? Straight "A's"? Be creative. The purpose is to see whether you can modify your own behavior by using your perks.

END NOTES

[1] Jessica Guynn "War Heats up for Top Silicon Valley Talent," *Los Angeles Times*, November 10, 2010, accessed May 23, 2011, from http://articles.latimes.com/2010/nov/10/business/la-fi-silicon-pay-war-20101111; D. Chow, "For SAS, Asia Presents Risks and Potential," *The Wall Street Journal*, November 21, 2010, accessed June 4, 2011, from http://online.wsj.com/article/SB10001424052748704170404575623952475539676.html; M. Hartley, "Business Software's 'Cadillac'; 'Tough Times are Good Times for Analytics,' SAS CEO Jim Goodnight Says," *Financial Post*, July 17, 2010, 3; D. Kaplan, "THE Best Company TO Work For," *Fortune*, February 8, 2010, 56–64; R. Lane, "Pampering the Customers, Pampering the Employees," *Forbes*, October 14, 1996, 74–80; S. Lohr, "SAS Tests Its Business Intelligence; Top Software Company Confronts New Threat from Heavyweight Rivals," *The International Herald Tribune*, November 23, 2009, 16; and A. Ricadeloa, "IBM vs. SAS: The Battle over Data Analysis Software," *Businessweek Online*, November 30, 2009), accessed June 4, 2011, from www.businessweek.com/technology/content/nov2009/tc20091129_192266.htm.

[2] T. Daniel & G. Metcalf, "Motivation: A Management Challenge," *T+D* 60 (November 2006): 11.

[3] J. P. Campbell & R. D. Pritchard, "Motivation Theory in Industrial and Organizational Psychology," in *Handbook of Industrial and Organizational Psychology*, M. D. Dunnette, ed. (Chicago: Rand McNally, 1976).

[4] D. Mattioli, "Rewards for Extra Work Come Cheap in Lean Times—With Raises and Promotions Scarce, Managers Are Generous With Low-Cost Incentives Like Thank-You Notes, Gift Cards," *The Wall Street Journal*, January 4, 2010, B7.

[5] J. Fried, "When the Only Way Up Is Out," *Inc.*, April 2011, 35–36.

[6] M. Kruse, "Can a Complete Novice become a Golf Pro with 10,000 Hours of Practice?" *St. Petersburg Times*, March 27, 2011, accessed May 31, 2011, from www.tampabay.com/features/can-a-complete-novice-become-a-golf-pro-with-10000-hours-of-practice/1159357.

[7] K. Ericsson, M. Prietula, & E. Cokely, "The Making of an Expert," *Harvard Business Review* (July–August 2007), accessed May 31, 2011, from http://hbr.org/2007/07/the-making-of-an-expert/ar/1.

[8] "The Plan," TheDanPlan.com, accessed May 31, 2011, from http://thedanplan.com/theplan.php.

[9] Amanda Greene, "9 Companies with the Best Perks," *Woman's Day*, April 26, 2010, accessed February 15, 2011, from www.womansday.com/Articles/Lifestyle/9-Companies-with-the-Best-Perks.html.

[10] E. A. Locke, "The Nature and Causes of Job Satisfaction," in *Handbook of Industrial and Organizational Psychology*, M. D. Dunnette, ed. (Chicago: Rand McNally, 1976).

[11] A. H. Maslow, "A Theory of Human Motivation," *Psychological Review* 50 (1943): 370–396.

[12] C. P. Alderfer, *Existence, Relatedness, and Growth: Human Needs in Organizational Settings* (New York: Free Press, 1972).

[13] D. C. McClelland, "Toward a Theory of Motive Acquisition," *American Psychologist* 20 (1965): 321–333; and D. C. McClelland & D. H. Burnham, "Power Is the Great Motivator," *Harvard Business Review* 54, no. 2 (1976): 100–110.

[14] J. H. Turner, "Entrepreneurial Environments and the Emergence of Achievement Motivation in Adolescent Males," *Sociometry* 33 (1970): 147–165.

[15] L. W. Porter, E. E. Lawler III, & J. R. Hackman, *Behavior in Organizations* (New York: McGraw-Hill, 1975).

[16] C. Ajila, "Maslow's Hierarchy of Needs Theory: Applicability to the Nigerian Industrial Setting," *IFE Psychology* (1997): 162–174.

[17] M. A. Wahba & L. B. Birdwell, "Maslow Reconsidered: A Review of Research on the Need Hierarchy Theory," *Organizational Behavior & Human Performance* 15 (1976): 212–240; and J. Rauschenberger, N. Schmitt, & J. E. Hunter, "A Test of the Need Hierarchy Concept by a Markov Model of Change in Need Strength," *Administrative Science Quarterly* 25 (1980): 654–670.

[18] E. E. Lawler III & L. W. Porter, "The Effect of Performance on Job Satisfaction," *Industrial Relations* 7 (1967): 20–28.

[19] Porter, Lawler, & Hackman, *Behavior in Organizations*.

[20] E. White, "Employers Increasingly Favor Bonuses to Raises," *The Wall Street Journal*, August 28, 2006, B3.

[21] Mike Rogoway, "Intel's Fourth-Quarter Sales Top Forecasts—Outlook Brighter Still," OregonLive.com. January 14, 2010, accessed August 29, 2010, from www.oregonlive.com/business/index.ssf/2010/01/intel_q4_numbers.html; and Mike Rogoway, "A Little More on Intel's New Bonuses," OregonLive.com., January 18, 2010, accessed August 29, 2010, from http://blog.oregonlive.com/siliconforest/2010/01/a_little_more_on_intels_new_bo.html.

[22]Porter, Lawler, & Hackman, *Behavior in Organizations*.

[23]J. Lublin, "Creative Compensation: A CEO Talks about His Company's Innovative Pay Ideas; Free Ice Cream, Anyone?" *The Wall Street Journal*, April 10, 2006, R6.

[24]J. Gibbs, "Atlassian Summit 2010 Highlights—FedEx Champions," Atlassian Blogs, accessed May 31, 2011, from http://blogs.atlassian.com/developer/fedex/.

[25]M. Cannon-Brookes, "Atlassian's 20% Time Experiment," Atlassian Blogs, March 10, 2008, accessed May 31, 2011, from http://blogs.atlassian.com/developer/2008/03/20_time_experiment.html; and RSA Vision, *Dan Pink—Drive*, video of a lecture by Daniel Pink at the Royal Society for the Encouragement of Arts, Manufacture, & Commerce, London, England, January 27, 2010, accessed July 29, 2010, from www.thersa.org/events/vision/vision-videos/dan-pink-drive.

[26]C. Caggiano, "What Do Workers Want?" *Inc.*, November 1992, 101–104; and "National Study of the Changing Workforce," Families & Work Institute, accessed May 31, 2005, from www.familiesandwork.org/summary/nscw.pdf.

[27]A. Brooks, "I LOVE my WORK," *American: A Magazine of Ideas* 6 (September–October 2007): 20–28.

[28]Anne Fisher "To Keep Employees Loyal, Try Asking What They Want," *Fortune*, January 27, 2011, accessed February 15, 2010, from http://management.fortune.cnn.com/2011/01/27/to-keep-employees-loyal-try-asking-what-they-want/.

[29]"America@Work: A Focus on Benefits and Compensation," Aon Consulting, accessed June 1, 2011, from www.aon.com/pdf/america/awork2.pdf [content no longer available online].

[30]Dolezalek, "Good Job!"

[31]J. Laabs, "Satisfy Them with More Than Money," *Personnel Journal* 77, no. 11 (1998): 40.

[32]R. Kanfer & P. Ackerman, "Aging, Adult Development, and Work Motivation," *Academy of Management Review* (2004): 440–458.

[33]E. White, "The New Recruits: Older Workers," *The Wall Street Journal*, January 14, 2008, B3.

[34]S. J. O'Malley, "Motivate the Middle: How Mid-Level Performance Can Bring Top Growth to the Bottom Line," *Bank Investment Consultant*, February 2007, 39.

[35]"Swiss Man Gets Record Fine," BBC News, January 7, 2010, accessed June 1, 2011, from http://news.bbc.co.uk/go/pr/fr/-/2/hi/europe/8446545.stm.

[36]"Swede Faces World-Record $1m Speeding Penalty," BBC News, August 12, 2010, accessed June 1, 2011, from www.bbc.co.uk/news/world-europe-10960230.

[37]S. Stecklow, "Fast Finns' Fines Fit Their Finances—Traffic Penalties Are Assessed According to Driver Income," *The Wall Street Journal*, January 2, 2001, A1.

[38]"Trends in CEO Pay," AFL-CIO, accessed August 11, 2011, from www.aflcio.org/corporatewatch/paywatch/pay/index.cfm; and "Employer Costs for Employee Compensation," Economic News Release, Bureau of Labor Statistics, June 9, 2010, accessed June 1, 2011, from www.bls.gov/news.release/ecec.nr0.htm.

[39]"CEO Pay: Average S&P 500 Chief Took Home $9.25 Million Last Year," Huffington Post, April 13, 2010, accessed February 15, 2010, from www.huffingtonpost.com/2010/04/13/ceo-pay-average-sp-500-ch_n_536113.html.

[40]Joann S. Lublin, "The Year's Top 10 Highest Paid CEOs," *The Wall Street Journal*, November 14, 2010, accessed June 2, 2011, from http://online.wsj.com/article/SB10001424052748704393960457561485219814427 6.html#project%3DSLIDESHOW08%26s%3DSB10001424052748704658204575610960521304890%26articleTabs%3Darticle.

[41]J. McGregor, "CEO Pay: Schwarzman Tops Corporate Library List," *Businessweek*, August 17, 2009, 10.

[42]Gil Rudawsky, "McDonald's CEO's $17 Million Pay Tied to Performance," DailyFinance, April 10, 2010, accessed February 15, 2010, from www.dailyfinance.com/story/mcdonalds-ceos-17-million-pay-tied-to-performance/19434075/.

[43]C. T. Kulik & M. L. Ambrose, "Personal and Situational Determinants of Referent Choice," *Academy of Management Review* 17 (1992): 212–237.

[44]World Bank, "GNI per Capita 2007, Atlas Method and PPP," [Online] accessed September 17, 2009, from http://siteresources.worldbank.org.

[45]J. S. Adams, "Toward an Understanding of Inequity," *Journal of Abnormal Social Psychology* 67 (1963): 422–436.

[46]J. Greenberg, "Employee Theft as a Reaction to Underpayment Inequity: The Hidden Costs of Pay Cuts," *Journal of Applied Psychology* 75 (1990): 561–568.

[47]R. A. Cosier & D. R. Dalton, "Equity Theory and Time: A Reformulation," *Academy of Management Review* 8 (1983): 311–319; and M. R. Carrell & J. E. Dittrich, "Equity Theory: The Recent Literature, Methodological Considerations, and New Directions," *Academy of Management Review* 3 (1978): 202–209.

[48]NBC News, "Ex-TSA Worker Charged with High-Tech Sabotage," MSNBC.com, March 10, 2010, accessed June 1, 2011, from www.msnbc.msn.com/id/35803009/ns/technology_and_science-security/t/ex-tsa-worker-charged-high-tech-sabotage/#.

[49]S. Dean, "Worker Accidentally Sends Sabotage E-mail to Boss who just Fired Her," *Houston Examiner*, 7 July 2009, accessed June 1, 2011, from www.examiner.com/page-one-in-houston/worker-accidentally-sends-sabotage-e-mail-to-boss-who-just-fired-her.

[50]"Anger at 30,000 Feet," *Fortune*, December 10, 2007, 32.

[51]M. Cimini, "Profile of the American Airlines' Pilot Sickout," *Compensation and Working Conditions* (Winter 1999): 21–26.

[52]J. Bendich, "When Is a Temp Not a Temp?" *Trial Magazine*, October 1, 2001, 42.

[53]U.S. Department of Labor, "2002 Statistics Fact Sheet: Back Wages for Fair Labor Standards Act Violations Increased by 29%," accessed March 25, 2009, from www.dol.gov/esa/whd/statistics/200212.htm; and M. Orey, "Lawsuits Abound from Workers Seeking Overtime Pay," *The Wall Street Journal*, May 30, 2002, B1.

[54]K. Maher, "Workers Are Filing More Lawsuits against Employers over Wages," *The Wall Street Journal*, June 5, 2006, A2.

[55]N. Maestri, "Supreme Court Lets Stand $36 Million Family Dollar Ruling," *Reuters.com*, October 5, 2009, accessed June 1, 2011, from www .reuters.com/article/domesticNews/ idUSTRE59447W20091005; and R. Montaigne, "Court Rejects Family Dollar Case; Store to Pay Up," *Morning Edition*, National Public Radio, October 6, 2009.

[56]C. Chen, J. Choi, & S. Chi, "Making Justice Sense of Local-Expatriate Compensation Disparity: Mitigation by Local Referents, Ideological Explanations, and Interpersonal Sensitivity in China-Foreign Joint Ventures," *Academy of Management Journal* (2002): 807–817.

[57]K. Aquino, R. W. Griffeth, D. G. Allen, & P. W. Hom, "Integrating Justice Constructs into the Turnover Process: A Test of a Referent Cognitions Model," *Academy of Management Journal* 40, no. 5 (1997): 1208–1227.

[58]S. Barr, "While the SEC Watches the Markets, the Job Market Is Draining the SEC," *The Washington Post*, March 10, 2002, C3.

[59]S. Needleman, "Burger Chain's Health-Care Recipe—Paying More for Insurance Cuts Turnover, Boosts Sales and Productivity," *The Wall Street Journal*, August 31, 2009, B4.

[60]D. Gullapalli, "Take This Job and . . . File It—Burdened by Extra Work Created by the Sarbanes-Oxley Act, CPAs Leave the Big Four for Better Life," *The Wall Street Journal*, May 4, 2005, C1.

[61]R. Folger & M. A. Konovsky, "Effects of Procedural and Distributive Justice on Reactions to Pay Raise Decisions," *Academy of Management Journal* 32 (1989): 115–130; and M. A. Konovsky, "Understanding Procedural Justice and Its Impact on Business Organizations," *Journal of Management* 26 (2000): 489–512.

[62]E. Barret-Howard & T. R. Tyler, "Procedural Justice as a Criterion in Allocation Decisions," *Journal of Personality & Social Psychology* 50 (1986): 296–305; and Folger & Konovsky, "Effects of Procedural and Distributive Justice on Reactions to Pay Raise Decisions."

[63]R. Folger & J. Greenberg, "Procedural Justice: An Interpretive Analysis of Personnel Systems," in *Research in Personnel and Human Resources Management*, vol. 3, K. Rowland & G. Ferris, eds. (Greenwich, CT: JAI, 1985); R. Folger, D. Rosenfield, J. Grove, & L. Corkran, "Effects of 'Voice' and Peer Opinions on Responses to Inequity," *Journal of Personality & Social Psychology* 37 (1979): 2253–2261; E. A. Lind & T. R. Tyler, *The Social Psychology of Procedural Justice* (New York: Plenum, 1988); and Konovsky, "Understanding Procedural Justice and Its Impact on Business Organizations."

[64]Nadine Heintz, "Building a Culture of Employee Appreciation," Inc, September 1, 2009, accessed November 4, 2010, from www.inc.com/magazine/20090901/building-a-culture-of-employee-appreciation.html.

[65]R. J. Bies & J. S. Moag, "Interactional Justice: Communication Criteria for Fairness," in *Research on Negotiation in Organizations*, R. J. Lewicki, B. H. Sheppard, & M. Bazerman, eds. (Greenwich, CT: JAI, 1986), 43–55.

[66]J. A. Colquitt, "On the Dimensionality of Organizational Justice: A Construct Validation of a Measure," *Journal of Applied Psychology* (2001: 86), 386–400; and J. A. Colquitt, D. E. Conlon, M. J. Wesson, C. Porter, & K. Yee Ng, "Justice at the Millennium: A Meta-Analytic Review of 25 Years of Organizational Justice Research," *Journal of Applied Psychology*, 86, 425–445.

[67]K. A. Dolan, "When Money Isn't Enough," *Forbes*, November 18, 1996, 164–170.

[68]V. H. Vroom, *Work and Motivation* (New York: John Wiley & Sons, 1964); and L. W. Porter & E. E. Lawler III, *Managerial Attitudes and Performance* (Homewood, IL: Dorsey & Richard D. Irwin, 1968).

[69]J. Galante, "Another Day, Another Virtual Dollar," *Bloomberg Businessweek*, June 21–27, 2010, 43–44.

[70]M. Polanco, "The Mill That Gives and Takes: Dedicated to the Job, Despite Heat, Dust and Danger," *The Hartford Courant*, January 29, 2007; G. P. Smith, "How Nucor Steel Rewards Performance and Productivity," ManagerWise.com, March 19, 2007, accessed June 1, 2011, from www..managerwise.com/article.phtml?id=172; C. Carpenter & M. Song, "Steel Is Beginning to Collect Rust in Stock Market," Bloomberg.com, March 25, 2007, accessed June 1, 2011, from www.bloomberg.com/apps/news?pid=20601109&refer=home&sid=avJsya9w6v84; and www.nucorfastener.com.

[71]S. Miller, "Countering the Employee Recognition Gap," SHRM Library, Society for Human Resource Management, February 2006, accessed March 25, 2009, from www.shrm.org.

[72]P. V. LeBlanc & P. W. Mulvey, "How American Workers See the Rewards of Work," *Compensation & Benefits Review* 30 (February 1998): 24–28.

[73]A. Fox, "Companies Can Benefit When They Disclose Pay Processes to Employees," *HR Magazine*, July 2002, 25.

[74]Joel Spolsky, "Why I Never Let Employees Negotiate a Raise," Inc.com, April 1, 2009, accessed February 15, 2010, from www.inc.com/magazine/20090401/how-hard-could-it-be-employees-negotiate-pay-raises.html.

[75]K. W. Thomas & B. A. Velthouse, "Cognitive Elements of Empowerment," *Academy of Management Review* 15 (1990): 666–681.

[76]J. Sandberg, "Been Here 25 Years and All I Got Was This Lousy T-Shirt," *The Wall Street Journal*, January 28, 2004, B1.

[77]C. Hymowitz, "When Meeting Targets Becomes the Strategy, CEO Is on Wrong Path," *The Wall Street Journal*, March 8, 2005, A8.

[78]E. L. Thorndike, *Animal Intelligence* (New York: Macmillan, 1911).

[79]S. Nassauer, "Now at Hotels: The $250 Cigarette; Major Chains Get Tough with Fines for Smoking; Busted for Butts in the Trash," *The Wall Street Journal*, February 21, 2008, D1.

[80]B. F. Skinner, *Science and Human Behavior* (New York: Macmillan, 1954); B. F. Skinner, *Beyond Freedom and Dignity* (New York: Bantam, 1971); and B. F. Skinner, *A Matter of Consequences* (New York: New York University Press, 1984).

[81]A. M. Dickinson & A. D. Poling, "Schedules of Monetary Reinforcement in Organizational Behavior

Management: Latham and Huber Revisited," *Journal of Organizational Behavior Management* 16, no. 1 (1992): 71–91.

[82]Valeirie Bauerlein, "PepsiCo Plans Recycling Initiative," *The Wall Street Journal*, April 22, 2010, accessed August 23, 2010, from http://online.wsj.com/article/NA_WSJ_PUB:SB100014240527487034040045751 98390481890492.html.

[83]L. Welch, "The Way I Work: Paul English of Kayak," *Inc.*, February 1, 2010, accessed June 2, 2011, from www.inc.com/magazine/20100201/the-way-i-work-paul-english-of-kayak.html.

[84]D. Grote, "Manager's Journal: Discipline without Punishment," *The Wall Street Journal*, 23 May 1994, A14.

[85]Hiroki Tabuchi, "After Tough Year, Pay Cuts and Forfeited Bonuses for Top Toyota Executives," *The New York Time*, June 24, 2010, accessed June 2, 2011, from www.nytimes.com/2010/06/25/business/global/25toyota.html?ref=akiotoyod.

[86]P. Dvorak, "Poor Year Doesn't Stop CEO Bonuses—Some Boards Use Discretion to Reward Top Executives Amid Signs Compensation Generally Fell in 2008," *The Wall Street Journal*, March 18, 2009, B1.

[87]E. Pedalino & V. U. Gamboa, "Behavior Modification and Absenteeism: Intervention in One Industrial Setting," *Journal of Applied Psychology* 59 (1974): 694–698.

[88]John R. Ryan, "Keeping Employees Happy in a Post-Recession World," *Bloomberg Businessweek*, August 31, 2010, accessed October 20, 2010, from www.businessweek.com/managing/content/aug2010/ca20100831_786655.htm.

[89]C. Cole, "Retooling Absentee Programs Bolsters Profits," *Workforce Management*, September 2002, accessed March 25, 2009, from www.workforce.com/section/09/feature/23/31/64.

[90]J. B. Miner, *Theories of Organizational Behavior* (Hinsdale, IL: Dryden, 1980).

[91]Dickinson & Poling, "Schedules of Monetary Reinforcement in Organizational Behavior Management."

[92]F. Luthans & A. D. Stajkovic, "Reinforce for Performance: The Need to

Go beyond Pay and Even Rewards," *Academy of Management Executive* 13, no. 2 (1999): 49–57.

[93]D. Anderson, *Up Your Business! 7 Steps to Fix, Build or Stretch Your Organization* (New York: Wiley, 2003).

[94]K. D. Butterfield, L. K. Trevino, & G. A. Ball, "Punishment from the Manager's Perspective: A Grounded Investigation and Inductive Model," *Academy of Management Journal* 39 (1996): 1479–1512.

[95]R. D. Arvey & J. M. Ivancevich, "Punishment in Organizations: A Review, Propositions, and Research Suggestions," *Academy of Management Review* 5 (1980): 123–132.

[96]R. D. Arvey, G. A. Davis, & S. M. Nelson, "Use of Discipline in an Organization: A Field Study," *Journal of Applied Psychology* 69 (1984): 448–460; and M. E. Schnake, "Vicarious Punishment in a Work Setting," *Journal of Applied Psychology* 71 (1986): 343–345.

[97]A. D. Stajkovic & F. Luthans, "A Meta-Analysis of the Effects of Organizational Behavior Modification on Task Performance, 1975–95," *Academy of Management Journal* 40, no. 5 (1997): 1122–1149; and A. D. Stajkovic & F. Luthans, "Behavioral Management and Task Performance in Organizations: Conceptual Background, Meta-Analysis, and Test of Alternative Models," *Personnel Psychology* 56, no. 1 (2003): 155–194.

[98]G. A. Yukl & G. P. Latham, "Consequences of Reinforcement Schedules and Incentive Magnitudes for Employee Performance: Problems Encountered in a Field Setting," *Journal of Applied Psychology* 60 (1975): 294–298.

[99]V. Harnish, "Five Ways to Get your Strategy Right," *Fortune*, April 11, 2011, 23.

[100]E. A. Locke & G. P. Latham, *Goal Setting: A Motivational Technique That Works* (Englewood Cliffs, NJ: Prentice-Hall, 1984); and E. A. Locke & G. P. Latham, *A Theory of Goal Setting and Task Performance* (Englewood Cliffs, NJ: Prentice-Hall, 1990).

[101]"Franchising—In with the New: As More Boomers Retire, Franchisers Set Their Sights on a Much Younger Crowd," *The Wall Street Journal*, September 28, 2009, R9.

[102]V. O'Connell, "Retailers Reprogram Workers in Efficiency Push," *The Wall Street Journal*, September 10, 2008, A1

[103]Ibid.

[104]G. P. Latham & E. A. Locke, "Goal Setting—A Motivational Technique That Works," *Organizational Dynamics* 8, no. 2 (1979): 68.

[105]Ibid.

[106]Z. Zhiwei, J. A. Wallin, & R. A. Reber, "Safety Improvements: An Application of Behaviour Modification Techniques," *Journal of Applied Management Studies* 15 (2000): 135–140.

[107]C. A. Arnolds & C. Boshoff, "Compensation, Esteem Valence, and Job Performance: An Empirical Assessment of Alderfer's ERG Theory," *International Journal of Human Resource Management* 13, no. 4 (2002): 697–719.

[108]Maslow, "A Theory of Human Motivation."

[109]Evan Ramstad & Jaeyeon Woo, "South Korea Works Overtime To Tackle Vacation Shortage," *The Wall Street Journal*, March 1, 2010, A1, 22.

[110]Eric Spitznagel, "Fantasy Football: The New Internet Porn," *Bloomberg Businessweek*, September 9, 2010, accessed February 18, 2010, from www.businessweek.com/magazine/content/10_38/b4195081511463.htm; Derek Thompson, "Fantasy Football is Not Sacking Productivity," *The Atlantic*, February 18, 2011, accessed February 18, 2011, from www.theatlantic.com/business/archive/2010/09/study-fantasy-football-is-not-sacking-productivity/63854/; and Henry Unger, "New Survey: Fantasy Football Does Not Sack Workplace Productivity," *Atlanta Journal Constitution*, September 30, 2010, accessed February 18, 2010, from http://blogs.ajc.com/business-beat/2010/09/30/new-survey-fantasy-football-not-sacking-workplace-productivity/.

[111]M. Boyle, "How to Cut Perks without Killing Morale," *Fortune*, February 19, 2001; and T. Pollock, "Managing for Better Morale," Automotive Manufacturing & Production, February 2001, accessed June 1, 2011, from www.autofieldguide.com.

BIZ FLIX

Friday Night Lights

In the small town of Odessa, Texas, everyone lives for Friday nights, when the high school football team, the Permian Panthers, takes the field. The town is proud of their Panthers, led by quarterback Mike Winchell (Lucas Black) and superstar tailback Boobie Miles (Derek Luke), and they're used to winning. They expect a state championship—and nothing less. When Boobie suffers a career-ending injury in the first game of the season, the team isn't sure they can win without him. But Coach Gary Gaines (Billy Bob Thornton) isn't ready to give up yet. In this scene, Coach visits the home of his QB Mike Winchell and tries to motivate him, even though it seems like all hope for the Panthers is lost.

© GreenLight

What to Watch for and Ask Yourself

1. This chapter defines motivation as "the set of forces that initiates, directs, and makes people persist in their efforts to accomplish a goal." Does Mike Winchell show the characteristics of this definition early in the sequence? Do you expect him to show any of the characteristics after the sequence ends and he returns to the team?

2. How does Coach Gaines try to motivate his QB? Do you think his approach is effective?

3. Apply the various parts of goal-setting theory to this sequence. Which parts of that theory appear in the sequence?

MANAGEMENT WORKPLACE

LivingSocial Escapes: Motivating Employees

LivingSocial Escapes, which offers a range of outdoor excursions, demands high commitment from employees. When hiring new workers, founder BramLevy offers only the most basic outline of job responsibilities. "Think about the brand and what we're trying to develop," Levy tells new recruits. "Now take it and formulate what you think will be best and run with it." The employees must then come up with creative ideas, and execute them. Though demanding, this approach to motivation has great benefits for employees, since employees can share in the financial rewards—even part time guides get special bonuses if trips are profitable.

© Cengage Learning

Discussion Questions

1. Which needs in Maslow's hierarchy are most important to the employees who work for LivingSocial Escapes, and how can managers use this information to develop a highly motivated workforce?

2. According to equity theory, how might a LivingSocial Escapes guide react if he or she feels underpaid or unappreciated?

3. What outcomes or rewards possess high valence for managers and guides who work at LivingSocial Escapes?

CHAPTER 14

Leadership

Learning Outcomes

1. Explain what leadership is.
2. Describe who leaders are and what effective leaders do.
3. Explain Fiedler's contingency theory.
4. Describe how path–goal theory works.
5. Discuss Hersey and Blanchard's Situational Leadership theory.
6. Explain the normative decision theory.
7. Explain how visionary leadership (i.e., charismatic and transformational leadership) helps leaders achieve strategic leadership.

what would **you do?**

Apple Headquarters, Cupertino, California[1]

CEO and cofounder Steve Jobs is synonymous with Apple. Fired from Apple in 1985, Jobs founded NeXT Computer, bought the Graphics Group from Lucasfilm, and transformed it into Pixar Studios, and then returned to Apple as CEO in 1995. In his absence, Apple lost billions and its share of the personal computer market dropped from 9 percent to 2 percent. Jobs saved Apple by procuring a $150 million investment from Bill Gates and Microsoft, and launching the iMac, a desktop machine that became one of Apple's leading sellers. Most importantly, though, Jobs directed the development of Apple's new operating system, OS X, an operating system that is speedy, simple to use, incredibly stable, and easy to write software for. OS X, in combination with easy-to-use software for film and picture editing, desktop publishing, presentations, and word processing, stabilized Apple's sales and market share, and put it in a financial position to eventually create the iPod, the iPhone, the iPad, and now iCloud. Today, Apple's 10 percent share of the personal computer market is growing, it has a large market share in smart phones, and a commanding market share in tablets and digital music. Furthermore, its combined stock value is greater than Intel and Microsoft combined.

Jobs was known for his highly demanding and influential leadership at Apple. When Apple's MobileMe service (which synchronized calendar and email and files across Macs, iPhones, and corporate networks) launched to terrible reviews and buggy performance, he berated the MobileMe team, telling them, "You've tarnished Apple's reputation. You should hate each other for having let each other down." He named a replacement manager on the spot. Jobs was also famous for saying "no." A former Apple executive says, "Over and over Steve talks about the power of picking the things you don't do." Jobs once said, "We're always thinking about new markets we could enter. But it's only by saying no . . . that you can concentrate on the things that are really important." Yet, despite his toughness and discipline, Jobs was able to inspire Apple's managers, software engineers, and designers to create elegant, simple, innovative products. Jeff Robbin, Apple's lead software designer for iTunes and the iPod said, "I remember sitting with Steve and some other people night after night from nine until one, working out the user interface for the first iPod. It evolved by trial and error into something a little simpler every day. We knew we had reached the end when we looked at each other and said, 'Well, of course. Why would we want to do it any other way?'"

Apple's future is bright, but Jobs' health was a long-term concern. In 2004 and 2009, he took medical leaves due to pancreatic cancer, a liver transplant, and an inability to maintain weight.

© Luay Bahoora/Alamy

study tips

Your professor and TA are the most valuable resources in your course. If you have questions on the fundamental concepts of leadership, visit them during office hours.

© iStockphoto.com/Alex Slobodkin

© iStockphoto.com/Ivan Burmistrov

In January 2011, he announced his third medical leave, telling Apple's 50,000 employees, "I love Apple so much and hope to be back as soon as I can. In the meantime, my family and I would deeply appreciate respect for our privacy." In October 2011, Jobs died, one month after handing the CEO job to long-time COO, Tim Cook.

Jobs' charismatic leadership was clearly central to Apple's success. But can Apple succeed without him? What steps should Apple take to increase its chances of continued success without Jobs as CEO? Are there ways to substitute for Jobs' leadership at Apple? Next, is Tim Cook the right leader to replace Jobs? Jobs was demanding, creative, and controlling. Cook is not. Should Tim Cook try to emulate Jobs or should he run Apple using a different leadership style? Should Cook focus more on managing or leading Apple? Finally, Jobs was at the center of all of Apple's key decisions over the last decade and a half. Jez Frampton, group CEO of Interbrand says, "Now the worry is the organization has to rewire itself and learn how to make decisions on its own." Should Apple become more participative, involving more managers and employees, or continue to use Jobs centralized approach to decision making, which was less participative and highly influenced by the founder and former CEO?

If you were in charge at Apple, what would you do?

If you've ever been in charge, or even just thought about it, chances are you've considered questions like these: Do I have what it takes to lead? What are the most important things leaders do? How can I transform a poorly performing department, division, or company? Do I need to adjust my leadership depending on the situation and the employee? Why doesn't my leadership inspire people? If you feel overwhelmed at the prospect of being a leader, you're not alone—millions of leaders in organizations across the world struggle with these fundamental leadership issues on a daily basis.

We begin this chapter by discussing what leadership is, who leaders are (meaning their traits and characteristics), and what leaders do that makes them different from people who aren't leaders. Next we examine four major contingency theories of leadership that specify which leaders are best suited for which situations or how leaders should change their behavior to lead different people in different circumstances. The chapter ends with a review of strategic leadership issues, such as charismatic and transformational leadership, which address how to work with others to meet long-term goals and how to create a viable future for an organization.

What Is Leadership?

How does an ensemble of 100 or more musicians, all playing different parts at different times on different instruments, manage to produce something as beautiful as Beethoven's Fifth Symphony? (Or, if Gustav Mahler's "Symphony of a Thousand" is on the program, a lot more people might be involved!) The conductor, like a CEO, is responsible for managing all of this complexity and ensuring a great performance. But conductors do much more than just keep the beat with a baton. According to Ramona Wis, author of *The Conductor as*

After reading the next two sections, you should be able to

1. *Explain what leadership is.*
2. *Describe who leaders are and what effective leaders do.*

Leader: Principles of Leadership Applied to Life on the Podium, conductors must also build connections between people, inspire them with vision, command their trust, and persuade them to participate in the ensemble at their very best.

Whether the end result is a stirring musical performance, innovation of new products, or increased profits, **leadership** is the process of influencing others to achieve group or organizational goals. The knowledge and skills you'll learn in this chapter won't make the task of leadership less daunting, but they will help you navigate it.

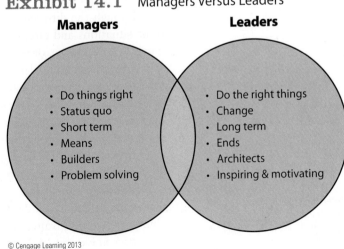

1 Leadership

In Chapter 1, we defined *management* as getting work done through others. In other words, managers don't do the work themselves. Managers help others do their jobs better. By contrast, *leadership* is the process of influencing others to achieve group or organizational goals. What, then, are the key differences between leaders and managers? Another question that gets at the nature of leadership is this: Is leadership required in every situation? Does leadership always matter? Or are there situations when leadership isn't needed or may even make things worse?

Let's learn more about leadership by exploring **1.1 the differences between leaders and managers** and **1.2 substitutes for leadership**.

1.1 Leaders Versus Managers

According to University of Southern California business professor Warren Bennis, the primary difference between leaders and managers, as shown in Exhibit 14.1, is that leaders are concerned with doing the right thing, whereas managers are concerned with doing things right.[2] In other words, leaders begin with the question "What should we be doing?" whereas managers start with "How can we do what we're already doing better?" Leaders focus on vision, mission, goals, and objectives, whereas managers focus on productivity and efficiency. Managers see themselves as preservers of the status quo, whereas leaders see themselves as promoters of change and challengers of the status quo in that they encourage creativity and risk taking. At **Maddock Douglas**, an Elmhurst, Illinois, firm that helps companies develop new products, President Louis Viton leads by encouraging creativity and risk taking with an annual "Fail Forward" award for ambitious ideas that end in disaster—even if they end up costing the company huge amounts of money. Viton says the latest "Fail Forward" winner produced "a new product design that was a total embarrassment. . . . But she was trying to do something new and different and better. She went for it, and she won an award for it."[3]

Another difference is that managers have a relatively short-term perspective, whereas leaders take a long-term view. Managers are concerned with control and limiting the choices of others, whereas leaders are more concerned with expanding people's choices and options.[4] Managers also solve problems so that others can do their work, whereas leaders inspire and motivate others to find their own solutions.

leadership the process of influencing others to achieve group or organizational goals.

< **"what's new" companies**

Exhibit 14.1 Managers Versus Leaders

Managers	Leaders
• Do things right	• Do the right things
• Status quo	• Change
• Short term	• Long term
• Means	• Ends
• Builders	• Architects
• Problem solving	• Inspiring & motivating

© Cengage Learning 2013

575

Finally, managers are also more concerned with *means*, how to get things done, whereas leaders are more concerned with *ends*, what gets done. When Ed Whitacre, formerly CEO of AT&T, was named cochairman of General Motors Board of Directors after it filed for bankruptcy, he said, "We're going to get this turned around. [And if current leadership can't fix the company] we'll find someone who can." Five months later, Whitacre and GM's board fired CEO Fritz Henderson, who had spent his entire career at the company. When the board asked Whitacre to take the reins, he accepted. In his first three months as CEO, he got rid of four top executives, moved 20 others into new positions, and brought in seven executives from outside of GM. Whitacre, who met just once per week with the new management team, evaluated their performance in six ways: market share, revenue, operating profit, cash flow, quality, and customer satisfaction.[5]

Although leaders are different from managers, organizations need them both. Managers are critical to getting out the day-to-day work, and leaders are critical to inspiring employees and setting the organization's long-term direction. The key issue for any organization is the extent to which it is properly led and properly managed. As Warren Bennis said in summing up the difference between leaders and managers, "American organizations (and probably those in much of the rest of the industrialized world) are under led and overmanaged. They do not pay enough attention to doing the right thing, while they pay too much attention to doing things right."[6]

1.2 Substitutes for Leadership: Do Leaders Always Matter?

One of the basic assumptions about leadership is that leaders always matter. According to this thinking, organizations are sure to fail without sound leadership. For example, as discussed in the opening case, when Apple CEO Steve Jobs took extended medical leaves and then died, journalists and investors worried that the company would suffer without its visionary leader. Donald Luskin, an investment officer with TrendMacro, said, "From the beginning, Apple has flourished when Jobs was present and declined when he was absent."[7] Other investment experts countered that Apple had enough resources and strategic momentum to flourish in the short term, but worried that any long-term absence of Jobs would jeopardize the company. Anthony Sabino, a professor of law and business at St. Johns University, noted that "Near-term effects will be small, but four quarters from now, investors will need to see that Apple remains on a successful strategic path." Still, others felt that Apple could succeed without Jobs. Stanford business professor Jeffrey Pfeffer said that new CEO Tim Cook, "Doesn't need to be Steve Jobs—he needs to be the best Tim Cook he can be.[8]

Although the difference that Steve Jobs made at Apple is inarguable, there are some situations and circumstances where leadership isn't necessary, likely to make much of a difference, or to blame for poor performance. These are known as leadership substitutes and leadership neutralizers.[9] Exhibit 14.2 lists a number of subordinate, task, or organizational characteristics that can act as leadership substitutes or neutralizers (some can act as both) for either people-related or task-related leader behaviors. Leaders' people-related behaviors—such as being approachable, supportive, or showing concern for employees—affect how satisfied people are with their jobs. Leaders' task-related behaviors—such as setting goals, giving directions, and providing resources—affect the extent to which people are able to perform their jobs well.

Leadership substitutes are subordinate, task, or organizational characteristics that make leaders redundant or unnecessary. For instance, when subordinates have ability, experience, training, and knowledge about their jobs (see subordinate characteristics in Exhibit 14.2), a subordinate's work performance is unlikely to improve

leadership substitutes subordinate, task, or organizational characteristics that make leaders redundant or unnecessary.

Exhibit 14.2   Leadership Substitutes and Neutralizers

Characteristics	People-Related Leadership Behaviors	Task-Related Leadership Behaviors
SUBORDINATE		
• Ability, experience, training, knowledge	Neutralize	Substitute, Neutralize
• Need for independence	Neutralize	Neutralize
• Professional orientation	Substitute, Neutralize	Substitute, Neutralize
• Indifference toward organizational rewards	Neutralize	Neutralize
TASK		
• Unambiguous and routine tasks	No effect	Substitute, Neutralize
• Performance feedback provided by the work itself	No effect	Substitute, Neutralize
• Intrinsically satisfying work	Substitute, Neutralize	Neutralize
ORGANIZATIONAL		
• Formalization, meaning specific plans, goals, and areas of responsibility	No effect	Neutralize
• Inflexibility, meaning rigid, unbending rules and procedures	No effect	Neutralize
• Highly specified staff functions	No effect	Neutralize
• Cohesive work groups	Substitute, Neutralize	Substitute, Neutralize
• Organizational rewards beyond a leader's control	Neutralize	Neutralize control
• Spatial distance between supervisors and subordinates	Neutralize	Neutralize

Source: S. Kerr & J. M. Jermier, "Substitutes for Leadership: Their Meaning and Measurement," *Organizational Behavior and Human Performance* 22 (1978): 375–403.

under task-related leader behavior that specifies goals, task assignments, and how to do the job. Think about it. Workers already have the capability to do their jobs. And the job itself provides enough information to let them know how well they're doing or what they might do to correct performance problems. In situations like this, where leadership substitutes are strong, leaders don't need to tell workers what to do or how to do their jobs.

Leadership neutralizers are subordinate, task, or organizational characteristics that can interfere with a leader's actions or make it impossible for a leader to influence followers' performance. Unlike substitutes, which simply take the place of leaders, leadership neutralizers create an "influence vacuum." In other words, leadership neutralizers actually create a need for leadership by preventing leadership from working. For example, when subordinates are indifferent toward organizational rewards (see subordinate characteristics in Exhibit 14.2), there may be nothing that a leader can do to reward them for good performance. Likewise, inflexible rules and procedures (see organizational characteristics in Exhibit 14.2) effectively neutralize the ability of leaders to reward workers. Such procedures include things like union contracts specifying that all employees be paid the same, organizational policies that reward employees by seniority, and salary and raise processes that don't give leaders enough money to substantially reward good performers.

Spatial distance (see organizational characteristics in Exhibit 14.2) can also neutralize leadership. Spatial distance arises when supervisors and subordinates don't work in the same place. This happens when people telecommute or work thousands of miles away in overseas offices. Spatial distance typically results in infrequent feedback, little or no face-to-face contact, and being "out of sight and out of mind," all of which make it very difficult for leaders to lead. Rieva Lesonsky, a small business consultant, says, "It's a loss of control thing for them." There are, however, a number of ways to address the challenges that spatial distance presents. Because managers

leadership neutralizers subordinate, task, or organizational characteristics that can interfere with a leader's actions or make it impossible for a leader to influence followers' performance.

often worry that employees who aren't in the office aren't getting work done, Lesonsky suggests giving new employees a probationary period. "Until you get more comfortable with having a disparate workforce, offer the ability to work from home one day a week or three days a month. [Then] see if there are any glitches," says Ms. Lesonsky. James Sinclair, CEO of Onsite Consulting, turned the management of his 65 employees to team leaders who, in turn, only supervise five or six workers. With a smaller number of people to manage, it's easier at a distance for each team leader to keep track of how well daily and weekly tasks are getting done.[10] Because of these challenges, some companies find telecommuting to be so disruptive to leadership processes that they require their telecommuters to come into the office at least once or twice a week.

So do leaders *always* matter? Leadership substitutes and neutralizers indicate that sometimes they don't. This doesn't mean that leaders never matter, though. Quite the opposite. Leaders do matter, but they're not superhuman. They can't do it all by themselves. And they can't fix every situation. In short, leadership is very important. But poor leadership isn't the cause of every organizational crisis, and changing leaders isn't the solution to every company problem.

Review 1

Leadership   Leadership is the process of influencing others to achieve group or organizational goals. Leaders are different from managers. The primary difference is that leaders are concerned with doing the right thing, whereas managers are concerned with doing things right. Furthermore, managers have a short-term focus and are concerned with the status quo, with means rather than ends, and with solving others' problems. By contrast, leaders have a long-term focus and are concerned with change, with ends rather than means, and with inspiring and motivating others to solve their own problems. Organizations need both managers and leaders. But in general, companies are overmanaged and under led. Although leadership is important, leadership substitutes and neutralizers create situations in which leadership isn't necessary or is unlikely to make much of a difference. Leadership substitutes are subordinate, task, or organizational characteristics that make leaders redundant or unnecessary. By contrast, leadership neutralizers are subordinate, task, or organizational characteristics that interfere with a leader's actions or make it impossible for a leader to influence followers' performance.

2 Who Leaders Are and What Leaders Do

Indra Nooyi, PepsiCo's CEO, talks straight, has a sharp sense of humor, and sings in the hallways wherever she is. Nooyi is an extrovert. By contrast, JC Penney's CEO, Mike Ullman, who is soft-spoken and easy to approach, is an introvert.[11] Which one is likely to be successful as a CEO? According to a survey of 1,542 senior managers, it's the extrovert. Forty-seven percent of those 1,542 senior managers felt that extroverts make better CEOs, whereas 65 percent said that being an introvert hurts a CEO's chances of success.[12] So clearly, senior managers believe that extroverted CEOs are better leaders. But are they? Not necessarily. In fact, a relatively high percentage of CEOs, 40 percent, are introverts. Sara Lee CEO Brenda Barnes says, "I've always been shy. . . . People wouldn't call me that [an introvert], but I am."[13] Indeed, Barnes turns down all speaking requests and rarely gives interviews.

So, what makes a good leader? Does leadership success depend on who leaders are, such as introverts or extroverts, or on what leaders do and how they behave?

Let's learn more about who leaders are by investigating **2.1 leadership traits** and **2.2 leadership behaviors**.

2.1 Leadership Traits

Trait theory is one way to describe who leaders are. **Trait theory** says that effective leaders possess a similar set of traits or characteristics. **Traits** are relatively stable characteristics such as abilities, psychological motives, or consistent patterns of behavior. For example, trait theory holds that leaders are taller and more confident and have greater physical stamina (i.e., higher energy levels) than nonleaders. Indeed, while just 14.5 percent of men are 6 feet tall, 58 percent of *Fortune* 500 CEOs are 6 feet or taller.[14] Author Malcolm Gladwell says, "We have this sense of what a leader is supposed to look like. And that stereotype is so powerful that when someone fits it, we simply become blind to other considerations."[15] Trait theory is also known as the "great person" theory because early versions of the theory stated that leaders are born, not made. In other words, you either have the right stuff to be a leader, or you don't. And if you don't, there is no way to get it.

For some time, it was thought that trait theory was wrong and that there are no consistent trait differences between leaders and nonleaders, or between effective and ineffective leaders. However, more recent evidence shows that "successful leaders are not like other people," that successful leaders are indeed different from the rest of us.[16] More specifically, as shown in Exhibit 14.3, leaders are different from nonleaders in the following traits: drive, the desire to lead, honesty/integrity, self-confidence, emotional stability, cognitive ability, and knowledge of the business.[17]

Drive refers to high levels of effort and is characterized by achievement, motivation, initiative, energy, and tenacity. In terms of achievement and ambition, leaders always try to make improvements or achieve success in what they're doing. Because of their initiative, they have strong desires to promote change or solve problems. Leaders typically have more energy—they have to, given the long hours they put in and followers' expectations that they be positive and upbeat. Thus, leaders must have physical, mental, and emotional vitality. Leaders are also more tenacious than nonleaders and are better at overcoming obstacles and problems that would deter most of us.

Successful leaders also have a stronger *desire to lead*. They want to be in charge and think about ways to influence or convince others about what should or shouldn't be done. *Honesty/integrity* is also important to leaders. *Honesty*, being truthful with others, is a cornerstone of leadership. Without it, leaders won't be trusted. When leaders are honest, subordinates are willing to overlook other flaws. For example, one follower said this about the leadership qualities of his manager: "I don't like a lot of the things he does, but he's basically honest. He's a genuine article, and you'll forgive a lot of things because of that. That goes a long way in how much I trust him."[18] *Integrity* is the extent to which leaders do what they say they will do. Leaders may be honest and have good intentions, but if they don't consistently deliver on what they promise, they won't be trusted.

Self-confidence, or believing in one's abilities, also distinguishes leaders from nonleaders. Self-confident leaders are more decisive and assertive and are more likely to gain others' confidence. Moreover, self-confident leaders will admit mistakes because they view them as learning opportunities rather than a refutation of their leadership capabilities. For example, in 2000, Netflix was working on a system that customers could use to download movies. However, it took 16 hours just to download one movie. Rather than forge ahead, Netflix CEO Reed Hastings killed the project.

Exhibit 14.3 Leadership Traits

© Cengage Learning 2013

trait theory a leadership theory that holds that effective leaders possess a similar set of traits or characteristics.

traits relatively stable characteristics, such as abilities, psychological motives, or consistent patterns of behavior.

Netflix took a different approach in 2003, building a branded Netflix box with a built-in hard drive. This time, a download only took six hours. Then, two years later, Hastings saw YouTube for the first time. He said, "It was immediately apparent that the click-and-watch approach was fantastic." So, he killed the box, and directed his software engineering team to find a way to stream movies to people's homes.[19] This also means that leaders have *emotional stability*. Even when things go wrong, they remain even-tempered and consistent in their outlook and in the way they treat others. Leaders who can't control their emotions, who anger quickly or attack and blame others for mistakes, are unlikely to be trusted.

Leaders are also smart. Leaders typically have strong *cognitive abilities*. This doesn't mean that leaders are necessarily geniuses—far from it. But it does mean that leaders have the capacity to analyze large amounts of seemingly unrelated, complex information and see patterns, opportunities, or threats where others might not see them. Finally, leaders also know their stuff, which means they have superior technical knowledge about the businesses they run. Leaders who have a good *knowledge of the business* understand the key technological decisions and concerns facing their companies. More often than not, studies indicate that effective leaders have long, extensive experience in their industries. Under the leadership of CEO Tim Solso, **Cummins Inc.**, an engine and power systems manufacturer based in Columbus, Indiana, has become a world leader in diesel-engine technology. Much of Solso's success can be attributed to his near four decades of experience with the company. In 1971, he got his first job with the firm, as Assistant to the Vice President of Personnel. Over the next several years, he took on positions such as Director of Development and Training, Executive Director of Personnel, and Executive Vice President of Operations, before being appointed CEO in 2000.[20]

> **"what's new" companies** >

2.2 Leadership Behaviors

Thus far, you've read about who leaders *are*. But traits alone are not enough to make a successful leader. They are, however, a precondition for success. After all, it's hard to imagine a truly successful leader who lacks most of these qualities. Leaders who have these traits (or many of them) must then take actions that encourage people to achieve group or organizational goals.[21] Accordingly, we now examine what leaders *do*, meaning the behaviors they perform or the actions they take to influence others to achieve group or organizational goals.

Researchers at the University of Michigan, Ohio State University, and the University of Texas examined the specific behaviors that leaders use to improve subordinate satisfaction and performance. Hundreds of studies were conducted and hundreds of leader behaviors were examined. At all three universities, two basic leader behaviors emerged as central to successful leadership: initiating structure (called *job-centered leadership* at the University of Michigan and *concern for production* at the University of Texas) and considerate leader behavior (called *employee-centered leadership* at the University of Michigan and *concern for people* at the University of Texas).[22] These two leader behaviors form the basis for many of the leadership theories discussed in this chapter.

Initiating structure is the degree to which a leader structures the roles of followers by setting goals, giving directions, setting deadlines, and assigning tasks. A leader's ability to initiate structure primarily affects subordinates' job performance. With intense competition from the Web, Taiwanese newspaper and magazine publisher Jimmy Lai decided that his stories would be more compelling if accompanied by visuals. Says Lai, "Images can transmit information so much faster." So he started **Next Media Animation**, a media company that produces computer animations of

initiating structure the degree to which a leader structures the roles of followers by setting goals, giving directions, setting deadlines, and assigning tasks.

> **"what's new" companies** >

what really works

Leadership Traits That Do Make a Difference

For decades, researchers assumed that leadership traits such as drive, emotional stability, cognitive ability, and charisma were *not* related to effective leadership. More recent evidence, however, shows that there are reliable trait differences between leaders and nonleaders. In fact, 54 studies based on more than 6,000 people clearly indicate that in terms of leadership traits, "successful leaders are not like other people."

Traits and Perceptions of Leadership Effectiveness

Several leadership models argue that in order to be successful, leaders must be viewed as good leaders by their followers. (This is completely different from determining whether leaders actually improve organizational performance.) Consequently, one test of trait theory is whether leaders with particular traits are viewed as more or less effective leaders by their followers.

Intelligence. On average, there is a 75 percent chance that intelligent leaders will be seen as better leaders than less intelligent leaders.

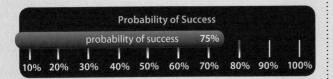

Dominance. On average, there is only a 57 percent chance that leaders with highly dominant personalities will be seen as better leaders than those with less dominant personalities.

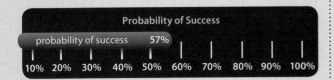

Extroversion. On average, there is a 63 percent chance that extroverts will be seen as better leaders than introverts.

Charisma and Leadership Effectiveness

As discussed at the end of the chapter, *charismatic leadership* is the set of behavioral tendencies and personal characteristics of leaders that creates an exceptionally strong relationship between leaders and their followers. More specifically, charismatic leaders articulate a clear vision for the future that is based on strongly held values or morals; model those values by acting in a way consistent with the company's vision; communicate high performance expectations to followers; and display confidence in followers' abilities to achieve the vision.

Charisma and Performance. On average, there is a 72 percent chance that charismatic leaders will have better-performing followers and organizations than less charismatic leaders.

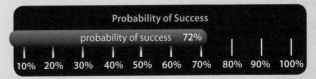

Charisma and Perceived Leader Effectiveness. On average, there is an 89 percent chance that charismatic leaders will be perceived as more effective leaders than less charismatic leaders.

(Continued)

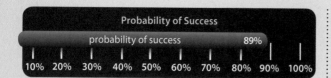

charismatic leaders will be more satisfied with their leaders than the followers of less charismatic leaders.[23]

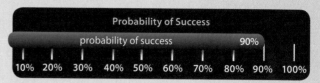

Charisma and Leader Satisfaction. On average, there is a 90 percent chance that the followers of

news events. When his animation team told him that it would take two weeks to produce an animated video of a new story, Lai told them they would have to figure out how to do it in two hours. They spent several months experimenting with stock digital faces and motion-capture technology and can now animate any news story in less than two hours.[24]

Consideration is the extent to which a leader is friendly, approachable, and supportive and shows concern for employees. Consideration primarily affects subordinates' job satisfaction. Specific leader consideration behaviors include listening to employees' problems and concerns, consulting with employees before making decisions, and treating employees as equals. When Gamal Azia became president of the **MGM Grand Hotel and Casino** in Las Vegas, he asked all employees, not just managers, to tell him how the hotel could improve. He was surprised to learn that hotel staff was not told what was happening in the hotel each day. Aziz listened and now the hotel's 10,000 employees start their work shift with a brief meeting, at which they are given a detailed overview of the conventions being held in the hotel, as well as the daily events and specials that the staff could offer to guests. The same approach has long been used in restaurants to let the waitstaff know about daily specials.[25]

Although researchers at all three universities generally agreed that initiating structure and consideration were basic leader behaviors, their interpretation differed on how these two behaviors are related to one another and which are necessary for effective leadership. The University of Michigan studies indicated that initiating structure and consideration were mutually exclusive behaviors on opposite ends of the same continuum. In other words, leaders who wanted to be more considerate would have to do less initiating of structure (and vice versa). The University of Michigan studies also indicated that only considerate leader behaviors (i.e., employee-centered behaviors) were associated with successful leadership. By contrast, researchers at Ohio State University and the University of Texas found that initiating structure and consideration were independent behaviors, meaning that leaders can be considerate and initiate structure at the same time. Additional evidence confirms this finding.[26] The same researchers also concluded that the most effective leaders were strong on both initiating structure and considerate leader behaviors.

This "high–high" approach can be seen in the upper right corner of the Blake/Mouton leadership grid, shown

"what's new" companies >

consideration the extent to which a leader is friendly, approachable, and supportive and shows concern for employees.

Exhibit 14.4   Blake/Mouton Leadership Grid

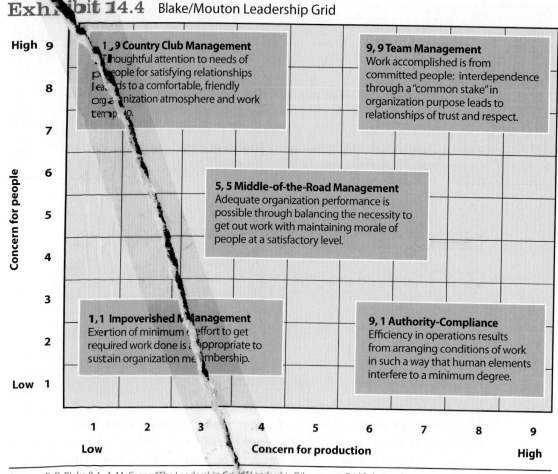

High 9   **1, 9 Country Club Management** Thoughtful attention to needs of people for satisfying relationships leads to a comfortable, friendly organization atmosphere and work tempo.

9, 9 Team Management Work accomplished is from committed people: interdependence through a "common stake" in organization purpose leads to relationships of trust and respect.

5, 5 Middle-of-the-Road Management Adequate organization performance is possible through balancing the necessity to get out work with maintaining morale of people at a satisfactory level.

1, 1 Impoverished Management Exertion of minimum effort to get required work done is appropriate to sustain organization membership.

9, 1 Authority-Compliance Efficiency in operations results from arranging conditions of work in such a way that human elements interfere to a minimum degree.

Concern for people (vertical axis, Low 1 to High 9)

Concern for production (horizontal axis, 1 Low to 9 High)

Source: R. R. Blake & A. A. McCanse, "The Leadership Grid," *Leadership Dilemmas—Grid Solutions* (Houston: Gulf Publishing Company), 21. Copyright © 1991, by Scientific Methods, Inc. Reproduced by permission of the owners.

in Exhibit 14.4. Blake and Mouton used two leadership behaviors, concern for people (i.e., consideration) and concern for production (i.e., initiating structure), to categorize five different leadership styles. Both behaviors are rated on a 9-point scale, with 1 representing "low" and 9 representing "high." Blake and Mouton suggest that a "high–high," or 9,9, leadership style is the best. They call this style *team management* because leaders who use it display a high concern for people (9) and a high concern for production (9).

By contrast, leaders use a 9,1 *authority–compliance* leadership style when they have a high concern for production and a low concern for people. A 1,9 *country club* style occurs when leaders care about having a friendly, enjoyable work environment but don't really pay much attention to production or performance. The worst leadership style, according to the grid, is the 1,1 *impoverished* leader, who shows little concern for people or production and does the bare minimum needed to keep his or her job. Finally, the 5,5 *middle-of-the-road* style occurs when leaders show a moderate amount of concern for both people and production.

Is the team management style, with a high concern for production and a high concern for people, the best leadership style? Logically, it would seem so. Why wouldn't you want to show high concern for both people and production? Nonetheless, nearly 50 years of research indicates that there isn't one best leadership style. The best leadership style depends on the situation. In other words, no one leadership behavior by itself and no one combination of leadership behaviors works well across all situations and employees.

Review 2

Who Leaders Are and What Leaders Do Trait theory says that effective leaders possess traits or characteristics that differentiate them from nonleaders. Those traits are drive, the desire to lead, honesty/integrity, self-confidence, emotional stability, cognitive ability, and knowledge of the business. Traits alone aren't enough for successful leadership, however; leaders who have these traits (or many of them) must also behave in ways that encourage people to achieve group or organizational goals. Two key leader behaviors are initiating structure, which improves subordinate performance, and consideration, which improves subordinate satisfaction. There is no single best combination of these behaviors. The best leadership style depends on the situation.

Situational Approaches to Leadership

After leader traits and behaviors, the situational approach to leadership is the third major method used in the study of leadership. We'll review four major situational approaches to leadership—Fiedler's contingency theory, path–goal theory, Hersey and Blanchard's Situational Leadership theory, and Vroom and Yetton's normative decision model. All assume that the effectiveness of any **leadership style**, the way a leader generally behaves toward followers, depends on the situation.[27] Stanford Business School professor Jeffrey Pfeffer agrees: "Situations differ, often wildly, in the extent to which one individual can make a difference and in the set of attributes required to be successful. . . . But utopia is impossible, which is why management consultants and authors should stop talking so much about how to find an ideal leader and instead focus on placing people into jobs that play to their strengths—and where their flaws won't be fatal."[28]

According to situational leadership theories, there is no one best leadership style. But one of these situational theories differs from the other three in one significant way. Fiedler's contingency theory assumes that leadership styles are consistent and difficult to change. Therefore, leaders must be placed in or matched to a situation that fits their leadership style. By contrast, the other three situational theories all assume that leaders are capable of adapting and adjusting their leadership styles to fit the demands of different situations.

After reading the next four sections, you should be able to

3. *Explain Fiedler's contingency theory.*
4. *Describe how path–goal theory works.*
5. *Discuss Hersey and Blanchard's Situational Leadership theory.*
6. *Explain the normative decision theory.*

3 Putting Leaders in the Right Situation: Fiedler's Contingency Theory

leadership style the way a leader generally behaves toward followers.

contingency theory a leadership theory that states that in order to maximize work group performance, leaders must be matched to the situation that best fits their leadership style.

Fiedler's **contingency theory** states that in order to maximize work group performance, leaders must be matched to the right leadership situation.[29] More specifically, as shown in Exhibit 14.5, the first basic assumption of Fiedler's theory is that

leaders are effective when the work groups they lead perform well. So, instead of judging leaders' effectiveness by what they do (i.e., initiating structure and consideration) or who they are (i.e., trait theory), Fiedler assesses leaders by the conduct and performance of the people they supervise. Second, Fiedler assumes that leaders are generally unable to change their leadership styles and that they will be more effective when their styles are matched to the proper situation. Ken Ottenbourg, former managing editor of the *Winston-Salem Journal*, agrees. After attending a weeklong course at the Center for Creative Leadership, a world-leading leadership institute, he struggled to implement the leadership ideas he learned. Says Ottenbourg, "It's easier to talk about changing behavior, and a lot harder to do it in the real world."[30]

Third, Fiedler assumes that the favorableness of a situation for a leader depends on the degree to which the situation permits the leader to influence the behavior of group members. Fiedler's third assumption is consistent with our definition of leadership as the process of influencing others to achieve group or organizational goals. In other words, in addition to traits, behaviors, and a favorable situation to match, leaders have to be allowed to lead.

Let's learn more about Fiedler's contingency theory by examining **3.1 the least preferred coworker and leadership styles, 3.2 situational favorableness,** and **3.3 how to match leadership styles to situations.**

Exhibit 14.5
Fiedler's Contingency Theory

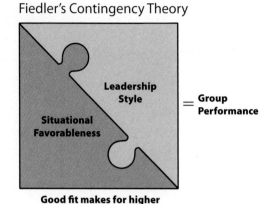

Good fit makes for higher performance levels.

© Cengage Learning 2013

3.1 Leadership Style: Least Preferred Coworker

When Fiedler refers to *leadership style*, he means the way that leaders generally behave toward their followers. Do the leaders yell and scream and blame others when things go wrong? Or do they correct mistakes by listening and then quietly but directly make their point? Do they take credit for others' work when things go right? Or do they make sure that those who did the work receive the credit they rightfully deserve? Do they let others make their own decisions and hold them accountable for the results? Or do they micromanage, insisting that all decisions be approved first by them? Fiedler also assumes that leadership styles are tied to leaders' underlying needs and personalities. Because personality and needs are relatively stable, he assumes that leaders are generally incapable of changing their leadership styles. In other words, the way that leaders treat people now is probably the way they've always treated others. So, according to Fiedler, if your boss's first instinct is to yell and scream and blame others, chances are he or she has always done that.

Fiedler uses a questionnaire called the Least Preferred Coworker (LPC) scale to measure leadership style; a sample of the scale is shown in Exhibit 14.6 (see the Self-Assessment at the end of this chapter for the full LPC scale). When completing the LPC scale, people are instructed to consider all of the people with whom they have ever worked and then to choose the one person with whom they have worked *least* well. Fiedler explains, "This does not have to be the person you liked least well, but should be the one person with whom you have the most trouble getting the job done."[31]

Would you describe your LPC as pleasant, friendly, supportive, interesting, cheerful, and sincere? Or would you describe the person as unpleasant, unfriendly, hostile, boring, gloomy, and insincere? People who describe their LPC in a positive way (scoring 64 and above) have *relationship-oriented* leadership styles. After all, if they can still be positive about their least preferred coworker, they must be people oriented. By contrast, people who describe their LPC in a negative way (scoring 57 or

Exhibit 14.6   Sample from Fiedler's Least Preferred Coworker Scale

Pleasant									Unpleasant
	8	7	6	5	4	3	2	1	
Friendly									**Unfriendly**
	8	7	6	5	4	3	2	1	
Supportive									**Hostile**
	8	7	6	5	4	3	2	1	
Boring									**Interesting**
	1	2	3	4	5	6	7	8	
Gloomy									**Cheerful**
	1	2	3	4	5	6	7	8	
Insincere									**Sincere**
	1	2	3	4	5	6	7	8	

Source: F. E. Fiedler & M. M. Chemers, *Improving Leadership Effectiveness: The Leader Match Concept,* 2nd ed. (New York: Wiley, 1984). Available at http://depts .washington.edu/psych/faculty/*cv/fiedler_cv.pdf, March 23, 2002. Reprinted by permission of the authors.

below) have *task-oriented* leadership styles. Given a choice, they'll focus first on getting the job done and second on making sure everyone gets along. Finally, those with moderate scores (from 58 to 63) have a more flexible leadership style and can be somewhat relationship oriented or somewhat task oriented.

3.2 Situational Favorableness

Fiedler assumes that leaders will be more effective when their leadership styles are matched to the proper situation. More specifically, Fiedler defines **situational favorableness** as the degree to which a particular situation either permits or denies a leader the chance to influence the behavior of group members.[32] In highly favorable situations, leaders find that their actions influence followers. But in highly unfavorable situations, leaders have little or no success influencing the people they are trying to lead.

Three situational factors determine the favorability of a situation: leader–member relations, task structure, and position power. The most important situational factor is **leader-member relations**, which refers to how well followers respect, trust, and like their leaders. When leader–member relations are good, followers trust the leader and there is a friendly work atmosphere. Of course, that's not always the case. After several years of quality and safety problems that led to highly negative publicity and a series of auto recalls, leader–member relations at Toyota have changed. Many Toyota managers and employees wonder if president Akio Toyoda can be a decisive leader. A top-level engineer complains, "The only way we find out anything about the [quality and safety crisis] is through the media." He worries, "Does Mr. Toyoda have the ability to lead?"[33] **Task structure** is the degree to which the requirements of a subordinate's tasks are clearly specified. With highly structured tasks, employees have clear job responsibilities, goals, and procedures. **Position power** is the degree to which leaders are able to hire, fire, reward, and punish workers. The more influence leaders have over hiring, firing, rewards, and punishments, the greater their power.

Exhibit 14.7 shows how leader–member relations, task structure, and position power can be combined into eight situations that differ in their favorability to leaders. In general, Situation I, on the left side of Exhibit 14.7, is the most favorable leader situation. Followers like and trust their leaders and know what to do because their tasks are highly structured. Also, the leaders have the formal power to influence

situational favorableness the degree to which a particular situation either permits or denies a leader the chance to influence the behavior of group members.

leader-member relations the degree to which followers respect, trust, and like their leaders.

task structure the degree to which the requirements of a subordinate's tasks are clearly specified.

position power the degree to which leaders are able to hire, fire, reward, and punish workers.

Exhibit 14.7 Situational Favorableness

Leader-Member Relations	Good	Good	Good	Good	Poor	Poor	Poor	Poor
Task Structure	High	High	Low	Low	High	High	Low	Low
Position Power	Strong	Weak	Strong	Weak	Strong	Weak	Strong	Weak
Situation	I	II	III	IV	V	VI	VII	VIII
	Favorable			**Moderately Favorable**			**Unfavorable**	

© Cengage Learning 2013

workers through hiring, firing, rewarding, and punishing them. Therefore, it's relatively easy for a leader to influence followers in Situation I. By contrast, Situation VIII, on the right side of Exhibit 14.7, is the least favorable situation for leaders. Followers don't like or trust their leaders. Plus, followers are not sure what they're supposed to be doing, given that their tasks or jobs are highly unstructured. Finally, leaders find it difficult to influence followers because they don't have the ability to hire, fire, reward, or punish the people who work for them. In short, it's very difficult to influence followers given the conditions found in Situation VIII.

> Followers like and trust their leaders and know what to do because their tasks are highly structured.

3.3 Matching Leadership Styles to Situations

After studying thousands of leaders and followers in hundreds of different situations, Fiedler found that the performance of relationship- and task-oriented leaders followed the pattern displayed in Exhibit 14.8.

Relationship-oriented leaders with high LPC scores were better leaders (i.e., their groups performed more effectively) under moderately favorable situations. In moderately favorable situations, the leader may be liked somewhat, tasks may be somewhat structured, and the leader may have some position power. In this situation, a relationship-oriented leader improves leader–member relations, which is the most important of the three situational factors. In turn, morale and performance improve. How did Gordon Bethune turn around Continental Airlines and its previously poisonous labor-management relations? He explains it this way: "When I was a mechanic, I knew how much faster I could fix an airplane when I wanted to fix it than when I didn't. I've tried to make it so our guys want to do it."[34]

By contrast, as Exhibit 14.8 shows, task-oriented leaders with low LPC scores are better leaders in highly favorable and unfavorable situations. Task-oriented leaders do well in favorable situations where leaders are liked, tasks are structured, and the leader has the power to hire, fire, reward, and punish. In these favorable situations,

Exhibit 14.8 Matching Leadership Styles to Situations

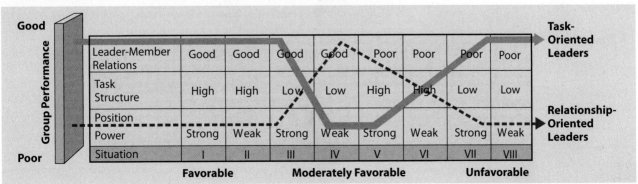

© Cengage Learning 2013

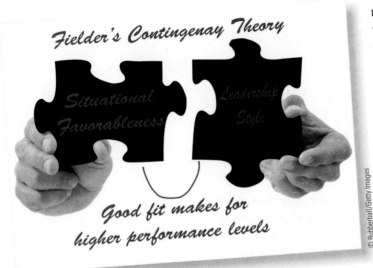

Fielder's Contingenay Theory

Situational Favorableness

Leadership Style

Good fit makes for higher performance levels

© Rubberball/Getty Images

task-oriented leaders effectively step on the gas of a well-tuned car. Their focus on performance sets the goal for the group, which then charges forward to meet it. But task-oriented leaders also do well in unfavorable situations where leaders are disliked, tasks are unstructured, and the leader doesn't have the power to hire, fire, reward, and punish. In these unfavorable situations, the task-oriented leader sets goals, which focus attention on performance and clarify what needs to be done, thus overcoming low task structure. This is enough to jump-start performance even if workers don't like or trust the leader.

Finally, though not shown in Exhibit 14.8, people with moderate LPC scores, who can be somewhat relationship oriented or somewhat task oriented, tend to do fairly well in all situations because they can adapt their behavior. Typically, though, they don't perform quite as well as relationship-oriented or task-oriented leaders whose leadership styles are well matched to the situation.

Recall, however, that Fiedler assumes leaders to be incapable of changing their leadership styles. Accordingly, the key to applying Fiedler's contingency theory in the workplace is to accurately measure and match leaders to situations or to teach leaders how to change situational favorableness by changing leader–member relations, task structure, or position power. Though matching or placing leaders in appropriate situations works particularly well, practicing managers have had little luck reengineering situations to fit their leadership styles. The primary problem, as you've no doubt realized, is the complexity of the theory.

In a study designed to teach leaders how to reengineer their situations to fit their leadership styles, Fiedler found that most of the leaders simply did not understand what they were supposed to do to change their situations. Furthermore, if they didn't like their LPC profile (perhaps they felt they were more relationship oriented than their scores indicated), they arbitrarily changed it to better suit their view of themselves. Of course, the theory won't work as well if leaders are attempting to change situational factors to fit their perceived leadership style rather than their real leadership style.[35]

Review 3

Putting Leaders in the Right Situation: Fiedler's Contingency Theory   Fiedler's theory assumes that leaders are effective when their work groups perform well, that leaders are unable to change their leadership styles, that leadership styles must be matched to the proper situation, and that favorable situations permit leaders to influence group members. According to the Least Preferred Coworker (LPC) scale, there are two basic leadership styles. People who describe their LPC in a positive way have relationship-oriented leadership styles. People who describe their LPC in a negative way have task-oriented leadership styles. Situational favorableness occurs when leaders can influence followers and is determined by leader–member relations, task structure, and position power. In general, relationship-oriented leaders with high LPC scores are better leaders under moderately favorable situations, whereas task-oriented leaders with low LPC scores are better leaders in highly favorable and unfavorable situations. Because Fiedler assumes that leaders are incapable of changing their leadership styles, the key is to accurately measure and match leaders to situations or to teach leaders how to change situational factors. Although matching or placing leaders in appropriate situations works well, reengineering situations to fit leadership styles doesn't, because the model is complex and difficult for people to understand.

4 Adapting Leader Behavior: Path–Goal Theory

Just as its name suggests, **path–goal theory** states that leaders can increase subordinate satisfaction and performance by clarifying and clearing the paths to goals and by increasing the number and kinds of rewards available for goal attainment. Said another way, leaders need to clarify how followers can achieve organizational goals, take care of problems that prevent followers from achieving goals, and then find more and varied rewards to motivate followers to achieve those goals.[36]

Leaders must meet two conditions for path clarification, path clearing, and rewards to increase followers' motivation and effort. First, leader behavior must be a source of immediate or future satisfaction for followers. The things you do as a leader must either please your followers today or lead to activities or rewards that will satisfy them in the future. For example, Kerri Brotherson started at Paducah Bank & Trust Company as a bank teller. But after three promotions, she is now a commercial loan officer. Paducah Bank & Trust does such a good job of developing its workers that 80 percent of its management jobs are filled from within. Each year, 6 to 8 of the bank's 140 employees are selected for an 18-month leadership development program. Says Brotherson, "They've always listened to me and helped me move into areas I wanted to move into."[37] She plans to spend her entire career with the bank.

Second, while providing the coaching, guidance, support, and rewards necessary for effective work performance, leader behaviors must complement and not duplicate the characteristics of followers' work environments. Thus, leader behaviors must offer something unique and valuable to followers beyond what they're already experiencing as they do their jobs or what they can already do for themselves. Exhibit 14.9 summarizes these basic assumptions of path–goal theory.

In contrast to Fiedler's contingency theory, path–goal theory assumes that leaders *can* change and adapt their leadership styles. Exhibit 14.10 illustrates this process, showing that leaders change and adapt their leadership styles contingent on their subordinates or the environment in which those subordinates work.

Let's learn more about path–goal theory by examining **4.1 the four kinds of leadership styles that leaders use, 4.2 the subordinate and environmental contingency factors that determine when different leader styles are effective,** and **4.3 the outcomes of path–goal theory in improving employee satisfaction and performance.**

path–goal theory a leadership theory that states that leaders can increase subordinate satisfaction and performance by clarifying and clearing the paths to goals and by increasing the number and kinds of rewards available for goal attainment.

directive leadership a leadership style in which the leader lets employees know precisely what is expected of them, gives them specific guidelines for performing tasks, schedules work, sets standards of performance, and makes sure that people follow standard rules and regulations.

4.1 Leadership Styles

As illustrated in Exhibit 14.10, the four leadership styles in path–goal theory are directive, supportive, participative, and achievement oriented.[38] **Directive leadership** involves letting employees know precisely what is expected of them, giving them specific guidelines for performing tasks, scheduling work, setting standards of performance, and making sure that people follow standard rules and regulations. GM CEO Daniel Akerson, who stepped in when Ed Whitacre stepped down, is known for being direct

Exhibit 14.9 Basic Assumptions of Path–Goal Theory

- Clarify paths to goals.
- Clear paths to goals by solving problems and removing roadblocks.
- Increase the number and kinds of rewards available for goal attainment.
- Do things that satisfy followers today or will lead to future rewards or satisfaction.
- Offer followers something unique and valuable beyond what they're experiencing or can already do for themselves.

Source: R. J. House & T. R. Mitchell, "Path–Goal Theory of Leadership," *Journal of Contemporary Business* 3 (1974): 81–97.

Exhibit 14.10 Path–Goal Theory

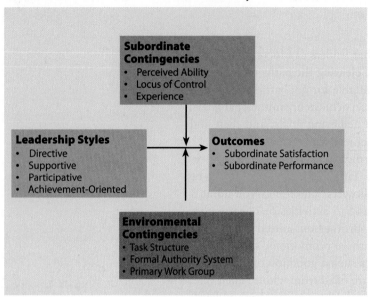

© Cengage Learning 2013

and demanding. Frustrated that his Detroit-based executives were focused on North America, he told them, "One of three people on this planet lives in China or India—we need cars for them." When he learned it would take four years to bring model cars to dealer showrooms, he replied, "During World War II, GM produced tanks and equipment within four years. Why should it take four years [with computer-aided design tools] to put a car out?" After reviewing engine plans with top managers, he asked, "Why do we have 18 types of engines? We have only four brands." When told it was GM's tradition to make a variety of engines, Akerson replied, "We have to break out of the old way of thinking around here," and directed his executives to benchmark how many engines Toyota made and then "take out complexity and save money." A year later, GM was producing only a dozen engines.[39]

Supportive leadership involves being approachable and friendly to employees, showing concern for them and their welfare, treating them as equals, and creating a friendly climate. Supportive leadership is very similar to considerate leader behavior. Supportive leadership often results in employee satisfaction with the job and with leaders. This leadership style may also result in improved performance when it increases employee confidence, lowers employee job stress, or improves relations and trust between employees and leaders.[40] When gas prices surged to over $4 a gallon, commuting costs took a toll on employee budgets and bank accounts. A survey at the time found that one-third of employees would quit to take a comparable job closer to home. Atlanta-based Lathem Time Corp. responded by changing from a five-day workweek to a compressed four-day workweek with ten-hour days. The change saved employees a tank of gas a month ($60 to $100 at the time) and greatly reduced commutes (by leaving work at 6:30 P.M., 90-minute commutes were reduced to 30 minutes). Lathem Time Corp. employee Jason Dupree said, "It's definitely improved my work. My stress level is down. Getting that break in the middle of the week is like a mini-weekend for me."[41]

Participative leadership involves consulting employees for their suggestions and input before making decisions. Participation in decision making should help followers understand which goals are most important and clarify the paths to accomplishing them. Furthermore, when people participate in decisions, they become more committed to making them work. Thomas Walter, the CEO of **Tasty Catering** in Elk Grove, Illinois, wanted to involve his employees in key company decisions. So he started two councils, one operating in English and the other in Spanish, to make strategic choices for the company. Each council is made up of eight employees representing the entire workforce—cooks, accountants, office staff, and drivers. When Walters and his two brothers, who own the company, wanted to provide health-care coverage, the councils decided to opt for a less costly package because most employees already had coverage through spouses. Anna Wollin, an account executive, says the councils "[put] us all on an even playing field. I have been with the company for less than a year, and my opinion was as important as an owner's opinion."[42]

Achievement-oriented leadership means setting challenging goals, having high expectations of employees, and displaying confidence that employees will assume responsibility and put forth extraordinary effort. Though he's an introvert, Google

supportive leadership a leadership style in which the leader is friendly and approachable to employees, shows concern for employees and their welfare, treats them as equals, and creates a friendly climate.

participative leadership a leadership style in which the leader consults employees for their suggestions and input before making decisions.

achievement-oriented leadership a leadership style in which the leader sets challenging goals, has high expectations of employees, and displays confidence that employees will assume responsibility and put forth extraordinary effort.

cofounder and CEO Larry Page is clearly an achievement-oriented leader. A former Google executive says, "When people come to Larry with ideas, he always wants it bigger. His whole point is that only Google has the kind of resources to make big bets. The asset that Larry brings [to the people he leads] is to say, 'Let's go and make big things happen.'" One example is with Franz Och, a top researcher responsible for Google's "machine-translation system," artificial intelligence, which uses complex statistics to translate websites from one language into another. Page spent a year trying to hire him for this task, and every time Och would tell Page that it couldn't be done. Says Och, "They were very optimistic, and I tried to tell them to be cautious. It's really complicated, extremely expensive, and you

need very large amounts of data." But, today, if you're using Google's Chrome web browser and you happen on a Chinese or German website, a button appears asking whether you want the website translated—and it works for 58 languages. Och says, "When I started at Google, if you told me that five years later we'd be able to translate Yiddish, Maltese, Icelandic, Azerbaijani, and Basque, I would have said, 'That's just not going to happen.' But [cofounders Larry Page and Sergey Brin] didn't believe me. And I guess they were more right than I was."[43]

4.2 Subordinate and Environmental Contingencies

As shown in Exhibit 14.10, path–goal theory specifies that leader behaviors should be adapted to subordinate characteristics. The theory identifies three kinds of subordinate contingencies: perceived ability, experience, and locus of control. *Perceived ability* is simply how much ability subordinates believe they have for doing their jobs well. Subordinates who perceive that they have a great deal of ability will be dissatisfied with directive leader behaviors. Experienced employees are likely to react in a similar way. Since they already know how to do their jobs (or perceive that they do), they don't need or want close supervision. By contrast, subordinates with little experience or little perceived ability will welcome directive leadership.

Locus of control is a personality measure that indicates the extent to which people believe that they have control over what happens to them in life. *Internals* believe that what happens to them, good or bad, is largely a result of their choices and actions. *Externals*, on the other hand, believe that what happens to them is caused by external forces beyond their control. Accordingly, externals are much more comfortable with a directive leadership style, whereas internals greatly prefer a participative leadership style because they like to have a say in what goes on at work.

Path–goal theory specifies that leader behaviors should complement rather than duplicate the characteristics of followers' work environments. There are three kinds of environmental contingencies: task structure, the formal authority system, and the primary work group. As in Fiedler's contingency theory, *task structure* is the degree to which the requirements of a subordinate's tasks are clearly specified. When task structure is low and tasks are unclear, directive leadership should be used because it

Exhibit 14.11   Path–Goal Theory: When to Use Directive, Supportive, Participative, or Achievement-Oriented Leadership

Directive Leadership	Supportive Leadership	Participative Leadership	Achievement-Oriented Leadership
Unstructured tasks	Structured, simple, repetitive tasks	Experienced workers	Unchallenging tasks
Inexperienced workers	Stressful, frustrating tasks	Workers with high perceived ability	
Workers with low perceived ability	When workers lack confidence	Workers with internal locus of control	
Workers with external locus of control	Clear formal authority system	Workers not satisfied with rewards	
Unclear formal authority system		Complex tasks	

© Cengage Learning 2013

complements the work environment. When task structure is high and tasks are clear, however, directive leadership is not needed because it duplicates what task structure provides. Alternatively, when tasks are stressful, frustrating, or dissatisfying, leaders should respond with supportive leadership.

The *formal authority system* is an organization's set of procedures, rules, and policies. When the formal authority system is unclear, directive leadership complements the situation by reducing uncertainty and increasing clarity. But when the formal authority system is clear, directive leadership is redundant and should not be used.

Primary work group refers to the amount of work-oriented participation or emotional support that is provided by an employee's immediate work group. Participative leadership should be used when tasks are complex and there is little existing work-oriented participation in the primary work group. When tasks are stressful, frustrating, or repetitive, supportive leadership is called for.

Finally, because keeping track of all of these subordinate and environmental contingencies can get a bit confusing, Exhibit 14.11 provides a summary of when directive, supportive, participative, and achievement-oriented leadership styles should be used.

4.3 Outcomes

Does following path–goal theory improve subordinate satisfaction and performance? Preliminary evidence suggests that it does.[44] In particular, people who work for supportive leaders are much more satisfied with their jobs and their bosses. Likewise, people who work for directive leaders are more satisfied with their jobs and bosses (but not quite as much as when their bosses are supportive) and perform their jobs better too. Does adapting one's leadership style to subordinate and environmental characteristics improve subordinate satisfaction and performance? At this point, because it is difficult to completely test this complex theory, it's too early to tell.[45] However, because the data clearly show that it makes sense for leaders to be both supportive *and* directive, it also makes sense that leaders could improve subordinate satisfaction and performance by adding participative and achievement-oriented leadership styles to their capabilities as leaders.

Adapting Leader Behavior: Path–Goal Theory   Path–goal theory states that leaders can increase subordinate satisfaction and performance by clarifying and clearing the paths to goals and by increasing the number and kinds of rewards available for goal attainment. For this to work, however, leader behavior must be a source of immediate or future satisfaction for followers and must complement rather than duplicate the characteristics of followers' work environments. In contrast to Fiedler's contingency theory, path–goal theory assumes that leaders can and do change and adapt their leadership styles (directive, supportive, participative, and achievement oriented), depending on their subordinates (experience, perceived ability, internal or external) or the environment in which those subordinates work (task structure, formal authority system, or primary work group).

Review 4

5 Adapting Leader Behavior: Hersey and Blanchard's Situational Leadership® Theory

Have you ever had a new job that you didn't know how to do, and your boss was not around to help you learn it? Conversely, have you ever known exactly how to do your job, but your boss kept treating you as though you didn't? Hersey and Blanchard's Situational Leadership® theory is based on the idea of follower readiness. Hersey and Blanchard argue that employees have different levels of readiness for handling different jobs, responsibilities, and work assignments. Accordingly, Hersey and Blanchard's **situational theory** states that leaders need to adjust their leadership styles to match followers' readiness.[46]

Let's learn more about Hersey and Blanchard's situational theory by examining **5.1 worker readiness** and **5.2 different leadership styles.**

5.1 Worker Readiness

Worker readiness is the ability and willingness to take responsibility for directing one's behavior at work. Readiness is composed of two components. *Job readiness* consists of the amount of knowledge, skill, ability, and experience people have to perform their jobs. As you would expect, people with greater skill, ability, and experience do a better job of supervising their own work. *Psychological readiness*, on the other hand, is a feeling of self-confidence or self-respect. Confident people are better at guiding their own work than insecure people are. Hersey and Blanchard combine job readiness and psychological readiness to produce four different levels of readiness in their situational leadership theory. The lowest level, R1, represents insecure people who are neither willing nor able to take responsibility for guiding their own work. R2 represents people who are confident and willing, but not able, to take responsibility for guiding their own work. R3 represents people who are insecure and able, but not willing, to take responsibility for guiding their own work. And R4 represents people who are confident, willing, and able to take responsibility for guiding their own work. It's important to note that a follower's readiness is usually task specific. For example, you may be highly confident and capable when it comes to personal computers but know nothing about setting up budgets for planning purposes. You would possess readiness (R4) with respect to computers, but not with respect to budgets.

situational theory a leadership theory that states that leaders need to adjust their leadership styles to match their followers' readiness.

worker readiness the ability and willingness to take responsibility for directing one's behavior at work.

5.2 Leadership Styles

Similar to Blake and Mouton's managerial grid, situational theory defines leadership styles in terms of task behavior (i.e., concern for production) and relationship behavior (i.e., concern for people). These two behaviors can be combined to form four different leadership styles: telling, selling, participating, and delegating. Leaders choose one of these styles, depending on the readiness a follower has for a specific task.

A *telling* leadership style (high task behavior and low relationship behavior) is based on one-way communication in which followers are told what, how, when, and where to do particular tasks. Telling is used when people are at the R1 stage. For instance, someone using a telling leadership style would identify all the steps in a project and give explicit instructions on exactly how to execute each one.

A *selling* leadership style (high task behavior and high relationship behavior) involves two-way communication and psychological support to encourage followers to own, or buy into, particular ways of doing things. Selling is used most appropriately at the R2 stage. For instance, someone using a selling leadership style might say, "We're going to start a company newsletter. I really think that's a great idea, don't you? We're going to need some cost estimates from printers and some comments from each manager. But that's pretty straightforward. Oh, don't forget that we need the CEO's comments too. She's expecting you to call. I know that you'll do a great job on this. We'll meet next Tuesday to see whether you have any questions once you've dug into this. By the way, we need to have this done by next Friday."

A *participating* style (low task behavior and high relationship behavior) is based on two-way communication and shared decision making. Participating is used with employees at R3. Because the problem is with motivation rather than ability, someone using a participating leadership style might solicit ideas from a subordinate about a project and let the subordinate get started, but ask to review progress along the way.

A *delegating* style (low task behavior and low relationship behavior) is used when leaders basically let workers run their own show and make their own decisions. Delegating is used for people at R4. For instance, someone using a delegating leadership style might say, "We're going to start a company newsletter. You've got ten days to do it. Run with it. Let me know when you've got it done. I'll email you a couple of ideas, but other than that, do what you think is best. Thanks."

In general, as people become more ready and thus more willing and able to guide their own behavior, leaders should become less task-oriented and more relationship-oriented. As people become even more ready, leaders should become less task-oriented *and* less relationship-oriented until people eventually manage their own work with little input from their leaders.

How well does Hersey and Blanchard's situational theory work? Despite its intuitive appeal (managers and consultants tend to prefer it over Fiedler's contingency theory because of its underlying logic and simplicity), most studies don't support situational theory.[47] Although managers generally do a good job of judging followers' readiness levels, the theory doesn't seem to work well except at lower levels, where a telling style is recommended for people who are insecure and neither willing nor able to take responsibility for guiding their own work.[48]

Review 5

Leader Behavior: Hersey and Blanchard's Situational Leadership® Theory According to situational theory, leaders need to adjust their leadership styles to match their followers' readiness, which is the ability (job readiness) and willingness (psychological readiness) to take responsibility for directing one's work. Job readiness and psychological readiness combine to produce four different levels of readiness (R1–R4). The levels vary based on people's confidence, ability, and willingness to guide their own work. Situational theory combines task and relationship behavior to create four leadership styles—telling (R1), selling (R2), participating (R3), and delegating (R4)—that are used with employees at different readiness levels.

6 Adapting Leader Behavior: Normative Decision Theory

For years, your company has insisted on formal business attire for men and women. Now, however, you want to make a change to casual wear. Do you make the decision yourself and announce it, or do you consult your employees before making the decision?

To keep up with the exponential growth in one of your sales regions, you're going to cut the region in half, add staff, and effectively reduce the earnings of its sales representatives and managers. Do you make the decision yourself, announce it, and then live with the backlash? Do you consult all of your regional managers before making this decision? Or do you go straight to the salespeople in the region to let them know about your concerns?

Many people believe that making tough decisions is at the heart of leadership. Yet experienced leaders will tell you that deciding *how* to make decisions is just as important. The **normative decision theory** (also known as the *Vroom-Yetton-Jago model*) helps leaders decide how much employee participation (from none to letting employees make the entire decision) should be used when making decisions.[49]

Let's learn more about normative decision theory by investigating **6.1 decision styles** and **6.2 decision quality and acceptance**.

6.1 Decision Styles

Unlike nearly all of the other leadership theories discussed in this chapter, which have specified *leadership* styles, that is, the way a leader generally behaves toward followers, the normative decision theory specifies five different *decision* styles, or ways of making decisions. (See Chapter 5 for a more complete review of decision making in organizations.) As shown in Exhibit 14.12, those styles vary from *autocratic decisions* (AI or AII) on the left, in which leaders make the decisions by themselves, to *consultative decisions* (CI or CII), in which leaders share problems with subordinates but still make the decisions themselves, to *group decisions* (GII) on the right, in which leaders share the problems with subordinates and then have the group make the decisions.

GE Aircraft Engines in Durham, North Carolina, uses a similar approach when making decisions. According to *Fast Company* magazine, "At GE/Durham, every decision is either an 'A' decision, a 'B' decision, or a 'C' decision. An 'A' decision is one that the plant manager makes herself, without consulting anyone."[50] Plant manager Paula Sims says, "I don't make very many of those, and when I do make one, everyone at the plant knows it. I make maybe 10 or 12 a year."[51] "'B' decisions are also made by the plant manager but with input from the people affected. 'C' decisions, the most common type, are made by consensus, by the people directly involved, with plenty of discussion. With 'C' decisions, the view of the plant manager doesn't necessarily carry more weight than the views of those affected."[52]

normative decision theory a theory that suggests how leaders can determine an appropriate amount of employee participation when making decisions.

Exhibit 14.12 Decision Styles and Levels of Employee Participation

Leader solves the problem or makes the decision

Leader is willing to accept any decision supported by the entire group

AI	AII	CI	CII	GII
Using information available at the time, the leader solves the problem or makes the decision.	The leader obtains necessary information from employees, and then selects a solution to the problem. When asked to share information, employees may or may not be told what the problem is.	The leader shares the problem and gets ideas and suggestions from relevant employees on an individual basis. Individuals are not brought together as a group. Then the leader makes the decision, which may or may not reflect their input.	The leader shares the problem with employees as a group, obtains their ideas and suggestions, and then makes the decision, which may or may not reflect their input.	The leader shares the problem with employees as a group. Together, the leader and employees generate and evaluate alternatives and try to reach an agreement on a solution. The leader acts as a facilitator and does not try to influence the group. The leader is willing to accept and implement any solution that has the support of the entire group.

Source: Adapted from V. H. Vroom & P. W. Yetton, *Leadership and Decision Making* (Pittsburgh: University of Pittsburgh Press, 1973).

6.2 Decision Quality and Acceptance

According to the normative decision theory, using the right degree of employee participation improves the quality of decisions and the extent to which employees accept and are committed to decisions. Exhibit 14.13 lists the decision rules that normative decision theory uses to increase the quality of a decision and the degree to which employees accept and commit to it. The quality, leader information, subordinate information, goal congruence, and problem structure rules are used to increase decision

doing the right thing

A Leadership Gap

The shift from one leader to another is one of the most crucial times for a company, and very few organizations have planned for the process. A smooth transition to a successor can help a company maintain, and even expand, the company's success. A rough transition, however, can throw the company into chaos as it struggles to find a coherent vision and strategy. This is the reason why 98 percent of global companies recently surveyed believed that a CEO succession plan was critically important to the organization. However, only 35 percent of responding companies actually have a plan set in place. It may sound strange, of course, to think about how you're going to find a new leader when you already have one. But CEOs don't just retire when you're ready for them to; they can resign suddenly, fall ill, or even be fired. So do the right thing, plan for the future, and set up a solid succession plan so that your company's stability isn't jeopardized.[53]

Exhibit 14.13 Normative Theory Decision Rules

Decision Rules to Increase Decision Quality
Quality Rule. If the quality of the decision is important, then don't use an autocratic decision style.
Leader Information Rule. If the quality of the decision is important, and if the leader doesn't have enough information to make the decision on his or her own, then don't use an autocratic decision style.
Subordinate Information Rule. If the quality of the decision is important, and if the subordinates don't have enough information to make the decision themselves, then don't use a group decision style.
Goal Congruence Rule. If the quality of the decision is important, and subordinates' goals are different from the organization's goals, then don't use a group decision style.
Problem Structure Rule. If the quality of the decision is important, the leader doesn't have enough information to make the decision on his or her own, and the problem is unstructured, then don't use an autocratic decision style.

Decision Rules to Increase Decision Acceptance
Commitment Probability Rule. If having subordinates accept and commit to the decision is important, then don't use an autocratic decision style.
Subordinate Conflict Rule. If having subordinates accept the decision is important and critical to successful implementation and subordinates are likely to disagree or end up in conflict over the decision, then don't use an autocratic or consultative decision style.
Commitment Requirement Rule. If having subordinates accept the decision is absolutely required for successful implementation and subordinates share the organization's goals, then don't use an autocratic or consultative style.

Source: Adapted from V. H. Vroom, "Leadership," in *Handbook of Industrial and Organizational Psychology* M. D. Dunnette (Chicago: Rand McNally, 1976); and V. H. Vroom & A. G. Jago, *The New Leadership: Managing Participation in Organizations* (Englewood Cliffs, NJ: Prentice Hall, 1988).

quality. For example, the leader information rule states that if a leader doesn't have enough information to make a decision on his or her own, then the leader should not use an autocratic decision style.

The commitment probability, subordinate conflict, and commitment requirement rules shown in Exhibit 14.13 are used to increase employee acceptance and commitment to decisions. For example, the commitment requirement rule says that if decision acceptance and commitment are important, and the subordinates share the organization's goals, then you shouldn't use an autocratic or consultative style. In other words, if followers want to do what's best for the company and you need their acceptance and commitment to make a decision work, then use a group decision style and let them make the decision.

As you can see, these decision rules help leaders improve decision quality and follower acceptance and commitment by eliminating decision styles that don't fit the particular decision or situation they're facing. Normative decision theory then operationalizes these decision rules in the form of yes/no questions, which are shown in the decision tree displayed in Exhibit 14.14. You start at the left side of the model and answer the first question, "How important is the technical quality of this decision?" by choosing "high" or "low." Then you continue by answering each question as you proceed along the decision tree until you get to a recommended decision style.

Let's use the model to make the decision of whether to change from a formal business attire policy to a casual wear policy. The problem sounds simple, but it is actually more complex than you might think. For instance, when Jim Holt, became president of **Mid American Credit Union** in Wichita, Kansas, the company dress code restricted women from wearing boots or backless shoes. Panty hose were also required, even when wearing pants. But when he attended a dress for success seminar, he was advised to relax the rule on women's shoes but require panty hose because

< "what's new" companies

Exhibit 14.14 Normative Decision Theory Tree for Determining the Level of Participation in Decision Making

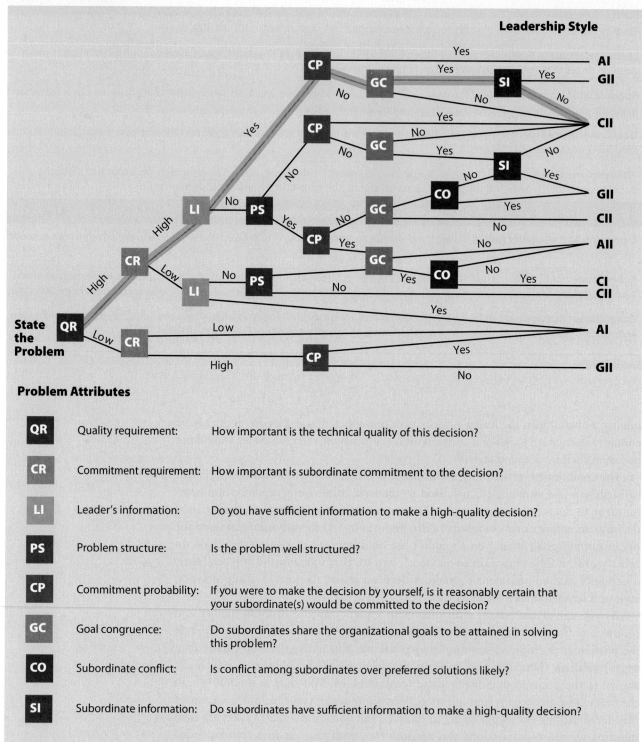

Leadership Style

Problem Attributes

QR	Quality requirement:	How important is the technical quality of this decision?
CR	Commitment requirement:	How important is subordinate commitment to the decision?
LI	Leader's information:	Do you have sufficient information to make a high-quality decision?
PS	Problem structure:	Is the problem well structured?
CP	Commitment probability:	If you were to make the decision by yourself, is it reasonably certain that your subordinate(s) would be committed to the decision?
GC	Goal congruence:	Do subordinates share the organizational goals to be attained in solving this problem?
CO	Subordinate conflict:	Is conflict among subordinates over preferred solutions likely?
SI	Subordinate information:	Do subordinates have sufficient information to make a high-quality decision?

Source: Figure 9.3 "Decision-Process Flow Chart for Both Individual and Group Problems" from *Leadership and Decision Making* by Victor H. Vroom and Philip W. Yetton, © 1973. Adapted and reprinted by permission of University of Pittsburgh Press.

bare legs aren't perceived as professional. When he wrote to a *Wall Street Journal* columnist to ask for input and his views became public, the backlash was intense. Online discussion groups called him Neanderthal Man." On reading the story, Washington, D.C., attorney Cyndi Lafuente, said, "It is not just that he is clinging to antiquated notions of femininity; it is also that he thinks he has the right to mandate femininity—antiquated or otherwise—in the office environment. Didn't we blow past that when we got the right to wear pants to work?"[54]

Follow the yellow line in Exhibit 14.14 as we work through the decision in the following discussion.

Problem: Change to Casual Wear?

1. *Quality requirement: How important is the technical quality of this decision?* High. This question has to do with whether there are quality differences in the alternatives and whether those quality differences matter. In other words: Is there a lot at stake in this decision? Although most people would assume that quality isn't an issue here, it really is, given the incredibly strong reactions that people have regarding the rules for casual wear at their companies.

2. *Commitment requirement: How important is subordinate commitment to the decision?* High. Changes in culture, like dress codes, require subordinate commitment or they fail.

3. *Leader's information: Do you have sufficient information to make a high-quality decision?* Yes. Let's assume that you've done your homework. Much has been written about casual wear, from how to make the change, to the effects it has in companies (almost all positive).

4. *Commitment probability: If you were to make the decision by yourself, is it reasonably certain that your subordinate(s) would be committed to the decision?* No. Studies of casual wear find that employees' reactions are almost uniformly positive. Nonetheless, employees are likely to be angry if you change something as personal as clothing policies without consulting them.

5. *Goal congruence: Do subordinates share the organizational goals to be attained in solving this problem?* Yes. The goals that usually accompany a change to casual dress policies are a more informal culture, better communication, and less money spent on business attire.

6. *Subordinate information: Do subordinates have sufficient information to make a high-quality decision?* No. Most employees know little about casual wear policies or even what constitutes casual wear in most companies. Consequently, most companies have to educate employees about casual wear practices and policies before making a decision.

7. *CII is the answer:* With a CII, or consultative decision process, the leader shares the problem with employees as a group, obtains their ideas and suggestions, and then makes the decision, which may or may not reflect their input. So, given the answers to these questions (remember, different managers won't necessarily answer these questions the same way), the normative decision theory recommends that leaders consult with their subordinates before deciding whether to change to a casual wear policy.

How well does the normative decision theory work? A prominent leadership scholar has described it as the best supported of all leadership theories.[55] In general, the more managers violate the decision rules in Exhibit 14.13, the less effective their decisions are, especially with respect to subordinate acceptance and commitment.[56]

Review 6

Adapting Leader Behavior: Normative Decision Theory The normative decision theory helps leaders decide how much employee participation should be used when making decisions. Using the right degree of employee participation improves the quality of decisions and the extent to which employees accept and are committed to decisions. The theory specifies five different decision styles or ways of making decisions: autocratic decisions (AI or AII), consultative decisions (CI or CII), and group decisions (GII). The theory improves decision quality via the quality, leader information, subordinate information, goal congruence, and unstructured problem decision rules. The theory improves employee commitment and acceptance via the commitment probability, subordinate conflict, and commitment requirement decision rules. These decision rules help leaders improve decision quality and follower acceptance and commitment by eliminating decision styles that don't fit the decision or situation they're facing. Normative decision theory then makes these decision rules more concrete by framing them as yes/no questions, as shown in the decision tree displayed in Exhibit 14.14.

Strategic Leadership

Thus far, you have read about three major leadership ideas: traits, behaviors, and situational theories. Leader *traits* are relatively stable characteristics such as abilities or psychological motives. Traits capture who effective leaders are. Leader *behaviors* are the actions leaders take to influence others to achieve group or organizational goals. Behaviors capture what effective leaders do (i.e., initiate structure and consideration). And *situational theories* indicate that the effectiveness of a leadership style, the way a leader generally behaves toward followers, depends on the situation. Situational theories capture what leaders need to do or not do in particular situations or circumstances. This final part of the chapter introduces a fourth major leadership idea—strategic leadership—and its components: visionary, charismatic, and transformational leadership.

Strategic leadership is the ability to anticipate, envision, maintain flexibility, think strategically, and work with others to initiate changes that will create a positive future for an organization.[57] Heidrick & Struggles (H&S), one of the world's largest executive search firms, helps companies find CEOs, board members, and senior executives. When the economy turned down, CEO Kevin Kelly realized it was time to dramatically change the company's strategy. Currently, 95 percent of its business is executive search. But with online resources like LinkedIn.com making it easier to find and identify talent, and NASDAQ's boardrecruiting.com charging just $350 per candidate to help companies find board members, Kelly wants to shrink search to just 50 percent of the business. In its place, he wants to grow leadership advisory services, such as executive retention and succession, to 40 percent. Says Kelly, "You can't pick up a newspaper today without seeing organizations that don't have proper succession planning in place. It's a major issue. What we're trying to become over the next three to five years is more of a leadership advisory firm, not only focusing on the acquisition of talent at the senior

After reading the next section, you should be able to

7. Explain how visionary leadership (i.e., charismatic and transformational leadership) helps leaders achieve strategic leadership.

level, but also focusing on helping them develop their own employees and retention [strategies]. Forty percent of executives who join firms from the outside last only 18 months. How do we as a firm help reduce that and help them with that turnover?"[58]

Thus, strategic leadership captures how leaders inspire their companies to change and their followers to give extraordinary effort to accomplish organizational goals.

7 Visionary Leadership

In Chapter 5, we defined a purpose statement, which is often referred to as an organizational mission or vision, as a statement of a company's purpose or reason for existing. Similarly, visionary leadership creates a positive image of the future that motivates organizational members and provides direction for future planning and goal setting.[59]

Two kinds of visionary leadership are 7.1 charismatic leadership and 7.2 transformational leadership.

7.1 Charismatic Leadership

Charisma is a Greek word meaning "divine gift." The ancient Greeks saw people with charisma as inspired by the gods and capable of incredible accomplishments. German sociologist Max Weber viewed charisma as a special bond between leaders and followers.[60] Weber wrote that the special qualities of charismatic leaders enable them to strongly influence followers. Jose Mourinho, coach of the Spanish soccer team Real Madrid, certainly qualifies as a charismatic leader. He has developed such a deep bond with his players that one of them was even quoted as saying that he would play for Mourinho on a broken leg. How was he able to form such ties? Former players and fellow coaches praise him for being confident, enthusiastic, and meticulous in his attention to detail. Above all, however, he shows his players that he cares for them. In a field where coaches often criticize their players for mistakes, Mourinho encourages them with personalized notes, emails, and text messages. He even does outrageous things to take pressure off of his players. Once, while preparing

strategic leadership the ability to anticipate, envision, maintain flexibility, think strategically, and work with others to initiate changes that will create a positive future for an organization.

visionary leadership leadership that creates a positive image of the future that motivates organizational members and provides direction for future planning and goal setting.

for a game against an archrival, Mourinho walked out on the pitch (i.e., the field) by himself. "I knew that I would get a thunderous reception in the negative sense, so I decided to go on the pitch alone before the team. There were 80,000 booing me but in off-loading that against me, they spared the team."[61]

Weber also noted that charismatic leaders tend to emerge in times of crisis and that the radical solutions they propose enhance the admiration that followers feel for them. Indeed, charismatic leaders tend to have incredible influence over followers who may be inspired by their leaders and become fanatically devoted to them. From this perspective, charismatic leaders are often seen as larger than life or more special than other employees of the company.

Charismatic leaders have strong, confident, dynamic personalities that attract followers and enable the leaders to create strong bonds with their followers. Followers trust charismatic leaders, are loyal to them, and are inspired to work toward the accomplishment of the leader's vision. Followers who become devoted to charismatic leaders may go to extraordinary lengths to please them. Therefore, we can define **charismatic leadership** as the behavioral tendencies and personal characteristics of leaders that create an exceptionally strong relationship between them and their followers. Charismatic leaders also

>> Articulate a clear vision for the future that is based on strongly held values or morals;

>> Model those values by acting in a way consistent with the vision;

>> Communicate high performance expectations to followers; and

>> Display confidence in followers' abilities to achieve the vision.[62]

Does charismatic leadership work? Studies indicate that it often does. In general, the followers of charismatic leaders are more committed and satisfied, are better performers, are more likely to trust their leaders, and simply work harder.[63] Nonetheless, charismatic leadership also has risks that are at least as large as its benefits. The problems are likely to occur with ego-driven charismatic leaders who take advantage of fanatical followers.

In general, there are two kinds of charismatic leaders, ethical charismatics and unethical charismatics.[64] **Ethical charismatics** provide developmental opportunities for followers, are open to positive and negative feedback, recognize others' contributions, share information, and have moral standards that emphasize the larger interests of the group, organization, or society. Jim McNerney, Boeing's CEO, believes that providing development opportunities for followers should be a leader's highest priority. Says McNerney, "I don't start with the company's strategy or products. I start with people's growth because I believe that if the people who are running and participating in a company grow, then the company's growth will in many respects take care of itself. I have this idea in my mind—all of us get 15 percent better every year. . . . Usually that means your ability to lead, and that's all about your ability to chart the course for [your employees], to inspire them to reach for performance—the values you bring to the job, with a focus on the courage to do the right thing. I tend to think about this in terms of helping others get better."[65] As you would expect, ethical charismatics produce stronger commitment, higher satisfaction, more effort, better performance, and greater trust.

By contrast, **unethical charismatics** control and manipulate followers, do what is best for themselves instead of their organizations, want to hear only positive feedback, share information that is only beneficial to themselves, and have moral standards that put their interests before everyone else's. Because followers can become

charismatic leadership the behavioral tendencies and personal characteristics of leaders that create an exceptionally strong relationship between them and their followers.

ethical charismatics charismatic leaders who provide developmental opportunities for followers, are open to positive and negative feedback, recognize others' contributions, share information, and have moral standards that emphasize the larger interests of the group, organization, or society.

unethical charismatics charismatic leaders who control and manipulate followers, do what is best for themselves instead of their organizations, want to hear only positive feedback, share only information that is beneficial to themselves, and have moral standards that put their interests before everyone else's.

mgmt:trends

When Leaders Step Down

After nearly a decade of struggles, including bankruptcy and a government-funded bailout, General Motors posted a quarterly profit of $1.3 billion and prepared for a public stock offering that would raise billions more for the company. It seemed, then, quite a strange time for CEO Ed Whitacre to announce that he would resign. But, from the day he took the job, Whitacre told GM's board that he viewed his job as temporary. The goal that he set for himself as leader of GM was to "return the company to greatness" by stabilizing its finances and ensuring that it would have a solid foundation for future growth. Once he felt he had accomplished that goal, he announced his resignation.[66]

just as committed to unethical charismatics as to ethical charismatics, unethical charismatics pose a tremendous risk for companies. According to *Fast Company*, "We're worshipful of top executives who seem charismatic, visionary, and tough. So long as they're lifting profits and stock prices, we're willing to overlook that they can also be callous, cunning, manipulative, deceitful, verbally and psychologically abusive, remorseless, exploitative, self-delusional, irresponsible, and megalomaniacal."[67]

John Thompson, a management consultant, warns, "Often what begins as a mission becomes an obsession. Leaders can cut corners on values and become driven by self-interest. Then they may abuse anyone who makes a mistake."[68] In terms of cutting corners and self-interest, it's hard to top the unethical charismatic behavior of former David H. Brooks, the former CEO of **DHB**, a military contractor that makes body armor for the military and police. Brooks was found guilty of 17 counts of fraud and of stealing nearly $190 million from the company. According to prosecutors, Brooks repeatedly used company funds to buy luxury items for himself and his family, including a Bentley, a Ferrari, purebred horses, family vacations, his wife's facelift, and a jewel-encrusted belt buckle worth more than $100,000. Along with Chief Operating Officer Sandra Hatfield, Brooks was accused of lying about the number of body armor units that were being shipped to the U.S. Army, ordering company accountants to produce false reports about the company's performance, and committing insider trading through an illegal sale of stock.[69]

< **"what's new" companies**

Exhibit 14.15 shows the stark differences between ethical and unethical charismatics on several leader behaviors: exercising power, creating the vision, communicating with followers, accepting feedback, stimulating followers intellectually, developing followers, and living by moral standards. For example, ethical charismatics account for the concerns and wishes of their followers when creating a vision by having followers participate in the development of the company vision. By contrast, unethical charismatics develop a vision by themselves solely to meet their personal agendas. One unethical charismatic said, "The key thing is that it is my idea; and I am going to win with it at all costs."[70]

What can companies do to reduce the risks associated with unethical charismatics? To start, they need a clearly written code of conduct that is fairly and consistently enforced for all managers. Next, companies should recruit, select, and promote managers with high ethical standards. Also, companies need to train leaders to value, seek, and use diverse points of view. Both leaders and subordinates need training

Exhibit 14.15 Ethical and Unethical Charismatics

CHARISMATIC LEADER BEHAVIORS	ETHICAL CHARISMATICS	UNETHICAL CHARISMATICS
Exercising power	Power is used to serve others.	Power is used to dominate or manipulate others for personal gain.
Creating the vision	Followers help develop the vision.	Vision comes solely from leader and serves his or her personal agenda.
Communicating with followers	Two-way communication: Seek out viewpoints on critical issues.	One-way communication: Not open to input and suggestions from others.
Accepting feedback	Open to feedback. Willing to learn from criticism.	Inflated ego thrives on attention and admiration of sycophants. Avoid or punish candid feedback.
Stimulating followers	Want followers to think and question status quo as well as leader's views.	Don't want followers to think. Want uncritical, intellectually unquestioning acceptance of leader's ideas.
Developing followers	Focus on developing people with whom they interact. Express confidence in them and share recognition with others.	Insensitive and unresponsive to followers' needs and aspirations.
Living by moral standards	Follow self-guided principles that may go against popular opinion. Have three virtues: courage, a sense of fairness or justice, and integrity.	Follow standards only if they satisfy immediate self-interests. Manipulate impressions so that others think they are "doing the right thing." Use communication skills to manipulate others to support their personal agenda.

Source: J. M. Howell & B. J. Avolio, "The Ethics of Charismatic Leadership: Submission or Liberation?" *Academy of Management Executive* 6, no. 2 (1992): 43–54.

regarding ethical leader behaviors so that abuses can be recognized and corrected. Finally, companies should celebrate and reward people who exhibit ethical behaviors, especially ethical leader behaviors.[71]

7.2 Transformational Leadership

Whereas charismatic leadership involves articulating a clear vision, modeling values consistent with that vision, communicating high performance expectations, and establishing very strong relationships with followers, **transformational leadership** goes further by generating awareness and acceptance of a group's purpose and mission and by getting employees to see beyond their own needs and self-interest, for the good of the group.[72] Like charismatic leaders, transformational leaders are visionary, but they transform their organizations by getting their followers to accomplish more than they intended and even more than they thought possible.

Transformational leaders are able to make their followers feel that they are a vital part of the organization and help them see how their jobs fit with the organization's vision. By linking individual and organizational interests, transformational leaders encourage followers to make sacrifices for the organization because they know that they will prosper when the organization prospers. As Exhibit 14.16 shows, transformational leadership has four components: charismatic leadership or

transformational leadership leadership that generates awareness and acceptance of a group's purpose and mission and gets employees to see beyond their own needs and self-interests for the good of the group.

idealized influence, inspirational motivation, intellectual stimulation, and individualized consideration.[73]

Charismatic leadership or idealized influence means that transformational leaders act as role models for their followers. Because transformational leaders put others' needs ahead of their own and share risks with their followers, they are admired, respected, and trusted, and followers want to emulate them. Thus, in contrast to purely charismatic leaders (especially unethical charismatics), transformational leaders can be counted on to do the right thing and maintain high standards for ethical and personal conduct. After Jim McNerney became Boeing's third CEO in three years, he pushed company lawyers to settle ethics violations that occurred under his predecessors. Under the settlement with the U.S. Justice Department, Boeing agreed to pay a $615 million penalty. But that wasn't enough for McNerney. He apologized before a Senate committee and refused to take a $200 million tax deduction to which Boeing was entitled for its costs in obtaining the settlement. Critics charge that McNerney's decision not to take the tax deduction wrongly cost Boeing shareholders $200 million. McNerney, who was responsible for restoring the company's commitment to ethical behavior, said, "I thought it was the right thing to do."[74] McNerney also instituted a new organization-wide ethics program and has linked bonuses and promotion to ethical behavior.

Inspirational motivation means that transformational leaders motivate and inspire followers by providing meaning and challenge to their work. By clearly communicating expectations and demonstrating commitment to goals, transformational leaders help followers envision future states, such as the organizational vision or mission. In turn, this leads to greater enthusiasm and optimism about the future. Medtronic's mission is "To contribute to human welfare by application of biomedical engineering in the research, design, manufacture, and sale of instruments or appliances that *alleviate pain, restore health, and extend life*."[75] Because Medtronic designs and makes life-altering products, it has an opportunity to inspire the managers and workers who work there. Every December for the holiday party, Medtronic flies in six patients to demonstrate that the company is accomplishing its mission to "alleviate pain, restore health, and extend life." The patients give testimonials describing the difference that Medtronic's products have made to them and their loved ones. Production supervisor Karen McFadzen says, "We have patients who come in who would be dead if it wasn't for us. I mean, they sit right up there and they tell us what their lives are like. You don't walk away from them not feeling anything." Medtronic quality systems manager Kirk Knock says, "We hear first-hand from the patients, including children, who we have helped. This is a very emotional and rewarding day for all of us."[76]

Intellectual stimulation means that transformational leaders encourage followers to be creative and innovative, question assumptions, and look at problems and situations in new ways, even if their ideas

Exhibit 14.16
Components of Transformational Leadership

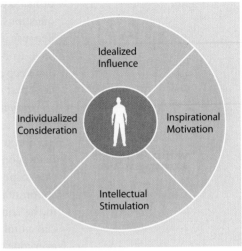

© Cengage Learning 2013

Jim McNerney, CEO of Boeing, took action to restore the company's commitment to ethical behavior.

© Fourmy Mario/ABACA/Newscom

605

are different from the leaders'. Carol Bartz, former CEO of AutoDesk, the industry leader in computer-aided design software, and now CEO of Yahoo!, pushes the people who work for her to think beyond their original assumptions by asking questions. Says Bartz, "All you have to do is ask questions. You just have to keep asking questions. You ask questions and guess what, they go, 'Oh, I never thought of that.' Because it unleashes so much power in people by just asking. Why do I [as the CEO] have to be the know-it-all? My God, I'm not that smart. But I'm smart enough to just keep asking questions and say, 'Is that the best you can do? Does that excite you? Will that excite the customer? Does this really have to work this way?'"[77]

Individualized consideration means that transformational leaders pay special attention to followers' individual needs by creating learning opportunities, accepting and tolerating individual differences, encouraging two-way communication, and being good listeners. At the **Sky Factory**, an Iowa company that installs ocean- and sky-scape ceilings and walls in hospitals, restaurants, and spas, founder Bill Witherspoon makes sure there is no hierarchy. He gives everyone the option to buy shares in the company. Every Friday, a company-wide meeting is held, during which financial numbers, quality issues, and the number of clients that visited is shared with everyone. Says Witherspoon, "Everyone is trained in financial literacy so he or she can make the best use of the information." Witherspoon is so committed to empowering his workers that when he wanted to expand to Europe but the group decided against it, he accepted their decision. "I argued my case for 15 minutes and then said, 'Clearly we don't have consensus, so we'll forget about it.' And we have."[78]

Finally, a distinction needs to be drawn between transformational leadership and transactional leadership. Whereas transformational leaders use visionary and inspirational appeals to influence followers, **transactional leadership** is based on an exchange process in which followers are rewarded for good performance and punished for poor performance. When leaders administer rewards fairly and offer followers the rewards that they want, followers will often reciprocate with effort. A problem, however, is that transactional leaders often rely too heavily on discipline or threats to bring performance up to standards. This may work in the short run, but it's much less effective in the long run. Also, as discussed in Chapters 11 and 13, many leaders and organizations have difficulty successfully linking pay practices to individual performance. As a result, studies consistently show that transformational leadership is much more effective on average than transactional leadership. In the United States, Canada, Japan, and India—and at all organizational levels, from first-level supervisors to upper-level executives—followers view transformational leaders as much better leaders and are much more satisfied when working for them. Furthermore, companies with transformational leaders have significantly better financial performance.[79]

"what's new" companies >

transactional leadership leadership based on an exchange process, in which followers are rewarded for good performance and punished for poor performance.

Review 7

Visionary Leadership Strategic leadership requires visionary, charismatic, and transformational leadership. Visionary leadership creates a positive image of the future that motivates organizational members and provides direction for future planning and goal setting. Charismatic leaders have strong, confident, dynamic personalities that attract followers, enable the leader to create strong bonds, and inspire followers to accomplish the leader's vision. Followers of ethical charismatic leaders work harder, are more committed and satisfied, are better performers, and are more likely to trust their leaders. Followers can be just as supportive and committed to unethical charismatics, but these leaders can pose a tremendous risk for companies. Unethical charismatics control and manipulate followers and do what is best for themselves instead of their organizations. To reduce the risks associated with unethical charismatics, companies need to enforce a clearly written code of conduct; recruit, select, and promote managers with high ethical standards; train leaders to value, seek, and use diverse points of view; teach everyone in the company to recognize unethical leader behaviors; and celebrate and reward people who exhibit ethical behaviors. Transformational leadership goes beyond charismatic leadership by generating awareness and acceptance of a group's purpose and mission and by getting employees to see beyond their own needs and self-interest for the good of the group. The four components of transformational leadership are charisma, or idealized influence; inspirational motivation; intellectual stimulation; and individualized consideration.

SELF-ASSESSMENT

Leadership Orientation

Think of everyone you have ever worked with in jobs, clubs, volunteer positions, student projects—everything. Now that you have all those situations in mind, try to identify the one person with whom you least liked to work. Who was the most difficult person to work with to get a job done? For whatever reason, you had trouble working with this person. The person can be a peer, boss, or subordinate. Once you have that person in mind, think of how you would describe him or her to another person. The Least Preferred Co-worker scale uses 18 oppositional adjective pairs to help you build your description.[80] For each pair, choose the number closest to the word that best describes your LPC.

Pleasant	8	7	6	5	4	③	2	1	Unpleasant
Friendly	8	7	6	5	4	③	2	1	Unfriendly
Rejecting	①	2	3	4	5	6	7	8	Accepting
Tense	①	2	3	4	5	6	7	8	Relaxed
Distant	1	2	③	4	5	6	7	8	Close
Cold	1	②	3	4	5	6	7	8	Warm
Supportive	8	7	6	5	4	3	2	①	Hostile
Boring	①	2	3	4	⑤	6	7	8	Interesting
Quarrelsome	1	2	③	4	5	6	7	8	Harmonious
Gloomy	1	②	3	4	5	6	7	8	Cheerful
Open	8	7	6	5	4	3	2	①	Guarded
Backbiting	①	2	3	4	5	6	7	8	Loyal
Untrustworthy	①	2	3	4	5	6	7	8	Trustworthy
Considerate	8	7	6	5	4	3	2	①	Inconsiderate
Nasty	①	2	3	4	5	6	7	8	Nice
Agreeable	8	7	6	5	4	3	2	①	Disagreeable
Insincere	①	2	3	4	5	6	7	8	Sincere
Kind	8	7	6	5	4	3	2	①	Unkind
TOTAL = _____									

Scoring

Determine your leadership style by totaling all the numbers you selected into a single sum. Your score will fall between 18 and 96. You can find the interpretation for your score at www.cengagebrain.com.

MANAGEMENT DECISION

To Cell or Not to Cell[81]

It's a bright Tuesday morning, and you're sitting in a rather exciting meeting in which your company's marketing team will present the new fall campaign. It's been an exciting time since you took over as CEO of this small electronics firm, and everyone is anticipating that the new product lineup that the company has been working on will bring new levels of success.

Just as the team is about to start presenting their thoughts on how to market the new products, your phone rings; it's Karen from distribution, asking whether you have five minutes to talk about truck maintenance. "No," you tell her, "I'm in a meeting." As you apologize for the interruption, your phone rings again; it's your assistant, and he wants to know when you can schedule a meeting with the president of a subcontractor. A few minutes after that, Gary from HR calls and asks when the new benefits package will be approved. After that you get calls from the mailroom, the president of the electricians' union, your chief accountant, and your teenage son, asking whether he can drive the car to school. And in between all of those calls, your phone has been buzzing nonstop with emails.

With all of these interruptions, a presentation that should have taken 30 minutes took more than two hours, and this isn't the first time something like this has happened either. Day and night, it seems, you're getting bombarded by phone calls and text messages and emails, almost to the point that you can't get any real work done. As you trudge back to your office, you remark to your assistant, "Maybe I should just get rid of this phone." And he says, "Maybe you should."

He mentions that he just saw a magazine article about executives who don't use cell phones, even high-powered people like Warren Buffett, Mikhail Prokhorov (owner of the NBA team New Jersey Nets), and Tavis Smiley, a TV and radio host. One manager quoted in the articles says that he got rid of his cell phone to increase his efficiency. With no cell phone, he could focus on one meeting at a time and give exclusive attention to whomever he is talking with. Tavis Smiley says that without a cell phone, employees of his company actually get more conversation time with him than before.

So maybe this is the solution to your problems: Without a cell phone, there would be no more interrupted meetings, no more urgent calls about stuff that isn't really urgent, no more 30-minute appointments that stretch to two hours. When you ask your managers and employees, however, there's a high level of anxiety. Will you be accessible at all? What if there is a real emergency?

Questions

1. Do you believe that the CEO of a company can effectively do his or her job of leading without being always accessible?
2. If you, as the CEO, were to get rid of your phone, how would ensure that lines of communication remain open?

MANAGEMENT TEAM DECISION

Setting Executive Salaries[82]

You are a member of the Board of Directors of a large, multinational bank that is looking to hire a new CEO. The previous CEO did as well as he could to guide your company through the recession, but everyone agrees that a new leader, with a fresh vision, is needed to lead the bank back to profitability.

You have been assigned to a committee that will create the new CEO's compensation package. Five years ago, this would have been a cakewalk assignment; put together a multimillion-dollar deal with cash, stock options, and tons of perks. But these are different times. You don't want to give out a lucrative package in the middle of the worst recession in 70 years. What would your employees think? What would the public think? At the same time, you're worried that if you don't offer extraordinary compensation, you'll never find the right person for the job.

One of the committee members shows up to a meeting with some recent research on CEO salaries. She reports that there are many CEOs who have taken drastic cuts in their pay during the past year. David Cote, the CEO of Honeywell, took a 57 percent salary cut. Vikram Pandit, the CEO of Citigroup, receives just $1 as a salary, and has publicly vowed not to take any additional compensation until the company returns to profitability. In fact, it appears that CEOs (and companies) across the country have lowered their expectations. A recent survey shows that CEO pay decreased by 8.6 percent from the previous year, and since 2000, CEO pay is down nearly 40 percent. This includes a 23 percent decrease in perks like private planes, security details, and country club memberships. Although you certainly don't except your next CEO to work for nothing, this does give you some hope that this person would be willing to lower his or her demands a bit.

But as the committee member continues her report, she points out a disturbing trend. Although the total package that CEOs receive is down, the amount that they receive in cash is up 8.3 percent, and their average cash bonus is up 7.9 percent, to $2.1 million, while the amount they receive in stock options is down nearly 30 percent. What does all of this mean? It means that more companies are placing less emphasis on long-term incentives. Instead of using stocks to link CEO pay to a company's performance, many companies are emphasizing short-term thinking by giving CEOs lots of cash. Even if the company does not perform well, their executives will still benefit financially.

You and the rest of the committee are left to wonder what the right approach is. Can you find the right CEO with a reduced salary package? Do you ask your new CEO to accept more stock options so that his financial well-being is tied to the company's? Or do you offer as much cash as possible, with the hopes of attracting top-flight talent? Form a group with three or four other students, and consider these issues as you discuss the questions below.

Questions

1. What are the advantages and disadvantages of tying an executive's pay to the company's performance?
2. How would you explain to concerned shareholders and employees why it is so important that the CEO receive a multimillion-dollar salary package?
3. How much input would you give company employees in making a decision on executive pay?

PRACTICE BEING A MANAGER

Changing Directions

Leadership is a highly prized process and capability. Organizations invest billions of dollars each year in recruiting and developing leadership talent. As more companies compete primarily on the basis of how well they employ their human capabilities, the importance of leadership continues to grow. This exercise will provide you with an opportunity to play coach to a leader entering a challenging situation.

Step 1: Get into groups. Your professor will assign you to pairs or small groups.

Scenario: PepsiCo is a company with a remarkable tradition of product and management innovations, but as the opening segment makes clear, over the past several years PepsiCo is facing increased competition from its archrival Coca-Cola and struggling to navigate the challenges of an ever-changing marketplace. As the new CEO scans the situation, it is difficult to know how to prioritize. Where to begin?

Assume that the members of your small team are a group of consultants working with Pepsi's new CEO. Your job is behind the scenes—you are simply helping the CEO brainstorm and think carefully about how to lead this company, improve performance, and restore the once-vibrant culture of creativity that made PepsiCo a leader in its industry.

Step 2: Outline leadership criteria. Work as a team to develop a set of leadership recommendations that are well matched to the PepsiCo situation. What do you think employees need most from their new leader?

Should the CEO help employees look back and learn from the company's past, or should the CEO encourage employees to move on and focus on the future? What are the trade-offs in each approach? The opening segment highlights some key areas of concern: (1) increased competition; (2) rising cost structures; (3) declining financial and marketing performance; (4) declining brand image (e.g., as a contributor to unhealthy eating habits and childhood obesity). So how would you recommend that the CEO prioritize these issues? Are there creative possibilities for tackling some of these concerns simultaneously?

Step 3: Determine a coaching plan. Prepare to coach the CEO during the process of transforming PepsiCo. How might path–goal thinking help the CEO guide PepsiCo employees through the transition? What should the CEO keep in mind regarding such situational factors as worker readiness, situation favorableness, and environmental contingencies? Assuming the CEO possesses charismatic capabilities, would you recommend relying upon a charismatic leadership style in this situation? Why or why not?

Step 4: Debrief as a class. Share some of the highlights of your recommendations, and discuss what leadership consultants/coaches need to know to effectively advise their clients.

DEVELOP YOUR CAREER POTENTIAL

The Role of Humility in Leadership

Everybody makes mistakes; today's media-saturated culture makes everyone's mistakes everyone else's news.[83] This is particularly true of leaders, who are less able (perhaps simply unable) to hide from the media microscope than in times past. We want our leaders to have an unshakable integrity, so when their mistakes turn into front-page news, it provides a unique look at the mettle of those who lead our governments, institutions, and businesses. One of the functions of leadership is to assume responsibility for company actions, even when those actions are dubious at best or downright shameful at worst. But how can leaders—who are supposed to always take the high road—work through mistakes that they or their organizations have made?

The answer is simple: a sincere apology. Okay, so the answer is not so simple. Everyone knows that apologizing is not so easy, as proved by the associated lump in the throat and the awful feeling that comes from knowing that something you did caused someone else pain, embarrassment, loss, or hardship. But as you read in the chapter, a critical element of what leaders do and how leaders succeed is consideration, which is akin to empathy, the engine of a sincere apology.

How do *you* apologize for mistakes? Do you use "sorry" so often that it is devoid of meaning? Or do you apologize profusely, which leads to the same effect? Do you wait until you have time to think things over, or do you apologize immediately, if briefly? The biggest mistake that leaders make when apologizing is passing the buck and using the word *regret* instead of *apologize*. Leaders take responsibility for actions and should assume blame even if it is not their own. Making an unqualified assumption of responsibility helps demonstrate that your apology is sincere, as does going beyond a basic "I'm sorry." According to Karen Friedman, a communication coach, "'I'm sorry' doesn't cut it. . . . It's empty, hollow, and quite frankly, pathetic: 'I'm sorry I cooked the books.' 'I'm sorry I beat my wife. I won't do it again.' You have to say, 'I made a terrible mistake. I offended people. I lied. I was stupid.'"[84] So, one of the marks of a true leader is not hubris, but humility. In other words, the best way to *appear* sincere is to *be* sincere.

Questions

1. Describe a time when something you did or said had a profound negative impact on a person, group, or situation.
2. Did you take responsibility for your actions, or did you try to blame circumstances or other people?
3. Did you apologize? How do you think the person who was receiving the apology took it?
4. What was the most difficult thing about apologizing?
5. Think about some high-profile blunders in recent news stories, whether in the world of sports, business, or entertainment. How do you think the company or individual involved did at delivering a public apology? Explain why you thought it was—or was not—sincere.

END NOTES

[1] J. Champy, "Apple's Arrested Development," *Forbes*, April 20, 1998, 132; A. Hesseldahl, "Was Apple 'Adequate but Late' on Jobs?" *Businessweek*, January 6, 2009, 2; Y. Kane, "Jobs, Back At Apple, Focuses on New Tablet," *Wall Street Journal*, August 25, 2009, B1; A. Lashinsky, "Apple: The Genius Behind Steve," *Fortune*, November 24, 2008, 70–80; and A. Lashinsky, "Inside Apple," *Fortune*, May 23, 2011, 125–134; and B. Schlender, "How Big Can Apple Get?" *Fortune*, February 21, 2005, 66–76.

[2] W. Bennis, "Why Leaders Can't Lead," *Training & Development Journal* 43, no. 4 (1989).

[3] L. Buchanan, "How the Creative Stay Creative," Inc., June 2008, 102–103.

[4] A. Zaleznik, "Managers and Leaders: Are They Different?" *Harvard Business Review* 55 (1977): 76–78; and A. Zaleznik, "The Leadership Gap," *Washington Quarterly* 6 (1983): 32–39.

[5] David Welch, "Ed Whitacre's Battle to Save GM from Itself," *Bloomberg Businessweek*. April 29, 2010, accessed August 27, 2010, from www.businessweek.com/magazine/content/10_19/b4177048204431.htm.

[6] Bennis, "Why Leaders Can't Lead."

[7] John Waggoner & Adam Shell, "Apple Falls, but Does Steve Jobs' Leave Merit a Pounding?" *USA Today* January 18, 2010, accessed June 5, 2011, from www.usatoday.com/money/perfi/stocks/2011-01-18-appleinvest18_ST_N.htm.

[8] G. Fowler, "Steve Jobs 1955–2011: Apple Must Face Rivals Without its Guru," *Wall Street Journal*, 6 October 2011, A7.

[9] J. P. Howell, D. E. Bowen, P. W. Dorfman, S. Kerr, & P. M. Podsakoff, "Substitutes for Leadership: Effective Alternatives to Ineffective Leadership," *Organizational Dynamics*, June 22, 1990, 20; and S. Kerr & J. M. Jermier, "Substitutes for Leadership: Their Meaning and Measurement," *Organizational Behavior & Human Performance* 22 (1978): 375–403.

[10] Diana Ransom, "6 Ways to Manage a Virtual Workforce," *Entrepreneur*, April 19, 2010, accessed February 21, 2011, from www.entrepreneur.com/humanresources/managingemployees/article206214.html.

[11] S. Berfield, "The Best of 2006: Leaders," *Businessweek*, December 18, 2006, 58.

[12] D. Jones, "Not All Successful CEOs Are Extroverts," *USA Today*, June 7, 2006, B1.

[13] Ibid.

[14] M. Gladwell, "Why Do We Love Tall Men?" *Gladwell.com*, accessed August 27, 2008, from www.gladwell.com/blink/blink_excerpt2.html.

[15] D. Sacks, "The Accidental Guru," *Fast Company*, January 1, 2005, 64.

[16] R. J. House & R. M Aditya, "The Social Scientific Study of Leadership: Quo Vadis?" *Journal of Management* 23 (1997): 409–473; T. Judge, R. Illies, J. Bono, & M. Gerhardt, "Personality and Leadership: A Qualitative and Quantitative Review," *Journal of Applied Psychology* (August 2002): 765–782; and S. A. Kirkpatrick & E. A. Locke, "Leadership: Do Traits Matter?" *Academy of Management Executive* 5, no. 2 (1991): 48–60.

[17] House & Aditya, "The Social Scientific Study of Leadership"; and Kirkpatrick & Locke, "Leadership: Do Traits Matter?"

[18] J. J. Gabarro, *The Dynamics of Taking Charge* (Boston: Harvard Business School Press, 1987).

[19] Michael V. Copeland, "Reed Hastings: Leader of the Pack," *Fortune*, November 18, 2010, accessed June 5, 2011, from http://tech.fortune.cnn.com/2010/11/18/reed-hastings-leader-of-the-pack/.

[20] "The Best CEOs," *Barron's*, March 29, 2010, accessed August 30, 2010, from http://online.barrons.com/article/SB126964409156568321.html; and "Cummins INC," *Bloomberg Businessweek*, no date, accessed August 30, 2010, from http://investing.businessweek.com/research/stocks/people/person.asp?personId=265255&ticker=CMI:US.

[21] Kirkpatrick & Locke, "Leadership: Do Traits Matter?"

[22] E. A. Fleishman, "The Description of Supervisory Behavior," *Journal of Applied Psychology* 37 (1953): 1–6; and L. R. Katz, *New Patterns of Management* (New York: McGraw-Hill, 1961).

[23] B. Fuller, C. E. P. Patterson, K. Hester, & D. Stringer, " A Quantitative Review of Research on Charismatic Leadership," *Psychological Reports* 78 (1996): 271–287; and R. G. Lord, C. L. De Vader, & G. M. Alliger, "A Meta-Analysis of the Relation between Personality Traits and Leadership Perceptions: An Application of Validity Generalization Procedures," *Journal of Applied Psychology* 71, no. 3 (1986): 402–410.

[24] Bruce Einhorn, "Innovator: Jimmy Lai," *Bloomberg Businessweek*, August 26, 2010, accessed September 9, 2010, from www.businessweek.com/magazine/content/10_36/b4193038847783.htm.

[25] N. Byrnes, "The Issue: Maintaining Employee Engagement," *Bloomberg Businessweek*, January 16, 2009, accessed August 20, 2010, from www.businessweek.com/managing/content/jan2009/ca20090116_444132.htm.

[26] P. Weissenberg & M. H. Kavanagh, "The Independence of Initiating Structure and Consideration: A Review of the Evidence," *Personnel Psychology* 25 (1972): 119–130.

[27] R. J. House & T. R. Mitchell, "Path-Goal Theory of Leadership," *Journal of Contemporary Business* 3 (1974): 81–97; F. E. Fiedler, "A Contingency Model of Leadership Effectiveness," in L. Berkowitz, ed., *Advances in Experimental Social Psychology* (New York: Academic Press, 1964); V. H. Vroom & P. W. Yetton, *Leadership and Decision Making* (Pittsburgh: University of Pittsburgh Press, 1973); P. Hersey & K. H. Blanchard, The *Management of Organizational Behavior*, 4th ed. (Englewood Cliffs, NJ: Prentice Hall,

1984); and Kerr & Jermier, "Substitutes for Leadership."

[28]J. Pfeffer, "In Defense of the Boss from Hell," *Business 2.0*, March 1, 2007, 70.

[29]F. E. Fiedler & M. M. Chemers, *Leadership and Effective Management* (Glenview, IL: Scott, Foresman, 1974); and F. E. Fiedler & M. M. Chemers, *Improving Leadership Effectiveness: The Leader Match Concept*, 2nd ed. (New York: Wiley, 1984).

[30]J. Walker, "Executives Learn New Skills To Improve Their Communication," *Wall Street Journal*, May 6, 2010, accessed June 5, 2011, from http://online.wsj.com/article/SB10001424052748704342604575222701379951106.html.

[31]Fiedler & Chemers, *Improving Leadership Effectiveness.*

[32]F. E. Fiedler, "The Effects of Leadership Training and Experience: A Contingency Model Interpretation," *Administrative Science Quarterly* 17, no. 4 (1972): 455; and F. E. Fiedler, *A Theory of Leadership Effectiveness* (New York: McGraw-Hill, 1967).

[33]N. Shirouzu, "Support Wavers At Toyota For Chief," *The Wall Street Journal*, February 23, 2010, A4.

[34]J. Helyar, "Why Is This Man Smiling?" *Fortune*, October 18, 2004, 130.

[35]L. S. Csoka & F. E. Fiedler, "The Effect of Military Leadership Training: A Test of the Contingency Model," *Organizational Behavior & Human Performance* 8 (1972): 395–407.

[36]House & Mitchell, "Path-Goal Theory of Leadership."

[37]K. Spors, "Top Small Workplaces 2008: Creating Great Workplaces Has Never Been More Important for Small Businesses; nor More Difficult; Here Are 15 Companies That Do It Well," *The Wall Street Journal*, October 13, 2008, R1.

[38]House & Mitchell, "Path-Goal Theory of Leadership."

[39]M. Langley & S. Terlep, "'I'm Not a Car Guy': On the Road With the New Man at GM's Wheel," *The Wall Street Journal*, January 8, 2011, A1.

[40]B. M. Fisher & J. E. Edwards, "Consideration and Initiating Structure and Their Relationships with Leader Effectiveness: A Meta-Analysis," *Proceedings of the Academy of Management*, August 1988, 201–205.

[41]A. Todorova, "Company Programs Help Workers Save on Gas," *The Wall Street Journal*, May 30, 2008, accessed June 18, 2009, from www.wsj.com/article/SB121216248602832943.html.

[42]Leigh Buchanan, "Letting Employees Run the Company," *Inc.*, June 8, 2010, accessed August 30, 2010, from www.inc.com/top-workplaces/2010/letting-employees-run-the-company.html.

[43]F. Manjoo, "Google: The Quest," *Fast Company*, April 2011, 69–120, 9p.

[44]J. C. Wofford & L. Z. Liska, "Path-Goal Theories of Leadership: A Meta-Analysis," Journal of Management 19 (1993): 857–876.

[45]House & Aditya, "The Social Scientific Study of Leadership."

[46]P. Hersey & K. Blanchard, *Management of Organizational Behavior: Leading Human Resources*, 8th ed. (Escondido, CA: Center for Leadership Studies, 2001).

[47]W. Blank, J. R. Weitzel, & S. G. Green, "A Test of the Situational Leadership Theory," *Personnel Psychology* 43, no. 3 (1990): 579–597; and W. R. Norris & R. P. Vecchio, "Situational Leadership Theory: A Replication," *Group & Organization Management* 17, no. 3 (1992): 331–342.

[48]Ibid.

[49]V. H. Vroom & A. G. Jago, *The New Leadership: Managing Participation in Organizations* (Englewood Cliffs, NJ: Prentice Hall, 1988).

[50]C. Fishman, "How Teamwork Took Flight: This Team Built a Commercial Engine—and Self-Managing GE Plant—from Scratch," *Fast Company*, October 1, 1999, 188.

[51]Ibid.

[52]Ibid.

[53]"Korn/Ferry Survey Reveals More Interest Than Action in CEO Succession Plan Among Companies" Korn/Ferry International. December 21, 2010, accessed June 6, 2011, from http://www.kornferry.com/PressRelease/11916.

[54]C. Binkley, "Style—On Style: Dress-Code Politics: Who Wears the Pants?; When a Man Regulates Attire at Work, Women Often See an Oppressor, Not a Mentor," June 19, 2008, D8.

[55]G. A. Yukl, *Leadership in Organizations,* 3rd ed. (Englewood Cliffs, NJ: Prentice Hall, 1995).

[56]B. M. Bass, *Bass & Stogdill's Handbook of Leadership: Theory, Research, and Managerial Applications* (New York: Free Press, 1990).

[57]R. D. Ireland & M. A. Hitt, "Achieving and Maintaining Strategic Competitiveness in the 21st Century: The Role of Strategic Leadership," *Academy of Management Executive* 13, no. 1 (1999): 43–57.

[58]CEO Insight: Kevin Kelly, "An Executive Recruiter's New Strategy," *Bloomberg Businessweek*, 15 January 2009, accessed June 6, 2011, from www.businessweek.com/managing/content/jan2009/ca20090115_508822.htm.

[59]P. Thoms & D. B. Greenberger, "Training Business Leaders to Create Positive Organizational Visions of the Future: Is It Successful?" *Academy of Management Journal* (Best Papers & Proceedings 1995): 212–216.

[60]M. Weber, *The Theory of Social and Economic Organizations*, trans. R. A. Henderson & T. Parsons (New York: Free Press, 1947).

[61]Jonathan Clegg, "The Way Mourinho Manages," *The Wall Street Journal*, June 2, 2010, accessed August 10, 2010, from http://online.wsj.com/article/NA_WSJ_PUB:SB1000142405274870396120457528085197233256.html.

[62]D. A. Waldman & F. J. Yammarino, "CEO Charismatic Leadership: Levels-of-Management and Levels-of-Analysis Effects," *Academy of Management Review* 24, no. 2 (1999): 266–285.

[63]K. B. Lowe, K. G. Kroeck, & N. Sivasubramaniam, "Effectiveness Correlates of Transformational and Transactional Leadership: A Meta-Analytic Review of the MLQ Literature," *Leadership Quarterly* 7 (1996): 385–425.

[64]J. M. Howell & B. J. Avolio, "The Ethics of Charismatic Leadership: Submission or Liberation?" Academy of *Management Executive* 6, no. 2 (1992): 43–54.

[65]M. Adams, "Boeing Bounces Back against Odds," *USA Today*, 11 January 2007, B.1.

[66]David Bailer & Kevin Krolicki "GM CEO Ed Whitacre Suddenly, Surprisingly Resigns, to Be Replaced by Dan Akerson," *Vancouver Sun*, August 12, 2010, accessed June 6, 2011, from http://www.vancouversun.com/Whitacre+suddenly+surprisingly+resigns+replaced+Akerson/3391052/story.html; and James R. Healey "GM CEO Ed Whitacre Says He'll Step Down Sept. 1," *USA Today*, August 12, 2010, accessed June 6, 2011, from http://content.usatoday.com/communities/driveon/post/2010/08/gm-ceo-ed-whitacre-says-hell-step-down-sept-1/1.

[67]A. Deutschman, "Is Your Boss a Psychopath?" *Fast Company*, July 2005, 44.

[68]P. Sellers, "What Exactly Is Charisma?" *Fortune*, January 15, 1996, 68.

[69]Sean Gardiner & Patricia Hurtado, "DHB Industries Ex-Chief David Brooks Looted Company, Jury Told," Bloomberg.com, January 26, 2010, accessed February 24, 2011, from http://www.bloomberg.com/apps/news?pid=newsarchive&aQw6hgpgZ9rE; and A. G. Sulzberger, "Military Contractor with $100,000 Belt Buckle Is Found Guilty," *The New York Times*, September 14, 2010, accessed June 6, 2011, from www.nytimes.com/2010/09/15/nyregion/15brooks.html.

[70]Howell & Avolio, "The Ethics of Charismatic Leadership."

[71]J. M. Burns, *Leadership* (New York: Harper & Row, 1978); and B. M. Bass, "From Transactional to Transformational Leadership: Learning to Share the Vision," *Organizational Dynamics* 18 (1990): 19–36.

[72]Bass, "From Transactional to Transformational Leadership."

[73]B. M. Bass, *A New Paradigm of Leadership: An Inquiry into Transformational Leadership* (Alexandra, VA: U.S. Army Research Institute for the Behavioral and Social Sciences, 1996).

[74]M. Adams, "Boeing Bounces Back against Odds," *USA Today*, January 11, 2007, B1.

[75]"Read the Medtronic Mission Statement to Learn about the Company Goals at Medtronic.com," Medtronic, accessed April 10, 2009, from www.medtronic.com/corporate/mission.html.

[76]C. Cross, "Medtronic Engineers the Patient Connection: Modern Medical Wonder," *Industrial Engineer*, July 2007, 28.

[77]K. Swisher, "A Question of Management: Carol Bartz on How Yahoo's Organizational Structure Got in the Way of Innovation," *The Wall Street Journal*, June 2, 2009, R4.

[78]L. Buchanan, "How to Build a Beautiful Company," Inc.com, June 8, 2010, accessed July 30, 2010, from www.inc.com/top-workplaces/2010/how-to-build-a-beautiful-company.html.

[79]Bass, "From Transactional to Transformational Leadership."

[80]F. E. Fiedler & M. M. Chemers, *Improving Leadership Effectiveness: The Leader Match Concept* (New York: Wiley, 1984).

[81]"The Cell-Free Club," *Bloomberg Businessweek*, August 9–15, 2010, 78–79.

[82]Jessica Silver-Greenberg, Tara Kawalski, & Alexis Leondis, "CEO Pay Drops, But . . . Cash Is King," *Businessweek*, April 5, 2010, 50–56.

[83]J. Zaslow, "Mistakes Were Made: What to Take Away from the High-Profile Blunders of 2006," *The Wall Street Journal*, December 26, 2006, D1; J. Brodkin, "Corporate Apologies Don't Mean Much: Data Breaches Force Company Executives to Apologize, But a Bad Apology Can Make Things Worse," *Network World*, March 14, 2007, 1; and L. Smith, "How Your Corporate Clients Can and Sometimes Must Apologize for Their Mistakes," *Of Counsel*, October 2005, 11–13.

[84]Zaslow, "Mistakes Were Made."

reel to real

BIZ FLIX

Doomsday

In the futuristic action thriller *Doomsday*, the "Reaper Virus" strikes the British Isles in 2007 and devastates the population in Scotland. Authorities go to desperate lengths to quarantine it, sealing off the borders and not allowing anyone to enter or leave the country. Social decay spreads, and cannibalistic behavior develops among the few remaining survivors. When the Reaper Virus reemerges in 2032, this time in London, England, classified satellite images show signs of life in Glasgow and Edinburgh. In this scene, Major Eden Sinclair (Rhona Mitra) is given the task of going into the city to find the scientist who they hope may have the cure for the virus. If she can't find him in time, she is told, "then you needn't bother coming back."

What to Watch for and Ask Yourself

1. Assess the behavior of both Major Sinclair and Michael Canaris. Which leadership traits does their behavior show?

2. Does this film sequence show any aspects of charismatic and transformational leadership? Draw some examples from the sequence.

MANAGEMENT WORKPLACE

Camp Bow Wow: Leadership

Although consistency and conformity are critical to the success of any chain, Camp Bow Wow seeks creative input from the franchisees who bought in to the system. To maintain a standard business template while encouraging fresh ideas, founder Heidi Ganahl keeps a door open for anyone who wants to meet and offer feedback. The policy has produced many visible improvements to the company, such as the new Tea Cup Pup Lounge, a play zone for small dogs. Because franchise companies attract hundreds of independent business owners into the system, Ganahl has to work with many strong leaders, which requires two-way cooperation and respect. She also has to manage personal relationships and keep every individual focused on business.

Discussion Questions

1. Does Camp Bow Wow CEO Heidi Ganahl possess qualities associated with contemporary leadership?

2. In what way is Heidi Ganahl's leadership charismatic and visionary? Give examples.

3. Where does Heidi Ganahl's leadership fall on the leadership grid discussed in the chapter? Explain.

CHAPTER 15

Communication

Learning Outcomes

1. Explain the role that perception plays in communication and communication problems.
2. Describe the communication process and the various kinds of communication in organizations.
3. Explain how managers can manage effective one-on-one communication.
4. Describe how managers can manage effective organization-wide communication.

what would you do?

Google Headquarters, Mountain View, California[1]

Founded in 1998, Google just had its most dominant year, with its search market share rising from 77 percent to 83 percent and revenues jumping 25 percent. Because most of the revenue came from search, Google is trying to diversify. But it faces intense competition in every market.

In traditional search, Microsoft's Bing search engine and Facebook, which passed Google as the most popular website in the world, pose threats as people desire more personalized and social media-related search information. Searches for local information, such as restaurant reviews or directions, are 20 percent of all Google searches and half of all mobile or smartphone searches. Yet, local-related search advertising is a weakness for Google, but a strength for Groupon, Facebook Places, Living Social, Foursquare, and Bing. Although Google's Android smartphones have more market share than Apple's iPhone, the Android software is open source, so Google makes no money except for built-in Google Ads and services. Likewise, Google trails Apple and Amazon in the number of publishers who use their software, devices (i.e., smartphones, tablets, book readers), and online stores to sell electronic versions of newspapers, magazines, books, music, TV shows, and movies. Finally, Google's Chrome web browser (13% market share) competes with Microsoft's Internet Explorer (55%), Mozilla's Firefox (22%), and Apple's Safari (7%).

In short, Google is trying to position itself for the day when people won't automatically use a Google search box to find information. Keith Woolcock, founder of 5thColumnIdeas, a technology research firm, doubts Google is up to the task, saying, "The problem for me as an investor is that Google looks a little too [much] like last year's model. It's the chicken in the sandwich—Apple and Facebook are on the opposing sides. Google is in the middle. Really, it looks to me as though it has become the Microsoft of its generation: big, bad and quickly becoming irrelevant."

Unfortunately, you fear that Woolcock might be right, which is why you replaced CEO Eric Schmidt, who now becomes executive chairman. When Google started, you were CEO for three years. But, as an introvert who prefers technology challenges to management issues, you were relieved to hire Schmidt from Sun Microsystems because of his extensive leadership experience. When Schmidt became CEO, Google was much smaller and still in start-up mode, so he focused on management and financial systems, while you and Sergey Brin focused on technology and product development. Google's philosophy was to hire really smart people and then let them do whatever they wanted. It was the norm for Google engineers to have 20 percent

© Felipe Trueba/ZUMA Press/Newscom

study tips

Close your book and write a list of the key concepts in this chapter.

Or create flashcards for key concepts (concept on one side, explanation and example on the other). Flashcards are great portable study aids that you can use over and over, in a group, with a partner, or on your own.

617

of their time to work on whatever they wanted. And it spawned great products like Gmail, which engineer Paul Buchheit designed in a day and then shopped around, to get other Google engineers to join his team. This approach worked well until Google hit 10,000 employees. But at Google's current size, 24,000 employees, with plans to hire another 6,000, it leads to confusion, poor coordination, and a lack of focus.

Today, Google is a much larger, more complicated company. But the biggest problem is that paralyzing bureaucracy has slowed the company. As technology companies grow, this happens. IBM, Apple, Microsoft, and HP weren't immune, and neither is Google. In fact, the key reason you became CEO again was to streamline decision making and communication, and create clearer lines of responsibility and accountability. But how do you do that in a company of 30,000 people? A related problem is that top management is increasingly isolated from middle- and lower-level managers and employees who are responsible for the research and project management that is key to Google's success. So, what might you do to improve upward communication within the company? Finally, what can Google do to communicate effectively on an organization-wide basis in an organization that has dozens of product lines and hundreds of research projects and that will soon have 30,000 employees?

If you were the new CEO at Google, what would you do?

It's estimated that managers spend over 80 percent of their day communicating with others.[2] Indeed, much of the basic management process—planning, organizing, leading, and controlling—cannot be performed without effective communication. If this weren't reason enough to study communication, consider that effective oral communication—achieved by listening, following instructions, conversing, and giving feedback—is the most important skill for college graduates who are entering the workforce.[3] Furthermore, across all industries, poor communication skills rank as the single most important reason that people do not advance in their careers.[4] Communication is especially important for top managers like Google's CEO. As Mark DeMichele, former CEO of Arizona Public Service Company, puts it, "Communication is the key to success. CEOs can have good ideas, a vision, and a plan. But they also have to be able to communicate those plans to people who work for them."[5]

This chapter begins by examining the role of perception in communication and how perception can make it difficult for managers to communicate effectively. Next, you'll read about the communication process and the various kinds of communication found in most organizations. In the last half of the chapter, the focus is on improving communication in organizations. You'll learn about one-on-one communication and then about how to effectively communicate and listen to others organization-wide.

What Is Communication?

Whenever Kristy Keith's boss said, "Today is a good day for change," she knew that bad news, be it layoffs or a lost client, was sure to follow. Keith says, "It was comforting to some people who didn't know better," but the experienced employees went "back to their offices and huddled" to discuss what her boss's announcement really meant (and it usually wasn't good).[6] Many bosses try to make bad news sound good with phrases like "rightsizing" for layoffs, "merger of equals" for acquisition by another company, "pursuing other interests" for employees who were fired, and "cost efficiencies" for outsourced jobs. Why do managers sugarcoat bad news? Because, says Dartmouth management professor Paul Argenti, they think "they'll get less flak."

Communication is the process of transmitting information from one person or place to another. Whereas some bosses sugarcoat bad news, smart managers understand that effective, straightforward communication between managers and employees is essential for success.

After reading the next two sections, you should be able to

1. Explain the role that perception plays in communication and communication problems.
2. Describe the communication process and the various kinds of communication in organizations.

1 Perception and Communication Problems

One study found that when *employees* were asked whether their supervisor gave recognition for good work, only 13 percent said their supervisor gave a pat on the back, and a mere 14 percent said their supervisor gave sincere and thorough praise. But when the *supervisors* of these employees were asked whether they gave recognition for good work, 82 percent said they gave pats on the back, while 80 percent said that they gave sincere and thorough praise.[7] Given that these managers and employees worked closely together, how could they have had such different perceptions of something as simple as praise?

Let's learn more about perception and communication problems by examining **1.1 the basic perception process, 1.2 perception problems, 1.3 how we perceive others**, and **1.4 how we perceive ourselves**. We'll also consider how all of these factors make it difficult for managers to communicate effectively.

1.1 Basic Perception Process

As shown in Exhibit 15.1, **perception** is the process by which individuals attend to, organize, interpret, and retain information from their environments. And because communication is the process of transmitting information from one person or place to another, perception is obviously a key part of communication. Yet perception can also be a key obstacle to communication.

As people perform their jobs, they are exposed to a wide variety of informational stimuli such as emails, direct conversations with the boss or coworkers, rumors heard over lunch, stories about the company in the press, or a video broadcast of a speech from the CEO to all employees. Just being exposed to an informational stimulus, however, is no guarantee that an individual will pay attention or attend to that stimulus. People experience stimuli through their own **perceptual filters**—the personality-, psychology-, or experience-based differences that influence them to ignore or pay attention to particular stimuli. Because of filtering, people exposed to the same information will often disagree about what they saw or heard.

communication the process of transmitting information from one person or place to another.

perception the process by which individuals attend to, organize, interpret, and retain information from their environments.

perceptual filters the personality-, psychology-, or experience-based differences that influence people to ignore or pay attention to particular stimuli.

Exhibit 15.1
Basic Perception Process

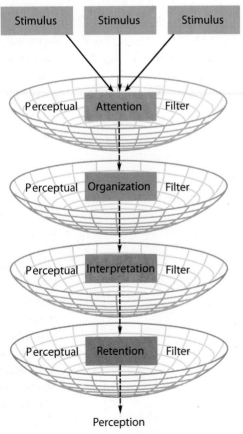

© Cengage Learning 2013

For example, every major stadium in the National Football League has a huge TV monitor on which fans can watch replays. As the slow-motion video is replayed on the monitor, you can often hear cheers *and* boos, as fans of competing teams perceive the same replay in completely different ways. This happens because the fans' perceptual filters predispose them to attend to stimuli that support their team and not their opponents.[8] The same perceptual filters that affect whether we believe our favorite team was "robbed" by the referees also affect communication, that is, the transmitting of information from one person or place to another. As shown in Exhibit 15.1, perceptual filters affect each part of the *perception process*: attention, organization, interpretation, and retention.

Attention is the process of noticing, or becoming aware of, particular stimuli. Because of perceptual filters, we attend to some stimuli and not others. For instance, a study at the University of Illinois asked viewers to watch people in black shirts and white shirts toss a basketball back and forth and to count the number of times someone in a black shirt tossed the basketball. Because their perceptual filters had narrowed to track the activities of people in black shirts, half of the viewers did not notice when the experimenters had someone in a gorilla suit walk through the midst of the people tossing the basketball back and forth.[9] *Organization* is the process of incorporating new information (from the stimuli that you notice) into your existing knowledge. Because of perceptual filters, we are more likely to incorporate new knowledge that is consistent with what we already know or believe. *Interpretation* is the process of attaching meaning to new knowledge. Because of perceptual filters, our preferences and beliefs strongly influence the meaning we attach to new information (e.g., "This decision must mean that top management supports our project."). Finally, *retention* is the process of remembering interpreted information. Retention affects what we recall and commit to memory after we have perceived something. Of course, perceptual filters affect retention as much as they do organization and interpretation.

For instance, imagine that you miss the first 10 minutes of a TV show and turn on your TV to see two people talking to each other in a living room. As they talk, they walk around the room, picking up and putting down various items. Some items, such as a ring, watch, and credit card, appear to be valuable, whereas others appear to be drug related, such as a water pipe for smoking marijuana. In fact, this situation was depicted on videotape in a well-known study that manipulated people's perceptual filters.[10] Before watching the video, one-third of the study participants were told that the people were there to rob the apartment. Another third of the participants were told that police were on their way to conduct a drug raid and that the people in the apartment were getting rid of incriminating evidence. The remaining third of the participants were told that the people were simply waiting for a friend.

After watching the video, participants were asked to list all of the objects from the video that they could remember. Not surprisingly, the different perceptual filters (theft, drug raid, and waiting for a friend) affected what the participants attended to, how they organized the information, how they interpreted it, and ultimately which objects they remembered. Participants who thought a theft was in progress were more likely to remember the valuable objects in the video. Those who thought a drug raid was imminent were more likely to remember the drug-related objects. There was no discernible pattern to the items remembered by those who thought that the people in the video were simply waiting for a friend.

In short, because of perception and perceptual filters, people are likely to pay attention to different things, organize and interpret what they pay attention to differently, and, finally, remember things differently. Consequently, even when people are exposed to the same communications (e.g., organizational memos, discussions with managers or customers), they can end up with very different perceptions and understandings. This is why communication can be so difficult and frustrating for managers. Let's review some of the communication problems created by perception and perceptual filters.

1.2 Perception Problems

Perception creates communication problems for organizations because people exposed to the same communication and information can end up with completely different ideas and understandings. Two of the most common perception problems in organizations are selective perception and closure.

At work, we are constantly bombarded with sensory stimuli: phones ringing, people talking in the background, computers dinging as new email arrives, people calling our names, and so forth. As limited processors of information, we cannot possibly notice, receive, and interpret all of this information. As a result, we attend to and accept some stimuli but screen out and reject others. This isn't a random process.

Selective perception is the tendency to notice and accept objects and information consistent with our values, beliefs, and expectations while ignoring or screening out inconsistent information. A classic case of selective perception occurred when Apple introduced the iPhone 4. Customers immediately complained that they were experiencing dropped phone calls and poor phone reception. The iPhone 4 has a metal antenna circling its edge, and touching any antenna reduces signal reception. Apple, however, didn't encounter this problem in real-world testing. Because it always cloaks its new phones in covers (so they can't be photographed before product launch) when it takes them out in public, those covers prevented testers from touching the phone's antenna and experiencing the problem. Within days, "Antennagate" had become a public relations crisis for Apple, as newspapers, TV news shows, and well-known computer websites, like cNet.com reported the problem. Furthermore, after conducting lab tests, *Consumer Reports* magazine recommended that customers not buy the iPhone 4.[11] What made matters worse was that Apple denied the problem. CEO Steve Jobs said, "This has been blown so out of proportion that it's incredible. There is no Antennagate." The iPhone 4, he said, was "perhaps the best product made by Apple."[12] Furthermore, Jobs, who didn't think there was an issue (i.e., selective perception), emailed customers who contacted him about the issue, to "avoid gripping it in the lower left corner in a way that covers both sides of the black strip in the metal [antenna] band, or simply use one of many available cases."[13] Within 10 days, Apple offered each of its iPhone 4 customers a free "bumper" or case that solved the problem by preventing contact with the antenna.

Once we have initial information about a person, event, or process, **closure** is the tendency to fill in the gaps where information is missing, that is, to assume that what we don't know is consistent with what we already do know. If employees are told that budgets must be cut by 10 percent, they may automatically assume that 10 percent of employees will lose their jobs too, even if that isn't the case. Not surprisingly, when closure occurs, people sometimes fill in the gaps with inaccurate information, which can create problems for organizations.

selective perception the tendency to notice and accept objects and information consistent with our values, beliefs, and expectations, while ignoring or screening out or not accepting inconsistent information.

closure the tendency to fill in gaps of missing information by assuming that what we don't know is consistent with what we already know.

For example, one of the first decisions faced by a new CEO was whether to approve a marketing campaign to launch a new product. Promotional materials, advertising, and a sales and distribution plan had all been completed. The only thing missing was the CEO's approval. Although he liked the campaign, he wanted to send a strong message that the company needed to change, so he killed the campaign. The marketing manager and team that had spent a year developing it were demoralized. Because they didn't know why the CEO canceled the marketing campaign, his top managers closed the gap by assuming that the CEO didn't have confidence in any of them either. Fearing that their decisions would be overturned too, they began seeking the CEO's approval on everything from capital expenditures to personnel decisions, to lower-level issues such as where, when, and whether to hold a conference for customers. After the marketing manager quit to take a job at another company, the CEO called his top managers together, assured them they had his confidence, told them he probably should have approved the marketing campaign, and said that he wouldn't repeat his mistake by doing anything to undermine their confidence or their authority.[14]

1.3 Perceptions of Others

Attribution theory says that we all have a basic need to understand and explain the causes of other people's behavior.[15] In other words, we need to know why people do what they do. According to attribution theory, we use two general reasons or attributions to explain people's behavior: an *internal attribution*, in which behavior is thought to be voluntary or under the control of the individual; and an *external attribution*, in which behavior is thought to be involuntary and outside of the control of the individual.

Have you ever seen someone changing a flat tire on the side of the road and thought to yourself, "What rotten luck—somebody's having a bad day"? If you did, you perceived the person through an external attribution known as the defensive bias. The **defensive bias** is the tendency for people to perceive themselves as personally and situationally similar to someone who is having difficulty or trouble.[16] When we identify with the person in a situation, we tend to use external attributions (i.e., features related to the situation) to explain the person's behavior. For instance, because flat tires are common, it's easy to perceive ourselves in that same situation and put the blame on external causes such as running over a nail.

Now, let's assume a different situation, this time in the workplace:

A utility company worker puts a ladder on a utility pole and then climbs up to do his work. As he's doing his work, he falls from the ladder and seriously injures himself.[17]

Answer this question: Who or what caused the accident? If you thought, "It's not the worker's fault. Anybody could fall from a tall ladder," then you interpreted the incident with a defensive bias in which you saw yourself as personally and situationally similar to someone who is having difficulty or trouble. In other words, you made an external attribution by attributing the accident to an external cause, or some feature of the situation.

Most accident investigations, however, initially blame the worker (i.e., an internal attribution) and not the situation (i.e., an external attribution). Typically, 60 percent to 80 percent of workplace accidents each year are blamed on "operator error," that is, the employees themselves. In reality, more complete investigations usually show that workers are responsible for only 30 percent to 40 percent of all workplace accidents.[18] Why are accident investigators so quick to blame workers? The reason is that they are committing the **fundamental attribution error**, which is the tendency

attribution theory the theory that we all have a basic need to understand and explain the causes of other people's behavior.

defensive bias the tendency for people to perceive themselves as personally and situationally similar to someone who is having difficulty or trouble.

fundamental attribution error the tendency to ignore external causes of behavior and to attribute other people's actions to internal causes.

Exhibit 15.2   Defensive Bias and Fundamental Attribution Error

© Cengage Learning 2013

to ignore external causes of behavior and to attribute other people's actions to internal causes.[19] In other words, when investigators examine the possible causes of an accident, they're much more likely to assume that the accident is a function of the person and not the situation.

Which attribution—the defensive bias or the fundamental attribution error—are workers likely to make when something goes wrong? In general, as shown in Exhibit 15.2, employees and coworkers are more likely to perceive events and explain behavior from a defensive bias. Because they do the work themselves and see themselves as similar to others who make mistakes, have accidents, or are otherwise held responsible for things that go wrong at work, employees and coworkers are likely to attribute problems to external causes such as failed machinery, poor support, or inadequate training. By contrast, because they are typically observers (who don't do the work themselves) and see themselves as situationally and personally different from workers, managers (i.e., the boss) tend to commit the fundamental attribution error and blame mistakes, accidents, and other things that go wrong on workers (i.e., an internal attribution).

Consequently, workers and managers in most workplaces can be expected to take opposite views when things go wrong. Therefore, the defensive bias, which is typically used by workers, and the fundamental attribution error, which is typically made by managers, together present a significant challenge to effective communication and understanding in organizations.

1.4 Self-Perception

Cindy Pruitt is a professional development and recruiting manager at the law firm of Womble Carlyle Sandridge & Rice. Pruitt works frequently with the firm's summer associates, law school students who are interning with the company during summer break. Pruitt was surprised when one of the summer associates broke down in tears after being told that the writing structure on a memo he had written was "a little too loose." Says Pruitt, "They're simply stunned when they get any kind of negative feedback. I practically had to walk him off the ledge."[20]

The **self-serving bias** is the tendency to overestimate our value by attributing successes to ourselves (internal causes) and attributing failures to others or the environment (external causes).[21] As the example with the upset summer law associate illustrates, the self-serving bias can make it especially difficult for managers to talk to employees about performance problems. In general, people have a need to maintain a positive self-image. This need is so strong that when people seek feedback at work, they typically want verification of their worth (rather than information about performance deficiencies) or assurance that mistakes or problems weren't their fault.[22] People can become defensive and emotional when managerial communication threatens their positive self-image. They quit listening, and communication becomes ineffective. In the second half of the chapter, which focuses on improving communication, we'll explain ways in which managers can minimize this self-serving bias and improve effective one-on-one communication with employees.

© iStockphoto.com/PeskyMonkey

Review 1

Perception and Communication Problems   Perception is the process by which people attend to, organize, interpret, and retain information from their environments. Perception is not a straightforward process. Because of perceptual filters such as selective perception and closure, people exposed to the same information stimuli often end up with very different perceptions and understandings. Perception-based differences can also lead to differences in the attributions (internal or external) that managers and workers make when explaining workplace behavior. In general, workers are more likely to explain behavior from a defensive bias, in which they attribute problems to external causes (the situation). Managers, on the other hand, tend to commit the fundamental attribution error, attributing problems to internal causes (the worker associated with a mistake or error). Consequently, when things go wrong, it's common for managers to blame workers and for workers to blame the situation or context in which they do their jobs. Finally, this problem is compounded by a self-serving bias that leads people to attribute successes to internal causes and failures to external causes. So workers may become defensive and emotional and not hear what managers have to say when they receive negative feedback from managers. In short, perceptions and attributions represent a significant challenge to effective communication and understanding in organizations.

② Kinds of Communication

Each year, on the anniversary of your hiring date, you receive a written assessment of your performance from your boss. This year, after receiving your performance appraisal, you gripe about it to your best friend, a coworker in a cubicle down the hall. Despite your griping, however, you appreciate that your boss cut you some slack, allowing you extra days off when you went through a divorce earlier this year. How did your boss know you were having personal problems? He knew something was wrong from your nonverbal communication—your rounded shoulders,

self-serving bias the tendency to overestimate our value by attributing successes to ourselves (internal causes) and attributing failures to others or the environment (external causes).

the bags under your eyes, and your over-all lack of energy. There are many kinds of communication—formal, informal, coaching/counseling, and nonverbal—but they all follow the same fundamental process.

Let's learn more about the different kinds of communication by examining **2.1 the communication process; 2.2 formal communication channels; 2.3 informal communication channels; 2.4 coaching and counseling, or one-on-one communication;** and **2.5 nonverbal communication.**

2.1 The Communication Process

Exhibit 15.3 The Interpersonal Communication Process

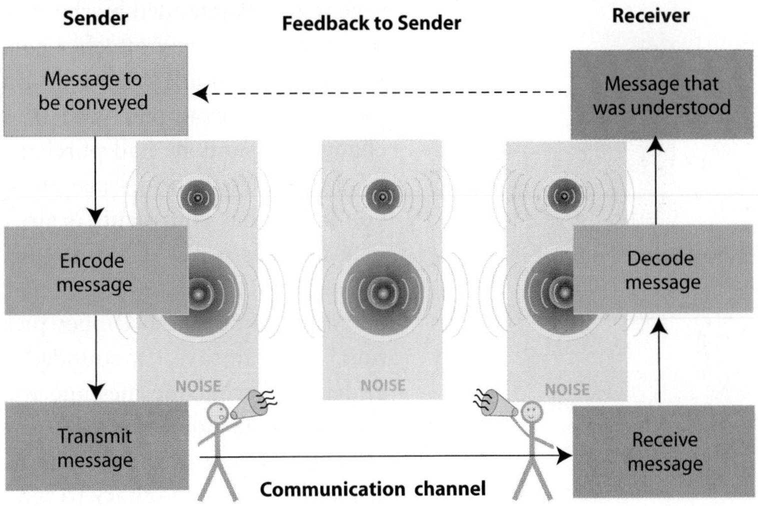

© Cengage Learning 2013

Earlier in the chapter, we defined *communication* as the process of transmitting information from one person or place to another. Exhibit 15.3 displays a model of the communication process and its major components: the sender (message to be conveyed, encoding the message, transmitting the message); the receiver (receiving message, decoding the message, and the message that was understood); and noise, which interferes with the communication process.

The communication process begins when a *sender* thinks of a message he or she wants to convey to another person. Throughout the world, customers expect to find lower prices when they shop at Walmart. Following the example of founder Sam Walton, Walmart's top executives, including the CEO, shop competitors to make sure Walmart's prices really are lower. So on a business trip to China, CEO Mike Duke shopped his Chinese competitors and noticed that they carried bananas from China, as well as imported bananas (which cost about 20% more). Walmart's Wanda supercenter in Beijing, however, only carried the more expensive imported bananas (but at a cheaper price than the competition). So, Duke wondered why they weren't carrying the cheaper Chinese-grown bananas.

The next step is to encode the message. **Encoding** means putting a message into a verbal (written or spoken) or symbolic form that can be recognized and understood by the receiver. The sender then *transmits the message* via *communication channels*. For example, Duke asked the store manager and the head of Walmart's China division why they only sold the more expensive imported bananas and not the less expensive bananas from China. With some communication channels such as the telephone and face-to-face communication, the sender receives immediate feedback, whereas with others such as email (or text messages and file attachments), fax, beepers, voice mail, memos, and letters, the sender must wait for the receiver to respond.

Unfortunately, because of technical difficulties (e.g., fax down, dead battery on the mobile phone, inability to read email attachments) or people-based transmission problems (e.g., forgetting to pass on the message), messages aren't always transmitted. If the message is transmitted and received, however, the next step is for the receiver to decode it. **Decoding** is the process by which the receiver translates the written, verbal, or symbolic form of the message into an understood message. In Duke's case, the message was decoded accurately, and the Beijing Wanda store had the cheaper bananas in stock within 24 hours. Within a week, all of Walmart's 49 northern China stores carried them. Within a month, shoppers could find the cheaper Chinese bananas in Walmart's 300 Wanda stores.[23]

encoding putting a message into a written, verbal, or symbolic form that can be recognized and understood by the receiver.

decoding the process by which the receiver translates the written, verbal, or symbolic form of a message into an understood message.

However, the message as understood by the receiver isn't always the same message that was intended by the sender. Because of different experiences or perceptual filters, receivers may attach a completely different meaning to a message than was intended. Technology can also contribute to misunderstood, or improperly decoded messages. For example, Nordstrom's customer Dan Sheeran had a tailor make some changes to pants he had purchased. When the pants were ready, the tailor left this hard-to-understand message on his voice mail in a thick accent, "Just wanted to let you know that your pants is already done and ready for pickup. Ok, then you can pick up your pants at Nordstrom." Google Voice, which automatically turns voice messages into text, translated that as, "Just wanted to know that your punches ordered the done in the Dipper pickup. Ok. Then you can pick up the French abortion." Sheeran says, "It sounded like a coded message for a drug deal," and didn't understand what the message was about until he clicked the link that played the voice message aloud.[24]

The last step of the communication process occurs when the receiver gives the sender feedback. **Feedback to sender** is a return message to the sender that indicates the receiver's understanding of the message (of what the receiver was supposed to know, do, or not do). Feedback makes senders aware of possible miscommunications and enables them to continue communicating until the receiver understands the intended message. Unfortunately, feedback doesn't always occur in the communication process.

Complacency and overconfidence about the ease and simplicity of communication can lead senders and receivers to simply assume that they share a common understanding of the message and, consequently, not use feedback to improve the effectiveness of their communication. This is a serious mistake, especially because messages and feedback are always transmitted with and against a background of noise. **Noise** is anything that interferes with the transmission of the intended message. Noise can occur in any of the following situations:

> » The sender isn't sure what message to communicate.
> » The message is not clearly encoded.
> » The wrong communication channel is chosen.
> » The message is not received or decoded properly.
> » The receiver doesn't have the experience or time to understand the message.

Jargon, which is vocabulary particular to a profession or group, is another form of noise that interferes with communication in the workplace. Do you have any idea what *rightsizing, delayering, unsiloing,* and *knowledge acquisition* mean? *Rightsizing* means laying off workers. *Delayering* means firing managers, or getting rid of layers of management. *Unsiloing* means getting workers in different parts of the company (i.e., different vertical silos) to work with others outside their own areas. *Knowledge acquisition* means teaching workers new knowledge or skills. Unfortunately, the business world is rife with jargon. Carol Hymowitz of *The Wall Street Journal* points out, "A new crop of buzzwords usually sprouts every three to five years, or about the same length of time many top executives have to prove themselves. Some can be useful in swiftly communicating, and spreading, new business concepts. Others are less useful, even devious."[25]

When managers wrongly assume that communication is easy, they reduce communication to something called the conduit metaphor.[26] Strictly speaking, a conduit is a pipe or tube that protects electrical wire. The **conduit metaphor** refers to the mistaken assumption that senders can pipe their intended messages directly into

feedback to sender in the communication process, a return message to the sender that indicates the receiver's understanding of the message.

noise anything that interferes with the transmission of the intended message.

jargon vocabulary particular to a profession or group that interferes with communication in the workplace.

conduit metaphor the mistaken assumption that senders can pipe their intended messages directly into the heads of receivers with perfect clarity and without noise or perceptual filters interfering with the receivers' understanding of the message.

Exhibit 15.4 Meanings of the Word *Fine*

1. If you exceed the 55 mph speed limit, you may have to pay a *fine* (penalty).

2. During the playoffs, Peyton Manning turned in a *fine* performance (excellent).

3. The machine has to run at a slow speed because the tolerance is extremely *fine* (tight).

4. Putting this puzzle together is difficult because many of the pieces are so *fine* (small).

5. Recently, experiments have been conducted on manufacturing certain drugs in space. It is hoped that these drugs, as compared with those manufactured on Earth, will be extremely *fine* (pure).

6. Be careful when you handle that antique book. Its pages are extremely *fine* (flimsy).

7. That's *fine* with me (okay).

© Cengage Learning 2013

the heads of receivers with perfect clarity and without noise or perceptual filters interfering with the receivers' understanding of the message. However, this just isn't possible. Even if managers could telepathically direct their thoughts straight into receivers' heads, misunderstandings and communication problems would still occur because words and symbols typically have multiple meanings, depending on how they're used. Exhibit 15.4 shows several meanings of an extremely common word, *fine*. Depending on how you use it, *fine* can mean a penalty; a good job; that something is delicate, small, pure, or flimsy; or that something is okay.

Managers who want to be effective communicators need to carefully choose words and symbols that will help receivers derive the intended meaning of a message. Furthermore, they have to be aware of all steps in the communication process, beginning with the sender (message to be conveyed, encoding the message, transmitting the message) and ending with the receiver (receiving the message, decoding the message, understanding the message, and using feedback to communicate what was understood).

formal communication channel the system of official channels that carry organizationally approved messages and information.

downward communication communication that flows from higher to lower levels in an organization.

2.2 Formal Communication Channels

An organization's **formal communication channel** is the system of official channels that carry organizationally approved messages and information. Organizational objectives, rules, policies, procedures, instructions, commands, and requests for information are all transmitted via the formal communication system or channel. There are three formal communication channels: downward communication, upward communication, and horizontal communication.[27]

Downward communication flows from higher to lower levels in an organization. Downward communication is used to issue orders down the organizational hierarchy, to give organizational members

© Blend Images/Jupiterimages

job-related information, to give managers and workers performance reviews from upper managers, and to clarify organizational objectives and goals.[28] Michael Beer, professor emeritus at Harvard Business School, says, "You can never over communicate. When you think you've communicated well, go out three or four more times and communicate again." Beer's consulting firm TruePoint studied 40 CEOs whose companies have been above average performers for over a decade. He found that, "Those remarkable leaders spend an enormous amount of time in communicating downward. They have a simple story, and that story gets out every place they go."[29]

Upward communication flows from lower levels to higher levels in an organization. Upward communication is used to give higher-level managers feedback about operations, issues, and problems; help higher-level managers assess organizational performance and effectiveness; encourage lower-level managers and employees to participate in organizational decision making; and give those at lower levels the chance to share their concerns with higher-level authorities.

"what's new" companies >

Barry Salzberg, the CEO of Big Four accounting firm **Deloitte & Touche USA**, facilitates upward communication through a series of regular town hall meetings in different locations. Says Salzberg, "I hold town hall meetings in which no question is out of bounds. I invite the audience to pass the mike and fire away—hardballs, softballs, anything goes. Everyone else in the organization is invited to dial in and listen. And the sessions and additional questions and answers are posted on a site available 24/7." So far, Salzberg has conducted a dozen meetings, with more than half of the firm's employees participating. Why take the time to hold these meetings? Says Salzberg, "[People] want to feel part of a caring community with leaders who, when making the hard choices, will balance the health of the organization with the best long-term interests of the workforce."[30]

Horizontal communication flows among managers and workers who are at the same organizational level, such as when a day shift nurse comes in at 7:30 A.M. for a half-hour discussion with the midnight nurse supervisor who leaves at 8 A.M. Horizontal communication helps facilitate coordination and cooperation between different parts of a company and allows coworkers to share relevant information. It also helps people at the same level resolve conflicts and solve problems without involving high levels of management. Although Zappos, the online shoe company, is located in Las Vegas, it was started in San Francisco. CEO Tony Hsieh moved the company to Las Vegas, bringing 70 of its 100 employees from San Francisco because of the lower cost of living, lower taxes, and restaurants and stores that were open 24 hours a day, the latter of which could easily accommodate the lifestyles of call center representatives who work evening and midnight-hour shifts. Another key factor, however, was that Hsieh wanted the company headquarters to be in the same location as the call center, for the purposes of better horizontal communication. Zappos takes advantage of this by having the company's buyers sit next to call center representatives in the office. Hsieh says, "A customer could be on the phone with someone in customer service and say, 'Is this style coming back in stock?' and [the customer service representative] can just put them on hold and speak to a buyer and get that information. And the buyers are finding out what the customers are asking for firsthand. It was an experiment, and it's something that we're going to be rolling out on a larger scale going forward."[31]

In general, what can managers do to improve formal communication? First, decrease reliance on downward communication. Second, increase chances for upward communication by increasing personal contact with lower-level managers and workers. Third, as at NuStar Energy, encourage much better use of horizontal communication. Finally, be aware of the problems associated with downward, upward, and horizontal communication, some of which are listed in Exhibit 15.5.

upward communication communication that flows from lower to higher levels in an organization.

horizontal communication communication that flows among managers and workers who are at the same organizational level.

Exhibit 15.5 Common Problems with Downward, Upward, and Horizontal Communication

DOWNWARD COMMUNICATION	UPWARD COMMUNICATION	HORIZONTAL COMMUNICATION
⊙ Overusing downward communication by sending too many messages	⊙ The risk involved with telling upper management about problems (i.e., fear of retribution)	⊙ Management discouraging or punishing horizontal communication, viewing it as small talk
⊙ Issuing contradictory messages	⊙ Managers reacting angrily and defensively when workers report problems	⊙ Not giving managers and workers the time or opportunity for horizontal communication
⊙ Hurriedly communicating vague, unclear messages	⊙ Not enough opportunities or channels for lower-level workers to contact upper levels of management	⊙ Not enough opportunities or channels for lower-level workers to engage in horizontal communication
⊙ Issuing messages that indicate management's low regard for lower-level workers		

Source: G. L. Kreps, *Organizational Communication: Theory and Practice* (New York: Longman, 1990).

2.3 Informal Communication Channels

An organization's **informal communication channel**, sometimes called the **grapevine**, is the transmission of messages from employee to employee outside of formal communication channels. The grapevine arises out of curiosity, that is, the need to know what is going on in an organization and how it might affect you or others. To satisfy this curiosity, employees need a consistent supply of relevant, accurate, in-depth information about "who is doing what and what changes are occurring within the organization."[32] Supervisor Paul McCann of Appleton Papers Inc., a specialty paper and packaging products company, agrees that when management doesn't explain what's happening in the company, "people will work together to develop their own reason."[33]

For example, at the University of Texas Medical Branch (part of the UT system), any of the 13,000 employees wanting to know the truth about rumors working their way through the campus grapevine can log on to the school's website and click on "Rumors or Trumors." Campus administrators comment on each posted rumor and rate it using the "kernel of truth" system. As shown in Exhibit 15.6, one

informal communication channel ("grapevine") the transmission of messages from employee to employee outside of formal communication channels.

Exhibit 15.6 "Rumors or Trumors" at the University of Texas Medical Branch

Rumor: I heard that the new "smart" ID badges will store all kinds of my private information, and worse, they can be used to track where I am at UTMB. True?

Rating:

TRUTH-O-METER

= Want to buy some swampland?

= A "kernel" of truth

= Maybe, but...

= The whole truth

Response: No, the cards will not contain anything but the most basic information, much as ID cards do today. No personal data, no employment history, no critical financial info or medical records. The cards will primarily verify identity (your photo and name help do that) and access, the same way magnetic strips and keys do now. In the future, they will also enable a user, at his/her discretion, to use them as a debit card for campus purchases, like a pre-paid phone card, and will help manage access to computer resources.

The cards can't track your location. The proximity readers are designed with a narrow sensitivity field (you wouldn't want doors unexpectedly unlocking because someone with access is walking in a nearby hallway). However, the system does register when you are in or out of a restricted area. This is no different than is currently the case with the magnetic key cards, and is an important aspect of maintaining security in sensitive research, clinical, and business areas.

Source: "Rumors or Trumors" at the University of Texas Medical Branch, www.utmb.edu. Reprinted by permission.

doing the right thing

One Thing at a Time

It's easier than ever for people to multitask. With blazing-fast computers and software, and the wealth of information from the Internet, we can work on lots of things at one time—writing memos, checking email, researching stock prices, or doing research, all while talking on the phone or meeting with colleagues. It seems like a great, efficient use of time, and a way to get employees to do more during the workday. But as efficient as all of this might seem, multitasking may actually be unethical. According to a study by scholars at Stanford University, while people who multitask can do many things at once, they don't to any of them well. In short, multitasking reduces the quality of our work. And sometimes, multitasking can even be dangerous. The Virginia Tech Transportation Institute found that truck drivers who multitask by texting on their phones were 23 times more likely to have an accident than those who just drove. So as a manager, you should do the right thing—set a good example by focusing on one task at a time, so that you (and your employees) will be better at what you're doing.[34]

kernel of corn indicates a little bit of truth. Two kernels indicate that more of the rumor is accurate, but it's still not entirely true. Three kernels indicate that the rumor is accurate. Wildly inaccurate rumors such as the one in Exhibit 15.6 about new ID tags being able to track the location of an employee are rated with a spaceship, indicating that they're too far out to be believed. Reaction thus far has been positive. Lecturer Sheryl Prather says, "It looks sincere. I've found that everything thus far has been pretty factual. It at least shows that somebody's listening to some of the talk that goes on around here and [is] putting it down on the computer where we can all see it."[35]

Grapevines arise out of informal communication networks such as the gossip or cluster chains shown in Exhibit 15.7. In a *gossip chain*, one highly connected individual shares information with many other managers and workers. By contrast, in a *cluster chain*, numerous people simply tell a few of their friends. The result in both cases is that information flows freely and quickly through the organization. Some believe that grapevines are a waste of employees' time, that they promote gossip and rumors that fuel political speculation and that they are sources of highly unreliable, inaccurate information. Yet studies clearly show that grapevines are highly accurate sources of information for a number of reasons.[36] First, because grapevines typically carry "juicy" information that is interesting and timely, information spreads rapidly. At Meghan De Goyler Hauser's former company, the word on the grapevine was that her boss drank on the job, the company accountant was stealing the company blind, and one of her coworkers was a nude model. She says, "The rumors all turned out to be true."[37] Second, because information is typically spread by face-to-face conversation, receivers can send feedback to make sure they understand the message that is being communicated. This reduces misunderstandings and increases accuracy. Third, because most of the information in a company

Exhibit 15.7 Grapevine Communication Networks

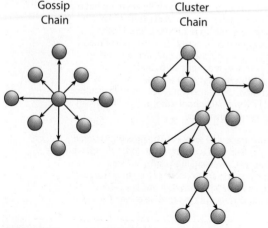

Gossip Chain

Cluster Chain

Source: K. Davis & J. W. Newstrom, *Human Behavior at Work: Organizational Behavior*, 8th ed. (New York: McGraw-Hill, 1989).

moves along the grapevine rather than formal communication channels, people can usually verify the accuracy of information by checking it out with others.

What can managers do to manage organizational grapevines? The very worst thing they can do is withhold information or try to punish those who share information with others. The grapevine abhors a vacuum, so rumors and anxiety will flourish in the absence of information from company management. Why does this occur? According to workplace psychologist Nicholas DiFonzo, "The main focus of rumor is to figure out the truth. It's the group trying to make sense of something that's important to them."[38] A better strategy is to embrace the grapevine and keep employees informed about possible changes and strategies. Failure to do so will just make things worse. An employee who works in a company where management maintains a culture of silence says, "They [management] think that not communicating the tough stuff will keep employees unaware of it. Of course, it doesn't work. It just fuels the grapevine."[39]

Finally, in addition to using the grapevine to communicate with others, managers should not overlook the grapevine as a tremendous source of valuable information and feedback. In fact, information flowing through organizational grapevines is estimated to be 75 percent to 95 percent accurate.[40] For this reason, managers should gather their courage and be willing to read the anonymous comments that angry, frustrated employees post on Internet gripe sites like untied.com (about United Airlines) or stainedapron.com (for griping restaurant workers), where employees post gripes about hundreds of different companies. Bob Rosner, who runs a gripe site called workingwounded.com, suggests managers look for themes rather than responding to any particular message. And Jeff Jarvis, author of the blog BuzzMachine, says, "There should be someone at every company whose job is to put into Google and blog search engines the name of the company or the brand, followed by the word 'sucks,' just to see what customers [and employees] are saying."[41] Indeed, there are over 20,000 Internet domain names that end in "sucks.com" and 2,000 that end in "stinks.com." As a preemptive strategy, 30 percent of *Fortune* 500 companies have purchased the "sucks.com" domain names affiliated with their company (i.e., Goldmansachssucks.com) or product names (i.e., michelobsucks.com).[42] Exhibit 15.8 lists that and other strategies that today's managers

Exhibit 15.8 Organizational Grapevines: Dealing with Internet Gripe Sites

1.	Correct misinformation. Put an end to false rumors and set the record straight. Don't be defensive.
2.	Don't take angry comments personally.
3.	Give your name and contact number to show employees that you're concerned and that they can contact you directly.
4.	Hold a town meeting to discuss the issues raised on the gripe site.
5.	Set up anonymous internal discussion forums on the company server. Then encourage employees to gripe anonymously on the company intranet, rather than on the web.
6.	If a mistake has been made, apologize; explain what happened and how the company will attempt to make it right.
7.	Stop the gripes before they start by having clear communication channels, web, phone, email, or mail, through which employees and others can communicate concerns to management.
8.	Purchase "IHateYourCompany.com" website domain names and then use them to invite and collect feedback from disgruntled employees and customers.

Sources: C. Martin & N. Bennett, "Business Insight (A Special Report): Corporate Reputation; What to Do About Online Attacks: Step No. 1: Stop Ignoring Them," *The Wall Street Journal*, March 10, 2008, R6; J. Simons, "Stop Moaning about Gripe Sites and Log On," *Fortune*, April 2, 2001, 181; and E. Steel, "How to Handle 'IHateYourCompany.com'; Some Firms Buy Up Negative Domain Names to Avert 'Gripe Sites,'" *The Wall Street Journal*, September 5, 2008, B5.

can use in dealing with gripe sites and blogs, the latest forms of the traditional organizational grapevine. See Section 4.2 for more on how managers can use blogs to do a better job of hearing what employees and customers think and feel about their companies.

2.4 Coaching and Counseling: One-on-One Communication

When the Wyatt Company surveyed 531 U.S. companies undergoing major changes and restructuring, it asked the CEOs, "If you could go back and change one thing, what would it be?" The answer: "The way we communicated with our employees." The CEOs said that instead of flashy videos, printed materials, or formal meetings, they would make greater use of one-on-one communication, especially with employees' immediate supervisors instead of with higher-level executives whom employees didn't know.[43]

Coaching and counseling are two kinds of one-on-one communication. **Coaching** is communicating with someone for the direct purpose of improving the person's on-the-job performance or behavior.[44] George Parsons, chief learning officer for Goldman Sachs says, "As soon as people become good managers, we want them to be good coaches too. You have to be good at getting and giving feedback so you can help individuals fully contribute."[45]

Managers tend to make several mistakes when coaching employees. First, they wait for a problem before coaching. Jim Concelman, manager for leadership development at Development Dimensions International, says, "Of course, a boss has to coach an employee if a mistake has been made, but they shouldn't be waiting for the error. While it is a lot easier to see a mistake and correct it, people learn more through success than through failure, so bosses should ensure that employees are experiencing as many successes as possible. Successful employees lead to a more successful organization."[46] Second, when mistakes *are* made, managers wait much too long before talking to the employee about the problem. Management professor Ray Hilgert says, "A manager must respond as soon as possible after an incident of poor performance. Don't bury your head. . . . When employees are told nothing, they assume everything is okay."[47] When Jay Whitehead, now president of Outsourcing Today, was a manager at a previous company, one of his employees accidentally copied an email to a customer that insulted the customer. Whitehead immediately talked to the employee, who offered to quit. Whitehead told him, "No, instead you're going to do something much harder. You're going to apologize." He did, and, according to White, "all was forgiven."[48] The key to this successful result was that Whitehead acted immediately to coach the employee on his mistake. In Section 3, you'll learn a number of specific steps for effective one-on-one communication and coaching.

By contrast to coaching, **counseling** is communicating with someone about non-job-related issues such as stress, child care, health issues, retirement planning, or legal issues that may be affecting or interfering with the person's performance. But counseling does not mean that managers should try to be clinicians, even though an estimated 20 percent of employees are dealing with personal problems at any one time. Dana Kiel, who works for **Cigna Behavioral Health**, says, "We call it the quicksand. If you're a good supervisor, you do care about your employees, but it's not your job to be a therapist."[49] Instead, managers should discuss specific performance problems, listen if the employee chooses to share personal issues, and then recommend that the employee call the company's *Employee Assistance Program (EAP)*. EAPs are typically free when provided as part of a company's benefit package. In

coaching communicating with someone for the direct purpose of improving the person's on-the-job performance or behavior.

counseling communicating with someone about non-job-related issues that may be affecting or interfering with the person's performance.

"what's new"
companies >

emergencies or times of crisis, EAPs can offer immediate counseling and support; they can also provide referrals to organizations and professionals that can help employees and their family members address personal issues. Cigna, a health services firm, provides counseling to its employees through its EAP. Whether they are struggling with substance abuse, domestic issues, or other personal issues, employees receive up to five free counseling sessions, either through in-house counselors or outside professionals. The program also sponsors frequent seminars that help employees deal with difficult issues. Recent seminars have included "Employees in Crisis: How Personal Finance Can Impact Job Performance" and "Working Through Difficult Times."[50] Exhibit 15.9 lists the standard services provided by EAPs.

Exhibit 15.9 Services Provided by Employee Assistance Programs (EAPs)

Problem or Need	Service Provided
Stress, depression, relationships, substance abuse	Counseling
Pregnancy, adoption, day care, nutrition, fertility	Child care
Health and nutrition, care options, Alzheimer's disease	Senior care
Wills, leases, estate plans, adoptions	Legal services
Referrals and discounts on chiropractic care, acupuncture, massage therapy, vitamins	Health/lifestyle assistance
Pet-sitting resources, obedience training, veterinarians	Pet care
Retirement planning, debt consolidation, budgeting	Financial services

Source: "You Can Do It. We Can Help," CIGNA Behavioral Health, available at www.hr.tcu.edu/eappages/core/html/default.html, March 30, 2002.

2.5 Nonverbal Communication

When people talk, they send both verbal and nonverbal messages. Verbal messages are sent and received through the words we speak, as when we congratulate a speaker by saying "That was a great presentation." By contrast, nonverbal messages are sent through body language, facial expressions, or tone of voice. Hearing "*That was a great* presentation!" is very different from hearing "Ahem [clearing throat], that was, ahem, ahem, a great presentation."

More generally, **nonverbal communication** is any communication that doesn't involve words. Nonverbal communication almost always accompanies verbal communication and may either support and reinforce the verbal message or contradict it. The importance of nonverbal communication is well established. Researchers have estimated that as much as 93 percent of any message is transmitted nonverbally, with 55 percent coming from body language and facial expressions and 38 percent coming from the tone and pitch of the voice.[51] Because many nonverbal cues are unintentional, receivers often consider nonverbal communication to be a more accurate representation of what senders are thinking and feeling than the words they use. If you have ever asked someone out on a date and been told "yes," but realized that the real answer was "no," then you understand the importance of paying attention to nonverbal communication.

Kinesics and paralanguage are two kinds of nonverbal communication.[52] **Kinesics** (from the Greek word *kinesis*, meaning "movement") are movements of the body and face.[53] These movements include arm and hand gestures, facial expressions, eye contact, folding arms, crossing legs, and leaning toward or away from another person. For example, people tend to avoid eye contact when they are embarrassed or unsure of the message they are sending. Crossed arms or legs usually indicate defensiveness or that the person is not receptive to the message or the sender. Also, people tend to smile frequently when they are seeking someone's approval.

It turns out that kinesics play an incredibly important role in communication. Studies of married couples' kinesic interactions can predict whether they will stay

nonverbal communication any communication that doesn't involve words.

kinesics movements of the body and face.

married with 93 percent accuracy.[54] The key is the ratio of positive to negative kinesic interactions of husbands and wives as they communicate. Negative kinesic expressions such as eye rolling suggest contempt, whereas positive kinetic expressions such as maintaining eye contact and nodding suggest listening and caring. When the ratio of positive to negative interactions drops below 5 to 1, the chances for divorce quickly increase. Kinesics operate similarly in the workplace, providing clues about people's true feelings, over and above what they say (or don't say). For instance, Louis Giuliano, former CEO of ITT (which makes heavy use of teams), says, "When you get a team together and say to them we're going to change a process, you always have people who say, 'No, we're not.' They usually don't say it out loud, but 'the body language is there,' making it clear that their real answer is 'no.'"[55]

Paralanguage includes the pitch, rate, tone, volume, and speaking pattern (use of silences, pauses, or hesitations) of one's voice. For example, when people are unsure what to say, they tend to decrease their communication effectiveness by speaking softly. When people are nervous, they tend to talk faster and louder. These characteristics have a tremendous influence on whether listeners are receptive to what speakers are saying. For example, Vinya Lynch believes that her "timid and sing-songy" voice is why others don't take her seriously and cut her off when she makes presentations. Lynch says, "When I listen to myself, it doesn't sound intelligent." She began working with a speech coach ($2,250 for 10 sessions) because, as she says, "I want my voice to be charismatic and confident all at the same time."[56] In short, because nonverbal communication is so informative, especially when it contradicts verbal communication, managers need to learn how to monitor and control their nonverbal behavior.

Review 2

Kinds of Communication Communication within an organization depends on the communication process, formal and informal communication channels, one-on-one communication, and nonverbal communication. The major components of the communication process are the sender, the receiver, noise, and feedback. The conduit metaphor refers to the mistaken assumption that senders can pipe their intended messages directly into receivers' heads with perfect clarity. With noise, perceptual filters, and little feedback, however, this just isn't possible. Formal communication channels such as downward, upward, and horizontal communication carry organizationally approved messages and information. By contrast, the informal communication channel, called the grapevine, arises out of curiosity and is carried out through gossip or cluster chains. Managers should use the grapevine to keep employees informed and to obtain better, clearer information for themselves. There are two kinds of one-on-one communication. Coaching is used to improve on-the-job performance, whereas counseling is used to communicate about non-job-related issues affecting job performance. Nonverbal communication such as kinesics and paralanguage accounts for as much as 93 percent of a message's content and interpretation. Because nonverbal communication is so informative, managers need to learn how to monitor and control their nonverbal behavior.

How to Improve Communication

paralanguage the pitch, rate, tone, volume, and speaking pattern (i.e., use of silences, pauses, or hesitations) of one's voice.

An employee comes in late every day, takes long lunches, and leaves early. His coworkers resent his tardiness and having to do his share of the work. Another employee makes as many as ten personal phone calls a day on company time. Still another employee's job performance has dropped significantly in the last three months. How do you communicate with these employees to begin solving these problems? Or suppose that you supervise a division of 50, 100, or even 1,000 people. How can you communicate effectively with everyone in that division? Moreover, how can top managers communicate effectively with everyone in the company when employees work in different offices, states, countries, and time zones? Turning that around, how can managers make themselves accessible so that they can hear what employees feel and think throughout the organization?

After reading the next two sections, you should be able to

3. *Explain how managers can manage effective one-on-one communication.*

4. *Describe how managers can manage effective organization-wide communication.*

When it comes to improving communication, managers face two primary tasks, managing one-on-one communication and managing organization-wide communication.

3 Managing One-on-One Communication

You learned in Chapter 1 that, on average, first-line managers spend 57 percent of their time with people, middle managers spend 63 percent of their time directly with people, and top managers spend as much as 78 percent of their time dealing with people.[57] These numbers make it clear that managers spend a great deal of time in one-on-one communication with others.

Learn more about managing one-on-one communication by reading how to **3.1 choose the right communication medium, 3.2 be a good listener, 3.3 give effective feedback**, and **3.4 improve cross-cultural communication**.

3.1 Choosing the Right Communication Medium

Sometimes messages are poorly communicated simply because they are delivered using the wrong **communication medium**, which is the method used to deliver a message. For example, the wrong communication medium is being used when an employee returns from lunch, picks up the note left on her office chair, and learns she has been fired. The wrong communication medium is also being used when an employee pops into your office every 10 minutes with a simple request. (An email would be better.)

There are two general kinds of communication media: oral and written communication. *Oral communication* includes face-to-face and group meetings through telephone calls, videoconferencing, or any other means of sending and receiving spoken messages. Studies show that managers generally prefer oral communication over written because it provides the opportunity to ask questions about parts of the message that they don't understand. Oral communication is also a rich communication medium because it allows managers to receive and assess the nonverbal communication that accompanies spoken messages (i.e., body language, facial expressions, and the voice characteristics associated with paralanguage).

Furthermore, you don't need a personal computer and an Internet connection to conduct oral communication. Simply schedule an appointment, track someone down in the hall, or catch someone on the phone. In fact, *Wall Street Journal* columnist

communication medium the method used to deliver an oral or written message.

635

Jason Fry worries that voice mail and email have made managers less willing to engage in meaningful, face-to-face oral communication than before. In fact, 67 percent of managers admit to using email as a substitute for face-to-face conversations.[58] Although there are advantages to email (e.g., it creates a record of what's been said), it's often better to talk to people instead of just emailing them. Jason Fry writes, "If you're close enough that the person you're emailing uses the plonk of your return key as a cue to look for the little Outlook envelope, [it's] best [to] think carefully about whether you should be typing instead of talking."[59] But the oral medium should not be used for *all* communication. In general, when the message is simple, such as a quick request or a presentation of straightforward information, a memo or email is often the better communication medium.

Written communication includes letters, email, and memos. Although most managers still like and use oral communication, email in particular is changing how they communicate with workers, customers, and each other. Email is the fastest-growing form of communication in organizations primarily because of its convenience and speed. For instance, because people read six times faster than they can listen, they usually can read 30 email messages in 10 to 15 minutes.[60] By contrast, dealing with voice messages can take a considerable amount of time. Fred DeLuca, founder of the Subway sandwich shop franchise, says, "I get about 60 messages a day from employees and franchisees, and I listen to all of them. For my sanity, I set a time limit of 75 seconds, because people can be long-winded when they're excited. When I hear, 'You have 30 messages,' I know right away that I'll spend 60 minutes on voice mail. I take two minutes per message, listening and returning or forwarding."[61]

Written communication such as email is well suited for delivering straightforward messages and information. Furthermore, with email accessible at the office, at home, and on the road (by laptop computer, cell phone, or web-based email), managers can use email to stay in touch from anywhere at almost any time. And because email and other written communications don't have to be sent and received simultaneously, messages can be sent and stored for reading at any time. Consequently, managers can send and receive many more messages using email than by using oral communication, which requires people to get together in person or by phone or videoconference.

Email has its own drawbacks, however. One is that it lacks the formality of paper memos and letters. It is easy to fire off a rushed email that is not well written or fully thought through. Another drawback to email is that it lacks nonverbal cues, making emails very easy to misinterpret. Kristin Byron, assistant professor of management at Syracuse University, says, "People perceive emails as more negative than they are intended to be, and even emails that are intended to be positive can be misinterpreted as more neutral. You get an email that's really short, with no greeting, no closing; it's probably because they were very rushed, or maybe they're not very good typists. But because of those things, people have a tendency to perceive the message as negative."[62]

Email is also not well suited to complex, ambiguous, or emotionally laden messages. Neal Patterson, CEO of Cerner Corporation, which develops health-care software, learned this lesson when he sent the following email to 400 company managers:

We are getting less than 40 hours of work from a large number of our KC-based EMPLOYEES. . . . The parking lot is sparsely used at 8 AM, likewise at 5 PM. As managers—you either do not know what your EMPLOYEES are doing or YOU do not CARE. You have created expectations on the work effort which allowed this to happen inside Cerner, creating a very unhealthy environment. In either case, you have a problem and you will fix it or I will replace you. NEVER in my career have I allowed a team which worked for me to think they had a 40-hour job. I have allowed YOU to create a culture which is permitting this. NO LONGER.[63]

Patterson continued: "We passed a Stock Purchase Program, allowing for the EMPLOYEE to purchase Cerner stock at a 15 percent discount, at Friday's BOD [board of directors] meeting. Hell will freeze over before this CEO implements ANOTHER EMPLOYEE benefit in this Culture."[64] He concluded by saying, "I will hold you accountable. You have allowed this to get to this state. You have two weeks. Tick, tock."[65]

Reaction to the message was so strong that, in just over a week, the email had been leaked to the entire company. And then someone, nobody knows who, posted the email on a Yahoo.com discussion board about Cerner. As word spread about the negative email, Cerner's stock price dropped from $44 to $31 per share in just three days. By the end of the week, Patterson issued another email, offering an apology. Not surprisingly, that email began, "Please treat this memo with the utmost confidentiality. It is for internal dissemination only. Do not copy or email to anyone else."[66] Emotionally laden and complex messages are better delivered through oral communication.

3.2 Listening

Are you a good listener? You probably think so. In fact, most people, including managers, are terrible listeners, retaining only about 25 percent of what they hear.[67] You qualify as a poor listener if you frequently interrupt others, jump to conclusions about what people will say before they've said it, hurry the speaker to finish his or her point, are a passive listener (not actively working at your listening), or simply don't pay attention to what people are saying.[68] On this last point—attentiveness— college students were periodically asked to record their thoughts during a psychology course. On average, 20 percent of the students were paying attention (only 12% were actively working at being good listeners), 20 percent were thinking about sex, 20 percent were thinking about things they had done before, and the remaining 40 percent were thinking about other things unrelated to the class (e.g., worries, religion, lunch, daydreaming).[69]

How important is it to be a good listener? In general, about 45 percent of the total time you spend communicating with others is spent listening. Furthermore, listening is important for managerial and business success, even for those at the top of an organization. When Carol Bartz became CEO of Yahoo!, the company was losing money and market share to Google and Microsoft. The first thing she did was listen—by holding 45-minute meetings with as many people as possible in all parts and levels of the company. Bartz said, "The first thing I did was just set up 45 min sessions with as many people as I could and just listened. I said, 'Okay, what do you think needs to be changed here? What's good? What's bad? What would you do if you were sitting in my seat?' And then I'd always ask, 'Who else should I talk to?' If you sit quiet long enough, you find out what people really think. I filled a whole notebook up in those first few weeks, just gently asking and listening."[70]

Listening is a more important skill for managers than ever, because Generation X employees tend to expect a high level of interaction with their supervisors. They want feedback on their performance, but they also want to offer feedback and know that it is heard.[71] In fact, managers with better listening skills are rated as better managers by their employees and are much more likely to be promoted.[72]

So, what can you do to improve your listening ability? First, understand the difference between hearing and listening. According to *Webster's New World Dictionary*, **hearing** is the "act or process of perceiving sounds," whereas **listening** is "making a conscious effort to hear." In other words, we react to sounds, such as bottles breaking or music being played too loud, because hearing is an involuntary

hearing the act or process of perceiving sounds.

listening making a conscious effort to hear.

© iStockphoto.com/PIKSEL

Active listening means assuming half the responsibility for successful communication.

active listening assuming half the responsibility for successful communication by actively giving the speaker nonjudgmental feedback that shows you've accurately heard what he or she said.

empathetic listening understanding the speaker's perspective and personal frame of reference and giving feedback that conveys that understanding to the speaker.

physiological process. By contrast, listening is a voluntary behavior. So, if you want to be a good listener, you have to choose to be a good listener. Typically, that means choosing to be an active, empathetic listener.[73]

Active listening means assuming half the responsibility for successful communication by actively giving the speaker nonjudgmental feedback that shows you've accurately heard what he or she said. Active listeners make it clear from their behavior that they are listening carefully to what the speaker has to say. Active listeners put the speaker at ease, maintain eye contact, and show the speaker that they are attentively listening by nodding and making short statements.

Several specific strategies can help you be a better active listener. First, *clarify responses* by asking the speaker to explain confusing or ambiguous statements. Second, when there are natural breaks in the speaker's delivery, use this time to paraphrase or summarize what has been said. *Paraphrasing* is restating what has been said in your own words. *Summarizing* is reviewing the speaker's main points or emotions. Paraphrasing and summarizing give the speaker the chance to correct the message if the active listener has attached the wrong meaning to it. Paraphrasing and summarizing also show the speaker that the active listener is interested in the speaker's message. Exhibit 15.10 lists specific statements that listeners can use to clarify responses, paraphrase, or summarize what has been said.

Active listeners also avoid evaluating the message or being critical until the message is complete. They recognize that their only responsibility during the transmission of a message is to receive it accurately and derive the intended meaning from it. Evaluation and criticism can take place after the message is accurately received. Finally, active listeners also recognize that a large portion of any message is transmitted nonverbally and thus pay very careful attention to the nonverbal cues transmitted by the speaker.

Empathetic listening means understanding the speaker's perspective and personal frame of reference and giving feedback that conveys that understanding to the speaker. Empathetic listening goes beyond active listening because it depends on our ability to set aside our own attitudes or relationships to be able to see and understand things through someone else's eyes. Empathetic listening is just as important as active listening, especially for managers, because it helps build rapport and trust with others.

The key to being a more empathetic listener is to show your desire to understand and to reflect people's feelings. You can *show your desire to understand* by listening, that is, asking people to talk about what's most important to them and then by giving them sufficient time to talk before responding or interrupting. Altera Corp., which makes computer chips, uses empathetic listening as the key sales tool for its

Exhibit 15.10   Clarifying, Paraphrasing, and Summarizing Responses for Active Listeners

Clarifying Responses	Paraphrasing Responses	Summarizing Responses
Could you explain that again?	What you're really saying is . . .	Let me summarize . . .
I don't understand what you mean.	If I understand you correctly . . .	Okay, your main concerns are . . .
I'm not sure how . . .	In other words . . .	To recap what you've said . . .
I'm confused. Would you run through that again?	So your perspective is that . . .	Thus far, you've discussed . . .
	Tell me if I'm wrong, but what you're saying is . . .	

Source: E. Atwater, *I Hear You*, revised ed. (New York: Walker, 1992).

sales force. When salesperson Mike Dionne first met with an information technology manager from a medical company, he told him he was there to find out how Altera could expand its business in the medical field. During the 90-minute meeting, Dionne rarely spoke and never said that Altera wanted to sell him computer chips. Instead, Dionne listened quietly and didn't interrupt as the manager described the kinds of technology (using computer chips) that his company wanted to buy. Dionne says, "You could tell [he] was jazzed. He was comfortable, leaning back in his chair and talking freely."[74]

Reflecting feelings is also an important part of empathetic listening because it demonstrates that you understand the speaker's emotions. Unlike active listening, in which you restate or summarize the informational content of what has been said, the focus is on the affective part of the message. As an empathetic listener, you can use the following statements to *reflect the speaker's emotions*:

> » So, right now it sounds like you're feeling . . . .
> » You seem as if you're . . . .
> » Do you feel a bit . . .
> » I could be wrong, but I'm sensing that you're feeling . . . .

In the end, says management consultant Terry Pearce, empathetic listening can be boiled down to these three steps. First, wait ten seconds before you respond. It will seem an eternity, but waiting prevents you from interrupting others and rushing your response. Second, to be sure you understand what the speaker wants, ask questions to clarify the speaker's intent. Third, only then should you respond first with feelings and then facts (notice that facts *follow* feelings).[75]

A word of caution, however: Not everyone appreciates having what they said repeated back to them. Manager Candy Friesen says that whenever she did that, "I seemed to engender animosity or hostility. . . . the person to whom you're speaking may not appreciate having his thoughts paraphrased one little bit."[76] So, when applying these listening techniques, pay attention to the body language and tone of voice of the person you're communicating with to make sure they appreciate your attempts to be a better listener.

3.3 Giving Feedback

In Chapter 11, you learned that performance appraisal feedback (i.e., judging) should be separated from developmental feedback (i.e., coaching).[77] We can now focus on the steps needed to communicate feedback one-on-one to employees.

To start, managers need to recognize that feedback can be constructive or destructive. **Destructive feedback** is disapproving without any intention of being helpful and almost always causes a negative or defensive reaction in the recipient. Kent Thiry is CEO of **DaVita**, which runs dialysis treatment centers. Thiry values receiving and giving feedback. For example, he holds 20 town hall meetings a year, and has his vice presidents do the same thing. Thiry likes town hall sessions because, "You can ask for a show of hands and find out immediately if your new scheduling software is terrible." When it comes to giving feedback, Thiry is overly zealous and tends to be too critical. As a result, in his 360 feedback, the executives who work for him regularly complain that he gives too much negative feedback. Says Thiry, "They say I'm not harder on them than I am on myself, but my negativity isn't constructive." To decrease his use of destructive feedback, Thiry gives himself "a daily score about feedback, to remind myself—and change." Avoiding destructive feedback is

< **"what's new" companies**

destructive feedback feedback that disapproves without any intention of being helpful and almost always causes a negative or defensive reaction in the recipient.

important. In fact, one study found that 98 percent of employees responded to destructive feedback from their bosses with either verbal aggression (two-thirds) or physical aggression (one-third).[78]

By contrast, **constructive feedback** is intended to be helpful, corrective, and/or encouraging. It is aimed at correcting performance deficiencies and motivating employees. When providing constructive feedback, Jenet Noriega Schwind, vice president and chief people officer of Zantaz, an e-business archiving company, tells employees, "What I'm going to tell you may be upsetting to you—but it's important to your success." She says, "When you are telling people things they don't necessarily want to hear, you have to deliver your message in a way that gets their attention and acceptance."[79]

For feedback to be constructive rather than destructive, it must be immediate, focused on specific behaviors, and problem oriented. *Immediate feedback* is much more effective than delayed feedback because manager and worker can recall the mistake or incident more accurately and discuss it in detail. For example, if a worker is rude to a customer and the customer immediately reports the incident to management, and if the manager, in turn, immediately discusses the incident with the employee, there should be little disagreement over what was said or done. By contrast, it's unlikely that either the manager or the worker will be able to accurately remember the specifics of what occurred if the manager waits several weeks to discuss the incident. When that happens, it's usually too late to have a meaningful conversation.

Specific feedback focuses on particular acts or incidents that are clearly under the control of the employee. For instance, instead of telling an employee that he or she is "always late for work," it's much more constructive to say, "In the last three weeks, you have been 30 minutes late on four occasions and more than an hour late on two others." Furthermore, specific feedback isn't very helpful unless employees have control over the problems that the feedback addresses. Giving negative feedback about behaviors beyond someone's control is likely to be seen as unfair. Similarly, giving positive feedback about behaviors beyond someone's control may be viewed as insincere.

Last, *problem-oriented feedback* focuses on the problems or incidents associated with the poor performance rather than on the worker or the worker's personality. Giving feedback does not give managers the right to personally attack workers. Although managers may be frustrated by a worker's poor performance, the point of problem-oriented feedback is to draw attention to the problem in a nonjudgmental way so that the employee has enough information to correct it. For example, if an employee has body odor, a surprisingly common workplace problem, don't leave deodorant, soap, or shampoo on the person's desk (for all to see) or say, "You stink." *HR Magazine* advises handling the problem this way: "Because this is a sensitive issue and the employee will likely be uncomfortable and embarrassed in discussing it, keep the meeting private and confidential. Be compassionate but direct. Treat it as you would handle any other job-related performance issue. Explain the problem and the need to correct it. Be specific about expectations. . . . If the employer has a dress and grooming policy, refer to the policy and provide the employee with a copy."[80]

constructive feedback feedback intended to be helpful, corrective, and/or encouraging.

cross-cultural communication transmitting information from a person in one country or culture to a person from another country or culture.

3.4 Improving Cross-Cultural Communication

As you know by now, effective communication is very difficult to accomplish. **Cross-cultural communication**, which involves transmitting information from a person in one country or culture to a person from another country or culture, is

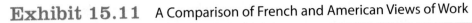

Exhibit 15.11   A Comparison of French and American Views of Work

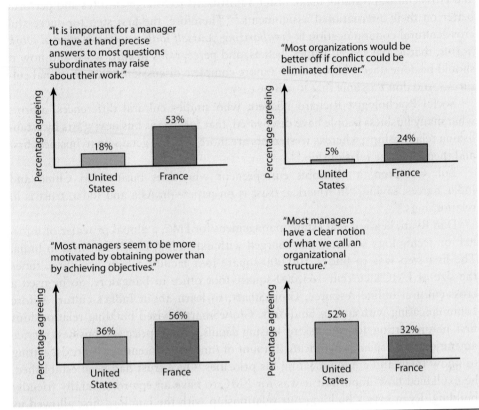

Source: Based on A. Laurent, "The Cultural Diversity of Western Conceptions of Management," in *International Studies of Management and Organization*, vol. 13, nos. 1 & 2 (Spring–Summer 1983), 75–96. From N. J. Adler, *From Boston to Beijing: Managing with a World View.* © 2002 South-Western, a part of Cengage Learning, Inc. Reprinted by permission. www.cengage.com/permissions.

even more difficult. For example, when a French company bought a U.S. company, it found that the American managers would not implement the new strategy that it recommended. As tensions grew worse, the American managers challenged their new French boss's strategy and explained why they hadn't followed it. Meanwhile, the French, who now owned the company, couldn't understand why the American managers, who, after all, worked for them, didn't just do as they were told.[81] Exhibit 15.11, which shows the rather different views that French and American workers have about work and gives us some insight into the difficulty of cross-cultural communication in this situation. Overall, the French are much more likely to believe that managers should have precise answers to subordinates' questions (53% vs. 18%), that organizations would be better off without conflict (24% vs. 5%), and that managers are more motivated by power than by achieving objectives (56% vs. 36%).[82] With such different views on these basic topics, no wonder there were communication difficulties.

You can do a number of things to increase your chances for successful cross-cultural communication:

>> Familiarize yourself with a culture's general work norms.

>> Determine whether a culture is emotionally affective or neutral.

>> Develop respect for other cultures.

>> Understand how address terms and attitudes toward time differ from culture to culture.

In Chapter 8, you learned that expatriates who receive pre-departure language and cross-cultural training make faster adjustments to foreign cultures and perform better on their international assignments.[83] Therefore, the first step for successful cross-cultural communication is *familiarizing yourself with a culture's general work norms*, that is, the shared values, beliefs, and perceptions toward work and how it should be done. (See Chapter 8 for a more complete discussion of international cultures.) And don't assume that it will be easy.

Social Psychologist Richard Nisbett, who studies cultural differences, affirms what many business people have discovered, that for Asians business starts by establishing relationships, whereas westerners are more likely to get down to business first and then build the relationship.[84]

Bob Compton, a Memphis entrepreneur who does business in China and India, agrees, saying, "In America, trust is on paper—in Asia and India, trust is in relationships."[85]

"what's new" companies >

Dan Ryan, head of real estate management for **EMC**, a global provider of information technology services, was charged with expanding EMC's business in India. The first step was to find a 500,000-square-foot facility, which was three times the size of EMC's current 165,000-square-foot office in Bangalore. So he used a cross-cultural online resource, GlobeSmart, to learn about India's culture before communicating with Indian landlords. GlobeSmart advised building relationships first, before getting down to asking leasing details, such as price and business service amenities. So he spent a significant amount of time with potential landlords, getting to know them and communicating his priorities. Once trust had been established, he explained how important it was for EMC to have an environmentally friendly building. Ryan says, "Building our relationship with the landlord first allowed us to get him to consider meeting those [environmental] standards. Now he's talking about doing all of his projects that way."[86]

So, no matter how difficult, you should work hard to learn different cultures and languages. Fortunately, books such as *Kiss, Bow, or Shake Hands: How to Do Business in 60 Countries* (by Terri Morrison, Wayne Conaway, George Borden, and Hans Koehler), *Do's and Taboos Around the World* (by Roger E. Axtell), and *Dun & Bradstreet's Guide to Doing Business Around the World* (by Terri Morrison, Wayne Conaway, and Joseph Douress) and websites such as BusinessCulture.com and ExecutivePlanet.com provide a wealth of information about countries, their cultures, and their work and communication norms.

Determining whether a culture is emotionally affective or neutral is also important to cross-cultural communication. People in **affective cultures** tend to display their emotions and feelings openly when communicating, whereas people in **neutral cultures** do not.[87] Although Italians are prone to strong bursts of emotion (positive and negative), Chinese don't show strong emotions because doing so is thought to disrupt harmony and lead to conflict. Likewise, a smiling American is displaying happiness, but a smiling Japanese may be trying to hide another emotion or avoid answering a question.[88] The mistake most managers make is misunderstanding the differences between affective and neutral cultures. People from neutral cultures aren't by definition cold and unfeeling. They just don't show their emotions in the same way or with the same intensity as people from affective cultures. The key is to recognize the differences and then make sure your judgments are not based on the lack or presence of emotional reactions. Exhibit 15.12 provides a more detailed explanation of the differences between affective and neutral cultures.

Respecting other cultures is also an important part of improving cross-cultural communication. Because we use our own culture as the standard of comparison,

affective cultures cultures in which people display emotions and feelings when communicating.

neutral cultures cultures in which people do not display emotions and feelings when communicating.

Exhibit 15.12   Affective and Neutral Cultures

In Affective Cultures, People	In Neutral Cultures, People
1. Reveal thoughts and feelings through verbal and nonverbal communication	1. Don't reveal what they are thinking or feeling
2. Express and show feelings of tension	2. Hide tension and only show it accidentally in face or posture
3. Let their emotions show easily, intensely, and without inhibition	3. Suppress emotions, leading to occasional "explosions"
4. Admire heated, animated, and intense expression of emotion	4. Admire remaining cool, calm, and relaxed
5. Are used to touching, gesturing, and showing strong emotions through facial expressions (all are common)	5. Resist touching, gesturing, and showing strong emotions through facial expressions
6. Make statements with emotion	6. Often make statements in an unexpressive manner

Source: F. Trompenaars, *Riding the Waves of Culture: Understanding Diversity in Global Business* (London: Economist Books, 1994).

it's very easy to make the common mistake of assuming that *different* means "inferior."[89] Take this example:

> *A Swiss executive waits more than an hour past the appointed time for his Spanish colleague to arrive and to sign a major supply contract. In his impatience, he concludes that the Spaniard must be lazy and totally unconcerned about business.*[90]

According to Professor Nancy J. Adler:

> *The Swiss executive has misevaluated his colleague by negatively comparing the colleague's behavior to his own culture's standard for business punctuality. Implicitly, he has labeled his own culture's behavior as good ("The Swiss arrive on time, especially for important meetings, and that is good.") and the other culture's behavior as bad ("The Spanish do not arrive on time and that is bad.").*[91]

According to Adler, "Evaluating others' behavior rarely helps in trying to understand, communicate with, or conduct business with people from another culture."[92] The key, she says, is taking a step back and realizing that you don't know or understand everything that is going on and that your assumptions and interpretations of others' behavior and motives may be wrong.

So, instead of judging or evaluating your international business colleagues, observe what they do. Also, delay your judgments until you have more experience with your colleagues and their culture. Last, treat any judgments or conclusions you do make as guesses and then double-check those judgments or conclusions with others.[93] The more patient you are in forming opinions and drawing conclusions, the better you'll be at cross-cultural communication.

You can also improve cross-cultural communication by *knowing the address terms* that different cultures use to address each other in the workplace.[94] **Address terms** are the cultural norms that establish whether you address businesspeople by their first names, family names, or titles. When meeting for the first time, Americans and Australians tend to be informal and address each other by first names, even nicknames. Such immediate informality is not accepted in many cultures. For instance, an American manager working in one of his company's British subsidiaries introduced himself as "Chuck" to his British employees and coworkers. Nonetheless, even after six months on the job, his British counterparts still referred to him as

address terms cultural norms that establish whether you should address businesspeople by their first names, family names, or titles.

"Charles." And the more he insisted they call him "Chuck," the more they seemed to dig in their heels and call him "Charles."[95] So, to decrease defensiveness, know your address terms before addressing your international business counterparts.

Understanding different cultural attitudes toward time is another major consideration for effective cross-cultural communication. Cultures tend to be either monochronic or polychronic in their orientation toward time.[96] In **monochronic cultures**, people tend to do one thing at a time and view time as linear, meaning that time is the passage of sequential events. You may have heard the saying, "There are three stages in people's lives: when they believe in Santa Claus, when they don't believe in Santa Claus, and when they are Santa Claus." The progression from childhood, to young adulthood, to parenthood (when they are Santa Claus) reflects a linear view of time. Schedules are important in monochronic cultures because you schedule time to get a particular thing done. Professor Frons Trompenaars, a noted researcher on international cultures and business, gives these examples of monochronic cultures:

> *In London I once saw a long queue of people waiting for a bus when it started pouring rain. They all stood stolidly, getting soaked even though cover was close by, lest they lose their sequential order. They preferred to do things right rather than do the right thing. In the Netherlands, you could be the queen, but if you are in a butcher's shop with number 46 and you step up for service when number 12 is called, you are still in deep trouble. Nor does it matter if you have an emergency; order is order.*[97]

By contrast, in **polychronic cultures**, people tend to do more than one thing at a time and view time as circular, meaning that time is a combination of the past, present, and future. Consider the following example from a polychronic culture:

> *In the Bahamas, bus service is managed similarly to many taxi systems. Drivers own their own buses and collect passenger fares for their income. There is no set schedule nor set time when buses will run or arrive at a particular location. Everything depends on the driver.*
>
> *Bus drivers in the Bahamas are present-oriented; what they feel like doing on a particular day at a particular hour dictates what they will actually do. If the bus driver feels hungry, for example, the driver will go home to eat lunch without waiting for a preset lunch hour. Drivers see no need to repeat yesterday's actions today, nor to set tomorrow's schedule according to the needs and patterns of yesterday.*[98]

As you can easily imagine, businesspeople from monochronic cultures are driven to distraction by what they perceive as the laxness of polychronic cultures, while people from polychronic cultures chafe under what they perceive as the strict regimentation of monochronic cultures. Conflicts between these two views of time occur rather easily. Let's go back to Trompenaars's butcher shop for an example:

> *At my local butcher shop in Amsterdam, the butcher calls a number, unwraps, cuts, rewraps each item the customer wants, and then calls the next number. Once I ventured a suggestion, "While you have the salami out, cut a pound for me, too." Customers and staff went into shock. The system may be inefficient, but they were not about to let some wise guy change it.*

Researchers Edward and Mildred Hall summed up the conflicts between these different views of time by saying, "It is impossible to know how many millions of dollars have been lost in international business because monochronic and polychronic people do not understand each other or even realize that two such different time systems exist."[99] Exhibit 15.13 provides a more detailed explanation of the differences between monochronic and polychronic cultures.

monochronic cultures cultures in which people tend to do one thing at a time and view time as linear.

polychronic cultures cultures in which people tend to do more than one thing at a time and view time as circular.

appointment time a cultural norm for how punctual you must be when showing up for scheduled appointments or meetings.

Exhibit 15.13   Monochronic versus Polychronic Cultures

People in Monochronic Cultures	People in Polychronic Cultures
• Do one thing at a time	• Do many things at once
• Concentrate on the job	• Are highly distractible and subject to interruptions
• Take time commitments (deadlines, schedules) seriously	• Meet time commitments only if possible without extreme measures
• Are committed to the job	• Are committed to people
• Adhere scrupulously to plans	• Change plans easily and often
• Are concerned about not disturbing others (privacy is to be respected)	• Are more concerned with relationships (family, friends, business associates) than with privacy
• Show respect for private property (rarely lend or borrow things)	• Frequently borrow and lend things
• Emphasize promptness	• Vary their promptness by the relationship
• Are accustomed to short-term relationships	• Tend to build lifetime relationships

Source: E. T. Hall & M. R. Hall, *Understanding Cultural Differences* (Yarmouth, ME: Intercultural Press, 1990).

Differences in monochronic and polychronic time show up in four important temporal concepts that affect cross-cultural communication: appointment time, schedule time, discussion time, and acquaintance time.[100] **Appointment time** refers to how punctual you must be when showing up for scheduled appointments or meetings. In the United States, you are considered late if you arrive more than 5 minutes after the appointed time. Swedes don't even allow 5 minutes, expecting others to arrive on the dot. By contrast, in Latin countries people can arrive 20 to 30 minutes after a scheduled appointment and still not be considered late.

Schedule time is the time by which scheduled projects or jobs should actually be completed. In the United States and other Anglo cultures, a premium is placed on completing things on time. By contrast, more relaxed attitudes toward schedule time can be found throughout Asia and Latin America.

Discussion time concerns how much time should be spent in discussion with others. In the United States, we carefully manage discussion time to avoid wasting time on nonbusiness topics. In Brazil, though, because of the emphasis on building relationships, as much as two hours of general discussion on nonbusiness topics can take place before moving on to business issues.

Finally, **acquaintance time** is how much time you must spend getting to know someone before the person is prepared to do business with you. Again, in the United States, people quickly get down to business and are willing to strike a deal on the same day if the terms are good and initial impressions are positive. In the Middle East, however, it may take two or three weeks of meetings before reaching this comfort level. The French also have a different attitude toward acquaintance time. Polly Platt, author of *French or Foe*, a book that explains French culture and people for travelers and businesspeople, says, "Know that things are going to take longer and don't resent it. Realize that the time system is different. Time is not a quantity for them. We save time, we spend time, we waste time; all this comes from money. The French don't. They pass time. It's a totally different concept."[101]

schedule time a cultural norm for the time by which scheduled projects or jobs should actually be completed.

discussion time a cultural norm for how much time should be spent in discussion with others.

acquaintance time a cultural norm for how much time you must spend getting to know someone before the person is prepared to do business with you.

© 878111805/Shutterstock.com

Review 3

Managing One-on-One Communication One-on-one communication can be managed by choosing the right communication medium, being a good listener, giving effective feedback, and understanding cross-cultural communication. Managers generally prefer oral communication because it provides the opportunity to ask questions and assess nonverbal communication. Oral communication is best suited to complex, ambiguous, or emotionally laden topics. Written communication is best suited for delivering straightforward messages and information. Listening is important for managerial success, but most people are terrible listeners. To improve your listening skills, choose to be an active listener (clarify responses, paraphrase, and summarize) and an empathetic listener (show your desire to understand, reflect feelings). Feedback can be constructive or destructive. To be constructive, feedback must be immediate, focused on specific behaviors, and problem oriented. Finally, to increase the chances for successful cross-cultural communication, familiarize yourself with a culture's general work norms, determine whether a culture is emotionally affective or neutral, develop respect for other cultures, and understand how address terms and attitudes toward time (polychronic vs. monochronic time; appointment, schedule, discussion, and acquaintance time) differ from culture to culture.

4 Managing Organization-Wide Communication

Although managing one-on-one communication is important, managers must also know how to communicate effectively with a larger number of people throughout an organization. When Bill Zollars became CEO of Yellow Corporation, a trucking company, he decided that he needed to communicate directly with all 25,000 of the company's employees, most of whom did not work at company headquarters in Overland Park, Kansas. For a year and a half, he traveled across the country conducting small, town hall meetings. Zollars says, "When I first got to Yellow, we were in a bad state. So I spent 85 percent of my time on the road talking to people one-on-one or in small groups. I would start off in the morning with the sales force, then talk to drivers, and then the people on the docks. At the end of the day I would have a customer dinner. I would say the same thing to every group and repeat it ad nauseam. The people traveling with me were ready to shoot me. But you have to be relentless in terms of your message."[102] Effective leaders, however, don't just communicate to others. They also make themselves accessible so they can hear what employees throughout their organizations are thinking and feeling.

Learn more about organization-wide communication by reading the following sections about **4.1 improving transmission by getting the message out** and **4.2 improving reception by finding ways to hear what others feel and think.**

4.1 Improving Transmission: Getting the Message Out

Several methods of electronic communication—email, collaborative discussion sites, televised/videotaped speeches and conferences, and broadcast voice mail—now make it easier for managers to communicate with people throughout the organization and get the message out.

Although we normally think of email, the transmission of messages via computers, as a means of one-on-one communication, it also plays an important role in organization-wide communication. With the click of a button, managers can send email to everyone in the company via distribution lists. After two quarters of poor financial performance, including an 18 percent drop in the company's stock, CEO John Chambers, sent a company-wide email to Cisco's managers and employees, saying, "As I've said, our strategy is sound. It is aspects of our operational execution that are not. We have been slow to make decisions, we have had surprises where we should not, and we have lost the accountability that has been a hallmark of our ability to execute consistently for our customers and our shareholders. That is unacceptable. And it is exactly what we will attack. That said, today we face a simple truth: we have disappointed our investors and we have confused our employees. Bottom line, we have lost some of the credibility that is foundational to Cisco's success—and we must earn it back."[103]

Many CEOs and top executives make their email addresses public and encourage employees to contact them directly. On his first day as the new CEO of Quest Communications, Richard Notebaert sent this simple email to his 50,000 employees: "I'm here. Talk to me." Since then he has received 200,000 emails, many of which he has reacted to by taking some action.[104]

Collaborative websites are another means of electronically promoting organization-wide communication. **Online discussion forums** use web- or software-based discussion tools to allow employees across the company to easily ask questions and share knowledge with each other. The point is to share expertise and not duplicate solutions already discovered by others in the company. Furthermore, because collaborative discussion sites remain online, they provide a historical database for people who are dealing with particular problems for the first time.

Collaborative discussion sites are typically organized by topic, project, or person and can take the shape of blogs that allow readers to post comments, wikis to allow collaborative discussions, document sharing and editing, or traditional discussion forums (see Chapter 17 on managing information for further explanation). At IBM, 26,000 employees have blogs (blogs are discussed later in the chapter) where they write about their work and invite others to contribute through standard blog comments. "Wiki Central" at IBM hosts 20,000 wikis for IBM teams and projects that have 100,000 users. Brian Goodman, who manages an IBM software development team, says that with his wiki, "I have a single view of the projects and their status without pinging each of them once a day."[105] Goodman's team wiki also uses a "polling widget" to let team members vote on specific issues as they design the software and a "rating widget" that is used by team members to rate proposals and ideas. And connecting all of this and IBM's employees is BluePages, IBM's employee-edited corporate directory. When you want to find out more about who authored a wiki or blog entry, click on the name (no anonymous entries or pseudonyms allowed within IBM) and you're taken to that employee's BluePages site (which looks a lot like a FaceBook page), which lists contact information, projects he or she is working on, jobs held, and other blog and wiki entries the person has written.

Exhibit 15.14 lists the steps companies need to take to establish successful collaborative discussion sites. First, pinpoint your company's top intellectual assets through a knowledge audit, and spread that knowledge throughout the organization. Second, create an online directory detailing the expertise of individual workers, and make it available to all employees. Third, set up collaborative discussion sites on the intranet so that managers and workers can collaborate on problem solving. Finally, reward information sharing by making online sharing of knowledge a key part of performance ratings.

Televised/videotaped speeches and meetings are a third electronic method of organization-wide

online discussion forums the in-house equivalent of Internet newsgroups. By using Web- or software-based discussion tools that are available across the company, employees can easily ask questions and share knowledge with each other.

Exhibit 15.14
Establishing Online Discussion Forums

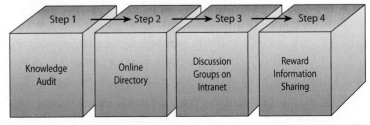

Source: Based on G. McWilliams & M. Stepanek, "Knowledge Management: Taming the Info Monster," *Businessweek*, June 22, 1998, 170.

communication. **Televised/videotaped speeches and meetings** are simply speeches and meetings originally made to a small audience that are either simultaneously broadcast to other locations in the company or videotaped for subsequent distribution and viewing by a broader audience. Cisco's John Chambers describes how, over his 15 years as CEO, he's added televised messages to his communication strategies:

> *I started off with classic communication methods when I got here 15 years ago. I'd walk around and talk to small groups and larger groups. I'd see who was here in the evening. To this day I can tell you whose car is out in the parking lot. Then email became very effective, because it gave me the ability to send a message to the whole group. But I'm a voice person. I communicate with emotion that way. I like to listen to emotion too. It's a lot easier to listen to a key customer if I hear how they're describing a problem to me. I'll leave 40 or 50 voice mails a day. I do them on the way to work and coming back from work. The newest thing for me is video on demand, which is my primary communication vehicle today. We have a small studio downstairs. We probably tape 10 to 15 videos a quarter. That way employees, and customers, can watch them when they want.*[106]

Voice messaging, or voice mail, is a telephone answering system that records audio messages. In one survey, 89 percent of respondents said that voice messaging is critical to business communication, 78 percent said that it improves productivity, and 58 percent said they would rather leave a message on a voice messaging system than with a receptionist.[107] Nonetheless, most people are unfamiliar with the ability to *broadcast voice mail* by sending a recorded message to everyone in the company. Broadcast voice mail gives top managers a quick, convenient way to address their workforces via oral communication, but only if people actually listen to the message, and that turns out to be a challenge with Generation Y workers. Jeff Schwarz, global talent leader at Deloitte & Touche, says, "If you send a message on voicemail or send an e-mail, they are likely to ignore it. It's very frustrating to our leaders, most of whom are boomers [and] some of whom are Gen X'ers. When they broadcast voicemail messages, big swaths of their organization are not hearing it. They're not even listening to it and they're not even sure it's directed to them because they don't think about being communicated with in that way. CEOs or HR leaders or business leaders think they're sending a direct message, but that is not the most effective way to communicate across the generations." Deloitte's solution—embed the broadcast voice mail in an email.[108]

4.2 Improving Reception: Hearing What Others Feel and Think

When people think of "organization-wide" communication, they think of the CEO and top managers getting their message out to people in the company. But organization-wide communication also means finding ways to hear what people throughout the organization are thinking and feeling. This is important because most employees and managers are reluctant to share their thoughts and feelings with top managers. Surveys indicate that only 29 percent of first-level managers feel that their companies encourage employees to express their opinions openly. Another study of 22 companies found that 70 percent of the people surveyed were afraid to speak up about problems they knew existed at work.

Withholding information about organizational problems or issues is called **organizational silence**. Organizational silence occurs when employees believe that telling management about problems won't make a difference or that they'll be punished or hurt in some way for sharing such information.[109] At **Jetstar Airways**, an

televised/videotaped speeches and meetings speeches and meetings originally made to a smaller audience that are either simultaneously broadcast to other locations in the company or videotaped for subsequent distribution and viewing.

organizational silence when employees withhold information about organizational problems or issues.

"what's new" companies >

Australia-based airline, pilots were afraid to speak up about fatigue from flying too many hours. Captain Richard Woodward, vice-president of the Australian and International Pilots Association, said that his organization had received dozens of complaints from Jetstar pilots, but that the pilots were afraid to complain to Jetstar management because "there was a culture of fear and intimidation at that airline."[110] One pilot scheduler told his pilots, "Toughen up, princesses! You aren't fatigued, you are tired and can't be bothered to go into work." A report from Australia's Civil Aviation Safety Authority concluded, "There remains reluctance from a number of flight crew to report fatigue risk and/or to say no to an extension of duty based on the perceived punitive nature of taking such actions."[111]

© Peter Dazeley/Getty Images

Company hotlines, survey feedback, frequent informal meetings, surprise visits, and blogs are additional ways of overcoming organizational silence. **Company hotlines** are phone numbers that anyone in the company can call anonymously to leave information for upper management. For example, Force Protection, which builds vehicles that protect armed forces personnel from explosions and ballistics, has a toll-free hotline for employees to call to report any kind of problem or issue within the company. Force Protection's policy states, "The Company Hotline is available 24 hours a day, 7 days a week and is serviced by an independent contractor. The Hotline will not be answered by an employee of Force Protection. You have the option to remain anonymous. No retaliation or reprisals will be taken against anyone utilizing this confidential service in good faith."[112] Hotlines are particularly important because 44 percent of employees will not report misconduct. Why not? The reason is twofold: They don't believe anything will be done, *and* they "fear that the report will not be kept confidential."[113] David Childers, CEO of EthicsPoint, which runs hotlines for corporations, says that companies can expect 1 to 1.5 percent of their employees to call their hotlines.[114] Company hotlines are incredibly useful, as 47 percent of the calls placed to them result in an investigation and some form of corrective action within the organization. Anonymity is critical too, because as those investigations proceed, 54 percent of the callers did not want their identities revealed.[115]

Survey feedback is information that is collected by survey from organization members and then compiled, disseminated, and used to develop action plans for improvement. Many organizations make use of survey feedback by surveying their managers and employees several times a year. **Guardian News and Media**, the publisher of the British newspaper *The Guardian*, conducts an annual survey of its employees to gauge their satisfaction and confidence in the company. After a recent restructuring, during which more than 100 journalists, editors, and editorial staff lost their jobs, the survey showed *Guardian* employees still had confidence in the company. Eighty-six percent of respondents reported that they were still proud to work at *The Guardian*, and 93 percent reported that they did extra work beyond what was required of them. Perhaps most importantly, 86 percent stated that they understood the need for cost-cutting measures and layoffs given the declining readership challenges facing the newspaper and the news industry. Managing director Tim Brooks said, "Some people—among them, friends of mine who do similar jobs to me in other media companies—thought we were bonkers to be conducting the staff survey at a time of major reorganization, cuts and redundancies. But why take someone's temperature when they are feeling fine? Taking it when they are stressed tells you much more. And actually what this survey tells us—both from the scores themselves, many of which are as high or higher than in previous surveys—and from the participation rate, which is only one percentage point below last time (and

> "what's new" companies

company hotlines phone numbers that anyone in the company can call anonymously to leave information for upper management.

survey feedback information that is collected by surveys from organizational members and then compiled, disseminated, and used to develop action plans for improvement.

much higher than the rate in most organizations)—is that although we are an organization under stress, we are fundamentally in very good health."[116]

Frequent *informal meetings* between top managers and lower-level employees are one of the best ways for top managers to hear what others think and feel. Many people assume that top managers are at the center of everything that goes on in organizations, but top managers commonly feel isolated from most of their lower-level managers and employees.[117] Consequently, more and more top managers are scheduling frequent informal meetings with people throughout their companies. Yogesh Gupta, CEO of **Fatwire** (now owned by Oracle), which makes software to manage business websites, says that managers must not get defensive during informal meetings. Says Gupta, "I've heard so many executives tell employees to be candid and then jump down their throats if they bring up a problem or ask a critical question."[118] Gupta has spent hundreds of hours in informal meetings with his 200 managers and nine executives. He meets with each privately because he believes that it encourages people to be candid. And he asks each these questions:

> » What am I doing wrong?
> » What would you do differently if you were running the company?
> » What's the biggest thing getting in the way of you doing your job well?

As a result of these meetings, Gupta learned that Fatwire was understaffed in marketing and product development.

Have you ever been around when a supervisor learns that upper management is going to be paying a visit? First, there's shock. Next, there's anxiety. And then there's panic, as everyone is told to drop what he or she is doing to polish, shine, and spruce up the workplace so that it looks perfect for the visit. Of course, when visits are conducted under these conditions, top managers don't get a realistic look at what's going on in the company. Consequently, one of the ways to get an accurate picture is to pay *surprise visits* to various parts of the organization. These visits should not just be surprise inspections, but should also be used as an opportunity to encourage meaningful upward communication from those who normally don't get a chance to communicate with upper management. Such surprise visits are now part of the culture at the Royal Mail, the United Kingdom's postal service. Chairman Allan Leighton frequently shows up unannounced at Royal Mail delivery offices. Leighton says the initial reaction is always the same, "Oh s***, it's the chairman." However, Leighton isn't there to catch his employees doing something wrong. He's there to find out, right or wrong, what's really going on. Says Leighton, "Those visits at half past five in the morning [with employees] are the most important part" of turning around the Royal Mail, which was once losing 1.5 million pounds a day.[119] Today, thanks in part to his communication with employees, the Royal Mail delivers 95 percent of first-class mail in one day, better than any other postal service in the world, and now *earns a profit* of 1.5 million pounds per day.

Blogs are another way to hear what people are thinking and saying, both inside and outside the organization. A **blog** is a personal website that provides personal opinions or recommendations, news summaries, and reader comments. At Google, which owns the blog-hosting service Blogger, hundreds of employees are writing *internal blogs*. One employee even wrote a blog for posting all the notes from the brainstorming sessions used to redesign the search page used by millions each day. Marissa Mayer, now Vice President, Search Products & User Experience, said, "Our

blog a personal website that provides personal opinions or recommendations, news summaries, and reader comments.

mgmt:facts

Tweet Tweet

Twitter can be a powerful communications tool, one that allows you and your company to communicate with hundreds and thousands of people in a split second. It can help you introduce new products, send out valuable updates, and hear from your existing customers. But to use Twitter effectively, you have to understand why people follow companies on Twitter at all. A survey from ExactTarget, a marketing agency specializing in social media and email, shows that 38 percent of people who follow companies on Twitter do so to get updates on future products. Thirty-two percent, on the other hand, say they follow a company's tweets to stay informed about what a company is doing. Saving money also seems to be a big motivation, as 31 percent said they follow a company to get a discount, 30 percent said they follow to get news of upcoming sales, and 28 percent said they follow to get free samples.[120]

legal department loves the blogs, because it basically is a written-down, backed-up, permanent time-stamped version of the scientist's notebook. When you want to file a patent, you can now show in blogs where this idea happened."[121]

External blogs and Twitter sites (micro blogs where entries are limited to 140 characters), written by people outside the company, can be a good way to find out what others are saying or thinking about your organization or its products or actions. But it means that someone in the firm has to actively monitor what is being said on web, blog, and Twitter sites. At Virgin America airlines, the interactive marketing team, public relations, and guest care departments all monitor Twitter for customer comments. And because it has wireless Internet access on all flights, customers sometimes tweet about poor service in the middle of a flight. Abby Lunardini, director of corporate communications, says, "We've had guests tweet about missing food service, and we sent a message to the plane's crew to assist [them]." Likewise, she said, "We got a tweet from someone en route to Boston who said he had been ignored on the flight and had some other service issues. Our team met him at the gate in Boston and asked if we could assist with anything or help him further."[122]

Managing Organization-Wide Communication Managers need methods for managing organization-wide communication and for making themselves accessible so they can hear what employees throughout their organizations are thinking and feeling. Email, collaborative discussion sites, televised/videotaped speeches and conferences, and broadcast voice mail make it much easier for managers to improve message transmission and get the message out. By contrast, anonymous company hotlines, survey feedback, frequent informal meetings, and surprise visits help managers avoid organizational silence and improve reception by hearing what others in the organization feel and think. Monitoring internal blogs and external blogs and Twitter sites is another way to find out what people are saying and thinking about your organization.

Review 4

SELF-ASSESSMENT

How Do You Listen?

Have you ever been eager to tell someone a funny story, only to have that person interrupt you repeatedly to ask for details or clarification? And have you ever said in exasperation, "Will you just listen?" Some people prefer an inquisitive listening style, whereas others prefer a contemplative listening style. What listening style best describes you? This listening styles inventory will help you establish a baseline to use as a foundation for developing your listening skills.

The following items relate to listening style.[123] Circle the appropriate responses. Please be candid.

1 Almost always

2 Often

3 Sometimes

4 Seldom

5 Almost never

1. I want to listen to what others have to say when they are talking.

   (5) 4 3 2 1

2. I do not listen at my capacity when others are talking.

   1 2 (3) 4 5

3. By listening, I can guess a speaker's intent or purpose without being told.

   (5) 4 3 2 1

4. I have a purpose for listening when others are talking.

   (5) 4 3 2 1

5. I keep control of my biases and attitudes when listening to others speak so that these factors won't affect my interpretation of the message.

   5 (4) 3 2 1

6. I analyze my listening errors so as not to make them again.

   5 (4) (3) 2 1

7. I listen to the complete message before making judgments about what the speaker has said.

   5 (4) 3 2 1

8. I cannot tell when a speaker's biases or attitudes are affecting his or her message.

   1 2 3 4 (5)

9. I ask questions when I don't fully understand a speaker's message.

   5 (4) 3 2 1

10. I am aware of whether or not a speaker's meaning of words and concepts is the same as mine.

    (5) 4 3 2 1

    SUBTOTAL = __5__ + __3__ + __5__ + __5__ + __4__ = 22

    GRAND TOTAL + __4__ 4 5 4 5

You can find the interpretation of your score at www.cengagebrain.com.

22

KEY TERMS

acquaintance time 645
active listening 638
address terms 643
affective cultures 642
appointment time 645
attribution theory 622
blog 650
closure 621
coaching 632
communication medium 635
communication 619
company hotlines 649
conduit metaphor 626
constructive feedback 640
counseling 632
cross-cultural
   communication 640
decoding 625
defensive bias 622
destructive feedback 639
discussion time 645
downward
   communication 627
empathetic listening 638
encoding 625
feedback to sender 626
formal communication
   channel 627
fundamental attribution
   error 622
hearing 637
horizontal
   communication 628
informal communication
   channel ("grapevine") 629
jargon 626
kinesics 633
listening 637
monochronic cultures 644
neutral cultures 642
noise 626
nonverbal
   communication 633
online discussion forums 647
organizational silence 648
paralanguage 634
perception 619
perceptual filters 619
polychronic cultures 644
schedule time 645
selective perception 621
self-serving bias 624
survey feedback 649
televised/videotaped
   speeches and
   meetings 648
upward communication 628

MANAGEMENT DECISION

A Communication Policy for the Internet Generation[124]

In your short tenure as the manager of a restaurant chain, you've come up with some brilliant ideas—the Super Bowl parties, unlimited wings night—and who could forget the 80's Karaoke Flashdance Fever? But one of your best ideas came a few months ago, when you decided that your company needed to be on Twitter. You've used it to announce promotions, concerts, special menu items, and even offer discounts. One day, you tweeted that the first 1,000 people to join your Twitter feed would get a free meal for four; about 2,700 people joined up in one hour. Your loyal Twitter followers have even spread word of your restaurants overseas. Just the other day, a huge tourist group from Hong Kong stopped at one of your eateries (and spent a ton of money) because they heard about it on Twitter.

Your venture into social media has been such a success that you want to use it for communication within the organization. Instead of phone calls, faxes, and memos, you envision sending a company-wide Tweet announcing policy changes, or identifying employees-of-the-month on the Facebook wall, or using text messages to alert chefs of menu changes. As you begin a trial run within the warehouse division, the possibilities seem endless. You get a sharp dose of reality, however, when some senior managers start calling you, frantically asking "What does FTW mean?" "Someone sent me a performance review that said KUTGW—what is that?" "Who the heck is @jimbo?" "One of my employees asked me to give them a 'tweet'—does that violate our sexual harassment policy?" One even told you about how she thought LOL meant "lots of love" and sent it as a text message to an employee whose grandfather had passed away.

All these questions made you aware of how much work was involved in integrating social media into your company's communications. It would not be as easy as giving people new computers or phones; they would have to learn a whole new language. All of the shorthand, abbreviations, and symbols that seemed so obvious to a generation raised on the Internet are a dark and mysterious code to a generation raised on phone calls, newspapers, and handwritten letters. These managers aren't ready to give up yet—they certainly see the vast potential for social media. But, they are asking—demanding—that you provide them with training so that they can tell the difference between FTW and WTF.

Questions

1. In your opinion, what is the most ideal way to train people who are unfamiliar with social media on how to use it for organization-wide communication?
2. Do you think it is appropriate to use tweets or text messages for organization-wide communication? Why or why not?

MANAGEMENT TEAM DECISION

Talking Across Time Zones

In the beginning, your company was run out of a small, drab building in the middle of Ohio. With just five employees, your little "factory" produced just a single product—small boat engines. Five years later, against all odds, you somehow landed a lucrative government contract to supply the U.S. Army with small engines for its unmanned vehicles program.

That date would prove to be a turning point, as the company would transform from a small local business into a global powerhouse. Gone are the days when the entire company was housed in a small, cramped, converted farmhouse. The entire manufacturing operation was moved to China several years ago. The R&D and engineering division operates out of a sparkling new building in Berlin, Germany. The marketing staff works out of Los Angeles, and the sales and customer service call center is based in Mumbai, India. As for the little farmhouse that you started out in, it's long gone, replaced by a glamorous modern building that's home to executive management.

With facilities located all over the world and an international staff, there have been few challenges that your company has not been able to overcome. It's been able to create low-cost, reliable engines that have been a hit in developing economies. Its alternative fuels research division is among the largest in the world and is poised both to introduce a hydrogen-powered engine and create an infrastructure to give consumers easy access to refueling stations. However, there remains one issue that your company has struggled with for some time. It doesn't have to do with dealing with environmental groups, suppliers, or competitor firms. Instead, it's about communication.

Your company has always emphasized speed—speed in discussing issues, speed in coming to decisions, and speed in executing them. And all this speed requires a great amount of efficient communication within the company. Back in the day, of course, this simply meant that Jo in engineering would walk across the hall to talk to Sam in marketing. But now that you have offices all over the world, it's become more difficult to make quick decisions and plans, because it's hard to find a way to get people together to talk. If it's 10 A.M. in Ohio, it's 7 A.M. in Los Angeles, 11 P.M. in Beijing, 8 P.M. in Mumbai, and 4 P.M. in Berlin.

So, how can we talk to each other quickly and efficiently? That's the question that the senior management team has been gathered to try to resolve. Their task is to find, or even create, a communication system that will allow timely, clear, and effective communication throughout the organization without forcing people to wake up at 3 A.M. for a videoconference.

Questions

1. In your opinion, what communication method would be ideal for an organization that has offices in many different countries?
2. Is it necessary to sacrifice speed in communication for the sake of a global presence? That is, can a company have both a global presence and an efficient, timely means of communication?
3. What cross-cultural issues should you keep in mind as you create a new communication system?

PRACTICE BEING A MANAGER

Avoiding Communication Breakdown

When problems occur in organizations, they are frequently attributed to a breakdown in communication. The communication process may get more than its share of the blame for some breakdowns that result from organizational or leadership problems. But there is some truth to the common perception that communication is problematic. In this exercise, you will have the opportunity to consider how you might improve your own communication from two sides of the table—coaching or disciplining an employee and receiving coaching or disciplining from a manager.

Step 1: Get into groups and read the scenario. Your professor will organize you in small groups of three or four students.

Scenario: Chalet is a fine-dining restaurant in a ski resort setting. The restaurant is well-known for its gourmet cuisine, fine wine selection, and outstanding service. Dinner for two at Chalet would typically cost $100 or more. A key management responsibility at Chalet is the training and development of waitstaff. Service quality is carefully monitored and standards, rigorously maintained. In exchange for meeting these

demanding standards, Chalet waitstaff are well compensated and enjoy good benefits. As time permits, you should complete conversations in which you play each of the following roles: Dennis/Denise (new waitstaff member with three months of experience at Chalet); Christy/Chris (service manager); and D.J./R.J. (communication consultant to Chalet).

Here are some basic facts of the situation:

- The service manager has not directly observed any problems with Dennis/Denise interacting with customers of the restaurant.

- Over this past busy weekend, three tables of customers reported problems with the service they received from Dennis/Denise. Only one other table received any negative feedback at all during the weekend, and that concerned the quality of a particular dessert item.

- The reports about Dennis/Denise were rather vague—"server seemed distant, unresponsive" and "acted aloof, like we were a bother."

- Christy/Chris, the service manager, did catch the tail end of what seemed like an argument between Dennis/Denise and one of the cooks on Friday night. When the cook was asked about the incident, she said, "It was nothing . . . usual cook versus server stuff."

- Dennis/Denise needs this job to pay for college and is taking a full load of classes.

The role-play should involve a brief conversation (5 to 7 minutes) initiated by Christy/Chris on Monday afternoon prior to opening. The focus of this conversation should be to coach and/or discipline regarding the concerns of the previous weekend. Those playing the role of communication consultant should take notes and provide feedback on the communication in this conversation (strengths and areas for improvement). As time allows, rotate roles after completing a conversation and hearing consultant feedback.

Step 2: Do the role-play. Complete a role-play conversation with one person playing the role of the service manager (Christy/Chris) and another person playing the role of the waitstaffer (Dennis/Denise).

Communication consultant(s) should listen and take notes in order to provide feedback to the two individuals who are role-playing the coaching/discipline conversation.

Step 3: Give feedback. Communication consultant(s) should give feedback to the role-players at the conclusion of the conversation, considering key aspects of communication discussed in this chapter.

Step 4: Switch roles. Switch roles and repeat the role-play conversation and post-conversation feedback as time allows.

Step 5: Debrief as a class. What challenges face the communicators in this scenario? Which role was most difficult for you, and why? Why is it important for managers to coach and discipline effectively? Why might managers avoid (or underutilize) this form of communication?

DEVELOP YOUR CAREER POTENTIAL

I Don't Agree, but I'm Listening

Being a good listener is a critical part of effective communication. Without it, you're unlikely to be a good manager. Therefore, the purpose of this assignment is to help you develop your listening skills. And there's no better way to do that than to talk to someone whose views are quite different from yours. In the best of situations, being a good listener is difficult. Because of perceptual filters, distractions, or daydreams, we retain only about 25 percent of what we hear. When we're talking with people who have very different views and opinions, it can be almost impossible to be good listeners. We tend to interrupt, jump to conclusions about what they'll say, and hurry them to finish their points (which we don't want to listen to anyway) so that we can "correct" their thinking with our own opinions.

To complete this assignment, you'll have to find someone who has different views or opinions on some topic (handgun control, abortion, capital punishment, and euthanasia are just some of the topics on which you can always find someone with a different viewpoint). Once you've found someone, conduct a 10-minute listening session, following this simple rule: Before stating your opinion, you must first accurately reflect or paraphrase the statement that your listening partner just made (be sure to reread Subsection 3.2 on listening). For example, suppose that your listening partner says, "Women shouldn't have to ask anyone for permission for what they do to their bodies. If they decide they want an abortion, they should go ahead and have it." Before making your point or disagreeing with your partner's, you will have to accurately paraphrase that statement in your own words. If you don't paraphrase it correctly, your listening partner will tell you. If you or your partner has difficulty accurately paraphrasing a statement, ask the other person to repeat the statement and try again. Also, don't parrot the statement by repeating it word for word. Good listening isn't mimicry. It's capturing the essence of what others have said in your own words. And before your listening partner responds, he or she too has to accurately paraphrase what you say. Continue this listening-based discussion for ten minutes.

Questions

1. Was this discussion different from the way you normally discuss contentious topics with other people? Why or why not?
2. Was it difficult to reflect or paraphrase your listening partner's perspectives? Explain and give an example.
3. Did active listening techniques or empathetic listening techniques lead to more effective listening for you? Explain.

[1]"Top Browser Share Trend," NetMarketShare, May 2011, accessed June 19, 2011, from www.netmarketshare.com/browser-market-share.aspx?spider=1&qprid=1; R. Adams & J. Vascellaro, "Google Digital Newsstand Aims to Muscle In on Apple," *The Wall Street Journal*, January 3, 2011, B1; L. Edmund & M. Learmonth, "What Larry Page Will Be up Against at Google," *Advertising Age*, January 24, 2011, 1; A. Efrati, "Google to Test Daily Deals That Challenge Groupon," *The Wall Street Journal*, January 22, 2011, B4; A. Efrati & J. Vascellaro, "Power Shifts Atop Google—Internet Giant Says Co-Founder Larry Page Will Replace CEO Eric Schmidt," *The Wall Street Journal*, January 21, 2011, A1; M. Farhad, "Google: The Quest," *Fast Company*, April 2011, 68–120, 9p; H. Jenkins, Jr., "The Weekend Interview with Eric Schmidt: Google and the Search for the Future," *The Wall Street Journal*, August 14, 2010, A9; M. Mangalindan, "Boss Talk: The Grownup at Google; How Eric Schmidt Imposed Better Management Tactics But Didn't Stifle Search Giant," *The Wall Street Journal*, March 29, 2004, B1; B. Saporito, "Refreshing Google," *Time*, February 7, 2011, 48–49; and J. Stewart, "WEEKEND INVESTOR—Common Sense: Will Google Survive Facebook?" *The Wall Street Journal*, January 29, 2011, B7.

[2]E. E. Lawler III, L. W. Porter, & A. Tannenbaum, "Manager's Attitudes toward Interaction Episodes," *Journal of Applied Psychology* 52 (1968): 423–439; and H. Mintzberg, *The Nature of Managerial Work* (New York: Harper & Row, 1973).

[3]J. D. Maes, T. G. Weldy, & M. L. Icenogle, "A Managerial Perspective: Oral Communication Competency Is Most Important for Business Students in the Workplace," *Journal of Business Communication* 34 (1997): 67–80.

[4]R. Lepsinger & A. D. Lucia, *The Art and Science of 360 Degree Feedback* (San Francisco: Pfeiffer, 1997).

[5]I. M. Botero, "Good Communication Skills Needed Today," *Business Journal: Serving Phoenix and the Valley of the Sun*, October 21, 1996.

[6]J. Sandberg, "Bosses Often Sugarcoat Their Worst News, but Staffers Don't Bite," *The Wall Street Journal*, April 21, 2004, B1.

[7]E. E. Jones & K. E. Davis, "From Acts to Dispositions: The Attribution Process in Person Perception," in L. Berkowitz, ed., *Advances in Experimental and Social Psychology*, vol. 2 (New York: Academic Press, 1965), 219–266; and R. G. Lord & J. E. Smith, "Theoretical, Information-Processing, and Situational Factors Affecting Attribution Theory Models of Organizational Behavior," *Academy of Management Review* 8 (1983): 50–60.

[8]M. Nicholson & R. Hoye, "Contextual Factors Associated with Poor Sport Spectator Behaviour," *Managing Leisure* 10 (April 2005): 94–105.

[9]D. Simons & C. Chabris, "Gorillas in Our Midst: Sustained Inattentional Blindness for Dynamic Events," *Perception* 28 (1999): 1059–1074.

[10]J. Zadney & H. B. Gerard, "Attributed Intentions and Informational Selectivity," *Journal of Experimental Social Psychology* 10 (1974): 34–52.

[11]"Lab Tests: Why Consumer Reports Can't Recommend the iPhone 4," *Consumer Reports*, July 12, 2010, accessed June 12, 2011, from http://news.consumerreports.org/electronics/2010/07/apple-iphone-4-antenna-issue-iphone4-problems-dropped-calls-lab-test-confirmed-problem-issues-signal-strength-att-network-gsm.html.

[12]G. Fowler & I. Sherr, "A Defiant Steve Jobs Confronts 'Antennagate,'" *The Wall Street Journal*, July 17, 2010, B1.

[13]J. Topolsky, "Apple Responds to iPhone 4 Reception Issues: You're Holding the Phone the Wrong Way," Engadget.com, June 24, 2010, accessed June 12, 2011, from www.engadget.com/2010/06/24/apple-responds-over-iphone-4-reception-issues-youre-holding-th/.

[14]M. Porter, J. Lorsch, & N. Nohria, "Seven Surprises for New CEOs," *Harvard Business Review* (October 2004): 62.

[15]H. H. Kelly, *Attribution in Social Interaction* (Morristown, NJ: General Learning Press, 1971).

[16]J. M. Burger, "Motivational Biases in the Attribution of Responsibility for an Accident: A Meta-Analysis of the Defensive-Attribution Hypothesis," *Psychological Bulletin* 90 (1981): 496–512.

[17]D. A. Hofmann & A. Stetzer, "The Role of Safety Climate and Communication in Accident Interpretation: Implications for Learning from Negative Events," *Academy of Management Journal* 41, no. 6 (1998): 644–657.

[18]C. Perrow, *Normal Accidents: Living with High-Risk Technologies* (New York: Basic Books, 1984).

[19]A. G. Miller & T. Lawson, "The Effect of an Informational Opinion on the Fundamental Attribution Error," *Journal of Personality & Social Psychology* 47 (1989): 873–896; and J. M. Burger, "Changes in Attribution Errors over Time: The Ephemeral Fundamental Attribution Error," *Social Cognition* 9 (1991): 182–193.

[20]D. Sacks, "Scenes from the Culture Clash," *Fast Company*, January 1, 2006, 72.

[21]F. Heider, *The Psychology of Interpersonal Relations* (New York: Wiley, 1958); and D. T. Miller & M. Ross, "Self-Serving Biases in Attribution of Causality: Fact or Fiction?" *Psychological Bulletin* 82 (1975): 213–225.

[22]J. R. Larson, Jr., "The Dynamic Interplay between Employees' Feedback-Seeking Strategies and Supervisors' Delivery of Performance Feedback," *Academy of Management Review* 14, no. 3 (1989): 408–422.

[23]Brian O'Keefe, "Meet the CEO of the Biggest Company on Earth," *Fortune*, September 9, 2010, accessed February 25, 2011, from http://money.cnn.com/2010/09/07/news/companies/mike_duke_walmart_full.fortune/.

[24]N. Wingfield, "Say What? High-Tech Messages Can Get Lost in Translation.

Devices Make Communicating Easier—Or Incomprehensible; Phone Doesn't Swear," *The Wall Street Journal*, May 4, 2011, accessed on June 17, 2011, from http://online.wsj.com/article/SB1000142405274870384190 4576256851860269320.html.

[25]C. Hymowitz, "Mind Your Language: To Do Business Today, Consider Delayering," *The Wall Street Journal*, March 27, 2006, B1.

[26]M. Reddy, "The Conduit Metaphor—A Case of Frame Conflict in Our Language about Our Language," in *Metaphor and Thought*, ed. A. Ortony (Cambridge: Cambridge University Press, 1979), 284–324.

[27]G. L. Kreps, *Organizational Communication: Theory and Practice* (New York: Longman, 1990).

[28]Ibid.

[29]J. Jusko, "A Little More Communication," *Industry Week*, March 1, 2010, 19.

[30]B. Salzberg, "Trusting a CEO in the Twitter Age," *Bloomberg Businessweek*, August 7, 2009, accessed August 10, 2010, from www.businessweek.com/managing/content/aug2009/ca2009087_680028.htm?chan=careers_managing+your+company+page_top+stories.

[31]J. McGregor, "Zappos' Secret: It's an Open Book," *Businessweek*, March 23, 2009, 62; and N. Zmuda, "Surfing for Sales: Zappos Execs Aim to Hit $1 Billion," *Footwear News*, August 21, 2006, 1–8.

[32]J. Sandberg, "Ruthless Rumors and the Managers Who Enable Them," *The Wall Street Journal*, October 29, 2003, B1.

[33]K. Moran, "Web Used to Answer Rumors: UT Medical Staff Gets Truth Quickly," *Houston Chronicle*, April 18, 1999, 35.

[34]Bruce Weinstein, "The Ethics of Multitasking," *Bloomberg Businessweek*, September 4, 2009, accessed October 10, 2010, from www.businessweek.com/managing/content/sep2009/ca2009094_935233.htm.

[35]W. Davis & J. R. O'Connor, "Serial Transmission of Information: A Study of the Grapevine," *Journal of Applied Communication Research* 5 (1977): 61–72.

[36]Sandberg, "Ruthless Rumors and the Managers Who Enable Them."

[37]K. Voight, "Office Intelligence," *Asian Wall Street Journal*, January 21, 2005, P1.

[38]Ibid.

[39]G. Hoover, "Maintaining Employee Engagement when Communicating Difficult Issues," *Communication World*, November 1, 2005, 25.

[40]Davis & O'Connor, "Serial Transmission of Information: A Study of the Grapevine"; and Hymowitz, "Managing: Spread the Word, Gossip Is Good," *The Wall Street Journal*, October 4, 1988, online, page number not available.

[41]D. Kirkpatrick & D. Roth, "Why There's No Escaping the Blog," *Fortune (Europe)*, January 24, 2005, 64.

[42]"The Power of Internet Gripe Sites," *Perspectives*, August 13, 2008, accessed June 25, 2008, from www.fairwindspartners.com.

[43]W. C. Redding, *Communication within the Organization: An Interpretive View of Theory and Research* (New York: Industrial Communication Council, 1972).

[44]D. T. Hall, K. L. Otazo, & G. P. Hollenbeck, "Behind Closed Doors: What Really Happens in Executive Coaching," *Organizational Dynamics* 27, no. 3 (1999): 39–53.

[45]P. O'Connell, "Goldman Sachs: Committed to the Next Generation," *Businessweek*, February 17, 2010, 12.

[46]J. Kelly, "Blowing the Whistle on the Boss," *PR Newswire*, November 15, 2004, accessed June 17, 2011, from www.prnewswire.com [content no longer available online].

[47]R. McGarvey, "Lords of Discipline," *Entrepreneur Magazine*, 1 January 2000, page number not available.

[48]S. Needleman, "Career Journal: Tips for Managers on Handling Their Workers' Personal Problems," *The Wall Street Journal*, April 25, 2006, B9.

[49]C. Hirschman, "Firm Ground: EAP Training for HR and Managers Improves Supervisor-Employee Communication and Helps Organizations Avoid Legal Quagmires," *Employee Benefit News*, June 13, 2005, accessed June 17, 2011, from http://www.benefitnews.com [content no longer available online].

[50]"Issue: Cigna's In-House Compassion," *Bloomberg Businessweek*, March 31, 2009, accessed February 25, 2011, from www.businessweek.com/managing/content/mar2009/ca20090331_920962.htm.

[51]A. Mehrabian, "Communication without Words," *Psychology Today* 3 (1968): 53; A. Mehrabian, *Silent Messages* (Belmont, CA: Wadsworth, 1971); R. Harrison, *Beyond Words: An Introduction to Nonverbal Communication* (Upper Saddle River, NJ: Prentice Hall, 1974); and A. Mehrabian, *Non-Verbal Communication* (Chicago: Aldine, 1972).

[52]M. L. Knapp, *Nonverbal Communication in Human Interaction*, 2nd ed. (New York: Holt, Rinehart & Winston, 1978).

[53]H. M. Rosenfeld, "Instrumental Affiliative Functions of Facial and Gestural Expressions," *Journal of Personality & Social Psychology* 24 (1966): 65–72; P. Ekman, "Differential Communication of Affect by Head and Body Cues," *Journal of Personality & Social Psychology* 23 (1965): 726–735; and A. Mehrabian, "Significance of Posture and Position in the Communication of Attitude and Status Relationships," *Psychological Bulletin* 71 (1969): 359–372.

[54]J. Gottman & R. Levenson, "The Timing of Divorce: Predicting When a Couple Will Divorce over a 14-Year Period," *Journal of Marriage & the Family* 62 (August 2000): 737–745; and J. Gottman, R. Levenson, & E. Woodin, "Facial Expressions during Marital Conflict," *Journal of Family Communication* 1, no. 1 (2001): 37–57.

[55]T. Aeppel, "Career Journal: Nicknamed 'Nag,' She's Just Doing Her Job," *The Wall Street Journal*, May 14, 2002, B1.

[56]J. Saranow, "A Personal Trainer for Your Voice," *The Wall Street Journal*, February 3, 2004, D1.

[57]A. Joyce, "Confidentiality as a Valued Benefit; Loose Lips Can Defeat the Purpose of an Employee Assistance Program," *The Washington Post*, May 11, 2003, F05.

58C. A. Bartlett & S. Ghoshal, "Changing the Role of Top Management: Beyond Systems to People," *Harvard Business Review*, May–June 1995, 132–142.

59E. Spragins, "Sending the Wrong Message," *Fortune Small Business*, July 1, 2003, 32.

60J. Fry, "When Talk Isn't Cheap: Is Emailing Colleagues Who Sit Feet Away a Sign of Office Dysfunction, or a Wise Move?" *The Wall Street Journal*, November 28, 2005, http://online.wsj.com [content no longer available online].

61T. Andrews, "E-Mail Empowers, Voice-Mail Enslaves," *PC Week*, April 10, 1995, E11.

62"The Joys of Voice Mail," *Inc.*, November 1995, 102.

63A. Rawlins, "There's a Message in Every Email," *Fast Company*, September 2007, accessed September 2, 2008, from www.fastcompany.com.

64E. Wong, "A Stinging Office Memo Boomerangs; Chief Executive Is Criticized after Upbraiding Workers by E-Mail," *The New York Times*, April 5, 2001, C1.

65Ibid.

66Ibid.

67Ibid.

68R. G. Nichols, "Do We Know How to Listen? Practical Helps in a Modern Age," in *Communication Concepts and Processes*, ed. J. DeVitor (Englewood Cliffs, NJ: Prentice Hall, 1971); and P. V. Lewis, *Organizational Communication: The Essence of Effective Management* (Columbus, OH: Grid Publishing Company, 1975).

69E. Atwater, *I Hear You*, rev. ed. (New York: Walker, 1992).

70K. Pattison, "Yahoo CEO Carol Bartz: 'I'm Just a Manager,'" *Fast Company*, August 11, 2010, accessed August 20, 2010, from www.fastcompany.com/1680546/yahoo-ceo-carol-bartz-im-just-a-manager; "Yahoo! Reports Second Quarter 2010 Results," MarketWatch, July 20, 2010, accessed August 20, 2010, from www.marketwatch.com/story/yahoo-reports-second-quarter-2010-results-2010-07-20?reflink=MW_news_stmp.

71C. Gallo, "Why Leadership Means Listening," Businessweek Online, January 31, 2007, accessed September 3, 2008, from www.businessweek.com.

72B. D. Seyber, R. N. Bostrom, & J. H. Seibert, "Listening, Communication Abilities, and Success at Work," *Journal of Business Communication* 26 (1989): 293–303.

73Atwater, *I Hear You*.

74C. Edwards, "Death of a Pushy Salesman," *Businessweek*, July 3, 2006, 108.

75J. Sandberg, "Not Communicating with Your Boss? Count Your Blessings," *The Wall Street Journal*, May 22, 2007, B1.

76P. Sellers, A. Diba, & E. Florian, "Get Over Yourself—Your Ego Is Out Of Control. You're Screwing Up Your Career," *Fortune*, 30 April 2001, 76.

77H. H. Meyer, "A Solution to the Performance Appraisal Feedback Enigma," *Academy of Management Executive* 5, no. 1 (1991): 68–76.

78C. Hymowitz, "Executives Who Build Truth-Telling Cultures Learn Fast What Works," *The Wall Street Journal*, June 12, 2006, B1.

79C. Hymowitz, "How to Tell Employees All the Things They Don't Want to Hear," *The Wall Street Journal*, 22 August 2000, B1.

80L. Anguish, N. Cossack, & A. Maingault, "Payroll Cuts, Personal Hygiene, Extra Leave," *HR Magazine*, June 1, 2003, 41.

81G. Gitelson, J. Bing, & L. Laroche, "How the Cultural Trap Deepens in Cross-Border Deals," *Dealmakers*, 1 December 2001, page number not available.

82N. J. Adler, *From Boston to Beijing: Managing with a World View* (Cincinnati, OH: South-Western, 2002), based on A. Laurent, "The Cultural Diversity of Western Conceptions of Management," in *International Studies of Management and Organization* 13, no. 1–2 (Spring–Summer 1983): 75–96.

83J. S. Black & M. Mendenhall, "Cross-Cultural Training Effectiveness: A Review and Theoretical Framework for Future Research," *Academy of Management Review* 15 (1990): 113–136.

84H. Alberts, "East Versus West," *Forbes Asia*, 11 May 2009, 64-65.

85H. Aperian, "Helping Companies Bridge Cultures," *Businessweek Online*, September 8, 2008 accessed June 17, 2011, from www.businessweek.com/technology/content/sep2008/tc2008095_508754.htm.

86H. Aperian, "Helping Companies Bridge Cultures."

87F. Trompenaars, Riding the Waves of Culture: Understanding Diversity in Global Business (London: Economist Books, 1994).

88N. Forster, "Expatriates and the Impact of Cross-Cultural Training," *Human Resource Management* 10 (2000): 63–78.

89Adler, *From Boston to Beijing: Managing with a World View*.

90Ibid.

91Ibid.

92Ibid.

93Ibid.

94R. Mead, *Cross-Cultural Management* (New York: Wiley, 1990).

95Ibid.

96Edward T. Hall, *The Dance of Life* (New York: Doubleday, 1983).

97Trompenaars, *Riding the Waves of Culture*.

98Adler, *From Boston to Beijing: Managing with a World View*.

99E. T. Hall & M. R. Hall, *Understanding Cultural Differences* (Yarmouth, ME: Intercultural Press, 1990).

100E. T. Hall & W. F. Whyte, "Intercultural Communication: A Guide to Men of Action," *Human Organization* 19, no. 1 (1961): 5–12.

101N. Libman, "French Tip: Just Walk the Walk and Talk the Talk, but Not Too Loud," *Chicago Tribune Online*, March 17, 1996.

102C. Tkaczyk & M. Boyle, "Follow These Leaders," *Fortune*, December 12, 2005, 125.

103C. Tuna, "Corporate News: Chambers Vows 'Fix' As Cisco Stumbles," *The Wall Street Journal*, April 6, 2011, B2.

[104]J. Lublin, "The 'Open Inbox'—Some CEOs Stay Up Late Reading Employee Emails; Replies Can Be Brief: 'Thanks,'" *The Wall Street Journal*, October 10, 2005, B1.

[105]W. Bulkeley, "Business Solutions; Playing Well With Others: How IBM's Employees Have Taken Social Networking to an Unusual Level," *The Wall Street Journal*, June 18, 2007, R10

[106]A. Lashinsky, "Lights! Camera! Cue the CEO!" *Fortune*, August 21, 2006, 27.

[107]M. Campanelli & N. Friedman, "Welcome to Voice Mail Hell: The New Technology Has Become a Barrier between Salespeople and Customers," *Sales & Marketing Management* 147 (May 1995): 98–101.

[108]Sam Ali, "Why No One Under 30 Answers Your Voicemail," Diversity-Inc, February 3, 2011, accessed February 22, 2011, from www.diversityinc.com/article/7967/Why-No-One-Under-30-Answers-Your-Voicemail/.

[109]E. W. Morrison, "Organizational Silence: A Barrier to Change and Development in a Pluralistic World," *Academy of Management Review* 25 (2000): 706–725.

[110]R. Willingham, "Jetstar Pilots 'Afraid to Report Risks,'" *The Age*, March 19, 2011, accessed June 17, 2011, from www.theage.com.au/travel/travel-news/jetstar-pilots-afraid-to-report-risks-20110318-1c0mi.html.

[111]A. Heasley, "Tired Jetstar Pilots Told to 'Toughen up Princesses,'" *The Age*, March 31, 2011, accessed June 17, 2011, from www.theage.com.au/travel/travel-news/tired-jetstar-pilots-told-to-toughen-up-princesses-20110331-1chh1.html.

[112]"Force Protection: Code of Conduct and Ethics," Force Protection, accessed June 26, 2009, from www.forceprotectioninc.com.

[113]K. Maher, "Global Companies Face Reality of Instituting Ethics Programs," *The Wall Street Journal*, November 9, 2004, B8.

[114]Ibid.

[115]"An Inside Look at Corporate Hotlines," *Security Director's Report*, February 2007, 8.

[116]J. Confino, "Guardian Employee Survey Maintains High Scores Despite Radical Restructuring," Guardian.co.uk, January 11, 2010, accessed July 15, 2011, from www.guardian.co.uk/sustainability/corporate-social-responsibility-employee-survey-employee-engagement-sustainability.

[117]C. Hymowitz, "Sometimes, Moving Up Makes It Harder to See What Goes on Below," *The Wall Street Journal*, October 15, 2007, B1.

[118]Ibid.

[119]J. Bevan, "Leadership, Clarity, and a Very Thick Skin," *Spectator*, 14 October 2006, 32.

[120]Mark Dollivbre, "Why Companies 'Click' on Twitter," *Adweek*, August 15, 2010, accessed February 13, 2011, from www.adweek.com/aw/content_display/data-center/research/e3i831a0b575c6cd1c617038e29f192cc92.

[121]Kirkpatrick & Roth, "Why There's No Escaping the Blog."

[122]M. Bush, "How Twitter Can Help or Hurt an Airline," *Advertising Age*, July 16, 2009, accessed August 1, 2010, from http://adage.com/digital/article?article_id=137977.

[123]C. G. Pearce, I. W. Johnson, & R. T. Barker, "Assessment of the Listening Styles Inventory: Progress in Establishing Reliability and Validity," Journal of Business and Technical Communication 17, no. 1 (2003): 84–113.

[124]Stephanie Raposo, "Quick! Tells Us What KUTGW Means," *The Wall Street Journal*, August 5, 2009. D1, 3.

© iStockphoto.com/Oner Döngel

© GreenLight

BIZ FLIX

Friday Night Lights

In the small town of Odessa, Texas, everyone lives for Friday nights when the high school football team, the Permian Panthers, takes the field. The town is proud of their Panthers, led by quarterback Mike Winchell (Lucas Black) and superstar tailback Boobie Miles (Derek Luke), and they're used to winning. They expect a state championship, and nothing less. When Boobie suffers a career-ending injury in the first game of the season, the team isn't sure they can win without him. But Coach Gary Gaines (Billy Bob Thornton) isn't ready to give up yet. In this clip from the film, Coach Gaines gathers the team around during the half-time break to talk about what success really means and how he wants them to achieve it.

What to Watch for and Ask Yourself

1. Both the speaker and the listener(s) are necessary components in the communication process. Coach Gaines is the speaker and each team member and the assistant coaches are listeners. Only Gaines spoke. Did he still meet the basic requirements of effective communication? Draw examples from his speech to support your conclusions.

2. How well do the members of the team and the assistant coaches seem to be listening to the message the coach is communicating to them? How can you tell?

3. Assess the effectiveness of the coach's communication to the team. How do you expect the team to play in the second half of the game as a result?

MANAGEMENT WORKPLACE

Plant Fantasies: Managing Communication

In a day when companies use Twitter and Facebook to communicate, Teresa Carleo of Plant Fantasies is a throwback—she doesn't use social media or email. It's not because she's out of touch with technology. Instead, leaders at Plant Fantasies tailor the communication methods they use to the situation they are in. Not all communication channels are equally suited for each situation. A quick tweet might be a great way to communicate with a landscaper, but a terrible way to reach a new client.

Discussion Questions

1. Why would Teresa Carleo and Steve Martucci favor face-to-face communication over email when dealing with customers?

2. Why would Carleo and Martucci prefer to use electronic communication methods for certain types of communication within the company?

3. In the video, Carleo says that she worries that at times she communicates too much. What steps could she take to confirm that her messages are being heard and understood by others?

© Cengage Learning

Controlling

what would **you do?**

Caterpillar Headquarters, Peoria, Illinois[1]

Caterpillar dominates the construction and earth-moving industry, with $50 billion per year in revenues. Komatsu, its next closest competitor, does $25 billion. However, Caterpillar has not been able to master the cyclical nature of its industry. When the heavy machinery industry booms, no one keeps up with demand, and everyone builds new factories and hires thousands of new employees. Indeed, Caterpillar doubled its workforce the last time global demand surged. But when the industry goes bust, factories are closed and tens of thousands of employees are laid off. What kind of dramatic swings does Caterpillar experience? A 43 percent spike in sales in April 2004 and a 52 percent decline in September 2009. Caterpillar's Doug Oberhelman had firsthand experience with an even larger sales swing in Argentina. He says, "We sold 1,200 machines a year in Argentina in the late '70s. In 1981, '82, and '83, while I was there, we sold four total."

In sudden downturns, Caterpillar learned to switch from selling new equipment to refurbishing used equipment. For customers, the advantages of taking apart, cleaning, repairing, and reassembling the engines, transmissions, and other major parts of heavy machinery are a new factory warranty and a 30 percent to 80 percent lower cost. Globally, the remanufacturing business is worth $100 billion a year, with profit margins as high as 40 percent. So, it has been a good way for Caterpillar to offset the boom-and-bust cycle to some extent.

The second way in which Caterpillar has dealt with sudden swings was to try to predict when they occurred. Company economists told your chief financial officer, "We've got good news and bad news. The good news is we found an indicator that predicts shifts in U.S. GDP with a lead time of six to nine months. The bad news is it's our own sales to users." The problem, though, was that while they could generally predict *when* a shift in sales would occur, they couldn't predict the *severity*. As a result, the last time a severe downturn occurred, Caterpillar laid off 35,000 managers and workers out of 120,000 worldwide. Furthermore, it cut executive compensation by 50 percent, senior manager pay by up to 35 percent, and manager and support staff pay by 15 percent. To reduce costs further, Caterpillar offered voluntary buyout packages to 25,000 salaried workers.

You've just been named Caterpillar's next CEO, and you've got six months before you take over from the current CEO. You've decided to use this time to pick your 16 top managers and work with them to analyze the company. Caterpillar has entered a lot of businesses in the last two decades and every part, good, bad, and ugly, is on the table for review. The critical issue is how to better manage the cyclical nature of your industry, particularly downturns. While you can see them coming, you can't predict their

"what's new" companies

- Bellagio Casino
- Intuit
- We Energies
- Marsh Groceries
- Progressive Insurance
- LoveMachine
- Winn Dixie
- Fresh Seasons Markets
- CitiStorage
- A. P. Moller-Maersk A/S
- The Lavergne Group
- Cows to Kilowatts Partnership Limited

study tips

The list of key terms on page 694 can be a valuable study aid. Write down the definition of each term on a separate piece of paper, without consulting the margin terms in the chapter.

severity. So, what can the company do to better prepare itself and its customers, suppliers, and dealers for the next severe downturn? Also, what are your goals for company performance for the next downswing? Second, severe upswings, though preferable, are disruptive and difficult to manage, particularly when it comes to hiring thousands of workers at one time, restarting mothballed production facilities, procuring the necessary parts from suppliers, and suddenly finding the cash to pay for it all. So, given that there's little warning to when this is coming, what can be done to make sudden increases in production more manageable for you and your suppliers? Finally, sudden upswings and downswings produce opportunities for your competitors to steal customers by undercutting price, delivering products faster, or designing better products. What can Caterpillar and its dealers do to decrease customer losses and defections? What can top management do to make sure it keeps a stronger focus on customers?

If you were the new CEO at Caterpillar, what would you do?

As Caterpillar's situation shows, past success is no guarantee of future success. Even successful companies fall short, face challenges, and have to make changes. **Control** is a regulatory process of establishing standards to achieve organizational goals, comparing actual performance against the standards, and taking corrective action when necessary to restore performance to those standards. Control is achieved when behavior and work procedures conform to standards and when company goals are accomplished.[2] Control is not just an after-the-fact process, however. Preventive measures are also a form of control.

We begin this chapter by examining the basic control process used in organizations. In the second part of the chapter, we go beyond the basics to an in-depth examination of the different methods that companies use to achieve control. We conclude the chapter by looking at the things that companies choose to control (finances, customer retention, and product quality, among others).

Basics of Control

"what's new" companies >

A thief robbed the **Bellagio Casino** in Las Vegas at gunpoint, speeding off with $1.5 million in casino chips that he thought could be cashed in at a later date. But, thanks to the Bellagio's security procedures (i.e., control), the chips that the thief stole were made worthless when the casino's stock of chips was completely replaced. According to Alan Feldman, spokesperson for MGM Resorts International, which owns the Bellagio resort, "The new set was put out probably a half an hour after the robbery took place."[3]

After reading the next section, you should be able to

1. Describe the basic control process.

control a regulatory process of establishing standards to achieve organizational goals, comparing actual performance against the standards, and taking corrective action, when necessary.

1 The Control Process

The basic control process **1.1 begins with the establishment of clear standards of performance; 1.2 involves a comparison of performance to those standards; 1.3 takes corrective action, if needed, to repair performance deficiencies; 1.4 is a dynamic,** cybernetic process; and **1.5 consists of three basic methods: feedback control, concurrent control, and feedforward control.** However, as much as managers would like, **1.6 control isn't always worthwhile or possible.**

1.1 Standards

The control process begins when managers set goals such as satisfying 90 percent of customers or increasing sales by 5 percent. Companies then specify the performance standards that must be met to accomplish those goals. **Standards** are a basis of comparison for measuring the extent to which organizational performance is satisfactory or unsatisfactory. For example, many pizzerias use 30–40 minutes as the standard for delivery times. Because anything longer is viewed as unsatisfactory, they'll typically reduce the price if they can't deliver a hot pizza to you within that time period.

So how do managers set standards? How do they decide which levels of performance are satisfactory and which are unsatisfactory? The first criterion for a good standard is that it must enable goal achievement. If you're meeting the standard but still not achieving company goals, then the standard may have to be changed. In the salmon industry, to maximize productivity it was standard procedure to grow as many fish as possible in fish farms and then deal with diseases (that spread from the fish being in such close proximity) through liberal use of antibiotics in fish food. This was effective until a few years ago, when the new Isa (infectious salmon anemia) virus, which is resistant to antibiotics, developed. Norwegian salmon farms, the largest in the world, sharply reduced the incidence of Isa by developing new production standards that involved the use of antiviral vaccines and no longer allowing overcrowded fish pens.[4]

Companies also determine standards by listening to customers' comments, complaints, and suggestions or by observing competitors. Walk into a busy Starbucks and you can generally count on a fast-moving line. The focus on speed, however, has also led to customer complaints about "average" quality and inconsistently prepared drinks, for example, a latte tasting differently from barista to barista or store to store. Starbucks is now addressing those concerns. Instead of grinding a day's worth of coffee beans first thing in the morning, beans will be freshly ground for each batch of coffee. Rather then steaming a pitcher of milk to be used in several drinks, baristas will steam just enough fresh milk for the drink they're preparing. Finally, baristas are to prepare only two drinks at a time—and even then, they're only to start the second drink while finishing the first. Starbucks believes these steps will address customers' concerns about quality. However, Starbucks baristas are worried that customers will begin to complain about long lines. Erik Forman, a Starbucks barista in Bloomington, Minnesota, says these new procedures have "doubled the amount of time it takes to make drinks in some cases," and lines have gotten longer. If customers complain about long waits, Starbucks may have to reconsider some of these changes and change its standards accordingly.[5]

Standards can also be determined by benchmarking other companies. **Benchmarking** is the process of determining how well other companies (though not just competitors) perform business functions or tasks. In other words, benchmarking is the process of determining other companies' standards. When setting standards by benchmarking, the first step is to determine what to benchmark. Companies can benchmark anything from cycle time (how fast), to quality (how well), to price (how much). For example, through national benchmarking studies of thousands of fire departments, firehouses are expected to respond to an alarm within 15 seconds 95 percent of the time. Additionally, 90 percent of the time it should take no more than 60 seconds to leave the firehouse, and then no more than four minutes to arrive at the scene.[6]

standards a basis of comparison for measuring the extent to which various kinds of organizational performance are satisfactory or unsatisfactory.

benchmarking the process of identifying outstanding practices, processes, and standards in other companies and adapting them to your company.

**"what's new"
companies** >

The next step is to identify the companies against which to benchmark your standards. The last step is to collect data to determine other companies' performance standards. When Brad Smith became CEO of **Intuit**, maker of financial software and websites such as QuickBooks, Pay Employees, TurboTax, and Quicken, a dinner with H-P's then CEO Mark Hurd and Intuit's founder, Scott Cook, gave him the idea to benchmark Intuit's performance against other companies, particularly in Silicon Valley where the top web and software companies are located. After learning how Google gave its engineers time each week to work on whatever they wanted, Smith created a similar program, where Intuit's software engineers could spend 10 percent of their time, about half a day each week, working on experimental projects. Smith spent time with Facebook's chief operating officer, Sheryl Sandberg, to learn how Intuit could build online communities for each of its products. In the end, Intuit benchmarked its spending and performance against hundreds of companies in procurement, marketing, legal services, information technology, and human resources.[7]

1.2 Comparison to Standards

The next step in the control process is to compare actual performance to performance standards. Although this sounds straightforward, the quality of the comparison depends largely on the measurement and information systems a company uses to keep track of performance. The better the system, the easier it is for companies to track their progress and identify problems that need to be fixed.

All passenger planes must pass rigorous certification and safety standards before going into service. When Boeing completed construction of its new 787 Dreamliner, it built six aircraft just for testing, at a cost of more than $1 billion. Two planes were designated for testing how the plane operated in extreme ice conditions. One plane was built solely to test interior systems, such as flight controls, climate control, and safety systems. Other tests included operations at extremely slow speeds, operations at extremely fast speeds (nearly 50% faster than normal cruising speed), takeoffs and landings in virtually every imaginable weather condition, measuring the stress and load on the wings and frame, and determining how long the plane could operate with just one engine. The tests, amounting to 3,100 test hours in the air and 3,700 test hours on the ground, were run on a 24-hour schedule closely mimicking the real-world schedules that airlines maintain. By comparing performance to rigorous performance standards, the testing process helps Boeing and the Federal Aviation Administration identify problems that were not uncovered in early design and manufacturing, thus ensuring a high-quality, fuel-efficient, safe passenger jet.[8]

1.3 Corrective Action

The next step in the control process is to identify performance deviations, analyze those deviations, and then develop and implement programs to correct them. This is similar to the planning process discussed in Chapter 5. Regular, frequent performance feedback allows workers and managers to track their performance and make adjustments in effort, direction, and strategies. When Denise Hill checked into a Phoenix hotel with her luggage and her 18-month-old grandson, only the desk clerk was on duty, so no one could help her take her belongings to her room. Upset with the lack of service, she rated the hotel a "one" out of five on TripAdvisor.com, and wrote, "After stacking luggage and grandson on a luggage cart, [I] was helped into the front door and elevator by other guests." She also complained about the housekeeping and that there weren't enough pool towels. Hotel owner Ben Bethel wrote a response two days later, promising changes would be made, including adding a second person to the front desk, having the assistant manager work evenings and weekends, and telling customers that bellhops would bring their bags to their rooms later (if bellhops were currently busy). Bethel admits that when Denise Hill checked in, "We just didn't have enough people," but he stated that the changes would prevent that from recurring.[9]

1.4 Dynamic, Cybernetic Process

As shown in Exhibit 16.1, control is a continuous, dynamic, cybernetic process. Control begins by setting standards, measuring performance, and then comparing performance to the standards. If the performance deviates from the standards, then managers and employees analyze the deviations and develop and implement corrective programs that (they hope) achieve the desired performance by meeting the standards. Managers must repeat the entire process again and again in an endless feedback loop (a continuous process). Thus, control is not a onetime achievement or result. It continues over time (i.e., it is dynamic) and requires daily, weekly, and monthly attention from managers to maintain performance levels at the standard (i.e., it is cybernetic). **Cybernetic** derives from the Greek word *kubernetes*, meaning "steersman," that is, one who steers or keeps on course.[10] The control process shown in Exhibit 16.1 is cybernetic because constant attention to the feedback loop is necessary to keep the company's activity on course.

Keeping control of business expenses is an example of a continuous, dynamic, cybernetic process. A company that doesn't closely monitor expenses usually finds that they quickly get out of control, even for the smallest things. In the first few months of 2011, the price of diesel fuel increased 27 percent, from $3.05 per gallon to $3.90 per gallon. With gas and diesel prices expected to continue rising, managers in all kinds of businesses suddenly needed to deal with this increased expense. PepsiCo addressed this by adding 176 all-electric trucks to its vehicle fleet. Because these trucks don't use diesel fuel, Pepsi will reduce fuel usage by 500,000 gallons per year, resulting in $1.9 million annually in fuel savings. Furthermore, the electric trucks will save PepsiCo an additional $700,000 per year in maintenance costs.[11] Sure, it's a cliché, but it's just as true in business as in sports: If you take your eye off the ball, you're going to strike out. Control is an ongoing, dynamic, cybernetic process.

1.5 Feedback, Concurrent, and Feedforward Control

The three basic control methods are feedback control, concurrent control, and feedforward control. **Feedback control** is a mechanism for gathering information about performance deficiencies *after* they occur. This information is then used to correct or prevent performance deficiencies. Study after study has clearly shown that feedback improves both individual and organizational performance. In most instances, any feedback is better than no feedback.

Exhibit 16.1 Cybernetic Control Process

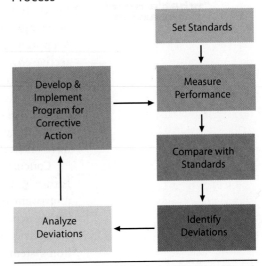

Source: H. Koontz & R. W. Bradspies, "Managing Through Feedforward Control: A Future Directed View," *Business Horizons*, June 1972, 25–36. Reprinted with permission from Elsevier.

cybernetic the process of steering or keeping on course.

feedback control a mechanism for gathering information about performance deficiencies after they occur.

If feedback has a downside, it's that feedback always comes after the fact. For example, 90 percent of the time an electrical transformer malfunctions on a neighborhood utility pole, the cause of the problem is a squirrel. Paul Gogan of **We Energies**, an energy provider in Wisconsin and Michigan's upper peninsula, says, "Trying to keep squirrels off poles is like trying to herd cats. We insulate the wires and put protective covers over the grounded equipment." Brian Manthey, a spokesperson for We Energies, says, "If they are on a wire and touch a piece of equipment that's grounded, the current flows through them. They're killed and sometimes the power to homes and businesses goes out." And there's never any warning until after the fact, and usually nothing left of the squirrel because of the electrical surge or because predators have taken the remains.[12]

Concurrent control addresses the problems inherent in feedback control by gathering information about performance deficiencies *as* they occur. Thus, it is an improvement over feedback because it attempts to eliminate or shorten the delay between performance and feedback about the performance. The Nissan Leaf, an all-electric compact car, provides concurrent control via its Intelligent Transportation system, which gives drivers instantaneous information about how much battery power is remaining, how many more miles the car can go before needing a recharge, and the location of the nearest charging station. When the car is plugged in for recharging, the system will even call the driver's mobile phone when charging is complete.[13]

Feedforward control is a mechanism for gathering information about performance deficiencies *before* they occur. In contrast to feedback and concurrent control, which provide feedback on the basis of outcomes and results, feedforward control provides information about performance deficiencies by monitoring inputs rather than outputs. Thus, feedforward control seeks to prevent or minimize performance deficiencies before they happen. Microsoft uses feedforward controls to try to prevent software problems before they occur. For example, when developing the latest version of its Windows Server software (for network and Internet computer servers), Microsoft taught 8,500 experienced programmers new methods for writing more reliable software code *before* asking them to develop new features for Windows Server software. Microsoft has also developed new software testing tools that let the programmers thoroughly test the code they've written (i.e., input) before passing the code on to others to be used in beta testing of Windows 7. Using feedforward control has shortened development time, and by the end of its development cycle, Windows 7 was expected to ship ahead of schedule.[14] Exhibit 16.2 lists guidelines that companies can follow to get the most out of feedforward control.

Exhibit 16.2   Guidelines for Using Feedforward Control

1. Thorough planning and analysis are required.
2. Careful discrimination must be applied in selecting input variables.
3. The feedforward system must be kept dynamic.
4. A model of the control system should be developed.
5. Data on input variables must be regularly collected.
6. Data on input variables must be regularly assessed.
7. Feedforward control requires action.

Source: H. Koontz & R. W. Bradspies, "Managing Through Feedforward Control: A Future Directed View," *Business Horizons*, June 1972, 25–36. Reprinted with permission from Elsevier.

concurrent control a mechanism for gathering information about performance deficiencies as they occur, thereby eliminating or shortening the delay between performance and feedback.

feedforward control a mechanism for monitoring performance inputs rather than outputs to prevent or minimize performance deficiencies before they occur.

1.6 Control Isn't Always Worthwhile or Possible

Control is achieved when behavior and work procedures conform to standards and goals are accomplished. By contrast, **control loss** occurs when behavior and work procedures do not conform to standards.[15] For example, 1,600 people in 17 states became seriously ill from eating eggs contaminated with salmonella bacteria that were processed by Wright County Egg and Hillandale Farms. Both issued massive recalls covering 500 million eggs sold nationwide. Government inspectors found 4- to 8-foot-high manure piles that pushed open doors, which likely allowed rats, one of the main causes of salmonella, to enter the egg-processing buildings. Furthermore, employees were not required to change protective clothing when moving between henhouses, as required by law. Because of these violations, Wright County Egg was banned from selling eggs for several months and then was only allowed to sell eggs after they had been removed from their shells and treated for potential salmonella infection.[16]

Maintaining control is important because control loss prevents organizations from achieving their goals. When control loss occurs, managers need to find out what, if anything, they could have done to prevent it. Usually, that means identifying deviations from standard performance, analyzing the causes of those deviations, and taking corrective action. Even so, implementing controls isn't always worthwhile or possible. Let's look at regulation costs and cybernetic feasibility to see why this is so.

To determine whether control is worthwhile, managers need to carefully assess **regulation costs**, that is, whether the costs and unintended consequences of control exceed its benefits. If a control process costs more than it benefits, it may not be worthwhile. For example, the European Union uses the metric system—kilograms and centimeters—to ensure standard pricing throughout its 27 member states. But because the United Kingdom uses the British imperial system (pounds, ounces, inches, miles, etc.), the EU regulation allows businesses to use both metric *and* imperial measures. So when Janet Devers, who runs a vegetable stall at the Ridley Road market in East London, only sold vegetables by the pound and

> "We have knifings. We have killings. And they're talking me to court because I'm selling [vegetables] in pounds and ounces."
>
> —JANET DEVERS, VEGETABLE MERCHANT

the ounce, she faced 13 criminal charges and fines totaling $130,000 for not also posting prices using the metric system. Devers could not believe she was being prosecuted: "We have knifings. We have killings. And they're taking me to court because I'm selling in pounds and ounces."[17]

Because everyone in Britain buys fruits and vegetables by the pound or ounce, the British public was outraged by the charges because the regulatory costs clearly outweighed their benefits. Innovations Secretary for the United Kingdom, John Denham, soon indicated that such prosecutions were not in the public interest. And the local government council that had spent $50,000 pursuing the case in court eventually dropped all the charges.[18]

An often overlooked factor in determining the cost of control is that *unintended consequences* sometimes accompany increased control. Control systems help companies, managers, and workers accomplish their goals. But although they help solve some problems, they can create others. For example, Six Sigma is a quality control system, originally developed by Motorola, that manufacturers use to achieve the goal of producing only 3.4 defective or nonstandard parts per million parts made. Clearly, manufacturers who reach Six Sigma consistently produce extremely high-quality products. But aligning the constrictive process needed to attain Six Sigma with the need for out-of-the box thinking and innovation can be difficult.

control loss the situation in which behavior and work procedures do not conform to standards.

regulation costs the costs associated with implementing or maintaining control.

For example, when George Buckley took over as CEO of 3M, he found that the company, long known for innovation, had lost much of its creativity. Under his predecessor, 3M focused on efficiency by streamlining processes, laying off 8,000 employees, and adopting Six Sigma practices. Although this reduced costs, it destroyed creativity in the company's research labs. CEO George Buckley observed, "Invention is by its very nature a disorderly process. You can't put a Six Sigma process into that area and say, well, I'm getting behind on invention, so I'm going to schedule myself for three good ideas on Wednesday and two on Friday. That's not how creativity works." Former 3M employee Michael Mucci said, "We all came to the conclusion that there was no way in the world that anything like a Post-it note would ever emerge from this new system [meaning Six Sigma]." Art Fry, the 3M scientist who invented the Post-it note, one of 3M's most successful products, said innovation is "a numbers game. You have to go through 5,000 to 6,000 raw ideas to find one successful business." Because the point of Six Sigma is to eliminate waste, that is, all of the ideas it takes to find that one great product or service, Fry believes that Six Sigma was destroying 3M's innovation culture. Said Fry, "What's remarkable is how fast a culture [of innovation] can be torn apart."[19]

Another factor to consider is **cybernetic feasibility**, the extent to which it is possible to implement each step in the control process: clear standards of performance, comparison of performance against standards, and corrective action. If one or more steps cannot be implemented, then maintaining effective control may be difficult or impossible.

**"what's new"
companies** >

For example, retail stores are struggling to find successful ways to provide discounts via the Web or social media. When Indianapolis-based **Marsh Groceries** used its Facebook site to give 3,100 customers who had signed up as its Facebook "friends" a $10 coupon and then encouraged them to share that coupon with their friends, the number of people who tried to redeem the downloadable coupons exploded and spiraled out of control, so Marsh had to halt the offer after four days. The company apologized on its website, saying, "We at Marsh recently stuck our toe in the water to try this whole social media thing. Unfortunately, we ended up stubbing it. Our recent $10 coupon offer on Facebook has instead left us red in the face and many of our loyal customers angry. Rightfully so. For that we are truly sorry. Needless to say, we're learning."[20] Likewise, when Oprah Winfrey mentioned that KFC was offering an online free grilled chicken meal coupon, 10 million coupons were downloaded and 4.5 million meals were given away in four days. Like Marsh, KFC had to stop honoring the coupon because it couldn't limit the number that could be redeemed. In both instances, there was no cybernetic feasibility.

cybernetic feasibility the extent to which it is possible to implement each step in the control process.

Review 1

The Control Process The control process begins by setting standards, measuring performance, and then comparing performance against the standards. The better a company's information and measurement systems, the easier it is to make these comparisons. The control process continues by identifying and analyzing performance deviations and then developing and implementing programs for corrective action. Control is a continuous, dynamic, cybernetic process, not a onetime achievement or result. Control requires frequent managerial attention. The three basic control methods are feedback control (after-the-fact performance information), concurrent control (simultaneous performance information), and feedforward control (preventive performance information). Control has regulation costs and unanticipated consequences and therefore isn't always worthwhile or possible.

How and What to Control

Auto insurance companies control costs by determining which drivers are higher or lower risks, and then increasing or decreasing auto insurance prices in accordance with that risk. Risk, in turn, is determined in part by your driving record, that is, whether you've had accidents or speeding tickets, and by pooling, that is, looking at the average risk of people similar to yourself. For instance, because male teenagers are much more likely to be in an auto accidents, their car insurance costs are generally higher than others. **Progressive Insurance** is changing the way it measures and controls driving risk through its Snapshot program, in which customers can have a small monitoring device installed in their cars. The device provides real-time information on driving distance, acceleration, speed, and how hard the brakes are applied. Progressive gets a much more accurate picture of how its customers drive, and thus how much risk it assumes when providing them auto insurance. A.T. Kearney consultant Joe Reifel says, "Snapshot is underwriting based on how people are actually driving. It clearly will make the pricing of insurance more accurate." In turn, Progressive can provide lower costs to its customers, while increasing profits.[21]

< **"what's new" companies**

After reading the next two sections, you should be able to

2. *Discuss the various methods that managers can use to maintain control.*

3. *Describe the behaviors, processes, and outcomes that today's managers are choosing to control in their organizations.*

2 Control Methods

Managers can use five different methods to achieve control in their organizations: **2.1 bureaucratic, 2.2 objective, 2.3 normative, 2.4 concertive**, and **2.5 self-control.**

2.1 Bureaucratic Control

When most people think of managerial control, what they have in mind is bureaucratic control. **Bureaucratic control** is top-down control, in which managers try to influence employee behavior by rewarding or punishing employees for compliance or noncompliance with organizational policies, rules, and procedures. Most employees, however, would argue that bureaucratic managers emphasize punishment for noncompliance much more than rewards for compliance.

For instance, one manager gave an employee a written reprimand for "leaving work without permission"—after she passed out in the bathroom and was whisked by ambulance to a nearby hospital. Another manager, a school principal, forced a teacher to work through the day even after the teacher said her arm was throbbing after she slipped on ice outside the school and fell. "He decided there was no way I could have broken my arm, probably just bruised it." The teacher said, "During first period, my arm hurt horribly, but I continued teaching. But when I reached for chalk, and my fingers would not move, I did go [to the hospital] where my broken arm was set."[22]

As you learned in Chapter 2, bureaucratic management and control were created to prevent just this type of managerial behavior. By encouraging managers to apply well-thought-out rules, policies, and procedures in an impartial, consistent manner to

bureaucratic control the use of hierarchical authority to influence employee behavior by rewarding or punishing employees for compliance or noncompliance with organizational policies, rules, and procedures.

Managers who use bureaucratic control often emphasize following the rules above all else.

everyone in the organization, bureaucratic control is supposed to make companies more efficient, effective, and fair. Ironically, it frequently has just the opposite effect. Managers who use bureaucratic control often emphasize following the rules above all else.

For instance, when visiting the company's regional offices and managers, the president of a training company, who was known for his temper, for micromanaging others, and for an extraordinary commitment to pressuring others to reduce or eliminate costs, would get some toilet paper from the restrooms and aggressively ask, "What's this?" When the managers answered, "toilet paper," the president would scream that it was two-ply toilet paper that the company couldn't afford. When told of a cracked toilet seat in one of the women's restrooms, he said, "If you don't like sitting on that seat, you can stand up like I do!"[23]

Another characteristic of bureaucratically controlled companies is that, due to their rule- and policy-driven decision making, they are highly resistant to change and slow to respond to customers and competitors. Recall from Chapter 2 that even Max Weber, the German philosopher who is largely credited with popularizing bureaucratic ideals in the late nineteenth century, referred to bureaucracy as the "iron cage." He said, "Once fully established, bureaucracy is among those social structures which are the hardest to destroy."[24] Of course, the national government, with hundreds of bureaus, agencies, and departments, is typically the largest bureaucracy in most countries. In the United States, because of the thousands of career bureaucrats who staff the offices of the federal government, even presidents and Congress have difficulty making changes. When General Dwight Eisenhower became president, his predecessor, Harry Truman, quipped: "Poor Ike. It won't be a bit like the army. He'll sit here and he'll say, 'Do this, do that,' and nothing will happen."[25]

2.2 Objective Control

In many companies, bureaucratic control has evolved into **objective control**, which is the use of observable measures of employee behavior or output to assess performance and influence behavior. Whereas bureaucratic control focuses on whether policies and rules are followed, objective control focuses on observing and measuring worker behavior or output. A waitress at Brixx Pizza in Charlotte, North Carolina, was fired for complaining about some customers on her Facebook page. She became frustrated when a couple who had stayed at one of her tables for three hours and forced her to work an extended shift only left her a $5 tip. So she criticized them on her Facebook page, calling them "cheap," along with some other choice words. Two days later, she was called in and fired for violating company policy that restricts employees from criticizing customers and making the restaurant look bad on social networks. One of the restaurant's owners, Jeff Van Dyke, said, "We definitely care what people say about our customers." Attorney Megan Ruwe says, "If you say something on social networks that puts your employer in a negative light, that's not very different than an employee standing on a corner and holding a sign or

objective control the use of observable measures of worker behavior or outputs to assess performance and influence behavior.

screaming it. It's public, and it's out there for the world to see. Individuals can forget that it is a very public forum."[26]

There are two kinds of objective control: behavior control and output control. **Behavior control** is regulating behaviors and actions that workers perform on the job. The basic assumption of behavior control is that if you do the right things (i.e., the right behaviors) every day, then those things should lead to goal achievement. Behavior control is still management based, however, which means that managers are responsible for monitoring and rewarding or punishing workers for exhibiting desired or undesired behaviors.

For example, companies that use global positioning satellite (GPS) technology to track where workers are and what they're doing are using behavior control. JEA, an electric utility located in Jacksonville, Florida, had a problem with employees who would show up to work, drive off in a service vehicle, then goof off for the rest of the day. A local TV station also caught JEA's employees selling company equipment. To make sure that employees are completing assigned projects and not wasting time, JEA has installed GPS tracking devices with cameras in its fleet of vehicles so that its managers can track how and where employees are spending their time. As a result of the new system, 17 workers were warned about their work habits, and 3 of those 17 were fired from their jobs.[27]

Instead of measuring what managers and workers do, **output control** measures the results of their efforts. Whereas behavior control regulates, guides, and measures how workers behave on the job, output control gives managers and workers the freedom to behave as they see fit as long as they accomplish prespecified, measurable results. Output control is often coupled with rewards and incentives.

Three things must occur for output control to lead to improved business results. First, output control measures must be reliable, fair, and accurate. Second, employees and managers must believe that they can produce the desired results; if they don't, then the output controls won't affect their behavior. Third, the rewards or incentives tied to output control measures must truly be dependent on achieving established standards of performance. For example, Erik Bedard, now with the Red Sox, was a pitcher for the Seattle Mariners. Due to a shoulder injury, he missed most of the 2009 season and was left without a contract at the beginning of the 2010 season. He ended up signing a one-year deal with the Mariners for $1.5 million, nearly $2 million less than the average Major League salary. The contract specified that he could earn up to $7.5 million more for meeting specific performance levels. Bedard could have earned $250,000 each time he was injury-free for 30 days (i.e., 60 days means $500,000, 90 days means $750,000, etc.). He could have made $500,000 each time he reached milestones, such as pitching in his 14th, 17th, 20th, 23rd, and 26th games. He could have earned $500,000 for pitching 75 innings and an additional $600,000 for every 25 innings after that. For output control to work with rewards, the rewards must truly be at risk if performance doesn't measure up. This was clearly the case with Erik Bedard's contract. Unfortunately, his shoulder injury prevented him from playing in 2010.[28]

2.3 Normative Control

Rather than monitoring rules, behavior, or output, another way to control what goes on in organizations is to use normative control to shape the beliefs and values of the people who work there. With **normative controls**, a company's widely shared values and beliefs guide workers' behavior and decisions.

Philip Rosedale, the founder and CEO of **LoveMachine**, an information technology firm, runs his company entirely on one value—transparency. He applies

behavior control the regulation of the behaviors and actions that workers perform on the job.

output control the regulation of workers' results or outputs through rewards and incentives.

normative control the regulation of workers' behavior and decisions through widely shared organizational values and beliefs.

< **"what's new" companies**

transparency to everything at the company. Every employee, contractor, and freelancer that works for the company has access to everything that others are working on, what others are earning, and what other freelancers are charging and how many hours it took them to complete a project. Even Rosedale's salary and benefits are openly available to everyone. Rosedale believes that this extreme level of transparency is vital for creating an open, collaborative environment in which there is a free exchange of information from one person to another.[29]

Normative controls are created in two ways. First, companies that use normative controls are very careful about whom they hire. Whereas many companies screen potential applicants on the basis of their abilities, normatively controlled companies are just as likely to screen potential applicants based on their attitudes and values. Billionaire Richard Branson, founder of Virgin, which has 300 branded companies (Virgin Airways, Virgin Mobile, Virgin Megastore, etc.) employing 50,000 people in 30 countries, hires entrepreneurial people with positive attitudes. He says, "We stumbled on this formula when we were launching our record store business in the late 1960s. We decided to look for employees who were passionate about music, because we thought their enthusiasm and knowledge would be as important a draw as the beanbag chairs, coffee and listening posts we planned to feature in our first stores and that turned out to be correct." Branson says, "When we launched Virgin Records a couple of years later . . . We put a lot of effort into finding and hiring the right people and then we made sure that they felt empowered to run the business as they saw fit—that's what we had hired them for. This approach helped us to attract and keep great talent. . . . Virgin has launched 400 businesses in more than 40 years of expansion; our focus on employees is one of the main reasons for our success."[30]

Second, with normative controls, managers and employees learn what they should and should not do by observing experienced employees and listening to the stories they tell about the company. Ed Fuller, the head of international lodging at Marriott International, loves to tell stories to illustrate Marriott's commitment to customer service. One of his favorites is when he was a general manager at a Marriott in Boston. A senior executive told him that Bill Marriott, the chairman of the company, was upset about something at his hotel. Fuller was positive that he was going to be fired for being $300,000 behind his catering sales goal. But when Marriott met with him, he wasn't upset about the sales; he was upset that a member of the Marriott family had been served cold clam chowder and that the restaurant

doing the right thing

Don't Cheat on Travel Expense Reports

Workers are often tempted to pad their travel expense reports. As one puts it, "After a while you feel that they owe it to ya, so the hell with 'em. I'm going to expense it." Frank Navran of the Ethics Resource Center says that people justify this by telling themselves, "I'm not really stealing from the company—I'm just getting back what I feel I'm entitled to." However, Joel Richards, executive vice president and chief administrative officer of El Paso Corporation, says, "You learn a lot about people from their expense reports. If you can't trust an employee to be truthful on an expense report, if you can't trust them with small dollars, how can you trust them with making decisions involving millions of dollars?" So, do the right thing: Don't cheat on your travel expense reports.[31]

manager handled the complaint poorly. Fuller says that the moral of the story is, "If [the family] is treated badly, we assume the customer is treated worse."[32]

Nevertheless, this story makes clear the attitude that drives employee performance at Marriott in ways that rules, behavioral guidelines, or output controls could not.

2.4 Concertive Control

Whereas normative controls are based on beliefs that are strongly held and widely shared throughout a company, **concertive controls** are based on beliefs that are shaped and negotiated by work groups.[33] Whereas normative controls are driven by strong organizational cultures, concertive controls usually arise when companies give work groups complete autonomy and responsibility for task completion (see Chapter 10, "Managing Teams," for a complete discussion of the role of autonomy in teams and groups). The most autonomous groups operate without managers and are completely responsible for controlling work group processes, outputs, and behavior. Such groups do their own hiring, firing, worker discipline, work schedules, materials ordering, budget making and meeting, and decision making.

Concertive control is not established overnight. Highly autonomous work groups evolve through two phases as they develop concertive control. In phase one, group members learn to work with each other, supervise each other's work, and develop the values and beliefs that will guide and control their behavior. And because they develop these values and beliefs themselves, work group members feel strongly about following them.

In the steel industry, Nucor was long considered an upstart compared with the "biggies" U.S. Steel and Bethlehem Steel. Today, however, not only has Nucor managed to outlast many other mills, the company has bought out 13 other mills in the past five years. Nucor has a unique culture that gives real power to employees on the line and fosters teamwork throughout the organization. This type of teamwork can be a difficult thing for a newly acquired group of employees to get used to. For example, at Nucor's first big acquisition in Auburn, New York, David Hutchins is a frontline supervisor, or "lead man," in the rolling mill, where steel from the furnace is spread thin enough to be cut into sheets. When the plant was under the previous ownership, if the guys doing the cutting got backed up, the guys doing the rolling—including Hutchins—would just take a break. He says, "We'd sit back, have a cup of coffee, and complain: 'Those guys stink.'" It took six months to convince the employees at the Auburn plant that the Nucor teamwork way was better than the old way. Now, Hutchins says, "At Nucor, we're not 'you guys' and 'us guys.' It's all of us guys. Wherever the bottleneck is, we go there, and everyone works on it."[34]

> "At Nucor, we're not 'you guys' and 'us guys.' It's all of us guys. Wherever the bottleneck is, we go there, and everyone works on it."
>
> —DAVID HUTCHINS, FRONTLINE SUPERVISOR, NUCOR

The second phase in the development of concertive control is the emergence and formalization of objective rules to guide and control behavior. The beliefs and values developed in phase one usually develop into more objective rules as new members join teams. The clearer those rules, the easier it becomes for new members to figure out how and how not to behave. Before Nucor finalizes an acquisition, it sends a team of long-time employees to the new plant. People at all levels, from managers to steelworkers, visit with their counterparts at the mill being acquired and tell them about the "Nucor way." Getting new employees on board quickly helps preserve everyone's bonus and performance-based pay. By following the program of working together and increasing output, Dave Hutchins saw his annual pay of $53,000 rise

concertive control the regulation of workers' behavior and decisions through work group values and belief

to $67,000 the year after Nucor acquired his plant, then to $92,000 only four years after that.[35] Again, the key difference in concertive control is that the teams—and not management—enforce these rules. A system based upon team equality is not just a feature of Nucor, but permeates the best companies.

Ironically, concertive control may lead to even more stress for workers to conform to expectations than bureaucratic control. Under bureaucratic control, most workers only have to worry about pleasing the boss. But with concertive control, their behavior has to satisfy the rest of their team members. For example, one team member says, "I don't have to sit there and look for the boss to be around; and if the boss is not around, I can sit there and talk to my neighbor or do what I want. Now the whole team is around me and the whole team is observing what I'm doing."[36] Plus, with concertive control, team members have a second, much more stressful role to perform: that of making sure that their team members adhere to team values and rules.

2.5 Self-Control

Self-control, also known as **self-management**, is a control system in which managers and workers control their own behavior.[37] Self-control does not result in anarchy, in which everyone gets to do whatever he or she wants. In self-control or self-management, leaders and managers provide workers with clear boundaries within which they may guide and control their own goals and behaviors.[38] Leaders and managers also contribute to self-control by teaching others the skills they need to maximize and monitor their own work effectiveness. In turn, individuals who manage and lead themselves establish self-control by setting their own goals, monitoring their own progress, rewarding or punishing themselves for achieving or for not achieving their self-set goals, and constructing positive thought patterns that remind them of the importance of their goals and their ability to accomplish them.[39]

For example, let's assume you need to do a better job of praising and recognizing the good work that your staff does for you. You can use goal setting, self-observation, and self-reward to manage this behavior on your own. For self-observation, write "praise/recognition" on a 3-by-5-inch card. Put the card in your pocket. Put a check on the card each time you praise or recognize someone. (Wait until the person has left before you do this.) Keep track for a week. This serves as your baseline or starting point. Simply keeping track will probably increase how often you do this. After a week, assess your baseline or starting point and then set a specific goal. For instance, if your baseline was twice a day, you might set a specific goal to praise or recognize others' work five times a day. Continue monitoring your performance with your cards. Once you've achieved your goal every day for a week, give yourself a reward (perhaps a CD, a movie, lunch with a friend at a new restaurant) for achieving your goal.[40]

As you can see, the components of self-management, self-set goals, self-observation, and self-reward have their roots in the motivation theories you read about in Chapter 13. The key difference, though, is that the goals, feedback, and rewards originate from employees themselves and not from their managers or organizations.

self-control (self-management) a control system in which managers and workers control their own behavior by setting their own goals, monitoring their own progress, and rewarding themselves for goal achievement.

Review 2

Control Methods The five methods of control are bureaucratic, objective, normative, concertive, and self-control (self-management). Bureaucratic and objective controls are top-down, management-based, and measurement-based. Normative and concertive controls represent shared forms of control because they evolve from company-wide or team-based beliefs and values. Self-control, or self-management, is a control system in which managers turn over much, but not all, control to the individuals themselves.

(continued)

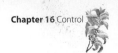

Exhibit 16.3 When to Use Different Methods of Control

BUREAUCRATIC CONTROL	• When it is necessary to standardize operating procedures • When it is necessary to establish limits
BEHAVIOR CONTROL	• When it is easier to measure what workers do on the job than what they accomplish on the job • When "cause-effect" relationships are clear, that is, when companies know which behaviors will lead to success and which won't • When good measures of worker behavior can be created
OUTPUT CONTROL	• When it is easier to measure what workers accomplish on the job than what they do on the job • When good measures of worker output can be created • When it is possible to set clear goals and standards for worker output • When "cause-effect" relationships are unclear
NORMATIVE CONTROL	• When organizational culture, values, and beliefs are strong • When it is difficult to create good measures of worker behavior • When it is difficult to create good measures of worker output
CONCERTIVE CONTROL	• When responsibility for task accomplishment is given to autonomous work groups • When management wants workers to take "ownership" of their behavior and outputs • When management desires a strong form of worker-based control
SELF-CONTROL	• When workers are intrinsically motivated to do their jobs well • When it is difficult to create good measures of worker behavior • When it is difficult to create good measures of worker output • When workers have or are taught self-control and self-leadership skills

Sources: L. J. Kirsch, "The Management of Complex Tasks in Organizations: Controlling the System's Development Process," *Organization Science* 7 (1996): 1–21; and S. A. Snell, "Control Theory in Strategic Human Resource Management: The Mediating Effect of Administrative Information," *Academy of Management Journal* 35 (1992): 292–327.

Bureaucratic control is based on organizational policies, rules, and procedures. Objective controls are based on reliable measures of behavior or outputs. Normative control is based on strong corporate beliefs and careful hiring practices. Concertive control is based on the development of values, beliefs, and rules in autonomous work groups. Self-control is based on individuals' setting their own goals, monitoring themselves, and rewarding or punishing themselves with respect to goal achievement.

Each of these control methods may be more or less appropriate depending on the circumstances. Examine Exhibit 16.3 to find out when each of these five control methods should be used.

3 What to Control?

In the first section of this chapter, we discussed the basics of the control process and the fact that control isn't always worthwhile or possible. In the second section, we looked at the various ways in which control can be obtained. In this third and final section, we address an equally important issue: What should managers control? Costs? Quality? Customer satisfaction? The way managers answer this question has critical implications for most businesses.

In grocery stores where profit margins are thin, competitors are aggressive, and customers are price sensitive, chains have long focused on controlling costs. By having beef carcasses presliced into larger segments and by switching to suppliers who

delivered prepackaged frozen poultry and pork, ready to put in display cases, they were able to shrink their meat-cutting staff and lower costs. But by controlling costs alone, grocery stores severed the traditional service relationship between meat cutters and customers. Realizing that they overcorrected on costs at the expense of service, many grocers are now putting their meat cutters back out front to help customers. **Winn Dixie's** meat cutters watch cooking videos. Supervalu's meat cutters now have thick "speak the language of beef" binders to teach them how to answer customers' questions. Paul Henry, a meat cutter at **Fresh Seasons Markets**, says that people ask him how to season roasts, how long to cook them, and what vegetables to serve with them. Says Henry, "I don't think people look at us as a chef, but they expect us to have the knowledge of a chef."[41]

"what's new" companies >

"what's new" companies >

If you control for just one thing, such as costs, as many grocers have done in their meat departments, then other dimensions like marketing, customer service, and quality are likely to suffer. But if you try to control for too many things, then managers and employees become confused about what's really important. In the end, successful companies find a balance that comes from doing three or four things right, like managing costs, providing value, and keeping customers and employees satisfied.

After reading this section, you should be able to explain **3.1 the balanced scorecard approach to control and how companies can achieve balanced control of company performance by choosing to control 3.2 budgets, cash flows, and economic value added; 3.3 customer defections; 3.4 quality;** and **3.5 waste and pollution.**

3.1 The Balanced Scorecard

Most companies measure performance using standard financial and accounting measures such as return on capital, return on assets, return on investments, cash flow, net income, and net margins. The **balanced scorecard** encourages managers to look beyond such traditional financial measures to four different perspectives on company performance. How do customers see us (the customer perspective)? At what must we excel (the internal perspective)? Can we continue to improve and create value (the innovation and learning perspective)? How do we look to shareholders (the financial perspective)?[42]

The balanced scorecard has several advantages over traditional control processes that rely solely on financial measures. First, it forces managers at each level of the company to set specific goals and measure performance in each of the four areas. For example, Exhibit 16.4 shows that Southwest Airlines uses nine different measures in its balanced scorecard in order to determine whether it is meeting the standards it has set for itself in the control process. Of those, only three—market value, seat revenue, and plane lease costs (at various compounded annual growth rates, or CAGR)—are standard financial measures of performance. In addition, Southwest measures its Federal Aviation Administration (FAA) on-time arrival rating and the cost of its airfares compared with those of competitors (customer perspective); how much time each plane spends on the ground after landing and the percentage of

balanced scorecard measurement of organizational performance in four equally important areas: finances, customers, internal operations, and innovation and learning.

Exhibit 16.4 Southwest Airlines' Balanced Scorecard

	OBJECTIVES	MEASURES	TARGETS	INITIATIVES
FINANCIAL	Profitability	Market Value	30% CAGR	
	Increased Revenue	Seat Revenue	20% CAGR	
	Lower Costs	Plane Lease Cost	5% CAGR	
CUSTOMER	On-Time Flights	FAA On-Time Arrival Rating	#1	Quality Management, Customer Loyalty Program
	Lowest Prices	Customer Ranking (Market Survey)	#1	
INTERNAL	Fast Ground Turnaround	Time on Ground	30 Minutes	Cycle Time Optimization Program
		On-Time Departure	90%	
LEARNING	Ground Crew Alignment with Company Goals	% Ground Crew Shareholders	Year 1: 70% Year 3: 90% Year 5: 100%	Employee Stock Option Plan Ground Crew Training
		% Ground Crew Trained		

Source: G. Anthes, "ROI Guide: Balanced Scorecard," *Computer World*, accessed May 5, 2003, from www.computerworld.com/managementtopics/rpo/story/0,10801,78512,00.html.

planes that depart on time (internal business perspective); and the percentage of its ground crew workers, such as mechanics and luggage handlers, who own company stock and have received job training (learning perspective).

The second major advantage of the balanced scorecard approach to control is that it minimizes the chances of **suboptimization**, which occurs when performance improves in one area at the expense of decreased performance in others. Jon Meliones, chief medical director at Duke Children's Hospital, says, "We explained the [balanced scorecard] theory to clinicians and administrators like this: If you sacrifice too much in one quadrant to satisfy another, your organization as a whole is thrown out of balance. We could, for example, cut costs to improve the financial quadrant by firing half the staff, but that would hurt quality of service, and the customer quadrant would fall out of balance. Or we could increase productivity in the internal business quadrant by assigning more patients to a nurse, but doing so would raise the likelihood of errors—an unacceptable trade-off."[43] Likewise, Toyota's president, Akio Toyoda, admits that the company's all-out push to become the world's largest car maker might have come at the expense of product quality, bloated inventories, and huge financial losses. As a result, he has vowed to rebalance Toyota's priorities.[44]

Let's examine some of the ways in which companies are controlling the four basic parts of the balanced scorecard: the financial perspective (budgets, cash flows, and economic value added), the customer perspective (customer defections), the internal perspective (total quality management), and the innovation and learning perspective (waste and pollution).

3.2 The Financial Perspective: Controlling Budgets, Cash Flows, and Economic Value Added

The traditional approach to controlling financial performance focuses on accounting tools such as cash flow analysis, balance sheets, income statements, financial

suboptimization performance improvement in one part of an organization but only at the expense of decreased performance in another part.

Exhibit 16.5   Basic Accounting Tools for Controlling Financial Performance

STEPS FOR A BASIC CASH FLOW ANALYSIS

1. Forecast sales (steady, up, or down).

2. Project changes in anticipated cash inflows (as a result of changes).

3. Project anticipated cash outflows (as a result of changes).

4. Project net cash flows by combining anticipated cash inflows and outflows.

PARTS OF A BASIC BALANCE SHEET (ASSETS = LIABILITIES + OWNER'S EQUITY)

1. Assets
   a. Current Assets (cash, short-term investment, marketable securities, accounts receivable, etc.)
   b. Fixed Assets (land, buildings, machinery, equipment, etc.)

2. Liabilities
   a. Current Liabilities (accounts payable, notes payable, taxes payable, etc.)
   b. Long-Term Liabilities (long-term debt, deferred income taxes, etc.)

3. Owner's Equity
   a. Preferred stock and common stock
   b. Additional paid-in capital
   c. Retained earnings

BASIC INCOME STATEMENT

SALES REVENUE
− sales returns and allowances
+ other income
= NET REVENUE
− cost of goods sold (beginning inventory, costs of goods purchased, ending inventory)
= GROSS PROFIT
− total operating expenses (selling, general, and administrative expenses)
= INCOME FROM OPERATIONS
− interest expense
= PRETAX INCOME
− income taxes
= NET INCOME

© Cengage Learning 2013

cash flow analysis a type of analysis that predicts how changes in a business will affect its ability to take in more cash than it pays out.

balance sheets accounting statements that provide a snapshot of a company's financial position at a particular time.

income statements accounting statements, also called "profit and loss statements," that show what has happened to an organization's income, expenses, and net profit over a period of time.

financial ratios calculations typically used to track a business's liquidity (cash), efficiency, and profitability over time compared to other businesses in its industry.

budgets quantitative plans through which managers decide how to allocate available money to best accomplish company goals.

ratios, and budgets. **Cash flow analysis** predicts how changes in a business will affect its ability to take in more cash than it pays out. **Balance sheets** provide a snapshot of a company's financial position at a particular time (but not the future). **Income statements,** also called profit and loss statements, show what has happened to an organization's income, expenses, and net profit (income less expenses) over a period of time. Exhibit 16.5 shows the basic steps or parts for cash flow analyses, balance sheets, and income statements. **Financial ratios** are typically used to track a business's liquidity (cash), efficiency, and profitability over time compared with other businesses in its industry. Exhibit 16.6 lists a few of the most common financial ratios and explains how they are calculated, what they mean, and when to use them. Finally, **budgets** are used to project costs and revenues, prioritize and control spending, and ensure that expenses don't exceed available funds and revenues. Exhibit 16.7 reviews the different kinds of budgets managers can use to track and control company finances.

Exhibit 16.6 Common Financial Ratios

RATIONS	FORMULA	WHAT IT MEANS	WHEN TO USE
LIQUIDITY RATIONS			
Current Ratio	Current Assets / Current Liabilities	• Whether you have enough assets on hand to pay for short-term bills and obligations. • Higher is better. • Recommended level is two times as many current assets as current liabilities.	• Track monthly and quarterly. • Basic measure of your company's health.
Quick (Acid Test) Ratio	(Current Assets − Inventories) / Current Liabilities	• Stricter than current ratio • Whether you have enough (i.e., cash) to pay short-term bills and obligations. • Higher is better. • Recommended level is one or higher.	• Track monthly. • Also calculate quick ratio with potential customers to evaluate whether they're likely to pay you in a timely manner.
LEVERAGE RATIOS			
Debt to Equity	Total Liabilities / Total Equity	• Indicates how much the company is leveraged (in debt) by comparing what is owed (liabilities) with what is owned (equity). • Lower is better. A high debt-to-equity ratio could indicate that the company has too much debt. • Recommended level depends on industry.	• Track monthly. • Lenders often use this to determine the creditworthiness of a business (i.e., whether to approve additional loans).
Debt Coverage	(Net Profit + Noncash Expense) / Debt	• Indicates how well cash flow covers debt payments. • Higher is better.	• Track monthly. • Lenders look at this ratio to determine if there is adequate cash to make loan payments.
EFFICIENCY RATIOS			
Inventory Turnover	Cost of Goods Sold / Inventory Average Value of Inventory	• Whether you're making efficient use of inventory. • Higher is better, indicating that inventory (dollars) isn't purchased (spent) until needed. • Recommended level depends on industry.	• Track monthly by using a 12-month rolling average.
Average Collections Period	Accounts Receivable / (Annual Net Credit Sales Divided by 365)	• Shows on average how quickly your customers are paying their bills. • Lower is better. • Recommended level is no more than 15 days longer than credit terms. If credit is net 30 days, then average should not be longer than 45 days.	• Track monthly. • Use to determine how long company's money is being tied up in customer credit.
PROFITABILITY RATIOS			
Gross Profit Margin	Gross Profit / Total Sales	• Shows how efficiently a business is using its materials and labor in the production process. • Higher is better, indicating that a profit can be made if fixed costs are controlled.	• Track monthly. • Analyze when unsure about product or service pricing. • Low margin compared with competitors means you're underpricing.
Return on Equity	Net Income/Owner's Equity	• Shows what was earned on your investment in the business during a particular period. Often called "return on investment." • Higher is better.	• Track quarterly and annually. • Use to compare what you might have earned on the stock market, bonds, or government Treasury bills during the same period.

Exhibit 16.7 Common Kinds of Budgets

Revenue Budgets—used to project or forecast future sales.	• Accuracy of projection depends on economy, competitors, sales force estimates, etc. • Determined by estimating future sales volume and sales prices for all products and services
Expense Budgets—used within departments and divisions to determine how much will be spent on various supplies, projects, or activities.	• One of the first places that companies look for cuts when trying to lower expenses
Profit Budgets—used by profit centers, which have "profit and loss" responsibility.	• Profit budgets combine revenue and expense budgets into one budget • Typically used in large businesses with multiple plants and divisions
Cash Budgets—used to forecast how much cash a company will have on hand to meet expenses.	• Similar to cash flow analyses • Used to identify cash shortfalls, which must be covered to pay bills, or cash excesses, which should be invested for a higher return
Capital Expenditure Budgets—used to forecast large, long-lasting investments in equipment, buildings, and property.	• Help managers identify funding that will be needed to pay for future expansion or strategic moves designed to increase competitive advantage
Variable Budgets—used to project costs across varying levels of sales and revenues.	• Important because it is difficult to accurately predict sales revenue and volume • Lead to more accurate budgeting with respect to labor, materials, and administrative expenses, which vary with sales volume and revenues • Build flexibility into the budgeting process

© Cengage Learning 2013

> By themselves, none of these tools—cash flow analyses, balance sheets, income statements, financial ratios, or budgets—tell the whole financial story of a business.

By themselves, none of these tools—cash flow analyses, balance sheets, income statements, financial ratios, or budgets—tell the whole financial story of a business. They must be used together when assessing a company's financial performance. Because these tools are reviewed in detail in your accounting and finance classes, only a brief overview is provided here. Still, these are necessary tools for controlling organizational finances and expenses, and they should be part of your business toolbox. Unfortunately, most managers don't have a good understanding of these accounting tools even though they should.[45] When Boeing's new chief financial officer attended her first company retreat with other Boeing executives, she assumed that her discussion of financial ratios, like those shown in Exhibit 16.6, would be a boring review for everyone present. Afterward, she was shocked when dozens of the 280 executives attending the retreat told her that for the very first time they finally understood what the formulas meant.[46]

If you, like those experienced executives, struggle to understand how financial ratios can be used where you work, you might find help in the following books: *Accounting the Easy Way*, by Peter J. Eisen; *Accounting for Dummies* and *How to Read a Financial Report: Wringing Vital Signs Out of the Numbers*, both by John A. Tracy; *Schaum's Quick Guide to Business Formulas: 201 Decision-Making Tools for Business, Finance, and Accounting Students*, by Joel G. Siegel, Jae K. Shim, and Stephen W. Hartman; *The Vest-Pocket Guide to Business Ratios*, by Michael R. Tyran; *Essential Managers: Managing Budgets*, by Stephen Brookson; or *Forecasting Budgets: 25 Keys to Successful Planning (The New York Times Pocket MBA Series)*, by Norman Moore and Grover Gardner.

Though no one would dispute the importance of cash flow analyses, balance sheets, income statements, financial ratios, or budgets for determining the financial health of a business, accounting research also indicates that the complexity and sheer amount of information contained in these accounting tools can shut down the brain and glaze over the eyes of even the most experienced manager.[47] Sometimes there's simply too much information to make sense of. The balanced scorecard simplifies things by focusing on one simple question when it comes to finances: How do we look to shareholders? One way to answer that question is through something called economic value added.

Conceptually, **economic value added (EVA)** is not the same thing as profits. It is the amount by which profits exceed the cost of capital in a given year. It is based on the simple idea that capital is necessary to run a business and that capital comes at a cost. Although most people think of capital as cash, once it is invested (i.e., spent), capital is more likely to be found in a business in the form of computers, manufacturing plants, employees, raw materials, and so forth. And just like the interest that a homeowner pays on a mortgage or that a college student pays on a student loan, there is a cost to that capital.

The most common costs of capital are the interest paid on long-term bank loans used to buy all those resources, the interest paid to bondholders (who lend organizations their money), and the dividends (cash payments) and growth in stock value that accrue to shareholders. EVA is positive when company profits (revenues minus expenses minus taxes) exceed the cost of capital in a given year. In other words, if a business is to truly grow, its revenues must be large enough to cover both short-term costs (annual expenses and taxes) and long-term costs (the cost of borrowing capital from bondholders and shareholders). If you're a bit confused, the late Roberto Goizueta, the former CEO of Coca-Cola, explained it this way: "You borrow money at a certain rate and invest it at a higher rate and pocket the difference. It is simple. It is the essence of banking."[48]

Exhibit 16.8 shows how to calculate EVA. First, starting with a company's income statement, you calculate the net operating profit after taxes (NOPAT) by subtracting taxes owed from income from operations (see Exhibit 16.5 to review an income statement). The NOPAT shown in Exhibit 16.8 is $3,500,000. Second, identify how much capital the company has invested (i.e., spent). Total liabilities (what the company owes) less accounts payable and less accrued expenses, neither of which you pay interest on, provides a rough approximation of this amount. In Exhibit 16.8, total capital invested is $16,800,000. Third, calculate the cost (i.e., rate) paid for capital by determining the interest paid to bondholders (who lend organizations their money), which is usually somewhere between 5 and 8 percent, and the return that stockholders want in terms of dividends and stock price appreciation, which is historically about 13 percent. Take a weighted average of the two to determine the overall cost of capital. In Exhibit 16.8, the cost of capital is 10 percent. Fourth, multiply the total capital ($16,800,000) from Step 2 by the cost of capital (10 percent) from Step 3. In Exhibit 16.8, this amount is $1,680,000. Fifth, subtract

© Image Source/Jupiterimages

economic value added (EVA) the amount by which company profits (revenues, minus expenses, minus taxes) exceed the cost of capital in a given year.

Exhibit 16.8 Calculating Economic Value Added (EVA)

1. Calculate net operating profit after tax (NOPAT).	$3,500,000
2. Identify how much capital the company has invested (i.e., spent).	$16,800,000
3. Determine the cost (i.e., rate) paid for capital (usually between 5 and 13 percent).	10 percent
4. Multiply capital used (Step 2) times cost of capital (Step 3).	(10% × $16,800,000) = $1,680,000
5. Subtract the total dollar cost of capital from net profit after taxes.	$3,500,000 NOPAT −$1,680,000 Total cost of capital $1,820,000 Economic value added

© Cengage Learning 2013

the total dollar cost of capital in Step 4 from the NOPAT in Step 1. In Exhibit 16.8, this value is $1,820,000, which means that our example company has created economic value, or wealth, this year. If our EVA number had been negative, meaning that the company didn't make enough profit to cover the cost of capital from bondholders and shareholders, then the company would have destroyed economic value, or wealth, by taking in more money than it returned.[49]

Why is EVA so important? First and most importantly, because it includes the cost of capital, it shows whether a business, division, department, profit center, or product is really paying for itself. The key is to make sure that managers and employees can see how their choices and behavior affect the company's EVA. For example, because of EVA training and information systems, factory workers at Herman Miller, a leading office furniture manufacturer, understand that using more efficient materials, such as less expensive wood-dust board instead of real wood sheeting, contributes an extra dollar of EVA from each desk the company makes. On its website, Herman Miller explains, "Under the terms of the EVA plan, we shifted our focus from budget performance to long-term continuous improvements and the creation of economic value. When we make plans for improvements around here, we include an EVA analysis. When we make decisions to add or cut programs, we look at the impact on EVA. Every month we study our performance in terms of EVA, and this measurement system is one of the first things new recruits to the company learn."[50] "The result is a highly motivated and business literate workforce that challenges convention and strives to create increasingly greater value for both customers and owners. Every month the company and all employees review performance in terms of EVA, which has proven to be a strong corollary to shareholder value."[51]

Second, because EVA can easily be determined for subsets of a company such as divisions, regional offices, manufacturing plants, and sometimes even departments, it makes managers and workers at all levels pay much closer attention to their segment of the business. When company offices were being refurbished at Genesco, a shoe company, a worker who had EVA training handed CEO Ben Harris $4,000 in cash. The worker explained that he now understood the effect his job had on the company's ability to survive and prosper. Because the company was struggling, he sold the old doors that had been removed during remodeling so that the company could have the cash.[52] In other words, EVA motivates managers and workers to think like small-business owners who must scramble to contain costs and generate enough business to meet their bills each month. And unlike many kinds of financial controls, EVA doesn't specify what should or should not be done to improve performance. Thus, it encourages managers and workers to be creative in looking for ways to improve EVA performance.

EVA is the amount by which profits exceed the cost of capital in a given year. So the more that EVA exceeds the total dollar cost of capital, the better a company has used investors' money that year. For example, Apple had an EVA of $10.03 billion in 2010, by far the largest EVA in the world. The next closest company was Google, at $5.28 billion. To put Apple's 2010 EVA performance in perspective, note that Apple had an average EVA of $1.7 billion a year from 2005–2009, and that was 2.5 times more what investors were expecting. Apple's EVA financial performance in 2010 was truly extraordinary.[53]

3.3 The Customer Perspective: Controlling Customer Defections

The second aspect of organizational performance that the balanced scorecard helps managers monitor is customers. It does so by forcing managers to address the question "How do customers see us?" Unfortunately, most companies try to answer this question through customer satisfaction surveys, but these are often misleadingly positive. Most customers are reluctant to talk about their problems because they don't know who to complain to or think that complaining will not do any good. Indeed, a study by the federal Office of Consumer Affairs found that 96 percent of unhappy customers never complain to anyone in the company.[54]

One reason that customer satisfaction surveys can be misleading is that sometimes even very satisfied customers will leave to do business with competitors. Another challenge is getting effective feedback when there is a problem. Norm Brodsky, founded and ran **CitiStorage**, a document-archive business based in Brooklyn, New York. Despite his success, he says, "I still remember the moment, many years ago, when I found out we'd lost one of our biggest customers. . . . One of my salesmen called me in my car and told me we'd just received a fax from the customer, a major law firm, announcing its intention to move its boxes out of our [storage] facility when the contract expired three months later." Brodsky, who was stunned and surprised, asked his sales representative why the law firm was leaving. Brodsky says, "The salesman didn't have an answer, and we couldn't get one from the customer. The people in charge at the law firm wouldn't see us or talk to us on the telephone. Our urgent messages brought perfunctory replies: 'The decision has been made, and it is final.'"[55]

< **"what's new" companies**

Rather than poring over customer satisfaction surveys from current customers, studies indicate that companies may do a better job of answering the question "How do customers see us?" by closely monitoring **customer defections**, that is, by identifying which customers are leaving the company and measuring the rate at which they are leaving. Unlike the results of customer satisfaction surveys, customer defections and retention do have a great effect on profits.

For example, very few managers realize that obtaining a new customer costs ten times as much as keeping a current one. In fact, the cost of replacing old customers with new ones is so great that most companies could double their profits by increasing the rate of customer retention by just 5 to 10 percent per year.[56] Retaining customers obviously means having more customers, but how many more?

Consider two companies starting with a customer base of 100,000 customers and an acquisition rate of 20 percent (i.e., yearly each company's customer base grows by 20%). Assuming company B has a higher retention rate of just 5 percent (90% retention rate for company B versus an 85% retention rate for company A), company B will double its customer base around the ninth year, whereas it will take company A slightly more than 15 years to double its customer base. On average, this means company B also profited by a higher percentage.[57] And if a company can keep a customer for life, the benefits are even larger. According to Stew Leonard, owner of the Connecticut-based Stew Leonard's grocery store chain, "The lifetime value of a customer in a supermarket is about $246,000. Every time a customer comes through our front door I see, stamped on their forehead in big red numbers, '$246,000.' I'm never going to make that person unhappy with me. Or lose her to the competition."[58]

Beyond the clear benefits to the bottom line, the second reason to study customer defections is that customers who have left are much more likely than current

> "The lifetime value of a customer in a supermarket is about $246,000. Every time a customer comes through our front door I see, stamped on their forehead in big red numbers, '$246,000.' I'm never going to make that person unhappy with me. Or lose her to the competition."
>
> —STEW LEONARD, FOUNDER, STEW LEONARD'S

customer defections a performance assessment in which companies identify which customers are leaving and measure the rate at which they are leaving.

customers to tell you what you are doing wrong. Perhaps the best way to tap into this source of good feedback is to have top-level managers from various departments talk directly to customers who have left. It's also worthwhile to have top managers talk to dissatisfied customers who are still with the company.

After CitiStorage's Norm Brodsky lost the law firm client (above), he said the lesson wasn't that they made mistakes. All firms do. So, Says Brodsky, "We decided that, from then on, we'd go to each customer 18 months before the end of the contract and offer to negotiate a new one. If the customer hesitated, we'd know right away that we had a problem—while there was still time to fix it." As they did this, he says they were surprised to discover they had unhappy customers. For example, one customer wanted a lower price because its storage volume had increased. The customer was right and they made the change. Another didn't like CitiStorage's inventory system for managing stored documents. So, they changed it. Says Brodsky, "In four months with the new policy, we made four improvements, pleased four customers, and locked up four accounts, and all these benefits came from one failure. In the long run, that failure proved to be one of the best things that ever happened to the company."[59]

Some might argue that it's a waste of valuable executive time to have upper-level managers interact with dissatisfied customers, but there's no faster way for the people in charge to learn what needs to be done than to hear it directly from customers who are unhappy with the company's performance.

Finally, companies that understand why customers leave can not only take steps to fix ongoing problems but also identify which customers are likely to leave and can make changes to prevent them from leaving.

3.4 The Internal Perspective: Controlling Quality

The third part of the balanced scorecard, the internal perspective, consists of the processes, decisions, and actions that managers and workers make within the organization. In contrast to the financial perspective of EVA and the outward-looking customer perspective, the internal perspective focuses on internal processes and systems that add value to the organization. For McDonald's, it could be processes and systems that enable the company to provide consistent, quick, low-cost food. For Toyota, it could be reliability—when you turn on your car, it starts, no matter whether the car has 20,000 or 200,000 miles on it. Yet no matter what area a company chooses, the key is to excel in that area. Consequently, the internal perspective of the balanced scorecard usually leads managers to a focus on quality.

Quality is typically defined and measured in three ways: excellence, value, and conformance to expectations.[60] When the company defines its quality goal as *excellence*, managers must try to produce a product or service of unsurpassed performance and features. Conde Nast Traveler magazine has been ranking global airlines for 23 years. For 22 of those years, Singapore Airlines was named the best airline in the world.[61] Whereas many airlines try to cram passengers into every available inch on a plane, Singapore Airlines delivers creature comforts to encourage repeat business and customers willing to pay premium prices. On its newer planes, the first-class cabin is divided into eight private mini-rooms, each with an unusually wide leather seat that folds down flat for sleeping, a 23-inch LCD TV that doubles as a computer monitor, and an adjustable table. These amenities and services are common for private jets but truly unique in the commercial airline industry.[62] Singapore Airlines was the first airline, in the 1970s, to introduce a choice of meals, complimentary drinks, and earphones in coach class. It was the first to introduce worldwide video, news, telephone, and fax services and the first to feature personal video monitors for movies, news, documentaries, and games. Singapore Airlines has had AC power for laptop computers for some time, and recently it became the first airline to introduce onboard, high-speed Internet access.

Value is the customer perception that the product quality is excellent for the price offered. At a higher price, for example, customers may perceive the product to be less of a value. When a company emphasizes value as its quality goal, managers must simultaneously control excellence, price, durability, and any other features of a product or service that customers strongly associate with value. One of the ways that Hyundai has succeeded in the U.S. auto market is by emphasizing value. For example, the 2011 Sonata comes standard with dozens of features that are optional in competitors' models, such as active head restraints, electronic stability control, and satellite radio and Bluetooth connectivity. Furthermore, the Sonata's engine leads its class in power and fuel-efficiency (averaging 33 mpg). With these extras, a price that is 10 percent to 20 percent less than a Honda Accord or Toyota Camry, and a 10-year warranty, Hyundai has positioned the Sonata to be a great value.[63]

When a company defines its quality goal as conformance to specifications, employees must base decisions and actions on whether services and products measure up to the standard. In contrast to excellence and value-based definitions of quality that can be somewhat ambiguous, measuring whether products and services are "in spec" is relatively easy. Furthermore, whereas conformance to specifications (e.g., precise tolerances for a part's weight or thickness) is usually associated with manufacturing, it can be used equally well to control quality in nonmanufacturing jobs. Exhibit 16.9 shows a checklist that a cook or restaurant owner would use to ensure quality when buying fresh fish.

© Munshi Ahmed/Bloomberg/Getty Images

value customer perception that the product quality is excellent for the price offered.

Exhibit 16.9 Conformance to Specifications Checklist for Buying Fresh Fish

QUALITY CHECKLIST FOR BUYING FRESH FISH		
FRESH WHOLE FISH	**ACCEPTABLE**	**NOT ACCEPTABLE**
Gills	✓ bright red; free of slime; clear mucus	✗ brown to grayish; thick, yellow mucus
Eyes	✓ clear, bright, bulging, black pupils	✗ dull, sunken, cloudy, gray pupils
Smell	✓ inoffensive, slight ocean smell	✗ ammonia or putrid smell
Skin	✓ opalescent sheen; scales adhere tightly to skin	✗ dull or faded color; scales missing or easily removed
Flesh	✓ firm and elastic to touch, tight to the bone	✗ soft and flabby, separating from the bone
Belly cavity	✓ no viscera or blood visible; lining intact; no bone protruding	✗ incomplete evisceration; cuts or protruding bones; off-odor

Sources: "A Closer Look: Buy It Fresh, Keep It Fresh," *Consumer Reports Online*, accessed June 20, 2005, from www.seagrant.sunysb.edu/SeafoodTechnology/SeafoodMedia/CR02-2001/CR-SeafoodII020101.htm [no longer available]; and National Fisheries Institute, "How to Purchase: Buying Fish," accessed June 20, 2005, from www.aboutseafood.com.

Exhibit 16.10 Advantages and Disadvantages of Different Measures of Quality

QUALITY MEASURE	ADVANTAGES	DISADVANTAGES
Excellence	Promotes clear organizational vision.	Provides little practical guidance for managers.
	Being/providing the "best" motivates and inspires managers and employees.	Excellence is ambiguous. What is it? Who defines it?
Value	Appeals to customers, who "know excellence when they see it."	Difficult to measure and control.
	Customers recognize differences in value.	Can be difficult to determine what factors influence whether a product/service is seen as having value.
	Easier to measure and compare whether products/services differ in value.	Controlling the balance between excellence and cost (i.e., affordable excellence) can be difficult.
Conformance to Specifications	If specifications can be written, conformance to specifications is usually measurable.	Many products/services cannot be easily evaluated in terms of conformance to specifications.
	Should lead to increased efficiency.	Promotes standardization, so may hurt performance when adapting to changes is more important.
	Promotes consistency in quality.	May be less appropriate for services, which are dependent on a high degree of human contact.

Source: Republished with permission of Academy of Management, PO Box 3020, Briar Cliff Manor, NY, 10510-8020. C. A. Reeves & D. A. Bednar, "Defining Quality: Alternatives and Implications," *Academy of Management Review* 19 (1994): 419–445. Reproduced by permission of the publisher via Copyright Clearance Center, Inc.

The way in which a company defines quality affects the methods and measures that workers use to control quality. Accordingly, Exhibit 16.10 shows the advantages and disadvantages associated with the excellence, value, and conformance to specification definitions of quality.

3.5 The Innovation and Learning Perspective: Controlling Waste and Pollution

The last part of the balanced scorecard, the innovation and learning perspective, addresses the question "Can we continue to improve and create value?" Thus, the innovation and learning perspective involves continuous improvement in ongoing products and services (discussed in Chapter 18), as well as relearning and redesigning the processes by which products and services are created (discussed in Chapter 7). Because these are discussed in more detail elsewhere in the text, this section reviews an increasingly important topic, waste and pollution minimization. Exhibit 16.11 shows the four levels of waste minimization, ranging from waste disposal, which produces the smallest minimization of waste, to waste prevention and reduction, which produces the greatest minimization.[64]

The goals of the top level, *waste prevention and reduction*, are to prevent waste and pollution before they occur or to reduce them when they do occur. For example, **A. P. Moller-Maersk A/S**, the world's largest shipping container company, recently placed an order for ten of the biggest container ships in the world. At 1,312 feet long and 193.5 feet wide, these ships can carry 18,000 twenty-foot containers, or 2,500 more than the largest ships currently in service. Thanks to an innovative hull design, as well as a heat-recovery system that reuses energy from engine exhaust, the ships produce 50 percent less carbon dioxide and consume 35 percent less fuel

"what's new" companies >

Exhibit 16.11
Four Levels of Waste
Minimization

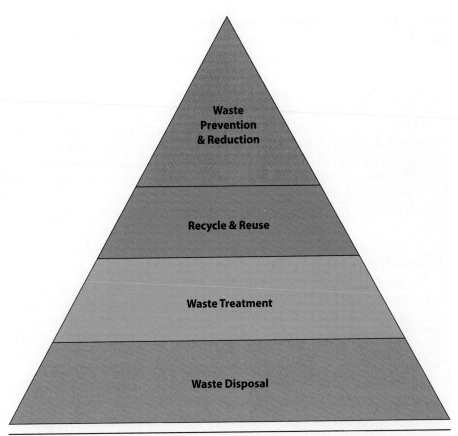

Waste
Prevention
& Reduction

Recycle & Reuse

Waste Treatment

Waste Disposal

Source: D. R. May & B. L. Flannery, "Cutting Waste with Employee Involvement Teams," *Business Horizons* September–October 1995, 28–38. Reprinted with permission of Elsevier.

mgmt:trends

Dell's Three C's

When Dell Computers set out to reduce the environmental impact of its packaging, it undertook a strategy focused on three "C's." The first "C" stands for cube, which meant using a smaller box, with more efficient packaging and less unnecessary material. By switching to smaller boxes, Dell was able to fit 17 percent more notebook computers per shipping pallet. The second "C" is content—Dell increased the amount of recycled and sustainable material that it used to produce its packaging material. So, for example, it used recycled foam; products derived from bamboo, which is a fast-growing, sustainable plant; and recycled milk jugs (over 9 million of them actually). The third "C" stands for curbside recyclability. Dell committed to educating both consumers and recycling companies about how to recycle the packaging material that the company uses. Dell also set a goal of making sure that 75 percent of its packaging can be recycled. In all, Dell's efforts to reduce waste have reduced the amount of packaging it uses by 18 million pounds in just two years.[65]

© iStockphoto.com/Kirsty Pargeter

than the average ship, despite their massive size. Maersk has even drawn up detailed plans for how the ships will be recycled when they are decommissioned.[66]

There are three strategies for waste prevention and reduction:

1. *Good housekeeping*—performing regularly scheduled preventive maintenance for offices, plants, and equipment. Examples of good housekeeping include fixing leaky valves quickly to prevent wasted water and making sure machines are running properly so that they don't use more fuel than necessary. UPS uses GPS and telematic tracking systems to improve the efficiency of its fleet of delivery trucks. The GPS tracker helps drivers find the most fuel-efficient route for deliveries, and the telematic device monitors more than 200 elements of a truck's condition, such as oil pressure, idling time, acceleration, and gas mileage. Routine maintenance used to be done based on fixed intervals (say, every 7,500 miles). But thanks to telematics information, maintenance is performed when needed, and needed repair work is detected and fixed much earlier, thus reducing downtime and repair expenses. Because of these steps, UPS reduced the amount of time that its U.S. trucks spend idling by 15 minutes per day, saving 1.4 million gallons of fuel per year. Donna Longina, a UPS spokesperson said, "Multiply results like that by more than 90,000 drivers worldwide, and you can see the potential."[67]

2. *Material/product substitution*—replacing toxic or hazardous materials with less harmful materials. As part of its Pollution Prevention Pays program over the last 30 years, 3M eliminated 2.2 billion pounds of pollutants and saved $1 billion by using benign substitutes for toxic solvents in its manufacturing processes.[68]

3. *Process modification*—changing steps or procedures to eliminate or reduce waste. **The Lavergne Group**, which recycles printer cartridges for HP, used to shred the cartridges to produce recyclable plastic. However, by dismantling the cartridges, it now recovers 50 percent more recyclable plastic from each printer cartridge, and recycles 1 million pounds of plastic each month. Since 2005, it has helped HP make 500 million printer cartridges using recycled plastic.[69]

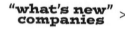
> **"what's new" companies**

At the second level of waste minimization, *recycle and reuse*, wastes are reduced by reusing materials as long as possible or by collecting materials for on- or off-site recycling. General Motors uses recycled plastics in the production of its hybrid electric car, the Chevy Volt. The plastic cover for the Volt's radiator fan is made from recycled consumer goods, recycled tires used at GM's test tracks, and the plastic booms that were used to contain the BP oil spill in the Gulf of Mexico. In 2011, GM will use 100,000 pounds of recycled plastics and 100 miles of plastic boom to make radiator fan covers for the Chevy Volt.[70]

A growing trend in recycling is *design for disassembly*, where products are designed from the start for easy disassembly, recycling, and reuse once they are no longer usable. Herman Miller, a manufacturer of office equipment, not only uses recycled material in its award-winning office chairs, it makes it easy to recycle them once they're no longer usable. It clearly labels which parts are recyclable, identifies the type of plastic used in each part, and then minimizes the different types of plastics used. Finally, it designs its chairs so that they are easy to take apart and includes detailed disassembly instructions. As a result, Herman Miller has won a number of Cradle-to-Cradle (C2C) certifications for it chairs, storage systems, and office systems.[71] Whereas Herman Miller is doing this

© Stephen Chernin/Getty Images

UPS uses GPS and telematic tracking systems to improve the efficiency of its fleet of delivery trucks.

voluntarily, the European Union requires companies to make most of their products and packaging recyclable. And because companies, not consumers, are held responsible for recycling the products they manufacture, they must design their products from the start with recycling in mind.[72] Under the EU's end-of-life vehicle program, companies will have to be able to recover and recycle 80 percent of parts from cars built in Europe since January 2002. The requirement rises to 85 percent for cars made since 2006, and will be 95 percent for cars made after 2015. Moreover, since 2007, the EU has required auto manufacturers to recycle all the cars that they made between 1989 and 2002.[73]

At the third level of waste minimization, waste treatment, companies use biological, chemical, or other processes to turn potentially harmful waste into harmless compounds or useful byproducts. In Africa, animal slaughterhouses often dump untreated animal waste into rivers and lakes. This spreads disease and generates methane and carbon dioxide—greenhouse gases that contribute to global warming. Unlike traditional treatment processes, **Cows to Kilowatts Partnership Limited** uses an advanced anaerobic reactor to turn animal blood and waste into biogas, which is then processed and compressed into cooking gas or fuel to run household generators. Even the leftover sludge can be reused as environmentally friendly fertilizer.[74]

< *"what's new"
   companies*

The fourth and lowest level of waste minimization is *waste disposal*. Wastes that cannot be prevented, reduced, recycled, reused, or treated should be safely disposed of in processing plants or in environmentally secure landfills that prevent leakage and contamination of soil and underground water supplies. Contrary to common belief, all businesses, not just manufacturing firms, have waste disposal problems. For example, with the average computer lasting just three years, approximately 60 million computers come out of service each year, creating disposal problems for offices all over the world. But organizations can't just throw old computers away, because they have lead-containing cathode ray tubes in the monitors, toxic metals in the circuit boards, paint-coated plastic, and metal coatings that can contaminate groundwater.[75] Many companies give old computers and computer equipment to local computer recycling centers that distribute usable computers to nonprofit organizations or safely dispose of lead and other toxic materials. A number of retailers and electronics manufacturers operate recycling programs to keep electronics out of landfills. For example, Customers can drop off computers, TVs, DVD players, batteries and other items at Best Buy stores. There is a $10 recycling fee for anything with a screen, but Best Buy offsets that with a $10 gift card. Best Buy will recycle 80 million pounds of electronics this year. But for those items that still function, Costco and NewEgg.com work with Gazelle.com, which buys, refurbishes, and resells 250,000 items overseas and on eBay. College student Bobby Lozano sold his used iPod Nano and LG EnV Touch phone to Gazelle because, he says, "I got an iPhone, so I no longer needed the other two." Gazelle wiped the devices of personal information and put $70 into his PayPal account.[76]

What to Control? Deciding what to control is just as important as deciding whether or how to control. In most companies, performance is measured using financial measures alone. However, the balanced scorecard encourages managers to measure and control company performance from four perspectives: financial, customers, internal operations, and innovation and learning. Traditionally, financial control has been achieved through cash flow analysis, balance sheets, income statements, financial ratios, and budgets. Another way to measure and control financial performance is through economic value added (EVA). Unlike traditional financial measures, EVA helps managers assess whether they are performing well enough to pay the cost of the capital needed to run the business. Instead

Review 3

of using customer satisfaction surveys to measure performance, companies should pay attention to customer defectors, who are more likely to speak up about what the company is doing wrong. Performance of internal operations is often measured in terms of quality, which is defined in three ways: excellence, value, and conformance to expectations. Minimization of waste has become an important part of innovation and learning in companies. The four levels of waste minimization are waste prevention and reduction, recycling and reuse, waste treatment, and waste disposal.

SELF-ASSESSMENT

Too Much Information?

Imagine that your professor handed back term papers, and the only mark on yours was the grade. Would you be content, or would you feel gypped? People have different comfort levels about receiving feedback: Some thrive on it; others are ambivalent. What about you? Would you rather see comments in the margins of your term paper or not? This self-assessment will give you insights into your perceptions of feedback. Understanding your preferences in this area will help you develop the skills you'll need as a manager.[77]

As you complete this feedback inventory, be candid as you circle the appropriate responses. "Extremely Untrue" is 1, and "Extremely True" is 6.

1. It is important for me to obtain useful information about my performance.

    1   2   3   4   5   6

2. If I receive negative feedback, I would have a negative attitude towards myself, so I try to avoid criticism.

    1   2   3   4   5   6

3. I am not really worried about what people will think of me if I ask for feedback about my performance.

    1   2   3   4   5   6

4. I like people to hear about my good performance at work (or at college).

    1   2   3   4   5   6

5. Receiving feedback about my performance helps me to improve my skills.

    1   2   3   4   5   6

6. Negative feedback doesn't really lower my self-worth, so I don't go out of my way to avoid it.

    1   2   3   4   5   6

7. I'm concerned about what people would think of me if I were to ask for feedback.

    1   2   3   4   5   6

8. Seeking feedback from my supervisor (instructor) is one way to show that I want to improve my performance.

    1   2   3   4   5   6

9. I would like to obtain more information to let me know how I am performing.

    1   2   3   4   5   6

10. Receiving negative feedback wouldn't really change the way I feel about myself.

    1   2   3   4   5   6

11. I am worried about the impression I would make if I were to ask for feedback.

    1   2   3   4   5   6

12. I want people to know when I ask for feedback so I can show my responsible nature.

    1   2   3   4   5   6

KEY TERMS

balanced scorecard 680
balance sheets 682
behavior control 675
benchmarking 667
budgets 682
bureaucratic control 673
cash flow analysis 682
concertive control 677
concurrent control 670
control 666
control loss 671
customer defections 687
cybernetic feasibility 672
cybernetic 669

economic value added (EVA) 685
feedback control 669
feedforward control 670
financial ratios 682
income statements 682
normative control 675
objective control 674
output control 675
regulation costs 671
self-control (self-management) 678
standards 667
suboptimization 681
value 689

13. I would like to receive more useful information about my performance.

   1   2   3   4   5   6

14. It's hard to feel good about myself when I receive negative feedback.

   1   2   3   4   5   6

15. I don't really worry about what others would think of me if I asked for feedback.

   1   2   3   4   5   6

16. I don't really care if people hear the good feedback that is given to me.

   1   2   3   4   5   6

17. I'm not really concerned about whether I receive useful information about my performance.

   1   2   3   4   5   6

18. I don't really worry about getting negative feedback because I still feel I am a person of worth.

   1   2   3   4   5   6

19. I don't really care if people know the type of feedback I get.

   1   2   3   4   5   6

20. When I receive praise, I don't really want others to hear it.

   1   2   3   4   5   6

21. Feedback is not really useful to help me improve my performance.

   1   2   3   4   5   6

22. I try to avoid negative feedback because it makes me feel bad about myself.

   1   2   3   4   5   6

23. If I sought feedback about my performance, I wouldn't want other people to know what type of feedback I received.

   1   2   3   4   5   6

24. I don't care either way if people see me asking my supervisor (instructor) for feedback.

   1   2   3   4   5   6

25. Obtaining useful feedback information is not very important to me.

   1   2   3   4   5   6

26. I worry about receiving feedback that is likely to be negative because it hurts to be criticized.

   1   2   3   4   5   6

27. I am usually concerned about other people hearing the content of the individual feedback I receive.

   1   2   3   4   5   6

28. I hope positive feedback about my performance will make a good impression on others.

   1   2   3   4   5   6

29. I don't really require more feedback to let me know how I am performing.

   1   2   3   4   5   6

30. Negative feedback doesn't really worry me because I still have a positive attitude toward myself.

   1   2   3   4   5   6

31. It doesn't worry me if people know how I've performed at something.

   1   2   3   4   5   6

32. I don't really need to impress others by letting them know about the positive feedback I receive regarding my performance.

   1   2   3   4   5   6

Scoring

Determine your average score for each category by entering your response to each survey item below, as follows. In blanks that say *regular score*, simply enter your response for that item. If your response was a 4, place a 4 in the *regular score* blank. In blanks that say *reverse score*, subtract your response from 7 and enter the result. So if your response was a 4, place a 3 ($7 - 4 = 3$) in the *reverse score* blank. Total your scores, then compute each average score.

Desire for Useful Information

1. regular score _____
5. regular score _____
9. regular score _____
13. reverse score _____
17. reverse score _____
21. reverse score _____
25. reverse score _____
29. reverse score _____
    TOTAL = _____

Ego Defense

2. regular score _____
6. reverse score _____
10. regular score _____
14. regular score _____
18. reverse score _____
22. reverse score _____
26. regular score _____
30. regular score _____
    TOTAL = _____

Defensive Impression Management

3. reverse score _____

7. reverse score _____

11. reverse score _____

15. reverse score _____

19. reverse score _____

23. reverse score _____

27. reverse score _____

31. reverse score _____

TOTAL = _____

Assertive Impression Management

4. reverse score _____

8. reverse score _____

12. reverse score _____

16. reverse score _____

20. reverse score _____

24. reverse score _____

28. reverse score _____

32. reverse score _____

TOTAL = _____

You can find the interpretation for your score at www.cengagebrain.com.

MANAGEMENT DECISION

Managing or Spying?[78]

Well, it's the last Friday of the month, and that can only mean one thing—time to process the invoices from the freelance workers you hired. A few months ago, your company was overloaded by the amount of data processing that needed to be done. There were a few days when the entire staff, even the janitors, stayed past 11pm to read through, sort, and organize all of your clients' account data. The work wasn't necessarily difficult. But it was time consuming, and you hated it when your employees and managers had to take time off of other important things to get the processing done. You thought you found a perfect solution when you decided to hire some freelancers—part-time outsiders that you could contract to do all of the processing, freeing up your staff to focus on other things.

What seemed to be a great solution, however, produced a few troubles of its own. It wasn't as if the work wasn't getting done—the freelancers actually did a pretty good job with their assignments. The problem was, though, how much time they seemed to be spending on the work. When you used to do the processing in-house, it usually took one person about 4-5 hours to go through the data for one client. Even employees who didn't have any specialized training could usually get through one client's account in less than 7 hours. Your freelancers, however, have been charging for more hours—a lot more. Six months ago, their time sheet showed that they spent an average of 16 hours per account. Three months ago, their time sheet showed that they spent an average of 19 hours per account. And as you open this month's invoices,

you see that they are reporting having spend an average of 21 hours per account.

You think to yourself "This can't be right?" You wonder if maybe they are just working extra slow. Or maybe they are billing you for hours they spend looking up YouTube videos.

As you worry about what the freelancers are doing, one of your managers says he has saw a solution on TV the other day. It's a service from a company called oDesk. The company, which helps businesses connect with freelance workers all over the world, also offers a software program that takes pictures of freelancers' computer screens and records their keystrokes and mouse clicks throughout the day. In short, it lets companies like yours know almost every single move that a freelancer makes.

"It's the perfect solution," your manager tells you. No more worries about what the freelancers are doing with their time and your money. You can know every single thing they do during the time they are billing you.

It does seem to be a great solution. But you have some hesitation—isn't this a bit too much like spying? Do I really want to spend my time constantly looking over someone else's shoulder?

Questions

1. Should this company use oDesk's feature to monitor its contractors? Why or why not?

2. In your opinion, do the benefits of using oDesk's surveillance feature outweigh the potential costs?

MANAGEMENT TEAM DECISION

Making Airports More Secure[79]

Everything you do as an official at the Department of Homeland Security is about control. Your task is to maintain strict security standards at all U.S. airports, while also trying to keep things running smoothly and efficiently. As the training program you created repeats emphatically, and as recent events have demonstrated, just one slip, one small mistake, can quickly escalate into a disaster. It is your responsibility to make sure that tragedy does not occur again.

The security measures that DHS has put in place have created a complex system of checks. Passengers are now required to show a valid photo ID and a boarding pass to proceed to the terminal. They cannot take knives or other sharp objects on board the plane, as a reaction to the events of 9/11. They need to take off their shoes at the x-ray machines, as a precaution against the shoe bomb plot of 2001. There are strict limits to how much liquid they can take on board, as a reaction against the liquid bomb plot of 2006. And at many major airports, they are subject to full body scans, as a reaction to the underwear bomb plot of Christmas 2009. In addition, the DHS maintains several lists of people who are either subjected to additional security or prevented from flying at all.

There are, however, many critics to these measures. They argue that scanning shoes or limiting liquids is only a reactionary step against tactics that future terrorists wouldn't think of using. They argue, further, that DHS's control methods are not refined enough. Mikey Hicks, an 8-year old boy from New Jersey, is included on a "selectee" list maintained by the government that subjects him to a high level of security every time he flies. Even when he was two years old, he was subject to pat downs, a thorough frisking, and even an interview with DHS screeners. There are many other stories about people who, because they have the same name as a suspected terrorist, are subjected to extraordinary delays. Even the late Senator Ted Kennedy found himself on a suspected-persons list! As congressmen William J. Pascrell comments "We can't just throw a bunch of names on these lists and call it security. If we can't get an 8-year-old off the list, the whole list becomes suspect."

Other critics argue that the primary effect of federal control methods is to heighten the sense of paranoia in the skies. In January of 2009, a US Airways flight heading to Louisville, KY, was diverted to Philadelphia because passengers saw a Jewish passenger wearing phylacteries, leather straps that Jews wrap around their heads and arms as part of a prayer ritual. After the underwear bomb plot of 2009, some airlines prohibited passengers from using blankets or toilet facilities for the last hour of the flight.

You have been assigned to a DHS team charged with refining the agency's control methods. How can you maintain security in the nation's airports while also proving passengers with an efficient and smooth experience? Is there a way you can prevent 8-year-old boys from ending up on a suspected terrorist list? From a group with three or four other students and discuss the questions below.

Questions

1. In your opinion, is there a way to you can maintain airport security without sacrificing efficiency? What would such a system look like?
2. How could you incorporate feedforward control (gathering information about performance deficiencies before they occur) into airport security measure?

PRACTICE BEING A MANAGER

In Control or Control Freak?

Control is one of the most controversial aspects of management. Exercising too much control can foster employee resentment and bureaucratic delays. Exercising too little control can raise employee stress and breed organizational chaos. And not only must managers work to achieve a healthy *level* of control but they must also strive to set controls around the *right targets*. The control process is about more than charts and feedback loops—it is about focusing personal and organizational efforts toward desired outcomes. This

exercise will allow you an opportunity to try your hand at developing a control system that is tailored to a particular company and type of work.

Step 1: Get into groups. Your professor will organize your class into teams of three or four students per team. One team will be designated as Company Leadership.

Scenario: Razor's Edge (RE) is a young and growing company that serves the needs of those who engage in extreme sports, adventure/exploration, and guiding services. Some examples of RE's core market include expert/professional mountain climbers, white-water rafting guides, and polar explorers. The founders of RE are the husband and wife team of Dan and Alice Connors, world-famous mountain climbers and explorers. Dan and Alice have both reached the summit of Mount Everest and each is well respected in the rather small and close-knit community of adventurers and explorers. RE is an eclectic company of employees who, like Dan and Alice, share a passion for adventure and extreme sports. The company not only designs and sells its own lines of specialized products such as mountain-climbing shoes and ropes but also develops software designed to support expedition planning, communication and navigation, and simulation and scenario response (i.e., training tools for guides and newer expedition members).

For the first five years of its development, RE did not worry too much about organizational policies or controls. Employees were encouraged to climb, trek, and guide, and attendance issues were addressed on a case-by-case basis. Although officially all employees were given two weeks of paid vacation, many employees were allowed to take up to two months off at half-pay so that they could complete an expedition. Sick days were jokingly referred to as "mountain flu" days, and it was not unusual for the small company to be thinly staffed on Mondays and Fridays. But in the past three years, RE has grown from 25 employees to 85. The company is too big, and the jobs too diverse, for Dan and Alice to deal with each employee request for "expedition time" away from work. And the "mountain flu" has occasionally weakened the company's response to customers. Dan and Alice have also become victims of their own success as they attracted other climbers to join their company—most climbers want time off in the peak climbing seasons. But this also happens to be a peak time for RE orders and service requests.

The company has organized all employees into teams and announced a contest. Each team should come up with an approach for controlling staffing levels to meet or exceed customer expectations for responsiveness, while at the same time preserving RE's tradition as a company of active adventurers and explorers. The company has announced that each member of the employee team that develops the winning solution will receive $2,500 worth of RE gear of their choice.

Step 2: Determine staffing levels. You are a team of workers at RE. Design an approach to controlling daily staffing levels so that RE is able to meet or exceed customer expectations for responsiveness without sacrificing its own identity as a company of adventurers and explorers. Keep in mind that RE is somewhat unusual in that even its accounting staff members (five full-time employees) are experienced adventurers and explorers and are expected to answer customer questions and handle their service needs. You should consider the following elements:

- Paid vacation
- Expedition time
- Sick days and "mountain flu" (Monday/Friday absences)
- Dealing with peak times, and/or most desirable times for vacation or expedition
- Knowing whether customers are pleased with RE's responsiveness to their needs

Step 3: Outline a proposal. Submit a one-page hand-written outline of your proposal to the Company Leadership team.

Step 4: Present the proposal. Each team will briefly present its proposal to the Company Leadership team, and members of the Company Leadership team may ask questions.

Step 5: Vote. The Company Leadership will confer, vote, and announce the winning proposal.

Step 6: Debrief as a class. What tensions confronted you as you worked to design an approach to staffing control for Razor's Edge? What trade-offs and challenges might you anticipate for the company when it implements the winning proposal? In what ways is control related to employee motivation? In what ways is control related to organizational culture? Do you think that the winning RE proposal would be well suited for use by a major outdoor and casual clothing company such as Lands' End? Why or why not?

DEVELOP YOUR CAREER POTENTIAL

Learning from Failure

There is the greatest practical benefit of making a few failures early in life.
—T. H. Huxley

No one wants to fail.[80] Everyone wants to succeed. Nevertheless, some businesspeople believe that failure can have enormous value. At Microsoft, founder Bill Gates encouraged his managers to hire people who have made mistakes in their jobs or careers. A Microsoft vice president says, "We look for somebody who learns, adapts, and is active in the process of learning from mistakes. We always ask, what was a major failure you had? What did you learn from it?" Another reason that failure is viewed positively is that it is often a sign of risk taking and experimentation, both of which are in short supply in many companies. Harvard Business School professor John Kotter says, "I can imagine a group of executives 20 years ago discussing a candidate for a top job and saying, 'This guy had a big failure when he was 32.' Everyone else would say, 'Yep, yep, that's a bad sign.' I can imagine that same group considering a candidate today and saying, 'What worries me about this guy is that he's never failed.'" Jack Matson, who teaches a class at the University of Michigan called Failure 101, says, "If you are doing something innovative, you are going to trip and fumble. So the more failing you do faster, the quicker you can get to success."

One of the most common mistakes that occurs after failure is the *attribution error*. To *attribute* is to assign blame or credit. When we succeed, we take credit for the success by claiming it was due to our strategies, how we behaved, and how hard we worked. When we fail, however, we ignore our strategies, how we behaved, and how hard we worked (or didn't). Instead, when we fail, we assign the blame to other people, or to the circumstances, or to bad luck. In other words, the basic attribution error is that success is our fault but failure isn't. The disappointment we feel when we fail often prevents us from learning from our failures.

This means that attribution errors disrupt the control process. The three basic steps of control are to set goals and performance standards, to compare actual performance against the performance standards, and to identify and correct performance deviations. When we put all of the blame on external forces rather than our own actions, we stop ourselves from identifying and correcting performance deviations.

Furthermore, by not learning from our mistakes, we make it even more likely that we will fail again. Your task in this exercise is to begin the process of learning from failure. This is not an easy thing to do. When *Fortune* magazine writer Patricia Sellers wrote an article called "So You Fail," she found that most of the people she contacted were reluctant to talk about their failures. She wrote:

Compiling this story required months of pleading and letter writing to dozens of people who failed and came back. "If it weren't for the 'F' word, I'd talk," lamented one senior executive who got fired twice, reformed his know-it-all management style, and considered bragging about his current hot streak. Others cringed at hearing the word "failure" in the same breath as "your career."

Questions

1. Identify and describe a point in your life when you failed. Don't write about simple or silly mistakes. The difference between a failure and a mistake is how bad you felt afterwards. A real failure still makes you cringe when you think about it years later. What was the situation? What were your goals? And how did it turn out?
2. Describe your initial reaction to the failure. Were you shocked, surprised, angry, or depressed? Initially, who or what did you blame for the failure? Explain.
3. One purpose of control is to identify and correct performance deviations. With that in mind, describe three mistakes that you made that contributed to your failure. Now that you've had time to think about it, what could you have done differently to prevent these mistakes? Finally, summarize what you learned from your mistakes that will increase your chances of success the next time around.

END NOTES

[1] I. Brat, "Caterpillar Gets Bugs Out of Old Equipment; Growing Re-manufacturing Division Is Central to Earnings-Stabilization Plan," *The Wall Street Journal*, July 5, 2006, A16; D. Cameron, "Corporate News: Caterpillar Wields Ax on Bonuses—Executive Compensation to Fall as Much as 50%; Other Cutbacks Are Set," *The Wall Street Journal*, December 23, 2008, B3; G. Colvin, "Caterpillar is Absolutely Crushing It," *Fortune*, May 23, 2011, 136–144; S. Oster, "Caterpillar, China Are to Promote Remanufacturing," *The Wall Street Journal*, September 15, 2006, A10; and T. Van Hampton, "Down to Earth," *Engineering News-Record*, March 21, 2011, 26–32.

[2] R. Leifer & P. K. Mills, "An Information Processing Approach for Deciding upon Control Strategies and Reducing Control Loss in Emerging Organizations," *Journal of Management* 22 (1996): 113–137.

[3] S. Mayerowitz, "Casinos Always Win, Even When Robbed," ABC News, January 4, 2011, accessed June 13, 2011, from http://abcnews.go.com/m/story?id=12531632.

[4] R. Grais-Targow, "Big Salmon Exporter Fights Virus—Chile's Share of Global Output Expected to Fall; Pickup Unlikely Until 2011," *The Wall Street Journal*, July 7, 2009, B6.

[5] Julie Jargon, "At Starbucks, Baristas Told No More Than Two Drinks," *The Wall Street Journal*, October 13, 2010, accessed April 5, 2011, from http://online.wsj.com/article/SB10001424052748704164004575548403514060736.html.

[6] P. Bryan & P. Pane, "Evaluating Fire Service Delivery," *Fire Engineering*, April 2008, 207–210.

[7] A. Ricadela, "Intuit Taps Hewlett-Packard and Google for Advice," *Businessweek*, October 1, 2008, 15.

[8] Michael Mecham & Guy Norris, "Boeing Plans 8.5 Months of 787 Testing," *Aviation Week*, December 18, 2009, accessed August 1, 2010, from www.aviationweek.com/aw/generic/story_channel.jsp?channel=comm&id=news/W787PLAN121809.xml.

[9] R. Yu, "Hotel Managers Monitor Online Critiques to Improve Service," *USA Today*, March 23, 2010, accessed June 13, 2011, from www.usatoday.com/travel/hotels/2010-03-23-businesstravel23_ST_N.htm.

[10] N. Wiener, *Cybernetics; Or Control and Communication in the Animal and the Machine* (New York: Wiley, 1948).

[11] Duane Stanford, "Sustainability Meets the Profit Motive," *Bloomberg Businessweek*, April 4–10, 2011, 25–26.

[12] M. Rohde, "Squirrelly Behavior: Critters Shock the System," *Daily Reporter*, January 4, 2011, accessed June 20, 2011, from http://dailyreporter.com/2011/01/04/squirrely-behavior-critters-shock-the-system/ Squirrelly behavior: Critters shock the system.

[13] Peter Lyon, "First Drive: 2011 Nissan Leaf Japanese Spec," *MotorTrend*, June 28, 2010, accessed July 16, 2010, from www.motortrend.com/roadtests/alternative/1006_2011_nissan_leaf_japanese_spec_drive/index.html.

[14] Paul Thurrott, "What You Need to Know About Windows 7 Beta 1," *Windows IT Pro Magazine*, February 1, 2009, 7.

[15] Leifer & Mills, "An Information Processing Approach."

[16] Alicia Mundy, "Flies, Birds, Mice Found at Egg Plant," *The Wall Street Journal*, August 31, 2010, accessed April 5, 2011, from http://online.wsj.com/article/SB10001424052748703369704575461881721525848.html; and Elizabeth Weise, "Hillandale Farms Can Sell Eggs Again after Salmonella Recall," *USA Today*, October 19, 2010, accessed April 5, 2011, from www.usatoday.com/yourlife/food/safety/2010-10-18-eggs-salmonella_N.htm.

[17] Cassell Bryon-Low, "Pound for Pound, a Veggie Takes on the EU—East London's Ms. Devers Snubs the Metric System; Selling by the Bowl Is Alleged," *The Wall Street Journal*, January 22, 2008, A1.

[18] Daily Mail Reporter, "'Metric Martyr' Case Dropped against 64-Year-Old Fruit and Veg Seller," *Mail Online*, January 13, 2009, accessed August 22, 2009, from www.dailymail.co.uk/news/article-1113242/Metric-Martyr-case-dropped-64-year-old-fruit-veg-seller.html.

[19] Marc Gunther, "3M's Innovation Revival," *Fortune*, September 27, 2010, 73–76.

[20] E. Smith, "Marsh Gets Clipped by Online Coupon Deal," *Indianapolis Star*, August 5, 2009, A1.

[21] Erik Holm, "Progressive to Offer Data-Driven Rates," *The Wall Street Journal*, March 21, 2011, accessed April 5, 2011, from http://online.wsj.com/article/SB10001424052748704433904576212731238464702.html.

[22] Andrea Coombes, "Bully for You: Hair-Raising Bad-Boss Stories, and Tips on How to Cope," MarketWatch, July 17, 2006, accessed July 30, 2009, from wwws.workplacebullying.org/press/mktw071706.html.

[23] S. Shellenbarger, "Is the Awful Behavior of Some Bad Bosses Rooted in Their Past?" *The Wall Street Journal*, May 17, 2000, B1.

[24] M. Weber, *The Protestant Ethic and the Spirit of Capitalism* (New York: Scribner's, 1958).

[25] L. Criner, "Politicians Come and Go, Bureaucracies Stay and Grow," *Washington Times*, March 11, 1996, 33.

[26] Eric Frazier, "Facebook Post Costs Waitress her Job," *Charlotte Observer*, May 17, 2010, accessed April 5, 2011, from www.charlotteobserver.com/2010/05/17/1440447/facebook-post-costs-waitress-her.html.

[27] David Hunt, "JEA Keeping a Closer Watch on Employees," Jacksonville.com/*The Florida Times-Union*, March 4, 2010, accessed June 17, 2011, from http://jacksonville.com/news/metro/2010-03-04/story/jea_keeping_a_closer_watch_on_employees.

[28] "Some Details on Bedard's Contract Incentives," *Seattle Post Intelligencer*,

February 9, 2010, accessed June 19, 2011, from http://blog.seattlepi.com/baseball/archives/193984.asp.

[29]Darren Dahl, "Breaking 3 Workplace Taboos," *Inc.*, March 1, 2011, accessed April 5, 2011, from www.inc.com/magazine/20110301/breaking-3-workplace-taboos.html; and Darren Dahl, "A Radical Take on the Virtual Company," *Inc.*, March 1, 2011, accessed April 5, 2011, from www.inc.com/magazine/20110301/philip-rosedale-on-freelancing-business-processes.html?nav=related.

[30]R. Branson, "Motivated Employees are your Greatest Asset," *The West Australian*, May 26, 2011, 38.

[31]M. Boyle, "Expensing It: Guilty As Charged—When Times Are Tough, Employees Become Even More Devoted to Mastering the Art of Self-Perking," *Fortune*, July 9, 2001, 179; and R. Grugal, "Be Honest and Dependable: Integrity—The Must-Have," *Investor's Business Daily*, April 11, 2003, A03.

[32]Vickie Elmer, "How Storytelling Spurs Success," *Fortune*, December 3, 2010, accessed April 5, 2011, from http://management.fortune.cnn.com/2010/12/03/how-storytelling-spurs-success/.

[33]J. R. Barker, "Tightening the Iron Cage: Concertive Control in Self-Managing Teams," *Administrative Science Quarterly* 38 (1993): 408–437.

[34]N. Byrnes, "The Art of Motivation," *Businessweek*, May 1, 2006, 56–62.

[35]Ibid.

[36]Barker, "Tightening the Iron Cage."

[37]C. Manz & H. Sims, "Leading Workers to Lead Themselves: The External Leadership of Self-Managed Work Teams," *Administrative Science Quarterly* 32 (1987): 106–128.

[38]J. Slocum & H. A. Sims, Typology for Integrating Technology, Organization and Job Design," *Human Relations* 33 (1980): 193–212.

[39]C. C. Manz & H. P. Sims, Jr., "Self-Management as a Substitute for Leadership: A Social Learning Perspective," *Academy of Management Review* 5 (1980): 361–367.

[40]C. Manz & C. Neck, *Mastering Self-Leadership*, 3rd ed. (Upper Saddle River, NJ: Pearson, Prentice Hall, 2004).

[41]T. Martin, "Choice Advice from Meat Cutters," *The Wall Street Journal*, August 12, 2009, D1.

[42]R. S. Kaplan & D. P. Norton, "Using the Balanced Scorecard as a Strategic Management System," *Harvard Business Review* (January–February 1996): 75–85; and R. S. Kaplan & D. P. Norton, "The Balanced Scorecard: Measures That Drive Performance," *Harvard Business Review* (January–February 1992): 71–79.

[43]J. Meliones, "Saving Money, Saving Lives," *Harvard Business Review* (November–December 2000): 57–65.

[44]John Murphy, "Toyota Boss Vows to Change Priorities," *The Wall Street Journal*, June 26, 2009, B2.

[45]S. L. Fawcett, "Fear of Accounts: Improving Managers' Competence and Confidence through Simulation Exercises," *Journal of European Industrial Training* (February 1996): 17.

[46]J. Cole, "New Boeing CFO's Assignment: Signal a Turnaround Quickly," *The Wall Street Journal*, January 26, 1999, B1.

[47]M. H. Stocks & A. Harrell, "The Impact of an Increase in Accounting Information Level on the Judgment Quality of Individuals and Groups," *Accounting, Organizations & Society* (October–November 1995): 685–700.

[48]B. Morris, "Roberto Goizueta and Jack Welch: The Wealth Builders," *Fortune*, December 11, 1995, 80–94.

[49]G. Colvin, "America's Best & Worst Wealth Creators: The Real Champions Aren't Always Who You Think. Here's an Eye-Opening Look at Which Companies Produce and Destroy the Most Money for Investors—Plus a New Tool for Spotting Future Winners," *Fortune*, December 18, 2000, 207.

[50]"About Herman Miller: Operational Excellence," Herman Miller, accessed June 20, 2011, from www.hermanmiller.com/About-Us/About-Herman-Miller/Operational-Excellence.

[51]M. Schurman, "A Herman Miller Primer," Herman Miller, accessed June 20, 2011, from www.hermanmiller.com/MarketFacingTech/hmc/about_us/News_Events_Media/Corporate_Backgrounder.pdf.

[52]E. Varon, "Implementation Is Not for the Meek," *CIO*, November 15, 2002, accessed September 5, 2008, from www.cio.com.au/article/176603/implementation_meek/.

[53]"EVA Momentum Ranking for S&P 500," EVA Dimensions, December 15, 2010, accessed June 20, 2011, from http://evadimensions.com/wp-content/rankings/ForbesEVAMomentumRank12142010_website.pdf; and S. Cendrowski, "Buying Apple Stock? Think Twice," CNNMoney, September 28, 2010, accessed June 20, 2011, from http://money.cnn.com/2010/09/09/pf/apple_stock.fortune/index.htm.

[54]"Welcome Complaints," Office of Consumer and Business Affairs, Government of South Australia, accessed June 20, 2005, from www.ocba.sa.gov.au/businessadvice/complaints/03_welcome.html.

[55]N. Brodsky & B. Burlingham, *The Knack: How Street-Smart Entrepreneurs Learn to Handle Whatever Comes Up* (New York: Portfolio Hardcover, 2008).

[56]C. B. Furlong, "12 Rules for Customer Retention," *Bank Marketing* 5 (January 1993): 14.

[57]Customer retention graphs, accessed August 1, 2009, from www.voxinc.com/customer-experience-graphs/impact-customer-retention.htm.

[58]M. Raphel, "Vanished Customers Are Valuable Customers," *Art Business News*, June 2002, 46.

[59]N. Brodsky & B. Burlingham, The Knack: How Street-Smart Entrepreneurs Learn to Handle Whatever Comes Up (New York: Portfolio Hardcover, 2008).

[60]C. A. Reeves & D. A. Bednar, "Defining Quality: Alternatives and Implications," *Academy of Management Review* 19 (1994): 419–445.

[61]Ben Mutzabaugh, "Virgin America Named USA's Top Airline; Singapore Tops Global Ratings," *USA Today*, October 15, 2010, accessed April 4, 2011, from http://travel.usatoday.com/flights/post/2010/10/virgin-america-singapore-top-airline-/127567/1.

[62]S. Holmes, "Creature Comforts at 30,000 Feet," *Businessweek*, December 18, 2006, 138.

[63]Michael Harley "Review: 2011 Hyundai Sonata a Sweet Addition to Mid-Size Sedan Segment," Autoblog.com., February 22, 2010, accessed June 19, 2011, from www.autoblog.com/2010/02/22/2011-hyundai-sonata-review/.

[64]D. R. May & B. L. Flannery, "Cutting Waste with Employee Involvement Teams," *Business Horizons*, September–October 1995, 28–38.

[65]Heather Clancy, "In Green Packaging, Little Things Mean a Lot," ZDNet, August 25, 2010, accessed April 5, 2011, from http://www.zdnet.com/blog/green/in-green-packaging-little-things-mean-a-lot/13757; and Leon Kaye, "Dell Reduced Packaging by 18 Million Pounds Since 2008," Triple Pundit, August 26, 2010, accessed April 5, 2011, from www.triplepundit.com/2010/08/dell-reduced-packaging-by-18-million-pounds-since-2008/.

[66]John W. Miller, "Maersk Orders 10 Huge Ships from Daewoo," *The Wall Street Journal*, February 22, 2011, accessed April 5, 2011, from http://online.wsj.com/article/SB10001424052748704476604576157871902178028.html.

[67]Shelley Mika, "Telematics Sensor-Equipped Trucks Help UPS Control Costs," *Automotive Fleet*, July 2010, accessed April 5, 2011, from www.automotive-fleet.com/Channel/GPS-Telematics/Article/Story/2010/07/GREEN-FLEET-Telematics-Sensor-Equipped-Trucks-Help-UPS-Control-Costs.aspx.

[68]"Sustainability in Depth: Pollution Prevention Pays (3P)," 3M, accessed April 13, 2009, from http://solutions9.3m.com/3MContentRetrievalAPI/BlobServlet?locale=en_US&lmd=1240969645000&assetId=11805816741

44&assetType=MMM_Image&blobAttribute=ImageFile; and M. Warner, "Plastic Potion No. 9," *Fast Company*, September 2008, 88.

[69]Jim Motavalli, "See How Printer Cartridges Are Recycled," The Daily Green, April 17, 2010, accessed June 29, 2010, from www.thedailygreen.com/living-green/blogs/cars-transportation/recycle-printer-cartridges-460410.

[70]Peter Valdes-Dapena, "GM Turning BP Oil Spill Booms into Volt Parts," CNNMoney, December 20, 2010, accessed April 5, 2011, from http://money.cnn.com/2010/12/17/autos/gm_volt_recycling/index.htm.

[71]"Herman Miller Earns Design for Recycling Award," GreenerDesign, May 12, 2009, accessed July 23, 2010, from www.greenbiz.com/news/2009/05/12/herman-miller-earns-design-recycling-award.

[72]M. Conlin & P. Raeburn, "Industrial Evolution: Bill McDonough Has the Wild Idea He Can Eliminate Waste. Surprise! Business Is Listening," *Businessweek*, April 8, 2002, 70.

[73]B. Byrne, "EU Says Makers Must Destroy Their Own Brand End-of-Life Cars," *Irish Times*, April 23, 2003, 52.

[74]Jennifer L. Schenker. "Cows to Kilowatts: A Bounty from Waste," *Businessweek*, December 3, 2008, accessed August 1, 2009, from www.businessweek.com/globalbiz/content/dec2008/gb2008123_181278.htm.

[75]"The End of the Road: Schools and Computer Recycling," Intel, accessed September 5, 2008, from www.intel.com/education/recycling_computers/recycling.htm.

[76]Mickey Meece, "Giving Those Old Gadgets a Proper Green Burial," *The New York Times*, January 6, 2011, accessed March 5, 2011, from www.nytimes.com/2011/01/06/technology/personaltech/06basics.html?ref=recyclingofwastematerials.

[77]M. Tuckey, N. Brewer, & P. Williamson, "The Influence of Motives and Goal Orientation on Feedback Seeking," *Journal of Occupational and Organizational Psychology* 75, no. 2 (2002): 195.

[78]Paul Davidson, "Watching over Freelancers," *USA Today*, September 13, 2010, accessed March 5, 2011, from www.usatoday.com/printedition/money/20100913/odesk13_st.art.htm.

[79]Lizette Alvarez, "Meet Mikey, 8: U.S. Has Him on Watch List," *The New York Times*, January 14, 2010, accessed April 5, 2011, from www.nytimes.com/2010/01/14/nyregion/14watchlist.html; and Daniel Trotta, "Religious Item Led to False Bomb Scare on US Plane," January 21, 2010, accessed April 5, 2011, from www.reuters.com/article/idUSN2122260520100121.

[80]S. Caulkin, "If You Want to Stay a Winner, Learn from Your Mistakes," *The Observer*, March 3, 1996, 7; J. Hyatt, "Failure 101," *Inc.*, January 1989, 18; B. McMenamin, "The Virtue of Making Mistakes," *Forbes*, May 9, 1994, 192–194; P. Sellers, "So You Fail," *Fortune*, May 1, 1995, 48–66; P. Sellers, "Where Failures Get Fixed," *Fortune*, May 1, 1995, 64; and B. Weiner, I. Freize, A. Kukla, L. Reed, S. Rest, & R. M. Rosenbaum, "Perceiving the Causes of Success and Failure," in E. Jones, D. Kanouse, H. Kelley, R. Nesbitt, S. Valins, & B. Weiner, eds., Attribution: Perceiving the Causes of Behavior (Morristown, NJ: General Learning Press, 1971), 45–61.

BIZ FLIX

Friday Night Lights

In the small town of Odessa, Texas, everyone lives for Friday nights when the high school football team, the Permian Panthers, takes the field. The town is proud of their Panthers, led by quarterback Mike Winchell (Lucas Black) and superstar tailback Boobie Miles (Derek Luke), and they're used to winning. They expect a state championship, and nothing less. When Boobie suffers a career-ending injury in the first game of the season, the team isn't sure they can win without him. But Coach Gary Gaines (Billy Bob Thornton) isn't ready to give up yet. In this clip from the film, Coach Gaines gathers the team around during the half-time break to talk about what success really means and how he wants them to achieve it.

© GreenLight

What to Watch for and Ask Yourself

1. The control process begins when managers set goals and create standards. In this scene, what does Coach Gaines state that he expects from the members of his team?

2. Based on the topics discussed in this chapter, what similarities could you draw between what a coach and the manager of a company must do to ensure success for their team?

3. Which method of control do you think most football coaches exert over their teams: bureaucratic, objective, normative, or concertive? Why?

MANAGEMENT WORKPLACE

Barcelona Restaurant Group

According to Andy Pforzheimer, food is only 50 percent of the experience at his restaurants. The rest is comprised of intangibles like ambience and conversation with the staff. To ensure consistent quality across the board, Barcelona uses five "feedback loops" that gauge restaurant performance: a "secret shopper" program, credit card rewards for customers who complete surveys, customer comment cards, emails and surveillance cameras. In addition these loops, the owners and general managers walk the floor constantly to advise wait staff and gather feedback from customers. There's plenty at stake if Barcelona fails to control its performance. Pforzheimer notes that disappointing one's customers is the quickest way to kill a business. However, failure is about more than losing money: it's also about losing face.

© Cengage Learning

What to Watch for and Ask Yourself

1. How do managers at Barcelona control the company's financial performance?

2. What is the "balanced scorecard" approach to measuring corporate performance, and in what ways does Barcelona utilize this approach?

3. Describe the feedback control model and describe an instance where Barcelona followed this process to improve its performance.

CHAPTER 17

Managing Information
Information

Learning Outcomes

1. Explain the strategic importance of information.

2. Describe the characteristics of useful information (i.e., its value and costs).

3. Explain the basics of capturing, processing, and protecting information.

4. Describe how companies can access and share information and knowledge.

what would **you do?**

Delta Air Lines Headquarters, Atlanta, Georgia[1]

All airlines and airports lose bags. After all, they must handle thousands of bags per day, sort through the bags on each plane like a 500-piece puzzle dumped on the table from a just-opened box, and then rush them to the right connecting planes or baggage carousels. The challenging logistics, however, don't make up for the impact of delays on passengers. There's the rabbi flying to Israel, whose lost bag is returned waterlogged, with his belongings covered in black mold. Or the administrative assistant headed to Buffalo, New York, for her cousin's wedding, whose lost luggage contained her bridesmaid dress and her boyfriend's tuxedo. She said, "I was in utter despair. I thought: 'How can I be in this wedding?' You're frustrated, you want to cry, and you're pissed off." Finally, there's the Canadian singer who, on finding his $3,500 guitar damaged, sought and was refused payment by the airline. So he exacted his revenge by making a video and posting it on YouTube, where it has been seen 3.5 million times.

In all, 31 million bags are delivered late worldwide each year, or about 1.4 percent. In the United States, 7 people per 1,000 passengers, or roughly 1 per plane, don't get their luggage on time, and they file 7.5 million mishandled baggage reports a year. Over the last decade, the three largest airlines, American, United, and—yes—**Delta Airlines**, are the worst offenders. Several key statistics stand out. First, Delta is 30 percent worse compared to the best airlines. Second, 28 percent more bags are delayed today compared to a decade ago. No wonder passengers are frustrated, especially when airlines charge a $25 handling fee for the first checked bag and $35 for the second. Nothing like paying extra to have the airline lose your bags, especially when Delta brings in $952 million a year in bag fees! Third, it costs $15 to transport each bag. Nine dollars is for labor, as ten people touch each bag, between check-in and the baggage carousel. U.S. Airways spends $250 million a year on labor for bags alone, or 11 percent of payroll. Four dollars is for sorting systems such as carousels, conveyors, carts, and tractors. Finally, fuel accounts for the remaining $2. And depending on oil prices, that's sometimes lower, but in the last three to five years, it has generally been higher. Fourth, besides the customer dissatisfaction and ill will created, delayed luggage costs airlines $90 to $100 per bag, or $3 billion to $4 billion a year.

Passengers are beginning to realize that bag fees bring in much more than the cost to deliver bags, so they have every right to expect Delta to do a better job delivering bags. With advances in technology, clearly there have to be ways to use information technology to track bags and sharply decrease the number of delayed bags. If Amazon

< **"what's new" companies**

study tips ⊗

Imagine you are the professor, and make up your own test for Chapter 17.

What are the main topics and key concepts that students should know? If you work with a study group, exchange practice tests. Work them individually, then "grade" them collectively. This way you can discuss trouble spots and answer each other's questions.

can send emails and texts notifying customers when their orders leave the warehouse, arrive at their local airports, and are delivered to their homes, then why can't Delta do the same thing with luggage that's supposed to never leave the airport, except in passengers' hands? Surely there are ways to do this. What information technology changes would have to be made at the counter; behind the counter as bags are sorted and routed to planes; and then on the tarmac, where bags are sorted one last time as they are put on or taken off planes? Grocery stores and Home Depot have been using self-checkout lanes for several years. What kind of information technology would be required to use self-tagging, where passengers put destination tags on their own bags, and would that help the baggage problem or make it worse? Finally, Delta baggage handlers were caught stealing cameras, laptops, iPods, and jewelry from passengers' bags. If we're going to use technology to get more bags delivered on time, how can we also use technology to deter theft among our own employees?

If you were in charge at Delta Airlines, what would you do?

A generation ago, computer hardware and software had little to do with managing business information. Rather than storing information on hard drives, managers stored it in filing cabinets. Instead of uploading daily sales and inventory levels by satellite to corporate headquarters, they mailed hard-copy summaries to headquarters at the end of each month. Instead of word processing, reports were typed on an electric typewriter. Instead of spreadsheets, calculations were made on adding machines. Managers communicated by sticky notes, not email. Phone messages were written down by assistants and coworkers, not forwarded in your email as a sound file with the message converted to text. Workers did not use desktop or laptop computers as a daily tool to get work done. Instead, they scheduled limited access time to run batch jobs on the mainframe computer (and prayed that the batch job computer code they wrote would work).

Today, a generation later, computer hardware and software are an integral part of managing business information. This is due mainly to something called **Moore's law**. Gordon Moore is one of the founders of Intel Corporation, which makes 75 percent of the integrated processors used in personal computers. In 1965, Moore predicted that computer-processing power would double and that its cost would drop by 50 percent every two years.[2] As Exhibit 17.1 shows, Moore was right. Computer power, as measured by the number of transistors per computer chip, *has* more than doubled every few years. Consequently, the computer sitting in your lap or on your desk is not only smaller but also much cheaper and more powerful than the large mainframe computers used by *Fortune* 500 companies 15 years ago. In fact, if car manufacturers had achieved the same power increases and cost decreases attained by computer manufacturers, a fully outfitted Lexus or Mercedes sedan would cost less than $1,000!

We begin this chapter by explaining why information matters. In particular, you will learn the value of strategic information to companies, as well as the cost and characteristics of good information. Next, you will investigate how companies capture, process, and protect information. Finally, you'll learn how information is accessed and shared with those both inside and outside the company and how knowledge and expertise (not just information or data) are shared too.

Exhibit 17.1 Microprocessor Transistor Counts 1971–2011 and Moore's Law

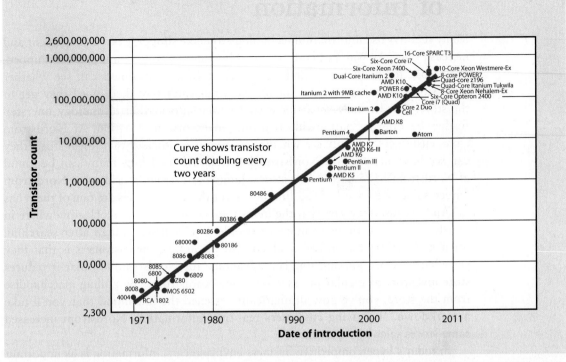

Source: W. G.Simon, "Microprocessor Transistor Count and Moore's Law - 2011," Wikipedia, May 13, 2011, accessed June 25, 2011, from http:// en.wikipedia.org/wiki/File: Transistor_Count_and_Moore%27s_Law_-_2011.svg.

Why Information Matters

Raw data are facts and figures. For example, 11, $452, 32, and 26,100 are some data that I used the day I wrote this section of the chapter. However, facts and figures aren't particularly useful unless they have meaning. For example, you probably can't guess what these four pieces of raw data represent, can you? If you can't, these data are useless. That's why researchers make the distinction between raw data and information. Whereas raw data consist of facts and figures, **information** is useful data that can influence someone's choices and behavior. One way to think about the difference between data and information is that information has context.

So what did those four pieces of data mean to me? Well, 11 stands for Channel 11, the local CBS affiliate on which I watched part of the men's PGA golf tournament; $452 is how much it would cost me to rent a minivan for a week if I go skiing over spring break; 32 is for the 32-gigabyte storage card that I want to add to my digital camera (prices are low, so I'll probably buy it); and 26,100 miles means that it's time to get the oil changed in my car.

> ## After reading the next two sections, you should be able to
>
> 1. *Explain the strategic importance of information.*
> 2. *Describe the characteristics of useful information (i.e., its value and costs).*

Moore's law the prediction that about every two years, computer processing power would double and its cost would drop by 50 percent.

raw data facts and figures.

information useful data that can influence people's choices and behavior.

1 Strategic Importance of Information

Many retailers use information technology to make shopping more convenient and increase sales. At Walmart.com, you can buy an item online and have it shipped, at no cost, for pickup at your local store. At Target, customers can see whether local stores carry items from the website, but can't buy them until they get to the store. Nordstrom's department stores take information technology one step further by offering nationwide real-time inventory information. At Nordstrom .com, customers not only see whether an item is in stock at their local store, they can see how many are in Nordstrom's warehouses and how many can be found at Nordstrom's 115 nationwide stores. Jamie Nordstrom, president of Nordstrom Direct, said, "We have 115 full-line stores out there — chances are one of them has it." And because they saw that the items they wanted were in stock somewhere in Nordstrom stores, the percentage of people who bought an item after searching for it at Nordstrom.com has doubled. The advantage for customers is that they get what they are looking for. The advantage for Nordstrom's is that it reduces store inventory at regular prices. Said Jamie Nordstrom, "By pulling merchandise from the store, you've now dramatically lessened the likelihood that you'll take a markdown." By giving customers real-time information, Nordstrom increased same-stores sales by 8 percent.[3]

In today's hypercompetitive business environments, information is as important as capital (i.e., money) for business success, whether it's about product inventory, pricing, or costs. It takes money to get businesses started, but businesses can't survive and grow without the right information. Information has strategic importance for organizations because it can be used to **1.1. obtain first-mover advantage** and **1.2. sustain competitive advantage once it has been created**.

first-mover advantage the strategic advantage that companies earn by being the first to use new information technology to substantially lower costs or to make a product or service different from that of competitors.

"what's new" companies >

© AVAVA/Shutterstock.com

1.1 First-Mover Advantage

First-mover advantage is the strategic advantage that companies earn by being the first in an industry to use new information technology to substantially lower costs or to differentiate a product or service from that of competitors. Texas-based **DG Fastchannel** revolutionized TV marketing when it built its own satellite and web-based distribution network. Whereas other companies were sending commercials to TV stations on videotapes, DG Fastchannel used its digital network to make commercials available just a few hours after it produced them. The speed of the network also allows the company to adjust commercials based on near-real-time feedback from consumers. When Universal Pictures began advertising *Despicable Me*, an animated movie about a criminal mastermind, DG Fastchannel's research showed that the movie trailer was not polling well among women over the age of 26. Literally overnight, the trailer was remixed to emphasize the heart-warming aspects of the movie, which went on to earn a "female-friendly" reputation and $200 million at the box office. DG Fastchannel has been growing at an average of 43 percent over the last three years and controls almost 65 percent of the ad delivery market in the United States.

First-mover advantages like those established by DG Fastchannel can be sizable.[4] On average, first movers earn a 30 percent market share compared to 19 percent for the companies that follow.[5] Likewise, over 70 percent of market leaders started as first movers.[6]

1.2 Sustaining Competitive Advantage

As described, companies that use information technology to establish first-mover advantage usually have higher market shares and profits. According to the resource-based view of information technology shown in Exhibit 17.2, companies need to address three critical questions in order to sustain a competitive advantage through information technology. First, does the information technology create value for the firm by lowering costs or providing a better product or service? If an information technology doesn't add value, then investing in it would put the firm at a competitive disadvantage to companies that choose information technologies that do add value.

Second, is the information technology the same or different across competing firms? If all the firms have access to the same information technology and use it in the same way, then no firm has an advantage over another (i.e., there is competitive parity). For example, a number of hotels and resorts, such as Marriott, now use social media to improve customer service. Staff members search for any mention of their hotel

Exhibit 17.2 Using Information Technology to Sustain a Competitive Advantage

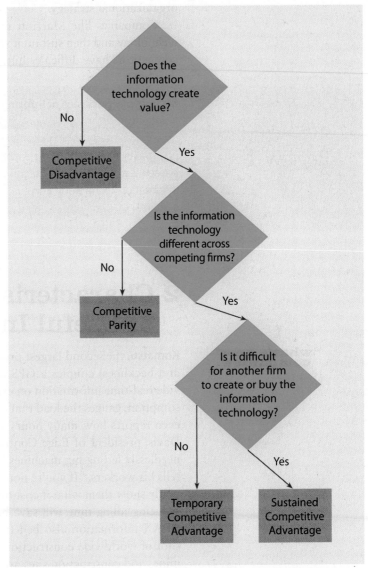

Source: Adapted from F. J. Mata, W. L. Fuerst, & J. B. Barney, "Information Technology and Sustained Competitive Advantage: A Resource-Based Analysis," *MIS Quarterly* 19, no. 4, December 1995, 487–505. © 1995, Regents of the University of Minnesota. Reprinted by permission.

on Twitter, Facebook, blogs, or websites like TripAdvisor, and other sites. When they find a complaint, they offer an immediate apology and, more often than not, perks like room upgrades and free meals to make up for the problem. When Paul Horan tweeted that his room at the Orlando Marriott World Center was "the crappiest room in the hotel," a member of the hotel's staff saw the tweet, immediately sent an apology note, and upgraded his room. By paying attention to social media, tech-savvy hotels have found a way to get near-instantaneous feedback from customers and quickly resolve problems.[7] But because this technology is available to all companies, it's unlikely that the technology will lead to a sustained competitive advantage.

Third, is it difficult for another company to create or buy the information technology used by the firm? If so, then the firm has established a sustainable competitive advantage over competitors through information technology. If not, then the competitive advantage is just temporary, and competitors should eventually be able to

duplicate the advantages the leading firm has gained from information technology. For more about sustainable competitive advantage and its sources, see Chapter 6 on organizational strategy.

Companies like Marriott that achieve first-mover advantage with information technology and then sustain it with continued investment create a moving target that competitors have difficulty hitting.

Review 1

Strategic Importance of Information The first company to use new information technology to substantially lower costs or differentiate products or services often gains first-mover advantage, which can lead to higher profits and larger market share. Creating a first-mover advantage can be difficult, expensive, and risky. According to the resource-based view of information technology, sustainable competitive advantage occurs when information technology adds value, is different across firms, and is difficult to create or acquire.

2 Characteristics and Costs of Useful Information

"what's new"
companies >

Komatsu, the second largest producer of heavy machinery (bulldozers, dump trucks, and backhoes) couples a GPS device and a web application, KOMTRAX, to provide real-time information on every machine it sells. KOMTRAX measures fuel consumption, gauges the load that each machine bears, provides maintenance alerts and even reports how many hours a machine was working, idling, or in transport. Jeff Davis, president of Edge Contracting Inc., keeps track of whether his workers are needlessly letting big machines idle in place too long, thus wasting fuel. Davis, who tells his workers, "If you're not using the machine, turn it off," says, "When I can actually show them what it cost the company, it starts to sink in." Davis estimates that reducing idling time will save between $50,000 and $100,000 a year.[8] The KOMTRAX information also benefits Komatsu by providing a detailed real-time snapshot of worldwide construction activity. As spokeswoman Natsuko Usami says, "If mines and construction sites are operating the equipment full-time, we know there's a chance that market demand will go up, and we can order our factories to ramp up production."[9]

As Kotmasu's KOMTRAX system demonstrates, information is useful when it is **2.1 accurate, 2.2 complete, 2.3 relevant,** and **2.4 timely**. However, there can be significant **2.5 acquisition, 2.6 processing, 2.7 storage, 2.8 retrieval,** and **2.9 communication costs associated with useful information.**

2.1 Accurate Information

Information is useful when it is accurate. Before relying on information to make decisions, you must know that the information is correct. But what if it isn't? For

"what's new"
companies >

example, in Japan, **7-Eleven** used to rely on centralized sales data to determine the kind and quantity of products that its 13,000 stores should stock on their shelves. The problem with that approach, however, is that a 7-Eleven in downtown Tokyo next to skyscrapers filled with office workers doesn't sell the same kind and number of products as a 7-Eleven in suburban Sapporo, which is one-tenth the size of Tokyo. So, to provide more accurate sales information to each store,

7-Eleven Japan is giving its 200,000 sales clerks detailed information about what sells in *their* stores. Based on those data, each clerk makes educated hypotheses each morning about what will sell that day and by the end of the day receives feedback on what actually sold. Twice a week, data analysts work with the clerks at each store to help improve their sales predictions. Thanks to more accurate information, Japan's 13,000 7-Eleven stores are now filled with the products that their local customers desire.[10]

2.2 Complete Information

Information is useful when it is complete. Incomplete or missing information makes it difficult to recognize problems and identify potential solutions. For example, doctors hate learning new technology, but they hate inaccurate and incomplete information even more. So, the University of Pittsburgh Medical Center (UPMC) set up a computerized medical system, eRecords, to replace paper medical charts and test results that were easily lost or misplaced and therefore not available when doctors and nurses needed them. eRecords automatically tracks vital signs, such as pulse, blood pressure, and respirations, and gives doctors and nurses immediate computerized bedside access to X-rays, medical test results, and patients' prescriptions. Dr. Ibrahim Ghobrial, UPMC's director of ambulatory services, says, "The applications within eRecord also enable the physician to complete clinical documentation, transcription, family histories, procedure histories, and a variety of other tasks online . . . online documentation is organized in clear, concise formats, which eliminates the task of interpreting handwritten notes sometimes placed in the margins of paper records or scattered throughout other parts of the paper forms."[11]

2.3 Relevant Information

You can have accurate, complete information, but it's not very useful if it doesn't pertain to the problems you're facing. Imagine that an earthquake destroys a large city in Japan or that a hurricane destroys cities and towns in a five-state area in the southeastern part of the United States. Usually when disaster strikes, the power goes out, and the authorities, first responders, and people affected lose access to what they need most, relevant information. Microsoft's Claire Bonilla is a senior director of field operations who coordinates Microsoft's resources to help people affected by disasters around the world (this is part of Microsoft's corporate social responsibility efforts). Bonilla says, "The core to the effectiveness of any disaster response is the ability to share information and coordinate the effort between the many organizations involved. Software can play a huge role in doing that. Whenever we hear about a disaster, the first step is to establish a connection with the lead response organization locally. Then we help with real-time communication and use mapping software to provide partners with situational awareness so that, for example, relief agencies can see the location of a shelter in need of medical supplies. We also give data-sharing capability to first responders and government agencies so they can share relevant information with outside organizations without compromising security."[12] For example, when an earthquake destroyed much of Wenchuan, China, and killed nearly 70,000 people, with another 18,000 listed as missing but presumed dead, a team of Microsoft employees developed and launched a missing people website that was up and running within 24 hours.[13] That website helped families and friends locate 500 missing people.

2.4 Timely Information

Finally, information is useful when it is timely. To be timely, the information must be available when needed to define a problem or to begin to identify possible solutions. If you've ever thought, "I wish I had known that earlier," then you understand the importance of timely information and the opportunity cost of not having it.

Several years ago, the I-35 bridge in Minneapolis collapsed during rush hour, killing 13 people and injuring hundreds. The collapse was caused by extra layers of concrete used to resurface the bridge over the years. In catastrophic accidents like this, investigators can usually determine the cause by gathering and analyzing information. But they rarely have timely information that could have prevented the disaster. That, however, is changing as researchers create smart structures—buildings, bridges, and tunnels equipped with wireless sensors that provide real-time information. For example, researchers from the University of California at Berkeley have installed sensors on the Golden Gate Bridge to monitor vibrations and analyze structural integrity. Humidity sensors installed on the Humber Bridge in East Yorkshire, England, now monitor the threat to its steel struts, which are susceptible to moisture. And to monitor future problems, the St. Anthony Falls Bridge, which replaced the fallen bridge in Minneapolis, is now equipped with temperature sensors that control antifreeze systems that prevent the bridge surface from freezing.[14]

2.5 Acquisition Costs

Acquisition cost is the cost of obtaining data that you don't have. Acxiom, a billion-dollar company, gathers and processes data for direct-mail marketing companies. If you've received an unsolicited, "preapproved" credit card application recently (and who hasn't?), chances are Acxiom helped the credit card company gather information about you. Where does Acxiom get that information? The first place it turns is to companies that sell consumer credit reports at a wholesale cost of $1 each. Acxiom also obtains information from retailers. Each time you use your credit card, websites and retailers' checkout scanners gather information about your spending habits and product preferences. Acxiom also uses publicly available information such as motor vehicle and real estate records, as well as website traffic.

So why pay for this information? Acquiring it can help credit card companies better identify who will mail back a signed credit card application and who will rip the credit card application in half and toss it in the trash. Likewise, Acxiom's information helps retailers by helping them categorize consumers into 70 demographic groups. For example, Nordstrom's, an upscale department store, would find it worthwhile to advertise to "Apple Pie Families," married homeowners between the ages of 46 and 65 who live in urban areas, earn $100,000 to $500,000, and have school-age children. Likewise, Walmart is better off advertising to "Trucks and Trailers," people between the ages of 30 and 45 who earn less than $100,000 and live in rural areas. Paying Acxiom to acquire this kind of data significantly increases the return that retailers and credit card companies get from advertising and direct marketing.

acquisition cost the cost of obtaining data that you don't have.

doing the right thing

Recycling and Disposing of Computer Equipment

With most companies replacing computers every four years, an estimated 250 million computers will be discarded over the next five years. Computers and computer monitors contain hazardous materials, however, so you can't just toss them in the trash. Doing that is not just wrong—it's against the law. Instead, contact your state's department of environmental protection for help in finding a recycling company. Or donate your old computers to deserving individuals or charitable organizations. Or sell the computers at a steep discount to your employees. And when you buy your new corporate computers, bargain with the vendor to make it responsible for recycling those computers the next time around.[15]

2.6 Processing Costs

Companies often have massive amounts of data, but not in the form or combination they need. **Processing cost** is the cost of turning raw data into usable information. For example, the Large Hadron Collider (LHC), the world's largest particle accelerator, which is used to conduct research on subatomic particles, generates 4 gigabytes of data per second, enough to fill 1.7 million DVDs per year. CERN, the agency that operates the LHC, created the Worldwide LHC Computing Grid (WLCG), a complex computer network connecting 130 research centers in 34 countries, to analyze, process, and distribute this massive amount of data. The total cost of building the WLCG was $640 million, and CERN will spend $18 million annually to maintain and process LHC's data so they can be turned into usable information for scientific research.[16]

2.7 Storage Costs

Storage cost is the cost of physically or electronically archiving information for later use and retrieval. For consumers who want to make sure they never lose their computer data, **Carbonite** offers an online backup service. For an annual fee, Carbonite gives users unlimited storage space on its servers so that clients can back up critical files they can't afford to lose. Over 100 million data files are added to Carbonite's servers each day. To make room for them, Carbonite opened a new server facility in Boston, at a cost of more than $46 million. The facility features multiple AC feeds (necessary for preventing the servers from overheating), an uninterruptable diesel generator in case the electricity ever goes out, and 24-hour security (complete with fingerprint scanners).[17]

< **"what's new" companies**

2.8 Retrieval Costs

Retrieval cost is the cost of accessing already-stored and processed information. One of the most common misunderstandings about information is that it is easy and cheap to retrieve once the company has it. Not so. First, you have to find the information. Then, you've got to convince whoever has it to share it with you. Then the

processing cost the cost of turning raw data into usable information.

storage cost the cost of physically or electronically archiving information for later use and retrieval.

retrieval cost the cost of accessing already-stored and processed information.

information has to be processed into a form that is useful for you. By the time you get the information you need, it may not be timely anymore.

For example, as companies move toward paperless office systems, how will employees quickly and easily retrieve archived emails, file records, website information, word processing documents, or images? One solution is Enterprise Content Management (ECM), which is a way of storing and providing access to unstructured information wherever it exists. Ulrich Kampffmeyer, former member of the board of directors of the **Association for Information and Image Management,** summed up the challenge of retrieval costs well when he said, "The most important job is to keep in-house information under control. The questions add up: where to put the thousands and thousands of emails, what to do with the electronically signed business correspondence, where to put taxation-relevant data, how to transfer information from the disorganized file system, how to consolidate information in a repository that everybody can use, how to get a single login for all the systems, how to create a uniform in-basket for all incoming information, how to make sure that no information is lost or ignored, etc. etc."[18]

"what's new" companies >

2.9 Communication Costs

Communication cost is the cost of transmitting information from one place to another. Flight data recorders, also called black boxes, are used to investigate accidents because they record flight data such as altitude, speed, and climb rate. Sometimes, however, as with Air France Flight 447, which crashed in the Atlantic Ocean in June 2009, the black box can't be found, leaving investigators little information about what caused the accident. To solve this problem, Star Aviation and AeroMechanical Services market a next-generation black box that provides airlines real-time flight data. However, at a cost of $3 to $5 per minute via satellite, this information doesn't come cheap. An airline operating hundreds of flights per day would spend several hundred million dollars to obtain real-time data.[19]

Review 2

Characteristics and Costs of Useful Information Raw data are facts and figures. Raw data do not become information until they are in a form that can affect decisions and behavior. For information to be useful, it has to be reliable and valid (accurate), of sufficient quantity (complete), pertinent to the problems you're facing (relevant), and available when you need it (timely). Useful information does not come cheaply. The five costs of obtaining good information are the costs of acquiring, processing, storing, retrieving, and communicating information.

Getting and Sharing Information

In 1907, Metropolitan Life Insurance built a huge office building in New York City for its brand-new, state-of-the-art information technology system. What was this great breakthrough in information management? Card files. That's right, the same card file system that every library in America used before computers. Metropolitan Life's information technology consisted of 20,000 separate file drawers that sat in hundreds of file cabinets more than 15 feet tall. This filing system held 20 million insurance

communication cost the cost of transmitting information from one place to another.

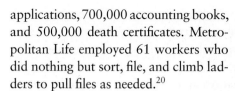

applications, 700,000 accounting books, and 500,000 death certificates. Metropolitan Life employed 61 workers who did nothing but sort, file, and climb ladders to pull files as needed.[20]

How we get and share information has clearly changed. The cost, inefficiency, and ineffectiveness of using this formerly state-of-the-art system would put an insurance company out of business within months. Today, if storms, fire, or accidents damage policyholders' property, insurance companies write checks on the spot to cover the losses. When policyholders buy a car, they call their insurance agent from the dealership to activate their insurance before driving off in their new car. And now, insurance companies are marketing their products and services to customers directly from the Internet.

From card files to Internet files, in just under a century the rate of change in information technology is spectacular.

After reading the next two sections, you should be able to

3. *Explain the basics of capturing, processing, and protecting information.*

4. *Describe how companies can access and share information and knowledge.*

3 Capturing, Processing, and Protecting Information

When you go to your local Rite Aid pharmacy to pick up a prescription, the pharmacist reviews an electronic file that shows all of the medications you're taking. That same system automatically checks to make sure that your new prescription won't create adverse side effects by interacting with your other medications. When you pay for your prescription, Rite Aid's point-of-sale information system determines whether you've written any bad checks lately (to Rite Aid or other stores), records your payment, and then checks with the computer of the pharmaceutical company that makes your prescription drugs to see whether it's time to reorder. Throughout the process, Rite Aid protects your information to make sure that your data are readily available only to you, your physician, and your pharmacist.

In this section, you will learn about the information technologies that companies like Rite Aid use to **3.1 capture**, **3.2 process**, and **3.3 protect information**.

3.1 Capturing Information

There are two basic methods of capturing information: manual and electronic. Manual capture of information is a slow, costly, labor-intensive, and often inaccurate process, which entails recording and entering data by hand into a data storage device. For example, when you applied for a driver's license, you probably recorded personal information about yourself by filling out a form. Then, after you passed your driver's test, someone typed your handwritten information into the department of motor vehicles' computer database so that local and state police could access it from their patrol cars in the event they pulled you over for speeding. (Isn't information great?) Consequently, companies are relying more on electronic capture. They use electronic storage devices such as bar codes, radio frequency identification tags, and document scanners to capture and record data electronically.

Bar codes represent numerical data by varying the thickness and pattern of vertical bars. The primary advantage of bar codes is that the data they represent can be read and recorded in an instant with a handheld or pen-type scanner. One pass of the

bar code a visual pattern that represents numerical data by varying the thickness and pattern of vertical bars.

scanner (okay, sometimes several) and "beep!"—the information has been captured. Bar codes cut checkout times in half, reduce data entry errors by 75 percent, and save stores money because stockers don't have to go through the labor-intensive process of putting a price tag on each item in the store.[21] Consumer product companies, like Unilever, are now partnering with grocery stores and technology companies to test bar code–based coupons that can be scanned directly from consumers' cell phones.[22] Likewise, all airlines use bar codes on boarding passes, either printed from your home computer or from the check-in kiosk at the airport. An increasing number of airlines, however, now send paperless bar codes to smartphones to be scanned in place of bar codes on printed boarding passes. The U.S. Transportation Security Administration says that paperless boarding passes are more secure "and will prevent fraudulent paper boarding passes that could be created and printed at home."[23] Besides saving time, and the cost of printing and paper, paperless boarding passes are likely to be popular with frequent travelers. Dan Green, a frequent business traveler who lives in Burlington, Vermont, says, "It's easier. I like to use my laptop, but I don't have a printer. Especially in hotels, where sometimes you don't have access to a printer, it makes not having a printer easier for those of us on the go."[24]

Radio frequency identification (RFID) tags contain minuscule microchips and antennas that transmit information via radio waves.[25] Unlike bar codes, which require direct line-of-sight scanning, RFID tags are read by turning on an RFID reader that, like a radio, tunes into a specific frequency to determine the number *and* location of products, parts, or anything else to which the RFID tags are attached. Turn on an RFID reader, and every RFID tag within the reader's range (from several hundred to several thousand feet) is accounted for.

Because they are now so inexpensive, RFID tags and readers are being put to thousands of uses in all kinds of businesses. Coca-Cola is testing a soft-drink vending machine, the Freestyle, which has 30 different flavor cartridges that can be used to make 100 different Coca-Cola brand drinks. A Coke, for example, is made by dispensing flavor concentrate from the cartridge into a cup, and then mixing it with a sweetener, water, and carbonation. Ice can be added if wanted. What makes this machine unique, however, is the use of RFID chips attached to each flavor cartridge. Thanks to RFID, Coca-Cola can track which drinks are selling, how much they're selling, and when. The RFID tags also indicate when cartridges are running low and must be replaced. Furthermore, RFID enhances functionality and security by showing whether a cartridge has been installed correctly or whether it is a genuine Coca-Cola product. In the case of a product recall, Coca-Cola can even stop particular cartridges from dispensing drinks until they can be pulled from the machines. Ray Crockett, Coca-Cola's director of communications says, "We consider Freestyle nothing short of a revolution in the fountain dispenser business."[26]

Electronic scanners, which convert printed text and pictures into digital images, have become an increasingly popular method of capturing data electronically because they are inexpensive and easy to use. The first requirement for a good scanner is a document feeder that automatically feeds document pages into the scanner or turns the pages (often with a puff of air) when scanning books or bound documents.[27] Text that has been digitized cannot be searched or edited like the regular text in your word processing software, however, so the second requirement for a good scanner is **optical character recognition** software to scan and convert original or digitized documents into ASCII text (American Standard Code for Information Interchange) or Adobe PDF documents. ASCII text can be searched, read, and edited with standard software for word processing, e-mail, desktop publishing, database management, and spreadsheets, and PDF documents can be searched and edited with Adobe's Acrobat software. **National EMS**, a Georgia-based ambulance and emergency response company, saves lives every day. But because of state, insurance, Medicare, and Medicaid

radio frequency identification (RFID) tags tags containing minuscule microchips that transmit information via radio waves and can be used to track the number and location of the objects into which the tags have been inserted.

electronic scanner an electronic device that converts printed text and pictures into digital images.

optical character recognition the ability of software to convert digitized documents into ASCII text (American Standard Code for Information Interchange) that can be searched, read, and edited by word processing software as well as other kinds of software.

"what's new"
companies >

requirements, so much paperwork (which must be kept by law for seven years) was being generated that the 12-person office staff couldn't keep up, and the file cabinets had to be emptied and moved to a warehouse every other month. However, after installing double-sided sheet-feeding scanners on each desk, along with document management software that automatically links documents to billing, and task routing software, the company will save 80 hours a week in document handling. It will also be able to do away with warehouse storage of its paper documents as well as its high-speed copiers and the costs associated with them.[28]

© Vartanov Anatoly/Shutterstock.com

3.2 Processing Information

Processing information means transforming raw data into meaningful information that can be applied to business decision making. Evaluating sales data to determine the best- and worst-selling products, examining repair records to determine product reliability, and monitoring the cost of long-distance phone calls are all examples of processing raw data into meaningful information. And with automated, electronic capture of data, increased processing power, and cheaper and more plentiful ways to store data, managers no longer worry about getting data. Instead, they scratch their heads about how to use the overwhelming amount of data that pours into their businesses every day. Furthermore, most managers know little about statistics and have neither the time nor the inclination to learn how to use them to analyze data.

processing information transforming raw data into meaningful information.

mgmt:trends

Smart Parking Meters

The city of San Francisco recently introduced "smart" parking meters that are equipped with sensors that can sense when a car is parked in a designated spot, and can communicate with other meters within a certain distance. Other cities have used similar systems to charge different rates at different hours, but San Francisco is the first city to use the real-time information from meters in an effort to reduce traffic congestion and pollution from emissions. Instead of endlessly circling around a block looking for an open parking space, drivers are able to use an application on their smartphones or laptops that shows the precise location of free parking spots. They can even use the application to "feed the meter" digitally.[29]

© iStockphoto.com/Kirsty Pargeter

One promising tool to help managers dig out from under the avalanche of data is data mining. **Data mining** is the process of discovering patterns and relationships in large amounts of data.[30] Data mining works by using complex algorithms such as neural networks, rule induction, and decision trees. If you don't know what those are, that's okay. With data mining, you don't have to. Most managers only need to know that data mining looks for patterns that are already in the data but are too complex for them to spot on their own. Surprisingly, Osco Drugs, based in Chicago, found that beer and diapers tended to be bought together between 5 and 7 P.M. The question, of course, was: Why? The answer, on further review, was fairly straightforward. Fathers, who were told by their wives to buy some diapers on their way home, decided to pick up a six-pack for themselves too.[31]

Data mining typically splits a data set in half, finds patterns in one half, and then tests the validity of those patterns by trying to find them again in the second half of the data set. The data typically come from a **data warehouse** that stores huge amounts of data that have been prepared for data mining analysis by being cleaned of errors and redundancy. The data in a data warehouse can then be analyzed using two kinds of data mining. **Supervised data mining** usually begins with the user telling the data mining software to look and test for specific patterns and relationships in a data set. Typically, this is done through a series of "what-if" questions or statements. For instance, a grocery store manager might instruct the data mining software to determine whether coupons placed in the Sunday paper increase or decrease sales. By contrast, with **unsupervised data mining**, the user simply tells the data mining software to uncover whatever patterns and relationships it can find in a data set. For example, State Farm Insurance used to have three pricing categories for car insurance, depending on your driving record: preferred for the best drivers, standard for typical drivers, and nonstandard for the worst drivers. Now, however, it has moved to tiered pricing based on the 300 different kinds of driving records that its data mining software was able to discover. This allows State Farm to be much more precise in matching 300 different price levels to 300 different kinds of driving records.[32]

Unsupervised data mining is particularly good at identifying association or affinity patterns, sequence patterns, and predictive patterns. It can also identify what data mining technicians call data clusters.[33] **Association or affinity patterns** occur when two or more database elements tend to occur together in a significant way. HEAT, short for Health Care Fraud Prevention and Enforcement Action Teams, is a multi-agency federal department charged with finding and prosecuting large-scale medical fraud, in which false medical claims are submitted to the U.S. and state governments for Medicare and Medicaid payments. Using data mining software, agent Rene Olivas knew that he had found a likely case of fraud. The data mining software found factors commonly associated with fraud for TA Medical Supply, in Los Angeles, which sold high quantities of durable medical equipment, like wheelchairs. First, most of the patients and referring doctors were out of state. Second, a very high percentage of patients ordered orthotics (to support or correct limb function) for more than one body part, which is rare. And, third, 96 percent of its patients ordered two braces at the same time, for both knees, both ankles, both elbows, or both wrists. The owner of TA Medical pleaded guilty to health-care fraud and was sentenced to 54 months in prison.[34]

Sequence patterns occur when two or more database elements occur together in a significant pattern in which one of the elements precedes the other. Most professional baseball teams set the price of tickets for each game at the beginning of the season, varying the price depending on the day of the week and the opponent. For example, the New York Yankees charge a higher price for a ticket to a weekend night game versus the Boston Red Sox, their hated rivals, than for a weekday game versus the Washington Nationals. The San Francisco Giants have taken things a step

data mining the process of discovering unknown patterns and relationships in large amounts of data.

data warehouse stores huge amounts of data that have been prepared for data mining analysis by being cleaned of errors and redundancy.

supervised data mining the process when the user tells the data mining software to look and test for specific patterns and relationships in a data set.

unsupervised data mining the process when the user simply tells the data mining software to uncover whatever patterns and relationships it can find in a data set.

association or affinity patterns when two or more database elements tend to occur together in a significant way.

sequence patterns when two or more database elements occur together in a significant pattern, but one of the elements precedes the other.

further by introducing dynamic pricing for all of its single-game tickets. Using data mining, the Giants re-price tickets on a daily basis by calculating the impact of various factors (i.e., database elements) that only become clear a few days before a game, such as the weather, winning streaks, and pitching matchups, all of which influence how many people will want to attend. Russ Stanley, vice president for ticket sales and services said, "The thing about baseball is that the product changes every day. You could be in first place one day and you'll be in fifth place the next." During the 2009 season, the Giants lowered and raised prices in a small section of seats, using this data, and were able to sell an extra 25,000 tickets, which increased revenue by $500,000. And for the 2010 season, when the Giants switched to dynamic pricing for all single-game seats, ticket revenues were up by 6 percent.[35]

Predictive patterns are just the opposite of association or affinity patterns. Whereas association or affinity patterns look for database elements that seem to go together, **predictive patterns** help identify database elements that are different. Banks and credit card companies use data mining to find predictive patterns that distinguish customers who are good credit risks from those who are poor credit risks and less likely to pay their loans and monthly bills. J. P. Martin, an executive at **Canadian Tire**, pioneered the use of purchase data to predict consumer behavior. By analyzing what customers were buying, he identified predictive patterns that accurately forecast whether consumers would pay their debts. For example, he found that people who bought generic motor oil were more likely to miss payments than those who bought more expensive, name-brand oil. People who bought felt furniture pads, which protect wood floors from scratches, were very unlikely to miss payments. And he found that 47 percent of the Canadian Tire customers who frequented the Sharx Pool Bar in Montreal missed an average of four credit card payments per year.[36]

< "what's new" companies

Data clusters are the last kind of pattern found by data mining. **Data clusters** occur when three or more database elements occur together (i.e., cluster) in a significant way. For example, after analyzing several years' worth of repair and warranty claims, Ford Motor Company might find that, compared with cars built in its Chicago plant, the cars it builds in Kansas City (first element) are more likely to have problems with over-tightened fan belts (second element) that break (third element) and result in overheated engines (fourth element), ruined radiators (fifth element), and payments for tow trucks (sixth element), which are paid for by Ford's five-year, 60,000-mile power train warranty.

Traditionally, data mining has been very expensive and very complex. Today, however, data mining services and analysis are much more affordable and within reach of most companies' budgets. And if it follows the path of most technologies, it will become even easier and cheaper to use in the future.

3.3 Protecting Information

Protecting information is the process of ensuring that data are reliably and consistently retrievable in a usable format for authorized users but no one else. For instance, when customers purchase prescription medicine at Drugstore.com, an online drugstore and health-aid retailer, they want to be confident that their medical and credit card information is available only to them, the pharmacists at Drugstore.com, and their doctors. So Drugstore.com has an extensive privacy policy (click "Privacy Policy" at www.drugstore.com to make sure this is the case).[37]

Companies like Drugstore.com find it necessary to protect information because of the numerous security threats to data and data security listed in Exhibit 17.3. People inside and outside companies can steal or destroy company data in various ways, including denial-of-service web server attacks that can bring down some of the

predictive patterns patterns that help identify database elements that are different.

data clusters when three or more database elements occur together (i.e., cluster) in a significant way.

protecting information the process of ensuring that data are reliably and consistently retrievable in a usable format for authorized users, but no one else.

Exhibit 17.3   Security Threats to Data and Data Networks

SECURITY PROBLEM	SOURCE	AFFECTS	SEVERITY	THE THREAT	THE SOLUTION
Denial of service, web server attacks, and corporate network attacks	Internet hackers	All servers	High	Loss of data, disruption of service, and theft of service.	Implement firewall, password control, serverside review, threat monitoring, and bug fixes, and turn PCs off when not in use.
Password cracking software and unauthorized access to PCs	Local area network, Internet	All users, especially digital subscriber line and cable Internet users	High	Hackers take over PCs. Privacy can be invaded. Corporate users' systems are exposed to other machines on the network.	Close ports and firewalls, disable file and print sharing, and use strong passwords.
Viruses, worms, Trojan horses, and rootkits	Email, downloaded and distributed software	All users	Moderate to high	Monitor activities and cause data loss and file deletion: compromise security by sometimes concealing their presence.	Use antivirus software and firewalls, and control Internet access.
Spyware, adware, malicious scripts, and applets	Rogue web pages	All users	Moderate to high	Invade privacy, intercept passwords, and damage files or file system.	Disable browser script support, and use security, blocking, and spyware/adware software.
E-mail snooping	Hackers on your network and the Internet	All users	Moderate to high	People read your email from intermediate servers or packets, or they physically access your machine.	Encrypt message, ensure strong password protection, and limit physical access to machines.
Keystroke monitoring	Trojan horses, people with direct access to PCs	All users	High	Records everything typed at the keyboard and intercepts keystrokes before password masking or encryption occurs.	Use antivirus software to catch Trojan horses, control Internet access to transmission, and implement system monitoring and physical access control.
Phishing	Hackers on your network and the Internet	All users, including customers	High	Fake but real-looking emails and websites that trick users into sharing personal information on what they wrongly thought was the company's website. This leads to unauthorized account access.	Educate and warn users and customers about the dangers. Encourage both not to click on potentially fake URLs, which might take them to phishing websites. Instead, have them type your company's URL into the web browser.
Spam	Email	All users and corporations	Mild to high	Clogs and overloads email servers and inboxes with junk mail. HTML-based spam may be used for profiling and identifying users.	Filter known spam sources and senders on email servers, and have users create further lists of approved and unapproved senders on their personal computers.
Cookies	Websites you visit	Individual users	Mild to moderate	Trace web usage and permit the creation of personalized web pages that track behavior and interest profiles.	Use cookie managers to control and edit cookies, and use ad blockers.

Sources: K. Bannan, "Look Out: Watching You, Watching Me," *PC Magazine*, July 2002, 99; A. Dragoon, "Fighting Phish, Fakes, and Frauds," CIO, September 1, 2004, 33; B. Glass, "Are You Being Watched?" *PC Magazine*, April 23, 2002, 54; K. Karagiannis, "DDoS: Are You Next?" *PC Magazine*, January 2003, 79; B. Machone, "Protect and Defend," *PC Magazine*, June 27, 2000, 168–181; "Top 10 Security Threats," *PC Magazine*, April 10, 2007, 66; and M. Sarrel, "Master End-User Security," *PC Magazine*, May 2008, 101.

busiest and best-run sites on the Internet; viruses and spyware/adware that spread quickly and can result in data loss and business disruption; keystroke monitoring in which every mouse click and keystroke you make is monitored, stored, and sent to unauthorized users; password-cracking software that steals supposedly secure passwords; and phishing, where fake but real-looking emails and websites trick users into sharing personal information (user names, passwords, account numbers) leading to unauthorized account access. On average, 19 percent of computers are infected with viruses, 80 percent have spyware, and only one-third are running behind a protected firewall (discussed shortly). Studies show that the threats listed in Exhibit 17.3 are so widespread that automatic attacks will begin on an unprotected computer just 15 seconds after it connects to the Internet.[38]

As shown in the right-hand column of Exhibit 17.3, numerous steps can be taken to secure data and data networks. Some of the most important are authentication and authorization, firewalls, antivirus software for PCs and email servers, data encryption, and virtual private networks.[39] We will review those steps and then finish this section with a brief review of the dangers of wireless networks.

Two critical steps are required to make sure that data can be accessed by authorized users and no one else. One is **authentication**, that is, making sure users are who they claim to be.[40] The other is **authorization**, that is, granting authenticated users approved access to data, software, and systems.[41] When an ATM prompts you

authentication making sure potential users are who they claim to be.

authorization granting authenticated users approved access to data, software, and systems.

doing the right thing

Password Dos and Don'ts

Anyone with access to sensitive personal (personnel or medical files), customer (credit cards), or corporate data (costs) has a clear responsibility to protect those data from unauthorized access. Use the following dos and don'ts to maintain a "strong" password system and protect your data.

» Don't use any public information such as part of your name, address, or birth date to create a password.

» Don't use complete words, English or foreign, that are easily guessed by password software using "dictionary attacks."

» Use eight or more characters and include some unique characters such as !@#$ to create passwords like "cow@#boy."

» The longer the password and the more unique characters, the more difficult it is to guess.

» Consider using "passphrases," such as "My European vacation starts July 8th," instead of shorter passwords. The longer password, including upper- and lowercase letters, spaces, and numbers, is easy to remember and much, much more difficult to guess using password-cracking software.

» Remember your password and don't write it down on a sticky note attached to your computer.

» Change your password every six weeks. Better yet, specify that your computer system force all users to change their passwords this often.

» Don't reuse old passwords.

Together, these basic steps can make it much more difficult to gain unauthorized access to sensitive data.[42]

to enter your personal identification number (PIN), the bank is authenticating that you are you. Once you've been authenticated, you are authorized to access your funds and no one else's. Of course, as anyone who has lost a PIN or password or had one stolen knows, user authentication systems are not foolproof. In particular, users create security risks by not changing their default account passwords (such as birth dates) or by using weak passwords such as names (e.g., Larry) or complete words (e.g., football) that are quickly guessed by password-cracker software.[43] (See Doing the Right Thing on password dos and don'ts to learn how to prevent this.)

This is why many companies are now turning to **two-factor authentication**, which is based on what users know, such as a password, and what they have, such as a secure ID card.[44] Amazon Web Services, a cloud computing platform, protects data by requiring all users to sign with an account name (usually an email address), a password (the first factor), and a six-digit code (the second factor) that is randomly generated from an Ezio Time Token, a handheld device given to the customer that, with the push of a button, creates a one-use random password that expires a few minutes after being generated.[45]

With **biometrics** such as fingerprint recognition or iris scanning, users are identified by unique, measurable body features.[46] Troy Appling, vice president of The Bankers Bank, says, "With fingerprint biometrics, we can reduce the risk of unauthorized people making millions of dollars off fraudulent transfers. And we don't have to spend up to 60 percent of our IT [information technology] time resolving lost or forgotten passwords."[47] Likewise, **24 Hour Fitness USA** has implemented "cardless check-in" by scanning its members' fingerprints. 24 Hour Fitness emphasizes, however, that it doesn't store images of fingerprints. "By scanning your finger, we chart the distance between a few distinct points [on your fingerprint] that are unique to you and come up with an identifying number based on those distances." And each time your finger is placed on the scanner, those distances are then compared to the identifying number in their system.[48]

Of course, because some fingerprint scanners can be fooled by fingerprint molds (probably not a big concern for 24 Hour Fitness), some companies take security measures even further by requiring users to simultaneously scan their fingerprint *and* insert a secure, smart card containing a digital file of their fingerprint. This is another form of two-factor authentication.

Unfortunately, stolen or cracked passwords are not the only way for hackers and electronic thieves to gain access to an organization's computer resources. Unless special safeguards are put in place, every time corporate users are online there's literally nothing between their personal computers and the Internet (home users with high-speed DSL or cable Internet access face the same risks). Hackers can access files, run programs, and control key parts of computers if precautions aren't taken. To reduce these risks, companies use **firewalls**, hardware or software devices that sit between the computers in an internal organizational network and outside networks such as the Internet. Firewalls filter and check incoming and

two-factor authentication authentication based on what users know, such as a password and what they have in their possession, such as a secure ID card or key.

biometrics identifying users by unique, measurable body features, such as fingerprint recognition or iris scanning.

firewall a protective hardware or software device that sits between the computers in an internal organizational network and outside networks, such as the Internet.

SecuriMetrics   PIER 2.3

Recog Image

© Peter Macdiarmid/Getty Images

outgoing data. They prevent company insiders from accessing unauthorized sites or from sending confidential company information to people outside the company. Firewalls also prevent outsiders from identifying and gaining access to company computers and data. Indeed, if a firewall is working properly, the computers behind the company firewall literally cannot be seen or accessed by outsiders.

A **virus** is a program or piece of code that, without your knowledge, attaches itself to other programs on your computer and can trigger anything from a harmless flashing message to the reformatting of your hard drive to a systemwide network shutdown. You used to have to do or run something to get a virus, such as double-clicking an infected email attachment. Today's viruses are much more threatening. In fact, with some viruses just being connected to a network can infect your computer. *Antivirus software for personal computers* scans email, downloaded files, and computer hard drives, disk drives, and memory to detect and stop computer viruses from doing damage. However, this software is effective only to the extent that users of individual computers have and use up-to-date versions. With new viruses appearing all the time, users should update their antivirus software weekly or, even better, configure their virus software to automatically check for, download, and install updates. By contrast, *corporate antivirus software* automatically scans email attachments such as Microsoft Word documents, graphics, or text files as they come across the company email server. It also monitors and scans all file downloads across company databases and network servers. So, although antivirus software for personal computers prevents individual computers from being infected, corporate antivirus software for email servers, databases, and network servers adds another layer of protection by preventing infected files from multiplying and being sent to others.

Another way of protecting information is to encrypt sensitive data. **Data encryption** transforms data into complex, scrambled digital codes that can be unencrypted only by authorized users who possess unique decryption keys. One method of data encryption is to use products by PGP (Pretty Good Privacy) (www.pgp.com) to encrypt the files stored on personal computers or network servers and databases. This is especially important with laptop computers, which are easily stolen. After a Boeing employee's laptop PC was stolen from his hotel room, the company implemented a training program that requires managers and employees to have data encryption software installed on their laptops and become certified in using it. Those not following the encryption procedures can be reprimanded and even fired.[49]

With people increasingly gaining unauthorized access to email messages—email snooping—it's also important to encrypt sensitive email messages and file attachments. You can use a system called "public key encryption" to do so. First, give copies of your "public key" to anyone who sends you files or email. Have the sender use the public key, which is actually a piece of software, to encrypt files before sending them to you. The only way to decrypt the files is with a companion "private key" that you keep to yourself. If you want to learn more or want to begin encrypting your own files, download a free copy of Pretty Good Privacy from http://web.mit.edu/pgp.

Although firewalls can protect personal computers and network servers connected to the corporate network, people away from their offices (e.g., salespeople, business travelers, telecommuters) who interact with their company networks via the Internet face a security risk. Because Internet data are not encrypted, packet sniffer software easily allows hackers to read everything sent or received except files that have been encrypted before sending. Previously, the only practical solution was to have employees dial in to secure company phone lines for direct access to the company network. Of course, with international and long-distance phone calls, the costs quickly added up. Now, **virtual private networks (VPNs)** have solved this problem by using software to encrypt all Internet data at both ends of the transmission process. Instead of making long-distance calls, employees connect to the Internet. But unlike

virus a program or piece of code that, without your knowledge, attaches itself to other programs on your computer and can trigger anything from a harmless flashing message to the reformatting of your hard drive to a systemwide network shutdown.

data encryption the transformation of data into complex, scrambled digital codes that can be unencrypted only by authorized users who possess unique decryption keys.

virtual private network (VPN) software that securely encrypts data sent by employees outside the company network, decrypts the data when they arrive within the company computer network, and does the same when data are sent back to employees outside the network.

typical Internet connections in which data packets are unencrypted, the VPN encrypts the data sent by employees outside the company computer network, decrypts the data when they arrive within the company network, and does the same when data are sent back to the computer outside the network. VPN connections provide secure access to everything on a company's network.

Alternatively, many companies are now adopting web-based **secure sockets layer (SSL) encryption** to provide secure off-site access to data and programs. If you've ever entered your credit card in a web browser to make an online purchase, you've used SSL technology to encrypt and protect that information. You can tell whether SSL encryption is being used on a website if you see a padlock icon (gold in Internet Explorer or Firefox; green in Google Chrome, silver in Safari), or if the URL begins with "https."

SSL encryption works the same way in the workplace. Managers and employees who aren't at the office simply connect to the Internet, open a web browser, and then enter a user name and password to gain access to SSL-encrypted data and programs. **MIM Software**, based in Beachwood, Ohio, recently introduced the Mobile MIM app for iPhones and iPads. Using the app, doctors can use their iPhones and iPads to view patients' CT, MRI, or nuclear imaging scans, allowing them to make quick treatment decisions even when not in the office. The scans are transferred from the hospital where the images were taken to the doctor's iPhone or iPad over MIM's Internet service, which is protected by SSL encryption.[50]

Finally, many companies now have wireless networks, which make it possible for anybody with a laptop and a wireless card to access the company network from anywhere in the office. Though wireless networks come equipped with security and encryption capabilities that, in theory, permit only authorized users to access the wireless network, those capabilities are easily bypassed with the right tools. Compounding the problem, many wireless networks are shipped with their security and encryption capabilities turned off for ease of installation.[51] Caution is important even when encryption is turned on because the WEP (Wired Equivalent Privacy) security protocol is easily compromised. If you work at home or are working on the go, extra care is critical because Wi-Fi networks in homes and public places like hotel lobbies are among the most targeted by hackers.[52] See the Wi-Fi Alliance site at www.wi-fi.org for the latest information on wireless security and encryption protocols that provide much stronger protection for your company's wireless network.

> **"what's new"**
> **companies** >

secure sockets layer (SSL) encryption Internet browser–based encryption that provides secure off-site web access to some data and programs.

Review 3

Capturing, Processing, and Protecting Information Electronic data capture (bar codes, radio frequency identification [RFID] tags, scanners, and optical character recognition) is much faster, easier, and cheaper than manual data capture. Processing information means transforming raw data into meaningful information that can be applied to business decision making. Data mining helps managers with this transformation by discovering unknown patterns and relationships in data. Supervised data mining looks for patterns specified by managers; unsupervised data mining looks for four general kinds of data patterns: association/affinity patterns, sequence patterns, predictive patterns, and data clusters. Protecting information ensures that data are reliably and consistently retrievable in a usable format by authorized users, but no one else. Authentication and authorization, firewalls, antivirus software for PCs and corporate email and network servers, data encryption, virtual private networks, and web-based secure sockets layer (SSL) encryption are some of the best ways to protect information. Be careful with wireless networks, which are easily compromised even when security and encryption protocols are in place.

4 Accessing and Sharing Information and Knowledge

Vendor Pulse, is a data sharing program started by grocery store chain Food Lion. Food Lion provides vendors, such as consumer goods company Unilever, with 14 kinds of sales metrics, ranging from point-of-sale statistics (even down to each cash register), store inventory (how much of each item is left in each store), distribution center inventory (how much of each item is in the warehouse), shrinkage (how much of each item has been stolen or misplaced), out-of-stocks (extent to which a product is out of stock in various locations), and reclamations (how much of each item has been returned). Troy Prothero, Food Lion's supply chain manager, says that the data are so rich in information that "there are no more data requests from suppliers [and the program]. Anything they would have requested comes to them daily."[53] How good is Food Lion's Vendor Pulse program? According to Andy Patel, manager of business capabilities for Unilever, "[F]ew have the rich and robust data of Food Lion. It's got 14 metrics around each individual UPC [Universal Product Code, which is unique to each product], while some other retailers have only got two." Tony Prothero, a supply chain manager for Delhaize Groups-USA, which includes Food Lion, says, "We're providing what suppliers wanted access to."[54]

Today, information technologies are letting companies communicate data, share data, and provide data access to workers, managers, suppliers, and customers in ways that were unthinkable just a few years ago.

After reading this section, you should be able to explain how companies use information technology to improve **4.1 internal access and sharing of information**, **4.2 external access and sharing of information**, and **4.3 the sharing of knowledge and expertise**.

4.1 Internal Access and Sharing

Executives, managers, and workers inside the company use three kinds of information technology to access and share information: executive information systems, intranets, and portals. An **executive information system (EIS)** uses internal and external sources of data to provide managers and executives the information they need to monitor and analyze organizational performance.[55] The goal of an EIS is to provide accurate, complete, relevant, and timely information to managers. With just a few mouse clicks and basic commands such as *find*, *compare*, and *show*, the EIS displays costs, sales revenues, and other kinds of data in color-coded charts and graphs. Managers can drill down to view and compare data by global region, country, state, time period, and product. Managers at **Colgate-Palmolive**, which makes dental (Colgate toothpastes), personal (Irish Spring soap and Speed Stick antiperspirants), and home care (Palmolive dish soaps) products, as well as pet nutrition (Hill's Science Diet), use their EIS, which they call their "dashboard," to see how well the company is running. Ruben Panizza, Colgate's Global IT Director of Business Intelligence, says, "These real-time dashboards are a change for people who are used to seeing a lot of numbers with their data. But they quickly realize they can use the information as it's presented in the dashboards to make faster decisions. In the past, executives relied on other people to

executive information system (EIS) a data processing system that uses internal and external data sources to provide the information needed to monitor and analyze organizational performance.

< **"what's new" companies**

© AP Images/Bob Leverone

725

Exhibit 17.4   Characteristics of Best-Selling Executive Information Systems

EASE OF USE	Few commands to learn.	Simply drag-and-drop or point-and-click to create charts and tables or get the information you need.
	Important views saved.	Need to see weekly sales by store every Monday? Save that "view" of the data, and it will automatically be updated with new data every week.
	3-D charts to display data.	Column, square, pie, ring, line, area, scatter, bar, cube, etc.
	Geographic dimensions.	Different geographic areas are automatically color-coded for easy understanding.
ANALYSIS OF INFORMATION	Sales tracking.	Track sales performance by product, region, account, and channel.
	Easy-to-understand displays.	Information is displayed in tabular and graphical charts.
	Time periods.	Data can be analyzed by current year, prior year, year to date, quarter to date, and month to date.
IDENTIFICATION OF PROBLEMS AND EXCEPTIONS	Compare with standards.	Compares actual company performance (actual expenses versus planned expenses, or actual sales by sales quotas).
	Trigger exceptions.	Allows users to set triggers (5 percent over budget, 3 percent under sales quota), which then highlight negative exceptions in red and positive exceptions in green.
	Drill down.	Once exceptions have been identified, users can drill down for more information to determine why the exception is occurring.
	Detect & alert newspaper.	When things go wrong, the EIS delivers a "newspaper" via email to alert managers to problems. The newspaper offers an intuitive interface for easily navigating and further analyzing the alert content.
	Detect & alert robots.	Detect & alert robots keep an extra "eye" out for events and problems. Want to keep an eye out for news about one of your competitors? Use a news robot to track stories on Dow Jones News Retrieval. Robots can also be used to track stock quotes, internal databases, and email messages.

Sources: "Business Intelligence Overview: Enterprise Services from Pilot Software," Accrue Software, www.pilots.com, February 9, 2002; Cornshare home page, www.cornshare.com. February 2002.

get custom reports and data. Now, they can look at the information themselves. They see the real data as it is in the system much more easily and quickly. For the first time, many of the company's business leaders are running BI [business intelligence] tools — in this case, dashboards — to monitor the business to see what's going on at a high level."[56] Exhibit 17.4 describes some of the basic capabilities found in EIS programs.

Intranets are private company networks that allow employees to easily access, share, and publish information using Internet software. Intranet websites are just like external websites, but the firewall separating the internal company network from the Internet permits only authorized internal access.[57] Companies typically use intranets to share information (e.g., about benefits) and to replace paper forms with online forms. Many company intranets are built on the web model as it existed a decade ago. **Duke Energy's** intranet, which it calls "The Portal," was recently named one of the ten best corporate intranets by the Nielsen Norman Group. The Portal not only provides the documents, forms, and information needed to get your work done at Duke, it also incorporates social media to help employees communicate with each other and management. A key feature is "My Site," a Facebook-like function that employees can use to share information. The Portal also allows employees to comment and

"what's new" >
companies

intranets private company networks that allow employees to easily access, share, and publish information using Internet software.

Exhibit 17.5   Why Companies Use Intranets

- Intranets are inexpensive.

- Intranets increase efficiencies and reduce costs.

- Intranets are intuitive and easy to use and web-based.

- Intranets work across all computer systems and platforms (web-based).

- Intranets can be built on top of an existing computer network.

- Intranets work with software programs that easily convert electronic documents to HTML files for intranet use.

- Much of the software required to set up an intranet is either freeware (no cost) or shareware (try before you buy, usually less expensive than commercial software).

© Cengage Learning 2013

communicate on nearly every part of the site. If management posts an article about a new work process, The Portal not only gives employees the article but allows them to respond to the article so that an interactive conversation can take place. Tom Shiel, from Duke's corporate communications department, said, "Our old system concentrated on top-down communication. Now when we have an article from senior management, employees can respond on the site. It is much more a tool for conversation back and forth."[58] Exhibit 17.5 further explains why companies use intranets.

Finally, **corporate portals** are a hybrid of executive information systems and intranets. Whereas an EIS provides managers and executives with the information they need to monitor and analyze organizational performance, and intranets help companies distribute and publish information and forms within the company, corporate portals allow company managers and employees to access customized information *and* complete specialized transactions using a web browser. Hillman Group is the company that sells the nuts, bolts, fasteners, keys, and key cutting machines that you find in Home Depot, Lowes, Ace, and nearly every other hardware store. Hillman's 1,800 employees produce products for 25,000 customers. Two years ago, Hillman hired a new CIO, Jim Honerkamp, to improve the quality of information that Hillman's managers and employees used to make decisions. Says Honerkamp, "Our executives were trying to piecemeal information together to make business decisions on spreadsheets." The first thing he did was to create a corporate portal that contained a real-time revenue report for every product that updated sales and production numbers on a continuous basis. The portal and the report were so useful that CEO Mick Hillman began using them on a daily basis. Says Honerkamp, "The first thing he [Hillman] does when he arrives at 6:30 A.M. is to get on the portal and start looking at reports. He picks up the phone and starts calling my peers, the SVP of operations or the VP of distribution or the CFO and starts asking questions based on what he's seeing."[59] Today, Hillman's portal contains 75 specialized reports that are accessed by 800 managers and employees.

4.2 External Access and Sharing

Historically, companies have been unable or reluctant to let outside groups have access to corporate information. Now, however, a number of information technologies—electronic data interchange, extranets, web services, and the Internet—are making it easier to share company data with external groups like suppliers and customers. They're also reducing costs, increasing productivity by eliminating manual information processing (70% of the data output from one company, like a purchase order,

corporate portal a hybrid of executive information systems and intranets that allows managers and employees to use a web browser to gain access to customized company information and to complete specialized transactions.

ends up as data input at another company, such as a sales invoice or shipping order), reducing data entry errors, improving customer service, and speeding communications. As a result, managers are scrambling to adopt these technologies.

With **electronic data interchange**, or **EDI**, two companies convert purchase and ordering information to a standardized format to enable direct electronic transmission of that information from one company's computer system to the other company's system. For example, when a Walmart checkout clerk drags an Apple iPod across the checkout scanner, Walmart's computerized inventory system automatically reorders another iPod through the direct EDI connection that its computer has with Apple's manufacturing and shipping computer. No one at Walmart or Apple fills out paperwork. No one makes phone calls. There are no delays to wait to find out whether Apple has the iPod in stock. The transaction takes place instantly and automatically because the data from both companies were translated into a standardized, shareable, compatible format.

Web services, as mentioned in the Food Lion example, are another way for companies to directly and automatically transmit purchase and ordering information from one company's computer system to another company's computer system. **Web services** use standardized protocols to describe and transfer data from one company in such a way that those data can automatically be read, understood, transcribed, and processed by different computer systems in another company.[60] Route One, which helps automobile dealers process loans for car buyers, was started by the financing companies of DaimlerChrysler, Ford, General Motors, and Toyota. Not surprisingly, each auto company had a different computer system with different operating systems, different programs, and different data structures. Route One relies on web services to connect these different computer systems to the wide variety of different databases and software used by various auto dealers, credit bureaus, banks, and other auto financing companies. Without web services, there's no way these different companies and systems could share information.[61]

Now, what's the difference between web services and EDI? For EDI to work, the data in different companies' computer, database, and network systems must adhere to a particular set of standards for data structure and processing. For example, company X, which has a seven-digit parts numbering system, and company Y, which has an eight-digit parts numbering system, would agree to convert their internal parts numbering systems to identical ten-digit parts numbers when their computer systems talk to each other. By contrast, the tools underlying web services such as extensible markup language (or XML) automatically do the describing and transcribing so that data with different structures can be shared across very different computer systems in different companies. (Don't worry if you don't understand how this works, just appreciate what it does.) As a result, by automatically handling those differences, web services allow organizations to communicate data without special knowledge of each other's computer information systems.

In EDI and web services, the different purchasing and ordering applications in each company interact automatically without any human input. No one has to lift a finger to click a mouse, enter data, or hit the return key. An **extranet**, by contrast, allows companies to exchange information and conduct transactions by purposely providing outsiders with direct, web browser–based access to authorized parts of a company's intranet or information system. Typically, user names and passwords are required to access an extranet.[62] Penske Truck Leasing, which leases truck fleets to companies (just like leasing a car), has created an extranet at MyFleetAtPenske.com for its U.S. customers. Fleet managers use the Penske extranet to track and schedule preventive maintenance, get updates on real-time emergency roadside assistance, generate detailed usage and cost reports, have their drivers participate in online safety training programs, and manage U.S. Department of Transportation safety compliance

electronic data interchange (EDI) when two companies convert their purchase and ordering information to a standardized format to enable the direct electronic transmission of that information from one company's computer system to the other company's computer system.

web services using standardized protocols to describe data from one company in such a way that those data can automatically be read, understood, transcribed, and processed by different computer systems in another company.

extranets networks that allow companies to exchange information and conduct transactions with outsiders by providing them direct, web-based access to authorized parts of a company's intranet or information system.

requirement (including drug and alcohol testing). [63]

Finally, companies are reducing paperwork and manual information processing by using the Internet to electronically automate transactions with customers; this is similar to the way in which extranets are used to handle transactions with suppliers and distributors. For example, most airlines have automated the ticketing process by eliminating paper tickets altogether. Simply buy an e-ticket via the Internet, and then check yourself in online by printing your boarding pass from your personal computer or from a kiosk at the airport. Internet purchases, ticketless travel, and automated check-ins have together fully automated the purchase of airline tickets. Use of self-service kiosks is expanding too. Grocery store shoppers in Houston and San Antonio, Texas, can use **Chirp** automated kiosks to buy designer handbags from Coach, Michael Cors, or DKNY. Other Chirp machines display high-def scenes from recent movies, while offering shoppers items like jewelry, perfume, or accessories inspired by the films. To buy, customers swipe a credit card, and like a typical vending machine, out comes your purchase. Typically, Chirp's prices are 30 percent to 75 percent below retail because it avoids the cost of retail employees or stores and buys discounted goods in small lots from designers like Gucci, Prada, and others. Returning goods is just as easy. Customers call a toll-free number and Chirp sends them a box with prepaid postage to mail the goods back. [64]

In the long run, the goal is to link customer Internet sites with company intranets (or EDI) and extranets so that everyone—all the employees and managers within a company as well as the suppliers and distributors outside the company—involved in providing a service or making a product for a customer is automatically notified when a purchase is made. Companies that use EDI, web services, extranets, and the Internet to share data with customers and suppliers achieve increases in productivity 2.7 times larger than those that don't. [65]

© c68/ZUMA Press/Newscom

< **"what's new" companies**

4.3 Sharing Knowledge and Expertise

At the beginning of the chapter, we distinguished between raw data, which consist of facts and figures, and information, which consists of useful data that influence someone's choices and behavior. One more important distinction needs to be made, namely, that data and information are not the same as knowledge. **Knowledge** is the understanding that one gains from information. Importantly, knowledge does not reside in information. Knowledge resides in people. That's why companies hire consultants and why family doctors refer patients to specialists. Unfortunately, it can be quite expensive to employ consultants, specialists, and experts. So companies have begun using two information technologies to capture and share the knowledge of consultants, specialists, and experts with other managers and workers: decision support systems and expert systems.

knowledge the understanding that one gains from information.

Whereas an executive information system speeds up and simplifies the acquisition of information, a **decision support system (DSS)** helps managers understand problems and potential solutions by acquiring and analyzing information with sophisticated models and tools.[66] Furthermore, whereas EIS programs are broad in scope and permit managers to retrieve all kinds of information about a company, DSS programs are usually narrow in scope and targeted toward helping managers solve specific kinds of problems. DSS programs have been developed to help managers pick the shortest and most efficient routes for delivery trucks, select the best combination of stocks for investors, and schedule the flow of inventory through complex manufacturing facilities.

It's important to understand that DSS programs don't replace managerial decision making; they *improve* it by furthering managers' and workers' understanding of the problems they face and the solutions that might work. Though used by just 2 percent of physicians, medical DSS programs hold the promise of helping doctors make more accurate patient diagnoses. A British study of 88 cases misdiagnosed or initially misdiagnosed (to be correctly diagnosed much later) found that a medical DSS made the right diagnosis 69 percent of the time.[67] With a medical DSS, doctors enter patient data such as age, gender, weight, and medical symptoms. The medical DSS then produces a list of diseases and conditions, ranked by probability, low or high, or by medical specialty, such as cardiology or oncology. For instance, when emergency room physician Dr. Harold Cross treated a 10-year-old boy who had been ill with nausea and dizziness for two weeks, he wasn't sure what was wrong because the boy had a healthy appetite, no abdominal pain, and just one brief headache. However, when the medical DSS that Dr. Cross used suggested a possible problem in the back of the boy's brain, he ordered an MRI scan that revealed a tumor, which was successfully removed two days later. Says Dr. Cross, "My personal knowledge of the literature and physical findings would not have prompted me to suspect a brain tumor."[68]

Expert systems are created by capturing the specialized knowledge and decision rules used by experts and experienced decision makers. They permit nonexpert employees to draw on this expert knowledge base to make decisions. Most expert systems work by using a collection of "if–then" rules to sort through information and recommend a course of action. For example, let's say that you're using your American Express card to help your spouse celebrate a promotion. After dinner and a movie, the two of you stroll by a travel office with a Las Vegas poster in its window. Thirty minutes later, caught up in the moment, you find yourselves at the airport ticket counter trying to purchase last-minute tickets to Vegas. But there's just one problem. American Express didn't approve your purchase. In fact, the ticket counter agent is now on the phone with an American Express customer service agent. So what put a temporary halt to your weekend escape to Vegas? An expert system that American Express calls "Authorizer's Assistant."[69]

The first "if–then" rule that prevented your purchase was the rule "*if* a purchase is much larger than the cardholder's regular spending habits, *then* deny approval of the purchase." This if–then rule, just one of 3,000, is built into American Express's transaction processing system that handles thousands of purchase requests per second. Now that the American Express customer service agent is on the line, he or she is prompted by the Authorizer's Assistant to ask the ticket counter agent to examine your identification. You hand over your driver's license and another credit card to prove you're you. Then the ticket agent asks for your address, phone number, Social Security number, and your mother's maiden name and relays the information to American Express. Finally, your ticket purchase is approved. Why? Because you met the last series of "if–then" rules. *If* the purchaser can provide proof of identity and *if* the purchaser can provide personal information that isn't common knowledge, *then* approve the purchase.

decision support system (DSS) an information system that helps managers understand specific kinds of problems and potential solutions and analyze the impact of different decision options using "what-if" scenarios.

expert system an information system that contains the specialized knowledge and decision rules used by experts and experienced decision makers so that nonexperts can draw on this knowledge base to make decisions.

Accessing and Sharing Information and Knowledge Executive information systems, intranets, and corporate portals facilitate internal sharing and access to company information and transactions. Electronic data interchange, web services, and the Internet allow external groups like suppliers and customers to easily access company information. All three decrease costs by reducing or eliminating data entry, data errors, and paperwork and by speeding up communication. Organizations use decision support systems and expert systems to capture and share specialized knowledge with nonexpert employees.

Review 4

SELF-ASSESSMENT

Computer Comfort

Computers are ubiquitous in modern society, but that does not mean that everyone embraces them. As with any innovation, some people are reluctant to adopt computer technology, for whatever reason. How comfortable are you with computer technology?[70] Be candid as you complete the assessment by circling the appropriate responses, from 1, strongly disagree, to 5, strongly agree.

1. I hesitate to use a computer for fear of making mistakes that I cannot correct.
   1   2   3   4   5

2. The challenge of learning about computers is exciting.
   1   2   3   4   5

3. I feel apprehensive about using computers.
   1   2   3   4   5

4. I am confident that I can learn computer skills.
   1   2   3   4   5

5. I feel insecure about my ability to interpret a computer printout.
   1   2   3   4   5

6. I look forward to using a computer on my job.
   1   2   3   4   5

7. I have avoided computers because they are unfamiliar and somewhat intimidating to me.
   1   2   3   4   5

8. Learning to operate computers is like learning any new skill—the more you practice, the better you become.
   1   2   3   4   5

9. It scares me to think that I could cause the computer to destroy a large amount of information by hitting the wrong key.
   1   2   3   4   5

10. If given the opportunity, I would like to learn about and use computers.
    1   2   3   4   5

11. I have difficulty in understanding the technical aspects of computers.
    1   2   3   4   5

12. I am sure that with time and practice, I will be as comfortable working with computers as I am working with a typewriter.
    1   2   3   4   5

KEY TERMS

acquisition cost 712
association or affinity
   patterns 718
authentication 721
authorization 721
bar code 715
biometrics 722
communication cost 714
corporate portal 727
data clusters 719
data encryption 723
data mining 718
data warehouse 718
decision support system
   (DSS) 730
electronic data interchange
   (EDI) 728
electronic scanner 716
executive information
   system (EIS) 725
expert system 730
extranets 728
firewall 722
first-mover advantage 708

information 707
intranets 726
knowledge 729
Moore's law 706
optical character
   recognition 716
predictive patterns 719
processing cost 713
processing information 717
protecting information 719
radio frequency identification
   (RFID) tags 716
raw data 707
retrieval cost 713
secure sockets layer (SSL)
   encryption 724
sequence patterns 718
storage cost 713
supervised data mining 718
two-factor authentication 722
unsupervised data
   mining 718
virtual private network
   (VPN) 723
virus 723
web services 728

13. You have to be a genius to understand all the special keys contained on most computer terminals.

   1   2   3   4   5

14. Anyone can learn to use a computer if he or she is patient and motivated.

   1   2   3   4   5

15. I do not think I would be able to learn a computer programming language.

   1   2   3   4   5

16. I feel computers are necessary tools in both educational and work settings.

   1   2   3   4   5

17. I dislike working with machines that are smarter than I am.

   1   2   3   4   5

18. I feel that I will be able to keep up with the advances happening in the computer field.

   1   2   3   4   5

19. I am afraid that if I begin using computers, I will become dependent upon them and lose some of my reasoning skills.

TOTAL = _____

Scoring

Reverse scores on even-numbered items. Reverse means, for instance, a 1 becomes a 5; a 4 becomes a 2, and so on. Using the reversed scores and the remaining scores, compute your score for the nineteen items by adding up the scores. You can find the interpretation for your score at www.cengagebrain.com.

MANAGEMENT DECISION

Switching to the iPad[71]

As part of the anti-recession stimulus bill, the federal government allocated $19 billion to subsidize the modernization of medical records. You've been considering making the switch to computer-based records for some time now, and the stimulus funds will certainly make that decision a little easier now. But which system will you buy? You've visited a number of other practices and hospitals to see what they're using, and you've found a dizzying variety—desktops, laptops, PDAs, smartphones, all running different software.

You've heard, though, that Apple's iPad might trump them all. Released in April 2010, Apple's tablet computer has an elegant design and an operating system so easy to use that a widespread YouTube video shows a two-year-old figuring out how to use it in just five minutes. With its great battery life, lightweight, and sharp display, many in the medical industry are practically giddy about how the iPad can revolutionize medical records. Already, insurance giant Kaiser Permanente, Harvard Medical Schools, and the prestigious Cedars-Sinai Hospital have conducted trial programs to test the iPad's functionality in medical facilities. Best of all, it's relatively cheap compared to other laptop computers, and it has a low learning curve, because most of the doctors in your practice already use the iPhone.

In addition to getting federal funding, then, the iPad can bring several first-mover advantages for your practice. Your medical records will be consolidated and more efficient than competitors, which will make your entire operation run more smoothly. Patients will have to spend less time waiting for you and your staff to retrieve their charts and review their history. And it never hurts to have a reputation for being a practice that uses cutting edge technology. But just as you're about to order iPads for everyone in the office, one of your colleagues has some warnings. Do you think that flimsy thing can handle the rigors of a medical setting, he asks? He doesn't think it would last more than a month in a pediatrician's office, much less a hectic emergency room. And what about security? What kind of features does it have that will protect patient confidentiality? And then, he drops this bomb on you: "You know, people who buy first-generation Apple products are suckers . . . ." He reminds you that the first iPhone sold for $600 but had a minimal number of applications. Just two months later, the price was cut to $400, and ten months after that, they sold the iPhone 3G, with faster network access and thousands of more apps, for just $300. You could buy the iPad now, he says, but why not wait until Apple releases a cheaper, faster iPad with better features? And then, he reminds you that HP, Google, and other competitors will soon be releasing their own tablet computers. What if those are even better for medical records and they become the industry standard. Do we want to be left behind?

Questions

1. Considering the various first-mover and second-mover advantages, would you switch to the iPad or wait?

2. How important is it that the medical records system you select for your practice reflects the industry standard?

3. Do the benefits of having a computerized medical records system outweigh the costs involved in setting that system up?

MANAGEMENT TEAM DECISION

How Much Should We Tell?[72]

As the latest meeting of the management team of your mobile phone company begins, the marketing team passes out the results of the latest customer survey they performed. There isn't much in the survey that is surprising, but the one thing that did stand out is that customers want some more information. They want data about the phones' reception - how well the phones pick up the signal, how well they hang on to the signal, how often they drop calls, or whether they are susceptible to certain kinds of problems.

As the marketing team explains, one of the reasons the customers want to know this is because of the iPhone 4, many customers of which noted that the phone dropped calls and lost signals when it was held a certain way. When consumers and journalists criticized Apple for producing a phone with a defect, CEO Steve Jobs claimed that the iPhone's reception problems were caused by people holding the phone the wrong way and that most other phones from other manufacturers had similar problems.

This claim was quickly rebuffed by executives from other mobile phone manufacturers. Jim Balsille and Mike Lazaridis of RIM, Sanjay Jha of Motorola, and Hui-Meng Cheng of HTC all claimed that their equipment performed much better than Apple's iPhone. The problem was, however, that no one ever provided any data. All customers received were some vague claims that their phones worked great, but no one ever gave them any solid data, research results, or statistics.

As your marketing team shows, customers want this data. They're spending a lot of money to buy phones, and they want to know that it's money well spent. It's not as if obtaining or providing this data presents any difficulties. Already, cell phone carriers regularly provide equipment manufactures with dropped-call rates and information about how well specific phones perform on their networks. It's just that no company makes this data public.

So the question facing your management team is how to respond to your customers' desire for more information. Do you take a radical step, doing what no other company in the industry does, and release information about phone performance to the public? Or do you just follow in the footsteps of everyone else and issue a vague assurance?

Questions

1. What are the advantages and disadvantages of releasing information about the signal reliability of your phones to the public?

2. How could you use this information to gain a competitive advantage over other manufacturers who do not publicize?

PRACTICE BEING A MANAGER

Information Pipeline

Information is the lifeblood of organizations and one of the keys to sustaining a competitive advantage. The tools for processing and sharing information have improved and proliferated rapidly over the past few decades. But growing sophistication has also meant growing challenges in maintaining quality and security across far-flung corporate information systems. And managers increasingly feel deluged by the rising

flow of email, text messages, and near-instantaneous reports. To thrive in the information-rich environment of modern business, managers must effectively utilize the various tools available. This exercise will give you an opportunity to consider which tools might work best for a given need.

Step 1: Get into groups and read the scenario. Your professor will organize you into pairs or groups of three.

Scenario: Suppose that you and your partner(s) are going into business together. Brainstorm about some new ventures that might interest you. Select one of the ideas that seems appealing, and then talk about how you might build a sustainable competitive advantage for your new business. (*Hint:* You may want to review the first few sections of the chapter.) With this initial sketch of your business plan in mind, discuss how you might use information systems and tools to accomplish the following tasks:

- Researching the likely competition that you will face
- Finding out what steps will be required to get the necessary permits, licenses, and/or regulatory approvals to open and maintain your business
- Determining what price you should charge for your product(s) or service(s)
- Deciding what computer and communication equipment you will need to buy to support your new venture
- Recruiting and hiring the best people for available jobs in your new company

Step 2: Discuss the issues. Discuss how you might develop the information system that your company needs to successfully launch and grow. Be sure to include security issues/concerns in your discussion.

Step 3: Debrief as a class. What are the major challenges in creating and maintaining a sustainable competitive advantage? What role does information and information technology play in successfully competing with other companies in a given market? Is it possible to secure sensitive information and at the same share information with employees and/or other key stakeholders (suppliers, customers)?

DEVELOP YOUR CAREER POTENTIAL

Learn to Talk Tech

Most people are intimidated by technology. But like many things, technology becomes easier if you familiarize yourself with the basics. One way to learn to "speak geek" is to subscribe to *PC Magazine*, the premier magazine about personal computing. Depending on your budget, it may be more feasible (and possibly more productive) if you spend a set amount of time each week perusing technology websites like www.cnet.com and flipping through a selection of magazines dedicated to technology. The important thing is to be patient, however. After several issues, you should begin to understand what they're talking about. After that, it's easy to stay current. Subscribe at http://pcmag.com. You can also sign up for the "Term of the Day" email newsletter at http://webopedia.com. Each day, Webopedia will email you a new technology term and its definition. Either way, you'll soon be able to "talk tech."

Why is talking tech so important? Information technology (IT) is an integral part of nearly every business, whether it's simple email applications or more complex networking, e-commerce, and operations software. Very few companies are able to get by without using IT regularly. This being the case, managers need to understand this critical component of their companies' operations. That's not to say that managers (other than IT managers, of course) need to know every last technical detail, but as a manager, you will need—and want—to know what your tech staff is talking about when they bring problems, concerns, or suggestions for improvement to your office.

Computers are becoming an integral part of all kinds of work, so you need to do more than just understand the terminology. You also need to be able to use technology effectively. The reason is that people with basic computer skills earn 15 percent to 30 percent higher lifetime incomes than those without them. What should you do to learn about computers? Subscribe to *PC Magazine*, *PC World*, or *Macworld*. Buy a book about Microsoft Office and then take tests to be Microsoft Office User certified (see the Microsoft website for more information) in Word, Excel, PowerPoint, or Access. Take more than the required computer classes for your degree. Unless you want less job security and earning power, start learning more about computers today.

Activities

1. If you are completely new to IT, you might be more comfortable reading about it in the context of your favorite business publication. Walter Mossberg has a regular technology column in *The Wall Street Journal*, as does David Pogue, see Pogue's Posts, in *The New York Times*. Articles in both publications are on the shorter side, so take an hour and read through a few weeks' worth of each.

2. The U.S. government operates a career website at http://information-technology.careerbuilder.com. Go there to learn more about the IT field, see which jobs are in demand, and get an industry overview. There are also industry videos and links. This will give you a wealth of ideas about where and what kind of IT training you may want to pursue in conjunction with your business degree.

END NOTES

[1]Research and Innovative Technology Administration, "Baggage Fees by Airline, 2010," Bureau of Transportation Statistics, accessed June 27, 2011, from www.bts.gov/programs/airline_information/baggage_fees/; and F. Levy, "The Airlines' Bag Reflex," *Businessweek Online*, July 31, 2008, 11, accessed June 27, 2011, from www.businessweek.com/lifestyle/content/jul2008/bw20080729_355085.htm; S. McCartney, "Middle Seat Mailbox: Travelers Blast Airlines for Lost Bags; Would Hefty Penalties for Lost Luggage Force Air Carriers to Find a Better Way?" *The Wall Street Journal*, January 18, 2007, accessed June 27, 2011, from http://online.wsj.com/article/SB116909017751179834.html; S. McCartney, "Welcome to London: Your Luggage Is Missing; Why British Airways Is Worse Than Even U.S. Airlines At Losing (and Finding) Bags," *The Wall Street Journal*, August 21, 2007, D1; S. McCartney, "The Middle Seat: Why Your Bags Aren't Better Off On a Big Airline," *The Wall Street Journal*, September 2, 2008, D1; S. McCartney, "The Middle Seat: What It Costs an Airline to Fly Your Luggage," *The Wall Street Journal*, November 25, 2008, D1; D. Michaels, "Airlines' Expert on Missing Bags Fights Lost Cause: Mr. Price's Luggage Keeps Getting Mislaid; Buy Insurance, He Says," *The Wall Street Journal*, August 13, 2009, A1; and C. Palmeri, "Broken-Guitar Hero," *Businessweek*, August 3, 2009, 17.

[2]R. Lenzner, "The Reluctant Entrepreneur," *Forbes*, September 11, 1995, 162–166.

[3]Stephanie Clifford, "Nordstrom Links Online Inventory to Real World," *The New York Times*, August 23, 2010, accessed October 10, 2010, from www.nytimes.com/2010/08/24/business/24shop.html.

[4]Richard McGill Murphy, "Rising Stars," *Fortune*, September 6, 2010, 110–116.

[5]R. D. Buzzell & B. T. Gale, The PIMS Principles: Linking Strategy to Performance (New York: Free Press, 1987); and M. Lambkin, "Order of Entry and Performance in New Markets," *Strategic Management Journal* 9 (1988): 127–140.

[6]G. L. Urban, T. Carter, S. Gaskin, & Z. Mucha, "Market Share Rewards to Pioneering Brands: An Empirical Analysis and Strategic Implications," *Management Science* 32 (1986): 645–659.

[7]S. Nassauer, "'I Hate My Room' The Traveler Tweeted. Ka-Boom! An Upgrade!" *The Wall Street Journal*, June 24, 2010, accessed August 14, 2010, from http://online.wsj.com/article/NA_WSJ_PUB:SB10001424052748704256304575320730977161348.html.

[8]J. Hagerty, "'Big Brother' Keeps an Eye on Fleet of Heavy Equipment," *The Wall Street Journal*, June 1, 2011, B1.

[9]Kenji Hall, "How Komatsu Innovations Keep Its Machinery Selling," *Bloomberg Businessweek*, October 1, 2009, accessed July 10, 2010, from www.businessweek.com/globalbiz/content/sep2009/gb20090930_232338htm?campaign_id=alerts.

[10]J. Ross & P. Weill, "Four Questions Every CEO Should Ask about IT," *The Wall Street Journal*, April 25, 2011, R3.

[11]"UPMC Creates Electronic Health Record," UPMC, accessed June 28, 2009, from www.upmc.com/aboutupmc/qualityinnovation/excellenceinpatientcare/pages/erecord.aspx.

[12]A. Palanjian, "Career Journal: Disasters Are Her Specialty," *The Wall Street Journal*, April 7, 2009, B12.

[13]"The Human Face of Technology: Using Information Technology to Manage Disaster Response," Microsoft PressPass, June 4, 2008, accessed June 28, 2009, from www.microsoft.com/presspass/features/2008/jun08/06-04recovery.mspx; and A. Jacobs & E. Wong, "China Reports Student Toll for Quake," *The New York Times*, May 7, 2009, accessed June 28, 2009, from www.nytimes.com/2009/05/08/world/asia/08china.html.

[14]"Superstructures," *The Economist*, December 11, 2010, 17–19.

[15]M. Santosus, "Technology Recycling: Rising Costs of High-Tech Garbage," *CIO*, April 15, 2003, 36.

[16]"What is the WLCG?" CERN—the European Organization for Nuclear Research, no date, accessed July 22, 2010, from http://lcg.web.cern.ch/LCG/public/overview.htm.

[17]"Carbonite Expands Boston Data Center," PressReleasePoint, November 2, 2009, accessed September 15, 2010, from www.pressreleasepoint.com/carbonite-expands-boston-data-center-0.

[18]M. Santosus, "Procter & Gamble's Enterprise Content Management (ECM) System," CIO, May 15, 2003, accessed September 12, 2008, from www.cio.com/article/31920/Procter_Gamble_s_Enterprise_Content_Management_ECM_System; Ulrich Kampffmeyer, "Trends in Records, Document and Enterprise Content Management," Whitepaper. S.E.R. conference, Visegrád, September 28, 2004.

[19]Nicola Clark, "Crash Spurs Interest in Real-Time Flight Data," The New York Times, July 21, 2010, accessed July 29, 2010, from www.nytimes.com/2010/07/22/business/global/22blackbox.html?_r=1&hp.

[20]S. Lubar, Infoculture: The Smithsonian Book of Information Age Inventions (Boston: Houghton Mifflin, 1993).

[21]Ibid.

[22]A. Lavallee, "Unilever to Test Mobile Coupons—In Trial at Supermarket, Cellphones Will Be the Medium for Discount Offers," The Wall Street Journal, 29 May 2009, B8.

[23]A. Pawlowski, "Paperless Boarding Takes Off at United," CNN.com, March 15, 2010, accessed March 10, 2011, from http://articles.cnn.com/2010-03-15/travel/mobile.boarding.passes_1_boarding-airport-gates-passes?_s=PM:TRAVEL.

[24]L. Loyd, "US Airways Introduces Paperless Boarding Passes in Philadelphia," The Inquirer Digital at Philly.com, March 9, 2011, accessed June 25, 2011, from www.philly.com/philly/business/20110309_US_Airways_introduces_paperless_boarding_passes_in_Philadelphia.html?c=r.

[25]B. Worthen, "Bar Codes on Steroids," CIO, December 15, 2002, 53.

[26]Claire Swedberg, "RFID to Revolutionize Coca-Cola's Dispensers," RFID Journal, June 10, 2009, accessed June 25, 2011, from www.rfidjournal.com/article/view/4967.

[27]M. Stone, "Scanning for Business," PC Magazine, 10 May 2005, 117.

[28]D. Smith, "Paperless Office Solution Rescues Ambulance Service," PC World, December 2, 2009, accessed June 26, 2011, from www.pcworld.com/businesscenter/article/183541/paperless_office_solution_rescues_ambulance_service.html.

[29]Ben Worthen, "New Meters Aim to Cure Parking Headaches," The Wall Street Journal, January 27, 2011, accessed June 16, 2011, from http://online.wsj.com/article/SB10001424052748703555804576102090737327466.html.

[30]N. Rubenking, "Hidden Messages," PC Magazine, 22 May 2001, 86.

[31]G. Saitz, "Naked Truth—Data Miners, Who Taught Retailers to Stock Beer Near Diapers, Find Hidden Sales Trends, a Science That's Becoming Big Business," Newark (NJ) Star-Ledger, August 1, 2002, 041.

[32]A. Carter & D. Beucke, "A Good Neighbor Gets Better," Businessweek, June 20, 2005, 16.

[33]Rubenking, "Hidden Messages."

[34]M. Schoofs & M. Tamman, "Using a Computer to Fight Medicare Fraud," The Wall Street Journal, December 22, 2010, accessed June 26, 2011, from http://online.wsj.com/article/SB10001424052748704851204576034332420051722.html.

[35]Joshua Brustein, "Star Pitchers in a Duel? Tickets Will Cost More," The New York Times, June 27, 2010, accessed June 26, 2011, from www.nytimes.com/2010/06/28/technology/28tickets.html.

[36]Charles Duhigg, "What Does Your Credit-Card Company Know About You?" New York Times Magazine, May 12, 2009, accessed June 16, 2010, from www.nytimes.com/2009/05/17/magazine/17credit-t.html?pagewanted=1.

[37]"Privacy Policy," accessed June 26, 2011, from http://www.drugstore.com.

[38]B. Gottesman and K. Karagiannis, "A False Sense of Security," PC Magazine, February 22, 2005, 72.

[39]F. J. Derfler, Jr., "Secure Your Network," PC Magazine, June 27, 2000, 183–200.

[40]"Authentication," Webopedia accessed September 12, 2008, from www.webopedia.com/TERM/a/authentication.html.

[41]"Authorization," Webopedia, accessed September 12, 2008, from www.webopedia.com/TERM/a/authorization.html.

[42]K. Karagiannis, "Security Watch: Don't Make It Easy," PC Magazine, April 8, 2003, 72; M. Steinhart, "Password Dos and Don'ts," PC Magazine, February 12, 2002, 69; and L. Seltzer, "Are Pa55.W0rd5 Dead?" PC Magazine, December 28, 2004, 86.

[43]L. Seltzer, "Password Crackers," PC Magazine, February 12, 2002, 68.

[44]"Two-Factor Authentication," Information Security Glossary, accessed June 28, 2009, from www.rsa.com.

[45]"Gemalto Releases OTP Device for Access to Amazon's Web Services," DigitalIDNews, September 10, 2009, accessed on May 29, 2010, from www.digitalidnews.com/2009/09/10/gemalto-releases-otp-device-for-access-to-amazons-web-services.

[46]B. Grimes, "Biometric Security," PC Magazine, April 22, 2003, 74.

[47]Ibid.

[48]"Cardless Check-In at 24 Hour Fitness," 24 Hour Fitness, accessed June 26, 2011, from www.24hourfitness.com/health_clubs/cardless_checkin/; and J. Hagerty, "Biometrics Firms Widen Net," The Wall Street Journal, September 20, 2010, accessed June 26, 2011, from http://online.wsj.com/article/SB10001424052748703376504575492371980339514.html.

[49]M. McQueen, "Laptop Lockdown," The Wall Street Journal, June 28, 2006, D1.

[50]Angela Townsend "Cleveland-Area Software Company Designs First FDA-Cleared Medical Imaging App for Mobile Devices," Cleveland Plain-Dealer, February 15, 2011, accessed March 11, 2011, from www.cleveland.com/medical/index.ssf/2011/02/cleveland-area_software_compan.html.

[51]C. Metz, "Total Security," PC Magazine, October 1, 2003, 83.

[52]J. DeAvila, "Wi-Fi Users, Beware: Hot Spots Are Weak Spots," The Wall Street Journal, 16 January 2008, D1.

[53]M. Garry & J. Gallagher, "Food Lion Expands Data-Sharing Program," Supermarket News, November 10, 2008, 28.

[54]D. Orgel, "Food Lion's Data and the Spider-Man Principle," SuperMarket

News, November 30, 2009, accessed June 26, 2011, from http://supermarketnews.com/viewpoints/food-lions-data-1130/.

[55]J. van den Hoven, "Executive Support Systems & Decision Making," *Journal of Systems Management* 47, no. 8 (March–April 1996): 48.

[56]D. Hannon, "Colgate-Palmolive Empowers Senior Leaders with Executive Dashboards," *InsiderProfiles*, April 1, 2011, accessed June 26, 2011, from http://insiderprofiles.wispubs.com/article.aspx?iArticleId=5720.

[57]"Intranet," Webopedia, accessed August 26, 2001, from www.webopedia.com/TERM/i/intranet.html.

[58]"Duke Energy Gives Its Employees a Portal on Company News," *Charlotte Business Journal*, January 21, 2011, accessed March 11, 2011, from www.bizjournals.com/charlotte/print-edition/2011/01/21/Duke-gives-its-employees-a-news-Portal.html.

[59]J. Ericson, "The Hillman Group Leverages Consolidated Reporting, Geographic Analysis to Support Its Hardware Manufacturing/Distribution Leadership," *Business Intelligence Review*, March 1, 2007, 12.

[60]"Web Services," Webopedia, accessed April 16, 2009, from www.webopedia.com/TERM/W/Web_Services.html.

[61]S. Overby, "This Could Be the Start of Something Small," *CIO*, February 15, 2003, 54.

[62]"Extranet," Webopedia, accessed September 12, 2008, from www.webopedia.com/TERM/E/extranet.html.

[63]Press Release, "Penske Truck Leasing Launches Improved Customer Extranet," Truckinginfo.com, February 4, 2009, accessed June 26, 2011, from www.truckinginfo.com/news/news-detail.asp?news_id=62365&news_category_id=52; and "Do You Need a Comprehensive Solution? Penske Is an Expert in Fleet Operations," *Penske Truck Leasing*, accessed June 26, 2011, from www.pensketruckleasing.com/leasing/.

[64]Vicki Vaughan, "Smart Little Retail Shops," *Houston Chronicle*, August 17, 2010, accessed March 11, 2011, from www.chron.com/disp/story.mpl/business/7157804.html.

[65]S. Hamm, D. Welch, W. Zellner, F. Keenan, & F. Engardio, "Down but Hardly Out: Downturn Be Damned, Companies Are Still Anxious to Expand Online," *Businessweek*, March 26, 2001, 126.

[66]K. C. Laudon & J. P. Laudon, *Management Information Systems: Organization and Technology* (Upper Saddle River, NJ: Prentice Hall, 1996).

[67]J. Borzo, "Software for Symptoms," *The Wall Street Journal*, May 23, 2005, R10.

[68]Ibid.

[69]R. Hernandez, "American Express Authorizer's Assistant," *Business Rules Journal*, August 2001, accessed June 26, 2011, from http://bizrules.info/page/art_amexaa.htm.

[70]R. Heinssen, Jr., C. Glass, & L. Knight, "Assessing Computer Anxiety: Development and Validation of the Computer Anxiety Rating Scale," *Computers in Human Behavior* (1987): 49–59.

[71]Dana Blankenhorn, "Medicine Is the Apple iPad Sweet Spot," ZDNet, January 28, 2010, accessed June 26, 2011, from http://healthcare.zdnet.com/?p=3257; and Martha C. White, "An Apple a Day," The Big Money.com, April 7, 2010, accessed June 26, 2011, from www.thebigmoney.com/articles/0s-1s-and-s/2010/04/07/apple-day.

[72]Farhad Manjoo, "How Often Does Your Phone Drop Calls?" Slate.com, July 22, 2010, accessed March 11, 2011, from www.slate.com/id/2261251/.

© GreenLight

BIZ FLIX

The Good Shepherd

In the 2006 film *The Good Shepherd*, Edward Wilson (Matt Damon) is an idealistic young man who values honor, morality, and discretion. As the head of the CIA counterintelligence, Wilson is in charge of covert operations during the Bay of Pigs. The agency suspects that Castro was tipped off about the invasion, and Wilson is looking for the mole. As he investigates, his idealism gives way to something else: distrust of everyone in his office, fueled by Cold War paranoia. In this clip from the movie, Wilson is being briefed in the Technical Services Division on the clues found in a photograph and in a recording of a woman's voice.

What to Watch for and Ask Yourself

1. Which parts of this scene show data?
2. Which parts of this scene show information?
3. These film scenes show the information technology used during the 1960s at the CIA. In what ways do you think this investigation might progress differently with modern technology?

© Cengage Learning

MANAGEMENT WORKPLACE

Numi Organic Tea

When Brian Durkee shows up at Numi Organic Tea every day to work as the director of operations, he's on a mission to make Numi a worldwide leader in sustainable supply chain management. Setting up and maintaining an efficient enterprise resource planning (ERP) system turned out to be much easier than converting Chinese suppliers to profoundly different farming methods and ways of doing business. Numi had just begun to implement an ERP system with integrated inventory management and accounting when Durkee joined the company. In this video, Durkee explains how Numi is dedicated to sustainable supply chain management, eliminating waste, and using recycled materials.

What to Watch for and Ask Yourself

1. What kinds of challenges does Numi face in managing information?
2. Why was it no longer sufficient for Numi to use programs like Excel and QuickBooks to manage its information?
3. What are some of the advantages Durkee mentions that have come with using the ERP system?

CHAPTER 18

Managing Service and Manufacturing Operations

Learning Outcomes

1. Discuss the kinds of productivity and their importance in managing operations.
2. Explain the role that quality plays in managing operations.
3. Explain the essentials of managing a service business.
4. Describe the different kinds of manufacturing operations.
5. Explain why and how companies should manage inventory levels.

what would you do?

Louis Vuitton Headquarters, Paris, France[1]

Louis Vuitton Moët Hennessy (LVMH) is the world's leading luxury goods company. Louis Vuitton, who was employed by wealthy women to pack their clothes, started his company in 1854 and revolutionized travel by offering flat-topped, waterproof trunks that replaced curved, domed-top trunks. Made by hand and with a lifetime guarantee (still so today), Vuitton's expensive trunks were purchased by royalty and well-to-do travelers. Counterfeiters soon produced fakes, forcing the company in 1876 to release a brown and beige striped trunk that was initially difficult to duplicate. By 1888, because of more counterfeiting, Vuitton introduced a patented checkered material that was the forerunner of the distinctive bags it sells today.

LVMH, however, is much more than Louis Vuitton. Among its best known brands, Kenzo, Givenchy, and Celine make up its fashion and leather goods division; Christian Dior, Givenchy, and Guerlain in perfumes and cosmetics; Dom Pérignon, Hennessy, Krug, and Moët & Chandon in wine and spirits; TAG Heuer, Chaumet, and Hublot in watches and jewelry; along with Sephora (perfume and cosmetics) and DFS group (duty-free stores).

Over the last decade, the worldwide luxury market has doubled to $220 billion a year, with much of that growth coming from China. Louis Vuitton's CEO, Yves Carcelle, said about China: "There are 1.4 billion people there who suddenly want to treat themselves, and it will continue." That growth has attracted fierce competition, and disagreements about what constitutes luxury. Coach, for example, with its $300 handcrafted bags, considers itself in the "accessible luxury" business. Peter Marino, who designs Louis Vuitton retail stores counters that, "Coach has nothing to do with luxury. It could be selling iron ore, but it just happens to sell handbags. This is not about girls in China with a sewing machine, but about workmanship, exclusivity, and the sheer gloriousness of the materials." Coach CEO Lew Frankfort responds, "When did they last speak to a consumer? Luxury has been democratized." He insists that Coach bags, "are as well made as products anywhere. We even source from some of the same tanneries as European houses. But because we manufacture in low-cost countries, we can pass the savings on to consumers."

In practice, LVMH, Coach, and their competitors all walk a tightrope between exclusivity and reaching out to a broader market through diversification. Francesco Trapani, CEO of Bulgari, a luxury Italian jeweler and watchmaker, says, "Diversification is the rule of the game, but you can't do everything. The danger is, you do something badly, and then you don't just lose money but your reputation." Or, you overexpose your product by selling so broadly that it no longer seems like a luxury item.

"what's new" companies

Louis Vuitton
Red Door Interactive
Trader Joe's
Southwest Airlines
Diapers.com
Boeing

< "what's new" companies

© Peter Horree/Alamy

study tips

Ⓧ

Form a study group. Photocopy the glossary at the end of this text, and cut the copies into strips, one term per strip. Put all strips into a large bowl. Divide into two teams and have one team at a time draw out a strip. Quiz the opposing team, and then read the correct answer. You can do the same with the chapter outlines at the beginning of each chapter.

© iStockphoto.com/Alex Slobodkin

Louis Vuitton expands production of its most popular products to meet demand, but also produces small numbers or limited editions of a large variety of high-quality luxury items. CEO Yves Carcelle says that "über-luxury" items are a small part of sales, but are growing quickly. He says, "There is demand for things that are incredible and unique. Our paradox is how to grow without diluting our image."

From a production standpoint, this creates a number of challenges. First, don't run out of the most popular products, yet also have the flexibility to produce small batches (i.e., limited editions) of a large number of different luxury goods. But how do you design factories to do both, and increase productivity? Second, because workers complete just one task, such as cutting leather, gluing and sewing, or stitching the lining, it generally takes 30 craftsmen eight days to produce just one Louis Vuitton bag. Production bottlenecks are common as the faster workers are forced to wait on the slower workers. So, how can you restructure production process to add more capacity without building any more factories?

If you were in charge of Louis Vuitton's factories and production system, what would you do?

As you read in the opening vignette, luxury good maker Louis Vuitton faces the challenges of adapting its operations, managing inventory, and improving productivity. In this chapter, you will learn about **operations management** —managing the daily production of goods and services. You will begin by learning about the basics of operations management: productivity and quality. Next, you will read about managing operations, beginning with service operations, turning next to manufacturing operations, and finishing with an examination of the types, measures, costs, and methods for managing inventory.

Managing for Productivity and Quality

You're "crossing the pond" in September to visit your company's European offices and suppliers. Because business is down, your boss has given you a limited budget of $1,600 for airfare. Your round-trip ticket from Chicago to London costs $839 on American Airlines, but that leaves only $761 for airfare in Europe. The total cost of flying from London to Dublin (via BMI), Dublin to Brussels (via Aer Lingus), Brussels to Venice (via Lufthansa), and Venice to London (via Alitalia) is $989—$228 more than your remaining budget and $150 more than your flight from the United States. At lunch, you're griping about the cost of European air travel when the company intern tells you to check out Ryanair, which she flew when she backpacked in Europe last summer. So, after lunch, you surf to www.ryanair.com and find that the total cost to travel to the same cities on the same dates and times is an amazing $176, or just 17.8 percent of the cost of flying the other major European airlines!

Modeled after U.S.-based Southwest Airlines, Ryanair achieves dramatically lower prices through aggressive price cutting and much higher productivity. Want a frequent-flier plan? You won't find one at Ryanair. It's too expensive. Want a meal on your flight? Pack a lunch. Ryanair doesn't even serve peanuts because it takes too much time (i.e., expense) to get them out of the seat cushions. Passengers enter

operations management managing the daily production of goods and services.

742

and exit the planes using old-fashioned rolling stairs because they're quicker and cheaper than extendable boarding gates. As a result of such cost-cutting moves, Ryanair does more with less and thus has higher productivity. Most airlines break even on their flights when they're 75 percent full, but Ryanair's productivity allows it to break even when its planes are only half full, even with its incredibly low prices. With this low break-even point, Ryanair attracts plenty of customers, who enable it to fill most of its seats (84%) and earn 20 percent net profit margins. Finally, because of its extremely low prices (and its competitors' extremely high prices), Ryanair has increased passenger traffic and profits for 19 straight years. Ryanair is the third-largest airline in Europe in terms of passenger numbers and the world's largest in terms of international passenger numbers.[2]

After reading the next two sections, you should be able to

1. *Discuss the kinds of productivity and their importance in managing operations.*

2. *Explain the role that quality plays in managing operations.*

1 Productivity

At their core, organizations are production systems. Companies combine inputs such as labor, raw materials, capital, and knowledge to produce outputs in the form of finished products or services. **Productivity** is a measure of performance that indicates how many inputs it takes to produce or create an output.

$$\text{Productivity} = \frac{\text{Outputs}}{\text{Inputs}}$$

The fewer inputs it takes to create an output (or the greater the output from one input), the higher the productivity. For example, a car's gas mileage is a common measure of productivity. A car that gets 35 miles (output) per gallon (input) is more productive and fuel efficient than a car that gets 18 miles per gallon.

Let's examine **1.1 why productivity matters** and **1.2 the different kinds of productivity**.

1.1 Why Productivity Matters

Why does productivity matter? For companies, higher productivity—that is, doing more with less—results in lower costs for the company, lower prices, faster service, higher market share, and higher profits. For example, every second saved in the drive-through lane at a fast-food restaurant increases sales by 1 percent. Furthermore, increasing the efficiency of drive-through service by 10 percent adds nearly 10 percent to a fast-food restaurant's sales. And with up to 75 percent of all fast-food restaurant sales coming from the drive-through window, it's no wonder that Wendy's (average drive-through time of 131 seconds per vehicle), Burger King (average time of 153 seconds per vehicle), and McDonald's (average time of 167.1 seconds per vehicle) continue to look for ways to shorten the time it takes to process a drive-through order.[3]

Productivity matters so much at the drive-through that McDonald's is experimenting with outsourcing. At roughly fifty McDonald's franchises around the country, drive-through orders are taken by someone at a California call center. An operator can take orders from customers at restaurants in Honolulu one minute and in Gulfport, Mississippi, the next. Although it seems counterintuitive, initial

productivity a measure of performance that indicates how many inputs it takes to produce or create an output.

results show the system has improved order-taking accuracy and improved productivity. During the 10 seconds it takes for a car to pull away from the microphone at the drive-through, a call center operator can take the order of a different customer who has pulled up to the microphone at another restaurant, even if it's thousands of miles away. According to Jon Anton, cofounder of Bronco Communications, which operates the call center for McDonald's, the goal is "saving seconds to make millions," because more efficient service can lead to more sales and lower labor costs.[4]

The productivity of businesses within a country matters to that country because it results in a higher standard of living. One way that productivity leads to a higher standard of living is through increased wages. When companies can do more with less, they can raise employee wages without increasing prices or sacrificing normal profits. For instance, when I wrote this chapter, recent government economic data indicated that companies were paying workers 2 percent more than in the previous year. But because workers were producing 1.8 percent more than they had the year before, real labor costs actually rose by 0.2 percent.[5] The average American family earned approximately $60,088 in 2009. If productivity grows 1 percent per year, that family's income will increase to $77,059 in 2034. But if productivity grows 2 percent per year, their income in 2034 will be $98,581, an increase of more than $22,000, and that's without working longer hours.[6]

Thanks to long-term increases in business productivity, the average American family today earns 19 percent more than the average family in 1980 and 40 percent more than the average family in 1967—and that's after accounting for inflation.[7] Rising income stemming from increased productivity creates other benefits as well. Productivity increased an average of 2.3 percent between 1995 and 2005, and then slowed to an average of 1.2 percent from 2005 to 2009.[8] And from 1998 to 2008, the U.S. economy created nearly 16.6 million new jobs.[9]

And when more people have jobs that pay more, they give more to charity. For example, in 2007 Americans donated over $306 billion to charities, 3.9 percent more than they gave in 2006. Did Americans become more thoughtful, caring,

Thanks to long-term increases in business productivity, the average American family today earns 19 percent more than the average family in 1980 and 40 percent more than the average family in 1967.

© iStockphoto.com/mark yuill

conscientious, and giving? Probably not. Yet, because of strong increases in productivity during this time, the average American income increased by 30 percent, from $35,190 in 2000 to $45,840 in 2007.[10] Because more people earned more money, they were able to share their good fortune with others by giving more to charity.[11] Likewise, charitable giving fell slightly from $306 billion in 2006 to $304 billion in 2009, as average income was essentially unchanged from $46,240 in 2006 to $46,360 in 2009, while unemployment rose dramatically from 4.6 percent in 2006 to 9.3 percent in 2009.[12]

Another benefit of productivity is that it makes products more affordable or better. For example, while inflation has pushed the average cost of a new car to $27,950, increases in manufacturing productivity have actually made cars cheaper. In 1960, the average family needed 26 weeks of income to pay for an average car. Today, the average family needs just 23.2 weeks of income—and today's car is loaded with accessories that weren't available in the 1960s, including air bags, power steering and brakes, CD and DVD players, seat warmers, air conditioning, and satellite navigation. So, in terms of real purchasing power, productivity gains have actually made today's $27,950 car cheaper than the 1960's car that sold for $2,000.[13]

1.2 Kinds of Productivity

Two common measures of productivity are partial productivity and multifactor productivity. **Partial productivity** indicates how much of a particular kind of input it takes to produce an output.

$$\text{Partial Productivity} = \frac{\text{Outputs}}{\text{Single Kind of Input}}$$

Labor is one kind of input that is frequently used when determining partial productivity. *Labor productivity* typically indicates the cost or number of hours of labor it takes to produce an output. In other words, the lower the cost of the labor to produce a unit of output, or the less time it takes to produce a unit of output, the higher the labor productivity. For example, the automobile industry often measures labor productivity by determining the average number of hours of labor needed to completely assemble a car. According to the most recent Harbour Report, the three Detroit-based automakers have reached near parity with their Japanese rivals in manufacturing efficiency. Toyota and Chrysler assemble a car in 30.37 hours; Honda, in 31.33 hours; GM, in 32.29 hours; Nissan, in 32.96 hours; and Ford, in 33.88 hours. The gap between the most and least productive automakers has narrowed from 10.51 labor hours in 2003 to just 3.5 labor hours in 2008.[14] Partial productivity assesses how efficiently companies use only one input, such as labor, when creating outputs. Multifactor productivity is an overall measure of productivity that assesses how efficiently companies use all the inputs it takes to make outputs. More specifically, **multifactor productivity** indicates how much labor, capital, materials, and energy it takes to produce an output.[15]

$$\text{Multifactor Productivity} = \frac{\text{Outputs}}{(\text{Labor} + \text{Capital} + \text{Materials} + \text{Energy})}$$

Exhibit 18.1 shows the trends in multifactor productivity across a number of U.S. industries since 1987.

With a 268 percent increase between 2002 (scaled at 100) and 2008 (when it reached a level of 368) and a thirtyfold increase since 1987, the growth in multifactor productivity in the computer and electronic products industry far exceeded the

partial productivity a measure of performance that indicates how much of a particular kind of input it takes to produce an output.

multifactor productivity an overall measure of performance that indicates how much labor, capital, materials, and energy it takes to produce an output.

Exhibit 18.1   Multifactor Productivity Growth Across Industries

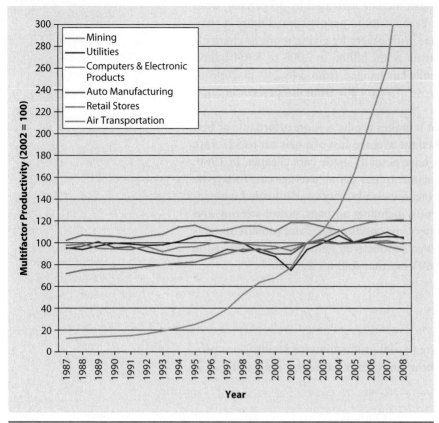

Source: "Industry Productivity Indexes, Detailed 4-Digit NAICS Industries for Multifactor Productivity," Bureau of Labor Statistics, accessed June 27, 2011, from www.bls.gov/mfp/tables.htm.

productivity growth in retail stores, auto manufacturing, mining, utilities, and air transportation as well as most other industries tracked by the U.S. government.

Of course, the surge in productivity in the computer and electronics industry isn't a surprise. Each round of technology advances brings significantly smaller and cheaper yet much more powerful electronic devices. Significantly less labor, capital, materials, and energy are needed today than in the past to produce computers and electronic products (including smartphones, iPads, and computer game devices such as the PlayStation 3). In 1981, the IBM PC Model 5150, featuring 16k of memory, a 4.7mhz processor, a floppy disk or cassette tape drive, and a monochromatic monitor, sold for $1,995, equivalent to about $4,800 in 2010. A 10mb hard drive and a four-color display were optional add-ons. Today, thanks to increased productivity in the computer industry, $1,995 would buy five IdeaPad netbooks from Lenovo, each of which is 300 times faster and nearly 50 pounds lighter than the original IBM PC. You'll even get hard drives and color screens.[16]

Should managers use multiple or partial productivity measures? In general, they should use both. Multifactor productivity indicates a company's overall level of productivity relative to its competitors. In the end, that's what counts most. However, multifactor productivity measures don't indicate the specific contributions that labor, capital, materials, or energy make to overall productivity. To analyze the contributions of these individual components, managers need to use partial productivity measures. Doing so can help them determine what factors need to be adjusted or in what areas adjustment can make the most difference in overall productivity.

Review 1

Productivity   At their core, companies are production systems that combine inputs (such as labor), raw materials, capital, and knowledge to produce outputs (such as finished products or services). Productivity is a measure of how many inputs it takes to produce or create an output. The greater the output from one input, or the fewer inputs it takes to create an output, the higher the productivity. Partial productivity measures how much of a single kind of input (such as labor) is needed to produce an output. Multifactor productivity is an overall measure of productivity that indicates how much labor, capital, materials, and energy are needed to produce an output. Increased productivity helps companies lower costs, which can lead to lower prices, higher market share, and higher profits. Increased productivity helps countries by leading to higher wages, lower product prices, and a higher standard of living.

2 Quality

With the average car costing $27,950, car buyers want to make sure that they're getting good quality for their money.[17] Fortunately, as indicated by the number of problems per 100 cars (PP100), today's cars are of much higher quality than earlier models. In 1981, Japanese cars averaged 240 PP100. General Motors' cars averaged 670, Ford's averaged 740, and Chrysler's averaged 870 PP100! In other words, as measured by PP100, the quality of American cars was two to three times worse than that of Japanese cars. By 1992, however, U.S. carmakers had made great strides, significantly reducing the number of problems to an average of 155 PP100. Japanese vehicles had improved too, averaging just 125 PP100.

Exhibit 18.2 shows the results of the 2011 J.D. Power and Associates survey of initial car quality. Overall quality improved to 107 problems per 100 vehicles (PP100) in 2011, down from 125 PP100 in 2007 and 118 PP100 in 2008 and 108 PP100 in 2010. Lexus, with just 73 PP100, had the best quality, followed by Honda with 86 PP100, Acura with 89 PP100, and

Exhibit 18.2 J.D. Power and Associates Survey of Initial Car Quality

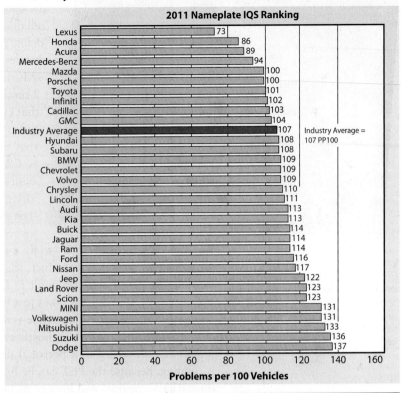

Source: Press Release, "J.D. Power and Associates Reports: Initial Quality of Recent Vehicle Launches is Considerably Lower than in 2010, While Carryover Model Quality is Better than Ever," JD Power and Associates, 23 June 2011, http://businesscenter.jdpower.com/news/pressrelease.aspx?ID=2011089 [accessed 27 June, 2011].

Mercedes-Benz with 94 PP100. At the bottom of the list were MINI and Volkswagen tied for 131 PP100, Mitsubishi with 133 PP100, Suzuki with 136 PP100 and Dodge with 137 PP100. In 2011, however, even the worst cars on the J.D. Power and Associates Survey of Initial Car quality beat the scores of the Japanese cars of decades ago. And category leaders like Porsche, Acura, Mercedes-Benz, Lexus, Ford, and Honda came in with scores under 100. That means there's less than one problem per car![18]

The American Society for Quality gives two meanings for **quality**. It can mean a product or service free of deficiencies, such as the number of problems per 100 cars, or it can mean the characteristics of a product or service that satisfy customer needs.[19] Today's cars are of higher quality than those produced 20 years ago in both senses. Not only do they have fewer problems per 100 cars, they also have a number of additional standard features (power brakes and steering, stereo/CD/MP3 player, power windows and locks, air bags, cruise control).

In this part of the chapter, you will learn about **2.1 quality-related characteristics for products and services, 2.2 ISO 9000 and 14000, 2.3 the Baldrige National Quality Award,** and **2.4 total quality management.**

2.1 Quality-Related Characteristics for Products and Services

As shown in Exhibit 18.3, quality products usually possess three characteristics: reliability, serviceability, and durability.[20] A breakdown occurs when a product quits

quality a product or service free of deficiencies, or the characteristics of a product or service that satisfy customer needs.

Exhibit 18.3
Characteristics of Product Quality

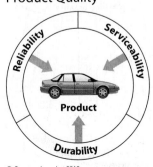

© Cengage Learning 2013

747

An electric REVA automobile drives along a city street during Bangalore's celebration of World Environment Day. REVA uses a computer diagnostic system that can sync to the owner's cell phone and indicate the type of service the vehicle needs.

Exhibit 18.4
Characteristics of Service Quality

© Cengage Learning 2013

working or doesn't do what it was designed to do. The longer it takes for a product to break down or the longer the time between breakdowns, the more reliable the product. Consequently, many companies define *product reliability* in terms of the average time between breakdowns. For example, Western Digital sells the WD RE4 2 TB hard drive, an extremely fast 2-terabyte (a terabyte is 1,000 gigabytes) hard drive that customers can use for gaming, multimedia, and video applications. The WD RE4 2 TB is so reliable that the estimated mean time between breakdowns is 1.2 million hours, or more than 28.5 years![21] Of course, this is just an average. Some WD RE4 hard drives will break down much sooner, but others will last even longer than 137 years.

Serviceability refers to how easy or difficult it is to fix a product. The easier it is to maintain a working product or fix a broken product, the more serviceable that product is. The REVA is an electric two-seater car built in India for city use. It goes 50 miles on a single battery charge (a recharge takes just five hours), and its operating costs per mile are one-third that of a typical gasoline-powered car. The REVA has high serviceability by virtue of a computerized diagnostic system that plugs into a portable electronic tool (PET), about the size of a personal digital assistant, that assesses how well the car is running. Because the PET can be linked to a phone, customers can easily transmit their REVA's operational history to instantly find out whether their car needs work and, if so, what kind. In many instances, a simple computer change downloaded to the PET and then to the REVA will fix the problem.[22]

A product breakdown assumes that a product can be repaired. However, some products don't break down; they fail. *Product failure* means products can't be repaired. They can only be replaced. *Durability* is defined as the mean time to failure. Typically, for example, when an LCD screen quits working, it "dies" and can't be repaired. Consequently, durability, or the average time before failure, is a key part of LCD quality. Why buy a great-looking LCD if it's only going to last a few years? Indeed, Toshiba is now producing thin-film transistor LCDs with a mean time between failures of 100,000 hours, or 11.4 years.[23]

Whereas high-quality products are characterized by reliability, serviceability, and durability, services are different. There's no point in assessing the durability of a service because services don't last but are consumed the minute they're performed. For example, once a lawn service has mowed your lawn, the job is done until the mowers come back next week to do it again. Services also don't have serviceability. You can't maintain or fix a service. If a service wasn't performed correctly, all you can do is perform it again. Rather than serviceability and durability, the quality of service interactions often depends on how the service provider interacts with the customer. Was the service provider friendly, rude, or helpful? As shown in Exhibit 18.4, five characteristics typically distinguish a quality service: reliability, tangibles, responsiveness, assurance, and empathy.[24]

Service reliability is the ability to consistently perform a service well. Studies clearly show that reliability matters more to customers than anything else when buying services. When you take your clothes to the dry cleaner, you don't want them returned with cracked buttons or wrinkles down the front. If your dry cleaner gives you back perfectly clean and pressed clothes every time, it's providing a reliable service.

Also, although services themselves are not tangible (you can't see or touch them), services are provided in tangible places. Thus, *tangibles* refer to the appearance of the offices, equipment, and personnel involved with the delivery of a service. One of the best examples of the effect of tangibles on the perception of quality is the restroom. When you eat at a fancy restaurant, you expect clean, if not upscale, restrooms. How different is your perception of a business, say a gas station, if it has clean rather than filthy restrooms?

Ten years ago, when Apple launched its retail stores, most experts predicted that they would fail given all of the other locations where consumers could buy computer and electronics equipment. This year, over a quarter billion people will visit Apple's 326 stores, or four times the number of visitors to Walt Disney Companies four largest theme parks. Why? Largely because of the quality characteristics of responsiveness, assurance, and empathy.

Responsiveness is the promptness and willingness with which service providers give good service. Ironically, at Apple stores this manifests itself in a sales philosophy of not selling. Instead, Apple store employees are trained to help customers solve problems. An Apple training manual says, "Your job is to understand all of your customers' needs—some of which they may not even realize they have." David Ambrose, a former Apple store employee says, "You were never trying to close a sale. It was about finding solutions for a customer and finding their pain points."

Assurance is the confidence that service providers are knowledgeable, courteous, and trustworthy. Apple "geniuses," who staff the "Genius Bars" in each store are trained at Apple headquarters and, according to Apple's website, "can take care of everything from troubleshooting your problems to actual repairs." Geniuses are regularly tested on their knowledge and problem-solving skills to maintain their certification. Other Apple store employees are highly trained too, and are not allowed to help customers until they've spent two to four weeks shadowing experienced store employees.

Empathy is the extent to which service providers give individual attention and care to customers' concerns and problems. The acronym, APPLE, instructs employees how to empathetically engage with customers: "**A**pproach customers with a personalized warm welcome," "**P**robe politely to understand all the customer's needs," "**P**resent a solution for the customer to take home today," "**L**isten for and resolve any issues or concerns," and "**E**nd with a fond farewell and an invitation to return." And when customers are frustrated and become emotional, the advice is to "Listen and limit your responses to simple reassurances that you are doing so. 'Uh-huh,' 'I understand,' etc."

The results from Apple's retail approach speak for themselves, as Apple retails sales average $4,406 per square foot, higher than Tiffany jewelry stores ($3,070), Coach luxury retail ($1,776), or Best Buy ($880), a full-service computer and electronics store.[25]

2.2 ISO 9000 and 14000

ISO, pronounced "eye-so," comes from the Greek word *isos*, meaning "equal, similar, alike, or identical" and is also an acronym for the International Organization for Standardization, which helps set standards for 162 countries. The purpose of this agency is to develop and publish standards that facilitate the international exchange of goods and services.[26] **ISO 9000** is a series of five international standards, from ISO 9000 to ISO 9004, for achieving consistency in quality management and quality assurance in companies throughout the world. **ISO 14000** is a series of international standards for managing, monitoring, and minimizing an organization's harmful effects on the environment.[27] (For more on environmental quality and issues, see Section 3.5 of Chapter 16 on controlling waste and pollution.)

ISO 9000 a series of five international standards, from ISO 9000 to ISO 9004, for achieving consistency in quality management and quality assurance in companies throughout the world.

ISO 14000 a series of international standards for managing, monitoring, and minimizing an organization's harmful effects on the environment.

The ISO 9000 standards publications, which are available from the American National Standards Institute (see the end of this section), are general and can be used for manufacturing any kind of product or delivering any kind of service. Importantly, the ISO 9000 standards don't describe how to make a better-quality car, computer, or widget. Instead, they describe how companies can extensively document (and thus standardize) the steps they take to create and improve the quality of their products. Why should companies go to the trouble to achieve ISO 9000 certification? Because their customers increasingly want them to. In fact, studies show that customers clearly prefer to buy from companies that are ISO 9000 certified. Companies, in turn, believe that being ISO 9000 certified helps them keep customers who might otherwise switch to an ISO 9000–certified competitor.[28]

To become ISO certified, a process that can take months, a company must show that it is following its own procedures for improving production, updating design plans and specifications, keeping machinery in top condition, educating and training workers, and satisfactorily dealing with customer complaints.[29] An accredited third party oversees the ISO certification process, just as a certified public accountant verifies that a company's financial accounts are up-to-date and accurate. Once a company has been certified as ISO 9000 compliant, the accredited third party will issue an ISO 9000 certificate that the company can use in its advertising and publications. This is the quality equivalent of the *Good Housekeeping* Seal of Approval. But continued ISO 9000 certification is not guaranteed. Accredited third parties typically conduct periodic audits to make sure the company is still following quality procedures. If it is not, its certification is suspended or canceled.

It's estimated that more than half of mid-sized U.S. manufacturers have achieved ISO 9000 certification. Two-thirds of the certified companies say they wanted certification because it increases customer satisfaction. Accordingly, most advertise their ISO certification in their promotional materials and mention or even post it on their website. For example, ACME Specialty Manufacturing, a maker of rugged tempered glass exterior mirrors and interior mirrors for manufacturers of a wide variety of types of vehicles, has posted its certificate at www.acmespecialty.com and states, "At ACME Specialty Manufacturing, our products are created using state-of-the-art equipment in our 70,000 square-feet, ISO-9001-2000 registered facility in Toledo, Ohio."[30] To get additional information on ISO 9000 guidelines and procedures, see the American National Standards Institute (http://webstore .ansi.org/default.aspx; the ISO 9000 and ISO 14000 standards publications are available here for about $400 and $300, respectively), the American Society for Quality (www.asq.org), and the International Organization for Standardization (www.iso.org).

2.3 Baldrige National Quality Award

The Baldrige National Quality Award, which is administered by the U.S. government's National Institute for Standards and Technology, is given "to recognize U.S. companies for their achievements in quality and business performance and to raise awareness about the importance of quality and performance excellence as a competitive edge."[31] Each year, up to three awards may be given in these categories: manufacturing, education, health care, service, small business, and nonprofit. Exhibit 18.5 lists the latest Baldrige Award winners.

The cost of applying for the Baldrige Award includes a $150 eligibility fee, an application fee of $7,000 for manufacturing firms and $3,500 for small businesses, and a site visitation fee of $20,000 to $35,000 for manufacturing firms and $10,000 to $17,000 for small businesses.[32] Why does it cost so much? Because you get a great deal of useful information about your business even if you don't win. At a minimum, each company that applies receives an extensive report based on 300 hours of assessment from at least eight business and quality experts. At $10 an hour for small businesses and about $20 an hour for manufacturing and service businesses, the *Journal for Quality and Participation* called the Baldrige feedback report "the best bargain in consulting in America."[33] Arnold Weimerskirch, former chair of the Baldrige Award panel of judges and vice president of quality at Honeywell, says, "The application and review process for the Baldrige Award is the best, most cost-effective and comprehensive business health audit you can get."[34]

Exhibit 18.5 Latest Baldrige National Quality Award Recipients

Sector	2010	2009
Manufacturing	MEDRAD Nestle Purina PetCare	Honeywell Federal Manufacturing Technologies
Education	Montgomery County Public Schools	—
Healthcare	Advocate Good Samaritan Hospital	AtlantaCare Heartland Health
Nonprofit	—	VA Cooperative Studies Program Clinical Research Pharmacy Coordinating Center
Small business	Freese and Nichols K&N Management Studer Group	MidwayUSA

Source: "1988–2010 Award Recipients' Contacts and Profiles," National Institute of Standards and Technology, accessed June 27, 2011, from www.quality.nist.gov/Contacts.htm.

The criteria for the Baldrige Award are different for business, education, and health-care organizations. Businesses that apply for the Baldrige Award are judged on a 1,000-point scale based on the seven criteria shown in Exhibit 18.6: leadership; strategic planning; customer and market focus; measurement, analysis, and knowledge management; work force focus; process management; and results.[35] Results are clearly the most important category, as it takes up 450 out of 1,000 points. In other words, in addition to the six other criteria, companies must show that they have achieved superior quality when it comes to products and services, customers, financial performance and market share, treatment of employees, work systems and processes, and leadership and social responsibility. This emphasis on results is what differentiates the Baldrige Award from the ISO 9000 standards. The Baldrige Award indicates the extent to which companies have actually achieved world-class quality. The ISO 9000 standards simply indicate whether a company is following the management system it put into place to improve quality. In fact, ISO 9000 certification covers less than 10 percent of the requirements for the Baldrige Award.[36]

> "The application and review process for the Baldrige Award is the best, most cost-effective and comprehensive business health audit you can get."
>
> —ARNOLD WEIMERSKIRCH, VICE PRESIDENT OF QUALITY, HONEYWELL

Why should companies go to the trouble of applying for the Baldrige Award? Earnest Deavenport, CEO of Eastman Chemical, explains, "Eastman, like other Baldrige Award winners, didn't apply the concepts of total quality management to win an award. We did it to win customers. We did it to grow. We did it to prosper and to remain competitive in a world marketplace."[37] Furthermore, the companies that have won the Baldrige Award have achieved superior financial returns. Since 1988, an investment in Baldrige Award winners would have outperformed the Standard & Poor's 500 stock index 80 percent of the time.[38] For additional information about the Baldrige Award, see the National Institute of Standards and Technology website at www.nist.gov/baldrige/.

Exhibit 18.6 Criteria for the Baldrige National Quality Award

2009 Categories/Items	Point Values
1 Leadership	**120**
Senior Leadership	70
Governance and Societal Responsibilities	50
2 Strategic Planning	**85**
Strategy Development	40
Strategy Deployment	45
3 Customer Focus	**85**
Customer Engagement	40
Voice of the Customer	45
4 Measurement, Analysis, and Knowledge Management	**90**
Measurement, Analysis, and Improvement of Organizational Performance	45
Management of Information, Knowledge, and Information Technology	45
5 Workforce Focus	**85**
Workforce Engagement	45
Workforce Environment	40
6 Process Management	**85**
Work Systems	45
Work Processes	40
7 Results	**450**
Product and Process Outcomes	120
Customer-Focused Outcomes	90
Workforce-Focused Outcomes	80
Leadership and Governance Outcomes	80
Financial and Market Outcomes	80
TOTAL POINTS	1,000

Source: "2011–2012 Criteria for Performance Excellence," Baldrige National Quality Program 2008, accessed June 27, 2011, from www.nist.gov/baldrige/publications/upload/2011_2012_Business_Nonprofit_Criteria.pdf.

2.4 Total Quality Management

Total quality management (TQM) is an integrated, organization-wide strategy for improving product and service quality.[39] TQM is not a specific tool or technique. Rather, TQM is a philosophy or overall approach to management that is characterized by three principles: customer focus and satisfaction, continuous improvement, and teamwork.[40]

Although most economists, accountants, and financiers argue that companies exist to earn profits for shareholders, TQM suggests that customer focus and customer satisfaction should be a company's primary goals. **Customer focus** means that the entire organization, from top to bottom, should be focused on meeting customers' needs. The result of that customer focus should be **customer satisfaction**, which occurs when the company's products or services meet or exceed customers' expectations.

At companies where TQM is taken seriously, such as Enterprise Rent-A-Car, paychecks and promotions depend on keeping customers satisfied.[41] Enterprise measures customer satisfaction with a detailed survey called the Enterprise Service Quality index. Enterprise not only ranks each branch office by operating profits and customer satisfaction but also makes promotions to higher-paying jobs contingent

total quality management (TQM) an integrated, principle-based, organization-wide strategy for improving product and service quality.

customer focus an organizational goal to concentrate on meeting customers' needs at all levels of the organization.

customer satisfaction an organizational goal to provide products or services that meet or exceed customers' expectations.

on above-average customer satisfaction scores. According to Andy Taylor, Enterprise's CEO, "Once we showed we were serious—a couple of star performers who had achieved good growth and profit numbers but had generated below-average satisfaction scores were passed over for promotions—all doubt about the importance of the scores vanished."[42] Not surprisingly, this emphasis on quality increased the number of completely satisfied Enterprise Rent-a-Car customers from the high 60 percent range to the high 70 percent range in just five years. As a result, Enterprise customers are three times more likely to rent an Enterprise car again than are

customers of other car rental companies, and Enterprise has topped J.D. Power & Associates' Rental Car Satisfaction ratings for five straight years.[43]

Continuous improvement is an ongoing commitment to increase product and service quality by constantly assessing and improving the processes and procedures used to create those products and services. How do companies know whether they're achieving continuous improvement? Besides higher customer satisfaction, continuous improvement is usually associated with a reduction in variation. **Variation** is a deviation in the form, condition, or appearance of a product from the quality standard for that product. The less a product varies from the quality standard, or the more consistently a company's products meet a quality standard, the higher the quality. At Freudenberg-NOK, a manufacturer of seals and gaskets for the au-

tomotive industry, continuous improvement means shooting for a goal of Six Sigma quality, meaning just 3.4 defective or nonstandard parts per million (PPM). Achieving this goal would eliminate almost all product variation. In a recent year, Freudenberg-NOK made over 200 million seals and gaskets, with a defect rate of 9 PPM.[44] As Exhibit 18.7 shows, this almost puts Freudenberg-NOK at Six Sigma, or 3.4 defective PPM. Furthermore, it represents a significant improvement from seven years previous when Freudenberg-NOK was averaging 650 defective PPM. General manager Gary Van Wambeke says, "The whole goal is variation reduction," so Freudenberg-NOK expects the quality of its products to continue to improve.[45]

The third principle of TQM is teamwork. **Teamwork** means collaboration between managers and nonmanagers, across business functions, and between the company and its customers and suppliers. In short, quality improves when

continuous improvement an organization's ongoing commitment to constantly assess and improve the processes and procedures used to create products and services.

variation a deviation in the form, condition, or appearance of a product from the quality standard for that product.

teamwork collaboration between managers and nonmanagers, across business functions, and between companies, customers, and suppliers.

Exhibit 18.7   Number of Defects per Million with Six Sigma Quality

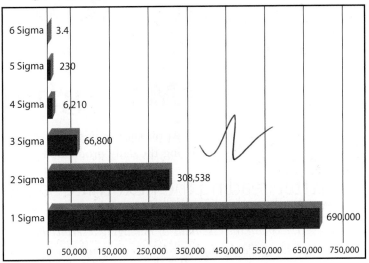

Defects per Million Parts

© Cengage Learning 2013

753

"what's new"
companies >

everyone in the company is given the incentive to work together and the responsibility and authority to make improvements and solve problems. Reid Carr, the president of **Red Door Interactive**, an Internet Presence Management firm, believes that teamwork is critical to his company's success. Therefore, his employees work collaboratively on multiple account teams made up of people from throughout the company. He says, "Forming teams made up of employees that perform different job functions allows staff to better understand how their colleagues contribute. Combining different skills sets and allowing staff members to work together to complete a client project that will produce better outcomes and allow individuals to recognize and appreciate what each person brings to the table." Furthermore, he says, "it's the formation of internal teams that yields ultimate results and leads to increased productivity among employees."[46]

Customer focus and satisfaction, continuous improvement, and teamwork mutually reinforce each other to improve quality throughout a company. Customer-focused continuous improvement is necessary to increase customer satisfaction. At the same time, continuous improvement depends on teamwork from different functional and hierarchical parts of the company.

Review 2

Quality Quality can refer to a product or service free of deficiencies or the characteristics of a product or service that satisfy customer needs. Quality products usually possess three characteristics: reliability, serviceability, and durability. Quality service involves reliability, tangibles, responsiveness, assurance, and empathy. ISO 9000 is a series of five international standards for achieving consistency in quality management and quality assurance; ISO 14000 is a set of standards for minimizing an organization's harmful effects on the environment. The ISO 9000 standards can be used for any product or service because they ensure that companies carefully document the steps they take to create and improve quality. ISO 9000 certification is awarded following a quality audit from an accredited third party. The Baldrige National Quality Award recognizes U.S. companies for their achievements in quality and business performance. Each year, up to three Baldrige Awards may be given for manufacturing, service, small business, education, and health care. Companies that apply for the Baldrige Award are judged on a 1,000-point scale based on leadership; strategic planning; customer focus; measurement, analysis, and knowledge management; work force focus; process management; and results. Total quality management (TQM) is an integrated, organization-wide strategy for improving product and service quality. TQM is based on three mutually reinforcing principles: customer focus and satisfaction, continuous improvement, and teamwork.

Managing Operations

At the start of this chapter, you learned that operations management means managing the daily production of goods and services. Then you learned that to manage production, you must oversee the factors that affect productivity and quality. In this half of the chapter, you will learn about managing operations in service and manufacturing businesses. The chapter ends with a discussion of inventory management, a key factor in a company's profitability.

After reading the next three sections, you should be able to

3. *Explain the essentials of managing a service business.*
4. *Describe the different kinds of manufacturing operations.*
5. *Explain why and how companies should manage inventory levels.*

3 Service Operations

Imagine that your trusty TiVo digital video recorder (DVR) breaks down as you try to record your favorite TV show. You've got two choices. You can run to Walmart and spend $250 to purchase a new DVR, or you can spend less (you hope) to have it fixed at a repair shop. Either way, you end up with the same thing, a working DVR. However, the first choice, getting a new DVR, involves buying a physical product (a good), whereas the second, dealing with a repair shop, involves buying a service.

Services differ from goods in several ways. First, goods are produced or made, but services are performed. In other words, services are almost always labor-intensive: Someone typically has to perform the service for you. A repair shop could give you the parts needed to repair your old DVR, but you're still going to have a broken DVR without the technician to perform the repairs. Second, goods are tangible, but services are intangible. You can touch and see that new DVR, but you can't touch or see the service provided by the technician who fixed your old DVR. All you can "see" is that the DVR works. Third, services are perishable and unstorable. If you don't use them when they're available, they're wasted. For example, if your DVR repair shop is back-logged on repair jobs, then you'll just have to wait until next week to get your DVR repaired. You can't store an unused service and use it when you like. By contrast, you can purchase a good, such as motor oil, and store it until you're ready to use it. Finally, services account for 59 percent of gross national product, whereas manufacturing accounts for only 30.8 percent.[47] So any review of operations management would be incomplete without an examination of how to manage service operations.

Because services are different from goods, managing a service operation is different from managing a manufacturing or production operation. Let's look at **3.1 the service–profit chain** and **3.2 service recovery and empowerment**.

3.1 The Service–Profit Chain

One of the key assumptions in the service business is that success depends on how well employees—that is, service providers—deliver their services to customers. But success actually begins with how well management treats service employees, as the service–profit chain, depicted in Exhibit 18.8, demonstrates.[48]

The key concept behind the service–profit chain is internal service quality, meaning the quality of treatment that employees receive from a company's internal service providers, such as management, payroll and benefits, human resources, and so forth. For example, HCL Technologies, an India-based technology services company, created an "Employee First" strategy to increase employee satisfaction with internal service quality, meaning the way they are treated by others in the company. The philosophy is simple, says CEO Vineet Nayar, "In our day and age, it's the employee who sucks up to the boss. We are trying, as much as possible, to get the manager to suck up to the employee."[49] One way in which HCL encourages better quality treatment of its employees is its online "smart service desk," where employees file "tickets" or complaints about any issue in the company, from overly cold air-conditioning,

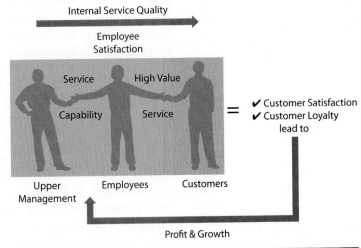

Exhibit 18.8 Service–Profit Chain

Internal Service Quality

Employee Satisfaction

Service Capability

High Value Service

= ✔ Customer Satisfaction
✔ Customer Loyalty lead to

Upper Management   Employees   Customers

Profit & Growth

Sources: R. Hallowell, L. A. Schlesinger, & J. Zornitsky, "Internal Service Quality, Customer and Job Satisfaction: Linkages and Implications for Management," *Human Resource Planning* 19 (1996): 20–31; and J. L. Heskett, T. O. Jones, G. W. Loveman, W. E. Sasser, Jr., & L. A. Schlesinger, "Putting the Service–Profit Chain to Work," *Harvard Business Review*, March–April 1994, 164–174.

Exhibit 18.9 Components of Internal Service Quality

Policies and Procedures	Do policies and procedures facilitate serving customers?
Tools	Has the organization provided service employees the tools they need to serve customers?
Effective Training	Is effective, useful, job-specific training made available in a timely fashion?
Rewards and Recognition	Are individuals rewarded and/or recognized for good performance?
Communication	Does necessary communication occur both vertically and horizontally throughout the organization?
Management Support	Does management aid (versus hinder) employees' ability to serve customers?
Goal Alignment	Are the goals of senior management aligned with the goals of frontline service employees?
Teamwork	Do individuals and departments engage in teamwork when necessary?

Sources: R. Hallowell, L. A. Schlesinger, & J. Zornitsky, "Internal Service Quality, Customer and Job Satisfaction: Linkages and Implications for Management," *Human Resource Planning* 19 (1996): 20–31.

to mistakes made in their paychecks, to complaints about the food sold in the cafeteria. And, to make sure the "smart service desk" matters, only employees who have filed the "tickets" can close them. So, tickets remain open until employees feel that their problems and issues have been fairly addressed.

Exhibit 18.9 defines the elements that constitute good internal service quality. For employees to do a good job serving customers, management must implement policies and procedures that support good customer service; provide workers the tools and training they need to do their jobs; reward, recognize, and support good customer service; facilitate communication; and encourage people and departments to work together as teams to accomplish company goals with respect to internal service quality and customer service. For example, companies that reward employees for low rates of customer complaints unwittingly encourage those employees to ignore dissatisfied customers so that their problems aren't acknowledged and counted (which would endanger employee bonuses).[50] Instead of ignoring customer complaints, the Ritz-Carlton Hotel (a luxury chain) gives their front-desk employees the tools to address them by authorizing each employee to credit up to $2,000 on a dissatisfied customer's account. This not only empowers its employees to fix customer problems, the high costs (up to $2,000) also encourages Ritz-Carlton workers to fix service failures before they happen.[51]

As depicted in Exhibit 18.8, good internal service leads to employee satisfaction and service capability. *Employee satisfaction* occurs when companies treat employees in a way that meets or exceeds their expectations. In other words, the better employees are treated, the more satisfied they are, and the more likely they are to give high-value service that satisfies customers. How employers treat employees is important because it affects service capability. *Service capability* is an employee's perception of his or her ability to serve customers well. When an organization serves its employees in ways that help them to do their jobs well, employees, in turn, are more likely to believe that they can and ought to provide high-value service to customers.

Finally, according to the service–profit chain shown in Exhibit 18.8, *high-value service* leads to *customer satisfaction* and *customer loyalty*, which in turn lead to *long-term profits and growth*.[52] What's the link between customer satisfaction and loyalty and profits? To start, the average business keeps only 70 percent to 90 percent of its existing customers each year. No big deal, you say? Just replace leaving customers with new customers. Well, there's one significant problem with that solution. It costs ten times as much to find a new customer as it does to keep an existing customer. Also, new customers typically buy only 20 percent as much as established customers. In fact, keeping existing customers is so cost-effective that most businesses could double their profits by simply keeping 5 percent more customers per year![53] How does this work? Imagine that keeping more of yours customers turns some of those customers into customers for life? How much of a difference would that make to company profits? Consider that just one lifetime customer spends $8,000 on pizza and over $330,000 on luxury cars![54]

One company that understands the relationship between high-value service, customer loyalty, and profits is **Trader Joe's**, a California-based chain of grocery stores, where everything employees do is focused on the customer. Perishable items, such as apples or bananas, are sold by the unit (for example, 75 cents per apple), rather than by the pound, so that customers know how much they are spending before checking out. When employees put products on the floor, they aren't told what the margin is on the products. So instead of stocking items according to what makes the most money, employees stock what's popular with customers. Refunds are made cheerfully—employees are encouraged to give full refunds on any and all products, no questions asked. Thanks to this great level of customer service, Trader Joe's is one of the hottest retail chains in the United States, with sales of $8 billion.[55]

< **"what's new" companies**

3.2 Service Recovery and Empowerment

When mistakes are made, when problems occur, and when customers become dissatisfied with the service they've received, service businesses must switch from the process of service delivery to the process of **service recovery**, or restoring customer satisfaction to strongly dissatisfied customers.[56] Service recovery sometimes requires service employees to not only fix whatever mistake was made but also perform heroic service acts that delight highly dissatisfied customers by far surpassing their expectations of fair treatment. When a Southwest Airlines flight from Fort Lauderdale to Denver was diverted because of storms, air traffic control sent the flight to the Pueblo, Colorado, airport. Upon landing, passengers learned that the wait, at a minimum, would be several hours, but that they would have to stay on the plane because the airport terminal had closed at 6 P.M. So passengers expected a long, unpleasant stay on the ground. They were pleased, however, when the pilot ordered pizza for the entire plane. Passenger James Mino said, "Flight attendants were VERY patient while distributing snacks and soft drinks, but no liquor [!] The flight crew went out of their way to make sure spirits were high through this ordeal. We arrived in Denver four hours late, but [we] had a memorable experience!" Chris Mainz, a spokesman for Southwest Airlines, said, "It's not uncommon for our employees to take the extra step to take care of our customers. We do reward and encourage our employees to do something on their own."[57]

service recovery restoring customer satisfaction to strongly dissatisfied customers.

© Joe Raedle/Getty Images

It's not uncommon for our employees to take the extra step to take care of our customers. We do reward and encourage our employees to do something on their own.

—CHRIS MAINZ,
SOUTHWEST AIRLINES.

doing the right thing

Protect Your Frontline Staff: The Customer Isn't Always Right

In 1909, Harry Gordon Selfridge, an American who founded London's famous Selfridge's department store, coined the phrase "The customer is always right." Though managers and employees should do what they can to provide great service and make up for mistakes with great service recovery, the customer isn't always right. Companies should fire customers who use foul language, make threats against employees or other customers, lie, demand unethical or illegal service, try to bully frontline employees into granting special favors, or are just generally belligerent. Management consultant John Curtis says, "If you don't [fire these customers], you're telling your employees and your other customers that you care more about money than the safety of the people in the business." So, do the right thing. Protect your frontline staff by telling bad customers that you won't tolerate these kinds of behavior. Ask them to leave. Close their accounts. Inform them that they'll need to go elsewhere.[58]

Unfortunately, when mistakes occur, service employees often don't have the discretion to resolve customer complaints. Customers who want service employees to correct or make up for poor service are frequently told, "I'm not allowed to do that," "I'm just following company rules," or "I'm sorry, only managers are allowed to make changes of any kind." In other words, company rules prevent them from engaging in acts of service recovery meant to turn dissatisfied customers back into satisfied customers. The result is frustration for customers and service employees, and lost customers for the company.

Now, however, many companies are empowering their service employees.[59] In Chapter 9, you learned that *empowering workers* means permanently passing decision-making authority and responsibility from managers to workers. With respect to service recovery, empowering workers means giving service employees the authority and responsibility to make decisions that immediately solve customer problems.[60]

"what's new" companies > At **Diapers.com**, all customer service agents are empowered to do whatever it takes to care of the customer, regardless of cost. As CEO Marc Lore describes it, "The concept is if Mom calls and there's an issue, do whatever is necessary to make her happy and really wow her." One customer tried to order a car seat for the weekend, but wouldn't receive it in time because of UPS's delivery schedule. So the customer service rep shipped to her own home (because UPS came to her house in the morning) and then delivered it to the customer's house. Lore says, "We're doing 6,000 orders a day, but that stuff still happens all the time." Empowering service workers does entail some additional costs, but they are usually less than the company's savings from retaining customers.[61]

In short, the purpose of empowering service employees is zero customer defections, that is, turning dissatisfied customers back into satisfied customers who continue to do business with the company. Empowering service workers does entail some costs, although they are usually less than the company's savings from retaining customers. For example, over a typical year, Hampton Inn will give back 0.5 percent of its room rental charges to dissatisfied customers. But according to Cordell, service recovery pays off because every dollar refunded to disgruntled customers results in a $7 payoff as those formerly dissatisfied customers return to Hampton Inn or

Exhibit 18.10 Costs and Benefits of Empowering Service Workers for Service Recovery

COSTS
1. Finding service workers who are capable of solving problems and dealing with upset customers increases selection costs.
2. Training service workers to solve different kinds of problems entails increased costs.
3. Higher wages are needed to attract and keep talented service workers.
4. A focus on service recovery may lead to less emphasis on service reliability, doing it right the first time. Ultimately, this could lead to slower delivery of services.
5. In their quest to please customers, empowered service workers may cost the company money by being too eager to provide "giveaways" to make up for poor or slow service.
6. Empowered service workers may unintentionally treat customers unfairly by occasionally being overly generous to make up for poor or slow service.

BENEFITS
1. Responses to customer complaints and problems are quicker.
2. Employees feel better about their jobs and themselves.
3. Employee interaction with customers will be warm and enthusiastic.
4. Employees are more likely to offer ideas for improving service or preventing problems.
5. Empowered employees who provide service recovery lead to great word-of-mouth advertising and customer retention.
6. Satisfied employees who take good care of customers are more likely to stay with the company.

Sources: D. E. Bowen & E. E. Lawler III, "The Empowerment of Service Workers: What, Why, How, and When," *Sloan Management Review* 33 (Spring 1992): 31–39; and S. Kundu & J. Vora, "Creating a Talented Workforce for Delivering Service Quality," *Human Resource Planning* 27 (January 1, 2004): 40.

recommend Hampton Inn to their friends.[62] Exhibit 18.10 describes some costs and benefits of empowering service workers to act in ways that they believe will produce service recovery.

Service Operations Services are different from goods. Goods are produced, tangible, and storable. Services are performed, intangible, and perishable. Likewise, managing service operations is different from managing production operations. The service–profit chain indicates that success begins with internal service quality, or how well management treats service employees. Internal service quality leads to employee satisfaction and service capability, which in turn lead to high-value service to customers, customer satisfaction, customer loyalty, and long-term profits and growth. Keeping existing customers is far more cost-effective than finding new ones. Consequently, to prevent disgruntled customers from leaving, some companies are empowering service employees to perform service recovery—restoring customer satisfaction to strongly dissatisfied customers—by giving them the authority and responsibility to immediately solve customer problems. The hope is that empowered service recovery will prevent customer defections.

Review 3

4 Manufacturing Operations

Ford makes cars, and Dell does computers. British Petroleum produces gasoline, whereas Sherwin-Williams makes paint. Boeing makes jet planes, but Budweiser makes beer. Maxtor makes hard drives, and Maytag makes appliances. The

Exhibit 18.11
Processing in Manufacturing Operations

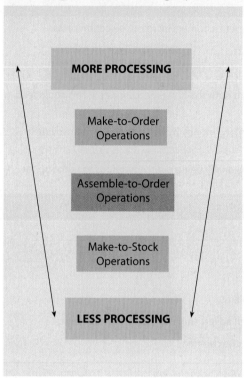

© Cengage Learning 2013

manufacturing operations of these companies all produce physical goods. But not all manufacturing operations, especially these, are the same. Let's learn how various manufacturing operations differ in terms of **4.1 the amount of processing that is done to produce and assemble a product** and **4.2 the flexibility to change the number, kind, and characteristics of products that are produced.**

4.1 Amount of Processing in Manufacturing Operations

As Exhibit 18.11 shows, manufacturing operations can be classified according to the amount of processing or assembly that occurs after a customer order is received. The highest degree of processing occurs in **make-to-order operations**. A make-to-order operation does not start processing or assembling products until it receives a customer order. In fact, some make-to-order operations may not even order parts until a customer order is received. Not surprisingly, make-to-order operations produce or assemble highly specialized or customized products for customers.

For example, Dell has one of the most advanced make-to-order operations in the computer business. Because Dell has no finished goods inventory and no component parts inventory, its computers always have the latest, most advanced components, and Dell can pass on price cuts to customers. Plus, Dell can customize all of its orders, big and small. So whether you're ordering 5,000 personal computers for your company or just 1 personal computer for your home, Dell doesn't make the computers until you order them.

A moderate degree of processing occurs in **assemble-to-order operations**. A company using an assemble-to-order operation divides its manufacturing or assembly process into separate parts or modules. The company orders parts and assembles modules ahead of customer orders. Then, based on actual customer orders or on research forecasting what customers will want, those modules are combined to create semicustomized products. For example, when a customer orders a new car, General Motors may have already ordered the basic parts or modules it needs from suppliers. In other words, based on sales forecasts, GM may already have ordered enough tires, air-conditioning compressors, brake systems, and seats from suppliers to accommodate nearly all customer orders on a particular day. Special orders from customers and car dealers are then used to determine the final assembly checklist for particular cars as they move down the assembly line.

The lowest degree of processing occurs in **make-to-stock operations** (also called build-to-stock). Because the products are standardized, meaning each product is exactly the same as the next, a company using a make-to-stock operation starts ordering parts and assembling finished products before receiving customer orders. Customers then purchase these standardized products—such as Rubbermaid storage containers, microwave ovens, and vacuum cleaners—at retail stores or directly from the manufacturer. Because parts are ordered and products are assembled before customers order the products, make-to-stock operations are highly dependent on the accuracy of sales forecasts. If sales forecasts are incorrect, make-to-stock operations may end up building too many or too few products, or they may make products with the wrong features or without the features that customers want.

These disadvantages are leading many companies to move from make-to-stock to build-to-order systems. Randy Meis, director of manufacturing for Dorner

make-to-order operation a manufacturing operation that does not start processing or assembling products until a customer order is received.

assemble-to-order operation a manufacturing operation that divides manufacturing processes into separate parts or modules that are combined to create semicustomized products.

make-to-stock operation a manufacturing operation that orders parts and assembles standardized products before receiving customer orders.

Dell operates one of the most advanced make-to-order operations in the computer industry.

© BABU/Reuters/Landov

Manufacturing, which makes conveyer systems used to move materials efficiently in factories throughout the world, says, "Even though we've got less inventory, we've been able to speed up our delivery rates for conveyers, in most cases, to just a few days from the time the order is received. Overall our BTO [build-to-order] process allows our employees to become more efficient in their jobs."[63]

4.2 Flexibility of Manufacturing Operations

A second way to categorize manufacturing operations is by **manufacturing flexibility**, meaning the degree to which manufacturing operations can easily and quickly change the number, kind, and characteristics of products they produce. Flexibility allows companies to respond quickly to changes in the marketplace (i.e., respond to competitors and customers) and to reduce the lead time between ordering and final delivery of products. There is often a trade-off between flexibility and cost, however, with the most flexible manufacturing operations frequently having higher costs per unit and the least flexible operations having lower costs per unit.[64] Exhibit 18.12 shows different types of manufacturing operations arranged in order from the least flexible to the most flexible: continuous-flow production, line-flow production, batch production, job shops, and project manufacturing.

Most production processes generate finished products at a discrete rate. A product is completed, and then—perhaps a few seconds, minutes, or hours later—another is completed, and so on. For instance, if you stood at the end of an automobile assembly line, nothing much would seem to be happening for 55 seconds of every minute. In that last 5 seconds, however, a new car would be started and driven off the assembly line, ready for its new owner. By contrast, in **continuous-flow production**, products are produced continuously rather than at a discrete rate. Like a water hose that is never turned off and just keeps on flowing, production of the final product never stops. Liquid chemicals and petroleum products are examples of continuous-flow production.

manufacturing flexibility the degree to which manufacturing operations can easily and quickly change the number, kind, and characteristics of products they produce.

continuous-flow production a manufacturing operation that produces goods at a continuous, rather than a discrete, rate.

Exhibit 18.12
Flexibility of Manufacturing Operations

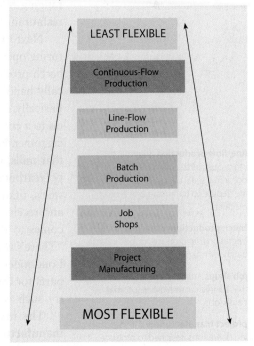

LEAST FLEXIBLE

Continuous-Flow Production

Line-Flow Production

Batch Production

Job Shops

Project Manufacturing

MOST FLEXIBLE

© Cengage Learning 2013

If you're still struggling with this concept, think of Play-Doh. Continuous-flow production is similar to squeezing Play-Doh into a toy press and watching the various shapes ooze out of the Play-Doh machine. With continuous-flow production, the Play-Doh machine would never stop oozing or producing rectangle- or triangle-shaped Play-Doh. Because of their complexity, continuous-flow production processes are the most standardized and least flexible manufacturing operations.

Line-flow production processes are preestablished, occur in a serial or linear manner, and are dedicated to making one type of product. In this way, the 10 different steps required to make product X can be completed in a separate manufacturing process (with separate machines, parts, treatments, locations, and workers) from the 12 different steps required to make product Y. Line-flow production processes are inflexible because they are typically dedicated to manufacturing one kind of product. For example, nearly every city has a local bottling plant for soft drinks or beer. The processes or steps in bottling plants are serial, meaning they must occur in a particular order. After empty bottles are sterilized, they are filled with soft drinks or beer, using a special dispenser that distributes the liquid down the inside walls of the bottle. This fills the bottle from the bottom up and displaces the air that was in the bottle. The bottles are then crowned or capped, checked for underfilling and missing caps, labeled, inspected a final time for fill levels and missing labels, and then placed in cases that are shrink-wrapped on pallets and put on trucks for delivery.[65]

The next most flexible manufacturing operation is **batch production**, which involves the manufacture of large batches of different products in standard lot sizes. A worker in a batch production operation will perform the same manufacturing process on 100 copies of product X, followed by 200 copies of product Y, and then 50 copies of product Z. Furthermore, these batches move through each manufacturing department or process in identical order. So, if the paint department follows chemical treatment, and chemical treatment is now processing a batch of 50 copies of product Z, then the paint department's next task will be to paint 50 copies of product Z. Batch production is finding increasing use among restaurant chains. To ensure consistency in the taste and quality of their products, many restaurant chains have central kitchens, or commissaries, that produce batches of food such as mashed potatoes, stuffing, macaroni and cheese, rice, quiche filling, and chili, in volumes ranging from 10 to 200 gallons. These batches are then delivered to the individual restaurant locations, which in turn serve the food to customers.

Next in terms of flexibility is the job shop. **Job shops** are typically small manufacturing operations that handle special manufacturing processes or jobs. In contrast to batch production, which handles large batches of different products, job shops typically handle very small batches, some as small as one product or process per batch. Basically, each job in a job shop is different, and once a job is done, the job shop moves on to a completely different job or manufacturing process for, most likely, a different customer. For example, Grauch Enterprises in Philipsburg, Pennsylvania, is a job shop that mills, turns, drills, paints, and finishes everything from plastics, such as nylon, polycarbonates, and laminates, to metals, such as brass, aluminum, stainless and alloy steels, titanium, and cast iron. It makes 650 different parts for one customer alone and receives one order to make 5,000 units out of 20,000 individual parts. When it comes to making different parts for different customers, owner Fred Grauch says, "There's very little we won't try. . . ."[66] Likewise, Millennium Precision, a job shop in Londonderry, New Hampshire, makes brass, titanium, and regular and stainless-steel parts for the aerospace industry. Millennium also makes parts for the medical industry, such as bone taps, bone drills, and parts to help stop leaky heart valves.[67]

The most flexible manufacturing operation is project manufacturing. **Project manufacturing** is an operation designed to produce large, expensive, specialized products like custom homes, military systems such as aircraft carriers and

line-flow production manufacturing processes that are preestablished, occur in a serial or linear manner, and are dedicated to making one type of product.

batch production a manufacturing operation that produces goods in large batches in standard lot sizes.

job shops manufacturing operations that handle custom orders or small batch jobs.

project manufacturing manufacturing operations designed to produce large, expensive, specialized products.

submarines, and aerospace products such as passenger planes and the space shuttle. Project manufacturing is highly flexible because each project is usually significantly different from the one before it, even if the projects involve the same general type of product, such as a submarine. Because of each project's size, expense, and high degree of customization, project manufacturing can take an extremely long time to complete. For example, **Boeing** will use project manufacturing to build a new line of refueling tankers for the United States Air Force. These aircraft, which will hold up to 200,000 pounds of fuel and can refuel two planes at the same time, will replace the Air Force's current generation of tanker aircraft that is more than 50 years old. According to the terms of the contract, the Air Force will purchase a total of 179 refueling tankers at a total cost of $35 billion.[68] Project manufacturing is required for making refueling tankers because of the tremendous cost (budgeted cost of $196 million each) and the complexity of the planes.

< "what's new" companies

Manufacturing Operations Manufacturing operations produce physical goods. Manufacturing operations can be classified according to the amount of processing or assembly that occurs after receiving an order from customers. Make-to-order operations, in which assembly doesn't begin until products are ordered, involve the most processing. The next highest degree of processing occurs in assemble-to-order operations, in which preassembled modules are combined after orders are received to produce semi-customized products. The least processing occurs in make-to-stock operations, in which standard parts are ordered on the basis of sales forecasts and assembled before orders are received.

Manufacturing operations can also be classified in terms of flexibility, the degree to which the number, kind, and characteristics of products can easily and quickly be changed. Flexibility allows companies to respond quickly to competitors and customers and to reduce order lead times, but it can also lead to higher unit costs. Manufacturing operations can be arranged in order from the least to the most flexible as follows: continuous-flow production, line-flow production, batch production, job shops, and project manufacturing.

Review 4

5 Inventory

Inventory is the amount and number of raw materials, parts, and finished products that a company has in its possession. When a devastating earthquake, and an accompanying tsunami, damaged factories throughout the eastern coast of Japan, inventory shortages, arising from destroyed or damaged Japanese factories, disrupted production around the world. For example, because Toyota's Japanese factories were producing limited car parts, Toyota's Indian division, Toyota Kirloskar Motor, had to limit car production to Tuesdays, Wednesdays, and Thursdays for nearly six weeks.[69] Likewise, Honda's Japanese facilities suffered so much damage that it temporarily stopped taking orders from U.S. Honda dealers. Furthermore, damage to a paint factory limited the number of colors that Honda factories could use in production. Finally, parts shortages were so severe that Honda's North American plants, which rely heavily on parts from Japan, were only running at half of their normal production volume.[70]

In this section, you will learn about **5.1 the different types of inventory, 5.2 how to measure inventory levels, 5.3 the costs of maintaining an inventory,** and **5.4 the different systems for managing inventory.**

inventory the amount and number of raw materials, parts, and finished products that a company has in its possession.

Exhibit 18.13 Types of Inventory

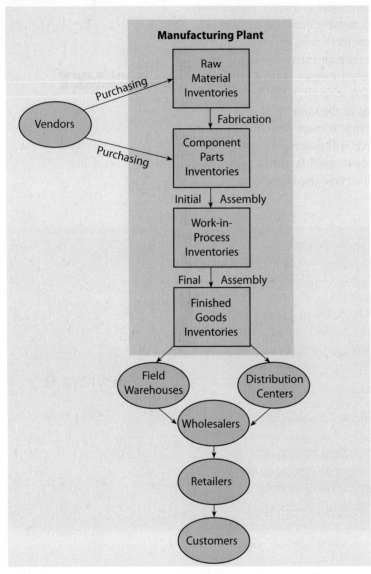

Source: R. E. Markland, S. K. Vickery, & R. A. Davis, *Operations Management,* 2nd ed. (Mason, OH: South-Western, 1998).

5.1 Types of Inventory

Exhibit 18.13 shows the four kinds of inventory a manufacturer stores: raw materials, component parts, work-in-process, and finished goods. The flow of inventory through a manufacturing plant begins when the purchasing department buys raw materials from vendors. **Raw material inventories** are the basic inputs in the manufacturing process. For example, to begin making a car, automobile manufacturers purchase raw materials like steel, iron, aluminum, copper, rubber, and unprocessed plastic.

Next, raw materials are fabricated or processed into **component parts inventories**, meaning the basic parts used in manufacturing a product. For example, in an automobile plant, steel is fabricated or processed into a car's body panels, and steel and iron are melted and shaped into engine parts like pistons or engine blocks. Some component parts are purchased from vendors rather than fabricated in-house.

The component parts are then assembled to make unfinished **work-in-process inventories**, which are also known as partially finished goods. This process is also called *initial assembly*. For example, steel body panels are welded to each other and to the frame of the car to make a "unibody," which comprises the unpainted interior frame and exterior structure of the car. Likewise, pistons, camshafts, and other engine parts are inserted into the engine block to create a working engine.

Next, all the work-in-process inventories are assembled to create **finished goods inventories**, which are the final outputs of the manufacturing process. This process is also called *final assembly*. For a car, the engine, wheels, brake system, suspension, interior, and electrical system are assembled into a car's painted unibody to make the working automobile, which is the factory's finished product. In the last step in the process, the finished goods are sent to field warehouses, distribution centers, or wholesalers, and then to retailers for final sale to customers.

raw material inventories the basic inputs in a manufacturing process.

component parts inventories the basic parts used in manufacturing that are fabricated from raw materials.

work-in-process inventories partially finished goods consisting of assembled component parts.

finished goods inventories the final outputs of manufacturing operations.

5.2 Measuring Inventory

As you'll learn next, uncontrolled inventory can lead to huge costs for a manufacturing operation. Consequently, managers need good measures of inventory to prevent inventory costs from becoming too large. Three basic measures of inventory are average aggregate inventory, weeks of supply, and inventory turnover.

If you've ever worked in a retail store and had to take inventory, you probably weren't too excited about the process of counting every item in the store and storeroom. It's an extensive task that's a bit easier today because of bar codes that mark items and computers that can count and track them. Nonetheless, inventories still differ from day to day. An inventory count taken at the beginning of the month will likely be different from a count taken at the end of the month. Similarly, an inventory count taken on a Friday will differ from a count taken on a Monday. Because of such differences, companies often measure **average aggregate inventory**, which is the average overall inventory during a particular time period. Average aggregate inventory for a month can be determined by simply averaging the inventory counts at the end of each business day for that month. One way that companies know whether they're carrying too much or too little inventory is to compare their average aggregate inventory with the industry average for aggregate inventory. For example, 72 days of inventory is the average for the automobile industry.

The automobile industry records inventory in terms of days of supply, but most other industries measure inventory in terms of *weeks of supply*, meaning the number of weeks it would take for a company to run out of its current supply of inventory. In general, there is an acceptable number of weeks of inventory for a particular kind of business. Too few weeks of inventory on hand, and a company risks a **stockout**—running out of inventory. For more than a decade, Lowe's significantly outperformed its key rival Home Depot, posting higher sales, larger profits, and opening more stores. Home Depot, however, is catching up because, unlike Lowe's, it has done a better job of avoiding stockouts. After a particularly stormy winter across the country, Home Depot's profits rose twice as fast as Lowe's, and its same-store sales rose four times as fast. The key was Home Depot's strong sales of snow blowers, shovels, salt, and other winter-weather items that were in high-demand. Lowe's, meanwhile, ran out of these products and lost sales.[71]

Another common inventory measure, **inventory turnover**, is the number of times per year that a company sells, or "turns over," its average inventory. For example, if a company keeps an average of 100 finished widgets in inventory each month, and it sold 1,000 widgets this year, then it turned its inventory ten times this year.

In general, the higher the number of inventory turns, the better. In practice, a high turnover means that a company can continue its daily operations with just a small amount of inventory on hand. For example, let's take two companies, A and B, which have identical inventory levels (520,000 widget parts and raw materials) over the course of a year. If company A turns its inventories 26 times a year, it will completely replenish its inventory every two weeks and have an average inventory of 20,000 widget parts and raw materials. By contrast, if company B turns its inventories only two times a year, it will completely replenish its inventory every 26 weeks and have an average inventory of 260,000 widget parts and raw materials. So, by turning its inventory more often, company A has 92 percent less inventory on hand at any one time than company B.

The average number of inventory turns across all kinds of manufacturing plants is approximately eight per year, as shown in Exhibit 18.14, although the average can be higher or lower for different industries.[72] The exhibit also shows the inventory turn rates for some of the best companies in each industry (i.e., companies in the 75th percentile). Whereas the average auto company turns its entire inventory 13 times per year, some of the best auto companies more than double that rate, turning their inventory 27.8 times per year, or once every two weeks.[73] Turning inventory more frequently than the industry average can cut an auto company's costs by several hundred million dollars per year. Finally, it should be pointed out that even make-to-order companies like Dell turn their inventory. In theory, make-to-order companies have no inventory. In fact, they've got inventory, but you have to measure it in hours. For example, Dell turns the inventory in its faculties 500 times a year, which means that on average it has 17 hours—that's *hours* and not days—of inventory on hand in its factories.[74]

average aggregate inventory average overall inventory during a particular time period.

stockout the point when a company runs out of finished product.

inventory turnover the number of times per year that a company sells, or "turns over," its average inventory.

Exhibit 18.14 Inventory Turn Rates Across Industries

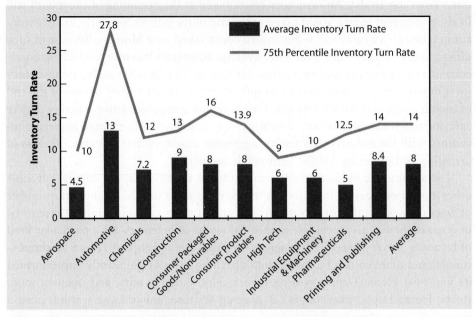

Source: D. Drickhamer, "Zeroing in on World-Class," *Industry Week*, November 2001, 36.

5.3 Costs of Maintaining an Inventory

Maintaining an inventory incurs four kinds of costs: ordering, setup, holding, and stockout. **Ordering cost** is not the cost of the inventory itself but the costs associated with ordering the inventory. It includes the costs of completing paperwork, manually entering data into a computer, making phone calls, getting competing bids, correcting mistakes, and simply determining when and how much new inventory should be reordered. For example, ordering costs are relatively high in the restaurant business because 80 percent of foodservice orders (in which restaurants reorder food supplies) are processed manually. One report, *Enabling Profitable Growth in the Food-Prepared-Away-From-Home Industries*, estimated that the food industry could save $14.3 billion if all restaurants converted to electronic data interchange (see Chapter 17), in which purchase and ordering information from one company's computer system is automatically relayed to another company's computer system. Toward that end, an industry-wide effort, Efficient Foodservice Response (EFR), is underway to improve efficiencies in the foodservice supply chain.[75]

Setup cost is the cost of changing or adjusting a machine so that it can produce a different kind of inventory.[76] For example, 3M uses the same production machinery to make several kinds of industrial tape, but it must adjust the machines whenever it switches from one kind of tape to another. There are two kinds of setup costs, downtime and lost efficiency. *Downtime* occurs whenever a machine is not being used to process inventory. If it takes five hours to switch a machine from processing one kind of inventory to another, then five hours of downtime have occurred. Downtime is costly because companies earn an economic return only when machines are actively turning raw materials into parts or parts into finished products. The second setup cost is *lost efficiency*. Recalibrating a machine to its optimal settings after a switchover typically takes some time. It may take several days of fine-tuning before a machine finally produces the number of high-quality parts that it is supposed to. Exhibit 18.15 illustrates the trade-off between setup costs, meaning downtime and lost efficiency, and manufacturing flexibility, or the number of *different* products (or inventory) that can be processed or assembled on a particular machine. The data

ordering cost the costs associated with ordering inventory, including the cost of data entry, phone calls, obtaining bids, correcting mistakes, and determining when and how much inventory to order.

setup cost the costs of downtime and lost efficiency that occur when a machine is changed or adjusted to produce a different kind of inventory.

Exhibit 18.15 Trade-Off Between Setup Costs and Manufacturing Flexibility

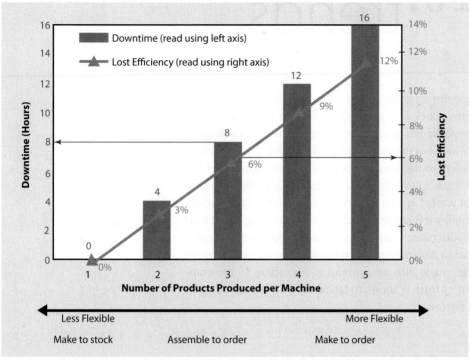

© Cengage Learning 2013

in Exhibit 18.15 assume that four hours of downtime and 3 percent lost efficiency occur each time a machine's setup has to be changed from one product to another. So, as shown in the exhibit, each time a machine has to be changed to handle a different kind of inventory, setup costs (downtime and lost efficiency) rise.

Holding cost, also known as *carrying* or *storage cost*, is the cost of keeping inventory until it is used or sold. Holding cost includes the cost of storage facilities, insurance to protect inventory from damage or theft, inventory taxes, the cost of obsolescence (holding inventory that is no longer useful to the company), and the opportunity cost of spending money on inventory that could have been spent elsewhere in the company. For example, it's estimated that U.S. airlines have a total of $44 billion worth of airplane parts in stock at any one time for maintenance, repair, and overhauling their planes. The holding cost for managing, storing, and purchasing these parts is nearly $11 billion—or roughly one-fourth of the cost of the parts themselves.[77]

Stockout costs are the costs incurred when a company runs out of a product, as happened to Apple when it failed to have enough iPods during the holiday shopping season. There are two basic kinds of stockout costs. First, the company incurs the transaction costs of overtime work, shipping, and the like, in trying to quickly replace out-of-stock inventories with new inventories. The second and perhaps more damaging cost is the loss of customers' goodwill when a company cannot deliver the products it promised. Stockouts occur more often than you might think. In the United States, the supermarket industry's average out-of-stock rate (the percentage of items that are unavailable at a given time) is 7.9 percent, according to research firm Market6. Highly promoted items have, as would be expected, a higher average out-of-stock rate of 13.1 percent. How costly is it for stores to run out of stock? Market6 estimates that running out of stock on the 25 best-selling product categories reduces a grocery store's revenue by an average of $200,000 per year, per store.[78] In general, retailers can increase sales 4 percent if they never run out of stock.

holding cost the cost of keeping inventory until it is used or sold, including storage, insurance, taxes, obsolescence, and opportunity costs.

stockout costs the costs incurred when a company runs out of a product, including transaction costs to replace inventory and the loss of customers' goodwill.

767

mgmt:trends

Beyond Recycling

The newest practice in making more efficient use of materials is upcycling. When a company recycles paper, it comes back as, well, paper. It's taken to a plant where it's processed, cleaned up, and repackaged as another paper product. Upcycling, by contrast, turns material that is thrown out into something else. So, for example, Worn Again, a clothing and accessories manufacturer in London, makes bags out of old mailmen's uniforms, and jackets made out of old hot air balloons. Upcycling is based on the concept of "designing out waste," in which plans are made for how a product will be recycled or reused even before it is made. Thus, effective upcycling could lead to a closed loop, in which all products are made to be easily dismantled and completely reused. Interface, an Atlanta-based carpet manufacturer, uses upcycling so that all of its old products can be made into new products. According to the company, it has reduced the amount of trash it sends to landfills by 80 percent and its greenhouse gas emission by 44 percent.[79]

© iStockphoto.com/Kirsty Pargeter

5.4 Managing Inventory

© iStockphoto.com/Luis Carlos Torres

Inventory management has two basic goals. The first is to avoid running out of stock and thus angering and dissatisfying customers. This goal seeks to increase inventory to a safe level that won't risk stockouts. The second is to efficiently reduce inventory levels and costs as much as possible without impairing daily operations. This goal seeks a minimum level of inventory. The following inventory management techniques—economic order quantity (EOQ), just-in-time inventory (JIT), and materials requirement planning (MRP)—are different ways of balancing these competing goals.

Economic order quantity (EOQ) is a system of formulas that helps determine how much and how often inventory should be ordered. EOQ takes into account the overall demand (D) for a product while trying to minimize ordering costs (O) and holding costs (H). The formula for EOQ is

$$EOQ = \sqrt{\frac{2DO}{4}}$$

For example, if a factory uses 40,000 gallons of paint a year (D), ordering costs (O) are $75 per order, and holding costs (H) are $4 per gallon, then the optimal quantity to order is 1,225 gallons:

$$EOQ = \sqrt{\frac{2(40,000)(75)}{4}} = 1,225$$

With 40,000 gallons of paint being used per year, the factory uses approximately 110 gallons per day:

$$\frac{40,000 \text{ gallons}}{365 \text{ days}} = 110$$

economic order quantity (EOQ) a system of formulas that minimizes ordering and holding costs and helps determine how much and how often inventory should be ordered.

Consequently, the factory would order 1,225 new gallons of paint approximately every 11 days:

$$\frac{1{,}225 \text{ gallons}}{110 \text{ gallons per day}} = 11.1 \text{ days}$$

In general, EOQ formulas do a good job of letting managers know what size or amount of inventory they should reorder to minimize ordering and holding costs. Mark Lore, CEO of Diapers.com, explains how his company uses EOQ formulas to decide precisely how much inventory to keep on hand. He says, "We built software with computational algorithms to determine what the optimal number of boxes to have in the warehouse is and what the sizes of those boxes should be. Should we stock five different kinds of boxes to ship product in? Twenty kinds? Fifty kinds? And what size should those boxes be? Right now, it's 23 box sizes, given what we sell, in order to minimize the cost of dunnage (those little plastic air-filled bags or peanuts), the cost of corrugated boxes, and the cost of shipping. We rerun the simulation every quarter."[80] As this example makes clear, EOQ formulas and models can become much more complex as adjustments are made for price changes, quantity discounts, setup costs, and many other factors.[81]

Whereas EOQ formulas try to minimize holding and ordering costs, the just-in-time (JIT) approach to inventory management attempts to eliminate holding costs by reducing inventory levels to near zero. With a **just-in-time (JIT) inventory system**, component parts arrive from suppliers just as they are needed at each stage of production. By having parts arrive just in time, the manufacturer has little inventory on hand and thus avoids the costs associated with holding inventory. By combining a JIT inventory system with its make-to-order production system, Dell turns its inventory more than 500 times a year, as mentioned above. John Egan heads Dell's inventory fulfillment center in Austin, Texas, and has this to say about Dell's JIT inventory system: "We used to measure our factory inventory in days; but now we manage it in hours. Our suppliers see demand changes every two hours. We try to achieve a perfect balance between the parts that are needed and what's already in the factory."[82]

To have just the right amount of inventory arrive at just the right time requires a tremendous amount of coordination between manufacturing operations and suppliers. One way to promote tight coordination under JIT is close proximity. Most parts suppliers for Toyota's JIT system at its Georgetown, Kentucky, plant are located within 200 miles of the plant. Furthermore, parts are picked up from suppliers and delivered to Toyota as often as 16 times a day.[83] A second way to promote close coordination under JIT is to have a shared information system that allows a manufacturer and its suppliers to know the quantity and kinds of parts inventory the other has in stock. Generally, factories and suppliers facilitate information sharing by using the same part numbers and names. Ford's seat supplier accomplishes this by sticking a bar code on each seat, and Ford then uses the sticker to route the seat through its factory.

Manufacturing operations and their parts suppliers can also facilitate close coordination by using the system of kanban. **Kanban**, which is Japanese for "sign," is a simple ticket-based system that indicates when it is time to reorder inventory. Suppliers attach kanban cards to batches of parts. Then, when an assembly-line worker uses the first part out of a batch, the kanban card is removed. The cards are then collected, sorted, and quickly returned to the supplier, who begins resupplying the factory with parts that match the order information on the kanban cards. Glenn Uminger, manager of production control and logistics at Toyota's Georgetown,

just-in-time (JIT) inventory system an inventory system in which component parts arrive from suppliers just as they are needed at each stage of production.

kanban a ticket-based JIT system that indicates when to reorder inventory.

Kentucky, plant, says, "We are placing orders for new parts as the first part is used out of a box." Because prices and batch sizes are typically agreed to ahead of time, kanban tickets greatly reduce paperwork and ordering costs.[84]

A third method for managing inventory is **materials requirement planning (MRP)**. MRP is a production and inventory system that, from beginning to end, precisely determines the production schedule, production batch sizes, and inventories needed to complete final products. The three key parts of MRP systems are the master production schedule, the bill of materials, and inventory records. The *master production schedule* is a detailed schedule that indicates the quantity of each item to be produced, the planned delivery dates for those items, and the time by which each step of the production process must be completed in order to meet those delivery dates. Based on the quantity and kind of products set forth in the master production schedule, the *bill of materials* identifies all the necessary parts and inventory, the quantity or volume of inventory to be ordered, and the order in which the parts and inventory should be assembled. *Inventory records* indicate the kind, quantity, and location of inventory that is on hand or that has been ordered. When inventory records are combined with the bill of materials, the resulting report indicates what to buy, when to buy it, and what it will cost to order. Today, nearly all MRP systems are available in the form of powerful, flexible computer software.[85]

Which inventory management system should you use? Economic order quantity (EOQ) formulas are intended for use with **independent demand systems,** in which the level of one kind of inventory does not depend on another. For example, because inventory levels for automobile tires are unrelated to the inventory levels of women's dresses, Sears could use EOQ formulas to calculate separate optimal order quantities for dresses and tires. By contrast, JIT and MRP are used with **dependent demand systems,** in which the level of inventory depends on the number of finished units to be produced. For example, if Yamaha makes 1,000 motorcycles a day, then it will need 1,000 seats, 1,000 gas tanks, and 2,000 wheels and tires each day. So, when optimal inventory levels depend on the number of products to be produced, use a JIT or MRP management system.

materials requirement planning (MRP) a production and inventory system that determines the production schedule, production batch sizes, and inventory needed to complete final products.

independent demand system an inventory system in which the level of one kind of inventory does not depend on another.

dependent demand system an inventory system in which the level of inventory depends on the number of finished units to be produced.

Review 5

Inventory There are four kinds of inventory: raw materials, component parts, work-in-process, and finished goods. Because companies incur ordering, setup, holding, and sometimes stockout costs when handling inventory, inventory costs can be enormous. To control those costs, companies measure and track inventory in three ways: average aggregate inventory, weeks of supply, and turnover. Companies meet the basic goals of inventory management (avoiding stockouts and reducing inventory without hurting daily operations) through economic order quantity (EOQ) formulas, just-in-time (JIT) inventory systems, and materials requirement planning (MRP).

EOQ formulas minimize holding and ordering costs by determining how much and how often inventory should be ordered. By having parts arrive just when they are needed at each stage of production, JIT systems attempt to minimize inventory levels and holding costs. JIT systems often depend on proximity, shared information, and the system of kanban made popular by Japanese manufacturers. MRP precisely determines the production schedule, production batch sizes, and the ordering of inventories needed to complete final products. The three key parts of MRP systems are the master production schedule, the bill of materials, and inventory records. Use EOQ formulas when inventory levels are independent, and use JIT and MRP when inventory levels are dependent on the number of products to be produced.

SELF-ASSESSMENT

How to Handle Disgruntled Customers

How a company manages its customers is an important indicator of its future success. But managing customers can be as difficult as it is critical. For example, one customer may like to be greeted by an employee and immediately helped upon entering the store. Another might find this approach a bit aggressive. What is your style? If you were responsible for interacting with customers, which approach would you use? The following assessment will evaluate your perspectives on the relationship a company has with its customers. Be candid as you respond to the items, using a scale from 1 to 9, in which 1 means you strongly disagree, 5 means you are neutral, and 9 means you strongly agree (other numbers indicate varying degrees of agreement or disagreement).[86]

1. I try to bring a customer with a problem together with a product/service that helps solve that problem.
   1 2 3 4 ⑤ 6 7 8 9

2. I keep alert for weaknesses in a customer's personality so I can use them to put pressure on them to agree with me.
   ① 2 3 4 5 6 7 8 9

3. I try to influence a customer by information rather than pressure.
   1 2 3 4 5 6 7 ⑧ 9

4. It is necessary to stretch the truth in describing a product to a customer.
   ① 2 3 4 5 6 7 8 9

5. I decide what product/service to offer on the basis of what I can convince customers to accept, not on the basis of what will satisfy them in the long run.
   1 2 3 4 ⑤ 6 7 8 9

6. I paint too rosy a picture of my product/service to make it sound as good as possible.
   1 2 3 4 ⑤ 6 7 8 9

7. I try to find out what kind of products/services will be most helpful to a customer.
   1 2 3 4 5 6 7 8 ⑨

8. I try to sell a customer all I can convince them to buy, even if I think it is more than a wise customer would buy.
   1 2 3 ④ 5 6 7 8 9

9. I begin talking about the product/service before exploring a customer's need with him or her.
   1 2 3 4 5 6 7 8 ⑨

10. I try to help customers achieve their goals.
    1 2 3 4 5 6 7 ⑧ 9

11. I try to figure out what a customer's needs are.
    1 2 3 4 5 6 7 ⑧ 9

12. A good employee has to have the customer's best interest in mind.
    1 2 3 4 ⑤ 6 7 8 9

13. I try to sell as much as I can rather than to satisfy a customer.
    1 2 3 4 ⑤ 6 7 8 9

14. I try to give customers an accurate expectation of what our product/service will do for them.
    1 2 3 4 5 6 7 ⑧ 9

15. I imply to a customer that something is beyond my control when it is not.
    ① 2 3 4 5 6 7 8 9

KEY TERMS

assemble-to-order operation 760
average aggregate inventory 765
batch production 762
component parts inventories 764
continuous-flow production 761
continuous improvement 753
customer focus 752
customer satisfaction 752
dependent demand system 770
economic order quantity (EOQ) 768
finished goods inventories 764
holding cost 767
independent demand system 770
inventory 763
inventory turnover 765
ISO 14000 749
ISO 9000 749

job shops 762
just-in-time (JIT) inventory system 769
kanban 769
line-flow production 762
make-to-order operation 760
make-to-stock operation 760
manufacturing flexibility 761
materials requirement planning (MRP) 770
multifactor productivity 745
operations management 742
ordering cost 766
partial productivity 745
productivity 743
project manufacturing 762
quality 747
raw material inventories 764
service recovery 757
setup cost 766
stockout costs 767
stockout 765
teamwork 753
total quality management (TQM) 752
variation 753
work-in-process inventories 764

16. I try to achieve my goals by satisfying customers.
    1   2   3   4   5   6   7   8   9

17. If I am not sure if our product/service is right for a customer, I will still apply pressure to get him or her to buy.
    1   2   3   4   5   6   7   8   9

18. I answer a customer's question about product/services as correctly as I can.
    1   2   3   4   5   6   7   8   9

19. I offer the product/service that is best suited to the customer's problem.
    1   2   3   4   5   6   7   8   9

20. I treat a customer as a rival.
    1   2   3   4   5   6   7   8   9

21. I spend more time trying to persuade a customer to buy than I do trying to discover his or her needs.
    1   2   3   4   5   6   7   8   9

22. I am willing to disagree with a customer in order to help him or her make a better decision.
    1   2   3   4   5   6   7   8   9

23. I try to get customers to discuss their needs with me.
    1   2   3   4   5   6   7   8   9

24. I pretend to agree with customers to please them.
    1   2   3   4   5   6   7   8   9

Scoring

Determine your score by entering your response to each survey item below, as follows. Total each column to derive two scores.

Customer Orientation

1. regular score	_____
3. regular score	_____
7. regular score	_____
10. regular score	_____
11. regular score	_____
12. regular score	_____
14. regular score	_____
16. regular score	_____
18. regular score	_____
19. regular score	_____
22. regular score	_____
23. regular score	_____
TOTAL =	_____

Selling Orientation

2. regular score	_____
4. regular score	_____
5. regular score	_____
6. regular score	_____
8. regular score	_____
9. regular score	_____
13. regular score	_____
15. regular score	_____
17. regular score	_____
20. regular score	_____
21. regular score	_____
24. regular score	_____
TOTAL =	_____

You can find the interpretation for your score at www.cengagebrain.com.

MANAGEMENT DECISION

Is Bigger Always Better?[87]

When you told your friends and family that you were starting your own business, they were thrilled. When you told them that it would be a food truck, well, they were less than thrilled. All they could imagine was a truck filled with cold sandwiches and watered-down coffee parked next to a construction site. But you used your culinary training to come up with fresh, delicious,

and healthy dishes that appealed to almost everyone. And instead of construction sites, you parked your truck next to busy office buildings and downtown intersections. In almost no time at all, there were hundreds of people lined up at your truck, waiting for one of your latest creations.

Ever since you opened, the business has been pretty small—just one truck, you manning the kitchen in the back, and your best friend taking orders and working the cash register. But all of that could soon change. A few weeks ago, a camera crew and producers from Food Network came by your truck to do a profile on the hottest dining trends in the country. They called your truck "adventurous," "cutting-edge," and a definite "must-eat." A little while after that, you were profiled on TV news and magazines, and you've lost track of the number of food bloggers who have stopped for a taste. And the attention hasn't come just from the media. Investors are calling left and right with offers to help you expand your business. They want to help you buy more trucks, hire more people, and increase your productivity so that you can sell food in more cities across the country. Some have even called with you offers of opening up a chain of restaurants.

This seems like a dream come true, taking a small business and growing it into a nationwide chain. However, your best friend has a word of warning. He says that growing so fast isn't always the best way to go. He tells you about Jim Picariello, who had a small business making all-natural ice pops. Picariello began making the pops himself, at home, but in just two years, he expanded into a 15-employee company with a 3,000-square-foot facility. But when the recession

hit, all of his funding dried up, he couldn't afford to make payments on his manufacturing equipment, and he eventually had to lay off all of his employees and declare bankruptcy. Then he tells you about Toyota. For decades, the company had a sterling reputation for making quality vehicles. But when it made rapid expansion its overall priority, the quality of its cars suffered and it was forced to recall 11 million vehicles. "Definitely not where you want to be," your best friend concludes.

So what should you do? You don't want to turn down an opportunity to expand your business and make more money. But you also don't want to lose what you have by growing too fast. What to do?

Questions

1. As the owner and manager of this small business, what pace of growth do you think is ideal—slow or rapid? Why?
2. What steps could you take to make sure that the quality of your products, and the customer service your employees offer, do not suffer with expansion of the business?

MANAGEMENT TEAM DECISION

Going Lean at Starbucks[88]

It started off as a day basically like any other. You went into the Starbucks that you manage, helped employees open, and thought about making a dent in the mountain of paperwork left over from the previous week. But then you got an unexpected visit from a team at the corporate office. They started talking about the need to lower labor costs, improve efficiency, and increase productivity. When you asked them how they planned on doing all that, they responded, "Lean production."

They informed you that lean production is a management philosophy derived from Toyota that is focused on reducing waste. Whether it's wasted motion, wasted time, or wasted parts, the goal of lean production is to eliminate waste so that all an organization can do its work efficiently. The executives then show you all the "waste" that's in your stores right now—baristas bending over to scoop coffee from a counter below, others waiting for coffee to fully drain before starting a new pot, one worker carrying trays

of pastries from storage to the display case, another spending ten seconds per drink to read the milk label. They even show you a map showing the winding trail that a barista takes in making a single drink. It looks like a big pile of spaghetti, you think to yourself.

With lean production, the executives tell you, you can reduce the amount of motion that employees spend making drinks and the amount of time they spend reaching for stuff, reading labels, or moving from here to there. This will make your store more efficient and productive so that the same number of employees can serve more customers.

You're intrigued by all of this, as nothing would please your supervisors more than increased revenue and lower costs. But you're also worried about how your employees will react. Many of them came to work at Starbucks because it wasn't like other fast-food chains that only focus on speed, speed, and speed. How will they feel once you tell them that they'll have to change the way they work to become faster? What if they feel like you just want them to be coffee-making robots, leaving them no time to interact

with customers or experiment with new drinks? Consider these issues with three or four other students as you discuss the questions below.

Questions

1. How would an increase in efficiency and production benefit your employees?

2. How would you address employees' concerns that they are being transformed into coffee-making robots?

3. What is the best way to ensure that the quality of your products does not decline with increased production speed?

PRACTICE BEING A MANAGER

Balancing Speed and Accuracy

Success in service and manufacturing operations requires managers to maintain high levels of both productivity and quality. High productivity ensures that the company is cost-competitive with rivals; and high quality helps the company to attract customers and grow revenues and profits. Because productivity and quality are basic drivers of company success, managers must be adept at measuring and improving both. This exercise will give you some practice in developing productivity and quality measures.

Step 1: Your professor will organize your class into small groups of three or four students.

Scenario: Your group is a management team working to improve productivity and quality in a pharmaceutical company. You have been assigned two units of this company as the focus of your improvement efforts. The first is a pill-packaging unit, and the second is a research and development (R&D) laboratory.

Workers in the packaging unit are responsible for checking to ensure that the pills in the box match the packaging and labeling, placing the appropriate labels and packaging information on each box, and then certifying with a stamp that the box of pills is ready for shipping to wholesale customers, for example, chains like Walgreens and Costco. Mistakes in packaging, if undetected by pharmacists, could have serious, even fatal, outcomes. These manufacturing workers are skilled and highly trained. If they detect a problem, they have the authority to halt production.

Workers in the R&D unit are responsible for developing new drugs and for testing their effectiveness and safety. The company relies for its success upon a steady pipeline of promising new products. At the same time, some basic research (e.g., study of progression of a particular type of cancer) is necessary in order to develop new drugs. These workers are mostly Ph.D.'s and highly skilled laboratory technicians.

Step 2: Develop metrics. Working as a team, develop some productivity and quality measures for (a) packaging unit workers and (b) R&D unit workers. Be sure to consider whether productivity and quality should be measured on an individual or unit basis, and why.

Step 3: Analyze the metrics. Critically examine your team's measures for each unit. What unintended consequences might develop as workers in each unit strive to improve on the measures you have designed? Are you more confident of your measures in one unit versus the other? Why or why not?

Step 4: Debrief as a class. What are some of the challenges of measuring productivity and quality? Are these challenges greater for particular types of work? Which level of measurement and accountability—individual or unit—is most likely to generate positive results? Why? What impact do productivity and quality systems of measurement and improvement have on workers? How can firms ensure productivity and quality without overloading workers and/or fostering unhealthy levels of stress?

DEVELOP YOUR CAREER POTENTIAL

Take a Factory Tour

Imagine that you arrive back at your dorm room one afternoon to find your roommate watching a *Mister Rogers* rerun. When asked why, your roommate replies, "Management homework." That may not be as crazy as it sounds. The late Fred Rogers, host of PBS's *Mr. Rogers' Neighborhood*, may well hold the record for factory tours. During his long career, he broadcast footage to millions of children showing how Cheerios, plastic drinking straws, raincoats, pasta, blue jeans, spoons, and a host of other products are made. He was even at Crayola when the one-billionth crayon rolled off the production line. (He also broadcast footage of how Crayola crayons are made and packaged.)

For years, John Ratzenberger (known for his role as Cliff Clavin on *Cheers* and as a regular voice in Pixar animated feature movies, most recently Mack the truck in *Cars 2*), hosted a cable television program titled *Made in America* that features nothing but factory tours around the United States. The Food Network also broadcasts a program that describes how all kinds of food products are manufactured. Beyond the world of television, however, each year thousands of people visit corporate facilities like these:

- The Boeing Everett Tour Center outside Seattle introduces visitors to how Boeing makes its 747, 767, and 777 passenger jets.

- Steinway & Sons in Queens, New York, offers a 2½-hour tour that is like a master class. Each Steinway piano takes about a year to build, so you will be able to see pianos at every stage of the production process.

- Ben & Jerry's in Waterbury, Vermont, offers tours accompanied with a scoop of whatever flavor ice cream was made that day.

- Tabasco Factory on Avery Island, Louisiana, is part factory tour, part nature preserve. You can see how the pepper sauce is aged in oak barrels and then step outside to see Bird City, a special structure devised by E. A. McIlhenny to provide a sanctuary for snowy egrets.

- Mack Truck has an assembly plant in Macungie, Pennsylvania. The production line is a mile and a half long, so wear comfortable shoes!

- Yuengling Brewery in Pottsville, Pennsylvania, also offers tours, which include a trip to the cave where the nation's oldest brewery used to age its beer.

- Louisville Slugger in Louisville, Kentucky (where else?), offers a factory tour at the end of which you receive a miniature Slugger bat to take home.

- Harley-Davidson plants in Milwaukee, Kansas City, and York, Pennsylvania, offer factory tours for teens and adults.

- Carousel Magic in Mansfield, Ohio, is one of the few remaining carousel horse manufacturers and restorers.

Many companies no longer open their factories for tours. Kellogg's in Battle Creek, Michigan, ceased giving factory tours in 1986, but now the company operates a museum/activity center called Cereal City. Other companies say they offer factory tours, but in reality the tour is just a marketing device. Budweiser in St. Louis has an enormous visitor center for its tours, but you won't be able to see any of the actual production—just videos and the various outbuildings on the Anheuser-Busch campus. Still other companies offer virtual tours of their operations. Just Born, maker of Marshmallow Peeps, Mike & Ikes, and Hot Tamales, offers a static tour of the Peep production line at www.marshmallowpeeps .com Hershey Foods also has an online tour at www .hersheys.com/chocolateworld/chocolate_tour.shtm.[89]

Your assignment is to take a factory tour. Use the Internet or other resources to locate a factory tour near you. The site Factory Tours USA www.factorytoursusa .com) organizes tours by state, so locating something interesting is easy.

Questions

1. What steps or procedures does the company take to ensure the quality of its products?
2. How does the company measure productivity, and how does its productivity compare with others in the industry?
3. Using the vocabulary from the chapter, describe the basic steps used to make the finished products in this factory.
4. What did you find most impressive about this company or its manufacturing processes? Based on what you read in the chapter, describe one thing the company could do differently to improve quality, increase productivity, or reduce inventory.

END NOTES

[1]"LVMH Moët Hennessy Louis Vuitton S.A.," International Directory of Company Histories, vol. 113, St. James Press, 2010. Reproduced in Business and Company Resource Center, Farmington Hills, MI: Gale Group, 2011, http://galenet.galegroup.com/servlet/BCRC; P. Gumbel & E. Levenson, "Mass vs. Class," Fortune, September 17, 2007, 82–88; W. Langley, "Louis Vuitton; Not My Bag," The Sunday Telegraph (London), August 16, 2009, Features 8; C. Passariello, "At Vuitton, Growth in Small Batches; Luxury-Goods Maker's New French Factory Adds to Capacity but Sticks to Strategy of Tight Rein," The Wall Street Journal, June 27, 2011, accessed June 30, 2011, from http://online.wsj.com/article/SB100014244052702303627104576409813842858304.html; and K. Walsh, "He's Got the Whole World in His Handbag," The Sunday Times (London), November 21, 2010, Business 7.

[2]"Ryanair Asks Passengers If They Will Stand on Short Flights," July 9, 29009, from accessed August 2, 2009, from www.breakingtravelnews.com/news/article/btn20090709121520864; "Ryanair Celebrates 20 Years of Operations," Ryanair, May 31, 2005, accessed September 12, 2008, from www.ryanair.com/doc/investor/2005/q4_2005.pdf.

[3]B. Baker, "America's Best Drive-Thru 2008 Is . . . Chick-fil-A! (Again)," QRS Magazine, accessed August 2, 2009, from www.qsrmagazine.com/reports.

[4]M. Richtel, "The Long-Distance Journey of a Fast-Food Order," The New York Times, April 11, 2006, accessed September 12, 2008, from www.nytimes.com/2006/04/11/technology/11fast.html.

[5]"Employment Cost Index News Release Text," Bureau of Labor Statistics, 29 April 2011, accessed June 27, 2011, from www.bls.gov/news.release/eci.nr0.htm; and "Productivity and Costs, First Quarter 2011, Revised," Bureau of Labor Statistics, June 2, 2011, accessed June 27, 2011, from www.bls.gov/news.release/prod2.nr0.htm.

[6]www.census.gov/hhes/www/income/data/historical/families/f07AR.xls;

"Historical Income Tables—Families: Table F-23—Families by Total Money Income, Race, and Hispanic Origin of Householder: 1967 to 2009," U.S. Census Bureau, accessed September 1, 2009, from www.census.gov/hhes/www/income/data/historical/families/f23.xls.

[7]"Historical Income Tables—Families: Table F-23—Families by Total Money Income, Race, and Hispanic Origin of Householder: 1967 to 2009," U.S. Census Bureau, accessed June 27, 2011, from www.census.gov/hhes/www/income/data/historical/families/f23.xls.

[8]The Conference Board Total Economy Data Base, Summary Statistics 1995–2010 "Table 3: Growth of Labor Productivity, Real GDP and Total Hours Worked by Region for Advanced Countries, 1995–2010," The Conference Board, September 2010, accessed June 27, 2011, from www.conference-board.org/retrievefile.cfm?filename=SummaryTables_Sep20101.pdf&type=subsite.

[9]"Employment Projections, Table 1: Civilian Labor Force by Sex, Age, Race, and Hispanic Origin, 1988, 1998, 2008, and projected 2018," in Employment Outlook: 2008–18; Labor Force Projections to 2018: Older Workers Staying More Active, Monthly Labor Review, November 2008, 30–51, accessed June 27, 2011, from www.bls.gov/opub/mlr/2009/11/art3full.pdf.

[10]"Key Development Data & Statistics: United States Data Profile," World Bank, accessed September 9, 2009, from http://web.worldbank.org/datacatalog.

[11]"Philanthropy in the American Economy," Council of Economic Advisers, February 19, 2002, accessed April 12, 2009, from http://clinton4.nara.gov/media/pdf/philanthropy.pdf.

[12]"GNI Per Capita, Atlas Method (Current US$)," World Bank, accessed June 27, 2011, from http://data.worldbank.org/indicator/NY.GNP.PCAP.CD; and "Where Can I Find the Unemployment Rate for Previous Years," in Labor Force Statistics from the Current Population Survey, Bureau of Labor Statistics, February 3, 2011,

accessed June 27, 2011, from www.bls.gov/cps/prev_yrs.htm.

[13]"Are Cars Becoming Less Affordable for the Average American Family? Cars.com, accessed March 23, 2010, from http://blogs.cars.com/kickingtires/2010/08/are-cars-becoming-less-affordable-for-the-average-american-family.html; and "Auto Affordability Flat in First Quarter of 2011, Comerica Bank Reports," Comerica, May 12, 2011, accessed June 27, 2011, from www.comerica.com/Comerica_Content/Corporate_Communications/Docs/Auto%20Affordability%20Index/Auto_Affordability_Index_Q12011.pdf.

[14]R. Harbour & M. Hill, "Productivity Gap Narrows across North America and Europe," The Harbour Report, accessed August 2, 2009, from www.theharbourreport.com/index2.jsp (also see www.oliverwyman.com/ow/automotive.

[15]"Profiles International: America's Most Productive Companies," Drug Week, May 15, 2009, 265; and "America's Most Productive Companies," accessed August 2, 2009, from http://article.wn.com/view/2009/04/28/Americas_Most_Productive_Companies/.

[16]Lenovo IdeaPad S Series Netbook, no date, accessed August 1, 2010, from http://shop.lenovo.com/us/notebooks/ideapad/s-series; and Product fact sheet, no date, accessed August 1, 2010, from www-03.ibm.com/ibm/history/exhibits/pc25/pc25_fact.html.

[17]"Study: Auto Makers Initial Quality Improves Considerably," Quality Digest, accessed August 2, 2009, from www.qualitydigest.com/inside/quality-insider-news/study-overall-initial-quality-improves-considerably.html; and "2008 Initial Quality Study Results," accessed August 2, 2009, from www.jdpower.com/autos/articles/2008-Initial-Quality-Study-Results.

[18]"2011 Initial Quality Study Results (IQS)," JD Power and Associates, June 23, 2011, "2008 Initial Quality Study Results," accessed June 27, 2011, from www.jdpower.com/autos/articles/2011-Initial- Quality-Study-Results.

[19]"Basic Concepts," American Society for Quality, accessed August 2, 2009, from www.asq.org/learn-about-quality/basic-concepts.html.

[20]R. E. Markland, S. K. Vickery, & R. A. Davis, "Managing Quality" (Chapter 7) in *Operations Management: Concepts in Manufacturing and Services* (Cincinnati, OH: South-Western College Publishing, 1998).

[21]"WD® Launches High-Performance, 7200 Rpm 2 Tb Hard Drives for Desktop and Enterprise Systems," Western Digital, September 1, 2009, accessed September 12, 2009, from http://hothardware.com/News/WD-Launches-HighPerformance-7200RPM-2TB-Hard-Drives/.

[22]REVA Electric Car Company, accessed August 2, 2009, from www.revaindia.com.

[23]"New Industrial LCD Panels with 100,000 Hour MTBF LED Backlight Systems from Toshiba America Electronic Components," *Your Industry News*, August 26, 2009 accessed September 12, 2009, from www.toshiba.com/taec/news/press_releases/2009/lcdb_09_576.jsp.

[24]L. L. Berry & A. Parasuraman, *Marketing Services* (New York: Free Press, 1991).

[25]Y, Kane & I. Sherr, "Penney Picks Boss From Apple—Secrets From Genius Bar: Full Loyalty, No Negativity," *The Wall Street Journal*, June 15, 2011, A1.

[26]"FAQs—General Information on ISO," International Organization for Standardization, accessed September 12, 2009, from www.iso.org/iso/support/faqs/faqs_general_information_on_iso.htm.

[27]"ISO 9000 Essentials," and "ISO 14000 Essentials," International Organization for Standardization, accessed September 12, 2009, from www.iso.org/iso/iso_catalogue/management_standards/iso_9000_iso_14000.htm.

[28]J. Briscoe, S. Fawcett, & R. Todd, "The Implementation and Impact of ISO 9000 among Small Manufacturing Enterprises," *Journal of Small Business Management* 43 (July 1, 2005): 309.

[29]R. Henkoff, "The Hot New Seal of Quality (ISO 9000 Standard of Quality Management)," *Fortune*, June 28, 1993, 116.

[30]Accessed August 2, 2009, from www.acmespecialty.com.

[31]"Frequently Asked Questions about the Malcolm Baldrige National Quality Award," National Institute of Standards & Technology, accessed September 12, 2009, from www.nist.gov/public_affairs/factsheet/baldfaqs.htm.

[32]"Baldrige Award Application Forms," National Institute of Standards & Technology, accessed September 12, 2009, from www.quality.nist.gov/public_affairs/factsheet/baldfaqs.cfm.

[33]"Frequently Asked Questions and Answers about the Malcolm Baldrige National Quality Award."

[34]Ibid.

[35]"Criteria for Performance Excellence," Baldrige National Quality Program 2008, accessed September 15, 2009, from www.quality.nist.gov/PDF_files/2008_Business_Criteria.pdf.

[36]Ibid.

[37]Ibid.

[38]"Baldrige Index Beaten by S&P 500 For Second Year," NIST Tech Beat, accessed September 12, 2009, from www.quality.nist.gov/Stock_Studies.htm.

[39]J. W. Dean, Jr., & J. Evans, *Total Quality: Management, Organization, and Strategy* (St. Paul, MN: West, 1994).

[40]J. W. Dean, Jr., & D. E. Bowen, "Management Theory and Total Quality: Improving Research and Practice through Theory Development," *Academy of Management Review* 19 (1994): 392–418.

[41]R. Allen & R. Kilmann, "Aligning Reward Practices in Support of Total Quality Management," *Business Horizons*, May 1, 2001, 77; and F. Reichheld & P. Rogers, "Motivating Through Metrics," *Harvard Business Review* (September 2005): 20–24.

[42]A. Taylor, "Driving Customer Satisfaction," *Harvard Business Review* (July 2002): 24.

[43]"J.D. Power and Associates Reports: Customer Satisfaction with Rental Cars Continues to Decline," J.D. Power and Associates, November 11, 2008, accessed September 12, 2009, from http://content4.businesscenter.jdpower.com/JDPAContent/CorpComm/News/content/Releases/pdf/2008244.pdf.

[44]R. Carter, "Best Practices: Freudenberg-NOK/Cleveland, GA: Continuous Kaizens," *Industrial Maintenance & Plant Operations*, June 1, 2004, 10.

[45]Ibid.

[46]Reid Carr, "Teamwork at Its Best," *Fast Company*, May 16, 2010, accessed March 23, 2011, from www.fastcompany.com/1648449/teamwork-at-its-best.

[47]"Table 647. Gross Domestic Product in Current and Real (2000) Dollars by Type of Product and Sector; 1990 to 2007," *The 2009 Statistical Abstract*, U.S. Census Bureau, accessed September 12, 2009, from https://docs.google.com/viewer?url=http://www.census.gov/compendia/statab/2008/tables/08s0647.pdf.

[48]R. Hallowell, L. A. Schlesinger, & J. Zornitsky, "Internal Service Quality, Customer and Job Satisfaction: Linkages and Implications for Management," *Human Resource Planning* 19 (1996): 20–31; and J. L. Heskett, T. O. Jones, G. W. Loveman, W. E. Sasser, Jr., & L. A. Schlesinger, "Putting the Service–Profit Chain to Work," *Harvard Business Review* (March–April 1994): 164–174.

[49]J. McGregor, "The Employee Is Always Right," *Businessweek Online*, November 9, 2007, 21.

[50]S. Michel, D. Bowen, & R. Johnston, "Customer Service: Making the Most of Customer Complaints," *The Wall Street Journal*, September 22, 2008, R4.

[51]Ibid.

[52]J. Paravantis, N. Bouranta, & L. Chitiris, "The Relationship between Internal and External Service Quality," *International Journal of Contemporary Hospital Management* 21 (2009): 275–293.

[53]G. Brewer, "The Ultimate Guide to Winning Customers: The Customer Stops Here," *Sales & Marketing Management* 150 (March 1998): 30; and F. F. Reichheld, *The Loyalty Effect: The Hidden Force behind Growth, Profits, and Lasting Value* (Cambridge, MA: Harvard Business School Press, 2001).

[54]J. Heskett, T. Jones, G. Loveman, E. Sasser, & L. Schlesinger, "Putting

the Service–Profit Chain to Work," *Harvard Business Review* 86 (July–August 2008): 118–129.

[55]Beth Kowitt "Inside the Secret World of Trader Joe's," *Fortune*, August 23, 2010, accessed June 28, 2011, from http://money.cnn.com/2010/08/20/news/companies/inside_trader_joes_full_version.fortune/index.htm.

[56]L. L. Berry & A. Parasuraman, "Listening to the Customer—The Concept of a Service-Quality Information System," *Sloan Management Review* 38, no. 3 (Spring 1997): 65; and C. W. L. Hart, J. L. Heskett, & W. E. Sasser, Jr., "The Profitable Art of Service Recovery," *Harvard Business Review* (July–August 1990): 148–156.

[57]Deb Stanley, "When Flight Diverted, Crew Ordered Pizza for Passengers," *Denver News*, May 21, 2010, accessed July 7, 2010, from www.thedenverchannel.com/news/23620842/detail.html.

[58]S. Hale, "The Customer Is Always Right— Usually—Some Are Just Annoying, but Others Deserve the Boot," *Orlando Sentinel*, April 15, 2002, 54.

[59]D. E. Bowen & E. E. Lawler III, "The Empowerment of Service Workers: What, Why, How, and When," *Sloan Management Review* 33 (Spring 1992): 31–39; and D. E. Bowen & E. E. Lawler III, "Empowering Service Employees," *Sloan Management Review* 36 (Summer 1995): 73–84.

[60]Bowen & Lawler, "The Empowerment of Service Workers: What, Why, How, and When."

[61]"The Way I Work: Marc Lore of Diapers.com," Inc.com, September 1, 2009, accessed September 2, 2010, from www.inc.com/magazine/20090901/the-way-i-work-marc-lore-of-diaperscom.html.

[62]Stoller, "Companies Give Front-Line Employees More Power."

[63]"No Speed Limit," *Industrial Maintenance & Plant Operation* (October 2007): 45–47.

[64]G. V. Frazier & M. T. Spiggs, "Achieving Competitive Advantage through Group Technology," *Business Horizons* 39 (1996): 83–88.

[65]"The Top 100 Beverage Companies: The List," *Beverage Industry*, July 2001, 30.

[66]"Job Shop Hit's Bull's Eye with Multitasking," *Manufacturing Engineering* (November 2008): 43–105.

[67]C. Felix, "Drafting New Players for Swiss Precision," *Production Machining* (December 2007): 34–37.

[68]Christopher Drew, "Boeing Wins Contract to Build Air Force Tankers," *The New York Times*, February 24, 2011, accessed March 29, 2011, from www.nytimes.com/2011/02/25/business/25tanker.html.

[69]S. Choudhury, "Toyota to Resume Normal India Factory Operations," *The Wall Street Journal*, May 16, 2011, accessed June 28, 2011, from http://online.wsj.com/article/SB100014240527487035091045763265725602338.html.

[70]M. Ramsay, "Honda to Halt Orders for Japan-Made Vehicles," *The Wall Street Journal*, May 2, 2011, accessed June 28, 2011, from http://online.wsj.com/article/SB10001424052748704436004576299091314633036.html.

[71]Miguel Bustillo, "For Lowe's, Landscape Begins to Shift," *The Wall Street Journal*, February 24, 2011, B3.

[72]D. Drickhamer, "Reality Check," *Industry Week*, November 2001, 29.

[73]D. Drickhamer, "Zeroing In on World-Class," *Industry Week*, November 2001, 36.

[74]J. Zeiler, "The Need for Speed," *Operations & Fulfillment*, April 1, 2004, 38.

[75]Efficient Foodservice Response (EFR), accessed August 3, 2009, from www.ifdaonline.org/webarticles.

[76]J. R. Henry, "Minimized Setup Will Make Your Packaging Line S.M.I.L.E.," *Packaging Technology & Engineering*, February 1, 1998, 24.

[77]J. Donoghue, "The Future Is Now," *Air Transport World*, April 1, 2001, 78; and D. Evans, "Aftermarket Outlook," *Aviation Maintenance Magazine*, May 1, 2006, accessed September 13, 2004, from www.aviationtoday.com.

[78]K. Clark, "An Eagle Eye for Inventory," *Chain Store Age*, May 2005, Supplement, 8A.

[79]Beth Gardiner, "Upcycling Evolves from Recycling," *The New York Times*, November 3, 2010, accessed June 27, 2011, from www.nytimes.com/2010/11/04/business/energy-environment/04iht-rbogup.html.

[80]"The Way I Work: Marc Lore of Diapers.com," Inc.com, September 1, 2009, accessed September 2, 2010, from www.inc.com/magazine/20090901/the-way-i-work-marc-lore-of-diaperscom.html.

[81]E. Powell, Jr., & F. Sahin, "Economic Production Lot Sizing with Periodic Costs and Overtime," *Decision Sciences* 32 (2001): 423–452.

[82]J. Bonasia, "Just-in-Time Cuts Costs, but Has Risks," *Investor's Business Daily*, October 3, 2002, 4.

[83]N. Shirouzu, "Why Toyota Wins Such High Marks on Quality Surveys," *The Wall Street Journal*, March 15, 2001, A1.

[84]Ibid.

[85]G. Gruman, "Supply on Demand: Manufacturers Need to Know What's Selling before They Can Produce and Deliver Their Wares in the Right Quantities," *Info World*, April 18, 2005, accessed April 15, 2009, from www.infoworld.com/t/data-management/supply-demand-680.

[86]J. A. Perriat, S. LeMay, & S. Chakrabarty, "The Selling Orientation—Customer Orientation (SOCO) Scale: Cross-Validation of the Revised Version," *Journal of Personal Selling & Sales Management* 24, no. 1 (2004): 49–54.

[87]Laura Petrecca, "Fast Growth Isn't Always Good," *USA Today*, September 13, 2010, 1B–6B.

[88]Julie Jargon, "Latest Starbucks Buzzword: 'Lean' Japanese Techniques," *The Wall Street Journal*, August 4, 2009, accessed June 27, 2011, from http://online.wsj.com/article/SB124933474023402611.html.

[89]J. Craddock, ed., *VideoHound's Golden Movie Retriever* (Farmington Hills, MI: Gale Group, 2000); "John Ratzenberger," accessed September 6, 2007, from http://www.wikipedia.org; Grainger David, "Day Trippers," *Fortune*, April 4, 2005, 108–118; www.marshmallowpeeps.com; www.tabasco.com; and www.factorytoursusa.com.

© iStockphoto.com/Oner Döngel

BIZ FLIX

In Bruges

The tagline for the award-winning 2008 film *In Bruges* was "Shoot first. Sightsee later." That's because it's the story of two hit men—Ray (Colin Farrell) and Ken (Brandan Gleeson)—who tragically botch the job of murdering a priest in a confessional by accidentally killing an innocent young bystander. Ray and Ken are ordered to hide out in the beautiful medieval Flemish city of Bruges, Belgium. They spend their days sightseeing, interacting with the locals, and bickering with each other while awaiting further orders from Harry, their boss (Ralph Fiennes). This video features two scenes that show Ken and Harry interacting with a ticket seller (Rudy Blomme), who makes it more difficult for them to visit a historic bell tower than they'd like.

© GreenLight

What to Watch for and Ask Yourself

1. Ken is the customer and the ticket seller responds to him as a customer. Do you perceive the ticket seller as having a customer focus as emphasized in this chapter? Why or why not?

2. As you were watching the ticket seller interact with Ken and Harry in the second part of this video, did you predict that his customer approach could result in negative results for him? Why or why not?

3. These scenes offer a lesson in customer focus. What did the ticket seller fail to understand about his customers? Could he have handled the situations better?

MANAGEMENT WORKPLACE

Barcelona Restaurant Group

At Barcelona Restaurant Group, quality is defined not just by the food, but by the service that the waitstaff delivers. To ensure consistent quality across the board, Barcelona uses five "feedback loops" that gauge restaurant performance: a "secret shopper" program, credit card rewards for customers, customer comment cards, e-mails, and surveillance cameras. In addition, general managers walk the floor constantly to advise wait staff and gather feedback from customers. There's plenty at stake if Barcelona fails to control its performance, since disappointing one's customers is the quickest way to kill a business.

© Cengage Learning

What to Watch for and Ask Yourself

1. How does Barcelona Restaurant Group's approach to customer service fulfill the quality-related characteristics of services?

2. How does Barcelona Restaurant Group's approach to customer service fulfill the three aspects of Total Quality Management?

3. Discuss how Barcelona Restaurant Group implements service recover and service empowerment.

Glossary

360-degree feedback a performance appraisal process in which feedback is obtained from the boss, subordinates, peers and coworkers, and the employees themselves

A

Absolute comparisons a process in which each decision criterion is compared to a standard or ranked on its own merits

Accommodative strategy a social responsiveness strategy in which a company accepts responsibility for a problem and does all that society expects to solve that problem

Achievement-oriented leadership a leadership style in which the leader sets challenging goals, has high expectations of employees, and displays confidence that employees will assume responsibility and put forth extraordinary effort

Acquaintance time a cultural norm for how much time you must spend getting to know someone before the person is prepared to do business with you

Acquisition the purchase of a company by another company

Acquisition cost the cost of obtaining data that you don't have

Action plan the specific steps, people, and resources needed to accomplish a goal

Active listening assuming half the responsibility for successful communication by actively giving the speaker nonjudgmental feedback that shows you've accurately heard what he or she said

Address terms cultural norms that establish whether you should address business people by their first names, family names, or titles

Adverse impact unintentional discrimination that occurs when members of a particular race, sex, or ethnic group are unintentionally harmed or disadvantaged because they are hired, promoted, or trained (or any other employment decision) at substantially lower rates than others

Advocacy groups concerned citizens who band together to try to influence the business practices of specific industries, businesses, and professions

Affective cultures cultures in which people display emotions and feelings when communicating

Affectivity the stable tendency to experience positive or negative moods

and to react to things in a generally positive or negative way

Affirmative action purposeful steps taken by an organization to create employment opportunities for minorities and women

Age discrimination treating people differently (e.g., in hiring and firing, promotion, and compensation decisions) because of their age

Analyzers companies using an adaptive strategy that seeks to minimize risk and maximize profits by following or imitating the proven successes of prospectors

Appointment time a cultural norm for how punctual you must be when showing up for scheduled appointments or meetings

Asia-Pacific Economic Cooperation (APEC) a regional trade agreement between Australia, Canada, Chile, the People's Republic of China, Hong Kong, Japan, Mexico, New Zealand, Papua New Guinea, Peru, Russia, South Korea, Taiwan, the United States, and all the members of ASEAN, except Cambodia, Laos, and Myanmar

Assemble-to-order operation a manufacturing operation that divides manufacturing processes into separate parts or modules that are combined to create semicustomized products

Assessment centers a series of managerial simulations, graded by trained observers, that are used to determine applicants' capability for managerial work

Association of affinity patterns when two or more database elements tend to occur together in a significant way

Association of Southeast Asian Nations (ASEAN) a regional trade agreement between Brunei Darussalam, Cambodia, Indonesia, Laos, Malaysia, Myanmar, the Philippines, Singapore, Thailand, and Vietnam

Attack a competitive move designed to reduce a rival's market share or profits

Attribution theory the theory that we all have a basic need to understand and explain the causes of other people's behavior

A-type conflict (Affective Conflict) disagreement that focuses on individuals or personal issues

Authentication making sure potential users are who they claim to be

Authoritarianism the extent to which an individual believes there should be

power and status differences within organizations

Authority the right to give commands, take action, and make decisions to achieve organizational objectives

Authorization granting authenticated users approved access to data, software, and systems

Autonomy the degree to which a job gives workers the discretion, freedom, and independence to decide how and when to accomplish the job

Average aggregate inventory average overall inventory during a particular time period

Awareness training training that is designed to raise employees' awareness of diversity issues and to challenge the underlying assumptions or stereotypes they may have about others

B

Background checks procedures used to verify the truthfulness and accuracy of information that applicants provide about themselves and to uncover negative, job-related background information not provided by applicants

Balance sheets accounting statements that provide a snapshot of company's financial position at a particular time

Balanced scorecard measurement of organizational performance in four equally important areas: finances, customers, internal operations, and innovation and learning

Bar code a visual pattern that represents numerical data by varying the thickness and pattern of vertical bars

Bargaining power of buyers a measure of the influence that customers have on a firm's prices

Bargaining power of suppliers a measure of the influence that suppliers of parts, materials, and services to firms in an industry have on the prices of these inputs

Batch production a manufacturing operation that produces goods in large batches in standard lot sizes

BCG matrix a portfolio strategy, developed by the Boston Consulting Group, that categorizes a corporation's businesses by growth rate and relative market share, and helps managers decide how to invest corporate funds

Behavior control the regulation of the behaviors and actions that workers perform on the job

Behavioral addition the process of having managers and employees perform new behaviors that are central to and symbolic of the new organizational culture that a company wants to create

Behavioral formality a workplace atmosphere characterized by routine and regimen, specific rules about how to behave, and impersonal detachment

Behavioral informality a workplace atmosphere characterized by spontaneity, casualness, and interpersonal familiarity

Behavioral substitution the process of having managers and employees perform new behaviors central to the "new" organizational culture in place of behaviors that were central to the "old" organizational culture

Behavior observation scales (BOSs) rating scales that indicate the frequency with which workers perform specific behaviors that are representative of the job dimensions critical to successful job performance

Benchmarking the process of identifying outstanding practices, processes, and standards in other companies and adapting them to your company

Biographical data (biodata) extensive surveys that ask applicants questions about their personal backgrounds and life experiences

Biometrics identifying users by unique, measurable body features, such as fingerprint recognition or iris scanning

Blog a personal Web site that provides personal opinions or recommendations, news summaries, and reader comments

Bona fide occupational qualification (BFOQ) an exception in employment law that permits sex, age, religion, and the like to be used when making employment decisions, but only if they are "reasonably necessary to the normal operation of that particular business." BFOQs are strictly monitored by the Equal Employment Opportunity Commission

Bounded rationality a decision-making process restricted in the real world by limited resources, incomplete and imperfect information, and managers' limited decision-making capabilities

Brainstorming a decision-making method in which group members build on each others' ideas to generate as many alternative solutions as possible

Budgeting quantitative planning through which managers decide how to allocate available money to best accomplish company goals

Budgets quantitative plans through which managers decide how to allocate

available money to best accomplish company goals

Bureaucracy the exercise of control on the basis of knowledge, expertise, or experience

Bureaucratic control the use of hierarchical authority to influence employee behavior by rewarding or punishing employees for compliance or noncompliance with organizational policies, rules, and procedures

Bureaucratic immunity the ability to make changes without first getting approval from managers or other parts of an organizaion

Business confidence indices indices that show managers' level of confidence about future business growth

Buyer dependence the degree to which a supplier relies on a buyer because of the importance of that buyer to the supplier and the difficulty of finding other buyers for its products

C

Cash cow a company with a large share of a slow-growing market

Central America Free Trade Agreement (CAFTA-DR) a regional trade agreement between Costa Rica, the Dominican Republic, El Salvador, Guatemala, Honduras, Nicaragua, and the United States

Centralization of authority the location of most authority at the upper levels of the organization

Chain of command the vertical line of authority that clarifies who reports to whom throughout the organization

Change agent the person formally in charge of guiding a change effort

Change forces forces that produce differences in the form, quality, or condition of an organization over time

Change intervention the process used to get workers and managers to change their behavior and work practices

Character of the rivalry a measure of the intensity of competitive behavior between companies in an industry

Charismatic leadership the behavioral tendencies and personal characteristics of leaders that create an exceptionally strong relationship between them and their followers

closed systems systems that can sustain themselves without interacting with their environments

Closure the tendency to fill in gaps of missing information by assuming that what we don't know is consistent with what we already know

Coaching communicating with someone for the direct purpose of improving

the person's on-the-job performance or behavior

Coercion the use of formal power and authority to force others to change

Cognitive maps graphic depictions of how managers believe environmental factors relate to possible organizational actions

Communication the process of transmitting information from one person or place to another

Communication medium the method used to deliver an oral or written message

Company hotlines phone numbers that anyone in the company can call anonymously to leave information for upper management

Company vision a company's purpose or reason for existing

Competitive advantage providing greater value for customers than competitors can

Competitive analysis a process for monitoring the competition that involves identifying competition, anticipating their moves, and determining their strengths and weaknesses

competitive inertia a reluctance to change strategies or competitive practices that have been successful in the past

Competitors companies in the same industry that sell similar products or services to customers

Complex environment an environment with many environmental factors

Complex matrix a form of matrix departmentalization in which managers in different parts of the matrix report to matrix managers, who help them sort out conflicts and problems

Component parts inventories the basic parts used in manufacturing that are fabricated from raw materials

Compression approach to innovation an approach to innovation that assumes that incremental innovation can be planned using a series of steps and that compressing those steps can speed up innovation

compromise an approach to dealing with conflict in which both parties give up some of what they want in order to reach agreement on a plan to reduce or settle the conflict

Concentration of effect the total harm or benefit that an act produces on the average person

Conceptual Skills the ability to see the organization as a whole, understand how the different parts affect each other, and recognize how the company fits into or is affected by its external environment

Conduit metaphor the mistaken assumption that senders can pipe their intended messages directly into the heads of receivers with perfect clarity and without noise or perceptual filters interfering with the receivers' understanding of the message

Conscientiousness the degree to which someone is organized, hardworking, responsible, persevering, thorough, and achievement oriented

Consideration the extent to which a leader is friendly, approachable, and supportive and shows concern for employees

Consistent organizational culture a company culture in which the company actively defines and teaches organizational values, beliefs, and attitudes

Constructive feedback feedback intended to be helpful, corrective, and/or encouraging

contingency approach holds that there are no universal management theories and that the most effective management theory or idea depends on the kinds of problems or situations that managers are facing at a particular time and place

Contingency theory a leadership theory that states that in order to maximize work group performance, leaders must be matched to the situation that best fits their leadership style

Continuous improvement an organization's ongoing commitment to constantly assess and improve the processes and procedures used to create products and services

Continuous reinforcement schedule a schedule that requires a consequence to be administered following every instance of a behavior

Continuous-flow production a manufacturing operation that produces goods at a continuous, rather than a discrete, rate

Controlling monitoring progress toward goal achievement and taking corrective action when needed

Conventional level of moral development the second level of moral development, in which people make decisions that conform to societal expectations

cooperative contract an agreement in which a foreign business owner pays a company a fee for the right to conduct that business in his or her country

Core capabilities the internal decision-making routines, problem-solving processes, and organizational cultures that determine how efficiently inputs can be turned into outputs

Core firms the central companies in a strategic group

Corporate-level strategy the overall organizational strategy that addresses the question "What business or

businesses are we in or should we be in?"

Cost leadership the positioning strategy of producing a product or service of acceptable quality at consistently lower production costs than competitors can, so that the firm can offer the product or service at the lowest price in the industry

Counseling communicating with someone about non-job-related issues that may be affecting or interfering with the person's performance

Creative work environments workplace cultures in which workers perceive that new ideas are welcomed, valued, and encouraged

Creativity the production of novel and useful ideas

Cross-cultural communication transmitting information from a person in one country or culture to a person from another country or culture

Cross-functional team a team composed of employees from different functional areas of the organization

Cross-training training team members to do all or most of the jobs performed by the other team members

C-type conflict (Cognitive Conflict) disagreement that focuses on problem- and issue-related differences of opinion

Customer defections a performance assessment in which companies identify which customers are leaving and measure the rate at which they are leaving

Customer departmentalization organizing work and workers into separate units responsible for particular kind of customers

Customer focus an organizational goal to concentrate on meeting customers' needs at all levels of the organization

Customer satisfaction an organizational goal to provide products or services that meet or exceed customers' expectations

Customs classification a classification assigned to imported products by government officials that affects the size of the tariff and imposition of import quotas

Cybernetic the process of steering or keeping on course

Cybernetic feasibility the extent to which it is possible to implement each step in the control process

D

Data clusters when three or more database elements occur together (i.e., cluster) in a significant way

Data encryption the transformation of data into complex, scrambled digital

codes that can be unencrypted only by authorized users who possess unique decryption keys

Data mining the process of discovering unknown patterns and relationships in large amounts of data

Data warehouse stores huge amounts of data that have been prepared for data mining analysis by being cleaned of errors and redundancy

Decentralization the location of a significant amount of authority in the lower levels of the organization

Decision criteria the standards used to guide judgments and decisions

Decision making the process of choosing a solution from available alternatives

Decision support system (DSS) an information system that helps managers understand specific kinds of problems and potential solutions and analyze the impact of different decision options using "what if" scenarios

Decoding the process by which the receiver translates the written, verbal, or symbolic form of a message into an understood message

Deep-level diversity differences such as personality and attitudes that are communicated through verbal and nonverbal behaviors and are learned only through extended interaction with others

Defenders companies using an adaptive strategy aimed at defending strategic positions by seeking moderate, steady growth and by offering a limited range of high-quality products and services to a well-defined set of customer

Defensive bias the tendency for people to perceive themselves as personally and situationally similar to someone who is having difficulty or trouble

Defensive strategy a social responsiveness strategy in which a company admits responsibility for a problem but does the least required to meet societal expectations

De-forming a reversal of the forming stage, in which team members position themselves to control pieces of the team, avoid each other, and isolate themselves from team leaders

Delegation of authority the assignment of direct authority and responsibility to a subordinate to complete tasks for which the manager is normally responsible

Delphi technique a decision-making method in which members of a panel of experts respond to questions and to each other until reaching agreement on an issue

De-norming a reversal of the norming stage, in which team performance begins to decline as the size, scope, goal, or members of the team change

Departmentalization subdividing work and workers into separate organizational units responsible for completing particular tasks

Dependent demand system an inventory system in which the level of inventory depends on the number of finished units to be produced

Design competition competition between old and new technologies to establish a new technological standard or dominant design

Design iteration a cycle of repetition in which a company tests a prototype of a new product or service, improves on that design, and then builds and tests the improved prototype

Destructive feedback feedback that disapproves without any intention of being helpful and almost always causes a negative or defensive reaction in the recipient

Devil's advocacy a decision-making method in which an individual or a subgroup is assigned the role of a critic

Dialectical inquiry a decision-making method in which decision makers state the assumptions of a proposed solution (a thesis) and generate a solution that is the opposite (antithesis) of that solution

Differentiation the positioning strategy of providing a product or service that is sufficiently different from competitors' offerings that customers are willing to pay a premium price for it

Direct competition the rivalry between two companies that offer similar products and services, acknowledge each other as rivals, and act and react to each other's strategic actions

Direct foreign investment a method of investment in which a company builds a new business or buys an existing business in a foreign country

Directive leadership a leadership style in which the leader lets employees know precisely what is expected of them, gives them specific guidelines for performing tasks, schedules work, sets standards of performance, and makes sure that people follow standard rules and regulations

Disability a mental or physical impairment that substantially limits one or more major life activities

Disability discrimination treating people differently because of their disabilities

Discontinuous change the phase of a technology cycle characterized by technological substitution and design competition

Discretionary responsibilities the social roles that a company fulfills beyond its economic, legal, and ethical responsibilities

Discussion time a cultural norm for how much time should be spent in discussion with others

Disparate treatment intentional discrimination that occurs when people are purposely not given the same hiring, promotion, or membership opportunities because of their race, color, sex, age, ethnic group, national origin, or religious beliefs

Disposition the tendency to respond to situations and events in a predetermined manner

Disseminator role the informational role managers play when they share information with others in their departments or companies

Distal goals long-term or primary goals

Distinctive competence what a company can make, do, or perform better than its competitors

Distributive justice the perceived degree to which outcomes and rewards are fairly distributed or allocated

Disturbance handler role the decisional role managers play when they respond to severe problems that demand immediate action

Diversification a strategy for reducing risk by buying a variety of items (stocks or, in the case of a corporation, types of businesses) so that the failure of one stock or one business does not doom the entire portfolio

Diversity a variety of demographic, cultural, and personal differences among an organization's employees and customers

Diversity audits formal assessments that measure employee and management attitudes, investigate the extent to which people are advantaged or disadvantaged with respect to hiring and promotions, and review companies' diversity-related policies and procedures

Diversity pairing a mentoring program in which people of different cultural backgrounds, sexes, or races/ethnicities are paired together to get to know each other and change stereotypical beliefs and attitudes

Dog a company with a small share of a slow-growing market

Dominant design a new technological design or process that becomes the accepted market standard

Domination an approach to dealing with conflict in which one party satisfies its desires and objectives at the expense of the other party's desires and objectives

Downsizing the planned elimination of jobs in a company

Downward communication communication that flows from higher to lower levels in an organization

Dynamic environment an environment in which the rate of change is fast

Dysfunctional turnover loss of high-performing employees who voluntarily choose to leave a company

E

Early retirement incentive programs (ERIPs) programs that offer financial benefits to employees to encourage them to retire early

Economic order quantity (EOQ) a system of formulas that minimizes ordering and holding costs and helps determine how much and how often inventory should be ordered

Economic responsibility a company's social responsibility to make a profit by producing a valued product or service

Economic value added (EVA) the amount by which company profits (revenues, minus expenses, minus taxes) exceed the cost of capital in a given year

Effectiveness accomplishing tasks that help fulfill organizational objectives

Efficiency getting work done with a minimum of effort, expense, or waste

Electronic brainstorming a decision-making method in which group members use computers to build on each others' ideas and generate as many alternative solutions as possible

Electronic data interchange (EDI) when two companies convert their purchase and ordering information to a standardized format to enable the direct electronic transmission of that information from one company's computer system to the other company's computer system

Electronic scanner an electronic device that converts printed text and pictures into digital images

Empathetic listening understanding the speaker's perspective and personal frame of reference and giving feedback that conveys that understanding to the speaker

Employee involvement team a team that provides advice or makes suggestions to management concerning specific ideas

Employee separation the voluntary or involuntary loss of an employee

Employee shrinkage employee theft of company merchandise

Employee stock ownership plan (ESOP) a compensation system in which a company pays a percentage of its profits to employees in addition to their regular compensation

Employee turnover loss of employees who voluntarily choose to leave the company

Employment benefits a method of rewarding employees that includes virtually any kind of compensation other than wages or salaries

Employment references sources such as previous employers or coworkers who can provide job-related information about job candidates

Empowering workers permanently passing decision-making authority and responsibility from managers to workers by giving them the information and resources they need to make and carry out good decisions

Empowerment feelings of intrinsic motivation, in which workers perceive their work to have impact and meaning and perceive themselves to be competent and capable of self-determination

Encoding putting a message into a written, verbal, or symbolic form that can be recognized and understood by the receiver

Entrepreneur role the decisional role managers play when they adapt themselves, their subordinates, and their units to change

Entrepreneurial orientation the set of processes, practices, and decision-making activities that lead to new entry, characterized by five dimensions: risk taking, autonomy, innovativeness, proactiveness, and competitive aggressiveness

Entrepreneurship the process of entering new or established markets with new goods or services

Entropy the inevitable and steady deterioration of a system

Environmental change the rate at which a company's general and specific environments change

Environmental complexity the number and the intensity of external factors in the environment that affect organizations

Environmental scanning searching the environment for important events or issues that might affect an organization

Equity theory a theory that states that people will be motivated when they perceive that they are being treated fairly

Ethical behavior behavior that conforms to a society's accepted principles of right and wrong

Ethical charismatics charismatic leaders who provide developmental opportunities for followers, are open to positive and negative feedback, recognize others' contributions, share information, and have moral standards that emphasize the larger interests of the group, organization, or society

Ethical intensity the degree of concern people have about an ethical issue

Ethical responsibility a company's social responsibility not to violate accepted principles of right and wrong when conducting its business

Ethics the set of moral principles or values that defines right and wrong for a person or group

Evaluation apprehension fear of what others will think of your ideas

Executive information system (EIS) a data processing system that uses internal and external data sources to provide the information needed to monitor and analyze organizational performance

Expatriate someone who lives and works outside his or her native country

Expectancy the perceived relationship between effort and performance

Expectancy theory the theory that people will be motivated to the extent to which they believe that their efforts will lead to good performance, that good performance will be rewarded, and that they will be offered attractive rewards

Experiential approach to innovation an approach to innovation that assumes a highly uncertain environment and uses intuition, flexible options, and hands-on experience to reduce uncertainty and accelerate learning and understanding

Expert system an information system that contains the specialized knowledge and decision rules used by experts and experienced decision makers so that nonexperts can draw on this knowledge base to make decisions

Exporting selling domestically produced products to customers in foreign countries

External environments all events outside a company that have the potential to influence or affect it

External locus of control the belief that what happens to you is largely the result of factors beyond your control

External recruiting the process of developing a pool of qualified job applicants from outside the company

Extinction reinforcement in which a positive consequence is no longer allowed to follow a previously reinforced behavior, thus weakening the behavior

Extranets networks that allow companies to exchange information and conduct transactions with outsiders by providing them direct, web-based access to authorized parts of a company's intranet or information system

Extraversion the degree to which someone is active, assertive, gregarious, sociable, talkative, and energized by others

Extrinsic reward a reward that is tangible, visible to others, and given to employees contingent on the performance of specific tasks or behaviors

F

Feedback the amount of information the job provides to workers about their work performance

Feedback control a mechanism for gathering information about performance deficiencies after they occur

Feedback to sender in the communication process, a return message to the sender that indicates the receiver's understanding of the message

Feedforward control a mechanism for monitoring performance inputs rather than outputs to prevent or minimize performance deficiencies before they occur

Figurehead role the interpersonal role managers play when they perform ceremonial duties

Financial ratios calculations typically used to track a business's liquidity (cash), efficiency, and profitability over time compared to other businesses in its industry

Finished goods inventories the final outputs of manufacturing operations

Firewall a protective hardware or software device that sits between the computers in an internal organizational network and outside networks, such as the Internet

Firm-level strategy a corporate strategy that addresses the question "How should we compete against a particular firm?"

First-line managers train and supervise the performance of nonmanagerial employees who are directly responsible for producing the company's products or services

First-mover advantage the strategic advantage that companies earn by being the first to use new information technology to substantially lower costs or to make a product or service different from that of competitors

Fixed Interval reinforcement schedule an intermittent schedule in which consequences follow a behavior only after a fixed time has elapsed

Fixed ratio reinforcement schedule an intermittent schedule in which consequences are delivered following a specific number of behaviors

Flow a psychological state of effortlessness, in which you become completely absorbed in what you're doing and time seems to pass quickly

Focus strategy the positioning strategy of using cost leadership or differentiation to produce a specialized product or service for a limited, specially targeted group of customers in a particular geographic region or market segment

Formal communication channel the system of official channels that carry organizationally approved messages and information

Forming the first stage of team development, in which team members meet each other, form initial impressions, and begin to establish team norms

Four-fifths (or 80 percent) rule a rule of thumb used by the courts and the EEOC to determine whether there is evidence of adverse impact. A violation of this rule occurs when the selection rate for a protected group is less than 80 percent or four-fifths of the selection rate for a nonprotected group

Franchise a collection of networked firms in which the manufacturer or marketer of a product or service, the franchisor, licenses the entire business to another person or organization, the franchisee

Functional departmentalization organizing work and workers into separate units responsible for particular business functions or areas of expertise

Functional turnover loss of poor-performing employees who voluntarily choose to leave a company

Fundamental attribution error the tendency to ignore external causes of behavior and to attribute other people's actions to internal causes

G

Gainsharing a compensation system in which companies share the financial value of performance gains, such as productivity, cost savings, or quality, with their workers

Gantt chart a graphical chart that shows which tasks must be completed at which times in order to complete a project or task

General Agreement on Tariffs and Trade (GATT) a worldwide trade agreement that reduced and eliminated tariffs, limited government subsidies, and established protections for intellectual property

General electric workout a three-day meeting in which managers and employees from different levels and parts of an organization quickly generate and act on solutions to specific business problems

General environment the economic, technological, sociocultural, and political trends that indirectly affect all organizations

Generational change change based on incremental improvements to a dominant technological design such that the improved technology is fully backward compatible with the older technology

Geographic departmentalization organizing work and workers into separate units responsible for doing business in particular geographic areas

Glass ceiling the invisible barrier that prevents women and minorities

from advancing to the top jobs in organizations

Global business the buying and selling of goods and services by people from different countries

Global consistency when a multinational company has offices, manufacturing plants, and distribution facilities in different countries and runs them using the same rules, guidelines, policies, and procedures

Global new ventures new companies that are founded with an active global strategy and have sales, employees, and financing in different countries

Goal a target, objective, or result that someone tries to accomplish

Goal acceptance the extent to which people consciously understand and agree to goals

Goal commitment the determination to achieve a goal

Goal difficulty the extent to which a goal is hard or challenging to accomplish

Goal specificity the extent to which goals are detailed, exact, and unambiguous

Goal-setting theory the theory that people will be motivated to the extent to which they accept specific, challenging goals and receive feedback that indicates their progress toward goal achievement

Government import standard a standard ostensibly established to protect the health and safety of citizens but, in reality, often used to restrict imports

Grand strategy a broad corporate-level strategic plan used to achieve strategic goals and guide the strategic alternatives that managers of individual businesses or subunits may use

Groupthink a barrier to good decision making caused by pressure within the group for members to agree with each other

Growth strategy a strategy that focuses on increasing profits, revenues, market share, or the number of places in which the company does business

H

Hearing the act or process of perceiving sounds

Holding cost the cost of keeping inventory until it is used or sold, including storage, insurance, taxes, obsolescence, and opportunity costs

Horizontal communication communication that flows among managers and workers who are at the same organizational level

Hostile work environment a form of sexual harassment in which unwelcome

and demeaning sexually related behavior creates an intimidating and offensive work environment

Human resource information system (HRIS) a computerized system for gathering, analyzing, storing, and disseminating information related to the HRM process

Human resource management (HRM) the process of finding, developing, and keeping the right people to form a qualified work force

Human resource planning (HRP) using an organization's goals and strategy to forecast the organization's human resource needs in terms of attracting, developing, and keeping a qualified work force

Human skills the ability to work well with others

I

Imperfectly imitable resource a resource that is impossible or extremely costly or difficult for other firms to duplicate

Income statements accounting statements, also called "profit and loss statements," that show what has happened to an organization's income, expenses, and net profit over a period of time

Incremental change the phase of a technology cycle in which companies innovate by lowering costs and improving the functioning and performance of the dominant technological design

Independent demand system an inventory system in which the level of one kind of inventory does not depend on another

Individualism-collectivism the degree to which a person believes that people should be self-sufficient and that loyalty to one's self is more important than loyalty to team or company

Industry regulation regulations and rules that govern the business practices and procedures of specific industries, businesses, and professions

Industry-level strategy a corporate strategy that addresses the question "How should we compete in this industry?"

Informal communication channel ("grapevine") the transmission of messages from employee to employee outside of formal communication channels

Information useful data that can influence people's choices and behavior

Initiating structure the degree to which a leader structures the roles of followers by setting goals, giving directions, setting deadlines, and assigning tasks

Innovation streams patterns of innovation over time that can create sustainable competitive advantage

Inputs in equity theory, the contributions employees make to the organization

Instrumentality the perceived relationship between performance and rewards

integrative conflict resolution an approach to dealing with conflict in which both parties indicate their preferences and then work together to find an alternative that meets the needs of both

Intermittent reinforcement schedule a schedule in which consequences are delivered after a specified or average time has elapsed or after a specified or average number of behaviors has occurred

Internal environment the events and trends inside an organization that affect management, employees, and organizational culture

Internal locus of control the belief that what happens to you is largely the result of your own actions

Internal motivation motivation that comes from the job itself rather than from outside rewards

Internal recruiting the process of developing a pool of qualified job applicants from people who already work in the company

Interorganizational process a collection of activities that take place among companies to transform inputs into outputs that customers value

Interpersonal skills skills, such as listening, communicating, questioning, and providing feedback, that enable people to have effective working relationships with others

Interviews a selection tool in which company representatives ask job applicants job-related questions to determine whether they are qualified for the job

Intranets private company networks that allow employees to easily access, share, and publish information using Internet software

Intraorganizational process the collection of activities that take place within an organization to transform inputs into outputs that customers value

Intrapreneurship entrepreneurship within an existing organization

Intrinsic reward a natural reward associated with performing a task or activity for its own sake

Inventory the amount and number of raw materials, parts, and finished products that a company has in its possession

Inventory turnover the number of times per year that a company sells or "turns over" its average inventory

ISO 14000 a series of international standards for managing, monitoring, and minimizing an organization's harmful effects on the environment

ISO 9000 a series of five international standards, from ISO 9000 to ISO 9004, for achieving consistency in quality management and quality assurance in companies throughout the world

J

Jargon vocabulary particular to a profession or group that interferes with communication in the workplace

Job Analysis a purposeful, systematic process for collecting information on the important work-related aspects of a job

Job characteristics model (JCM) an approach to job redesign that seeks to formulate jobs in ways that motivate workers and lead to positive work outcomes

Job description a written description of the basic tasks, duties, and responsibilities required of an employee holding a particular job

Job design the number, kind, and variety of tasks that individual workers perform in doing their jobs

Job enlargement increasing the number of different tasks that a worker performs within one particular job

Job enrichment increasing the number of tasks in a particular job and giving workers the authority and control to make meaningful decisions about their work

Job evaluation a process that determines the worth of each job in a company by evaluating the market value of the knowledge, skills, and requirements needed to perform it

Job rotation periodically moving workers from one specialized job to another to give them more variety and the opportunity to use different skills

Job shops manufacturing operations that handle custom orders or small batch jobs

Job specialization a job composed of a small part of a larger task or process

Job specifications a written summary of the qualifications needed to successfully perform a particular job

joint venture a strategic alliance in which two existing companies collaborate to form a third, independent company

Just-in-time (JIT) inventory system an inventory system in which component parts arrive from suppliers just as they are needed at each stage of production

K

Kanban a ticket-based JIT system that indicates when to reorder inventory

Kinesics movements of the body and face

Knowledge the understanding that one gains from information

L

Leader role the interpersonal role managers play when they motivate and encourage workers to accomplish organizational objectives

Leader-member relations the degree to which followers respect, trust, and like their leaders

Leadership the process of influencing others to achieve group or organizational goals

Leadership neutralizers subordinate, task, or organizational characteristics that can interfere with a leader's actions or make it impossible for a leader to influence followers' performance

Leadership style the way a leader generally behaves toward followers

Leadership substitutes subordinate, task, or organizational characteristics that make leaders redundant or unnecessary

Leading inspiring and motivating workers to work hard to achieve organizational goals

learning-based planning learning better ways of achieving goals by continually testing, changing, and improving plans and strategies

Legal responsibility a company's social responsibility to obey society's laws and regulations

Liaison role the interpersonal role managers play when they deal with people outside their units

licensing an agreement in which a domestic company, the licensor, receives royalty payments for allowing another company, the licensee, to produce the licensor's product, sell its service, or use its brand name in a specified foreign market

Line authority the right to command immediate subordinates in the chain of command

Line function an activity that contributes directly to creating or selling the company's products

Line-flow production manufacturing processes that are preestablished, occur in a serial or linear manner, and are dedicated to making one type of product

Listening making a conscious effort to hear

local adaptation modifying rules, guidelines, policies, and procedures to adapt to differences in foreign customers, governments, and regulatory agencies

Locus of control the degree to which individuals believe that their actions can influence what happens to them

M

Maastricht Treaty of Europe a regional trade agreement between most European countries

Machiavellian the extent to which individuals believe that virtually any type of behavior is acceptable in trying to satisfy their needs or meet their goals

Magnitude of consequences the total harm or benefit derived from an ethical decision

Make-to-order operation a manufacturing operation that does not start processing or assembling products until a customer order is received

Make-to-stock operation a manufacturing operation that orders parts and assembles standardized products before receiving customer orders

Management getting work done through others

Management by objectives (MBO) a four-step process in which managers and employees discuss and select goals, develop tactical plans, and meet regularly to review progress toward goal accomplishment

Manufacturing flexibility the degree to which manufacturing operations can easily and quickly change the number, kind, and characteristics of products they produce

Market commonality the degree to which two companies have overlapping products, services, or customers in multiple markets

Materials requirement planning (MRP) a production and inventory system that determines the production schedule, production batch sizes, and inventory needed to complete final products

Matrix departmentalization a hybrid organizational structure in which two or more forms of departmentalization, most often product and functional, are used together

Maximize choosing the best alternative

Mechanistic organization an organization characterized by specialized jobs and responsibilities; precisely defined, unchanging roles; and a rigid chain of command based on centralized authority and vertical communication

Media advocacy an advocacy group tactic that involves framing issues as public issues; exposing questionable, exploitative, or unethical practices; and forcing media coverage by buying media time or creating controversy that is likely to receive extensive news coverage

Meta-analysis a study of studies, a statistical approach that provides one of the best scientific estimates of how well management theories and practices work

Middle Managers responsible for setting objectives consistent with top management's goals and for planning and implementing subunit strategies for achieving these objectives

Milestones formal project review points used to assess progress and performance

Modular organization an organization that outsources noncore business activities to outside companies, suppliers, specialists, or consultants

Monitor role the informational role managers play when they scan their environment for information

Monochronic cultures cultures in which people tend to do one thing at a time and view time as linear

Mood linkage a phenomenon in which one worker's negative affectivity and bad moods can spread to others

Moore's law the prediction that about every two years, computerprocessing power would double and its cost would drop by 50 percent

Motion study breaking each task or job into its separate motions and then eliminating those that are unnecessary or repetitive

Motivation the set of forces that initiates, directs, and makes people persist in their efforts to accomplish a goal

Motivation to manage an assessment of how enthusiastic employees are about managing the work of others

Multifactor productivity an overall measure of performance that indicates how much labor, capital, materials, and energy it takes to produce an output

Multifunctional teams work teams composed of people from different departments

multinational corporation a corporation that owns businesses in two or more countries

N

National culture the set of shared values and beliefs that affects the perceptions, decisions, and behavior of the people from a particular country

Needs the physical or psychological requirements that must be met to ensure survival and well-being

Needs assessment the process of identifying and prioritizing the learning needs of employees

Negative affectivity a personality trait in which individuals tend to notice and focus on the negative aspects of themselves and their environments

Negative reinforcement reinforcement that strengthens behavior by withholding an unpleasant consequence when employees perform a specific behavior

Negotiator role the decisional role managers play when they negotiate schedules, projects, goals, outcomes, resources, and employee raises

Neutral cultures cultures in which people do not display emotions and feelings when communicating

Noise anything that interferes with the transmission of the intended message

nominal group technique a decision-making method that begins and ends by having group members quietly write down and evaluate ideas to be shared with the group

Nonsubstitutable resource a resource that produces value or competitive advantage and has no equivalent substitutes or replacements

Nontariff barriers nontax methods of increasing the cost or reducing the volume of imported goods

Nonverbal communication any communication that doesn't involve words

Normative control the regulation of workers' behavior and decisions through widely shared organizational values and beliefs

Normative decision theory a theory that suggests how leaders can determine an appropriate amount of employee participation when making decisions

Norming the third stage of development, in which team members begin to settle into their roles, group cohesion grows, and positive team norms develop

Norms informally agreed-on standards that regulate team behavior

North American Free Trade Agreement (NAFTA) a regional trade agreement between the United States, Canada, and Mexico

O

Objective control the use of observable measures of worker behavior or outputs to assess performance and influence behavior

Objective performance measures measures of job performance that are easily and directly counted or quantified

Online discussion forums the in-house equivalent of Internet newsgroups. By using Web- or software-based discussion tools that are available across the company, employees can easily ask questions and share knowledge with each other.

Open office systems offices in which the physical barriers that separate workers have been removed in order to increase communication and interaction

open systems systems that can sustain themselves only by interacting with their environments, on which they depend for their survival

Openness to experience the degree to which someone is curious, broad-minded, and open to new ideas, things, and experiences; is spontaneous; and has a high tolerance for ambiguity

Operational plans day-to-day plans, developed and implemented by lower-level managers, for producing or delivering the organization's products and services over a 30-day to six-month period

Operations management managing the daily production of goods and services

Opportunistic behavior a transaction in which one party in the relationship benefits at the expense of the other

Optical character recognition the ability of software to convert digitized documents into ASCII text (American Standard Code for Information Interchange) that can be searched, read, and edited by word processing and other kinds of software

Options-based planning maintaining planning flexibility by making small, simultaneous investments in many alternative plans

Ordering cost the costs associated with ordering inventory, including the cost of data entry, phone calls, obtaining bids, correcting mistakes, and determining when and how much inventory to order

Organic organization an organization characterized by broadly defined jobs and responsibility; loosely defined, frequently changing roles; and decentralized authority and horizontal communication based on task knowledge

Organization a system of consciously coordinated activities or forces created by two or more people

Organizational change a difference in the form, quality, or condition of an organization over time

Organizational culture the values, beliefs, and attitudes shared by organizational members

Organizational decline a large decrease in organizational performance that occurs when companies don't anticipate, recognize, neutralize, or adapt to the internal or external pressures that threaten their survival

Organizational development a philosophy and collection of planned change interventions designed to improve an organization's long-term health and performance

Organizational heroes people celebrated for their qualities and achievements within an organization

Organizational innovation the successful implementation of creative ideas in organizations

Organizational plurality a work environment where (1) all members are empowered to contribute in a way that maximizes the benefits to the organization, customers, and themselves, and (2) the individuality of each member is respected by not segmenting or polarizing people on the basis of their membership in a particular group

Organizational process the collection of activities that transform inputs into outputs that customers value

Organizational silence when employees withhold information about organizational problems or issues

Organizational stories stories told by organizational members to make sense of organizational events and changes and to emphasize culturally consistent assumptions, decisions, and actions

Organizational structure the vertical and horizontal configuration of departments, authority, and jobs within a company

Organizing deciding where decisions will be made, who will do what jobs and tasks, and who will work for whom

Outcome/Input (O/I) ratio in equity theory, an employee's perception of how the rewards received from an organization compare with the employee's contributions to that organization

Outcomes in equity theory, the rewards employees receive for their contributions to the organization

Outplacement services employment-counseling services offered to employees who are losing their jobs because of downsizing

Output control the regulation of workers' results or outputs through rewards and incentives

Overreward a form of inequity in which you are getting more outcomes relative to inputs than your referent

Overt integrity test a written test that estimates job applicants' honesty by directly asking them what they think or feel about theft or about punishment of unethical behaviors

P

Paralanguage the pitch, rate, tone, volume, and speaking pattern (i.e., use of silences, pauses, or hesitations) of one's voice

Partial productivity a measure of performance that indicates how much of a particular kind of input it takes to produce an output

Participative leadership a leadership style in which the leader consults employees for their suggestions and input before making decisions

Path-goal theory a leadership theory that states that leaders can increase subordinate satisfaction and performance by clarifying and clearing the paths to goals and by increasing the number and kinds of rewards available for goal attainment

Perception the process by which individuals attend to, organize, interpret, and retain information from their environments

Perceptual filters the personality-, psychology-, or experience-based differences that influence people to ignore or pay attention to particular stimuli

Performance appraisal the process of assessing how well employees are doing their jobs

Performance feedback information about the quality or quantity of past performance that indicates whether progress is being made toward the accomplishment of a goal

Performing the fourth and final stage of team development, in which performance improves because the team has matured into an effective, fully functioning team

Personal aggression hostile or aggressive behavior toward others

Personality the relatively stable set of behaviors, attitudes, and emotions displayed over time that makes people different from each other

Personality-based integrity test a written test that indirectly estimates job applicants' honesty by measuring psychological traits, such as dependability and conscientiousness

Personality tests tests that measure the extent to which applicants possess different kinds of job-related personality dimensions

Phased retirement employees transition to retirement by working reduced hours over a period of time before completing retiring

Piecework a compensation system in which employees are paid a set rate for each item they produce

Planning choosing a goal and developing a strategy to achieve that goal

Planning determining organizational goals and a means for achieving them

Policies a standing plan that indicates the general course of action that should be taken in response to a particular event or situation

Policy uncertainty the risk associated with changes in laws and government policies that directly affect the way foreign companies conduct business

Political deviance using one's influence to harm others in the company

Political uncertainty the risk of major changes in political regimes that can result from war, revolution, death of political leaders, social unrest, or other influential events

Polychronic cultures cultures in which people tend to do more than one thing at a time and view times as circular

Pooled interdependence work completed by having each job or department independently contribute to the whole

Portfolio strategy a corporate-level strategy that minimizes risk by diversifying investment among various businesses or product lines

Position power the degree to which leaders are able to hire, fire, reward, and punish workers

Positive affectivity a personality trait in which individuals tend to notice and focus on the positive aspects of themselves and their environments

Positive reinforcement reinforcement that strengthens behavior by following behaviors with desirable consequences

Postconventional level of moral development the third level of moral development, in which people make decisions based on internalized principles

Preconventional level of moral development the first level of moral development, in which people make decisions based on selfish reasons

Predictive patterns patterns that help identify database elements that are different

Primary stakeholder any group on which an organization relies for its long-term survival

Principle of distributive justice an ethical principle that holds that you should never take any action that harms the least fortunate among us: the poor, the uneducated, the unemployed

Principle of government requirements an ethical principle that holds that you should never take any action that violates the law, for the law represents the minimal moral standard

Principle of individual rights an ethical principle that holds that you should never take any action that infringes on others' agreed-upon rights

Principle of long-term self-interest an ethical principle that holds that you should never take any action that is not in your or your organization's long-term self-interest

Principle of personal virtue an ethical principle that holds that you should never do anything that is not honest, open, and truthful and that you would not be glad to see reported in the newspapers or on TV

Principle of religious injunctions an ethical principle that holds that you should never take any action that is not kind and that does not build a sense of community

Principle of utilitarian benefits an ethical principle that holds that you should never take any action that does not result in greater good for society

Private spaces spaces used by and open to just one employee

Proactive strategy a social responsiveness strategy in which a company anticipates responsibility for a problem before it occurs and does more than society expects to address the problem

Probability of effect the chance that something will happen and then harm others

Problem a gap between a desired state and an existing state

Procedural justice the perceived fairness of the process used to make reward allocation decisions

Procedures a standing plan that indicates the specific steps that should be taken in response to a particular event

Processing cost the cost of turning raw data into usable information

Processing information transforming raw data into meaningful information

Product boycott an advocacy group tactic that involves protesting a company's actions by persuading consumers not to purchase its product or service

Product departmentalization organizing work and workers into separate units responsible for producing particular products or services

Product prototype a full-scale working model that is being tested for design, function, and reliability

Production blocking a disadvantage of face-to-face brainstorming in which a group member must wait to share an idea because another member is presenting an idea

Production deviance unethical behavior that hurts the quality and quantity of work produced

Productivity a measure of performance that indicates how many inputs it takes to produce or create an output

Profit sharing a compensation system in which a company pays a percentage of its profits to employees in addition to their regular compensation

Project manufacturing manufacturing operations designed to produce large, expensive, specialized products

Project team a team created to complete specific, one-time projects or tasks within a limited time

Property deviance unethical behavior aimed at the organization's property or products

Prospectors companies using an adaptive strategy that seeks fast growth by searching for new market opportunities, encouraging risk taking, and being the first to bring innovative new products to market

Protecting information the process of ensuring that data are reliably and consistently retrievable in a usable format for authorized users, but no one else

Protectionism a government's use of trade barriers to shield domestic companies and their workers from foreign competition

Proximal goals short-term goals or subgoals

Proximity of effect the social, psychological, cultural, or physical distance between a decision maker and those affected by his or her decisions

Public communications an advocacy group tactic that relies on voluntary participation by the news media and the advertising industry to get the advocacy group's message out

Punctuated equilibrium theory the theory that companies go through long periods of stability (equilibrium), followed by short periods of dynamic, fundamental change (revolution), and finishing with a return to stability (new equilibrium)

Punishment reinforcement that weakens behavior by following behaviors with undesirable consequences

Purchasing power the relative cost of a standard set of goods and services in different countries

Purpose statement is a statement of a company's purpose or reason for existing

 Q

Quality a product or service free of deficiencies, or the characteristics of a product or service that satisfy customer needs

Question mark a company with a small share of a fast-growing market

Quid pro quo sexual harassment a form of sexual harassment in which employment outcomes, such as hiring, promotion, or simply keeping one's job, depend on whether an individual submits to sexual harassment

Quota a limit on the number or volume of imported products

R

Racial and ethnic discrimination treating people differently because of their race or ethnicity

Radio frequency identification (RFID) tags tags containing minuscule microchips that transmit information via radio waves and can be used to track the number and location for the objects into which the tags have been inserted

Rare resource a resource that is not controlled or possessed by many competing firms

Rate buster a group member whose work pace is significantly faster than the normal pace in his or her group

Rater training training performance appraisal raters in how to avoid rating errors and increase rating accuracy

Rational decision making a systematic process of defining problems, evaluating alternatives, and choosing optimal solutions

Raw data facts and figures

Raw material inventories the basic inputs in a manufacturing process

Reactive strategy a social responsiveness strategy in which a company does less than society expects

Reactors companies using an adaptive strategy of not following a consistent strategy, but instead reacting to changes in the external environment after they occur

Reciprocal interdependence work completed by different jobs or groups working together in a back-and-forth manner

Recovery the strategic actions taken after retrenchment to return to a growth strategy

Recruiting the process of developing a pool of qualified job applicants

Reengineering fundamental rethinking and radical redesign of business processes to achieve dramatic improvements in critical measures of performance, such as cost, quality, service, and speed

Referents in equity theory, others with whom people compare themselves to determine if they have been treated fairly

Refreezing supporting and reinforcing new changes so that they "stick"

Regional trading zones areas in which tariff and nontariff barriers on trade

between countries are reduced or eliminated

Regulation standards the costs associated with implementing or maintaining control

Reinforcement the process of changing behavior by changing the consequences that follow behavior

Reinforcement contingencies cause-and-effect relationships between the performance of specific behaviors and specific consequences

Reinforcement theory the theory that behavior is a function of its consequences, that behaviors followed by positive consequences will occur more frequently, and that behaviors followed by negative consequences, or not followed by positive consequences, will occur less frequently

Related diversification creating or acquiring companies that share similar products, manufacturing, marketing, technology, or cultures

Relationship behavior the establishment of mutually beneficial, long-term exchanges between buyers and suppliers

Relative comparisons a process in which each decision criterion is compared directly with every other criterion

Resistance forces forces that support the existing state of conditions in organizations

Resistance to change opposition to change resulting from self-interest, misunderstanding and distrust, or a general intolerance for change

Resource allocator role the decisional role managers play when they decide who gets what resources

Resource scarcity the abundance or shortage of critical organizational resources in an organization's external environment

Resource similarity the extent to which a competitor has similar amounts and kinds of resources

Resources the assets, capabilities, processes, employee time, information, and knowledge that an organization uses to improve its effectiveness and efficiency, create and sustain competitive advantage, and fulfill a need or solve a problem

Response a competitive countermove, prompted by a rival's attack, to defend or improve a company's market share or profit

Results-driven change change created quickly by focusing on the measurement and improvement of results

Retrenchment strategy a strategy that focuses on turning around very poor company performance by shrinking the size or scope of the business

Retrieval cost the cost of accessing already-stored and processed information

Rules and regulations standing plans that describe how a particular action should be performed, or what must happen or not happen in response to a particular event

S

S.M.A.R.T. goals goals that are specific, measurable, attainable, realistic, and timely

Satisficing choosing a "good enough" alternative

Schedule of reinforcement rules that specify which behaviors will be reinforced, which consequences will follow those behaviors, and the schedule by which those consequences will be delivered

Schedule time a cultural norm for the time by which scheduled projects or jobs should actually be completed

Scientific management thoroughly studying and testing different work methods to identify the best, most efficient way to complete a job

S-Curve pattern of innovation a pattern of technological innovation characterized by slow initial progress, then rapid progress, and then slow progress again as a technology matures and reaches its limits

Secondary firms the firms in a strategic group that follow strategies related to but somewhat different from those of the core firms

Secondary stakeholder any group that can influence or be influenced by a company and can affect public perceptions about the company's socially responsible behavior

Secure sockets layer (SSL) encryption internet browser-based encryption that provides secure off-site web access to some data and programs

Selection the process of gathering information about job applicants to decide who should be offered a job

Selective perception the tendency to notice and accept objects and information consistent with our values, beliefs, and expectations, while ignoring or screening out or not accepting inconsistent information

Self-control (Self-management) a control system in which managers and workers control their own behavior by setting their own goals, monitoring their own progress, and rewarding themselves for goal achievements

Self-designing team a team that has the characteristics of self-managing teams but also controls team design, work tasks, and team membership

Self-serving bias the tendency to overestimate our value by attributing successes to ourselves (internal causes) and attributing failures to others or the environment (external causes)

Semi-autonomous work group a group that has the authority to make decisions and solve problems related to the major tasks of producing a product or service

Sequence patterns when two or more database elements occur together in a significant pattern, but one of the elements precedes the other

Sequential interdependence work completed in succession, with one group's or job's outputs becoming the inputs for the next group or job

Service recovery restoring customer satisfaction to strongly dissatisfied customers

Setup cost the costs of downtime and lost efficiency that occur when a machine is changed or adjusted to produce a different kind of inventory

Sex discrimination treating people differently because of their sex

Sexual harassment a form of discrimination in which unwelcome sexual advances, requests for sexual favors, or other verbal or physical conduct of a sexual nature occurs while performing one's job

Shadow-strategy task force a committee within a company that analyzes the company's own weaknesses to determine how competitors could exploit them for competitive advantage

Shared spaces spaces used by and open to all employees

Shareholder model a view of social responsibility that holds that an organization's overriding goal should be profit maximization for the benefit of shareholders

Simple environment an environment with few environmental factors

Simple matrix a form of matrix departmentalization in which managers in different parts of the matrix negotiate conflicts and resources

Single-use plans plans that cover unique, one-time-only events

Situational (SWOT) analysis an assessment of the strengths and weaknesses in an organization's internal environment and the opportunities and threats in its external environment

Situational favorableness the degree to which a particular situation either permits or denies a leader the chance to influence the behavior of group members

Situational theory a leadership theory that states that leaders need to adjust their leadership styles to match their followers' readiness

Skill variety the number of different activities performed in a job

Skills-based diversity training training that teaches employees the practical skills they need for managing a diverse work force, such as flexibility and adaptability, negotiation, problem solving, and conflict resolution

Skill-based pay compensation system that pays employees for learning additional skills or knowledge

Slack resources a cushion of extra resources that can be used with options-based planning to adapt to unanticipated change, problems, or opportunities

Social consensus agreement on whether behavior is bad or good

Social integration the degree to which group members are psychologically attracted to working with each other to accomplish a common objective

Social loafing behavior in which team members withhold their efforts and fail to perform their share of the work

Social responsibility a business's obligation to pursue policies, make decisions, and take actions that benefit society

Social responsiveness refers to a company's strategy to respond to stakeholders' economic, legal, ethical, or discretionary expectations concerning social responsibility

Soldiering when workers deliberately slow their pace or restrict their work output

Specificability tests (aptitude tests) tests that measure the extent to which an applicant possesses the particular kind of ability needed to do a job well

Specific environment the customers, competitors, suppliers, industry regulations, and advocacy groups that are unique to an industry and directly affect how a company does business

Spokesperson role the informational role managers play when they share information with people outside their departments or companies

Stability strategy a strategy that focuses on improving the way in which the company sells the same products or services to the same customers

Stable environment an environment in which the rate of change is slow

Staff authority the right to advise, but not command, others who are not subordinates in the chain of command

Staff function an activity that does not contribute directly to creating or selling the company's products, but instead supports line activities

Stakeholder model a theory of corporate responsibility that holds that management's most important responsibility, long-term survival, is achieved by satisfying the interests of multiple corporate stakeholders

Stakeholders persons or groups with a "stake" or legitimate interest in a company's actions

Standardization solving problems by consistently applying the same rules, procedures, and processes

Standards a basis of comparison for measuring the extent to which various kinds of organizational performance are satisfactory or unsatisfactory.

Standing plans plans used repeatedly to handle frequently recurring events

Star a company with a large share of a fast-growing market

Stepladder technique a decision-making method in which group members are added to a group discussion one at a time (like a stepladder). The existing group members listen to each new member's thoughts, ideas, and recommendations; then the group shares the ideas and suggestions that it had already considered, discusses the new and old ideas, and makes a decision

Stock options a compensation system that gives employees the right to purchase shares of stock at a set price, even if the value of the stock increases above that rate

Stockout the point when a company runs out of finished product

Stockout costs the costs incurred when a company runs out of a product, including transaction costs to replace inventory and the loss of customers' goodwill

Storage cost the cost of physically or electronically archiving information for later use and retrieval

Storming the second stage of development, characterized by conflict and disagreement, in which team members disagree over what the team should do and how it should do it

Strategic alliance an agreement in which companies combine key resources, costs, risk, technology, and people

Strategic dissonance a discrepancy between a company's intended strategy and the strategic actions managers take when implementing that strategy

Strategic group a group of companies within an industry against which top managers compare, evaluate, and benchmark strategic threats and opportunities

Strategic leadership the ability to anticipate, envision, maintain flexibility, think strategically, and work with others to initiate changes that will create a positive future for an organization

Strategic objective a more specific goal that unifies company-wide efforts, stretches and challenges the organization, and possesses a finish line and a time frame

Strategic plans overall company plans that clarify how the company will serve customers and position itself against competitors over the next two to five years

Strategic reference points the strategic targets managers use to measure whether a firm has developed the core competencies it needs to achieve a sustainable competitive advantage

Structural accommodation the ability to change organizational structures, policies, and practices in order to meet stretch goals

Structural interviews interviews in which all applicants are asked the same set of standardized questions, usually including situational, behavioral, background, and job-knowledge questions

Subjective performance measures measures of job performance that require someone to judge or assess a worker's performance

Suboptimization performance improvement in one part of an organization but only at the expense of decreased performance in another part

Subsidies government loans, grants, and tax deferments given to domestic companies to protect them from foreign competition

Subsystems smaller systems that operate within the context of a larger system

Supervised data mining the process when the user tells the data mining software to look and test for specific patterns and relationships in a data set

Supplier dependence the degree to which a company relies on a supplier because of the importance of the supplier's product to the company and the difficulty of finding other sources of that product

Suppliers companies that provide material, human, financial, and informational resources to other companies

Supportive leadership a leadership style in which the leader is friendly to and approachable, shows concern for employees and their welfare, treats them as equals, and creates a friendly climate

Surface-level diversity differences such as age, sex, race/ethnicity, and physical disabilities that are observable, typically unchangeable, and easy to measure

Survey feedback information that is collected by surveys from organizational members and then compiled, disseminated, and used to develop action plans for improvement

Sustainable competitive advantage a competitive advantage that other companies have tried unsuccessfully to duplicate and have, for the moment, stopped trying to duplicate

Synergy when two or more sub systems working together can produce more than they can working apart

System a set of interrelated elements or parts that function as a whole

T

Tactical plans plans created and implemented by middle managers that specify how the company will use resources, budgets, and people over the next six months to two years to accomplish specific goals within its mission

Tariff a direct tax on imported goods

Task identity the degree to which a job, from beginning to end, requires the completion of a whole and identifiable piece of work

Task interdependence the extent to which collective action is required to complete an entire piece of work

Task significance the degree to which a job is perceived to have a substantial impact on others inside or outside the organization

Task structure the degree to which the requirements of a subordinate's tasks are clearly specified

Team diversity the variances or differences in ability, experience, personality, or any other factor on a team

Team leaders managers responsible for facilitating team activities toward goal accomplishment

Technical skills the ability to apply the specialized procedures, techniques, and knowledge required to get the job done

Technological discontinuity the phase of an innovation stream in which a scientific advance or unique combination of existing technologies creates a significant breakthrough in performance or function

Technological lockout the inability of a company to competitively sell its products because it relied on old technology or a nondominant design

Technological substitution the purchase of new technologies to replace older ones

Technology the knowledge, tools, and techniques used to transform input into output

Technology cycle a cycle that begins with the "birth" of a new technology and ends when that technology reaches its limits and is replaced by a newer, substantially better technology

Televised/videotaped speeches and meetings speeches and meetings originally made to a smaller audience that are either simultaneously broadcast to other locations in the company or videotaped for subsequent distribution and viewing

Temporal immediacy the time between an act and the consequences the act produces

Testing the systematic comparison of different product designs or design iterations

Threat of new entrants a measure of the degree to which barriers to entry make it easy or difficult for new companies to get started in an industry

Threat of substitute products or services a measure of the ease with which customers can find substitutes for an industry's products or services

Time Study timing how long it takes for good workers to complete each part of their jobs

Top Managers executives responsible for the overall direction of the organization

Total quality management (TQM) an integrated, principle-based, organization-wide strategy for improving product and service quality

Trade barriers government-imposed regulations that increase the cost and restrict the number of imported goods

Traditional work group a group composed of two or more people who work together to achieve a shared goal

Training developing the skills, experience, and knowledge employees need to perform their jobs or improve their performance

Trait theory a leadership theory that holds that effective leaders possess a similar set of traits or characteristics

Traits relatively stable characteristics, such as abilities, psychological motives, or consistent patterns of behavior

Transactional leadership leadership based on an exchange process, in which followers are rewarded for good performance and punished for poor performance

Transformational leadership leadership that generates awareness and acceptance of a group's purpose and mission and gets employees to see beyond their own needs and self-interests for the good of the group

Transient firms the firms in a strategic group whose strategies are changing from one strategic position to another

Transition management team (TMT) a team of 8 to 12 people whose full-time job is to manage and coordinate a company's change process

Two-factor authentication authentication based on what users know, such as a password and what they have in their possession, such as a secure ID card or key

Type A personality a person who tries to complete as many tasks as possible in the shortest possible time and is hard driving, competitive, impatient, perfectionistic, angry, and unable to relax

Type A/B personality dimension the extent to which people tend toward impatience, hurriedness, competitiveness, and hostility

Type B personality a person who is relaxed, easygoing, and able to engage in leisure activities without worrying about work

U

Uncertainty extent to which managers can understand or predict which environmental changes and trends affect their businesses

Underreward a form of inequity in which you are getting fewer outcomes relative to inputs than your referent is getting

Unethical charismatics charismatic leaders who control and manipulate followers, do what is best for themselves instead of their organizations, want to hear only positive feedback, share only information that is beneficial to themselves, and have moral standards that put their interests before everyone else's

Unfreezing getting the people affected by change to believe that change is needed

Unity of command a management principle that workers should report to just one boss

Unrelated diversification creating or acquiring companies in completely unrelated businesses

Unstructured interviews interviews in which interviewers are free to ask the applicants anything they want

Unsupervised data mining the process when the user simply tells the data mining software to uncover whatever patterns and relationships it can find in a data set

Upward communication communication that flows from lower to higher levels in an organization

V

Valence the attractiveness or desirability of a reward or outcome

Validation the process of determining how well a selection test or procedure predicts future job performance. The better or more accurate the prediction of future job performance, the more valid a test is said to be

Valuable resource a resource that allows companies to improve efficiency and effectiveness

Value customer perception that the product quality is excellent for the price offered

Variable interval reinforcement schedules an intermittent schedule in which the time between a behavior and the following consequences varies around a specified average

Variable ratio reinforcement schedule an intermittent schedule in which consequences are delivered following a different number of behaviors, sometimes more and sometimes less, that vary around a specified average number of behaviors

Variation a deviation in the form, condition, or appearance of a product from the quality standard for that product

Virtual organization an organization that is part of a network in which many companies share skills, costs, capabilities, markets, and customers to collectively solve customer problems or provide specific products or services

Virtual private network (VPN) software that securely encrypts data sent by employees outside the company network, decrypts the data when they arrive within the company computer network, and does the same when data are sent back to employees outside the network

Virtual team a team composed of geographically and/or organizationally dispersed coworkers who use telecommunication and information technologies to accomplish an organizational task

Virus a program or piece of code that, without your knowledge, attaches itself to other programs on your computer and can trigger anything from a harmless flashing message to the reformatting of your hard drive to a systemwide network shutdown

Visible artifacts visible signs of an organization's culture, such as the office design and layout, company dress code, and company benefits and perks, like stock options, personal parking spaces, or the private company dining room

Visionary leadership leadership that creates a positive image of the future

that motivates organizational members and provides direction for future planning and goal setting

Voluntary export restraints voluntarily imposed limits on the number or volume of products exported to a particular country

W

Web services using standardized protocols to describe data from one company in such a way that those data can automatically be read, understood, transcribed, and processed by different computer systems in another company

Whistleblowing reporting others' ethics violations to management or legal authorities

wholly owned affiliates foreign offices, facilities, and manufacturing plants that are 100 percent owned by the parent company

Work sample tests tests that require applicants to perform tasks that are actually done on the job

Work team a small number of people with complementary skills who hold themselves mutually accountable for pursuing a common purpose, achieving performance goals, and improving interdependent work processes

Worker readiness the ability and willingness to take responsibility for directing one's behavior at work

Work force forecasting the process of predicting the number and kind of workers with specific skills and abilities that an organization will need in the future

Work-in-process inventories partially finished goods consisting of assembled component parts

Workplace deviance unethical behavior that violates organizational norms about right and wrong

World Trade Organization (WTO) the successor to GATT; the only international organization dealing with the global rules of trade between nations. Its main function is to ensure that trade flows as smoothly, predictably, and freely as possible

Wrongful discharge a legal doctrine that requires employers to have a job-related reason to terminate employees

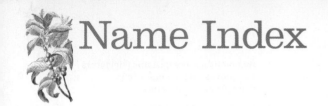

Name Index

A

A. P. Moller-Maersk A/S, 690, 692
A&W Restaurants, 309
AARP (American Association of Retired Persons), 493
AB InBev, 96, 346
ABC, 93, 94, 209, 210
ABC Fine Wine & Spirits, 444
Abercrombie & Fitch, 147, 488
Abledata, 499
ABM Industries, 436
Abrams, Julie, 560
Academy of Management, 47
Academy of Management Perspectives, 47
Accenture, 506
Accord, 689
Accounting for Dummies, 684
Accounting the Easy Way, 684
Accu-Screen, 444
Ace Hardware, 112, 217–218, 727
Acer, 238
Acme Markets, 232
ACME Specialty Manufacturing, 750
Activision-Blizzard, 92
Actonel, 348
Acura, 280, 747
Acxiom, 712
Adams, Ed, 508
Addessi, Joan, 131–133
Addessi, Richard, 131–133
ADF Companies, 114
Adidas, 100
Adidas-Salomon, 308
Adler, Nancy J., 643
Administrative Science Quarterly, 47
Advocate Good Samaritan Hospital, 751
AES, 355–356
Aflac, 536–537, 539
Agility, 149
Agnello, William, 367
AIG, 14
Air Lease Corporation, 312
Air Products & Chemicals, 352–353
Airbus, 299
Akerson, Daniel, 589–589

Akio Toyoda, 215, 351, 552, 586, 681
Akraya, 91
al-Farabi, 45
al-Ghazali, 45
Albaugh, Jim, 408
Albertsons, 232
Alderfer, 534
Alibaba Group Holdings, 296
Allaire, Paul A., 513
Allan, Paul, 209
Alok Shende, 308
Alteon Websystems, 192
Altera Corp., 638–639
Amazon, 5, 89, 178, 213, 215, 238, 617
Ambrose, David, 749
American Airlines, 32, 542, 705
American Association of Retired Persons (AARP), 493
American Civil Rights Institute, 489
American College Testing, 454
American Council of the Blind, 499
American Customer Satisfaction Index, 112
American Express, 121–122, 730
American Federation of Teachers, 463
American Heart Association, 243
American Honda, 182
American Hospital Association, 99
American Humane Society, 99
American Idol, 307
American Motors Corporation, 273
American National Standards Institute, 750
American Society for Quality, 747, 750
American Society for Training and Development, 453, 457
American Society of Engineers, 46
American Society of Mechanical Engineers, 51
Amgen, 533
Amos, Dan, 536–537
AMP, 323
Anadarko Petroleum, 231
Anchor Blue, 355
Anderson, David, 555
Andreessen, Marc, 427

Andrew, Jim, 21
Android, 255, 272, 617
Angelini, Greg, 554
Angry Birds, 83
Anheuser-Busch, 96, 228
Ann Taylor, 560
Antartica, 346
Anton, Jon, 744
Antoncic, Madelyn, 191
Apex Companies, 441
A-Power Energy Generation Systems, 307
Apple, 20, 82, 83, 101, 150, 185, 271–272, 304, 351, 369, 401, 427, 573–574, 576, 617, 618, 621, 686, 728, 732, 733, 749, 767
Apple Computer, 210–213, 216, 223, 238
Applebaum, Stuart, 74
Appleton Papers Inc., 629
Appling, Troy, 722
Arcos Inc., 468
Are We There Yet?, 491
Argenti, Paul, 619
Aricept, 232
Arizona Public Service Company, 618
Arkin, Alan, 378
Arkwright, 45
Arm & Hammer, 176–177
Armstrong, Neil, 178
The Art of War, 44
Ascentius, 308
Asian Enterprise, 488
Association for Information and Image Management, 714
Astro Zeneca, 231
Asurion Corporation, 240
A.T. Kearney, 673
AT&T, 8, 25, 64, 94, 101, 275–276, 311, 393, 576
ATK, 429
AtlantaCare, 751
Atlassian, 536
Aubuchon Hardware, 218
Austalian Wool Innovation, 147
Australian and International Pilots Association, 649
Autodesk, 348, 606
Avero LLC, 16
Avon, 178, 436, 495

Subject Index

See separate index for names.

What Would You Do?

What Really Works

Doing the Right Thing

Management Facts

Management Trends

Self Assessment